GUSTAV MAHLER

GUSTAV MAHLER

VOLUME 3

VIENNA: TRIUMPH AND DISILLUSION
(1904–1907)

HENRY-LOUIS DE LA GRANGE

OXFORD

UNIVERSITY PRESS

OXFORD
UNIVERSITY PRESS

Great Clarendon Street, Oxford OX2 6DP

Oxford University Press is a department of the University of Oxford.
It furthers the University's objective of excellence in research, scholarship,
and education by publishing worldwide in

Oxford New York

Athens Auckland Bangkok Bogotá Buenos Aires Calcutta
Cape Town Chennai Dar es Salaam Delhi Florence Hong Kong Istanbul
Karachi Kuala Lumpur Madrid Melbourne Mexico City Mumbai
Nairobi Paris São Paulo Singapore Taipei Tokyo Toronto Warsaw

with associated companies in Berlin Ibadan

Oxford is a registered trade mark of Oxford University Press
in the UK and in certain other countries

Published in the United States
by Oxford University Press Inc., New York

British Library Cataloguing in Publication Data

Data available

Library of Congress Cataloging in Publication Data

La Grange, Henry-Louis de, 1924–
[Gustav Mahler. English]
Gustav Mahler/Henry-Louis de La Grange,
p. cm.
Rev., enl., and updated translation of the French ed. published in
3 v.: Paris: Fayard, c1979–c1984.
Includes bibliographical references and index.
Contents:—v. 3. Vienna: Triumph and Disillusion (1904–1907)
1. Mahler, Gustav, 1860–1911   2. Composers—Austria—Biography.
I. Title.
ML410.M23L3413 1999   780´.92—dc20 [B] 94–18322

ISBN 0–19–315160–X (v. 3: acid-free paper)

1 3 5 7 9 10 8 6 4 2

Typeset in Bodoni by
Cambrian Typesetters, Frimley, Surrey

Printed in Great Britain
on acid-free paper by
Biddles Ltd
Guildford & King's Lynn

ACKNOWLEDGEMENTS

To the list of people I thanked for their kind help in preparing my second volume, I must add Stewart Spencer and Alfred Clayton, not only for their excellent translations of my French text of several chapters of this volume, but also for their enlightened comments and suggestions; Stephen McClatchie for his extensive work on the Rosé collection (UWO), for checking the dates I had previously ascribed to the letters I had read in the 1950s and 1960s, and for sending me his transcriptions of others, previously unknown to me. Claude Meylan has contributed much to the knowledge of Mahler by studying and transcribing new documents discovered by him among William Ritter's papers in the Bibliothèque Nationale Suisse in Berne, Switzerland. They include copies of his letters to Mahler, previously unknown articles, and long passages in Ritter's private diaries concerning Mahler, his personality, and his rehearsals. He was most generous in allowing me to read these, as was the Berne Library in permitting me to quote from them. My thanks should also be extended to Stéphan Buchon for checking a number of sources at short notice in Vienna. Finally I am grateful to Lewis Foreman, Richard Landau, Michael Burden, Tony Duggan, and Chris Goddard for their last-minute research in London, to Paul Moor for putting me in contact with them, and to Colman W. Kraft for translating from the Russian Alexander Ossovsky's review, written after Mahler's St Petersburg concerts of October–November 1907, one of the most interesting and substantial critical articles ever written about him as a conductor.

This volume was based on *Gustav Mahler: L'âge d'or Vienne 1900–1907* and *Gustav Mahler: Le génie foudroyé 1907–1911* by Henry-Louis de La Grange originally published in French in 1983–4 by Librairie Arthème Fayard, Paris © 1983, 1984 Librairie Arthème Fayard.

CONTENTS

LIST OF ILLUSTRATIONS

(between pp. 336–337 and 688–689)

All photographs courtesy of the Bibliothèque musicale Gustav Mahler, Paris, unless otherwise indicated.

ABBREVIATIONS

ABB   Anton Bruckner, *Gesammelte Briefe*, ed. Max Auer (Bosse, Regensburg, 1924).

AML   Alma Mahler, *Mein Leben* (Fischer, Frankfurt, 1960); *And the Bridge Is Love*, shortened English version, trans. E. B. Ashton (Harcourt Brace, New York, 1958).

AMM1   Alma Mahler, *Gustav Mahler: Erinnerungen und Briefe* (Bermann Fischer, Vienna, 1949).

AMM2   Alma Mahler, *Gustav Mahler: Erinnerungen und Briefe* (Propyläen-Ullstein, Frankfurt, 1971).

AMM3   Alma Mahler, *Gustav Mahler: Memories and Letters*, English version, trans. Basil Creighton, ed. Donald Mitchell and Knud Martner (Sphere Books, London, 1990).

BDB   Kurt Blaukopf, *Mahler: Sein Leben, sein Werk und seine Welt in Zeitgenössischen Bildern und Texten* (Universal Edition, Vienna, 1976).

BGA   *Ein Glück ohne Ruh': Die Briefe Gustav Mahlers an Alma*, ed. Henry-Louis de La Grange and Günther Weiss (Siedler, Berlin, 1995).

BME   Anna Bahr-Mildenburg, *Erinnerungen* (Wiener Literarische Anstalt, Vienna, 1921).

BMG   Ludwig Karpath, *Begegnung mit dem Genius* (Fiba, Vienna, 1934).

BMS   Paul Bekker, *Gustav Mahlers Sinfonien* (Schuster & Loeffler, Berlin, 1921).

BSP   Paul Stefan (ed.), *Gustav Mahler: Ein Bild seiner Persönlichkeit in Widmungen* (Piper, Munich, 1910).

BWB   Bruno Walter, *Briefe 1894–1962* (Fischer, Frankfurt, 1969). Trans. supervised by Lotte Walter Lindt (Knopf, New York, 1959).

BWM   Bruno Walter, *Gustav Mahler* (Reichner, Vienna, 1936).

BWT   Bruno Walter, *Thema und Variationen* (Fischer, Berlin, 1950). *Theme and Variations*, trans. James A. Galston (Knopf, New York, 1946).

DMM1   Donald Mitchell, *Gustav Mahler: The Early Years* (Rockliff, London, 1958). 2nd edn., rev. by Paul Banks and David Matthews (Faber, London, 1980).

DMM2   Donald Mitchell, *Gustav Mahler: The Wunderhorn Years* (Faber, London, 1975).

DMM3   Donald Mitchell, *Gustav Mahler: Songs and Symphonies of Life and Death* (Faber, London 1985).

DNM   Dika Newlin, *Bruckner, Mahler and Schoenberg* (King's Crown, Morningside Heights, New York, 1947).

EDM   Ernst Decsey, *Musik war sein Leben: Lebenserinnerungen* (Deutsch, Vienna, 1962).

EDS1   Ernst Decsey, *Stunden mit Mahler*, *Die Musik*, Berlin (Gustav Mahler-Heft), 10 (1911): 18, 352 ff.

EDS2   Ernst Decsey, *Stunden mit Mahler*, *Die Musik*, Berlin (Gustav Mahler-Heft), 10 (1911): 21, 143 ff.

EON   Ernst Otto Nodnagel, *Jenseits von Wagner und Liszt* (Ostpreussische Druckerei, Königsberg, 1902).

ESM   Erwin Stein, 'Mahler and the Vienna Opera', in Harold Rosenthal (ed.), *The Opera Bedside Book* (Gollancz, London, 1965).

EWL   Egon and Emmy Wellesz, *Egon Wellesz, Leben und Werk*, ed. Franz Endler (Zsolnay, Vienna, 1981).

FPM   Ferdinand Pfohl, *Gustav Mahler: Eindrücke und Erinnerungen aus den Hamburger Jahren*, ed. Knud Martner (Musikalienhandlung, Hamburg, 1973).

GAB   August Göllerich, *Anton Bruckner: Ein Lebens- und Schaffens-Bild*, ed. and completed by Max Auer (9 vols., Bosse, Regensburg, 1936).

GAM   Guido Adler, *Gustav Mahler* (Universal Edition, Vienna, 1st edn., 1911; 2nd edn., 1916).

GEM   Gabriel Engel, *Gustav Mahler, Song Symphonist* (Bruckner Society of America, New York, 1932).

GWO   Max Graf, *Die Wiener Oper* (Humboldt, Vienna, 1955).

HHS   Hans Heinz Stuckenschmidt, *Schönberg: Leben, Umwelt, Werk* (Atlantis, Zurich, 1974).

HFR   Hans Ferdinand Redlich, *Bruckner and Mahler* (Dent, London, 1955).

HMW   Hans Moldenhauer, *Anton von Webern: A Chronicle of his Life and Work* (Gollancz, London, 1978).

JFP   Josef Bohuslav Förster, *Der Pilger* (Artia, Prague, 1955).

JRM   Josef Reitler, '*Ein jugendlicher Mahler—Enthusiast*' and '*Gustav Mahler*'. Unpublished manuscripts obtained from Reitler's nephew, Frederick Reitler.

KIW   Julius Korngold, *Die Korngolds in Wien: Der Musikkritiker und das Wunderkind* (Musik & Theater, Zurich, 1991).

KMA   *The Mahler Album*, ed. Gilbert Kaplan (The Kaplan Foundation, New York, in association with Thames and Hudson Ltd., London, 1995).

KMO   Karl Maria Klob, *Musik und Oper: Kritische Gänge* (Heinrich Kerler, Ulm, 1953).

LEM   Max Graf, *Legende einer Musikstadt* (Österreichische Buchgemeinschaft, Vienna, 1949).

LKR   Liselotte Kitzwegerer, 'Alfred Roller als Bühnenbildner', Ph.D. thesis (Vienna, 1959).

LSM   Ludwig Schiedermair, *Gustav Mahler: Eine biographisch-kritische Würdigung* (Seemann Nachfolger, Leipzig, n.d. [1901]).

MAB   Max Auer, *Anton Bruckner: Sein Leben und Werk* (Musikwissenschaftlicher Verlag, Leipzig, 1941).

MAY   Zoltan Roman, *Gustav Mahler's American Years 1907–11* (Pendragon, Stuyvesant, New York, 1989).

MBR1   Gustav Mahler, *Briefe 1879–1911*, ed. Alma Mahler (Zsolnay, Vienna, 1924).

MBR2   Augmented and revised edn. of MBR1, ed. Herta Blaukopf (Zsolnay, Vienna-Hamburg, 1982).

MBRS   Gustav Mahler, *Unbekannte Briefe*, ed. Herta Blaukopf (Zsolnay, Vienna, 1983).

MFM   Friends of Music, *Gustav Mahler: The Composer, the Conductor and the Man*, appreciations by distinguished contemporary musicians, publ. on the occasion of the first performance of Mahler's Eighth Symphony in New York, 9 Apr. 1916.

MKB   Max Kalbeck, *Johannes Brahms* (8 vols. Deutsche Brahms Gesellschaft, Berlin, 1921).

MKW   Max Morold, *Wagners Kampf und Sieg* (2 vols. Amalthea, Zurich, 1930).

MMR   Max Mell, *Alfred Roller* (Wiener Literarische Anstalt, Vienna, 1922).

MSB   Gustav Mahler and Richard Strauss, *Briefwechsel 1888–1911*, ed. Herta Blaukopf (Piper Verlag, Munich, 1980).

NBL1   Natalie Bauer-Lechner, *Erinnerungen an Gustav Mahler*, ed. Johann Kilian (Tal, Leipzig, 1923).

NBL2   *Gustav Mahler, Erinnerungen von Natalie Bauer-Lechner*, ed. Herbert Killian, Anmerkungen und Erklärungen von Knud Martner (Wagner, Hamburg, 1984).

OKM   Otto Klemperer, *Meine Erinnerungen an Gustav Mahler* (Atlantis, Zurich, 1960).

OR   original.

PSE   Paul Stefan, *Gustav Mahler's Erbe* (Weber, Munich, 1908).

PSG   Paul Stefan, *Das Grab in Wien* (Reiss, Berlin, 1913).

PSM   Paul Stefan, *Gustav Mahler* (Piper, Munich, 1st edn., 1910; 2nd edn., 1912).

RBM   Alfred Roller, *Die Bildnisse von Gustav Mahler* (Tal, Leipzig, 1922).

RHM   Theodor Reik, *The Haunting Melody* (Farrar, Strauss & Young, New York, 1953).

RMA   Edward R. Reilly, *Gustav Mahler und Guido Adler: Zur Geschichte einer Freundschaft* (Universal Edition, Vienna, 1978). Engl. version: *Gustav Mahler and Guido Adler: Records of a Friendship* (Cambridge Univ. Press, Cambridge, 1982).

RMH   Reeser Eduard, *Gustav Mahler und Holland: Briefe* (Universal Edition, Vienna, 1980).

RSM1   Richard Specht, *Gustav Mahler* (Gosse und Tetzlaff, Berlin, n.d. [1905]).

RSM2   Richard Specht, *Gustav Mahler* (1st edn., illustr., Schuster & Loeffler, Berlin, 1913).

RWM   Arnold Schoenberg *et al.*, *Mahler* (Rainer Wunderlich, Leins, Tübingen, 1966).

SBE   Richard Strauss, *Briefe an die Eltern* (Atlantis, Zurich, 1954).

SWE   Paul Stauber, *Das wahre Erbe Mahlers* (Hubert & Lahme, Vienna, 1909).

SWO   Richard Specht, *Das Wiener Operntheater: Erinnerung aus 50 Jahren* (Knepler, Vienna, 1919).

TAF   Theodor Wiesengrund Adorno, *Quasi una fantasia*, Musikalische Schriften II (Suhrkamp, Frankfurt, 1963).

TAFe   Theodor Wiesengrund Adorno, *Quasi una fantasia: Essays of Modern Music* (Verso, London, 1992).

TAM — Theodor Wiesengrund Adorno, *Gustav Mahler: Eine musikalische Physiognomik* (Suhrkamp, Frankfurt, 1960).

TAMe — Theodor Wiesengrund Adorno, *Mahler: A Musical Physiognomy* (University of Chicago Press, Chicago, 1992).

THE — Theodor Helm, *Erinnerungen eines Musikkritikers*, ed. Max Schönherr (Verlag des Herausgebers, Vienna, 1977).

VKM — Vladimir Karbusicky, *Gustav Mahler und seine Umwelt* (Wissenschaftliche Buchgesellschaft, Darmstadt, 1978).

WKL — Wilhelm Kienzl, *Meine Lebenswanderung: Erlebtes und Erlauschtes* (Engelhorn, Stuttgart, 1926).

WLE — Felix Weingartner, *Lebens-Erinnerungen* (2 vols. Orell Füssli, Zurich, 1928–9).

WMW1 — Franz Willnauer, *Gustav Mahler und die Wiener Oper* (Jugend und Volk, Vienna, 1979).

WMW2 — Franz Willnauer, *Gustav Mahler und die Wiener Oper* (Löcker, Vienna, 1993).

WRE — William Ritter, *Études d'Art étranger* (Mercure de France, Paris, 1906).

Reference abbreviations for unpublished sources

AMS — Alma Mahler, 'Ein Leben mit Gustav Mahler' (Manuscript, BGM).

AMT — Alma Mahler, Tagebuch (Manuscript, UPL).

KMI — Knud Martner, personal communication to the author.

NBLS — Natalie Bauer-Lechner, *Mahleriana* (partly unpubl. manuscript, BGM).

Fidelio
First Performance of the Fifth Symphony
Second Journey to Holland
Mahler as Diplomat
The Third Symphony in Leipzig and Vienna

(August–December 1904)

> Oh! If only I could give my symphonies their first
> performances fifty years after my death! . . .

MAHLER'S summer holidays with his family in Maiernigg invariably ended with his returning alone to Vienna, leaving Alma and the children to enjoy further weeks away from the hustle and bustle of the capital. These separations always gave rise to a stream of letters or postcards from Mahler to Alma. There is no trace of such correspondence at the end of the summer of 1904. For once, therefore, Alma must have returned at the same time as her husband. He no doubt wanted to have her by his side while he was preparing two major events scheduled to take place in the early autumn—the new production of *Fidelio*, and the first performance of his Fifth Symphony in Cologne, rehearsals for which were to begin in Vienna. *Fidelio* was for Mahler the finest work in the entire repertory. He devoted all his strength and 're-creative' genius to this 'opera of operas', and had set the date of the première to coincide with the Emperor's name day celebrations on 4 October.

Alma watched the rehearsals from the director's box while Mahler and Roller dealt with every detail of the staging and lighting, both of which were even more elaborate and refined than those of the previous year's *Tristan*. After two years of operatic stage designing, Roller had now fully mastered the possibilities of integrating visual representation with the shifting moods and

episodes of the music. The new production, many aspects of which were
initially viewed as the height of audacity and modernism, was so often copied
round the world that it came to be regarded as another major event in the
history of opera production.[1] Several of its main, and at first most controversial
features, like the new positioning of the *Leonore* Overture No. 3 and the scene
change in the middle of the first act, established a new tradition.

For the first scenes, with their domestic, workaday character, Mahler and
Roller decided to provide a more intimate setting than that of the prison: they
showed the interior of the jailer's modest dwelling. The subsequent change of
scene to the prison courtyard thus fitted in perfectly with the change in the
style of the music which, in the middle of the first act, abandons the prosaic
Singspiel for the noble and tragic mood of *opera seria*. After the Overture,
therefore, the curtain rose on a little room with worn furnishings. A few details
emphasized the rustic atmosphere: a picture of a Madonna on the wall; a bunch
of flowers on a cabinet; an ironing board balanced across two chairs and piled
with linen; clothes over the stair rail. The setting was well suited to the domestic comedy scenes between Marzelline, Jaquino, and Rocco. Mahler, faithful
subscriber to the Romantic and optimistic view of human nature, simply cut
out Rocco's first-act aria in praise of gold, thus at a stroke speeding up the
action and making the old jailer's character less venal. To eliminate everything which undermined the essentially tragic character of the work, Mahler
gave the role of Marzellina to a lyric soprano, Berta Förster-Lauterer, rather
than to a light soprano as had usually been done before.[2] He also reduced
Jaquino's 'silly teasing' to a strict minimum.

The lighting, and with it the mood on stage, changed as soon as Leonore-
Fidelio entered. From the first note of the orchestral introduction to the quartet 'Mir ist so wunderbar', and on to the final note of the quartet itself, Mahler
had the four singers stand perfectly still, 'because, during that time, they all
have but one single thought which is expounded in glorious detail by the miracle of music. But each is thinking the thought to himself in his mind, which
means that any action, the slightest movement even, during that "moment of
thought", would be preposterous.'[3]

The contrast between Mahler's conception, based overridingly on expressiveness, and that of other conductor-directors became increasingly evident
after his departure from Vienna. When his successor, Felix Weingartner, came
to this episode in the first act and was told about the 'sacred stillness (*heilige*

---

[1] As early as Nov. 1903, when Mahler first approached the Intendant for the grant for the new production, he submitted Roller's estimate of 31,000 kronen (HOA, G.Z.X. 65.3878/1903). The painter had indicated at that time that he had prepared the estimate so carefully that there would be no significant increase.
In fact, the total was reduced to 26,400 kronen in June 1904 (ibid., G.Z.X. 37.2571/1904).

[2] JFP 698.

[3] Bernard Paumgartner, *Erinnerungen*, 64. The influence of the quartet in *Fidelio*, or rather of its
introductory bars, is clearly perceptible on the opening of the Adagio of Mahler's Fourth. The resemblance
goes much further than the tonality, or the writing for divided strings. One could almost construe the whole
movement as a huge development and amplification of these few bars of Beethoven's.

Stille)' Mahler had imposed on stage during the quartet, he said: 'What a strange idea. Such a long instrumental episode, the introduction and even more so the Quartet, need some action on the stage, or the audience will hardly be able to stand it!' To liven things up, Weingartner had Jaquino come in with a basket of laundry just before launching into his part in the canon.[4] In Mahler's staging, the four characters formed a trance-like tableau; the only 'action' was the ray of sunlight that fell through the bars of the ivy-covered window, illuminating the bouquet of flowers with a 'supernatural glow' from above.[5] Charged with meaning, like everything that happened on the stage in Mahler and Roller's productions, it seemed like 'a ray of hope', a presentiment of the opera's happy ending.

The scene change that followed immediately after the trio[6] remedied one of the worst improbabilities in Beethoven's final version of *Fidelio*: the ironing of the laundry in the vast prison courtyard. Beethoven had originally planned a break in his first version of the opera, *Leonore*.[7] The musical continuity was not broken, for the opening bars of the March served as an interlude. Nobody missed the soldiers parading up and down the stage pounding the floor at every step with their lances. When the curtain rose again, the spectator was confronted with a massive, dark, grey-blue picture, all uniforms, frock-coats, and three-cornered hats, setting off Pizarro's black old-style military habit, red coat, black three-cornered hat with its golden rosette, and military boots. While he sang his aria, the soldiers, not daring to move, stood watching and commenting on his words.

In the second scene, Roller tried to evoke 'all the formidable tyranny of the prisons of old Spain'. A surprisingly realistic massive tower dominated stage left. 'Pallid, chilly' daylight filled the courtyard, which looked as though it had been 'hollowed out of the high walls' surrounding it. The atmosphere was dank and suffocating. The great blocks of masonry, pierced by a scattering of barred windows, seemed designed as much 'to stifle groans and conceal dreadful tortures' as to prevent escape. Upstage at left centre a broad archway opened onto Rocco's quarters which were reached by a flight of steps leading up to a small door on the other side of the stage. More steps led to a massive iron door, secured by heavy lateral bars, the entrance to the dungeons. Upstage right, another flight of stairs led up to an even larger door, the prison's main entrance. Over the wall above it a glimpse of blue sky, a cypress, and a flowering vine bathed in sunlight contrasted with the sinister bleakness below. Everywhere prison guards in uniform marched mechanically back and forth.

The traditional staging required the chorus to emerge for no particular

---

[4]   See below, Vol. iiii, Chap. 2. Roller's long description in a letter to Mahler on 22 Jan. 1908 (AMM1, 421) of Weingartner's revival, which more or less did away with his predecessor's production.

[5]   According to Max Kalbeck. *Neues Wiener Tagblatt* (11 Oct. 1904).

[6]   Number 5 in the score.

[7]   This three-act version was performed for the first time on 20 Nov. 1805. The second act opened with the soldiers' march.

reason from the wings and group themselves in a semi-circle under full spotlights for the hushed mystery of the prisoners' chorus, 'O welche Lust'. They
then knelt as one man for the G major passage and rose to their feet for the
invocation to freedom. Mahler's innovation was to have them emerge slowly
from the dungeon through two small gaps between iron bars during the orchestral introduction. It was apparently Roller who wanted to have the prisoners
enter haltingly from those dark holes, one by one or in small groups, stumbling
'and feeling their way along the walls', 'poor miserable earthworms', 'blinded
by daylight and intoxicated by fresh air'.[8] Because the orchestral passage was
so brief and the doors narrow, Mahler decided that there was only enough time
for a double vocal quartet[9] or at the most a much reduced chorus to enter. The
new staging shocked the Opera staff, especially the chorus master who had
always used this most celebrated of bravura pieces to show off his singers,
assembled at maximum strength. When, in similar cases, people tried to
convince Mahler that he was in the wrong, they invariably invoked 'tradition'
to sway him, reportedly provoking one of his best known aphorisms: 'Tradition
ist Schlamperei' (tradition is sloppiness). Like many famous sayings, this one
was probably never uttered, at least not in this form. According to Ludwig
Karpath and Alfred Roller, Mahler's actual words on this occasion were: 'Was
Ihr Theaterleute Eure Tradition nennt, das ist nichts anderes als Eure
Bequemlichkeit und Schlamperei!' (What you theatre people call your tradition is nothing but your inertia and sloppiness!)[10] Actually Mahler had already
made similar pronouncements before the *Fidelio* rehearsals. In Hamburg, he
had said several times in the presence of Ferdinand Pfohl that 'Tradition nichts
anderes sei als Schlamperei' (Tradition is nothing else than sloppiness).[11]
'Beim Theater bedeutet die "Tradition" Schlamperei!' ('In the theatre, "tradition" means sloppiness') is also cited as one of his favourite expressions[12] in a
book published by Ernst Otto Nodnagel in 1902. Paul Stefan quoted still

---

[8]   Alfred Roller, quoted by Ludwig Karpath, BMG 126.
[9]   Here contemporary witnesses must have exaggerated, for it would seem impossible to do justice to
this powerful chorus with so few singers. Yet Roller, in a long letter to Mahler (AMMl, 421) quoted in Vol.
iiii, Chap. 2 notes that the chorus has been increased to forty under Weingartner, which indicates that it was
considerably less before.
[10] BMG 126 and *Musikblätter des Anbruch, Mahler Heft*, 2 (1920): 7/8, 273. Roller undoubtedly heard
Mahler say exactly this, since his version is practically identical with Karpath's.
[11] See above, Vol. i, Chap. 20.
[12] Justine Rosé's family believed that the authentic version of this bon mot was: 'Dies ist Tradition, dies
ist Schlamperei.' (This is tradition, this is sloppiness.) Strangely, the Berlin choral conductor Siegfried Ochs
claims in his memoirs *Geschehenes, Gesehenes* (Grethlein Leipzig, 1922, 354), that he was the inventor of the
famous phrase. He recalls a conversation he had with Mahler in 1906 concerning the première of the Eighth
Symphony. 'When he said to me in the course of conversation that the new work would overturn all previous
symphonic traditions, I replied: "Tradition ist Schlendrian" (tradition means the same old routine), a slogan
I had been proclaiming since the days of the Hochschule. Mahler liked it so much that he asked me to make
him a present of it. When I asked him what he meant, he assured me that he would spread the phrase
throughout the world, until everyone regarded it as self-evident. So I generously made his wish come true
and made him a present of the saying.' We need not give much credence to this strange tale, since Nodnagel
noted the phrase as early as 1902.

another version more likely to have been uttered in conversation than in the theatre: 'There is no such thing as tradition. There is only genius or stupidity'. (*Es gibt keine Tradition, nur Genius und Stupidität.*)[13]

Whatever words Mahler actually used, he and Roller successfully overcame the resistance of the Hofoper's traditionalists. According to some witnesses, the prisoners' appearance on stage made some of the audience 'shed tears'. At the end of the great crescendo, the prisoners lifted their arms toward the sky, symbol of the liberty they were invoking. The threatening silhouette of a sentry pacing the stage left wall made them lower their voices, and they ended in a barely audible murmur. Roller designed the first-act costumes with the utmost care. Instead of the usual knitted page's tunic the heroine wore trousers, a simple Sevillian peasant's blouse, gaiters, and a big plain brown waistcoat of the same cut as Jaquino's, though Jaquino's was embroidered in pink and mauve. Rocco, too, wore an ample waistcoat over a long greyish peasant smock and gaiters. Marzelline wore a dark blue Spanish dress with a pleated skirt patterned in red and gold, and a flowered apron. The prisoners were still wearing their former court clothes, but these were now mouldering and threadbare.[14] Florestan's coat, for example, was 'in the old style' with a broad belt, and, after the wear and tear of long months of captivity, 'practically falling off his back'.

For the underground vault in the second act, Mahler rejected Roller's original sketch which he found 'too spacious, too much like Nibelheim'. Roller, inspired by the engravings of Piranesi, had planned a large, dark prison with staircases, catwalks, and columns,[15] but the final project was far simpler: a huge natural vault or cistern which looked as if it 'had been formed by an earthquake'. To those who criticized its vast dimensions, Roller replied that it was meant to supply the whole fortress with water and that it was much more in keeping with the story of the opera than the spacious and brightly lit hall of the former production.[16] The cistern's roof was a crude rock face descending obliquely from stage-left to stage-right. No masonry was to be seen except the upstage staircase which led to a small barred door halfway up in the middle of the wall. Florestan's aria was sung in oppressive, almost total, darkness, which shocked some critics[17] who had earlier been scandalized by the dimly lit second act of *Tristan*. Many people, including some of Mahler's intimates,

---

[13] PSM 58.   [14] *Neue Musik-Zeitung*, 12: 4, 55.   [15] BMG 127.

[16] Alfred Roller, 'Die Fidelio Bühne', *Kunst und Volk*, Eine Festgabe der Kunststelle zur 1000. Theaterausführung (Leopold Heidrich, Vienna, 1923), 12–15.

[17] At the time of Mahler's death, Maximilian Muntz wrote an obituary that was critical of Mahler's achievements as Director of the Hofoper. He claimed that Roller had ordered quantities of black velvet to line the walls in the prison scene, but discovered during the first rehearsal that it completely absorbed the voices and the instruments. The article contains so many errors of fact (Mahler is credited with a son and daughter instead of two daughters) that nothing in it can be taken at face value. In fact it seems most likely that Roller did indeed achieve the oppressive and sinister atmosphere achieved in this scene thanks to the use of the black velvet he had already employed in *Tristan* (LKR 45).

apparently felt the same way. Berta Zuckerkandl recalled that Alma, for one, was convinced that 'one should be able to <u>see</u> the actors, otherwise the dramatic tension is destroyed'. Mahler sympathized with this point of view, but as usual where Roller was concerned, he pointed out that: 'I always defend my own ideas with the utmost conviction, and I would rather put up with being attacked than tie the hands of an artist who is currently responsible for a true renaissance of stagecraft.'[18] Thus in *Fidelio*, at the beginning of the second act, the huge cliff-like walls on stage-right and left of the stage were barely discernible in the dim light of a single oil lamp near the prisoner. Rocco's lantern started as a small pinpoint of light at the top of the stairs, projecting ghostly shadows on the roof of the vault. At the end of the first scene, after the duet 'O namenlose Freude', Mahler restored a passage of long-discarded spoken dialogue. Rocco comes to announce that the Minister has arrived with a list of prisoners to be summoned before him. Florestan's name is not included, since his imprisonment was an arbitrary act by Pizarro. Raising his arm, Rocco asks Leonore and Florestan to follow him up the steps; it is therefore to him they will owe their freedom. These words are immediately followed by the beginning of the great *Leonore* Overture No. 3, whose first G carries over naturally from the one in the final chord of the preceding duet.

Beethoven's powerful symphonic poem had usually been played before the first act, an ill-suited introduction to the comedy scenes that followed. Later Otto Nicolai inserted it between the acts, establishing a tradition which Hans Richter followed in 1875. Because the E major overture (*Fidelio*) is infinitely more appropriate to the light comedy of the opening scenes, and since the transition from the brilliant conclusion in major of *Leonore* No. 3 to the slow introduction in F minor of the prison scene was rather awkward,[19] Mahler decided to insert it on this occasion between the two scenes of the second act, where it provided a splendid introduction to the Finale. According to Berta Zuckerkandl, he justified this insertion to the orchestra musicians in the following words: 'From now on, gentlemen, we shall play the third *Leonore* Overture after the dungeon scene, because this work compresses the drama's whole gamut of emotions into a great climax. Only thus will the triumph of good over the forces of evil seem overwhelming.'[20] The composer Egon Wellesz, who

---

[18] Bernhard Paumgartner, *Erinnerungen*, 64.

[19] In Munich, Hermann Zumpe had for the same reason placed it at the very end of the work, as a sort of epilogue or symphonic postlude. Hermann Levi did the same, first in his Rotterdam production (1863), then in Munich and elsewhere.

[20] Berta Zuckerkandl, *Österreich intim*, 40. 'The overture is so great,' Mahler had explained to Natalie a few years earlier, 'that it contains in concentrated form the content of the entire work, so that it can only be there as a sort of epilogue, and nothing can follow it but the jubilant scene of the Finale. It's impossible to have the simple music of the first act starting up after the whole essence of the work has been expressed. It would be like finding oneself obliged, at the end of one's life, to start all over again from the beginning' (NBLS). However Mahler apparently failed to mention the main drawback for inserting the great overture between the two scenes of Act II, that the trumpet signal is heard twice, which is questionable both musically and dramaturgically (cf. *Internationale Mahler Gesellschaft, Nachrichten zu Mahler-Forschung* no. 19).

was soon to join Schoenberg's circle, suggested another reason why Mahler's innovation was a stroke of genius:

His interpretation of *Fidelio* turned a hitherto rarely performed work into the opera of operas. Anyone who has seen a production of *Fidelio* knows that the work reaches its dramatic conclusion with Florestan's release from the dungeon. The last scene simply enables us to share in the joy of those who have been freed and to witness the reward of the righteous and the punishment of the tyrant. It has always been a problem on the stage to transform the dungeon into the sunlit castle courtyard fast enough so that, after the curtain falls to hide the scene change, the applause, the lights and the inevitable chatter do not break the tension; otherwise the final scene would merely seem a friendly and almost conventional conclusion. Such considerations prompted Mahler's bold decision to start the opera with the short *Fidelio* Overture, which matches the mood of the first scene. After the dungeon scene, without allowing for a break, he inserted the third *Leonore* Overture, thereby allowing the spectator to relive all that he has just seen and heard, and, with the last bar of the overture, embarked on the final scene, which, with its choruses, followed the instrumental episode to become the culmination of the work. It is gratifying to note that today this version of *Fidelio* continues to be played in Vienna and elsewhere.[21]

In fact, Mahler's decision to insert the *Leonore* Overture in that position had another, more practical reason: Roller's set was so heavy and so complicated that getting it in place took the entire duration of the overture. Some critics were shocked, but many musicians agreed with Strauss in thinking that *Leonore* No. 3 'had finally found its rightful place', as Strauss put it after attending one of the Vienna performances of *Fidelio*:[22] 'No matter what prompted Mahler and Roller to do what they did, it was in any case exactly the right thing. The overture simply belongs where it is now and I would never again put it anywhere else.' History proved to be on Mahler's side; until lately, many opera houses still inserted the overture in the middle of the second act and no more appropriate place has yet been found for it in the opera.[23]

[21]   Egon Wellesz, 'Erinnerungen an Gustav Mahler und Arnold Schoenberg', *Urbis Musicae*, Tel Aviv, 1 (1971): 1, 72.   [22]   LKR 92.

[23]   According to Irvin Kolodin ('*The Great Fidelio Mystery*', programme note for the Metropolitan Opera, New York), the *Leonore* Overture No. 3 had already been placed between the two scenes of the second act of *Fidelio* in performances conducted by Anton Seidl at the Met in 1890, but it is not known which overture he played at the beginning of the work (see Harold Rosenthal and John Warrack, *The Oxford Dictionary of Opera* (Oxford University Press, Oxford, 1992) and Denis Arnold and Nigel Fortune (eds.), *The Beethoven Companion* (Faber & Faber, London, 1971)). At the time, Seidl published an article in the *Musical Courier* (subsequently quoted in the *New York Times*) justifying this insertion. Harold Rosenthal also discovered an account of a performance conducted in London in 1851 (at Her Majesty's Theatre) by the composer Michael William Balfe, with the great overture in the same place, although Covent Garden at that time usually placed it at the beginning of the second act. *The Oxford Dictionary of Opera* further notes that Carl Anschütz inserted the great overture in the middle of Act II in Amsterdam (Apr. 1849) and at Drury Lane in London (19 May 1849). It seems that in 1896 Walter Damrosch put it in the same place, rather than at the beginning of the second act as he was to do in 1900–1. From contemporary press reports, it is impossible to ascertain the placing of the *Leonore* Overture in Wagner's Zurich production of 1851. Mahler's example was followed by Otto Klemperer (Cologne, 1919), Richard Strauss (Vienna, 1920), and Arturo Toscanini (Milan, 1927), etc. Robert Hirschfeld notes in one of his articles that the violinist-composer Joseph Wasilewski also inserted the great overture in the middle of Act II in Bonn, in 1884.

Mahler always allowed plenty of time for applause after the Leonore–Florestan duet, but at the end of the overture he kept both arms raised in order to go directly into the orchestral introduction to the last scene. At one time he even considered cutting this introduction and moving straight from the overture's triumphant ending to the 'Heil sei dem Tag' chorus, but ultimately decided that he could not allow himself so great a liberty with regard to Beethoven's text.[24]

In his set for the Finale, Roller tried to symbolize 'the emergence from darkness into light' by designing a broad esplanade in front of the main gate of the prison, instead of the customary banal town square with the troops parading around the king's statue.[25] In the new set, a high, massive, crenellated rampart with an imposing baroque gateway rose at stage right; it has been described as 'ancient Egyptian in style' on account of its gently sloping wall, which distantly recalled the portals of the great temples of Luxor and Karnak. At the back of the set was a low crenellated rampart with cannon in the battlements. A terrace along it was reached by a few steps. Beyond there stretched as far the eye could see a vast resplendent plain where yellows and blues blended happily with the green of trees and meadows and the brilliant white of villages in the summer sun. In this way the painter evoked 'a free and happy life' so effectively that the backdrop seemed a further extension of the drama. Korngold said it was 'painted in C major'. The peasants wore blouses and the women brightly coloured dresses and aprons, and scarves about their heads. Don Fernando, the minister, wore a grey-blue court costume picked out in gold, a broad blue sash, lace sleeves, a flowered waistcoat, and an eighteenth-century white wig appropriate to the Age of Enlightenment, as opposed to Pizarro's 'old-style' seventeenth-century costume.

As with *Tristan* the year before, Roller's aim had been not only to 'design suitable décors'; but to make the drama come alive visually. Similarly, Mahler wanted to make it live for the ear. His overall musical interpretation, full of subtle nuance, had all the restraint and delicacy of chamber music. He created striking contrasts between the violence and cruelty embodied by Pizarro and the great hymn to freedom of the Finale. According to Erwin Stein, he

---

[24] BMG 127. According to Karpath, Mahler inveighed against the 'snobs' who answered the applause with boos and catcalls after Florestan's aria. In his opinion, 'time comes to a standstill during such an aria along with the drama. Then, the applause is justified since it relieves the tension. It is a liberating force which restores attention.' After Mahler's departure, Weingartner, anxious to assert his own personality, replaced the *Fidelio* Overture at the beginning of the opera with *Leonore* No. 2 and took out *Leonore* No. 3, thus making it impossible to use Roller's final set. 'Not that I blamed him,' he writes in his memoirs, 'but Beethoven was more important to me than a set!' (WLE, ii. 157, see below, Vol. iiii, Chap. 2). Wilhelm Furtwängler supported the insertion of the *Leonore* Overture No. 3 in the middle of the second act, and underlined the parallel thus created with Siegfried's Funeral March, which serves as an interlude between the two scenes of the third act of *Götterdämmerung* (Wilhelm Furtwängler, *Ton und Wort, Aufsätze und Vorträge* 1918–54, (Brockhaus, Wiesbaden, 1955), 173).

[25] It seems that the last scene had sometimes even been performed against the same set as Act I, scene ii, the prison courtyard.

did not try to smooth over, as is the usual practice, Beethoven's occasional oddities and abruptnesses, but made the music sound as strange as it is conceived. The purpose of Beethoven's many unexpected halts and sudden modulations was realised: they throw the drama into keen relief. To give one example of many, the motley *allegro molto* section of the first Finale, including Pizarro's furious entry and Rocco's apologetic stammer, was not only dramatically, but also musically plausible, because tempo and rhythms were not dictated by the bar lines, but by the music's dramatic sense which a sweeping *rubato* helped to secure.[26]

One day when he was rehearsing the orchestra in the gloomy last act Prelude, Mahler told them: 'These are sighs, these are groans (*Stöhnen*)'. Later on, in a passage of Florestan's aria ('Und die Ketten sind mein Lohn', And chains are my reward), he remarked to the second violins: 'That is really a picture—in music.'[27]

Although illness prevented her from taking part in the première of the new production, Mildenburg, in subsequent performances, 'lived' the part of Leonore with intense feeling and matchless sincerity. In a lecture she gave many years later, she provided a fascinating glimpse of the way Mahler behaved when dealing with talented singers. In the first scene of the second act he became very angry and upset because she and Hesch did not share his view of a certain passage in the dialogue.

We repeated the few words fifteen times without being able to please him; we were told we were without talent, intellectually lazy, indolent and spiritless, and of course, this did not help any . . . Finally he gave up, contemptuously averting his eyes from us. The rehearsal went on. Afterwards Hesch and I waited for him backstage because it seemed impossible for us to part in disagreement. At first we got a chilly reception, then we were shouted at but listened to—and five minutes later it turned out that actually the three of us had meant the same thing all along.[28]

Schmedes, as Florestan, never failed to move the audience. According to Erwin Stein, 'restraint imposed upon his heroic voice and appearance often brought his finest artistic instincts to the fore.' Hesch's 'black' voice gave breadth to the character of Rocco, while Weidemann brought to Pizarro the inexhaustible resources of his dark voice and 'demonic expression', making this character 'not a bloodstained, eye-rolling tyrant, but a courtier intoxicated with ambition to the point where he would use any means to satisfy it'. In this role, his 'sombre and authoritative voice, swollen with fury, lost its beautiful sonority and attained a raging power'.[29] Mayr, as the Minister, was the very incarnation of goodness and justice.[30]

[26]   ESM, in *Opera Bedside Book*, 310.   [27]   BMG 127.

[28]   Anna von Mildenburg, unpublished manuscript of a lecture given in 1946 (Library of the Performing Arts, Lincoln Center, New York).

[29]   Richard Specht, 'Friedrich Weidemann', *Die Schaubühne*, 3 (1907): 24, 597.

[30]   According to Erwin Stein cast changes later introduced by Weingartner weakened the production's dramatic tension. The phlegmatic Demuth replaced Weidemann as Pizarro, Weidemann being given the part

As usual, the days leading up to the première were marked by quarrels and tensions. During one of the final rehearsals, Weidemann came forward almost to the orchestra pit to sing his great aria with such a troubled expression that Mahler interrupted the orchestra to ask him: 'My dear Herr Weidemann! Why do you look so worried and upset? Are you the Director of the Opera?' Mildenburg was much admired by all during the final rehearsals but she 'caught a cold' and reported sick the day before the première. Mahler reminded her that the performance was to be given in honour of the Emperor's name day, and she agreed to appear in spite of her sore throat. But for once perhaps her illness was genuine, because at about four o'clock that afternoon her doctor decided that she was in no condition to go on. As Sophie Sedlmair was also indisposed and Lucie Weidt not yet up to the role, Mahler had to resign himself at the last moment to delaying the performance for three days, even though the gala had been in preparation for several months. Embarrassing scenes occurred in the foyer, with opera-goers in evening dress vainly demanding their money back. But the majority of the audience only found out about the change of programme when Bruno Walter mounted the podium instead of Mahler, and launched into the 'majestic sounds' of the overture to Goldmark's *Die Königin von Saba*. The next day, rumour had it in the salons of Vienna that Mildenburg was not really indisposed, but 'had not felt quite ready'. It was also suggested that Sophie Sedlmair had refused to sing solely because she resented being a stand-in. Whatever the real reason for Mildenburg's absence, the première was postponed until 7 October, when Lucie Weidt sang the title role. Those must have been three harrowing days for Mahler!

The production had an even better reception than the *Tristan* of the year before, but here and there it aroused similar indignation because of its new and revolutionary features. As usual, Robert Hirschfeld savagely attacked 'this fresh sacrilege', this 'furious determination' to do something new at any price. He felt that Beethoven's spirit was 'still alive' in Vienna, and that 'one did not have the right to make mistakes like these'. He denounced as scandalous the self-centred urge merely 'to be different, to see differently, to interpret differently. . . . Now begins the analysis of sound, a modern activity that owes its origins to science. One hears how Beethoven's storms are made up of small particles of wind, how note upon note combine in the master's melodic arch, one can count the scale steps of every run . . .'. The exaggerated staccatos resulted in a kind of 'musical goose-step'. The precision thus obtained belonged to the realm 'of the machine' and 'not to art'. Under Mahler's baton,

of Don Fernando. The role of Rocco was given to the amiable Mayr (see below Vol. iiii, Chap. 2). The principal sources concerning Mahler's new production of *Fidelio* are articles by Oskar Bie (BSP 30 ff.) and Erwin Stein (ESM); a pamphlet by Paul Stefan (SME 35 ff.); and the books by Paul Stefan (PSM 72 ff.) and Richard Specht (RSM2, 140 ff.). Other details are provided by American newspaper accounts of 1908, when Roller's sets were taken over to the United States (*New York Herald Tribune*, 21 May, *Boston Evening Transcript*, 3 Apr.).

Beethoven's music was reduced to 'a rustling murmur': 'the sounds seem to come fluttering gently from individual desks'. The orchestra was shrouded in a 'silken veil', the chorus uttered 'almost inaudible whispers' and the score became 'no more than an accompaniment to spasmodic miming'. 'Each note of this *Fidelio* is imbued with Mahler's spirit, a Mahlerian chiaroscuro atmosphere quivers throughout the work.' Mahler's touch shrouded and muffled much of the work, so that what remained was 'essentially a personal work of art (*Sonderkunstwerk*) by Mahler based on Beethoven'. What would happen if this production were entrusted to someone else? As Mahler was inimitable, the result would be the same as with *Die Meistersinger:* it would become a caricature.

As for the sets, Hirschfeld acknowledged that Roller had attempted and often succeeded 'in accentuating and deepening' the various moods in *Fidelio*. Despite this, he found that Roller's contribution to the new production attracted far too much attention at the music's expense. In *Fidelio* the music 'is not continually derived from the stage nor formed by it'. This striving 'to reconstruct a musical drama posthumously' and to give visual expression to 'the mood of Beethoven's music' was 'embarrassing and painful'. Since Hirschfeld always listened to the first act quartet with his eyes closed,[31] he simply refused to believe 'that a ray of light' had fallen on to the stage. Furthermore, there should not be a change of scene in the middle of the act since this only underlined a weakness already inherent in the work. As for the new place chosen for the *Leonore* Overture No. 3, which was, he conceded, magnificently played, he thought it quite inappropriate.

Hirschfeld's persistently negative attitude and evident desire to denigrate Mahler make it difficult to take most of his criticisms seriously. The only other critic who was so persistently hostile was Maximilian Muntz, who at least had the excuse that he worked for an anti-Semitic paper. Like Hirschfeld, he said that *Fidelio* had undergone 'an extensive revision along Mahlerian lines'. Mahler, 'for all his inventiveness', had in the end betrayed the spirit of Beethoven. Muntz was particularly critical of the darkness in Florestan's cell (although in fact it is called for in the libretto and suggested by the music). He also felt there had been errors in casting: Lucy Weidt lacked the heroism so indispensable to the title role, Hesch's characterization of Rocco was in itself 'a mistake', and Förster-Lauterer wasn't 'naive enough' for the part of Marzelline. In the *Allgemeine Zeitung*, Gustav Schönaich called *Fidelio* a flawed work, a series of set pieces rather than a well-constructed opera. In his opinion, Roller's 'fertile imagination and intellectual energy' had come up with both marvels and excesses, like the 'unprecedented darkness', which made the plot seem to unfold 'in a tunnel'.

On the other hand, Max Kalbeck, though essentially a conservative,

---

[31] Can one really blame Mahler and Roller for having put on a production for theatregoers who prefer to keep their eyes open?

lavished praise on the new production. For him clarity was the highest virtue of a musical performance. He preferred those interpreters whose 'didactic energy revealed the authentic or imagined aims of a work of art' and who, 'without misrepresentation or distortion, can reveal the work with total objectivity in its true light, with the purity and immediacy it possessed when it left the hands of its creator'. He thought the 'revival' of *Fidelio* was just such an achievement, a work of 'clarification and enlightenment (*Klärung und Aufklärung*)' in which Mahler 'at one fell swoop had banished entrenched errors and ageing prejudices', and done away with the sloppiness that had previously gone by the name of tradition'. He had shed light on the peculiar nature of the work, which even its admirers had underrated. Kalbeck approved almost all Mahler's innovations; the scene change in the first act, the placing of the grand overture in the middle of the last act, and especially the immobility of the characters and the ray of sunlight during the quartet, which linked this musical episode with the work's basic concept, anticipating not only the light which later illuminated the prisoner's cell but also the drama's happy outcome. Every scenic and musical detail contributed toward the success of the whole. The chorus and the orchestra obeyed Mahler's every gesture, and the singers surpassed themselves to meet his demands.[32] In Kalbeck's opinion, Mahler deserved the gratitude of the Viennese public for 'having brought Beethoven's spiritualized music from its gleaming heavenly heights down through the colourful haze of our atmosphere to the blossoming earth'. In Roller's sets, that earth 'breathes love' and the air 'drinks freedom', his horizon 'stretches to eternity', 'because Beethoven leads him on, and he Beethoven'.

Julius Korngold, in the *Neue Freie Presse*, voiced certain reservations about the staging which he felt played too prominent a role in the production. Nevertheless he praised it for its expressiveness, which matched Beethoven's music. Inspired by Appia, Roller had developed the stage set into another element of art, which was to 'enter into a symbolic relationship with the two other moodmaking elements (*Stimmungselemente*), action and music'. He had 'rendered Beethoven in terms of painting', bringing, as it were, 'additional trombones or flutes onto the stage'. The first-act scene change was perhaps debatable. Mahler might have tried too hard to interpret 'a score that is inwardly dramatic rather than conceived for visual presentation on the stage'. And perhaps voices with the right singing technique (*Gesangskunst*) for this idiosyncratic German opera did not exist. Korngold admitted that all these points could be argued, but felt that the score of *Fidelio* had never been better performed or interpreted in Vienna, with the possible exception of the two finales, in which Mahler had somewhat 'restrained and fragmented the powerful flow' of the music. His genius 'had completely absorbed the hallowed

---

[32] Kalbeck informed his readers that Schmedes had had to lower the key of his aria from A flat to G flat, and that 'not one of the singers overacted, not even Weidemann'.

score', and everywhere enhanced the dramatic element.[33] Each bar was proof of his incredible mastery, particularly in the quartet (whispered rather than sung), the prisoners' chorus, and the Rocco–Leonore duet. The importance of the production went far beyond momentary 'sensation'. It could already be included among the most precious treasures of the Vienna Opera.

In *Die Zeit*, Richard Wallaschek praised Roller's 'four poetic and evocative sets', whose visual beauty did not set out to seduce but was firmly subordinated by him to the essence of the music. Although he did not approve of the new positioning of the big overture, Wallaschek conceded that its effectiveness silenced all arguments. Max Graf, on the other hand, like many of his colleagues, felt that Mahler had turned Beethoven into 'Wagner's precursor' and transformed *Fidelio* into a 'music drama'. 'At this point,' he said, a 'Romantic semi-darkness' reigned rather than 'the full light of classic feeling'. Thus, the score's slightest measure, the libretto's slightest word revealed the work's 'dramatic soul'. Everything combined to support the drama: the sets, the lighting, and the costumes. Mahler wanted 'the stage to dominate and the music to serve it'. Most of his innovations were valid. Perhaps the work had been sung by more glorious voices, but never had it been so imbued musically and dramatically with life.[34]

In the Austrian and German music journals opinions ranged from indignation to wonder. For Max Vancsa, critic of the *Neue Musikalische Presse*, who liked to consider himself 'modern', it was horror which predominated in the face of such an 'insult to tradition', an 'improvement' of Beethoven's work. He disliked and condemned all the innovations, including the change of scene in the first act and above all the insertion of the *Leonore* Overture in the middle of the second, which seemed to him a 'barbaric' idea. Certainly Mahler was right to underline the intimate aspect of the work, certainly he had created some moments of real magic, like the first-act quartet, but he was wrong to tone down Pizarro's wickedness and Marzelline's and Jaquino's gaiety, and to make of Rocco a lachrymose old man. Vancsa considered that every one of the roles had been miscast. But above all, Mahler and Roller had blundered in creating so much visual beauty for such an inward-looking work. In the *Neue Musik-Zeitung*, Armin Friedmann took a similar view. Mahler's penetrating mind had revealed hitherto unsuspected refinements; but everything which in Beethoven was great, simple, and modest had here become 'complicated and confused'. 'Each ray of Beethoven's genius, traversing the prism of Mahler's artistic sensibility, is refracted into the colours of its spectrum.' In this *Fidelio*, everything was 'veiled, covert, attenuated'. 'All dynamism was held back until the final jubilation in light and freedom.' All in all, the old *Fidelio* was 'much stronger and more profound'. In the same journal, another article went so far as to

---

[33] Korngold stressed the efforts undertaken to improve the singers' diction in the spoken dialogue.

[34] The cast for the 7 Oct. performance: Förster-Lauterer (Marzelline); Weidt (Leonore); Schmedes (Florestan); Maikl (Jaquino); Weidemann (Pizarro); Mayr (Don Fernando); Hesch (Rocco).

suggest that there was a fundamental contradiction between the work and its presentation.[35]

Fortunately there were also a great number of forward-looking Viennese who admired and supported the revolution brought about by the Secession in opera production. When Roller left the Vienna Opera in 1909, Richard Specht summed up the revelation that this 'Secessionist' *Fidelio* had been for him and for so many others in the following words:

all the pain of enslaved, groaning humanity, a helpless prey to the cruelty of the mighty, cries out—or, as I must now unfortunately write, cried out—from this frightful prison yard with its black, dank, massive walls—into whose gloom Pizarro's scarlet robe erupted like a brutal fanfare—its mean, heavily barred vents and gloomy, sunless atmosphere pitilessly shutting out all light, air and joy. And at the end, all longing, all pent-up joy, streaming toward the light through the dark gates, was embodied in the bright ramparts, the jubilant daylight, the bright heaven and the broad, endless view over the sun-filled plain. To destroy this picture and limit the scene again to the prison yard means simply to go back to the 'opera finale' which the words of the libretto express. Whereas Beethoven's music reaches out far beyond those words. In his music we can hear all the joy of freedom, the all-embracing love that knows no barriers and liberates from shameful bondage. And that is exactly what the stage setting expresses, with an incomparable strength and clarity which have nothing to do with theatrical convention.[36]

In a long article later included in *Buch der Jugend*, Hermann Bahr, the Secession's most influential theorist, emphasized what he considered to be the greatest merit of Roller's work, a merit which some seemed determined not to recognize: the beauty he created was 'significant', at its peak it 'reinforced dramatic expression', it was 'modelled in conformity with the essence of the drama'. After a long series of more or less successful experiments thanks to Adolphe Appia, Gordon Craig, Josef Olbrich, Peter Behrens, and Max Reinhardt, 'the problem of theatre design is solved'. To end his article, Bahr first used the phrase which for him best characterized Roller's theatrical work: 'stage design as expression'.[37]

Confident that he had achieved one of the most outstanding triumphs in his entire operatic career, Mahler left Vienna on 12 October for Cologne to wage a far more hazardous battle: the launching of a new gigantic symphony, the first in fifteen years in which he had not relied on the direct appeal of the human voice. With his Fifth, Mahler had everything to fear. He knew that none of his previous works had ever been understood when it was first performed. This time, he had waited two years and had chosen Cologne, where the orchestra was excellent and the audiences appeared to be particularly interested in both him and his work. But had he chosen well? True, no one thought of him any

[35] *Neue Musik-Zeitung*, Stuttgart, 26 (1904): 3, 55 ff.

[36] Richard Specht, 'Rollers Scheiden', *Die Schaubühne*, 5 (1908–9): 3, 73.

[37] Hermann Bahr, 'Fidelio. December 1904', in *Buch der Jugend* (Hellen, Wien, 1908), 19.

more as an obscure composer of *Kapellmeistermusik*. In the preceding two years, his earlier symphonies had won over a large public, and also a small number of faithful admirers in the ranks of his profession. What would those who had 'digested' the first four symphonies think of the more abstract Fifth, and its richer, denser polyphony? Not long after the première of the Fifth, Mahler wrote to Specht: 'In spite of sporadic successes (which I owe perhaps simply to incidental and external circumstances) it seems to me that a long, hard road still lies before my works, and perhaps even more so before my future works.'[38]

There was another source of concern: for the first time in Mahler's life he had doubts and misgivings concerning the orchestration of his new work. As usual he had planned a reading rehearsal with the Vienna Philharmonic, but had in this case asked for two. That the musicians should have agreed to play for him is somewhat surprising in view of the spectacular break which had occurred between Mahler and the orchestra a year earlier. It was during a general meeting which took place on 16 September 1904 that Arnold Rosé had submitted a request 'that Herr Direktor Mahler be allowed two rehearsals of his Fifth Symphony, which is soon to be published and which will be performed in Cologne in October, and which for these reasons he would like to hear in advance. Naturally these services would be remunerated . . .'. Nobody having asked permission to speak, the flautist Alois Markl declared in the name of the Committee that the musicians granted Herr Direktor's request, that he was free to invite the musicians he wished, and that they had agreed to play the rehearsals without fee.[39]

The two rehearsals took place on 17 and 26 September. Shortly before the first, the Czech composer Josef Bohuslav Förster visited Mahler at the Opera.[40] Mahler was not in his office, so Förster sat down at the piano and improvised for several minutes. Without his intending it, a theme from the Fifth Symphony, the score of which Mahler had just sent him, found its way into his improvisation. The door burst open and Mahler, without even greeting him, said: 'What do you think you're playing? That's the opening of my new symphony!' A moment later, having read the facts of the matter in the eyes of his old friend, he was laughing heartily. A few days later, Förster received from Mahler the following card: 'Tomorrow, at nine o'clock, I rehearse the Fifth Symphony in the Tonkünstlersaal. Greetings.' Score in hand, Förster went to the rehearsal and sat down after greeting Schoenberg and Zemlinsky. When Mahler appeared, Förster waved to him. Mahler saw him open his score, and called

---

[38] MBR1, no. 238; MBR2, no. 336.

[39] HOA, GZ. 150/1904. See Clemens Hellsberg, *Demokratie der Könige, Die Geschichte der Wiener Philharmoniker* (Schweizer Verlagshaus, Zurich, 1992), 317.

[40] JFP 696. Förster relates that the incident took place when he came to take leave of Mahler before the summer holidays. However his memory fails him, for the score of the new symphony was not published until Sept. At that time Förster was the Viennese correspondent for several foreign papers and it was normal that Mahler should have sent him one of the first copies of the miniature score.

him over to tell him that he had already changed his orchestration and would soon be sending him the new version. During the rehearsal, Förster observed that he was continually making further changes.[41]

Besides Förster, who was an invited guest, another listener attended the reading incognito: Ludwig Karpath, who that evening wrote to Theobald Pollak the following lively account of his experiences:

Think what I did today: I furtively slipped into the Musikvereinssaal to hear the Fifth. I was almost caught, because the orchestra was seated near the entrance to the hall, which was something I hadn't known about. I therefore had to revise all my original plans and try to get to the organ without being seen, something I luckily managed to do. But every trespasser must pay for his sins, and so I completely spoiled my coat by sitting down on a freshly painted step, where I remained stuck. I no sooner thought myself in safety than Mahler requested the orchestra to change its seating. I thought the gentlemen were going to come up to the organ and dislodge me from my hiding place. But again my guardian angel was watching, for they didn't come all the way up and in the end I was able to sit there completely undisturbed. I don't think anyone saw me. The symphony lasted exactly an hour and a half. That is the actual playing time, without any pauses. It is clear; without any artifice. Of course that applies only to modern ears. But even the 'older ones' will hardly be able to complain of extravagances. I haven't the time at the moment to go into detail, I'd like to say only one thing: in the symphony there is an Adagio, in F major (I don't think I'm mistaken about the key) for strings only, and it is one of the most beautiful things I have ever heard in my life. It's not only the beauty of the sound that captivates, but more the tender intimacy (*Innigkeit*) of a great melody that really has no end and that simply overwhelms you. So full of sweetness, exaltation and nostalgia that tears poured from my eyes. I've no reason to be ashamed of them, especially as no one saw them. Please keep this to yourself, too.[42]

Apparently, Karpath did not notice any weakness in the orchestration of the Fifth, unlike another listener more discreetly seated on the balcony:

I, who had heard all the melodies as I copied them, could no longer hear them, because Mahler had assigned so much importance to the percussion and the snare-drum that one recognized little except the rhythm. I ran home, crying aloud. He followed me. For some time I couldn't even speak. Then, at last, sobbing, I said: 'You have written a symphony for percussion'. He laughed, then took up the score and crossed out with a red pencil most of the snare-drum part and almost half the percussion. He already knew it himself, but my passionate pleading clinched the matter. The completely altered score is still in my possession.[43]

---

[41]   JFP 696. According to Förster, Nedbal had a similar experience when he planned to conduct the Third in Prague. Knowing that Mahler was never satisfied with his scores, he came to him to ask which one to use. Mahler ended up by lending him his own, in which 'scarcely ten pages stood uncorrected'. This must refer to the performance of the Second Symphony in Dec. 1903, since Nedbal never conducted the Third in Prague during Mahler's lifetime. Fritz Stiedry, whose career later took him to the USA and the Metropolitan Opera, recalled the rehearsals with the Vienna Philharmonic, in which, still a music student, he played the triangle (see below, Chap. 5).

[42]   Letter from Karpath to Pollack, dated 24 Sept. 1904, Schweizerische Nationalbibliothek, Berne.

[43]   AMM1, 95; AMM2, 100.

Alma, as usual, exaggerates somewhat. How could Mahler possibly have written such an all-important part for the snare-drum, only to cut it out later in one go? She is right, though, in claiming that the Fifth's orchestration underwent extensive revisions before and even after the first performance. Bruno Walter later claimed that most of the money advanced to Mahler by his new publisher, Peters, went towards the engraving of the new plates.[44] Strange as it may seem, the letters written by Mahler to his publisher, Henri Hinrichsen, do not confirm either Alma's or Bruno Walter's assertions. Throughout this correspondence, Mahler shows himself to be extremely meticulous with regard to detail. He even goes so far as to request three different sets of proofs for the orchestral score and the piano transcriptions. Yet the only passages that mention revisions were written in September, immediately after the reading rehearsal with the Vienna Philharmonic: 'I found the percussion rather overloaded, which would have been to the detriment of the general effect', then, later: 'I am very sorry to give you all this extra trouble, but in a work which is so polyphonic it is impossible to foresee everything down to the last detail . . .' To Fritz Steinbach, who was already rehearsing the Fifth in Cologne, Mahler wrote in almost identical terms: 'I've just played through my work and made a number of small changes. In particular I have decided that the percussion is overloaded, and that the whole thing lacks the desired clarity. I hope that you too will be content.'[45]

Nor do Mahler's letters written after the première suggest that he had made such extensive changes. On 1 November 1904, he wrote to Hinrichsen: 'Now that everything is done, down to the last detail, we can hand over the work to the "world". We both have the time and patience to wait and see what it will make of it . . .' Neither here nor anywhere else is there any allusion to changes being made to the engraved score. It is true that that the publisher's replies have disappeared, but it is difficult to imagine anything that would greatly alter the existing picture.[46]

The fact that Mahler had so easily found a new publisher for the Fifth and that he had obtained 15,000 marks instead of the 10,000 he had originally intended to ask for suffice to show that he was now considered one of the major composers of his time. Another proof of his changed status was that he and his works were now the subject of several critical studies. The first of these was by

[44] BWT 170. Mahler did not behave in this way with all his scores. In Oct. 1904, he sent Mengelberg a score of the Fourth in which he had just marked important changes in red ink. In an article on Mahler which was published in 1936, Walter states that Mahler 'returned to the publisher' the whole of the 15,000 marks he had received, so that the score of the Fifth could be re-engraved with the new instrumentation.

[45] Undated letter to Fritz Steinbach (end of Sept. 1904), Library of Congress, Washington, DC.

[46] Concerning the autograph score of the Fifth Symphony and other versions of the score, see above, Vol. ii, Appendix 2, and Erwin Ratz's introduction to the critical edition of 1964. The catalogue of the Düsseldorf Mahler Exhibition (1979–80, Arno Volk Verlag, Cologne, 1979) reproduces two pages of the orchestral score and one from the second violin part which belonged to Bruno Walter. The orchestration here is lightened by the removal of the horn parts and by rests in the second violins (Abb. No. 25 to 27). The bassoon part of this same score was sold by Stargardt in 1981.

Ludwig Schiedermair, a young musicologist who later gained considerable renown as the editor of Mozart's letters and was the founder of the Beethoven Archives in Bonn. Entitled simply *Gustav Mahler: Eine biographisch-kritische Würdigung* (a biographical and critical appreciation), it was published in Leipzig in 1901.[47] It is brief (only 38 pages) and relatively superficial, but Schiedermair should be given credit for being the first critic to write and publish a monograph on Mahler and his music. After retracing the main steps of his conducting career, he lists his early works and quotes the well-known condemnation of 'programmes', pronounced at a banquet after the Munich première of his Second Symphony.[48] Schiedermair then very briefly analyses the works so far published, Symphonies 1 to 3 and *Das klagende Lied*. His comments on the symphonies are brief and superficial. Mahler felt obliged to ask him to correct one of his most glaring errors concerning the 'programme' of the Third Symphony, which Schiedermair described as 'a purification of the soul, following struggles, renunciation and suffering, and ending in victory and a positive view of life *(Daseinsbejahung)*'. In a letter addressed to Bernard Schuster, the director of the Berlin review *Die Musik*,[49] Mahler deplores the fact that his most enthusiastic followers were often the least enlightened:

As for Sch[iedermair], who is evidently well intentioned and whom I certainly wouldn't like to denounce, I must tell you that I can't read his trite and quite uncomprehending attempts to flatter me without feeling furious. My God, many people praise me to the skies—but I have yet to read one reasonable word about myself. Never anything but high-sounding, nebulous, self-indulgent outpourings. My natural reaction is the same as for hate and mockery—simply to ignore it. For I am profoundly convinced that great effects take time to emerge, they quietly go on maturing. What Schiedermair [has written] about my First Symphony is as lacking in understanding as the witticisms of the Berlin critics. Just to give you one example—the third movement which he finds so overwhelmingly cheerful is <u>heart-rending</u>, <u>tragic irony</u>, and is [to be understood] as exposition and preparation for the sudden outburst of despair in the last movement— a deeply wounded and broken heart.

Schiedermair's comments on another of his works (the Third, no doubt) 'made my hair stand on end' and Mahler concludes: 'I would have preferred not to have to bother about such things, to have confidence in my interpreters

[47] The publisher was Hermann Seemann and the publication bears no date (it appeared in 1901). Ludwig Schiedermair (1876–1957) was born in Regensburg and studied German philology in Munich, where he also studied musicology with Adolf Sandberger. A pupil of Hugo Riemann in Leipzig and Hermann Kretschmar in Berlin, he wrote an extensive thesis on Giovanni Simone Mayr for Marburg University in 1906. He later settled in Bonn, where he directed the Musicological Seminar at the University. Mahler corresponded with him in 1900 on the subject of the Fourth (see above, Vol. ii, Chap. 9). And he wrote to him, doubtless in 1904, announcing the publication of the Fifth (BSM, Munich, sign. 8006a). Schiedermair also wrote an article on Mahler in the *Neue Zeitschrift für Musik* of 10 May 1905, as part of a series about 'contemporary composers' (see below, Chap. 4).

[48] In *Musikalische Begegnungen* (Staufen, Cologne, 1948), Schiedermair also recalls Mahler's famous public declaration at the Parkhotel in Munich, and quotes passages from letters he received from him at the time.

[49] RSM2, 37

(*Mittler*), and simply go on composing'.[50] This feeling of isolation which Mahler got from the undiscerning praise of people like Schiedermair is touchingly expressed in a letter he wrote to the German composer Ernest Bloch, who had been present at the rehearsals and performance of the Second Symphony at Basle in 1903:

My dear Herr Bloch, Your letter really gladdened my heart. Please don't think that I am insensitive to such warm-hearted approval, or to the refined way in which it is expressed. I live in the world like a stranger, it's seldom that the voice of someone who thinks as I do reaches my ears. How could I not be moved by such intimate under-standing and generous sympathy? If you think it would be proper and useful to express in public your opinion of me and my work, I would be delighted. For I cannot see why the right to write about me in newspapers should be reserved only for people who don't understand me and know nothing about me.[51]

A year later, in 1902, the *Münchner Neueste Nachrichten* music critic, Arthur Seidl, published a short book called *Moderne Dirigenten* (Modern Conductors) in which four pages are devoted to Mahler, his conducting and his compositions. His much publicized 'dictatorial' character and his perfection-ism are mentioned (with examples), but later, Seidl praises his 'wonderful imagination (*geniale Phantasie*)' as a composer.[52] The same year, Ernst Otto Nodnagel, the former *Berliner Tageblatt* critic, 'the inevitable Nodnagel' as Mahler called him, who had moved to Königsberg in East Prussia, published a book of 'Profiles and Perspectives' called *Jenseits von Wagner und Liszt* which contains two whole chapters about Mahler (about 25 pages).[53] He recalled

[50] Mahler does not actually refer to Schiedermair by name at this point, although he may have done so in the original letter, which has for the time being disappeared. Specht only gives the first three letters (Sch) of the name, but this can only mean Schiedermair since, in his analysis of the third movement of the First Symphony, written later, he wrote: 'And yet, what humour gladdens us here!' (*Mahlers Symphonien*, ed. Edgar Istel, 17) Schiedermair's analysis of the Third is given in the same collection (ibid. 54 seq.), but the sentence Mahler reproached him with is not there, no doubt because he had corrected the first version of his text.

[51] Letter from Mahler to Ernest Bloch (undated, summer 1903, Ernest Bloch Society Bulletin, no. 10, 1977). Bloch also possessed a postcard written in Maiernigg in Aug. 1904, in which Mahler informs him of the first hearing of the Fifth in Cologne (Suzanne Bloch Bulletin). Ernest Bloch (1880–1959), born in Geneva, was a pupil of Émile Jaques Dalcroze. He completed his studies in Frankfurt and Munich, where he took lessons with Ludwig Thuille, and in Paris. Returning to Switzerland, he conducted concerts there and lectured at the Geneva Conservatory (1911–15). At the end of the First World War he moved to the United States, where he taught at the Mannes School of Music and conducted concerts. He acquired US nationality in 1924. Bloch directed first the Cleveland Institute of Music (1920–5) and then the San Francisco Conservatory (1925–30) and later taught at the University of California. His best-known works are *Schelomo* (1916); the *Concerto Grosso* No. 1 for strings and piano (1925) and the opera *Macbeth*.

[52] For biographical information on Arthur Seidl, see above, Vol. i, Chap. 23. Seidl also lectured on Mahler and published another article about him in 1904 in the first edition of *Der Moderne Geist in der Deutschen Tonkunst* (The Modern Spirit in German Music).

[53] Ernst Otto Nodnagel (1870–1909), writer and Lieder singer, born in Berlin, studied law and music in Heidelberg (under Philipp Wolfrum). He later attended the Königliche Hochschule in Berlin and started writing for the *Berliner Tageblatt* in the early 1890s. In 1899 he moved to Königsberg where he remained for four years, reviewing and teaching singing at the Conservatory. He was also active as a composer (symphonic works, orchestra/Lieder, etc.) and wrote a number of books, including a novel, and essays (on Max von Schillings, Arnold Mendelssohn, Mahler, and others).

having received his first revelation of the music in 1894 when he attended the disastrous third performance of the First Symphony at the Allgemeiner Deutscher Musikverein festival in Weimar. He told the detailed story of the subsequent Berlin performances of the three early symphonies, took his colleagues of the Berlin press to task for their vicious disparagement of these works, summed up the 'programmes' and the titles originally appended to them, and finally gave a brief analysis of each. Mahler, who had a pretty low opinion of Nodnagel's intelligence and quickly tired of his enthusiasm, often tried to discourage him from writing his lengthy analyses.[54] However, while Nodnagel was perhaps neither the most perceptive of critics nor the most subtle of stylists, he must be credited with having been the first wholehearted advocate of all aspects of Mahler's genius, at a time when this required courage. Here are the closing words of his article:

The passionate intensity which from the very beginning characterized the clashing opinions aroused by Mahler's art immediately suggested that something of real importance had just emerged; usually such battles break out only over something truly outstanding. Moreover, the strong fascination which his works exert on both the general public and unprejudiced professionals definitely points to the work of a great artistic personality possessed of powerful originality. His C-minor Symphony has been the most powerful artistic experience in my life up to now. I have no doubt that Gustav Mahler is a 'candidate for posterity'.[55]

The second of Nodnagel's chapters on Mahler is an enthusiastic report of the recent première of the Fourth Symphony, in which the author contrasts Mahler's 'logic' with Strauss's 'anarchy and revolution' and describes the Fourth as 'more artistic and convincing' in its simplicity than any work by Strauss. For Nodnagel, the slow movement of the Fourth is one of the greatest ever written. (He ranks it with those in Schumann's Second, Brahms's First, and Bruckner's Seventh.) These judgements show that, despite Mahler's low opinion of him, Nodnagel was a man of courage and insight, a true pioneer. Nevertheless, the first truly important monograph on Mahler appeared only in 1905 and was written by Richard Specht, a 35-year-old Viennese critic who deserves a place in musical history for this and even more for his later full-length study of Mahler's personality, works, and theatrical career. Specht's 1905 essay is a manifesto, a pamphlet written to defend Mahler's music against virulent criticism. But it is also the first publication, after Schiedemair's brief monograph, which, though not comprehensive, was devoted entirely to him.[56]

---

[54] Mahler forbade Nodnagel to publish detailed analyses of the Second and Fifth Symphonies in *Die Musik*. However, an analysis of the Fifth was issued separately by Peters.

[55] EON 19. The same work contains essays on Hugo Wolf, Arnold Mendelssohn, Max von Schillings, Siegfried Wagner, and Richard Strauss (62 pages, more than double the number of pages devoted to Mahler).

[56] Richard Specht's little monograph appeared undated in Berlin, but its publication by Gose und Tetzlaff was announced by the *Neue Freie Presse* on 22 Oct. 1905. Mahler had asked him to make a few changes in his text. In particular, he did not wish his father to be described as an innkeeper (MBR1, no. 238; MBR2, no. 336). Richard Specht (1870–1932), son of a textile manufacturer and a musically gifted

It is obvious that most of the material of this small monograph was provided by Mahler himself. Thus its importance far exceeds its length. Some of Specht's statements on sensitive subjects, such as the influence of Bruckner, folk music, and military bands, as well as the exact date of his discovery of the *Wunderhorn* anthology, can be taken as reflecting Mahler's own statements.

After analysing the early symphonies in some detail, Specht draws a parallel between the Second and Fifth Symphonies, both of which move from funereal gloom to powerful, optimistic affirmation. Specht does not hesitate to make some negative criticisms: for instance, he considers the *Klagende Lied* an uneven work, especially in the second part, which he feels 'needs the stage and decorative art of a Roller'. While admitting that Mahler's compositions are undoubtedly controversial, Specht concludes: 'Mahler's art is striding forward with such wonderful maturity (*köstliche Reife*), completely "lost to the world" (*der Welt abhanden gekommen*); his art for me is an incomparable experience and discovery (*Erkenntnis*). I may be wrong. But I would rather support this music for the wrong reasons than attack it for the right ones.' These brave words undoubtedly touched Mahler. After he received a typescript of Specht's text, he wrote to thank him: 'I am very pleased with the whole thing. I am amazed to see how deeply you have penetrated the very essence of my being. Your understanding is doubly precious to me since it approaches the man through the works.'[57]

Another result of the recognition Mahler had by then gained as a composer was C. F. Kahnt's plan to publish the Sixth Symphony and the *Rückert-Lieder*. Kahnt also considered for a time reissuing the score of *Die Drei Pintos*, which in the previous years had been performed in Weimar (November 1899, under Rudolf Krzyzanowski), Prague (November 1900), and Frankfurt (October 1901). Kahnt pleaded with Mahler to compose a new overture, but he refused: 'It is impossible for me to plunge myself back into the atmosphere of the work after so long an interval.'[58]

mother, became known as a poet, playwright, and librettist, and was a member of the Café Griensteidl circle (together with Artur Schnitzler, Hermann Bahr, Hugo von Hofmannsthal, and Felix Salten). He first studied architecture before turning to music criticism under the guidance of Brahms, Goldmark, and Ignaz Brüll, with whom the Specht family spent several summers on the Attersee. After writing for several years on the theatre, literature, and visual arts, he was hired by *Die Zeit* as assistant music and theatre critic to Richard Wallaschek from 1903 until 1907. He later wrote regularly for the journal *Die Musik* between 1908 and 1915, and in 1909 founded *Der Merker* with Richard Batka and Julius Bittner, and later taught at the Vienna Akademie für Musik. But after being branded as a member of the 'Mahler Clique' he could never obtain another post as a music critic. He wrote a large number of books and monographs on Mozart, Beethoven, and Brahms as well as Johann and Richard Strauss, Julius Bittner, Erich Wolfgang Korngold, Franz Schreker, Wilhelm Furtwängler, Arthur Schnitzler, Emil Nikolaus von Reznicek, Giacomo Puccini, and Franz Werfel. After this 57-page monograph, he wrote the first major full-length book on Mahler (1913, revised in 1924), as well as thematic analyses of the Third (Universal Edition, 1916), Sixth (Kahnt, 1906), and Eighth (Universal Edition, 1912) Symphonies. (See Herta Blaukopf, 'Amsterdam 1920: Sechs zeitzugen feiern Mahler', *Muziek & Wetenschap*, 5 (1995–6): 3, 347 ff.).

[57]   MBR1, no. 238; MBR2, no. 336.
[58]   Reply to a letter dated 28 Mar. 1904 (HOA).

As seen above, the correspondence between Mahler and Henri Hinrichsen[59] provides a complete record of the publication of the Fifth. The first proofs were corrected by the composer between January and June 1904. He insisted in advance that they be sent to him piecemeal, or at least movement by movement, so that he would be able to spend all the time he needed over them. Having foreseen that he would want to make changes after the reading rehearsal and the première, Mahler requested that the printing of the orchestral parts be delayed until after the première.[60] Hinrichsen wrote on 24 January warning Mahler that the chances of a German première were 'slight' because of the conflict between the German Genossenschaft (to which Mahler and he both belonged) and the symphonic societies, a conflict which was terminated by the end of the year at a time when the situation had become intolerable. In his opinion, the best solution was that the première should form part of the Festival of the Allgemeiner Deutscher Musikverein in Frankfurt at the end of May. But Mahler preferred to wait until the autumn, which would give him time to choose carefully from among the different offers he had received.[61]

In February, Mahler wrote again to Peters, saying that he 'found himself in the distressing situation of having to refuse to conduct his own works in all sorts of places because of the Genossenschaft conflict'.[62] On 1 March, Hinrichsen announced that the page proofs were about to be sent and agreed in principle to send a third set of proofs in order to avoid 'a posteriori corrections' at any price (he was still far from anticipating the difficulties which were to arise from Mahler's successive revisions). In the same letter he passed on to Mahler a proposal from the publisher Ernst Eulenburg, organizer of the Neue Abonnements-Konzerte (New Subscription Concerts), for a première in Leipzig, in a hall seating 2,500, the Albert Halle. Hinrichsen considered that this première, conducted by the composer, was much to be desired 'under present circumstances', but Mahler did not share his opinion. In his view it was better not to be in a hurry and 'in both our interests, to let the summer go by'. In any case, Leipzig

is, for the time being, the least appropriate for our purposes. 1. The Winderstein Orchestra (which I know) is of poor quality and definitely not in a condition to do full justice to this very demanding work (an absolute necessity for a première of such potential importance). 2. The Leipzig public knows absolutely nothing about me thus

<hr/>

[59]　Eberhardt Klemm's article ('Geschichte') contains a letter from Alma to Hinrichsen written in 1921, in which she complains that she is receiving no income from performances of the Fifth Symphony, even though it was frequently performed, because her husband had sold all the rights to the publisher. The anonymous author claims that Peters paid her the sum of 5,000 marks as ex gratia royalties.

[60]　Undated letter of Nov. 1903 (Eberhardt Klemm, 'Geschichte', 25). In his reply on 21 Jan., Hinrichsen conceded on this point because he always preferred 'not to correct plates' already engraved (ibid. 26).

[61]　Ibid. 27. In Feb., Mahler sent the director of Peters the text of his new version of Weber's *Euryanthe* in the hope that he would publish it, since several theatres had expressed the intention of staging it. Hinrichsen wrote in his own hand on Mahler's letter: 'Nein! 20.II'.

[62]　See above Vol. ii, Chap. 14, 590 ff.

far, and is therefore in no position to understand the most advanced of my works. Furthermore, I have in front of me a whole list of proposals which seem to me to be worthy of consideration: <u>Prague</u> (the German or the Czech Philharmonic), <u>Amsterdam</u>, <u>Mannheim-Heidelberg</u>, <u>Cologne</u>, where I am to conduct my <u>Third</u> on Palm Sunday— as seems to have been agreed—and above all the <u>Berlin Philharmonic</u>, which wants the première at any price.[63]

At the end of March, after the relative success of the Third in Cologne, Mahler finally decided to accept the offer of the Gürzenich Concerts.[64] Max Singer, a member of the Peters firm, came to Vienna in May to talk with Mahler about the piano transcriptions.[65] In June and July Mahler revised and corrected these arrangements. He devoted considerable time to this because 'I know from experience that such transcriptions . . . are of crucial importance in making a work known'. It was a formidable task 'because as it originally stood it would have been impossible to form any proper idea of the whole from the piano transcription. Often, subsidiary material was given prominence while the central theme was obscured.'[66] On 8 July, Singer wrote to Peters complaining of Mahler's demands:

It is a complete disaster. From day to day he changed his mind about the necessity of certain alterations, and ended up approving what initially he was about to reject, without taking any account of the mature reflection I had already given to each bar. In the last two movements, he at first decided every note was in place. Why then in the end did he change his view so radically? Once before I have had to withdraw my name from a transcription because I did not wish it to be misused to cover up for the clumsy bowd-lerizations a young composer had foisted on to my work. Is it really going to be necessary for me to do that again?[67]

In his reply, Hinrichsen tried to console Singer by reminding him that it was better for corrections to be made before, rather than after, the printing of the transcription, that the composer's corrections were principally in the last two movements and that it was mainly a matter of bringing out the trumpet part.[68]

Relations between Mahler and the Vienna Philharmonic had improved a great deal, to the point where the orchestra decided to include his Third Symphony in a Gesellschaftskonzert at the end of the year. Writing to Hinrichsen on 2 June, Mahler commented: 'It might be possible, under certain circumstances, to envisage a first performance with the magnificent Philharmonic <u>here</u>!' Mahler was overjoyed to hear that Hinrichsen had also decided to publish a pocket score of the Fifth (as Bote und Bock had done with the *Domestica* of Strauss) because it would 'encourage the dissemination of the

---

[63] Undated letter (of 12 Mar.), Klemm, 'Geschichte'.
[64] Undated letter (of 29 Mar.), and Hinrichsen's reply of 30 Mar.
[65] Undated Letter (postmarked 26 July).
[66] Klemm, 'Geschichte' 107, Doc. No. 76, n. 1.
[67] Ibid. 54.
[68] Ibid. letter of 13 July. The first edition of the four-hand piano transcription comprised 600 copies (Klemm, 'Geschichte', 94, n. 52).

work and help it to be understood'. But he insisted that the orchestral parts be printed only <u>after</u> the première, for 'as regards quality of performance, it is essential that the insertion (of dynamic marks) should not be left to individual initiative'.[69]

In another postcard, dispatched from Maiernigg in the middle of the summer, Mahler replied to a request concerning the key of the symphony. He did not want this to appear on the cover. Normally one would have put the key of the main movement (A minor). But in this particular symphony the main movement was preceded by another (the Funeral March).[70]

At the end of July, Mahler drew Hinrichsen's attention to the fact that certain pages of the pocket edition of the *Symphonia Domestica* were illegible and 'hurt the reader's eyes'. He suggested following Schott's procedure for the miniature scores of the Wagner operas, where the score was spread across two pages laterally, with half the instruments on the upper halves and the others below. But in the end this method was not adopted for the Fifth. The final proofs were returned to Peters on 31 July.[71]

Mahler also exchanged a number of letters with Fritz Steinbach, conductor of the Gürzenich Concerts, concerning the première of the Fifth Symphony. In April, he promised him that Peters would send the orchestral parts in the beginning of June and accepted the same fee for conducting the première as he had received in March in Cologne for the Third. Then, later in the same month, Mahler informed his colleague that some difficulties had arisen concerning the performing rights. He had asked Steinbach to get in touch with the Committee of the Berlin Genossenschaft and agreed to urge them beforehand not to charge an additional sum for the <u>first</u> performance. Despite all his efforts, the percentage asked for must have been larger than expected because Steinbach again asked Mahler to bargain for a lower fee. However, Mahler reminded him that he no longer owned the performance rights and that Steinbach must use his influence with the Genossenschaft, otherwise the performance would simply have to be cancelled.[72] The problem must have been settled quickly, for it was not mentioned again.

---

[69] Letter of 4 June (Klemm, 'Geschichte', 33).   [70] Ibid.

[71] Telegram to Hinrichsen from Maiernigg, explaining that the parcel had been waiting to be posted, probably for several days, as the result of a misunderstanding (Klemm, 'Geschichte', 37).

[72] In a letter of 5 May, Joseph Stritzko, director of the firm Waldheim-Eberle which published Mahler's early symphonies, warned him that he could henceforth 'no longer successfully defend his interests' since he had left the Austrian Society and joined the Berlin Genossenschaft. The Viennese publisher thought that Mahler had acted against his own interests by doing so, since the Genossenschaft was trying to attract as many composers as possible in order to dominate the German symphonic societies. Even if he were now to leave the Genossenschaft, Mahler's early symphonies would remain among the works under its protection. Since the German Society persisted in demanding rights ranging from 250 to 400 marks per performance, these works would no longer be played. Thus Stritzko's suggestion was that Mahler should persuade Strauss and the other directors of the Genossenschaft either to release his works, or to reduce their demands to 50 to 100 marks per performance (Klemm, 'Geschichte', 58.) The original of this letter has disappeared, but a manuscript copy has survived in Peters's archives. Probably Mahler showed it to Hinrichsen, who had it copied for his own reference.

At the beginning of September, Hinrichsen worried because nothing had been heard for some time from Steinbach and he was now arranging a second performance in Leipzig under Stavenhagen, and one in Berlin under Nikisch. Two days later, a telegram from Mahler informed the publisher that Steinbach's letters had simply been mislaid and that the première was indeed to go ahead on 18 October as planned.[73] What was more, rehearsals had already begun, and the parts contained very few errors. But Mahler still wanted to have all the material in his hands in Vienna for the reading rehearsal.

After this working session, Mahler sent an over-optimistic report to his publisher:

To judge from the first reading, the first two movements are difficult to play and will present the listener with several hard nuts to crack. The last two movements seem to catch on even with the unprepared listener, so I'm hoping that they at least will go down well with the audience at the première. . . . You need to be aware right from the start that works of this sort need time to win over the public, and are certainly unlikely to have immediate success.[74]

The proofs for the pocket edition delighted Mahler: 'So much for Schott, Bote und Bock, etc.! I am convinced that this small score will do more to disseminate my work than all other publications together!'[75] A few days before the Cologne première, Mahler worried about the Fifth Symphony's press reception: 'Don't you have a friend or acquaintance among the critics who would be sufficiently interested in the première of my work to undertake the trip to Cologne? In my opinion it would be very important not to leave ourselves entirely in the hands of the Cologne press. And it is difficult for me to issue such an invitation!'

Several of Mahler's letters to Peters concern the final changes to be made to the score and the orchestral parts after the reading rehearsal. On 28 September he apologized for their being so numerous, drawing the publisher's attention to the fact that the polyphonic nature of the work called for particular care in its orchestral scoring. Other letters concerned the planned performance in Leipzig:

Would it not be possible to find a conductor other than Stavenhagen (who will certainly massacre my work—I can say that from experience)? I could recommend Herr Kapellmeister Walter, for example, who knows well what I am trying to do and who is willing to conduct if only his travelling expenses are paid. It would be a pity if this second performance were a complete failure![76]

The Third's failure in Munich, under Stavenhagen, in February, must have left Mahler with bitter memories, for his next letter mentions him again:

[73]   Letters and telegram sent by Mahler on 5 and 9 Sept. Letter from Hinrichsen on 7 Sept.

[74]   Undated letter (27 Sept. 1904).

[75]   According to Peters's letter of 3 Oct., the miniature score was put on sale at a price of 6 marks, the same price as that of the *Symphonia Domestica* (Klemm, 'Geschichte', 43). The first edition comprised 500 copies. The first edition of the full score comprised 100 copies (Klemm, 'Geschichte', 94, n. 49).

[76]   Undated letter to Hinrichsen (middle of Sept.).

Herr Stavenhagen has already programmed my Fifth for Munich! And <u>Munich</u> in particular is of the greatest importance to me in the immediate future. In Hamburg I am confronted with a very Philistine subscription audience, in Berlin with a hostile press. So we must pay particular attention to Munich, which has a wonderful public and a modernist press. I would almost advise a performance conducted only by myself or Walter. Or else Mottl or Weingartner, who are naturally 'hors concours' and who would certainly do the work no harm.[77]

At the end of September, Bruno Walter was officially invited by Ernst Eulenburg to conduct the Fifth in Leipzig,[78] in one of the Neue Abonnements-Konzerte. But the performance never took place, because of the conflict between the Genossenschaft and the symphonic societies, a conflict in which Eulenburg took a very active part, rallying many opponents of the Genossenschaft by canvassing and writing letters.[79]

In January 1905, Stavenhagen was once again the subject of a telegram from Mahler to his publisher: 'Under these conditions, performance will certainly be bad. . . . Essential to delay Stavenhagen's performance until after Berlin.' Mahler must have succeeded in discouraging the Munich conductor, for none of the performances he had planned came to fruition. After Mahler's performance in Hamburg in March, the Third was given in Berlin, under Nikisch, but it was so coldly received that it convinced Mahler once again of the extreme care required when it came to choosing the right performers.

Before he left for Cologne, Mahler wrote to a few of his most faithful admirers, including Mengelberg[80] and the critic Arthur Seidl, asking them to attend the première. To Seidl he wrote that his presence would be

reassuring, as Cologne is a bit out of the way and it is quite possible that some catch-phrase will be put around, the sort of thing which sometimes determines the attitude to a work for a long period of time. My Fourth suffered for a long time from a snap judgement put about by incomprehending hacks. So let me be bold and invite you to be there![81]

It had been agreed for some time that Alma would accompany Mahler and

---

[77] This letter is one of several which are wrongly numbered in Peters's archives (no. 27). It was certainly written after the Cologne concert and should therefore carry the number 40 or 41. Similarly a letter dated (by Peters) 10 Dec. has the number 10, though in fact it is the 42nd or 43rd in the collection. Letters of several pages have two successive numbers, one for each double page.

[78] Letter from Mahler, 1 Oct.

[79] Letters from Peters to Ernst Eulenburg, 4, 5, and 15 Oct. (Klemm, 'Geschichte', 60). In Feb., Hinrichsen corresponded with the Genossenschaft about plans for the Leipzig performance (letters of 26 and 29 Feb., ibid. 57). The composers' society first suggested a modest royalty of 50 marks (Peters was requesting 100 marks for the hire of score and parts) but hesitated to give its consent 'because of his [Eulenburg's] extraordinary campaign against our organization' (ibid. 59, letters of 3, 4, and 5 Oct. 1904). To avoid 'fanning the blaze', Friedrich Rösch finally gave the Genossenschaft's consent for the performance, while admitting that he would have preferred the work to be performed in the Gewandhaus or Winderstein Concerts, which had just joined the Genossenschaft. The Genossenschaft requested Eulenburg to put an end to his attacks, and he finally made a definitive decision not to programme the Fifth (letters from the Genossenschaft to Eulenburg, 15 Oct., ibid. 61).

[80] Undated postcard postmarked 7 Sept. 1904 (RHM 48).

[81] MBR1, no. 312; MBR2, no. 337.

attend the first performance of this work, which he had completed with her at his side. The score had been copied out by her, and the Adagietto was, according to Mengelberg, a 'declaration of love to her', though she herself never mentioned it as such. First, however, she had to wean little Gucki, and the change in the nursing regime proved so difficult that she had to take to bed with a high fever. Consequently Mahler had to leave without her, and it was agreed that she would join him for the general rehearsal, and then go on with him to Holland.

On the evening of 12 October, Mahler left home by tram, but a power failure forced him to switch to a horse-drawn cab. At the station he scribbled a few lines to Alma, and did so again between trains in Frankfurt the following morning. He had a sleeping compartment to himself, and enjoyed a reasonably comfortable trip. In Cologne, Fritz Steinbach met him at the station, took him to the Dom Hotel, and invited him to come, with Alma, to lunch the following week. The same evening, Mahler went to the station to post his first letter to Alma.[82] The next afternoon he wrote again to describe the first rehearsal:

O how happy to be a cobbler! With variations! . . .[83] Everything went reasonably well. The Scherzo is a devil of a movement! What a long and painful history awaits it! For the next fifty years conductors will play it too quickly, and make a nonsense of it. And the audience—heavens!—what a face it is bound to pull at this chaos which constantly gives birth to a new world only to destroy it moments later, at these sounds of a primeval world, this howling, booming, roaring sea, this host of dancing stars, these breathtaking, iridescent, glittering waves? What can a herd of sheep do but bleat when confronted by a 'singing contest of the fraternal spheres'![84] O how happy to be a tailor! Would to God I had been born a clerk and later become a baritone at the Vienna Opera![85] Oh, if only I could give my symphonies their first performances fifty years after my death![86]

Anticipating no doubt that Mahler would make still more changes to his score, Hinrichsen asked him to conduct the première from a corrected copy of the pocket score which the publisher could then take away with him in order to transfer the latest changes to the large orchestral score.[87] Mahler agreed straight away, knowing he was bound to make a number of further changes. After the rehearsal he relaxed by taking his favourite form of exercise:

Now I'm going for a walk along the Rhine—the only resident in Cologne who will keep going peacefully on his way without calling me a monster after the première! Would to God that I were 'just like mother, just like father!'[88] 'O how happy to be a locksmith'

[82] BGA, nos. 104, 105, and 106.
[83] Paraphrase of an aria from *Zar und Zimmermann*.
[84] A quote from Goethe's *Faust*.
[85] A reference to Leopold Demuth.
[86] BGA, no. 107.
[87] Letter to Mahler from Hinrichsen, 3 Oct., and Mahler's reply, 5 Oct.
[88] Reference to Strauss's *Symphonia Domestica*.

and then to become a tenor at the Vienna Opera![89] This evening, I must go to the theatre to hear a singer.[90] They are giving Giordano's *Fedora*. Oh, would that I were an Italian chestnut seller! Would that I were a Russian police spy! Oh, if only I were a town councillor in Cologne with my own box at the Stadttheater and the Gürzenich and could despise all modern music! Oh, if I were only a university professor[91] so that I could give lectures on Wagner and publish them! I expect you without fail on Sunday! There must be at least one person there to whom my symphony will give pleasure![92]

The next day Mahler learned by telegram that Alma had a cold and had not been allowed to leave her bed. He 'threw a tantrum' but still hoped she would get there in time for the concert. Fortunately, the second rehearsal went better than the first. Up to now, the greatest satisfaction of his trip had been the orchestra's growing enthusiasm. They are 'my greatest (if not my only) admirers', Mahler wrote from Amsterdam several days later.[93] The morning of the 18th he wired Alma, who by then had been forced to give up the idea of coming at all: 'Dress rehearsal very satisfactory. Performance good. Audience on edge, at first surprised, finally enthusiastic. Hinrichsen has already asked for the Sixth.'[94] The following day he amplified his wire with a letter:

After the Scherzo, a few catcalls. Adagietto and Rondo seem to have got through to them. Many musicians, conductors, etc. have arrived from abroad. Hinrichsen is most enthusiastic and with the greatest excitement has already reserved my Sixth . . . You not being here, Almschi, has spoiled the whole thing for me, and I almost couldn't care less what happens![95]

Bruno Walter, Arnold Berliner, and Ernst Otto Nodnagel[96] had just arrived, and Mahler sent Alma another report the day after the concert: 'Walter will come to see you immediately to tell you all the details. Hinrichsen remains enthusiastic and refuses to be influenced by adverse criticism. In any case, I think it made a really significant impact . . . The diversity of opinions on the work is most amusing. Each movement has its partisans and its enemies.'[97] The next morning, before boarding the train for Amsterdam, Mahler wrote to his sister Emma: 'Yesterday evening went rather well. The audience was at first put off . . . but by the end went along with it'.[98]

Much later, in his memoirs and monograph on Mahler Bruno Walter recalled that changes made the previous spring had not succeeded in clarifying the

[89] A reference to Leo Slezak.

[90] This was Frieda Felser (cf. Hermann Kipper's article in the *Volkszeitung*, 17 Oct.). Mahler went back to the Cologne Opera the next day to hear *Der Fliegende Holländer*.

[91] A reference to Guido Adler.

[92] BGA, no. 107.   [93] BGA, no. 113.   [94] BGA, no. 109.

[95] BGA, no. 110.

[96] Nodnagel's lengthy analysis of the Fifth, which later appeared as a separate monograph, was published in two successive issues of *Die Musik* (15 Nov. and 1 Dec. 1904). The same analysis was published by Peters in Jan. 1905. Nodnagel received a fee of 300 marks (Klemm, 'Geschichte', letters of 17 and 19 Feb. 1904, 54 and 107).

[97] BGA, no. 111.

[98] Undated letter to Emma Mahler, written on Dom Hotel notepaper, copy in BGM.

work's polyphony, and that he had been obliged to confirm Mahler's own anxieties in this respect. 'I'll never succeed in fully mastering my orchestration!' Walter quotes him as saying, when he had decided to send his score back to Peters so that some of the pages could be reset.[99] But once again there is no trace of this in Mahler's letters to Hinrichsen.

As Mahler had feared, the Fifth Symphony not only disconcerted most of the German critics but aroused their indignation. Only the *Kölnische Zeitung* greeted it with the same enthusiasm as it had the Third six months earlier. The author of the unsigned review, clearly Otto Neitzel,[100] rejoiced in the discovery of a composer who 'goes his own way and delights in surprises'. With this symphony, 'the Titan we left behind after the first movement of the Third reappears, the powerful master of forms, the Caesar of instrumentation and the art of building up movements, whose motto seems to be: *"Sic volo, sic jubeo"* ("Thus I will, thus I ordain").' Sometimes he 'loses himself, as if overcome by a desire to fling himself into an abyss,' but elsewhere, as in the Finale, 'he rediscovers terra firma'. Mahler is not a 'programme composer'. His art comes from his innermost being. His mastery of form and structure (*Gestaltung*) compensates for what he lacks in 'force and originality of invention'. It makes him 'one of the greatest men of our time'. Neitzel was sorry nonetheless not to find in the two sections of the first part the same 'logic' as in the first movement of the Third. He deplored the return in the Allegro to the funeral atmosphere of the March, and felt that there were 'dead' moments in the Scherzo. But the Finale, that 'pearl of the new literature', soothed the spirit, and at the end of the concert in the Gürzenich, the music-lovers of Cologne had applauded warmly. However, he thought they needed to hear the symphony again before trying to judge the whole, since the work contained 'thorns' as well as 'fragrant roses'. In any event, he said, an artist of such calibre is 'worth meeting halfway'.

In an article written some time later for the journal *Signale für die Musikalische Welt*, the same Otto Neitzel, whose enthusiasm had apparently grown meanwhile, claimed that the symphony showed 'progress on all fronts' in relation to its predecessors, even though there might be a 'slight weakness' in the quality of the inspiration. He stressed even more than before the polyphonic nature of the writing, and the fabulous subtlety of the instrumentation, notably in the mixing of timbres; and he admired the 'absolute sureness with which Mahler achieves his goal', a sureness which he thought was 'unique today'. He thought it absurd that anyone should complain of the absence of programme, for listeners to this symphony had no need of 'poetic images' to understand what they were hearing. 'For this reason, the work is well suited to disarming the criticism Mahler has often provoked in the past. It is of a sufficiently high standard to be taken into consideration by all the principal concert

[99] BWT 170; BWM 47.   [100] See Otto Neitzel's biography above, Vol. i, Chap. 23.

societies, particularly since, despite its modernity, it belongs to the realm of absolute music that contemporary composers tend to neglect.'[101]

In the *Kölner Volkszeitung*, Hermann Kipper made no effort to hide his disappointment. To his mind, the work had a 'hidden programme' and he quoted a remark to that effect that Mahler had made to the orchestra during rehearsals: 'Think of a man whose ideals have been destroyed'. The symphony was what Gustave Charpentier called a 'musical novel'. Mahler's style was as incongruous as ever and his orchestral colour had become even harsher. The first movement was much too long and the second contained many passages that sounded 'unmusical'. That Mahler belonged to a 'hypernervous and pessimistic age, . . . that his brain seemed to be in perpetual turmoil', was evident when one saw him 'walking in the street bare-headed, hat in hand'. If the performance was not entirely beyond reproach, it was because he wilfully imposed difficulties upon the players, sometimes forcing the instruments to play at pitches in which they sounded shrill. He had only himself and 'his atrocious cacophonies' to blame for the misunderstandings his music aroused. His work would gain both from being explained, 'softened', or, better still, abridged. Many listeners asked themselves after the Adagietto 'why he didn't always write such beautiful music'.

But a Mahler première was now an event important enough to be reported on by the main newspapers in Berlin, Leipzig, and Munich. The *Berliner Tageblatt* and the *Leipziger Tageblatt* carried brief and hostile reviews. In the Berlin paper, the anonymous critic (probably Leopold Schmidt) considered that, in the Fifth, 'the train of thought is as incomprehensible as the style is enigmatic'. 'Pretty details' and 'refined instrumentation' were not enough to justify 'the numerous dissonances and dreadful oddities'. The Leipzig paper drew attention to the coolness of the audience's reception and to the hisses, which proved that 'Rhinelanders, with their joie de vivre, are of all people the least likely to understand the more or less shadowy labyrinths of the Mahlerian muse'.

However, Mahler received great comfort from an unexpected source. The Berlin critic Rudolph Kastner published in the *Münchner Neueste Nachrichten*, Munich's leading newspaper, a courageous eulogy of Mahler explaining and justifying his aesthetic aims and means. Many passages in the symphony did indeed make an 'absurd and bizarre' first impression. 'However, the bizarre should never deter one when judging a work: look at Berlioz.' 'The essence of Mahler's symphonies has never seemed unclear to me, and what most people consider to be "disconcerting" is for me the composer's most delightful characteristic.' With 'a little more objectivity and good will,' Kastner wrote, it was impossible not to see that Mahler was composing not only for his own time but for the future, that he was 'an essentially sound musician of vigorous imagination and brilliant insight'.

---

[101] *Signale für die musikalische Welt*, 62 (1904): 65–6, 1192.

His creativity was rooted in a 'pure, pristine and genuine feeling for truth that emanated from an innermost conviction'. After the monumental Funeral March, 'a divine inspiration in itself' and 'written with his heart's blood', the work reached its apogee in the second movement. Then, in the Finale, there reigned 'a severe and compelling logic'. The Adagietto recalled a painting by Hans Thoma,[102] 'a sunset landscape at harvest time'. The composer of such a piece could only be 'one of the greatest masters of his art'. Only a thorough study of the score could give an exact idea of his 'inexhaustible skill at variation', 'of the eminent refinement of the orchestration'. Since the *Neueste Nachrichten* had always denigrated his symphonies, Mahler wrote to Kastner: 'You have really given me a great pleasure. I think you understand me as few others do and I wish you would write at greater length about my whole approach to music. The world needs that! Must one wait until one is dead before people grant one the right to live?'[103]

Kastner's review indeed stood out against an overwhelming majority of adverse criticisms. The music monthlies were no less scathing than the daily press. Paul Hiller,[104] correspondent for *Die Musik*, the *Neue Zeitschrift für Musik*, and *Musikalisches Wochenblatt*, found that the symphony contained no genuine musical ideas. As a 'clever but not convincing' composer Mahler made use of the resources of his craft merely 'to create sensations', 'a jumble of sounds lacking any kind of musical logic'. The work was an accumulation of 'absurdities, and revels in utterly bizarre oddities'. Only the Adagietto really belonged to the realm of music. The general effect was 'more disconcerting and repellent than pleasurable', an unsuccessful attempt to score a 'triumph of technique (*Mache*)'.

In the *Neue Musikalische Presse*, Eccarius Sieber expressed the 'bitter disappointment' of all those who had admired Mahler's earlier works and were not prepared for something so different. The evolution of his creative powers was completely 'unpredictable'. Clearly his intentions were 'sincere and honest'. 'He loves clarity. And clarity reigns everywhere in his Fifth. . . . He feels the need to express himself clearly in order to make the listener understand (what he himself calls) the "transhuman" nature of his creative process.' Thus Mahler's individuality had never been so clearly exposed, nor his 'Achilles heel', the 'weakness of his musical invention'. For this reason, 'the numerous dissonances and the merciless harshness of utterance . . . seem doubly wounding' and 'at times spoil the pleasure of listening to an unbearable degree'. In developing themes by 'powerful crescendos' 'thickly' and 'deafeningly' scored, leading to 'evolutions, conclusions, "catastrophes"', Mahler 'now stands alone, often as "the enemy of the culture" of our time'.

---

[102] Hans Thoma (1839–1924), painter, lithographer, and engraver, was one of the members of Munich's avant-garde.

[103] MBR1, no. 316; MBR2, no. 339.

[104] Paul Hiller (1853–1934), music critic of the *Rheinische Zeitung*, and son of the composer and critic Ferdinand Hiller, had received from Peters a miniature score of the Fifth (Klemm, 'Geschichte', 114).

In Sieber's eye, the first movement seemed to be an 'epic on the death not of a single human being, but of a whole generation', and ended in 'despairing cries and demoniac weeping'. The march theme, with its 'almost banal, Magyar-sounding second theme' and altogether 'affected popular style', was bound to disturb even Mahler's most loyal admirers. 'But strangely enough, all their doubts were dispelled by the soothing, soulful melodies' of the Adagietto. Mahler was

like a fanatical preacher who casts the faithful to the ground with his searing condemnations, but then raises them up again with comforting words . . . He arouses the audience's . . . antagonism and disagreement, and then effects a reconciliation. This act of reconciliation begins with the concessions the Adagietto makes to our artistic sensibility. To these tender and moving sounds he adds a second reconciling element, his contrapuntal refinements which inspire the listener with respect for the composer's skill. . . . Masterly in form, structure, content and decorative instrumentation, the Finale celebrates the triumph of man's tireless activity over the miseries of earthly existence.

And by the end of the performance Mahler took leave of his audience as 'a kindly composer' who had convinced and reconciled his public.[105]

Fortunately Mahler did not have time to become aware of the extent of the Fifth's failure before he left Cologne. The afternoon after the concert, he took the train to Amsterdam, where Mengelberg had invited him for the second time to conduct two of his symphonies. Although he was firmly resolved to stay at a hotel rather than accept once again his colleague's hospitality, the Mengelbergs met him at the station and he finally gave in to their entreaties to stay with them, probably because he felt lonely without Alma. The chambermaid who unpacked his case was surprised to find in it two bedsheets from the Dom Hotel in Cologne, which in the excitement of departure he had inadvertently rolled up and brought along with him.[106]

Between Mahler's first and second visits to Holland, a small revolution had occurred at the Concertgebouw. The concert hall had been erected between 1883 and 1888 by a group of wealthy philanthropists and influential music-lovers who at the same time assumed financial responsibility for the salaries of the orchestra and the conductor, and also the soloists' fees. At this time the Dutch government did not subsidize the arts, and the Association's sole

[105] After the Fifth Symphony, the first Gürzenich Konzert of the 1904/5 season ended on 18 Oct. with the following works, conducted by Fritz Steinbach: Schubert, *Ständchen* for female chorus and alto solo, 'Zögernd Leise' D. 920; 3 Lieder ('Bei Dir', 'Nacht und Träume', and 'Das Lied im Grünen'), both with Lula Mysz-Gmeiner, alto; Beethoven, *Leonore* Overture No. 3.

[106] Interview with Willem Mengelberg, 'Intimes von Gustav Mahler', *Neues Wiener Journal* (7 Nov. 1930). Several years later, Alma Mahler wrote to Mengelberg, to announce she was giving him the autograph score of the Seventh Symphony. In the same letter she told him that Mahler hated any contact with strange linen and that he liked to travel with his own sheets, pillowcases, and even towels, which he then rolled up and threw in his case when he left to return to Vienna. According to Alma, he had on one occasion left his own sheets in a hotel. (Letter from Alma Mahler to Willem Mengelberg, 21 Jan. 1938, sent from Capri, Mengelberg archives).

revenue came from ticket sales and subscriptions. Until 1904 the post of administrator was held by Willem Hutschenruyter, the orchestra's principal hornplayer, whose brother was the conductor of the Utrecht Orchestra.[107] For him, Willem Mengelberg's independent mind, and his absolute authority over the players, were a constant source of exasperation. He fought tooth and nail to have the orchestra's finances separated from those of the building and to reduce the musical director's powers. In 1904, after the management committee had finally rejected his proposals, Hutschenruyter resigned. A significant number of musicians took his side and resigned with him, along with the assistant conductor André Spoor. The vacant posts were filled with new musicians, and the committee appointed a new administrator, Hendrik de Booy, a former naval officer, to whom Mahler took an instant liking, nicknaming him 'Seeheld' (hero of the sea).[108]

Mahler's second stay in Holland was preceded by a long exchange of letters with Mengelberg who was now 'the master in his own house' (*der Herr im Hause*, as Mahler put it).[109] The Concertgebouw dates had been arranged to follow that of the Cologne première of the Fifth, but despite his horror of travelling, Mahler had been prepared to make a special journey.[110] In a letter written to Mengelberg on 12 June 1904, Mahler expressed his pleasure at returning to Amsterdam and 'reaffirming our newly fledged friendship', for 'the days in Amsterdam [in 1903] were among the happiest I have ever spent with a fellow artist (*Kunstgenossen*)'.[111] Mahler's initial plan had been to conduct in Amsterdam, besides the Second Symphony, the second performance of the Fifth, which he asked his colleague to come and hear in Cologne, but Mengelberg finally chose the Fourth, no doubt because he found it more approachable. Mahler asked him to include only well-known works in the programme with it, so that he could use all the rehearsal time for his symphony.[112]

---

[107] See above, Vol. ii, Chap. 15.

[108] RMH 12 (letters nos. 32, 71, to Willem Mengelberg, 12 June 1904). The committee's final decision must have been taken during the two preceding months. Before it was made Mengelberg considered leaving his post, and Mahler assured him of his 'great concern', and tried to have him appointed head of the Musikverein Orchestra.   [109] Letter no. 5 to Mengelberg, RHM 44.

[110] The letter is reproduced in abridged form in MBR1, no. 303; MBR2, no. 329. It mainly concerns two Dutch musicians, the flautist Ary van Leeuwen and the cellist Willem Willeke, whom Mengelberg wanted back in Holland, doubtless to replace musicians resigning from the orchestra. Both had been engaged at the Vienna Opera in 1903 and Mahler was reluctant to let them go. In a further letter, he said he would yield only if his friend Mengelberg insisted, but he asked that the whole affair remain absolutely secret, for otherwise the consequences for him could be very serious (RMH 46). Willem Willeke eventually remained in Vienna until 1907 and Ary von Leeuwen until 1920. This is the letter written at the end of June and first published in RMH, in which Mahler writes that he has just 'started work again on something old' which is a certain indication that he had decided to finish the *Kindertotenlieder* (see above, Vol. ii, Appendix 2).

[111] RMH 45.

[112] Letter of 11 or 12 Oct. Mahler announced that the bells had been sent from Vienna for the Finale of the Second and requested a supplementary rehearsal for the off-stage instruments (4 trumpets, 4 horns, and timpani) in the 'Last Trump'. In a postscript he also asked Mengelberg to transcribe the violin solo in the Scherzo of the Fourth for a normally tuned instrument, as he wanted to find out how it sounded.

Upon his arrival in Amsterdam, he rehearsed 'the vocal solos' in the evening with Alida Oldenboom-Lütkeman, a Dutch soprano[113] whom he described to Alma as 'A short, buxom woman, a bit like Cilli [one of the Mahlers' cooks], but she sings divinely and her voice is as pure as a bell.'[114] Very soon, Mahler received the first press clipping concerning the première of the Fifth Symphony. 'So far I haven't seen any others,' he wrote, enclosing it in a letter to Alma. 'I can imagine how they will go on about it! The *Neue Freie Presse* in particular will go to town on the matter!'[115] And he added a day later: 'I still don't know whether I will come back to Vienna in disgrace or not. Have I failed or succeeded?'[116] After he read the rest of the reviews, he wrote:

I realize now how wrong I was to introduce one of my works in Cologne, where the public had already responded to my Third in such a cool way. Its reaction always ends up influencing the newspaper hacks, who are unprincipled and wholly incapable of having any ideas of their own. It was silly to have undertaken all the inconvenience and hardship of such a long journey just for that. I could have obtained the same result in Vienna with far less trouble! With the Sixth, I'll try to be a bit more intelligent![117]

The kindness of the Mengelbergs ('simple and charming') and of the Dutch people in general made up to a large extent for Mahler's disappointment.

'Here, the people are a real delight,' he wrote to Alma.

Just think of the programme for next Sunday:

    1. Fourth Symphony, G. Mahler
       Interval
    2. Fourth Symphony, G. Mahler

How do you like that? They have simply put my work on the programme twice! After the interval, we begin all over again from the beginning! I'm rather curious to see whether the audience will warm to the work the second time round.[118]

Holland was paying him a unique tribute with this double performance, and Mahler was overwhelmed at every rehearsal by the orchestra's enthusiasm and the 'wonderful purity' of its playing, thanks to previous rehearsals under Mengelberg. More and more, he felt that he had found in Amsterdam 'the musical home I had hoped to discover in that stupid town, Cologne'. The other side of the coin was, as always, too long an absence from Vienna:

It's an atrocious life, sitting around in foreign parts! However warmly one is welcomed, one ends up being embarrassed in every way, and in the end feels abandoned. . . . I wasn't born for constant travelling, however necessary it may be. The only moments of

---

[113]   Alida Oldenboom-Lütkeman sang the Finale of the Fourth as well as the soprano part in the Second. Originally Mahler had recommended engaging Stephanie Becker, the Mainz soloist, since he had been very pleased with her, but she seems not to have been free (RMH 49).

[114]   BGA, no. 112 (20 Oct.).   [115]   BGA, no. 113 (21 Oct.).

[116]   BGA, no. 114 (21 Oct.).   [117]   BGA, no. 115 (22 Oct.).

[118]   BGA, no. 113. The day after the concert Mahler wrote to his brother-in-law Arnold Rosé, communicating the same news, adding that the Fifth 'did not seem to have been very well understood' in Cologne (card dated 24 Oct., Rosé Collection, University of Western Ontario).

such a journey when I feel really comfortable are the rehearsals. If only I had reached the stage at which conductors understood the style of my works! I could go for a stroll through Heiligenstadt instead.[119]

Thanks to Eduard Reeser's recently published collection of letters and documents concerning Diepenbrock,[120] Mahler's second trip to Holland is well documented. Diepenbrock called on Mahler at the Mengelbergs' on 20 October, on the day of his arrival. They greeted each other affectionately, and went for a long walk in the town, after which Diepenbrock played his 'Te Deum' to Mahler, who was 'enthusiastic'.[121] The two composers saw each other daily thereafter. Diepenbrock was seated near Mahler, as always, at the supper the Mengelbergs gave after the double performance of the Fourth. Once the other guests were gone, Mahler asked him to stay on. 'He then said some marvellous things about the nature of music,' Elisabeth Diepenbrock writes. 'It was an unforgettable moment. Fons[122] kept on drawing him out and he became really enthusiastic. Fons calls him Orpheus and says he has an ancient Greek way of looking at music.' The next day, while visiting the banker Hendrik Johan de Maresz Oyens, Mahler once again asked for Diepenbrock to be seated next to him. On being invited to dinner by the president of the Concertgebouw, Jerome Alexander Sillem,[123] this time without the Diepenbrocks, he exclaimed: 'What is the point of going if my friends aren't there?'

On the day of the first performance of the Second, Mahler lunched at the Diepenbrocks with the Mengelbergs and Elisabeth writes in her diary:

He felt completely at home, said at once where he wanted to sit (he prefers to be on the left). He spoke at length about his childhood, about the home in which he was born, not a single window was unbroken, and about his brothers, the earthworms. He also said that he would like to have four children but not quadruplets.

The following day they all took lunch in the country, at the home of the sculptress Sara de Swart in Laren, east of Amsterdam.[124] Mahler set off early in the morning with Mengelberg and Diepenbrock to walk from Hilversum to Laren.

Mahler often walked on ahead, alone, bareheaded and saying nothing. Sometimes he dropped back and talked. He loved the countryside, and the village, and also Sara's house. Over lunch he had some fascinating things to say about the content of his

---

[119] A reference to Beethoven's favourite vacation village, now a suburb of Vienna near Grinzing. BGA, nos. 114, 115.

[120] See above Vol. ii, Chap. 15.

[121] Elisabeth Diepenbrock's private diary, 20 Oct. 1904, RMH 12. Mahler was to take up the cudgels on behalf of his friend, trying to persuade Franz Schalk to conduct the 'Te Deum' for the Musikverein (letter from Mahler to Diepenbrock, 10 Oct. 1905, and another undated letter, RMH 56). According to the article from the *Weekblad vor Muziek* already quoted, the planned performance never materialized, and Schalk returned the manuscript to the Dutch composer without comment.

[122] This was Elisabeth Diepenbrock's nickname for her husband.

[123] Dr Sillem had been a friend of Brahms and one of the founders of the Concertgebouw, of which he was president from 1905 until his death in 1912.

[124] Sara de Swart (1861–1951) lived in a villa in Laren with her friend, Emilie van Kerckhoft.

Second Symphony. Afterwards, we walked back . . . Fons went on another long walk with Mahler on the 23rd. On the 26th, after the performance they went with some of the musicians to the American Hotel. Not a successful party on the whole, but afterwards Fons had a few moments with Mahler and talked about his own music. He told him that he often used motifs, melodies or reminiscences, perfectly aware of where they came from, but that this didn't worry him at all because all music was linked with earlier music, and all that mattered was <u>what</u> one did with it, and whether that was new and personal. 'Of course', said Mahler, and taking Fons by the hand he said: 'this is not a sheep, nor an ox, it is none other than Diepenbrock'. Those were lovely festive days, filled as much with an entrancing personality as with wonderful music and the warm, friendly relationship.[125]

On 24 October, Mahler went to Haarlem with Mengelberg and Diepenbrock to visit the Frans Hals Museum.[126] Unfortunately they found it closed and Mahler was so disappointed that he contemplated missing a rehearsal on the day of the first performance of the Second, taking the electric train to Zandvoort on the North Sea, and stopping at Haarlem on the way, but it seems this plan came to nothing, since he does not even allude to it in his letters to Alma.

Hendrik de Booy,[127] the new administrator of the Concertgebouw Orchestra, also recorded some memories of Mahler's visit:

It was difficult to go for a walk with Mahler, because sometimes he went on ahead, at other times he hung back, so absorbed in his own thoughts that conversation was impossible. What is more, he always went out bareheaded, which at that time was unheard of in Amsterdam, so that some street boy would immediately pop up and ask curiously: 'Mister, where's your hat?' and stand looking at him.

We came to the Damrak, to Berlage's Stock Exchange, opened in 1903. Mahler expressed his admiration, without at first knowing what the building actually was.[128] When Diepenbrock told him, adding that he was not one of its admirers, Mahler defended his initial reaction by asserting that a stock exchange, where business is transacted, and where cupidity predominates, should not have the outward aspect of a temple. He asked to be told the name of the architect and said: 'Tell him I think he's a great architect'.[129]

[125] Elisabeth Diepenbrock's diary, 'Brieven', 14.

[126] From there, Diepenbrock sent his pupil Johanna Jongkindt a postcard that was also signed by Mahler and Mengelberg (ibid. 17).

[127] Hendrik de Booy, 'Menschen die ik ontmoette', unpublished manuscript quoted above, RMH 18 (see above Vol. ii, Chap. 15).

[128] Hendrik de Booy is mistaken here, because Mahler alluded to the Berlage Stock Exchange building in a letter he wrote to Alma on 21 Oct. 1903 (BGA, no. 49) 'I saw the Stock Exchange yesterday. It's imposing, but the people here don't seem very keen on it! Just like Vienna!' (see above Vol. ii, Chap. 15). It would be possible to believe that the incident mentioned by de Booy took place the previous year, except that Mahler had probably not made his acquaintance yet. Perhaps de Booy later came to believe he had been present at a conversation which had in fact been related to him by Diepenbrock.

[129] Henrik-Petrus Berlage (1856–1934), co-designer of the Amsterdam Panoptikon (1882) and pioneer of the modern style in Holland, was one of the greatest architects of his time. He wished to combine traditional craftsmanship with industrial production and 'rethink the basis of architecture'. In his time he was thought of as the leader of the Dutch architectural renaissance, and exercised great influence, notably on Mies van der Rohe. 'The Amsterdam Exchange, his masterpiece, was conceived and constructed with the vigour, formal concentration and the technological economy of a Roman temple.'

Afterwards we went to Jodenbreestraat, where Mahler stood a long time, bare-
headed, before Rembrandt's house, surrounded by lively young inhabitants of the
Jewish quarter, who said things to him to which he paid not the slightest attention. He
just stood looking at the house, and finally said: 'Those are the windows he looked
through . . .' Then, heaving a sigh, he said he hoped to die as soon as he could make
no further progress in knowledge and skill.

On this occasion De Booy noticed Mahler's dislike of concert promoters. He
had inadvertently dropped on the pavement a letter addressed to the impresario Norbert Salter, whereupon Mahler commented: 'A letter to a concert
promoter can never look dirty enough!'

At an official dinner, de Booy saw Mahler pick up a voluminous table
centrepiece made up of fruit and flowers, and place it on a nearby buffet. This
'unusual action' holds no surprise for us, given the many similar tales about his
behaviour in society during the Hamburg era and his early Vienna years. Later
that evening the conversation turned, as the year before, to the writer
Multatuli[130] and his famous anti-colonialist novel *Max Havelaar*, which Mahler
and Alma had both read and much enjoyed. When someone remarked that
Multatuli himself had not fulfilled his duties with much zeal in the East Indies,
Mahler stoutly defended him, saying that he would have regarded it as a great
honour to meet and talk with him. 'Whereupon he stood up from the table and
bowed low before the imaginary guest . . .: "Herr Multatuli, I have the greatest
admiration for you, and like you I hate all Droogstoppels (Philistines)!" '[131]

In his memoirs Richard van Rees, another member of the committee of the
Concertgebouw Orchestra, compared Mahler with Brahms, whom he had
frequently met around 1880 at the house of Jerôme Sillem: 'Mahler too could
be very moody, unceremonious and awkward, but he was also much more
excitable, lively, witty and brilliant. In any case he was not the man for dinners
and company. He ate little, and liked to light up a big cigar right in the middle
of the meal,'[132] a breach of etiquette which people were quite prepared to
accept as part of his outstanding personality.

Contemporary witnesses agree that the atmosphere at rehearsals was as
warm in 1904 as it had been the previous year. On the first day Mahler heard
a wrong note and immediately stopped the orchestra. It turned out to be due to

---

[130]   Eduard Douwes Dekker (1820–87), who used the pseudonym Multatuli, was 40 when he published
his first book, *Max Havelaar, or The Sale of Coffee by the Netherlands Commercial Society*, a work both autobiographical and violently anticolonialist in character. It caused a great stir and even led to a commission
of inquiry into the administration of the Dutch East Indies. As a result of his opposition in West Java to the
Javanese Regent's exploitation of his fellow-countrymen, with the connivance of the Dutch Resident, Dekker
was dropped from the Civil Service, subsequently returning to Europe and settling in Brussels, where he
wrote his famous novel. Dekker defined himself as a 'bundle of contradictions', which might well be one of
the reasons why his book fascinated Mahler, who was well aware of his own contradictions (see above, Vol.
ii, Chap. 15).
[131]   Droogstoppel was an Amsterdam coffee merchant, the anti-hero of *Max Havelaar*.
[132]   Richard van Rees, 'Herinneringen, Ervaringen op musikaal gebied', 1924, unpublished manuscript
in the Gemeentemuseum in The Hague (RMH 19).

a misprint in the score. Instead of merely correcting it and carrying on, Mahler would not be satisfied until a Concertgebouw employee had been called to telegraph the publisher of the Fourth in Vienna about the mistake: 'Otherwise, everyone will repeat the error!'[133]

Alphons and Elisabeth Diepenbrock noticed how lively and expressive Mahler's gestures were when he was on the podium during rehearsals, and how precisely he indicated everything. 'Beethoven must have conducted like that,' said Diepenbrock. The Dutch writer Balthasar Verhagen[134] later recalled the following incident:

One memorable evening, on Sunday 23 October 1904, Mahler conducted his Fourth twice in succession before a small but appreciative audience. The following Tuesday, with my head still full of this divine, and for me entirely new, music, I arrived for my Latin lesson with Diepenbrock. Naturally we talked about Mahler. When Diepenbrock told me that the maestro was rehearsing his Second at the Concert-gebouw . . . we soon agreed that we should be there and that Virgil could wait for a week. We went into the hall, Diepenbrock joined his friends, and I went up alone to the gallery, near the podium. The rhythms of the enormous orchestra sounded through the dark empty hall. Then a door was cautiously opened, and a trumpeter tried to creep unnoticed behind the chorus to his place. But what could possibly escape Mahler's attention? He tapped crossly with his baton, and there was dead silence. 'Well, sir, so you've decided to look in. If you please, I've been here for some time'. What a voice! All of us, orchestra, chorus and the small handful of listeners, trembled for the unfortunate latecomer. Those who have heard Mahler speak could never forget his voice!

'The rehearsal continued. But it was not going well any more, the players were making mistakes and complaining of the inadequate lighting, which made it difficult to read their complicated parts. Again Mahler stopped, and again came that terrifying silence. He turned and directed his flashing spectacles at . . . me, sitting up there alone in the darkness. 'Could you not please give us some light?' Startled out of my intoxication with the work's overwhelming riches of melody and sound, I stared at him thunderstruck. He repeated his question more sharply and angrily, and, helpless as a soldier struck dumb before Napoleon, I longed for the darkness in the hall to swallow me up. How I blessed the member of staff who came to my assistance![135]

Between rehearsals, Mahler attended a concert conducted by Mengelberg and heard an 'excellent performance' of Schumann's Fourth Symphony. As he listened, an anonymous admirer sketched his portrait.[136] Mahler's work took up so much time and energy that he had no time left for more sightseeing. He was rather worried about the public's reaction to the double performance of the Fourth ('a very heavy meal for an Amsterdam stomach, one which they could

[133] J. Poppelsdorf, *Mahler repeteert de Vierde Symphonie*, in *Programmbuch*, Holland Festival, 1960, 11.

[134] Balthasar Verhagen (1881–1950), who was to make a name for himself as a poet and playwright, played an important part in Dutch cultural life.

[135] Balthasar Verhagen, 'Herinneringen aan Gustav Mahler', *De Amsterdammer*, 4 June 1911, 2 (RMH 16).   [136] BGA, nos. 115, 228.

find hard to digest!') Still, he was more optimistic than usual: 'In Holland there is a great interest in my music. Perhaps it is because of my kinship with the old Dutch masters (*alten Niederländern*).'[137] Mengelberg had undoubtedly taken a big risk, but the result exceeded their wildest hopes, as Mahler reported to Alma.

It was an astonishing evening. The audience was attentive and understanding from the start, and grew warmer from movement to movement. During the second performance the enthusiasm grew and grew, and at the close the same thing happened as in Krefeld. The singer performed her solo with simple and touching expressiveness, and the orchestra accompanied her like sunbeams. It was a painting with a golden background.[138]

The contemporary witnesses were unanimous in agreeing that the audience was even more enthusiastic than after the previous year's Third Symphony. Prompted by its success, Mengelberg immediately decided to perform the Fourth again a few months later.[139]

Why did Alma claim that one of the two 23 October performances was conducted by Mengelberg, who 'adhered to Mahler's intentions so closely that it seemed it was Mahler himself conducting?' Could Mahler have heard a rehearsal of the Fourth conducted by his Dutch colleague, and later mentioned it to his wife? Or did Alma confuse it with the performance of Schumann's Fourth Symphony? There is ample evidence that Mahler himself conducted both performances of the Fourth: the Concertgebouw programme, the reviews, an entry in Alphons Diepenbrock's diary[140] and finally this phrase from a recently published card to Alma: 'I'm leaving now for the concert, where I'm going to conduct the Fourth twice in succession.'[141]

The tone and content of the accounts by Dutch critics show that, unlike most of their German colleagues, they did not consider the Fourth Symphony 'scandalous'. To be sure, Anton Averkamp was astounded to hear a simplicity 'borrowed from another age'. He wondered whether Mahler had not deliberately wanted 'to disavow his previous compositions' and resurrect the spirit of Haydn and Schubert, or whether he had merely wanted to relax perhaps after some hard work. In his opinion, the Fourth revealed a completely new aspect of its composer. Although it contained a few 'caprices', the general impression was 'joyous, cheerful and naive' and one listened to it with 'unusual pleasure'. Of all the movements, the Adagio with its Beethovenian melodies was certainly the most enchanting. The Scherzo was inferior, a humourless, 'coarse burlesque'. As for the Finale, it was full of atmosphere and in perfect harmony with the chosen text. The orchestra played to perfection, and the two

---

[137] BGA, no. 117 (23 Oct.). [138] BGA, no. 118 (24 Oct.).
[139] Mengelberg conducted the Fourth in The Hague on 15 Feb. 1905 and the following day in Amsterdam. [140] RMH 14. [141] BGA, no. 117 (23 Oct.).

successive performances inspired the most lively interest. Averkamp felt, however, that since the Fourth was neither complex nor profound, it hardly had to be played twice the same evening.

Simon van Milligen of the *Handelsblad*, on the other hand, felt that the quality of the work, and particularly the 'masterly orchestral portrayal' in the last movement, amply justified the two performances. He also felt that the musicians had played with more assurance and freedom the second time round. The Fourth was certainly simpler, clearer, and more naive than most contemporary symphonies. The Finale in particular revealed such mastery and was 'so characteristic that it was impossible to compare it with any other work by any other composer'. The first time Milligen heard the first movement, its development had seemed 'too complicated'; later, he found it 'more natural'. With a kind of naive 'transfiguration' which illuminated the entire work, Mahler was perhaps trying to 'say that it is high time to stop following the path towards immense complexity in our modern music'. Nevertheless, he had made use of all the instrumental refinements of his time. The limpid and poetic expression in his work was extremely engaging. He was a highly original composer, one who had something to say and was a master of his means of expression. The Fourth Symphony deserved a secure place in the repertory of the Concertgebouw Orchestra.

In *Het Nieuws van den Dag*, Daniel de Lange also approved the idea of a double performance, because the work presented 'thoughts and impressions' in a manner almost reminiscent of Haydn, though 'in modern dress'. It was the 'true image' of a soul which after great struggles 'has found all that it needs and that it holds to be true'. Mahler had handled and mastered his material admirably. His music flowed so naturally than one did not even notice the score's 'great polyphonic feats'. Without doubt, the excellent quality of performance had made it easier to understand the sound-combinations, and with Mahler on the podium 'one did not think, one did not begin to reflect or deliberate; one entered into the musical events, one participated in the birth of the soul that was taking place at that very moment'. With this work perhaps, Mahler had uttered the 'first word for the beginning of a new (musical) era'. At any rate de Lange looked forward to further performances of a work that exhaled 'an artistic vernal fragrance' that was balm to the hearts of music lovers.

Thus, in Holland, one of Mahler's most disputed works had won him respect and admiration from the majority of critics, a rare event in his thorny career as a composer. The one discordant note came as no surprise. The *Telegraaf*'s Otto Knaap began by declaring that his opinion of Mahler's music had 'remained unchanged', that he could appreciate only those movements written in traditional form and that 'tone painting' (*Tonmalerei*) was anathema to him. And if the music was composed solely to show off its interesting counterpoint, this would imply that it was 'the interesting grammar of a literary work that constitutes its merit'. Mahler's music was never beautiful or moving: it inflicted severe punishment upon the ears. Knaap had been unable to discover a trace of unity in the work and had left before the second performance. In his humble opinion, an Adagio that constantly changed tempo was simply devoid of style.

One of the letters Mahler wrote to Alma from Amsterdam shows how carefully he had read the Dutch reviews and how pleased he had been by them, knowing that the future of his works greatly depended on them:

Please, dearest Almschi, read the attached review and give it to Mama, who is a much better audience for such things and drinks this kind of brew with far more understanding. Whatever one thinks of such efforts, the sympathy and the candour of such comments is pleasing all the same. The other reviews are all written in this tone.[142]

Rehearsals for the Second Symphony were as reassuring as they had been for the Fourth. The orchestra continued to display goodwill and growing enthusiasm. At the end of the final rehearsal, all the performers and a sprinkling of listeners gave Mahler a warm ovation. At the concert, the first three movements were warmly received, and after the Finale it seemed as though the applause would never end. 'Yesterday the Second,' Mahler wrote to Alma. 'It has completely lived up to expectations! Overall impression as in Basle and Krefeld! This evening, the second performance and then home again—to you!'[143]

Surprisingly enough, the critics did not take to the Second as they had to the Fourth. Averkamp found the 'contrasted feelings' and divergent, even irreconcilable moods and attitudes disconcerting. Moving from the 'naivety of a child', to the 'tyranny of a despot', Mahler, in his Second, provided a 'kaleidoscopic display of moods and emotions': an 'idyllic naivety' in the Andante that made one think of Schumann; 'lively, rousing movement and sometimes a transparency of instrumentation reminiscent of Berlioz' in the Scherzo; in the first three movements, decidedly ugly orchestral effects with percussion and piccolo; 'an infernal noise with brutal effects' in the Finale. True, a work needed contrasts in order to avoid undue monotony, but it should not give the impression of having been composed by 'several different people'. Only the Andante with its 'pure lyricism', and the simplicity of the 'Urlicht' had been really impressive. The effect of the backstage instruments in the Finale 'was purely superficial'. Mahler could not, after all, be compared to the great masters: for each of them had been 'all of a piece', and he was not.

The contrasting moods of the Second Symphony perplexed Milligen, though he had been much impressed by the last two movements and the titanic crescendo leading up to 'supreme ecstasy' of the final chorus. Mahler's music made great demands on the listener, but he expressed a 'rich, original talent'

[142] Undated letter, BGA, no. 120 (25 Oct.).   [143] BGA, no. 122, 27 Oct.

and a strongly individual sensivity. Daniel de Lange strongly objected to the 'theatrical, even cinematic' procedures, and various 'tricks' such as the first entrance of the alto voice and the off-stage instruments. He had perceived no 'deeply felt, noble emotions' in the symphony, nothing but 'sounds, sounds, sounds'. Masters like Bach, Beethoven, or Brahms did not care what effect their works might have on the world; they wrote music because they were unable to remain silent. But in spite of what might be said for or against this symphony, it would take its place in history because Mahler had 'done what he had to do as an artist'.

Otto Knaap's review repeated all the tired clichés of contemporary German criticism. The only original touch was that he put them into the mouth of his 'younger brother' newly arrived from Chicago, whom he had invited to attend the concert with him. This 'brother' had been alternately incensed or reduced to laughter by the composer's 'offensive dissonances', 'infernal noise', or 'nonsense', and had reached the conclusion that 'this music can't be meant to be taken seriously'. He called Mahler a 'poseur' for remaining seated between movements with his back to the audience and his head in his hands, and surmised that his music was designed to 'épater les bourgeois'. However, it had been nothing but 'torture' for Knaap's 'brother'. He guessed that the enthusiastic applause came from 'decadent', 'degenerate' people anxious to 'swim with the tide' and afraid of being called fuddy-duddies.[144]

The usual reactions of the press had thus been stood on their head. The incredible success of the Fourth had prejudiced that of the Second, although this was the symphony which had brought Mahler his first triumphs. Luckily the reservations of the Dutch critics about the Second could do nothing to spoil Mahler's memories of the ecstatic audience, the adoring orchestra, the eminent colleague ready to do anything in his power to make his work better known, and a press which for the first time had managed to unravel the 'enigmas' of the Fourth. In Holland, for the first time in his life, he had experienced what all composers dream of. Not surprisingly, he began to think of Amsterdam as his 'second musical home',[145] and on his return he wrote to Mengelberg:

I am especially grateful to you for . . . your youthful zest and initiative, your congenial conducting and penetrating understanding of my works—these are some of the things which, as we agreed on the occasion of a convivial gathering, can be deeply felt, though one can never express one's gratitude for them. And so in spirit I grasp your friendly hand, and beg you to keep these attitudes to me in the future, attitudes all the more precious because they are so rare, all the more worthy of admiration because only they can nurture living art, something in which I have recognized you to be an enthusiastic adept.[146]

---

[144] For the two performances of the Second Symphony on 26 and 27 Oct. 1904, the soloists were Alida Oldenboom-Lütkemann, soprano, and Martha Stapelfold, contralto.

[145] Mahler used this term in a letter to Mengelberg later in the same year after returning from Holland (MBR1, no. 304; MBR2, no. 338).

[146] Mahler also asked Mengelberg to pass on to the chorus and orchestra 'his deep gratitude for achievements which only they [he and Mengelberg] were able to appreciate'.

As an example of the fervent admiration Mahler inspired in his Dutch friends, two letters written at the end of October by Alphons Diepenbrock should be quoted. They were occasioned by an unsigned article, entitled 'A View of Mahler, by a Friend of Art' which appeared in the *Weekblad voor Muziek* on 30 October 1904[147] and which ran as follows:

A musician of some authority (his identity is irrelevant here) has written to say what a torture it would have been for him if, last Sunday, he had sat through two consecutive performances of Mahler's Fourth Symphony. He left during the interval.

He cannot understand an educated public's predilection for such a work. 'Are people really so stupid, or is the homage they paid merely the result of the shameful circumstances which allow such a thing to happen?'

A long, infernally boring work, devoid of musical ideas, which demonstrates in the most absurd fashion how *not* to use instruments. Mahler is extremely good at calling forth from instruments sounds they do not actually possess.

All that a genius like Richard Strauss needs for his giant ideas is a simple voice and an admittedly large, but natural and simple orchestra. But a charlatan like Mahler needs for his mindless clamour the most impossible instruments, which on top of everything else he causes to toot and blow in a manner quite at odds with their character. Fortunately for healthy artistic sensibility, his success was purely superficial. The first three movements are totally bogus, insincere, impotent. The shorter fourth movement made a better impression, but only because Mahler, probably much to his regret, was unable to place a mute in the mouth of the soprano (Frau Oldenboom-Lütkemann).

And they had the effrontery—may Apollo forgive them—to ape von Bülow's distinguished example and put on this boring spectacle twice in the same evening!

Diepenbrock was furious when he read this, and wrote an indignant letter to the editor-in-chief of the magazine, Hugo Nolthenius.[148] He accused the anonymous critic of having devoted his own article to *Mignon*, contenting himself with the judgement of a self-styled 'friend of art' for the Mahler concerts. He had ignored 'the greatest living composer' and the 'Beethoven of our time'. How could he merely have accepted someone else's report?

Mahler is the greatest musical genius alive today. He is a true tone poet (*Tondichter*) in the real sense of the word, such as music has known from Orpheus to Beethoven and Wagner. He thinks of his art in terms of a priesthood. We shall have cause to be grateful to him if the descendants of our miserable epoch manage to find something other than the supremacy of 'backward' plebeians. And thus, because he is a genius and cannot meet the weaknesses of his contemporaries half-way, the plebeians hate him. Sicut erat in principio et nunc et semper.[149] And you should be ashamed to make common cause with these plebeians![150]

[147] 11 (1904): 44, 418. Eduard Reeser attributed it to a pupil of Bernard Zweers, Willem Landré (1874–1948), who at the time was writing articles in a similar vein for *Die Nieuwe Courant* in The Hague.

[148] Hugo Nolthenius (1848–1929), founder and editor of the *Weekblad voor Muziek*, which appeared regularly between 1894 and 1910. A classics master at the Grammar School in Utrecht, he was a self-taught musician who particularly admired Wagner and Strauss. His attitude to Mahler always remained sceptical.

[149] 'As it was in the beginning, is now and ever shall be.'

[150] Diepenbrock, *Brieven*, ed. Eduard Reeser, 295.

It seems this letter was never sent, unlike the other one Diepenbrock wrote the same day to his friend, the composer Bernard Zweers, whom he apparently suspected of being connected with the offending review. He asked him if he knew who the author was, and reproached him with having expressed his antipathy towards Mahler in front of his students at the Conservatory, instead of inculcating respect for 'genius', or 'if you don't consider him to be one, for an artist who approaches his duty as an artist and pursues his ideals with unbelievable seriousness and ardour.'[151] Zweers passed on the letter to Nolthenius, who published in the following issue of the *Weekblad* a short paragraph recognizing that 'in Amsterdam opinions are very divided' on the subject of Mahler and his concerts, and that 'certain composers, who were no less competent' than the person whose negative views had appeared in the previous number, considered him to be 'the Beethoven of our time' and 'the greatest living composer'.[152]

But Zweer's disparaging remarks, which had previously been the rule, now became the exception, especially in Holland. The fact that Mahler had gained the support of eminent musicians like Mengelberg and Diepenbrock was entirely new in his life and its importance cannot be overestimated. After the second concert on 27 October, Mahler's stay in Amsterdam ended with a farewell dinner given by the editor of the *Algemeen Handelsblad*, Charles Boissevain. The talk was local gossip, which aroused Diepenbrock's indignation: 'Awful,' he wrote, 'better not to think of such things, especially after the final chorus (of the Second).'

Mahler returned from Holland on 29 October after a long journey and a fortnight's absence, and was immediately engrossed in problems at the Opera which absorbed all his energies[153] despite the fact that no new production or important staging was in prospect until the beginning of the following year. The only exception was *Lakmé*, whose Viennese première took place on 14 November under Bruno Walter and with Selma Kurz in the title role. Several Viennese critics complained as before that Kurz was not 'a true coloratura'; Schönaich, on the other hand, thought her coloratura well-nigh perfect but accused her of having 'a warm voice and an icy heart'. The majority verdict, however, was that she had 'developed her great natural gifts', and that her technique was 'less cold and less objective than previously'. Contrary to Schönaich, Kauders maintained that she was not simply a singer with a lifeless silvery flute in her throat but that her voice, despite its phenomenal technique, showed

---

[151] Letter to Bernard Zweers, Diepenbrock, *Brieven*, 296. Further on in the book, an extract from Elisabeth Diepenbrock's diary describes a meal she had with her husband and Hutschenruyter at the Zweers' after Mahler's departure. In the course of the evening Zweers had declared that Mahler was 'not a composer'.

[152] *Weekblad voor Muziek*, 11 (1904): 45, 430.

[153] The days immediately after his return must have been particularly busy, because he had to send Peters the score of the Fifth with his final corrections, something he had not had time to do in Amsterdam. He sent it from Vienna on 1 Nov., with a telegram and a further letter (Klemm, 'Geschichte', 44). The large full score containing his final changes appeared in the same month.

deep-felt emotion. Most of Vienna's 'infernal judges' tore Delibes' opera to shreds. Kalbeck called it a 'object of fashion'. Kauders described it as a 'cleverly arranged trapeze designed to show off a diva's virtuosity', containing a few 'successful numbers', a few 'agreeable and attractive melodies', some 'spicy rhythms', but very little 'genuine feeling'. For six years in succession, *Lakmé* served as a vehicle for Selma Kurz, and even though Max Vancsa found the music 'worthy of an operetta', it remained in the Vienna repertory until 1918.[154]

Though all Mahler's friends, acquaintances, family, and collaborators commented on his occasional bad temper, his uncompromising artistic demands and his fanaticism, his enemies sometimes accused him of being utterly ruthless in achieving his ends, even if this meant using deceit or the occasional ruse. Although he was often blamed for losing his temper and treating the singers roughly, it is obvious that he could not have spent ten years running one of the greatest opera houses in Europe unless he had been also capable of tact and diplomacy. This was especially true for Vienna, where polite manners were considered to rank among the major virtues. It is equally obvious that the Director of the Hofoper was often forced to disregard his own deepest sympathies and artistic tastes. We know for example that his relations with the famous Munich conductor Felix Mottl were never warm. In 1904, Mottl came to Vienna almost every week to conduct the Philharmonic concerts, which, since Josef Hellmesberger's resignation, had no permanent conductor. Mahler's and Mottl's diplomatic behaviour was commented upon by the *Neues Wiener Journal* on 12 November:

Recently the public has been keeping a close eye on two men. One is Director Mahler, the other Herr Felix Mottl. They have called on each other. Herr Mottl went to a performance of *Die Zauberflöte* at the Hofoper.[155] This in itself is not particularly noteworthy, but there are those in Vienna who still believe that Mottl will be Mahler's successor. True, for the moment Mahler does not have the slightest intention of resigning from his position, and Mottl has never been seriously thought of as his successor. Nonetheless, it is surmised that the two are rivals. Thus, during Herr Mottl's recent visit to *Die Zauberflöte* his face and hands were carefully observed. Alas, everyone was disappointed. His face expressed total rapture and he applauded vigorously at the end of every act. When the all-powerful Musikdirektor from Munich left the Opera at the end of the performance, he provided his friends with the following critique: 'It was simply superb! No opera company in the world is capable of giving a better performance of *Die Zauberflöte* . . . Marvellous . . . Marvellous . . .'

The paper also disclosed that on the previous Sunday Mahler had attended a Philharmonic concert conducted by the Munich conductor.[156] A letter from

---

[154] Cast for the performance of 14 Nov., conducted by Bruno Walter: Kurz (Lakmé), Kittel (Mallika), Elizza (Ellen), Michalek (Rosa), Petru (Mrs Bentson), Slezak (Gerald), Mayr (Nilakantha), Moser (Friedrich), Preuss, Boruttau, Pacal, Marian. The work was performed eight times in 1904 and nine times in 1905. The review in the *Neue Musik-Zeitung* complains bitterly of the 'effrontery' of the claque on the first night.

[155] On 2 Nov.

[156] On 6 Nov. Mottl conducted Mozart's 38th Symphony, a *Scherzo* in C minor by Pfitzner dating from 1887 and Beethoven's 'Eroica' Symphony.

Mottl to Mahler has survived[157] in which he declined an invitation to dine at Auenbruggergasse because he had a chill. As the two musicians were trying to outdo one another in expressions of courtesy, there is no reason to suppose that Mottl's illness was merely an excuse. Even if their relations never went beyond simple politeness, it is likely that the invitation to dinner was taken up later in the season during another of Mottl's trips to Vienna.

Another incident demanded tactful handling by Mahler. The Intendant of the Munich Opera, Ernst von Possart,[158] wrote to Mahler asking him to engage his daughter Poppi, a light soprano. It is clear from Mahler's reply that his opinion of the girl's talent was not very high, yet he took great pains not to offend Possart. The nearly complete draft of Mahler's answer, which has survived among Alma's papers, shows that he made several false starts. The young girl had, he said, made an excellent impression during the audition, 'not only on account of her voice, but especially on account of her cultivated artistry. I have never met anything comparable in a beginner, and it is obviously not acquired, but inherited.' Nevertheless, Mahler told Possart that the Opera did not need another light soprano for the moment; Poppi could be hired only if she agreed to appear first as a guest. After a guest appearance (during which she could sing whatever she pleased), 'the outcome . . . is not entirely in my hands, yet I ask you to remain assured of my warmest solicitude, and I am ready in the event to discuss with you in person all details and prospects beforehand.' Thus Mahler could be tactful and diplomatic when the interests of the Opera were at stake. Obviously, the excuse he gave for not engaging Possart's daughter was a diplomatic lie, for in fact he was soon to engage a new lyric and coloratura soprano, the 22-year-old Austrian Berta Kiurina.[159] But because of her youth he thought it would be some time before she would be able to sing all the roles in her category. The situation at the Opera was becoming critical, for Rita Michalek had put on weight and lost most of her vocal freshness.[160] A warmly recommended guest artist from Leipzig, Alda Gardini, failed to convince. The problem was not solved until 1906, when Mahler engaged another light soprano Gertrud Förstel.[161]

But the Opera was also short of dramatic sopranos, and Mahler put his hope in Charlotte von Seebock, another pupil of Rosa Papier. Her auditions had

---

[157]   A copy of this letter, dated 16 Nov., is in AMS.

[158]   Ernst von Possart (1841–1921), actor and elocutionist, Intendant of the Königliche Hoftheater in Munich from 1895 to 1905. Strauss dedicated *Enoch Arden* Op. 38 and *Das Schloss am Meer* (1899) to him.

[159]   Berta Kiurina (1882–1933) made her first guest appearance on 28 Feb. 1905. She became a member of the Hofoper from 1 Sept., and for twenty-five years was one of the most popular of Viennese singers. Born in Linz, she had studied with Gustav Geiringer at the Vienna Conservatory. Her best roles were Cherubino, Nedda, Leonora (in *Trovatore*). She also triumphed in coloratura roles. Her salary for the first year was 8,000 kronen, with a yearly increase of 2,000 kronen from the second year onwards (letter of 17 Nov. 1904, HOA, Z. 1097/1904).

[160]   A registered letter from Mahler to Intendant Plappart, dated 25 June 1903, concerns Michalek, and explains that 'if the natural consequences of her recent marriage are to occur, she will become useless for her appointed tasks'. (The envelope of this letter is in Alma's hand, HOA.)

[161]   Letters from Mahler, 1 Mar. 1905, HOA, Z. 295/1905.

been promising, and he offered her a contract commencing in September 1905 so as to dissuade her from accepting one from Berlin. It is obvious, however, that Seebock failed to live up to expectations, for she left the Opera at the end of her second season.[162]

Having renewed the contract of the principal comic tenor (*Spieltenor*) of the Hofoper, Hans Breuer, and raised his salary, Mahler engaged a new Heldentenor, Hubert Leuer.[163] Because Hesch was ill again and Moritz Frauscher was about to leave Vienna, he also engaged two new basses, Willi von Wissiak[164] in June and Alexander Haydter[165] the following year.

In 1904, plans to engage Ernestine Schumann-Heink, an international star who had already sung with Mahler in Hamburg, came to nothing. The great contralto had been living in the United States since 1898 and her European agent, Eugen Frankfurter, told Mahler 'in strict secrecy' in 1903 that 'exceptional conditions' might persuade her to accept an engagement. Mahler immediately replied by telegram: 'Urgently await your proposals. Ready for big concessions except for contractual leave.'[166] No doubt the regal prima donna found the Vienna Opera's 'concessions' insufficient to induce her to leave the United States, where salaries were considerably higher than in Europe. She never sang at the Vienna Opera, and was heard by the Viennese public only in 1906, in a series of guest performances at the Volksoper.

Despite the rule which he had set and most of the time observed, Mahler sometimes granted a singer leave to appear in other theatres. He did this in 1904 in the case of Gutheil-Schoder, who had been invited to Leipzig for a week by Max Staegemann. Mahler explained his decision to the Intendant: he had yielded to the singer's request in this case because 'in the near future, he [Staegemann] may well be asked to do a similar favour'.[167] So for once the singer's salary was not cut during her absence.

Mahler's diplomacy also had its limits and it sometimes happened that his position and the power he wielded put him in embarrassing situations, when composers sent him operas which he found unworthy of the Vienna stage, or writers' libretti which he found unworthy of being set to music. In 1898, a few months after he had become director, he received from the German poet Julius

---

[162] Letters from Mahler to the Indendant, 28 May and 19 June 1904, and a letter from Rosa Papier, 28 May, HOA, Z. 598/1904. Mahler asked the Intendant to pay Seebock 400 kronen a month, starting on 1 June, in order to 'keep this fine talent and this splendid voice' in Vienna.

[163] Hubert Leuer (1880–1969), born in Cologne, studied singing in his native city. He was engaged by the Vienna Opera on 1 Aug. 1904, where he remained until 1920 and sang most of the great Wagnerian roles, Herod in *Salome*, and the title role in Verdi's *Otello*. He was married to Berta Kiurina.

[164] HOA, Z. 701/1904. Wissiak was a member of the Opera until 1908.

[165] Alexander Haydter (1872–1919), born in Vienna, studied at the Vienna Conservatory with Gustav Geiringer and Josef Gansbächer. He made a brilliant debut in Zurich in 1896, and sang both baritone and bass parts at the Vienna Opera from 1 Sept. 1905 until his death. His main parts were Alberich, Beckmesser, Rocco, and Klingsor.

[166] Telegram of 27 May 1903.

[167] Letter of 15 Jan. 1904, HOA, G.Z. 100/1904.

Wolff[168] a draft libretto based on a long octosyllabic narrative poem (85 pages!) entitled *Renata*, which he had published in Berlin and which had met with considerable success. This no doubt explains both the courtesy and the attention to detail of Mahler's firm reply:

Honoured Sir, forgive me for having kept you waiting so long for an answer. I am sure you will understand how busy my duties keep me. Besides which it is always difficult to bring oneself to say 'no' if I am not to do you a real disservice. This is not a question of making a literary judgement; in an operatic performance, the very thing that gives the work coherence and sense would be lost. That it is not the wine, but the shape of the goblet out of which it is drunk that has the magic effect—that, on the stage, would hardly be apparent even to the most perceptive opera-goers. The public at large would only see that a drink produces general bewilderment. They wouldn't be interested in the bewilderment as such, or know what it signified. The explanation and the end however produces, to put it mildly, a disconcertingly dramatic dénouement, not the exposition of an idea. Represented in flesh and blood, this as spoken drama might have an impact on a small group who understand and are interested in the tensions between the ancient and the medieval worlds and their reconciliation in the Renaissance. But even they would not be very enthusiastic, and their numbers would be small.

To come now to some points of detail. The magic potion theme is a difficult one to handle—when, as here, it is so harped upon and used as the sole driving force of the action. In *Götterdämmerung*, Siegfried, before he establishes a relationship with a human being, before he becomes fully human, must forget the realm of the Gods in which Brünnhilde and he have their origins. With Tristan and Isolde, we see the physical attraction for each other long before they drink the potion; and the fact that they believe they have drunk a deadly poison is what loosens their tongues. In *Renata* however we are supposed to be interested in the potion, or rather the goblet, as such and with that as a sole viewpoint, understand the whole story—not in itself an interesting one—and get carried away by it. But that won't happen—not even with the few people who are capable of a subtle construction and interpretation. The spirit of the Renaissance cannot be got over to us from the stage by means of the shape of the goblet. But what else is there to get it over? What is there to bring out the contrast between the Christian Middle Ages and the new way of life? The fact that she now loves this young man rather than that one, and that he loves this rather than that girl? That Jucunda falls head over heels for a grey beard obsessed with the future? That a

[168] Julius Wolff (1834–1910) was born in Quedlinburg (Prussia). He came from a prosperous middle-class family. After completing his university studies in Berlin, he joined the family business. In 1869 he founded a newspaper, *Harz-Zeitung*. He fought as an officer in the Franco-Prussian war, and then moved to Charlottenburg, where he devoted himself exclusively to literature. He published a collection of poems based on his wartime experiences, and then wrote a number of epic poems, some of them inspired by Wagner. They include *Till Eulenspiegel* (1874), *Der Rattenfänger* (1876), *Tannhäuser* (1880), *Der fliegende Holländer* (1892), and *Assalide* (1876). He also wrote several novels. The poetry of Julius Wolff, Rudolf Baumach, and Joseph Victor von Scheffel has often been criticized as attempting to revive a long-defunct Romantic tradition. Paul Heyse, in 1884, referred to it as *Butzenscheibenpoesie* (pseudo-Gothic or, translated literally, lattice window poetry), its principal characteristics are the treatment of historical, and especially medieval themes in a style inspired by that of the Middle Ages; primitive psychology; and avowed nationalist tendencies. Wolff was on good terms with Richard Strauss and Engelbert Humperdinck, whose *Festgesang*, a work for chorus and orchestra, makes use of one of his poems.

boisterous crowd drinking wine (the public sees no more than that!) is overcome by a certain sensuality? There is nothing in any of that to indicate the rebirth of Antiquity. The merchant in the midst of the festivities—it is he who has donated the goblet—can no more represent outmoded medievality and withdrawal from life than the journeyman who was so quick to renounce the world can represent a life-thirsty Renaissance man . . .

If at least a number of emaciated ascetics, under the influence of the drink or the goblet, were to throw back their hoods and defrock themselves! That would have shown us something like love of the world and flight from the world.

Should I mention smaller details? The Gothic style, for instance, which is described at the end as a frightening contrast to Antiquity? Yet the Votivkirche[169] is as beautiful and cheerful as any Greek temple. An element of perversity and outrage is produced by such observations, even in the really quite heart-warming final conclusion. And yet it is in Gothic churches (and in the equally 'sinister' gloom of the stained-glass windows) that the Pagan spell is cast: It is on the high altar itself that the goblet must stand. Renata, inspired by a Hellenic thirst for life, has a vision of Christian saints and it is they who arrange in advance the coming together of the two Renaisance characters, who are then specifically summoned to unite in the words of the spell. And so forth. The result is that the idea is not developed, and we don't get the feeling of contrast which is supposed to be the essence of the play. Instead the idea, on which everything depends produces confusion and bewilderment inasmuch as it arouses expectations which are not fulfilled. I hope you will one day succeed in getting what is really an original and interesting play put on the stage. If underlying it there is a fine and profound idea, that in itself won't harm the play, but only on condition that any abstract elucidation of the idea is rendered superfluous by the action and the characters themselves.

I hope you will accept this detailed criticism as proof of my esteem with which I remain yours

Gustav Mahler[170]

Mahler's harsh judgement was undoubtedly well founded, and it is amazing that he should have taken such trouble reading and analysing in such detail what appears to have been a particularly poor libretto, one which would probably never even have been set to music. However he obviously wished to show some consideration for a correspondent whom he did not wish to offend with a curt refusal, and that is why he took the time to define his position, based upon a thorough knowledge and a long experience of the musical stage, and to express his essential beliefs about the role, nature, and limitations of an opera libretto.

Because of his position in Vienna, Mahler was constantly badgered by composers, authors, and singers, and the situation could become more embarrassing when he was dealing with a composer and sometimes a respected

[169] The church built in Vienna in the second half of the nineteenth century in Gothic style by Emperor Franz-Joseph to commemorate his escape from a murder attempt.

[170] Letter to Julius Wolff, 20 May 1898, *Revue Mahler Review*, 1 (1987), BMG, Paris, 9 ff. Translation by Roy MacDonald Stock. *Renata: Eine Dichtung*, published in 1893 by the Berlin publisher Grote.

colleague who was hoping to have his opera performed at the Hofoper. Max von Schillings, for one, had gained considerable repute in Germany[171] as a composer of 'national' and 'neo-romantic' music. Hermann Behn, who counted both Mahler and Schillings among his friends, had recommended Schillings' *Ingwelde* to him, but Mahler could not be persuaded to perform the work. Schillings complained in a letter to Behn:

And now you are working on Mahler. If I could think of an advocate for *Ingwelde*,[172] it would be you, for you know how to preach enthusiasm with reason. In any case, I have little hope in the case of Mahler, either now or in the future. I am of the opinion that his music has its origins in an area that is altogether different from mine, so that it is probably impossible for him to understand me. If the principal obstacle for refusing the opera was his antipathy to the text, then this could be countered with reasonable arguments. Are the faults of the text really worse than those of many new works performed in Vienna and whose music is not '*Ingwelde*' music?[173]

Wilhelm Raupp, Schillings' biographer, believed that Mahler's aversion to Schillings and his music was really racial, and that Schillings was the victim of the 'Jewish machinations (*Machenschaften*)' that had acquired control over German music.

In the case of *Der Moloch*, Schillings' third opera, Mahler apparently decided to make up for his rejection of *Ingwelde* and accept it without seeing the score or even knowing what the libretto was about. It was in fact based on an unfinished play by the great German poet Friedrich Hebbel. The central character is Hiram, the Carthaginian high priest of Moloch who has left his native country for the German island of Thule, where he has installed his idols and resurrected his ancestral religion in order to take vengeance on the Romans. At the end of the opera he is shown to be a charlatan, and commits suicide. For mysterious reasons, Hiram's Carthaginian religion was identified with Judaism, and Schillings' opera was interpreted as a violent attack on Jews and Jewry. Before he had even read the libretto, Mahler wrote to Schillings in the autumn of 1905:

At this time I cannot think of a more appropriate place than Vienna for the première of your work or of a place where fewer obstacles of any kind would be erected in the path of a work that is exceptional in every way. The ideal conditions for the birth of a dramatic work include the fulfilment of the material conditions necessary for a successful performance, and also that there should be time to apply the final artistic polish to the work itself in the course of rehearsals. Unlimited time and care are needed.[174]

---

[171]　In 1911, however, the *Bilder Atlas zur Musikgeschichte* claimed that 'his [Schillings'] melody lacked convincing warmth, his musical imagination any strongly pulsating life, those qualities which compel the listener to take an interest in a work and are of decisive significance for its survival.' See above, Vol. ii, Chap. 15, for the biography of Max von Schillings.

[172]　The work had been performed in 1896, in Karlsruhe.

[173]　Wilhelm Raupp, *Max von Schillings*, 63

[174]　Ibid. 104. This letter is dated 19 Nov. 1905.

In January 1906 Mahler confirmed his decision after reading the libretto, and proposed to give the world première in Vienna. 'I would rather not judge the libretto, since for the moment I have not the slightest idea of its musical treatment. But it seems to me that you have the right blood in your veins for a grand musical realization of this powerful material.'[175] Later on, some delay must have occurred, for Mahler wrote, 'it is not my ambition to be the first (at most it is to be the best)' and that Schillings should feel free to give the world première elsewhere. With *Feuersnot*, Mahler had assumed an identical attitude, yet Schillings' latent anti-Semitism immediately led him to believe that some Machiavellian intrigue was being directed against him and his work. At least this is what his openly anti-Semitic biographer, writing during the Nazi era, leads us to believe. Nevertheless, Mahler continued his preparations and even suggested going to Munich to see Schillings, together with Bruno Walter, who was to conduct the work in Vienna. The casting of the principal roles, particularly the high priest Hiram, a baritone, posed certain problems, and Schillings was asked to come to Vienna in May 1905. He played the whole work to Mahler on the piano and left convinced that all difficulties had been overcome and that rehearsals would soon start in time for an autumn première.

That plans for the première had reached an advanced stage is proved by a series of documents from the Schillings archives.[176] Roller had already designed the sets.[177] Then, just as rehearsals were about to commence, the *Neue Freie Presse* published a vitriolic review by Oscar Bie of the recent Dresden première of *Der Moloch*.[178] It tore the opera to shreds and called it an 'unpardonable error'. The characters were no more than 'marionettes, or symbols', 'shadows' to which Schillings' music failed to give the slightest trace of life, with its 'reserve', its 'distinguished air', its 'lack of power', its 'intellectualism' and its 'cold and empty' motifs. The Dresden Opera was 'the Moloch's latest victim'. According to Raupp, Bie denounced the work's anti-Semitic tendencies, but in fact the article merely hints at them. Because the *Neue Freie Presse* was run by Jews, Schillings once more received the impression of being a victim of the 'Jewish clique', an impression confirmed when he received the following letter from Mahler: 'The local press has for some weeks carried on such a shameless campaign against your work—such a prelude to a forthcoming première is unheard of, even going by what is usual here—that the public is now completely biased and will come to the première full of prejudices.'

[175] Letter of 5 Jan. 1906; ibid. 108.

[176] Österreichische Nationalbibliothek, Vienna. It seems that Mahler also intended to produce Schillings' *Der Pfeifertag*. According to the contract signed by the Opera and the composer, Schillings was to receive 1,000 kronen as 'royalties of the première' plus 5 per cent of the gross takings. But the Hofoper refused to name a date for the two premières. It was specified that the score of *Der Pfeifertag* should arrive in Vienna before 1 Sept. 1906 (letter from Schillings to Mahler, 24 Jan. 1906, and Mahler's reply of 29 Jan. Draft contract dated Feb. 1906).

[177] Ludwig Hevesi writes that he saw the finished models for the sets in Roller's studio at the beginning of 1907 (*Altkunst, Neukunst* (Konegen, Vienna 909), 265).

[178] 22 Dec. 1906.

Thus, the performance was cancelled[179] and Schillings' anger and frustration are understandable, although *Der Moloch* had a rather undistinguished fate and its lack of success elsewhere seems to indicate that it was anything but a masterpiece.[180] Mahler's heroic battle for *Salome* in 1906 and 1907 proves that he was quite willing to fight and overcome many obstacles, even to the extent of endangering his own position, when he knew he was fighting for something important.

Towards the end of 1904, Franz Schmidt, one of Mahler's solo cellists at the Opera, was persuaded by one of his orchestral colleagues to play to Mahler on the piano his first opera, which was based on Victor Hugo's *Notre Dame de Paris*. He had so far hesitated to do so, mainly because, as was well known, he was one of Mahler's most determined opponents in the orchestra. According to Schmidt's biographer Carl Nemeth, he was very nervous on the morning of his appointment with Mahler and wanted to cancel it. However, around nine, he appeared in the big rehearsal room adjoining Mahler's office and played the whole opera on the piano. Mahler remained silent the whole time; then, at the end, he said: 'Very beautiful, but I deplore the lack of big ideas in your music.'[181] All the same, he praised Schmidt's piano-playing and offered him a post as Korrepetitor, which the young man refused. A few days later Mahler passed on to him the offer of another post, that of Kapellmeister in Mannheim. This prompted Nemeth to accuse Mahler of trying to get rid of Schmidt whilst seeming to be promoting his career. Schmidt refused to leave Austria and the Mannheim post was, it seems, subsequently taken by Arthur Bodanzky.[182]

During this final stage of Mahler's directorship, another new opera was offered to him by Ethel Smyth, the English composer, who is remembered both for her music and her feminist activities. She had already gained wide recognition after the great success, in 1893, of her *Mass* and the performances of her first two operas, and had met Mahler briefly in Leipzig when she was studying composition and he was a conductor at the local opera house. Their meeting must have been very brief indeed, for Smyth's report of Mahler's love affair with

[179] The production of *Der Pfeifertag* was cancelled too, but this time for financial reasons, Mahler having been reprimanded by the Intendant for having significantly exceeded his own expenditure estimates (WMW1, 220; WMW2, 85 ff.).

[180] *Der Moloch* was first performed in Dresden, under Ernst von Schuch, in 1906. It was staged in recent times at Oberhausen, in the Ruhr, in 1989 (*Neue Zeitschrift für Musik*, 7 (1989), 55).

[181] *Notre Dame de Paris* was definitively refused, and its score returned to the composer, on 18 May 1907 (HOA, Z. VI.36/1907). In 1906, Mahler suggested Schmidt for the title of Hofmusiker, which was granted to him on 1 Oct. (letter of 21 Aug., HOA, Z. 939 and Z. 3077/1906).

[182] Carl Nemeth, *Franz Schmidt*, 86. Schmidt's *Symphonisches Zwischenspiel* (Symphonic Interlude) had been conducted by Ernst von Schuch at the Vienna Philharmonic on 6 Dec. 1903. Schmidt's biographer claims that Mahler's 'jealousy' had been aroused in 1902 by the success of the Vienna performance of Schmidt's First Symphony (ibid. 52). Franz Schmidt (1874–1939), born in Pressburg, studied violoncello, organ, and composition at the Vienna Conservatory between 1889 and 1896. He became a cellist at the Opera at the age of 22 and stayed there until 1910, when he accepted a position as professor of piano at the Academy of Music, whose director he later became in 1925. His works include two operas (*Notre Dame*, performed at the Hofoper in 1914, and *Fredegundis*), four symphonies, an oratorio, *Das Buch mit sieben Siegeln*, several works for piano and organ, and chamber music.

Marion von Weber is based entirely on hearsay.[183] In 1906, Smyth had just had a 'cruel experience' in Prague, where *The Wreckers* (performed under the name *Strandrecht*) had been badly received by the audience at the German Opera House, and torn to pieces by the press. Unshaken, she decided to go to Vienna and try her luck there.

I knew there was one man big enough to serve my turn, Gustav Mahler, now in charge of the Viennese Opera. But how to get his ear? For I had not met him since the old, old Leipzig days when I was slightly known to him as one of the reactionary anti-Wagner Herzogenberg group! I wrote to him boldly, however, and when Harry and I arrived at Vienna I found I had been given an appointment. But it appeared that full of distrust of this composing English woman's opera Mahler had deputed his second-in-command to hear it and report.[184]

Thus Smyth met Bruno Walter, not Mahler. However, the encounter proved a success on both sides, as Walter later recalled:

Before me stood a gaunt Englishwoman of about forty-eight clad in a nondescript baggy dress. She told me she had formerly studied in Leipzig, that Brahms had been interested in her chamber music, her opera *Der Wald* had had its première in Dresden, and now she was here in Vienna to make us acquainted with her latest opera, based on Henry Brewster's *The Wreckers*. I was apprehensive about our meeting, but she had hardly played for ten minutes, singing the vocal parts in an unattractive voice, when I made her stop, rushed over to Mahler's office and implored him to come back with me; the Englishwoman was playing her work to me and she was a true composer. Mahler was unfortunately unable to spare the time, so I had to go back alone. We spent the whole morning on her opera, and when we parted I was wholly entranced by her work and her personality. I asked her to my home and we saw as much as possible of each other while she was in Vienna.[185]

Many years later, Ethel Smyth wrote to Walter to confirm the details of this story. Mahler, it seems, had asked to meet her, surely towards the end of 1906, shortly before he left Vienna, for he eventually refused to accept *The Wreckers* for the Hofoper, 'so as not to tie the hands of his successor'.[186]

Although there were many occasions when Mahler conformed to the traditional conventions of courtesy and diplomacy when offered a new opera, he

---

[183]   See above, Vol. i, Chap. 12.

[184]   Ethel Smyth, *What Happened Next* (Longmans, Green, London, 1940), 277.

[185]   BWT 154.

[186]   Christopher St. John, *Ethel Smyth: A Biography* (Longmans, London, 1959), 110 and 283. Ethel Smyth (1858–1944) was born in London, the daughter of an English general and a French mother, and studied in Leipzig, where she was a pupil of Brahms's friend Henrich von Herzogenberg. It was there that she first made a name for herself with her chamber music. She then returned to England where, after 1890, her first orchestral works were performed. But her real reputation was made with a number of operas, the texts of which she wrote herself: *Fantasio* (Weimar, 1898); *Der Wald* (Dresden, 1901); *The Wreckers* (Leipzig, 1906); *The Boatswain's Mate* (London, 1916); *Fête Galante* (Birmingham, 1923); and *Entente Cordiale* (Bristol, 1926). In 1911 in the course of her untiring support for women's suffrage, she composed a *March for Women*, which was often played at feminist meetings. It later appeared in the opera *The Boatswain's Mate*. The rest of her output included a *Horn Concerto* (1927), a symphony with chorus, songs, and numerous chamber works. At the end of her life she went deaf and stopped composing, but she published about a dozen books, autobiographies, and travel reminiscences.

sometimes came straight to the point. For instance, in June 1904, after Alfred Wernicke, the conductor of the Mannheim Opera, whom he had met there at the beginning of the year, sent him the score of his opera, he wrote back:

Although I acknowledge the intrinsic musical quality of your work, I must, alas, inform you that I am unable to recommend its acceptance by our theatre. I think it is not effective enough for the stage and the musical style is far too old-fashioned. Please do not take offence at my frankness. With my best wishes, Gustav Mahler.[187]

On another occasion, he wrote even more curtly to the Viennese composer Karl Weinberger in 1907: 'The undersigned management herewith returns the material—score, vocal score and libretto—of the opera *Schlaraffenland* with thanks. Unfortunately a performance of the said work at the Imperial and Royal Court Opera cannot be considered.'[188] In 1899 Hermann Grädener, a composer whose conservative style was well thought of in Vienna, had submitted a symphony to Mahler in the hope of a performance by the Philharmonic. Mahler's reply was brief, and to the point: 'In reply to your letter, please come and play your work to me some time in December. The impression which I get from that will decide whether or not it can be accepted for performance in the second half of the season. Yours etc.'[189]

To his friend Countess Wydenbruck, Mahler was also quite frank in explaining why he was unable to put on a new opera by Josef Reiter, whose *Der Bundschuh*[190] he had produced in 1900: 'Naturally I am always prepared to do something for Herr Reiter, as long as it lies within my powers. To perform his opera because I feel sorry for him is <u>not</u> within my powers. The Hofoper is not my private property, it is a public institution for whose running I am fully responsible. I don't believe his opera is fit for performance, but that is not quite my final judgement, since I usually take a further look, even at a rejected work.'[191]

The situation could be even more embarrassing when the composer had been a close friend of Mahler, as was the case with Edmund von Mihalovich.[192] The Hungarian composer had for several years tried to persuade him to perform his third opera, *Toldi Szerelme*. In April 1904 and again in the following October Mahler promised to come to Budapest to see a performance but on

[187] Undated card, addressed to Herr Kammermusiker Wernicke (postmark 27 June). It was probably written in 1904, since Mahler had met Alfred Wernicke in Feb. when he conducted the Third Symphony at the Mannheim opera (Stadtarchiv Mannheim, Nachlass Wernicke).

[188] Letter to Karl Weinberger, Stadtbibliothek, Vienna, Z. 144/1907, I.N. 175.954.

[189] Letter of 15 Oct. 1899, to Hermann Grädener, Stadtbibliothek, Vienna, I.N. 176.380. Hermann Grädener (1844–1929), violinist, conductor, and composer, was the son of a famous Hamburg cellist and composer, whose pupil he had been before entering the Vienna Conservatory (1862). A violinist at the Opera from 1864 to 1869, Grädener taught harmony at the Conservatory from 1874 and received the title of professor in 1882. In 1886 he was appointed director of the Academic Society for Orchestral Music and of the Academic Gesangverein. In 1899 he succeeded Bruckner in the chair of harmony and counterpoint at the University of Vienna. He wrote mainly chamber and orchestral music, but also one opera, *Die heilige Zita*, which was performed in Vienna in 1918.　　　　　　　　　　　　[190] See above, Vol. ii, Chap. 9.

[191] Undated letter to the Countess Wydenbruck-Esterhazy (postmarked 21 June 1902, BMG, Paris).

[192] See above, Vol. i, Chap. 13.

both occasions he cancelled his trip at the last moment. 'That you still have the same old friendly feelings for me gives me the greatest pleasure,' Mahler wrote to Mihalovich in April. 'I don't have to tell you that it's the same on my side.' Six months later he added: 'I am still moved when I remember the times when you were practically the only one, after that unfortunate performance of my First, who did not "tactfully" avoid me . . .' While trying to spare the feelings of such a faithful and loyal friend as Mihalovich, Mahler no doubt felt it unnecessary to travel as far as Budapest to prove that 'an apple tree cannot produce oranges',[193] particularly as he was undoubtedly familiar with the score of *Toldi Szerelme* and knew there was no place for such a work in the Vienna repertory.[194]

Mahler had already experienced an embarrassing situation of this kind in 1901. Ignaz Brüll,[195] whom he had visited many years earlier on the Altersee and whose opera *Gloria* he had conducted in Hamburg, wanted him to revive *Das goldene Kreuz* (The Golden Cross), premièred in Berlin in 1875 and in Vienna in 1876, the only one of his operas to have ever been really successful. In 1899, after taking the matter up with Justi, Brüll believed he had won his case: 'She noted all my suggestions and I left in the certainty that my opera would be revived,' Brüll wrote to Mahler in 1901. 'I was wrong, and I resent the fact that you have not deigned to explain the reason for your change of heart! . . . The absence of any work of mine from the repertory for so long is a serious moral injury.' It is obvious that Mahler did not want to revive *Das goldene Kreuz* immediately, but in this case he was tactful and gave as an excuse the recent departure of Theodor Bertram. Brüll replied that Hesch could perfectly well replace him and that Demuth had assured him that he would be willing to sing the role of Bombardon. Mahler finally gave way and performed the work in 1902 and 1903 and again in 1907.[196]

In January 1902, another opera composer, the famous pianist and Liszt pupil, Eugen d'Albert,[197] had written to Mahler about *Die Abreise*, a work which

---

[193] A lapidary phrase used by Mahler when he refused to perform Count Bela Zichy's opera, *Meister Roland* (see below, Chap. 5).

[194] Mahler's letters of 22 Apr. and Oct. 1904 to Edmund von Mihalovich (Library of the Budapest Academy of Music).

[195] Ignaz Brüll (1846–1907), born in Prosnitz in Moravia, was an excellent pianist, well known as an interpreter of the works of Schumann. He taught at the Horaksche Klavierschule in Vienna. Two of his other operas were performed at the Hofoper, *Der Landfriede* (1877) and *Gringoire* (1892). Each received a number of performances, but neither held its place in the repertory. According to Theodor Helm, his music frequently borrowed from the past, and from such rococo composers as Dittersdorf and Monsigny (THE 336). See also Hartmut Wecker, *Der Epigone, Ignaz Brüll, ein jüdischer Komponist im Wiener Brahms-Kreis* (Centaurus, Pfaffenweilen, 1994).

[196] *Das goldene Kreuz* was performed three times in 1902, once in 1903 and five times in 1907. Letters from Ignaz Brüll to Mahler, dated 14 and 18 Nov. 1901, HOA, Z. 812/1901.

[197] Born in Glasgow of Italian stock in 1864, and later student at the Berlin Conservatory, Eugen d'Albert (1864–1932) began his career as a piano virtuoso in his native country. Later he settled in Germany where he became one of Liszt's last pupils. He became known for his transcriptions and editions of Bach and Beethoven. The influence of Brahms remained preponderant in his piano and chamber music. His operas include *Der Rubin* (1893), *Ghismonda* (1895), *Gernot* (1897), *Die Abreise* (1898), *Kain* (1900), *Der*

is going the rounds of all the German opera houses and has become a repertory piece in the big cities . . . *Kain* has also been performed on almost all the German stages. Even theatres mainly interested in 'box-office successes', such as Hamburg, Leipzig, Breslau, etc., have felt obliged to put it on. Why is Vienna not interested in my works?[198]

Since the 1890s, d'Albert's career as an opera composer had indeed been a successful one, but Mahler remained one of the few Opera directors who had not yet yielded and produced one of his stage works. A month after he had written about *Die Abreise*, d'Albert invited Mahler to the première of his new opera, *Der Improvisator*, but Mahler declined the invitation because he had to conduct the première of Forster's *Der dot mon* in Vienna.[199]

Early in 1903, d'Albert visited Vienna with his second wife, the singer Hermine Finck. On this occasion, he played *Tiefland* to Mahler, who apparently did not fully appreciate the new opera's exceptional qualities. It had its first performance in Prague on 15 November 1903 and was soon performed in all the main German opera houses. Mahler finally made up his mind to accept *Tiefland* in the autumn of 1907, but the first Vienna performance took place two months after he had left Vienna. It was one of the most memorable triumphs in the history of the institution, but it was Mahler's successor, Felix Weingartner, who got the credit for it.

In the meantime, d'Albert had returned to Vienna to give a new series of recitals and had played for Mahler another full-length opera, *Tragadalbas*.[200] As he often did in such circumstances, Mahler praised the score but regretted that 'the libretto made the work impossible to produce'. To compensate, however, he accepted d'Albert's earlier one-act work, *Die Abreise*, which he put on in 1905.[201]

At the beginning of the 1904–5 season, Mahler was invited to Brno by the Austrian Minister for Czech Affairs, Ottokar, Baron Prazak, for the première of a Czech opera *Jeji Pastorkyna* (*Her Foster-Daughter*) (known outside the Czech Republic as *Jenůfa*). He also received a letter from the composer himself:

Sir, The attached reviews from the Prague papers . . . concerning the production of my opera *Jeji Pastorkyna* say more about my person than I could briefly do myself, I invite you to come to Brno for the performance . . . on 7 December, or else for one of the later ones, I hope you have received an invitation from Baron Prazak. Yours faithfully and respectfully, Leos Janáček, Director, Brno Organ College.[202]

Improvisator (1902), and *Tiefland* (1903). Thirteen others followed, among which only *Die toten Augen* (1916) was a real success. Only one opera, *Tiefland*, has survived in the current repertory in Germany. D'Albert's six successive marriages were the subject of much comment at the time.

[198] Letter dated 11 Jan. 1902, HOA, Z. 58/1902. See below Chap. 3.
[199] Charlotte Pangels, *Eugen d'Albert* (Atlantis, Zurich, 1981).
[200] Wilhelm Raupp, *Eugen d'Albert* (Koehler & Amelang, Leipzig, 1930), 187 and 199. *Tragadalbas* was first performed in 1907 in Hamburg, but soon disappeared from the repertory.
[201] See below, Chap. 3.　　　　　[202] WMW 60.

The work, completed some time after March 1903, had been offered to the director of the Prague National Theatre, but was rejected without comment. Next year in Brno it had scored an exceptional success, but only at the provincial level.

As might have been expected, Mahler's reply was a polite refusal. He mentioned 'important business' in Vienna but asked Janáček to send him a piano score with a German translation.[203] Mahler thus missed the opportunity of discovering one of the outstanding personalities of twentieth-century opera. But Janáček himself later admitted that he had never sent his score to Vienna because the German translation was not complete. In any case, it is not certain that Mahler would have taken an immediate interest in *Jenůfa*. Janáček revised his score extensively for its first performance at the National Theatre in Prague, on 16 May 1916. In any case, if Mahler, like so many others, had rejected it after playing it through, it would not have been on account of its progressive tendencies. In 1904, by wholeheartedly supporting Schoenberg's Vereinigung and defending his works against the advice of some of his friends he had proved that nothing in music frightened him, even the most radical modernity. According to Alma several warnings in this respect had come from Guido Adler. In her *Erinnerungen*, she describes Adler as an 'arch-conservative' and fails to mention the fact that it was Guido Adler who introduced the Vereinigung to the Viennese public in the *Neue Freie Presse* and who arranged Mahler's first meeting with its two founders. A note from Schoenberg to Adler dated 11 November 1904 is proof that the three musicians met that same afternoon at the Auenbruggergasse.[204] Alma reports that the climate at these meetings was gradually becoming warmer and more congenial. One evening when 'Eisele and Beisele'[205] came for dinner, Mahler offered them his favourite beer, Spatenbräu. The conversation went smoothly enough until Schoenberg suddenly launched into his usual 'paradoxes' and Mahler lost his temper: 'Stop talking our ears off with your beery fantasies!' (the Austrian expression for 'nonsense' is '*Bierschwefel*'). Schoenberg retorted at once: 'It's really not my fault if there isn't any wine!'[206] But the dispute was as short-lived and superficial as the froth on the beer. Mahler was won over to the cause of the young musicians.

The first Vereinigung concert was scheduled for 23 November, and Schoenberg decided to turn it into a great event by programming the latest work by the head of the *neu-deutsch* school, Richard Strauss. The *Symphonia Domestica* had had its première in New York, on 31 March. Shortly afterwards, the first European performance had been the main attraction at the last festival of the Allgemeiner Deutscher Musikverein in Frankfurt. Strauss's star was

---

[203] HOA, Z. 1196/104. See *Mitteilungen des Österreichischen Staatsarchivs*, 25 (1972), 409, Jaroslav Vogel, *Janacek* (Artia, Prague, 1958), 312, and John Tyrell, *Janacek's Operas* (Faber, London, 1992), 61 ff.

[204] Stadtbibliothek, Vienna, J.N. 203.008.   [205] See above, Vol. ii, Chap. 16.

[206] AMM1, 199 ff.; AMM2, 111 ff.

then at its zenith. In 1903, London had held a festival of all his symphonic works from *Aus Italien* to *Ein Heldenleben*, and in 1904 there had been several concerts of his music in New York. The performances of the new *Domestica* had been important events everywhere, primarily because Strauss was giving up heroic or literary subjects, and turning instead to the theme of his own daily life. 'Why shouldn't I compose a symphony about myself,' he had been known to say, 'I find myself just as interesting as Napoleon or Alexander.' Strauss had imparted epic proportions to the intimate events of his family life, and the work was even longer than *Ein Heldenleben*, the longest of his symphonic poems. Mahler himself was always so reticent about his own private life that it is easy to imagine his feelings, when faced with such shameless exhibitionism. Strauss had planned to conduct the Viennese première of the *Domestica* himself, but changed his mind at the last minute. Mahler was thus able to demonstrate both his friendship for Strauss and his support for the Vereinigung, and it was he who conducted the Konzertverein Orchestra in the first Viennese performance of the new work. In defiance of the composer's explicit instructions, he excluded his 'programmatic' allusions from the concert programme. Two of Schoenberg's young students, Egon Wellesz and Anton Webern, were allowed to attend all the rehearsals and Egon Wellesz later wrote:

I was very impressed to note that Mahler made adjustments to the score of the *Symphonia Domestica*. The instrumentation of the work is masterly, but the adjustments were justified. Their sole aim was to facilitate the execution of a few passages, and they did not alter the sound in any way whatsoever. In fact I have never heard a more beautiful, transparent performance of the work than at that unforgettable concert. As was normal with Mahler, every detail had been meticulously worked out. But the broad lines were always brought out, so that the structure of the work became clearly apparent. Richard Strauss paid much less attention to detail, and was only concerned to maintain the impetus (*Schwung*), to stress the general line. Although Mahler probably felt no particular affection for the work, he later copied one detail of the instrumentation. In the symphony Strauss includes an oboe d'amore, whose soft, middle register corresponds to the low notes of the ordinary oboe, but without the hard quality that characterizes that instrument. The sound of the rarer instrument pleased Mahler so much that, in the performance of his Third Symphony which took place a few weeks later, he assigned the initial theme of the second movement, the minuet, to an oboe d'amore, and noted in the score that this should be done whenever the instrument was available.[207]

According to Robert Hirschfeld, Mahler conducted on 23 November with 'an uncanny composure' that 'aroused not only great surprise but even terror':

There was something demoniac about him. The baton in his right hand gives barely perceptible signs. His presence of mind demands and achieves everything . . . Out of an almost inextricable tangle of wittily intertwined parts and inexhaustible instrumental jokes, Mahler brings out the leading lines which reveal the progress of the

---

[207] EWL 43. The indication in question does not appear in the critical Mahler Gesellschaft edition.

motifs ... As if by magic he kindles the scintillating lights of the score ... Strauss as composer and Mahler as conductor had reached the highest summit of modern musical technique.

Hirschfeld called Strauss's score 'an exaggerated and protracted orchestral joke, pushed to the point of madness'. In the *Neues Wiener Tagblatt* Kalbeck attacked the very concept of the Vereinigung. 'The strong are always more powerful when they are alone', he wrote, and noted sadly that 'today's youth does not have the time to wait for immortality.' He went on to describe the *Domestica* as a 'bad joke', despite its undeniable thematic unity and the richness of its original sound. He felt that such a 'triumph of technique' could not conceal its lack of invention and 'inner warmth.' Wallaschek however, preferred the *Domestica* to Strauss's other symphonic poems, despite its 'heterogeneous elements'. He felt that Strauss 'had achieved more than when he tried to be profound'.

Max Graf defended the Vereinigung by recalling the difficulties that had confronted Brahms, Bruckner, and Hugo Wolf in Vienna, while Helm defended Strauss as usual in the *Wochenblatt*, praising 'the exquisite humour and astonishing polyphony of the *Symphonia Domestica*'.[208] Most of the critics recognized the obvious discrepancy between the vast orchestral means and the intimate nature of the family scenes it sought to depict. Thus the reviews of the *Symphonia* were almost as negative as those of Mahler's symphonies. However, Strauss, who had probably heard favourable reports of the concert, wrote to Mahler on 27 November: 'Having just arrived home. I wish to thank you and the Vereinigung committee for the kind telegram and most especially for your marvellous performance of my work. However thankless such a task may be in the face of short-lived "Viennese enthusiasm", I myself shall never forget what you have given me.'[209]

Strauss's reputation was by now firmly established internationally, while Mahler's was just beginning to attract attention and to make some headway on the other side of the Atlantic. In February 1904, a Boston musicologist, named Arthur Elson, wrote to Mahler to ask for his biography and list of works[210] because Walter Damrosch was planning to include the Fourth Symphony in the next programmes of the New York Symphony Orchestra. On the morning of the concert, Richard Aldrich published a detailed analysis of the work in the *New York Times*,[211] together with an article telling how Damrosch, hearing Mahler

---

[208] The remainder of the concert was made up of Hermann Bischoff's three Lieder for voice and orchestra to poems by Richard Dehmel and Emil von Bodmann (sung by the baritone Anton Moser, who replaced the indisposed Friedrich Weidemann), followed by the *Dionysische Phantasie* by Siegmund von Hausegger, conducted by Zemlinsky. Siegmund von Hausegger (1872–1948), born in Graz, was the son of a well-known musicologist. He composed his first opera, *Zinnober*, before embarking on a career as a conductor. After directing the Kaim Orchester he was appointed musical director of the Museum Konzerte in Frankfurt (1903–6). His music was much appreciated for its brilliant orchestral colour and progressive, *neudeutsch* tendencies. [209] Letter from Strauss to Mahler, dated 27 Nov. 1904, MSB 88.

[210] HOA, 25 Feb. 1904. In his reply, Mahler advised Elson to get in touch with Nodnagel.

[211] In the issue of 6 Nov. 1904.

conduct in Hamburg several years earlier, had sent him a congratulatory letter, to which Mahler had replied 'that he had never received one from a colleague before'. After the New York concert on 6 November, the New York press accused Mahler of 'lacking invention', and claimed that the audience had been disconcerted by the contrast between the 'simplicity' of the thematic material and the 'hypermodern complexity' of its development. But the performance itself must have been partly to blame for the listeners' disappointment, for Damrosch was not a virtuoso conductor and had no real feeling for Mahler's music, as he himself acknowledges in his memoirs:

His moments of real beauty are too rare, and the listener has to wade through pages of dreary emptiness which no artificial connection with philosophical ideas can fill with real importance. The feverish restlessness characteristic of the man reflects itself in his music, which is fragmentary in character and lacks continuity of thought and development. He could write cleverly in the style of Haydn or Berlioz or Wagner, and without forgetting Beethoven, but he was never able to write in the style of Mahler.[212]

Despite many adverse reactions in the press, the Fourth Symphony was well received by the public, and by Richard Aldrich, whose unsigned review appeared in the *New York Times*, New York's most important paper then as now.[213] He praised Mahler's 'impressive mastery' and his 'exceptional originality and resources' but refused to arrive at a definitive judgement, mainly because of the 'numerous reminiscences and quotations of popular melodies' in the work. On the other hand, the *Daily Tribune*[214] unhesitatingly condemned the Fourth as 'anarchic, enigmatic, fragmentary and disjointed'. Despite the astonishing ingenuity it showed, it was 'wearing and irritating because incapable of stimulating the imagination'. The anonymous critic of the New York magazine, the *Musical Courier* outdid all his colleagues:

It is not fair to the readers . . . to take up their time with a detailed description of that musical monstrosity which masquerades under the title of Gustav Mahler's Fourth Symphony. There is nothing in the design, content or execution of the work to impress the musicians, except its grotesquerie . . . The writer frankly admits that to him it was one hour or more of the most painful musical torture to which he has been compelled to submit.

By 1904, few critics in Europe would have maintained that Mahler had no talent for composition. Most German critics had by then heard the work which,

---

[212] Walter Damrosch, *My Musical Life*, (Scribner, New York, 1923), 334. As usual, Damrosch analysed and commented on the work from the podium before conducting it. On Walter Damrosch, his biography and his dealings with Mahler in New York, see below, Vol. iiii, Chaps. 2 and 3. Programme of the New York Symphony's concert on 6 Nov. Elgar: *In the South* Overture; Liszt: *Hungarian Rhapsody* No. 4; Gluck: Aria 'Alceste' (Ella de Montjau, sop.); Bassani: Aria 'Dormi Bella'; Duparc: Mélodie; Strauss: Song: Caecilia; Mahler: *Symphony* No. 4 (Ella de Montjau).

[213] See below, Vol. iiii, Chap. 1. The articles in the daily New York press were often unsigned.

[214] The newspaper's main critic was Henry Krehbiel, who later was to play an important—and highly destructive—part in Mahler's New York career.

in 1903, had changed his status as composer, the Third Symphony. One of the few exceptions was Leipzig, the city of Bach, Mendelssohn, and Schumann, where he had been a conductor at the Opera for two years, but where his own works had never had any real success. This no doubt prompted him to change his plans at the last minute and undertake the long journey there to conduct the scheduled performance of the Third himself. Yet Hinrichsen had warned him by telegram that the Winderstein Orchestra was inferior to that of the Gewandhaus and that the performance had serious competition in the form of a subscription concert the same day conducted by Felix Weingartner.[215] But the Gewandhaus's policy remained steadfastly conservative, not to say reactionary, and Mahler was undoubtedly grateful to Hans Winderstein[216] for including the première of his longest symphony in the programme of one of his subscription concerts. In the event, Hinrichsen had painted too dark a picture: the Winderstein orchestra was a well-disciplined ensemble and it included many excellent musicians.[217]

Mahler left Vienna on 25 November, three days after the performance of the *Symphonia Domestica*. Once in the train, he found to his horror that all the other berths in his compartment were occupied, so that he had to lie down fully dressed. When he reached Leipzig late the next morning he was thoroughly exhausted, as much by his wretched night as by his recent schedule, for the *Symphonia Domestica* rehearsals had come on top of those at the Opera. He was greeted at the station by the concert master of the Winderstein Orchestra, who assured him that 'the musicians were excited about my work and that I would find they had rehearsed with great care'. 'Whenever I hear this,' Mahler wrote to Alma, 'it gives me a twinge and I think to myself—damn it, Almschi could have come along after all.'[218] On the day of his arrival, he conducted a first rehearsal of the chorus, then the following day, after a good night's sleep, the first orchestral rehearsal. He was at first discouraged and dismayed but his misgivings soon proved unfounded: 'What seemed a ruinous heap of unrelated sounds has now become a well-proportioned building. The stones assembled themselves willingly at the sound of Arion's voice and I look forward to today's performance with a certain confidence.'[219]

The critic of the *Leipziger Tageblatt*, Paul Zschorlich, described Mahler's tireless rehearsing with the orchestra in an article published at the time of Mahler's death:

[215] Telegram from Mahler, 21 Nov., and telegraphed reply from Peters on the same day (Klemm, 'Geschichte').

[216] Hans Winderstein (1856–1925), composer and conductor, born at Lüneburg, studied at the Leipzig Conservatory and later conducted the Winterthur orchestra in Switzerland. He then moved to Nuremberg, where he founded the Philharmonic Verein. He conducted the Kaim Concerts in Munich from 1893 to 1896 and founded the concert series which bears his name in Leipzig.

[217] Mahler had also disparaged the orchestra in a letter to Hinrichsen wirtten in March.

[218] BGA, no. 124, undated (26 Nov. 1904).

[219] BGA, no. 126, undated (28 Nov. 1904).

An enormous amount of effort and patience were required until the symphony sounded the way Mahler wanted it to sound. If this short, excitable man had not been such a famous and controversial figure and if all the musicians, without exception, had not felt that they were playing under a conductor who, for all his crotchety ways, was a genius, then there would certainly have been an explosion (*Eclat*).[220]

Zschorlich recalled that, at one point in the symphony, in a soft chord by the brasses, a wrong note kept creeping in. After eight unsuccessful attempts, Mahler rehearsed the horns alone, but the wrong note was still there. He asked each player what note he was playing, and each had the right one. No one could figure out what had gone wrong until Winderstein realized that it must have been a harmonic note from the horns, barely audible under normal circumstances, but which had been amplified by some acoustic quirk and become perceptible to Mahler's uniquely fine and discerning ear.[221]

Fortunately for Mahler, the dress rehearsal was much more satisfactory than the preceding one. 'These poor devils have behaved splendidly. They allowed me to torment them yesterday and today for four whole hours, and then took leave of me with unimpaired enthusiasm. The whole town is taking an enormous interest in the work. The leading critics attended both rehearsals and it's a good thing I came myself for this performance!'[222] The 'inevitable' Nodnagel appeared as soon as the rehearsals started, having come all the way across Germany expressly to hear the work. The same day, Mahler lunched with his sister Emma, who had come along with her husband for the last rehearsals and the concert. Afterwards he paid a visit to Max Staegemann, who still directed the Leipzig Opera, and who 'received him with great friendliness'.[223] In the evening he dined with Henri Hinrichsen, and they played a four-hand arrangement of a Bruckner symphony. Obviously the director of Peters was particularly fond of Bruckner, and Mahler had to promise to send him the 'old' score of the Third Symphony (the one his four-hand transcription was based on) as well as the new one.[224] It seems that Mahler did not enjoy this Bruckner evening. 'Secretly, I considered it a sacrifice, or payment of a debt of gratitude for his generosity, and a small compensation for what the failure of the Fifth had cost the poor devil!' Still the same day, Kahnt, the publisher of *Die drei Pintos*, came to his hotel to make a firm offer for his *Lieder und Balladen*.[225] On the day of the concert, Mahler lunched with Nikisch, who asked him to play

[220]   The rest of Zschorlich's description is quoted below, Chap. 5.

[221]   'Gustav Mahler als Dirigent' by Paul Zschorlich, *Strassburger Post* (25 May 1911).

[222]   BGA, no. 126.

[223]   Staegemann died two months later on 29 Jan. 1905, at the age of 61.

[224]   Letter to Hinrichsen received on 6 Dec. Mahler acknowledges receipt of the 'magnificent edition' of the score of the Fifth, as well as a Reger score which he promises to study 'with great care' (*heisse Bemühungen*). These last words are in quotation marks, which indicates that Mahler and Hinrichsen must have joked about the 'care' one had to take in order to understand Reger's music.

[225]   Kahnt was to publish in 1905 all of Mahler's last orchestral Lieder, the two additional *Wunderhorn-Lieder*, the five *Kindertotenlieder*, and the four *Rückert-Lieder*, as well as 'Liebst du um Schönheit', with piano accompaniment.

the Fifth Symphony to him on the piano for he was still unfamiliar with the work, which he was to conduct in Berlin.[226]

In the evening after the concert, Mahler cabled Alma: 'Total success. Greetings Gustav.'[227] The public's response had indeed been very warm. The final ovation had lasted 'a good quarter of an hour,' swelling every time a small group tried to boo. This did not prevent the Leipzig critics from tearing the symphony apart because the public's applause had made them furious. Alex Winterberger in the *Leipziger Neueste Nachrichten* called the Third a 'kaleidoscope', an 'oriental symphony', which, if supplied with a plot for 'a fantastical tragic ballet', would make 'a sensational entertainment'.

Adding or removing a few implausibilities would not matter as long as a sensation-seeking audience is given the visual fare for which it craves. Of course, Nietzsche, Saint Peter and the angels would have to be replaced by odalisques and pirates bold which, as is well known, are in plentiful supply in the Orient. Since the field has already been far too heavily exploited, we cannot blame a composer in search of a subject for casting about for one in distant lands and among strange people, cleverly appropriating everything he needed for his oriental symphony . . . There was not a single bar in which the composer's intentions were not immediately apparent. Whenever he tries to plumb the depths of his own heart, as in the fourth, fifth and sixth movements, and especially in the last, he is enmeshed in a Wagnerian net which holds him so tightly that he tosses and turns in every direction in order to escape, but in vain. In the field of speculative music, Mahler is a past master beyond compare. Speaking of the performers, who in fact is able to elicit mystery, gaiety or even impudence from inner emptiness? It is always impossible to render such moods in a merely superficial manner . . . Mahler knows his public exactly and knows exactly what he must do . . . to astonish it.

Since Krefeld, nothing so completely damning had been written by a critic about the Third Symphony, or any other work of Mahler for that matter. Similar wrath was expressed by Arthur Smolian[228] in the *Leipziger Zeitung*. He accused Mahler of ignoring a basic artistic precept, economy of means. The Third was 'monstrous on account of its excesses and its lack of style . . . and any unifying higher idea.' The first movement, 'overloaded with brass instruments', was 'incapable of being understood on account of its frightful variety of styles'. Certain themes were 'worthy of an operetta' and the whole 'evoked a dreadfully violent and murderous battle'. The Scherzo was the kind of 'oriental dance one

---

[226] BGA, no. 126, undated (28 Nov.).   [227] BGA, no. 127.

[228] Arthur Smolian (1856–1911) was born in Riga. After studying at the Königliche Musikschule in Munich (with Franz Wüllner and Joseph Rheinberger) he conducted in Berlin, Basle, and Stettin and then was director of the Leipzig Männergesangverein until 1890, during which time he built a career as a critic. He moved to the Rhineland, where he taught at the Karlsruhe Conservatory and wrote regularly for the *Karlsruher Zeitung*. From 1900 he was editor of the Eulenburg pocket scores of Berlioz. In 1901 he returned to Leipzig, where he joined the *Leipziger Zeitung*, the *Musikalisches Wochenblatt*, and the *Neue Musikalische Presse* and became editor of the *Musikführer* and *Opernführer* (H. Seemann Nachf.). He wrote many analyses of romantic and classical works; two books, *Vom Schwinden der Gesangkunst* (On the Disappearance of the Art of Singing) and *Stella del Monte* (based on the memoirs of Berlioz); and a number of Lieder.

finds in operas'; the posthorn solo recalled '*Die Post im Walde*' and other musical vulgarities, the Nietzschean solo 'lacked real emotional depth', while the
Finale was made up of nothing but reminiscences.

The articles in the musical journals were equally condemnatory. They trotted out the same old time-honoured clichés: 'lack of originality', 'vulgar and
trivial' themes, 'unimaginative development', 'banality', 'borrowings', 'oddities', 'sudden changes of mood', 'lack of balance between form and content'.
Nearly all the critics admitted that the symphony had been a stunning success
with the public, but they assured their readers that this was only 'superficial'
and certainly 'ephemeral'. Only the *Musikalisches Wochenblatt* was prepared to
recognize that, in the Finale, Mahler's music emanated from the depths of his
heart, and not from cold calculation. The music was 'solemn, euphonious,
deeply felt and profoundly thought out'. Only one critic, Paul Zschorlich, who
wrote for the important *Leipziger Tagblatt*, refused to follow the general trend,
defending Mahler with eloquence and discernment. After carefully studying
the score of the Third Symphony, he declared:

Condemning a work is not in itself a critical achievement . . . It takes far more time
and effort to understand it. As difficult to judge the art of one's own time as to contemplate a landscape when you are right in the middle of a wheat field. Next to Reger,
Mahler is the most misunderstood (and also the least accessible) contemporary
composer. The insults hurled at him over the years, personal and otherwise, would
have been enough to silence any ordinary mortal. Mahler has replied to words with
deeds . . . Mindless of the insinuations from left and right, deaf to the insulting
pronouncements of his enemies, he goes his own way. This stubbornness commands
respect. Even if we thought we were able to prove that he is pursuing the wrong path.

Zschorlich explained that when he had heard the Fourth Symphony three
years earlier in Berlin, he had not condemned it. Most of the other critics had
joined in 'sounding its death knell'. He had sensed in Mahler a marriage of
spiritual greatness and artistic bad taste, though he admired his 'powerful
ideas' and 'prodigious and masterful technique'. But he had found Mahler's
whole manner 'repellent'. Still, he had had the courage to admit that he was
incapable of judging it after a single hearing, whereupon he was accused of
'critical impotence'. If more journalists had reacted with similar honesty, both
Mahler and Strauss would have been spared a lot of heartache.

Having attended two long rehearsals and one performance of the Third,
Zschlorlich finally felt qualified 'to write something positive'.

Mahler is a truly important personality as a composer. He is not a mere follower of
Wagner, but is a composer of our time. He writes new works, in every sense of the word
. . . he is a master of polyphonic orchestral technique . . . there is no doubt that the
artistic content of the Third Symphony is immense . . . One is not in a position to judge
if the work has only swept over one on a single occasion. It must be studied closely. In
doing so we touch on a question that seems to lie at the centre of Mahler's work. With
few exceptions, critics have already said they were baffled by the work. So how is the

public supposed to find its way? . . . Only when this work joins Mahler's other symphonies in the repertory will the public begin to understand it . . . Those who decide to study Mahler seriously will soon be convinced that he offers something more than intellectual and technical refinement.

Nevertheless Zschorlich felt that the Third Symphony was programme music, not absolute music. He singled out for praise the 'Song of Midnight' based on Nietzsche's words.

The atmosphere is so genuine and so convincing that the listener is overwhelmed. This cannot be mere calculation. Similarly, the last movement has such noble voice-leading, and a clarity and transparence quite unlike Mahler, that it goes directly to the heart, as soon as the listener's consciousness has absorbed its organic unity. . . . Is Mahler original? That is a particularly delicate question. He's certainly not original in the way Strauss is: one might say that he is, taken as a whole, but not when it comes to specific details.

After drawing up a list of Mahler's 'reminiscences' Zschorlich ended his article with these discerning words:

And those who go so far as to say that Mahler is only capable of thinking thoughts others have thought of before him have understood nothing of his greatness . . . Mahler is a problem, at least for those of us living in the year 1904. . . . Anyone attempting to hand down a quick and definitive judgement is nothing but a charlatan.[229]

Thus Zschorlich was one of the very few critics who admitted that he had at first been wrong, and that Mahler's works could not be judged on the basis of the first hearing. He was also one of the very rare people who at the time understood the real difficulties which for many years had stood in the way of a proper understanding of Mahler's art. His review is remarkable for its anticipation of the judgement of posterity and for the courage which must have been necessary to adopt a position that ran counter to that of all his Leipzig colleagues. Mahler was to find another enlightened defender in a rather modest periodical, the *Blätter für Haus- und Kirchenmusik*. This was Max Arend,[230] for whom the first hearing of the Third had been 'an artistic event of outstanding importance':

Mahler's sense of form (*Gestaltungskraft*), his counterpoint and his amazing instrumentation were irresistible and overwhelming. . . . There are orchestral colours no musician has ever presented, wonderful moments of inspiration. Perhaps the most wonderful thing of all is the refinement of effects that would seem completely vulgar in any other context: I am thinking for example of the Flügelhorn in the distance and

---

[229] The Third Symphony took up the entire programme of the fourth symphonic concert given in Leipzig on 28 Nov. 1904. It was performed by the Winderstein Orchestra, supplemented by players from the band of the 107th Regiment; Marie Hertzer-Deppe, alto; and the children's chorus from the Singakademie.

[230] Max Arend (1873–1944) was a student of Hugo Riemann at the Cologne and Wiesbaden Conservatories. Later, he studied law at the University of Leipzig, took up an administrative post, wrote a monograph and many articles on Gluck, edited two of his stage works, and founded two societies for the dissemination of his music.

its cantilena, accompanied by violins in the high register. . . . One thing is certain: here is someone who can do something, who, if you follow him, allows you to feel the heart-beat of our age. . . . For in fact all art of the past interests us only from the viewpoint of the present. That Mahler is part of the music of our time cannot be doubted by any perceptive person who has come under his influence!

Arend wound up this courageous defence of Mahler by condemning the conservative policy of the Gewandhaus, which 'should have performed this symphony long ago'.[231]

Leipzig was not the only large German-speaking city which had not been given the opportunity to hear the Third Symphony. There was at least one other—of essential importance for Mahler since he lived in it and felt he belonged to it, and that was Vienna, which seemed determined not to take him seriously as a composer, or even to acknowledge his success elsewhere. For some months and particularly since the reading rehearsal of the Fifth, his rela-tions with the Philharmonic musicians had been improving, to the point where he had been able to write to Hinrichsen that, 'under certain conditions', the first performance of his new symphony might be given in Vienna.[232] This improvement in relations may have been connected with the fact that at the time he was attempting to convince the Oberhofmeisteramt that the salaries of the Opera's musicians should be increased. To support their claim he had had a comparative table made showing the much higher salaries paid to the court musicians of Dresden or Berlin and added: 'The undersigned, your most obedi-ent Director, who is primarily responsible for the artistic direction of the insti-tute, can thus in all such cases only allow himself to be guided by the consideration that he must ensure that the artistic personnel required for the work in hand are content, especially as regards their material needs.'[233]

After the rehearsals of the Fifth Symphony, Mahler had been so delighted that he 'could find no words strong enough' to express his satisfaction to the players.[234] As head of the Gesellschaft der Musikfreunde, Franz Schalk had announced an 'extraordinary concert' for the 14 December, with the première of Mahler's Third Symphony. The Philharmonic musicians usually took part in these Gesellschaftskonzerte but, in this case, they would have been within their rights had they refused to participate, for the concert had been announced <u>before</u> they had been officially approached. In fact, at the general meeting of 4 November, they voted not to participate. 'Herr Direktor Mahler declared that he had very recently received proof of the orchestra's goodwill, and said that he could only consider its conduct as reasonable.'[235] Fortunately Franz Schalk, director of the Gesellschaft, assumed full responsibility for the

---

[231] *Blätter für Haus- und Kirchenmusik*, 9 (1904–5): 5, 80.
[232] See above.
[233] Letter of 2 Nov. 1904, HOA, G.Z. 1020/1904.
[234] According to the *Neues Wiener Journal* of 12 Nov. 1904.
[235] Minutes of the Philharmonic, G.Z. 255/904.

undiplomatic oversight, and duly presented his apologies in writing to the Philharmonic and to the committee. The matter was at last unanimously agreed upon at a further general meeting.[236]

Six weeks earlier, Vienna had heard another work by Mahler, the first in two years. Receiving its second hearing in the capital, the First Symphony was conducted by Ferdinand Löwe, who had obtained the score from Mahler's publisher and had not informed the composer beforehand of the planned performance. According to several Viennese daily papers, Mahler was so offended that he flatly refused to attend the rehearsals and could not even be persuaded to go to the concert.[237] In *Die Zeit*, Richard Specht noted that the reaction at the end of the performance was a mixture of applause and opposition. He was unable to tell 'to what extent this was aimed at the work itself and how much was due to the politics of the Vienna art world'. Were Mahler's enemies demonstrating against his music as usual, or were his friends voicing their indignation at Löwe's behaviour and objecting to what Specht himself considered to be his 'ill-chosen tempos'? The response was in any case much warmer than at the first performance conducted four years earlier by Mahler himself with the Philharmonic. Hirschfeld also noted the mixed reception at the end of the performance, but made the following comment: 'ironic music is bound to elicit ironic applause.' He did not wish to reopen the old 'critical argument' about this 'cuckoo's *Eroica*'. He felt that the work had been 'written for the future when there will no longer be any shortage of sensitive spiritual antennae for the most delicate ironies and enigmas in sound'.

According to Maximilian Muntz, the task of the Konzertverein was to 'present the noblest and highest masterpieces of musical art', whereas Mahler's work 'is ironic and caricaturizes, parodies and satirizes what is sacred to believers, plunging them into complete disarray'. All those who considered the concert hall as a 'sacred temple of art' had expressed their displeasure at this 'musical museum piece' and its oddities, borrowings, pastiches, and witticisms, which in the Finale became an 'assault on the ears'.[238]

Concerning the rehearsals of the Third Symphony for a performance which was to open a new phase in Mahler's Viennese career as a composer, two anecdotes have come down to us. The Philharmonic's librarian, Rudolf Effenberger remembered having strolled with Mahler before the concert through the corridors of the Musikvereinsaal, looking for a good place for an off-stage trumpet (probably a replacement for the flügelhorn) in the Scherzo. Having rejected

[236] Cf. Clemens Hellsberg, *Demokratie der Könige*, 317.

[237] *Neues Wiener Tagblatt*, 12 Nov., and Richard Specht's article published the same day in *Die Zeit*. Relations between Mahler and Löwe had been strained ever since Löwe had left the Opera (see above Vol. ii, 188). Yet it was Löwe who, in 1909, conducted the first Viennese performance of the Seventh Symphony (see below, Vol. iiii, Chap. 5).

[238] The concert took place at 7.30 p.m. on Tue. 8 Nov. at the Musikvereinsaal with the following programme: Mahler: Symphony No. 1; Beethoven: Piano Concerto No. 5 (soloist: Frédéric Lamond); Brahms: *Academic Festival* Overture.

several possible locations, Mahler noticed a narrow stairway leading up at the side of the first balcony on the left. To achieve an echo effect, he decided to position another trumpet at the corresponding place on the right. Before Effenberger had a chance to object, Mahler had headed for the opposite staircase. When the librarian finally caught up with him, Mahler was standing at the open door of a narrow cubicle, looking down at a wood-rimmed hole whose function was only too obvious. If Effenberger's memory is to be relied on, only one off-stage instrument was finally employed for the two concerts.[239] Another anecdote concerns the rehearsals themselves. After Mahler's death, Ludwig Karpath remembered his telling the Philharmonic players not to 'ennoble' a certain passage which was certainly one of the marches in the first movement.[240]

If ever a Mahler performance created a stir in the Austrian capital, it was this one. Writing in the *Musikalisches Wochenblatt*, at the beginning of 1905, Theodor Helm drew a bold parallel between the rivalry of Strauss and Mahler in Vienna and that of Gluck and Piccini in Paris at the end of the eighteenth century. It was a rather far-fetched comparison, for it is hard to imagine Piccini conducting the first performance of Gluck's *Orpheus* or *Armide*, as Mahler had the *Symphonia Domestica*. Its only justification might have been the recent performance of three works by Strauss, the *Symphonia Domestica* (23 November), *Don Quixote* (at the Konzertverein, 17 November), and *Ein Heldenleben* (at the Philharmonic under Mottl on the 18th), while Mahler's Third was to meet with such extraordinary enthusiasm that one day in the street Strauss hailed him as 'Vienna's famous man'.[241] Indeed, the Third Symphony proved to be such a triumph at the 'extraordinary concert' on 14 December that the Philharmonic committee decided to repeat it a week later. Consequently the critics, while persisting in their attacks found themselves in the embarrassing position of having to explain this sudden craze for Mahler, a composer they had always condemned. In his *Wochenblatt* article, Theodor Helm proffered an ingenious explanation. Mahler's concerts, he thought, were attended largely by women, and his audiences were 'favourably disposed' towards him and 'looked upon him as a god' while his opponents 'normally stayed away from such events'.[242]

Robert Hirschfeld did not conceal his indignation after seeing so many people who seemed to enjoy the Third Symphony when so few of them had yet

---

[239] Rudolf Effenberger: *Fünfundzwanzig Jahre Dienstbarer Geist im Reiche der Frau Musika*, reproduced in Alexander Witeschnik, *Musizieren geht übers Probiren* (Paul Neff, Vienna, 1967, 48).

[240] Ludwig Karpath, 'Gustav Mahler', *Strassburger Post*, 'Unterhaltungsblatt' (29 Jan. 1905).

[241] AMM1, 128; AMM2, 128. Alma speaks of the kind of success in Vienna that the Third did. This scene, which Alma assigns to Essen in May 1906, probably took place in Strasbourg in May 1905, five months after the double performance of the Third.

[242] The *Neue Freie Presse* made things easy for Mahler's enemies by publishing a particularly superficial article, by Gill Bara, on Christmas Day. It devoted more space to what the women in the audience were wearing and how they had behaved than to Mahler's music, which was discussed in a particularly mindless manner.

'learned to penetrate the profundity of Brahms or to feel the beating of Bruckner's heart'. What could one say of 'these weak and impressionable men and women who accept compromises so readily', who cared only for 'novelty' and who mistook this music for 'an organically developed world of sounds'? Albert Kauders was amazed that such a success should follow so many failures. It had to be admitted, he said, that it was the audience which had changed, for Mahler had remained faithful to himself. Finally, Maximilian Muntz reproached the Philharmonic musicians for the 'impropriety' of adding their applause to that of the audience after the two concerts.

The immediate result of the Third's triumph in Vienna was to provoke the critics to unprecedented levels of denigration. Felix Salten recalled that one of them rushed up to Mahler after the concert and exclaimed: 'Anybody who has committed such a deed deserves a couple of years in prison!' Mahler's 'sentence' was indeed served on him by the Viennese reviewers with their pens, which many of them could wield with considerable effect. Theodor Helm found Strauss's recently performed *Ein Heldenleben* and *Don Quixote* 'far more likeable' and 'convincing' than the Third, which was 'bizarre, full of reminiscences', and 'lacking in unity and logic'. In almost identical terms Maximilian Muntz denounced Mahler's 'absurdities', his desire 'to deceive and shock', and his lack of inventiveness, which his technical prowess failed to conceal. The first movement was 'a physical and mental strain on the ear', 'a chaos of shrieks and dissonances' followed by 'unheard-of vulgarities' and 'jokes worthy of an operetta'. Later Mahler put aside his 'superman' persona to show 'his true self' in the minuet. 'Decadent and sentimental', it was still preferable to the banality of the Scherzo, to the 'theatrical angels' of the choral movement, and to the vocal solo, the mood of which was quite foreign to 'the philosophical and poetical spirit of Nietzsche'. As for the Finale, it derived from Mozart (!) and Bruckner, and was totally lacking in authenticity.

In the *Wiener Abendpost*, Hirschfeld rose to the occasion with a bravura piece in his most flamboyant vein. Torn between a love for Beethoven and a taste for 'little folk songs', Mahler could only string together 'eight bars of triviality, sixteen of Titanic defiance, then again the hankering for banality, and again a touch of Prometheus'. This 'self-indulgent music keeps posturing as if in front of a mirror, this pose for sublimity, that for passion, this for renunciation, that for remorse'. As in the case of Bernard Shaw, one never knew whether Mahler was being ironic about himself or about others. The Minuet was ballet music, the Scherzo worthy of a military band, and the Finale nothing more than an 'excellent Wagnerian sketch' . . .

But Hirschfeld did not stop there. He later published in the journal *Österreichische Rundschau* under the title 'Mahler and Strauss in Vienna' an attack on three of his colleagues who had written favourably of Mahler.[243] He accused

---

[243] They were Julius Korngold, Richard Wallaschek, and David Joseph Bach (see below).

them of accepting all they thought 'original' or 'personal' 'to avoid being considered old-fashioned'. What could a flawed work of art express except a flawed personality?[244] All that Mahler did was to 'reawaken heart-felt feelings engendered by others ... Mozart, Beethoven, Wagner, Bruckner and band-stand music.' This was the article in which Hirschfeld launched a new anti-Mahlerian slogan which subsequently caught on like wildfire. Mahler's symphonies, he said, 'were not progress, they were a regression, a return to Meyerbeer, though Meyerbeer's music showed a richer, stronger inventive-ness'. Like Meyerbeer, Mahler had a hundred different and contrasted styles and was able to switch suddenly from one to another. Like Meyerbeer, he was fond of instrumental solos. Like him, he heaped banality upon banality. His use of popular songs resembled Meyerbeer's use of a Lutheran chorale in *Les Huguenots*. Like Meyerbeer's, his music was 'clear and easy to grasp' because, 'it was all on the surface ready to be caught'. His counterpoint was merely an arbitrary effect since the centre of interest was always 'tone colour and instru-mental surprises'. The very essence of his music was trickery. His refusal to rely on programmes made his works 'symphonies *à clef*', 'symphonic riddles'. How could one be expected to take these 'musical witticisms' seriously, as some people obviously do? At least Strauss's jests were 'more honourable' because they had 'their own style, themes and polyphony'.[245]

While more restrained than Hirschfeld in his indulgence in polemics, Max Kalbeck nevertheless portrayed Mahler as a restless, artistic mind, a 'big sophisticated child who forces those other children—the audience—to listen to him'. The Third Symphony could not be understood without a programme because the various movements 'do not coalesce as subsidiary parts of the same structure'. The music was theatrical and superficial, worthy at best of a play or a ballet. Over and over again, in the first movement, one heard

the noise of a market place, an approaching band beating the tattoo, the tumult of a battleground. . . . sounds from nature, exclamations, fanfares, transitions, smaller and larger motifs all hoping to become part of the thematic material. . . . Mahler can make the flute rage, the kettledrum sing, the trombones joke, the trumpets croak, turn the basses into violins and human voices into bells. He thus shows his unlimited domina-tion over the terrified orchestra so why shouldn't he one day rape the listeners?

Kauders too thought that these 'excesses, oddities, absurdities' had just one aim: to cover up for a lack of melodic invention. Nonetheless Kauders bestowed some praise on the last movements, and particularly the Finale, which he found 'substantial and heartfelt', 'its theme developing into an expression of violent fervour (*gewalttätige Inbrunst*)'. Gustav Schönaich also declared himself deeply moved by the Finale, which 'few recent works can rival'. Mahler 'had reached a level of achievement at which he could afford to

---

[244] Wallaschek and Korngold both agreed 'that no one but Mahler could have written such music'.
[245] *Österreichische Rundschau*, 1 (1904–5): 10, 537 ff.

ignore his enemies' scorn. His musical inventiveness was inexhaustible and he had shown himself to be a 'symphonic' composer who was far more serious, substantial, and significant than Strauss. If Schönaich had not soon shifted his stand in a second article for the *Allgemeine Zeitung* and another for *Die Musik*, one might have believed that he had been won over to Mahler's cause: but now the Third Symphony's success disturbed him, especially when he thought back to the time when the public had booed Liszt's Sonata and *Faust Symphony*. The final Adagio still seemed to him to 'sing from the depths of the soul' but its melody 'rested on the shoulders of Beethoven and Wagner': he was worried by the 'baroque' nature of the work, the 'enormous number of performers', and the '*chiaroscuro* aesthetic'.

Only three critics were bold enough to disagree with the majority of the 'infernal judges': Julius Korngold in the *Neue Freie Presse*, Richard Wallaschek in *Die Zeit*, and David Joseph Bach in the *Arbeiter-Zeitung*. Korngold failed to understand why it had taken such a long time for Mahler to gain acceptance, especially as his music combined Bruckner's religious faith and certain features reminiscent of Berlioz—sublimity, irony, and a penchant for big sound. Mahler, he wrote, carried on the tradition of Berlioz, just as Strauss carried on that of Liszt. His partiality for folk music went too deep to be insincere. However, Korngold joined the opposing camp in disapproving Mahler's refusal to disclose his programmes, 'the occasional lack of originality in his themes', and the 'pot pourri' of marches in the first movement. For him the composer's personality was revealed in the thematic development rather than in the themes themselves. The melodic invention of the choral (fourth) movement was 'personal, lively and natural', though the last Adagio, a 'synthesis of Beethoven and Wagner', remained the work's crowning glory. 'Currently', no one but Mahler was 'capable of creating such a work of art'. Korngold felt that much could be expected from him as a composer, and predicted a difficult though brilliant future. 'Using realistic means, he has broken away from the musical realism of his time.' And then, had not the music of Berlioz been considered just as mad, bizarre, and extravagant in Leipzig seventy-five years earlier?

In *Die Zeit*, Richard Wallaschek, who had never previously been one of Mahler's supporters, was clearly won over by the Third Symphony, including even the first movement. Cutting short the argument about 'pure' versus 'programme' music, he said that one of the advantages of the Third was that, while Mahler no doubt wanted it to be approached as pure music, in fact 'it left to our individual inclinations "the free play of the imagination", as Kant would have said.' As for the first movement, he had at first been apprehensive about its length. 'Even the greatest master would have found it difficult to retain our attention with pure music for so long.' But Mahler had done the trick, and moreover

has so entertained us, so that this first part doesn't seem a moment too long. This kind of success cannot be achieved by workmanship alone or indeed by mere technical facility. Here a strong personality has a vital role to play. One also feels that Mahler has written each measure ... with his heart's blood; one is hearing the innermost thoughts of the composer ... who never asks himself whether what he is writing is agreeable, but has the courage to show himself as he is. ... One thing, finally, must be said: Mahler has succeeded in gripping our attention uninterruptedly for two hours and bringing us to a state of glowing enthusiasm.

David Joseph Bach[246] also firmly defended Mahler. Among modern composers, only Bruckner had until now inspired him, though Mahler's compositions were 'far clearer, stricter and more consistent'. As for the widely held opinion that his music was based on poetic and philosophical ideas, he conceded that Mahler 'felt poetically and thought philosophically'. However, he transformed everything into music, 'not in order to provide a musical illustration for a given programme, but, out of all the elements of his inner being, to create music, for he cannot create anything else. Indeed, the essence of his being is harmony, and harmony alone.' His music, whether sad or exuberant, always showed the same underlying, easily recognizable rhythm of *joie de vivre* and self-assured serenity. Bach thought that Mahler had understood and served Nietzsche perfectly in the fourth movement, and that in the Finale he had created an 'enchanted sea'.

Max Vancsa, the progressive-minded critic of the *Neue Musikalische Presse*, a leading member of the Hugo Wolf-Verein, began his review with a word of praise. The Third was the first important work ever to have its première at a Gesellschaftskonzert, and it was also 'the least eccentric, the least irritating, the most unified and for this reason probably the most successful' of Mahler's symphonies. A number of reservations followed: there was a great disparity of style between the opening movement and the others. The first was the only one that resembled his other symphonies in displaying 'a concatenation of little motifs, little orchestral ideas and witticisms', brief instrumental solos, and 'empty noises' in the manner of a pointillist painting. By comparison, the other movements seemed thoroughly classical. Mahler often confused the 'popular' with the 'banal'. Like Arthur Smolian in Leipzig, Vancsa noticed a kinship between the flügelhorn solo in the Scherzo and *Die Post im Walde*. The Finale had assured the success of the work, yet it was the least original of the six movements and the closest to Wagner and Bruckner. In spite of all his reservations, Vancsa regarded the Third as

---

[246]　David Josef Bach (1874–1947), born in Vienna, studied philosophy, art history, and science as well as music at the University there. Completing his studies in Berlin, Leipzig, and London, he was recruited in 1904 by Victor Adler for the socialist *Arbeiter-Zeitung* upon the death of Josef Scheu on 12 Oct. In 1905 he founded the Arbeiter Simphoniekonzerte (the first concert was held on 28 Dec., in the Musikvereinsaal), then later the Freie Volksbühne (Free People's Theatre). He also ran the Verein für Volkstümliche Musikpflege. After the First World War he edited the literary and artistic column of the *Arbeiter-Zeitung* and, with Julius Bittover, founded the journal *Der Merker*, which lasted until 1922. In 1911 he wrote a book about the Vienna Volksoper and in 1923 a volume entitled *Tausend!* (Thousand!) that celebrated the anniversary of Social Democracy. A close friend of Schoenberg and Webern, he emigrated after the Anschluss to England, where he died in 1947.

a very important achievement, the work of a genius full of imagination and wit and with complete mastery of all the available modern technical means. What it lacks, in order to be a great work, is the power of genuine personal artistic conviction . . . Gustav Mahler's character is marked by conflict: as a true modern man, he is inwardly divided, and impelled to extremism. He has many artistic ideals and he worships them and sometimes himself, in spasmodic ecstasies as if they were idols, only in order to scoff at them and smash them to smithereens a moment later. The most basic trait of his character is irony, corrosive, devastating irony. The listener, who has allowed himself to be borne along, finds he is being led by the nose, becomes disenchanted and completely loses the thread. The artist does not believe in himself and the listener does not believe in him.

Thus another critic was totally baffled by Mahler's 'irony' and unable to find his way among his 'heterogeneous' styles. Once again, the Viennese critics at large instinctively rejected a composer to whom the public had obviously taken. In fact, Mahler's native country was to be among the last to recognize his stature. According to Max Graf, each performance of his symphonies in Vienna did even more to swell the ranks of his enemies than the 'scandals' at the Opera. Graf thus ascribes Mahler's increasing stubbornness and irritability during his last Vienna years to the unending partisan disputes about him and his work, and which affected him all the more because he had been at first universally admired. According to Graf, he himself confessed that the critics' hostility affected him less than the malevolence of 'theatre reporters', who 'revel in, magnify and orchestrate the most minor incident at the Opera and poison the air I breathe'.[247]

Despite all the destructive animosity unleashed by the critics after the performance of the Third, Mahler had for once had the deep satisfaction of seeing that one of his works had been a complete success with the Viennese public, so much so that it had to be repeated eight days later. At last the old dream had come true, the dream which had led him to compose the *Klagende Lied* when he was 20 years old. No less gratifying was the Philharmonic Orchestra's dedication, and its applause at the end of the concert. On 20 December, between the two performances of the Third, Mahler gave the 115 musicians a banquet at the 'Zur Goldene Birne' restaurant on the Mariahilferstrasse in order to show them how grateful he was. He arrived late, having been to the first chamber concert of the Vereinigung.[248] The steins and plates were already empty, so he went off to the kitchen to order more food and

---

[247]   GWO 92. The 'extraordinary' Gesellschaftskonzert with the Philharmonic took place on 14 Dec. at 8.00 p.m. and was repeated on the 22nd. The women's chorus was borrowed from the Singverein, the children's chorus from the Löwenburg'schen Konvict. The contralto soloist was Hermine Kittel. The final rehearsal was held on 12 Dec. at three in the afternoon.

[248]   The programme was made up of five Lieder by Gerhard von Keussler, Pfitzner's Trio performed by Arnold Rosé (violin), Bruno Walter (piano), and Friedrich Buxbaum (cello), four Lieder by Rudolph Stefan Hoffmann, and six by Kurt Schindler. According to Bruno Walter's letter to Hans Pfitzner, dated 26 Dec. 1904 (BWB 76), the Trio was a smashing success (*Bombenerfolg*) and even Max Kalbeck, the most reactionary of all Vienna critics, wrote about it 'with deep respect'.

drink.[249] After large quantities of beer had been consumed and everyone was beginning to unbend, the bass clarinettist provoked a roar of laughter when he remarked: 'This afternoon, Herr Direktor, you heard everything one can get out of a bass clarinet. Now you're seeing everything that can go into one!'[250] The evening was so gay and relaxed, that several newspapers reported shortly afterwards that Mahler was planning once again to take over the conductorship of the orchestra.[251] However, he was now far too busy, travelling with a view to establishing a tradition for the interpretation of his own works. And according to Ludwig Karpath the euphoria soon evaporated, since two or three rehearsals at the theatre were enough to create new tension. 'You see,' Mahler said sadly to the *Tagblatt* critic, 'it's quite impossible. . . . Whatever I do, as soon as I prolong a rehearsal, it's all over! Once again I am a tyrant in the eyes of the Philharmonic and that's all there is to it.'[252]

Even Mahler's worst enemies had to acknowledge the fact that the enthusiasm aroused by the two performances of the Third Symphony indicated a new trend in Viennese musical taste. Many Viennese became aware for the first time of Mahler's true stature as a composer, particularly the younger musicians around Arnold Schoenberg. Egon Wellesz[253] recalled a quarter of a century later what he and his friends had felt after hearing the Third Symphony for the first time, shortly after Strauss's *Domestica*. Wellesz went to the library of the Institute of Musicology, where he was a student, and located a score of the new work, together with a four-hand transcription which he immediately played with his friend Anton von Webern. After they had played the whole score several times, Webern expressed certain reservations: the second theme, for flutes, oboes, and clarinets[254] seemed to him to be 'too Viennese' and he asked Wellesz, 'Wouldn't it be better to treat the bassoon part as the principal voice?' According to Wellesz, who for his part had already been converted, Webern, in his innermost nature, was too much of a sensitive poet, 'closest in those days to Rilke, and thus found it difficult to come to terms with the romanticism of the work and its popular character'.[255] For Wellesz, 'a new world' had opened up:

The statement of the first theme, with the full might of eight horns; the entry of the fifths in the sixth bar, played by all the strings, timpani, bassoons, which were joined by two trombones, bass tuba, side and bass drums on the third beat; then the fortissimo cymbal clash in the ninth bar: and the fading sound of the closing pianissimo *morendo* phrase in the horns' deepest register: nothing of this kind had ever been heard

[249]   BMG 276. The invitation Mahler sent to the secretary of the orchestra, Franz Heinrich, is in the archives of the Vienna Philharmonic.

[250]   Alexander Witeschnik, *Musizieren* n. 239 above, 48.

[251]   Theodor Helm hinted as much in the *Musikalisches Wochenblatt* 36 (1905): 1, 12–13, and Korngold in his article on the Third Symphony.   [252]   BMG 176.

[253]   See below, Chap. 2.   [254]   Probably on pages 28–9 of the pocket score.

[255]   *Egon Wellesz: Leben und Werk*, completed by Emmy Wellesz and edited by Franz Endler (Zsolnay, Vienna, 1981), 42.

before . . . Whenever I turn over the pages of the score, I remember how new and amazing it all seemed to the few who attended the rehearsals of this symphony, and how the orchestra gradually had to become accustomed to a new style of interpretation and ensemble playing that required from each player an unprecedented degree of attention and intensity, not only in the loud passages, but also, and even more, in the softer ones, where the slightest slackening of tension would have meant a break in the continuity.[256]

Another witness, the Graz critic Ernst Decsey, who had attended one of the Vienna performances, went to some trouble to describe the astonishing 'scandal' of the Third Symphony:

When the eight horns played the principal theme, which was a spitting image of the old folk song 'Wir hatten gebaut ein stattliches Haus', when the podium literally trembled to the blows of the bass drum and the furious runs of the basses, the musician next to us ran his hand through his hair in horror. When the nasal trumpets played their sneering D minor motif, which ends on the sarcastic C# leading note, when the high-pitched clarinets played their strident chords and when the much disparaged second theme (*Gesangsthema*) finally appeared, the theme described by some as *Burgmusik* (military band music) and by others as *Pülchermusik* (vagabonds' music), which deliberately introduces a banal element into the picture, it was almost too much for our honest musician. He began to cast looks of despair at the ceiling, drew circles on his forehead to show what he thought of this musical insanity, began to laugh out loud, and once more ran his hand through his hair. His agitation knew no bounds. . . . However, then came the second part. First the delightful minuet in A, then the good-natured scherzando with the posthorn solo, the nocturne in which the human voice participates solely on account of its musical beauty, the women's and boys' choruses with their chiming bells, and then finally the D major Adagio, a hymn to love that grows and burgeons in extent and complexity from a quite simple violin melody. Our musician had recovered his composure. He had stopped running his hand through his hair, had stopped casting looks of horror, and had totally changed his opinion. 'It's magnificent,' he murmured several times. 'Magnificent!' And with the same impetuosity with which he had at first rejected the music, he began to praise it to the skies. He sat down and wrote the composer an enthusiastic letter of thanks, and this is all the more praiseworthy since he is himself a composer.[257]

The hero of this story could well have been the author of the following letter, sent to Mahler on the evening of the general rehearsal of the Third Symphony, on 12 December 1904:

Dear Herr Direktor, in attempting to formulate some kind of description of the wholly unprecedented impression your symphony made on me, I cannot speak as a musician to a fellow musician, but as one human being to another. The fact is: I have seen your

---

[256] Egon Wellesz, 'Mahler's Instrumentation', *Musikblätter des Anbruch* 12 (1930): 3, 106.

[257] This description serves as preface to an article written in Dec. 1906 by Ernst Decsey before the performance conducted by Mahler in Graz two days later (*Tages Post, Morgenblatt*, 1 Dec. 1906). The composer he describes could well be Schoenberg, who is known to have been lukewarm about Mahler's music until he heard the Third Symphony on that occasion. Wellesz, who was Schoenberg's pupil at that time, noted that at the beginning of the final rehearsal neither he, nor Zemlinsky, nor Webern seemed to be very convinced by what they heard.

soul in its nakedness, its utter nakedness. It was spread out in front of me, like a wild and mysterious landscape, full of terrifying chasms and ravines, and next to them, serene and charming, sunlit meadows, idyllic places of repose. I felt it was like an awesome phenomenon of nature, with its terrors and calamities and its transfiguring, comforting rainbows. What difference does it make if, when I was subsequently told about your 'programme', this did not seem to correspond to my emotions? Is it of importance whether I am good or bad at interpreting the emotions that an experience has excited within me? Must I understand correctly, when I have experienced and felt? And I believe I felt your symphony. I felt the battle against illusions; I sensed the pain of one who has lost them; I saw the forces of good and evil engaged in combat; I saw a human being struggling in agitated torment for inner peace; I felt a human being, a drama, *truth*, the most ruthless truth!

I had to get this off my chest; forgive me, but I do not go in for middle of the road emotions. Either—or!

Yours faithfully, Arnold Schoenberg.[258]

---

[258] AMS and AMM1, 335. This letter, dated Sun. 12 Dec. 1904, appears only in the first edition of Alma's book. It was probably written after the general rehearsal of the Third, which took place on that day at half past two. Among Mahler's letters to Schoenberg is a brief postcard (postmarked 13 Dec.) thanking him for his 'dear lines' and offering him a seat at the concert the following day. This is undoubtedly a reply to the young composer's long letter. In another card probably dating from the same time, Mahler apologizes for being unable to give the young man seats for the Opera that evening (Library of Congress, Washington, DC, see MBRS 182).

2

Mahler in Vienna (XVIII)—*Das Rheingold*
Mahler and Viennese Society
Première of the *Kindertotenlieder*
Meeting with Webern—End of the Vereinigung
The Fifth in Dresden, Berlin, Prague, and Hamburg

(January–March 1905)

> Believe me! I can understand and forgive the anger I provoke far more
> easily than my enemies can tolerate my equanimity!

WITH their production of *Tristan* Mahler and Roller had ushered in a new era in the presentation of Wagner operas. They now turned to the *Ring*, the stage settings for which had remained unchanged since the first Vienna production (1877–9). The initial plan was to restage the four operas in close succession: *Das Rheingold* in January 1905, *Die Walküre* in April, *Siegfried* in the autumn, and *Götterdämmerung* early the following year. The estimates for *Die Walküre* had even been approved by the Intendant.[1] Mahler stressed that the four new productions should be completed in a short space of time, 'since once *Das Rheingold* has been restaged, complete performances of the cycle would no longer be possible until the other *Ring* dramas have also been restaged'.[2]

Later on, probably in early 1905, the new *Walküre* was postponed until September, only to be cancelled later on, when Mahler decided to devote the funds to three new Mozart productions originally planned for 1906: *Don*

---

[1] The total budget for each new production was estimated at 30,000 kronen (ÖTM, HOA: Roller's letter of 18 June 1904). The cost of the new Mozart productions planned for 1906 was originally to have come entirely from the 'Mozart Year' budget, until it was decided to begin the Mozart cycle at the end of 1905 with productions of *Così* and *Don Giovanni*.

[2] Mahler's letter of 18 June 1904 (HOA, G.Z. 690/1904).

Giovanni, Così fan tutte, and *Die Entführung*.[3] The *Neuinszenierung* of *Walküre* was thus put off, first until 1906, then until early 1907. For nearly two years, therefore, the complete *Ring* cycles given at the Hofoper included only one new production, the Roller *Rheingold*.[4]

Rehearsals of the new *Rheingold* at the end of 1904 and the beginning of 1905 were marked by the usual tensions, quarrels, and setbacks. A score of musicians went down with flu and had to be replaced. Then, rehearsing the descent to Nibelheim, Mahler asked a clarinettist to raise the bell of his instrument in order to increase the effect of a crescendo. The resulting volume was still inadequate, so Mahler asked the musician to play standing up. This time the sound he produced was satisfactory, but was greeted with a burst of laughter from the orchestra musicians: their colleague had shot up and immediately sat down again as though someone had prodded him in a delicate part of his anatomy.[5]

On another occasion, at the entrance of Fasolt and Fafner, Mahler was dissatisfied with the forte produced by the timpanist, Franz Weber. He made Weber repeat the passage again and again, and then, still not satisfied, suddenly rushed up to him, wrested the drumstick from his grasp, and had a go at the passage himself—ending up a few seconds later with a broken drumstick dangling from his hand. 'I could have managed it that way myself', thought Weber, whose face must have betrayed him, since from that day on, says Otto Strasser, he was *persona non grata* with Mahler.[6] Later in the same scene Mahler interrupted the rehearsal to ask Fasolt and Fafner 'why they didn't carry Freia on their shoulders as called for in the score'. The strapping and powerfully muscled Mayr and Hesch explained sheepishly that they found this impossible. Whereupon Mahler leapt onto the stage, picked Gutheil-Schoder up, and trotted round holding her out at arm's length![7] Max Graf later recalled a conversation he had had with Mahler at the Café Imperial, at the time of the *Rheingold* rehearsals. Graf was amazed at the naivety of Mahler's approach to the opera. 'It's just a fairy tale', he kept repeating. Graf explained that for him, on the contrary, 'Loge's recitative marked the beginning of modern psychology'. Mahler rejected this out of hand, and took to greeting Graf as 'the quibbler' in subsequent encounters at the Café Imperial.[8]

Now that Lefler had left the Hofoper for the Burgtheater, Roller had a free hand. He had already modernized several outmoded sets such as that for *Les Contes d'Hoffmann*. For *Das Rheingold* he experimented boldly, using the new

---

[3]　Mahler's proposal is dated 23 Sept.; the Intendant's approval, 2 Oct. The estimate for *Don Giovanni* was 25,000 kronen; for *Entführung* 15,000 (HOA, Z. 3572/1905). *Entführung* was finally postponed until 1906.

[4]　Mahler passed on to Roller the Intendant's final letter of refusal with MBR1, no. 299; MBR2, no. 331.

[5]　This and other anecdotes were published in the 29 Jan. issue of the *Fremden-Blatt*.

[6]　Otto Strasser, *Und dafür wird man noch bezahlt: Mein Leben mit den Wiener Philharmonikern* (Paul Neff, Vienna, 1974).

[7]　Leo Feld, 'Die wunderlichen Geschichten des Kapellmeisters Gustav Mahler', *Neues Wiener Journal* (1 Apr. 1923).　　　　　　　　　　　　　　　　　　　　　　　　　[8]　GWO 79.

lighting techniques and the resources of impressionistic painting to achieve a combination of realism and stylization. His efforts aroused particular interest since until then no German opera house had dared to turn its back on the model provided by Bayreuth.[9] Roller's central idea was to suggest 'nature before the fall', which he felt was the true inspiration and hence the only suitable framework for *Das Rheingold*. To ensure that scene shifts could be carried out within the time allotted by the score, he decided to use the revolving stage installed some years previously for *Così fan tutte*. But the size and weight of the sets called for not just one but two circular platforms which turned on themselves 180 degrees, like mill wheels.[10] The new set-up allowed rapid shifting of the three sets needed for the opera's four scenes, but some critics felt that the resulting stage space was too cramped, both scenically and for the singers.

While ensuring that the huge papier-maché rocks looked as real as possible, Roller no more wanted to create the 'illusion' of reality in *Das Rheingold* than he had in *Tristan* or *Fidelio*. The curtain thus rose on a scene that effectively suggested the watery depths of the Rhine, but Roller also used it to evoke the opera's overall atmosphere and symbolize the main 'themes' of the plot. He used sea-greens not only to suggest the 'Rhine's delightful depths' but also to express 'innocence before sin'. The stage was taken up with three gigantic rocks and flanked by two slanting asymmetrical rock walls. The earlier traditional staging with trolleys only allowed the three Rhinemaidens to go through the most rudimentary motions of swimming. Now, reclining on their backs, they hovered over the stage in huge 'baskets' suspended by cables. Mahler planned their movements so carefully that they seemed to be floating in a state of total weightlessness. Unfortunately, Roller's baskets were not comfortable, perhaps because they lacked padding, and the singers protested that nobody could expect them to sing in attitudes which were not only awkward but downright dangerous. During one rehearsal, Jenny Pohlner (Wellgunde) felt her wig catch on a rock, and tore out some of her own hair freeing it. After which she tried to organize a general protest.[11] As was his wont, Roller took stern measures to restore order. He succeeded, but aroused

[9] If Ludwig Karpath is to be believed, Roller said to him years later that if he had been to Bayreuth before designing Wagner sets 'he would have done many things differently' (BMG 124).

[10] Each metal platform was 11 metres in diameter and 13 centimetres thick (the old platform, in use since 1900, was 30 centimetres thick). The new platforms cost 14,000 kronen out of an overall budget of 50,000 kronen, later increased to 65,000 (Roller's letter to the Intendant of 20 Oct. 1904). In August, Mahler and Roller obtained a further 8,000 kronen to expand one of the revolving stages to 16 metres, which meant it could be used on its own in the autumn for Wolf Ferrari's *Die neugierigen Frauen* and later for *Così fan tutte*, *The Marriage of Figaro*, and *Die lustigen Weiber von Windsor* (HOA, Z. X 29/1905: reports by theatre inspector Richard Bennier and Roller of 24 Aug.; Mahler's letter to the Intendant of 29 Aug.). The two revolving stages, the flying machinery, and the five new spotlights installed in the flies finally cost 24,753 kronen instead of the 20,000 allocated at the end of 1904.

[11] Testifying in connection with the suit brought against the Opera by the baritone Neidl after his accident in 1899, Mahler cited *Das Rheingold* as an example of what could happen to singers. He noted that even when the Rhinemaidens had been wafted about on trolleys these sometimes overturned. To compensate the Opera stage crew, Mahler asked the Intendant in early Mar. to grant them a 1,383 kronen bonus (HOA G.Z. 322/1905).

further resentment in the process. Mahler felt obliged to stand by him, thus encouraging rumours that Roller now had him firmly under his thumb. Mahler freely acknowledged his stage-designer's influence but justified it by maintaining that he would never dream of 'tying the hands' of his chief collaborator.

Since childhood, Roller had been an admirer of natural beauty. He had spent his summers in the Dolomites, and now used a landscape of those mountains as inspiration for his setting for the second scene of *Das Rheingold*, a sloping alpine meadow covered with flowers and framed by pine trees and steep cliffs.[12] Through field and forest the view stretched to the Rhine, gleaming in the distance. On the horizon, the other side of the river, was Valhalla, looking more like a 'fortified town in southern Tunisia' than a medieval fortress. The jumbled, unreal heap of Cyclopean blocks, not unlike Appia's design, changed colour with the lighting. Ludwig Hevesi described Valhalla as 'a pink castle at dawn, a golden city at dusk, sometimes glittering in the flush of morning—while the world below dreams in shadowed sleep—and sometimes seen from the other side, with a rainbow descending to the land of mortals'.[13] Most of the time it was softly blurred in a shifting but predominantly pink haze. The sky shone in impressionist tones of pale green. Here too, Roller employed colour symbolically as well as decoratively. Lighting was used to evoke Freia's abduction: the landscape turned greyish, colour draining away until Valhalla was 'almost invisible, wrapped in a damp white mist'. Then all vanished in the sudden onset of 'a universal grey-green autumn'.[14] Lighting effects of this kind obviously worked better when applied to mobile, adjustable elements than to *trompe-l'oeil* flats.

Peter Altenberg was one of the most colourful figures in the Vienna of that time. Essayist, writer, a friend of Adolf Loos, Arthur Schnitzler, and Alban Berg (who set some of his short prose poems to music), and above all a lover of life in all its aspects and an attentive witness of all the events of his time, he devoted one of his essays to the new *Rheingold*, in the form of an impressionist vignette. He was struck above all by the omnipresence of nature, as much in Mahler's conducting as in Roller's designs.

This strange tension at *Rheingold*: we waited with an almost anxious longing for the first note and the murmur of the Rhine. Never had an audience been so absorbed! What if the murmur, the flow, the shimmer of the water engulfed everything that the puny gods and puny mortals experience, suffer, and believe important. The *Pànta rèi*[15] tragedy begins: everything in the world is flowing and in transforming movement. It

---

[12] Two 'plastic', i.e. three-dimensional, rocks were ordered from a sculptor named Albert Stozek for 230 kronen (HOA, Z. 70/1905).

[13] Ludwig Hevesi, *Altkunst, Neukunst: Wien 1894–1908* (Konegen, Vienna, 1909), 265.

[14] Ibid. A painstaking technician as well as an artist and poet, Roller made extremely detailed watercolour sketches of the high points of each opera so that he could obtain the precise effect he wanted by means of lighting (Alfred Roller's original sketches are now in ÖTM, Vienna). His set and costume designs for *Das Rheingold* were shown in 1908 at the first *Kunstschau* exhibition.

[15] 'Everything flows.'

begins with the murmur, the flow, the shimmer of the Rhine . . . Roller the painter had put prehistoric pines to the left, in the corner, with bare, broken branches: and they too look down in quiet containment as the tragedy unfolds . . . Today, thanks to Roller the painter, I have seen nature like a wise chorus solemnly following the fate of those who are its victims. The deep Rhine waters, the old pines, the vaporous, misty valley of the Rhine embraced the wretched destinies, brought about by love and greed . . . Erda emerged from a crevasse to warn Wotan. Her singing was so much like nature, as if the Rhine, the pines, the misty valleys were to warn of trivial human matters! We, the onlookers, the listeners, tremble when Erda warns! Severe and impartial Nature eternally warns us in the same urgent, mysterious way of our own follies . . . But still we build castles on earth and castles in the air! Still we construct our Valhalla with cheating wretches, whom we ourselves cheat.[16]

Roller's costumes were another break with Bayreuth tradition. The Rhinemaidens were veritable sirens with long fishtails covered in greenish scales. Their coiffures were stylized corollas made up of three irregularly shaped petals. Fricka wore a long white tunic draped in classical style and fastened by a chain over a bodice of open-weave knitted fabric. The pattern in her cloak was a Roller design. Wotan had a full beard, a grey tunic, a breastplate, bound leggings of cloth, and a sweeping blue cloak. His spear was a long stick with a crude iron tip lashed on with strips of leather. Erda entered directly from the wings and not, as before, through a trapdoor in the floor. She seemed to be the prisoner of the long, flower-garlanded hair that spilt down over her long blue tunic.

The costumes of the other gods were inspired sometimes by ancient Greece, sometimes by German legend. Freia's robe with its red and green flowers and wide sleeves was borrowed from antiquity, like her Grecian coiffure and its double garland of flowers. Her wide belt was a cord wound several times round her waist, its ends trailing around her feet. Froh, also garlanded with flowers and foliage, wore leggings and a wide white tunic of vaguely Grecian cut. Donner, god of thunder, had red hair and beard and wore a belt and gauntlets of steel, a white tunic and a bearskin beneath a grey-blue mantle. Loge, the god of fire, wore a red wig and a tunic hung with hundreds of scarlet flames. Fasolt and Fafner were swathed in fur, as befits denizens of the forest—Fafner with red hair and beard, Fasolt with a tigerskin draped over his head. For the descent into Nibelheim, Wagner's painted scrim was abandoned. It appears that Roller planned to replace it with a kind of black-velvet curtain, but it failed to work properly on the night of the dress rehearsal.[17] Roller and Mahler therefore simply lowered a double curtain of green velvet which, Mahler decided, made it easier for the audience to 'concentrate on the music'.

[16] 'Rheingold', in *Das grosse Peter Altenberg Buch* (Zsolnay, Vienna and Hamburg, 1967), 310 ff.

[17] Writing in the *Allgemeine Zeitung* and *Die Musik*, Schönaich reported that despite this hitch 'the Intendant refused to postpone the première so that he wouldn't have to refund the tickets already sold'. For Max Graf, all the 'charm of passing from one world to another' was lost. Erik Schmedes relates that Mahler ordered felt slippers for the stagehands, to prevent their footsteps being heard in the auditorium (*Neues Wiener Tagblatt*, 21 June 1931).

Shadowy Nibelheim was 'drowned in infernal vapours' flickeringly lit by the distant forge. As in Florestan's cavern in *Fidelio*, the looming rocks were represented by masses of black velvet which made it easier for Alberich, an ape-like gnome in black fur, to appear and disappear. For the last scene, Roller discarded the wooden bridge over which the gods had formerly crossed to Valhalla. Now they proceeded in a cortège upstage while a gigantic rainbow appeared behind the rocks, projected onto the backdrop. The staging as a whole showed a particular concern for sobriety and stylization.[18] The Rhinemaidens' water ballet and the rocks of Nibelheim constituted concessions to the illusion of reality, but in other respects Roller's presentation came closer to Appia's principles by discarding the papier-mâché dragon in Alberich's metamorphosis scene and, later, the wooden bridge.

Erwin Stein observed that Mahler's interpretation of the score was predominantly lyrical, as it was later to be in the *Walküre* of 1907. The emphasis was no longer placed solely on the spectacular passages—the entry of the gods into Valhalla in *Das Rheingold*, the magic fire and the ride of the Valkyries in *Die Walküre*. There were as many piano and cantabile passages as there were shattering tuttis. 'The score', wrote Stein, 'toned down to the softness of an accompaniment, revealed many new colours and shades and, most important, the vocal line of the singers. Even Schmedes's Siegfried had not penetrated the thick sound of Schalk's orchestra.'[19] It is worth noting that after the asceticism of the Wieland Wagner era, Mahler's and Roller's conceptions of the *Ring* have been revived at Bayreuth itself in Boulez's 'chamber-music' interpretation of the score and Patrice Chéreau's naturalistic-symbolic staging of 1976.

The prodigies of ingenuity and poetry Roller achieved were not always appreciated by the critics, whose verdicts were less favourable than they had been for *Tristan* and *Fidelio*, probably because, nearly thirty years after the Vienna première of the *Ring*, the Bayreuth tradition still weighed heavily on the style and details of the staging. In particular, the critics accused Roller of cluttering up the stage with huge rocks. They also as usual, disliked the 'orgies of darkness' which forced the singers to 'wander about like blind men' in the Nibelheim cavern. A few critics also decried the disappearance of traditional props and Wagner's famous mobile scrim.

One of the most implacable enemies of the new production was the drama critic of the daily *Deutsche Zeitung*, Albert Leitich, who used the occasion to launch yet another attack on Mahler's overall management policy. Leitich thought that the Hofoper repertory now included too many 'worthless' works like *Lakmé*, *Cavalleria Rusticana*, and *Les Contes d'Hoffmann*, whereas the operas of Weber, Gluck, Marschner, and Kreutzer had completely disappeared. Mahler, he said, was devoting all his energies to new productions which were

---

[18] *Neues Wiener Journal*, 19 and 26 June 1921. In this connection Graf cites Mahler's first production of *The Magic Flute* in 1897, when he had the animals enter one by one, attracted by Tamino's flute.
[19] ESM 304.

'gross frauds' because they failed to attract audiences—an unfair accusation, since the *Tristan* and *Fidelio* productions and their sets remained in the repertory long after Mahler's departure. Leitich accused Mahler of failing to find replacements for the major singers he had 'banished', people like Van Dyck, Renard, and Reichmann, so that he was continually 'forced' to resort to guest performances of new singers. He advised readers that they would be better off 'tossing seat money out of the window than going to the Opera'. He felt that the former production of *Das Rheingold* was far preferable to Mahler's, and that Roller was wrong to ignore the precedent of Bayreuth and, therefore, Wagner's intentions. In the first scene, he noted, the 'baskets' carrying the Rhinemaidens could be seen from some seats, and as the singers lay there on their backs they looked more like seals than sirens. As for their much talked-about 'swim', it amounted to no more than a couple of turns around a rock. After that, the maidens remained immobilized upstage, suspended much too high for Alberich ever to reach them. In any case, the surrounding gloom was so deep that you couldn't make out *what* he was trying to do. Leitich felt the production owed more to 'pedantics' (*Schulmeisterei*) than to art, a 'mistake' all the more 'unforgivable' in that it cost 60,000 kronen. Because of the exiguous stage, the 'vistas were too short' and 'it looked as if the gods had their noses pressed up against Valhalla'. He disliked the huge rocks, the 'floral display', and the lighting change during Freia's abduction, which he called 'an antiquated and almost childish' effect. Valhalla looked to him like 'a quarry after an explosion' or a 'cluster of armour-plated blockhouses'. This 'dwelling-place with neither doors nor windows' was 'more suitable for frogs or scorpions than gods'. Yet Wagner's music 'depicts a noble and majestic castle'.[20]

Leitich's damning criticisms appeared in the anti-Semitic *Deutsche Zeitung* several days after the première. But in the meantime the paper's music critic, Maximilian Muntz, had already condemned the new *Rheingold* in much the same terms, claiming that 'the dramatic requirements were subservient to those of the painter'. At times Roller's feeble imagination produced décors 'lacking both the form and effects of perspective': the characters remained for the most part stationary in the midst of overwhelming rocky masses. The 'staging' was simply a 'series of *tableaux vivants*'.[21] Hirschfeld also thought that Roller's imagination 'often clashed with the drama's inner requirements'.[22] The cramped stage continually forced singers to bunch up so that they couldn't all be seen at once. The high sidewalls were too close together and 'seem to have

[20] Leitich said that Mahler had pursued 'naturalistic pedantry' to such lengths that he made Wotan sing the invocation to Valhalla with his back to the audience.

[21] Muntz also took exception to the 'dark and muffled' playing of the orchestra, due, he felt, both to the lowered pit and to the 'gaudy, indecent' sound of the brass, 'which too often drowned the rest of the instruments'.

[22] Hirschfeld accused Mahler of betraying one of his own principles by giving *Das Rheingold* four times independently of the rest of the tetralogy. It is hard to see how he could have done otherwise, however, since the funds needed for *Die Walküre* had been refused.

been designed without any thought for the characters, . . . the scene depicted destroys life, and turns the singers into figurines'. Hirschfeld criticized the darkness which obscured the Rhine and Nibelheim, and thought that Roller's colour symphonies, although beautiful in themselves, often seemed 'unrelated to the plot'. The contrast of the red wigs of the singers against the violet background was magnificent but did not reflect, as far as he was concerned, corresponding 'sound colours' in Wagner's music. The very beauty of the scenic pictures contained a disturbing element which 'prevents the Wagner listener from feeling at one with the Roller viewer'. Mahler had succeeded brilliantly in adapting Wagner's orchestra to Roller's colours. When Mahler had first arrived in Vienna, he had captivated his listeners in an entirely different way, transmitting his fiery temperament to the orchestra and singers in 'an orgy of movement': 'the gleams of torchlight flickered over the whole orchestra'. 'Today,' concluded Hirschfeld, 'the emphasis has changed to resignation, asceticism of sound, twilight, liquefaction'. Whatever 'marvellous effects' Mahler might thus obtain, such 'nocturnal spells' were more indicative of 'the art and artistic progress of Gustav Mahler than the essence of *Fidelio* or *Das Rheingold*.[23] 'Not everybody is capable of changing his artistic conception with the change of the year, jettisoning with the old calendar the conception he had so far passionately defended.'

Apart from Hirschfeld and Muntz, for whom an anti-Mahler stance was now the rule, Viennese critics liked the production. Wallaschek thought it Mahler's and Roller's greatest success. In particular, he felt that the Rhinemaidens' 'swim' was far more graceful and realistic than before, though in his view Valhalla in no way resembled the giants' description of it, and the Nibelheim cavern was definitely too crowded. In the *Fremden-Blatt*, Kauders noted that for once Roller had 'prevented too much ratiocination from making him heavy-handed', and had created scenery which 'breathed poetry and eternity'. He thought that very little could be held against him, and spoke with admiration of his superb sets and the 'noble style' of his costumes. Even more surprising praise came from the chief defender of Wagnerian orthodoxy in Vienna, Schönaich, who called Mahler's *Das Rheingold* 'a welcome development' and 'the climax of contemporary decorative art'.[24] Max Graf marvelled in similar terms at the subtlety of the lighting, which sometimes blurred, sometimes changed the outlines of the imposing mass of Valhalla as though it were 'a huge toy'. No other German theatre, he felt, could boast sets comparable to Roller's.[25]

[23] The vast majority of critics nevertheless admitted that since the beginning of his career Mahler had always tried to lighten Wagner's orchestral accompaniment.

[24] Schönaich's reviews in the *Allgemeine Zeitung* and *Die Musik* were full of praise. He congratulated Gutheil-Schoder for finally releasing Freia from the 'soubrette' treatment to which the role was too often subjected.

[25] Graf especially liked Roller's designs for the weapons and armour of the gods, singling out Wotan's spear for particular mention.

In the *Arbeiter-Zeitung*, David Joseph Bach had only two minor reservations, and these concerned the lighting. He thought that the water in the first
scene lacked movement and that the gleams of sunlight on the Nibelung treasure in the second scene should not have spread over the whole stage.
Korngold felt that Roller had created both 'nature and fairy-tale pictures',
while Karpath thought that 'Mahler's achievements' with Wagner would assure
him of 'immortal glory in the history of the Hofoper'. He also singled out the
flower meadow of *Das Rheingold* as 'a masterpiece of plastic and theatrical
art'.[26] But a year later the same Karpath delivered the severest and most definitive verdict of all on Roller's Wagnerian productions, accusing him of 'sinning
against the spirit of our greatest composer, Richard Wagner, in order to obtain
the pictorial effects he wanted':

He has recreated *Das Rheingold* and *Lohengrin*, he has communicated impressions
hitherto unknown and occasionally of striking beauty, but he has ignored all of
Wagner's indications in a way that arouses indignation. This is particularly true of *Das
Rheingold*, whose new production in itself is above reproach but which, from the point
of view of Richard Wagner, who indicated his intentions more carefully than any other
composer, deserves the strongest possible disapproval.[27]

Shortly before the première of the new *Rheingold*, Lilli Lehmann arrived in
Vienna to give her annual Gastspiel, this time limited to two performances,
Norma and *Fidelio*. She seems to have fitted perfectly into Mahler's new
production of *Fidelio*, wearing the long brown waistcoat and white Spanish
peasant shirt Roller had designed for Leonore with a totally natural air. The
Neue Freie Presse lauded the singer's 'noble radiance', a product, wrote the
anonymous critic, of 'the stylistic aptness, brilliance and refinement' of her
performance.

Mahler's sensational *Rheingold* was followed by two important premières:
Pfitzner's *Die Rose vom Liebesgarten* and an evening of two one-act operas, Leo
Blech's *Das war ich* and Eugen d'Albert's *Die Abreise*. The 1904–5 season
closed with a revival of Rossini's *Guillaume Tell*, conducted by Franco
Spetrino. But as before, Mahler's interpretations of his own works absorbed an
increasing amount of his time and energy. After two concerts of his Lieder in
Vienna in late January 1905, he conducted his Fifth Symphony in Hamburg in
March, and at the Strasbourg festival in May. This was followed by a Beethoven
concert, also in Strasbourg, and finally, in early June, another concert of his

[26] Features Karpath disapproved of included Roller's 'orgies of darkness' and certain costume details,
like Freia's 'Grecian' hairdo and Erda's crinoline-type gown. Cast for the performance of 23 Jan. 1905:
Gutheil-Schoder (Freia); Mildenburg (Fricka); Elizza, Pohlner, and Kittel (Rhinemaidens); Petru (Erda);
Schmedes (Loge); Breuer (Mime); Leuer (Froh); Weideman (Donner); Haydter (Alberich); Demuth (Wotan);
Mayr (Fasolt); Schwarz (Fafner). The role of Freia was originally meant to be sung by Förster-Lauterer. Franz
Schwarz replaced the ailing Wilhelm Hesch at the last moment. Weidemann and Demuth were to have alter-
nated in the roles of Wotan and Donner. According to Erwin Stein, Schmedes was such a fine Loge that the
God of Fire acquired a new dimension (ESM 304).

[27] *Bühne und Welt*, 2 (1906): 8, 801.

Lieder in Graz. To cut down on the time he spent away from the Hofoper, Mahler had as usual had to forgo conducting several other premières of his own works.

How much time and energy did this hectic schedule allow him to devote to his family, and in particular to Alma? Many women would of course have been happy and proud simply to share in the life of so famous a husband—but not Alma! Though she was flattered in the early days by the love she had awakened in so 'important' a personality, it wasn't long before she began to feel embarrassment and confusion under the inquisitive and insistent gaze of the gawking Viennese. She began to feel that people regarded her as a mere 'appendage' of Gustav, and what she wanted was not that: she wanted to express her own self and have her own triumphs. Yet some psychiatric observers have thought they could detect in Alma's memoirs a certain masochistic pleasure in such self-effacement.[28] Her writings do in fact reveal the ambiguity of her feelings. All Vienna recognized Mahler immediately, even at a distance, as he strode along bareheaded, with energetic, irregular steps, his pale face framed by abundant jet-black hair. He and Alma could never get very far in the streets before someone would turn around, smile and nudge his companion, or perhaps exclaim, 'That's Mahler and his wife!'

Mahler noticed nothing. His obliviousness was often quite grotesque. One day, for instance, we were in the Tivoli at Schönbrunn. Suddenly he got up, attracting innumerable inquisitive glances. After a time he returned, burst out laughing, and told me something totally intimate and private. Then he took a carafe of water from the table, poured it over his hands, washed them very carefully, rubbing them together, and wiped them with a café napkin . . .[29] Once we were waiting for the electric tram on the Prater, everybody watching. As the tram hove into view Mahler suddenly decided to disappear into a nearby toilet. Everybody smiled with embarrassment and stared at me. At times like that I wished for the earth to swallow me up. In restaurants too, he would never fail to draw the waiter's attention to a dish some other customer was eating. If necessary, he would stand up, point to the lucky man who had ordered the coveted dish, and call out: 'Waiter! What is that gentleman over there eating?'[30]

Around this time, an anonymous paragraph appeared in the satirical gossip column of a Viennese daily. It reported a scene that had recently taken place in a second-class compartment of the Stadtbahn (Vienna's municipal railway) full of dashing officers and elegant women in light summer dresses.

Suddenly the door was flung open to reveal a highly nervous gentleman with his hair brushed straight back, a very high forehead, and a crumpled felt hat. He scrutinized the other passengers, noticed a corner seat free near a window and settled into it. The train started. All at once the intellectual gentleman began to scrape his foot and wriggle restlessly. He did not seem in the least bothered by the reproving glances he

---

[28] The hypothesis is put forward by several psychoanalysts, among them Dr Stuart Feder, author of several studies of Mahler, notably *Mahler Dying*.
[29] AMM1, 98; AMM2, 102 and AMS.   [30] Ibid.

attracted, but continued to fidget. Finally, under the horrified gaze of the women, he raised his foot. Worse still, he removed his shoe and rapped it against the window until—a pebble fell out! The strange gentleman then resumed his seat, calmly put the shoe back on, and got off at the Karlplatz station. The women turned up their noses; the gentlemen declared his behaviour 'shocking'. One of them, however, leaned forward with a smile in an attempt to appease the other passengers! 'Don't be hard on him!' he explained. 'That was Gustav Mahler. Is there any reason why, for a little matter of etiquette, he should get along any worse than . . . the Hofoper.'[31]

Such displays of absent-mindedness were for years a staple subject for Viennese gossip about Mahler. Few people took offence, but Alma nonetheless felt cruelly humiliated, particularly on the occasions when she was present. Another facet of Mahler's character remained equally incomprehensible to her. It was something he was perfectly aware of, if only because so many friends, Natalie in particular, had brought it to his attention: his lack of consistency and abrupt changes of opinion. He of course owned up to them, but justified them by pointing out that there was no such thing as absolute truth, not in science or philosophy or art. From the same experiences one might draw, within a few hours, different and even opposite conclusions. 'But Gustav! You told me the exact opposite yesterday', Alma would sigh. Mahler would try to conceal his irritation, reminding her as gently as possible that he had always reserved the right to change his mind. Alma found this hard to accept: 'I could never be absolutely sure of his opinions,' she complains. 'And then,' she notes in her memoirs, writing at some time in the mid-1920s, 'there were many other odd traits in his nature which I cannot and do not yet want to talk about. It's still too soon!'[32]

She was undoubtedly alluding to sexual matters. She later complained bitterly that Mahler had been a 'puritan', and that sex had played only a very small part in his life. On one occasion she even told the author that 'her children were immaculately conceived'. At first sight this is an extraordinary statement for someone to make who was pregnant with her and Mahler's first child when she married him. Their second child was born two years later. But at the time of their marrige Alma was 22 years of age, and Mahler was 41. Alma's diary entries describing Mahler's first attempts to make love to her portray him as anything but a potent and practised lover, although we now know of his past and stormy premarital affairs. And yet Alma was young, and beautiful, and willing. The evidence would suggest that Mahler's powers to make physical love were at fault at this time, probably because of the misgivings and remorse which he felt at the idea of marrying a woman so much younger than him. Had he not in his letters to Alma during their engagement mentioned Eva and

---

[31] The press cutting, from which the name and date of the paper have been omitted, was in possession of Fritz Löhr.

[32] AMM1, 98; AMM2, 101 and AMS. A short sentence in AMS proves that the first MS of her *Erinnerungen* was written approximately ten years after Mahler's death.

Sachs, Sachs who was so much more worthy of Eva's love than Walther? Although the first unsuccessful attempt was quickly overcome and although Alma does not mention any other similar failure in her diary, her statement to the author implies that her physical relationship with Mahler had always been disappointing. It should however be borne in mind that Alma's remarks in her *Erinnerungen* were made at a time when she was writing her memoirs and felt compelled both to mention her liaison with Gropius and to find extenuating circumstances for having so quickly fallen into his arms. Mahler's failure to satisfy her sexually was surely the best excuse she could find for her behaviour in June 1910.

Today, all evidence seems to suggest that Alma's central problem was not sex but a much wider dissatisfaction and uncertainty about herself and her life with Mahler. Every day, in fact, she reflected on her 'bad' nature (this was the word she herself used in her diary), by which she meant the side of herself that was both frivolous and selfish. Every day she chafed under the duty of self-effacement which she had imposed on herself, of having to play a subordinate role and having constantly to curb her dominating temperament. She feared that she could not long tolerate the life she had chosen. Even the marriage of one of her former sweethearts, Gustav Klimt, awoke in her ambigous feelings, a mixture of jealousy, regret, and self-pity:

And yet I am happy that everything is as it is. I wouldn't want it to be otherwise. I could not bear the constant burning and singeing. I owe him a lot. I owe him my awakening. But I need calm. Klimt married! And she is flawless, immaculate! He is right! She is the one he needs for his life, for his art. Her beauty, her charm, all that is perfect: apart from that, she is nothing. As for me, nothing is perfect, not my face nor my mind nor my talent! . . .[33] I'm neither happy nor unhappy. But I have suddenly realized that I am leading only a semblance of a life. Inwardly I feel completely frustrated, I am not free! I am suffering—I don't know why and for what . . . MY SHIP IS IN PORT, BUT IT IS LEAKING . . .

Thus Alma continued to have doubts about herself. The only way she could quieten such doubts was to prove that she still exerted a hold over others. She was painfully conscious of her two tumultuous and opposing aspirations. On 1 January 1905 she wrote:

I blame myself, and yet! (The lioness licks up a single drop of blood and yet gets more out of it than the puny male does gobbling up a whole human being.)[34] We are in fact two people and we ought to be one! I am no longer capable of the least enthusiasm. Nothing really interests me—serious things tire me out. I drag myself wearily from hour to hour—weary in body and soul. In my make-up there is too much of something—or not enough!

'My children are ill,' Alma added four days later:

---

[33] See above, Vol. ii, Chap. 16, 713 ff.
[34] The passage in brackets was later deleted by Alma in the typewritten copy of AMT.

Putzi is better, but Gucki is going through it. Sad as it is, it has given me back my strength. I have found that the more you make demands on yourself, the more strength you find. All the morning I wrapped Gucki in cold sheets, took her temperature, etc. I've rarely been so cheerful and good-humoured. I suddenly realized why I'm on this earth. My children need me. Gustav needs me too. But I can't give him what he needs. Why not, in fact? Yesterday we talked about the old days and in passing I told him that in the early stages of our intimacy I found his body odour offensive. He said to me, 'That is the key to a lot of things! You acted against your nature!' I alone know how right he is. He was a stranger to me, many things are still strange for me and, I think, will always be so, and I have already suffered so much from that! And that's why there is much that I can't understand—or sometimes, when I could, it drives me away from him. I'm surprised that after realizing this one can go on living together. Duty? Children? Habit? No, no, I know that I really love him and that at the moment I couldn't live without him. For he has taken so much from me that his presence is now my only support. It seems impossible to me now to go back to my former life. The watchword now must be: chin up and get the best I can out of the short span that is <u>life</u>. And what I mean by the *best* is to <u>become so good, so useful, so calm, content and self-contained</u> that I can achieve my happiness from that.

But Alma well knew that she would never find the strength to keep her reso-lution. Less than three weeks later, her diary entry dated 23 January 1905 reads:

So little happens, I mean inside me, that there's no point in writing about it. My life is utterly calm. The children—Gustav! Gustav—the children! What goes on at the theatre doesn't interest me. Zemlinsky was here recently. He told me that he still could not bring himself to destroy a single one of my letters. He has saved every scrap. So have I. We talked a lot about the past. I told him that I read his letters again recently and that—

The diary stops short here—the following page has been removed—and, then carries on intermittently until the beginning of the summer, when it again comes to a halt.[35] From all this it becomes obvious that Alma often succeeded in resigning herself to her husband's powerful hold over her, but in truth could never accept it and ultimately found it impossible to live only for and through him. She could not forgive him for all that she had given up for his sake: a bril-liant social life with friends who were devoted to her, and of course musical composition—which for her was much more than a pastime. Sometimes Mahler would grow impatient at seeing his wife in the throes of yet another depression. Yet he respected her independent spirit: it was what had struck him most about her when he first met her at the Zuckerkandls. Curiously, he loved her all the more for the spirit of contradiction she often displayed, unlike most of the women who had surrounded him before his marriage. He had also got into the

---

[35] Typescript of Alma's private diary (UPL, Philadelphia). Page 14 has been removed. Page 15 begins: 'das Hauptmann merkwürdigerweise . . .' (AML 338). The last two pages of the copy of Alma's diary are dated 6 July 1906. It resumes after Mahler's death. Only the few excerpts published in AML (39) survived but Alma almost certainly made changes in the original before publication, as was her custom.

habit of listening to what she had to say, even on occasion heeding her advice, particularly when she tried to 'open his eyes' to the pernicious influence Arnold Rosé exercised on his relations with the Philharmonic, or to Roller's 'excesses'. She often agreed with the newspaper tirades against Roller's 'orgies of darkness', since she felt that a production could not be dramatic unless the actors' faces were clearly visible. She continually reproached Gustav for yielding to the painter's influence too easily. But to this Mahler would always reply that he 'had the greatest respect for Roller's integrity and preferred to expose himself to attacks rather than tie the hands of an artist responsible for a true regeneration of the theatre'.[36]

In an attempt to render their day-to-day existence more agreeable, Alma claims she entered into a pact with Gustav: if there was any bad news in the morning, she took care not to mention it when he returned from the Opera for lunch. While they ate she would chatter gaily on as though nothing at all was amiss. She would wait until he was rested and relaxed after his afternoon nap before telling him what had gone on while he was out, knowing that he would be better able to decide what had to be done. There is no doubt that during this period the management of their finances was a major preoccupation. Alma had to limit their expenditures so that Mahler could gradually repay what he had borrowed from his sisters to build the house in Maiernigg. From the start, he decided to trust his young wife completely in this matter. Like Adolar in *Euryanthe* ('Ich baue auf Gott und meine Euryanthe'), he would say, 'I put my trust in God and you to pay our debt off soon'.[37] However Mahler's income had increased in recent times thanks to the fees he earned as guest conductor of his own work. He had also received 10,000 gulden (20,000 kronen) from Peters for the Fifth Symphony and 15,000 (30,000 kronen) from Kahnt for the Sixth. The couple now lived on a comfortable footing, sparing themselves few pleasures or comforts. A note which has recently come to light was sent by Mahler to Alma in 1904. It refers to a sum of 2,000 kronen, which would allow her to run the Maiernigg household during July and August. For a family of four, with two servants, this was a generous provision.[38] Nevertheless, Alma claimed that the strict economy she had to impose on herself prevented her from buying the clothes she needed to make a proper showing in society, so that she had to refuse most of the invitations they received. But her *Erinnerungen*, one of whose early typescripts also contains the reminiscences of Erica Tietze-Conrat, mentions several dinner parties, some of which took place during this very winter of 1904–5.

On one occasion, for example, the Mahlers were invited to dine at the

---

[36] Bertha Zuckerkandl, *Österreich intim*, 68.   [37] AMM1, 93; AMM2, 98.

[38] BGA, no. 139 undated (12 July 1904). According to information obtained on 8 Dec. 1994 from the Austrian Bureau of Statistics 1,000 kronen of 1904 more or less equalled 8,000 marks of 1995, or $5,550 or £3,600 (see BGA, p. 247).

house of a wealthy family, that of Kommerzialrat Bernhard Wetzler.[39] As usual, Gustav arrived late from the Opera; the other guests were already at table. No sooner had he taken his place than he selected an apple from one of the fruit-dishes garnishing the table, carefully inspected it and sniffed its perfume, and then put it down next to his plate, much to the astonishment of the other guests. He then quickly polished off the main course and, without waiting for the dessert, got up and went into the smoking room where, despite his vehement protests, the master of the house and his daughter felt obliged to take turns in keeping him company. Later, probably out of remorse, he consented to listen to a singer named Muhr who wished to profit from the occasion to get the Director of the Opera to hear him. The singer had overestimated Mahler's patience, however, for hardly had the accompanist begun to play than Mahler rose and left the room. As soon as the first Lied was over, he bade his hosts a particularly curt farewell. Even if Alma has exaggerated some of the details, it must be recognized that Mahler on this occasion at least transgressed the limits of the most elementary good manners, deliberately, no doubt, since he felt a trap had been laid for him. It must also be said that his host was also gravely at fault in putting him, the Director of the Hofoper, in a very awkward position.

Clearly, Mahler never felt he had to observe the rules and conventions of a society he did not feel part of. This may explain why he so frequently caused 'dismay' and 'embarrassment': it was, Alma wrote in the manuscript of her memoirs, 'as though there was a corpse under the table'. He remained open to intimate and friendly exchange, to straightforward and enthusiastic discussion among chosen friends, but he was never at ease in society. On one occasion they accepted an invitation to dine with the Prince von Thurn und Taxis,[40] a cultured Viennese aristocrat. As they discussed the evening on the way home, they decided that with the money they had spent on clothes and a carriage they could have gone off on a short holiday together. Then they discovered that each had put up with the evening as a favour to the other. They solemnly decided to refuse such invitations in future, and dine out only with close friends. Among these were the Reininghauses,[41] who often entertained the artists of the Secession. Mahler liked visiting them, and also Josef

[39] The name Wetzler is mentioned only in AMS. The address of Bernhard Wetzler, Ehrenbürger von Kiralyhida was Trautsohngasse 6, in the 8th Bezirk, according to the *Wiener High Life Almanach* (Wiener High Life, Verlag, Vienna, 1905).

[40] The prince's family, originally from Bergamo, had lived in Austria since the sixteenth century and comprised a number of branches. The head of the family, Albert, born in 1867, was the eighth prince of the line and married to a princess of imperial blood. Prince Karl Ludwig, born in 1863, was married to a Braganza princess.

[41] AMS, beginning of 1904. Carl Reininghaus, a wealthy industrialist born in Graz, patron of Klimt and Schiele, whose *Beethovenfries* he purchased, and thus saved from destruction at the close of the 1902 exhibition, lived in Vienna at Schmalzhofgasse 24. Reininghaus's collection included a famous van Gogh and seven Hodlers which he bought at a Secession Exhibition of 1903–4. As a token of his gratitude for his purchase of the *Fries*, Klimt gave him all the preparatory drawings. (See Alessandra Comini, *The Changing Image of Beethoven* (Rizzoli, New York, 1987), 466, n. 51.)

Strzygowski,[42] founder of the first Art History Institute at the University of Vienna.

During most of his Viennese tenure, Mahler kept the members of the Viennese aristocracy at a distance, if only so that he would be better able to resist the pressures they sometimes brought to bear on him. When he came face to face with the uncrowned queen of Viennese society, Princess Pauline Metternich-Sandor (famous in the annals of music for the part she played in preparing the Paris première of *Tannhäuser*), Alma said that he felt an unease which undoubtedly arose from his desire to remain polite without making the slightest concession.'One day', Alma writes,

I was walking with him in the Michaelerplatz when we had to take flight because Princess Pauline Metternich, that famous ghost from the Second Empire, had spotted him from her carriage and was coming after him. She caught up with us at the end of the Kohlmarkt. I hid in a gateway while Mahler went up to the carriage. He spoke with her for quite a long time. She was always wanting to push forward some protégé or else to be first with the latest news from the Director's office. At last he rejoined me, fuming with rage. 'That horrible woman! Those mauve lips!' The worst invective he could think of was not strong enough for him. He could be driven to absolute fury by such bad taste, and had to get it out of his system; he was used to reacting strongly and immediately to any vexation.[43]

At the time of the Philharmonic's concerts in Paris in 1900 he had been in daily contact with the Princess Metternich.[44] Some time afterwards she sent him, via a writer called Richard Voss, the libretto *Die Aphrodite*, a 'ballet of landscapes and atmospheres, figures and colours', based on one of her own ideas. A glance showed Mahler that it wasn't suited to the Hofoper and he returned it to Prince Montenuovo without comment. Six months later, the Princess sent Mahler the following letter:

Dear Herr Director, Since the somewhat too detailed libretto which Herr Richard Voss composed on my idea for a ballet did not find favour, and you rejected it out of hand, I must ask you to return the manuscript with a few accompanying lines to the author. He occupies an outstanding place in the world of letters, and has taken serious offence at the treatment he was subjected to by the Hofoper. I am very upset because it was I who asked him to put my idea into a form suitable for the stage. The fact that he did not succeed in no way justifies discourtesy on the part of the Institute. Herr Lefler has not replied, despite a request to do so. I would have thought, nevertheless, that there

[42]   Josef Strzygowski (1862–1941) was born in Bielitz, in Galicia. He was one of the first historians to study the influence of the Orient on the development of Western art, and he invented a new method and new schemas for the scientific study of the arts. Strzygowski wrote many works, mainly on oriental subjects. He acquired an international reputation, and was awarded the Austrian title of Hofrat. AMS contains a letter he wrote from Graz, on 17 Feb. 1908, to Alma Mahler in New York. The historian gave a pessimistic description of the state of things in Austria, where the clergy had 'completely taken over' and 'hypocrisy' reigned everywhere.   [43]   AMM1, 81; AMM2, 64.
[44]   According to Josef Reitler ('Gustav Mahler', unpublished essay put at my disposal by the author's nephew Frederick Reitler, 66) Mahler had come into violent conflict with the Princess in Paris in 1900, on finding out that he was expected to conduct in the Trocadéro, which had appalling acoustics. The Princess never forgot the incident: he had made a 'henceforth implacable enemy'.

must be someone in the Hofoper administration who could write a few lines <u>on behalf of</u> at least. With the assurance of my highest esteem, and the aforementioned <u>urgent</u> request to return the manuscript in question. Metternich Sandor-Sandor. P.S.: Surely you must have a secretary—that would be the answer?[45]

When he saw the letter, Prince Montenuovo delivered a severe reprimand. Mahler wrote the following note in reply:

Your Excellency, Your Excellency's secretary asked me on 14 Apr. whether the manuscript of Herr Voss's composition (*Elaborat*) had been returned to him. Since the affair had already been taken out of my hands and put into those of Herr Lefler some time previously, I considered that no further action was required from me, and no longer concerned myself with the matter, since both sides had decided that the Hofoper could not use the poem in its present form! At the request of your Excellency's secretary, the manuscript was returned to Herr Voss 'with thanks' and the affair therefore seemed to me closed as far as the Opera was concerned. I do not know what else Your Excellency would have expected me to do, and what I have done to merit Your Excellency's reprimand. I surely don't need to point out that I am far too busy to be expected to compose formulas (*Enunciationen*) for Herr Voss which would have informed him in a consoling manner about what was for him the depressing outcome of our perusal . . .[46]

The most surprising aspect of the affair is not that Mahler felt no need to be diplomatic about turning down an inferior ballet scenario but that he allowed himself to reply in this tone to one of the highest personages in the Austrian Empire.[47]

Though he may not have worried unduly about what the Princess Metternich-Sandor or any other member of the nobility thought of him, he did have one real friend among its ranks, and that was Countess Misa Wydenbruck-Esterhazy, daughter of Count Franz Esterhazy and therefore of Hungarian origin. Like her close friend the Princess, Misa Wydenbruck spent most of her time working for charity (people called her 'General Pauline's aide-de-camp'). The activities to which she gave her active support included the Viennese Public Welfare (*Wohlfahrtspflege*), which she and the Princess Metternich had founded with the Princess Rosa Croy and Countess Anastasia Kielmannsegg; a large dressmaking workshop; the Vienna Polyclinic; and an artists' Welfare Society (*Kunstfürsorge*). A refined, distinguished little woman of 50, Misa took an enthusiastic interest in the arts in general but above all in music. She had studied singing with Mathilde Marchesi and displayed real gifts as an amateur actress. She also frequented writers such as Arthur Schnitzler, and musicians, including Mahler and his brother-in-law Alfred Rosé, for whom she sponsored a subscription to enable him to buy an old violin. Her life's ruling passion was to do all she could to help her artist friends. She regularly organized charity balls, concerts, and galas, calling on the talents of singers like Marie Gutheil-Schoder and Erik Schmedes.

[45] HOA, Z.VI. 51/1902.   [46] Ibid.
[47] That Mahler was also capable of the greatest tact in matters of this sort is shown by the letter he wrote in May 1898 to the Berlin librettist Julius Wolff, explaining in detail the weaknesses of his text *Renata*. See above, Chap. 1.

Misa married Count August Wilhelm Wydenbruck in 1883 and bore him three children. The eldest, Clementine, or Tinette, was a favourite of Mahler's, who sent her a photograph of himself in 1900, when Tinette was 16: the inscription was in verse and included a musical quotation from the first act of *Die Walküre*.[48] Another gift to the Countess was an early text of the finale of the Second Symphony, dated 13 June 1894.[49] Misa Wydenbruck lived very near Mahler at No. 1A Rennweg, which meant that most of the twenty-seven letters and postcards she received from him between 1897 and 1909 were delivered by hand.[50] They were usually accompanied by tickets or invitations to dress rehearsals of new opera productions or to concerts Mahler was conducting. When rehearsals were closed to the public, Mahler would sometimes invite the Countess to watch discreetly from the rear of a box and to drop into his office beforehand. Some of Mahler's letters gave or withheld permission for various singers to perform at one of her benefits. All betray much warmer and more spontaneous feelings than he usually showed for members of the aristocracy. A page handwritten by Alma and inserted in one of the original versions of her first *Erinnerungen* tells how the unfortunate Countess once had to play the ungrateful role of chaperone when the Baron Albert von Rothschild one day decided to take a series of 'artistic' photographs of Alma. Although she hated posing, Alma accepted on condition that she be accompanied. The Countess had to be a 'slave', holding out a shawl, then a boa.[51]

Fifteen years after Mahler's death, the Countess Wydenbruck paid him vibrant homage:

Both as an artist and as a man he was one of the few truly great. I consider myself fortunate to have been able to come closer to him than most, to know and plumb the depths of his nature, unfortunately inaccessible to many and so utterly misunderstood during his lifetime. It is only today, many years after his death, that the clouds which

[48] BGM, Paris. The poem is written in Roman script on the back of a Hamburg photo of Mahler. It is preceded by a 6 bar-musical quotation in A major from Act I of *Die Walküre* (p. 41 of the Schott miniature score, immediately after Siegmund's line 'Die Sonne lacht mir nun neu'). Above it Mahler quotes Wagner's annotation: *Anmuthig bewegt* (with graceful movement), which is one of the 'themes' of the poem.

Wie diese Klänge selig aufwärts schweben,	Just as these sounds do joyously upsoar,
Von uns'ren hehren Sänger licht gestaltet:	sung in our lofty singer's accents pure,
so holder Melodie sei voll dein Leben,	so be thy life with noble melody replete,
von <u>Anmuth</u> nur <u>bewegt</u>, die dir so reich	<u>moved</u> only by that <u>grace</u> of which thou'lt have so
gegeben,	much,
Wenn einst die Knospe sich zur Ros' entfaltet!	when once the bud unfolds itself to rose.

[49] Ibid.   [50] Ibid.

[51] AMS. Albert Salomon Anselm Freiherr von Rothschild (1844–1911), grandson of the founder of the Rothschild dynasty, had studied in Bonn and become head of the Viennese bank in 1872. When his wife died in 1892, he went into part retirement, and devoted much of his time to his art collections, to mountain-climbing, chess, and photography, and sponsorship on which he wrote many articles. The session probably took place in the Baron von Rothschild's palace on Prinz Eugen Strasse. Albert's brother, Nathaniel (1836–1905) was even more famous as an art collector but, since he died as early as 1905, he was probably not the subject of Alma's anecdote. According to her, Albert von Rothschild tried to get the unfortunate Countess out of the way so that he could show Alma—not his stamp collection, but his house and paintings, with the ill-disguised object of seducing her (AMS; see above, Vol. ii, Chap. 16, an account of Mahler's visit to Albert von Rothschild in the hope of obtaining money for the Vereinigung).

incomprehension, and also perhaps ill-will and envy, created around him are beginning to lift. Thus the image of the artist and the man is now gradually appearing in all its grandeur and purity.[52]

Despite Mahler's affection for Misa Wydenbruck, he was never a regular visitor to her salon. On the other hand, he did pay fairly frequent visits to another household, at least in 1904 and 1905; that of Erica Tietze's parents, Hugo and Ida Conrat. One evening he had accepted their invitation, but warned them that he might be late for dinner. The meal was ready, but the guests continued waiting until the telephone rang. It was Mahler, asking them to sit down without him: he was obliged to attend part of the evening's performance at the Opera to pass judgement on a new soprano.[53] The party proceeded into the dining room, having prudently wrapped themselves in shawls because of the icy weather and the poorly heated room. Halfway through the meal, the phone rang again. This time it was Hassinger, Mahler's factotum, wanting to know the Conrats' address—his chief had forgotten the house number. Finally Mahler burst in, exhausted from a day's work which included two rehearsals as well as the first act of *Die Königin von Saba*. As Erica recorded later,

Suddenly, something occurred to him and he began to talk—about a piece of music, he compared it to something in painting. He spoke with great earnestness, moving his hands expressively—nothing theatrical, simply his intense personality—and when he had finished, he calmly turned to his chicken cutlet and asked about the vegetables. As far as he was concerned he hadn't said anything out of the ordinary: it was all self-evident. The guests had been holding their breath, bending forward in their chairs and not taking their eyes off him. . . . When he had finished, they leaned back, sighed, and relaxed smiling . . . And the mistress of the house: did she cast a look of triumph around her, as though to say, 'What more can I offer you? Isn't this better than oysters and Chablis, the foie gras with truffles, or even the enormous bunches of grapes tied in blue ribbon from the Hotel Sacher? What's more, he never goes out anywhere else!' No! Nothing of the kind! The mistress of the house was paralysed with worry, worry that he might upset his cranberries on to the tablecloth; worry that somebody might ask him a question that would annoy him; fear that he might say rude things about somebody, worry about what would be said next, and worry about the silence which might ensue.[54]

Unfortunately, a few pages are missing from Erica's recollections, and some passages have been carefully deleted, yet the major part has survived. In her story of the dinner at her parents' home, she describes Alma as drinking 'large quantities of strong wine' (*Alma trinkt viele, schwere Weine*) so that it could be difficult to curb her verbal flights of fancy. Only Mahler could manage her: 'He

---

[52]   Quoted in the Countess's obituary in the *Neues Wiener Journal*, published a few days after her death on 24 Aug. 1926.

[53]   Frieda Felser, who sang Goldmark's *Die Königin von Saba* on 9 Dec. 1904. She was given a contract but stayed only a year at the Opera.

[54]   A typewritten copy of Erika Conrat Tietze's 'Erinnerungen an Gustav Mahler' survives in AMS. See also Vol. ii, Chap. 16.

made up for all the gaffes his wife committed (*was die Frau verbrochen*) with his wit and amiability, but it was an effort and he became even more tired. So he sat down by the window and read an article attacking the Michelangelo Crucifix Henry Thode had discovered':[55] 'Because I'm always glad when that man gets a box on the ears!' The hostess sat down next to Alma on the sofa, but she too found it hard to quieten her down. The others were silent in their big armchairs. A little while later, around eleven thirty, Mahler asked for a glass of his favourite beer, Spaten, and Erica sent a housemaid out to a bar in the Schwarzenbergstrasse.

Alma's *Erinnerungen* contain, surprisingly enough, two completely different, not to say contradictory, versions of the same earlier social occasion, this time in the Auenbruggergasse: a supper in the spring of 1904 given in honour of the Hamburg poet Richard Dehmel.[56] Richard Dehmel enjoyed considerable celebrity as poet and dramatist. A number of composers, particularly Schoenberg, had set his poems to music: Schoenberg even named his early String Sextet after one of them, *Verklärte Nacht*. 'I don't care for him myself,' Mahler remarked when he told Alma that Dehmel was in Vienna, 'but I know you're interested in him. Do you want me to bring him to see you?' As a writer, Dehmel was subject to a wide variety of influences ranging from Heine to Nietzsche by way of Ibsen, the French symbolists and even the *poètes maudits*. His inability to choose among these influences is often cited as his major shortcoming, but because of the ardour and verbal violence of his work he is usually ranked as one of the precursors of expressionism. Shortly after his second marriage he published in 1902 a verse 'romance' about his life with Frau Isi, in the form of three cycles of 36 ballads each of 36 lines: *Zwei Menschen—Roman in Romanzen*. Alma mentions having read this work aloud to Mahler. Finally Mahler and Alma decided to invite the Dehmels to lunch with the Molls, Klimt, Roller,

---

[55] Henry Thode (1857–1920), poet, translator, and professor of art history at Heidelberg, married Daniela von Bülow, one of Cosima Wagner's daughters, in 1886. Author of a two-volume work on Michelangelo (1902) and monographs on Wagner, Liszt, and Boecklin, as well as Giotto and Tintoretto, Thode undoubtedly angered Mahler with his German nationalist views. His discovery of a new crucifix, a work he attributed to the young Michelangelo, in the choir of the church of Santo Spirito, in Florence, had just been announced with fanfares in an article he wrote for the *Frankfurter Zeitung* of 1 May 1904. It was taken up and quoted in Germany's leading art journals. The real Michelangelo wooden crucifix seems to have been discovered as recently as 1962, in the Santo Spirito Convent in Florence (cf. Margrit Lisner, *Il Crocifisso di Santo Spirito: Atti del Convegno di Studi Michelangioleschi*, (Prestel, Munich, 1964).

[56] AMM1, 152; AMM2, 148. Richard Dehmel (1893–1920) was the son of a Silesian forester, of Slav and German origins. He attended the Sophie Gymnasium in Berlin, completed his secondary studies in Danzig, and finally obtained his degree from the University of Leipzig with a thesis on insurance. From 1891 on, he devoted his life wholly to literature and published his first collection of verse. He met Strindberg, with whom he founded the literary group 'The Black Piglet' and, in 1892 married a rabbi's daughter named Paula Oppenheimer, a writer in her own right. Dehmel's early poetry was inspired by the erotic excitement of this first marriage, which lasted eight years. He latter married another Jewish woman, Ida Auerbach—Frau Isi—a childhood friend of the poet Stefan George. After moving restlessly from country to country all over Europe, Dehmel settled down at Blankenese, near Hamburg, close to his best friend, the poet Detlev von Liliencron. An ardent patriot, he volunteered for the First World War and won the Iron Cross.

and Kolo Moser.[57] 'It was one of those days', Frau Dehmel recorded in her diary,

when all the senses were gratified so that they retain a feeling of agreeable satisfaction even in our recollection. That beautiful, fair-haired, radiant woman, making no attempt to conceal her pregnancy; the cheerful, comfortable, luxurious apartment; the good food and excellent wines. And people of whom every single one has the right and the courage to say, 'I am what I am'. Compared with the effeminate lot we had been meeting in Vienna, this was strong stuff.[58]

The mistress of the house, however, seems to have retained quite a different impression of the gathering. She notes in her memoirs that Mahler got into a bitter argument with Dehmel over Wagner. As usual, Mahler defended him warmly, while Dehmel's attitude towards him was 'cool, with a typically modern hardness'. The conversation was already taking a disagreeable turn when Dehmel exclaimed: 'And anyway, Wagner reminds me of a poppy, and I can't stand poppies!' This unexpected judgement, surrealist before its time, put a damper on the proceedings, and it was impossible to restore even a semblance of cordiality.[59] The Dehmels, however, as Frau Isi's diary suggests, seem to have forgotten the heated exchange.

What Alma does not record is that Mahler and Dehmel had met some years earlier, probably in Hamburg, as the following letter bears witness. Written in 1897 or 1898, it acknowledges a book of poems that Dehmel had sent to Mahler:

Dear Herr Dehmel, Thank you with all my heart for the confidence you place in me, a confidence which both honours and pleases me. I certainly feel an elective affinity for your verses and I cannot conceive any higher task than making them live by adding the poetry of my music. But don't you know that for the moment I'm the director of a theatre? It's an unhappy chapter of my life, but I really must see it through. It will certainly take two years before I can concentrate on a work of my own. Things have got to such a pitch that simply thinking about a task of this sort becomes a painful thorn in my side. So I must refuse your offer even before I have read your book, but be assured that this is one of the sacrifices imposed by the privilege of being 'director': a privilege envied by most of my colleagues but accursed as far as I am concerned. Once more, thank you for your friendly offer. Perhaps one day it will become the egg from which a sturdy chicken (Damn! But I must complete the metaphor I've so unfortunately begun) emerges! If, happy man, your travels should bring your to these parts, remember please that your visit would give me the same pleasure as that of a happy wanderer to a poor prisoner . . .[60]

---

[57] The supper was held after a 'correct but bad' performance of the Berlioz *Requiem* conducted by Ernst von Schuch at the Nicolai Konzert on 13 Mar. 1904. The Staats- und Universitätsbibliothek in Hamburg owns a note from Mahler to Dehmel inviting him 'to the Auenbruggergasse after the concert'. Dehmel had been in Vienna at least since 6 Mar., when there was an evening at the Ansorge-Verein of Lieder by several composers, all based on his poems. Mahler and Alma were in the audience. Parts of Frau Dehmel's diary are quoted in Alma's *Erinnerungen*.   [58] AMM1, 116; AMM2, 118.

[59] AMM1, 103; AMM2, 106. As we shall see later, Dehmel took particular exception to the Wagner who had been the instigator of the 'nationalist' theses then in fashion among German literary and art critics.

[60] Letter to Richard Dehmel, 1897 or 1898. Staats- und Universitätsbibliothek, Hamburg.

Apparently Mahler cared far more for the Dehmels than Alma claims for, a year later, in Hamburg, he invited them to attend the rehearsals of the Fifth Symphony, talking to them openly and cordially, as the record of their meetings in Frau Isi's diary shows.[61] Dehmel was, however, neither Mahler's favourite poet nor an intimate friend, unlike the playwright Gerhart Hauptmann, with whom the bonds of friendship grew progressively closer. In October 1904 Hauptmann spoke of Mahler to Isi Dehmel with the same warmth he had expressed earlier to Burckhard, and with a feeling she described as 'close to being under a spell'. Hauptmann called Mahler 'the very embodiment of genius', admitting however that he knew nothing about his music. His visit to a performance of Mahler's production of *Tristan und Isolde*, with Roller's sets, was 'one of the most intoxicating artistic joys of my whole life'. Whenever he heard that Mahler was scheduled to conduct one of his own symphonies somewhere, Hauptmann had to restrain himself from jumping aboard the next train that would take him there.

Yet Alma claimed that Mahler could not quite return Hauptmann's enthusiasm. At times, she said, he found the 'slowness' of his thinking and his slightly impeded speech irritating.[62] He nonetheless admired the poet as much as the man, whose kindness he found moving. This is shown by two hitherto unpublished letters. The first was probably written in 1904 in reply to Hauptmann's letter of 28 February:[63]

Caught up in a whirl of distracting and preoccupying activity which does not allow me fully to appreciate how deeply moved I was to read your words, let alone find an adequate reply, I would like to send you today this short note to thank you for your kind letter, a godsend which has accompanied me on my rounds for the past few days. What we want to say to each other—so as not to forget it in the course of our respective lives which unfortunately keep us apart for long periods—is that we belong to each other and that we intend and want the bond, so quickly forged between us almost before we knew it, to live on. If you only knew how lonely my life here is, with absolutely no one I can really talk to, you would understand how precious a habit it became in those few days to be together with you and talk and think over everything that has been stored up in me over the years. And that was only a beginning, simply a first attempt to understand each other's ways of feeling and speaking, like two people who after a long sea voyage meet on a distant shore and discover with inexpressible joy that they are from the same country. These last few days I felt every afternoon as if I was going to fetch you at the Hotel Sacher for a stroll through the streets and squares, savouring the pleasure of the moment without a thought for the morrow. Goodbye for now and thank you once more for your letter. When we meet again, we will begin where we left off. That too will show us that we are friends. My wife, who like myself is so fond of you and with whom I speak of you daily, joins me in sending our heartfelt greetings to you and your friend. Your devoted Gustav Mahler.

---

[61]   See below.

[62]   In her memoirs, Alma explains that Hauptmann had a slight stutter, especially when he had been drinking (AML 177).   [63]   See above, Vol. ii, Chap. 16.

Hauptmann later wrote, in an autobiographical sketch:

He was prodigal in friendship towards me, and this was one of the greatest favours thus far offered me by life. Those who never saw Gustav Mahler cannot know what greatness and inspired energy the human personality can attain. There was nothing one could do about it: everything seemed small beside him. Neither my own work, exhausting and exciting, nor my illness could prevent me from remaining with him, after the theatre, until dawn, walking with him deep in conversation all night through the streets and squares of Vienna.[64]

The affinity between the two men even extended to politics, as shown by this autobiographical note by Hauptmann, referring to the same period: 'The soul immersed in music, in that ocean of sound that is *Tristan.* . . . People in festive mood (*festliche Menschen*), men and women exalted in festiveness, existence (*Dasein*) raised to the grandeur of art: a divine socialism of art.'[65]

As artists, Mahler and Hauptmann were both animated by a sense of social solidarity with people of humble status; Hauptmann's literary work, like Mahler's music, has been accused of banality and sentimentality. The similarities between their respective roles in the history of their art have been stressed:

Both of them, composer and poet, were nature fanatics who aspired to transcendence. They regarded art as sacred and were situated, within the neo-romanticism and mysticism of their era, at the turning point from old to new, echoing the past and heralding the future. They were at once repositories of a heritage and innovators, and this often lends their work a feeling of rupture. . . . They shared a taste for the texts and melodies of popular song. . . . In *Hanneles Himmelfahrt* and the fifth movement of the Third Symphony, they even used versions of the very same folk song.[66]

These similarities make it easy to understand how fruitful the contact between the two men could be. It was probably in February 1905 that Mahler wrote Hauptmann a second letter, as affectionate as the first. At Hauptmann's request, Mahler addressed him in the familiar '*du*' form:

My dear Gerhart, Today I must simply note that I am deeply ashamed that I haven't replied either to your letter or your kind gift. I am well aware of the main reason for this silence: so far we have spoken so little to each other that I still can't manage to find the appropriate, natural tone; hence my inner reluctance to do as my conscience keeps telling me. I don't want to reply by an ordinary letter to such a sign of affection. And you certainly know yourself that a letter once postponed keeps on being postponed. So

[64] From Gerhard Hauptmann, *Tagebücher 1897 bis 1905*, edited by Martin Machatzke (Propyläen, Vienna, 1987), 728. The editor explains that Hauptmann suffered from a fever which kept his temperature between 38 and 39 degrees C, during the whole of his Viennese visit of Feb. 1904.

[65] Ibid. The term 'socialism', surprising in this context, undoubtedly reflects the discussions Hauptmann had with Mahler on the subject. I have referred above, Vol. ii, Chap. 12 to the political commitment and social criticism in Hauptmann's plays.

[66] This was *Es sungen drei Engel*, taken by Mahler from *Des Knaben Wunderhorn*, whereas Hauptmann found it in a collection of *Silesian Folk Songs* brought out by Hoffmann von Fallersleben. Cf. Martin Machatzke in Gerhard Hauptmann, *Tagebücher*, 730.

permit me today to greet you, to thank you, and to assuage my guilt. I was on the point one day of pouring my heart out to you, full as it was of your *Florian Geyer*, which I had then just discovered. Of all your works, there is none I value more or even as much. This way of reproducing life through art seems new to me and heralds perhaps a higher stage for drama in the future. It seems to me that, like *Faust in his chrysalid state*,[67] you have already reached a higher embodiment—and yet are still making fresh growth. My wife and I talk about you both so often, we feel so intensely that we are akin! Ought we not to be able to journey together again on life's path? My relationship to you—I feel more and more—is based on feelings—just like a teenage friendship. The mind takes time to catch up and still needs some life together. That is why an exchange of letters is so difficult! Don't you find it's the same for you? You certainly don't hold my negligence against me (in any case, in addition to this important reason there are one or two others I could mention. I have been a poor correspondent for years). Once more we send your wife and yourself all our most cordial greetings. Yours, Gustav Mahler.[68]

Though these letters are convincing evidence of the admiration and affection Mahler bore Hauptmann, the feelings he harboured for Gerhart's wife Margarethe Marschalk were much more ambiguous. In Hamburg, in March 1905, Ida Dehmel told him about a poem her husband had written into Grete Marschak's diary when she was 15. The way in which he had described her as a 'mermaid or forest fairy' had strongly influenced her development. The anecdote provoked in Mahler something close to rage and his comment was:

Every person is the product of many generations. One's character is fixed before one comes into the world. Absolutely no one can claim self-determination because everyone is subject at all times to ineluctable constraints. Grete Hauptmann would do well to get rid of whatever is 'elfin' (*Nixenhaft*) about her, in other words, her cold-hearted egoism. Poor Gerhart, I'm sorry for him, because he is far too good for her. If she were my wife, she would definitely have to pipe down.[69]

Such harsh words were hardly calculated to please Frau Dehmel, who obviously didn't share Mahler's opinion of Grete Hauptmann, but they clearly reflect Mahler's view of the relationship between a married couple, particularly when the husband is a creative artist. He outlined his stand very lucidly in his famous letter to Alma of December 1901, knowing full well that Alma would never share it.[70]

Towards the end of March 1905, Hauptmann went to Vienna where he attended, on the 25th, a performance of *Fidelio* conducted by Mahler. It made a strong impression on him and he noted in his diary:

Astonishing to see how he [Mahler] puts us in the presence of the original idea (*ursprüngliches Gebilde*). Sound blocks articulated (articulation of genius, producing a

[67] An allusion to a line (verse 11982) from the final scene of Goethe's *Faust* which is spoken by the 'Choir of Blessed Children': 'We receive him with joy in the chrysalid state' (*im Puppenstand*).

[68] Undated letter to Hauptmann, Staatsbibliothek, Berlin, Preussischer Kulturbesitz: the same collection also contains a picture postcard of the Vienna Karlskirche dated 26 Jan. 1906, addressed to the Hauptmanns by Mahler and Alma. 'I am ashamed not to have the courage to write you a letter,' Mahler writes. 'Don't hold it against me!'   [69] AMM1, 122; AMM2, 122.

[70] See above, Vol. ii, Chap. 12.

sound rhythm of unparalleled magnificence!) with crystalline sharpness and logic. (The crystal of music in movement.) The passage leading from darkness into light in the Overture to the last act. The impression powerfully surpassed all those that this Overture had previously given me. Something miraculous, yet obedient to laws, provoking astonishment, as when the eye leaves the grand edifice of the world and turns, full of presentiment, to the starry sky. Master of sound. Master. The compelling power and beauty of form. Nothing blurred or diluted. The immaterial stands almost materially before the soul. It stands there upright from the first note onwards, until the last note has died away. Nowadays no-one can do this like Mahler. Mahler and Pfitzner afterwards, at supper.[71] Spoken passages in music drama. When the music starts, said Mahler, one is suddenly somewhere on Mars etc, far from earth. Oscillations. Radiation of music into the infinite.[72]

Three days later, Hauptmann noted the emotions he had experienced again, listening to Mahler conduct at the Opera:

The last great artistic impression in Vienna was *Rheingold*, which Mahler conducted. Theatre of demons (*Dämonentheater*). The prelude was superhuman emotionally. River! Transparent river! Flowing ceaselessly through millenia, elemental. Sounds suggesting a silent process. Something that never stops, never in all eternity!—that forever flows! flows! flows! For long moments all sense of time disappears from the small theatre and its occupants. All was dissolved, all became a transparent flowing current. The crystal soul of this current. Propelled from within itself, turning upon itself, travelling further, noisily filled with forces now calmer, now stronger, passing like worlds in rotation. Resonance in itself, moving, rushing, rushing, sinking, rising, and flowing, always flowing, flowing! Minutes in which one perceives the hidden movement of all things. 'The ineffable is inaudible'—here, this law seems to be broken.— It is so grand, so new, not only musically, it opens up such perspectives, such possibilities—it is so indisputably a revelation that it permits limitless hopes for the future of man. I closed my eyes and saw only the river. I was not aware that the curtains were opening. All at once I heard other voices reverberating, sweet and overwhelming like an annunciation. I was astonished, I trembled, I waited . . . But the great things in Wagner, even this Prelude, are greater than his admirers can imagine.—Art means the divine life of Nature![73]

After that evening, Hauptmann returned home to Agnetendorf (today Jagniatkov), Silesia, in the Riesengebirge, south of Hirschberg. A few weeks later, at Easter, Mahler and Alma considered paying him a visit there, but changed their plans, probably to go to Abazzia again. Documentary proofs of their visit to the Adriatic are rare but conclusive: in a card sent to Oskar Fried[74] at the end of April, Mahler writes: 'since I was away from Vienna for the Easter holidays'. Furthermore, Rudolf L. Ernst, a nephew of the Hungarian journalist Siegmund Singer who later founded a Mahler Society in Sydney,

---

Australia, claimed to have seen Mahler at Abazzia in 1905.[75] The youthful Ernst was there with the Singers and their daughter Magrit, and made his debut as a reporter by photographing Mahler and Alma with his new camera.[76]

Not long after Easter, Hauptmann again wrote to Mahler, thanking him for the 'strong impressions made on me by your human nature and your friendship, unique in the world'.[77] In June, the poet returned to Vienna for a further series of performances of his play *Rose Bernd*,[78] one of which Mahler made a point of attending. An awkward scene took place in Mahler's box when Roller burst in after the first act. Taking no heed of Mahler's frantic gesturing and winking, he began to castigate the play as boring and inept. Finally Mahler got him out of the box, hoping that Hauptmann hadn't overheard.[79]

Alma, who felt 'instinctively' that Hauptmann was good for Mahler, often invited him to the Auenbruggergasse. He was then writing his novel *Emanuel Quint*,[80] and one evening at the Hotel Erzherzog Karl the two friends discussed the figure of Christ. One would like to know the gist of what they said, but Alma unfortunately neglects to tell us. She simply records that Mahler held forth for a long time in 'wonderful exaltation' while the poet 'listened quietly', and writes: 'I was quite sure that the two demons of darkness and of light were bound to harmonize and produce a beautiful chord.' When Mahler left the table, Hauptmann turned to Alma and said, 'Your husband expresses clearly everything I feel dimly. No other person has given me as much as he did!'

For Mahler the composer, the new year had started with a major event: an evening of his Lieder, many of them in world première, organized in Vienna by the Vereinigung der Schaffender Tonkünstler. After the triumph of the Third Symphony a month earlier, Mahler had every reason to hope that his more accessible compositions for voice would meet with equal success. During the rehearsals, the last of which, on 28 January 1905, was open to the public,[81] Mahler attended the final rehearsal of the Vereinigung's second orchestral concert

[75] Easter Sunday, 1905, fell on 23 Apr. That year, as every year, the Opera was closed for most of Holy Week, from Tue. 18 Apr. to Fri. 22 Apr. inclusive. Mahler could have left Vienna on the 15th or 16th, when the theatre closed. He had to be back by 25 Apr. at the latest, because he was conducting a performance of *Die Rose vom Liebesgarten* that evening in Vienna.

[76] Rudolf Ernst died not long after he had sent me a letter containing these recollections. In 1920 he claims to have given the negatives to a Viennese publisher who wanted to commemorate the tenth anniversary of Mahler's death with a book, but he was never able to recover them.

[77] A typescript of Hauptmann's letter, dated 14 Apr., is included in AMS, together with that of a subsequent letter of 16 May. Alma claims that Hauptmann went with Pfitzner to a performance of *Das Rheingold* conducted by Mahler on 26 Apr. (see also AML 38) but no doubt this was the performance of 26 Mar., described by Hauptmann in his diary on the 28th.

[78] Alma claims that the performances were held in the Burgtheater, but in fact they were given on 13 and 14 June at the Deutsches Volkstheater, by a troupe from Berlin. The Viennese censor had banned Hauptmann's play from the Burgtheater (see below, Chap. 5).

[79] Alma had already left for Maiernigg, where Mahler no doubt told her about the incident when he joined her there a day or two later.

[80] The full title of this work, finished in 1910 and published the following year, was *Der Narr in Christo Emanuel Quint* (The Fool in Christo Emanuel Quint) (Fischer, Berlin, 1910).

[81] On 24 Jan. the papers announced that since the concert on the 29th was sold out, tickets would be sold for the rehearsal the evening before.

(scheduled for the 27th, the evening before Mahler's Lieder concert) which featured three new works: Zemlinsky's symphonic poem *Die Seejungfrau* ('The Mermaid', based on Hans Christian Andersen), five Lieder with orchestra by Oscar Posa, and Schoenberg's symphonic poem *Pelleas und Melisande*, Op. 5.[82] Again, details of what Mahler thought about the latter work are lacking.[83] According to Alma's diary, it seems that he was less than enthusiastic about Zemlinsky's *Seejungfrau*. It is an irony of fate that, at this very same time, Zemlinsky should have been totally won over by the Third Symphony, which he had heard Mahler conduct at the end of December. Judging by the first of the letters he sent Alma on the subject, he assumed that Mahler expected an immediate 'critical analysis', but explained that this was impossible for him because the musician, like the layman, needed time for calm reflection which would allow him to 'subject the details of the work to the criteria of his own taste'. Nevertheless 'you must have realized that the symphony I have just heard compels my admiration'.[84]

In a further letter, addressed to Alma, Zemlinsky describes his impressions in detail:

I am writing to you rather than to the Director because what I feel bound to express today is terribly difficult for me to say or write directly to the person concerned. It relates to the impression the Third Symphony made on me yesterday at the public rehearsal. I am really happy to be able to tell you that the work completely opened my eyes to the magnificent originality and colossal stature of Mahler's art. I continually had the impression of hearing music which plumbed the most profound mysteries of nature. I can honestly say that I have never heard such power or depth, as for instance in the beginning of the first movement or in the last two movements, except by the greatest masters, and so precise and expressive a structure (*Gliederung*), and development only with Beethoven and Brahms (if I leave out Beethoven's predecessors). Yet the second movement is all grace and charm itself, turned into music in its ultimate, most perfect possible form. The tiniest note added or taken away would damage this perfection. I am no music critic, and for that reason (or despite it) I find it difficult to describe my impression. But one thing I can say which will tell you the impression it made on me. What I long suspected has now become a certainty for me, and, as I said yesterday to my friends: 'That's a Composer with a capital C!' and we were terribly excited to have been present at an event in the future history of music. Perhaps what I wanted to say to you is badly expressed, but you will know and understand that I don't say such things lightly. If you think my letter will interest your husband, then please let him read it, if not, then please pass on to him my greatest respect. A final request: could I borrow a score of the symphony for a few days?[85]

Alma's remarks about Schoenberg after the concert on 25 January are more complimentary than those about Zemlinsky: 'He's an extremely interesting

---

[82] At this time, Schoenberg was writing his First Quartet, which he was to finish the following summer at Gmunden on the Traunsee.

[83] In an undated letter, probably written at this time, Alma invites Schoenberg to come and spend an evening at the Auenbruggergasse and to bring with him the score of *Pelleas* (LOC, Washington, DC).

[84] UPL.   [85] Ibid.

character,' she writes, 'but very muddled (*verworren*)!' That says everything, and nothing! According to Alma, who went alone to the actual concert as Mahler was conducting *Rheingold* that evening but had attended the final rehearsal, many among the audience booed during the performance and others left at the end, slamming the doors. 'But I found his talent convincing', she concludes.[86] If *Pelleas und Melisande* struck Mahler as 'confusing' it is probably because the performance, with the composer conducting the mediocre Konzertverein orchestra, left much to be desired. According to Egon Wellesz there would have been terrible scenes with the orchestral musicians if Mahler had not appeared during the rehearsal.

He was standing in the middle of the hall with his coat still on and his fur cap on his head. The score was in his hands and he called out all of a sudden: 'Where's the second English horn? I can't hear it!' It is hardly surprising that Schoenberg failed to notice the absence of the instrument: the original version of the score, now in my possession, is so complicated and over-orchestrated that even at the performance it was difficult to hear the principal parts, and Mahler had trouble following the polyphonic fabric. One can understand why the work did not impress the public or the press. Schoenberg later revised this youthful work.[87]

It is unfortunate that Mahler did not conduct the work himself, for according to the 25 January *Fremden-Blatt* he had considered doing so as a striking tribute to his young colleague. The unsigned article claimed that he finally decided not to conduct this 'very daring symphonic poem' because 'his presence would have commanded respect, and what the Vereinigung really needed so that it could prosper and get itself talked about was to be hooted down for a resounding flop!' It seems unlikely that Mahler ever uttered any such words, especially since he had accepted the post of honorary president of the new Society and he experienced only too often the bitter taste left by a 'resounding flop'. However, Schoenberg probably did ask him to conduct in view of his own lack of experience. The true reason for Mahler's refusal was that he would never have found the time to learn and rehearse such a complex score at the height of the opera season. He was conducting not only the final rehearsals of *Das Rheingold* but also rehearsing his own Lieder, whose première was three days after *Pelleas und Melisande*. Moreover, although he certainly believed in Schoenberg and his outstanding talent, he did not always share all his ideas nor follow him along the new paths he was exploring.

Two years later, of course, he came out in wholehearted support of the First Quartet, which was even more advanced than *Pelleas*. He still felt, however, that some of Schoenberg's innovations were arbitrary and gratuitous, though this did not prevent him from standing up for him at every opportunity, for he still remembered how his own works were heaped with abuse in his early

---

[86] In the same passage in AMS Alma claims to have resumed her composition lessons with Zemlinsky.

[87] EWL 44. Wellesz explains that the original 1911 score was replaced in 1920 by a new one, with improved orchestration and altered dynamics.

attempts to become known as a composer. He would always hesitate to admit that he did not grasp what Schoenberg was doing, which would have played into the hands of the young revolutionary's many enemies. It is even possible that the Seventh Symphony, which Mahler wrote the following summer, perhaps the most 'advanced' of all his works, owed something to the stimulating influence of the Vereinigung's concerts and his many discussions with Schoenberg that year.

As far as Zemlinsky's contribution to the programme was concerned, Alma's diary simply records that she—and we can surmise Mahler as well—found Zemlinsky's score 'inadequate, suitable for a ballet at best, despite the many small but ravishing melodic ideas it contains'.[88] Thus Mahler's reaction was, at least according to Alma, largely negative, as it had been in 1900 about *Es war einmal* when he conducted the first performance at the Hofoper.[89] She reports that he found Zemlinsky's music lacking in originality or character—'chinless' like his face—and that his imagination was 'paralysed' by his technical knowledge. Hirschfeld's verdict was strangely similar in the *Wiener Abendpost*: he praised Zemlinsky's orchestration and compositional technique, but deplored his 'weak imagination'. But the other critics disagreed. Korngold in particular praised his musical style as 'less modern' and less radical than Schoenberg's. Karpath called his new work 'very pleasant' and, like Kauders, Graf, and Wallaschek, proceeded to lavish on Zemlinsky the praise withheld from Schoenberg. They all, in fact, felt that Schoenberg had gone totally astray. Theodor Helm called *Pelleas* a 'suicidal wallowing in every sort of dissonance and cacophony', the 'demise of all intelligible melody', a 'musical (or rather, anti-musical) moaning and whining spun out over a good three quarters of an hour'. Korngold alone stood up for Schoenberg's deep conviction and absolute integrity, pointing out that the principles underlying his work hadn't wavered since *Verklärte Nacht*—to which Vienna had, at least once, extended a warm welcome. He confessed, however, that he was unable to make out the architecture of the new work, whose 'atmospheric impressionism', like Debussy's, 'dethrones melody to the advantage of harmony', producing a 'formless, nebulous, crepuscular' art.

[88] In AML, Alma concludes—somewhat prematurely as it turns out—that Zemlinsky never became a great man because of his sickly constitution inherited from childhood rickets. 'An unhealthy shoot, however precious, can never grow into a great tree' (AML 30). The score of *Die Seejungfrau* has been rediscovered among Zemlinsky's papers and the work has now been recorded twice, under Riccardo Chailly (in 1996), and James Conlon. In a recently published letter to Schoenberg dated 19 Mar. 1903, Zemlinsky wrote that Mahler had been present with Alma the previous evening, when he conducted his *Ballet-Suite* (from *Der Triumph der Zeit*) during the fifth concert of the Wiener Konzertverein. Mahler had come 'merely to hear it' and had 'applauded heartily'. See Alexander Zemlinsky, *Briefwechsel mit Arnold Schönberg, Anton Webern, Alban Berg und Franz Schreker*, ed. Horst Weber (Wissenschaftliche Buchgesellschaft, Darmstadt, 1995), 39.

[89] Since *Es war einmal*, Mahler had played the role of artistic mentor to Zemlinsky, even advising him on the choice of his libretti. In an unpublished letter from Zemlinsky to a librettist named Ernst Hutschenreiter, dated by the recipient, 21 Apr. 1903, the composer mentions having obtained Mahler's opinion concerning a libretto that Hutschenreiter must have offered him. Mahler's opinion having been unfavourable, Zemlinsky abandoned the project (Gesellschaft der Musikfreunde, Vienna).

In the *Abendpost*, Hirschfeld started off by praising Schoenberg's 'solid talent' and 'eccentric but purely musical nature', he added that, once again, he had abused both to the point of 'madness'. He drove the audience 'as mad as himself' by subjecting them to an interminable composition built uniquely around a few poverty-stricken motifs'. Kauder's review would qualify for a place in an anthology of invective in musical criticism. For him, *Pelleas und Melisande* was a 'perverse creation, spurning beauty, abominating art', a 'monstrous manifestation of the most unrestrained ugliness and megalomania. Eventually the ear becomes blunted to the insults, but after twenty minutes of this excruciating game, we long for one thing only: the end.' The audience, delivered up defenceless to such merciless terrorizing, showed 'its goodwill in not exacting any reprisals'. In *Verklärte Nacht*, Kauders recalled, Schoenberg had announced his remarkable talent. If he observed the rules and constraints of musical composition, much good work could be expected from him. For in the last resort a thoughtful musician was bound to recognize that the ways of progress could not possibly lead back to chaos, the primeval state of things. Likewise the *Allgemeine Zeitung* called *Pelleas und Melisande* 'utter nothingness', an 'interminable mishmash of sound (*Klangbrei*), which was varied in every possible and impossible way by the instruments and might have kept on going until the day after tomorrow'.

Wallaschek thought Schoenberg's score amounted to one 'inexpressive dissonance' after another—'interminable, in uniformly moderate tempo, undeserving of the name of art'. Karpath, while recognizing 'Schoenberg's considerable talent', declared that either he 'had lost his mind or else he took his listeners for fools'. Of course, the young composer did have his 'partisans and admirers'. But on this occasion 'those who condemn Schoenberg have ears, and those who deify him do not'. What he had created was nothing more than a single unresolved dissonance stretched out over fifty minutes. Should Schoenberg thus persevere along the path of 'aberration', then the 'art of music would be doomed to annihilation'. How many times in history have critics thus prophesied the certain death of the art!

Even Max Vancsa, the Vereinigung's courageous defender and apologist in its early days, had some very unkind things to say about *Pelleas* in the *Neue Musikalische Presse*. After noting that Schoenberg had been unfairly handicapped by the ban 'on programmes for programme music' imposed by the Vereinigung, 'in deference to its lord and master, Mahler', so that the audience had not had the slightest chance of appreciating the enormous care Schoenberg had taken to reflect the strange moods and spirit of Maeterlinck's drama, he continued:

While Zemlinsky clearly had talent, Schoenberg has—not genius, that would be going too far—but certain dodges, a certain craziness that comes close to genius; whether it is curable or not I do not know. He is the more original of the two, and the one with more technique (*Können*). His counterpoint is breathtaking and the harmonies he discovers, the sound effects that he draws from the instruments, sometimes marvellous, sometimes convoluted, fill me with amazement.

Alas, the critic could discern 'no artistic discipline, no sense of balance, no clearly defined structure, no organic development, no moderation, no beauty. When fantasy is given free rein under such conditions, one can imagine the result: a monstrosity!' One point alone showed Vancsa's perceptiveness: the playing of the Konzertverein Orchestra under the inexperienced baton of the composer was certainly awful. Schoenberg would surely have done better, as Vancsa suggested, to allow his more expert and more experienced brother-in-law and friend Zemlinsky to conduct.

Mahler may have lent a less than attentive ear to *Pelleas und Melisande* than posterity, always on the lookout for historic encounters, might have wished, for he was in the throes of preparing a Lieder concert. The programme consisted mainly of first performances: the five *Kindertotenlieder* (finished the previous year), the four *Rückert-Lieder* of 1901, four of the *Wunderhorn-Lieder* composed between 1893 and 1898, and the last two written in 1899 and 1901. Given the intimate, non-symphonic character of these works, Mahler insisted that the concert be given in the small Musikvereinsaal. For the occasion he chose three of the Opera's best male singers, the tenor Fritz Schrödter and the baritones Anton Moser and Friedrich Weidemann,[90] a fact that deserves to be stressed because nowadays some of these Lieder are often sung by women. The small orchestra was made up of players from the Philharmonic. According to Bruno Walter, the rehearsals took place in a friendly atmosphere due to the presence of a group of young musicians from the Vereinigung, all staunch admirers of Mahler.[91]

The final rehearsal at 2.30 on the afternoon of 28 January was opened to the public because the concert itself had been sold out. The audience reacted very favourably. The next day the concert began at 7.30 but the small hall was packed long before and many had to be turned away. The audience's attentive and respectful attitude soon showed that the battle was won. Mahler had asked

---

[90] That evening Weidemann sang ten out of the sixteen songs, including the *Kindertotenlieder*. The programme, as drawn up by Mahler before the concert and preserved among Alma's papers, was as follows: Schmedes: 'Revelge' (1), 'Lied des Verfolgten im Turm' (2), 'Um Mitternacht' (3); Weidemann: Five *Kindertotenlieder* (4), 'Blicke mir nicht in die Lieder' (5), 'Ich bin der Welt' (6), 'Der Tamboursg'sell' (7), 'Der Schildwache Nachtlied' (8); Moser: 'Trost im Unglück' (9), 'Des Antonius von Padua Fischpredigt' (10), 'Lob des hohen Verstandes' (11), 'Rheinlegendchen' (12), 'Verlor'ne Müh'' (13), 'Wer hat dies Liedlein' (14). In the event, Schmedes did not take part in either of the two concerts, Schrödter sang 'Revelge' in his place and 'Ich atmet'' was added to the programme. The final arrangement was therefore: Moser, 2, 10, 9, 12; Weidemann, 8, 7; Schrödter, 1, for the *Wunderhorn-Lieder*. Next, nine *Rückert-Lieder*: Weidemann, 4; Moser, 'Ich atmet'' and 5; Weidemann, 6 and 3. According to the original plan reproduced above, Mahler had also intended to call on the services of Hermine Kittel. On 3 Feb., the order of the *Wunderhorn-Lieder* was changed: Weidemann, 8; Moser, 2, 10, 9, 12; Weidemann, 7; Gutheil-Schoder, 13, 11, 14; Schrödter, 1; followed by Weidemann, 4, 6; Moser, 5 and 'Ich atmet''; Weidemann, 3. This shows that three Lieder were added to the programme for 3 Feb.: 'Verlor'ne Müh'', 'Lob des hohen Verstandes', and 'Dort oben am Berg' (that is, 'Wer hat dies Liedlein erdacht'). They were sung by Marie Gutheil-Schoder.

[91] BWM 49.

that there should be no applause between songs, so the tension mounted steadily. Partisan or non-partisan, all contemporary accounts agreed that the evening was 'the only real triumph of the whole series of Vereinigung concerts'. 'Mahler's Lieder touched everyone,' Paul Stefan wrote 'We exulted with him, were sad with him, childlike, cheerful or pensive. One revelled in his skill and mastery of the small form, the beautiful realization of beautiful poems.'[92]

Mahler entrusted the most expressive of the Lieder to Friedrich Weidemann, and who had become his favourite interpreter and Richard Specht drew attention to the baritone's astonishing ability to modify his voice to characterize a role or a Lied. His high notes were a little insipid and cautious, but for 'inwardness', 'restrained grief' and 'grandeur in pain' he was unequalled, even by the famous Dutch baritone Johannes Messchaert.[93]

The following morning, one of the younger members of the Schoenberg circle, no less a person than Anton von Webern, confided to his diary:

Mahler's *Wunderhorn-Lieder* are marvels. The melody is popular and everything to be divined between the lines of the poems is brilliantly understood and expressed in a perfectly convincing manner. The Lieder based on the poems by Rückert were less satisfactory. Some of them seemed sentimental to me. I cannot explain this occasional sentimentality which, coming from so strong and authentic a personality, seems incomprehensible, unless these compositions represent an outpouring, on the spur of the moment, of intense feeling which in its exuberance is tinged now and then with sentimentality . . . What I admire about all these Lieder is their beauty of vocal expression, which is sometimes of overwhelming inwardness (*Innerlichkeit*). I'm thinking in particular of the fourth of the *Kindertotenlieder*, or of the 'Ich atmet' einen linden Duft'. His orchestral sonority is true throughout.[94]

For the young composing genius that Anton von Webern already was, this was a memorable day, particularly as it ended with a whole evening spent in Mahler's company. Webern was born in Vienna on 3 December 1883, to a Carinthian father of the minor nobility who was first a soldier and later a civil servant, and a mother of humbler origins. His parents having moved to Carinthia, he studied piano, cello, counterpoint, and composition in Klagenfurt with a local composer called Edwin Komauer. In 1901, when he was 18 and still living in the family house near Klagenfurt, he had discovered Mahler's music and made a careful study of the score of the Second Symphony, which he at first thought 'bizarre and contrived'. He was nevertheless profoundly indignant at the ill-will shown by the Viennese press after the first performance of the Fourth: 'The assumption that Mahler is writing parodies and is poking fun with his symphonies, or similar nonsensical statements, seems to me

[92] PSG 55.

[93] Richard Specht, 'Friedrich Weidemann', *Die Schaubühne*, Berlin, 3: 24 (13 June 1907), 596 ff. For Johannes Messchaert see below, Chap. 8.

[94] Friedrich Wildgans, 'Gustav Mahler und Anton von Webern', *Österreichische Musikzeitschrift, Mahler Heft*, 15 (1960): 6, 22 ff.

completely ridiculous. For me, he is a great and highly gifted conductor and a serious, deeply introspective composer whom I regard with veneration. I am filled with a burning desire to get to know his further works!'[95]

In 1902, Webern's father was appointed to the Ministry of Agriculture in Vienna. His son moved with him to the capital, and went regularly to the Opera and to concerts. The previous summer he had gone with quickened pulse to Bayreuth, like most young 'modern' musicians of the time with any curiosity. It was then that he had decided to continue his musical studies, and enrolled at the Musicological Institute of the University where he attended lectures by Guido Adler (History of Music), Hermann Grädener (Harmony), and Karl Navratil (Counterpoint), while continuing to study the piano and cello privately. He joined the Wagner-Verein, and attended the première of Bruckner's Ninth Symphony, which overwhelmed him, and most of the Hofoper's Wagner productions: he saw *Die Meistersinger* no less than five times during his first four months in the capital.

It was then that the young composer first encountered Mahler as a conductor, at the first night of *Zaide* (under Bruno Walter), which was followed by Bizet's *Djamileh*. 'Gustav Mahler conducted. I saw the man for the first time. An artist! Long black hair, closely shaven face, spectacles. How he leads the orchestra! He extracts everything from the score!'[96] On 22 February 1903, Webern attended Hugo Wolf's funeral at the Votivkirche. The previous day he had been in the 'gods' at the Hofoper for the first night of the Mahler–Roller *Tristan*, which he described at length in his diary.[97] At the same time he was hearing his first Strauss symphonic poems, which he described as 'magnificent works, highly inventive creations of a true genius'.

Webern's first surviving compositions, some Lieder, date from 1900. Like the chamber music pieces Mahler composed while he was at the Conservatory, many of them are unfinished. One of his earliest finished scores, dated August 1904, is *Im Sommerwind*, subtitled 'Idyll for a large orchestra'. But Webern's studies at the University of Vienna were nearly over, and he decided to look for a composition teacher who would stimulate him and help him to progress. His friend Josef Polnauer relates how at this point Webern went with Heinrich Jalowetz to Berlin and introduced himself to Hans Pfitzner. Unpleasant remarks made by the German composer about Mahler and Strauss resulted in the immediate flight of the two potential students.[98] In autumn 1904, chance brought into Schoenberg's circle his two great pupils, Alban Berg and Anton Webern, when they read a short paragraph in the press announcing lectures which Schoenberg was about to give at the school run by Eugenia Schwarzwald, philanthropist and pedagogue, in the Wallnerstrasse. Schoenberg and Zemlinsky were to teach there for some time, and Webern,

---

[95] Anton Webern, letter to his cousin Ernst Diez, 20 Feb. 1901, quoted in HMW 39.
[96] Webern's private diary, HMW 56.   [97] See above, Vol. ii, Chap. 14.
[98] See above, Vol. ii, Chap. 16.

who had already studied the score of *Verklärte Nacht*, responded immediately to their call. More than anything it was Schoenberg's personality and the originality of his music which made him decide to study under him, for Schoenberg was only nine years older than Webern, with no university diploma of any kind to back up his new career as a teacher. In autumn 1904 it seems that Webern was the first student Schoenberg worked with. He was soon joined by Karl Horwitz,[99] Heinrich Jalowetz, Alban Berg, and Erwin Stein. Schoenberg had left the Schwarzwald School by the time Egon Wellesz came into the group a year later. Webern had known Wellesz at the University, where he was completing his studies in law and Byzantine music, and the two young men attended the rehearsals of Mahler's Third Symphony in December 1904, having first played the four-hand version together.

Wellesz had long been an admirer of Mahler. At the age of 14 he had decided to devote himself to music after hearing him conduct *Der Freischütz* and Beethoven's Ninth Symphony. As we have seen, Webern, raised in a Wagnerian atmosphere, was not immediately convinced by the Third Symphony: the popular melodies and the 'linear orchestration' had worried him. But he was beginning to put his doubts aside, and Wellesz was happy to observe his 'gradual transformation'.[100] Even Schoenberg was still slightly disconcerted by the Third, as can be sensed on reading the nevertheless very admiring letter he wrote to Mahler the day after attending the final rehearsal.[101] He was not totally won over to Mahler until the Lieder concert in January 1905.

To satisfy concert-goers who were unable to get seats for the Lieder concert on 29 January, the Vereinigung repeated the programme on 3 February, this time with the participation of Marie Gutheil-Schoder, who sang three additional *Wunderhorn-Lieder*. After the concert, Mahler gave a dinner at the Annahof restaurant for the young Vereinigung musicians, that is to say, Schoenberg and his pupils. That long evening together created a lasting bond between Mahler and the men who were to determine the future of Viennese music after his death. A glance at Webern's account of the evening's talk shows the immense prestige the Director of the Opera and composer of the *Kindertotenlieder* enjoyed in his eyes:

These hours spent in his presence will always remain in my memory as exceedingly happy ones, since it was the first time that I got an immediate impression of a truly great personality. Almost all his words that I could hear are embedded in my memory. . . . At first there was a discussion of Rückert's lyric poetry. Mahler said: 'After *Des Knaben Wunderhorn* I could only compose more Rückert—which is lyricism at first hand, all the rest is lyricism at second hand.' He also mentioned that he did not understand everything in the *Wunderhorn* texts. The discussion turned to counterpoint, after Schoenberg had said that only the Germans knew how to handle counterpoint. Mahler drew our attention to the old French composers—Rameau, etc.—and ranked only Bach, Brahms and Wagner as the greatest contrapuntalists among Germans. 'Nature is for us the model in this realm. Just as in nature the entire universe has developed out of the primeval cell, through plants, animals, and men to God, the Supreme Being, so in music a larger structure should develop from a single motif in which is contained the germ of everything that is to come.' With Beethoven, he said, one almost always found a new motif in the development. The entire development should, however, be argued out from a single motif; that was why Beethoven was not a great contrapuntalist. Variation was the most important factor in a musical work. A theme would have to be really especially beautiful, some of Schubert's for example, for its return unchanged to be still enjoyable. For him, Mozart's string quartets ended at the double bar (repeat sign). The task of contemporary composers was to combine the contrapuntal skill of Bach with the melodiousness of Haydn and Mozart.[102]

In Alma's memoirs, Mahler is frequently quoted as making such *ex cathedra* pronouncements, couched in lapidary terms invariably prefaced by 'I'm telling you . . .' However, his opinions had nothing in common with those of an authentic and qualified theorist like Schoenberg: he knew himself too well ever to forget that he was simply expressing thoughts on the spur of the moment and that he was capable of almost immediately arguing the opposite. Usually, such pontifications were triggered by a recent experience or by something he had just read, or even, in the give-and-take of conversation, by a desire to put the other side of the case or put his interlocutor back on the right track—if necessary, at the cost of seeming paradoxical. Still, there are no paradoxes in what Webern reports him as saying. These remarks are couched in such general terms, so striking, so astonishing even, and in many ways so prophetic, that they seem to challenge, to demand detailed commentary, particularly in the light of the subsequent evolution of music in general and Mahler's in particular.

Nothing of what he said on this occasion is, of course, incompatible with anything he had said in the past at Steinbach, as recorded by Natalie. It should be borne in mind, however, that both the broad and narrow meanings he gives to the terms 'counterpoint' and 'polyphony' are quite different from the orthodox definitions. It is odd to see him include Rameau in his list of great polyphonists, since the French master composed primarily for the theatre, and was a harmonist far more than a polyphonist, and in this respect much closer to Monteverdi than to Palestrina. It is equally surprising that Mahler excludes from his approved list of polyphonists Beethoven, whom he venerated, sometimes to the point of deification—allegedly because Beethoven often introduced a new thematic element into his developments, which is in fact rarely the case, despite the famous example in the first movement in the *Eroica*. It is

[102] Friedrich Wildgans, 'Mahler und Webern', 24.

all the more surprising here since Mahler includes in his top three Brahms, whom he constantly denigrated in his letters (but perhaps Schoenberg, a fervent admirer of Brahms, might have influenced him on this occasion?).

If the remarks quoted above had been reported by another witness, one might perhaps have doubted their accuracy. But given Webern's personality and his almost mystical interest in Mahler as man and musician, we can take their authenticity for granted. To return, however, to Mahler's exclusion of Beethoven. This should perhaps not be taken too literally, but regarded simply as a theoretical symptom of the evolution of Mahler's compositional technique. Since the only justification Mahler gives for not ranking Beethoven among the 'polyphonists' is because he sometimes introduces new themes in his developments, it is obvious that the notion of 'polyphony' remains closely (and somewhat strangely) linked in Mahler's mind to that of the sonata form. Of course, the 'sonata' as actually practised in the classical period by no means always adhered to the pattern taught in schools of music: in Haydn, Mozart, and even Beethoven, there are innumerable movements which do not conform to it, either because they are monothematic (this is often the case with Haydn) or because the transitional section takes on its own thematic value (the first movement of Mozart's Quintet in G Minor is a good example) or because the opening theme is itself made up of both 'masculine' and 'feminine' elements (Mozart's 'Jupiter' Symphony) or even because the two elements, though contrasted, are thematically related (Beethoven's 'Appassionata'). To satisfy the two basic and conflicting requirements of musical composition—unity and diversity—classical composers proved themselves capable of boundless ingenuity in coming up with one new solution after another. Thus the traditional pattern doesn't really account for more than a limited number of classical movements: as Charles Rosen has recently noted,

The Sonata form could not be defined until it was dead. It was not until about 1840 that Czerny proudly claimed that he was the first to define it, but by then it was already part of history. Like the fugue it [the sonata] is a way of writing, a feeling for proportion, direction, and texture, rather than a pattern.[103]

But although it is easy to prove that these 'rules' for the sonata form were formulated *a posteriori*, it is nonetheless true that the sonata remained throughout the nineteenth century the musical form *par excellence*, and that it counted for a great deal with all Romantic and post-Romantic composers. And, for Mahler as for his predecessors, it served as a criterion, a canon, a requirement to be met, indeed, a kind of moral law imposed on any 'major' composer seeking to write a major work. It is all the more remarkable therefore that the first sonata movement which Mahler considered worthy of himself, the opening Moderato of the First Symphony, is almost entirely monothematic. The Finale of the same work, however, like all the major symphonic movements which

---

[103]   Charles Rosen, *The Classical Style* (Faber, London, 1971), 30.

were to follow, adheres quite closely to the classical pattern, which proves that Mahler still considered himself, at least where form was concerned, as heir to classicism and the Beethovenian sonata. In his early works Mahler thus accepted this legacy of sonata form without at first imposing any significant modifications, at least at first sight. For it takes close scrutiny indeed to perceive that, from the Third Symphony onwards, he transformed and reworked it until he had introduced into it what can be called, without exaggeration, a new method of composition. That, at least, is what Theodor Wiesengrund Adorno has so convincingly argued.

Sonata form strictly defined consists of three distinct sections—exposition/development/recapitulation—but it is also a succession of musical passages with contrasting characteristics—masculine/feminine, dynamic/lyric, rhythmic/melodic, strong/soft, rapid/slow, tonic/dominant, major/minor. (This is even truer of the rondo, where the special character of the rondo-theme is traditionally contrasted to that of the couplets).[104] These contrasting characteristics, which satisfy the basic need for diversity, have their origin in Renaissance dances, in which slow and fast tempos traditionally alternated to allow the dancers to catch their breath. This contrast of animation and calm, dynamic and lyric, is typical of all Romantic music, and Mahler himself, with a few changes in the order of the movements, continued throughout his life to alternate such contrasting passages in the macrocosms of his symphonies.

It should also be noted that with Beethoven it is usually the contrast between *two* main elements within each movement that provides the dynamic. Mahler gradually broke away from the constraints of this formal pattern which had nourished and sustained more than a century of music. Instead, he embarked on a new path, which Adorno has strikingly described as the 'novelistic' form. He struck a new balance between abstract, predetermined design and the 'hand' of the composer, his spontaneous acts, going so far as almost to do away with the conscious authority of the 'whole' over the details—or at least giving the overall form a more flexible and ambiguous character than hitherto.

True, Mahler had already found in the 'dramatic symphony' of Wagnerian opera a striking example of compositional freedom, since Wagner always varied his themes to suit the evolution of the characters and the plot. Undoubtedly it was the example of the Wagnerian drama which encouraged Mahler to endow his symphonies with vaster dimensions than ever before. And undoubtedly it was the same example which encouraged him to multiply the themes, independent episodes, and individual impulses until they became as numerous as the characters in a novel, thus sidestepping the traditional obligations of contrasts and symmetries. Mahler's multi-thematic approach was of course free of the functional character of Wagner's system of leitmotivs. But

---

[104] In the Classical period, the rondo was strongly influenced by the sonata, one of the episodes increasingly resembling development, the first episode, in the dominant, often being recapitulated later in the tonic.

with Mahler, this accumulation of musical material, this interplay of so many forces, made the need for unity even more imperative. This led Mahler to turn to nature, so dear to him from childhood onwards, and which in Iglau and Maiernigg had already taught him the true meaning of the word 'polyphony'.[105] Now he was saying that, in music as in nature, the whole must develop from the original 'cell', the original motif. This intellectually satisfying but somewhat abstract conception was one Mahler never applied literally. But Adorno was right when he said that:

The history of music since Mahler, even in its most recent phase, has maintained this trend towards integration and even taken it to extremes. The principle of motivic elaboration, which goes back to Bach, Beethoven, and Brahms, has been extended to the point where every element of the music is determined by a latent element common to them all. Hence it has virtually excluded the idea of a variety which is to be synthesized. An individual musical fact is viewed from the outset as a functional part of a totality, and hence sheds its own substantiality. Unity, however, is undermined as soon as it ceases to unify a plurality. Without a dialectical counterpart, it threatens to degenerated into an empty tautology.[106]

Mahler, said Adorno, had created a new concept of compositional unity, which was no longer imposed in advance from above, but from below, and based on details belonging in an entirely natural way to the 'novelistic' narrative. Adorno contrasts Beethoven's 'dramatic' symphony with Mahler's 'novelistic' symphony, pointing out that 'For him, as it did for Luther', greatness in composition consists 'in commanding the notes where they belonged . . .'[107]

The dynamic of musical discourse thus no longer depends on contrast, or on obedience to or departure from a predetermined scheme. It is found within the discourse itself. Thanks to the variant, now the basic principle of Mahlerian composition, energy is self-generating: variants 'do not suspend time but are both produced by it and produce it on the principle that you cannot immerse yourself twice in the same river'. Adorno adds that 'Mahlerian duration is dynamic',[108] a formula which might very well be reversed: the Mahlerian dynamic is duration.

But the distinction Adorno makes between the Mahlerian 'variant' and classical 'variation' is fundamental, and makes it possible to listen to Mahler in a way that gives deeper insight into his compositional logic. To define this logic, Adorno refers to the great models of the past:

If in Beethoven's thematic process, it is precisely the smallest motivic cells of the themes that determine their elaboration into qualitatively different theme complexes; if in that composer the thematic macrostructure is a technical result, in Mahler, by contrast, the musical micro-organisms are incessantly modified within the unmistakable outlines of

---

[105] See above Vol. ii, Chap. 8, Natalie's account of a walk Mahler took with Arnold Rosé in Maiernigg.
[106] TAF 132; TAFe 94.
[107] TAF 136 ff.; TAFe 96. Adorno is referring to a comment of Luther's on the music of Josquin.
[108] TAM 120; TAMe 89.

the main figures. . . . The nature of Mahler's themes qualifies them to work better on the level of themes than of motives. Their smallest elements are blurred to the point of irrelevance, because the wholes themselves do not sufficiently represent fixed values to be split up into differentials.[109]

Thus, the melodic intervals of the themes no longer predetermine the forms their future reappearances will take, and sonata form is in consequence renewed to its very foundations. Not only are the musical materials flexible, and literal recapitulations henceforth excluded, but the opening of a movement is no longer, properly speaking, an 'exposition' but rather a thematic 'proposition'. Adorno points out that just at the time when Freud was defining and analysing the unconscious and its laws, and Joyce was on the verge of inventing the stream of consciousness, Mahler was subjecting the returns of his themes to the kind of changes the memory applies to the past.

Still, all Mahler had really done was to rephrase the question that had obsessed all the Romantics before him: how to adapt the lyric, and inherently static material proper to Romanticism to the dynamic process, inherited from Classicism and basic to the sonata, of thematic (or, rather, 'motivistic') elaboration? How to develop those long, expressive melodies, already complete in themselves, which required such subtle, complex, and mobile harmonies that they disturbed and threatened the elementary tonal relationships which are the foundation of the sonata form? Strange that it should have been Mahler, a born melodist, one of the greatest in the history of music, who did more than many others to free music from its enslavement to melody. Nothing remains fixed or unchangeable in Mahler: everything changes, and the dynamic of these changes becomes the musical discourse itself. Though he employed a harmonic vocabulary inherited from the past (and, thanks to the influence of folk music, often deliberately simple), Mahler followed a newer and more 'radical' path than most composers of his generation. Faithful to the principle of irreversibility (*Nichtumkehrbarkeit*), he created a continuous stream of music in which themes 'reappear, then vanish again', never repeating themselves exactly, just as stories and songs are continuously modified by oral tradition.[110] Adorno also, and again rightly, compares this flexible and endlessly changeable thematic evolution to Schoenberg's twelve-tone method, which 'deliberately fills rhythmically stable patterns (*Muster*) with notes from mobile serial sets'.[111] It can be seen that, although Mahler himself never applied this fascinating concept of absolute unity and arborescent development from a single cell, he took it far enough to obviate the fundamental duality of Classical and Romantic composition (a legacy of the Renaissance and its discovery of an abstract 'classical' order). He created a music which proliferates like plants in nature, not fearing disparity, even seeking it. Even when it repeats itself, it is

[109] TAM 117; TAMe 87. [110] TAF 134; TAFe 95.
[111] TAM 118; TAMe 88.

a music that is always different, always seen in a new light with subtle modifications of rhythm, tempo, harmony, instrumentation, and even intervals. And far from destroying the fundamental unity of its unfolding, this luxuriant proliferation actually reinforces it, manifesting nature's supreme attribute: energy. Even when Mahler appears to be introducing a new thematic element, he later justifies it by revealing its relationship to a previous motif. In this way recapitulated elements are always recognizable—and always different. That is the meaning of the Mahlerian 'variant', which Adorno also calls 'deviant' (*Abweichung*).

'Development' now proceeds along natural lines in an organic growth based on cells which, as Adorno shows, often defy analysis, and on themes which evolve like characters in a novel:

In variation (*Variante*) technique each functional element is fixed in a recognizable shape; the structure of the themes and shapes is preserved. However, particular features are modified; . . . minute variations are introduced into the repetition of the original melody that transform the identical into the non-identical. Mahler is the composer of deviation (*Abweichung*), right down to the technicalities. Variations (*Die Varianten*), however, the *unexpected* is the opposite of the kind of effect used by the school of Berlioz, Liszt, and Strauss to achieve the *imprévu*. Nowhere do Mahler's variations (*Varianten*) introduce difference (*Abwechslung*) for its own sake.[112]

With Mahler, the miracle is that the most unexpected of these 'deviants' is always so inevitable that it is impossible to say which is the most accomplished and definitive form or version of a theme or which is the source of the other. What is more, unlike classical 'variations', which 'very often come as a disappointment after the theme in that they persist in stripping it of its essence without amplifying it until it becomes something truly different', and which often even go so far as to 'disfigure' (*verschandelt*) it,[113] the Mahlerian variant destroys nothing of its beauty or expressiveness, even though it constantly alters it, and even though the succession of musical incidents is rarely what would normally be expected.

It is in Mahler's last works that he most fully realizes his ideal arborescent growth springing from a parent cell. One of these cells (the phrase A, G, E) recurs, for instance, throughout the *Lied von der Erde*. Another (F sharp, A, B) runs through the first movement of the Ninth Symphony. While Mahler thus appeals to the remote past of liturgical polyphony and the *cantus firmus*, with music created from moment to moment on a common base, latent or expressed, but emancipated from compositional predetermination, he also heralds the entirely modern concept of an omnipotent and unique energy which is the essential source of all forms of matter. Mahler's music can be understood as a liberation of energy rather than a concrete interplay of sound elements.

---

[112] TAF 134; TAFe 95. The translator has used the common word 'variation' as equivalent to Adorno's 'variant', a term which is to my mind untranslatable and should not be altered in any translation from the German.   [113] TAM 121; TAMe 90.

Finally, in reference to this ideal of a higher musical unity in which everything develops from a parent cell, in which everything is nourished by one and the same motif, it is strange that if anyone ever achieved it, it was Webern himself, the man who recorded Mahler's remarks, in a form later called 'developing variation'. It is this, moreover, which gives Webern's music its unique appeal and prestige, and explains why it so influenced post-World War II composers, and why it has lost none of its fascination for us today.[114]

Adorno drew the basic ideas, summarized and much simplified here, primarily from his study of Mahler's symphonies. He set them out in 1960 in his Mahler monograph and centenary speech, for future generations, who, to my mind, can never afford to ignore them even if their view of his music has changed considerably.[115] But his analysis is just as applicable to the microcosm of the mature Mahler Lied which contains the same principles of the 'developing variation' and organic growth from one melodic cell. Needless to say, none of the Viennese critics fully realized the historical importance of the 29 January concert. At best, Theodor Helm was able to note in the *Musikalisches Wochenblatt* that the concert was 'highly interesting, and in parts even moving'. He said that the *Wunderhorn-Lieder*, mostly taken from military life, possessed a 'fresh and dashing' humour and that the orchestral accompaniment 'perfectly suggests the atmosphere without in any way overwhelming the voice'. Of course, Helm also discerned occasional reminiscences, of Bruckner and Johann Strauss in particular. Yet he admired the 'terrifying and ghostly atmosphere' of 'Revelge' and the 'deeply moving' expressiveness of the *Kindertotenlieder*. Although Mahler had so often been accused of striving for 'superficial effects', these five elegies seemed to have been written with his heart's blood.

An anonymous critic in the *Neue Musikalische Presse* speculated about the origin of Mahler's melodies:

The songs, their sequence, and their performance offered the highest state of polished refinement. . . . It does not matter to him (Mahler) or to the listeners whether the melodies are suffused with juicy banalities or borrowed from Bruckner's Romantic (Symphony) or Flotow's *Martha*. He makes the accompaniment progress in the time-honoured manner, stepwise with the voice, but casts over the whole a glittering orchestral web, full of clever ideas and piquant effects.

Here, for once, the henceforth standard reproach of eclecticism did not prevent sincere admiration for this 'group of brilliant and characteristic musical pictures'.[116]

---

[114] On the subtle relationship which can be detected between the music of Mahler and Webern, see Elmar Budde, 'Bemerkungen zum Verhältnis Mahler-Webern', in *Archiv der Musikwissenschaft*, 33 (1976): 3, 159. In particular, the author draws a wholly convincing parallel between the theme of the *Langsamer Satz für Streichquartet* of 1905 and the second theme of the slow movement of Mahler's Fourth Symphony.

[115] Adorno illustrated his main ideas in a striking analysis of the first movement of the Fourth Symphony in which he followed the evolution, or 'adventures', of a motif whose role he compared to that of a joker in a pack of cards (TAM 122; TAMe 91).

[116] *Neue Musikalische Presse* 14 (1905): 4, 53, quoted by John W. Finson, 'The Reception of Gustav Mahler's Wunderhorn Lieder', in *Journal of Musicology*, 5 (1987): 1, 104.

David Joseph Bach, who always showed a sympathy and comprehension for Mahler's art exceptional for the time, noted the originality in the relationship of the music to words: 'With him, words do not create the atmosphere. It is more as if, in order to create it, he needs the text as much as the music.' Julius Korngold began his review with a reservation: he felt that Rückert's intimate art was ill-suited to orchestral accompaniment, however 'noble, sensitive and poetic' Mahler's setting might be. Korngold thought however that the concert revealed a new aspect of the composer's talent: a deeper, richer musical sensitivity. In certain songs he had managed in a masterly fashion to combine the naivety of folk tunes with a description of gruesome situations. In 'Revelge', the listener is, so to speak, forced to follow the soldier to the dreadful reveille. In the *Kindertotenlieder*, the 'tone of deep grief' and the 'tender, modest and restrained feeling' of the music admirably suited the poems. Korngold rightly remarked that Mahler's treatment of this folk material was linked in many ways with operatic technique; he must surely have been thinking along these lines when he wrote the dramatic dialogue in 'Wo die schönen Trompeten', or the vocalise in the refrain of 'Wer hat dies Liedlein'.[117]

Similar praise for the *Kindertotenlieder* appeared in Kauders' review. He rejoiced that the Vereinigung, after so many 'insidious outbursts (*hinterhältige Eruptionen*)' and 'fraudulent extortions (*hinhaltende Extorsionen*)', had finally 'devoted a whole evening to an authentic "creative artist" '. Mahler's 'primary instincts and feelings seemed to be profoundly orchestral'; the song emanated from the orchestral accompaniment, though having a life of its own. Colour was a determining factor in the atmosphere prevailing in his compositions, and ensured their organic unity, but his 'military songs' also offered 'a wealth of musical finesse and piquancy'.

Wallaschek was also won over by the *Kindertotenlieder*, some of which he deemed 'entirely worthy of the poems'. He was deeply moved by this music 'which sings with body and soul', and which feared neither syllabic repetition, nor accentuations proper to the laws of melody but contrary to the sense of the words. Among the other Lieder, he preferred those which were 'graceful and friendly', such as 'Rheinlegendchen', and considered the folk-song style to be the most apt for Mahler. Nonetheless, the article ended negatively, for in Wallaschek's opinion Mahler lacked 'creative power'. 'As the French saying goes', it was 'a talent at the level of its time', 'one of those talents that the present should not underestimate' but not one of those which 'blaze new paths and lead us beyond the achievements of our age'. He thought that the 'lighter' Lieder did not gain from repeated hearings, though the first four *Kindertotenlieder* did.

Gustav Schönaich also acknowledged that he had been 'moved and captivated' by the *Kindertotenlieder*. In spite of the funereal character of so many of

---

[117] Cf. John W. Finson, 'Reception', 107.

Mahler's 'sensitive and skilfully written songs', even one of the love songs, the interest of the audience never flagged, thanks to the wonderful variety of the orchestral accompaniment. As for Robert Hirschfeld, he would not admit to having been moved, not even by the *Kindertotenlieder*. They 'have in no way modified my opinion of Mahler', for 'even an eccentric mind can, on occasion, aspire to a more interior and concentrated expression'. The composer of these doleful Lieder 'seeks an aesthetic pleasure in his own suffering, or else in his sympathy for the most terrifying of sufferings'. With 'refined and contrived instrumental effects and innumerable colour combinations', Mahler gave the orchestra 'the tender and intimate colours of chamber music'. 'Aspiring to lyricism, he idealizes the waltz, the Ländler and the military march.' Unfortunately, when the 'instrumental illustration' failed to carry the day, certain Lieder such as 'Ich atmet' und 'Ich bin der Welt' fall back into mediocrity.

Hirschfeld later returned to the charge, with even more insidious comments, in the *Österreichische Rundschau*. Mahler's Lieder were, in fact, 'orchestral pieces', with 'dazzling, exquisitely tender instrumentation, to which the Lieder had been added'. These 'Mahlerian paint-pots' (a pun on Mahler's name: *Maler* is the German word for *painter*) had become the centrepiece, around which the Schaffender Tonkünstler performed their 'grotesque dances'. The Lieder showed a 'veneer' of genius, but the brilliance of his orchestration distracted the listener. The genre of the Lied could not survive such refinements; was it not an art 'close to dying' which superimposed such technical subtleties on the naive feelings of the *Wunderhorn* and on the cruel suffering of the *Kindertotenlieder*? And a sign of his coldness and affectation: before consenting to start the performance, Mahler signalled with his baton for an usher to leave the hall, thereby allowing his 'personal ego to take precedence over his artistic ego. Never would the great composers of yesteryear have acted in this fashion! How great, therefore, is the weakness of contemporary composers, who attach more importance today to preserving the "illusion" of the listener than to the quality of the performances!' Surely it needed a great deal of ill-will to reproach Mahler with objecting to an usher continuing to show people to their seats, even at the back of the hall, when the music was about to begin.

Adopting a more general and also more objective point of view, Karpath remarked in the *Neues Wiener Tagblatt* that 'the current in Vienna which until recently ran against Mahler the composer was reversed after the performance of the Third Symphony'. Henceforth, the mere appearance of his name on a poster would suffice to guarantee a full house and a complete success. The new Lieder heralded, undeniably, a new period in his work; certainly 'the essentials of his nature have not changed, but the expressive means are transformed'. These were no longer 'the emanations of a spirit in the midst of combat, but rather the emotions of a soul which has come through purgatory, and has attained greatness in thought and feeling'. Despite their profound complexity,

these 'sound pictures' had all the appearance of simplicity; and the
Kindertotenlieder, an 'epic of sentimentality (*des Schwärmerischen*)', surpassed
all the other songs on the programme.

A month later, in the magazine *Signale für die musikalische Welt*, Karpath
added that 'the Vereinigung has done itself a great disservice in revealing to
the public these new works by its honorary president' because, in the context
of the 'confused' music of the association's members, Mahler appeared as a
'conservative', a 'normal musician', oriented henceforth toward 'melodic
beauty' rather than the 'extravagant and the bizarre'. In the same article,
Karpath declared: 'Mahler is to my knowledge the first to have revealed the
moving beauty of *Des Knaben Wunderhorn*, and to have put into music a
considerable number of these flowers of German poetry.' (The editor-in-chief
of the magazine reinforced the restrictive force of the expression 'to my knowledge' by adding a question mark in parentheses.) On the following page,
Karpath offered the warmest praise to the *Wunderhorn-Lieder* of the young
Viennese composer, Theodor Streicher.[118] Their 'conscious melodic simplicity', their 'clever union of word and sound' were 'a veritable balm for all
uncorrupted ears'. Hearing them, the critic felt he was 'finally emerging from
the impenetrable forest in which the evil spirits of impotent Lieder-makers had
for too long imprisoned' him. He was 'at last breathing deeply of the pure air
of the mountain tops'.

Mahler thought little of these Lieder by Streicher, which he had discovered
in rather unpleasant circumstances. He could therefore consider Karpath's
praise of Streicher only as indirect criticism and an additional offence. After
the appearance of the *Signale* article, which Karpath sent him accompanied by
a letter,[119] Mahler, stung by the phrase 'to my knowledge', wrote back:

To my knowledge, previous *Wunderhorn-Lieder* have been only isolated compositions,
so the fact that, up to the age of forty, I chose my texts exclusively from this collection
with the sole exception of those I wrote myself (and even they, in a certain sense,
belong to the *Wunderhorn*), does make a slight difference. However, it is not worth
insisting on my having been the first in this field. What is more important is that I have
given myself over heart and soul to this poetry because of its style and tone (which is,
in essence, quite different from all other 'literary poetry' and could be described as
nature and life, i.e. the very source of all poetry, rather than art). There is no doubt that,
after being jeered at for years for this choice, I've ended up as the initiator of this fashion. What is strange is that my works based on these texts should remain the least
known and most rarely played, while those of my imitators have become famous and
much performed.[120]

In the following issue of the same magazine, Karpath specified that Mahler,
if not the first composer to set these poems to music, was at least the first to

---

[118]   See below.
[119]   Karpath's letter to Mahler, accompanying the article, is dated 2 Mar. (MBR1, no. 230; MBR2, no.
341).   [120]   MBR1, no. 230; MBR2, no. 341.

bring his *Wunderhorn-Lieder* together in a collection. At the same time, he sent a letter of apology, to which Mahler replied that he felt 'not in the slightest offended', and proposed that they 'bury the hatchet'. He then added a deliberately ambiguous paragraph:

In any case, I have never taken your animosity seriously enough to hold it against you. You know from experience that I am not very susceptible in this domain. Whoever follows a path as clearly marked as mine cannot be upset by unjust reproach or stupid praise. And believe me, I can understand and forgive the wrath I unleash far more easily than my enemies can admit or excuse my indifference. So, I hope everything is all right again . . .[121]

Actually, things were not 'all right again'. Indeed, Karpath's half-concealed hostility towards Mahler was reinforced by this incident. The critic of the *Neues Wiener Tagblatt* certainly read between the lines and understood that Mahler was saying that he didn't really care whether Karpath's articles about him were favourable or unfavourable. The very unfavourable one he had written in 1904 for *Bühne und Welt* on 'Mahler and the Vienna Opera' was clearly intended to wound, despite frequent protestations of a desire to be fair and objective. In it he admitted to having been 'at war with him [Mahler] for some years', after having had 'at certain times, the advantage of being at his side almost daily'. Mahler was then accused of having become a bad Opera director, 'lacking control over his temper', and also 'consistent in his inconsistency', changing his opinions much too often. 'An Opera director must be a subtle diplomat, an experienced strategist.' Mahler was neither, and his 'lack of calm' detracted from his personality. Karpath added that 'anyone who insists on the unconditional acceptance of his authority must be without reproach in his actions, nine times out of ten'.[122] Fortunately this new attack had no more effect than the preceding ones, for Mahler enjoyed the full confidence of the higher authorities at the Opera, and in particular that of Prince Montenuovo.

In 1905, the first near-complete performance of the *Wunderhorn-Lieder* made Mahler more conscious than ever of his debt to the celebrated anthology, for fifteen years the principal source for his musical output. Six weeks later he returned to the subject of the *Wunderhorn* in the course of a conversation with Isi Dehmel, the wife of the poet and she recorded his words in her diary.

He always felt there was something barbaric in the way musicians chose poems of perfect beauty to set to music. It was as if a great sculptor had hewn out a marble to daub it with colour. He, Mahler, had only taken over for his purpose a few poems from the *Wunderhorn*; since his early childhood, he had had a special relationship with this book. They were not perfectly finished poems, but rather stone blocks which everyone could shape as he would.

[121]   MBR1, no. 231; MBR2, no. 342.
[122]   *Bühne und Welt*, Berlin, 6 (1904): 17, 705 ff.

In saying that he had known the collection since early childhood, Mahler would seem to be contradicting himself, since we know that he told Natalie and Richard Specht that he had not discovered the famous anthology until he was 27, in Leipzig. Nonetheless the conversation with Frau Dehmel expresses a deeper truth, and that is his lifelong passion for German folk poetry, already manifest in his own early poems, in 'Hans und Grethe', the *Lieder eines fahren-den Gesellen*, or in *Das Klagende Lied*.

Paradoxically, Mahler was right in believing that he had started a fashion with his *Wunderhorn-Lieder*. A new movement called the *Wandervogel* had been formed in Germany, with the still wholly romantic ideal of 'escaping from the artificial life of the big cities and returning to nature'. Its members called themselves 'Bacchantes', and dressed in the manner of the 'fahrenden Gesellen' (travelling apprentices) of former times. The group were of course keen practitioners of the *Volkslied*, its 'simplicity' forming part of their artistic ideal. The German Emperor went as far as to set up a commission of scholars and folklorists to make choral arrangements which would respect the 'Germanness' and 'folk' character of the songs, retaining the 'singing quality' of the vocal lines and keeping the accompaniments simple.

In 1903, the Berlin literary magazine *Die Woche*[123] published a collection of thirty 'modern popular songs' entitled *Im Volkston*, prefaced by Engelbert Humperdinck, Joseph Joachim, and Karl Krebs. Among the thirty composers were Eugen d'Albert, Ignaz Brüll, Friedrich Gernsheim, Siegfried Ochs, Leo Blech, Wilhelm Kienzl, Engelbert Humperdinck, Max von Schillings, Hans Sommer, Karl Reinecke, Siegfried Wagner, Hans Pfitzner, Ludwig Thuille, and our old acquaintance from Hamburg, Count Hochberg, author of the unforget-table *Der Wärwolf*. The name of Mahler was, of course, absent, even though three of the poems in the collection came from *Des Knaben Wunderhorn*.[124]

At the same time a jury of five musicians was appointed, with the task of awarding a yearly prize of considerable value for a *Volkslied* written 'in the spirit' of the popular song. Other prizes were instituted for Lieder in the same style, but in their case the tribunal was to be the public itself.[125] Even the 'learned' Reger wrote *Schlichte Weisen* (Simple Melodies, or Airs), while Wilhelm Kienzl, Max von Schillings, Conrad Ansorge, and Joseph Haas

---

[123] *Die Woche*, 11 (1903): 19.

[124] The others belonged to the famous folk collections of Herder (*Stimmen der Völker*), Becker (*Rheinischer Volksliederborn*), and Böhme (*Altdeutsches Liederbuch*). The less-known composers included in the collection were as follows: Reinhold Becker, Wilhelm Berger, August Bungert, Johannes Doebber, Philipp Fürst zu Eulenburg, Adalbert von Goldschmidt, Hans Hermann, Eugen Hildach, Robert Kahn, Arno Kleffel, Thomas Koschat, Henning von Koss, Eduard Lassen, Georg Schumann, Bogumil Zepler, and Hermann Zumpe. In the same year (1903) the new Austrian music publisher Universal Edition, which for the previous two years had been issuing scholarly editions of repertoire works and was soon to purchase all rights in the symphonies of Bruckner and Mahler, published a large (283 pages) album of folk songs en-titled *Das Lied im Volke*, and announced a vast project (never to be realized): for a series of collections of 'Popular songs of all the nations which are part of Austria'.

[125] Nearly 9,000 Lieder were composed in 1904, and 120,000 copies of the three prize-winning Lieder were sold.

composed *Ernte Lieder* (Harvest Songs). Schoenberg too composed some *Wunderhorn-Lieder* (in 1903, 1904, and 1905),[126] and Webern after him in his opus 15 (1924) and 18 (1927).[127]

In these circumstances it is easy to understand Mahler's irritation. He felt, rightly, that he had 'discovered' the anthology at a time when no one else was interested in it. On 29 January, that is, on the very evening that the premières of his Lieder were being performed at the Vereinigung, Eugenia Schwarzwald, directress of the school of music which had engaged Schoenberg and Zemlinsky as teachers, commemorated in Vienna the hundredth anniversary of the publication of Brentano's and Arnim's first anthology, with a lecture illustrated by readings of the poems, and a performance of *Wunderhorn-Lieder* by Mendelssohn, Schumann, Brahms, Strauss, and Theodor Streicher. The singer, Marie Gutheil-Schoder, also selected two Mahler songs from among his early collection for voice and piano: 'Ablösung im Sommer' and 'Ich ging mit Lust'.

Of the young composers who embraced this 'new' fashion of the *Wunderhorn*, one of the best known was Theodor Streicher, a largely self-taught musician and friend of Schoenberg and Zemlinsky. Mahler met him once, by chance according to Alma, on the shores of the Wörthersee, where Streicher spent each summer. He and his wife then paid several 'neighbourly' calls to the Mahler villa, but Mahler never quite understood the motive underlying their persistence. This only became clear later, in Vienna, the day when Schoenberg and Zemlinsky, invited to dine at the Auenbruggergasse with the young conductor Klaus Pringsheim,[128] asked Mahler if they might bring along Streicher, who wanted to play his most recent Lieder to Mahler.

Greeting their guests at the door, the Mahlers noticed with some disquiet a bundle of manuscripts in Streicher's overcoat pocket. Disquiet turned to consternation when Mahler learned that these were *Wunderhorn-Lieder*. As soon as the meal was over, Alma signalled to her husband that the moment had come to invite the young composer to the piano. Mahler smiled, and merely shrugged his shoulders. The conversation dragged on, the silences became longer and longer while the unfortunate Streicher exchanged worried and surprised looks with his wife. Towards midnight, Alma managed to get Mahler to come into another room, where she reminded him of his promise. Reluctantly, he did finally invite Streicher to play. In a glacial silence, the young man played one, two, three Lieder while Mahler, increasingly impatient, twitched his face nervously. Schoenberg and Zemlinsky, 'lacking courage' (according to Alma's account), went to the piano and voiced their admiration, approving this or that

---

[126] They include *Sehnsucht*, Op. 8, No. 3 and *Das Wappenschild*, Op. 8, No. 8.

[127] Between 1908 and 1913 the *Wandervogel* had 25,000 members. Once again the search was on, as it had been a century earlier at the time of Arnim and Brentano, for folk songs not yet written down. In 1909 Breuer's collection *Der Zupfgeigenhänsl* was much in demand, selling 100,000 copies over the next four years. Most of the information about this folk-song renaissance at the turn of the century comes from Edward Kravitt's article, 'The Trend toward the Folklike', *Chord and Discord* (1969), 40.

[128] Concerning Klaus Pringsheim (1883–1973), see below Chap. 6.

nice detail. Streicher, for his part, committed the 'unpardonable': he went on playing! Even worse, he began to read each poem before singing it, and even stopped from time to time in the middle to point out the passages that he felt he had handled particularly well. Alma hardly dared look at any of the guests, for fear of bursting out laughing. In an atmosphere of chilly embarrassment, the Streichers finally decided to take their leave. Once they had gone, the Auenbruggergasse apartment echoed to gales of uncontrollable mirth.[129]

On at least one other occasion Alma caught her husband in the act of being less than frank out of consideration for someone's feelings. Bruno Walter came one day to play for Mahler his new symphonic poem *Peer Gynt*. Its 'anaemic sterility' shocked Mahler, but his affection for the young conductor was such that he encouraged Walter in spite of everything to go on composing, just as he had done earlier when Rosé played Walter's Quartet. Later, he admitted to Alma that he had merely wanted to avoid hurting the young man's feelings, and that he had hated himself for being so hypocritical. As we shall see, he attended several premières of Walter's pieces knowing full well that there was no future for him as a composer.[130] It was also friendship that led Schoenberg and Zemlinsky to include Walter's Piano Quintet in the last but one concert of the Vereinigung.

After the triumph of Mahler's Lieder, which had been performed to a full house on two occasions, it might have been thought that the future of the young Vereinigung was assured. But Mahler had demanded four rehearsals, as costly as they were long. Some lasted well beyond the agreed time, and it was there-fore necessary to pay overtime to the Philharmonic musicians. Since the small Musikvereinsaal[131] chosen by Mahler for the performances had not enough seats to cover the expenses, the guarantee fund collected by subscription the preceding year was completely exhausted. On 5 February, an article in the *Fremden-Blatt* announced that a 'generous patron' had decided to pay the deficit and subsidize the following year's concerts. In fact, as we have seen, Schoenberg was merely hoping to obtain the help of the banker Albert von Rothschild, whom Mahler had promised to solicit personally. However, accord-ing to a letter that Schoenberg sent to Guido Adler two days later, nothing had yet been decided. Rothschild had let it be known to Schoenberg and Robert

---

[129]   Theodor Streicher (1874–1940), grandson of a friend of Friedrich von Schiller and son of a piano-manufacturer, studied singing and acting before devoting himself to music. A student of Heinrich Schulz-Beuthen in Dresden (counterpoint) and of Ferdinand Löwe in Vienna (piano and orchestration), though largely self-taught, he wrote mostly vocal works, among them thirty-one *Wunderhorn-Lieder*, in a style akin to that of Hugo Wolf. An entire concert of Streicher's *Wunderhorn-Lieder* had recently been given in Vienna, where his songs were published as a collection by Lauterbach and Kühn, who were soon to publish Mahler's Seventh Symphony (see below, Vol. iiii, Chaps. 2 and 3). Concerning Streicher, see also Edward F. Kravitt, *The Lied Mirror of Late Romanticism* (Yale University Press, New Haven, 1996), 114 and 269, and Richard Bruce Wursten, 'The Life and Music of Theodor Streicher: Hugo Wolf Redivivus', Dissertation, University of Wisconsin, 1980. According to Kravitt, the musical style of Streicher's *Wunderhorn-Lieder* were strongly influenced by Hugo Wolf's, which in itself explains why Mahler disliked them.

[130]   AMS.   [131]   Today it is called Brahmssaal.

Gound that they would obtain nothing from him without the intervention of Mahler, and the latter had promised to do what was expected of him. As for the 'other Rothschild', they had so far had no answer from him.[132]

After the two concerts in January, the members of the Vereinigung were obliged to meet twice, at the Lilienfeld Bierhaus and at the Museum Café: they came to pessimistic conclusions. The orchestral concert announced for 11 March[133] had to be cancelled and the group's activities came to an end after two evenings of chamber music, on 20 February (the Bruno Walter Quintet and a Sonata for Piano and Violin by Reger)[134] and 17 April (Lieder by Pfitzner, Reger, Joseph von Wöss, and Richard Strauss).[135]

For Mahler, the success of the two Vienna concerts had no doubt dispelled the painful memory of the Cologne première of the Fifth. Yet he was now aware that he had entered upon a new phase in his career as composer, and was therefore not surprised when the fate of the Fifth began to look as hazardous as that of the Fourth a few years earlier. The next two performances, conducted in Dresden and Berlin by two of the most celebrated conductors of the time—Ernst von Schuch and Arthur Nikisch—confirmed his misgivings. On the very day of the final rehearsal of his Lieder in Vienna, on 28 January, the 'accursed' Fifth puzzled and shocked the audience in the Dresden Königliche Kapelle. The review *Die Musik* was alone in its claim that the applause was 'warm'. The *Musikalisches Wochenblatt* condemned the music but praised the performers: only a first-class conductor and orchestra could get at least something enjoyable out of such a work, such a mixture of the beautiful, the ugly, and the pretentious. Once again, in the *Dresdner Nachrichten*, Hermann Starcke judged the new symphony to be 'absolutely incomprehensible without a programme'. It was, for him, only an immense 'chaos of sounds and chords, of combinations of bits and pieces cobbled together', a racket lasting one and a quarter hours which 'exhausts the nerves and tries the patience of the listeners', revealing in the last resort 'more pretension than creative gifts'. Despite his zeal, despite his 'skilful and refined compositional technique', Mahler composed 'without inner necessity'. He had 'nothing, or almost nothing, to say'. For Starcke, it was 'Ernst von Schuch's patience and devotion, his spirit of sacrifice' and the expenditure of spiritual and physical power required to come to grips with this work, which

[132] The 'other Rothschild' was no doubt Baron Albert's brother, Nathaniel (see above). See letter from Schoenberg to Guido Adler, 7 Feb. 1905 (Stadt-Bibliothek, Vienna).

[133] They had originally intended to present the *Sonata for orchestra* by Joseph von Wöss (see above, Vol. ii, Chap. 11, for this musician's biography), the monologue from the last act of Strauss's *Guntram* and some Lieder with orchestral accompaniment by Pfitzner and Franz Dubitzky.

[134] Reger's Sonata No. 4, in C major, Op. 72 was performed by the composer at the piano and Arnold Rosé on the violin. For his own Quintet in F Minor, Bruno Walter took the piano part, accompanied by the Rosé Quartet. In Jan. 1907, when his Trio had its première in Vienna (see below, Chap. 8), Walter also played the piano part. Mahler was seized with a fit of 'convulsive yawning' during the performance (AMS).

[135] According to the *Musikbuch aus Österreich*, 2 (1906), the programme of the third chamber music concert was originally intended to include Reger's Quartet No. 3, in D minor instead of his Sonata for Piano and Violin, and some Gesänge by Streicher. One may perhaps assume that the evening at the Mahlers' home caused the directors of the Vereinigung to change the programme.

won his admiration. Indeed, the applause at the end of the concert was addressed to him and the orchestra, not to Herr Mahler and his symphony.[136]

A month later, Nikisch conducted the same work in Berlin, before a relatively attentive audience in which a few dissenters nonetheless voiced their disapproval, from the end of the Scherzo on. A card from Strauss to Mahler,[137] and another from Mahler to Frau Luise Wolff (who had replaced her husband, deceased in 1902, as the head of the Berlin Concert Bureau), show that Mahler firmly intended to go to Berlin for the concert, and even promised to attend the dinner given afterwards in his honour by Frau Wolff. The day before the concert, however, he wrote to Frau Wolff: 'I am under such terrible strain here, due to unforeseen circumstances, that I don't know where to turn . . .'[138] Please give my warmest greetings to Nikisch and thank him, on my behalf, for all the trouble he has taken.' Alas, Mahler soon learned that the performance of his work had left much to be desired. The 'unforeseen circumstances' which kept him from leaving Vienna were doubtless the two one-act operas by Leo Blech and Eugen d'Albert, premièred on 28 February, which he finally had to conduct himself. It could also have been a simple excuse: knowing that the Berlin press had been prejudiced against him from the start, Mahler may have cancelled at the last moment in order to be able to go to Hamburg two weeks later—where he planned to conduct the same work himself.

Sure enough, the Berlin critics remained true to form, and found little good to say of the new work. The critic on the *Börsenzeitung* was alone in finding the piece 'interesting and significant', and that primarily because Mahler now revealed himself as much less of a 'heaven-stormer' than in his earlier symphonies. Its 'thematic material' was of 'great simplicity', and it was only 'the unusual contrapuntal art with which that material was developed that made the music seem rather complicated and hard to understand'. But the writer found, in the Fifth, the usual Mahler tendency to 'make rather too much noise' and to 'exceed the limits of the symphonic genre'. As before, it was the Finale which drew the most admiration and made the rest of the work acceptable. Oskar Eichberg, one of the earliest Mahler enthusiasts, found the Finale infinitely superior to the rest of the symphony. But he regretted in his *Börsen Courier* article the absence of any 'programme' or analysis. According to him, the listener felt he was faced with an arbitrary collection of incongruous fragments, packed with daring but gratuitous 'experiments' in the musical material.

Leopold Schmidt, who like Eichberg had sometimes passed favourable

[136] The Fourth Subscription Concert took place at 7 p.m., on 27 Jan., with the participation of the Belgian cellist Jean Gérardy, who performed Haydn's Concerto in D (without the Finale, according to the press). At the beginning of the concert, Schuch conducted Weber's *Jubel* Overture.

[137] On this card of 15 Feb. 1905, Strauss invites Mahler to lunch the day of the concert. The typed copy has been preserved in AMS (MSB 89). On 14 Feb. Mahler asked the Intendant's permission to go to Berlin for two days—18 and 19 Feb.—in order to hear 'two young altos, a dramatic soprano, a coloratura soprano, a heroic baritone, etc.' (HOA, G.Z. 229/1905).

[138] Letter of 27 Feb. 1905 (BGM, Paris).

judgements on Mahler's music, now once again declared that he had 'somewhat' changed his mind. He even blamed Nikisch for putting 'so much knowledge and such an outstanding artistic will at the service of such an ephemeral work'. The Funeral March, somewhat operatic but very effective—due to purely technical means—was the only good part of the symphony; the Scherzo was full of 'Viennese jokes', the Adagietto 'unpleasantly sweet, and worthy of Gounod', and the Finale 'completely formless'. The whole revealed, in his opinion, a 'painful contradiction between the composer's will and his capacities'. With an amazing mastery of counterpoint and orchestration, Mahler aspired to depth and originality; he was unfortunately incapable of 'creating a form' or of 'constructing organically the mosaic of his musical ideas'.

Adolf Schultze's judgement in the *Musikalisches Wochenblatt* was more or less the same. Mahler's Fifth was, in his opinion, 'inferior to all his other symphonic works'. It was full of longueurs, 'none of them heavenly';[139] the instrumentation was 'lustreless and dull'. A dissenting voice amid this chorus of disapproval was Friedrich Geissler's brief review in *Die Musik*. For him Mahler's Fifth revealed—as had his previous works—a composer who, though taking up where Bruckner had left off, 'seeks and finds his own way as far as invention, construction and expression are concerned'. But his works needed to be played more often in order to be fully appreciated and understood.

The anonymous critic in *Der Tag* condemned the Fifth with the same sarcastic tone that he had used earlier against the Fourth, ridiculing 'these absurd people who for years have been proclaiming at the top of their voices that Mahler should be taken seriously'.[140] Only one writer in Berlin came to Mahler's defence, and that was Otto Lessman, who, luckily for Mahler, had great influence as a member of the Allgemeiner Deutscher Musikverein. In the Verein's review, the *Allgemeine Musik-Zeitung*, Lessman denounced the 'uncouthness of spectators who don't hesitate to boo a work of such seriousness and power', a work which moreover seemed to him to be 'far clearer and easier to understand than those which preceded it'. He preferred not to express a definitive opinion after hearing the work only once. According to his first impressions, some 'italianizing' turns of phrase had crept into the thematic content of the first movement, which 'increased its graphic appeal but were not particularly convincing'. The Scherzo revealed the double influence of Schubert and Berlioz, and the Adagietto really captivated 'with its glow of feeling and magical sonority', even though 'Mahler's handling of the orchestra seemed less sensitive than usual'.[141]

In the same journal Mahler's faithful supporter Ernst Otto Nodnagel, who later published a detailed analysis of the new symphony,[142] wrote at great

---

[139] A reference to Schumann's comment on Schubert's C major Symphony, D. 944.
[140] Quoted by Ernst Otto Nodnagel (*Allgemeine Musik-Zeitung*, 32: 9 (3 Mar. 1905), 164 ff.).
[141] According to Lessmann, Nikisch's performance lasted one hour and twenty minutes.
[142] His thirty-seven-page analytical booklet was published by Peters that year.

length about Mahler's compositional techniques, and ridiculed those who accused the work of being 'formless' and incomprehensible without a programme. In his opinion, the architecture and the general conception were perfectly clear, and conformed to the most rigorous criteria, with the 'Dionysiac joy' of the Finale balanced by the 'agreeable and tender' character of the Scherzo. To him, the latter was a model of the genre, unsurpassed by Beethoven, Bruckner, or Strauss (*Till Eulenspiegel*). 'While the Scherzo was a triumph of Mahlerian polyphony', 'an embarrassment of riches', Nodnagel considered that the Adagietto was the weakest piece Mahler had ever written 'although for the public it is at present the highlight of the symphony'. He had not hesitated to say as much to the composer, he wrote. Given the poor opinion Mahler had always had of Nodnagel's intellectual capacity, and his undoubted affection for the Adagietto, one can easily imagine his private reaction to this candid statement. Luckily all the foolishness he had heard concerning his works, as much from friends as from enemies, had taught him 'long ago not to let myself be put off, either by unjust reproach or stupid praise'.[143]

But with the Berlin press in full cry, Mahler was not in any position to quarrel with his most ardent defender. In the journal *Musikalisches Wochenblatt*, Adolf Schultze[144] stated bluntly that the Fifth was 'the weakest of all this Viennese composer's works', and deplored the disproportion which existed, in his view, between the length of the work and its 'spiritual content'. Only the Adagio was judged 'pleasant if not imposing'. Hugo Leichtentritt,[145] correspondent of the Leipzig *Neue Zeitschrift für Musik*, also wrote that he had been 'terribly disappointed', especially after having liked the Second Symphony so much. In his opinion, this time neither the melodic invention nor the handling of the orchestra held one's interest. Even the Funeral March sometimes tended towards the 'burlesque', the second movement was disconcerting; the Scherzo was nothing but a string of Viennese waltz tunes; the Adagietto was padded out with reminiscences of *Tristan* and Tchaikovsky; and the Finale, after a good start, got lost 'in digressions'. The whole 'lacked character', with the brass being given too important a role. The hostile reception which the work had met everywhere could not even be attributed to lack of understanding, for 'the harmony is easy to grasp, the melodies are very pleasant and the rhythms are not particularly complicated . . .'.

Thus contemporary listeners, professional as well as laymen, continued to dismiss the Fifth as incomprehensible. Even Mahler's admirers thought of the Adagietto as a weakness and a regrettable concession to public taste. Richard

---

[143]   See above, Mahler's letter to Ludwig Karpath (n. 116).

[144]   Adolf Schultze (1853–1923) had been director of the Luisen-Konservatorium in Berlin since 1890.

[145]   Hugo Leichtentritt (1874–1951), a German musicologist, began his studies in the United States and completed them at the Hochschule für Musik in Berlin. Later he taught at the Klindworth-Scharwenka Conservatory. After a monograph on Chopin (1905) he published a *History of the Motet* in 1908, then a *Busoni* (1916), an analysis of Chopin's piano works (1920), and an important *Händel* (1924). He emigrated to the United States in 1933 and taught for several years at Harvard.

Strauss, writing to Mahler on 5 March after the Berlin concert, shared this opinion:

Your Fifth Symphony again brought me great joy recently, at the final rehearsal, a pleasure only slightly diminished by the little Adagietto. That this movement should have pleased the audience most serves you right. The first two movements especially are marvellous. The brilliant Scherzo seemed to be a bit too long (*wirkte nur etwas zu lang*), but how much that was due to a somewhat inadequate performance I could not tell. At the dress rehearsal your work was a great success from beginning to end. I am told that at the concert itself the audience seemed somewhat less inclined to make the necessary intellectual effort, but that is not new to either of us. Nikisch put a lot of hard work into the symphony, and in my opinion did a good job, considering that German music is not really his line.[146]

In Prague, the first performance of the Fifth was conducted on 2 March by Leo Blech.[147] Despite the readiness of the citizens of the capital to hear modern music, the work was no more successful there than in Berlin or Dresden. The first and second parts of the Symphony were greeted with utter silence, while the final applause was described by the *Prager Tagblatt* as having been 'hesitant' and 'not undisturbed by signs of dissent'. However, both critics in the German language press noted that the 'storm' of applause which later greeted the Weber Overture was 'a sign that the audience wished to show its disapproval of Mahler's very long symphony'. Richard Batka, the music critic of the German-language newspaper *Bohemia*,[148] began his review with a description of the atmosphere in the hall, both before and during the concert:

What agitation at the Philharmonic Concert after Mahler's Fifth! It is a long time since a composition excited our audience as much as this one! During the performance some people were showing every sign of helpless despair; others' faces were lit up with rapture. In the corridors and the foyer there were passionate debates for and against. Some, wringing their hands, described how they had endured an hour and a half of musical torment; others gesticulated energetically to express the ecstasy they had felt. Some complained and protested, others praised and admired. 'Can that stuff really be called music?' 'Sheer agony for the ears! Nothing behind it all!' 'You would be in a better position to judge if you had listened more attentively!' Some struck their brows and admitted wearily: 'Actually, I didn't understand a thing!' Someone else claimed to have recognized quite clearly in the Finale the capture of Port Arthur. But it cannot be

---

[146] AMS and MSB 90. The letter also discusses arrangements for a concert of Mahler Lieder to take place the following June in Graz, as part of the festival of the Allgemeiner Deutscher Musikverein. The programme of the eighth Philharmonic Concert conducted by Arthur Nikisch on 20 Feb. was as follows: Mahler: Symphony No. 5; Cornelius: scene from the first act of *Gunlod*; Wagner: *Liebestod* from *Tristan und Isolde* (Katerina Fleischer-Edel, soprano). Nikisch had previously planned to conduct the Fifth Symphony in Dec. 1904, but the work had been dropped from the programme at the last minute.

[147] Programme of the fourth German Philharmonic Concert, at 7.30 p.m. on 2 Mar., conducted by Leo Blech: Mahler: Fifth Symphony; Giordani: aria: 'Caro mio ben'; Buononcini: aria: 'Per la gloria' (soloist Therese Behr, contralto); Weber: *Oberon* Overture; Schubert: Lieder, 'Der Zwerg' and 'Liebe schwärmt auf allen Wegen'; Wolf: Lieder, 'Die Zigeunerin' and 'Der Freund' (same soloist). As an encore, Therese Behr sang Tchaikovsky's song, 'Amid the Din of the Ball', Op. 38, No. 3.

[148] See above, Vol. ii, Chap. 16.

denied that on this occasion the majority was not on the composer's side. I cannot hold it against them; it is hard for the listener to find his way through this symphony.[149]

Batka declared himself incapable, after only one hearing, to pass judgement on 'such an ambitious, gigantic monument in sound' as the Fifth Symphony. He nevertheless proceeded to describe his impressions at considerable length. In the A flat episode of the Funeral March, it had seemed to him that 'in the midst of the most popular Traviata-style frivolities the veterans are also marching in the procession', and, in the following B flat minor episode, 'the violins shriek in a frenzied outburst of pain and the whole orchestra is shaken to its depths with howls and lamentations'. He confessed that he had been shocked, in the Allegro, by the recurrence of the 'Veteranmelodie' in the middle of 'the most solemn, passionate moments' of the whole movement. The Scherzo seemed to him to be the hardest of the five movements to understand: 'the frequent starting and stopping again soon makes one lose track of what is going on'. In the Adagietto, the 'voice of love', the 'quietly blissful and then utterly overwhelming feeling of almost religious adoration' had obviously captivated him. Like many of his contemporaries, he had experienced as a 'catharsis' in the Finale the alternating moods, 'vigorous double-fugue' and 'sweet kindliness', it had brought 'consolation and encouragement' after the violent emotions of the two first movements.

Despite Batka's reservations, he had attempted objectively to describe the feelings awakened in him by the Fifth Symphony, whereas the unsigned article in the *Prager Tagblatt*[150] merely condemned 'this extremely demanding, long drawn-out and over-elaborated' work and spoke of a 'tit-for-tat' arrangement between Mahler and Blech, whereby Blech had performed the Fifth only because his opera had just been performed by the Hofoper. It was wrong, the Prague critic claimed, to call Mahler's music 'difficult to understand' because so many of its features were traditional. Of the Funeral March, he writes: 'Whereas the contrapuntal texture of the first movement makes a thoroughly harmonious impression, it then becomes forced and over-clever, affected and almost cynically doctrinaire. The ear does not want and cannot stand so much over-refinement.' Only the Adagietto's lovely melody and the contrapuntal intricacies in the Finale are praised by the anonymous critic, but with the following reservations: 'But even for these [intricacies] one would rather quietly read the score, than have to listen to them, for music of this texture, coming as it does at the end of such a long spun-out work, could hardly find a fresh, unwearied ear left in the auditorium.'

The Czech musical journal *Dalibor* sounded a more favourable note. Assuredly, some passages in the symphony displayed 'the grossest banality and triviality' but they were to be taken as ironic. In the second theme of the

[149]   *Bohemia* (4 Mar. 1905), 2.
[150]   The article is signed 'Dr v. B'.

Funeral March, the anonymous critic discerned a Czech influence. But the climax of the whole work was undoubtedly the Scherzo, in which the motifs were 'finely and brilliantly elaborated', whereas the Adagietto undoubtedly belonged to 'the weakest moments' in Mahler's compositions. The article praised the Finale for its 'elegance', its 'internal strength', its 'emotional richness', its 'temperamental sweeps', its 'marvellous instrumentation', and 'its clarity in the use of the musical material'. The whole symphony was undoubtedly 'one of the greatest symphonic masterpieces of the recent years'.[151] The open-mindedness of the Czech press was no doubt what persuaded Mahler, three years later, to accept the offer he was to receive from Prague for the première of his Seventh Symphony.

For one listener at least, this concert confirmed an admiration born out of initial violent resistance some years earlier in Munich, at the first performance of the Fourth Symphony. William Ritter was then living in Prague and, unlike the majority of listeners, his devotion to Mahler was not diminished by the Fifth:

Those two performances [the Third in February 1904 and the Fifth in March 1905] obliged us to set foot in the German Theatre where, as passionate Czechophiles in this city, we could not really feel at ease. And this breach of our Czech rules of behaviour was expensive . . . But for Mahler . . .! And henceforth our admiration for this Master— whose acquaintance we still claimed we did not wish to make—took on a really *demonic* character . . . a word Mahler liked and which was, for him, synonymous with *dionysiac*. We wished to know only the work, the man was not on our side. And in those days we were stubborn. . . . But we were only retreating the better to advance. Already the Mahler chapter in our *Études d'Art étranger*, which had just come out, was bound to lead to the establishment of a personal relationship, which a very kind letter . . . plus a package containing the score of the Second Symphony 'as I didn't know it yet'— rendered inevitable.[152]

Ritter does not describe the audience's adverse reactions, as he had at the time of the Munich première of the Fourth. Yet, according to the *Prager Tagblatt*, whose opening dispairing remarks were quoted above, 'the audience did not allow itself to be swayed by the exhausted expression on the faces of the musicians'. The critic ridiculed the analysis of the work which had been circulated in Prague before the concert, in which Nodnagel claimed that Mahler had long been 'misunderstood' by the critics and by a few 'envious' people. What this music 'brought us and taught us was not as new as all that', the critic commented. The opening Funeral March, though 'modelled on that of *Siegfried*', was by far the best part; then, in the first of the following movements, the contrapuntal fabric took on 'forced airs of genius, became affected,

---

[151] *Dalibor*, 27 (1904–5), 17.
[152] William Ritter, 'Souvenirs sur Gustav Mahler', *Revue Musicale Suisse*, 101 (1960, I/II), 33. At this time, Ritter had met his life companion, Janko Cadra, a Slovak with whom he attended in 1906 all the rehearsals of the Sixth Symphony in Munich (see below, Chap. 7).

almost cynically doctrinaire. The ear does not want, and simply cannot stand, so much nauseating art.' As for the 'wild pandemonium', the masterly contrapuntal writing and 'brilliant colours' of the Finale, one would have preferred quietly to study the score rather than listen to them: coming as they did at the end of such a 'spun-out' work, they could not be absorbed by the exhausted listener.

Thus, the Prague performance was yet another failure to be debited to the account of the Fifth Symphony; and anybody other than Mahler might have been discouraged. Fortunately, the invitations to conduct his work which he continued to receive from all quarters proved to him that interest in it was far from waning. He was rarely able to accept these invitations, even though he knew full well that the chances of success with someone else conducting were minimal. In Moravia, Janáček's homeland, his music made its first appearance in the Philharmonic Concerts of Brno (Brünn) with a performance of the Second Symphony conducted by Karl Frotzler a few days before the Prague concert. According to the *Neue Musik-Zeitung*, the local press and public greeted the performance as a great event and considered the work 'monumental and exceptional in every way, grandly conceived, and full of colourful dramatic life, especially in the first and last movements, which are particularly original and which indicate Mahler's tremendous mastery and his ceaseless striving towards the highest ideals'.[153]

In February, the First Symphony was also badly received in Munich. Conducted by Bernhard Stavenhagen—whose interpretations Mahler had long since learned to distrust—the performance was doubtless poor. This concert provided yet another occasion for Rudolf Louis to affirm his German 'nationalist' opinion and to express his 'thorough dislike' of a composer who remained an 'eclectic' through and through. In Louis's eyes, Mahler's originality was for the most part not 'primary', i.e. not the result of special characteristics peculiar to his musical idiom, but 'secondary', i.e. it consisted of the masterly way in which he succeeded in blending the obvious 'foreign' elements in his musical discourse into a unified whole, and the skill with which he amalgamated the heterogeneous influences he had undergone (Beethoven, Schubert, Berlioz, Meyerbeer, Bruckner, Vienna folk music) and produced something specifically Mahlerian from the mixture. The symphony to his mind was 'interesting, witty, amusing, never boring—but unauthentic in the most profound sense of the word, artistic pinchbeck'. This became obvious immediately afterwards, upon hearing a work by Pfitzner (Dietrich's monologue from *Der arme Heinrich*), with which one returned to 'authentic and great art'.[154]

In a similar vein, Martin Kroyer, the Munich correspondent of *Die Musik*, considered Mahler's First 'a repulsive baroque banter in which a few gullible listeners once thought they perceived the dawn of a new era . . . What jokers!'

---

[153] The programme also included *L'Apprenti Sorcier* by Paul Dukas, and the soloist for 'Urlicht' was, as in Vienna in 1899, Marcella Pregi.   [154] *Münchner Neueste Nachrichten* (25 Mar. 1905).

In Berlin, on 13 April, the same First Symphony, led by the same conductor, was no better received: 'We have recently discovered a tableau more pathological than interesting, drawn out to infinite lengths, like an earthworm, which comes from the same source as the Fifth,' wrote the critic of the magazine *Roland von Berlin.*[155]

With so many failures behind him, Mahler's frame of mind must have been comparable to that in which he wrote, five or six years earlier, the following message to one of those rare listeners who had enjoyed one of his symphonies:

Dear Mr Trepplin, your letter gave me much pleasure, and I confess that I need such generous, unconditional approval, even though it may come only from a handful of people. May I tell you one thing: our time has been thoroughly spoiled for genuine music (I can see that from someone like you). Are there no people left who can hear a note of music without immediately asking what relationship it has to the real world. I beg you always to accept my music as nothing but music, which is the highest (and sometimes also the lowest) of ourselves which we feel we must communicate to others. Do as I do: make your mind a complete blank when you are listening, and leave the notes completely free to get over to you what they have to say. After a time you will comprehend the things in his life that compelled the composer to communicate with others.

What does music know of 'time'—the Middle Ages, etc.?

But I am grateful to you. The unspeakable lack of response from audiences is beginning to get me down, alas! So it gives me a nice warm feeling to have an example of what perhaps many others are thinking who don't trouble to get in touch with me.[156]

Good news nevertheless came to Mahler from an unexpected source. On the American continent, the first performance of the Fifth Symphony had been much better received in the month of May under the baton of Franz van der Stucken in Cincinnati. Unfortunately, the New World—and this far-off city of which Mahler had barely heard—meant little for him as yet.[157] An unsigned

---

[155] On 14 Apr. 1905, Kalman Feld conducted in Budapest the first Hungarian performance of Mahler's Third Symphony. The orchestra and chorus were those of the Hungarian National Opera and the soloist Therese Behr. Mahler later recommended Kalman Feld to Wilhelm Mengelberg, who needed an assistant conductor (see below, Chap. 7, n. 216).

[156] Thanks to the kindness of its present owner, Dr Wolfgang Heberlein, of Jona, Switzerland, I obtained a copy of this letter written to a certain correspondent named Georg Trepplin, of whom nothing further is known. It is undated, but since it mentions Barerstrasse, an important street in Munich, this Trepplin must have lived in Munich.

[157] The Fifth was performed twice in Cincinnati: on 24 Mar. 1905 as a matinee, and on the 25th in the evening. The programme included, after Mahler's symphony, the Piano Concerto in F Minor, Op. 16, by Georg Henselt (1814–89) (Fanny Bloomfield-Zeisler, soloist) and Wagner's *Kaisermarsch*. Franz van der Stucken (1858–1929), the second to conduct Mahler in the United States (after Walter Damrosch), was a conductor whose intercontinental career seems worth relating. Of Belgian origin—but with a German mother—he was born the son of a Confederate captain in Fredericksburg, Texas. Moving to Europe at the age of 8, he became a student of Carl Reinecke, and then of Peter Benoit in Belgium. While conducting at the Breslau Opera, he attracted the interest of Liszt and Grieg with his first compositions. Returning to the United States in 1884, he conducted the male choir of the Arion Concerts in New York, then the Novelty Concerts and finally the Symphony Concerts, until 1888. In 1889 he conducted the first European concert of American music at the International Exposition in Paris. From 1895 to 1907, he was permanent conductor of the Cincinnati Orchestra. He then moved back to Europe, where he toured frequently as a guest conductor.

article in the *Cincinnati Enquirer* gives the impression that this first hearing had been quite an event in this large industrial town with a strong German tradition. The critic, having first alluded to the controversy raging in Germany around the figure of Mahler, congratulated Van der Stucken on his promptness in putting on a work, 'which has just received its première with the Berlin Philharmonic, conducted by Nikisch'. For him, the symphony was not difficult to understand, for 'despite all this expansion there is no complexity, and the intentions of the composer are clear'. Yet 'the real inventive genius of Mahler and his command of poetic resources seem to have been best declared in the Adagietto, which is full of soul and romance and as lofty a slow movement as was ever written.' His 'wonderful command of orchestral colour' was as obvious as his 'flights of genius', even if at times 'there is a lack of proportion and of ultimate capacity to accomplish his intentions'.

The *Commercial Tribune* unhesitatingly described the Fifth Symphony as 'the most impressive and meritorious novelty' that Van der Stucken and his orchestra had ever presented. As for the *Times Star*, it admired the composer's 'marvellous cleverness' even if 'his too-frequent orchestral combinations cause the sincerity of the work to be questioned'. Only the German-language papers reproduced more or less word-for-word the clichés of their brethren across the Atlantic: 'reminiscences', 'orchestral din', 'an excess of technique', and 'contempt for aesthetic rules' in the *Freie Presse;* 'enigmatic', 'almost unbelievable dissonances and cacophony' in the *Volksblatt*, which nevertheless acknowledged the melodic charm of the Adagietto. Obviously, the German critics in Cincinnati were familiar with what their colleagues across the Atlantic had written, whereas the English-language reviewers, as in New York, had listened to the Fifth with an open mind and a fresh ear. Given this promising start, and the real successes obtained by this work the following year in Boston, New York, and Philadelphia during a tour by the Boston Symphony Orchestra,[158] it is surprising that no other symphony by Mahler had been performed in the United States before his arrival in New York two years later.

In Europe, Mahler was still attempting to conduct as many performances of his new symphony as possible without jeopardizing his position at the Vienna Opera. Two weeks after the Berlin concert he went to Hamburg, rejoicing to find an audience which had been his for six years, as well as more open-minded critics than in Berlin. Between two trains on his way through the Prussian capital, he spoke with Arnold Berliner, doubtless about the Nikisch concert and the recent failures of the Fifth. Alma, who once again had not been able to join him, was one of their main subjects of conversation.[159] Despite the migraine headache which had tormented him ever since his departure from Vienna, Mahler went to the Stadttheater as soon as he arrived in Hamburg and was no doubt moved, after eight years of absence, to return to an institution

---

[158]　See below, Chap. 5.　　　　　[159]　BGA, no. 128, dated 8 Mar. 1905.

which held so many memories for him. That evening *Carmen* was conducted by Gustav Brecher, but the cast was so mediocre that even the phlegmatic Demuth 'seemed like God the father'.[160] Mahler left the theatre after the second act to have dinner with his old friend, the actor Karl Wagner, and Gustav Brecher joined them at the end of the evening.

Three days later, Mahler attended a performance at the Schauspielhaus Theatre of *The Double Suicide*, a realist play by the Austrian author, Ludwig Anzengruber,[161] after which he dined again with Karl Wagner and the director of the Schauspielhaus, Alfred von Berger. At the time of Mahler's death, Berger, whose memories of the evening were still fresh six years later, described the 'fascinating spiritual fervour' with which he had conducted his Fifth Symphony, and recalled the 'enthusiasm—naive and unsoured by any pretention of criticism'—with which Mahler described his impressions of Anzengruber's play and expressed his views on theatre in general. Every word 'radiated intelligence and authentic artistic feeling'.[162]

The day after his arrival, Mahler went through the driving rain to the first rehearsal of his symphony. 'Today,' he wrote, 'I told myself over and over again: "O happy, oh happy a cobbler to be!"'[163] The Fifth is an accursed work. Nobody understands it! Fortunately, everything began to improve at the end.'[164] The same afternoon, Mahler set off, as he had promised his mother-in-law to do, in search of her sister, Alma Bergen, and her brother Willy. The search took a long time in the pouring rain, for he had been given a wrong house number and the street was a long one. When he finally met Alma Bergen, he was struck by her resemblance to Alma's mother, whom he held in great affection. His account of the visit could not have pleased Alma, who was ashamed of her mother's petit bourgeois origin and called her uncle Willy 'ein öder Philister' (a dull Philistine).[165] However, the exchanges between Mahler and Alma's relatives must have been limited in scope for he stayed away from them when they visited Vienna later that year. On the other hand, renewing acquaintance with his old friend and admirer Hermann Behn was a happy experience. Behn 'has visited me with all his cordiality of earlier days' and constantly 'looks after me like a father'. He also saw the Hertzes, other old friends from Hamburg days, who kept looking at him 'with tears in their eyes', so happy were they to see

---

[160] BGA, no. 129, undated (9 Mar. 1905). The Carmen was Katerina Fleischer-Edel, and the Micaëla, Ottilie Metzger (who had sung guest performances at the Vienna Opera in 1901). The Don José, Josef Thyssen, had also appeared as a guest there in Jan. 1905.

[161] Ludwig Anzengruber (1839–89) was born in Vienna, the son of a modest employee of peasant origins. Before he became a writer, he worked in a travelling theatrical company. His works, on folk subjects, are rough and naive in manner. They include fourteen plays, as well as short stories and novels.

[162] *Neue Freie Presse*, 19 May 1911. Alfred von Berger was appointed director of the Burgtheater in 1908. He had hoped to meet Mahler again in Vienna, only to learn that he had already left for New York.

[163] Paraphrase of an aria from *Zar und Zimmermann* by Lortzing (see above, Chap. 1).

[164] BGA, no. 130, undated (10 Mar. 1905).

[165] The members of Alma's family then living in Hamburg included Anna Moll's brother Willi and his wife Martha, Anna's sister, Alma, and a younger sister named Bertha.

him again.[166] Gustav Brecher attended all the rehearsals of the Fifth, and Mahler felt that the young conductor had improved in every way since his early setback and departure from Vienna, in 1901.[167]

When he had agreed to come and conduct what was to be his second performance of the Fifth, Mahler demanded four rehearsals in addition to those conducted before his arrival by Max Fiedler.[168] The first two were particularly difficult, not through any fault of Fiedler's, who had done his work conscientiously, but because of the mediocrity of the orchestra itself. Yet, as usual, Mahler had found it 'extremely important' that the performance should be impeccably prepared, for the Hamburg public was 'critical and still totally unfamiliar with my creative side (*meiner Muse*)'.[169] Fortunately, the psychological conditions were excellent. 'Yesterday, the musicians were still a bit disturbed. Today they were perfectly at ease and showed real enthusiasm. The seats are sold out, for the interest caused by my concert is, of course, greater than usual; after all, for six years I was at the centre point of musical life here.'[170] He was delighted with the final rehearsal: 'the orchestra has behaved superbly, and is already completely won over to my work,' he wrote to Alma.[171]

In Hamburg, Mahler spent much of his time with the poet Richard Dehmel and his wife, Isi, who were living in Blankensee, on the outskirts of the city, and who had postponed a trip they had planned in order to attend the rehearsals and the concert.[172] It is thus clear that the unpleasant scene reported by Alma had not cast any shadow on their relationship. A few days before leaving for Vienna,[173] Mahler wrote to the poet:

[166]   BGA, no. 130, undated (9 Mar. 1905). Concerning Gustav Brecher, see above Vol. ii, Chap. 4.
[167]   Ibid.
[168]   On Max Fiedler, see above Vol. i, Chap. 20. Ferdinand Pfohl, in his reminiscences on Mahler, expatiates on relations between Mahler and Fiedler, claiming that Mahler had developed a strong dislike for him when he was in Hamburg, and called him a 'Schlaucherl' (Mr Fixit). Fiedler, who taught piano at the Bernuth Conservatory, was at that time just beginning to conduct. He had founded a women's choir of society ladies which occasionally gave concerts. According to Pfohl, Mahler found this irritating, and was wont to call him 'an arrivist, an incompetent and a charlatan, trying to push his way into Hamburg society and make a name for himself through the influence of rich women, with the aim of preparing his future position as an orchestral conductor'. According to Pfohl, Fiedler later proved how unfair Mahler had been to him when he took over the Philharmonic Orchestra. As usual, Pfohl's statements are unreliable, since he had taken such a dislike to Mahler in recent years.
[169]   Undated letter from Mahler to Henri Hinrichsen, 10 Dec. 1904. This is the letter in which Mahler had warned his publisher against letting Stavenhagen conduct the Fifth Symphony in Leipzig and Munich (see above, Chap. 1). Mahler had at first intended to conduct a concert in Hamburg on 11 Apr. the preceding year, but the plan came to nothing (ÖTM, HOA, G.Z. 318/1904). Mahler expressed anxiety about the reception he was likely to get in Hamburg 'from a totally Philistine subscription audience', and in Berlin 'where the press is ill-disposed toward me'.
[170]   Unpublished, undated letter to Anna Moll (9 Mar. 1905), copy in BGM, Paris.
[171]   BGA, no. 131, undated (10 Mar. 1905).
[172]   In a letter to Mahler of 5 Mar. 1905, Dehmel plans a rendezvous after the rehearsal on Sat. 11 Mar. The message he addressed to Alma at the end of the letter is characteristic of his somewhat precious style: 'I raise to my lips the fingertips of her soul' (AMM1, 117 and 118).
[173]   Despite the number and warmth of the letters exchanged between the Mahlers and the Dehmels at the beginning of 1905, their friendship was short-lived. At the beginning of Sept., a month before a projected visit to Vienna, Dehmel sent Mahler a letter and the score of a comic opera set to a text of his by the Frankfurt composer Hermann Zilcher (1881–1948). He gave a great deal of information about the work,

Dear Mr Dehmel! I have long felt a twinge of contrition at my failure to give you any sign of life since your friendly Christmas package. Your wife's kind letter proves that you don't hold my ingratitude against me. I send you my heartfelt thanks, for the package and for your indulgence. Perhaps you know already from your own experience (assuming that you are just as bad a correspondent as I) that such a letter, once put off, is never written at all. I delayed my apologies until my arrival in Hamburg and relied on seeing you there. I am most grateful to you for postponing your departure on my account. What would I do with the Hamburg audience if you were not among them?[174]

At first Mahler was invited to dine with the Dehmels on 11 March at the Hotel Streit, but he asked them by telegram to postpone the meeting until the next day, before the final rehearsal, because of a 'frightful migraine'. Frau Dehmel has fortunately left a detailed summary of the discussion that she and her husband had with Mahler on that occasion. One of the main topics was the ever-recurring notion of 'national' feeling in art. The art critic Julius Meier-Gräfe,[175] a close friend of the Dehmels, had been exasperated by the constant harping by art critics and others on the ill-defined concept of 'Germanness' (which Meier-Gräfe called 'Deutschtümelei'). He decided, together with Dehmel, to draw up a list of questions to be sent to a number of artists, critics, and even politicians, whose answers would then be published in book form. The stated aim of the two authors was to 'ask questions in a way that will bring out clearly the degree to which national sentiment should, or should not, play a part in aesthetic questions'. 'In fact,' wrote Meier-Gräfe to Dehmel, 'the point is naturally to combat Wagnerian ideas directly, inasmuch as they are not based on music but on silly notions, to combat Thode as well,[176] and to decide to what extent certain foreign influences can be accepted.' Meier-Gräfe sent to Dehmel the proofs of the introductory text and the questionnaire itself, suggesting that Dehmel ask Hauptmann, and a fourth person still to be chosen, to add their signatures.

In a lengthy introduction, the signatories noted that:

among the arguments used today in cultural matters, none recur so often, and in so many areas of thought, as the concept of nationality, . . . as if it were an absolute, and not a relative, notion, . . . something permanent and immutable. Such a notion must

which he suggested could have its première in Vienna at the time of the carnival in Feb. 1906, with designs by Roller; Mahler's answer was negative (AMS and AMM1, 354). The Dehmel archive in the Hamburg Staats- und Universitätsbibliothek contains three further notes from Mahler written on 26, 27, and 28 Oct. 1905 in Vienna concerning a meal at the Auerbruggergasse, to which he had invited the poet and his wife, and which did not take place. Finally the Dehmels left Vienna without seeing the Mahlers.

[174] Undated letter from Mahler, on which the poet or his wife wrote '5 Mar.' (Staats- und Universitätsbibliothek, Hamburg).

[175] Julius Meier-Gräfe (1867–1935), historian and critic, specialist in nineteenth-century French painting and zealous champion of Impressionism, is today known mainly for having rediscovered El Greco. He founded in 1894 the 'Pan' Society, and the review of the same name, with Dehmel and Bierbaum. His principal work is an *Entwicklungsgeschichte der modernen Kunst* in three volumes (1914–24), but he also wrote books on Böcklin, Delacroix, Corot, Renoir, Degas, Manet, Valloton, Cézanne, and van Gogh.

[176] See above (in this chapter) the biography of Henry Thode.

necessarily cast its shadow on important cultural issues, on many questions of politics and social economy, and above all on the world of thought and culture, and it will seriously prejudice all attempts at clarifying such problems. We find that it is in the most confused cultural sphere in Germany—namely art—that the dogma is most clearly formulated. Indeed, it is perhaps the cause of the confusion. We may suppose therefore, that by elucidating the situation, we could clarify many ideas. If Menzel's words are correct, that 'an improvement of criticism would also improve art,' then we might raise our sights even higher, especially if we do not limit the range of our reflection to art and art criticism . . .

The famous questionnaire contained a number of questions designed to bring out the absurdity of nationalistic considerations. For example:

'Are forms of culture stable? If not, which is the stronger factor in their development: the racial character of each nation, or the international, humane, cosmopolitan ideal?' 'Have there ever been exclusively national cultures? Or does every mature culture aspire to cosmopolitan importance?' 'Is there a typically German culture today? What are its characteristics?' 'Do Wagner's artistic creations show evidence of his nationalistic dogmas? Have they advanced German music? Or perhaps, German culture?'

Events showed that Meier-Gräfe and Dehmel had touched a particularly sensitive nerve, since Germany at the time was already in the process of forging, on the basis of Wagner's well-known 'doctrines', and of Nietzschean philosophy as misrepresented by his heirs, a new ideology which was later to have the most terrifying consequences. If the artists and politicians solicited had answered sincerely, the questionnaire would have pinpointed the disastrous consequences of Wagnerism and of the anti-Semitism which already characterized a large section of contemporary criticism, and of which Mahler was so frequent a victim. But the very idea of responding to such a document elicited violent reactions from the Germans, and Meier-Gräfe, himself a Jew, was soon obliged to abandon the project, and to declare his profound disgust for 'German hypocrisy' and 'the incredible cowardly meanness with which I am treated here'.[177]

In the realm of music, the nationalist theories propounded during the Romantic era were raised to the level of dogma by Wagner. In Mahler's time, however, neo-Romantic composers such as Pfitzner and Schillings still fervently adhered to them. During his socialist period Mahler pushed his Wagnerian convictions to some lengths, even to the point of becoming a vegetarian, but by now he had overcome such youthful aberrations. He knew he was Jewish and, brought up in a German cultural context, he had always admired Czech, Russian, Italian, and French music enough not to consider Germany as the sole source of all truth and beauty. It would be hard to imagine Mahler, for example, making the statement Schoenberg made (on inventing twelve-tone

[177] Two letters from Meier-Gräfe to Dehmel, dated 26 Feb. and 26 June 1905, have survived among the poet's papers at the same Hamburg Library, along with copies of the questionnaire.

music): 'I have made a discovery which will ensure the supremacy of German music for the next hundred years.'[178]

Quite apart from his Jewishness—a greater burden for Mahler than for Schoenberg—and even though his admiration for Wagner the musician and the man never diminished, Mahler was too much a citizen of the world to share the reactionary views of the Pfitzners and Schillings. It would be interesting to know details of the conversations he had at this time, not only with Dehmel but also with Hauptmann or Pfitzner. Frau Isi informs us that his position was 'firm and precise', and that it pleased both the Dehmels, but that he disapproved of all surveys like Meier-Gräfe's, because he found them 'superfluous'. In any case, he refused to take sides because, as a Jew, he would immediately be attacked on all sides. In any event, his own mode of expression is 'in music rather than words, which I wield with frightening clumsiness, and against my will'. 'Perhaps I would write more often if I wrote better,' he added, 'but I don't think so: Wagner's example puts me off! What use are all his volumes of writings? To love and appreciate Wagner's genius at his true value you must forget them completely.'

The same evening, Mahler complained to the Dehmels of the 'endless journeys' he had to make. 'But you do it all the same, in order to look after your children', Frau Dehmel told him. To which he replied:

Do you mean those of my body, or those of my mind? For I have to look after both. Actually, I would be happy to live only from my musical compositions, and frankly I am beginning to neglect my duties at the Opera. But I must make up for the reduction in my high earnings as conductor at the Hofoper in some other way, for instance through guest conducting.[179] I am really curious to know if the performance of my works will ever bring me a penny. That is one of the reasons for my journeys, but there is another: the Fifth was recently performed in Prague and Berlin, and both times it had no effect whatsoever. So I thought: 'You must figure out whether this is the fault of the symphony or of the conductor!' Now I know, for in Hamburg it made a big impression. We musicians are worse off than poets in this respect; everyone can read, whereas the printed score is a book with seven seals. Even the conductors who can read it present the work to the public impregnated with their own, different, conceptions. So a tradition has to be created—and only I can do that![180]

At the Hamburg concert the Dehmels were encountering Mahler's music for the first time. They attended the rehearsals as well as the concert, and the

---

[178] See Willi Reich, *Arnold Schönberg oder der Konservative Revolutionär* (Molden, Vienna, 1968), 173, and Hans Heinz Stuckenschmidt, *Schönberg, Leben, Umwelt, Werk* (Atlantis, Zurich, 1974), 252.

[179] Mahler's statement here is somewhat obscure. Indeed, if he had travelled less he could have conducted more performances at the Opera, which would have augmented the 'performance' allowances to his fixed salary. We have seen that during his first three seasons as director he conducted 111, 105, and 97 performances respectively. In the 1900–1 season, that of his haemorrhage and his operation, the number fell to 53, a total which he thereafter only exceeded once, during the Mozart year. The totals for performances conducted by him at the Hofoper from 1901 onwards were: 1901–2—36; 1902–3—53; 1903–4—38; 1904–5—41; 1905–6—57; 1906–7—44.

[180] AMM1, 119; AMM2, 120.

whole experience was for them a veritable 'revelation', as witness Frau Isi's enthusiastic comments:

If at first Mahler the man made me believe in Mahler the musician, I now believe so firmly in the musician that I forgive him his all too human weaknesses. As a musician I would call him a genius, sparing as I am with the term. The Fifth Symphony led me through the whole gamut of emotions (*Empfindungswelten*). In it I heard the mature man in his relationship to everything that lives; I heard him cry out in his solitude to other beings, to one being, to a homeland, to God: I saw him almost succumb; I heard him laugh defiantly and felt him serious in victory. In the second movement I cried for the first time in my life before a work of art, as if some strange contrition were forcing me to my knees. I could have done without the Adagietto, and the effort of comprehension required for the last movement interfered somewhat with my enjoyment. Yet this symphony is a masterpiece of the highest order and it was precisely in the Finale that I became passionately interested, after hearing it a second time—I devoured every note.

Earlier, Mahler had explained to the Dehmels that the Scherzo, composed before the rest of the symphony, would doubtless appear incomprehensible to them, for 'no critic has yet been able to understand it'. But Brecher and Dehmel were 'profoundly impressed', as were most of the public, whose reaction was particularly warm, both at the final rehearsal and at the concert. The applause at the end drowned out the catcalls of a few malcontents. The following day, the tone of the reviews was, with few exceptions, courteous, and often even admiring. Emil Krause, who ten years earlier had so often fulminated against Mahler the conductor, now stood resolutely by the composer and ranked him in the *Fremden-Blatt* with Richard Strauss among the representatives of the 'extreme avant-garde of contemporary artistic creation'. Krause discerned in Mahler the influence of Bruckner, 'with the same sprightly wealth of modulation, the same liberty in the construction of parts within the whole, the same energy in the accomplishment of his aim'. For Krause, 'the summit of all of Mahler's music and of all music today' was the first movement of the Second Symphony: the composer of such a piece deserved 'a leading place among the great men of our time'. Mahler's freedom of expression was 'the fruit of the inspiration of the moment', and each thought was born 'with its own strength'. Of course, Mahler wanted at all costs to 'create something new and break with the past', but thanks to his 'spiritual richness', and to 'that warmth that comes from the heart', each of his compositions was 'a manifestation of some degree of genius'. And the same could be said of his orchestral conducting.

After having described the new work in detail, Krause expressed his preference for the first movement, 'the most accomplished of all'. The second movement, with its 'passionate theme', seemed 'studied rather than natural'. Krause praised the Scherzo and 'the endless new counterpoints which surround its themes', then the Adagietto, 'captivating and full of inner warmth'.

Finally, he felt that no objective witness could fail to see in the Fifth a 'powerful work', a 'veritable instrumental poem which expresses only itself'. Mahler never introduced a motif 'without developing it and leading it to its conclusion'. 'When invention is lacking and Mahler evokes other styles, his genius for development (*Ausgestaltung*) takes over.' Difficult as it might be to predict the durability of a work, this one was in any event 'worthy of the highest regard'.

In the *Hamburger Nachrichten*, Ferdinand Pfohl, who had been Mahler's friend ten years earlier in Hamburg, but whose memoirs bear witness to the gradual souring of their relationship,[181] took up a position opposite to that of all the other critics, praising Mahler as a 'great musician', a 'phenomenal master of all the technical means of his art', and a soul imbued with

magical powers, with a touching inwardness (*Innigkeit*), with clear simplicity and with the most subtle refinement—but also with the superb deceitfulness of a pathos springing from the consciousness of his own power. The vehemence of his feelings and of his explosive temperament is such that it stirs up the sediment and all the yeast in the corners of his nature, and this rises unchecked and spreads in cloudy veils through the clear torrent of his music. Mingled into the tragedy of man's suffering and redemption, eternal theme of his symphonies, there is, strangely enough, a bitter, sulphuric grace and a mephistophelian irony—a violent and sometimes malicious humour which degenerates into the comic and grotesque.

Pfohl then evoked in this context the Callot 'fantasies', 'a strong influence' in Mahler's works and a reflection of his personality, about which Pfohl had many reservations, as we already know.

The man who in these works holds a dialogue with himself is not a happy one . . . Mahler, a genius? Certainly an outstanding personality, an exceptionally gifted artist . . . But in his humanity or his music I find nothing of that high moral sense, of stark truth or of powerful necessity which are the holy marks of a genius. Of all his works, the Fifth is one of the weakest. It parades the poverty and insignificance of its ideas with the pride and ostentation of a king who puts on rags in order to impress his subjects all the more once he appears in full vestimentary pomp, with sceptre and crown.[182]

In the Fifth Pfohl ultimately admired only the 'dazzling, marvellous, sunlit' virtuosity of the Finale, which was the 'most important and the most satisfying' movement. He characterized all the rest as 'dreary, unpleasant, atrocious, awkward', 'the painful combat of a titanesque will with a faltering creative power'. Mahler borrowed from everywhere 'without choice and without scruple', using even 'street songs'. The theme of the first movement, 'a funeral march for *Der Trompeter von Säkkingen*', was 'an error of taste without equal in

[181] See above, Vol. i, Chap. 20 and Vol. ii, Chap. 9.
[182] Ferdinand Pfohl, *Gustav Mahler: Eindrücke und Erinnerungen aus den Hamburger Jahren*, ed. Knud Martner (Musikalienhandlung, Hamburg, 1973), 72.

all symphonic literature'. With its Verdian sixths and thirds, it could have been composed for 'an Italian opera tenor'. 'Second- or third-hand music, ugly and barren', 'unbearable', a 'desecration of the sacred spirit of music', 'grimaces, tragi-comic distortions . . .'. Pfohl's attitude seemed unchanged since the unflattering portrait he painted in his memoirs of Mahler in Hamburg. It is not surprising that he refused Behn's invitation to a dinner given in Mahler's honour, and that he even brushed off Behn's overture to him—made through Gustav Brecher—with the following words, as he later recalled himself: 'I am too accustomed to pure air to wish to be in a room with Mahler, breathing the same pestilential atmosphere.'

The underlying causes of this transformation of what had been friendship, or at least camaraderie, into implacable hate, are still somewhat mysterious. It seems that towards the end of Mahler's time in Hamburg, Pfohl had the impression that Mahler was manipulating him or using him, notably in the unfortunate affair of the lawsuit brought against Josef Sittard.[183] But it is also possible that his animosity had another, secret cause, for the reasons Pfohl enumerates are insufficient to account for his violent animosity. When Behn, on hearing from Brecher of the *Nachrichten* critic's reply, went to see him and to ask for an explanation, Pfohl advised him to 'watch out for Mahler, and for your own gullibility where he is concerned'. The following year, in Essen, he was staying in the same hotel as Mahler when by chance he caught sight of him in one of the corridors, deep in conversation with their mutual friend Otto Neitzel. 'I put on a completely hostile attitude, feigning icy indifference. Otto Neitzel rushed over, saying, "Have you met Gustav Mahler?" I declined his introduction with the words, "Only too well, unfortunately" and turned away.'

At the end of his *Erinnerungen* Pfohl acknowledges that when he heard of Mahler's premature death he regretted the way he had behaved, 'which was not nearly so much a manifestation of my nature as a response, a very understandable echo, arising from Mahler's conduct, not towards me, but towards many worthy people and worthwhile artists'. Thus Pfohl's dislike was, in his own view, due to the way Mahler had treated his old Hamburg friends after his appointment to Vienna. However, their relationship had become cool well before his departure for Austria, and that this coolness probably stemmed from a basic incompatibility of character, for other old Hamburg friends, like Berliner and the Behns, remained loyal to Mahler to the end.

On this occasion, however, Pfohl's disparagement was the exception rather than the rule among the Hamburg critics. Writing for the *Hamburgischer Correspondent*, Max Julius Löwengard[184] defended the symphony with great

---

[183] See above, Vol. i, Chap. 20.

[184] Max Julius Löwengard (1860–1915), student of Joseph Raff in Frankfurt, began his career as a conductor. Appointed professor at the Wiesbaden Conservatory and then at the Scharwenka Conservatory in Berlin (where he remained until 1904), critic for the *Börsenzeitung* and then replacement for Sittard in the *Correspondent* of Hamburg, Löwengard was also the author of several books on the theory of music.

conviction. He congratulated the composer of the Fifth on 'following his own path without looking to the right or to the left':

In Mahler, some can never pardon the master of monumental thematic structure and of orchestral expression for suddenly composing totally naive music and contenting himself with the most primitive means of expression. Others resent him because—with all his love for naive music—he treats them to profound problems, with violent bursts of passion, and that in a language which is anything but naive. The essential greatness of Mahler lies exactly in this apparent juxtaposition of fundamentally different means of expression. To those who possess facile inventiveness and a strong melodic vein, great art is generally denied. Their melodic instinct keeps them close to the surface, and does not allow them to penetrate to the most profound depths. Conversely, those who want to dig to the very foundations of their art and build only with blocks of hewn stone easily lose the sense of happy melodic construction—if ever they had it in the first place. This is why some doubt the authenticity of an art which presents itself as both naive and profound, why they suspect one or other tendency to be insincere. They refuse to admit and to understand in Mahler what they eventually accepted in Bruckner.

Here, identified and analysed with exemplary lucidity by Löwengard in 1905, is one of the most disturbing aspects of Mahler's music, this fundamental paradox which it always presents, and which at the time was considered the most obvious proof of his creative impotence. Indeed, some considered Mahler a naive composer who had strayed into that most serious and profound of all genres, the symphony, while others considered him an over-intelligent, hyper-sophisticated composer and peerless orchestral technician who went against his nature by writing falsely naive music. As for the absence of a 'programme', Löwengard points out that 'all true art is based on personal experience', and that in that sense Mahler's music did have a programme. 'But that does not mean that each of his symphonies describes a chapter in the life of an opera director. The Fifth is not a *roman à clef*: it is true, authentic music, born of powerful emotion, moulded (*gestaltet*) by a powerful mind and a strong hand.' His counterpoint, authentic and made up of truly independent voices, did not engender 'fortuitous encounters' but rather led with 'compelling logic towards the harmonic unities'. The most outstanding aspect of his 'brilliant treatment of the orchestra' is that, even where he obtains the most breathtaking sound effects, one feels 'only the emotion that has produced them and not that they were honed to produce a certain effect'.

For the first time the majority of the Hamburg critics sided with Mahler, and pronounced the Fifth a masterpiece, which had never happened before. Even Heinrich Chevalley, whose article in *Die Musik* proves that he understood nothing of the new work, congratulated his fellow citizens for having fêted their 'great man of former times' and having accorded him a 'colossal personal success' less than ten years after 'crowning him with thorns'.[185]

---

[185] The second part of the programme of the fourteenth Philharmonic Concert on 13 Mar. included Beethoven's Eighth Symphony, conducted by Max Fiedler.

Returning to Vienna via Berlin, Mahler travelled with Isi Dehmel on the train and told her of his joy at the first true success of his Fifth, and also that it had happened in Hamburg, a city of capital importance in his life and career. Their conversation then turned to Strauss. Mahler regretted that the salesman in Strauss should so often have taken precedence over the artist, and that in the case of a conflict between these two sides of him, the former nearly always got the upper hand. Frau Dehmel read in Mahler's words a touch of envy at Strauss's triumphs, particularly his material success. Mahler went on to speak 'with scorn, with disgust even' of Strauss's relationship with his wife Pauline; the puritan in him was shocked by the 'masochism—there was no other word for it'—which seemed to characterize Strauss' attitude to his wife.

Frau Dehmel then told Mahler of a recent visit she had made to Pauline in Pankow in the company of Harry Graf Kessler[186] and Hugo von Hoffmannsthal. Pauline had surpassed herself that day in 'tactlessness, indiscretion, and bad manners'. She declared that the main thing was for her 'to keep men firmly on the leash', and added that each year, when she and her husband and child spent two months on her parents' estate 'and lived off my money', she made sure to make up for it on their return to Berlin by skimming the equivalent off her husband's salary in order to buy jewellery ('You understand, HIS money,' she underlined). Then, when she heard Kessler speaking with Strauss in the next room and praising *Also sprach Zarathustra*, she exploded with fury: 'And they've got the nerve to encourage him to write pieces no one wants to play? Whom do they please? One or two people! In any case not me, because I can't make any sense of them at all. He should sit down and write pieces that will be played everywhere!'

Given the number of anecdotes of this kind which have come down to us, it is tempting to speculate whether Pauline had not deliberately decided, not without a twisted sense of humour, to play the role of the untamed shrew.[187] However, Willy Schuh, Strauss's biographer, when questioned by the author of these lines about Pauline's character, declared her behaviour always to have been the genuine, direct, and totally uninhibited expression of a fiery temperament. Nothing in the writings of Alma, in Mahler's letters, or Isi Dehmel's diary, indicates that Pauline's contemporaries ever suspected her of putting on an act. Most of them speak of her with profound and righteous indignation.

Leaving the subject of the Strauss couple, Mahler and Isi began talking about the Hauptmanns, and Mahler said that he found Grete selfish and cold.[188] Finally they came to speak of Alma, and Isi's comments must have

---

[186] Harry, Graf Kessler (1868–1937), diplomat and writer, art collector and patron of art, was an intimate friend of Richard Strauss and co-author, with Hoffmannsthal, of the libretto of the ballet, *Josephs-Legende*.

[187] According to people who knew Pauline, Strauss's very detailed portrait of her in his libretto for *Intermezzo* was absolutely accurate (see below, Chap. 8). In it, she appears totally devoid of humour, at least concerning herself.

[188] 'Such statements are not agreeable for me to hear,' writes Frau Dehmel in her diary (later published by Alma in her *Erinnerungen*), for she was doubtless a good friend of Grete Hauptmann.

later on delighted Mahler's widow for she subsequently reproduced them in her *Erinnerungen*.

I had already spoken to him of his wife for her sunny nature had left us with a wonderful impression. He accepted this with pleasure and added that she had also made all the piano versions of his symphonies.[189] Some might find that marvellous, but I found it a little too utilitarian. In short, the man I took for a genius considers himself a highly sensitive instrument and, for that reason, protects himself with the spiked collar of egotism.[190]

In fact, Mahler's main concern when waxing idyllic about his relationship with Alma was to conceal the hidden conflicts and intimate problems he was facing and the worries these caused him. He never said a word on the subject to anyone other than his closest friends, and was to take with him to his grave most of the secrets which only Alma's diary permits us to glimpse here and there. However egocentric he might have been—and that is one of the leitmotivs of Alma's diary—he always shunned, in front of others, any exercise of masculine authority over her, and even more, of artistic authority. He wanted to be seen to treat her and to think of himself as treating her always as his equal. Finally, and more or less consciously, he no doubt hoped that the image which Alma and he presented to the world might become a model to which both of them would henceforth have to conform, an irreversible step as it were towards that harmony *à deux* which he so ardently desired.

[189] Here Isi Dehmel's memory is of course at fault. Alma had copied the orchestra scores of Symphonies No. 5 and 6, but had never transcribed any of Mahler's symphonies for piano.

[190] AMM1, 122; AMM2, 123.

3

Mahler in Vienna (XIX)—Pfitzner in Vienna—
Die Rose vom Liebesgarten—The Strasbourg Festival
(March–May 1905)

When a tempo seems wrong to you, just prod me in the back and put me
right. Don't worry about me losing face in front of the orchestra. After
all, you know it better than I—you composed it.

DURING the long weeks of preparation for the first Viennese performance of Pfitzner's opera *Die Rose vom Liebesgarten*, two one-act comic
operas, both based upon rococo librettos, were premièred at the Hofoper by
Mahler. The first, *Das war ich*, was composed by Leo Blech,[1] whom Mahler
a few years earlier had considered engaging as a conductor at the Hofoper
because he had given up hope of persuading Bruno Walter to take on the
job. The second was a 'musical conversation' entitled *Die Abreise* by Eugen
d'Albert, whose *Tragadalbas* Mahler had earlier refused. D'Albert had
proposed the little work to him in 1902,[2] and Mahler had no doubt searched
for another one-act opera which could successfully share the bill with *Die
Abreise* and it was only in 1904 that he had found it in Blech's *Das war ich*.
When the two operas were first performed on 28 February 1905, *Das war
ich* was greeted with catcalls by the audience and condemned by the critics. Blech was reproached for his 'surfeit of polyphony' and 'symphonic
megalomania' (Korngold), the 'colourless' themes (Wallaschek), his 'pretentious style' (Schönaich), his 'contrived humour' and 'lack of inventiveness'
(Graf). Karpath accused him of using 'the heavy artillery of an exaggerated
neudeutsch orchestra'. Hirschfeld thought that Blech 'had studied Wagner in
a manual written by Humperdinck', and that he had caused his singers to

---

[1] See above, Vol. ii, Chap. 16, for Leo Blech's biography and a list of his operas. On 30 Jan. 1905,
Mahler asked the Intendant for the money required (100 kronen) to invite Blech to attend the final rehearsals
of *Das war ich* and conduct the première (ÖTM, HOA, Z. 430/1905). He finally conducted the première
himself.   [2] See above, Chap. 1.

'shout' unpleasantly. Only Max Kalbeck called Blech a 'musician of distinction whom one can reckon with in future'.[3]

Die Abreise, on the other hand, was well received by the audience and the critics. Hirschfeld found that, though d'Albert's music lacked personality, it was perfectly constructed and appealed to 'the inner musical sense'. Schönaich found it 'refined (*vornehm*) but not affected'; 'ironic music' of 'no great originality', though 'subtle and cultivated'. Wallaschek judged it to be 'too lacklustre and monotonous to touch the heart, but nevertheless honest and decent, like the subject'. For Max Graf, *Die Abreise* was a 'pleasant, charming work by a musician of taste and culture', and he particularly praised the performance: 'full of grace, charm and agility', it reminded one 'of the Burgtheater'.[4]

A few months later d'Albert wrote to Mahler:

Thank you from the bottom of my heart for the great joy you gave me in producing *Die Abreise* in Vienna. I found the performance perfect in every respect. Under your masterly direction the orchestra achieved a magic sonority. All was so clear and transparent, in a way I have never heard before. The rendition of the three roles literally enchanted me. As I have already said, I cannot imagine a more ideal performance, and I hope all the more ardently that another work of mine may be performed under your direction.[5]

D'Albert's wishes would have been fulfilled if Mahler had conducted *Tiefland* in 1908. Unfortunately, he had already left Vienna at the time of its Viennese first performance.

During the 1904–5 season the usual conflicts occurred at the Hofoper, this time only with singers who had been refused leave of absence to sing elsewhere. Despite previous disputes, few of which had turned out to his advantage, Leo Slezak was determined to appear as a guest in other houses and thus earn extra money. In April, at the height of the season, he wrote directly to the Intendant to ask for five weeks' leave, because his Vienna salary no longer enabled him to make ends meet. He threatened to resign immediately if his request was refused. Since his contract had four more years to run, Mahler was obviously not going to give way. He reminded Slezak that he had never refused to grant him sick leave; he could not now dispense with his services for five weeks, especially since he had already several times given him permission to sing abroad.[6]

---

[3] Cast for *Das war ich* on 28 Feb. 1905: Kiurina (Röschen); Pohlner (Martha); Petru (Neighbour); Leuer (Peter); and Moser (Paul). The libretto was written by the Austrian critic Richard Batka. This performance marked Berta Kiurina's debut at the Hofoper. The evening concluded with the première of the ballet *Die roten Schuhe* by Raoul Mader (1856–1940), a sometime répétiteur at the Vienna Opera.

[4] The cast for the performance on 28 Feb. included: Gutheil-Schoder (Luise), Schrödter (Trott), Weidemann (Gilfen). Mahler cut out the final scene in which husband and wife, now reconciled, take tea together.

[5] Letter from Eugen d'Albert to Mahler, 27 Nov. 1905 (HOA, Z. 1233/1905). Mahler conducted d'Albert's *Flauto Solo* in Nov. 1906 (see below, Chap. 7).

[6] The Intendant forwarded Slezak's letter to Mahler on 15 Apr. 1904. Mahler replied the same day, explaining to the Intendant his grounds for refusing Slezak's request. On 22 Apr. the Intendant sent Slezak a letter refusing either to grant him an increase in salary, or to release him from his contract (HOA, Z. 1886/1904 and Z. 1464, 2 Apr. 1904).

Many years later, Slezak, with his usual sense of humour, described the scene which took place every time he asked Mahler for leave of absence:

With a beating heart I entered his office. Sensing the reason for my visit, the Director immediately assumed a reserved and distant air. 'What can I do for you?' 'Herr Direktor, I should like to sing in Graz for two evenings and request four days' leave.' 'Are you crazy? You have only just been away!' 'No, you are mistaken, I haven't been away for weeks.' On his desk was a board with about twenty-five or thirty buttons, underneath them little plates bearing the names of the opera officials. Mahler lunges furiously towards them, depressing twelve or fifteen at once with the palm of his hand. He wants Professor Wondra, who keeps a record of all leaves of absence, to show me that I am wrong. Doors open on all sides. Lenerl Sgalitzer rushes in breathlessly with her shorthand pad. 'Herr Direktor?' 'No, not you! Get out!' Deathly pale, Lenerl Ranninger arrives with the keys to all the music lockers; she too is expelled immediately. Secretary Schlader, stage managers, men in charge of the props rush in and even the house fire fighters respond to his call, appearing in full array, ready to start dousing the flames. Only Wondra fails to answer! One word leads to another, the confrontation comes to a head, and my patience is exhausted. Furious, I leave the battlefield, stepping on Hassinger's toes. Colleagues with similar requests waiting outside the Director's door dissolve into thin air and take their leave. I go home in a rage and swear to Elsa by all the saints in heaven that I can't take it any longer. A few hours later, everyone starts to calm down. We stand on the stage, he sits on the podium and conducts. Rancour and fury dissolve like March snow in the spring sun. This game is repeated several times a year, a month, a week . . .[7]

In the autumn of 1904, however, Slezak's request for leave of absence to sing at La Scala had caused more serious repercussions than usual. As early as April, even though his first request had been refused, he had quite simply accepted the proposed engagement. Behaving as if he had forgotten the refusal, he tried again on 6 September, asking to be freed from his obligations in Vienna between 1 January and 6 February in order to sing *Tannhäuser* at La Scala. He insisted on the importance of this guest appearance 'for my future' and on 'my need to earn extra money for my family, given the taxes and deductions which constantly diminish my salary'.[8] The following day he received Mahler's predictable response: 'I deeply regret that I cannot transmit your request for five weeks' leave for a guest appearance at La Scala in Milan to the higher authorities. You will no doubt understand that your services cannot be dispensed with for such a long period at the height of the season.'[9]

Yet Slezak was not discouraged. He wrote a second letter, this time directly to the Intendant, in which he claimed that other great German theatres, such as Berlin and Munich, granted their artists prolonged periods of leave and that the tenors Ernst Kraus and Heinrich Knote sang regularly in England, the United States, and even Russia. In such cases the Munich Intendant Possart

---

[7] Leo Slezak, 'Gustav Mahler', in *Moderne Welt*, 3 (1921–2): 7, 16. The article is reproduced in Slezak's *Meine sämtliche Werke*.   [8] HOA, Präs. 6 Oct. 1904.
[9] HOA, Z. 85/1904.

always recognized that 'the fame of one of its artists abroad invariably reflects credit on the institution to which he belongs'.[10]

Because in Vienna I am sadly conscious of the fact that I shall <u>always</u> be indispensable when asking for leave, for Director Mahler never grants leave on principle and because since April I have felt bitter and disgusted, I urgently beg to be given my freedom. Indeed, I fear I shall go mad if this joyless existence, worthy of a prison inmate, continues. During the whole of this summer, I have suffered greatly from the impressions and emotions aroused by my conflict with the Director; my health has taken a turn for the worse, considerable deductions from my salary have forced me to ask for an advance, thereby exacerbating my problems. As a final blow, His Highness retracted the small crumb of comfort he had offered me. So I was the loser and the brutal things I had suffered were swept aside. I beg the Generalintendanz in all humility to release me from my Hoftheater contract. I cannot believe that a royal institution of the first order would forcefully retain a singer against his will merely because he signed a contract he would certainly never have signed if he had understood how things really stood. No, that I cannot believe and I <u>confidently</u> await the acceptance of my request, for the forcible insistence upon the maintenance of appearances would be unworthy of an imperial institute . . .[11]

Slezak's excitement was such that he forgot the simplest rules of style and even of grammar. This was a far cry from the humorous way in which he would later describe his conflicts with Mahler! On 15 September Mahler returned the singer's new request to the Intendant, pointing out that he had always granted him leave on grounds of illness, and that in this case he had already refused on 20 April. He therefore asked to be spared the necessity of commenting anew 'on the enclosed demand which I herewith return with the request that a decision be taken as His Highness sees fit'.[12]

The real reason for Slezak's persistence emerged at last. On 10 October Mahler informed the Intendant that he had discovered that the tenor had already signed a contract for the guest appearance at La Scala and that he would be obliged to pay a heavy fine if he refused to honour it. Thus leave had to be granted. Nonetheless, the Director recommended that his salary be suspended during his absence and that the tenor be obliged to pay a fine equal to another month's salary 'for accepting an engagement in contravention of his contract'.[13]

In a third letter to the Intendant dated 31 October Mahler concludes by defending Slezak, explaining that he was 'a very popular and very useful member of the Opera and that in order to help him get out of the very awkward

---

[10] Mahler himself frequently used the same argument with Prince Montenuovo when being reproached for his frequent absences from Vienna.

[11] HOA, Z. 3074/1904. Letter of 14 Sept. 1904. [12] HOA, G.Z. 886/1904.

[13] Mahler's letter to the Intendant of 10 Oct. 1904 (HOA, G.Z. 986/1904). Another official letter from Mahler to Slezak dated 2 Feb. 1905 'regrets' that the tenor is still not in a position to 'fulfil his obligations' and warns him that as a result and until further notice his 'activity allowance' would no longer be paid. No doubt Slezak had prolonged his stay in Milan.

situation into which he had manœuvred himself, the much-discussed leave had been granted subject to the above-mentioned penalties'.

And with that the matter ended, and Slezak remained at the Opera. The whole story of their relationship shows that he held Mahler in great esteem and affection, something that invariably enabled him to overcome his resentment. It is equally obvious that Mahler respected him. Indeed, despite his careless-ness and his very faulty sense of rhythm, Slezak was undoubtedly one of the foremost singers of his time. He never failed to arouse the enthusiasm of connoisseurs of bel canto by the richness of his timbre, the resonance of his middle register, and the brilliance of his top notes, especially his famous high Cs, whose vibrations he could slow down or accelerate at will.

Occasionally, a note of humour did creep into Mahler's relationship with the star tenor of the Hofoper. Slezak recounts how he once thought he had found a way of getting around Mahler's ban on Opera singers giving recitals without his written approval: he gave his accompanist top billing, drafting the announcement as follows: 'Piano recital by Oskar Dachs (with the accompaniment of Leo Slezak).' But he had not counted with his impresario, who promptly had Dachs' name printed in tiny letters and Slezak's in gigantic ones. And so one day Mahler confronted the tenor with the poster in his hands. 'Do you know what this is? It's not a poster for a concert! It's a puzzle entitled "Where is Dachs?" '[14]

At the end of 1904, yet another popular member of the Opera threatened to resign. This was Selma Kurz, whose relationship with Mahler had considerably deteriorated since she had sung his Lieder at the Vienna Philharmonic in 1900 and he had fallen in love with her. In December the now famous coloratura wrote to Mahler concerning the role of Rachel in *La Juive* which she refused to learn although she had formally accepted it. At the same time, she apparently wanted to teach Mahler a lesson in administrative procedure, which he resented, to judge by his reply:

You will certainly be in no doubt that I am fully aware of the procedure governing professional relations between the Director and the artists [of the Opera] and I there-fore consider your comment that I should adhere to Article 19 of the contract entirely superfluous, to say the least. Your point of view, furthermore, is incorrect, for in no way can the assignment of a role be considered 'an important professional negotiation' (you left out the word 'important' in your letter): if this were the case, and if all administra-tive instructions had to be given in writing, then every member [of the Opera] would be equally entitled to demand that in the event of a cancellation or change in programme every last-minute order to replace another member should be given in *writ-ing*.

According to Para. 1 of the Regulations, all members coming under the authority of the Director are obliged to comply with the Director's official orders or those of the

---

[14] Alexander Witeschnik, *Musizieren geht übers Probieren*, 46. Later on, relations between the Director and his star tenor became less strained. Thus Mahler wrote to Angelo Neumann on 14 Oct. 1905 informing him that Slezak had been granted leave for 1 Nov., for a *Gastspiel* in Prague (Jewish National and University Library, Jerusalem).

departmental heads acting in his name. The rest of the paragraph, and Para. 2 of the Regulations, clearly indicate the procedure to be followed in the event of objections to such orders. You have discovered the procedure *only today* and, quite appropriately, you have submitted a request, with reasons, that the Director should release you from the role of Rachel.

In consideration of the reasons you advance, I accede to your request and release you from the role. I must insist, however, that you have no right to tell me how official orders are to be given.[15]

Thus, when occasion demanded it, Mahler knew how to employ the laboriously stilted style of contemporary Viennese bureaucracy. Offended by Mahler's response, Kurz reported sick early in February.[16] At the end of the month she approached the Intendant to demand the cancellation of her contract, complaining that she was never given new roles, that she was 'on bad terms with the Director' and therefore utterly deprived of his artistic influence. She could no longer stand his offensive behaviour towards members of the Opera, which was often the cause of complaints. It had plunged her into a state of perpetual agitation that had ruined her health, and into a nervous overexcitement confirmed by her doctors. She was certain that to continue to work at the Hofoper under the current management would gravely endanger her health.[17]

The Intendant sided with Mahler against Selma Kurz, pointing out that when her contract was renewed two years earlier she had not complained against the Director, and that nothing had occurred since which could explain either her being on 'bad terms' with him or her 'nervous overexcitement'. Mahler himself reminded Kurz in his letter of 31 March that during the past two years she had sung two new roles, Mimi in *La Bohème* and Lakmé. He had even planned to revive the *Barber of Seville* for her, in all probability planning to conduct the work himself. Moreover, he pointed out a strange contradiction in her letter: she complained of being 'deprived of her Director's artistic influence', and yet sought to resign, which would for ever remove her from that influence! As far as being on 'bad terms' with the Director was concerned, if she so desired, she would be treated just the same as the other members of the Opera, who, 'faithful to their duties, never give the least occasion for complaint'.

If the attitude and behaviour of a member of the Opera has no other object than to evade, under idle pretexts, the fulfilment of his obligations, when this member continually causes the worst difficulties and never fails to make demands which he well knows cannot be met, then the Director's attitude is bound to be different from that which he adopts towards those members who perform their contractually defined tasks with zeal and good will.[18]

[15]   Letter of 30 Dec. 1904: HOA, Z. 1287/1904.
[16]   Mahler's letter of 1 Feb. noted that the singer was 'not in a position to fulfil her contractual obligations', and added that, while the proposed medical certificate was not necessary, her 'activity allowance' would be withdrawn until she was able to resume her duties.
[17]   Undated letter from Selma Kurz (HOA, Z. 830/1905).
[18]   HOA, Z. 282. Letters of 27 Feb. and 31 Mar. 1905.

On 23 March 1905, the *Neue Freie Presse* announced that Mahler had refused to grant Selma Kurz an increased salary and to accept the cancellation of her contract, for which she had offered to pay a penalty of 44,000 kronen to the Hofoper. The dispute seems to have lasted into April, as can be seen from a letter Selma Kurz wrote to her confidante Hermine Baum from Baden bei Wien, where the singer was taking the waters: 'Yesterday I wrote my final letter to the management of the Opera, and my decision will depend on the reply.'[19] But ultimately, again, the matter was forgotten. In 1906, as he had promised, Mahler revived the *Barber of Seville* (after the *Marriage of Figaro*), conducting the first two performances himself. He was far from underestimating Selma Kurz's talent, and yet his behaviour to her, as indeed to Slezak, Demuth, and other bel canto singers, showed that he thought of them as 'stars' who were more concerned with their voices and technique[20] than with the psychology of a character or with dramatic expression on the stage.[21]

He behaved quite differently with 'singing actors' like Gutheil-Schoder, Mildenburg, or Weidemann. But even with them relations were not always easy. In the case of Mildenburg, the main problem was her frail health and the frequency with which she reported sick at the last moment. The most serious recent case had been her last-minute withdrawal from the première of *Fidelio* on 4 October 1904, the Emperor's name-day. Three days later, on the day of the postponed première in which Lucy Weidt was now to sing the title role, Mildenburg wrote to Mahler to inform him of the cause of the chill which had forced her to withdraw from the performance. She had caught a cold on stage during one of the last rehearsals, and was therefore obliged to request convalescent leave to spend a few days in the country. She complained that this chill, like the chills of many of her colleagues, was caused by draughts on the stage during the rehearsals. No measures had been taken to remedy this situation, even temporarily. She thought it only fair to ask that during her sick leave her salary should not be reduced on account of shortfalls due to personal negligence, as had been the case the previous year.[22]

Two letters from Mahler to the Intendant show that he had taken the problem to heart. In fact, he himself had noticed the growing number of singers catching colds. 'I am really quite nonplussed', he then wrote to Mildenburg, asking her to intervene directly and forcefully with the Intendant. 'I know that nothing I can do will come to anything, as has always been the case up to now.

[19] Letter of 28 Apr. 1905, Fonds Desi Halban, BGM.

[20] This was certainly true of Demuth. Selma Kurz later told her daughter, Desi Halban, that the great baritone 'stepped on the weighing scales daily. The idea of losing weight abhorred him [*sic*]. His theory was that the vocal chords should be embedded in fat. If he lost a few ounces he would immediately have some cream and butter. What would our modern singers say to this?' (Desi Halban, *My Mother Selma Kurz*. Lecture given 29 Feb. 1972, British Institute of Recorded Sound, Jan. 1973, 135).

[21] Letter of 28 Apr. 1905, Fonds Desi Halban, BGM.

[22] HOA, G.Z. 975/1904.

I would even welcome a scandal if it could improve this intolerable situation, which is obviously the responsibility of the Intendant.'[23]

Mildenburg then wrote a formal letter to Prince Montenuovo on 29 December 1904 in which she requested the creation of a 'stage police', the outside doors in the wings having been found open 'and even fastened in that position'. Mahler admitted that there was a perceptible draught, and other artists such as Lucy Weidt and Winkelmann had had to cancel their performances and suffer a reduction in their salaries as a result.

Mahler had probably completely forgotten the problem of the draught when, at the beginning of 1905, he and Mildenburg had a lively altercation after the singer claimed that no first performance and no new production had ever been cancelled due to her fault, with the single exception of *Fidelio*. Mahler was furious: he accused her of bad faith and told her quite bluntly that her cancellations would be less frequent if she took better care of her health (he was certainly well acquainted with her habits, having lived on intimate terms with her for over a year). The next day Mildenburg gave vent to her indignation in writing:

Dear Herr Director, I must ask you to read the following lines with patience, for, suffering from constant headaches, I can dictate only with great difficulty. Ever since you told me, I know not why, that I always use highflown language, I am even less able to reply in a manner that befits the occasion.

Yesterday, when I denied ever having cancelled a première before *Fidelio*, . . . you replied: 'That's because you always forget everything.' That is absolutely untrue. If you went into the matter, you would be amazed at my reliability. I once told you that six *Ring* cycles had been performed during the 1900–1901 season. You called the secretary, who only knew of five: a pardonable error on his part. However, I can prove, with dates, that there were six! Whereas this merely makes me smile, I must take seriously what happened yesterday. I am unreliable and forget everything! And recently, when I proved a fact in black and white you told me: 'I won't put up with all your lies!'

Demuth cancelled the new production of *Ernani*. Last year *Tristan* had to be called off because of Schmedes, and even after the postponement he could barely sing to the end, and so on. My God, I don't want to brag about my good luck prior to *Fidelio*! Cancellations are not uncommon. However, I have cancelled no more than many other people, and I can prove it. My voice is fundamentally healthy, and has lately recovered with remarkable speed.[24] My life is full of self-denial, the sole purpose of which is to safeguard my profession. You know perfectly well what can damage an artist leading this sort of life. Before *Fidelio*, and recently again before *Euryanthe*, you yourself acknowledged the circumstances against which I have been fighting a difficult and

---

[23] Undated manuscript letter to Mildenburg (ÖTM).

[24] At the end of Feb. 1905 Mahler on several occasions obliged Mildenburg, who was suffering from a cold, to sing the role of Fricka, which she considered unworthy of her. She was eventually forced to cancel a performance of *Götterdämmerung*. Subsequently she requested several days of convalescent leave in order to learn the leading role of *Die Rose vom Liebesgarten*. On the strength of a medical certificate this leave was extended. She again reported sick shortly before the première of Pfitzner's opera, and only resumed the role at a later stage (HOA, Z. 256/1905).

unpleasant battle for two years. Perhaps someone might actually say that one must be 'overly sensitive' to catch a cold after being hit by a draught of cold air on stage in the middle of a performance, but no one really believes it. (He would raise hell if anyone ventured to open a window in a train in winter, even if he weren't particularly hot!)

And on top of the moral, artistic and physical effect of these illnesses and cancellations (not to mention the deductions from my salary for 'shortfalls due to personal negligence', as the contract puts it!), on top of all the trouble it costs me to fight and defend myself, on top of all the exasperation caused by things one does not even want to talk about (for yesterday wasn't the first time) I have to listen to the Director saying again and again 'You're going to report sick. You always cancel premières'. Me! So it is my fault?! Even lecturers catch a cold on stage sometimes without even realizing it (while I live prudently, with greater care and only for my work). Shortly after *Fidelio*, Weidt caught a cold on stage and had to cancel; likewise Schmedes and Weidemann . . . Must I draw up a list of all the cancellations? That certain well-meaning people are only too happy to have a go at Mildenburg on an occasion like *Fidelio*—not her again, 'she always cancels'—, is not in itself surprising. However, that you should reproach me for catching a cold and reporting sick leaves me absolutely speechless.

I would have sung *Fidelio*, I would have sung Eglantine if only the necessary measures had been taken in time. Three weeks ago you spoke of fastening the wings of the doors. . . . Perhaps we will finally succeed, if we take enough trouble, in persuading people not to leave doors wide open in the wings, up above and at the rear during the rehearsals and not to carry in motors from the street—in short, so that people no longer do whatever they like without the slightest consideration for others! . . . The day after your justified outburst of rage, I still felt horrible draughts during the rehearsal. . . .

To get rid of the draughts which she deemed responsible for all her ills, Mildenburg again requested Mahler to institute a 'stage police', which would be more effective 'than to forbid her to sing in the last rehearsal before the première'.[25] After twenty years of experience with opera, Mahler was certainly accustomed to such outbursts. He was familiar with the psychology of opera singers. Mildenburg's illness and last-minute cancellations had caused him grave difficulties, but he also knew that artists of her rank were scarce and virtually irreplaceable. So he spared neither effort nor sacrifice to keep them at the Vienna Opera.

A few years earlier (the two letters quoted above are difficult to date with precision),[26] another incident had given Mildenburg occasion to protest. At the time she had written to Mahler to complain that she had received a letter from Wondra on 18 August, the day the Opera reopened, demanding her immediate return to Vienna, for otherwise the activity allowance (*Funktionzulage*) would

[25] HOA, Z. 23/1905. In the same letter Mildenburg implores Mahler not to force her to sing Fricka. On receipt of her letter of 29 Dec., Plappart requested Mahler to ensure that the doors leading out from the wings should remain closed during rehearsals (HOA, Z. 4844/1904).

[26] Mildenburg's letter is in Alma Mahler's archives in UPL. Mahler's reply is among those Mildenburg bequeathed to the Nationalbibliothek in Vienna (now ÖTM). Both were written after 1901, when the reopening of the Hofoper was postponed until 18 Aug.

be deducted from her salary. This was stipulated by the regulations when a singer sang less than a certain number of performances 'due to personal negligence'. Yet according to Mildenburg, Mahler himself had assured her at the beginning of the summer that she would not have to appear on stage before the beginning of September. Thus she had rented an apartment in Maiernigg until the end of August:

Put yourself in my place, I would have to leave tomorrow morning at the latest, and move into a hotel in Vienna, for a singer should not and cannot live in an apartment full of dust and mothballs—in short, I would have to spend the next few days harassed and in a state of agitation, which would make even a healthy person nervous and tired, let alone someone like me, in constant battle with my dreadful nerves. I beseech you to give me eight more days. Despite the fact that I shall then be expecting my monthly period and unable to go on stage, I will report to work . . .

Mahler replied by return that because of the regulation he could not possibly grant more than three additional days of vacation. 'By overstepping my powers I would expose myself to serious trouble and I cannot afford to take this risk.' Although he had forgotten this regulation when she had come to see him before the summer, <u>she</u> should have remembered it. He had not put her down for any roles, but could not grant her official leave, either; and if she stayed in Vienna she might be called on in the event of another singer cancelling a performance. But this was an official letter dictated to one of the secretaries at the Hofoper. Mahler sent her another letter, handwritten and private, probably dating from the same period:

Your news is rather depressing for me. Through my efforts, you have had three months' summer vacation. You know your colleagues, and you are well aware of what they say each time you are, so to speak, favoured. What you have written to me about the repertoire would, under normal circumstances, be unacceptable for an Opera Director (such as I am and must be). I bow to necessity, accept the consequences, and give you a free hand! Come when your doctor permits you to do so, and sing when you feel up to it. N.B. I am writing this very <u>briefly</u>, in <u>haste</u>, and without the <u>slightest</u> irritation.

The storms which broke periodically at the Hofoper, and which pitted one or another of the great singers against Mahler, often had positive rather than negative consequences. They often cleared the air, or acted as lightning conductors. Unfortunately the Viennese press, always eager to pick up scandals, often helped to aggravate them by interviewing singers as soon as news of a conflict filtered out of the Opera.

In 1905, before engaging the new members he needed for his ensemble, Mahler did his utmost to extend existing contracts. He did not at that time manage to convince Slezak (who increasingly resented refusals of permission to sing abroad), but he did succeed in persuading Schmedes to agree to an extension of his contract, which already ran until 1908. His already high salary (40,000 kronen per year) was increased by 8,000 kronen in order to enable him finally to pay off his debts. Mahler urged the Intendant to give him this preferential treatment, for 'it would be impossible to find an acceptable replacement at a lower salary'. He even suggested that the Opera grant Schmedes an 'ex gratia' payment of 2,000 kronen to 'reward him for accepting the renewal of his contract'. [27]

Mahler also requested and eventually obtained permission to extend Elise Elizza-Limlay's contract. Her hitherto modest salary (12,000 kronen) was to be raised progressively to 16,000 kronen over a period of a few years, for she had always been of 'great utility' in high soprano roles.[28] Thus, far from being engaged in constant strife with his singers, he often protected them, at times even against themselves. He knew from experience that they easily went sick before performances out of stage fright, and in June he actually refused to permit Weidemann to sing the role of Hans Sachs. The young baritone had insisted on taking the role that evening in order to retain his 'activity allowance', but Mahler, knowing that he had been suffering for some time from 'vocal indisposition', feared that his voice might suffer permanent damage. Demuth was too busy to replace him, so Mahler engaged the Leipzig baritone Hans Schütz as guest singer.[29]

Of the guest singers at the end of that season, only three were sufficiently successful to warrant firm contracts: the young lyric tenor Alfred Boruttau;[30] Gertrud Förstel,[31] who was excellent in the roles of Eva and Sulamith (in *Die Königin von Saba*) on 11 April 1905, and Alexander Haydter, who had been warmly applauded as Alberich in *Das Rheingold*.[32] Furthermore, Mahler obtained from the Intendant grants to finance the training of two young Viennese singers whom he hoped to recruit, the tenor Walter Wesskopf and the bass Nikolaus Zec, 'to avoid their being engaged by another theatre'. In both cases, his hopes were later disappointed.[33]

[27]   HOA, G.Z. 1148/1905, letter of 28 Aug. 1905.

[28]   HOA, G.Z. 43 and 186/1905. Letters of 11 Jan. and 19 Feb. 1905.

[29]   HOA, G.Z. 727/1905. Letter of 10 June. Schütz was paid 800 kronen for the performance. Renewals of the contracts of several other sopranos at the Opera made Mahler decide not to renew that of Frieda Felser. She thus spent only one year at the Vienna Opera. (Ibid., G.Z. 101/1905.)

[30]   Mahler furnished the Prague director, doubtless at his request, with information about the vocal and artistic abilities of the recently engaged young lyric tenor, Alfred Boruttau, who had sung Fenton in *Falstaff*. (Letters to Angelo Neumann of 9 Apr., 1 Nov., 9 Nov., and 12 Dec. 1904, Jewish National and University Library, Jerusalem). Alfred Boruttau was a member of the Vienna Opera for only one year, from 1 Sept. 1905, to 21 Aug. 1906.

[31]   Gertrud Förstel (1880–1950) was born in Leipzig and made her debut at the Prague Opera in *La Sonnambula* in 1900. After a guest appearance at the Vienna Opera in Apr. 1905, she was engaged from 1 Sept. 1906 until 1912. She initially received a yearly salary of 20,000 kronen. This was increased annually until, after six years, it had reached 30,000 kronen. Her principal roles were Papagena, Eva, Marguerite (*Faust*), Sophie (*Der Rosenkavalier*), and *Madame Butterfly*.

[32]   See above, Chap. 1. Already the previous year Mahler and Angelo Neumann had corresponded concerning the engagement of Haydter. Mahler had asked Neumann to grant the singer leave to attend rehearsals of *Rheingold*, originally planned for the beginning of January 1905, then put off for a week.

[33]   HOA, G.Z. 49/1905 and Z. 1342/1905, and G.Z. 430/1906. Letters of 12 Jan. and 12 Dec. 1905 and 29 Mar. 1906. In Mar. 1905, Mahler suggested that Wesskopf's retainer (*Sustensionsgage*) be 'raised from 1,600 to 3,000 kronen per year, for he has made great progress and is fast becoming an exceptional lyrical coloratura tenor'.

In the meantime, Roller had not been idle in his job of chief stage designer. The previous year he had noticed that 'despite all the warnings and fines', the women in the chorus continued to do their hair as they saw fit, even when the opera they were appearing in was 'historical' and required a single style. Since most of them eventually declared themselves unable to create the appropriate hairstyle, Roller designed wigs and had them made. Sixteen women in the chorus thought that they could continue to create 'period hairstyles' themselves but finally realized that the wigs saved their colleagues a lot of time and energy. After submitting a long handwritten report dated 25 February 1905, Roller finally obtained the 480 kronen needed to make the additional wigs for these women.

But by far the most important and most carefully prepared event of the 1904–5 Hofoper season was the production of Hans Pfitzner's[34] second opera, *Die Rose vom Liebesgarten*. Mahler had turned down his *Der arme Heinrich* in 1898 and had sharply criticized *Die Rose* in a letter to Alma in 1904. How is one to account for his sudden change of mind? Why did he accede to the request of a composer for whom a performance in Vienna represented the summit of his career? For once, Alma admits to having exerted a conscious and deliberate influence on her husband. Her own enthusiasm had been aroused by one of Mahler's closest friends and collaborators, Bruno Walter. While he was in Hamburg, Walter had discovered Pfitzner's first stage work, *Der arme Heinrich*, and had immediately brought it to Mahler's attention. Subsequently he had conducted the first performance in Berlin, where he formed a close friendship with the young composer.[35] As soon as *Die Rose vom Liebesgarten* had been completed in 1901, Pfitzner approached the Hofoper. Walter had no doubt promised to use his influence with Mahler.

On 20 February 1901, Mahler had asked the Intendant for 200 kronen to enable Pfitzner, 'this gifted composer, whose first work has been performed by the Berlin Opera', to come to Vienna to play the score of his new opera to him.[36] The request was granted, though Pfitzner's visit was delayed by Mahler's illness and operation.[37] Three days later, Pfitzner, who was living in Munich at the home of his friend and patron Paul Cossmann,[38] offered to come to Vienna

[34] Hans Pfitzner, the son of an orchestral musician, was born in Moscow in 1869. After studying at the Frankfurt Hochschule für Musik he became a pupil of Hugo Riemann in Wiesbaden. He taught at the Coblenz Conservatory (1892–3), was a conductor at the Mainz Opera (1894–6) and then at the Theater des Westens in Berlin. He then taught at the Stern Konservatorium (1897–1907). His contemporaries considered him to be a 'romantic' musician, a lover of nature, a composer in the Wagnerian tradition who evinced a taste for fantastic, fairy-tale subjects, whose exceptional gifts had permitted him to liberate himself from the influence of Wagner: the richness of his harmonic and thematic style was especially admired, as was the refinement of his compositional technique. Although he also composed chamber music, his principal works were for the stage. He wrote numerous Lieder, choral works, incidental music, and five operas: *Der arme Heinrich* (1895), *Die Rose vom Liebesgarten* (1901), *Das Christelflein* Op. 20 (1906), *Palestrina* (1917), and *Das Herz* Op. 39 (1931).   [35] MBR1, nos. 250 and 251; MBR2, nos. 284 and 285.

[36] HOA, Z. 392/1901.

[37] Letter from the Intendant to Pfitzner, 1 Mar. 1901 (HOA, Z. 198/1901).

[38] Paul Nikolaus Cossmann (1869–1942), son of the cellist and music teacher Bernhard Cossmann, was a journalist and religious theorist as well as a poet. Pfitzner referred to him as his 'lifelong friend' (*Urfreund*) and dedicated his opera *Der arme Heinrich* to him. Cossmann was one of the first to support

to play his opera to Mahler. A week later he even suggested coming to Abbazia where Mahler was convalescing after his operation.

> . . . I daily await news from Vienna. . . . I must now decide whether to give the first performance rights to Vienna or to one of the other theatres with whom I am at present negotiating. . . . I surely do not have to tell you that I would far rather have my work premièred at the Vienna Hofoper, for a good production requires large dramatic and orchestral forces, a large chorus, and suitable soloists. Moreover, I suspect that for you, too, putting on the first performance it is not altogether a matter of indifference. In any case, it is my greatest wish that you should now become acquainted with it. That is why I am offering to come to wherever you are to play it to you . . .[39]

The letter also indicates that Mahler had already suggested (via Bruno Walter) that Pfitzner should spend several weeks in Vienna for rehearsals of *Die Rose*, but Pfitzner asked for a firm offer before making up his mind whether to accept either Mahler's proposal or an engagement at the Stadttheater.

Unfortunately Pfitzner enclosed with his letter a copy of the libretto of *Die Rose*, which Mahler read with dismay. At his very first encounter with Pfitzner in his office at the Vienna Opera, Mahler asked casually, 'as if he were asking where I had bought my watch': 'Where did you dig up this text?' Poor Pfitzner muttered something in reply, finding the occasion scarcely appropriate for the defence of his libretto, which had been written at his prompting by a childhood friend, James Grun.[40] Mahler nevertheless asked the young composer to play the work to him. After making a few critical comments, he added that in his opinion the text was responsible for the work's shortcomings. Pfitzner concluded that Mahler considered him to be 'completely devoid of literary judgement'; however he himself believed that the libretto was no worse than that of *Euryanthe*, and in any case, the music had been written to that text and could not be transferred to another.[41] Posterity would judge whether or not his music deserved to survive its 'bad' text.

As to its chances of survival, the opera's record to date was inconclusive. It had first been performed at Elberfeld on 9 November 1901, and later in Mannheim (1904), Munich (1904), Bremen (1904), and Hamburg (1905), but

---

Pfitzner's music at the turn of the century. From 1926 he was president of the Hans-Pfitzner-Verein für deutsche Tonkunst. From 1904 he exercised considerable influence on cultural life in sourthern Germany by publishing the *Süddeutsche Monatshefte*, a cultural, artistic, and political review whose contributors included the liberal politician Friedrich Naumann, the economist Lujo Brentano, the writers Schnitzler, Hofmannsthal, Thomas Mann, Hermann Hesse, and Ricarda Huch, the philosopher Ludwig Klages, and the musicians Reger, Mottl, and Weingartner. Cossmann's imperialist, ultra-nationalist politics strongly influenced Pfitzner. In Apr. 1933 Cossmann was arrested as a Jew by the Gestapo; he was freed in 1934 thanks to Pfitzner's intervention. Re-arrested in 1941, he died in the Theresienstadt concentration camp (cf. Hans Pfitzner, *Briefe*, vol. ii (Schneider, Tutzing, 1991), 32).

[39]   Pfitzner's letter to Mahler of 23 Mar. 1901 (HOA, Z. 198/1901).

[40]   Born in England, James Grun, librettist of *Die Rose* and *Der arme Heinrich*, was one of Pfitzner's fellow students at the Frankfurt Conservatory. The subject had been suggested to him by a painting by the Munich painter Hans Thoma, *Der Hüter vom Liebesgarten*.

[41]   Hans Pfitzner, *Reden, Schriften, Briefe* (Luchterhand, Berlin, 1955), 282.

never more than two or three times in each theatre. During the Krefeld festival in 1902, Mahler had had a visit from Pfitzner, and had once again rejected the work, this time in abrupt and apparently final terms. It was on this occasion that Alma intervened, pressing the young composer's hand and giving him to understand that he had found an important ally.[42] Moreover, Bruno Walter had been trying for some time to convince Mahler that Pfitzner really was a great composer. On 18 December of the same year he played Pfitzner's Quartet on the piano to Mahler and Rosé, and wrote to Pfitzner two days later:

Mahler was absolutely delighted and could hardly find words to express his appreciation. He thought the Adagio was the most impressive movement. . . . The masterly structure of the whole quartet greatly impressed him. I had scarcely finished when he sat down at the piano to go over the score, picking out those passages which had especially pleased him . . . He is making all sorts of plans to make the work known. He considers it one of the most delightful he has ever come across. You have a very special friend in Frau Mahler, who is extremely musical; as Mahler put it, she literally devoured your quartet and I had to leave her the score so that she could continue to enjoy it . . .[43]

Mahler himself suggested that the Rosé quartet should give a first performance of the work. Even before Rosé had read the score, Mahler insisted: 'You can accept a work of Pfitzner's with your eyes closed, since I vouch for it.' He even considered giving the final rehearsal in his Auenbruggergasse apartment in the presence of a number of 'connoisseurs' and 'patrons', but it finally took place in January 1903 and Walter reported to Pfitzner three days after the rehearsal in one of the Opera's rehearsal halls, 'Mahler has become one of your most zealous friends'. But in his memoirs, Bruno Walter continued the story:

In the final rehearsal, in Rosé's room, the weaknesses in the performance (unfortunately) were not apparent. The ample acoustics of the room greatly contributed to its success, as did Mahler's silent but electrifying presence. . . . After the rehearsal he walked around in the snow with me for an hour, in a state of great animation. 'Don't you see, he's really an awkward customer (*herber Kerl*),' he kept on saying, 'but not awkward à la Schillings. This is a brilliant work,' he said over and over again, and then, completely spontaneously 'Damn it all! I'm going straight back to tackle *Die Rose*, once more.' Later, he confessed that he had 'the best possible opinion' of *Die Rose*, but added 'If only the libretto were more or less tolerable, I would have put it on already.'[44]

Thus the libretto remained the main obstacle. Even Bruno Walter recognized that it was the opera's principal weakness, and made Pfitzner promise never to set a text to music again without letting him read it first. In January 1904 Mahler finally attended a performance of *Die Rose* at the Mannheim Opera and, in a letter to his wife, drew up a veritable indictment of the work.[45] All seemed

[42] See above, Vol. ii, Chap. 13.   [43] BWB 59.
[44] BWB 62 and 63, letter of 16 Jan. 1903.   [45] See above, Vol. ii, Chap. 16.

lost. But way back in March 1902 Bruno Walter had already written to Pfitzner explaining Mahler's 'explosive' way of abruptly changing his mind:

With regard to *Die Rose*. It has become a sort of child of sorrow (*Schmerzenkind*) for me. Mahler has an astounding antipathy (it could almost be called an aversion) to your whole manner and we have already had quite serious quarrels about the *Rose*. You mustn't think that he deals with it lightly. On the contrary—he thinks about it a great deal. Yet despite his violent aversion I am still hoping I can help to bring about a performance here precisely because it depends exclusively on Mahler. Those who know him (and love him), as I do, know that with him every change of position is explosive. It is therefore not impossible that if, in a propitious moment, I manage to point out a passage in *Die Rose* whose beauty is quite apparent, he will insist on a production with the same vehemence with which he at present refuses it.[46]

Bruno Walter's letters and memoirs thus indicate that he had committed himself to a covert but persistant campaign in Pfitzner's favour, having no doubt recruited Alma as his ally. In 1904, the explosion he hoped for finally took place. One day, 'with a friendly and promising smile I shall never forget', Mahler informed Pfitzner that he had decided to put on his opera before the end of the year.[47] To ensure a first-rate performance, he did not hesitate to postpone the première three times, from December 1904 to January 1905, then to March, and finally to 6 April. Few operas have ever been prepared with such care, even during Mahler's tenure. The rehearsal halls at the Opera were not always available, so extra rehearsals took place in the small hall of the Musikverein. The costume makers worked day and night.[48]

Bruno Walter's letters to Pfitzner abound in details about the rehearsals, the décor, the singers, and their enthusiasm. 'The intensity of the preparations can only be compared with Bayreuth', he wrote. The production would certainly be 'the best possible', for Mahler was 'all fire and flame' for the opera.[49] Walter himself had already prepared for the 'siege' of Vienna, assuring Pfitzner of the support of certain critics, notably Gustav Schönaich and Ludwig Karpath (soon to become Pfitzner's close friend).[50] Both were prepared to champion the opera at all costs.

In view of his theatrical experience, Pfitzner, like Strauss, at first wanted to conduct the work himself, but Walter dissuaded him:

Just think: people will immediately interpret this as if Mahler were trying to get out of it and they will conclude that he has an unfavourable opinion of your work. You are not

---

[46] BWB 57.

[47] Pfitzner's letters to Alma indicate that he received the first official notification from the Opera in May 1904.

[48] Clemens Höslinger, 'Pfitzner und die Wiener Hofoper', *Musikerziehung*, 24 (1970–1), 69.

[49] BWB 74–5, 25 Sept. 1904.

[50] In a long letter to Pfitzner, Karpath discusses the performance of *Die Rose* which had taken place on 6 Oct. 1905 under Bruno Walter. The number of strings in the orchestra had been reduced that evening. Walter had later assured him that this had been due to a 'misunderstanding' and that the normal strength would be re-established in subsequent performances (ÖTM).

familiar with the singers or the orchestra. If Mahler conducts the rehearsal and the première, it will ensure that the singers will want to surpass themselves and the public will see it as a sign of the quality of the opera and performance. Furthermore, you can be sure—and I vouch for it—that Mahler will devote himself heart and soul to the precise execution of your intentions. In short, I am positive that Mahler can succeed much better than you in achieving a perfect performance which wholly corresponds to your ideals. (Even I would be more of a success though of course I do not inspire the trembling respect which Mahler can command, and which enables him to obtain incomparable artistic results . . .)[51]

On 20 February, Mahler wrote a note to the Intendant to explain that *Die Rose* was proving to be an 'unusually difficult' opera to prepare for production, and that to be certain that the composer's intentions were respected, Pfitzner should be invited to Vienna to conduct the final rehearsals and perhaps also the first two performances.[52] The same day he sent Pfitzner an official invitation, adding a private message:

We are working diligently and hope it will be to your satisfaction. I am as yet uncertain about a few tempos, but it is to be hoped that everything will quickly fall into place when you are here. Moreover, I take pleasure in telling you that with every rehearsal I am becoming more and more conscious of the great beauty of your work and am even beginning to reconcile myself to your text. How this has come about I shall tell you in person. . . .[53]

For Pfitzner the Vienna production of *Die Rose* was all important. According to Alma's memoirs he was in an almost pathological state of nervousness when he arrived in Vienna a fortnight before the première (about 20 March). The various delays had increased his impatience, and his anxiety at times bordered on despair. In the musical world he had already acquired a reputation for bad temper, and during the rehearsals he seemed intent on living up to it: 'He timed every late arrival at rehearsals of every member of the Opera to the minute', wrote Alma. 'I was the only person who could calm him down then.'[54]

But Pfitzner later acknowledged that the entire Vienna Opera had seemed animated by a single desire, to satisfy him and serve his work. And whereas everyone had told him that Mahler was an implacable, tyrannical despot, he found, to his amazement, from the first rehearsals onwards that Mahler was eager to respect and accomplish his every wish. Mahler even requested him to sit directly behind him in the front row of the stalls during the rehearsals so that he could indicate immediately the changes in tempo he desired. Pfitzner suggested that it would be sufficient if he noted them down and told him afterwards, but Mahler insisted: 'No, no. Sit down right behind me. When a tempo

[51] Letters from Bruno Walter to Hans Pfitzner of 26 Dec. 1904 (BWB 76–7). In a letter to Alma dated 21 Apr. 1903, Pfitzner had written: 'no one conducts my works as well as I do, at least the most recent ones.' On 21 Mar. 1905, he wrote to Paul Cossmann: 'Dear Paul, It's Mahler himself who is conducting, and what a conductor!' (Nationalbibliothek, Vienna, *Pfitzner Nachlass*). While Mahler was in Strasbourg, Pfitzner conducted a single performance, on 17 May 1905.   [52] HOA, G.Z. 250/1905.
[53] Ibid.   [54] AMM1, 105; AMM2, 108.

seems wrong to you, prod me in the back and put me right. Don't worry about me losing face in front of the orchestra. After all, you know it better than I— you composed it!'[55]

Pfitzner's stay in Vienna provided him with some of the happiest recollections in his tormented existence. Every instant of the rehearsals was to remain etched in his memory. 'It was the first time in my life that a great and distinguished conductor devoted himself to a work of mine with all his heart, sparing no effort in the process.' Until then he had encountered nothing but 'vanity and arrogance' from those who performed his music. The great conductors always seemed to be conscious of the honour they were bestowing upon his 'wretched scribbling by bringing it to life with their magic wand'. They always seemed to be expecting expressions of undying gratitude:

Even a request for a faster or slower tempo was an offence against the divine rightness of the great man, an insult that came close to blasphemy. And yet in many cases I was not even sure that the demigod had even studied the work or cast a glance at the score . . . I once asked Schuch to take a tempo in the *Christelflein Overture* a little faster. The result was that he told a friend of mine that he would never perform anything of mine again, for I was never satisfied.

In this case Mahler's behaviour was all the more admirable since Pfitzner made no secret of his contempt for Mahler's music, proclaiming to all and sundry that it was 'fundamentally distasteful' to him. Furthermore, the amorous advances he repeatedly made to Alma were hardly conducive to domestic harmony in the Auerbruggergasse apartment. As one might have expected, Pfitzner's stay in Vienna occupies a large place in Alma's diary and she also preserved the many letters Pfitzner addressed to her from 1903 onwards.[56] Alma's influence had clearly played a crucial role in Mahler's sudden change of mind, and Pfitzner thanks her profusely for exerting it. He also writes about his new compositions and forthcoming performances of his music, but inevitably he keeps coming back to the Vienna production of *Die Rose*, 'which is more important . . . than anything else'.

Mahler's artistic zeal and magnanimity were never more in evidence than during the hectic and difficult weeks leading up to the performance. Not only was he wholeheartedly promoting a work which he had described the previous year as 'jelly and protoplasm' (*Gallert und Urschleim*) now going so far (according to Alma) as to exclaim after the first act that 'nothing as sublime has been written since the first act of *Die Valkyrie*',[57] but he also refused to make the slightest cut ('It's a masterpiece, not a single note should be taken away!').[58]

---

[55] Hans Pfitzner, *Reden*, 284–5.

[56] Eight letters date from 1903 (12 and 17 Mar., 21 Apr., 30 June, 27 July, 21 Aug., 9 Nov., and 2 Dec.), five from 1904 (3 Mar., 28 Apr., 25 May, 8 Aug., and 5 Oct.) and twelve from 1905 (16 and 20 Jan., 14 and 20 Apr., 13 and 14 May, 14 June, 5 July, 14 Aug., and 12 Sept.). Alma and Pfitzner went on corresponding after Mahler's death; Pfitzner regularly informed Alma of his performances of Mahler's works (UPL).

[57] AMM1, 107; AMM2, 110.   [58] OKM 22.

He covered up for Pfitzner's tactless blundering, defended him vigorously against the complaints of his collaborators. Although it cannot have been pleasant for Mahler when Pfitzner so openly paid court to his wife, he did not complain, even when he visited her in his absence at the Auenbruggergasse. On 21 March, she had written in her diary:

Yesterday, at Pfitzner's request, I played him my early Lieder. He found them excellent and joyfully declared that I definitely had a talent for composition and a sound sense of melody. 'How I would like to work with you for a while . . . It's a pity about you!' What wistful joy came over me then! A brief moment of happiness!

Even Alma sometimes found Pfitzner difficult to get on with. Her diary entry for 22 March reads:

Lovely days with Hauptmann. It is splendid to listen to him and Gustav together! Yet yesterday evening was somewhat spoilt by Pfitzner's presence. How narrow-minded he is in certain respects. He said that the most profound and truest aspect of Wagner was his German-ness. Hauptmann and Gustav were both of the opinion that the greater the artist, the more he had to be <u>above</u> the national questions. Pfitzner wriggled around like a worm and soon went away offended. Since then, he has changed completely. This was after a performance of *Fidelio*,[59] during which Pfitzner and I stayed at home playing his and then my Lieder. We had arranged to join Hauptmann and Mahler after the performance in the Meissl and Schadn wine cellar. Absorbed in the music, we had lost track of time and arrived late, though no one held it against us. Pfitzner had played each of his Lieder at least ten times, repeating them until I was wholly taken with them so that I should learn to appreciate them. Today Mahler and Pfitzner quarrelled yet again on the subject of 'the eternal feminine'. It is difficult to imagine a more unpleasant conversation. Each misunderstood the other <u>on purpose</u>, and in the end both felt insulted. Added to which, Mahler is jealous.[60]

Since the day when Alma had come out from behind the curtain in Krefeld to shake Pfitzner's hand and console him for her husband's harsh words, a somewhat ambiguous complicity had sprung up between them. Pfitzner quickly understood that the young woman was an ally who could be used to overcome Mahler's reluctance. And Alma, ever since adolescence, was familiar with the sort of relationship in which gifted men became mentors, admirers, and potential lovers. When, in 1903, she began to correspond regularly with Pfitzner, she clearly hoped to create a bond of that kind: it would be an antidote to her frequent feelings of 'uselessness' and her nostalgia for her past, with all its erotically charged friendships. On several occasions she regretted the fact that she and Pfitzner lived in different cities.

Mahler must have long since discerned the inner workings of his wife's

---

[59] In between the rehearsals for *Die Rose* Mahler conducted *Fidelio* on 16 and 25 Mar. 1905. Alma also alludes to a performance of *Das Rheingold*, the first Hauptmann had seen, after which he, Pfitzner, and Mahler discussed 'nationalism' in art. Pfitzner alone defended this principle and Alma wondered whether his 'German-ness' was perhaps the main reason why he was so little known outside German-speaking countries.   [60] AMM1, 105 and 106; AMM2, 109.

psyche. He knew about her early life and understood that, for her, seduction, conquest, and sense of power over men, were vital needs. Also, since he had written the fateful letter in which he forbade her to compose, he was loath to impose any further constraints upon her. Some psychologists have interpreted his behaviour as masochistic. Without going that far, it is perhaps conceivable that he was unconsciously punishing himself for having married such a young and beautiful woman, and for having taken advantage of the fascination which his genius and fame held for her.

Pfitzner never concealed the fact that he was attracted to the beautiful Alma. In the summer of 1903 he had written:

. . . in a certain sense, it is not entirely without danger for you to write to me, for it is my nature to take things literally and to act accordingly. Do you know the passage I am referring to? You write '. . . and you can always depend on me.' Have you considered what might happen if I really depended on you for something? Someone like me with so many sides to my complicated personality needs just as many different people to do justice to them. Without drawing a comparison, I am led to think of Wagner. No one single person was fully enough for him. Cosima was there for one aspect of his personality, Liszt for another, Minna Planer yet another. For other facets there were countless friends of both sexes, who nonetheless had nothing in common with one another. That Cosima, for example, never had the vaguest notion of what was most profound in Wagner, namely his German-ness, is quite clear to me: yet those who sensed that side of Wagner had perhaps no inkling of his universal greatness, and so on. Do you understand me? All those who were close to Wagner and played a role in his life received, from nature as it were, a specific function to perform, and all together combined to further the development of this extraordinary, complicated organism. These are the thoughts that came to me as I read that passage in your letter: what role could you play in my destiny, you who are as close as is humanly possible to somebody who must naturally lay claim to your whole inner and outer being? But now I believe that we did not make each other's acquaintance in vain.[61]

Pfitzner, it would seem, was suggesting that Alma should become his muse, a sort of latter-day Mathilde Wesendonk. In any case, the extramarital intimacy he proposed was clearly incompatible with the ordered life which Alma had so far imposed upon herself as Mahler's wife. Her answer and most of her other letters have disappeared, but she obviously let Pfitzner know that he had gone too far. 'I am terribly sorry', Pfitzner replied, 'that certain passages in my letter annoyed you! This was certainly not my intention. I would like to say only pleasant things to you. Please reread my letter with that in mind. Can't one be serious occasionally?'[62]

Although two years earlier Alma had protested at Pfitzner's analogy between his own and Wagner's emotional needs, his remarks had struck a not unresponsive chord in her. A greater intimacy between them might have come

---

[61] Letter of 27 July 1903.   [62] Letter of 21 Aug. 1903.

about long before if the circumstances had been different. And now Pfitzner was actually in Vienna for three weeks. Alma's diary describes Pfitzner's advances and Mahler's jealousy:

Pfitzner, that evening, acted as though he were in love. Why so suddenly . . .? I don't know. I only know that he tried to approach me, touched me with his hands whenever he could, and finally asked me with a burning voice for a photograph (we were alone in the drawing room). I was pleased. I felt my skin tingling with pleasure, for the first time in a long time. And yet I saw him go without regret, for he did not want to dine with Gustav, the Hauptmanns and me. Yesterday morning I missed the rehearsal. He was so angry that he seemed completely changed. I note, once again without regret, that Gustav is jealous. But he no longer has reason to be . . . I was not nice to him. In the middle of our walk he turned around and returned to the theatre. I walked on alone in the city. Night fell and I suffered so much from my own lovelessness that tears almost came to my eyes. A young man followed me—I noticed it with wistful pleasure. That evening, Gustav was disgruntled and uncommunicative. He said that I always sided with the others. He is right. Deep down we are now strangers to each other. He lay down next to me in bed—neither of us quite knew why. He said, 'Read the *Kreutzer Sonata!*'[63] I am terrified when I think of my future life. I no longer have any courage.

To overcome his own jealousy Mahler pursued a 'strange tactic', and this reveals a new aspect of his character. He constantly invited Pfitzner to the Auenbruggergasse apartment and left him alone with his wife. Alma recalls an episode which took place on 1 May, three weeks after the opening of *Die Rose.*

Superb spring day. Rehearsal at the Opera. *Die Rose.* Afterwards Mahler held a brief rehearsal of his Lieder with the Opera orchestra (and Weidemann). Mahler invited Pfitzner, who of course was present at the rehearsal of *Die Rose*, to stay for the Lieder. But once *Die Rose* was over, Pfitzner did not dream of staying on out of consideration for Mahler; he mumbled some excuse about urgent business and ran out. To see me. On the way he bought a red rose, which he placed on the piano without saying a word. He was agitated and angry. It was 1 May,[64] and he had run into the workers' demonstration on the Ring. Full of rage against these 'proletarian faces' (*proletenhafte Gesichter*) he had dodged into a side street, but the impression of being pursued remained with him, even in my room. A short time later Mahler arrived. With a mixture of humour and vexation he now understood the reason for Pfitzner's precipitous departure. But today it didn't matter to him. He was much too happy to care! He too had run into the workers' demonstration on the Ring and had followed it for a while. They had all looked at him in such a brotherly fashion! They really *were* his brothers! These men

---

63   The famous novel by Tolstoy. (See incomplete typescript version of Alma's diary, UPL).

64   According to the rehearsal schedule in the Opera Archives, Mahler rehearsed the chorus on 1 May at 10.30 a.m. (see Clemens Höslinger, 'Pfitzner', 73). This was no doubt connected with the evening performance, for the première had taken place more than three weeks earlier. The Lieder which he then rehearsed must have been 'Das irdische Leben' and 'Ich bin der Welt'. They were subsequently performed in Graz, and had not been included in the Vienna programmes. In *Musik in Wien* (Molden, Vienna, 1970, 185), Kurt Dieman claims that Mahler encountered a procession of workers *before* the première of *Die Rose* on 6 Apr., and that it was only a demonstration for the right to vote. Since Pfitzner was staying in Berlin in the middle of Apr., and the *Neue Freie Presse* of 13 May announced that he had just arrived in Vienna for a stay of two weeks, it in fact seems unlikely that he could have been in Vienna on 1 May.

were the future! A quarrel ensued! Once again, hours of arguing. With not the slightest goodwill on either side, and me in the middle.[65]

This passage from Alma's memoirs has been the subject of much comment. Those who wonder at Mahler's sympathy for the workers should be reminded of his youth,[66] his membership of the Viennese socialist and vegetarian movements, and the keen social conscience which later led him to defend the claims of the orchestral musicians in Hamburg and the members of the chorus at the Vienna Opera. He had been profoundly influenced by Dostoevsky, and the spectacle of human misery had always moved him deeply. Yet the fact that his social conscience should have expressed itself with such force on this particular day is characteristic. In this respect, he was again the odd man out, and quite untypical of the majority of the Vienna bourgeoisie. Stefan Zweig's memoirs describe how they panicked in the face of working-class demonstrations, particularly since the first day that the workers had marched with their families into the main avenue of the Prater, normally the preserve of the aristocracy and privileged classes of Vienna. On that day the shops had remained closed, the police were stationed all along the route, ready to shoot at the slightest sign of disturbance and the privileged entrenched themselves in their apartments, fully expecting pillaging, looting, and every imaginable atrocity.[67]

A brief look at the origins of these social movements will help to explain the mortal fear of the bourgeoisie and the heated nature of the argument between Pfitzner and Mahler. In 1889, a hundred years after the fall of the Bastille, the Second International had been founded. At a time when the twelve-hour day and the seven-day week were still considered normal, when scarcely a fifth of the workers had Sundays off and worked less than nine or ten hours a day, proletarian revolt should not have surprised anyone. It happened more or less simultaneously in various countries, and met with brutal repression. In 1891, in the town of Fourmies, in northern France, the police killed ten workers during a demonstration for the eight-hour day. The whole of the 'third estate' rose in revolt and Clemenceau declared in the Chamber of Deputies: 'We must pay attention to the Dead!' In 1893, in Belgium, a demonstration for universal suffrage led to a general strike in which two people were killed by the police. In the United States, the brutal intervention in the Pullman strike led to ten deaths when the police took the railway carriages by storm.

In the Austrian Empire, Viktor Adler, Mahler's old friend, had been the leader and pioneer of the Second International. Having tried on himself in his youth working conditions as a bricklayer, he had studied the effects of malnutrition on the working class, and visited Germany, Switzerland, and England to

---

[65] AMM1, 106; AMM2, 110. 'Fifteen years after the event, I still don't know which of them was right' wrote Alma in AMS, incidentally revealing that the first version of 'Ein Leben mit Gustav Mahler' was written about 1920. It is interesting to recall that, on 1 May 1905, Mahler completed the fair copy of the score of the Sixth Symphony.   [66] See above, Vol. i, Chap. 5.

[67] Stefan Zweig, *Die Welt von Gestern* (Fischer, Pocket Books, Frankfurt, 1970), 55.

study social legislation and the living conditions of the workers. His programme for the Austrian socialists had been: 'health, culture, freedom, and dignity'. He believed that the advance of capitalism entailed the pauperization of the masses. Thin and frail, with a thick mop of hair and a moustache, a pale complexion and the gold-framed spectacles of an intellectual, he had little of the demagogue or prophet about him. For him revolution was an ultimate goal, but his immediate objectives were reforms which would improve the conditions of the working class.

1905 was a crucial year for the international socialist movement. In St Petersburg in January the people gathered under the windows of the Winter Palace to call for 'freedom, happiness or death', and a series of political crises led to the October Revolution later that year. Meanwhile, Adler called for a general strike in Austria. A dense crowd paraded on the Ringstrasse with red flags and clenched fists, demanding universal suffrage. The Austrian government, deeply worried, promised to accede to the workers' demands.[68]

In 1905 the 1st of May fell on a Monday. The strike order was widely followed, and ninety-six groups of workers from the various suburbs (Alsergrund, Hernals, Währing, and Döbling), converged on the centre of Vienna at midday, and moved towards the Ring, where a gigantic procession formed up with irreproachable order and discipline. Moving along the Josefskai, it crossed the Ferdinand Bridge towards the Prater, where it arrived towards 2.30. A wreath was laid at the Tegetthoff Monument. Some of the demonstrators began to sing the Austrian workers' hymn, the 'Lied der Arbeit',[69] but were called to order by their own stewards. All were wearing red badges and ribbons, and carrying red paper flowers and red flags. The women workers were dressed in red, entire rows marching in identical red smocks. Social Democratic slogans were blazoned across enormous red banners: 'Long live the social revolution!', 'Long live the eight-hour day!', 'Down with capital!', and 'Up with the underprivileged!' (*Hoch die Lumpen*) (on errand boys' bicycles decorated with flowers and ribbons). Three furniture vans were manned by removal men dressed in white, singing the 'Lied der Arbeit', and accompanying themselves on various instruments.

Forty to fifty thousand workers then spread out across the Prater, whose customary upper-class clientele had fled. They filled its forty-six restaurants and cafés, and sang and played music until 6.00 in the evening. The nervousness of the ruling classes, writes Stefan Zweig, was easy to understand. When the return procession formed up, the police tried to divert the marchers away from the Prater's main avenue, but the threatening mood of the demonstrators prevented them from doing so, and the triumphant marchers continued along

---

[68] See Barbara Tuchman, *The Proud Tower* (Macmillan, New York, 1962), 407. Universal suffrage was only introduced in Austria in 1907.

[69] 'Das Lied der Arbeit' (Hymn of Labour) with words by Josef Zapf, was composed in 1868 by Josef Scheu, who later held the post of music critic of the *Arbeiter-Zeitung*. He was a violent opponent of Mahler's from the start of his engagement in Vienna (see Vol. ii, Chap. 10).

the Praterstrasse. The most serious incident was a scuffle when police tried to snatch a banner from some of the demonstrators.[70]

This then was the momentous event which had elicited such completely different reactions from Pfitzner and Mahler. Mahler's socialist views are further confirmed by the unpublished testimony of Adler's wife Emma:

Gustav Mahler always kept politics and party membership at a distance. Yet everyone who came in contact with him knew that he took social issues to heart.[71] During the 1901 elections Gustav Mahler, the 'k.u.k. Direktor der k.u.k. Hofoper' made no secret of the fact that he was voting for the social democrat candidate of his constituency. The candidate's name was Viktor Adler. The Christian Social Party fumed with rage, and the *Deutsches Volksblatt* could hardly find words to express its hatred.[72]

In two successive issues, on 7 and 8 January 1901, the *Deutsches Volkblatt* vented its fury against the Jewish liberals, 'who have abandoned the last vestiges of their self respect . . . to support Dr Adler, the "Jewish Social Democratic" ' candidate in the second district of Vienna. The anti-Semitic press claimed that the Jewish bourgeoisie had spent hundreds of thousands of gulden to support Adler, that it had not shrunk from all kinds of dishonesty, even resorting to 'violence and terrorism' to help its candidates to victory, and that in the last resort the battle was 'between Christianity and Judaism'. 'Jewry and the Jewish liberal party', it was asserted, 'have publicly declared themselves the supporters of a revolutionary party whose aim is the establishment of a communist republic.'[73]

The 1901 elections themselves had been the occasion for violent clashes between 'the anti-Semites and their adversaries'. Adler's opponent, Julius Prohaska, the incumbent member and an 'anti-Semite', was finally elected with 26,533 votes to Adler's 25,193. The *Deutsches Volkblatt* published a list of the names of the university professors who had publicly supported Adler. It

---

[70] *Neue Freie Presse, Neues Wiener Tagblatt,* and *Neues Wiener Journal,* 2 May 1905. The description of demonstrations in other European cities (taking up a whole page in the *Journal*) indicates that they were on a smaller scale than those which took place in Vienna, the only city where the strike order was generally observed.

[71] Every year he donated free opera tickets to the Workers' Movement, and on one occasion became involved in a dispute with its 'musical director', Richard Wallaschek, over which opera they should thus be invited to attend.

[72] Emma Adler, typescript biography of Viktor Adler in the Viktor Adler Archives (Verein für Geschichte der Arbeiterbewegung). The same passage is cited in an article in the socialist review *Kunst und Volk* 1 (1929): 1a, 6 signed D.J.B. (probably David Josef Bach, music critic of the *Arbeiter-Zeitung* and close friend of Webern, who describes attending the final rehearsal of Mahler's Third Symphony with Adler in Dec. 1904). The most powerful enemy of the Arbeiterbewegung was Karl Lueger as head of the Christian Social Party since 1887. He had turned it into a mass movement for the middle and lower classes. Mayor of Vienna 1897–1910, he too claimed to be improving the lot of the workers (RSM2, 27 n. 1).

k.u.k.: 'kaisenlich und königlich' was the title of officials employed by the emperor or a title conferred by him on persons or institutions.

[73] A Gallup poll published in Vienna on 24 Oct. 1991, revealed that between 20 and 30 per cent of the Austrian people interviewed had 'a negative attitude to Jews', and 31 per cent did not wish to 'have a Jewish neighbour' (*Le Monde,* Paris, 27 Oct. 1991). The article noted, however, that anti-Semitism was no longer current among 'young people between 18 and 30'.

did not mention Mahler by name, however. Could he have been on another, earlier, list of Adler supporters? In any case, Emma Adler's testimony as to Mahler's socialist sympathies is not open to doubt. He did not hesitate publicly to support his childhood friend, candidate of the left, at a time that could well have jeopardized his standing with the court officials on whom he depended as director of the Opera.

But the most significant expression of Mahler's thoughts and feelings is not contained in what he said or wrote, but in his music, as he himself continually reminded those who tried to encourage him to write articles. Theodor Adorno has pointed out that Mahler's music, with its constant use of folk songs, military marches, and trumpet calls, is of a fundamentally 'plebeian' nature. Similarly, his Lieder frequently illustrate the life of the 'humble' and the 'oppressed', whereas the music of his contemporary, Richard Strauss, has something of the 'feudal lord' about it, 'heralding the imperialism of William II'.[74] Adorno made the following comments on this subject: 'This music transgresses the taboos of civilisation, it refuses to follow the rules of contemporary bourgeois society', which for that reason 'rejected it for so long'. 'It rages against the bourgeois, private, conventional, narrow view of music' and 'champions those excluded from the community'. In their simplicity his themes and his motifs symbolize 'the downtrodden and humiliated, those oppressed by society'.[75]

Mahler's 'socialism' had its limits of course. These had come to light when he refused to transmit to the Intendant the demands of the Opera technicians, on the grounds that they were incompatible with the discipline required in an Opera house, and when he demanded and obtained the dismissal of the 'agitators'.[76] But even if he rarely made pronouncements on this subject, no doubt so as not to compromise his position at the Opera, his liberal convictions and socialist sympathies were never in doubt. Pfitzner, on the other hand, professed a particularly reactionary form of nationalism. It is just possible that, in leaving Alma free to spend as much time as she wished with Pfitzner, Mahler did not take the German composer as a serious rival and was sure that she would come to realize her husband's superiority. In any case, Mahler never accepted the idea of becoming a habit for his wife, or worse still a fetter.

One source of tension between the two men was certainly Pfitzner's dislike of Mahler's music. Mahler also suspected that Alma had a secret predilection for Pfitzner's post-Romanticism, which was probably closer to her Wagnerian ideals. Nevertheless, she never failed to defend Mahler's music warmly to Pfitzner. In 1903, in one of his letters to Alma, Pfitzner had claimed that Mahler had 'understood nothing' of one of his Lieder, and had totally rejected

---

[74] Ulrich Schreiber, 'Une musique des contradictions sociales', in *Critique*, Paris, Sept. 1975.

[75] Theodor Adorno, 'Die Wiener Rede', in *Musikalische Schriften* i–iii (Suhrkamp, Frankfurt, 1978), ii. 120 ff.

[76] See Anna von Mildenburg, 'Cosima Wagner in ihren Briefen au mich', *Neue Freie Presse* (Vienna), 4 May 1930.

Die Rose vom Liebesgarten. But Mahler had the rare, even unique gift of utterly identifying himself with the works he had decided to perform. During the rehearsals he devoted himself wholeheartedly to *Die Rose* and to its author so that Pfitzner himself later described the Viennese performance as

the true première . . . a unique example of a truly gratifying interpretation of the work and of exemplary submission of the performer to the composer's will.[77] . . . And moreover I must say . . . that the period of the Vienna rehearsals—and not only the last ones, when it is really too late to change anything—was the only time I can remember when no discordant element marred the staging of my work, the only total fulfilment of this kind I have experienced. I truly felt that during those weeks only my work and its successful realization counted.[78]

Writing to Max Schillings shortly after the première, Pfitzner explained how he had grown to 'appreciate and even love . . . a great man' in Mahler, though he was fully aware that the harmony between them—i.e. between a composer he disliked and a performer of genius who had totally espoused his cause—was only transitory.[79] For Mahler's fiftieth birthday, Pfitzner wrote the following tribute:

In Vienna in 1905 I witnessed for the first time performance of a work of mine by a kindred spirit. Not only was it staged by a kindred spirit, it was also a lasting success, in the repertory for three seasons and nineteen performances. What made it possible? Germany has opera houses which, if they want to, can compete with the Vienna Hofoper in the use of lavish presentation, money and talent. But even if Vienna surpassed them, that would not be the reason for my success, especially at a time when my music was hardly ever performed in Austria. Indeed, there was something that went beyond all this, something which is chronically lacking in all our artistic practice, something without which, at least for me, that practice is unpleasant and inimical to art (*kunstfeindlich*): and that is love. At the beginning, Mahler was hostile to *Die Rose vom Liebesgarten* and actually refused to put it on. It is possible that among the great living conductors there are many who are closer to my music than Gustav Mahler. But that is where his greatness comes in: he lets himself be convinced and, once convinced, he became completely engrossed in the work. The artist who cannot on occasion completely enter into the spirit of another is not worthy of the name . . .[80]

On the other hand, Pfitzner was so obsessed with the question of 'Germanness' in art that Mahler's music always remained a closed world to him, as he acknowledged in the following text:

Judgement on him as a creative artist, as a composer is something quite different and belongs on a different plateau. Naturally here I have had to pass a refined judgement,

---

[77] Abendroth, *Pfitzner*, 138. Pfitzner contrasted the Vienna production to the one in Munich, where he thought he had been 'boycotted'.

[78] BSP 40 and Hans Rutz, 'Pfitzner in Österreich', *Österreichische Musik-Zeitschrift*, 4 (1949): 3/4, 59 ff.

[79] Pfitzner's letter to Schillings of 11 Apr. 1905, quoted by Abendroth, *Pfitzner*, 34.

[80] *Süddeutsche Monatshefte*, Munich (Aug. 1910).

such as would not be done in a pure eulogy. I have formulated my judgement on Mahler as a composer in the following way: he is subjectively sincere (*echt*) and objectively dishonest (*unecht*), that is, what he writes is always filled with the most perfect devotion, is always written with his heart's blood, but he cannot do anything beyond his nature. When he resorts to old German texts in his symphonies, for instance (like 'es sungen drei Engel'), he has (so one feels) a warm love for this world, but what stands on the music paper is by no means an adequate expression of the intended feeling. With this I believe that I have clarified what I meant by 'subjectively sincere, objectively dishonest'.[81]

Elsewhere, Pfitzner added: Mahler 'valiantly struggled to attain something which his being could not master, and this gave his music an "affected" quality'.[82]

Given his nationalist convictions, Pfitzner was bound to object to Mahler's 'heterogeneous' style. In return for Mahler's heroic efforts for the Viennese production of *Die Rose*, he might at least have kept his opinions to himself. Yet in May 1905, at the Molls', he did not hesitate to declare to Alma that 'Mahler's music was not music' and 'that it was embarrassing for him to be on such good terms with a man whose work was so foreign to him'.[83] When he wrote to Alma to ask for the score of a work of Mahler's 'which was new to him', she did not even bother to answer, and he surmised that she suspected him of pretending to take an interest in Mahler's music out of a sense of 'moral duty', merely because Mahler had championed *Die Rose*. In another letter he claimed that she was quite wrong: he would not hesitate to tell her the whole truth even if Mahler's art continued to seem 'foreign' to him![84]

Further letters exist which show that Pfitzner constantly offended his most fervent partisans and friends. A serious quarrel arose several months later with Bruno Walter, the most devoted of his Viennese friends and supporters, and it is obvious that in this case Alma had added fuel to the flames. Walter reproached Pfitzner with completely 'ignoring' him during his last stay in Vienna in autumn 1905, and of discussing their conflict with Alma, who was quite capable of 'using what she knew against them'. In another letter, he accused him of not speaking to him and even refusing to reply one evening when they had met by chance in a restaurant. To make things worse, Pfitzner had curtly requested him to return his scores, and then left Vienna without saying goodbye.[85]

[81] See John Williamson, 'Mahler and Pfitzner: A Parallel Development', in Philip Reed (ed.), *On Mahler and Britten: Essays in honour of Donald Mitchell on his Seventieth Birthday* (Boydell, London, 1995), 123. Williamson points out that Pfitzner was not an anti-Semite for reasons of 'biology or vulgar racism', but defined the Jewish spirit 'in terms of opposition to the "Platonic idea of Germany" '.

[82] Ludwig Schrott, *Hans Pfitzner* (Atlantis, Zurich, 1959), 122. Pfitzner nonetheless admitted liking certain movements like the Scherzo of the Third Symphony, which he later conducted at Strasbourg.

[83] Handwritten note at the bottom of Pfitzner's letter of 13 June 1905.

[84] Undated letter from Pfitzner to Alma (summer 1905), UPL.

[85] BWB 84–5. Another letter from Bruno Walter (18 Mar. 1907) shows that two years later the two were once again on good terms. Walter wrote: 'You were born to give suffering to yourself and joy to others' (BWB 90–1). Two letters from Alma to Pfitzner from the same period seem to imply that her indiscretions were largely the cause of the quarrel.

It would seem, indeed, that Pfitzner's personal and professional life was constantly spoilt by his catankerous temperament, something of which he himself does not seem to have been fully aware. In her *Erinnerungen*, Alma describes his conflicts with Mahler about socialism, but also about nationalism in art, and Goethe's concept of the 'eternal feminine'. Elsewhere she mentions one of their most unpleasant disputes, which was about Shakespeare. On 20 March 1905 Pfitzner conducted Mendelssohn's music in the first Viennese performance of the Berlin production of Shakespeare's *A Midsummer Night's Dream*, directed by Max Reinhardt, of which six performances were to be given in Vienna.[86] Afterwards, in Pfitzner's presence, Mahler and Reinhardt talked at length about their work. Both were deeply moved by the encounter.

In artistic matters they were not only in agreement about Alfred Roller. Their work, as performers, however personal and individual, and however different from that of others, was representative of their era and inner needs. Both Mahler and Reinhardt were men determined to resist the corroding power of day-to-day theatrical life and the kind of laziness that has become a habit.[87]

Thus perfect harmony reigned that evening between Mahler and Reinhardt. Once again, the only discordant note was struck by Pfitzner. Referring to *A Midsummer Night's Dream*, Mahler suggested that the richness and profundity of the play were such that it could only be a mature work. Pfitzner broke in to insist that, 'for a genius like Shakespeare, age and experience were of no importance'. The conversation grew heated. Pfitzner refused to yield an inch, and later wrote to Alma that he had proof that Shakespeare was only thirty years old when he wrote *A Midsummer Night's Dream*.[88]

The tragedy of Pfitzner's life was that he always felt himself to be a marginal artist and, much more than Mahler, an 'idealist' in a corrupt age, an artist 'out of season'. The consciousness of being isolated, misunderstood, and unappreciated constantly exacerbated his irritability and hostility toward musicians who had achieved acceptance. He saw himself as the bearer of the German romantic tradition. As such he was the sworn enemy of all '*neudeutsch*' tendencies, of 'musical progressivism', of 'the new Weimar school', and of the disciples of Liszt, whose music was contemptuously dismissed as *Afterkunst* (anal art) and *pseudosymphonik* by Pfitzner's biographer, Walter Abendroth. But most of all Pfitzner loathed Richard Strauss, the most successful of his contemporaries. His hostility apparently dated from a concert in Berlin in which *Ein*

---

[86]   This is the production which established Max Reinhardt's international reputation. It was presented in all the main cities of Germany and Austria and had led to Reinhardt's appointment as director of the Deutsches Theater in Berlin.

[87]   BWT 243 and LKR 111. Reinhardt had engaged Roller to design the sets for Hofmannsthal's *Oedipus and Sphinx* at the Deutsches Theater in Berlin. The first performance took place on 2 Feb. 1906. But, try as he might, he could not convince Roller to abandon Mahler and the Vienna Opera. In 1901, Roller collaborated with Reinhardt in the famous production of *Faust I*, for which he used a revolving stage.

[88]   Letter to Alma of May–June 1905. Interestingly enough, literary criticism now dates the writing of *A Midsummer Night's Dream* as 1594–5, the beginning of Shakespeare's career.

Heldenleben had been greeted with frenzied applause, whereas the second act of *Die Rose vom Liebesgarten* fell flat. He ceaselessly denounced the 'futuristic peril' and 'corrupting force' which Strauss allegedly represented, and claimed that his music showed even more symptoms of truly pathological degeneration than that of Bruckner or Mahler. Thus Abendroth's biography of Pfitzner, published in 1935, never ceases to attack Strauss. In the preface Abendroth establishes a parallel between Wagner's quarrel with 'the Jew Jacob Liebmann-Beer, alias Meyerbeer', and that which pitted Pfitzner (the pure German) against Strauss. Strauss's music was highly suspect to him if only because of the widespread success it enjoyed. He vilified and berated Strauss whenever he could, until Strauss finally broke off relations with him.[89] The difference in the temperaments of Pfitzner and Strauss—the one anxiety-ridden, dreamy, romantic, the other pragmatic, balanced, with both feet firmly on the ground, is well illustrated by a single anecdote: when told of the agonies Pfitzner went through while composing, Strauss was known to have replied: 'Poor fellow! If composing comes so hard for him, why didn't he learn another trade?'

Although she wrote in *Mein Leben* that 'spending two weeks with Pfitzner is like being constantly obliged to drink vinegar'. Alma Mahler remained loyal to Pfitzner to the end of her life, at least as far as his music was concerned.[90] In 1907, he went so far as to write to her demanding that she admit, once and for all, that she disliked his work, with the exception of *Die Rose* and the Quartet.

Why don't you come out with it and <u>tell me</u> that all the rest displeases you? Despite my high esteem for your highly trained musical capabilities, trained at the best possible school, it wouldn't change my own judgement! But from you it would be a sign of frankness and friendship. That would be <u>something</u>! But for the moment, all I sense is incomprehension and cowardice. Why don't you write me that you don't like the text and music of *Christelflein*? Walter hasn't got the courage to do so either. So don't be afraid! Don't imagine, dear Alma Mahler, that I am stupid enough not to know that fundamentally you make fun of me, and that this letter will make you laugh. So why (you will ask yourself) do I write it?

Pfitzner considered sincerity to be the very essence of integrity and, needless to say, his unwanted bouts of frankness never ceased to increase the number of his enemies, hence his isolation. Much later, in the 1920s, he even fell out with his best friend and patron, Paul Cossmann, who had financed the performance and publication of all his works, and this solely because

---

[89] Walter Thomas, *Richard Strauss und seine Zeitgenossen* (Langen-Müller, Munich, 1964), 202.

[90] AML 192. The passage was inspired by Pfitzner's stay at Alma's house in Breitenstein on the Semmering in 1927. A few years earlier, descending upon her uninvited at the Hohe Warte, Pfitzner had been especially troublesome, demanding constant attention and expecting affection and tenderness from Alma which she had no desire to give. Among Pfitzner's letters to Alma are four undated handwritten notes throwing light on the erotic element in their strange relationship: Pfitzner seems after all to have received from Alma, who behaved quite 'maternally' towards him, a certain degree of reassurance and understanding. Nevertheless, Pfitzner left Alma complaining that she had wanted to 'toy with him' (AML 69). During his stay, he played her the first sketches of his principal opera, *Palestrina* (cf. Hans Pfitzner, *Briefe*, i. 80).

Cossmann, a Jew, had converted to Catholicism.[91] His letter to Mahler, written in 1908, is another sad example of his obsessive need to be frank:

Dear and honoured friend! I may no doubt address you thus after the unexpected pleasure of your letter. I would have written back immediately, but I was unable to express at once everything that was going through my mind. Even though I still cannot write everything, the idea of leaving you without some sort of reply was beginning to torment me. I hope I will soon have the opportunity to explain it all in person. So I must ask you to bear with me. As I do not want you to think it is anything specific, I must say that a man like me—who is burdened with what (for me) is the curse of deadly sincerity—cannot be insincere to you, especially after your recent letter. I feel an irresistible need to be completely honest with you, even if it is at the price of alienating you at the very moment when you are beginning to draw closer to me. Of course, you are naturally entitled only to seek or permit the intimacy of those who unreservedly esteem you as a composer. I have never had the opportunity of discussing this with you in detail and such matters are not settled with a yes or a no. I only wish to say this: if, after studying one of your scores in detail, I do not come to appreciate your work in the manner that you seem to consider indispensable to a close personal relationship, you must permit me to be open about it, and not to deceive you by evading the issue.[92] But all this is to anticipate—please put it down to my clumsiness that I bother you with it now, and don't misunderstand me—I've received so many hard knocks from people that I'm always afraid that anything I say which is not utterly conventional will be resented. But there is surely no danger of that with you![93]

One wonders how Mahler reacted to this strange epistle, which conceded so much but explicitly withheld the essential. In any case, his efforts to meet this hypersensitive man's demands seem all the more admirable. Towards the end of his life Pfitzner became embittered and suffered from a veritable persecution mania. He briefly embraced Nazi ideology, but soon became disillusioned. His state of mind thereafter could aptly be described as one of 'inward emigration' (*innere Emigration*). The rest of his unhappy life was spent in a 'struggle against a world which persecuted, hated, and refused to understand me'.[94] After the final collapse of Hitler's Germany, Pfitzner's 'naive patriotism' became his only consolation and refuge. He wrote to Bruno Walter:

Now, at the end of my life here I sit: neglected, unwanted and oppressed, in an old people's home . . . But despite everything, I remain faithful to this land, the land of Luther, which has brought forth the *B minor Mass* and *Faust*, *Freischütz* and

---

[91]   In a letter dated 19 Mar. 1905, Pfitzner informed Cossmann that Mahler had reserved a box for the opening of *Die Rose* for the Cossmanns, the Walters, and the famous Vienna collector August Lederer (ÖNB, Musiksammlung, Nachlass Pfitzner).

[92]   It must be assumed that Pfitzner managed to overcome at least some of his reservations towards Mahler's music, since one of his first actions as Musikdirektor at the Opera and director of the Conservatory at Strasbourg was to conduct, on 11 Nov. 1908, Mahler's Second Symphony (see below, Vol. iiii, Chap. 3). After Mahler's death he performed the Fourth Symphony (25 Oct. 1911) and *Das Lied von der Erde* (1913) there; he pressingly invited Alma to these concerts, and was deeply disappointed when she didn't come (cf. Pfitzner, *Briefe*, 80).   [93]   AMM1, 432, letter of 18 Aug. 1908 (not included in AMM2).

[94]   Walter Thomas, *Strauss*, 193.

Eichendorff, the *Pastorale* and *Die Meistersinger* . . . To this land I shall remain faithful unto my dying breath.[95]

And yet, neither Germany nor his adopted Austria treated him well after his death, but allowed him to sink gently into semi-oblivion. Had he lived, he would surely have branded as a sign of decadence the glittering enduring fame of Strauss and the steep rise in the popularity of Mahler, whom he obstinately considered as 'alien to the German genius'.[96]

Mahler deserves a great deal of credit for having fulfilled Pfitzner's every wish, and for having overcome his own misgivings and allowed *Die Rose* for once to succeed in the Opera. To achieve this aim, he spared no effort. The original estimate of the cost of the production had been 52,000 kronen, but the Intendant had cut it down to less than 10,000. During the rehearsals, Mahler and Roller changed many of the costumes 'to fulfil the wishes of the composer who is present', which cost the Opera an additional sum of 4,300 kronen.[97]

A few days before the première of *Die Rose*, fixed for the end of March, Mildenburg reported sick yet again (after waiting, no doubt, to be sure that the work was viable and the role a 'good' one). According to Bruno Walter, no one at the Vienna Opera was capable of replacing her and a dramatic soprano had to be recruited as a guest for the Graz Opera. In fact, it was Berta Förster-Lauterer, who stepped in and took on the role of Minneleide.[98] But Pfitzner was becoming increasingly apprehensive, and Walter spent much time and effort comforting him and reading to him from Siegfried Lipiner's *Hippolytos*.

After Mildenburg, it was Schmedes' turn to have a sore throat. Mahler had induced him to give up horse-riding, his favourite sport, after he caught chills in the Prater. But Schmedes missed the fresh air and bought himself a handsome motorcycle, in which he took great pride:

It was just before the première of *Die Rose* . . . that I thought that an excursion to the Semmering would be the best remedy for a light catarrh (*sic*). When I arrived up at the top, I had completely lost my voice. Naturally I was desperate and telephoned my doctor. 'My God, what have you done now', he asked. 'Me? Nothing at all. I've only come up here on my motorcycle.' A few minutes passed before he recovered his speech. 'In this weather! With a catarrh! On a motorcycle? My dear fellow, have you taken leave of your senses?' And thereafter the motorcycle was also sacrificed to my profession.[99]

[95] Ibid.

[96] At Salzburg, despite the prominent place he occupied in the early programmes of the festival, Pfitzner's centenary in 1969 went unnoticed; not one of his works was played.

[97] HOA, G.Z. XVI. 4/1905, reports dated 3 and 26 June 1905. Pfitzner's stay in Vienna and the extraordinary attention he received were the subject of much gossip and rumour. The newspapers even announced that he was to be taken on at the Vienna Opera, and Mahler had to deny this in a letter to the Theater des Westens in Berlin, where Pfitzner was Kapellmeister (HOA, G.Z. 520/1905, letters of 22 and 28 Apr.). The following year, the Berlin press once again wrongly announced that he would be engaged by the Vienna Opera (undated letter of Alma, 1906, UPL).

[98] BWT 176. Berta Förster-Lauterer may well have been making a guest appearance at the Graz Opera at that time.   [99] *Neues Wiener Tagblatt*, 'Sonntags-Beilage', 28 June 1931.

Alas, no replacement could be found for Schmedes, who later admitted that the second cancellation of the première of *Die Rose* was his responsibility. Every day Mahler and Pfitzner visited him to make sure he was taking his medicine and that his condition was improving. The première finally took place on 6 April. It was a great success, and Pfitzner himself took a dozen curtain calls at the end of the last act. However, in his memoirs Theodor Helm calls the success 'somewhat odd', because most of the applause was prompted by the fairy-tale beauty of the décors. Schmedes was also applauded, partly because the audience realized he was struggling to overcome his hoarseness, but Helm was shocked by the display of enthusiasm of Pfitzner's partisans, which apparently prompted some opposition.[100]

In his memoirs, Egon Wellesz also describes the opening of *Die Rose* which he attended with other Schoenberg students. The first bars of the introduction in particular made a 'great impression' on both him and Webern because of the held notes which were passed from one instrument to another and created an effect which seemed daring for the time and which he considered to be one of the models for Schoenberg's *Klangfarbenmelodie*.[101]

After the première, Mahler and Alma gave a reception at the Auerbruggergasse to which all of Pfitzner's closest friends were invited: the Berlin banker Willi Levin, the Paul Cossmanns, Max Reinhardt, and also the Rollers, Zuckerkandls, Molls, and the Rosés. The dinner slowly proceeded, and Mahler grew impatient and rose before the end of the meal and went to read in his study. Since he always left the door open, took part in the conversation from a distance and later joined his guests, they usually forgave him. This time, however, the stout Berlin banker, who hardly knew him, felt mortally offended and swore that he would never set foot in the house of such a boor again.[102]

Bruno Walter calls *Die Rose vom Liebesgarten* one of the greatest achievements of the Hofoper under Mahler: 'On the stage Roller managed to create an atmosphere of heavenly beauty and joy with shades of blue and gold',

---

[100] THE 322.

[101] EWL 28. The prelude of *Die Rose* begins with a *piano* horn call starting on F sharp and descending to D. This D passes from the horn to the flute and then to the trombone, after which the F sharp is repeated by two horns and then by four. Thereafter the D is twice taken up by two trombones, by three trombones, and three trumpets in the course of a crescendo. Wellesz claimed to detect the influence of *Die Rose* in Mahler's use of the brass in the Finale of the Sixth Symphony. A detailed study has been published of the influence of *Die Rose* upon Mahler and the composers of the Viennese School. Its author also finds traces of Pfitzner's influence in Mahler's Fifth Symphony (see Wolfgang Osthoff, 'Hans Pfitzners *Rose vom Liebesgarten*, Gustav Mahler und die Wiener Schule', in *Festschrift Martin Ruhnke: zum 65. Geburtstag* (Hänssler, Neuhausen, Stuttgart, 1986), 265–93; see also Rainer Riehn, 'Zu Mahlers instrumentalen Denken', *Musik-Konzepte 91, Gustav Mahler: Der unbekannte Bekannte* (Jan. 1996), 65 ff.). John Williamson also draws a parallel between the 'almost classical form', and a number of other features in Pfitzner's First String Quartet, and Mahler's Fourth Symphony (Williamson, 'Mahler and Pfitzner', 127–8).

[102] According to Alma, nobody ever dared to disturb Mahler when he retired to his study. On this particular evening, however, Emil Zuckerkandl called out 'What's happening out there?' (*Was ist draussen?*) Mahler, who was sitting near an open window, replied 'It's cold', and Zuckerkandl riposted: 'Well, come back in!' (AMS).

harmonizing perfectly with the ecstatic, mystical music.[103] Paul Stefan's recollections, in *Das Grab in Wien*, also described the magical effect of Roller's set:

in all its blue, so German, and contemporary splendour! A fairy tale was told, a dream was woven, an emotional depth achieved. It was not the words that moved us, but the work as a whole: the sacred legacy of romanticism, the song of a soul filled with yearning. Nothing for the general public. But Mahler deliberately challenged public taste, and put it on again and again, especially on Sundays, and compelled people to come. And they came . . .[104]

The main virtue of this production was that it had successfully concealed the opera's main shortcoming, its abstract subject, symbolic characters, and lack of action. Pfitzner had spent much time and effort looking for a libretto and, like Hugo Wolf before him, had finally been ill-inspired in his choice. To Ida Dehmel, Mahler had confessed a few weeks earlier that he found Pfitzner's long search downright ludicrous because, in his opinion, in a

perfect drama, music was bound to be superfluous. A true playwright would never leave a work incomplete in order to provide scope to the musician, and even the most marvellous music could never make a great work of art out of a bad drama. Thus, those who did not possess both gifts, like Wagner, would be well advised to steer clear of it.[105]

Even Pfitzner's staunch admirers like Clemens Höslinger, the author of a very substantial article about 'Pfitzner and the Vienna Opera', have had to admit the 'turgidity' of Jacob Grun's libretto, his 'pure eclecticism', Wagnerian reminiscences, 'laboriously archaic German', and lack of dramatic 'know-how'.[106] The plot is indeed simple to a fault. Siegenot, the hero, possesses a talisman, a red rose, with which he is supposed to protect the 'garden of love', forbidding entry 'to all whom the light of beauty has not touched'. Thus, he has to turn away Minneleide, the Queen of the Elves, because she is 'still unworthy of supreme love'. Minneleide consequently falls into the hands of the King of the Mountain, who exiles her to the Kingdom of Shadows. There Siegenot, a new Orpheus, meets his death while trying to free her. The opera concludes with the redemption of the two lovers, 'who awaken to new life'.[107]

Most of the Viennese critics castigated the libretto's naivety, the gratuitous obscurity, the heavy-handed symbolism, and the lack of a plot capable of sustaining the interest of the audience. Hirschfeld accused the librettist of indiscriminately mixing 'all the symbols of romanticism, allegories, secrets, allusive names, figures, and ideas' stolen from *The Magic Flute*, *Lohengrin*,

---

[103] PSE (Paul Stefan, *Gustav Mahlers Erbe* (Hans von Weber, Munich, 1908), 39).
[104] PSG 56. [105] AMM1, 110–20 and AMM2, 121.
[106] Clemens Höslinger, 'Pfitzner', 69.
[107] On the libretto of *Die Rose*, its origins, its symbolism, and the form of the opera, see Reinhard Ermen, 'Der Lyriker als Musikdramatiker', in Wolfgang Osthoff, (ed.), *Hans Pfitzner und die Musikalische Lyrik seiner Zeit: Bericht über das Symposium Hamburg 1989* (Schneider, Tutzing, 1990), 185–93.

The Ring, and *Parsifal*. Pfitzner's music lent the work 'value, if not dramatic life'. Its exceptional qualities were inwardness, magical sonorities, technical perfection, a penchant for polyphonic richness, seriousness, and profundity. These aroused admiration and would ensure its survival for a long time. However, Pfitzner had an unfortunate tendency to add to every chord 'alterations, dissonances, augmentations and diminutions of the natural intervals', creating effects which 'both troubled and tortured the nerves by their wilfulness'. In conclusion, Hirschfeld labelled Pfitzner 'a sickly offshoot of the Wagnerian tradition'. Far from attaining to 'perfection, exaltation, and a full flowering', his art revealed a 'determination to cultivate music which produced both healthy and unhealthy growth'. Mahler had conducted it with 'obvious pleasure', imbuing every note with poetry. In the *Österreichische Rundschau* the same Hirschfeld, who as usual grew more critical with the passage of time, asserted that 'works such as *Die Rose* were without value in this world for they did not increase the pleasures of life nor did they permit us to look into the depths of art'. With Pfitzner technique took the place of expression, his characters, already fully developed by the time they left the wings, did not come alive on the stage, and their life or death were matters of total indifference.

Like most of his colleagues, Korngold noted that *Die Rose* had some thorns. The libretto was without the slightest psychological interest and was too obviously based upon Wagnerian models. The vocal writing 'exhausted the ear' with its wide intervals, the score lacked 'new and personal melodies'. Nevertheless it did contain some 'beautiful and original ideas' and revealed a harmonic and polyphonic imagination which in itself was sufficient to sustain interest.

In the *Fremden-Blatt* Kauders also regretted the virtual disappearance of dramatic action under the crushing weight of words, sounds, and, above all, images. The music expressed 'every nuance of melancholy, happiness, and terror', becoming 'especially forceful and convincing when the action stood still or was dispensed with altogether'. A musician capable of composing such music was 'rich enough to pay off the debts of others and make up for the shortcomings of the libretto'. Wallaschek praised the score of *Die Rose* and the 'sublime nuances' of Mahler's interpretation. Only Schönaich defended the libretto, and its 'both gentle and powerful effects'. His praise, however, was mainly for the composer, a 'rich man', because of the nobility of his melodic invention, the technical mastery of his symphonic development, the 'dramatic vigour' and the magical atmosphere which he depicted with feeling and imagination. One day, with a suitable libretto, such a musician might produce a masterpiece. For Max Graf, *Die Rose* displayed 'the imagination of a painter' rather than that of a man of the theatre and one soon tired of its 'nebulous' figures and 'pompously boring' dolls.

Nevertheless, in Vienna, as elsewhere, many professionals and amateurs took Pfitzner for an authentic genius, 'the most powerful since Wagner's death'.

Karpath, for one, warmly championed *Die Rose* and claimed that, despite the confusion of its libretto, Pfitzner had brought it to life on the stage because he was a born dramatist, as well as an accomplished and original composer. In the fourth column of his interminable eulogy, Karpath only regretted that he 'could not describe the work in greater detail'. The music's 'tender and poetic charm' had convinced even the most reluctant members of the audience.

Theodor Helm obviously had Karpath in mind when he derided an overzealous 'little group of impassioned admirers' of this 'weak and largely obscure imitation' of a Wagnerian opera. Pfitzner was not the 'pioneering genius' they claimed him to be. The score had exceptional qualities and the performance was beyond compare, but the subject would have been more suitable for 'a spectacular ballet'. Surprisingly Maximilian Muntz, writing in the nationalist and anti-semitic *Deutsche Zeitung*, also came out against Pfitzner, who was nevertheless soon to become one of the idols of German nationalists. Neither the production nor Pfitzner's harmonic imagination and 'lyrical gift', to which he gives but faint praise, could compensate for the 'lack of dramatic power'. Muntz said however that he preferred Pfitzner's 'natural' orchestration to that of 'the most refined technicians of the modern orchestra'—an obvious reference to Mahler and Strauss. In conclusion, the same critic praised the production, whose perfection had almost brought the opera to life.

Thus Mahler had every reason to be proud. He had lavished a huge amount of time and energy on a work alien to his own taste. His reward had been the only success that this ill-fated opera ever obtained, and the awareness of having thus successfully promoted and launched the Viennese career of one of the epoch's most talented composers. In 1905 and 1906, *Die Rose* was performed eighteen times. It led the way in Vienna to what was to be Pfitzner's one and only theatrical success, *Palestrina* (1917). After seven performances, Mahler handed the baton to Bruno Walter, whose 'dreamy and romantic nature', according to Richard Specht, was even better suited to the work.[108]

One month after the Viennese première of *Die Rose vom Liebesgarten*, the centenary of Friedrich von Schiller was commemorated at the Hofoper by a performance of Rossini's *Guillaume Tell*, the only work based on one of Schiller's plays then in the repertory.[109] For the occasion, Mahler cast new singers in most of the roles, and the performance was conducted by the Hofoper's Italian conductor, Francisco Spetrino. Certain critics complained of

[108] Cast for the 6 Apr. performance: Förster-Lauterer (Minneleide); Kiurina (Schwarzhilde); Forst, Michalek (soloists in the chorus); Kittel (Rotelse); Schmedes (Siegenot); Preuss (Moorman); Weidemann (Nachtwunderer); Demuth (Waffenmeister); Zawilowski (Sangesmeister). Later, the principal roles were given by Sembach (Siegenot), Mildenburg and Weidt (Minneleide), Stehmann and Mayr (Waffenmeister), Moser (Sangesmeister), Petru (Rotelse), and Wissiak (Nachtwunderer). The opera was given 14 times in 1905, 7 performances were conducted by Mahler, 6 by Bruno Walter, and one by the composer (on 17 May 1905). It was performed 4 times in 1906 and again in 1908 and 1910.

[109] As we have seen, the repertory included neither Verdi's *Don Carlos*, nor *Luisa Miller*, nor Donizetti's *Maria Stuarda*. Between 5 Mar. and 8 May, a series of concerts also commemorated Schiller. These included two performances of Beethoven's Ninth Symphony (THE 325).

the libretto and called it a 'parody of Schiller's play' and regretted that there should be 'no other opera based on Schiller's plays' (*sic*). The anonymous critic of the *Neues Wiener Journal*, approved the changes in the cast, but regretted that Spetrino should have been satisfied merely with 'doing his duty'. *Die Zeit* found the work 'dated', despite 'several passages of undeniable force, whose liveliness withstood the test of time'. Korngold, however, admired its 'indestructible freshness', underlined its historical significance and warmly praised the performance, though he acknowledged that it 'lacked atmosphere'.[110]

On 3 May, a week before the revival of *Guillaume Tell*, a large audience was sitting in the auditorium watching a performance of *The Magic Flute* conducted by Mahler. During the final chorus of Act I, the flying chariot carrying the three boys caught fire as a result of a short circuit. The wings were plunged into darkness, and the lights in the corridors and the boxes started flashing. Perceiving blue flashes above the stage, several ladies in the orchestra rose from their seats screaming 'Fire!' Smoke began to drift into the auditorium and there was a rush towards the exits. Fortunately, just as the audience was about to panic, the big chandelier lit up again. Leo Slezak, who had sung his aria to the end, walked to the front of the stage and with Anton Moser at his side, shouted that the danger was past. Neither of them succeeded in making himself heard in the confusion, so people continued to scramble for the doors. Soon however the majority of the audience understood that the danger was over, and order was restored. After going into the wings to check that everything was all right, Mahler resumed with the chorus exactly where he had left off. The public clapped vigourously, shouting 'Bravo Mahler!' At the end of the performance he was cheered once again. After the curtain had been lowered, he appeared on the stage to congratulate the singers on their composure.[111]

Two days later, the *Illustrirtes Wiener Extrablatt* carried a sketch of the incident by a member of the audience who wanted to demonstrate that 'certain accounts of the event had been exaggerated'. This sketch raises (and apparently answers) an interesting question which has never been conclusively answered until this day, that of the position of Mahler's podium at the Opera. It shows the first rows of the orchestra, the orchestra pit, and Slezak next to the prompt box haranguing the crowd as several members of the audience scramble for the exits. However, one of the interesting details of the sketch is the position it gives for Mahler's podium, which is in the *front* of the pit, near the footlights. Mahler is shown as having risen from the chair on which he

---

[110] Cast for the 11 May performance (instead of 9 May 1905, the anniversary of Schiller's death): Kiurina (Jemmy); Forst (Mathilde); Hilgermann (Hedwige); Slezak (Arnold); Maikl (Rudolph); Pacal (Rudi); Demuth (Tell); Wissiak (Melchthal); Moser (Leuthold); Mayr (Walter Früst); and Hesch (Gessler).

[111] The article in the 4 May issue of the *Neues Wiener Journal* adds that the rest of the opera was performed to a half-empty house. Cast for *The Magic Flute* of 3 May: Forst (Queen of the night); Michalek (Papagena); Gutheil-Schoder (Pamina); Slezak (Tamino); Moser (Papageno); Hesch (Sarastro). Weidemann (the Speaker), Breuer (Monostatos). Afterwards, Forst was occasionally replaced by Elizza, and Gutheil-Schoder by Forster-Brandt.

normally sat facing the stage. He is standing on the podium facing the audience, his left hand on the back of the chair. The amateurish perspective of the
sketch leaves the exact position of the podium unclear, but it appears to be
very near the footlights. At least one row of musicians are shown seated facing
the stage, with their backs to the balustrade separating them from the audience. This is proof enough that the conductor's podium was somewhere in
among the players, and not yet up against the balustrade, as it is today. Otto
Strasser, who joined the Philharmonic some years after Mahler's death, tells a
different story, derived from his older colleagues' reports: 'The conductor's
podium was originally placed in the middle of the pit, but he [Mahler] moved
it back to the railing, where it remains to this day.'[112]

If both the sketch and Otto Strasser's reminiscence are to be believed,
Mahler must have moved the podium back to the balustrade, but only in the
last years of his tenure, i.e. after the performance of *The Magic Flute* in May
1905. According to the official post-war historian of the Vienna Opera, Marcel
Prawy:

Gustav Mahler had the podium raised and moved it back to just in front of the strings.
His predecessor Jahn still sat on a round, wickerwork chair in the middle of the
orchestra. Earlier still the conductor's podium was right next to apron stage. The musicians sat behind him and he was almost exclusively concerned with the singers and
the events on the stage. A broad platform behind him made it possible for him to turn
to the orchestra if necessary. The present position of the podium, which to us seems
the norm and even natural, only dates from the time of Felix von Weingartner, Mahler's
successor.[113]

Two contemporary testimonies bear out Marcel Prawy on this point: in a
review dated 24 January 1908, of a performance of *Fidelio* conducted by
Weingartner the previous evening, Ludwig Karpath stated that Weingartner
was the first Director of the Vienna Opera to conduct with the entire orchestra
in front of him; and a letter from Roller to Mahler describes in detail the same
production.

He [Weingartner] has completely changed the position of the conductor's desk. From
now on all the musicians sit facing the audience, and he himself sits right against the
balustrade in front of the orchestra stalls. So we don't see sheets of music any more,
which is an improvement. Instead we see the faces of all the musicians, a more doubtful improvement perhaps. He himself has the bad habit of standing up to conduct ff
passages. It looks very odd! Perhaps he won't do it during the performance itself.[114]

So the bulk of the evidence seems to show that while Mahler brought the
conductor's podium back to 'just in front of the strings', it was Weingartner who
shifted the conductor's desk right back to the balustrade. According to several

---

[112] Otto Strasser, *Und dafür wird man noch bezahlt* (Paul Neff, Vienna, 1974).
[113] Marcel Prawy, *Die Wiener Oper* (Molden, Vienna, 1969), 63.
[114] AMM1, 421. See below, Vol. iii, Chap. 2.

reviews of the New York performance of *Don Giovanni* on 23 January 1908, Mahler also conducted there from the middle of the pit, where he placed the piano he used for the recitatives, with some of the musicians behind him.

The fire at the performance of *The Magic Flute* gave rise to another of Slezak's anecdotes. Mahler had reprimanded him a number of times for his faulty rhythms and intonation, especially in *The Magic Flute*, where he always made the same mistake during the scene in which he was supposed to play the flute. While congratulating him on stage for his presence of mind during the fire, he said: 'Slezak, do you realize that this is the first time you have sung that scene without making a mistake?' Then, turning to the other singers, he added, 'For Slezak to sing in tune, the house has to burn down!'[115]

The season at the Hofoper ended with a revival of Massenet's *Manon*, an opera which had been very popular during Jahn's tenure, but had disappeared from the repertory for three years. This time, Schalk conducted and Gutheil-Schoder made her debut in the title role which had been Marie Renard's speciality. Like most of his colleagues, Max Graf criticized her small and lack-lustre voice, and found her interpretation of the role lacking in unity and conviction. On the other hand, Richard Specht, who had just started writing for *Die Zeit*, compared Gutheil-Schoder to one of those old portraits 'which express the genius of an epoch', but acknowledged that she lacked warmth, spontaneity, and seductiveness. Both Korngold and Kauders accused the new Manon of 'misrepresenting a personage whose soul she had failed to compre-hend'. In any case, the opera which had charmed Vienna for so many years was now 'dead' and could only awaken wistful memories.[116]

At the end of the season, the Viennese press drew attention to Mahler's frequent absences and suggested that he was neglecting the Opera because he was planning to leave it. The 'ill health' of the Hofoper had already been diag-nosed the year before in the *Österreichische Rundschau* by Hirschfeld.[117] His report had been as usual highly unfavourable. He had drawn attention to the 'gaps' in the repertoire, the neglect of Gluck, Mozart, and Marschner. In his opinion even the Wagner operas needed to be thoroughly revised. Instead of celebrating Berlioz's centenary, Mahler had put on *La Juive*, and *La Bohème*, and 'the faded outpourings of the Italian School'. The ensemble no longer had the feeling of 'permanence' so essential for its well-being, and incessant changes destroyed its balance. Mahler was not blessed with that 'quiet strength' which was the most important attribute of an Opera Director. He contributed 'inspiration and vigour' in the case of new productions, but otherwise there was

---

[115] Leo Slezak, 'Mahler', in *Moderne Welt*, 3 (1921/2): 7, 17. The anecdote appears also in Slezak's *Meine sämtlichen Werke*, 144. Slezak also tells how he met Mahler one day when he was walking in the park with his 3-year-old son. Greeting the Director, Slezak momentarily let go the hand of his little boy, who fell over. 'Don't panic,' called Mahler, 'one upset (*Umschmiss*) won't stop a Slezak!'

[116] Cast for the performance on 26 May: Gutheil-Schoder (Manon); Kiurina (Poussette); Michalek (Javotte); Kittel (Rosette); Slezak (des Grieux); Moser (Lescaux); Mayr (Comte des Grieux); Felix (Stehmann).   [117] *Österreichische Rundschau*, 1 (1904–5): 2, 107.

a lack of cohesion. Even in the case of certain revivals (such as *Die Meistersinger*), the exceptional quality of the première had not been maintained in subsequent performances.[118]

A ballet evening entitled 'Chopin Dances' gave Hirschfeld a new opportunity to attack Mahler. He now accused him of permitting a ballet orchestra 'to trample on Chopin's musical flowers', whereas in other works 'a slightly delayed triple crochet would upset him' and 'in his symphonies, one bar could contain up to seven performance indications'. The virulence of Hirschfeld's attacks makes them suspect, but some of them have a ring of truth. Mahler's temperament certainly lent itself more readily to great bursts of energy for premières or new productions than to the humdrum, everyday work required to maintain the level of productions already in the repertoire. In March 1905, Hirschfeld complained again that the repertoire was poor and monotonous, and that the ensemble lacked resources. It included no first-class Venus, no adequate Elisabeth, except Frau Sedlmair, who 'at least sang with praiseworthy routine', no comic bass since Mayr's voice had been 'ruined' by overwork. Guest appearances, instead of being 'artistic events', had become sorry occasions indeed. The announcement that there was going to be one was enough to put the public off.

Furthermore, Hirschfeld went on, there was no longer any style to talk about at the Hofoper. Even an excellent singer like Demuth was at fault in this respect. The most one could hope for was 'a performance in accordance with the rules'. In fact, the Opera no longer took an interest in diction and style, except in the case of a première or a new production. Roller's costumes and phantasies absorbed the audience's attention, a 'violet light projector in the wings' or a wreath on a singer's head, had become more important than musical phrasing. To restore public confidence, a complete reorganization of the Opera was needed. The much publicized 'uncut performances' tired the audiences; the darkness which Roller insisted upon prevented people from reading the text.[119] Often the audience could not understand a single word. The fact that *Rheingold* had become a box-office attraction, sometimes performed several times in one week without the other *Ring* operas, symbolized for Hirschfeld the total decadence of the Opera.[120]

The majority of Hirschfeld's criticisms are obviously unfair, futile, even ridiculous. However, at the end of the 1904–5 season Helm expressed a number of similar reservations in the *Musikalisches Wochenblatt*. In his opinion, Mahler's 'highly-strung' temperament was responsible for the frequent changes among the singers, and the brilliant opening nights of his new productions were flashes in the pan, for the quality of the performances fell away as

---

[118] Hirschfeld claimed that Slezak's singing of the title role had gone from bad to worse, and that his acting was increasingly perfunctory. In the same article, Hirschfeld hints that Roller may have been responsible for the lowering of the orchestra pit.

[119] A strange remark! Should the audience be allowed to read the text during opera performance?

[120] *Österreichische Rundschau*, ibid.

his enthusiasm waned. Furthermore, the performances which he conducted himself were far superior to the others. Whatever the truth of these claims, the record of performances for the season makes nonsense of Hirschfeld's complaint about the 'poverty of the repertoire'; no opera house today can rival it for breadth and depth.

The most frequently performed opera in what Hirschfeld termed a 'poor' season was *Lakmé*, which was given fifteen times. *Fidelio*, a work considered 'unpopular', achieved a record thirteen performances. Wagner's operas were performed more frequently than in the preceding year, with five complete *Ring* cycles and the new production of *Rheingold*. On the other hand, there were few performances (10) of Mozart, though this was to be expected before the start of the Mozart anniversary in Oct. 1905. The repertoire included *Rheingold*, *Bohème*, *Pagliacci*, and *Cavalleria* (14 performances); *Fidelio* and *Les Contes de Hoffmann* (13); *Carmen* (12); *Tannhäuser* and *Die Rose vom Liebesgarten* (11); *Die Königen von Saba* (10); *Die Meistersinger* (9); *Aida*, *Mignon*, and *Die Fledermaus* (8); *Der fliegende Holländer* and *Die Abreise* (7); *Siegfried*, *Falstaff*, and *Les Huguenots* (6); *Walküre*, *Götterdämmerung*, *Rigoletto*, *Trovatore*, and *La Juive* (5); *Magic Flute*, *The Marriage of Figaro*, *Freischütz*, *Faust*, and *Das war ich* (4); *Tristan*, *Lustige Weiber*, *Hansel und Gretel*, *Guillaume Tell*, *Manon*, and *Le Postillon de Longjumeau* (3); *Don Giovanni*, *Rienzi*, *The Bartered Bride*, *Die Opernprobe*, *Czar und Zimmermann*, *Heilige Elisabeth*, *Norma*, *Lucia*, *Les Dragons de Villars* (2); *Euryanthe*, *Der Waffenschmied*, *Feuersnot*, Goldmark's *Das Heimchen am Herd*, *Pique-Dame*, *Louise*, *Le Prophète*, *La Dame blanche* (1).

The financial balance for the Hofoper in 1905 was less favourable than that for 1904, the best year financially during Mahler's tenure.[121] The plans he had made for the coming season were particularly ambitious since they included not only new productions of Mozart's greatest operas, but also of the two first *Ring* operas. *Siegfried* would follow in the autumn of 1905 and *Götterdämmerung* at the beginning of 1906.[122] One of Mahler's difficulties arose each year from the fact that, although the artistic season began in August, and ended in July of the following year, the budget covered the calendar year. 'Forecasting the estimated income from the box-office and ticket subscriptions was sometimes tricky, particularly when trying to gain the maximum return for frequent performances of new productions outside the subscription series. . . . This required some informed guesses on Mahler's part based on income from the box office during the previous season.'[123] Production

---

[121] Receipts Kr. 2,857,500 were Kr. 54,000 down on 1904, while expenditure increased by Kr. 245,000 to Kr. 3,286,000. Thus the estimated deficit of Kr. 170,100 which had been approved by the Intendant was exceeded by more than 150 per cent and amounted to Kr. 428,500 (WMW1, 218; WMW2, 180 ff.). In view of the large deficit, ticket prices were increased for 1906 (see WMW 215, for Roller's estimate of costs for 1905. He requested 282,000 kronen for the sets alone).

[122] The plan was rejected by the Lord Chamberlain as too costly.

[123] Evan Baker, 'Alfred Roller's Production of Mozart's "Don Giovanni" ', Dissertation, New York University, 1933, 28. See also Franz Willnauer, *Gustav Mahler und die Wiener Oper* (Löcker, Vienna, 1993) (WMW), 157 ff.

costs were of course carefully examined by the office of the General Intendant and had to be approved by him. *Così fan tutte* was finally selected to begin the Mozart season in October 1905, no doubt because the production was only five years old (1900)[124] and because Lefler's sets and costumes could be refurbished by Roller for little extra cost. Although *The Marriage of Figaro* had at first been planned to open the 1906 Mozart year proper at the end of 1905,[125] it was later postponed until the spring of the following year and a completely new production of *Don Giovanni* was chosen to replace it. Mozart's first Da Ponte opera had been considered his masterpiece throughout the nineteenth century. It had opened the brand new Hofoper in 1869 with sets by Carlo Brioschi,[126] and in October 1887 a new production had been commissioned by Wilhelm Jahn from Brioschi's son Anton on the occasion of the 100th anniversary of the opera. In 1905, it was to end the calendar year at the Hofoper in a completely new production which was to be one of the finest—and most controversial—of all of those prepared by Alfred Roller.

The first reference to a new Mozart production appeared in the Opera archive in October 1904. It was budgeted at 25,000 kronen but *Don Giovanni* had not yet been selected. The events leading to the new production have been described by Evan Baker: in the first part of 1905 the season progressed well, scoring artistic successes with the new productions, especially with *Das Rheingold* in January. But as the spring progressed, a situation developed which, if unresolved, would not leave sufficient funds for the production of *Don Giovanni*. When the expenditures for new productions and maintenance of the current repertory for the first half of 1905 were added together, a shortfall appeared in the budget projection for the second half of the season to begin 17 August. But because the combined costs of the settings, costumes, and special machinery for *Das Rheingold* totalled an extraordinary 56,892 kronen (an overrun of more than 13,000 kronen), this left only 13,000 for *Die Walküre*. Despite this, Mahler and Roller decided to take a calculated risk, and on 26 June 1905, a cost estimate for a total of 43,649 kronen for the production of *Die Walküre*[127] was submitted to the General Intendant for approval. If the requested additional funding of 17,000 kronen for the costs of [Wolf-Ferrari's] *Die Neugierigen Frauen* as well as the 25,000 kronen for the Mozart opera were to be included, the production deficit would rise to more than 70,000 kronen. In a letter dated 14 July,[128] Plappart angrily refused to consider exceeding the production budget, as he was certain the Lord Chamberlain would refuse any application for additional funds from the imperial treasury. Since the box office receipts were well below the projected estimates, he suggested cutting out one of the productions planned for the remaining part of the season.[129]

[124] See above, Vol. ii, Chap. 9.
[125] A notice to that effect appeared in the *Neue Freie Presse* of 11 June 1905.
[126] The 1869 production had had 113 performances in the course of 18 years.
[127] The estimated cost was 17,000 kronen.   [128] HOA, G.I. 2771 ex 1905.
[129] Baker, 'Roller', 128 ff.

Replying on 25 July, Mahler suggested that the production costs for the Mozart opera be accounted for in the budget of the 1906 fiscal year. However, innumerable difficulties arose with the planning of the new production of *Die Walküre*, which now appeared impossible within the confines of a restricted budget, and it was decided, towards the end of August 1905 to postpone the production to the following year (1907),[130] allowing funds previously allocated for the Wagner opera to be used for *Don Giovanni*. Roller began to draw preliminary design sketches in June 1905, completing the final set and costume designs by the end of the summer.

Meanwhile, Mahler's relations with the orchestra, which had improved after the reading rehearsal of the Fifth Symphony and the two performances of the Third in 1904, had changed once again for the worse. After other conflicts of lesser importance, the appointment of a new solo cello provoked a new storm of jealousy and backbiting. One after another, in 1900 and 1901, Reinhold Hummer, Ferdinand Hellmesberger, and Joseph Sulzer had left the orchestra. In 1902 Mahler had engaged Rudolf Krasselt, a young cellist from the Berlin Philharmonic. The other musicians were indignant that such a young man should immediately be given the rank of soloist, and they made life so hard for him that he resigned after only six months. Pending the appointment of a successor, Franz Schmidt was given the solo parts, without being officially appointed to the post. When Mahler finally felt obliged to appoint a new first cello, he bypassed Schmidt. His first choice was Friedrich Buxbaum, a member of the Rosé Quartet, who was followed by a Dutchman named Wilhelm Willecke,[131] and then by a young Czech, Wilhelm Jeral. The musicians naturally assumed that Schmidt, known to be *persona non grata* with Mahler, was being victimized. Rumour had it that on this occasion Mahler had acted 'under the influence of someone else known for his mercurial temperament'.[132] That someone else was evidently none other than Arnold Rosé, whom the entire orchestra accused of being Mahler's all-powerful adviser and the chief influence on him in all matters concerning the orchestra.

Franz Schmidt gives vent to his frustrations and accuses Arnold Rosé in his autobiographical sketch. As we have already seen, his biographer, Carl Nemeth, traces the origin of Schmidt's problems with Mahler to 1902, and to the successful first performance of Schmidt's First Symphony. The press then played off Schmidt against Mahler, who apparently suspected Schmidt of turning the Vienna critics against him—a most unlikely story, given what we know about Mahler's character. At any rate, Schmidt was, by 1904, playing most of the cello solos at the Opera, at least when Mahler conducted, for the two other first-desk players, Reinhold Hummer and Josef Sulzer, contrived not to play on those particular evenings. According to Schmidt, Mahler firmly intended at that time to appoint him to the post of soloist,

---

[130]   Baker, 'Roller', 130 ff.   [131]   See above, Chap. 1.
[132]   The incident was reported by Paul Bekker (*Allgemeine Musik-Zeitung*, 9 June 1905). The paper later published a 'reply' by a certain Erich Herpa.

but Arnold Rosé, his brother-in-law and friend, obstinately fought against it. As first concert master, Rosé had been invested with extraordinary powers by Mahler, and his use of them was not always exemplary. He had fallen prey to a sort of power complex and reigned over the orchestra with despotic brutality and narrow-mindedness. His insufferably arrogant behaviour led to a rift with Hummer, who finally left first the Rosé Quartet and then the Opera. Since I was Hummer's close friend, Rosé transferred his hatred and suspicion to me. Consequently, I was not chosen to replace Hummer in his quartet, as everyone had expected. Buxbaum, who had lost the trial competition I had won, . . . was appointed to the Opera orchestra. Rosé personally assured him that he would be appointed to the post of soloist.[133]

Schmidt claims that Mahler continued to ask him to take the solo parts every time he was conducting. Nevertheless, he soon began to understand that he was no longer *persona grata*:

Contrary to what it had been in the past, Mahler's behaviour towards me grew ice-cold. Rosé became ruder than ever, and the conductors Franz Schalk and Bruno Walter, among others, were gradually influenced by the all-powerful concert master, and made disapproving and even hostile remarks about my solo performances. I was almost ready to give up playing solos, for which I had never received additional remuneration. If I had, I would never again have been able to apply for the post. At that point, this would not have mattered to me. However, I did not wish to risk anything, because it was Mahler's express order that I should play the solos when he conducted, and at that time he conducted very often, easily half the performances.[134] I was sure that Mahler would have dismissed me if at that time I had stopped. This intolerable situation continued until the day when, in Mahler's absence, Rosé launched a frontal attack. On that evening *Lohengrin*, an opera without cello solos, was on the programme. Before the beginning of the performance I was sitting at the first desk, as usual, when the orchestral attendant came to tell me, on Rosé's behalf, that I was to give up my seat immediately. From now on the solos were to be played alternatively by Messrs Buxbaum and Jeral. I went to see Rosé who was in the musicians' room, and asked him to explain the reason for this sudden demotion and told him that he could have communicated his decision in a less insulting manner.

Rosé replied that he was not obliged to furnish any explanations and, raising his voice so that all the other musicians could hear him, he added: 'My decision remains unchanged. I no longer want to hear this gentleman play!' Schmidt was wounded to the quick, because both Buxbaum and Jeral, although they were older, were less experienced than he was. He declared himself ill for several days, and when he returned he took the last desk in the cello section. One afternoon Mahler, who was conducting *Die Walküre* that evening, let Schmidt know that he wanted him to resume his place as solo cellist. Schmidt immediately asked to see him in his office and told him that he would consent

[133] Carl Nemeth, *Franz Schmidt*, 52. The same passage occurs in Schmidt's 'Autobiographical Sketch', 16.

[134] In fact, during the 1904–5 season, Mahler conducted only 41 out of 296, less than a seventh of the total number of performances.

only if he were certain that he would be officially appointed as soloist. He complained about Rosé, and the discussion took an unpleasant turn. Mahler jumped up and yelled: 'What are you saying? Are you trying to lay down conditions? Are you trying to push up the price?' Schmidt accused Rosé of having insulted him, and Mahler, exasperated, finally exclaimed: 'My patience is at an end! Be careful! If you refuse to do your duty or say another word, consider yourself fired! I'm warning you!'[135]

After pondering this threat all day long, Schmidt arrived at the Opera that evening and took one of the back seats in the cello section. Neither an official request from the attendant nor threats from Rosé could persuade him to move, and Buxbaum finally sat down at the first desk. As soon as Mahler stepped into the pit he realized what had happened, but he 'started to conduct without batting an eyelid'. The performance began, and Schmidt realized that he had not been fired. But thereafter he vegetated for ten whole years in the ranks of the Vienna Hofoper as 'homo suspectus' while the post of solo cellist remained unfilled, despite a series of brief and unsuccessful experiments with Krasselt, Wilhelm Willeke, Cornelius von Vliet, and Ludwig Herkenrath.

Schmidt's recollections are of interest because they shed light on Arnold Rosé's character and behaviour. Without giving concrete examples, Alma alludes several times to the pernicious influence of Rosé on Mahler's relationship with the orchestra, and Schmidt's story corroborates her. Of course, Bekker's article in the *Allgemeine Musik-Zeitung* only gives Schmidt's version of the story. Although he does not say so specifically, Schmidt surely never made the slightest effort to be on good terms with either Mahler or Rosé, and in fact he opposed them secretly whenever and wherever he could. Nor does he explain why neither of the two Directors who succeeded Mahler appointed him to the solo post to which he considered himself entitled, especially as Rosé's[136] all-powerful position did not survive Mahler's departure. This painful incident certainly caused resentment within the orchestra and once again spoiled Mahler's relationship with the musicians. In the elections for a permanent conductor for the Vienna Philharmonic on 26 May 1905, Mottl and Muck each obtained eighty-eight votes, while Mahler only received two.[137]

The chronicle of the Vienna 1905 season would be incomplete without some reference to a new development in the field of the visual arts, which had become an important element in Mahler's daily life since his marriage. For some time serious conflicts had arisen within the ranks of the Secession. The

[135] Schmidt, 'Skizze' (unpubl. MS), 18, and Nemeth, *Schmidt*, 53. As another example of Rosé's 'will to power', Schmidt describes his ill-treatment of the cellist Wilhelm Willeke, who finally left the orchestra in 1907 to become a member of the Kneisel quartet in the United States.

[136] Arnold Rosé (1863–1946) had been appointed to the post of Konzertmeister of the Vienna Philharmonic Orchestra in 1881. He founded his famous quartet in 1883 and led it until 1938. Its numerous first performances included the quartets of Schoenberg (see below). Professor at the Vienna Conservatory until 1924, he fled to England in 1938, and died in London in 1946.

[137] Nine musicians abstained. According to HOA, each musician received an income of Kr. 560 for the Philharmonic concerts at the end of the 1904–5 season (Z. 471/1905). The money was paid by the Opera.

founding of the Wiener Werkstätte in 1903, and the importance which the most active members of the group gave to the decorative arts, was not welcomed by the other members, and the *Nur-Maler* or *Nicht-Stilisten* (partisans of 'pure' painting) went into opposition against the 'Klimt Group' or *Stilisten*. Klimt and his friends continued to believe that art should be present in all areas of life, and that decoration should somehow influence the life of modern man. The *Nicht-Stilisten*, gathering around the post-impressionist painter Josef Engelhart, scornfully labelled their colleagues *Raumkünstler* (space artists) and protested against the presence of architects such as Josef Hoffmann and Otto Wagner in the Secession. The conflict had almost come to a head in 1904, when the Austrian government asked the leaders of the Secession to organize an exhibition of avant-garde Austrian art for the St Louis World Fair in the United States. Their selection of paintings by Klimt, two sculptures, and a room decorated by Hoffmann did not seem sufficiently representative to the Viennese authorities, who cancelled the project. The other members of the Secession took umbrage at this and began openly to challenge the authority of Klimt and Hoffmann.

Thus, seven years after the rift which had divided the artists of the Künstlerhaus and resulted in the Secession, another battle between 'ancients' and 'moderns' was developing at the very heart of the new movement. The dispute came out into the open early in 1905. Klimt and his group had realized that the educational purpose of the Secession exhibitions, which had led them to show the best of the foreign avant-garde, was ultimately detrimental to Viennese artists, who, overwhelmed by the competition, were practically unable to exhibit their works. When the famous Othmar Miethke Gallery in the centre of Vienna was put up for sale, the 'Klimt group' suggested that the Secession should purchase it, and use it to present regular exhibitions of the works of its Austrian members.

The General Meeting was informed of the project, but the necessary funds were lacking. Klimt then asked one of his wealthiest friends, the jeweller Paul Bacher, to buy the Miethke Gallery and Bacher accepted on condition that Karl Moll should be its artistic director. Thus the Secession would continue to present 'thematic' exhibitions based on educational criteria, while the Miethke would exhibit Austrian painters of the past and present. All this was discussed in great detail by Klimt, Moll, and several other people, who were convinced that their enthusiasm for the project would be shared by all the members of the Secession. It seemed obvious to them that everyone would benefit from the Secession's association with the Miethke, since the private gallery could now take over the task of 'defending the material interests' of the members. Serious opposition to the project among the 'Secessionists' was not envisaged. However, this was just the opportunity Klimt's opponents had been waiting for.

After some hesitation, mainly on account of the additional duties that his dual involvement in the Secession and the Miethke Gallery would entail, Moll finally accepted Bacher's offer. The gallery had already organized several exhibitions under his direction: in 1904, Beardsley, Anton Romako, and Ferdinand Georg Waldmüller, and in 1905 the Belgian sculptor Georges Minnes and 'Austrian portraits of the first half of the nineteenth century'. The success of these ventures had irritated the adversaries of Klimt and Moll within the Secession. Asserting that the initial and essential aim of the Secession had been 'freedom from commercial constraints', they now claimed that Moll's strictly 'commercial' activities—competed with those of the Secession, and were thus incompatible with his post as the secretary of the group. Moll was asked to choose between Miethke and the Secession. Klimt pointed out that the Berlin Secession and its president, Max Liebermann, had for a long time worked together with the Cassirer Gallery, but the *Nicht-Stilisten* were intractable and persisted in their determination to exclude Moll.

Realizing that the rebellion was directed above all against himself, Klimt put the question to a vote during a general meeting in May 1905. He knew that the opposing groups were equally balanced, and everyone expected the ballot to end in a dead heat. However, a telegram arrived at the last minute from a member in Berlin, and this gave the 'conservatives' the majority they needed. Klimt immediately submitted his resignation, and was quickly followed by Otto Wagner, Josef Hoffmann, Karl Moll, Kolo Moser, Alfred Roller, and twelve other members[138] who subsequently constituted the 'Klimt Group'. The news was greeted with consternation in Vienna, for the departure of the Secession's strongest artistic personalities made the movement's future doubtful. It managed in fact to survive for a few years, but it was only much later, in 1918, that the Secession recovered some of its old dynamism with the famous Egon Schiele exhibition, for which Schiele himself designed the poster. After the Olbrich building had fallen into the hands of the conservatives, Hevesi's famous motto, which belonged to the founders of the Secession, that is, to the Klimt Group, was erased from its façade. For several years to come Klimt and his friends now had to organize exhibitions at the Miethke Gallery or at the Wiener Werkstätte. When they finally founded the Kunstschau and hastily erected a new building in 1908, Mahler had already left Vienna.[139]

At the same time a modest event, but one which was closely linked to the daily life of the Hofoper, underlined the salutary effect the Secession had had on Viennese artistic life. It also showed that the conservatives had not yet given up the fight. At 10 a.m. on 16 May 1905, the very day when the press announced the resignation of Klimt and his group from the Secession, two huge street lamps were inaugurated in front of the Opera, a gift to the City of Vienna by a recently deceased patron of the arts named Albert Böhler. The pedestals were adorned with two groups of sculpture depicting scenes from *Siegfried* and

---

[138] They included the sculptors Richard Luksach and Franz Metzner, and the painters Wilhelm Bernatzik, Adolf Böhm, Max Kurzweil, Wilhelm Liszt, Felician Myrbach, Emil Orlik, Hans Schwaiger, and Adolf Hölzel.   [139] See below, Vol. iiii, Chap. 2.

the finale of *Don Giovanni*. The sculptor was a certain Fritz Zäritsch (or Zerritsch-Almeroth, according to the *Neue Freie Presse*), and his thoroughly academic, eclectic style matched that of the Opera. The press criticized the small scale of the figures in relation to the majestic size of the lamps themselves. However, it did not question their thoroughly old-fashioned style. The battle for 'modernism' was indeed far from being won.

At the Hofoper, Mahler's frequent absences towards the end of the season to conduct his own works provided his enemies with an excuse for renewed attacks. He was in fact still turning down many of the offers he received. In March 1905 the disturbances in Russia provided him with an excuse to cancel a projected journey: 'one's personal security cannot be guaranteed', he wrote, 'and in any case artistic activity is utterly impossible.'[140]

By this time some of Mahler's works had been performed in America and England, as well as in Holland and Belgium. But nothing of his had been heard in France. A group of admirers, who were soon to become his close friends[141] decided that the time had come for a French performance of one of his symphonies. Sophie Clemenceau, Berta Zuckerkandl's sister, visited Madame Ménard-Dorian, a well-known patron of the arts, with a view to organizing a première of a Mahler symphony. In the autumn of 1904, Mahler accordingly received a letter from Alfred Cortot,[142] who offered to place his orchestra at Mahler's disposal for a performance of the Fifth Symphony in his 'Alfred Cortot' concert series. However, the date proposed, 25 May, was impossible for Mahler, who had insisted on a minimum of four rehearsals before the performance of the same work in Strasbourg on 29 May. Apparently, Cortot did not propose another date, and so five more years were to elapse before Mahler finally made his debut in Paris as composer-conductor.[143] Two years later, the letters he exchanged with a young Viennese journalist who was then living in Paris[144] did not lead to a French performance either, but, as Mahler wrote to Max Marschalk in April, he now had 'lots of patience and little ambition' concerning performances of his own works, in contrast with the youthful impatience he had felt ten years earlier.[145]

---

[140] Unfinished and undated draft of a letter to the Hermann Wolff Concert Agency in Berlin, HOA, cited in BDB 244.   [141] On Paul Clemenceau, see above, Vol. ii, 268 and 418.

[142] In 1902, Alfred Cortot (1877–1962) had conducted a sensational season of Wagner operas, which included *Tristan und Isolde* and the Paris première of *Götterdämmerung*. In 1905, he gave up composing, took up conducting, and, following the advice of Léon Blum, founded the Cortot-Thibaud-Casals Trio. The 'Alfred Cortot Concerts' were inaugurated on 1 Dec. 1904 and continued until 1 Apr. 1906. At this time Cortot, who had succeeded Vincent d'Indy, also conducted the Société Nationale de Musique. Three years later, in 1909, Cortot virtually gave up conducting after introducing the Parisian public to a great number of new orchestral works.

[143] Cortot's letter of 29 Oct. 1904 and Mahler's reply on 4 Nov. are preserved in HOA (Z. 1.079/1904).

[144] This was Josef Reitler (see below, Chap. 6).

[145] Undated letter to Max Marschalk. This letter was published only in the East German edition of Mahler letters (Mahler, *Briefe*, ed. Mathias Hanse (Reclam, Leipzig, 1981), no. 162). It is undated but accompanied reviews, apparently favourable, of a Berlin concert, conducted by Bernard Stavenhagen on 13 Apr. 1905 which gave Mahler's First Symphony as well as works by Schillings and Liszt.

Nevertheless, on 26 February 1905 Mahler's name made its first, timid appearance on a Parisian concert programme, not with a symphony but with three of the *Lieder eines fahrenden Gesellen*.[146] They were sung by Nina Faliero-Dalcroze in a Lamoureux Concert conducted by Camille Chevillard and were warmly applauded. In *Le Soir*, B. de Lomagne[147] wrote that 'Mme. Faliero-Dalcroze had successfully sung three songs by a German (*sic*) musician little known in France, Mr. Malher (*sic*)', but does not seem to have realized that the 'little known German musician' had conducted the Vienna Philharmonic five years earlier in Paris, and was Director of the Vienna Opera. In *Le Figaro*, Gabriel Fauré sensitively described the second song as 'a picture of an early morning, fresh and scented . . . particularly pleasing' and praised the 'simplicity and intelligence' of the singer's interpretation.[148] In *Gil Blas*, Louis Schneider considered that the songs lacked melodic originality but commended the 'interestingly multicoloured and extremely precise notation' of the orchestration. However, *Le Gaulois* found Mahler's songs totally uninteresting and their orchestration 'consistently imitative', while *Le Ménestrel* felt them to be much 'too intimate for our big concerts'.

As usual, 'l'Ouvreuse', who has been identified for 1905 as Émile Vuillermoz,[149] embellished his article in *L'Écho de Paris* with untranslatable and intricate puns, mainly on Mahler's name:

Chevillard's programme announced a *Wayfarer* who looked new to me (*qui mah ler nouveau*) (once doesn't make a habit), so I hurried over to the rue Blanche (*je me rue (bis) rue Blanche*). Anyway, even if Camille . . . only managed to put on the old stand-bys, I would run to the Nouveau Théâtre to cheer *Antar*, which drives me wild! . . . But we'd better get back to Gustav Mahler's songs. Sung—every cloud has a silver lining (*à quelque chose malher est bon*)—with charm and truly admirable expressive intensity by Mme. Nina Faliero-Dalcroze (more delicious than ever in pink chiffon spangled

---

[146] The first, second, and last songs of the cycle were first performed in Paris on 26 Feb. 1905 at the Nouveau Théâtre. The programme was as follows: Weber: Overture to *Der Freischütz*; Rimsky-Korsakov: Symphony No. 2, *Antar*; Mahler: *Lieder eines fahrenden Gesellen* (three Lieder sung by Nina Faliero-Dalcroze, soprano); Le Borne: *Fête populaire*. Nina Faliero-Dalcroze, who died in 1946, married the Geneva composer Émile Jaques-Dalcroze in 1899. The contemporary press reveals the richness of Parisian musical life during this period. In one and the same week the following major concerts took place: Wanda Landowska gave a piano and harpsichord recital at the Salle Pleyel under the title 'Voltes et Valses' (from William Byrd, Michael Praetorius, to Chopin, Schumann, and Berlioz); Ferrucio Busoni gave a recital of Bach, Beethoven, and Liszt at the Société Philharmonique; Johannes Messchaert sang Schumann's *Dichterliebe*; and Alfred Cortot conducted Liszt's *Sainte Elizabeth* at the Nouveau Théâtre.

[147] See above, Vol. ii, 261. B. de Lomagne was the joint pseudonym of two French musicologists Albert Soubies and Charles Malherbe.

[148] Fauré also expressed a desire to hear a Mahler symphony in Paris.

[149] Jacques Lonchampt, the French music-critic, discovered while examining Vuillermoz's papers in BGM, Paris, that Vuillermoz had for two whole years, 1905 and 1906, ghost-written for Willy the famous 'Lettres de l'Ouvreuse' published by *L'Echo de Paris*. Emile Vuillermoz (1878–1960) was born in Lyon. He studied composition with Gabriel Fauré at the Paris Conservatory and became the most famous and influential music critic in France, writing mainly for *Excelsior* (1922–39), *Candide* (1924–42), *Comoedia*, and *Paris-Presse* (1951–60). He was also co-founder of the Jeunesses Musicales de France and published several books, *Musiques d'aujourd'hui* (1923), *Histoire de la musique* (1949), *Ravel par quelques-uns de ses familiers* (1939), *Debussy* (1957), and *Fauré* (1960).

with silver), they were applauded politely. But just try and have them sung by anyone else . . .! Adorned with clever orchestration, wreathed with phoney sensitivity and genuine sentimentality, these little trifles combine Humperdinck's orchestration and Paul Delmet's inspiration: 'Little Gretel with the gentle eyes!' Nothing is omitted: neither the nightingale flute, nor the violin solo, oh Sechiari! neither the shower of pizzicati, nor the dripping harp. It all simpers around with the old-world graciousness of spurious adolescents. Jaques-Dalcroze makes every effort to convince me that this pretentious nonsense smells of good country air, of Gemüth and of Schubert! Dash it! I am not going to fall for that stuff (*pour ce nibé-là*) !¹⁵⁰

Thus the Parisian musical world had failed to recognize the unique musical personality displayed in these three short Lieder. It should be borne in mind, however, that France at the time was in the grip of the most narrow-minded chauvinism, and also that critical reactions in Germany had been equally negative towards Mahler. Yet in Strasbourg, a French province that had been ceded to Germany after the Franco-Prussian War thirty years earlier, Mahler was greeted like a hero, which seems odd at a time when his music still aroused so much controversy in Germany. The musical life of the Alsatian capital had been very active since 1871, thanks largely to Franz Stockhausen, an Alsatian musician of high international culture, who conducted the Municipal Concerts and also directed the Conservatory.¹⁵¹ Son of a German virtuoso harpist, younger brother of the famous baritone who had been one of Brahms's best friends, Franz had first been Charles Valentin Alkan's piano pupil in Paris, and then Ignaz Moscheles's at the Leipzig Consevatory. He had taught at the Hamburg Conservatory before returning to his native province in 1871. There he had deliberately and carefully preserved the double, French and German, tradition of Alsace which had just then fallen into German hands. Among the teachers he engaged at the Conservatory were Ignaz Jan Paderewski and Ernest Münch, who had studied in Leipzig under Philipp Spitta and greatly contributed to the revival of Johann Sebastian Bach's works in Strasbourg, at a time when they were not yet frequently played in Paris. Another important event in the musical life of the Alsatian capital had been the appointment of Norbert Salter as cello solo of the orchestra, and who had earlier been a member of the Budapest Opera orchestra under Mahler.¹⁵²

At this time, Strasbourg had already been visited by several great orchestras, the Berlin Philharmonic under Nikisch in 1897, the La Scala Orchestra under Mascagni in 1899, the Kaim Orchestra under Felix Weingartner in 1900. In 1902, Salter had founded a Concert management bureau and it was he who

¹⁵⁰ See above, Vol. ii, 258. The word 'nibé' is probably an abbreviation of 'Nibelungen', in which case Vuillermoz would be humorously alluding to the German-ness of the *Gesellen-Lieder*.

¹⁵¹ Franz Stockhausen (1839–1926) was born in Guebwiller. His older brother, Julius, the famous baritone and friend of Brahms, took care of his musical education. As director of the Strasbourg Conservatory (1871–1906) and conductor of the municipal orchestra he was in fact in charge of the musical life of Strasbourg until he retired in 1906.

¹⁵² Norbert Salter had played in the Opera orchestra in Budapest from October 1890 to May 1892, before (probably) following Mahler to Hamburg. (KMI).

conceived the whole plan of the festival, together with Stockhausen.[153] In 1904, a new 1,200-seat concert hall, the Palais des Fêtes, had been inaugurated. It had been financed by a subscription among the city's wealthiest citizens.

It was no doubt Salter who had persuaded Stockhausen to ask Mahler to conduct one of his own works in Strasbourg, during the three-day festival of 1905. Several plans had earlier been made but none had come to fruition. The first Fête musicale d'Alsace-Lorraine seemed like an ideal occasion to invite him, together with Richard Strauss. Besides these two leading figures in the German musical world, a number of French artists were also to attend the festival. A chorus of 240 had been assembled for the Finale of Beethoven's Symphony (to be conducted by Mahler), and for César Franck's *Les Béatitudes* (to be conducted by Camille Chevillard), and the size of the local orchestra had been increased to 108 by importing a number of musicians, among them a violin solo from Amsterdam and a trumpet player from Cologne.

Stockhausen had conducted a great number of local premières in Strasbourg. Saint-Saëns, Dvořák, Tchaikovsky, and Max Bruch had been invited to conduct their own works, but composers such as Eugen d'Albert, Gustave Charpentier, Jean-Guy Ropartz, Ernest Chausson, Paul Dukas, and Claude Debussy had also been performed.[154] Several of Strauss's symphonic poems had also been played, and Strauss himself had been invited in 1899 to conduct *Also sprach Zarathustra* and *Tod und Verklärung*. From then on, one or more of his works were included on the programmes each year. Not so, of course, with Mahler, who had warned Salter that he would not come to Strasbourg if one of his works was not included in the programme. He proposed the Fifth, but the organizing committee understandably hesitated at the idea of including a seventy-minute symphony in the programme. That the very daring (and costly) decision was finally taken is evidence of the enterprising spirit of both Stockhausen and Salter.[155] Mahler and Strauss were advertised beforehand as 'the greatest symphonic composers of the contemporary school' but it had obviously been a mistake, as far as the public was concerned, to include the Fifth Symphony and the *Symphonia Domestica* on the same programme. According to the *Hamburger Fremdenblatt* critic, Emil Krause, both composers were greeted in Strasbourg with 'boundless admiration' as welcome helpers in the fight against 'stagnation and laisser-aller in the artistic life' of Strasbourg.[156] The festival was to close with a Beethoven concert, its highlight being

---

[153]   Geneviève Honegger, head of the Strasbourg library, pointed out that Franz Stockhausen, the head of the Municipal Concerts in Strasbourg for 30 years, was an ardent defender of contemporary music.

[154]   When Stockhausen retired in 1906, he was replaced by Hans Pfitzner and there was an immediate shift in emphasis in the programmes from French to German music.

[155]   See Geneviève Honegger, 'Mahler et Strauss à Strasbourg', paper delivered at the Mahler symposium in Strasbourg in June 1993.

[156]   *Musikalisches Wochenblatt*, 36 (1905), 23. This was of course untrue, and Krause was obviously not well informed about the very active musical life of Strasbourg. As music critic of the *Strassburger Post*, Gustav Altmann was the most influential critic of the Alsatian capital. In his review of the festival in *Die Musik*, he also speaks of the 'rather stagnant artistic life' of Strasbourg.

the Ninth Symphony conducted by Mahler. In fact, he had almost cancelled the entire project when he heard from Salter that the Strasbourg authorities were hesitating to include his Fifth Symphony in the festival programme.[157]

As early as 29 January, the city's main newspaper, the *Strassburger Post* had introduced Mahler with a full-page article in the 'Unterhaltungsblatt' (Entertainment Page) section by the *Neues Wiener Tagblatt* critic Ludwig Karpath, who has probably interviewed the director of the Hofoper before writing it. It was a mistake, he wrote, to call Mahler a Bruckner pupil, for he had never been taught by him. The older composer's influence had been 'superficial' and Mahler had 'never been able to come to terms with some esoteric aspects of Bruckner's compositions'. Karpath emphasized the 'iron will' with which Mahler had overcome all the obstacles on his path, the absolute calm of his gestures on the podium, as opposed to the 'eccentricity' and the 'nervousness' of his former conducting, and drew up a list of the damning adjectives used by the critics to denigrate his music, pointing out the many famous musicians who denied Mahler all talent without having ever heard a single note of his music.

The critic of the *Neues Wiener Tagblatt* further pointed out the huge success, the frenetic applause which had greeted the two Viennese performances of Mahler's Third Symphony at the end of 1904. They had seemed to prove that his music had at last conquered the heart of the Viennese. He mentioned the influence on his compositions of Hoffmannesque irony, of Bohemian folk-music, and also of unadulterated nature. The article is that of a convinced Mahlerian, but Karpath's praise acquires an ironic undertone in the light of his rapid change of mind, as a result of the conflict which soon broke out because of the article Karpath wrote about Mahler's Lieder. Also ironically, the Vienna concert took place on the very day when the *Strassburger Post* published his encomium.

As always, Mahler was concerned about the quality of the local orchestra and demanded a large number of rehearsals. The local conductor Maximilian Wilhelmi[158] was given the task of preparing the orchestra for a full week of rehearsals under Mahler.[159] Mahler insisted that his symphony be placed at the beginning of the concert, 'so that the audience is fresh and has a better chance

---

[157]   Mahler's letters of 1904 and 1905 to Norbert Salter (Bayrische Staatsbibliothek, Munich).

[158]   The name of the Strasbourg conductor who rehearsed the orchestra before Mahler's arrival is not mentioned in any letter or document. Romain Rolland, in his article on the festival (see below), claims that Ernest Münch was in charge of all the preparations for the festival. However Münch was mainly a conductor of choruses and religious music, and it is more likely that the preliminary rehearsals of Mahler's Fifth Symphony took place under Albert Gorter, the first Kapellmeister of the Strasbourg Theatre (see below, Chap. 4).

[159]   In a letter written in Maiernigg in the summer of 1904, Mahler asked for a fee of 1,200 marks per concert and offered to accompany the Beethoven Lieder cycle *An die ferne Geliebte* on the piano. In the same letter, Mahler stressed the importance of training the horn-player for his symphony, and asked Salter to prepare a rehearsal for the evening of his arrival on 15 May, and to plan for others if necessary. He also stated that he would be bringing his own orchestral material for Beethoven's Ninth and *Coriolan* Overture.

of understanding it'.[160] But even when all these conditions were met he was still worried and wrote to his young friend Oskar Fried[161] just before leaving for Strasbourg:

I really don't know if I should encourage you to come. On such occasions, one has to 'let things take their course' and go on conducting through thick and thin. But it goes against the grain with people 'like us' not to work out all the details, but the modern masters call it 'painting with a broad brush'! Anyway, if you want to take the risk, let me know so that I can have a room and a ticket reserved in time.[162]

Mahler left Vienna for Strasbourg on the evening of 14 May for ten days of intense rehearsing. Alma accompanied him, so there are no letters from him to her describing his impressions of Alsace or what he did between the rehearsals. His wife's account in her *Erinnerungen* is, as usual, very succinct. The whole festival took place in the large and modern Sängerhaussaal. For the opening concert of 20 May, Richard Strauss conducted the overture to Weber's *Oberon*,[163] after which Camille Chevillard replaced him on the podium for César Franck's *Les Béatitudes*[164] and Gustav Charpentier's *Impressions d'Italie*,[165] followed by three songs with orchestra by Jean Sibelius, Hugo Wolf, and Armas Järnefelt,[166] sung by the Finnish soprano Maikki Järnefelt and accompanied by her husband. Strauss reappeared at the end of the concert to conduct the final scene of *Die Meistersinger*.[167]

For the second concert on the following evening, a substantial and remarkably heterogeneous programme had been chosen. Mahler's Fifth Symphony was the first item. It was followed by Brahms's *Alto Rhapsody* sung by Adrienne

[160] As we shall see below, Strauss later complained that the orchestra was badly rehearsed. He might also have complained about the place of his symphony on the programme, and perhaps would have if he had read a letter which Mahler wrote to Norbert Salter: 'Strauss's symphony does not need this [to be played at the beginning of the concert] as much as mine, both because of his [greater] renown and because his symphony is shorter than mine and easier to understand.' (Draft of a letter to Salter, HOA.)

[161] See below, Chap. 4.

[162] Undated letter to Oscar Fried, May 1905 (PML). Later on, Mahler wrote from Strasbourg to Fried, inviting him to attend the opening of the Graz Festival on 1 June, where he was to conduct a concert of his Lieder (undated letter, Jewish National and University Library, Jerusalem).

[163] Gustav Altmann complained in his report in *Die Musik* that Strauss 'seemed quite exhausted', and 'failed to render correctly the tenderly romantic passages' of Weber's Overture. He also censured Strauss's habit of hastening the tempo during crescendos.

[164] *Les Béatitudes* had already been performed in Strasbourg in 1896, under Franz Stockhausen. For Camille Chevillard's performance in 1905, the soloists were Maikki Järnefelt (soprano); Berthe Weber (mezzo); Adrienne von Kraus-Osborne (alto); Emile Cazeneuve (tenor); and Paul Daraux (bass-baritone).

[165] Many of the French critics, like Romain Rolland, complained of what they regarded as a poor choice of works to represent the music of their country (cf. Yves Simon, 'Les Premières Tribulations de Mahler en France', in *Gustav Mahler: un homme, une œuvre, une époque* (Association Gustav Mahler, Paris, 1985), 164).

[166] 'Fährmanns Bräute' by Sibelius, 'Gesang Weylas' by Wolf, and 'Sonntagsmorgen' by Järnefelt. The latter, conductor of the Stockholm Royal Opera Orchestra and husband of the singer, also conducted.

[167] The soloists were Felix von Kraus (Sachs), Maikki Järnefelt (Eva), and Karl Jörn (Walther). According to William d'Gelly, critic of the *Journal d'Alsace-Lorraine*, Jörn had 'stepped in for M. Anthes at the last moment'. Strauss was sharply criticized in Strasbourg for having included in his programme a scene in which Wagner's hero praises German art ('Ehrt eure deutschen Meister').

von Kraus-Osborne[168] and conducted by Ernest Münch. Strauss then appeared on the podium to conduct Mozart's Violin Concerto in G major, with Henri Marteau as soloist. The mammoth concert ended with the *Symphonia Domestica*. No wonder the exhausted orchestra was no longer at the top of its form to perform a difficult modern work which had not been adequately rehearsed!

As he appeared on the stage Mahler was greeted with a fanfare and rewarded after the performance with thunderous applause.[169] For the second half of the concert, Mahler and Alma sat at the end of a balcony not far from the artists' dressing room. After Brahms' *Alto Rhapsody*, the enthusiastic audience called for an encore (only the choral coda was repeated), at which point Mahler and Alma overheard Strauss uttering a flood of invective:

'What a bunch of circus artists! That cow should sing in "Venedig in Wien", not in a serious concert! Go on, repeat the end, repeat the end, tire out my oboists, they're already at the end of their tether! No wonder, with a bigwig like Brahms! If I ended my works with such a C major chord I'd be just as successful!'

According to Alma, Strauss's offensive words were repeated to the singer's husband, baritone Felix von Kraus,[170] and during the interval (after the Mozart Concerto) he stormed up to Strauss's box and shouted; 'At least *my* wife doesn't sing in department stores!'—a reference to the fact that Pauline Strauss had recently given a concert with her husband at Wanamaker's. Kraus demanded that Strauss apologize to her. He drew up a written statement of what had been said, and asked Alma and Mahler to sign as witnesses.[171] At the end of the interval, Mahler was still trying to calm Kraus while Strauss, still fuming with rage, had to interrupt the argument to go on stage and conduct the *Symphonia Domestica*. According to Alma, the performance was not very good, since the orchestra was tired and, as seen above, inadequately rehearsed, Strauss having apparently judged two rehearsals sufficient.

With regard to this last point, Strauss's own testimony has fortunately survived, written forty years later in the margins of a copy of Alma's *Erinnerungen* which had been lent to him by the critic and musicologist Willi

---

[168]   Adrienne von Kraus-Osborne (née Eisbein) was born in Buffalo to parents of German origin. She studied singing in Leipzig with August Götze and made her debut at the Leipzig Opera. She became famous for her Wagnerian roles, her concert performances, and especially for her interpretation of Brahms's *Alto Rhapsody*. She sang the parts of Erda and Waltraute at Bayreuth from 1902 to 1909, toured Holland, England, and the United States. Mahler considered engaging both her and her husband at the Hofoper in 1907 (see below, Chap. 8).   [169]   *Neue Zeitschrift für Musik*, 72 (1905): 24, 523.

[170]   Felix von Kraus (1870–1937) was born in Vienna. The son of a general practitioner, he studied philology and music history at the University, and then harmony with Bruckner and theory with Eusebius Mandyczewski. After studying singing on his own and with Julius Stockhausen, he embarked on his career in 1896, singing recitals, oratorios, and Lieder, especially Brahms's *Vier ernste Gesänge*. In 1899 he made his debut at Bayreuth, where, until 1909, he sang the roles of Gurnemanz, Hagen, Marke, and the Landgraf in *Tannhäuser*. In 1899 he married the contralto Adrienne Osborne. Between 1908 and 1935 Kraus taught at the Music Academy in Munich. Gustav Altmann, in *Die Musik*, found the part of Hans Sachs too high for Kraus and criticized him for 'singing in his score rather than for the public'.

[171]   AMM1, 110; AMM2, 112.

Schuh.[172] Concerning the performance of the *Domestica* in Strasbourg, his marginal note reads: 'It was understood that I should arrive for the last rehearsals and that I would find the symphony well rehearsed. But that was to prove impossible, for Mahler monopolized the whole of the rehearsal time.' Be that as it may, Strauss had certainly been unwise to request only two rehearsals while Mahler had demanded at least four. Strauss's wounded feelings and dismay when he read Alma's descriptions of his wife and some of the comments in Mahler's letters can be easily understood, for it seemed to him that both of them had entirely forgotten the help that he had given to Mahler at the beginning of his career as composer. 'What astonishes me personally is that Mahler, whom I profoundly admired as an artist and to whom I had always behaved amicably, apparently was not in the least grateful for all I had done to help him achieve success.'[173] Furthermore, Strauss wanted posterity to believe that Alma had made up every one of the lively incidents involving him and his wife which she describes in her *Erinnerungen*, such as his conflict with Felix von Kraus. However the descriptions are so realistic and the details so vivid that it seems highly unlikely that they could have been invented, even though they might have been exaggerated.

To return to the performance of the *Domestica*, Alma claims that it was so badly received that the booing could easily be heard above the applause.[174] Still fuming with rage, Strauss left the stage and paced up and down the corridors 'like a tiger', cursing 'all music festivals and their organizers'. Some members of the organizing committee bustled around him, reminding him that he was expected to attend the banquet to be given in his and Mahler's honour. Strauss categorically refused to attend, so Alma and Mahler returned with him to the hotel, where they tried to calm him down, reminding him that he alone was responsible for the poor performance and that he had been 'raving like a madman'. Strangely enough, the reproach delighted Strauss, who wanted to write to Pauline immediately about the incident, for 'she never believes me when I tell her how angry I can be! You too must tell her all about it, to frighten her a bit!' Mahler eventually persuaded him to come along with him to the banquet to make up for the bad impression his early departure had made on their Strasbourg hosts. Alma stayed at the hotel, where Mahler joined her some time later, laughing heartily: he and Strauss had been received first

---

[172] Willi Schuh was kind enough to lend me this copy and allowed me to make photocopies of the pages containing Strauss's handwritten notes. Strauss carefully noted the place and date on which he finished reading the book: Baden, 28 Dec. 1946.

[173] Strauss here draws up a list of the performances of Mahler which he had brought about. The list contains several errors, which is not surprising since almost forty years had passed since Mahler's death. See also below, Chap. 8.

[174] According to Gustav Altmann, correspondent of *Die Musik*, 4 (1904–5): 18, 458 ff., there had only been a single rehearsal, and it was therefore inevitable 'that the otherwise excellent orchestra was not at its best on this occasion', whereas Mahler had prepared his two concerts with a full week of rehearsals. By the end of the concert, the orchestra musicians must have been absolutely exhausted, for they had played right through the public final rehearsal that same morning.

with astonishment, and then with cordiality. Strauss had proceeded to harangue the members of the festival committee and Mahler, having been totally forgotten, had managed to slip away unnoticed.[175]

The morning after the concert, a group of distinguished French personalities[176] whom Mahler had met in Paris in 1900, arrived in Strasbourg for the second concert: Georges Picquart, Paul Painlevé,[177] Paul Clemenceau,[178] the brother of the famous statesman, his wife, Berta Zuckerkandl's sister, and another officer, Guillaume de Lallemand.[179] The four Frenchmen were renowned for their liberalism, their pro-Dreyfus opinions and their love of music. Georges Picquart, who was soon to become Mahler's close friend, had been the hero of the Dreyfus Affair. A year after Dreyfus's second trial, he was appointed head of the counter-espionage service and discovered documents proving Dreyfus's innocence and Esterhazy's guilt. In the name of truth and justice he felt compelled to open his superiors' eyes. But for them, whether Dreyfus was guilty or not was of little importance, provided that the honour of the army was preserved. 'No one will know he is innocent if you keep quiet', he was told.

Picquart, although initially not untinged with anti-Semitism, was a man of integrity and his insistence on justice was to make a hero of him. More or less

---

[175] According to the *Strassburger Neueste Nachrichten*, the banquet took place at the 'Roten Haus' and 'on behalf of the artists present Strauss and Mahler made witty speeches of thanks for the honour done to them'.

[176] Berta Zuckerkandl had nicknamed Picquart, Painlevé, Clemenceau, and Lallemand the 'Dreyfus Quartet'.

[177] Paul Painlevé (1863–1933) had already acquired fame as a mathematician, professor at the École Polytechnique, and aviator when, at the age of 40, he embarked upon a political career. An ardent 'Dreyfusard', he was elected to the Chamber of Deputies as an 'independent socialist' in 1910. Later on, he occupied several posts as cabinet minister and was twice appointed Prime Minister.

[178] Born in Nantes, Paul Clemenceau (1865–1945), was fifteen years younger than his more famous brother Georges. (The youngest brother, Albert, had been Dreyfus' lawyer.) After studying engineering, he worked for the Schneider Company at Creusot, after which he became President and General Director of Nobel Dynamite, a post he retained until his death. A music lover and, like his brother Georges, a great connoisseur of modern painting, in 1886 he married Sophie, Berta Zuckerkandl's sister and daughter of Moriz Szeps, a Viennese journalist of Polish origin (see above, Vol. ii, 218). Moriz Szeps was passionately pro-French and dreamed of an Austro-French alliance. With this in mind he got to know several important French politicians like Gambetta and Clemenceau. Sadly, the close ties between Paul Clemenceau and his wife's country of origin later clouded his relationship with his brother Georges, who never forgave him for making contact with Austria in Switzerland during the First World War through his wife and his sister-in-law, in the hope of concluding a separate peace treaty. Paul and Sophie Clemenceau formed a sort of *ménage à trois* with Paul Painlevé, though the couple never separated.

[179] Walter Jean Frédéric Guillaume, Baron de Lallemand du Marais (1860–1931) was at this time a captain, but died a general. He had reluctantly entered the army under pressure from his father. His main interests were music and literature. An amateur pianist of great talent, he had taken some lessons in composition with César Franck in his youth. He maintained close links with Vincent d'Indy, Ernest Chausson, Albéric Magnard, Claude Debussy, Gustave Samazeuilh, Edouard Lalo, Gabriel Fauré, and especially Paul Dukas, his close friend until his death. His daughter, Elisabeth de Lallemand (Madame Pierre Raindre) to whom Fauré later dedicated his *Préludes*, was the godmother of the author of this biography. In the Zuckerkandl family the story ran that Picquart and Clemenceau had made Lallemand's acquaintance purely by chance, in the streets of Reims. One day, through an open window, they heard a Mahler symphony being played on the piano. Overcome with curiosity, they finally rang the bell to ascertain the identity of the pianist. It was Guillaume de Lallemand.

exiled to Tunisia, he revealed the truth of the affair to his lawyer before his departure, and left a letter in Paris that was to be made public in the event of his death. When this act of disloyalty to his superiors became known, he was recalled, arrested, tried, and finally discharged from the army. In 1898, he was imprisoned for 'making public secret documents'. His case divided France. Workers distributed tracts and collected signatures outside the Cherche-Midi prison where he was imprisoned. The review of the Dreyfus case led to his release and he was permitted to return to the army. However, until the official rehabilitation of Dreyfus in 1906 his position remained delicate, and he had returned on this occasion to Strasbourg, his birthplace, incognito and without requesting official permission to leave France.[180]

Alma describes Picquart in highly emotional terms. In her eyes he was 'not so much a human as a seraphic being', with eyes as blue and clear as a mountain spring. He 'spoke little, but what he said was wisdom itself'! Anyone who met him realized at once his strength of character, his genius. Picquart spoke German fluently and was much better acquainted with contemporary German literature than Mahler, who rarely found time to read. Contemporary German music interested him equally, and he had played Mahler's symphonies on the piano with Guillaume de Lallemand.

The time Mahler spent in Strasbourg with the members of the 'Dreyfus quartet' was exceptionally gratifying for him. They had plenty to talk about and he admired their intelligence and feelings as much as their liberalism and their knowledge of music. The day after their arrival, the Frenchmen went on an excursion to Sesenheim, following in the footsteps of Goethe,[181] while Mahler and Alma stayed in Strasbourg with Strauss. The occasion was nothing less than historic, for that afternoon Strauss insisted on playing to Mahler his new opera, *Salomé*, which he had just finished. As a libretto, he had used the original text of Oscar Wilde's play, written in French. It had been banned in London in 1894,[182] and its provocative eroticism was considered to be the most audacious example of Wilde's love of the scandalous—a penchant which Strauss shared to some extent.

The French première, directed by Lugné-Poe (without Sarah Bernhardt) had not been a great success. In Germany, on the other hand, where the need to protest against the bourgeois order was perhaps stronger, its triumph was instantaneous, and some 200 performances were given in several cities within a few months. Two years earlier, when Strauss had first mentioned his plan to make an opera of it, Mahler had done his best to persuade him to drop the idea,

---

[180]   Alma claims that Georges Picquart (1854–1914) had 'recently' been obliged to resign because of his pro-Dreyfus opinions, but she is doubtless thinking of the events of 1898. In 1906, Clemenceau appointed him War Minister (see below, Chap. 7). He died in 1914 after a riding accident.

[181]   While studying at the University of Strasbourg, Goethe met Herder, whose influence led him to devote himself to literature. There he fell in love with Friederike Brion, daughter of the pastor of Sesenheim.

[182]   Sarah Bernhardt played the leading role and the rehearsals were well advanced when the play was banned.

for in his opinion such an opera would be 'unperformable in Catholic countries'. Strauss had defended his project with vehemence and passion, and Mahler quickly realized it was no use continuing the argument. 'It was', Alma wrote, 'as if you had tried to persuade a man not to marry his sweetheart.'[183]

Since then, Strauss had worked on his new work with feverish intensity. Hoping that the première might take place at the Vienna Opera, he took Mahler and his wife to the showrooms of the Strasbourg music dealer Wolf to play it. It was there, in a room crowded with pianos, that Mahler, thunderstruck, discovered what is arguably Strauss's masterpiece, while curious passers-by pressed their noses to the windows, hoping to hear something of what was going on. According to Alma, Strauss 'played and sang with incomparable skill'. Arriving at the penultimate scene, he came to a halt, admitted that he had not yet composed the 'Dance of the Seven Veils' and then went on to play the final scene. Mahler asked him if he was not afraid that he might now be unable to recapture the mood of the work but Strauss only laughed his carefree laugh, and said: 'I'll manage it somehow.' 'But he didn't manage it', Alma wrote later, 'for the dance was the only weakness in the score, a sort of compilation of the rest.'[184] Be that as it may, Mahler was so 'utterly convinced' by the work in which Strauss's genius had made 'the unbelievable believable' that he was soon to find himself fighting one of the hardest battles of his career as Director.

On 22 May, Mahler's second concert, an all-Beethoven programme, began with one of his favourite pieces, the *Coriolan* Overture, which was followed by the Fourth Concerto with Ferrucio Busoni as soloist. A Berlin tenor, Ludwig Hess, then sang the *An die ferne Geliebte* cycle with piano accompaniment[185] and the long programme came at the end with the Ninth Symphony.[186] Several anecdotes have survived about Mahler's sometimes stormy relationship with Busoni,[187] who had previously played under his baton in Hamburg and Vienna, but in Strasbourg they seemed to have got on famously.

---

[183]   AMS. On 5 Sept. 1904 Strauss wrote to Ernst von Schuch to announce the completion of his outline for *Salomé*, 'an almost literal transposition into music of Oscar Wilde's drama' (Stargardt autograph catalogue).

[184]   AMM1, 114; AMM2, 116.

[185]   Although Mahler's name had been announced as accompanist for the Beethoven cycle on the festival poster, he was finally replaced by Kapellmeister Koch, from the local theatre, no doubt because he could not spare the time to rehearse with the singer. According to Gustav Altmann, Hess had 'when singing such an impossibly unsteady voice and a tone at times so thick and rough that in spite of his exemplary diction the vocal effect is often embarrassing'. Charles Eckert's review, in *Der Elsässer*, was equally critical of the tenor: 'He sings with a tremolo and affects an exaggerated expressiveness, which deprives his voice of the steadiness necessary to develop the note. He also has a vulgar habit, when linking two notes over a large interval in a downward direction, of descending in a continuous chromatic slide which sounds horribly tearful. Thirdly, he puts an unnecessary flourish at the end of every long-held note, and that too is a bad habit.'

[186]   The vocal soloists were Johanna Dietz (soprano); Adrienne von Kraus-Osborne (alto); Ludwig Hess (tenor, replacing Otto Mařák, the Prague tenor listed in the programme); and Felix von Kraus (baritone).

[187]   A little-known episode was related by Busoni himself to his pupil, the conductor Rudolf Ganz. Busoni had apparently arrived late for one of the rehearsals of the eighth Concert of the Vienna Philharmonic which was to take place on 19 Mar. 1899. Mahler was angry and introduced him unceremoniously to the orchestra as 'Herr Professor Busoni'. Later on, when Busoni slowed down the tempo for a passage in the first

Mahler's performance of Beethoven's Ninth, Alma remembered as

the most beautiful I have ever heard in my life. The audience went wild and from my seat it even looked as though Mahler's life was in danger. The entire audience converged Bacchante-like upon him as if down a funnel, and he disappeared from view. Picquart, Clemenceau, and I ran out into the street and round the back to look for him. There he was, running, hat in hand, pursued by a huge crowd. When he saw us he heaved a sigh of relief. Clemenceau had hailed an old, comfortable landau, and just before the enthusiasts, who were threatening to unharness the horses, reached us, we were off. Then, in a small, out-of-the-way bistro, all incognito, we ate our supper.

Once again one might suppose that Alma was exaggerating. But Gustav Altmann, the music critic of the *Strassburger Post*, corroborates what she writes:

I have never before heard Beethoven's Ninth like that, and Strasbourg has never before heard such a storm of applause as followed the fascinating urgency with which the Finale displayed its power. That indeed was Mahler, the conductor, the Napoleon of the baton, who, with his indefatigable ability to recreate the spirit of a work, has not been equalled since Bülow. And for this his name—however unrecognized or belittled it might be now, especially in 'leisurely' Vienna—will shine in the artistic firmament of the future.[188]

The *Strassburger Neueste Nachrichten*, in a lengthy but unsigned review,[189] praised every aspect of Mahler's conducting and interpretation to the skies:

Mahler conducting! Without question he was the central point of the three days of the Festival, the artistic phenomenon which had the most profound, most overwhelming, most fascinating impact on all who heard him. Not through showy effects—Mahler is in fact most impressively calm, with him violent movements always indicate mistakes which have been made—but through his extraordinary seriousness and the greatness of his artistry. For Mahler music is something sacred, but he himself is the fanatical guardian of it. That is why he as a conductor is ruthlessly strict with himself and others, and why it's all the same to him whether he is correcting a prima donna or a drummer. The musicians of our orchestra can testify to his incredibly sensitive ear. At rehearsals—and it is typical of him that two or three rehearsals were not enough, he had up to twelve—it happened more the once that in some indistinct supporting part, for example the 4th horn, he would spot a mistake. The player in question would begin by denying it; but during the repeat his fault would be revealed, and Mahler proved right. There are plenty of stories of this kind. But this extraordinary concentration, this

movement of Beethoven's 'Emperor' Concerto, Mahler stopped the orchestra and said: ' "Herr Professor, here in Vienna, we play in time. Let's begin again." Busoni later said to Ganz: "I could have strangled him, the way he looked at me!", but henceforth he played in time.' (From a radio interview of Rudolf Ganz by Studs Terkel, broadcast by WDMT, Chicago, in 1964, sent to the author by Prof. Jeanne Colette Collester).

[188] Gustav Altmann, 'Mahler Erinnerungen', in *Strassburger Post* (27 May 1911).

[189] Thanks to Geneviève Honegger, I was able to identify the author of this important review. He was Max Bendiner (1853–?), a historian, author of a monograph on Strasbourg Cathedral, and member of the Festival committee. Born in Dresden, he was a fervent German nationalist and admirer of Wilhelm II. In 1907 he left Strasbourg for Zurich where he stayed at least until 1909, after which there is no further trace of him.

indefatigable schooling of the orchestra, was only the infrastructure. The full majesty of his greatness Mahler revealed in the performances themselves. This short swarthy little man with his forest of unruly hair and sharply cut features, and his deep harsh voice, he grew to giant size when he stood in front of the orchestra. Outwardly—as we said—calm, but his eyes flashed lightning, hot full-blooded life spurted from his fingertips. A mighty explosive temperament must be seething and foaming inside him, but he hardly shows it, one feels the stream of fire under the surface. And that's the way he handles the orchestra too. In the *Coriolan* Overture during the Beethoven evening, and in the first three movements of the Ninth, every suggestion of violence was avoided, in proud majesty these immortal works of art rose up like gigantic mountain peaks. But it was as if, touched by Mahler's magic wand, the covering fell which shrouded them, and one could see into the innermost parts of the mountains and watch the gold of life running through their veins like a stream of fire! And especially the Ninth in Mahler's interpretation will remain unforgettable for us. Never yet, we believe—and the writer of these lines has heard the Ninth Symphony performed under the most famous masters of the baton—has the monumentality of this divine work sunk so deeply into us, never before did the triumphal song to Joy really become such a joyful experience for us, too! A truly Elysian festival with the lovely round dances one can see on Greek vase paintings. Reflecting on the basic features of this performance it soon becomes clear that it was the extraordinarily strict and richly differentiated rhythms which gave it life. The second movement and the Finale were particularly convincing examples of this. The last movement with the chorus had the effect of the sunrise, as if Phoebus Apollo himself was appearing in his fiery chariot, filling the universe with the fiery glow! Anyone who was not there can have no idea of the enthusiasm with which the orchestra, the chorus and the soloists followed their conductor spellbound. Strasbourg has never before experienced such a storm! And that was the full-toned closing chord to the whole magnificent splendidly successful music festival!

Strangely enough, Charles Eckert, in the Colmar newspaper *Der Elsässer*, was disappointed by this performance which had so delighted the Strasbourg audience; he thought that by then the orchestral musicians were simply tired out. This he had found particularly noticeable in the famous cello and double-bass recitative at the beginning of the Finale.[190] However, most reviewers agreed that Mahler had been more successful and more popular with the Strasbourg public than any other conductor who had taken part in the festival. Furthermore, most of them felt that their local orchestra had never performed so splendidly as it had under him.

Nevertheless the Beethoven concert, which had aroused such unbridled enthusiasm, was as usual severely castigated by some critics. Not the least of them was the French writer Romain Rolland, an eminent member of the Paris intelligentsia. Although he had been a friend of Richard Strauss for many years—and was therefore receptive to certain forms of modernism—Rolland was obviously suffering from an acute case of chauvinism—not surprising at

---

[190] Since Mahler always rehearsed this recitative with the greatest care, it is possible that Eckert mistook for a weakness in the performance what was in truth a very personal way of phrasing.

that period in any Frenchman other than the author of *Jean Christophe*, and perhaps heightened by the spectacle of an Alsace-Lorraine which had now been German for thirty-five years. Had the performance of Franck's *Les Béatitudes* not convinced him that 'French art is silently taking the place of German art'?

In Mahler, Rolland thought he could see

the legendary type of one of those German musicians à la Schubert who have something of the schoolmaster or the minister about them: a long, cleanshaven face, dishevelled hair on a pointed skull, bald at the temples, eyes blinking behind glasses, a strong nose, a wide, thin-lipped mouth, hollow cheeks, and an ascetic, ironic and ravaged appearance. He is excessively highly-strung and in Germany shadow-theatre caricatures of him have popularised his mimicry of a scalded cat on the conductor's rostrum . . .

I could never have imagined that a German orchestra, conducted by the foremost *Kapellmeister* of Austria, could have been capable of such a wrongdoing. Incredible tempi. The scherzo with no impetus. The adagio taken post-haste, without lingering over a moment of dreaminess. Pauses in the finale, which interrupted the whole development: breaks in the thought. The different sections of the orchestra tumbling over each other. Constant uncertainty and lack of balance. I have, in the past, criticized Weingartner's neoclassical stiffness. How I appreciated his robust balance and his striving at accuracy, on hearing this neurasthenic Beethoven!—No, it is no longer Beethoven, or Mozart, whom we can hear in Germany today: it is Mahler or Strauss.[191]

In his diary, published long after *Musiciens d'aujourd'hui* (Musicians of today), Rolland made further comments in the same vein: 'But how one feels in Mahler the tiresome fascination with Germanic strength and brutality, pulverising a Vienna temperament which is if anything dreamy and agreeable, basically somewhat whimsical and soft-hearted. That adds even more to the impression of Germanic heaviness.'[192] The rest of the concert did not improve his humour. Busoni's 'brilliant and superficial virtuosity . . . let nothing remain of Beethoven's noble G major Concerto, and in *An die ferne Geliebte*, Ludwig Hess 'shouted at the top of his voice'. Rolland was not alone in condemning Mahler's Beethoven, which others found so admirable. The Hamburg critic Emil Krause, who had come all the way from his home town to attend the concert, was equally indignant at an 'interpretation full of personal touches and changes in instrumentation'.[193] The Strasbourg critic, Gustav Altmann, in

---

[191] 'Musique française et musique allemande', *Richard Strauss and Romain Rolland: Correspondance et fragments de Journal*, 205 (Albin Michel, Paris, 201).   [192] Ibid. 144 ff.

[193] Egon Wellesz describes hearing Mahler conduct Beethoven's Ninth in 1900 or 1901. One of his fellow-pupils showed him a score on which he had written in Mahler's retouchings, which permitted Wellesz to 'learn orchestration'. According to Wellesz, Mahler's tempo for the Trio of the Scherzo was indeed particularly slow. The English composer Charles Villiers Stanford apparently told him that he had seen the original printer's plates, and the metronomic tempo was ♩=116 and not ♩.=116. In London in the summer of 1970, Otto Klemperer conducted the symphony with Mahler's tempos (Egon Wellesz, 'The Vienna School of Modern Music, Erinnerungen an Gustav Mahler und Arnold Schoenberg', *Urbis Musical*, Tel Aviv University, 1 (1971), 1). The first metronome indication Beethoven sent to his publisher on 13 Oct. 1826

Die Musik, thought that the clarity and colouring (*Plastik und Färbung*) of the orchestral playing showed Mahler to be at the height of his conducting powers, though he too vehemently objected to the tempos of the symphony. The first movement lacked 'majesty' (maestoso), the second 'fiery pungency' (*feuriges Prickeln*) in the 3/4 rhythms, and the Adagio, in an over-hasty tempo, failed to bring out the contrast between 3/4 and 4/4. Only the Finale had been, to his mind, 'ideal' in a manner he 'had practically never heard before': 'The whole ensemble was animated, like a living being, following the rhythm of the spirit with which it was imbued. The conducting was truly grandiose, melting into the noble genius of the work.'

An anonymous correspondent of the Vienna *Neue Freie Presse* praised Mahler's conducting for 'the great fervour of his emotions and the dramatic power with which he expresses it'. But he went on to express his disappointment with Mahler's interpretation of Beethoven's Ninth: the first movement never moved towards a climax, the second lacked liveliness, and the third lacked calm. Only the Finale created a massive overall effect, so 'indescribable' that it fully deserved the endless ovation which followed it. Finally, William d'Gelly, the spritely music critic of the French-language *Journal d'Alsace-Lorraine*, pointed out many 'shortcomings' in the orchestra, but credited Mahler with 'a striking success ... in making the Ninth live and move, in inspiring the Scherzo and Finale with his verve, and bringing all his sensitivity to bear upon the Introduction (*sic*) to the Andante'. However, d'Gelly found Mahler 'extremely nervous' in the *Coriolan* Overture, which 'scarcely appeared to interest him, for he seemed anxious to get it over with as quickly as possible'.[194] In the Beethoven concerto Mahler 'almost fell asleep over his score while Busoni valiantly pegged away at a thankless trill. Busoni is an accomplished, first-class musician and when he happens upon an engaging piece he conquers the audience,' d'Gelly continued, 'but in the Concerto he only achieved an 'honourable success'. Only Stanislas Schlesinger, correspondent of the *Neue Zeitschrift*, defended the great pianist and praised 'the tender, poetic perfume' and 'refined simplicity' of his interpretation.[195]

Romain Rolland not only disliked Mahler's conducting, he also disliked his Fifth Symphony. 'But between ourselves', he wrote to Strauss after the Strasbourg Festival, 'isn't German music "going through a bad patch at present?" (as we say here). I was very disappointed by Mahler's Symphony. Which contemporary compositions do you consider interesting? I have the greatest desire to do justice to German works; but I must confess that I find

specifies $\downarrow$=116 for the Scherzo (and also for the Trio, barred as C). However, as it is in 3/4 time, it seems normal that it should have always been read as $\downarrow$.=116.

[194]   In fact, this overture was one of Mahler's favourite works.

[195]   The festival orchestra was the Strassburger Städtisches Orchester: with 108 musicians it was nearly double its normal size. Besides the Cologne trumpet soloist mentioned above, the first violin, Herr Kossmann, had been brought from Amsterdam (*Freie Presse*, Strasbourg, 22 May 1905).

very few worthy of interest!'[196] A few years later, in *Musiciens d'aujourd'hui*,[197] he attempted to paint a more comprehensive picture of Mahler's symphonies:

They are enormous, massive and cyclopean structures. The melodies upon which they are built are rough-hewn blocks of mediocre quality: they are banal, imposing only because of the solidity of their foundations and the obstinate repetition of the rhythmic patterns, which are adhered to with all the tenacity of an *idée fixe*. These musical agglomerates, learned and barbarous, with harmonies at once coarse and refined, rely for their effect on sheer massiveness. The orchestration is heavy and loud: the brasses dominate, adding their crude metallic sheen to the opaque colours of the main body of sound. The thinking is basically neo-classical, somewhat softened and diffused. The harmonic structure is composite: in it the styles of Bach, Schubert and Mendelssohn mingle with those of Wagner and Bruckner; with its pronounced taste for canon form (*sic*) it even reminds one of the music of Franck. It is opulent and brash bric-à-brac. The most characteristic feature of these symphonies is the use of the chorus with orchestra.[198]

Thus, for Romain Rolland, Mahler's personality was more interesting than his art.

Studying his works, it becomes clear that he is that rare thing in present-day Germany, a mind concentrated upon itself, sincere in its emotions; however, its emotions and thoughts do not succeed in expressing themselves in a truly personal and sincere manner; they come to us through a veil of reminiscences, a classical atmosphere. I believe that the root of the problem is in Mahler's activity as Director of the Vienna Opera, and the saturation in music that the job involves. Nothing is as deadly for the creative spirit as too much reading of other composer's scores, especially if you cannot choose what you read and if you are forced to absorb more than you can assimilate. In vain Mahler tries to protect his inner solitude: it is violated by the foreign thoughts besieging him from all sides, and which, instead of rejection, his conscience as a conductor compels him to take in and even embrace. Frantically busy, weighed down with responsibilities, he never stops working and has no time to dream. Mahler will only really be Mahler the day he can leave his administrative tasks, put away his books of scores, look into his own mind and patiently wait to be alone with himself. Unless by then it is too late.[199]

Major French writers have seldom written anything very enlightened about music. Stendhal, Balzac, André Gide, François Mauriac, and most recently Jean-Paul Sartre, have all had their say, and their paradoxes, pretentious naiveties, and platitudes only serve to remind us of the gulf separating the art of music from that of literature. But one would have expected better from Romain Rolland, a writer who was also a musicologist, and author of a famous

[196] Strauss seems to have wanted to revive Rolland's esteem for Mahler. When Rolland made some observations to him about the programme of the *Domestica*, Strauss replied: 'Perhaps you're right. . . . You're in agreement with Gustav Mahler, who utterly condemns programmes in general' (letter to Romain Rolland of 5 July 1905).

[197] In the same article, Rolland also commented upon the Second and Third Symphonies.

[198] *Musiciens d'aujourd'hui* (1922), 185.   [199] Ibid. 188.

'musical' novel, *Jean-Christophe*. Yet here he is unconsciously repeating all the most hackneyed clichés of German musical criticism. While he grudgingly admits that Mahler's choral symphonies (the Second and the Third) possess certain qualities, he echoes his German colleagues in regretting the lack of an explanatory 'programme' for the Fifth. Of course, Mahler wanted people to listen to his music as 'pure' music, but that was impossible because the work was

excessively long (it lasts an hour and a quarter), and no inner necessity justifies its length: aiming at the colossal, it is empty for most of the time. Its themes are hackneyed: after a tritely tempestuous funeral march in which Beethoven is tempered by Mendelssohn, comes a *scherzo*, or rather a Viennese waltz in which Chabrier joins hands with old Bach. The *adagietto* is sweetly sentimental, and the final *rondo* begins like an idea of César Franck's; it is the best bit. It gets carried away in a rapturous whirlwind, from which a chorale rises up amidst outbursts of joy; but it gets lost in repetitions which weigh it down and stifle it. Throughout the entire work there is a mixture of pedantic rigour and incoherence: aimless ramblings, abrupt breaks which interrupt the development, parasitic ideas with no musical logic which suspend the life of the work.

Most of all, I fear Mahler is coming under the hypnotic influence of that idea of strength which is currently infatuating all German artists. Mahler seems to me a hesitant soul; ironic, sad, quivering, and weak: the soul of a Viennese musician striving for Wagnerian grandeur. No one knows as well as he does the gracefulness of the Ländler and refined waltzes, of elegiac reverie. Perhaps no one else would be better suited to rediscover the secret of Schubert's touching and voluptuous melancholy, Schubert whom he resembles by certain of his virtues as well as certain of his faults. But it is Beethoven or Wagner that he wants to be. He is wrong: he lacks their balance and their Herculean strength, as was only too clear when he conducted the *Choral Symphony*. However this may be and whatever my disappointment with him at the Strasbourg Festival, I would never speak of him lightly or irreverently. I believe in him, I am sure that a musician of such lofty conscience will some day compose the work that is his by right.[200]

Once again Romain Rolland's comments reveal not so much the 'inadequacy of Mahler's aesthetics as the inadequacy of the "aesthete" who is disparaging them'.[201] Since the age of 20 Mahler had composed the music 'that was his by right', and only the incurable myopia of contemporary critics prevented them from realizing it. Rolland's only perceptive remarks are those concerning Schubert's influence and the incoherence and 'parasitic ideas' in the Finale of the Fifth. Evidently, as a close friend and fervent admirer of Richard Strauss, it was difficult for Rolland not to share Strauss's opinion of Mahler's music. Other reviewers, in Strasbourg and elsewhere, shared most of Rolland's opinions. Gustav Altmann, critic of the *Strassburger Post* and correspondent of *Die Musik*, who had admired the Second Symphony in Basle,

---

[200]   Ibid. 189.   [201]   Theodor Adorno was the author of this play on words.

regarded Mahler's Fifth as 'Kapellmeistermusik of a superior order', a clever
compilation of borrowed themes and melodic ideas. Yet, to his mind, all the
movements—the Funeral March (which he dubbed 'for the death of a bad
Kapellmeister'), the Scherzo, 'with its varied *Fledermaus* motifs' and the
'unpleasantly sweet Adagio', and the 'generously contrapuntal Finale, but with
every line endlessly repeated and heavily underlined by brass instruments'—
used themes typical of Austrian-Viennese 'Gemütlichkeit' with even a hint of
banality. As for the Hamburg critic, Emil Krause, who had valiantly defended
the Fifth after the Hamburg concert, he only spoke this time of Mahler's
conducting—'brilliant, incandescent, and warmly alive'—and of the ovation,
which 'even he [Mahler] could not have expected'.[202]

The critic of the *Strassburger Neueste Nachrichten*, who had been so
completely won over by Mahler's Beethoven interpretations, found his Fifth
Symphony 'rich in content, overflowing beauties, thoughts and moods', so
much so that 'mere words seem inadequate to the writer of these lines to do
justice to the excellence of this grandiose tone-poem'. All the elements present
in Mahler's earlier works were also to be found in his new symphony: 'the
moving sincerity and limpid simplicity of his melodic inventiveness, mingled
with grandiose pathos and with the fiery vehemence of an all-too-explosive
temperament, and with all the extraordinary mastery of everything technical,
which he uses to transform his symphonies into paintings in colours of such
intensity and depth that the listener is filled with admiring astonishment', a
description of Mahler's style which could have been written nowadays!
However the writer was still not convinced that everything in the new work
'really stemmed from an inner necessity of his spiritual life'.

Despite the passages which seem to come from the depths of the soul, one cannot rid
oneself of the thought that a highly developed refinement is also at work here. That
something which puts the sacred seal of genius on what is otherwise only a splendid
talent and an admirable technical skill, namely the naked truth, the compulsion of
necessity—this one does not always find in Mahler. Not always—one must not push
this caution too far, as Mahler's enemies do when they refuse to credit him with any
genuine feeling whatsoever and declare everything to be clever window-dressing.
Anyone who approaches Mahler's symphonies without prejudice but with a discerning
ear for modern music will unquestionably often feel himself to be transported to the
loftiest heights of emotion, and experience moments when he trembles under the
impact of passion or in delight at pure beauty. Mahler's intentions are always titanic,
aimed at perfect grandeur. But one would be guilty of idle boasting if one sought to
deny that occasionally the originality, the natural inevitability of his music seems to
switch off and be replaced by brilliant technical ability alone.

However, the unsigned article found that such moments were easily forgotten in view of 'the many, many inexhaustibly rich beauties of the work'. The
critic pointed out excesses in the various movements, for instance in the

second Trio of the Funeral March and the following Allegro, but he had nothing but praise for the Adagietto and particularly for the Rondo-Finale, with its 'sparkling wit', its 'twinkling humour', 'beaming joy of life', and 'cheerful optimism'.

Charles Eckert, in *Der Elsässer*, lauded Mahler's 'beautiful, distinguished' themes and his 'effective orchestration', the 'elegant', 'melodious' and 'sunny' Scherzo, the 'tenderness' and 'loving soulfulness' of the Adagietto, and the 'song of jubilation' of the Finale, as well as the 'formal perfection' of the whole work. As for the Strasbourg *Freie Presse*, its unsigned review commented that 'the splendour of the structure, the grandeur of the feeling leave no doubts as to Mahler's genius!' The anonymous critic uses the word 'frantic' to describe the applause which had greeted the Fifth Symphony both after the general rehearsal in the morning and after the concert in the evening. In the French-language *Journal d'Alsace-Lorraine*, William d'Gelly felt that putting the two long symphonies by Mahler and Strauss in the same programme had been 'unbelievably stupid', for the public had proved incapable of appreciating the second. He found Mahler's symphony 'absolutely remarkable': 'It is a very powerful work, ingeniously orchestrated and perfectly clear, no matter what people say. The Scherzo sparkles with colour and daring fantasy; the enchanting Adagietto, with its murmur of distant harmonies, and the lively final Rondo, produce an irresistible effect on the unsuspecting listener.' D'Gelly's only criticism concerned the too frequent use of the brass, 'for the ear quickly tires of their powerful sound. Gustav Mahler loves the trumpet like the Italians love macaroni: to distraction.'[203]

In the French and German musical reviews the reports by the various musical correspondents were not as enthusiastic as those of the local press (except for that of Altmann in *Die Musik*). The correspondent of the Parisian *Guide Musical* thought that the Fifth Symphony 'was highly interesting on the whole' and 'destined to please more and more with each new hearing'.[204] In the *Neue Zeitschrift*, Stanislas Schlesinger compared the opening Funeral March with those of Beethoven's *Eroica* and Wagner's *Götterdämmerung*, and praised both the delightful Scherzo and the huge Finale.[205]

For many years to come, French critical opinion chose to ignore or disdain Mahler's works. The journal of the SIM (Société Internationale de Musique), for example, said that it was rumoured that the thunder and 'frightful cataclysms of San Francisco and Naples' would shortly be making their musical debut in Mahler's Sixth Symphony. The *Revue Musicale de Lyon* published an anonymous, 'unconfirmed' list of the percussion instruments used by Mahler in this

---

[203] D'Gelly reported that Mahler was 'so delighted with the trumpet player brought from Cologne (Herr Werke according to the *Neueste Nachrichten*) that he hired him on the spot'. He also states that Strauss played his latest opera, *Salomon* (*sic*) to Mahler in the 'salons of Wolf'. He discloses the fees paid to the three conductors—Chevillard 400 marks, Strauss 1,500, and Mahler 2,400 for the two concerts.

[204] The article is signed A. Oberdoeffer. See *Le Guide Musical*, 51 (1905): 24/25, 469 ff.

[205] *Neue Zeitschrift*, 72 (1905): 24, 523 ff.

same work, an inventory ending with 'a few other sound machines, utterly devoid of all connection with music such as we have understood it thus far'.[206]

Only the three German-language newspapers of Strasbourg reviewed Mahler's Fifth favourably. The *Strassburger Post* (the unsigned article was certainly not by Gustav Altmann, who had written an unfavourable review of the symphony in *Die Musik*) recalled its harsh reception by the Berlin press, but found it unfair because the Fifth, though at first not easy to understand, was 'the fruit of real sensitivity and deep necessity'. Mahler's greatness and strength lay in the development and transformation of the (often simple) thematic material, and in the simultaneous presentation of themes. For this reason, the symphony had to be studied carefully, for otherwise 'the most carefully prepared passages might at first seem arbitrary'. The audience however, had 'recognized the true musician behind this work: it had sensed the natural ardour of his expression, the seductive charm of his melodies, and the force of his genuine emotions, even if certain passages seemed strange and incomprehensible'. The Strasbourg *Freie Presse* praised the Fifth's 'architectural splendour' and 'emotional grandeur' which 'left no doubt about Mahler's genius', and called the 'frenetic applause' well deserved. The *Neueste Nachrichten* critic had been captivated, not only by Mahler's skill, but also by 'the rich substance and abundance of beauty, ideas and moods' in the new symphony, although words were hard to find to 'suggest or describe this grandiose poem in sound' in which at times 'the force of passion and the felicity of pure beauty make one tremble'.

On balance, however, the general verdict on Mahler the composer after the Strasbourg concerts showed once again that the 'Noes' largely outnumbered the 'Yes' or even the 'Yes, but' votes. Clearly, Mahler would still have to content himself with scattering his seeds to the wind, in the hope, as he often said, that ultimately, somewhere, they would take root and flourish

---

[206]   See Simon, 'Tribulations', 165

4

Mahler in Vienna (XX)—The Graz Festival
Correspondence with Cosima Wagner—Completion of the Seventh Symphony
The Battle for Salome—The Second Symphony in Berlin: Oskar Fried
The Fifth Symphony in Trieste, Vienna, and Breslau—Preparation of the Mozart Year
(June–December 1905)

In artistic matters form is the important thing, not content.

A WEEK after leaving Strasbourg, the 'two most famous [contemporary] symphonists'[1] came together once again at the Allgemeiner Deutscher Musikverein Festival, which for the second time in its history was being held in Austria, this time in Graz. The choice of Graz, the capital city of the province of Styria, was not dictated by purely musical reasons, but must be understood in the context of the time as a political gesture by the nationalist German bourgeoisie. This is made clear in the speeches by local officials and manufacturers (who were financing the festival) reproduced in the *Grazer Tagblatt* of 1 June 1905. Since January the *Tagespost*, another local paper, had been publishing a series of articles entitled *Meister des Taktstocks* (masters of the baton) including an essay on Mahler written by the young Paul Bekker.[2] The programmes, dates, and choice of artists gave rise to an exchange of letters

---

[1]   See *Strassburger Neueste Nachrichten* (23 May 1905).

[2]   The third article in the series *Meister des Taktstocks*, it was published on 7 Mar. 1905. This was probably the first study of Mahler made by Bekker, who was later to become an influential critic and writer on music. See Gösta Neuwirth, 'Zur Geschichte der 4. Symphonie', Rudolf Stephan (ed.), *Mahler-Interpretation* (Schott, Mainz, 1985), 106.

between Strauss and Wilhelm Kienzl,[3] composer of the popular *Evangelimann*, who lived in Graz and, as a member of the Verein, was in charge of the local organization of the festival. The main interest of this correspondence is that it shows something of what went on behind the scenes in the organization of a music festival in 1905. Among other things, Strauss and Kienzl discussed the possibility of concluding the Graz events at the Vienna Opera with a performance of *Der Corregidor*, but Wolf's opera was finally replaced by *Feuersnot*, followed by *Die Rose vom Liebesgarten*. Strauss was also worried about the choice of the orchestra, but eventually had to be satisfied with the local Graz Opera Orchestra, supplemented by winds and strings from the Vienna Philharmonic. It was arranged that *Don Quichote*, Kienzl's most recent opera, written in 1897, would be performed at the Graz Opera after the festival's opening concert in the town earlier the same evening. Originally, Strauss suggested including Mahler's Fifth Symphony and Schoenberg's *Verklärte Nacht*, 'an extremely interesting sextet which the Rosé Quartet plays admirably', but neither appeared in the final programmes.

Later on, after Ferdinand Löwe had been appointed Festival Conductor, the conductor of the Graz Orchestra Richard Wickenhauser[4] wrote to Mahler complaining bitterly that while he would have to conduct most of the rehearsals he would not be allowed to conduct the concert performances.[5] Strauss himself initially baulked at putting one of his own works on the programme since Mahler had decided to conclude the festival in Vienna with *Feuersnot*, but ultimately he let himself be persuaded to conduct *Ein Heldenleben*. As usual, the soloists were reimbursed for their expenses but did not receive a fee.

The final selection of programmes and artists was made only twenty days before the opening of the festival, and Strauss upbraided Kienzl for not tackling the organizational problems 'with all the necessary coolness and attention to detail'. As director of the institution, Mahler had to refuse to allow musicians

---

[3] Wilhelm Kienzl (1857–1941), pianist, conductor, composer, critic, and musicologist, was born in Waizenkirchen in Upper Austria. Son of a lawyer who later became mayor of Graz, Kienzl studied music in Graz, Prague, and Munich (with Josef Rheinberger). Later, in Vienna, he became a pupil of Hanslick and obtained his doctorate in philosophy with a thesis entitled 'Musical Declamation' (1880). After a stay in Bayreuth, where he became fairly close to the Wagner family, he began in 1879 a career as an opera conductor in Amsterdam and then in Krefeld, Hamburg, and Munich. In 1893, he settled in Graz, where he composed and wrote music criticism until 1917. He eventually retired to Vienna where he died in 1941. Of Kienzl's nine operas (*Uvasi*, 1886; *Heilmar der Narr*, 1892; *Der Evangelimann*, 1895; *Don Quichote*, 1898; *In Knecht Rupprechts Werkstatt*, 1906; *Der Kuhreigen*, 1911; *Das Testament*, 1916; *Hassan der Schwärmer*, 1925; *Sanctissimum*, 1925), only *Der Evangelimann* achieved lasting success. Kienzl also composed works for orchestra, chorus, and chamber music, and wrote a lengthy autobiography, *Meine Lebenswanderung*, as well as an essay on Wagner (1903). See above, Vol. i, Chap. 15, etc.

[4] Richard Wickenhauser (1867–1936) was born in Brünn in Moravia and studied first in his home town, then in Leipzig and Vienna. Chorus master in Brünn from 1895, he was appointed artistic director of the Graz Musikverein in 1902. In 1907, he settled in Vienna where he conducted the Singakademie until 1911. Wickenhauser composed a number of works mostly for chorus and wrote a monograph for Universal Edition on Bruckner's symphonies.

[5] Letter from Richard Wickenhauser to Mahler, dated 24 Sept. 1905 (BGM).

from the Vienna Opera to take part,[6] and they were replaced by twenty-three members of the Konzertverein Orchestra and 'professors from the Steiermärkischer Musikverein'. Finally, in one of his last letters, dated 8 May, Strauss asked Kienzl to avoid at all costs letting composers conduct their own works: through inexperience, they inevitably prolonged the rehearsals, which meant a steep increase in costs. The final programme for the Graz Festival was as follows:

1 June, at 6 p.m.: Opening Concert:
    Roderich von Mojsihovics: *Romantic Fantasy* for organ, Op. 9 (Otto Burkert, organ)
    Guido Peters: Symphony No. 2 in E minor: 1st and 4th movements (cond. Ferdinand Löwe)
    Gustav Mahler: Thirteen Lieder. Cond. Gustav Mahler
    Paul Ertel: *Der Mensch*, Symphonic Poem, Op. 9, with organ (Alois Kofler, organ; cond. Ferdinand Löwe).

2 June, at 11 a.m.: Chamber Music Concert:
    Max Reger: *Variations and Fugue on a theme by Bach*, Op. 81 (August Schmid-Lindner, piano)
    Émile Jaques-Dalcroze: Serenade for string quartet (Rosé Quartet)
    Otto Taubmann: Three Lieder (Josef Loritz, baritone; August Schmid-Lindner, piano)
    Max Reger: *Variations and Fugue on a theme by Beethoven*, Op. 86, for two pianos (Max Reger and A. Schmid-Lindner, pianos)
    Rudolf Buck: Two Choruses: *Gotenzug* (Procession of the Goths) and *Wilde Jagd* (Wild chase), for male chorus.

2 June, at 6 p.m.: Symphony Concert:
    Anton Bruckner: Symphony No. 8 (cond. Ferdinand Löwe)
    Otto Naumann: *Der Tod und die Mutter* for soloists and chorus (Leopoldine Ullmann, soprano; Theo Drill-Orridge, contralto; Josef Loritz, baritone; Max Gillmann, baritone).

4 June, at 11 a.m.: Chamber Music Concert:
    Felix Draeseke: Quintette, with violotta[7] (Rosé Quartet with Franz Jellinek, violotta)
    Hans Pfitzner: Quartet, Op. 13, in D major (Rosé Quartet)
    Hugo Wolf: Fourteen Lieder (Amalia Löwe, soprano; Ludwig Hess, tenor; Anton Dressler, baritone; Ferdinand Löwe, piano).

4 June, at 6 p.m.: Symphony Concert:
    Franz Liszt: *Die Ideale*, symphonic poem no. 12 (cond. Ferdinand Löwe)
    Max von Schillings: *Dem Verklärten*, Hymnal Rhapsody, Op. 21, for baritone, chorus, and orchestra (Josef Loritz, baritone; cond. Max von Schillings)
    Richard Strauss: *Ein Heldenleben*

---

[6] According to Kienzl's diary (Stadtbibliothek, Vienna), seven wind-instrument players and five strings came from Vienna. Strauss's letters to Kienzl (12 and 26 Dec. 1904, 2 Feb., 13 Mar., 19 and 28 Apr., and 8 May 1905) are also in the Vienna Stadtbibliothek.

[7] The violotta is a kind of large viola.

Ernst Boehe: *Odysseus's Heimkehr*, episode from a Symphony in four movements (cond. Boehe)

Siegmund von Hausegger: *Lieder der Liebe*, for tenor and orchestra (Ludwig Hess, tenor)

Theodor Streicher: Two *Kriegerchöre* (Warrior Choruses) for chorus and wind instruments: *Der Churmainzer Kriegslied* and *Weinschröterlied*[8]

Julius Weissmann: *Fingerhütchen*, for baritone, chorus, and orchestra (Anton Dressler, baritone; cond. Ferdinand Löwe)

Richard Wagner: *Kaisermarsch*.

It is sad to find on this programme so many composers who have since fallen into oblivion, but it also more than likely—and a reflection of the evolution of musical taste—that a festival programme of contemporary music today will surely produce a similar impression some ninety years hence!

Mahler's Lieder were the subject of a long exchange of letters between him and Strauss.[9] First the total number of Lieder to be performed was reduced from sixteen to thirteen. Then in early May Strauss announced that he would have to leave Graz on 4 June,[10] which precluded his conducting both *Ein Heldenleben* that same day and the performance in Vienna of *Feuersnot*. He continued:

This brings me to the main point of my letter. Several times already, the gentlemen at Graz have informed me that you wished your songs, which last an hour and a quarter, to be performed in Graz in a separate concert of their own. I took this for overzealousness on the part of the Graz opera composers vis-à-vis the Director of the Vienna Opera. I took it all the less seriously as you yourself had never expressed such a desire to me. On the contrary: you even asked me not to perform the Fifth Symphony in Graz so that you could support the Festival without being suspected by your superiors of egotistical self-promotion. And yet such would certainly be the case were I to allocate an entire concert for a series of songs lasting an hour and a quarter. Two years ago already I was accused by a number of deservedly unperformed fellow artists of giving preferential treatment to compositions by Mahler and I am therefore all the more anxious to avoid even a semblance of preferential treatment. As President, I have obligations toward the entire membership and, most important of all, the special position you desire does not seem in this instance justified by any artistic necessity.[11]

Strauss then proposed inserting Mahler's Lieder between a symphonic poem by Liszt and Wagner's *Kaisermarsch*. In conclusion, he repeats that he can

---

[8] A third chorus by Streicher, *Kriegslied gegen Karl V* (Song of war against Charles the Fifth) was 'vetoed by the censor', probably because Charles the Fifth was a Habsburg. Paul Ehlers, correspondent of the *Neue Musikzeitung*, also reveals that Wagner's *Kaisermarsch* had to be played without the choral part, because the text was a hymn glorifying the German emperor.

[9] Mahler suggested to Strauss that Bruno Walter's Piano Quartet, premièred in Vienna shortly before, be included in one of the chamber music programmes, but nothing came of the proposal. Walter's work was performed at the next festival, in Essen, the following year. Strauss also exchanged a number of letters with Max von Schillings concerning the Graz Festival. See *Richard Strauss—Max von Schillings: Ein Briefwechsel*, ed. Roswitha Schlötterer (Ludwig, Pfaffenhofen, 1987), 121 ff.

[10] He was needed in Berlin to conduct the final scene of *Die Meistersinger* at the Crown Prince's betrothal ceremony.

[11] AMS and MSB 93.

neither prolong the festival for him, nor give him an entire concert, even in the morning, since the rest of the programme was already settled.

The insinuation that Mahler had put pressure upon 'the Graz opera composers' (an obvious reference to Kienzl) anxious to ingratiate themselves with him, in order to have his songs performed at a separate concert, was not allowed to pass unrefuted, especially since Strauss specifically referred to 'the special position you desire'. Mahler replied by return of post:

Dear Friend! I do not desire a 'special position'! That would be a great misunderstanding on your part. Only a small hall for my chamber music-style songs. And just because I do not want to monopolize an entire evening's concert, I suggest a matinée. Also in the interest of the whole it does not seem appropriate to me to conclude the festival with a few simple Lieder.

Please think again about the whole matter! 'Preferential treatment' for Mahler? Should an artistic association really have democratic principles? Or have these gentlemen construed your intercession on my behalf as cameraderie? I dislike both suppositions! You know better than anyone that I am not pushing myself forward, and that I really am not vain. Here (in Vienna), for artistic reasons (despite all the pressure of 'commercial' considerations), I have put on these Lieder only in the small hall, and that is where they belonged. To perform them in a large hall as the conclusion of a festival would be decidedly lacking in taste and really would expose us both to those reproaches. For the rest (as I in no way wish to cause embarrassment, for believe me, I would like very much to withdraw completely) I bow to your decision but do ask you to consider my reasons carefully.

And in a postscript, Mahler added:

I would have wished to be entirely free in Graz, both in order to devote myself more fully to my tasks in Vienna,[12] and also, as you say, so as not to seem to be pushing myself. Since Schillings, however, felt he had to insist on performing something of mine in Graz, I suggested the Lieder as a most modest contribution requiring less effort to prepare. Now, since they are going to be performed, the style of presentation must be right. So, only in the small hall! Obviously, I would cut a better figure in a big festival concert (*Festkonzert*). My preference for a matinée in the small hall cannot therefore be due to a desire to 'show off'.[13]

The irony of this last sentence must have been obvious to Strauss, but in view of what he had himself written, he could hardly take offence. An agreement must have been reached between them by 8 March, when a letter written by Strauss to Mahler mentions the name of the three soloists then intended for Mahler's Lieder (only Johannes Sembach was later replaced by Fritz Schrödter, and Schmedes added to the list). Strauss wanted to make sure that Marie Gutheil-Schoder and Hermine Kittel were not to appear in the concert. In a

---

[12] Mahler is referring here to Liszt's *Saint Elizabeth*, *Feuersnot*, and *Die Rose vom Liebesgarten*, which were given in Vienna at the close of the festival for the members of the Verein.

[13] Undated letter from Mahler to Strauss (beginning of May 1905), MSB 95. Additional letters were found in the Archiv des Allgemeiner Deutscher Musikverein in Weimar (folder no. 70/104).

telegram dated 15 May, Mahler says he has decided to cut three Lieder from the original programme, 'Ich atmet', 'Blicke mir nicht', and 'Lob des hohen Verstandes'.[14] Thirteen Lieder were ultimately performed at the opening festival concert, which took place on 1 June at 6 p.m.[15] in the small Stephaniensaal, as Mahler had wished. The same programme also included contemporary works by three particularly obscure members of the Verein, Roderich von Mojsihovics, Guido Peters, and Paul Ertel.[16] A few members of the Philharmonic, including his brother-in-law, the violinist Arnold Rosé and the harpist Alfred Holy, accompanied him to Graz, together with four singers from the Opera, three of whom had already participated in the Vienna concert four months earlier, including Friedrich Weidemann, who had become Mahler's favourite singer for his Lieder.

Before leaving for Graz with Anna Moll, Bruno Walter, Kolo Moser, and Richard Strauss, Mahler put Alma and their two daughters on the train for Klagenfurt, where they were going to spend the month of June in the country. Presumably to make up for his May letter, Strauss's behaviour during the voyage was 'very pleasant, as in the past'. After the opening concert, all the Verein composers attended a performance of Wilhelm Kienzl's *Don Quichote* at the Graz Opera. During the intermission, a telegram informed Strauss of his father's death at the age of 83, and he left precipitately for Bavaria. Three days later, Ferdinand Löwe conducted *Ein Heldenleben* in his place. Mahler also attended *Don Quichote* but left the performance with Guido Adler during the second intermission, much to Kienzl's annoyance. 'It put me in a very bad mood,' he confided to his diary.[17]

In Strauss's absence, the members of the Verein assumed towards Mahler 'the sugary (*picksüssen*), over-refined (*superfeinen*), politely evasive tone' he knew so well. According to Alma, even Schillings's behaviour was 'oddly ambiguous'.[18] Yet in a letter to Strauss quoted above, Mahler states that it was

---

[14]   See James A. Deaville, 'The Tonkünstlerfest of the Allgemeiner Deutscher Musikverein in Graz, 1905. New light on Strauss, Mahler, the ADMV, and the issues of Pan Germanism and Austrianness in Music', paper read at the Austria 1000 Conference, Ottawa, Jan. 1996. On 25 May, Mahler changed the dates of the three performances which were to conclude the Graz Festival at the Vienna Opera on 5, 6, and 7 June.   [15]   The dress rehearsal took place the same day at 9 a.m.

[16]   See above the complete programme of the concert.

[17]   Kienzl had announced the completion of the score of *Don Quichote* to Mahler in a letter written on 9 Oct. 1897 (Vienna Stadtbibliothek). In the hope of a possible Hofoper performance, he had offered to come to Vienna to play it for him (ÖTM, HOA 135, Z. 452/1897, see above, Chap. 3). Mahler's reply and Kienzl's subsequent letter reveal that Mahler first accepted and then refused Kienzl's offer, preferring to see the Berlin première before hearing the work on the piano (Mahler's letters of 11 and 18 Oct., and Kienzl's letter of 15 Oct.). Kienzl's diary describes a visit to Mahler on 29 Dec. 1897 to discuss his new opera. Mahler apparently said he would 'come and hear it in Prague or Berlin', but a reading of the score was probably enough to convince him that *Don Quichote* did not merit a production in Vienna (TME 283).

[18]   AMM1, 112; AMM2, 114. Alma claims that, already in Strasbourg certain members of the Verein, in particular Rösch and Schillings, 'had formed a separate clique', keeping Mahler at a distance for anti-Semitic reasons, but her statement is contradicted by several documents. In any case, it seems unlikely that many members of the Verein attended the Strasbourg festival. After the Graz festival, Schillings wrote to Strauss: 'Hats off to Mahler the opera director! You already know *Feuersnot* in their "version", but *Elisabeth* too was performed, in all essential respects, with startling beauty' (Letter from Schillings, 14 June 1905).

Schillings who insisted that a work of his be performed and he also wrote to Alma from Graz stressing Schillings's amiability and expressing his 'sympathy and friendship' for him. Their relationship had probably improved since Mahler had decided to produce *Der Moloch* at the Vienna Opera.[19] But in such an association of composers as the Verein, it was only to be expected that Mahler's growing success should meet with some resentment by a number of composers of lesser rank. This did not prevent the Verein from making an exceptional effort a year later by organizing the first performance of the Sixth Symphony.

During the rehearsals in Graz, Erik Schmedes, first Wagnerian tenor at the Hofoper, thought up a mischievous prank to play on Mahler. Knowing how delighted he was when his music was appreciated, Schmedes taught a young admirer the main melody of *Um Mitternacht* and asked him to whistle it while following Mahler in the street. Hiding behind a street lamp, Schmedes had the pleasure of seeing Mahler beaming with joy.[20] As star and guest of honour at the Graz Festival, Mahler had every reason to believe in the authenticity of his anonymous admirer.

Ernst Decsey[21] tells another anecdote connected with the same Graz Festival: between rehearsals, Mahler went for walks with friends in the woods surrounding Graz. One day, in the Hilmwald, they came upon a blind organ grinder playing alone in the middle of a clearing. To make him stop playing, a member of Mahler's party put a coin in his bowl, but Mahler insisted that he be allowed to play. 'He is the image of the [condition of] the artist in the world? Only the trees are listening to him! Altogether he is the image of the world with the sound of music at its centre.'[22]

For the festival's opening concert, the Stephaniesaal was decorated with drapes and greenery by a member of the Verein, Paul Marsop.[23] Like Wolfrum in Heidelberg, Marsop was carried away by his decorative zeal: the performers

[19]   See above, Chap. 1, and Wilhelm Raupp, *Max von Schillings*, 104. In 1907, Eugène d'Harcourt noticed the score of *Der Moloch* still in Mahler's office at the opera.

[20]   A similar incident took place in the summer of 1903. In the presence of Albine Adler and Frau Marie Singer, mother of Siegmund, Mahler played the melody of the second movement of the Third Symphony to the young Rudolf L. Ernst. To Mahler's great joy, the boy's face lit up and Mahler asked him to sing him the melody (personal reminiscence related to the author in the 1960s by Rudolf L. Ernst, Sydney, Australia).

[21]   Ernst Decsey (1870–1941) was one of Hugo Wolf's earliest biographers (4 vols., 1903–6). Of Hungarian origin and the son of a watchmaker, he was born in Hamburg and studied at the Vienna Conservatory with Robert Fuchs and Bruckner. From 1899 to 1908 he was music critic of the Graz *Tagespost* of which he later became editor-in-chief. After 1920, he settled in Vienna, wrote for the *Neues Wiener Tagblatt*, taught at the New Conservatory and wrote several monographs (*Bruckner, Johann Strauss, Debussy*) and novels. At Mahler's death he published in *Die Musik* some captivating reminiscences under the title *Stunden mit Mahler* (EDS), one of the richest source of information about Mahler's personality and ideas.

[22]   Ernst Decsey, *Die Spieldose* (Tal, Leipzig, 1922), 94.

[23]   Paul Marsop (1856–1925), born in Berlin, had been a pupil of Hans von Bülow, and lived in Munich and in Italy. A writer and art critic, he was known for his proposed reforms to the stage, the concert hall, programmes, etc. Author of numerous articles and pamphlets on various subjects, he founded a chain of popular music libraries in Germany. He was a friend of Hans Pfitzner from 1892, and one of the first champions of his music.

were hidden behind a sort of screen of greenery backed with olive green cloth. In a letter written to Kienzl before the festival,[24] Strauss opposed the whole project, and quoted his own letter to Ernst Decsey saying that the idea of hiding the orchestra and dimming the lights in the auditorium was 'devoid of significance and interest':

If you want to organize such a performance privately, outside the framework of the festival, you are free to do so, but as I said before, I cannot take responsibility for it. Furthermore, I must point out that Dr Marsop is not in any way authorized to interfere in the organization of the festival. He unfortunately neglected to communicate his wishes to the committee of the Allgemeiner Deutscher Musikverein in due time, and now there is nothing more to be done.

Despite Strauss's opposition, it seems that Marsop was allowed to go ahead with his project. Afterwards, in *Die Musik*, he proudly described the two dense 'thickets' and shrubs surrounding the podium, which transformed the concert hall into a 'veritable garden'.[25] According to him, everyone was delighted—the audience, the musicians, even the conductors, with the sole exception of Mahler, who disliked being only partly visible to the audience. Dr Marsop does not say how the singers were fitted into this pastoral setting, but reveals that Mahler, who liked to have a full view of his soloists and musicians, would not allow the lights to be lowered. 'What an ass!' Mahler exclaimed, while discussing Marsop's efforts with Richard Wickenhauser, who had conducted the preliminary rehearsals of the Lieder. 'The music must be so beautiful that the audience can no longer see anything, that it is blinded! It all depends on the performance, not on the concert hall!'[26] Ernst Decsey, critic for the *Grazer Tagespost* and source of the anecdote, recalls one of the rehearsals when Mahler conducted 'Ich bin der Welt abhanden gekommen'. With his head bowed, his eyes closed, and making the infinitesimal gestures characteristic of his conducting, he was as if 'transported into the world he had created, and oblivious to his surroundings just like the author of the poem'.

At the opening concert on 1 June, the first two numbers on the programme, by Mojsihovics and Guido Peters, were a complete failure. Mahler's Lieder followed, sung by four members of the Vienna Opera. Friedrich Weidemann began with three *Wunderhorn-Lieder*: 'Der Schildwache Nachtlied', 'Das ird-ische Leben' and 'Der Tamboursg'sell' followed by Rückert's 'Ich bin der Welt abhanden gekommen'. Anton Moser then sang the 'Lied des Verfolgten im Turm' and the 'Fischpredigt'. Finally Schrödter's 'Revelge', which was almost encored, was followed by Schmedes' 'Um Mitternacht'.[27] To conclude

---

[24] Letter dated 8 May, Stadtbibliothek, Vienna (IH. 177.603).
[25] *Die Musik*, 5 (1905): 15, 255.   [26] Ernst Decsey, *Die Spieldose*, 75.
[27] Marie Gutheil-Schoder and Hermine Kittel had also originally been scheduled to take part in the concert. According to Helm, Mahler intended to have the last two songs also sung by Johannes Sembach, a tenor he had engaged at the Opera in Oct. 1904, but who had broken his contract two weeks before the concert. Sembach nevertheless came back to the Opera in Oct. 1905.

Weidemann sang the five *Kindertotenlieder*, which he had premièred in Vienna four months earlier. With authoritative gestures, his back to the audience, Mahler discouraged applause at the end of each song. It broke out all the more enthusiastically at the end of each group of songs: 'Few eyes remained dry in the concert hall', wrote the *Grazer Volksblatt* later. 'The audience surrounded this strangely small and yet great artist with acclamation, flowers, laurel wreaths, gratitude, and genuine love . . .'[28] The acclaim was so spontaneous and enthusiastic that Mahler's habitual critics and the other composers whose works were performed that evening took umbrage. Sometime later, Mahler commented on this backlash of envy to Ernst Decsey:

I had to wait until I was 45 before I had my first successes. And now certain Vienna papers seem to think that that is too soon, and that there must be something wrong with so much public acclaim. I must be playing to the gallery! But woe to me if somebody boos once during a concert! Straight away they say that the work was booed off. I know it all too well. I have many 'respectable' friends who think it vulgar to applaud; but my enemies are not 'respectable'; they boo alright![29]

Delighted with his success, but only too aware of all these undercurrents of envy, Mahler decided not to attend the official banquet given by the festival organizers at the Schlossberg. Once again, as in Strasbourg, he claimed that 'no one noticed his absence', and dined peacefully at his hotel with Anna Moll, Bruno Walter, Guido Adler, and Kolo Moser and his wife Edytha. One of the more fortunate consequences of the concert was that the Leipzig editor C. F. Kahnt, who had already included Mahler's Lieder in his catalogue,[30] offered him 15,000 gulden for the Sixth Symphony. 'I'm now in a dilemma as to how to handle Peters', he wrote to Alma. 'I shall sleep on it for a few nights, but I'm certainly not going to let slip the advantage that has thus fallen into my lap.'[31]

Mahler had no difficulty resolving the problem of his obligation to Peters. On 15 May, Hinrichsen wrote to inform him that he would attend the Graz Festival in order to hear his Lieder, and asked whether they were 'still available' for publication.[32] Two days later, from Strasbourg, Mahler replied that they were already in print: 'Had I known that you were interested in them I

---

[28] Article published in 1911 at the time of Mahler's death.   [29] EDS2, 145.

[30] Mahler received the first copies in June (see below).

[31] The contract with Kahnt for Mahler's six Lieder of 1901, i.e. *Rückert-Lieder*, two additional *Wunderhorn-Lieder*, and *Kindertotenlieder*, is dated 15 Apr. 1905. On receipt by the editor of each score, Mahler was to receive 500 marks. On 15 July, in Maiernigg, Mahler signed the contract Kahnt had drawn up for the Sixth Symphony. All rights henceforth belonged to the publisher, except the right of performance (*Aufführungsrecht*). Kahnt agreed to print the entire score and orchestral parts, as well as a pocket score 'resembling the one which Peters printed of my Fifth in both type and format'. For 'Liebst du um Schönheit' Mahler signed a new contract on 8 Dec. 1906 specifying 'with piano accompaniment'. The subsequent orchestration of this Lied was the work of Max Puttmann (see Vol. ii, Appendix no. 1). Mahler received 30,000 kronen for the symphony and 600 marks (464 kronen in 1910) for 'Liebst du um Schönheit'. It is useful to compare these amounts with the 24,000 kronen per annum which Mahler received during his first four years at the Vienna Opera (salary: 12,000; activity allowance: 4,000; travel allowance: 4,000; and accommodation allowance: 4,000). As seen above (Vol. ii, Chap. 10), his yearly income from the Opera had been raised to 36,000 kronen in 1901.   [32] Eberhardt Klemm, 'Geschichte', 47.

would have waited. But I concluded from your attitude in Leipzig that you had no intention of including them in your catalogue.'[33] Two weeks later Hinrichsen, in another letter, hoped that Mahler's Lieder 'would enjoy great popularity'. He congratulated Mahler on the 'enormous enthusiasm' his concerts had aroused in Strasbourg, and added that he would unfortunately be unable, after all, to make the trip to Vienna and Graz. However, he promised to attend the festival in Essen the following year, for the 'chief attraction' would undoubtedly be Mahler's Sixth Symphony, which he 'would consider a very great honour to publish'.[34]

Mahler replied to Hinrichsen upon his return from Graz. After thanking him for his 'unswerving confidence in his works', he came to the heart of the matter. 'On this subject, permit me a frank question. Are you able and willing to offer me a fee of 15,000 florins (30,000 kronen), the amount which I have been offered from another quarter? My most fervent wish would be to see my Sixth Symphony also published by your distinguished firm. You have always treated me with such great generosity that I would like to show you similar consideration. On the other hand, you will understand that (since I am not a wealthy man) I must begin to think of my future, and so long as my ability to compose remains undiminished I would like to make the most of it.'[35]

In his reply, Hinrichsen declared that Mahler's letter had come 'like a bolt from the blue ... shattering his fondest hopes'. Given the small number of times the Fifth had been performed, he had not expected that Mahler would raise his fee. 'Without wishing to be mean', he felt that as an experienced publisher he had to set some limit to fees. He would therefore withdraw his offer to publish the Sixth.[36] On 12 August, Mahler replied:

I was—to my great regret, I must add—obliged to accept Kahnt's offer. I want to express once again my satisfaction and gratitude for the generosity and care you showed regarding my Fifth. I still hope that someday, perhaps with a future work of mine, we can resume our relationship, and above all that you may not regret our earlier association.[37]

In Graz, the articles in the press and musical reviews confirm contemporary accounts of the triumph Mahler achieved with his Lieder. Ernst Decsey called them the 'high point' of the first concert. In the *Tagespost*, and later in *Die Musik*, he wrote that although Mahler's personality 'might both fascinate and repel', each song was incontestably a 'phenomenon' unto itself, if only because of the 'absolutely unprecedented (sonority) of his chamber orchestra'. Its very sophistication, according to Decsey, aroused the suspicions of certain other critics, who reproached Mahler for 'tickling the nerves' rather than aiming at expressiveness. For Decsey, the 'Fischpredigt' was no less than an 'inspired

---

[33] Klemm, 'Geschichte', 47.   [34] Ibid.   [35] Ibid. 48.
[36] Letter dated 9 June 1905, Klemm, 'Geschichte', 49.
[37] Letter dated 12 Aug., Klemm, 'Geschichte', 49.

humoresque' which had conquered the audience as much as had the *Kindertotenlieder* and 'Ich bin der Welt'. Even those who preferred 'more elementary' art were forced to recognize its exceptional qualities.[38]

The anti-Semitic *Grazer Tagblatt* also praised Mahler's 'musical paintings' and the 'instrumental colouring', produced not by the number but by the choice of instruments, which imparted a strange personal charm and 'at times spoke an almost unheard-of language'. The choice of rhythms seemed as personal as the 'piquant churchyard atmosphere (*pikante Friedhofsstimmung*)' of most of the *Gesänge*. For Hans Kleindienst, critic of the *Grazer Volksblatt*, the entire evening had been dominated by Mahler's strong personality, which had 'been the centre of interest'. Some people were for him, some against him, but everybody was fascinated. Kleindienst pointed out that writing Lieder with orchestral accompaniment had become the fashion, 'and quite rightly so since the orchestra, with its thousands of potential instrument combinations, is more likely to do justice to the lyrical content of a poem than a piano'. Mahler's Lieder, at least as far as the instrumentation was concerned, achieved the highest possible degree of refinement:

You listen with bated breath—how did he manage to do that? Nuances, combinations of tones, effects of sound all strike the ear, and you cannot get over your astonishment and admiration. You are fascinated, thrilled by this diabolical art. You want to deny it, but are compelled to yield, in any case it is an extraordinary mind that can subjugate us to that extent.

Yet although Mahler's economy of means was, in the same writer's opinion, prodigious, his musical ideas were sometimes 'smothered' by the weight of his art. He had shown brilliance in finding exactly the right tone for the *Wunderhorn* texts. In the deeply moving 'Ich bin der Welt' and the *Kindertotenlieder* his music became secret magic and he 'forgot he was Mahler and turned into a poet'. He 'conducts with a tranquility which almost seems like nonchalance, but in fact every fibre of his being is vibrating and nothing escapes his ear'.

The anonymous correspondent of the *Musikalisches Wochenblatt* was the kind of critic who found Mahler's work 'interesting', with its 'personal drolleries', 'nervous idiosyncrasies', and 'effects lacking cause or reason'. In his opinion, Mahler's 'eclectic art' exhausted the listener by playing upon his 'nerves', for 'intellectual refinement often replaced naive feeling and intuitive creation'. 'Revelge', intended to sound popular, was if anything banal and 'Nun seh' ich wohl' was borrowed from *Tristan*. Nevertheless, all the songs contained remarkable sound effects.

The house organ of the Verein, the *Allgemeine Musik-Zeitung*, published an

---

[38] Decsey recalled in his review the first Mahler performance in Graz, that of the First Symphony under Martin Spörr in 1899, 'from which the public was virtually absent' and which was nevertheless loudly booed (see above, Vol. ii, Chap. 11).

article by the Berlin critic Paul Bekker which was far from favourable either for the conductor ('he is thought-provoking, perplexing, but he does not enthuse us. His light does not warm us. Strauss, Weingartner, Nikisch affect us directly, he only indirectly'), or for the composer:

This strange bundle of nerves who can clothe a theme of almost Haydnish simplicity in the most bizarre harmonies, only to end up in naive folk-poetry once more (he has a predilection for composing Lieder from 'Des Knaben Wunderhorn') shows us Mahler as the typical image of the modern, nervous, distorted man. Lacking a stable, ideal objective he keeps rushing from one extreme to the other and can never find peace and quiet anywhere.

This early and highly derogatory estimation of Mahler's art takes on a somewhat ironic light in view of Bekker's later change of mind and his espousing Mahler's cause to the extent of writing the first major study of his symphonic production, a book which is still in print, still read, and often quoted from today.

Thus once again, no first performance of Mahler's music ever failed to have at least one critic attacking him either for the 'banality' of his inspiration or the excessive refinement of its construction. Paul Ehler's article for the *Neue Musik-Zeitung*, on the other hand, was unusually perceptive.

Gustav Mahler presents the sharpest and most deliberate contrast to the nebulous hyper-ecstasy of the present day. . . . Mahler's opposition to the prevailing modernism shows itself in various ways: in his themes, with their sharp outlines, mostly simple melodies and energetic rhythms; in his utterly personal brand of orchestration, with its enthralling austerity (*Herbheit*) and quite new combinations; and in an often wilful negation of the laws of prosody and of general conviction in expression. What has always struck me as remarkable with Mahler, and again in these songs, is how he absorbs and reworks strong impressions he has received from other composers in such a way that they become typically Mahlerian. Thus in one of the *Kindertotenlieder* you think you hear Brahms, and yet in every bar it is Mahler. All in all, these compositions are captivating, both by their utterly musical content, and their form, but emotionally they remain, at least for the time being, alien to me. Mahler's wit (a virtue not to be underestimated) is obvious at every instant in his songs.

In general, whatever the critical bias, none of these articles fails to communicate the profound and lasting impression which these thirteen Lieder made upon the audience in Graz.

That same summer yet another festival included a work by Mahler in its programme, once again with mixed reception. His Second Symphony was performed at the Düsseldorf Niederrheinisches Musikfest, conducted for the second time by Julius Buths on 12 June 1905.[39] Once again, reactions were mixed, but in the majority hostile. According to the *Generalanzeiger*, the symphony had been the chief attraction of the evening and had won over

---

[39]   The first Düsseldorf performance of the Second Symphony had taken place in Apr. 1903.

even Mahler's greatest detractors. True, his inventiveness was generally considered to lag behind his truly astounding capacity for development, but Mahler was without doubt 'an outstanding personality, a powerful intellect, one of the most brilliant and gifted artists of our time'. For the *Tageblatt*, however, Mahler, despite his great technical know-how, was incapable of realizing his aspirations, for he lacked 'the divine spark of inspiration'. The *Düsseldorfer Zeitung* criticized him for 'taking himself for a composer and deploying such enormous orchestral means'. He wanted to surpass Wagner but lacked a sense of proportion, and the characteristics of his model were 'exaggerated, deformed and contorted'. His 'pompous muddle of styles' included borrowings from Brahms and Mendelssohn. The audience showed respect for the composer's technical knowledge but was clearly aware of his shortcomings.[40]

Thus the style, tone, and contents of most of the reviews of Mahler's music had not changed much with the passing years, even though the news of the triumph earned by his Third Symphony in Vienna and by his Lieder in Vienna and Graz had reached the four corners of the German-speaking world. However, this event led in 1905 to a new sign of recognition of Mahler as a composer in the form of two articles published in Germany's most prestigious music magazine, the *Neue Zeitschrift für Musik*. The first of them appeared on 10 May 1905 and was written by Ludwig Schiedermair, a specialist of opera and a Beethoven scholar who was then 29 years old and had published three years earlier a small monograph on Mahler.[41] Mahler, he claimed, was a born symphonist, although his concept of the genre, the way in which he expressed his feelings, were as new as the increased number of movements in each work. He had been, up to now, misunderstood as a composer of programme music, although programmatic tendencies could indeed be detected in his works. Their main characteristics were strong contrasts in dynamics and tempo, melodies of folk origin (*volkstümliche*), an original treatment of wind instruments and the prominent role of the human voice, expressing Mahler's need, at a certain point, for the word as a means of expression. To those who questioned Mahler's calling as a composer and accused him of 'reflecting more than feeling', it could be answered that his music was not that of a mere virtuoso, but that of a poet. Furthermore, only unimportant composers failed to arouse controversy.

Later on in the same year another long article, this time about Mahler's

---

[40] The same critic reveals, however, that the second movement had to be encored. The concert of 12 June 1905 was the high point of the 82nd Niederrheinische Musikfest. After a Bach cantata, *Also hat Gott die Welt geliebt*, Julius Buths conducted a 'Symphony for two flutes, two violins, viola and cello' by Wilhelm Friedemann Bach. Tartini's sonata 'Le Trille du Diable', played by Fritz Kreisler, was followed by Brahms's Second Piano Concerto (soloist Ernö von Dohnanyi). After a forty-five-minute intermission, Mahler's Second Symphony occupied the second half of this marathon concert, which lasted from 6 to 10.30 p.m. Irene Abendroth, soprano, and Muriel Foster, contralto, were the soloists.

[41] See above, Chap. 1.

Lieder, appeared in three issues of the same magazine,[42] written by its chief editor, a young musicologist whose contribution to the field of baroque and Renaissance studies and particularly to the field of interpretation, later made history. Contrary to Schiedermair, Arnold Schering, a fervent admirer of Richard Strauss, thought that Mahler indeed wrote programme music, but that his programmes would need clearer eludication. His works nevertheless displayed a coherent and unified artistic conception as well as new paths in composition. In his Lieder, Mahler followed Wagner's method, the voice reciting and the orchestra arousing emotions. Schering praised his economy of means and his use of instrumental effects, which were justified either by the form or by the musical substance. Thus his songs were accomplished art works, typical of the modern 'way of expressing feeling' without bombast, with simple melodies. Thus they provided a useful key to his symphonic music. These two serious and substantial musicological articles now set the tone for the future treatment of Mahler's music in the *Neue Zeitschrift*.

Mahler returned to Vienna from Graz on 2 June. Alma, before leaving for Maiernigg, had shut up the Auenbruggergasse apartment, and he spent the final days of the season at Frau Moll's on the Hohe Warte, rehearsing the special production of *Feuersnot* to be performed for the members of the Allgemeiner Deutscher Musikverein on 5 June. The cast included a new soprano, one of the youngest members of the Hofoper, Gertrud Förstel, who took the leading role of Diemut. Mahler must have accomplished miracles in three days for Schönaich found the performance was unforgettable: 'unprecedented . . . without the slightest flaw'. 'The soloists, décor, lighting and orchestra all combined to create perfection.'[43] 'Yesterday *Feuersnot*—to the amazement of the German critics and the envy of German opera composers', wrote Mahler to Alma. 'But then they were all consoled by *Der faule Hans* [ballet by Nedbal], and wept tears of pain and joy.'[44]

---

[42] Schering's article appeared in three issues of the *Neue Zeitschrift* between 30 Aug. and 27 Sept.1905 (see Helmut Kirchmeyer, 'Mahlers Berichterstattung der "Neuen Zeitschrift für Musik" zwischen 1898 un 1911', in Mathias Theodor Vogt (ed.), *Das Gustav-Mahler-Fest Hamburg 1989* (Bärenreiter, Kassel, 1990), 199 ff.). Arnold Schering (1877–1941) was born in Breslau and studied the violin with Joseph Joachim in Berlin before turning to musicology. While pursuing his studies with Hermann Kretschmar in Leipzig, he completed his Ph.D. thesis on 'Die Geschichte des instrumental Konzerts'. He was chief editor of the *Neue Zeitschrift* (1903–5) and later of the *Bach Jahrbuch*. He taught musicology at the Leipzig Conservatory and from 1928 until his death, at the Berlin University. His most famous works are *Geschichte der Musik in Beispiele* (1931), *Aufführungspraxis alter Musik* (id.), *Das Symbol in der Musik* (1941), as well as several volumes devoted to Johann Sebastian Bach.

[43] Schönaich continued with the assertion that he had been 'entirely won over' by a work 'full of atmospheric magic and bold realism, even if it appealed to the intellect rather than to feeling'. Korngold found that Mahler had been less careful than before 'to soften and restrain the flow of sound'. Cast for the 5 June performance: Förstel (Diemut); Kiurina, von Thann, Kittel (Margret, Elsbeth, Wigelis); Breuer (Burgvogt); Preuss (Tulbeck); Demuth (Konrad); Felix (Marian); Mayr (Sentlinger). According to a letter written by Mahler to Strauss in Apr. (MSB 92), Gertrud Förstel was originally supposed to sing the role of Diemut and Weidemann the role of Konrad in the 5 June performance. The evening concluded with a ballet *Der faule Hans*, conducted by Oskar Nedbal, the composer.

[44] GAB, no. 135, undated (6 June 1905).

The following day, despite the torrid weather, Mahler attended the official lunch given by the committee of the Allgemeiner Deutscher Musikverein at the Hotel Sacher, and Bruno Walter conducted a special performance of *Die Rose vom Liebesgarten* for the Verein in the evening. The cast was slightly altered, with Mildenburg in the principal role. Schönaich found the performance slightly inferior to the one Pfitzner himself had conducted two weeks earlier,[45] but it was nevertheless warmly acclaimed. The festival ended the following day, 7 June, again at the Hofoper, when Franz Schalk conducted a stage performance of the Oratorio *Saint Elisabeth* by Liszt, the founder and first President of the Verein.[46]

As always at this time of the year, Mahler had but one thought: to leave Vienna for Maiernigg, where he could start composing once more. This year, however, Prince Montenuovo had informed him that his presence was required to conduct a gala performance for the Shah of Persia on about 20 June. Compelled to remain in Vienna, he wrote to Alma every day, as he always did in the summer when they were separated. Fortunately Willem Mengelberg was in the capital for a few days, and Mahler made a special effort to return his generous hospitality. To escape the gala, he consulted a doctor who provided a certificate stating that he needed rest. But once again, his plans were almost foiled—this time, by the death of Countess Kinsky, sister of Prince Liechtenstein and mother-in-law of Prince Montenuovo, which could well have obliged him to stay in Vienna to attend a committee meeting. Eventually everything worked out, however, and he was able to leave for Maiernigg on 14 June. Three days before leaving, he became very concerned when he opened the iron box where he kept his manuscripts and could not find the 'drafts I had put aside for this year'—of the Seventh Symphony, in all probability.[47] Fortunately Alma was able to tell him that he had left them in Maiernigg.

Leaving for Carinthia on 15 June,[48] Mahler missed an important Viennese event, the première of Frank Wedekind's new play *Die Büchse der Pandora*. This was the second play that Wedekind had written around the character of Lulu, and the one that Alban Berg later used for the second part of his opera. The subject was considered so improper that the play was initially banned by

---

[45] Pfitzner's biographer, Walter Abendroth, attributes the 'cool reception of the Vienna performance' to the fact that the members of the Verein had already heard the opera in Mannheim and 'thought they were sufficiently acquainted with it'. Pfitzner was then a member of the committee of the Society.

[46] A letter from Mahler to Kahnt discloses the fact that in 1889 the Hofoper had bought the exclusive stage rights to the Oratorio. In 1903, after the Kaiserjubiläumstheater had also acquired the rights, Mahler proposed cutting Kahnt's share in the receipts from 5 to 3 per cent (Opera Archives; G.Z. 663/1903, letter of 28 Aug. 1903).

[47] BGA, no. 138, undated (11 June 1905).

[48] On 16 June, Mahler sent a card to Fritz Steinbach, conductor of the Gürzenich Konzerte of Cologne, in which he said that he had arrived in his 'summer retreat . . . several days ago'. And yet in a letter addressed to Alma from Vienna on the 13th (BGA, no. 140) he indicated that he would join her in Maiernigg two days later. In the card he apologized to Steinbach for having 'left him in the lurch' because Weidemann had cancelled his participation in a concert. He obviously stretched the truth about the date of his arrival in Maiernigg because he felt remorse at not answering his colleague sooner.

the police. It was finally put on privately on 29 May at the Trianon Theater, with Frank Wedekind himself in the role of Jack the Ripper and Karl Kraus playing Kongu Ponti. Alban Berg attended the première and Karl Kraus personally invited Schoenberg to the second, which took place on 15 June. Two more years were to pass before Mahler finally became acquainted with Wedekind's work in Berlin, where he attended a performance of *Frühlingserwachen*, an equally 'scandalous' play, for which he expressed admiration in a letter to Alma.[49]

A few days before leaving Vienna, Mahler received a long letter from Cosima Wagner. On first reading, it seems to be strictly concerned with getting information about Anna von Mildenburg, but its real purpose was quite different. Since their first meeting in Leipzig in 1889,[50] Mahler's relationship with Wagner's widow had been friendly, if not close. In 1894 she wrote to Hermann Levi: 'I am in close correspondence with Mahler and have nothing but the warmest praise for his person and his actions. Which reminds me that it was you who first recommended him to me.'[51]

In 1897 and 1900, Mahler and Cosima had corresponded about Mildenburg and other members of the Vienna Opera who were singing at the Bayreuth Festival. In a letter to her intimate friend Countess Marie von Wolkenstein, Cosima had written in 1899: 'I have the best possible relationship with Mahler, and I am very happy to know that he is in Vienna. In nearly every one of his letters, he assures me of his interest (*Teilnahme*) in Bayreuth and he has shown it many times.'[52] Writing to Mildenburg in 1900, she repeated the comment: 'Director Mahler has always been so kindly disposed toward Bayreuth.'[53] And yet in the autumn of 1899, as we have seen, Mahler's cuts in the score of Siegfried Wagner's *Bärenhäuter* had aroused great indignation in Bayreuth. Cosima had written to Mahler to protest against this 'inadmissible procedure', and it had been privately considered that Mahler, a Jew, was both incapable of understanding a 'German' work and totally 'devoid of religious feeling'.[54]

---

[49] *Frühlingserwachen* was first performed in 1891. Its characters include a pregnant 14-year-old girl, a young boy who commits suicide, and another who is seen masturbating in front of an engraving of Venus, which he subsequently throws down the toilet (see below, Chap. 8). Frank Wedekind (1864–1918) was born in Hanover the same year as Strauss. Actor, journalist, advertising agent, involved with the circus, cabaret singer, he was the son of an American actress and a German doctor in the service of the Sultan of Turkey. Beginning in 1891, he wrote a series of fierce, sinister, disconcerting plays, in which he defied all the sexual taboos of contemporary bourgeois society. His most fascinating character is of course Lulu, heroine of two plays and later of Berg's opera: *Erdgeist* (Spirit of the Earth), 1895, and *Die Büchse der Pandora* (*Pandora's Box*), 1901.

[50] See below, Vol. i, Chap. 12. On 16 Nov. 1887, in Leipzig, Mahler had conducted a performance of *Tannhäuser* in Cosima's presence. From a theatrical point of view, she found it 'worse than anything I ever imagined possible'. Mahler, however, struck her as 'not without a certain impressiveness' (letter to Hermann Levi dated 19 June 1889, in Cosima Wagner, *Das zweite Leben: Briefe und Aufzeichnungen 1883–1930* (Piper, Munich, 1980), 191). See also Eduard Reeser, 'Gustav Mahler and Cosima Wagner', in MBRS 211 ff.   [51] Letter dated 8 May 1894, *Das zweite Leben*, 797.

[52] Richard Du Moulin Eckart, *Cosima Wagner, Die Herrin von Bayreuth* (Drei Masken, Munich, 1931), ii. 574 ff.   [53] Letters of 26 Feb. and 12 Dec. 1900, in *Das zweite Leben*, 510 and 562.

[54] See above, Vol. ii, Chap. 5.

At the end of 1899 another incident occurred which led Siegfried and his doting mother to believe that the 'Semite' Mahler was hatching sinister plots against that pure Aryan hero, the composer of *Der Bärenhäuter*. Mahler had invited Siegfried to conduct his opera in Vienna, with all the cuts restored,[55] and had informed him officially on 22 October that the performance would be a benefit for the Opera's Pension Fund. However, Siegfried was told the evening before the performance that the benefit had been cancelled and that the event would be a normal subscription performance because 'the time of year was unfavourable and the house would otherwise have been empty'.[56] According to Cosima, Siegfried had been so angry that he had very nearly left Vienna, but he finally decided that he would donate part of his royalties for the evening to the Pension Fund. After he had publicly informed the members of the Opera of his generous plan, Cosima wrote to one of her friends that they 'were deeply moved because they realized that he had changed the spiteful intention [of Mahler] to harm him into kindness'.[57]

However, in the meantime, Mahler had written to Siegfried the morning before the performance to make it clear that he had had no part in the decision: 'I am as furious as you are. This high-handed action of bureaucracy shows you better than anything else what I have to suffer here. . . . Don't let it, I beg of you, spoil this splendid evening. Remember, my dear friend, that all Vienna, and especially all of us here at the Opera, are thinking of you today with affection and gratitude.'[58]

Cosima's letter quoted above proves that she did not believe in the sincerity of Mahler's explanation. However, she felt she could not afford to spoil her relationship with him. She attended Siegfried's Vienna performance, and dined afterwards with Mahler. She wrote at the end of the year to thank him for 'preserving my son's work so faithfully at the Hofoper that he was able to conduct it with such assuredness after only one trial run-through'. And she offered Mahler once again to be of help to him whenever possible, and to 'prepare this or that artist in the *Einstudierung* of a part'.[59] Mahler had obviously told her during the dinner in Vienna that he enjoyed snowy weather for she adds in a very cordial ending: 'With the abundant snow we have now been granted I imagine you must be in a good humour, and that is what I wish you in your exacting job.'[60]

[55] In a telegram dated 2 Dec. 1899, Mahler had offered Siegfried four piano rehearsals before the performance, plus a two-hour orchestra rehearsal. Siegfried had asked for a rehearsal as 'practice for some of the choral passages' (HOA, Z. 595/1899).

[56] Letter from Cosima to Marie von Wolkenstein, in Du Moulin Eckart, *Cosima Wagner*, ii. 591. See Eduard Reeser, 'Gustav Mahler und Cosima Wagner', in MBRS 220 ff.

[57] Cosima Wagner, ibid. Cosima nevertheless concedes that 'the whole [Vienna] performance' had 'a fluency the like of which one rarely experiences' and that the sound of the orchestra was unique (Du Moulin, *Cosima Wagner*, ii. 592).   [58] Letter of 11 Dec. 1899, MBRS 220.

[59] A copy of this letter is preserved in the Bayreuth archives.

[60] Letter of Cosima to Mahler, dated 28 Dec. 1899. See Du Moulin, *Cosima Wagner*, ii. 591, and Reeser 'Mahler and Cosima', in MBRS 221.

Mahler soon responded to Cosima's offer of help and sent her Mildenburg, who was about to sing her first Isolde at the Vienna Opera on 13 February 1900.[61] Mildenburg remained in Bayreuth for three weeks and Cosima reported to Felix Mottl as follows: 'Mahler has a contract for life. Mildenburg, who adores him and never stops saying how wonderful he is, also says, like everyone, that he is also hated. Recently, when he appeared on the podium, someone yelled; "Here comes the bogey man, the black Devil." A quite remarkable phenomenon, especially in Vienna, this personality.'[62]

An important link and intermediary between Mahler and the Wagner family was Gustav Schönaich, a fervent Wagnerian and close friend of Cosima and Siegfried, and at the same time an objective, honest critic who recognized Mahler's merits and maintained friendly if not close relations with him. It was undoubtedly Schönaich who described the November 1899 revival of *Die Meistersinger* to Cosima in glowing terms and induced her to write to Mahler a year later:

I thank you from the bottom of my heart, dear Herr Director, for supporting our strenuous efforts to establish the style in which our works should be performed, by preserving and furthering in Vienna what artists have learned here, and teaching them the main features of our stage production methods. We must build on such support if our work is to succeed elsewhere.[63]

One might well wonder whether such specious praise pleased Mahler, Cosima thus giving him clearly to understand that outside Bayreuth there was neither style nor staging method for Wagner worthy of the name. Fortunately he was determined to follow his own ideas.

The letter Cosima wrote to Count Keyserling[64] in 1903 leaves no doubt as to her intransigence concerning the way Wagner's operas should be staged. Her letter indicates that Keyserling had written to tell her how much he had admired a production in Paris by Adolphe Appia of a scene from the second act of *Carmen*, and Byron's *Manfred*, set to music by Schumann.[65] Apparently, he had even dared to hint that Appia's pioneering genius could well be put to good use in the Wagnerian repertory. This was too much for Cosima. A month earlier, she had already had the troubling news from Vienna of Mahler's and Roller's departure from the traditional staging for *Tristan*, and in her answer she gave Keyserling a sound dressing down. She could certainly approve of Appia's staging of Bizet's work without decor but

---

[61] In her memoirs, Mildenburg tells much about her three-week work session in Bayreuth (*Erinnerungen* (Vienna-Berlin, 1921), 69 ff.).

[62] Cosima Wagner, *Das zweite Leben*, 503, and MBRS 222.

[63] Letter from Cosima to Mahler, 19 Nov. 1900, *Das zweite Leben*, 557.

[64] Hermann Count Keyserling (1880–1946) was a philosopher and writer of Baltic German origin, and a friend of Houston Chamberlain. His entire work consisted of a critique of occidental civilization and praise of Oriental culture and values. He visited the East several times.

[65] The performances took place on 25, 27, and 28 Mar. 1903, in the Princess of Béarn's palace.

she could hardly remember the scene Keyserling alluded to.[66] After going on to express her distaste for Schumann's 'formless, ponderous' music, full of unaesthetic repetitions,[67] and her surprise that Keyserling should have been impressed by it, she went on:

But to come to the main point, can Herr Appia's ideas be applied to our art. And here, dear Count, you forget one thing: the creator of our works, the man who has created the drama out of the spirit of the music, has given the most precise indications as to how his works are to be presented. Even the lighting of individual characters or groups at different moments is specified. You only need to follow the instructions marked in the score. And thank God the master himself has staged each of his operas and told us what was effective and what not in the performances. There is, therefore, no room for invention here—only for improving details. For the creator of these dramas would certainly not have required or contrived anything detrimental to the drama. . . . Isolde's tent, the view of the sea in the third act of *Tristan*, Siegfried's forest—in short, everything must remain as indicated by the creator, leaving, as I have already said, only details to be improved. . . . The lighting effects too are indicated with precision. There is no room for invention here. . . .[68]

She goes on to suggest that a more appropriate field for Appia's experiments would be the plays of Shakespeare or Goethe, but concludes: 'I can no more approve of the suppression of stage scenery and its replacement by lighting effects than I can approve of the re-instrumentation of Beethoven's symphonies by clever conductors.' Mahler was obviously foremost on Cosima's mind as one of the 'clever conductors' who retouched Beethoven's scores. Concerning Wagnerian mise-en-scène, he was fully aware of Cosima's ideas and her belief in her mission as guardian of the Bayreuth tradition. The tone of his letters reveals above all his respect for the wife of a venerated artist, but stops short of warmth or cordiality. He certainly did not forget that in 1897 Cosima had done her best to have her protégé Felix Mottl[69] appointed as Director of the Hofoper. She had failed only because of the confidential nature of the negotiations and the rapidity with which the decision was made. He also knew that she shared her illustrious husband's anti-Semitism: Houston Chamberlain's letter cited above epitomizes the state of mind which still prevailed in contemporary Bayreuth.[70]

Mildenburg's schooling in Bayreuth had been highly successful and she later reported to her 'Meisterin' about the performance in Vienna. Shortly after, Cosima wrote to Mahler to recommend a Romanian baritone named Demeter Popovici, (she later admitted that she had been grossly over-generous in her

---

[66] Cosima's sincerity here may be doubted. In view of Nietzsche's famous change of mind when he repudiated Wagner and praised *Carmen*, the score of this opera must have been well-known at Bayreuth.

[67] Cosima says that in his *Manfred* music Schumann includes too many *sogenannten Schusterflecken oder Rosalien*. The two words mean the same thing: the repetition of a melody in a higher tone, with exactly the same intervals. [68] Letter of 11 Apr. 1903, *Das zweite Leben*, 629.

[69] See Cosima's letters to Mottl, *Das zweite Leben*, 503.

[70] See above, Vol. ii, Chap. 14.

assessment of him).[71] In the same letter she also recommended Franz Beidler, a young conductor who was then engaged to Wagner's and Cosima's eldest child, Isolde: 'My future son-in-law is a young and skilled musician who, for several years now, has proved himself capable and in whom I hope to find a competent support. Should you need an assistant or a volonteer conductor, I would be happy to have him spend some time with you.'[72] Mahler did not engage Beidler, who soon fell from grace in Bayreuth. He was scheduled to conduct the *Ring* in 1904 and *Parsifal* in 1906, but proved incapable of doing either, and behaved generally so unsatisfactorily that Cosima broke completely with him in 1906.[73]

At the end of 1900, Mildenburg was invited to sing Kundry at the 1901 festival but she had to refuse because at the end of a tiring opera season she was always in need of a rest. Cosima wrote to Mahler himself on 10 December asking him if he would grant her a leave after the Bayreuth Festival instead of before. 'Direktor Mahler has always shown himself so friendly toward Bayreuth', she wrote at the same time to Mildenburg. 'I feel as if what we accomplish here were present and preserved on the Vienna Opera stage.'[74] Cosima was much disappointed when this request was also refused. Siegfried again suspected Mahler of foul play and sent the following telegram to Anna: 'What is wrong again, Anderl? Is that a renewed affirmation of your faithful nature, the gratitude for your study of Isolde? God only knows what lies hidden behind this, because our faithful Anderl is incapable of such a heartless deed, let your faithful Siegfried remain convinced of this.'[75]

In fact, Mahler knew better than anyone in Bayreuth how fragile Mildenburg's voice and general health was, and how prone to last-minute cancellation she had been, and he would have been acting against the Opera's interests had he granted her leave to appear in Bayreuth. Cosima was more tactful than her son. She immediately wrote to Mildenburg that it was necessary for her to rest after the season, and that she should not hold it against Siegfried, whatever the contents of his telegram had been. She assured her once again 'of her deep gratitude to Direktor Mahler for preserving and promoting in his theatre the things his artists experience and acquire here'.[76]

In 1901, Mahler's relationship with Richard Wagner's widow waxed almost cordial. In April 1901 the German Reichstag debated whether or not to prolong the time span for the protection of authors' copyright from thirty to fifty years. The extension was strongly supported by Bayreuth, who coupled it with a demand for the extension of its exclusive right to perform *Parsifal*, in accordance with Richard Wagner's express wish during his lifetime. A special

[71] Cosima's letter to Mahler of 16 Jan. 1901, copy in the Bayreuth archive.
[72] Cosima Wagner, *Das zweite Leben*, 557.
[73] See letter from Cosima to Beidler of 11 Aug. 1906 in Cosima Wagner, *Das zweite Leben*, 685.
[74] Letter of Cosima Wagner to Anna von Mildenburg, *Das zweite Leben*, 562 and MBRS 223.
[75] Anna von Mildenburg, 'Cosima Wagner in ihren Briefen an mich', *Neue Freie Presse*, Vienna (4 May 1930), 36, and MBRS 225.   [76] Mildenburg, 'Cosima Wagner', ibid.

clause (para. 33) providing for this was inserted into the draft law. The Social Democrats in the Reichstag strongly opposed this clause, considering it to be simply a device for protecting the financial interests of the Wagner family. When paragraph 33 was rejected by the Reichstag, Cosima Wagner sent a circular letter dated 9 May 1901 to all Reichstag deputies, in which she tried to counter the many arguments of the opposition and to show that they were based on ignorance of the real situation. She even offered to renounce the royalties for Wagner's works after thirty years provided Bayreuth was able to retain exclusive rights to perform *Parsifal*.

She sent a copy of her circular to Mahler, and added a note expressing the hope that 'artists [will] help me to protect the exclusivity of *Parsifal*, and that you might know or can think of ways in which a demonstration of artists could be organized in Austria . . . I believe that this is <u>something</u> on which artists have <u>something</u> to say.'[77]

Mahler replied at once:

I doubt that you could find anyone more ready to support you in this matter. As far as diplomatic means are concerned, I find it hard to suggest how a campaign for such a perfect cause as *Parsifal* could be initiated and organized. Nonetheless, I am body and soul at your disposal. If you were to give me a hint as to how I can be of use to you, I will spare and disdain no effort to help with all my physical and intellectual strength to attain our goal (permit me, from now on to consider it our common cause). If a petition from artists or intellectuals in general would be useful, I am sure that there would be no defaulters. And if you want the Austrian authorities to be brought into it, I will find ways and means of approaching them.[78]

Would it be wrong to detect a suggestion of irony now and again in Mahler's high-flown protestations of devotion? If so, it was directed at Cosima, not at the Wagnerian cause itself.

In another letter, Mahler forwarded to Cosima the advice of an 'expert friend of mine' (certainly Emil Freund) who had pointed out to him that there was no point in undertaking anything until a new 'Authors' Society' had been founded, for the Reichstag would certainly not agree to reopen a debate on a law which had already been passed and which would undoubtedly be approved by the Kaiser. The new Society would stress two points: first that the publishers would no longer be the main beneficiaires of an extension of the time-limit for protection of rights, and second, that German composers could leave the French Société des Auteurs and reclaim their rights when the time limit for the protection was extended to fifty years in Germany and Austria. But the Bayreuth circle decided not to remain inactive: they prepared an appeal and sent it around the world during the 1901 festival. It was signed by strange bedfellows indeed—the composer Engelbert Humperdinck, the painter Hans Thoma, the

[77] Cosima Wagner, *Das zweite Leben*, 583
[78] Letter from Mahler to Cosima Wagner, May 1901, ibid. 849.

writer Houston Chamberlain, and others, asking that *Parsifal* be henceforth considered an exceptional case and remain protected for a longer period than the law prescribed.[79]

However, all attempts to obtain such exceptional treatment for one stage work failed and Cosima could do nothing to prevent the 'rape of the Holy Grail' (*Gralsraub*), with performances of *Parsifal* in New York in 1903, and then in Holland in 1905, neither country having signed the Berne Treaty. After the New York performance, the singers who took part were banned from ever appearing again on the Bayreuth stage.[80] After 1913, in fact, *Parsifal* was likewise 'desecrated' (*entweiht*) in every provincial theatre in Europe and elsewhere.

In 1901, Mahler and Cosima exchanged four more letters concerning the baritone Theodor Bertram, who was then at the beginning of his career at the Hofoper, and who had failed to arrive in Bayreuth on the appointed date;[81] and Erik Schmedes, whom Cosima wanted to retain in Bayreuth until the end of the festival. Cosima's name appears only once in Mahler's correspondence as at present known, accompanied by a scarcely flattering allusion to her personality. This is in a letter addressed to Arnold Berliner dated 4 October 1903, which contains the following paragraph: 'Frau Cosima's letter is a factum humanum in the history of culture. From (being) Pope Gregory, the lady has turned little by little into Leo X. The Church in Bayreuth only lacks a Tetzel. Borgia would already feel at home there.'[82]

To return to the letter which Mahler received in June 1905; he quickly sensed that the request for information about Mildenburg was only a pretext, but duly responded to Cosima's request. As the soprano had not sung at Bayreuth since 1897, Cosima had heard 'conflicting' reports, and asked Mahler to inform her of the facts as quickly as possible. Mahler telegraphed that as an artist she was incomparable, but 'physically unreliable'. But the real purpose of Cosima's letter, as Mahler must have immediately realized, concerned a project especially dear to her: she wanted to see her son Siegfried's most recent opera, *Bruder Lustig*, being premièred in Vienna.

After the resounding success of *Der Bärenhäuter* in Vienna in 1899, Mahler had asked Siegfried Wagner to send him the score of his next work. At that time, Siegfried had already signed a contract with the Munich Opera for his second work, *Herzog Wildfang*. Mahler subsequently realized that the work was not up to Vienna standards.[83] Undiscouraged, Siegfried sent the score of

[79] Cosima Wagner, ibid. 851.   [80] See below, Vol. iiii, Chap. 1.

[81] Bertram had promised to be in Bayreuth on 29 Apr., but only arrived on 8 June (HOA, ZXV. 1901, letters of 24 and 26 May and 5 June 1901.

[82] MBR1, no. 283; MBR2, no. 365. The two names 'Cosima' and 'Bayreuth' are omitted in MBR1. Hans Dietz, alias Johannes Tetzel (1465–1513), a German dominican friar who advocated and practised the selling of indulgences. Luther's attack on him in 1517 sparked off the Reformation.

[83] In a telegram of 4 Mar. 1901, Siegfried invited Mahler to the opening of *Herzog Wildfang* (HOA, Z. 260/1901).

his third opera, *Der Kobold*, which Mahler found equally unsuitable for the Vienna stage. This time Siegfried was mortified,[84] and he asked his mother to serve as a go-between for his fourth opera, *Bruder Lustig*. Cosima accordingly bombarded Mahler with letters during June 1905. 'To spare (her son's) pride and susceptibility,' she even asked Mahler to 'be so good as to give an answer by telegram, even before seeing the score ... otherwise he (Siegfried) will consider himself free to accept another offer.' Mahler sent her a telegram on 10 June.

In accordance with your wishes, I am telegraphing to assure you, in case the slightest doubt remains in your mind, that it was only for technical reasons that I accepted *Der Bärenhäuter* and declined *Kobold*. I am awaiting a new work of your son's with the greatest interest. Naturally, I could only decide to accept it after careful consideration.[85]

Instead of leaving things at that, Cosima persisted in her campaign. Given Siegfried's position as poet, composer, conductor, and stage manager (*Bühnenmeister*) of the Bayreuth Festival, she claimed it was Mahler's duty to present his works to the public, 'beyond all considerations of whether or not they would please'. Hadn't he 'more or less accepted in advance' the opera which had come after *Der Bärenhäuter*, and couldn't he do the same now? If he had judged *Kobold* unworthy of performance in Vienna, he would certainly never have expressed 'interest' in its author's subsequent works. Therefore Cosima continued to hope that 'this interest would awaken [in Mahler] the warm confidence of an artist, and triumph over the critical, prudent director'. She asked him to reply by telegram, and said that she would consider his silence equivalent to a refusal.[86]

Such persistence seems pathetic coming as it did from the proud wife of Richard Wagner, the daughter of Franz Liszt. After all, she had never gone out

---

[84] The Vienna opening of *Der Kobold* at the Kaiserjubiläumstheater was a complete flop. In a telegram sent from Venice on 10 Oct. 1903, Siegfried had asked Mahler to make up his mind as quickly as possible. Mahler telegraphed his reply: 'Deeply regret I cannot acquire rights for opening. Excuse delay replying, but I thought opening already decided for Leipzig.'

[85] HOA, Z. 730/1905. In fact, Mahler had already been accused by Bayreuth in 1900 of having ended the scheduled performances of *Der Bärenhäuter* long before its success had run out. It was said that this was because of Mahler's animosity towards the Wagner family and because he had never been invited to conduct at the Bayreuth Festival. Mahler was certainly aware of this (THE 279).

[86] AMM1, 351. The letter is missing in AMM2, but can be found in the English translation, 268. Siegfried continued to pursue his prolific career as composer of operas with picturesque titles: *Sternengebot* (1908), *Banadietrich* (1910), *Schwarzschwanenreich* (1915), *Sonnenflammen* (1918), *Der Heidenkönig* (1915), *Der Friedensengel* (1915), *An allem ist Hütchen* (1917), *Der Schmied von Marienburg* (1920), *Rainulf und Adelasia*, and *Die heilige Linde*. *Banadietrich* was performed at the Hofoper in 1912 with only moderate success. The last two were never staged anywhere. Cosima's two letters to Mahler are dated 8 and 13 June (HOA, Z. 730/1905). No trace of a reply to the second can be found in the Opera Archives. Mahler probably chose not to reply, even at the risk of a rupture with the Wagner family. However, Cosima wrote to him again in Nov., asking him to allow Weidemann to come to Bayreuth to work with her on the role of Wotan for the coming festival. On that occasion she thanked Mahler for the 'friendly reception you always give to my requests', and considered it 'a further token of the importance you attach to my work at Bayreuth' (HOA, Z. 1212/1905).

of her way to do anything for Mahler. She probably resented the fact that he had never attended the Bayreuth Festival since he had come to Vienna, for she had written to him in 1901: 'I very much regret that we have never had the honour of welcoming you here. I believe that our performances would be a source of great satisfaction to you, and I would especially like to put on *The Flying Dutchman* for you, for my son's production has given this noble work new life.'[87] Cosima certainly knew that in 1897 one of the first productions Mahler had put on at the Vienna Opera had been a new *Flying Dutchman*. In any case, it was a tactical error on her part to try to hustle Mahler into taking an artistic decision against his own judgement and conscience. Could Siegfried the apple tree grow oranges? Even if this famous quip, which he made a few years earlier about Count Zichy's opera, did not occur to him,[88] Mahler never agreed to put on a work before examining the score. He was never to regret his decision, for when Siegfried Wagner's *Herzog Wildfang* and *Der Kobold* were performed at the Kaiserjubiläums Stadttheater (the former Volksoper) in December 1904, neither met with success.

After long, hot days of intensive work at the Opera, after committee meetings and discussions about the programme for the coming season, Mahler finally got away to the refreshing coolness of the family house on the Wörthersee on 15 June.[89] A few days before his arrival, Alma had knocked over an oil lamp while copying the score of his Sixth Symphony. The fire quickly spread to the carpet and the sofa, only a few feet from the children's rooms, but with the help of the cook and the chambermaid it was smothered with quilts and blankets.

Alma's diary entries before Mahler's arrival reveal that she was by no means idle, with her reading, score copying, children, and household chores, but that nevertheless she was again prey to bouts of anxiety and frustration.[90] As usual, the diary tells us little about daily life at Maiernigg during the summer of 1905, visiting friends, or Mahler's work. The following are its final pages which have been preserved (in a typewritten copy):

2 June. Maiernigg. I have not written much. I have lost the habit of conversing with myself. In my heart I was unfaithful to Gustav—only in my heart, but he knows it! It is over now. Only the memory weighs on me. One thing remains—Gustav!

5 June. Oh, if only I could write everything that I think and feel, as I used to . . . The two children are in the room, and yet I have just had again the feeling of intellectual freedom and fruitfulness—if only I could be alone longer—and really on my own a lot.

Later: I have worked all day. Copied for Gustav, looked after the children, played the piano: in the evening I finally found some inner peace. I walked to Maiernigg on my own—wished and am still wishing Gustav were here. Out of the lake... out of the

[87] HOA, letter dated 17 Aug. 1901.   [88] See below, Chap. 6.
[89] On 9 June Mahler officially requested permission to begin his holidays on the 16th (HOA, G.Z. 726/1905).
[90] AMT, typewritten copy of entries dated 2 and 5 June and 6 July 1905.

woods... his image comes up before me everywhere. When we are apart I see things as they are. I really live <u>only</u> in him. I copy for him, I play the piano to impress him, I learn and read all for the same reason... And yet when he is here, I spoil most of my pleasure through my hypersensitivity! It is simply reprehensible! Always the old pride that rears its head, the old desire to dominate, boundless ambition and thirst for glory! All this instead of striving to make HIS life happy and easy, which is the only reason I am on this earth, and the only justification for my existence. And my darling brats (*Fratzen*)! I am very worried—I have not heard from him for several days.

As soon as she had arrived in Maiernigg, Alma had written to Gustav 'positive' words, but also about her fits of depression. In reply, he wrote her a long letter full of general reflections and encouragements which were at the same time affectionate and indirect reproaches.

Now you are on the right road, I notice. When we have been alone for a considerable time, we achieve a <u>unity</u> with ourselves and with <u>nature</u>, which of course is a more comfortable environment than the people who normally surround us. We then become positive (instead of as usual getting stuck in negation) and finally productive. This is the usual path. It leads us away from ourselves whereas solitude leads us <u>to ourselves</u>; and from ourselves to God is only one step. You are full of this mood (*Stimmung*) and I am delighted to see it, for I never doubted that you had it in you.

How petty our daily life then seems to us, bogged down as it is in negation and 'criticism'. The same thing, you see, is true of your reading. Shakespeare is <u>positive</u>, <u>productive</u>; Ibsen nothing but analysis, negation, sterility. It is the same difference between you *now* and you in Vienna, when you get so annoyed over the theatre or that sort of thing. Now you will understand when I strive to preserve my <u>positive</u>, <u>productive</u> mood amidst the confusion of everyday life, and so I often take a bird's eye view of something while you remain stuck in the middle of it. Don't be misled if once again (whether through physical depression or a bout of irritation) negation gets hold of you temporarily and the prospect looks bleak for a time.[91] Don't imagine that the <u>positive</u> is not there, or is not the important thing. Just tell yourself that the sun is just behind the clouds and the weather for the moment is dark, cold and unfriendly. But the sun <u>will</u> <u>come out</u> again![92]

Alma often used her diary as a safety-valve to let off steam when things threatened to become unbearable. She was sometimes brutally frank with herself. How much of this got through to Mahler in her letters we shall never know, since later she destroyed all her letters to him. But his letters to her show that she must have told him at least something of her unease and depression. Judging from the entries in her diary written before Mahler's arrival, her mood was relatively peaceful during the first days she spent alone in Maiernigg. As always, things began to go wrong when Gustav arrived. On 6 July she wrote:

With Gustav, I often can't find anything to talk about. I know too well from the start every word he is going to say. The last few weeks have been so atrociously hot that I

---

[91] The preceding sentence was omitted by Alma in the published version of her *Erinnerungen*.
[92] BGA, no. 135, undated (6 June 1905).

haven't felt like doing anything. So I haven't read, nor worked—nor anything else. I could yearn for a man—for I <u>haven't got one</u>—but I am too lazy even for that!

A few visits enlivened their 'splendid isolation' in Maiernigg and helped to distract Alma while Gustav spent more and more time in the Häuschen. First of all, the faithful Theobald Pollak arrived,[93] then Roller and his wife Mileva.[94] Then the banker Paul Hammerschlag, who had rented a house not far from Maiernigg at Sekirn, came to visit. Sometimes he called and took Mahler for walks and outings.[95] And then, in August, came two friends from Graz, the critic and musicologist Ernst Decsey,[96] and the choral conductor Julius von Weis-Ostborn.[97] Arriving without warning, they came upon Mahler as he was going out, 'dressed for bicycling, agitated but friendly'. Their conversation was 'calm and relaxed':

The hours I spent with Mahler were incomparably richer than any I have experienced with any other artist. Mahler was a man who gave of himself (*er war ein Gebender*), he never spoke in empty fifths (*nie leere Quinten*): he was productive even in friendly discourse, and one never left him without feeling stimulated in a strangely powerful way, often followed by a temptation to play the Eckermann to him. (*Eckermannsche Anwandlungen*) . . .[98] This relationship, which I so much enjoyed, began with an argument, a violent argument about Hugo Wolf. To be exact, Mahler argued with himself over Wolf, while I just sat and listened most of the time.[99] Mahler grew so violent that I said to myself 'Watch out! The roof's on fire! He's really worried about Wolf!' He talked about *Weylas Gesang* in a scornful tone: 'It's not song at all in the artistic sense of the word—in what sense are these arpeggiated chords in quavers, with just a thread of melody above them, a song?' He probably sensed its greatness but didn't want to admit it: the natural egotism of genius struggled hard against his intelligence. Before I got up and left I wanted to point out to him the impressionistic, the Böcklinesque fantastic quality of the deliberately simple rhythm. With that, the thatch really began to blaze. He did not let me finish. 'Yes, I know! Anyone can produce tone painting (*Tonmalen*)! But I don't ask a song to tinkle when a bird appears or to rumble in the bass when the wind blows! I ask for theme, development of theme, thematic elaboration, and singing, not de-cla-ma-tion!' And he hammered each word home with the back of one hand against the palm of the other. I had the feeling: any minute now he is going to explode. His nature is like iodine-nitrogen: touch it with a feather and it explodes. The atmosphere grew oppressive.

Furiously silent, he sat down in his chair; the sun's reflection on the Wörthersee sparkled blindingly in the room. But I was glad that he had said what he thought was true so bluntly, without trying to flatter his visitor, while so many great men wag their

---

[93] AMT and AMM1, 451.   [94] Letter from Alma to Pfitzner, UPL, Philadelphia.
[95] A detail furnished by one of Hammerschlag's daughter, Elisabeth Duschnitz-Hammerschlag.
[96] See above, n. 21.
[97] Julius von Weis-Ostborn (1862–1927), privy councillor and member of the Graz finance department, was also the founder of the Deutscher Akademischer Gesangverein 'Gothina' who gave the first Graz performance, in Mar. 1910, of *Das klagende Lied* (see below, Vol. iiii, Chap. 57).
[98] Johann Peter Eckermann, assistant and close associate of the ageing Goethe. He published a large volume of his 'Conversations with Goethe' in 1836.
[99] At this time Decsey had already published part of his biography of Wolf.

tails in front of the most insignificant critic. And so I stayed. I liked this man who struggled so naively with himself, and who, moreover, had got it completely wrong. In Wolf's work as well as in his own, some songs have a thematic elaboration, and others don't, but Mahler did not seem to realize it or did not want to know. In short, Wolf was his raw nerve...[100] But after this outburst, as if by tacit agreement, the subject was dropped. He stuck to this modus vivendi with admirable tact.[101]

Elsewhere, however, Decsey described the end of the discussion. When Decsey praised Wolf's prosody, Mahler burst out again:

'Where is the thematic follow-through? Of all his Lieder, perhaps two, three, or six will survive: those which are being sung today!' 'In that case,' I [Decsey] replied, 'according to you, only half a dozen of Loewe's ballads will survive!'—'Certainly no more! Those are the good, worthwhile ones which the public instinct has selected!'—'The public! My God!'—'Yes indeed! The public, I say! The public is right: Vox dei!'[102]

Wolf was not the only subject of Decsey's conversations with Mahler although he occupied a large place in them. They also discussed one of Mahler's favourite subjects, artistic creation. 'A developing intellect never stops developing . . . (*Ein Werdender wird niemals fertig*). This saying of Goethe's applies to no one better than to Goethe himself. He never finished developing: he remained an apprentice to the end of his days. That is his well-known secret.' Mahler smiled fiercely, several devils twisted his features. 'The average man, the German opera-goer, only knows—his life's work—Goethe's *Faust* through Gounod's *Margarethe*... In this form it is familiar to him. And the dangerous thing about that *Margarethe* is—that it is so well done!'

At that time Mahler did not like speaking about his own work. He touched upon 'Ich bin der Welt abhanden gekommen', which Decsey had greatly admired at Graz, remarking that he had composed it several years before in the 'most profound solitude' of the woods of Maiernigg.[103] Then, when Decsey praised certain harmonic details and also commented on the concluding passage of 'Der Schildwache Nachtlied', in which a 'strange development and transformation of the dominant had produced an ever-increasing tension', Mahler did not agree: 'Nonsense! Dominant! Why don't you take things naively, as they are intended?'[104] The same day, the conversation concluded with a discussion of criticism in general. Mahler, Decsey realized, felt genuinely bitter about the reproaches he now received for his public successes. 'It's not fair!' he exclaimed. 'At first, my works were failures. Of course, they could only be bad! Whence their lack of success. Now, since last season they are acclaimed—So they must be bad! Of course! For they are successful. So how can they be good?'

---

[100] Mahler could certainly not have forgotten the painful quarrel he had had in 1897 with Wolf, who had been a fellow-student at the Conservatory. He must also sometimes have wondered whether this painful incident had been a contributory factor in Wolf's subsequent insanity and tragic death.

[101] EDS2, 143 ff. [102] Ernst Decsey, *Die Spieldose*, 93.

[103] 'Six years earlier', Mahler said. It was in fact only four. [104] EDS2, 144–5.

Unusually for him, Mahler also spoke of the past. For example, he mentioned the 1892 Berlin concert at which Amalie Joachim sang Lieder, including 'Der Schildwache Nachtlied', which made people laugh. In Graz, however, the same song was greeted with applause. Decsey suddenly realized that Mahler was changing, becoming 'increasingly patient'. He could now 'afford to wait', keeping his scores in his drawer for years if necessary. Then, if he still liked them, he would produce them to the public. Decsey continues:

That reminded me of Bach's naive way of writing music. His principal concern was not his future immortality but the forthcoming public holiday for which he had to compose a cantata. It also reminded me of Bruckner's holy patience. This is no longer the custom. For nowadays composers race to the publisher with their scores before the ink is even dry and curry favour with journalists to get reviews. But Mahler—we have come to understand—creates for himself. And only someone who creates for himself creates for others... As his naive rudeness and naive patience both show us, Mahler is a profoundly honest artist.[105]

On his arrival in Maiernigg in June, one of Mahler's first tasks was to send the first copies of the *Rückert-Lieder*, which he had just received from Kahnt, to a few friends. Among them was Kolo Moser's wife, who had been enthusiastic in Graz and to whom he sent 'Ich bin der Welt abhanden gekommen' with the following inscription: 'To Frau Edytha Moser, who should become lost to the world though only for a short time, and will then reappear with her beloved.'[106] But contrary to his custom, that summer Mahler could not devote himself entirely to his creative work, for he had to plan the coming season and the cycle of performances in celebration of Mozart's 150th birthday. He read scores and exchanged letters with Max Kalbeck, whom he had commissioned to prepare the new German-language versions of *Don Giovanni* and *The Marriage of Figaro*.[107] 'In the meanwhile, I have found my "*Don Juan*",' wrote Mahler to his old friend Henriette Mankiewicz, 'and I can now add a fine new storey to my edifice. Next year we will tackle the Mozart cycle.'[108]

But despite everything, Mahler did manage to finish the Seventh Symphony,

---

[105] These passages were published by Decsey in the *Triester Tagblatt* on 22 Nov. 1905, one week before the first Trieste performance of the Fifth Symphony.

[106] *Frau Edytha Moser, welche der Welt aber nur für kurze Zeit, abhanden kommen soll und hierauf mit ihrem Liebsten wieder zum Vorschein.* Edytha Moser (b. 1883) was probably leaving Vienna for the summer with her husband. She came from a wealthy Jewish family of Viennese brewers and philanthropists, of Bohemian origin, the Mauthner von Markhofs. Her father was Karl Ferdinand Mauthner von Markhof (1834–96), her mother, his second wife, née Editha, Freiin Sunstenau von Schutzenthal (1846–1918) was another musician, benefactor and founder of a famous secondary school for girls. Edytha Mauthner's sister was married to the painter Josef Engelhart. The Mauthner von Markhof family lived in a palace which was situated on the Landstrasse Hauptstrasse no. 138, next to the house inhabited by Alfred Roller.

[107] MBR contains several letters written by Mahler to Max Kalbeck (MBR1, nos. 273–8; MBR2, nos. 283, 292, 327–8, 343, 345, and 365). Handwritten copies of other unpublished letters from the same period to the same addressee are in BGM, Paris. They were a present to the author from Anna Mahler.

[108] Postcard to Henriette Mankiewicz (Library of Congress). Mahler crossed out 'Direktor' on the card's letterhead ('Der Direktor der k.k. [kaiserlich und königlich] Hofoperntheater') and replaced it with 'Sklave' (Slave).

which he had begun the year before 'in one furious burst'. According to Alma, 'in composing the two "Nachtmusiken", he had Eichendorfian visions, bubbling fountains, German Romanticism. Otherwise this symphony has no programme.' Yet Willem Mengelberg has suggested another source of inspiration for the Seventh: Rembrandt's famous *Nightwatch*, which had overwhelmed Mahler two years earlier at the Amsterdam museum. Alma does not mention this, nor does she record the anxiety Mahler had again experienced before settling down to work. Yet in September, in one of his letters to her, he spoke of having suffered that summer from violent digestive troubles which he himself suspected were of psychosomatic origin.[109] Fortunately Mahler's correspondence fills the gaps in Alma's memoirs. At the end of June, as usual, Mahler left for the Dolomites, in a depressed state of mind because he had still not begun the first movement of the Seventh. Upon arriving at Schluderbach, south of Toblach, on the road to Cortina, he wrote to his wife on the 22nd:[110]

My Almschi! After sticking doggedly to my compartment in Lienz in order to avoid the restaurant car, a feeling of numbness warned me that a migraine was unavoidably in the offing, and it came upon me in all its splendour yesterday in Schluderbach. I tried lying down, but in vain, it continued to mount, driving me from the sofa into the street—for two and a half hours I ran around the lake[111] and it was almost gone when I arrived here, where I settled in for the night. During my 'run' (through a forest of dwarf pines) I kept thinking: if only Almschi were here! How you would like it! What a shame! For just now the holiday makers are gone—though today, Corpus Christi, the peasants and soldiers (from the Landro fortress) made such a racket that the house shook. But two steps from the inn and the row is gone. A thousand kisses. Tomorrow I shall go to Misurina.[112]

And so once again Mahler had come to the shores of Lake Misurina in search of the inspiration he needed, this time for his Seventh. Unfortunately he failed to find it there. Five years later, writing to Alma, he recalls the circumstances in which the theme of the first movement finally came to him.

For two weeks I tortured myself into a state of depression, as you surely remember—until I escaped to the Dolomites! There, the same thing all over again, until I finally gave up and made my way home, convinced that the summer had been wasted.

I hadn't sent word of my arrival, so you weren't waiting for me at Krumpendorf. I got into the boat to cross the lake. With the first stroke of the oars the theme (or rather the rhythm and style) of the introduction to the first movement came to me—and within four weeks the first, third, and fifth movements were ready![113]

---

[109] The two sentences in question, in one of Mahler's letters following his return to Vienna, were later struck out by Alma (See BGA, no. 145, undated, 25 Aug. 1905).

[110] AMM1, 342; AMM2, 302. Schluderbach should not be confused with Alt-Schluderbach, where Mahler and Alma later rented the Trenkerhof for the summer. Corpus Christi fell on Thursday 22 June that year but it was celebrated as usual on the Sunday following. The undated postcard was therefore probably written on 25 June.

[111] This is undoubtedly the Dürrensee, which is situated a short distance to the north of Schludenbach.

[112] BGA, no. 141, undated (22 June 1905). The last sentence has been cut out of the editions of Alma's *Erinnerungen*.

[113] BGA no. 303, undated (8 June 1910).

On 15 August Mahler wrote, in Latin, to Guido Adler in Aussee, to announce the completion of his new work. 'Septima mea finita est. Credo hoc opus fauste natum et bene gestum. Salutationes plurimas tibi et tuis etam meae uxoris. G.M.' (My Seventh is finished. I believe it has been well conceived and born under favourable auspices. Many greetings to you and yours from my wife and me. G.M.).[114] Four days later, as he was taking the train for Vienna, he announced the same news to Richard Strauss, though in less mock-solemn fashion.

After six or seven weeks of intensive work (and not four, as he claimed in his 1910 letter), he added to the two 'Nachtstücke' of the previous year a dark and tense first movement with long stretches of blissful reverie; a ghostly Scherzo, and a Finale which purports to celebrate the triumph of light over darkness but which is perhaps the most bizarre and disconcerting piece Mahler ever wrote. As always, he completed the score in Vienna during the following winter and spring. In accordance with the newly acquired 'patience' which Decsey had discerned in him, he put the thick manuscript away in a drawer. It was to remain there for three years, for he no doubt feared that his most 'advanced' and 'modern' work would strike its first audiences as even more disconcerting and difficult to accept than his earlier works.

In 1905, Mahler returned to Vienna earlier than planned, on 22 August, probably because of the additional work caused by the cancellation of the new production of *Die Walküre* and the preparations for the Mozart year. The day of his departure from Maiernigg he spent hours shopping and visiting in Klagenfurt, which left him tired out but hungry. He ate a dish of pancakes in the station restaurant before boarding the train, where he was disappointed to find another traveller in his sleeping compartment, which usually meant that he would have a sleepless night. Hassinger, his right-hand man at the Opera, met him at the station in Vienna, and he went straight away to the Auenbruggergasse to lock the completed manuscript of the Seventh in his iron box.[115] With the help of Johanna, the chambermaid, who had opened the apartment, he changed his clothes, packed a small bag, and went to the Opera. There he saw Roller ('as cordial as ever'), Wondra, and Przistaupinski, his closest collaborators, and wrote to Alma about his trip.[116] The Lord Chamberlain and the Intendant were still away on vacation.

Once the important business had been taken care of, he asked Hassinger to book a room for him for a few days in Edlach an dem Rax, in the Semmering mountains south of Vienna. A storm was in progress when he arrived in Edlach the same evening. He spent the following day walking and reading, becoming engrossed in Fechner's *Esthetics*, (volume ii only; he had left volume i behind, probably in the train from Klagenfurt). In his letters to Alma, he told her as

---

[114] RMA 46.

[115] Three days later, he asked Alma to send him the manuscript of the Sixth by registered post, so that he could give it to his copyist.   [116] BGA, no. 142, undated (23 Aug. 1905).

usual how sorry he was she was not with him, for these last days of summer in Vienna were the only ones that he could spend as he wished, 'without care and without obligations to fulfil'.[117] The digestive problems which had plagued him continually in Maiernigg were no more than a bad memory. 'If you could see how healthy and relaxed I already feel today,' he wrote, 'you would be relieved, for I am entirely aware of the limits to my strength.' He urged her to forget the advice which their friend Alfons von Rosthorn,[118] the doctor who had visited him in Maiernigg, had given. Rosthorn had advised him to reduce his workload, but Mahler knew that he could not stand the thought of being idle.

During the following days, he spent the mornings in his office at the Opera and returned to Edlach in the afternoon. At the Hotel Edlacherhof the food was excellent and he took long walks, even in pouring rain, for four or five hours at a time. But if the bad weather persisted he would move back to Vienna, and then come to the Hochschneeberg as soon as the sun came out again. Although he had meant to avoid social life in Edlach, he had run into some of the Schindler family's more tiresome friends and acquaintances at the principal café. Among them was a Frau Horwitz, 'who soon slid over to my table, despite the fact that I firmly avoided the welcoming glances she cast from her table', a certain Doctor Seewald and one Ludwig Grünfeld. 'So there I was, in most amusing company,' Mahler writes ironically. When his wife was not with him, this sort of sociability never appealed to him. The day after this encounter, after finishing at the Opera, he fetched his things from Edlach and moved into Theobald Pollak's apartment in Vienna pending a second departure for the Schneeberg. He missed Alma more and more, and meals in restaurants were beginning to trouble his digestion.[119]

Mahler's arrival at the Hochschneeberg in the middle of a torrential rainstorm delighted him. It was 'the most beautiful, the most magnificent' of places: 'I don't understand where I had left my eyes and my head the last time I came here. The problem was obviously Arnold, whose presence weighed upon me like a dark cloud, oppressing my heart and soul. What an ass I am! Why didn't I come here right away instead of going to Edlach?'[120] The view was splendid, the food excellent, the prices moderate. In September, he insisted, Alma definitely had to come with him for a rest in this blessed place. Unfortunately, the rain continued to fall and Alma's silence worried him. Unaware that he had left Edlach, she probably continued to address her letters there. Already he longed for the day when they would be together again in Vienna and he would sip his glass of Munich beer at his wife's side.[121] As he

---

[117] BGA, no. 144, undated (23 Aug. 1905).

[118] BGA, no. 145, undated (25 Aug. 1905). Alfons von Rosthorn (1857–1909), came from a family ennobled by Joseph II in 1790. He had studied medicine in Vienna under Theodor Billroth. A renowned gynaecologist, he was director of a womens' clinic, privy counsellor, and professor at the University. He owned a property near Viktring, not far from the Wörthersee.

[119] BGA no. 146, undated (26 Aug. 1905).   [120] BGA, no. 147, dated 26 Aug. 1905.

[121] BGA, no. 148, undated (postmark, 27 Aug. 1905).

had done in Edlach, he went for walks in spite of the rain and managed to find a sheltered path with a wide view of the splendid landscape.[122] He met Alma on 31 August (her birthday) at Payerbach Station at the foot of the Semmering mountains and accompanied her to Vienna.

After Alma had returned from Maiernigg, she and Mahler decided once again to enjoy the country air, and paid a short visit to their friends Fritz and Emmy Redlich[123] in their small baroque *Schloss* at Göding (today Hodonin) in Moravia, a few kilometres from the Austrian frontier and an hour and a half from Vienna by train. Alma had stayed behind in Göding with the children when Mahler, back in Vienna, received a visit from a young Berlin conductor Oskar Fried[124] who sought advice for the performance of the Second Symphony which he was soon to conduct in Berlin. Several months earlier, in March, Schalk had invited Fried to Vienna to attend rehearsals of his cantata for voice, chorus, and orchestra, *Das trunkene Lied*, based on the same Nietzsche text which Mahler had set in the Third Symphony, a work which had already acquired a certain notoriety and which was to be performed in a Gesellschaftskonzert.[125] On that occasion, Schalk had encouraged Fried to call on Mahler, but out of diffidence and 'respect for an artist he venerated', Fried did not do so. Nevertheless, the day of the final rehearsal, he heard from Schalk that Mahler himself had expressed the desire to meet him, and hastened to the Director's office.

When he, the unjustly feared and decried master of the house, himself stood before me, I had an impression, to begin with, which I can only call wonderful, a strong impression of a human personality. The man who peered through his severe, forbidding glasses with a childlike curiosity and an unfeigned candour which above all sought to probe and penetrate the human qualities of his fellow men, this man indeed, with his childlike and yet extremely manly head, I found truly handsome. His look penetrated everything, laying bare what is innermost. His voice was beautiful, deep and bell-like. His finely drawn mouth betrayed unshakeable energy, while its almost feminine line hinted at kindness and inner warmth, the intensity of his gestures and his manner— all this made him irresistible. I confess, I took to him right away. He was particularly

[122]   BGA, nos. 147 to 149, undated (postmark, 26, 27, 28 Aug. 1905).

[123]   Fritz Redlich (1868–1921), owner of a sugar refinery and several other businesses and industries in the Göding (Hodonin) region, was a great patron of the arts and collector, and as such had made the acquaintance of Karl Moll, who had advised him on his purchases. His brother Joseph Redlich (1869–1936) later played an important political role in the Austrian monarchy. Joseph's son Hans-Ferdinand Redlich (1903–68) wrote a pamphlet at the age of 16 entitled *Gustav Mahler: Eine Erkenntnis*, dedicated to his uncle Fritz Redlich, which Joseph Redlich had published in 1919. Hans-Ferdinand Redlich emigrated to England before the Second World War and became a well-known musicologist, author of *Bruckner-Mahler* (Dent, London, 1955).   [124]   See below.

[125]   This concert, conducted by Franz Schalk, took place in Vienna on 6 Mar. 1905. The programme consisted of Goldmark's *Frühlingshymne* for contralto solo, chorus, and orchestra; Bach's *Magnificat*, and Oskar Fried's *Das trunkene Lied* (soloists: Hermine Kittel, contralto, and Richard Mayr, bass). The day after the concert, Julius Korngold published a four-column-long review in the *Neue Freie Presse*, giving full rein to his enthusiasm for this 'very imposing example of modernism'. For the first time, he declared, 'modern style has made its entrance into the field of choral music'. He felt that the catcalls of the audience could not have been directed at the 'musical quality of the work', but possibly at its length and 'overrichness'.

nice to me, treating me with a measure of cordiality I had not expected, and by the time we started talking we had won each other over. Soon we were speaking like good old friends, for whom nothing would be so unpleasant and tasteless as the cultivation of one another's favour by lavish flattery and complacent courtesy. So, in our first conversation we discussed our respective artistic plans and intentions.[126]

This first meeting was the beginning of a long friendship. The tone of Mahler's many letters to Fried reveals the exceptional cordiality and frankness of their relationship. Fried was then 34 years old. His origins remain somewhat mysterious and many of the details of his little-known biography, as told by William Malloch,[127] are so bizarre as to appear born of the imagination of a writer of fiction. It is hinted that he may have been a natural child. However, he is known to have come from a Jewish family in Berlin where his father was a shopkeeper. He left school when he was very young, trying his hand at various trades and odd jobs. He studied music on his own and more or less by chance became a horn player. For several years he belonged to a group of itinerant musicians who played at weddings and other family celebrations, travelling through Germany, Italy, and even as far as Russia. He then left the group and worked for a while in a circus as clown, stable-boy, and dog trainer.

After breaking off relations with his family he settled in Frankfurt for a few years, playing the horn first in a beer saloon band and later in the Opera orchestra. It was there that he met Humperdinck, who taught him composition and musical theory, and for whom he carried out a number of arrangements and piano transcriptions. After leaving Frankfurt in 1894 he moved to Düsseldorf, where he studied painting and art history and was taken under the wing of Julius Buths, the local conductor. He then spent three years in Munich, where he made friends with three writers, Frank Wedekind, Knut Hamsun, and Otto Julius Bierbaum (with whose wife he later eloped). He also became the protégé of Hermann Levi, who commissioned him to write the incidental music for Bierbaum's play *Die vernarrte Prinzessin* (The Infatuated Princess), a score which was never published or even performed.

After these three years in Munich Fried went to Paris, where he led a bohemian life, frequenting several famous cafés, always short of money. In 1898 he returned to Berlin, got married, and turned seriously to composition. He studied counterpoint with Xavier Scharwenka, who was the first to speak to him of Mahler, and wrote *Das trunkene Lied*, a 'Romantic Fantasy for chorus and orchestra'. Its first performance, conducted by Karl Muck, brought Fried to public attention and he found a publisher for several of his works.[128] Contemporary criticism emphasized Bach's influence on his polyphonic style and Wagner's on his orchestration.

---

[126] Oskar Fried, 'Erinnerung an Mahler', in *Musikblätter des Anbruch*, 1 (1919): 1, 16 ff.

[127] The main source, concerning Fried's youth, is William Malloch's biographical notes included in the first LP edition of Fried's recording of Mahler's Second Symphony (Bruno Walter Society: 1975).

[128] *Verklärte Nacht*, for two voices and orchestra, Op. 9 (on the same poem of Dehmel's which inspired Schoenberg's Sextet); *Erntelied*, Op. 15, for male chorus and orchestra (also on a text by Dehmel); *Prelude and Double Fugue* for orchestra; and numerous Lieder.

The success of the première of *Das trunkene Lied* was such[129] that in the autumn of 1904, although he had no appropriate experience of conducting, Fried was offered Friedrich Gernsheim's position as conductor of the Stern'schen Gesangverein. His brusque, emotional, irascible temperament, combined with his often sharp comments, aroused strong opposition from some members of the chorus, but his talent as a conductor was such that he was allowed to dismiss the dissidents and reorganize the Gesangverein according to his wishes. His first deed as conductor was a performance in March 1905 of Liszt's *Saint Elisabeth*, a work then virtually unknown in Berlin which earned him a triumph.[130] Liszt's oratorio was one of the subjects of Fried's first conversation with Mahler who, at this time, was planning to put it on again at the Hofoper.[131] The vehemence and conviction with which the younger musician discussed the problems of its interpretation so impressed Mahler that, according to Fried, he asked him to conduct his Second Symphony in Berlin. This is Mahler's record of his meetings with Fried, in the two letters he wrote to Alma, who had remained in Göding with the children:

Fried lunched with me [today]. Afterwards, we went through my Second. He inspired me with great confidence in his ability. I consider this Berlin performance [8 November] extremely <u>important</u>, and plan to attend it <u>with you</u>. . . . I spent yesterday evening with Fried, who is a very original, strange customer. I think he has a great future before him, and he will be <u>very</u> valuable to me. A pity you have not met him. I *must* go to Berlin and <u>you must</u> come with me.[132]

Fried was indeed going to play an important part in ensuring that Mahler's works were performed throughout Europe.[133] But the major article of reminis-

---

[129]   Hugo Leichtentritt published a long analysis of *Das trunkene Lied* in 1904. Paul Stefan and Paul Bekker also wrote monographs on Fried in 1907 and 1910.

[130]   In the series of 'New Concerts' which he founded, Fried broke with the conservative tradition of the Stern'schen Gesangverein and conducted many premières and little-known works such as Mahler's Second Symphony, Liszt's *Gran Mass*, Haydn's *Seasons*, Beethoven's Fantasy for piano, chorus, and orchestra, Brahms's *Alto Rhapsody*, Mendelssohn's *Midsummer Night's Dream*, and many first performances.

[131]   In fact, Mahler put on *Saint Elisabeth* every year at the Hofoper as a memorial to Empress Elisabeth of Austria on the anniversary of her death. He had organized another theatrical performance of Liszt's oratorio in June 1905 for the members of the Allgemeiner Deutscher Musikverein.

[132]   BGA, nos. 150, 151, and 152 (Sept. 1905).

[133]   Fried later performed Mahler's Symphonies in Germany, Hungary, France, Russia, England, Italy, Holland, and Denmark. In the early 1920s, he made the first complete recording (for Polydor) of a Mahler symphony, the Second. He was engaged as conductor of the Berlin Gesellschaft der Musikfreunde in the autumn of 1907, and with that orchestra gave first performances of Borodin, Sibelius, Delius (*A Mass of Life*), Busoni (*Brautwahl* and *Turandot Suite*), Scriabin (*Le Poème de l'extase*), Sibelius (the Fourth Symphony), Schoenberg (*Pelleas und Melisande*), and Stravinsky's (*Firebird* and *Rite of Spring*). At that time, he was the only Berlin conductor who regularly gave first performances of contemporary works, but he was never appointed permanent conductor of an orchestra for any length of time. In 1925, he conducted the Berlin Symphony Orchestra but for only one season. In 1934, he left Nazi Germany for Soviet Russia where, in 1922, he had been the first foreign conductor invited to conduct since the Revolution, and had been met on arrival at the station by Lenin himself. For some time he conducted the Tiflis Opera and was later named conductor of the Orchestra of Radio Moscow. He acquired Soviet citizenship and died in Moscow on 5 July 1941. During the 1920s Fried recorded not only Mahler's Second Symphony, but Bruckner's Seventh, Brahms's First, Strauss's 'Alpine' Symphony, and (twice) Berlioz's *Fantastique*, for a long time one of his favourites. After the advent of electronic recording, he also recorded Beethoven's Ninth, Tchaikovsky's 'Pathétique', Liszt's *Mazeppa*, and Stravinsky's *Firebird Suite*.

cences he later wrote about him[134] shows that the two men shared many tastes and affinities. A frail young man, he was no more concerned with appearances and conventions than Mahler. With his broad forehead, imperious nose, and ironic mouth, he gave the impression of knowing both what he wanted and how to get it. No wonder then that in September 1905 Mahler devoted considerable time to him and played him the whole of his Second Symphony.

During Alma's absence, Mahler also took long walks with Fritz Löhr, one of his closest friends from the past whom Alma had not taken to. He much needed such moments of calm, for his duties at the Opera were as exhausting as ever. Many performances had had to be cancelled at the last minute, the conflict with the imperial censor over *Salome* was developing into a pitched battle, and the preparation of the Mozart cycle required considerable effort. For the celebration of the Emperor's name-day, on 4 October, Mahler chose a work which was not likely to offend the Viennese audience, a comic opera which attempted to revive the style of the eighteenth-century opera buffa. Its composer, Ermanno Wolf-Ferrari, was then only 30 years old. He was born in Venice, the first of five sons of a German Jewish painter, August Wolf, and his Venetian wife Emilia Ferrari. Following in his father's footsteps, he was studying painting when, at the age of 13, he discovered his musical vocation during a trip to Bayreuth. Faithful to his dual origins, he then studied composition at the Munich Conservatory with Josef Rheinberger, but he finished his studies in Venice with Don Lorenzo Perosi. Wolf-Ferrari's entire life and career were divided in the same manner between Germany and Italy. In the country of his birth he studied Renaissance and baroque music, met Verdi and Boito, and married young. He was only 24 years old in 1900, when his first opera, *Cenerentola*, had its première at la Fenice in Venice. It was not a great success, but two years later a new German version triumphed in Germany, where his subsequent operas were now premièred. For the next one, he himself adapted a play by his eighteenth-century compatriot, Carlo Goldoni, *Le Donne Curiose*. This first of his Goldoni operas had had a triumphant première in Munich on 27 November 1903, and was subsequently performed in Kassel, Schwerin, Breslau, and Düsseldorf, in a German version and under the title *Die neugierigen Frauen.*[135]

---

[134] See above, n. 124.

[135] Wolf-Ferrari's next operas were *I Quattro Rusteghi* (1906), *Il Segreto di Susanna* (1909), *I Gioielli della Madonna* (1911), and *l'Amore Medico* (1913). During the whole of this period Wolf-Ferrari was virtually unknown in his home country, although he was appointed Director of the Liceo Benedetto Marcello in Venice (1903–9). But after the First World War several other operas were premièred in Italy: *Gli Amanti Sposi* (1925); *La Vedova Scaltra* (1931); *Il Campiello* (Munich and Milan, 1936). Others were *Das Himmelskleid* (Munich 1927); *La Dama Bobu* (1939), and finally *Der Kuckuck von Theben* (1943). The United States were the scene of Wolf-Ferrari's greatest glory, when Toscanini conducted *Le Donne Curiose* (1912) and *l'Amore Medico* (1914) and Maria Jeritza premièred *I Gioielli della Madonna* (1925) at the Metropolitan Opera. Wolf-Ferrari spent his later life in relative obscurity in Munich, with his second wife Wilhelmine Funck. During the Second World War he emigrated to Switzerland and died of a heart attack in his native city of Venice in 1948.

A colourful anecdote concerning the rehearsals of *Le Donne Curiose* has survived. Roller[136] had designed a magnificently embroidered rococo costume with lace cuffs for Richard Mayr, the young bass who played Ottavio, a wealthy Venetian bourgeois. In one of the scenes in the opera, Mayr was supposed to remove the jacket but, as was customary at the Opera, the cuffs were sewn onto the sleeves of the jacket, and the male singers wore nothing but a sleeveless shirt underneath. So on the evening of the first dress rehearsal, the spectators were treated to the sight of a pair of muscular plebeian arms which, far from recalling rococo Venice, rather suggested 'all the crude vitality of Henndorf' (Mayr's native village near Salzburg, where his father ran a brewery).[137] At the last minute therefore, Roller was obliged to have a long-sleeved shirt made for Mayr, allowing him to retain the appearance of a Venetian bourgeois of the enlightened century even in his shirtsleeves. Most of the Viennese critics found *Le Donne Curiose* meagre fare. Indeed, the subject matter is scanty: it revolves around the ruses invented by several 'curious' wives as they try to penetrate the mysteries of the 'club' founded by their husbands to get away from them. A lively, very 'Italian' comedy, it succeeded in diverting the audience, at least until the end of the second act. Kalbeck considered its success 'well merited': it was 'light as well as healthy musical fare'.[138]

Hirschfeld praised Wolf-Ferrari's sparkling wit, which kept the audience in excellent mood: Mahler had succeeded 'not only in showing us this amusing work, but also the spirit of Goldoni and his times'. Richard Wallaschek, on the other hand, criticized Mahler for choosing a work of so little musical originality and imagination, especially since the subject, entertaining though it was, was utterly 'foreign to the music', the action slow and poor, and its comic aspects outmoded. However, 'elegant and discreet orchestration', a refreshing change from the currently fashionable 'thick instrumental pap', was evidence of the composer's individuality and independence and gave rise to hopes for his future development.[139]

As usual, Korngold, in the *Neue Freie Presse*, took an intermediate position between the admirers and detractors of the new work. While acknowledging that Wolf-Ferrari lacked imagination and borrowed from *Falstaff*, Rossini, Cornelius, Smetana, and even Wagner and Mozart, and finding his merry-making restless and somewhat 'contrived', he lauded his success in 'modernizing the old comic opera style', and his real gift for the theatre. His 'music reinforced the action even as the action reinforced the music'. Max Graf also

---

[136] Roller sent in his estimate for the Vienna production on 29 June 1905: 5,260 kronen for the costumes, 150 kronen for the wigs, 2,300 for set construction, 1,650 for accessories, and 7,616 for the décors, for a total of 16,976 kronen. One of *Das Rheingold*'s revolving stages was enlarged for the occasion.

[137] Otto Kunz, *Richard Mayr* (Bergland, Vienna, 1933), 106.

[138] Kalbeck also congratulated Mahler on having placed the overture, as an intermezzo between the first two scenes.

[139] Wallaschek further complained that the performances of Marie Gutheil-Schoder bordered on caricature and even suggested operetta.

defended the 'freshness and vivacity' of this 'attractive and entertaining' work and praised its 'witty, if not original', inventiveness.

Schönaich went further, proclaiming Wolf-Ferrari's comic genius exceptional for the time. He knew how to illuminate the action 'with an abundance of musical spotlights' and succeeded in stimulating and maintaining the interest of the audience. He certainly showed great promise, despite the comparative weakness of his musical invention. The *Fremden-Blatt* confined its praise to the cast[140] and the quality of the performance as a whole. Even Muntz, who found fault with both the libretto and the music, and called Wolf-Ferrari a 'genius for compiling', found the comedy 'so tasteful' that its faults were 'inoffensive' in comparison, as its reception by the public showed. Such was also the opinion of the public. The success of *Die neugierigen Frauen* was however short-lived: after twelve performances in 1905, of which all but the last two were conducted by Mahler himself, it was never put on again.

In a letter written in Maiernigg and dated 19 August 1905, Mahler informed Strauss of the completion of his Seventh Symphony, and discussed one of his dearest projects, the première of *Salome* at the Hofoper. On the way back to Vienna a few days later, he was determined to defeat the violent opposition which the project had unleashed at the Opera. Since he had discovered it in Strasbourg the preceding May, he had firmly resolved to put it on but had underrated the opposition which the project was to encounter. The imperial censor immediately declared Wilde's text 'scandalous' and relegated it to the 'domain of sexual psychopathology'. Mahler, however, taking the artist's point of view, refused to yield because in his eye Strauss's music had ennobled and transfigured Wilde's play.

In the twenty years since they had first met, Mahler's relationship with Strauss had always been courteous and even amicable, but stopped short of real friendship. It is obvious from the many letters they exchanged that it was the interests they had in common and the similarities in the pattern of their careers that brought them together so often. They were poles apart in character and motivation, and were constantly aware of this. Mahler perhaps more so than Strauss. However, they had both long sensed the extent to which their destinies were linked, and each tried always to be helpful to the other. Strauss never hid the fact that he did not fully understand or admire Mahler's music.[141] Although he later conducted two Mahler symphonies, the First and the Fourth, he once said to Fritz Busch, in his Bavarian accent: 'Sö, Busch, der Mahler,

---

[140] Except for Slezak, whose voice was considered to be 'too heroic' for the role of Florindo. The cast for the performance on 4 Oct. 1905 was: Gutheil-Schoder (Colombine); Felser (Eleonore); Forst (Rosaura); Kittel (Beatrice); Slezak (Florindo); Weidemann (Pantalone); Mayr (Ottavio); Stehmann; Wissiak; Haydter (Leandro). For the second performance, Hesch replaced Mayr as Ottavio and Kiurina replaced Forst as Rosaura. Wolf-Ferrari himself attended the rehearsals and the opening.

[141] In a brief homage drafted for the BSP published in 1910 in honour of Mahler's fiftieth birthday, Strauss praised him only for 'the exemplary plastic qualities of his instrumentation' (BSP 66). For a detailed account of the Strauss–Mahler relationship, see below, Chap. 8.

dös is überhaupt gar ka Komponist. Dös is bloss a ganz grosser Dirigent. (You know, Busch, Mahler isn't a composer at all. He's merely a very great conductor).'[142] Mahler, on the other hand, had always recognized the richness, flamboyance, and powerful vitality of Strauss's music, even when he criticized its illustrative tendencies.

However Strauss's private performance of *Salome* in the showroom of the Strasbourg piano-dealer Wolf, had been a revelation to Mahler. He was convinced he had discovered the greatest German dramatic composer of his time, and felt it his duty to stage *Salome* in Vienna. The numerous notes and letters he addressed to Strauss testify to the vigour and constancy of his efforts. Some of Strauss's replies have also been preserved, in the form of copies made on Alma's orders.[143] On 18 August Strauss read in the Berlin paper *Der Tag* that Mahler intended to stage *Salome* at the beginning of the new season, and promised him the piano score for September and the orchestral parts for November. The choice of the cast seemed obvious to him: Herod—Schmedes; Herodias—Mildenburg; Jochanaan—Weidemann; Narraboth—Slezak. For the title role, strange as it may seem, Strauss thought of Selma Kurz and questioned Mahler about her voice and acting talent.[144] Probably because of rumours he had heard about Roller's 'decorative whims', he added a postscript asking that 'instructions for the decors should be as short as possible, and designed to help the acoustics'.

The following day, Mahler replied, apologizing for not being able to set the date for the première. Obviously he had underestimated the difficulties he was going to encounter, for at that time he still intended to hold the première of *Salome* on the Emperor's name-day, 4 October.[145] He was anxiously awaiting a copy of the libretto, for the Intendant refused to approve the slightest expenditure before it had been read and accepted by the censor. He disagreed with some of Strauss's suggestions for the cast. Selma Kurz was incapable 'in every respect' of singing Salome, and for the moment he considered giving the role to a young dramatic singer named Elsa Bland.[146] He also suggested that Demuth might perhaps replace Weidemann. But for Narraboth Slezak was quite unacceptable. He might be good enough for *William Tell* and *Il Trovatore*, but he 'does not exert himself, sings negligently, deforms the rhythm and by the third performance is useless'.

---

[142] Fritz Busch, *Aus dem Leben eines Musikers* (Rascher, Zürich, 1949), 169.

[143] AMS. The originals seem to have disappeared with all the letters addressed to Mahler when the library on the top floor of Alma's house on the Hohe Warte was damaged by a bomb or a grenade.

[144] Letter of 18 Aug. 1905, MSB 99. Strauss also thanked Mahler for conducting *Feuersnot* in Vienna for the members of the Verein, and described the performance of *Tristan* he had attended in Cologne with four Viennese singers in the cast: Schmedes, Mildenburg, Kittel, and Mayr. He had been very disappointed by Mildenburg's voice, intonation, and diction, except in the first act.

[145] If not on that date, Mahler warned Strauss, the première would have to be put off until Jan. 1906 as the new Mozart productions could not be postponed since they were to celebrate the 150th anniversary of the Salzburg composer's birth.

[146] She had been engaged on 1 June 1905 and spent three years at the Hofoper.

Mahler received the libretto of *Salome* at the end of August and immediately forwarded it to the censor, Emil Jettel von Ettenach. He then told Strauss that his 'affair was going well', but recommended the 'greatest discretion'. For the time being the 'only obstacle' came from a high court personage with authority over the Opera, but *Salome* could still be put on that autumn. Mahler promised to attend the Dresden première, and advised Strauss to continue his negotiations with Rainer Simons, director of the Kaiserjubiläumstheater,[147] for 'they would help him [Mahler] in his efforts'. But on 22 September Mahler drafted a letter to Strauss[148] officially informing him that *Salome* had been rejected by the censor on 'religious and moral grounds' and could therefore not be performed. However, the letter was never sent for Mahler changed his mind and on the same day dispatched a telegram to Strauss asking him for several copies of the score for the singers to learn their parts, thus showing that he still hoped to overcome the censor's opposition.[149]

On 26 September, Mahler wrote to the Intendant requesting that he ask the censor to indicate the passages he considered offensive, so that they could be changed. On 10 October Strauss wrote to Mahler enclosing a letter[150] from Simons to the effect that *Salome* would not be accepted by the Hofoper censor, and that he (Simons) would like to perform it. Strauss added that the date for the Dresden première had been fixed for the end of November and that the censorship in Saxony had posed no problems. In his reply of 11 October Mahler confirmed the 'sad truth' of the refusal but promised to move heaven and earth to have this 'bêtise' reversed. He had not yet identified the 'influence' responsible for the decision. 'The letter [from Simons]', he continued, 'will be very useful. *Salome* cannot possibly be performed at the Jubiläumstheater, but I intend to show it as being possible.' He advised Strauss to continue negotiating with other theatres. He had envisaged putting on the opera in January or February, and was still hoping that its performance at so catholic a court as Dresden would count in its favour.

You would not believe all the trouble I have gone through ever since my return from Strasbourg, where I spoke of my project, full of enthusiasm *Salome* is the best thing (*Höhepunkt*) you have done so far! Nothing you have written before can compare with it.[151] You know that I do not go in for empty phrases, even less with you than with others. But this time, I feel I must tell you, every note is in the right place. I have always known it: you are the born dramatist! I must confess that it is only thanks to your music that this work by Wilde has become comprehensible to me. I hope to be able to attend the première in Dresden. Let me know if you agree with my plan of

---

[147] The former and later Vienna Volkstheater, as mentioned above.

[148] HOA, Z. 1019/1905, cited MSB 103 and WMW1, 230; WMW2, 193 ff.

[149] Ibid.

[150] Strauss asked Mahler to return the letter, which is today in the Strauss archives in Garmisch (MSB 104).

[151] Egon Wellesz, then Schoenberg's young composition pupil, noticed the score of *Salome* on his master's piano (around this time), a gift from Mahler.

campaign. You have my word that I will leave no stone unturned and will never weary of championing this incomparable, thoroughly original masterpiece.

The events that followed were to prove Mahler's sincerity. A note addressed by Mahler to Strauss in mid-October informs him that the acceptance of *Salome* in Dresden and Rainer Simon's offer seem to have had a positive effect upon the censorship bureaucrats in Vienna.[152] At the end of the month Schuch wrote to Mahler asking him if the news of the Vienna censor's refusal was correct. By return, Mahler confirmed that it was, but added that he was trying to have the decision reversed. 'In the interests of a successful outcome,' he wrote to Schuch, 'I must ask you to keep all this very secret. . . . Every day, I am more delighted with this masterpiece: in my opinion, it is the summit of all Strauss's work.'[153]

The Opera archives testify to Mahler's strenuous efforts on behalf of Strauss's opera. At the end of October, an interview with the censor inspired new hopes, and Mahler wrote to Strauss that 'the difficulties have been over-come and *Salome* is accepted'. Strauss would receive a copy of the libretto in which the words to be changed had been underlined. The censor had promised that 'nothing essential would be modified', but insisted, among other things, upon the deletion of the name Jochanaan. Mahler was already considering four alternative casts. None of the Hofoper's sopranos seemed to him to be entirely up to the principal role. For the moment he considered Gutheil-Schoder the best choice. Strauss immediately thanked him for his selfless efforts and comforting letter:

Your recognition of my work, words which one so rarely hears from colleagues and yet so badly needs, caused me almost more pleasure than the news of your all-knowing censor's withdrawal of his refusal. Naturally, I agree to all the changes you wish: the change of name for John, whose perilous story every schoolboy knows, is heavenly![154]

Strauss then wrote saying that the Dresden première was postponed until early December because the prima donna was indisposed, and that he would be leaving for Russia after 13 December. The Vienna première would therefore have to take place between those two dates or be postponed until January. When further delays occurred in Dresden, Strauss wrote to Schuch triumphantly that 'everything was going well in Vienna'. But the following week all Mahler's hopes were again dashed by a new letter, dated 31 October, from the censor. After a fresh examination of the text, he considered that 'all allusions to Christ must be deleted', or drastically revised, as would 'the Hebrew name of John the Baptist'. Apart from these considerations he simply could not come to terms with the repulsive nature of the subject as a whole, and added:

---

[152] MSB 107.
[153] Letter to Ernst von Schuch dated 26 Oct. 1905 (HOA, Z. 1170).
[154] AMS and MSB 109.

I can only repeat that the staging of events which belong to the field of sexual pathology is not suited to our Imperial stage. I regret that a work whose musical impact, as you say, is so powerful, should come to grief because of the text on which it is based but, from my point of view as a censor, I cannot reach any other conclusion.

However Mahler should allow the press to believe that the 'question was still open'.[155] Mahler wrote to Strauss immediately about the changes requested:

He [the censor] has just returned the libretto with a long disquisition (I'll bring the letter to you in Berlin, where I shall be the 7th and 8th November), and is talking again about 'the staging of events which belong to the field of sexual pathology and are not appropriate for our Court Theatre . . .' Another damned ramble in the realm of generalities, against which there are no weapons! I beg you, dear Strauss, let's from now on keep all this to ourselves, otherwise our cart will get stuck. On Tuesday, I am going to pay him another personal visit and take the bull by the horns. I won't give in, and consider your Salome my own personal affair.[156]

Unfortunately, the newspapers got wind of this new refusal. On 23 October, it was announced in the press, and certain journals even tried to justify it. The *Illustrirtes Wiener Extrablatt* recalled that during Jahn's tenure the censor had pronounced reservations about three works: Giordano's *André Chénier*, which dramatized episodes from the French Revolution; Leoncavallo's *I Medici*, in which a murder is committed in a church, and Massenet's *Hérodiade*, because of its 'biblical' subject. But in the case of *Salome*, it was not reservations, but a stark 'refusal'. The same article reminded its readers that the Hofoper was a 'court theatre' built and financed by the Emperor, and its audience included the Emperor and his family: it was therefore not any ordinary theatre, directed by a mere impresario, whose principal aim was to attract the public. Not only the 'unbridled sensuality' and perversity of *Salome*, but also repeated references to Christ and the presence of personages like Saint John the Baptist made it unfit for an imperial theatre. The article concluded:

In artistic circles, it is said that the decision was directed against Mahler (personally). According to our information, such is not the case. No director of a Viennese court theatre has ever drawn such personal conclusions from a negative decision of the *Literarische Aufsichtbehörde* (Literary Surveillance Office). The distressing *Rose Bernd* affair is still in everyone's memory. Director Schlenther, who was closer to Gerhart Hauptmann than Mahler is to Strauss, did not make an 'issue' out of it.

This 'well-informed' article was probably inspired or even dictated by the censor to justify his intransigence. Indeed it was by means of censorship that the court had always been able to exert its influence over the two official theatres. The day in 1901 when Mahler and Alma had met at the

---

[155] The letter of the censor, Dr Emil von Jettel von Ettenach, is accompanied by Plappart's definitive refusal, dated 5 Nov. (HOA, Z. 1168 and 1170/1905).

[156] *Österreichische Musikzeitschrift*, 15 (1905): 6, 312, and MSB 110.

Zuckerkandls', conversation had turned to this subject, and to the banning of a play at the Burgtheater during Max Burckhard's tenure. Then the archdukes and archduchesses frequently attended the theatre, and it was common knowledge that the prohibition of Hauptmann's *Rose Bernd* was the result of the direct intervention of one of the Emperor's daughters, Archduchess Marie Valerie, to whom Theodor Helm also attributed, in his memoirs, the refusal of *Salome*.[157] Later, in 1908, Archduke Franz Ferdinand objected to the performance of Karl Schönherr's *Königsreich*, and at the beginning of the First World War in 1914, Archduchess Blanca had a play by the same author, *Weibsteufel*, banned.[158] At the Opera, it was obviously a rarer event for the censor to express reservations of a 'moral' order about a libretto, but it had happened before, as we have seen above.

In his letter to Strauss informing him of the censor's definitive refusal, Mahler had blamed 'these accursed newspaper scribblers who have spoilt everything'.[159] He was determined to continue his efforts but feared that the postponement of the Dresden première would be interpreted by the Vienna authorities as also being due to 'censorship' difficulties. Throughout October he remained firmly convinced that he would be able to produce *Salome*, as shown in a letter he wrote to Engelbert Humperdinck, who had offered him his latest opera, *Heirat ohne Willen* (The Enforced Marriage): between *Salome* and the imminent Mozart festival, he wrote, he could not consider another new production.[160] When he wrote again to Strauss on 1 November, Mahler was still far from having lost hope. The confidential inquiry which Herr Jellinek, another member of the *Literarischen Aufsichtbehörde*, had addressed to Ernst von Schuch about the attitude of the Dresden censor even struck him as a encouraging sign. Schuch replied that Strauss's libretto had not elicited the slightest objection.

In Dresden, the opening of *Salome* on 9 December 1905 was one of the greatest successes in the history of opera, with thirty-eight curtain calls for the artists and the composer. It obliged the Berlin censor to back down and authorize the performance of the work, despite the reluctance of the Empress herself, who had banned other works in the past. The influence of the new General Intendant, Georg von Hülsen-Häseler,[161] was decisive, and the only condition imposed upon Strauss was that the star of Bethlehem should shine at the moment of Salome's death. In Berlin, as in Dresden, the opera was a great success, and no less than fifteen performances were given in the year following the première.

---

[157] THE 305.

[158] Hilde Spiel, in *Du*, 266 (Apr. 1963), 51. Karl Schönherr (1867–1943) was a doctor from South Tirol who wrote realistic, moving dramas based on peasant life in that region.

[159] MSB 110.

[160] The exchange of letters took place between Aug. and Oct. 1905 (HOA, Z. 893 and 1175/1905). Mahler encouraged Humperdinck to continue his negotiations with the Director of the Kaiser-jubiläumstheater, but there, too, the imperial court proscribed a performance of this work.

[161] He was the son of former Intendant Botho von Hülsen (see above, Vol. i, Chap. 17).

In Vienna, Mahler had apparently given up hope. A handwritten draft of a letter dated early December has survived in the Opera Archives. Weary of the petty arguments he was constantly confronted with, Mahler seems to have tried at least once to raise the level of the debate:

Permit me to insist briefly that in artistic matters form is the important thing, not content, at least from a higher standpoint; only the way in which a subject is treated and developed matters, not what it is about. A work of art should be taken seriously when the artist has mastered the subject matter by purely artistic means, and succeeded in absorbing it entirely by the 'form' [Gestalt appears in brackets after Form, and is followed by: 'You can interpret this expression in the Aristotelian sense']. According to this principle, serious works of art include operas like *Don Juan* (in which a libertine wages war upon God and mankind), or the *Ring*, in which incest, etc. becomes not only a tragic subject (*tragiert*) but is rendered comprehensible. It is my unshakeable conviction that such works do not profane even the holiest holy day. On the other hand, works like *Der Evangelimann*[162] (in which Christ and all the saints become daily fare) and all the Mary-Magdalene and Saint John tragedies in which the subject matter is supposed to excite the tear glands, are in my opinion not serious works of art. Consequently they are not fit for any holy day, and are on the whole not fit for anything . . .[163]

The fact that this letter was never sent would suggest that Mahler was beginning to doubt the efficacy of his own arguments. At the end of December, he acknowledged in a letter to Strauss that the Vienna première could not possibly take place before the autumn of 1906. 'I will succeed,' he added, 'trust me. But you must be patient. . . . Things here are deplorable. I am dreadfully sorry not to be able to put on this magnificent work immediately. But you will enjoy it once it is put on here.'[164]

As we shall see, the Austrian première of *Salome* ultimately took place in Graz.[165] Vienna discovered *Salome* only in 1907 at the Deutsches Theater, during a season of the Breslau Vereinigtes Theater ensemble between 25 May and 20 June. It was subsequently performed at the Kaiserjubiläumstheater in 1910, and was only produced at the Hofoper (which had meanwhile become the Staatsoper) on 14 October 1918, after the fall of the Habsburgs. In the meantime, the opera continued to excite a controversy which was not always to its advantage. In New York, the first Metropolitan Opera production was banned the day after the dress rehearsal, 21 January 1907 (which enabled the rival Hammerstein Opera to put on a memorable production with Mary Garden in the title role).[166] In London, the royal censor demanded radical changes in the libretto. In the 'revised' Covent Garden version, Salome's passion for the prophet was purged of its sexual element. She summoned him to her presence

---

[162] By Wilhelm Kienzl (see above).

[163] Draft of a letter from Mahler (probably to the Intendant or the censor), HOA, cited by BDB 246.

[164] This letter, dated 22 or 23 Dec. (MSB 115), replies to a telegram in which Strauss asks Mahler to send a Vienna soprano to Munich for the role of Diemut in *Feuersnot*.

[165] See below, Chap. 7.   [166] See below, Vol. iiii, Chaps. 1 and 4.

as her father confessor and sang her last solo with an empty platter in her hands. Viewed in retrospect, Strauss succeeded brilliantly in challenging the clerical and bourgeois morality of his time . . . and reaped considerable financial benefit in the process, as he later recalled in his *Erinnerungen*: 'One day, William II said to his Intendant: "I am sorry Strauss composed that 'Salome'. He is really a very nice fellow, but that will do him a lot of harm!" Well, from the harm it did me I was able to build my villa in Garmisch!'[167]

In his letter of 1 November, which was mainly about *Salome*, Mahler suggested meeting Strauss a few days later in Berlin, for he had promised to be there on 8 November, the date on which Fried was to conduct the Second Symphony in one of the Neue Symphonische Konzerte he had recently instituted.[168] Before leaving for Berlin, Mahler presented his old friend Guido Adler with the manuscript of 'Ich bin der Welt abhanden gekommen' for his fiftieth birthday on 1 November.[169]

Outside Austria and Germany, Mahler's music had already been performed in Belgium,[170] France (a few Lieder only),[171] and several times in the United States.[172] It had also been heard on one occasion in England thanks to Henry Wood, the insatiably inquisitive conductor and founder (in 1895) of the London Promenade Concerts.[173] The English première of the First Symphony had taken place on 21 October 1903 at the Proms. Wood 'cannot have been much encouraged by the critical reception accorded to his initiative', as witness the following review published in the *London Times*:[174]

From time to time the name of Gustav Mahler has come before those who follow the course of musical events attentively as that of a composer who had not only done great

---

[167] Richard Strauss, *Betrachtungen und Erinnerungen*, ed. Willi Schuh (Atlantis, Zurich, 1949), 227.

[168] As seen above, the four Neue Symphonische Konzerte took place with the participation of the Berlin Philharmonic orchestra and the Stern'schen Gesangverein. Originally, Fried had planned to perform some of Mahler's Lieder in the same programme with Emily Destinn and Martha Stapelfelt, the soloists of the Second Symphony, but he ultimately replaced them by Reger's *Choral Cantata* No. 3.

[169] Edward Reilly, *Gustav Mahler und Guido Adler* (Universal Edition, Vienna, 1978), 46. The manuscript which was probably the draft orchestral score, has disappeared. It was dedicated: 'To my faithful friend Guido Adler (may he never become lost to me) (*der mir nie abhanden kommen möge*), on his fiftieth birthday.'

[170] Symphony No. 2 in Liège in 1898 under Sylvain Dupuis, and in 1899 under Mahler (see above, Vol. ii, Chaps. 3 and 5).

[171] Three *Lieder eines fahrenden Gesellen* in 1905 under Camille Chevillard (see above Chap. 3).

[172] Symphony No. 4 under Walter Damrosch in New York in 1904 (see above, Chap. 1); Symphony No. 5 under Franz von der Stucken in Cincinnati (see above, Chap. 2).

[173] Henry Wood (1869–1944) was born in London, the son of a modest artisan. He studied at the Royal Academy of Music and started his career as an organist, singing teacher, and opera conductor. In 1895 he founded the famous Promenade Concerts which he led until 1940. During those years he performed a vast number of English premières, by Strauss, Debussy, Reger, and Scriabine, and also Shostakovitch's Seventh Symphony and Schoenberg's Five Orchestral Pieces. Although not a great conductor by international standards, he exerted a powerful influence on the musical life of his country. Henry Wood had married Olga Urussov, a young soprano who had been his pupil. In 1933 he conducted the first English performance of Mahler's Eighth Symphony.

[174] The review is unsigned, but the paper's chief music critic from 1889 to 1911 was John Alexander Fuller-Maitland (1856–1936). See Donald Mitchell, 'The Mahler Renaissance in England: Its Origins and Chronology', in Donald Mitchell and Andrew Nicholson (eds.), *The Mahler Companion* (Oxford University Press, Oxford, 1997), 6 ff.

things already, but was expected to accomplish even greater. By those, however, who remember him as the 'completer' of Weber's unfinished opera *Die Drei Pintos*, which was heard in Leipzig and one or two other German towns some 15 years ago, the news of his late-developed creative faculty was received with feelings of doubt; and now that his First Symphony (in D) has been heard in England—it was given at the Promenade Concert last night—the doubt is resolved into a certainty that Herr Mahler has little or no creative faculty. It is, in fact, quite impossible, however willing one may be, to find any genuinely good point in the symphony, which is a work commonplace and trite to an almost infantile degree, contains no germ of real inventive ability, and is not even well scored, but is imitative of Weber, Mozart, Wagner, and other composers, and when 'original' is naive to childlessness. To English hearers some amusement was caused by *quasi* references to 'Three Blind Mice' and 'Hot Cross Buns' in the first and the slow movements; but even these were cases in a desert of incongruous and inconsecutive dullness; and at the end of three-quarters of an hour which the symphony occupies in performance, one found oneself still wondering what the composer set out to say.

The views expressed by the musical journals were hardly more enlightened. The anonymous critic of the *Musical Standard*[175] did not 'think it necessary to write much about [the work]':

The music struck me as utterly impossible. Nearly sixty minutes of dreadful monotony and weakness were spent listening to a composition that appeared to have more childishness than charm. There is nothing daring in the symphony beyond the fact that the composer asks us to listen to yards of stuff that seems to be of the least imaginable musical value. When the music is not coarsely loud and confused, it is generally of a baby-like simplicity. The orchestral colouring is often the composer's own, and he has certainly written a symphony that is unlike any other work in the same form. But for all that I doubt whether any rational musical being wants to become acquainted with it. It matters not to me what 'programme' the composer had before him: for the music is bad—at least, that is my opinion. Very likely the later symphonies may be infinitely better. I cannot say.[176]

A week later, the *Musical Times* was equally disparaging:

Herr Gustave [*sic*] Mahler's Symphony (No. 1) was heard for the first time in England on the 21st ult. It proved to be a clever, scholarly work, but so over-developed as to frequently give rise to a sense of weariness before the hour, less eight minutes, occupied by the performance had expired. Most of the themes are couched in folk-tune phraseology, and their treatment is reminiscent of the style of Humperdinck, though less polyphonic than that composer's. The most memorable movement of the symphony is the Andante, which, though more gruesome than charming, possesses distinctiveness.[177]

Henry Wood's determination was unshaken by this critical onslaught, and two years later he included another Mahler symphony, the Fourth, on his

[175] The article is signed J.H.G.B. [176] *Musical Standard* (24 Oct. 1903).
[177] *Musical Times* (1 Nov. 1903).

programmes. This time, the press did not call Mahler untalented, yet once again none of the English 'infernal judges' guessed that they were dealing with a major composer. The *London Times* proclaimed that the performance next day of Granville Bantock's Orchestral Variations, *Helena*, had proved 'the great superiority of the average English composer of the day over the average German composer'. Nowhere had Mahler's compositions 'won him undisputed success'. In the Fourth Symphony,

it is difficult to see why the three earlier movements should have been written at all, as their thematic material is nearly all used again in the Finale. All the subjects are studiedly, not to say affectedly, simple to the verge of baldness; but when it comes to the question of developing them the composer has little to offer us but a series of noises in the manner of Richard Strauss, which assort so ill with the themes themselves as to produce the most incongruous impression.

In this reviewer's opinion, Wood's choice of the piece was difficult to comprehend, and only his wife's performance of the last movement justified it. The critic of the *Morning Post* was obviously uninformed about musical life on the Continent since he claimed that Mahler was 'at present Director of the Imperial Opera in Hamburg'. The symphony had left the critic with an impression of 'inequality', which had been redeemed only by the Finale. The Scherzo was 'discursive' and lacking in thematic interest, the Adagio 'long and worked out to an exhaustive degree', and the whole score full of 'instrumental devices, some effective and some distractive'.

The *Athenaeum* critic found that, although Mahler had displayed 'remarkable fertility of resource', his symphony was 'too long', and 'weariness came before the end was reached'. However, he called the Adagio 'the most attractive movement', and praised one of Mahler's most profound slow movements for its 'charming theme' and 'clever variations'. For him as for his colleagues the vocal Finale was the 'chief feature' of the work. The *Westminster Gazette* considered Mahler's 'technical mastery more apparent than any very obvious inspiration'. He was assuredly 'a master of the art of writing for the orchestra', and his scores were 'marvels of learning and ingenuity'. Like his German colleagues, this critic found it hard to explain 'the curiously naïf character and the half-humorous archaisms which abound in conjunction with much that is ultra-modern'. However, the 'work contains undoubtedly some splendid music, and if it were not so inordinately long one would hope to hear it again'.

Only the *Musical Standard* dismissed the Fourth as a 'keen disappointment':

We expected something fine, but with the exception of a passable but unoriginal slow movement we had to put up with yards of whimsical fooling. It may be the composer's wish to go back in the art—possibly he desires to give us glorified prehistoric music. Seriously we don't mind simple-minded people having symphonies written for them, but it is rather hard to expect rational music lovers to listen to them. Mahler is truly original, though not melodically—but is he talented? His 4th Symphony does not show he is. That is all we shall say now.[178]

On 3 November 1905, just as Mahler was preparing to leave for Berlin, another performance of the Fourth Symphony was given in Graz, under Richard Wickenhauser, conductor of the local Musikverein. Mahler had met Wickenhauser in June, during the Allgemeiner Deutscher Musikverein Festival, and the plans for this concert had probably been made at that time. Mahler had written to him in September, informing him of the numerous changes he had made to the work, and suggesting that he send back the score so that they could be written in.[179] The day of the concert, Ernst Decsey published in his newspaper, the *Graz Tagespost*, a long article about Mahler. The reviews after the concert were in the main quite favourable. The *Grazer Tagblatt* mentioned that 'Mahler has written into the score used by maestro Wickenhauser many important instructions concerning particularities of nuance and rhythm', and informed its readers that the symphony had been greeted 'with the greatest interest', the first and last movements 'with exceptional warmth'.[180]

But the main event of the autumn of 1905 was clearly the Berlin performance under Fried of the Second Symphony. Mahler had enjoyed meeting this young— and highly gifted conductor who raved about his work and he expected much of him, as he had written to Alma in September.[181] Since the spring of 1905, Mahler had exchanged a number of letters with Fried regarding the forthcoming performance of the Second Symphony in Berlin. Fried's replies have disappeared, like most of the letters addressed to Mahler, but it is usually possible to guess their contents. At the end of April, returning from Abbazia[182] Mahler complained about the negligence of his first publisher, Weinberger, who had not yet forwarded the score of the symphony to Fried. Sometime later, in Strasbourg, he again wrote to the young conductor expressing his 'tremendous joy at having been so [fully] understood by you'. These first two letters begin 'Mein lieber Herr Fried', but they probably met again shortly afterwards in Strasbourg for the following letters open with 'Lieber Freund' (Dear Friend). As we have seen, Mahler had hesitated over advising Fried to come to Strasbourg because he had feared that the performance of the Fifth would be inadequate.

---

[178] *Musical Standard* (28 Oct. 1905). Programme of the penultimate Promenade Concert, conducted by Henry Wood on 25 Oct. 1905, at 8 p.m., in Queen's Hall: Tchaikovsky: *Capriccio Italien*; Tchaikovsky: Suite No. 3: Variations; Gluck: *Alceste*: Aria; Mahler: Symphony No. 4 (Mrs Henry Wood, sop.); George Henschel: *Morning Hymn*; Tchaikovsky: *Marche slave*; Schubert: *Rosamunde* Overture; Berlioz: *La Damnation de Faust: Marche hongroise*.

[179] Letter to Richard Wickenhauser of 24 Sept. 1905, BGM. This printed score, annotated by Mahler in red ink, is now in the Library of the Grazer Landeskonservatorium. Most of these changes were carried into the pocket score published by Universal the following year.

[180] See Neuwirth, '4. Symphonie', *Mahler-Interpretation*, 105–10.

[181] See BGA, no. 150.

[182] Eight of the nine surviving letters Mahler wrote to Oskar Fried in 1905 are in the Pierpont Morgan Library in New York, the gift of Robin Lehmann.

The following note, written in May or June[183] reveals that Fried wanted to include some of Mahler's Lieder in the same programme with the Second, using the same soloists. Mahler, however, was opposed to the idea, because he did not want his songs sung by female voices.

My songs (*Gesänge*) are all conceived for the male voice. If you like, you could have the man who sings them here in Vienna[184] for the price of his travel expenses. Wouldn't it be possible, though, to perform the work, which lasts more than an hour and a half, on its own (as I myself have done everywhere in the past). This is only a tentative suggestion, for you know better how things are in Berlin!

In his next letter, Mahler suggested Fried might include 'Revelge', a Lied 'which I regard as very moving'.[185] Then, at the end of August, he informed Fried that he had completed the Sixth Symphony, and asked him to send back his score of the Second for the final changes in orchestration. Mahler had previously advised Fried to rehearse the small instrumental group of the Finale of the Second separately, to accustom the musicians to playing out of his sight. This probably explains Fried's request for 300 marks for an additional rehearsal. Mahler replied that he would pay the sum 'with pleasure', adding: 'I am as happy as a sandboy [at the prospect].' The last two postcards addressed to Fried indicate that two soloists had been engaged: Emmy Destinn, soprano, and Martha Stapelfeld, contralto. Mahler advised Fried to assign a certain soprano passage to the contralto as he felt suspicious about the whims of the 'prima donna assoluta' Fried had mentioned (certainly Emmy Destinn).[186]

All these letters show that Mahler thought that he had found in Fried the ideal interpreter of his works, at least in Germany. Of course he had still not heard him conduct but the young man's personality had obviously made a deep impression on him. In the words of one of his contemporaries,[187] Fried

was certainly the kind of character 18th century writers called 'an original'. He was . . . temperamental in the extreme; he had the arrogance, impertinence, and cock-sureness of the self-made man (overcompensation for feelings of insecurity as a Jew and man of humble origins and early deprivations?). . . . His manner was brusque, tactless, frequently offensive. He did not beat about the bush in conversations; . . . his remarks were often cutting and sometimes witty. In late youth and early middle age he was somewhat of a *poseur*, a monocled, utterly unsentimental, mocking, sceptical, iconoclastic Jewish Berliner with an ironic smile fixed on his lips.

---

[183] This card, which formerly belonged to the author of this biography, was given to Dietrich Fischer-Dieskau several years ago but has apparently disappeared since then.

[184] Obviously Friedrich Weidemann.

[185] For this Lied, Mahler recommended 'a tenor who has a good middle and low range'. Fried ultimately included three of Mahler's Lieder in the programme of the 'New Concert' of 19 Dec.: 'Revelge', 'Um Mitternacht', and 'Ich bin der Welt'. The soloist was the tenor Ludwig Hess, who had sung in Mahler's performance of Beethoven's Ninth Symphony in Strasbourg.

[186] See below, Vol. iiii, Chap. 4, the biography of Emmy Destinn.

[187] William Malloch, notes for Fried's recording of the Second Symphony (see above).

In many ways, then, Fried's character differed greatly from Mahler's. Yet he resembled him in one crucial respect: he, too, was ready to give himself over, body and soul, to another composer's work. This 'self-made *enfant terrible*', as Richard Specht describes him,[188] 'passionate and full of fire', whose 'demands knew no limits', who seemed 'unable to control his terrible temper', this auto-crat, this eccentric, was, like Mahler, capable of subordinating his own will to that of another, especially that of a composer. And as conductors, they shared many qualities: both had the powerful will, the flamboyant intensity, the desire to tackle problems head on, the gift of galvanizing the musicians of the orches-tra into giving their best, the scrupulous respect for the smallest detail and a taste for pronounced dynamic contrast.

Mahler arrived in Berlin full of hope, early in the morning on 7 December. Unfortunately the final rehearsal was disappointing. Fried had apparently forgotten almost everything that they had worked out together in September. His youthful gusto had got the upper hand and the tempos were much too fast. 'Happy, oh happy to be a shoemaker!', wrote Mahler once again in a short note to his wife at the end of this 'sombre day'.[189] But all was not lost and Mahler was even touched by the young conductor's eagerness to please. 'Fried is very willing and my broad hints (*Winke mit Zaunpfählen*) may do some good. In any case, I will see whether or not he has talent (yesterday everything was too fast by half!).' In the same long letter recounting his first day in Berlin, Mahler wrote: 'Dear heart, Here I am, sitting again at the same table from which I bombarded you daily with letters about four years ago, and I realize that my feelings have not changed. I think of you with the same love and joy, and have as much pleasure in telling you so now as then.' He goes on to describe the visits he paid to Gerhart Hauptmann, Karl Muck, Siegfried Ochs, and Count von Hülsen (Intendant of the Opera), and the 'quite pleasant' evening he spent with Strauss discussing *Salome* and the censor's refusal. Once again, Mahler complained of 'a certain coldness and blasé quality' in Strauss. The latter gave him his new edition of Berlioz's, *Traité d'orchestration*, with his comments and promised him a signed score of *Salome*. 'But I would have preferred a little more warmth', Mahler writes.[190]

A young conductor, who was soon to make his mark, and whom Fried had chosen to lead the instrumental group located in the wings for the Finale of the Second Symphony, much later wrote a captivating description of the dress rehearsal and concert in Berlin. Then 20 years old, Otto Klemperer had won the first prize for piano at the Klindworth-Schwarenka Conservatory in Berlin and had been engaged as an accompanist by Fried for the Stern'schen Gesangverein. For him Mahler had long been a legendary figure. One day, as a little boy in Hamburg, on the way home from school, he had seen the well-known conductor of the Stadt-Theater walking in the Grindelallee, in the

[188] Richard Specht, 'Oskar Fried', in *Musikblätter des Anbruch*, 2 (1920): 16, 573–7.
[189] BGA, no. 154, dated 7 Nov. 1905.   [190] BGA, no. 155, undated (8 Nov. 1905).

district in which he then lived. This 'strange' man was walking jerkily, hat in hand, and appeared to have a club foot. 'At that time he used to make faces which had a terrible effect on me. For ten minutes I ran shyly beside him, drinking him in with my eyes like a sea monster (*ein Meerwunder*).'[191] The boy had straightaway guessed that this was Mahler, because his opera-loving parents had often spoken about him, and Xaver Scharwenka, the Director of the Berlin Conservatory, had later praised Mahler's music in his presence.

Klemperer had to conduct the instrumental group in a place from which he was unable to see Fried, and Mahler's presence made him nervous, particularly because of the tempo changes. At the end of the rehearsal, he hurried into the hall to see if Mahler was satisfied:

'It was awful,' he replied, 'much too loud.' I permitted myself to remark that the indication on the score was 'with great resonance' (*sehr schmetternd*). 'Yes,' he answered, 'but from a great distance.' I left things at that and for the performance, I had the musicians play very softly (since we were much too close and unable to move further away).

After the concert, Mahler came backstage and assured him that it had been 'very good'.[192]

Klemperer also describes Mahler's disapproval of Fried's tempos. As we have seen, two works preceded the Second on the programme: Reger's *Cantata* and two Lieder by Liszt. Fried spent so much time rehearsing the *Cantata* that he had barely arrived at the second movement of Mahler's Symphony when the three allotted hours of rehearsal were over:

When he [Fried] heard that he had to stop, he fell into a frightful rage, grabbed hold of the nearest chair and hurled it with all his might into the audience (it was sheer luck that no one was hurt). Mahler remained quite unruffled and composed, took Fried along to his hotel, and there discussed everything with him. Before the beginning of the concert on the following evening, Fried appeared before the musicians and said: 'Gentlemen, everything I have done and rehearsed with you was wrong. Tonight I shall use entirely different tempos; please follow me.'[193]

According to Klemperer, the musicians were not alone in 'following' Fried. The public too responded to the first two movements of the Second with warm applause, and the third movement, which had so often disconcerted its audience, gave rise to such enthusiasm that the beginning of 'Urlicht' was delayed for several minutes. Mahler, who was seated in the second row of a box at the rear of the hall and whose presence increased the interest of the audience, 'plunged his nose into his programme, and refused to acknowledge all those who were cheering him, . . . as if all this were none of his business'. At the end

---

[191] Letter from Klemperer to Alma (c.1911/12), UPL, Philadelphia.

[192] Klemperer had been so impressed by Mahler's personality that he longed to be engaged by him at the Vienna Opera. To that end, Oskar Fried advised him to do a piano reduction of the Second, for Mahler was always sensitive to the attention and admiration of young musicians (OKM 6 and Peter Heyworth, *Conversations with Klemperer*).
[193] OKM 15–16.

of the performance, there was a storm of applause. An unending ovation from the audience obliged Mahler to make several curtain calls with Fried, and the musicians, singers, and chorus joined in the applause. Mahler, who had hitherto met only with failure in Berlin, particularly a short time before with his Fifth, was flabbergasted. When he finally appeared on stage, Fried rushed over, hugged him, and dragged him by the hand to the conductor's podium to take a bow. 'Whatever one thinks of this symphony,' stated the *Neue Freie Presse* correspondent, 'for many years past no other piece of music has been acclaimed in Berlin with such paroxysms of joy.'

For once, the cheers of the crowd failed to provoke the strictures of the critics. Most of them recognized that in ten years, since the first disastrous performance of the Second in Berlin, music in general and Mahler's situation in particular had 'significantly changed'.[194] In the *Berliner Tageblatt*, Leopold Schmidt called the Second by far Mahler's greatest work. It 'transcended all limitations of form' to the point of 'truly inspiring and at times deeply moving the listener'; it showed 'the depth of his artistic sentiment' and demonstrated the composer's 'total mastery of all the problems of musical development'. Schmidt detected Bruckner's influence in the first movement, with its beautiful, wide-sweeping themes, full of character . . . even if they were repeated rather than developed'. He also praised the graceful, spirited Andante, 'inspired by Austria and Schubert', and the 'humour' and 'piquant rhythms' of the Scherzo. But in the Finale, he thought, Mahler had tried to go too far. He was only capable of 'playing at Titanism', and 'Meyerbeer-like histrionics' were the result. The whole symphony was a 'technical triumph' with many 'arbitrary, unconnected' passages, apart from the '*Auferstehen*' itself, the choral coda, with its 'intended simplicity and profoundness'. It was a 'bizarre monstrosity', but it nevertheless secured for Mahler a place among contemporary composers.[195]

The brief article in the *Vossische Zeitung* also recalled the negative attitude of the press in 1895 and noted the 'evolution of public opinion' since then with satisfaction. Mahler was now placed with Strauss at the summit of the 'modern school', both far outclassing all their other contemporaries.[196] In the *Neue Freie Presse*, Oscar Bie also stressed the transformation of the Berlin musical audience and the exceptional nature of the ovations which ended the evening. He

---

[194] Schering's long article about Mahler's Lieder had just appeared in three issues of the *Neue Zeitschrift für Musik* (see above). It had particular impact because at the time Schering was editor-in-chief of this influential magazine.

[195] Schmidt included this article in his book *Aus dem Musikleben der Gegenwart*. Leopold Schmidt (1860–1927) was born in Berlin, where he studied at the Hochschule für Musik and at the University. Conductor in Heidelberg (1887), Berlin (1888–9), Zurich (1891), and Halle (1895–7), he was engaged as critic for the *Berliner Tageblatt* in 1897. From 1900 to 1915 he taught history of music at the Stern'sche Konservatorium and the Klindworth-Scharwenka Conservatory in Berlin. Author of monographs on Mozart, Beethoven, and Meyerbeer, Schmidt also wrote numerous analyses of musical compositions, edited letters of Brahms and Beethoven, and published several volumes of his own articles. He also composed some vocal and chamber music.

[196] The same anonymous critic praised the extraordinary talent of Oskar Fried, who, 'in a miraculously short time seems to have learned all the secrets of his trade'.

himself, ten years ago, had written about the symphony's 'jumbled up tonalities and other revolutionary audacities'. This time it seemed clear, simple and direct. 'Its impact was crushing, even unmusical people found their faith.'

With equal honesty, Otto Lessmann in the *Allgemeine Musik-Zeitung* reminded his readers of his article written in 1895. At that time he had said that Mahler's 'enormous know-how' was only 'the outward finery disguising the poverty of his imagination and that his demented wallowing in dissonances did not deserve the name of music'. Since then, his views had changed: what seemed 'confused and painful' in 1895 now struck him as 'clear and logical', for in the meantime he had heard 'much worse'. Despite its peculiarities, the Second Symphony made a great impression on him. Even the first and fifth movements, which he had previously considered contrived, now moved him profoundly. Liszt's symphonic poems, Lessmann continued, had been initially criticized as 'confused' and 'unimaginative'. Now that his successors had gone far beyond Liszt's innovations, one recognized the 'clarity, simplicity and intelligibility of his works'. The same applied to Mahler, hence the enthusiastic acclamation at the end of the concert.[197]

Had Fried's performance really met with Mahler's complete approval? Afterwards, Fried wrote that 'the success was unprecedented—and Mahler was delighted' but since Fried had not even had time to conduct the whole of the symphony in Mahler's presence during the final rehearsal, and had improvised the new tempos on the basis of a few general comments by Mahler, it is likely that the performance was far from perfect! Max Friedländer, the famous musicologist who edited Schubert's Lieder, later stated he had attended the concert with Mahler, that Mahler had refused to shake Fried's hand in the wings, and finished the evening with Friedländer in a restaurant. Mahler had not even mentioned the performance until Friedländer frankly asked him for his opinion, whereupon he responded in his 'resonant baritone voice: "Oh! Ah! I turned in my grave." '[198]

Like so many anecdotes told long after the event, this one probably embroiders on the truth. The descriptions provided by the press at that time are categorical: Mahler hugged Fried on the stage with a warmth which was certainly not feigned. Even if he was not entirely pleased with the performance, its

---

[197]   The 8 Nov. concert was one of the Neue Symphonische Konzerte series conducted by Oskar Fried in the concert hall of the Philharmonic. The programme was as follows: Reger *Choral Cantata* No. 3, 'O Haupt voll Blut und Wunden' (soloists: Destinn, soprano; Brieger-Palm, contralto; Briefemeister, tenor; Brieger, bass); Liszt: two Lieder with orchestra: 'Der Fischerknabe' and 'Die Loreley' (soloist: Emmy Destinn); Mahler: Symphony No. 2 (soloists: Emmy Destinn, soprano; Martha Stapelfeld, contralto).

[198]   The source of this anecdote is the conductor Harold Byrns, a close friend of Alma Mahler's in Los Angeles. He had heard it from Franz Röhn, Max Friedländer's son. In 1930 William Mengelberg claimed that Mahler had uttered the same words in Berlin while discussing a bad performance of one of his symphonies in Prague. However, Mahler never heard any of his symphonies under another conductor in Prague, and it is likely that Mengelberg was referring to Oskar Fried. Mengelberg might have changed the story to avoid hurting Fried's feelings, who was still alive. (See 'Intimes von Gustav Mahler', an interview with Mengelberg in London, published in the *Neues Wiener Journal* on 7 Nov. 1930).

triumphant reception must have touched and delighted him and to a certain extent made him forget his disappointment. Moreover, it is unlikely that, as the hero of the evening, he could have refrained from attending the reception Frau Luise Wolff gave in his honour after the concert as Friedländer seems to imply. Be that as it may, the Berlin concert in no way shook his confidence in Fried, otherwise he would not have continued to encourage him to conduct his works for two important premières, the Sixth in Berlin, and the Second in St Petersburg, both in 1906.

Many years later, in a letter to Alexander Zemlinsky, Schoenberg claimed that Fried—whom he calls 'a sickening rascal'—had only pretended to admire Mahler's music:

I cannot understand how he could have succeeded in so completely fooling Mahler whom he certainly does not think much of. . . . In any case I can remember exactly that Mahler told me that it was very necessary for him to be present at the rehearsals for his Third [*sic*] Symphony[199] which Fried was conducting, for there was a lot that was bad! When I looked surprised at this, he alas praised him a little. But I noticed that that was only because he did not want to drop Fried entirely, since Fried had been one of the first to perform him, and had managed to persuade him that he was an admirer of his works.[200]

However, Schoenberg's low opinion of Fried as a man and artist could have been motivated by the young conductor's reluctance to perform Schoenberg's own works or some other personal reason, for it seems impossible that Fried should have so long defended and conducted works in which he did not believe. Furthermore, the articles Fried wrote are among the most moving testimonies we possess about Mahler as a man and creative artist. They were written after Mahler's death and they could not possibly have been elicited by anything but sincere admiration.

Shortly after the performance of the Second Symphony, Mahler replied to a letter from Fried describing a bad performance in Berlin of the *Kindertotenlieder* (by Weidemann, conducted by Nikisch):

Well, that's a fine thing (*Das ist recht hübsch*)—and unfortunately not surprising. Nikisch hadn't looked it over beforehand and, as Weidemann tells me, rehearsed superficially. My God, we must all be prepared for such things (think of Schalk and your work!)[201]—but then there are evenings like yours, and people like you, a ray of hope (*Lichtblick*) . . .[202] which make up for all the rest . . . Someday you will resurrect these things too (the *Kindertotenlieder*) from the tomb into which Nikisch (as before with the Fifth) has thrown them. I am tremendously happy about the appreciation which the public has shown for your talent and your personality, and which is now

[199] Schoenberg's memory is of course playing him false. Fried only conducted Mahler's Second Symphony in the composer's presence.

[200] Alexander Zemlinsky, *Briefwechsel mit Arnold Schönberg, Anton Webern, Alban Berg und Franz Schreker*, ed. Horst Weber (Wissenschaftliches Buchgesellschaft, Darmstadt, 1995), 69 ff.

[201] He refers no doubt to the performance of *Das trunkene Lied* at a Gesellschaftskonzert in Vienna on 6 Mar. 1905.   [202] Two words are illegible.

presumably solidly established in Berlin.—I am now once again bogged down in the stifling atmosphere of the Opera quagmire![203]

These are not the words of a composer who feels he has been betrayed by a conductor of his works! That Mahler had great confidence in Fried's ability is apparent from the fact that he was as keen as ever to persuade him to include his Lieder in his programmes, as witness the following postcard:

One day you must perform all those songs (*Gesänge*) which didn't succeed with Nikisch and a small orchestra (the Philharmonic without extra instruments), in a small hall (N.B.). I am convinced we would get as much of a surprise as the other day with my C Minor! [. . .] N.B.: Though 'Revelge' and 'Mitternacht' are really written for a large ensemble and meant to be showpieces.

As seen above, Fried followed Mahler's suggestion and performed three Lieder on 19 December, including 'Um Mitternacht'and 'Revelge'.[204]

Thus, after Fried's triumph with the Second, even Berlin seems to have laid down its arms and chosen to forget the 1895 disaster. And yet five days later, when Nikisch, Weidemann, and the same orchestra premièred nine of Mahler's Lieder (five *Kindertotenlieder*, 'Ich bin der Welt', and three *Wunderhorn-Lieder*),[205] a section of the audience booed vociferously and the hisses 'finally drowned the applause'. Was this due to a clique of Mahler's adversaries, exasperated by the recent success of his symphony? For once the critics proved more open-minded than the public. Mahler's previous refusal to authorize performances of his Lieder in large concert halls is confirmed by Otto Lessmann who, as a member of the Allgemeine Deutscher Musikverein, knew how hard he had fought for a small hall for the Graz performance. Lessmann found that the Philharmonic Hall had destroyed the songs' intimate character. It seemed to him that Weidemann 'had sung more slowly' than in Graz, almost tediously, while Nikisch conducted 'with indifference' (we know from Mahler's letter quoted above that the Lieder had been insufficiently rehearsed). Yet to Lessmann, they appeared as they had in Graz: 'eclectic, but full of spirit and marvellous sonorous effects', as well as 'beautiful sensitivity'.

---

[203] Undated letter (Nov. 1905), PML (Lehmann deposit). At the beginning of this letter, Mahler asks Fried to remember everything he said 'during the rehearsals'. He is probably referring to the performance of the Second Symphony, which the young man was scheduled to conduct in Russia the following year.

[204] See below, Chap. 5. Undated letter-card to Oskar Fried (beginning of Dec. 1905), Notar Hertz collection, Hamburg. Mahler starts by replying to Fried's question concerning the lower B on the double bassoon, which according to Mahler does not exist on that instrument (he is probably referring to a passage from 'Um Mitternacht' where the double bassoon does in fact go down to lower B in bar 72). Mahler also asks Fried to send him his copy of a score, most likely that of the Second. A pocket edition was about to be published in Vienna and Mahler wanted to add all the changes, particularly those in 'the famous "Walküre" passage'. Were these perhaps the bars in the first movement which are strikingly reminiscent of Hunding's entrance in the first act of Wagner's opera (see above, Vol. i, Appendix 1 on the Second Symphony).

[205] On 13 Nov., the third Philharmonic concert began with the Overture to Méhul's *La Chasse du Jeune Henri*, followed by Reger's *Sinfonietta*. Mahler's Lieder constituted the focal point of the programme. Among the *Wunderhorn-Lieder* Nikisch chose 'Der Schildwache Nachtlied' (first performed by Amalie Joachim at the Berlin Philharmonic in 1892), 'Fischpredigt' and 'Das irdische Leben'. The concert ended with the overture to Schumann's opera *Genoveva*.

The unsigned article in the *Vossische Zeitung* expressed the same reservations about Weidemann's 'almost tedious' interpretation and about the wisdom of an orchestral accompaniment for Lieder, but he declared himself won over by 'the simplicity and naturalness of feeling' and in particular by the 'profound authenticity' of 'Ich bin der Welt'. The evening had been a 'victory' for Mahler, a musician who 'without the slightest artistic vanity' aspired to 'expressing his soul', and created music of 'refreshing simplicity' despite its technical refinement. The coherence of form and content was stupefying, as was the total originality of these 'masterpieces'. If the public's reception had been 'cooler' than in Graz, it was only because it had been a mistake to include an entire hour of Lieder in a symphony concert programme. Only the *Börsenzeitung* maintained its usual opinion of Mahler. After grudging praise for 'the marvellous simplicity of certain *Volkslieder*', the critic deplored the 'pretentiousness of the orchestral accompaniment', which robbed the other songs of 'their essence and character. . . . The modest violet is transformed into a cabbage rose (*Zentifolie*), and the modest, lyrical folk style gives way to pretentious dramatic pathos.'

It is obvious, in comparing the critical reception of these two concerts, that Fried had understood and performed Mahler's music with far more love and care than the great Nikisch, and the public had reacted accordingly. On his way back to Vienna from Berlin, Mahler stopped for a few hours in Leipzig, where he had an appointment with the inventors of a new music recording process of great future potential, and which had already caused a stir in Germany and even abroad. The Welte 'Mignon' piano roll recording system had been developed by the firm of Welte of Freiburg-im-Breisgau, who called it 'Mignon' to underline its compactness compared to the more cumbersome devices the firm had built and hitherto marketed.

The adventure had begun in 1832 in Vöhrenbach, a little village in the Black Forest, when Michael Welte (1807–80), founder of the Welte dynasty, had developed the mechanism of a musical clock which played elaborate tunes on a set of little wooden organ pipes. Soon after Welte, a great lover of music, expanded his workshop and decided to improve the 'Viennese mechanical organ', the instrument which had acquired the summit of respectability when Mozart wrote two compositions for it at the end of his life. After three years of work, Michael Welte had created a monumental instrument, the 'Orchestrion', with no less than 1,100 pipes, which he presented at the international exhibition in Karlsruhe in 1849 and later throughout the world. This instrument, a veritable masterpiece of contemporary technique, laid the groundwork for all the organs and mechanical pianos of the late nineteenth century.

In 1872, the firm moved to Freiburg-im-Breisgau, capital of the Grand Duchy of Baden. Around 1885 Berthold, Michael's son, developed a new system, later called the 'Pianola' in its American version, in which the music box cylinder (the 'Orchestrion' had three) is replaced by a paper roll whose perforations release streams of air which activate the keys of a piano through a system of pneumatic transmission. For the next fifteen years, the paper rolls were made by hand by an artisan who traced on the paper with ink the positions and lengths of the future perforations by calculating with a metronome the exact timing and duration of each note in the score, and without any attempt to introduce artistic or personal considerations.

In those days, recording techniques, whether cylinders or records, still required the horn. They remained primitive, particularly for the piano (Edison's 'talking machine' was mainly destined for the spoken or singing voice). For the purposes of recording, pianists were obliged to play fortissimo, without felt dampers, and the result was consequently very disappointing. Emil Welte (1841–1923), his son Edwin (1876–1958), and his Alsatian son-in-law, Karl Bockisch (1874–1952), therefore concentrated their efforts on improving Berthold Welte's mechanical piano so as to reproduce not only the notes, but the other traits particular to the performing pianist: attack accentuation, dynamics, pedal. Bockisch worked on the problem from 1901 to 1904, and in liaison with the principal German piano manufacturers developed an entirely new system capable of capturing all the nuances of a pianist's performance. 'The freedom of movement, the natural flow, the impetus of conception, the often surprising and yet enchanting change of tempo, in short . . . the things that make a performance "artistic", "personal".' The two inventors felt their new and revolutionary machine was able to reproduce all these delicate features.[206] The patent for the 'Reproduktionsclavier' was registered on 21 May 1904. Thereafter, the firm concerned itself with building up a repertory for the Welte 'Mignon'. Its creators showed both taste and imagination by appealing not only to the leading pianists of the time but also to the most famous composers, who were thus given the opportunity of setting an authoritative example for the interpretation of their works.

Mahler's distress over the lack of understanding of his work by contemporary conductors explains his acceptance of Welte's invitation. The greatest pianists of the era were already listed in Welte's catalogue in 1905 and 1906,[207] and the composers included Gabriel Fauré, Edvard Grieg, Engelbert Humperdinck, Ruggiero Leoncavallo, Wilhelm Kienzl, Max Reger, Camille Saint-Saëns, and Richard Strauss. Welte had already set up recording studios in Leipzig, Paris, and St Petersburg, and by 1911, 140 artists had left living testimonies of their art to posterity on Welte-Mignon rolls. They remained

---

[206]   Werner König, 'Über frühe Tonaufnahmen der Firma Welte und die Werke für das Welte-Mignon-Reproduktionsklavier', *Jahrbuch des Staatlichen Instituts für Musikforschung Preussischer Kulturbesitz* (Merseburger, Berlin, 1978), 31 ff. The author of this article points out that the main weakness of the Welte-Mignon was in reproducing the original dynamics. It was unable for instance to differentiate between the various notes of a single chord, and between the bass and treble registers.

[207]   Eugen d'Albert, Ferrucio Busoni, Fannie Bloomfield-Zeisler, Teresa Carreno, Ernö von Dohnanyi, Carl Friedberg, Alfred Grünfeld, Theodor Leschetitzky, Frederic Lamond, Vladimir de Pachmann, Ignace Jean Paderewski, Raoul Pugno, Alfred Reisenauer, Emil von Sauer, and Xavier Scharwenka.

expensive for the prospective purchaser, who had to buy a piano equipped with an apparatus patented by Welte before the First World War. The rolls themselves cost approximately fifteen dollars each.[208] Nevertheless they were in great demand, especially in the United States. Edwin Welte and his brother-in-law Karl Bockisch toured Europe with their *Vorsetzer*[209] in order to reproduce for concert audiences the playing of pianists and composers in their catalogue.[210]

All the archives of the Welte Company disappeared during the bombing of Freiburg, so no documents remain describing Mahler's stopover in Leipzig on 9 November 1905, nor the recording session which probably took place in the showrooms of Popper and Company[211] on the Reichstrasse, using a Feurich piano. That autumn, many series of rolls by different artists were recorded, and it is likely that Edwin Welte or Karl Bockisch welcomed the renowned Director of the Vienna Opera and directed the recording session in person.

What happened during the recording session? According to texts published by the Welte company, the artist was seated before a grand piano equipped with the Welte system. A bath of mercury, in which electrodes connected to each key were immersed, was located beneath the keyboard, and behind the piano a long, narrow wooden box was placed just above the keyboard.[212] Each key was provided with a little carbon rod which, when depressed, dipped more or less deeply into the mercury. The electric contact was prolonged as required by the *Vorsetzer*, which simultaneously printed an ink mark of corresponding size on a matrix band. On top of a flat surface next to the piano was a black box with two holes apparently (according to contemporary photographs) covered with a membrane, not unlike present-day loudspeakers. Connected to

---

[208] See album notes by Walter Heebner (Recorded Treasures, North Hollywood, 1972), and those included in the Telefunken LP album of 1970. The roll of Busoni's interpretation of the transcription by Liszt of Beethoven's song 'Adelaïde' cost $12.50 in the United States, and that of Mahler playing the Funeral March from the Fifth Symphony $14.50 (24 marks in Germany), as did the Finale from the Fourth.

[209] See below for a description of the apparatus.

[210] After these promising beginnings, the future of the Welte Company was gravely compromised, first by the First World War, then by the economic crisis of 1929–31, and finally by the microphone and electric recording process which allowed an increasingly faithful reproduction of the sound of a piano without the need for the instrument itself. In 1940 the Freiburg factory was commandeered for the production of optical bombs, and was completely destroyed by Allied bombardments in 1944–5. Edwin Welte and Karl Bockisch survived, and thanks to their efforts some 500 master rolls hidden in an underground storehouse in the Black Forest were recovered after the war, as well as many others scattered all over the world, and several *Vorsetzer*. The Mahler rolls include two Mahler Lieder, 'Ich ging mit Lust' and 'Ging heut' Morgen übers Feld', the second of the *Gesellen-Lieder* (Welte rolls nos. 768 and 769), as well as the Finale of the Fourth Symphony ('Das himmlische Leben') and the Funeral March of the Fifth (nos. 769 and 770). For details of the Welte recording process and the extent to which these rolls constitute reliable documents, see Vol. iiii, Appendix. Mahler's four piano rolls were recently transferred onto CD by Gilbert Kaplan.

[211] Hugo Popper, director of the firm, was Karl Bockisch's close friend. He was in charge of all Welte's sales of machines and rolls in Germany and of contracts with artists.

[212] Gregory Benko, founder and former director of the International Piano Archives, maintains that most of the details furnished by Ben M. Hall, author of an article accompanying the LP album 'Welte Legacy of Piano Treasures', are purely imaginary, particularly the mercury bath and ink imprint on the master band. Furthermore, he claimed that the famous allegedly original artistic 'expression' had been added subsequently by an 'editor'.

the piano by wires, it completed the ultra-secret, patented invention of the Weltes. Unfortunately the secret of this mechanism is only partly disclosed, since all the original recording instruments were destroyed during the bombardments.

Once the matrix band was imprinted by a marking crayon, the artist was invited to wait in an adjacent hall for the colloidal graphite ink to 'fix'. Then he returned to hear the roll played back by the *Vorsetzer*. Karl Bockisch's extraordinary invention resembled a dresser or very low upright piano. It contained the same number of felt 'fingers' as the piano keyboard, each as long as a human finger measured from the wrist to the tip of the nail. It was also furnished with two felt-shod 'feet' which worked the pedals. The *Vorsetzer* then read the matrix band and reproduced the artist's playing. To judge from the enthusiastic comments in the company's visitors' book, most of the artists were greatly impressed by the faithfulness of the reproduction. Once the artist had approved the original band, an artisan copied each perforation by hand onto a roll which was then sold, to be played either by a *Vorsetzer* or by a mechanism fitted into the piano itself. Mahler's comments in Welte's visitor's book are briefer than those of most of Welte's other recording artists, but nevertheless show that he was deeply impressed: 'In astonishment and admiration, I join those who have preceded me [in this book]. Gustav Mahler.'[213]

After this experience, of whose importance he was probably not fully aware, Mahler returned to Vienna early on 10 November to resume preparations for the Mozart Festival, scheduled to open two weeks later with *Così fan tutte*. Before the end of the year, four more performances of Mahler's works were scheduled, of which only the first took place in Mahler's absence, in Strasbourg. The success of the May concerts there had probably encouraged Franz Stockhausen[214] to include the Third Symphony in the programme of a Städtisches Orchester subscription concert, on the same day that the Second was performed in Berlin. Stockhausen was in poor health at this time, he was about to retire, and he was replaced by the conductor of the Strasbourg Opera, Albert Gorter.[215] The press reacted to the work with all the customary reservations. As always, the Finale was the movement that was most admired. The *Strassburger Bürger-Zeitung* considered it to be 'musically the most substantial' and the 'most impressive'. It also mentioned the kaleidoscope-like combination

---

[213] This handwritten note is reproduced in the booklet which accompanies the Recorded Treasures LP album, but the date (19 Nov. 1905) is doubtful. Mahler probably signed the register in Leipzig on 9 Nov., immediately after hearing the *Vorsetzer* play back the pieces he had just recorded, unless the book was sent to him in Vienna. Before accepting Welte-Mignon's offer, Mahler wrote to a member of the Berlin Genossenschaft der deutschen Tonkünstler that he intended to 'record three short compositions on a pianola (if such indeed is the name of the instrument)' and asked him if, as a member of the society, he had the right to do so (undated catalogue of autograph dealer Rosen).					[214] See above, Chap. 3.

[215] Albert Gorter (1862–1936) came from Nuremberg, studied at the Akademie der Musik in Munich, and held posts successively in the theatres of Regensburg, Stuttgart, Karlsruhe, Leipzig, and Strasbourg. From 1910 to 1920 he was Generalmusikdirektor in Mayence. Author of several operas and orchestral scores, he later retired near Munich.

of themes which had been interwoven and orchestrated with astonishing skill. However, the numerous 'reminiscences' of Wagner, Brahms, Bizet, Mendelssohn, Delibes, and Nicolai, on the one hand, and popular, banal, and 'sentimental' tunes on the other, were proof of Mahler's lack of discrimination. According to *Der Elsässer*, Mahler wrote 'problem' music rather than programme music: the juxtaposition of simple, popular themes and 'great symphonic phrases' was simply incomprehensible. Even Mahler's effective orchestration failed to give an impression of unity.

The *Strassburger Zeitung* took a much more positive attitude. Unlike many younger composers, it said, who were trying to impress by outward means, for Mahler the idea was the dominating factor and he employed powerful means only for the purposes of description. What made this symphony a genuine work of art were the grandiose contrasts which clearly demonstrated the composer's spiritual richness. His style was at times complicated, but never confused, and often of enchanting simplicity. All movements showed great warmth of expression, and the power and impact of the Finale was worthy of Beethoven. In the *Freie Presse* an unsigned article called Mahler one of the most misunderstood and enigmatic artists of the day. He was certainly no epigone but an innovator; he overwhelmed and surprised with the power of his ideas and strange sound combinations. Although the critic regarded himself as familiar with contemporary art, he had found the first movement the most puzzling. Its first bars fascinated the audience, but, later on, when with powerful effects and startling contrasts three utterly different and unrelated themes were developed, one had the impression of being 'faced with a hieroglyphic writing without any clues'. The third movement, too, was a 'hard nut to crack'. Again it was probably the 'majestic force' of the Finale that saved this obviously perplexed critic from judging the symphony too harshly. In the *Strassburger Post*, Gustav Altmann once again attacked Mahler for his 'borrowings' and 'lack of scruples'. Despite 'the skill with which his themes are elaborated', his music lacked logic and unity and, with the exception of the Finale, contained many 'vulgar and undistinguished traits'. While listening to Mahler one often felt 'transported into the alcohol-reeking atmosphere of a noisy popular gathering at which a loud-mouthed demagogue was showing off'. The most hostile review appeared in the *Revue alsacienne*, which mocked the symphony's 'incoherent style', 'vulgar themes', 'overblown orchestration', and 'poor imagination', and scoffed at a concert which had offered nothing but 'disappointment and boredom'.

Two other Strasbourg papers took a more positive stand. The *Strassburger Neueste Nachrichten* considered Mahler's main characteristics to be, first, his tendency towards the gigantic, not only with regard to the dimension of the work, but also its poetic ideas and their musical expression; and second, his unswerving independence and originality. The Scherzo and Finale were praised, the first movement was described as the 'music of a desperate Faust' and 'the struggle of a torn soul longing for peace, light and reconciliation'. The symphony as a whole was judged 'profoundly imposing'. This last opinion was shared by William d'Gelly who, in the *Journal d'Alsace-Lorraine,* declared himself entirely convinced, for 'the breadth of the impression overshadows discussion and analysis'. Nonetheless, like many of his Strasbourg fellow critics, he had preferred the Fifth Symphony. The Third, he thought, was more 'astonishing than moving'; it lacked 'that something which renders works definitive, that soul-uplifting breath of clarity'. 'Inspired by Nietzsche', it was marred by the same 'lack of true feeling which, despite all explanations, rendered its emotional understanding irritating and artificial'. And yet 'in its opulence, this superb, massive, harmonic creation leaves a trail of admiration in its wake for the great artist who conceived it'.[216]

Despite his busy schedule at the Opera, Mahler was able that autumn to conduct three other performances of the Fifth Symphony. Scarcely two weeks after returning from Berlin he left Vienna for Trieste, where his symphony was going to be performed by the local orchestra at the instigation of one of the principal members of the city's Philharmonic Society, Heinrich (or Enrico) Schott, a rich patron of the arts and passionate music lover.[217] As usual, Mahler had asked the conductor of the Triestiner Orchester, Mario Vittorio Banzo, to conduct the first rehearsals. He himself arrived on the morning of 29 November, in time to conduct the final rehearsal. He had been worried about the quality of the orchestra and its preparation, but for once he had a pleasant surprise: the level of the musicians was 'entirely adequate'. They were full of 'fire and zeal' and extremely well prepared by the Italian conductor. The concert was already sold out when he arrived in Trieste. His sole disappointment, since he had been looking forward to fine, warm weather, was the continuous rain which obliged him to arm himself with umbrella and galoshes on his walks. Heinrich Schott took him to Miramare, the white-stone castle which Archduke Maximilian had had built on a seaside rock between 1856 and 1870, in the neo-Gothic style of the English palaces of the late Renaissance. Emperor Franz-Joseph's younger brother, the ill-starred Emperor of Mexico, had not lived to see his castle finished and it had retained a romantic aura linked with his tragic death in 1867. Mahler and Schott walked for two hours in the famous park, 'a lovely resort with cypress and laurel trees, everything green, ponds with swans, and heavenly quiet'.[218] Pan-European city if ever there was one, Trieste had a glorious past. Its Italian inhabitants had sought and obtained the protection of the Austrian Emperor Leopold III in 1382 against its ambitious Venetian neighbours, and eventually became integrated into the Austrian Empire. Since 1718, when it had been declared a free port

---

[216] The second subscription concert took place on 8 Nov. in the main hall of the Aubette. The Dutch singer Tilly Köhnen sang the contralto solos.

[217] The concert was billed as 'the first Symphony concert of the Orchestrale Triestina'. It took place at the Politeama Rossetti (1878), one of the two main theatres in Trieste (today Theatro Stabile).

[218] BGA, no. 156, undated (30 Nov. 1905).

by Charles VI, Trieste had been the only harbour of the Austrian Empire, and was now its third largest city, after Vienna and Prague. It was inhabited by roughly equal numbers of Austrians proper, Czechs, and Italians, all united in a passionate love of the arts, and music in particular. Unfortunately the hotel—dirty, noisy, and badly run—was 'torture' to Mahler and he regretted that two members of the committee felt obliged to show him over the town. 'They don't leave me a moment to myself—such seems to be their conception of hospitality.'[219]

A long article in the *Indipendente*, published on the day of Mahler's arrival, introduced him to the Trieste public. The article contained one or two errors of fact (for example that Bruckner had been Mahler's teacher at the Vienna Conservatory, and that he had taken his exams at the Gymnasium in Prague before completing his education at Vienna University), but went on to say that as composer he belonged both to the 'Vienna school' and the '*Neu Deutsch*' school, and thus had a 'musically double nature', which contrasted him favourably with 'the isolated artistic personality of Max Klinger'. The anonymous critic said that the Fifth 'was rich in the finest melody in the poetic, not pictorial sense'. The underlying intention of the symphony was to symbolize 'the capacity of the human soul to find, even in the greatest sorrow, a way through to consolation and joy'.

The *Triester Zeitung* reported that the hall was full on the evening of the concert, not so much to hear Mahler's most recent work but to see and hear the conductor, the famous Opera director, whose 'despotism' and artistic fanaticism were already legendary. The audience was not disappointed. The 1 December concert opened with the Overture to *Coriolan* followed by Mozart's 'Jupiter' Symphony, whose 'fresh and light' first movement gave the critic of the *Triester Zeitung* the impression of a 'soul-refreshing little breeze'. Had they played the Mozart *after* the Mahler symphony, whose restlessness made him long for peace and quiet, he would have enjoyed it even more. 'Yet, let's be fair! Nowadays we listen perhaps with greater interest to Mahler than to these Mozart harmonies' which at certain moments 'are out of keeping with our modern feeling . . . too much rococo!' After Mahler's Fifth Symphony it was once again the conductor, not the composer, who had been rewarded with enthusiastic applause and crowned with a laurel wreath. The critic had pledged himself to listen to the work 'without any preconceptions', and so had declined to attend the rehearsals, and to read the score, in order 'not to be influenced'. But he had had to recognize the futility of his efforts, Mahler's 'conscience had to wrestle with the powerful impressions he had received from

---

[219] The rehearsals took place from noon to two o'clock in the afternoon, and then from eight to eleven o'clock in the evening, so Mahler had a good deal of free time. The two undated letters he sent to Alma from the Hôtel de la Ville in Trieste were written on 30 Nov. and 1 Dec. (BGA nos. 156 and 157). A score of the Fifth Symphony has survived in the Library of the Trieste Conservatory. It has many corrections pencilled in by Mahler himself (see Quirino Principe, 'Zur Mahler Reception in Italien', *Nachrichten zur Mahler Forschung*, no. 33 (1995), 3 ff.).

his studies', and he could not free himself from the influence of all he had learned from Bach to Mozart, Beethoven, Brahms, Bruckner, and Wagner. Consequently, reminiscences kept occurring, probably without the composer being aware of them. Mahler sought to be original at all costs, but lacked the essential quality of naivety. What 'comprehensible images' could one employ to describe this 'powerful torrent of sound'? The disquiet aroused by this music 'tortures the listener to death', and compels him to 'rebel'. At one moment the critic had even suspected Mahler of playing a 'horrible joke', but a few moments afterwards the Adagietto, 'the loveliest music of the evening', convinced the public that it was indeed listening to a symphony.

The *Osservatore Triestino* described Mahler as calm and sparing in gesture; a 'splendidly precise and brilliant' interpreter of Mozart and 'an artistic personality of the first order'. The Fifth had immediately displayed 'l'alto intelletto e la profonda dottrina' of the composer, but it was nevertheless full of studied, bizarre effects (*stranezze*), 'arabesques and the strange zigzags' which typify modern art and replace nowadays the 'coherence and sublime inspiration' of the great classical masters. In the *Gazzettino*, another anonymous critic had vainly sought in Mahler's Fifth Symphony 'the clarity and simplicity of form, so unsurpassably exemplified by Beethoven' and the 'logical consistency of each musical thought'. Instead he had found 'unpredictable and unusual dissonances, the most contrived counterpoints, and sudden blasts of the brass instruments which threatened to drown all the other instruments with their tumult! All this surely impressed the public, but did not help it to follow the musical argument. Only the "Adagio" had seemed successful to this disappointed listener, because its refined technique (*Faktur*) and noble melodic thought were worthy of Wagner and gave immediate pleasure.'

If Trieste was ill-prepared for its first hearing of the Fifth, Vienna was only too ready to tear the new work to pieces when Mahler conducted the local première six days later. Franz Schalk, who directed the Gesellschaftskonzerte, suggested this première performance to Mahler and organized a 'special concert' for the occasion, like the one for the Third which had been a resounding success the year before. The concert took place on 7 December, once again in the main hall of the Musikverein. Egon Wellesz, who attended some of the rehearsals with the other Schoenberg students, was struck by the number and importance of the changes Mahler made in the dynamic markings and even in the orchestration itself.[220] Schalk opened with the Bach Motet 'Singet dem Herrn ein neues Lied' (Sing a New Song to the Lord).[221] Theodor Helm, who seems to have had a wrong impression about the reception awarded to the Fifth in Cologne, claims that the 'paeans of jubilation' had heightened the public's expectations. Thus they had hardly listened to Bach's 'New Song', so impatient were they to hear Mahler conduct his own 'new

[220] EWL 45.
[221] It will be remembered that he studied the Bach Motets just before composing the Fifth Symphony.

song'. Clapping between movements was discreet, but at the end 'thunderous applause' burst forth, which (according to Theodor Helm), 'was almost obligatory after every Mahler première'. 'It is doubtful', the critic wrote, 'whether this strange symphony would have met with such success if it had been by another composer.' Its triumph, oddly enough, 'had left a powerful, immortal master standing modestly in the background', namely Bach.

In her memoirs, Berta Zuckerkandl asserts that a veritable cabal had 'carefully prepared' a genuine Viennese 'scandal' for this première. The word 'scandal' seems exaggerated however, for no critic mentions any catcalls or other manifestations of hostility like those which had greeted the first hearing of the Fourth three years earlier. But near the Zuckerkandls' box was seated Bela Haas, a notorious Viennese practical joker and humorist. During one movement she noticed him busily scribbling on his shirt cuffs. In the pause at the end of the movement, he proclaimed loudly: 'To punish Gustav Mahler's fifth misdeed, I gladly sacrifice my cuffs. Tomorrow a couple of deadly jibes will destroy the eruption of a swindler.'[222]

Though Mahler certainly did not expect the critics to hail the Fifth as an unqualified success, he could not have foreseen the extremes of hostility their reviews would display. Robert Hirschfeld was especially vehement in the three articles he wrote for the *Abendpost* and the *Österreichische Rundschau*. For him, the Fifth Symphony sadly reflected 'an era which has lost all sense of beauty'. Respect for norms, laws, or aims in art had been discarded. Nobody dared to condemn sudden, unmotivated harmonic sequences, or question changes of key: they were accepted uncritically as simply being characteristic of a particular composer. People who at one time had rejected any form of contemporary music other than Brahms now willingly sided with those who acclaimed a Mahler symphony as a symphony because they had never happened to hear another symphony or to think about it. The Fifth, Hirschfeld continued, contained no new or meaningful themes, 'but his supporters claim that Mahler does not want to invent, but only to re-form, re-colour something that already exists, to surprise and stun the listener with orchestral sonorities of resplendent magnificence, of intimate charm'. The main theme of the Funeral March was nothing but 'a variation on the theme of the Allegretto from Brahms's Third Symphony'.[223] The Symphony had moments of frightening banality, 'a series of sound effects which change with every bar, too amusing to make you think of a symphony or wish for symphonic themes'. In the first movement, Mahler 'scoffs at sadness'; in the Scherzo 'at Viennese gaiety'; and finally, in the

---

[222]   Berta Zuckerkandl, *Osterreich intim*, 68. A. F. Seligmann's article, 'Silhouetten aus der Mahler-Zeit', contains another anecdote about Bela Haas. During a concert of 'Secession' music, Max Burckhard sat listening with his hands over his eyes; Haas tapped him on the shoulder and whispered: 'You're mistaken, Herr Direktor. It's at the Secession that you cover your eyes. Here, one plugs one's ears!' See *Moderne Welt*, 3 (1922–3): 7, 11.

[223]   The first four notes of the string melody (bars 34 to 37) are in fact identical, as well as the dotted rythm, although the similarity has not been detected by recent commentators.

Adagietto, he scoffs at himself by trivializing a quotation from one of his *Kindertotenlieder*[224] 'in the manner of a composer of drawing room music who had reached his Opus 700'. In the Finale, Mahler employed 'all the sources of musical gaiety from Haydn to Humperdinck. A self-confident counterpoint seems to proclaim in every bar: "Look what I can do! And I can do even better!" '

In the December issue of the *Österreichische Rundschau*, Hirschfeld reminded readers that on a previous occasion[225] he had dubbed Mahler 'the Meyerbeer of the Symphony'. He now went further in the same vein. In making 'this comparison (he had not) meant to hurt Meyerbeer, whose melodic imagination was at least commensurate with his aspirations', but his principle of 'sacrificing the thing to its wrapping, its essence to its effect' continued to live in Mahler's works. Art, like Nature, produced 'retrogressive types'. After Gluck, Mozart, Beethoven, Weber, opera appeared to have reached the limits of its inner resources. Meyerbeer therefore tried to approach this art from the outside, i.e. by means of sophisticated effects. The same applied to the contemporary development of the symphony. The literary sources of inspiration for programme music had been exhausted. The summits reached by the last two giants of the classical symphony, Brahms and Bruckner, who had proclaimed the power of thought in symphonic creation, 'could not be surpassed and therefore had to be outflanked by people not blessed with such powers'. Hence Mahler, like Meyerbeer, concentrated on timbre and effect to hide the poverty of his themes.[226]

Hirschfeld lambasted everything in the Fifth: he called the opening March a 'funereal joke' and detected in it the influence of Italian opera. 'Critics,' he added, 'should strive to be witty, but symphonies should not!' He condemned the 'ironic glorification of trite sentimentality' in the Second movement, and the parody of Viennese waltzes in the Scherzo. As for the Adagietto, it was a 'classic example of trivial thematic invention', a travesty of insipid drawing-room music. There were now five Mahler symphonies offering these 'puzzling sentiments', these 'feelings in fancy dress'. It was as if, in a comedy, the fool were to take the role of hero. This 'neurasthenic' symphony, despite its many beautiful and gripping passages, inflicted 'a veritable torture on healthy minds', for it was unable to 'sustain the same manner, direction, or timbre for more than four bars without becoming trite'. 'There was a time', Hirschfeld concluded, 'when freaks of nature like giants, six-legged calves, and Siamese twins, only awakened curiosity . . . Today

---

[224] The reference to the *Kindertotenlieder* actually occurs in the Funeral March, and the resemblance between the theme of the Adagietto and 'Nun seh' ich wohl' is less striking than its similarity to 'Ich bin der Welt'.

[225] One year earlier, after the Viennese première of the Third Symphony.

[226] In the same article in the *Österreichische Rundschau*, Hirschfeld praised the first orchestral work, a suite by a young 'Hungarian who skilfully uses modern orchestral means and stylized popular themes', adding that it had found great favour with the audience. It was Bela Bartok's first Orchestral Suite.

the public has totally lost its appreciation of what is healthy in art, and is interested mostly in freaks.'

The other critics were hardly more positive than Hirschfeld. Wallaschek also detected signs in the Fifth that Mahler was facing a crisis. He seemed undecided as to what style to adopt. His work showed reminiscences of old Italian opera, of Bizet, Wagner, old popular tunes, and military band music. It contained paraphrases of drawing-room pieces, but 'we miss the strong personality capable of forging these diverse elements into a new artistically valuable whole!' Mahler's works exhibited 'boundless enthusiasm' and 'prodigious artistic intelligence', but also an absence of critical discernment in the choice of material. The work as a whole left an impression of incoherence: the Funeral March was a mixture of Donizetti, modern French opera, Romantic chromaticism, and the tragic revolt of Liszt or Berlioz; the Scherzo, starting with a popular tune, degenerated into 'old-fashioned drawing-room music'. Mahler could please either as a 'Tyrolian' or as a 'drawing-room man', but not as a 'drawing-room Tyrolian'.[227] The Adagietto was disappointing, the initially attractive Finale turned into a 'Straussian polka' followed by continuous 'changes of style and atmosphere'. If the symphony were an Opus No. 1, Wallaschek concluded, one could have hoped that the composer would develop and acquire his own musical personality. But given Mahler's age, Wallaschek predicted that his symphonies would have the same fate as Herbeck's, falling into oblivion after being considered 'the sum total of an era's musical knowledge'.

Kauders abstained from such dire predictions, but he too was far from appreciating Mahler's new work. In the 'interminable funeral procession' of the opening moment, all he saw was desperate monotony and 'the pale dawn of a November morning', and, in the second movement, a touch of 'beer-garden music' in the succession of thirds and sixths. For him, what had been buried was 'the powerful conviction which previously permitted him to believe in the artistic vocation, and even mission, of Gustav Mahler', whose lack of aesthetic sense was now all too clear. However, in the course of the third movement Kauder's buried conviction was 'gradually exhumed' and the electrifying impressions of the Finale made it live more vigorously than before. For him it was 'one of the masterpieces of symphonic literature', with its 'spontaneous, natural, naive, humour', 'irresistible affability', 'captivating temperament', 'masterful composition', 'abundant imagination', and manifold thematic variations. It seemed to 'combine Brahms and Bruckner, with their specific genius, as well as the Wagner of the Prelude to *Die Meistersinger* and the Schumann of the Fourth Symphony'.

Schönaich on the other hand remained unconvinced, even by the Finale. He expressed amazement that, unlike Liszt and Wagner, Mahler 'had never had to fight for recognition of his work' (*sic*). Apparently he had already forgotten the

---

[227] A play of words on the title of an operetta by Gustav von Moser (which had been performed in Kassel during Mahler's stay), *Der Salon-Tiroler* (see above, Vol. i, Chap. 9).

fiascos of the first Viennese performances of the First, Second, and Fourth, only three years earlier. Korngold, on the other hand, contrasted the ovation the Fifth had received with the derision and failures Mahler's symphonies had encountered on previous occasions, and praised Mahler for 'having the strength nevertheless to continue composing'. Even David Josef Bach confessed that he was incapable of unravelling the 'many enigmas' in the new work.

Like Hirschfeld, Maximilian Muntz claimed that the reception which a 'fashionable audience' gave the Fifth could not hide 'the ghost of a general disappointment' at Mahler's weakening imagination and inability to progress. The Fifth Symphony could no longer be described as 'ironical' like an earlier one, but as 'cynical': it revealed a 'decadent personality' which was trying to conceal the conflict between its ethical and technical creative powers by means of refined and unnatural stimulants; a composer who cynically used music to mock music. Every sentiment degenerated into parody or caricature, content and form continually repudiated each other as if intended as 'a furious mockery, not only of the listener but of the very essence of music'. The extravagant display of technical means and shrill orchestral colouring aggravated the impression of inner incoherence of the symphony to the point of making it unbearable. The cynical character of the work manifested itself above all in the first movement in which Mahler jeered at the suffering of naive and sensitive men in a Funeral March full of 'trivial tunes and pompous, stodgy orchestration', the tragedy of death became 'a war veteran's funeral' with Turkish music and malicious orchestral jokes. In the second [third] movement he scoffed at Viennese popular music with equal cynicism, robbing it of its innocence and naivety by recasting it 'in modern orchestral colours' and 'contrapuntal cancans'. After the 'superficial and sentimental' Adagietto, the Finale was nothing but 'symphonic anarchy', 'vulgar noise', 'scornful laughter', and 'popular ditties'.

Max Graf had been so incensed by the public's enthusiasm that he had compiled no less than twenty-three quotations from famous writers, including Goethe, Hebbel, Schiller, Lessing, Wilde, and Plato, all of which were meant to show the fatal weaknesses Mahler had displayed when composing the Fifth Symphony. Thus, by implication, Mahler's 'technique was an absurdity', for he lacked 'moral and aesthetic clarity'; he had 'imagination but no taste', and had composed a work 'without unity, and which would soon be forgotten'. With other tendentious statements like 'genius should not flaunt itself, but hide behind art', and 'a fake presented with artistry surprises and dazzles, but truth persuades and conquers' (Vauvenargues), Graf suggested that Mahler deliberately adopted a 'mannered style, and cultivated obscurity in order to hide his confusion'. His talent was above all a 'technical' one, his art one of constant change in thought and expression. As Wilde had written, 'artists who impress by their manner are bad artists'.

Theodor Helm had at least 'carefully examined the score' of the Fifth, which had inspired him with 'profound respect for Mahler's prodigious virtuosity, if not for his thematic invention', which was 'even scantier than in his earlier works'.[228] The Allegro (the second movement) disconcerted the listener even more than the March, for he doubted whether the 'orgies of dissonance' expressed deep-felt sentiments. Helm considered the Scherzo to be an 'audacious exhibition of eccentric counterpoint', with 'orgies of grotesque and burlesque dances'. Unlike his colleagues, he refrained from calling the Adagietto a piece of 'salon music' but he too regarded the Finale as the sole symphonic passage in the traditional sense of the word, and claimed that it alone was responsible for the symphony's success.

Finally, Hans Liebstöckl, the witty critic of the *Illustrirtes Wiener Extrablatt*, detected and also denounced the ambiguous and unhealthy element in Mahler's new work: 'No doctor would prescribe it for his patient, for ... he would not sleep well, it would give him bad dreams and leave him depressed in the daytime.' This superficially democratic, but fundamentally mystical and reactionary symphony 'noisily displays the late-flowering strength of a decaying culture, saturated with artistry and decorative themes, ... unintentionally reminiscent of Huysmans[229] and his satanic characters, or the contrite piety of a Gilles de Rais'. Mahler, Liebstöckl continued, was a phenomenon: he commanded attention, intrigued his listeners, made them 'see spirits'. The fashionable ladies who came to hear his works were no doubt proud to be present, thereby showing that they felt capable of understanding 'this most difficult and serious music'. The audience, composed of young people from the Conservatory, the best society, professional musicians, writers, and even politicians, resembled the 'birth of the first Christian community'. 'A beat of the tom-tom, a sigh of violins and solidarity is established. But the magic vanishes once a cynic makes his appearance. ... The veils fall away, and two, three people suddenly realize that music should really want to do much less if it were to be good music.'

Never before had the Viennese critics displayed so much imagination and talent, or taken such pains to denigrate a work by Mahler. Only two or three isolated voices dared to swim against the tide and suggest that perhaps a closer look might lead to a different verdict. Korngold, in particular, saw the Fifth as 'the work of a serious and original artist, the extravagant and brilliant sister of his first symphonies'. The critic might be puzzled by the confusing interplay of attraction and repulsion 'but then, that is what novelty does'. A work should be judged exclusively on the musical impression it makes and not on its deviation from classical form, which, in the last resort, was nothing but the shape in

---

[228] According to Helm, a Berlin critic named Wilhelm Kleefeld had suggested a highly imaginative programme for the Fifth Symphony, the first movement representing the 'burial of the Carnival Prince', and the last his 'resurrection'.

[229] The French writer Joris-Karl Huysmans (1848–1907), of Dutch origin, mixed occultism and sensuality in a character of *Là-bas* (1891) called Durtal. A few years later (1895) he became a fervent Catholic.

which the last generally recognized artist had imposed a new content. That content, to be truly symphonic, must not only set out musical thought and argument, but reflect both the grave and happy movements of the human heart, of human life, and this was undoubtedly what Mahler's Fifth did. Nor could Mahler be reproached with lack of imagination: on the contrary, his solidly diatonic themes were of generous proportions, at a time when others preferred to employ thematic fragments. They were also profoundly original, lyrical, and close to folk language. Their popular character did not by any means make them unworthy of a symphony. All music, Korngold recalled, originated in folklore, and Mahler in any case used mostly stylized themes. His methods of development constituted a 'genuine (musical) enrichment', like his 'fabulous instrumental technique' and his 'unequalled sonorous imagination'. The Fifth showed 'hypertrophied counterpoint', 'brutal individualism in contrapuntal style', and 'immoderate emotional contrasts'—all symptoms of 'excessive feverishness'. But it was absurd to question the authenticity of a composition, every note of which so utterly reflected the personality of the man and the artist. The public was 'under the spell of this fascinating minstrel (*Spielmann*)'. And to the question, so often asked, 'what exactly was going on in these strange symphonies' Korngold replied: 'The twentieth century is going on, with its mysterious impulsions, with its nerves and, we hope, also with its determination to master them.'[230]

Thus Korngold showed a perspicacity and open-mindedness unique in the Viennese music criticism of 1905. Despite his essentially conservative nature, Max Kalbeck also tried to achieve a measure of critical objectivity. In his opinion, Mahler had reached a turning-point in his dizzying climb, which opened up prospects of a happy future. He had created a work whose 'rich, beautiful and interesting content' far surpassed that of his previous symphonies. Until now, Mahler had allowed himself to be influenced by the opera. He had used the human voice as a 'sonorous, talking tool' which had had a disintegrating effect on his symphonies. Mahler the poet produced a poetic text. At last, the musician in him had torn up the programmes he had once used. In his Fifth Symphony, the 'declared or concealed' programme had been replaced by an underlying, basic thought capable of being expressed by music, namely the powers of life and death confronting each other. But other elements had crept in: the 'lugubrious pomp' of the initial Funeral March seemed to be accompanied by a critical second self giving either 'ironic smiles or impatient sighs'—it is 'the street ditty which follows the mournful melody of the march': 'grieving tension turning into nervous gaiety.'

For Kalbeck Mahler was above all a 'master of magic atmosphere', an unequalled virtuoso of orchestral sonority, whose artistic genius 'revealed itself by necessary, yet surprising changes of mood without ever losing control over

[230]   A few lines later Korngold singles out three other composers as 'modern': Siegfried Wagner, Hans Pfitzner, and Bela Bartok.

the form'. In the Scherzo, he had not made things easy for himself or the public, but had guided it by a masterly hand through its enthralling and entertaining episodes. Despite its sources in folk music, the Scherzo was certainly not meant to imitate the banalities of a 'Heuriger'.[231] This was proved by the care taken over its intricate construction, and even more by the presence of 'unrestrained, demonic elements' betraying the 'restlessness of a Faustian mind'. As for the Adagietto, its melody was 'enthralling, bewitching, and soothing in its gentleness'. The Finale, the Fifth's 'triumphant crown', the most perfect of all Mahler's symphonic movements, had 'brilliantly vanquished all resistance'.

Although it had disarmed Kalbeck, the Finale had not altered the other critics' verdicts: Schönaich, for example, attacked Mahler's 'lack of form', 'inflated, chubby, town-crier themes' and 'convulsive' aesthetics. The Fifth's public success was an illusion: it was due solely to the composer's personality and his 'clever instrumental jokes'. Mahler's works and their themes were not difficult to understand. However, the arbitrary order of the movements and their irrational structure allowed people to put on a thoughtful expression and to pretend things to be obvious which were, in fact, 'utterly incomprehensible'. The Adagietto reminded Schönaich of those 'pretty pious images which fashionable priests use as visiting cards and give to aristocratic young ladies'.

Thus once again, with quasi-unanimity and only one major exception, the Viennese press declared that Mahler as a composer was either a lunatic or a charlatan. He must by now have understood that a favourable terrain for his art was not to be found in Austria, at least not among the Viennese musical professionals of the older generation, and he conducted only one more local première of one of his symphonies there. Luckily, there were other cities where the ears and minds of the musical establishment had not been poisoned by prejudice. Barely two weeks after the Vienna concert, Mahler went to Breslau where, thanks to his friend, the famous dermatologist Albert Neisser, he had been invited to conduct his Fifth Symphony. As the capital of the German province of Silesia, Breslau had become an important centre of commerce and industry, largely because of its geographical location at a crossroads between Northern and Southern Europe and, more important still, between the Eastern (Slav) and Western (German) world. Thanks to its prosperity, it had also become a cultural centre, where science and the arts flourished and music occupied a privileged position. Mahler's friend, Albert Neisser, taught at the University in Breslau and exerted a powerful influence on the musical activities of the city. He had invited Mahler to stay at his home and Mahler had accepted on the following conditions:

I shall arrive in Breslau early on Sunday. I have one great favour to ask of you: that you neither fetch me at the station nor get up to let me in at so early an hour. It is crucial to my feeling at ease that my early morning arrival shall disturb no one's sleep, and you have promised me that I would feel at home in your house, and not a 'guest'. Therefore

---

[231] Traditionally the *Heuriger* (or new wine) is drunk in taverns in the Vienna suburbs to strains of *Schrammelmusik*, popular tunes which Mahler often stylized in his Scherzos.

I do ask you to let me make my way to the Fürstenstrasse on my own. There, a servant or chambermaid will let me in and take me to my room, where I shall make myself as presentable as my nature permits. From there, I shall betake myself full of arduous longing to the breakfast room, where I shall help myself to coffee and bread and butter, and await the beginning of events with a cigar and some reading.

So, please, you will be so kind as to take no notice whatever of my arrival, won't you, and just come down to breakfast at your usual hour . . .[232]

Breslau had changed hands several times in the course of its complicated history. It had at first belonged to Poland, but had been annexed by the Kingdom of Bohemia in 1335 and then by the Habsburgs, before becoming Prussian in 1745. Its University, built at the beginning of the eighteenth century, had been enlarged, transformed, and reorganized in 1811. Thanks to it, Breslau had become one of the scientific and cultural centres of Europe. Mahler's friend, Arthur Neisser, taught there and there he had studied various microbes and discovered that of gonorrhoea.[233] According to Mahler's report in a letter to Alma,[234] the Neissers were 'lavish hosts and lived in a superb house'. Arnold Berliner, Mahler's old friend from Hamburg and Arthur Neisser's cousin, had come from Berlin for the performance. Every afternoon, Mahler posed for the artist Fritz Erler who, at Neisser's request, painted his portrait and later used it as the basis for an engraving.[235] Erler was well known in Germany for his interior decoration and for his portraits. His décors for the Munich Künstlerhaus and collaboration with Georg Fuchs, the celebrated stage director,[236] had added to his fame. He was a close friend of the Neisser family, had decorated their music room, and painted several portraits of Frau Neisser. His design for the Neissers' music room had become a famous example of the new style of interior decoration. He adorned the walls with his frescos, and designed all the wood fittings, including the light-fixtures, organ case, music stands, seats, door-locks, etc. Mahler must have felt very much at home in this very contemporary décor, which surely reminded him of the Hohe Warte.[237]

---

[232] MBR1, no. 324; MBR2, no. 348. The 1906 date assigned to this letter in MBR1 is incorrect. Mahler alludes to the première of *Salome*, which had taken place in Dresden a few days earlier.

[233] Breslau (Warslaw) is now the fourth city in Poland.

[234] BGA, no. 158, undated (18 Dec. 1905).

[235] Erler's engraving, dated 1905, is reproduced in RBM (no. 85), BDB (no. 225), and KMA (no. 219). When it was sent to Mahler in the autumn of the following year, he wrote to Berliner: 'He seems to have added details from memory after I had left—alas!' (MBR1, no. 283; MBR2, no. 365).

[236] See above, Vol. ii, Chap. 14.

[237] Fritz Erler (1868–1914) was born near Breslau, where he had been the pupil of Albrecht Bräuer. During a two-year stay in Paris (1892–4), he attended the Académie Julian, and came under the influence of Albert Besnard. In addition to German fairy-tale scenes he painted, while in Paris, a series of Brittany landscapes and designed vases and posters. He returned to Germany in 1896, and became one of the founders of the Munich review *Jugend* (the model for *Ver sacrum*), for which he designed the first cover featuring a young ice-skater bearing a branch of mistletoe in one hand and a torch in the other. Erler's work after 1900 is usually considered less vigorous, particularly as his compromise between naturalism and decorative stylization was less successful. Aside from the frescos painted for private clients and administrative buildings, he was renowned above all for his portraits, especially of Sarasate and Richard Strauss (1898). At the end of his life, he collaborated with Fuchs in several famous Künstlertheater productions, notably *Faust* and *Hamlet* (1908).

Rehearsals in Breslau would have been a pleasure, had Mahler not been constantly plagued by 'very disagreeable' news from Vienna, where Demuth had deeply resented the fact that the title role of *Don Giovanni* had been given to his rival, Friedrich Weidemann.[238] The Breslau performance of the Fifth Symphony was to be the main attraction of the sixth concert of the Silesian city's Orchesterverein. The first rehearsals had been conducted by the Breslau conductor, Gorg Dohrn. Mahler's previous experience had taught him that applause between movements spoilt the effect of the Fifth. He consulted the directors of the Orchesterverein, who explained that it could scarcely be avoided because it was a tradition. Mahler did however manage to discourage it at the concert by keeping his arms raised at the end of each movement as if to hold a chord,[239] before giving the signal for the following movement.

The Breslau press gave Mahler an exceptionally favourable reception, thus once again proving to him that the Viennese press had probably attacked the Director of the Opera rather than the composer of the Fifth Symphony. Most of the critics were favourable. Emil Bohn[240] and Ernst Flügel[241] compared Mahler to Bruckner, Flügel even claiming that he surpassed his 'former master' by 'his originality, maturity of technique ... and logical development of thematic ideas'. He found the Fifth superior to the Fourth, which had been heard in Breslau recently, and claimed that Mahler's mastery of development equalled that of Brahms while his orchestration certainly surpassed it. There was 'dazzling light and rays of sunshine in Mahler's music', compared with Brahms's 'clair-obscur'. Indeed, his 'daring juxtapositions of sonorities' and 'scorn for tradition' could be compared to those of Richard Strauss.[242] For Flügel, understanding the Fifth presented no problems to the well-disposed listener, for the conception was all of one piece, and the themes were 'admirable, fascinating, and generously conceived', even when reminiscent of others. The force of the development and the power of the crescendos revealed in themselves 'a masterpiece'. 'Eccentric youth will love it [the Fifth] and calm, reflective old age will esteem it', Flügel concluded. Mahler had conducted it with 'pleasing and imposing calm'.

In the *Breslauer Zeitung*, Emil Bohn was more reticent. Mahler's themes, in his opinion, were not up to Bruckner's, but their development was 'stupefying'. Mahler lacked perhaps 'the brilliant power of the creator who elicits something unheard of and unthought of out of nothing', but he remained a musician of astounding technical virtuosity, 'whose penetrating thought dominates all the

---

[238] See below, Chap. 5.

[239] *Fremden-Blatt*, Vienna, 'Aus der Theaterwelt' (6 Jan. 1907). Nevertheless, Mahler probably allowed pauses between the various 'parts' of the symphony.

[240] Emil Bohn (1839–1909), born near Neisse, studied music and philology in Breslau. Organist, founder of a chorus and a series of historical concerts, critic of the *Breslauer Zeitung*, and author of many works on music, he taught at the University of Breslau and was highly reputed in Germany and abroad.

[241] Ernst Flügel (1844–1912) was born in Halle. After studying with Bülow and Geyer he became an organist like his father. Appointed Kantor and Musikdirektor in Breslau, he wrote a number of choral works.

[242] Certain chords and whole-tone scales seemed to him particularly daring.

resources of his art and whose sovereign touch subordinates them to his unbending will'. Serious and profound, the Fifth had impressed him as a whole. It represented considerable progress over Mahler's earlier symphonies. Bohn was particularly impressed by the 'idealized Viennese waltz of the Scherzo', and its 'most daring counterpoint'. He praised the conciseness of the Adagietto, 'expressing gentle, tranquil happiness . . . tender without being sentimental'. In the Finale there was also a great deal to be admired. However, it lacked 'the happy proportions or equilibrium which alone allow a work of art to survive the fashions of the day'.

The *Schlesische Volkszeitung* portrayed Mahler as an adversary of programme music and as such the antipode of Strauss. He was a composer whose thinking was clear for anyone 'sensitive to the atmosphere of a piece of music'. Mahler composed 'pure music . . . with all the resources of a big, modern orchestra': 'it all flows without interruption or rest, with every instrument speaking its own language and participating individually in the general debate.' Mahler 'really imagined' his themes, instead of constructing them, and, even when they lacked 'originality or intrinsic value'; they never failed to create the desired atmosphere. The only reproach one might make was the abundance of ideas, 'which sometimes overgrow the general form and hide the architecture'.[243] The opening march, despite its 'fits of despair', was a victory over the forces of darkness, and the Scherzo was 'daring in conception and superbly performed'. The critic praised 'the tenderness and magic intimacy of the Adagietto' and the overflowing energy of the Finale. The work and its brilliant interpretation had made a deep impression on the Breslau public, which although not usually receptive to modern music, had applauded enthusiastically and without reservation.

When the Neissers forwarded these hymns of praise to Mahler several days after the concert, he admitted his delight and suggested he might soon be consecrated 'Breslau's national composer'. News of the triumph filled the German periodicals. In the *Neue Zeitschrift*, Fritz Kaatz[244] congratulated Mahler for returning to classical form, renouncing programmes, and developing generously conceived (*grosszügige*) themes, 'powerful and virile', even if they were sometimes 'already known'. For Robert Ludwig, of the *Musikalisches Wochenblatt*, it was the combinations of these themes which provided the most compelling example of Mahler's 'prodigious art'; they did 'not emanate from the intelligence alone' but were surrounded by musical atmosphere. Finally, *Die Musik* more speciously praised the 'witty and clever traits of the work', its general architecture, and the succession of themes in each movement.[245]

---

[243] The anonymous critic claimed that Mahler used the trumpet and horn to counteract this multiplicity of ideas. He had brought the two players with him from Vienna.

[244] Fritz Kaatz was Director of the Breslau Conservatory.

[245] To conclude the sixth concert of the Breslauer Orchesterverein, on 20 Dec., Georg Dohrn conducted Beethoven's *Leonore* Overture No. 3.

As seen above, Mahler's journeys away from Vienna to conduct his own works led to frequent accusations that he was neglecting his duties as Director of the Opera. That autumn, however, his duties in Vienna had been onerous indeed. Although his battle for *Salome* seemed definitively lost, he refused to admit defeat. The opera had finally had its première in Dresden on 9 December and Strauss had found the production 'absolutely exceptional', thanks mainly to the tenor Karl Burian, the Dresden Opera Orchestra and its conductor Ernst von Schuch. The first three performances had been sold out. In its review of the opening, the German *Neue Musikalische Presse* remarked that the Viennese ban had been ill-inspired, and that it would probably have the opposite effect to that intended in that it would stimulate curiosity about the 'prohibited opera'. Strauss was still impatiently awaiting good news from the Vienna Opera. It was all the more important to him since smaller opera houses could not do justice to *Salome*: 'Who will put on this horribly difficult opera if those houses which are really capable of performing it refuse to do so?'[246]

In the meantime, the Mozart anniversary season was about to begin, as seen above, with *Così*, which was to be followed by *Don Giovanni*. However, Mozart was not the only composer whose works needed to be restaged at the Hofoper. Mahler's efforts to obtain the necessary funds for the new production of the *Ring* had been interrupted after *Das Rheingold*, but he thought he might at least be allowed, during the Mozart year, to restage *Lohengrin* which had long been Wagner's most popular opera in Vienna. A gala performance—or 'théâtre paré, as the Viennese called it—was to be offered on 14 November 1905 by the Emperor to Alfonso XIII, King of Spain. This provided Mahler with a golden opportunity to request credits for a new production of *Lohengrin*, of which the first act was to be performed for the royal visitor. In honour of the distinguished guest, Mahler conducted Act I of *Lohengrin* and a few selected scenes from *Lakmé*. The rest of the evening consisted of the first act of Josef Bayer's ballet *Excelsior*, conducted by the composer.

Alma, for whom an artistic event was something sacred, was outraged that evening by the casual behaviour of the members of the Imperial Court, and embarrassed to see her husband waiting at the podium for Prince Montenuovo's permission to start the performance. The Prince was standing in the large 'incognito box', himself waiting for a signal from Alma's uncle Wilhelm Nepalleck, the Master of Protocol,[247] who was to raise a white cane when His Imperial Majesty and the royal visitor arrived. After noisily taking their seats, the Emperor and his guests conversed aloud during the performance. Scornful and exasperated, Alma observed the antics of the gala audience and the

---

[246] Letter of 15 Dec. 1905 (MSB 112).

[247] After Alma's grandfather on her father's side had died, Alma's grandmother took a second husband, Wilhem Nepalleck, and had a son, Wilhelm Friedrich Nepalleck, who later became Master of Ceremonies at the Imperial Court. Though their relationship was thus remote, Alma chose to call him her 'Wahl-Onkel' (Elective Uncle). (KMI)

courtiers until she could stand it no longer and left the Director's box. Afterward, she told Mahler that she had had the impression of 'having a flunkey for a husband'.[248]

Yet Mahler had never concealed, even from the court authorities, his distaste for these glacial performances given on the occasion of state visits to Vienna of royal personages from foreign countries. In fact he tried to avoid them whenever he could. During the same visit of Alfonso XIII of Spain, he also had to conduct a performance of Eugen d'Albert's *Die Abreise* in the theatre of the Schönbrunn Palace. As soon as it was over, he rushed away, although he well knew that the Emperor had invited all the artists to join him afterwards.[249]

[248] AMM1, 143; AMM2, 141. The date Alma gives for the gala is inaccurate: no gala performance took place at the Hofoper on 11 Mar. 1907. Cast for the first act of *Lohengrin* on 14 Nov. 1905: Weidt (Elsa); Mildenburg (Ortrud); Schmedes (Lohengrin); Demuth (Telramund); Mayr (King); Haydter (Herald). The new production was performed in its entirety in Feb. 1906 (see below). The scenes from *Lakmé* were sung by Selma Kurz and Leo Slezak.

[249] From an unidentified press clipping in the Vondenhoff collection (ÖNB, Vienna).

5

Mahler in Vienna (XXI)—The Mozart Year—*Così fan tutte* and *Don Giovanni* *Die Entführung* and *Figaro*—*The Magic Flute*— Antwerp and Amsterdam Concerts Mahler as Administrator, Stage Director, and Conductor (December 1905–April 1906)

> Others take care of themselves and destroy the Opera. I take
> care of the Opera and destroy myself.

T HE Mozart Year, 1906, began five weeks ahead of the calendar at the Hofoper. On 24 November 1905, after a three-year absence, *Così fan tutte* reappeared in the Spielplan with a production which was largely, though not entirely new. Mahler had planned to commission Roller to design new sets for all of Mozart's great operas. But, as seen above, the funds made available to him were insufficient, and for *Così*, *Die Entführung*, and *The Magic Flute* he had to refurbish the existing sets. The only productions he was able to renew from scratch were *Don Giovanni* and *The Marriage of Figaro*.[1] Mahler's first problem was the German text, at a time when the performance of Mozart's Italian operas in the original language was out of the question in Vienna. In *Figaro*, the original recitatives had been replaced by a spoken German text of no literary value. Shortly after his arrival in Vienna Mahler had commissioned Max Kalbeck, the author of the German version used in Vienna since 1887, to

---

[1] Theodor Helm (THE 325) recalls that in 1891, for the centenary of Mozart's death, Jahn had presented all the great operas from *Idomeneo* to *The Magic Flute*, with an eighth evening devoted to *Bastien und Bastienne* and *La Finta Giardiniera*. Obviously Mahler's requirements with regard to new productions were altogether different from those of his predecessor.

translate the recitatives in full, and these were now to be sung to piano accompaniment.[2]

The same work had now to be done for *Don Giovanni*. 'As you probably know', Mahler wrote to Kalbeck at the end of spring,

I am finally getting ready to approach that monster, Don Juan. You already know the way, and I am definitely counting on the fact (at least our conversations led me to this belief) that you will accompany me now, as so often before. I am planning to visit you sometime during the next few weeks; please let me know when I can do so, without disturbing you of course.[3]

Shortly afterwards, Mahler thanked Kalbeck for his work:

I have just finished reading your new translation and cannot deny myself the pleasure of sending you word from afar of my joy and my total agreement with your rendering. In fact I consider the problem solved. I have checked your version against the original and can vouch for its accuracy, and considering the unseemly haste with which the whole thing has to be done (preparing the parts and studying them) I would prefer not to lose any more time with the further verification you suggested.

In the end Mahler asked Kalbeck to make things easier for the singers, who were suffering from overwork, by keeping to his 1887 text for the best-known arias. As before, he made many suggestions and worked closely with Kalbeck in order to achieve 'a *Don Giovanni* which will live and outlive us'.[4] They continued to make changes during the rehearsals, and only agreed on the final version shortly before the opening night.[5]

Concern for historical authenticity led Mahler to request permission from the Intendant and High Chamberlain on 25 August to order a harpsichord ('*Mozart-Spinett*') from Pleyel-Wolff in Paris. A few days later, however, he heard that an old spinet from the time of the Emperor Joseph, 'which had been played by Mozart' and could be restored, was still being kept at the Augarten Palace.[6] Mahler asked to see it. One day, when the Czech composer Josef Bohuslav Förster came to his office, he pointed with emotion to the yellowing

---

[2]   The new translation of *The Marriage of Figaro*, for which Kalbeck received 300 gulden (600 kronen), was completed in 1899. Theodor Helm claimed that the recitatives were unsingable in German, and Mahler had previously hesitated to include them (THE 325).

[3]   Copies of these and several other unpublished letters from Mahler to Kalbeck were made available to the author by Anna Mahler.

[4]   MBR1, no. 276 ; MBR2, no. 343. In a letter dated 18 Aug. 1905 (ÖTM, HOA), Kalbeck informed Mahler that his new translation was finished, adding that he only hoped 'no one would notice how much effort I put into it'. As agreed with Mahler, his new German text closely followed the original Italian libretto of 1787. Act I was now divided into twenty scenes and Act II into fifteen. Kalbeck asked Mahler whether he intended to pay a flat fee or royalties on each performance. Mahler replied that Kalbeck himself should decide, for 'the work deserved to be properly recompensed'. At Mahler's request Kalbeck received a fee of 750 gulden (1,500 kronen), plus 250 florins (500 kronen) for revising the 1899 translation of *The Marriage of Figaro*.   [5]   MBR1, no. 277; MBR2, no. 345.

[6]   Augarten Palace, formerly the summer residence of Joseph II, is situated between the Danube and the Danube Canal.

keys on which the youthful Mozart had played before the Empress Maria Theresia.[7]

Unfortunately Mahler discovered that its pitch was too low, and that raising it to modern standards might damage it. He therefore reverted to his original plan and ordered a Pleyel spinet. After a first trial, during the 24 November performance of *Così fan tutte*, it was purchased and subsequently used at the Hofoper for all Mozart operas.[8] For the revival of *Così fan tutte*, the revolving stage of 1900 was enlarged during the course of the summer.[9] The cast was slightly different: Slezak replaced Naval and Kurz Saville. The critics greeted the production favourably, but still refused to consider the opera one of Mozart's masterpieces. Paul Stefan later spoke of the 'divine lightness' and 'utter perfection' of Mahler's interpretation, and the Prague critic Felix Adler considered that Mahler had 'brought a musical comedy to life, endowing it with deep philosophical meaning'.[10] Only Korngold regretted that this opera, so full of treasures, had never become part of the Hofoper repertoire.[11] He recalled the exquisite performance in 1900[12] when the recitatives with accompaniment had finally replaced the spoken dialogues. The new performance was of the same high quality; it was impossible to imagine a better production, he concluded.

As usual, Mahler took a certain number of liberties with the score. He altered the orchestration here and there and added a number of nuances in order to enhance the dynamic contrasts (especially *pp* and even *ppp*). He deleted some arias and ensembles[13] and made some cuts within particular episodes. As a prelude to Act Two, he continued to use the Allegro Molto of the Finale of Mozart's Divertimento for strings and two horns, K. 287. And between the recitative following Don Alfonso's aria and the finale of the second act, he repeated the 14 opening bars of the Overture (Andante) in order to keep 'the audience from clearing their throats and shifting around in their seats'.[14]

The general attitude of the critics towards the opera itself remained one of

---

[7]   JFP 695. Förster wrongly believed that it had been used in the performances.

[8]   HOA, G.Z. 821/1905. Letters of 25 Aug., 8 Sep., 7 Oct., and 20 Dec. 1905. Richard Strauss subsequently seems to have used the same instrument for the *Don Giovanni* he conducted at the Redoutensaal (Otto Strasser, *Und dafür wird man noch bezahlt. Mein Leben mit den Wiener Philharmonikern* (Neff, Vienna, 1974), 33). Curiously, the French writer Eugène d'Harcourt thought that the spinet used for this production was a Bösendorfer (*La Musique actuelle en Allemagne et en Autriche-Hongrie*, (Durdilly, Paris, 1908), 155).

[9]   This revolving stage, which was made up of 30 wooden elements, could be erected upon the stage of the Opera without any change in the flooring. Thirty metres in diameter, it could be put up or taken down within an hour.

[10]   PSG 68, and Felix Adler, 'Gustav Mahler', in the programme of two concerts which the Mannheim Philharmonic Society dedicated to Mahler's memory (11 and 12 May 1912).

[11]   Between 1897 and 1907, *Figaro* was performed 62 times, *Don Giovanni* 48 times, and *Così fan tutte* only 15 times.   [12]   See above, Vol. ii, Chap. 9.

[13]   Including the Ferrando–Guglielmo duet, 'Al fato don legge', no. 7 of the first act; Guglielmo's aria, no. 15; and Ferrando's arias, nos. 24 and 27 of the second act.

[14]   Bernhard Paumgartner, 'Gustav Mahlers Bearbeitung von Mozarts Cosi fan Tutte für seine Aufführung an der Wiener Hofoper', *Musik und Verlag: Karl Vötterle zum 65. Geburtstag* (Bärenreiter, Kassel, 1968), 476.

extreme reserve, as it had been in 1900. Maximilian Muntz, for instance, was in a particularly unpleasant mood in reviewing the new *Così fan tutte*. Not only did he call it 'one of Mozart's weaker works', but he accused Mahler, in preparing the new cast, of having allowed personal considerations to take preference over his professed artistic aims. In the role of Despina, Gutheil-Schoder tried to compensate for her 'ludicrous and ruined voice' with a plethora of 'mannered grimaces and gestures' which were entirely out of place in a Mozart opera. Like Muntz, Wallaschek attributed *Così*'s long neglect to the weakness of the libretto. While recognizing that Mahler had an 'affinity' for Mozart, he too disagreed with the choice of the cast,[15] and disliked the sonority of the spinet used to accompany the recitatives. However, the *Fremden-Blatt* critic, Kauders, appreciated its 'archaic quality', finding it much better suited to the work than the 'insipid' sound of the pianoforte. He shared Muntz's low opinion of Gutheil-Schoder, but considered nevertheless that she knew how to 'put the audience into a good humour'.[16] As for Mahler, he had never 'seemed so great'. Schönaich also thought that Mahler was 'unsurpassable in Mozart': with his 'delicacy of nuance and infallible sense of tempo', he 'brought out the many treasures in *Così* and cast a spell over the listener'. Max Graf marvelled at the way Mahler could create a comic atmosphere, and at the same time moderate the sound while giving it a thousand different shades of colour, 'as though it were chamber music'.[17]

But *Così fan tutte* was still, in Mahler's day, regarded as a minor opera—telling a story that was cynical, decadent, and even of questionable morality. On the other hand, ever since E. T. A. Hoffmann, *Don Giovanni* had been acclaimed as the operatic masterpiece of the rococo period and perhaps of all time. For the new production of December 1905, Mahler and Roller demonstrated tremendous passion, ingenuity, and zeal, and achieved a resolutely new and indeed avant-garde result. Yet Mahler's primary concern was to return to Mozart's original score as often as possible, and to restore passages which had previously been cut. As we have seen, Max Kalbeck prepared a new translation, and after some hesitation he and Mahler decided to leave the title in the original Italian: *Don Giovanni* instead of *Don Juan*. The principal reason was the impossibility of finding an adequate translation of the Commendatore's famous lines: 'Don Giovanni, a cenar teco . . .'

The estimate of cost for the production had been prepared in September and presented to the Intendant on the 23rd. It then reached a total of 25,000

---

[15] Wallaschek expressed doubts about the 'purity' of the voices of the two heroines, but considered Slezak an 'authentic' Mozart singer and Gutheil-Schoder 'exquisite' as Despina.

[16] In Schönaich's opinion, she transcended her role as soubrette to give a perfect rendering of a depraved eighteenth-century chambermaid. Enthusiastic about Hesch's 'performance', Graf nonetheless claimed, as did many of his colleagues, that the 'outmoded' subject of *Così* had not inspired Mozart, who for once 'had proved incapable of joking about love'.

[17] According to Graf, the impression was such that the relative 'weakness' of the second act passed unnoticed. Cast of the 24 Nov. 1905 performance: Kurz (Fiordiligi); Hilgermann (Dorabella); Gutheil-Schoder (Despina); Slezak (Ferrando); Demuth (Guglielmo); Hesch (Alfonso).

kronen. In October, a new estimate was prepared with the help of the set-painter, Anton Brioschi, the technical director Richard Bennier, and the costumier, Alexander Blaschke. It was presented to the Intendant on 27 October with a detailed list and the total now amounted to 50,000 kronen: 15,000 of the additional money was to be obtained by lowering the production costs of *Die Entführung* and the remaining 10,000 would require new funds from the 1905 budget. Roller enclosed a letter from Mahler explaining that:

The high costs for the production of *Don Giovanni* are due to that fact that, after much consideration, we have decided to set the opera in the period of the late Renaissance—a period when luxurious display was fashionable—and very few of the costumes we now have in stock are appropriate for that purpose.

If we were forced to, we could make the costumes ourselves with very cheap materials, but this would be at the expense of durability. After a short period of time, to repair or recreate the costumes would necessarily cost twice as much in terms of material and labour.

Another reason [for the increased estimate] is that we are planning to have a new style of staging (the Shakespeare stage). This can be used to fulfil other artistic purposes, and will thus enable us to reduce costs [in the long run].

The Directorate believes that this new 'staging style' may be used for all the classical and older Italian operas [such as those by Donizetti and Bellini], and for new productions. It will therefore be profitable in the future and lead to reductions in expenditure and preparation time. Therefore, with this first attempt, no expense should be spared to make this renewal of the staging style acceptable to the public.[18]

Permission for the extra funding came from the Obersthofmeister at the beginning of November, but the sum requested for the costumes of the second cast was not granted. Moreover, the production of *Die Entführung* was postponed until the following year.[19]

Feverish agitation and conflict marked the months preceding the opening night of *Don Giovanni*, scheduled for 21 December. After Reichmann's departure and subsequent death, Leopold Demuth had taken over the principal role of *Don Giovanni*. His splendid voice and impeccable technique had won him public acclaim. Mahler was not persuaded, however, and continued to criticize his lack of temperament and stage presence. Furthermore, in Friedrich Weidemann, the chosen interpreter of his most expressive Lieder, Mahler had discovered an excellent baritone and an artist after his own heart. While Weidemann was most at ease in dramatic rather than comic roles, Mahler hoped that with practice and his assistance he would gradually acquire the

---

[18]   Letter from Mahler to the General Intendant HHstA G.Z. 14030/Oper X-35 ex 1905. See Evan Baker, 'Alfred Roller's production of Mozart's "Don Giovanni": A break in the scenic traditions of the Vienna Court Opera', Dissertation, New York University, 1993. In fact the towers were used for the second and last time in *Die Entführung* in January.

[19]   Minute dated 30 Oct., HHStA OMEA 19/C/5 ex 1905 and G.I. 4030–I ex 1905, dated 5 November. After a second appeal from Mahler the additional funds for the costumes were granted in November, but were attributed to the 1906 production budget.

charm, seductiveness, and exuberant vitality that the role required. And thus the Vienna Opera would have two Don Giovannis instead of one.

Demuth already suspected that Mahler was inclined to favour his young rival. Nevertheless, he considered that he had a legitimate claim to the role and expected to sing in the new production, at least on the opening night. On 12 October, while reading the *Neue Freie Presse*, he learned that Weidemann was to have that honour. That evening he wrote to Mahler, asking him 'not to force (him) to learn the new version'. Mahler replied that no decision had been reached, and wondered 'why Demuth imagined that the part belonged to him alone', since no such exclusive rights existed at the Hofoper. As Director, he would consider it unacceptable if Demuth 'refused to sing the role after Weidemann'. Demuth gave in and participated in all the rehearsals. However, he remained convinced that Mahler would give him the role despite the fact that the name of his rival had already been announced for the première.

To spare Demuth's feelings, Mahler arranged to have him sing on the evening of the dress rehearsal, when all the critics were in attendance. For the first time in the history of the Hofoper, this took place five days before the opening night, because Mahler was leaving Vienna to conduct in Breslau. There, between two rehearsals of the Fifth Symphony, he learned that Demuth had announced his intention of leaving the Hofoper if he did not sing in the première.[20] Mahler immediately telegraphed Wondra, proposing to postpone the opening night until the next public holiday and to hold a second dress rehearsal at which Weidemann would sing the title role, thus eliminating Demuth's cause for complaint. He also reminded Demuth of a recent letter in which he agreed to sing the role at the dress rehearsal. Mahler claimed that by entrusting the dress rehearsal and the opening night for the first time to two different artists, he had satisfied Demuth's request.

Like many singers before him, Demuth tried unsuccessfully to push Mahler into a corner. On 21 December, the day of the first performance, he finally realized that the Director was not going to change his mind, and sent him a letter of resignation in which he complained of the 'deep and painful wound' that had been inflicted upon him during rehearsals. Mahler replied that he had 'never dreamed of hurting [him]', and repeated that he 'never granted any singer, however excellent, exclusive rights over all the roles suited to his voice'. He reminded Demuth that when he had been Reichmann's young and dangerous rival some years ago, Mahler had given him 'all the attention and encouragement he merited'. Was it not natural that he should now behave in the same way with Weidemann? He added that Demuth's voice and personality struck him as better suited to heroic (*Heldenpartien*) than to comic parts (*Spielpartien*)—though that, of course, had not prevented him from obtaining as great a success as Reichmann in *Don Giovanni*. Perhaps Weidemann would

[20] Demuth's statement appeared in the *Neue Freie Presse* on the 19 Dec., when Mahler was already in Breslau.

come to equal him. At any rate, the selection of Weidemann for the première was in no way a personal attack.

Four days later, on Christmas Day, Demuth wrote another letter in which he once again complained of the 'insult' he had suffered. While admitting that he was not an ideal Don Giovanni, he 'at least deserved to be treated with respect by the Director, since [he] had sung the role for seven years'. Yet Mahler 'had never once complimented [him], except after Falstaff'.[21] No other singer had ever been so maltreated in full view of the public and the press, and none had ever been hurt so often by the Director's indifference during rehearsals. For, while Mahler personally supervised certain singers in rehearsal day after day and week after week, he had never imparted his wisdom to Demuth. And so Demuth again pleaded with him to accept his resignation, for 'it was impossible to continue to work at the Vienna Opera, where [he] did not feel appreciated either artistically or morally'.[22]

Demuth's splendid voice, so deeply admired by Viennese lovers of bel canto, was obviously indispensable to Mahler. But Mahler never felt the same human or artistic affinity for him as for Mildenburg, Gutheil-Schoder, or Weidemann. One of the articles published at the time of his death by the *Illustrirtes Wiener Extrablatt* even claims that when Demuth asked him what he thought of his interpretation of Wotan, he replied: 'Once a clerk, always a clerk.' It is highly unlikely that Mahler ever insulted his first baritone thus, but the anecdote is nonetheless revealing, for it is known that in private Mahler often referred to Demuth's former profession.[23]

The staging rehearsals with the first cast began on 29 November on the stage.[24] As usual for the new productions, Mahler personally directed the staging. Evan Baker, the author of an important dissertation on the Mahler–Roller *Don Giovanni*, has compiled a staggering amount of information about the new production. It seems that seven piano rehearsals, four orchestral/stage rehearsals, and one technical rehearsal were held before the final dress rehearsal, which took place on 16 December, just before Mahler left for Breslau to conduct his Fifth Symphony. On the morning of the première, on 21 December, he held a quick run-through with the orchestra, soloists, and chorus at noon.[25]

---

[21] Demuth added that 'Weidemann had recently been favoured more at his expense than [he] had been at Reichmann's', for upon his arrival at the Hofoper Weidemann had been given roles which Demuth had obtained only after several years. Armed with a host of examples, he also challenged the distinction Mahler had made between 'comic' and 'heroic' roles.

[22] HOA, Z. 1379, 1415, and 1124/1905. Demuth's contract was due to expire in 1907. He accused Mahler of 'not replying' when he had spoken of renewing it. According to Karpath and Korngold, the hisses heard on the night of the revival of *Don Giovanni* came from Demuth's admirers.

[23] This story was related in several articles published at the time of Mahler's death (see Mahler's letters to Alma during the rehearsals for the first performance of the Fifth in Cologne, BGA, nos. 107 ff.).

[24] See Baker, 'Roller', 134. Mahler was conducting his Fifth Symphony in Trieste and therefore not present for several of the first rehearsals of *Don Giovanni*, leaving Roller to supervise the Hofoper's stage-director, August Stoll. Mahler returned to Vienna on 3 Dec. and took command again. On 9 Dec., Roller travelled to Dresden to attend the première of Richard Strauss's *Salome* (Baker, 'Roller', 140).

[25] Ibid. 140.

With *Tristan*, *Fidelio*, and *Rheingold*, Roller had met the challenge of great opera in the heroic style with sets which were both 'symbolic' and 'dramatic'. This time, *Don Giovanni* gave him the opportunity to tackle Italian opera, the heir to the *commedia dell'arte*, a genre whose inherent historical and stylized conventions must be both respected and renewed by every new generation. In *Don Giovanni* the basic problem was a practical one: the necessity for rapid set changes. Considering the revolving stage of *Così fan tutte* to be incompatible with the monumental scenery required for *Don Giovanni*, Roller turned to a device borrowed from antiquity by the Elizabethans. A 'Shakespeare stage' had been used in Germany as early as 1831 in Düsseldorf by one Karl L. Immermann, who used a single unit set with no ornamentation and indicated locales by simply painted drops.[26] In 1889, Karl von Perfall, Intendant of the Munich Court Theatre, together with his stage director, Jocsa Savits, and technical director, Karl Lautenshläger, presented Shakespeare's *King Lear* on a *Reformbühne* in which the 'emphasis was placed on a fixed and simple architectural frame', while a 'simply painted backdrop "indicated" (*deuten*) the locale'. Thus, 'rapid and open changes of scenery were effected without breaking the continuity of the action, and production costs kept low'.[27] In the Munich *Reformbühne*, the variable dimensions of the stage had been determined by curtains of a neutral colour within a fixed rectangle defined by two stylized 'towers'. But whereas in Munich the towers had no dramatic function, in Roller's set for *Don Giovanni* they were transformed by the lighting and played different roles in each scene. Changes of scenery took place in record time, and lasted twenty to thirty seconds at the most. As Ludwig Hevesi wrote in the *Fremden-Blatt*: 'the whole thing is too practical not to be welcome'.

Later on Roller explained his aims in reviving a late Renaissance theatrical tradition:

The most remarkable element in the structure of this kind of theatre was the 'Proscenium'. Situated behind the main curtain, it is part of the stage; framed by the boxes overlooking the stage, it is also part of the auditorium and thus creates an architectural link between the two. It is reserved for the solo actor, while the back of the stage is for the sets, entries, dances and crowd scenes. In a refreshingly naive manner what is *heard* is placed in front of what is *seen*. The 'orchestra' [in the Greek sense of the word] is situated *behind* the proscenium.

The Romantics lost the feeling for this arrangement. They did away with the proscenium, transplanting the actor from his ideal space, where anything or nothing may be represented, into the scenery itself. The clash between the actor, with his three-dimensional body, and the make-believe world of the scenery, creates relationships which are grotesque and often tasteless to the point of absurdity.[28]

[26] Baker, 'Roller', 135   [27] Ibid.
[28] Alfred Roller, 'Bühne und Bühnenhandwerk', *Thespis Theaterbuch* (1930), 137, quoted in Liselotte Kitzwegerer, 'Alfred Roller als Bühnenbildner', (Ph.D. Diss., Vienna, 1959), 66.

At the time, Roller's epoch-making idea of the grey towers for *Don Giovanni*[29] seemed so extraordinary that Mahler hesitated for a long time before giving his consent, and did so only after Roller had explained their significance and usefulness.[30] This last factor was of overriding importance, as the painter Koloman Moser, who participated in many conversations with Mahler and Roller about this production, recounted in his diary:

Swift changes of scenery! That indeed is the crux of the matter, although the critics all missed the point. Roller told me that, when Mahler was planning to add Mozart to the repertoire, he had found an excellent solution to his demand for a stage which would do justice to the music of these works.

With the exception of *The Magic Flute*, he intended to perform all of Mozart's stage works in this way. This is the reason for the 'towers' and the simple background. Only at the end of *Don Giovanni*, when the music, as Mahler so beautifully explained, becomes highly dramatic, is the full extent of the stage utilized. . . . In short, it must be said that Mahler and Roller derived the conception of the set from the work itself; there was no other reason.[31]

At first, Mahler feared that the new sets would be too elaborate and distracting for the audience. To convince him, Roller reminded him of Renaissance theatre, giving as an example Palladio's 'Teatro Olimpico'.[32] His 'towers' consisted of two pairs of tall square buttresses[33] covered with a neutral grey fabric. Their principal function was to define the scenic space. The towers were movable from the centre of the stage, either up or down stage.[34] A set of grey legdrops hung in front of the downstage towers and acted as an adjustable second proscenium. They were intended to mask the off-stage side of the towers and occasionally the downstage windows. The back of the stage was a simple painted canvas whose flatness Roller made little effort to disguise by exaggerated effects of perspective. The characters stood out in sharp relief against this backdrop,[35] never merging into it. The stage's flooring was a sort of chequerboard pattern of the kind favoured by the Secession, of the same neutral greyish colour as the towers. Different lighting effects transformed it into street pavement, parquet flooring, or even flagstones (in the cemetery scene).[36]

---

[29] He eventually adapted the same idea for the spoken theatre in his celebrated stagings of Shakespeare at the Burgtheater.   [30] BMG 125.

[31] The manuscript of Koloman Moser's diary is in the Vienna Stadtbibliothek.

[32] Ludwig Karpath, *Bühne und Welt*, 8 (1906), 793.

[33] It seems that Roller originally intended to have three pairs of towers, the first, downstage, pair framing the stage curtain. But the final designs drawn by him include ground plans which clearly indicate two pairs.

[34] Evan Baker gives the measurements of the towers: 2.50 m. wide and 1.80 m. deep. He estimates their height at 9 m.

[35] Christof Bitter, in *Wandlungen in den Inszenierungsformen des Don Giovanni, 1787–1928* (Bosse, Regensburg, 1961), 124, compares this set to the *Reliefbühne* of the Munich Künstlertheater. He thought the painter was trying to create a scenic space in the antique style, focusing all the interest of the audience on the characters.

[36] Ludwig Hevesi, *Altkunst, Neukunst, Wien 1894–1908* (Konegen, Vienna, 1908), 261.

The towers could present blank walls of masonry, be masked by hangings or tapestries, or show windows opening out of first-floor rooms or balconies required by the action. In the serenade scene, for example, Elvira's window was located on the first floor of one of the towers.[37] In the preceding act, Don Giovanni and Leporello invited the masqueraders to the ball from the opposite tower window. When the windows were not in use, they were covered by hangings or tapestries. The towers themselves could be either visible or concealed by curtains. Turned to one side, they could become entrances to houses or passageways to the street. They also contained staircases and platforms which were invisible when not required by the action. The successive backdrops showed Don Giovanni's park, his palace, the farm, the tavern, the ballroom, and the cemetery.

The first set depicted a terrace in front of the Commendatore's palace, the presence of which was suggested by the two stage-right towers. Between them, the last steps of a staircase were brightly illuminated, with a long ray of light on the chequered floor, while on the right the other two towers were plunged in darkness. In the background, a practical cut-out balustrade decorated with five evenly spaced potted, bright-red rose bushes[38] overlooked a flower garden, which also remained in darkness. The jagged outline of lofty cypresses[39] stood out threateningly against a turquoise blue velvet sky[40] in which the Great Bear could be perceived. The entire dramatic effect arose from the contrast between the illuminated staircase, the red bushes in the shadows on both sides and in the background, the nocturnal garden which seemed to stretch out to infinity under the immense sky and the lofty cypresses, whose blackness brought out the colour of the bushes. Except for the flowers and the bright red azaleas, which symbolized the 'sensuality of the seducer', all the colours were neutral.

For the second tableau, a 'country road with an inn and Don Giovanni's palace in the distance', chairs with high backs (*Sprossenlehnen*), and an open door surrounded by a tunnel of vines (Masetto's hiding place) were placed between the two towers on stage-right.[41] A large tree with dense foliage rose above the low 'plaster and tile' wall marking the back of the set, and behind it a brightly painted drop depicting a woodland scene with cypresses in the distance. The entire set was in strong tones of blue and green, brightly lit by the midday sun.

---

[37] Each tower had two interior platforms, the highest 2 m. from the floor, and windows 3 m. high, and about 1.50 m. by 1 m. on the downstage and on-stage sides. Grey curtains 'opened and closed' the windows on the inside and additional curtains could mask the outside of the tower (Baker, 'Roller', 146).

[38] Other potted red rose-bushes were placed around the front pair of towers.

[39] They were made of black velvet glued on to the drop.

[40] Hevesi emphasized the 'stifling', 'voluptuous', and 'velvety' effect Roller obtained with this black sky and the total obscurity created by the black backdrops which appeared grey under the lights. The 'star' drop, borrowed from the earlier production of *Tristan*, was a canvas drop with numerous holes cut through. Lighting instruments were set behind the drop to create the stars (Baker, 'Roller', 148).

[41] According to the ground plan, it was relocated during the rehearsals to the opposite end of the stage (Baker, 'Roller', 151).

For the champagne aria and the preceding recitative (Scene iii) Roller created a backdrop which was hung between the upstage and downstage towers. Don Giovanni's garden, this time full of flowers, with a labyrinth of box-trees clipped in the French manner, green hedges, all vividly illuminated by the hot late afternoon sun. The stage was shallow, framed by only one tower on each side, high cypresses (again in black velvet) and a bright blue sky. On the backdrop, the resplendent white Renaissance-style palace was inspired by the Villa d'Este in Tivoli, to which Roller added a large arcaded loggia. On both sides two huge reddish oleander bushes reached up to the rectangular windows of the towers. In this scene, Roller sought to suggest the natural environment of a libertine: 'with an orgy of immodest colours', . . . 'a powerful triad of blue, green and yellow',[42] he wanted to evoke a guilty eroticism, heavy and stifling. Here again, the scarlet of the oleanders anticipated the use of the same colour in the two Finales.

The following tableau (Scene iv) showed another corner of Don Giovanni's garden at nightfall, with a fountain in the centre, surrounded by trees, the towers were covered with dark violet. While the windows on stage-left were in total darkness, those on stage-right were brightly lit. The hero and his valet appeared at one of them to welcome the guests and invite the three masqueraders to the ball. Once again, 'in the foreground, two luxuriant bushes shone brightly with fiery red flowers. Red, the colour of blood and love, was also the colour of the great erotic hero'.[43] The colours were somewhat softened by the darkness and took on unusual tones under a greenish yellow late afternoon sky, against which big beech trees stood up. Clipped box-tree hedges provided enough hiding-places for the staging of the argument between Zerlina and Masetto. They bordered a pond, and a staircase on stage-right, between the two towers, led to Don Giovanni's abode.

The full depth of the stage was seen only at the end of the act, in Scene v, the Ball Scene. A spacious red hall, brightly lit, was divided rear-stage centre by an extra tower, used here for the first and only time. In front of it stood the main musicians' platform. The whole stage was dominated by an enormous chandelier.[44] The sumptuous and yet severe style of the late Renaissance inspired the sobriety and the symmetry of the principal lines.[45] Staircases on both sides led to the tower windows, which had become loges lined with red brocade for the spectators. The musicians of the three orchestras, in scarlet livery, were grouped on platforms carpeted in red velvet, each of which provided a distinct space for

---

[42] Ludwig Hevesi, *Altkunst*, 262.   [43] KIW 106.

[44] Although this was obviously the most intricate of all the sets and the hardest to prepare, it seems that it did not take more time than the others to install. The platforms were more than likely already prepared backstage (Baker, 'Roller', 155 ff.).

[45] Christof Bitter (*Wandlungen*, 110) notes that Brioschi's former sets were consistently monumental in style, alternating between the pseudo-oriental lavishness of Don Giovanni's palace, with its flower motifs and nude caryatids rather obviously referring to his sensuality, and the neo-Gothic ambience of Donna Anna and her father, the Commendatore. Thus the opera had become an 'ideological drama' of Wagnerian inspiration, in which spirit (and faith) did battle with matter and the senses (as in *Tannhäuser*).

the different dance episodes. Three sets of garlands of foliage adorned with red ribbons and hung from the ceiling spanned the entire width of the playing space. The hangings, the rugs, the red livery, and the ruffs of the musicians and the lackeys all shone under the blazing light of the chandelier and ten gigantic candelabra. The backdrop, two Gobelin tapestries in pastel shades of grey, over the side-platforms, served as a foil, intensifying the effect of the whole.[46] In this set, Roller's admirers perceived an amplification of the themes of the music through light and colour. The conclusion of the act was one of the scenes most often rehearsed by Mahler.[47]

The *Fremden-Blatt* published an interesting report of a rehearsal of the end of Act I:

Throughout the scene, the chorus, dancers, stage orchestras, and supernumeraries populated the entire acting space upstage of the front towers. The soloists occupied the space between and downstage of the front towers. At the moment when the Trio of the Masks revealed themselves, the position of the soloists would be as follows:

Zerlina/Masetto/Leporello/Don Giovanni/Ottavio/Donna Anna/Donna Elvira

After the storm sequence of thunder and lightning, Don Giovanni attempted to flee, but 'the weak kneed' Ottavio 'boldly raised his sword,' and tried to hold him back. But Don Giovanni 'struck the sword from his hand'. Mahler, at this point, so that 'the remaining soloists do not appear to stand around like supernumeraries with nothing to do,' attempted to give them each a specific action for the remaining eight bars of music. Masetto and Leporello exchanged blows as Zerlina comes to Masetto's assistance. As Don Giovanni and Ottavio fight their duel, Donna Anna 'should look on horrified, and—so suggested Roller—sink in a faint into the arms of Donna Elvira (so that she too will have something to do). Anna von Mildenburg, the Donna Anna, would have nothing to do with this particular staging. Mildenburg protested that 'Donna Anna is a valiant and great character! She can calmly watch Ottavio's blood run, and she needs no smelling salts!' Mahler, after some consideration, sided with her point of view.[48]

In the second act, the street in front of Elvira's house resembled the first set. The dominant colour was the same dark violet. In the background, tall cypresses again towered above a thick wall, and a large building loomed in the background towards stage-left.[49] Elvira's room was no doubt in the stage-left tower, with a floor lamp illuminating the inside, and a ray of light streaming out of her window. Another floor-light, backstage, lit up the staircase to Elvira's dwelling, between the two towers. Mahler used the harpsichord's lute stop to accompany the Serenade.

---

[46] Evan Baker gives the measurement of the central tower, placed between the two platforms, with a large window in the middle overlooking the stage, 3 m. wide by 1.60 m. deep. The side platforms were 5.80 m. deep by 5.50 m. wide. The central platform which was occupied by the main stage orchestra, was 3.30 m. wide, 1.50 m. deep, and 83 cm. high (Baker, 'Roller', 156).   [47] Ibid. 157.

[48] *Fremden-Blatt*, 24 Dec. 1905, quoted by Baker, 'Roller', 159 ff.

[49] Evan Baker describes the drop which depicted 'a large villa encompassed by cypresses and bushes', but adds that, for lack of time and money, it was not painted at the time of the première, and thus not incorporated into the setting before 1907. Thus the Act I, Scene i backdrop was used again for this scene in 1905–6.

Unlike the preceding scene, which was dominated by vertical lines, the set for the sextet (no. 19 in the score) was based on a horizontal axis, with a low drop coming down to just above the tower windows. Instead of a room in the palace, which Leporello would have had difficulty in reaching, the 'atrio terreno in casa di Donna Anna' specified by da Ponte was now a courtyard.

In the dusk a huge, dark, square gateway. A rectangle within a rectangle, the one darker than the other. No accessories, no articulation, geometry pure and simple. Then a casement opens, a dazzling beam of light shines down onto the middle of the stage, and the torch bearers penetrate the gloom from the right and the left. Mahler's insistence that the orchestra lights be dimmed is easy to understand, although it caused considerable difficulty. Bright lights on the music stands would have destroyed the Rembrandtian chiaroscuro.[50]

Only the front stage towers were visible. A flight of stairs led to the Commendatore's palace, behind the stage-right tower. Grey and dark brown hangings covered the back wall around the studded door, accentuating the atmosphere of solitude and sadness characteristic of the Commendatore's abode. When the back door was opened, the stream of blue light which spilled across the stage floor created a 'tremendous' effect according to several critics.[51]

Mahler inserted 'Mi tradi' (no. 21b), Elvira's great aria composed by Mozart for the Vienna production, in its original place, just before the cemetery scene.[52] Roller's setting was a simple brown drop,[53] upstage of the front towers, with opened suitcases and scattered clothes in monotonous shades of brown and fawn and one or two touches of brighter colour. Elvira has come to confront her seducer, cursing him and pondering her fate in the light of a little lantern on the ground.

Act II, Scene iii: The cemetery (no. 22). This was no doubt the most famous of all Roller's designs during his collaboration with Mahler. The day after the première, Julius Korngold proclaimed the cemetery scene to be his 'masterpiece'. So powerful was the atmosphere of this scene, in fact, that the spectator imagined 'coffins and corpses where nothing was to be seen at all'. Cold bright moonlight shimmering between the towers on stage-right bathed the whole scene in greyish blue light and emphasized the ghostly whiteness of the statue and the black and white flagstones on the ground. 'One is, as it were, at the end of the world, and face to face with infinity', wrote Richard Specht.[54] The great marble horseman, presented in profile on an ornate baroque

---

[50] Ludwig Hevesi, *Fremden-Blatt* article reprinted in *Altkunst*, 263.

[51] Baker, 'Roller', 162.

[52] Mahler had originally wanted to move this aria to Act I, after the catalogue aria, but he finally restored it to its original place, where it was very useful because Roller's set for the cemetery took longer to install than planned.

[53] The drop was originally intended for a ballet, *Fanny Elsler*, but had been recycled (Baker, 'Don Giovanni', 162, n. 80).

[54] Richard Specht, 'Wiener Mozartspiele', *Die Schaubühne* (1906), 185.

pedestal, occupied the centre of the stage.[55] Sitting astride a large Andalusian horse, with armour and helmet, he held a field-marshal's baton. Behind the monument there were two memorial tablets on a low wall. The looming silhouettes of four large cypresses (again black velvet cutouts) made it almost impossible to see the starry sky (of deep blue velvet), and gave a hint of the punishment that lay ahead. To the right and left, in front of the front towers, one caught a glimpse of two monumental recumbent effigies, while the remaining towers were covered with two tall funerary bas-reliefs. They later awakened Korngold's admiration: 'A few sarcophagi . . . were illuminated by pale moonlight. The dead were literally coming closer and closer to the viewer . . . [It is as if] we could touch the stone sepulchers, and it gives us the creeps.'[56] As in *Tristan*, the darkness had a symbolic value. Up to this point, the sets for the hero were brightly coloured and well lit: Mahler insisted that as soon as the curtains opened on the cemetery the spectator should realize that 'everything was going badly for him'. Mahler and Roller fought hard to reduce the spill from the bright lamps on the music stands and even considered extinguishing for this scene the exit lights in the auditorium, but had to abandon the idea.[57] Hevesi approved of their efforts to preserve 'the Rembrandt-like play of shadow and light'.[58]

The same funereal darkness dominated the following scene (no. 23) in the high, narrow antechamber where the Commendatore's body had lain and where Donna Anna came every day to meditate in front of his portrait. Roller used only the downstage towers, with their curtains closed. Hung with heavy draperies and thick black curtains, the room had two square Renaissance-style monumental doors. In the middle, the great life-size portrait of the Commendatore was hung over a black velvet drop and faintly illuminated by the flickering light of six tall chandeliers. The upper part of the drop represented the upper portion of the wall and ceiling in forced perspective. A prie-dieu occupied the centre of the room, and the only ornament was a large golden silk panel with a floral pattern at the back above the doors. Bluish light streamed in onto the floor from one of the tower windows.

As in the case of the Finale of the first act, the final scene took place in a vast baroque hall dominated by the same scarlet, which imparted to the music its poetic significance by symbolizing 'the wild, unbridled passions' of the hero.[59] In the background, three red-carpeted steps led to an imposing studded door covered with gilt and framed by two huge Gobelin tapestries in faded shadings of grey, red, and green. This upstage space was framed by the two towers with their windows closed by curtains. Two tables with white tablecloths

[55]   In order to impart a supernatural quality to the statue in the final scene, Roller had the idea of making a suit of armour of white felt soaked in a phosphorescent substance, (Hevesi, *Altkunst*, 272). The same substance, used as make-up for the singer, added to the air of unreality.

[56]   Julius Korngold, *Neue Freie Presse* (22 Dec. 1905).   [57]   Baker, 'Roller', 166.

[58]   Ludwig Hevesi, *Altkunst*, 263.

[59]   Marie Gutheil-Schoder, 'Mahler bei der Arbeit', *Der Merker* 3 (1912): 5, 165.

embroidered with gold and silvergilt dishes were placed in front of the towers, two others, seen laterally, were at stage-right and left, on platforms of red velvet and surrounded by red-cushioned chairs.[60] Four candlestands from the First Act Finale were also used. Though shallow, the set exuded wealth and voluptuousness. Under the tapestries, a frieze painted by Roller himself portrayed Eros in the middle of nude nymphs dancing and bearing garlands of flowers,[61] while the side panels were covered with purple rugs.

Roller did away with the scantily-clad women and superficial commotion of previous productions, and Don Giovanni now faced his fate alone. After giving him one final warning, Elvira rushes to the door in the background, staggers to a halt, turns, and, with a terrible scream, crosses the entire stage and disappears through the other door. In nineteenth-century productions Don Giovanni disappeared through a trapdoor and the whole palace collapsed.[62] Roller decided to simplify the ending, making him disappear behind a black velvet curtain that represented 'infernal night rising up out of the bowels of the earth'. But his plan for the ending did not function: 'After the exit of the Commendatore through the trap, large swaths of black velvet were to rise from the floor, covering not only Don Giovanni, but engulfing the entire stage as well.'[63]

Statements by Alma Mahler, David Joseph Bach, and Ludwig Hevesi, who all attended the general rehearsal of 16 December, explain why Roller's original plan was not carried through, at least not for the first performances. Alma writes that Roller 'had black velvet rolled over the whole stage, to give the impression of the Don being devoured by darkness. It was a good idea, but it did not come off.'[64] Bach adds: 'Hell rose up, that is, a shadowy, black wall that awakens all the fears of the underworld. But it rises far too slowly, too evenly to sustain the interest.'[65] Hevesi also noted that the black velvet curtains expected to appear from everyhere had been dropped and that instead 'the usual fires from hell appeared and consumed the sinner'.[66] Like Mozart himself in the Vienna production, Mahler left out the final Sextet. The Romantics had already considered it an unworthy ending to this 'tragedy of vanity and desire'.[67]

In many other respects, however, Mahler had gone back to Mozart's original

[60] Baker, 'Roller', 68 ff.

[61] Roller painted this portion of the drop himself after the conclusion of the stage rehearsals (see letter of Roller to Anna von Mildenburg of 5 Dec. 1905, quoted by Evan Baker, 'Roller', 169).

[62] See above, Vol. ii, Chap. 3.

[63] Baker, 'Roller', 171.

[64] AMM1, 117; AMM2, 117.

[65] *Arbeiter Zeitung*, 30 Dec. 1905, quoted by Evan Baker, 'Roller', 171.

[66] Ludwig Hevesi, quoted by Evan Baker, 'Roller', 171. The production of steam for stage effects had been found problematic at the Hofoper and Richard Bennier had recommended the purchase of a 'mechanical device for producing clouds of fog by chemical means'. The purchase was proposed and approved in the final budget for 1905 (ibid. 172–3).

[67] However several recent productions of *Don Giovanni* had included it, notably that of Ernst von Possart in Munich (cf. Bitter, *Wandlungen*, 118).

score. In the ballroom scene, the song 'Viva la libertà' had formerly been transformed into a sort of revolutionary hymn sung by the entire chorus, although
Mozart had written it for seven soloists. During Donna Anna's second aria (no.
23), 'Non mi dir', Don Ottavio no longer appeared on stage and Donna Anna
voiced her feelings while writing a letter (hence the title 'Letter Aria' in
German-speaking countries), probably to obviate the need for a new set at this
juncture. Mahler restored the recitative dialogue between Donna Anna and
Ottavio just before her great solo, and inserted afterwards the aria 'Il mio
Tesoro' (which, in Mozart's original, concludes the *Atrio terreno* scene and
follows the Sextet). Then came Elvira's great aria, 'Mi tradì' (it had previously
followed the Catalogue aria, no. 4 in the first act),[68] which now preceded the
Finale.

In contrast with the relative simplicity of the sets, Roller's costumes were
sumptuously decorative and designed to have dramatic and symbolic significance. During the first act, the hero wore a ruff, a black silk doublet with
slashed sleeves revealing a beige silk lining, and a plumed black felt hat (as
specified in the libretto)—all worthy of a 'womanizer on the warpath'.[69] For the
champagne aria and the subsequent merry-making, he sported a spangled
costume of golden brocade lined with yellow silk, a light beige velvet cloak
embroidered with pearls arranged in the shape of flames, and a felt hat
crowned with an enormous ostrich feather. For the last act, Roller was inspired
by a famous portrait of Sir Walter Raleigh, and Don Giovanni's white costume
was splendidly embroidered with a motif of urns filled with acanthus leaves.

As for Leporello, he wore the same costume throughout the opera: a white
waistcoat with red slashed sleeves, a white felt hat and a many-coloured cloak
in the Neapolitan style. After the pink *déshabillé* of the first scene, Donna
Anna changed into a dress of sumptuous red brocade for the ball. It had a white
collar and was embroidered with floral motifs reminiscent of the era of
Mazarin. Elvira's attire was more modest: a grey and white dress with a transparent collar. Don Ottavio wore a magnificent gold-embroidered Spanish
nobleman's costume, a felt hat and a dark grey cloak. Zerlina's Andalusian
peasant costume and bonnet were adorned with flowers; she wore a white
apron, and wide orange-yellow sleeves.[70]

Like Roller's sets and costumes, Mahler's mise-en-scène relied upon stylization and symbolism rather than realism. During the ballroom scene, when
Don Giovanni ran back onto the stage with Zerlina to accuse Leporello, all the
guests stepped back in order to focus attention on the protagonists and the
music. The masks were no more than stylized suggestions. In the second act,

---

[68] In Mozart's Vienna version, Elvira's E flat aria followed the Leporello–Zerlina duet (no. 21a) and
Leporello's aria, 'Ah, pietà, signori miei!' (no. 20). Mahler restored Leporello's aria, but cut the duet. See
Robert Werba, 'Mahlers Mozart Bild am Beispiel des Don Giovanni', *Wiener Figaro, Mozartgemeinde Wien*,
42 (1975), 10.

[69] Ludwig Hevesi, *Altkunst*, 264.

[70] The sketches of the sets and costumes are in ÖTM.

the *Atrio terreno* provided no hiding place for Elvira and Leporello. Thus they would probably have been discovered very quickly by Anna and Ottavio. However, as we have already noticed, Mahler attached no importance to this. He thought it only natural that the spectator should be aware of events which the actors were supposed to ignore.

He also departed from tradition with regard to the characters themselves. His idea of Donna Anna, 'mourning, vengeance, honour, hope, and sensual love',[71] was inspired by Hoffmann, whose famous story depicted her secretly in love with the conquering, suborning scoundrel; a woman whose revengeful fury would quickly subside if Don Giovanni, twice a murderer, prevailed over pallid Ottavio. Mildenburg masterfully conveyed all the nuances of the character and her secret conflict. Her acting expressed both tragic duty and repressed desire, though her singing, especially her vocalizing and legato, left much to be desired, particularly in the second aria. To make things easier for her, Mahler agreed to transpose both arias down a tone.[72] While acknowledging that she was not in fact suited to Mozart, Ludwig Speidel wrote after her first Viennese appearance in the role in 1898:

She is effective, for example, in the recitative of the 'revenge' aria (*Or sai che l'onore*), even if she occasionally sings with more violence than passion . . . It is noteworthy that she understands the art of listening to music at least as much as the art of making it. While Herr Naval sang Don Ottavio's first aria . . . she stood before him and listened . . . listened to him with such acute understanding that one was entranced by the richness and subtle delicacy of her acting.[73]

But in Mahler's eyes Elvira, the opera's principal female role, was also 'most noble'. 'Her hatred arose from too great a love',[74] and thus she 'ought not to be portrayed as pitiable and laughable'. For this production, her name immediately followed that of Don Giovanni on the programme, and instead of the traditional tearful, tragicomic character whose ridiculousness almost justified Don Giovanni's betrayal, Gutheil-Schoder incarnated, in Specht's words, 'the first true Elvira', a woman 'profoundly troubled, terribly hurt, full of murderous pride, wounded dignity, and repressed desire'.[75] She represents noble sorrow and love betrayed, passion and dignity, renunciation and sacrifice—in a word, she is 'all of womanhood betrayed'. 'Here at last we have a woman with whom we suffer, and for whom we have sympathy because we understand her', wrote David Josef Bach in the *Arbeiter-Zeitung*. Contemporary witnesses were unanimous with regard to Gutheil-Schoder's prodigious ability to identify convincingly with the most disparate characters. Until she took on the role, the forsaken Elvira had always been abandoned by the audience as much as by

[71] PSG 69. [72] Robert Werba, *Wiener Figaro* (Dec. 1979), 5.

[73] *Fremden-Blatt* (5 Nov. 1898).

[74] In an article, 'Mahlers Opernregie' (BSP 35), Marie Gutheil-Schoder recalled that Mahler came to this novel conception of the character only during rehearsals of the new production. It was also at that stage that he decided to give an important place to Elvira. [75] RSM2, 107 ff.

Don Giovanni, standing as she did between the passion of Donna Anna and the coquetry of Zerlina. 'Gutheil-Schoder restored to the anguish of abandonment its proper nobility. This role alone assures her a leading place on the German stage. . . . The noble sorrow of her face immediately captures imagination.'[76]

As we have already seen, Weidemann's portrayal of the title role was never one of the glories of the Hofoper. It was not without elegance and charm, but it lacked the exuberant vitality, the smiling cynicism, and the diabolical seductiveness of the 'burlador'. Rather, Weidemann's Don Giovanni was a romantic lover and a somewhat tearful tragic figure. His musicality and the beauty of his voice (which Korngold judged a little too light for the work, especially in the final scene) nonetheless compelled admiration, and he was in his element in this production, which emphasized the tragic aspect. Yet in the following year Richard Specht wrote that his interpretation remained 'incomplete', still lacking the 'satanic domination' required by the role, and added: 'It is questionable whether this role is suited to his temperament, indeed, whether it is at all possible for him to express the many disparate sides of this character, human, superhuman, and subhuman.'[77]

As Leporello, Mayr was supposed to symbolize 'the silent, malignant revolt of the fourth estate' (the proletariat) instead of the traditional cowardly, caddish valet.[78] Johannes Sembach played Ottavio: although not yet 25 years old, his voice was already much too full. His striking virility was not exactly what the role required. Grete Forst as Zerlina probably possessed the prettiest and most accomplished voice in the cast, but she was criticized for a certain dryness and a lack of charm that was out of keeping with this skittish character.

There are several accounts of the musical interpretation. Perhaps the most interesting one is by the French critic Eugène d'Harcourt:

Mahler, who . . . conducted, had just restaged the opera. One of the novelties. . . is the use in the recitatives of a harpsichord, . . . with a delicious sonority. This harpsichord was placed in front of Mahler, who played it with great charm, and almost always accompanied by a solo cello and a double bass. Mahler moved from harpsichord to baton with great dexterity and it was absolutely impossible to discern the slightest break between the instrument and the orchestra. The latter's precision and subtlety were marvellous from start to finish. . . . Such a performance gives an impression of utmost vitality and youth. To tell the truth, rarely has a work been put on with such care, perfection, and artistic sensitivity.[79]

---

[76] L. Andro, 'Marie Gutheil-Schoder', *Allgemeine Musik-Zeitung*, Berlin, 37 (1910): 6, 134. L. Andro was the pseudonym of Therese Rie, a Viennese writer who published several books and monographs, as well as translations: *Das entschwundene Ich* (1924), *Die Komödiantin* (1920), *Lilli Lehmann* (1923), *Marie Gutheil-Schoder* (1923), etc.

[77] Richard Specht, 'Friedrich Weidemann', *Die Schaubühne*, Berlin, (1906), 537.

[78] RSM2, 136. When Mayr returned to the role in 1921 under the baton of Richard Strauss, Korngold recalled that in 1905 he had 'lacked humour' and 'agility'. Since then he had come to understand all aspects of the role and now succeeded in bringing Leporello to life on stage.

[79] Eugène d'Harcourt, *Musique actuelle*, 155. Eugène d'Harcourt (1859–1918), a pupil of Massenet and Savard, studied at the Paris Conservatory and in Berlin. Founder of the 'Concerts éclectiques popu-

Erwin Stein also commented upon Mahler's interpretation of *Don Giovanni*:

Mahler was the ideal Mozart performer. He was capable of the exceedingly subtle *rubato* that is implied in Mozart's melodies and does justice to both the high degree of their organisation and the perfect balance of their phrases. Accent and duration of each note resulted from its place within the phrase, beyond the time signature, and in spite of the tempo which nevertheless seemed straight. But his mind was ahead of the tempo. I have never again heard such quiet yet animated *adagios*, or such quick yet deliberate *prestissimos*. There was always time for the music to sound and for the singer to sing. Perhaps I could not then judge each of these details, but later on, when I heard other performances, my memory discovered what I was missing—and finding.[80]

Mahler's conducting of Mozart's operas, and especially of *Don Giovanni*, became a sort of model of Mozart interpretation. The praise it constantly received finally exasperated Richard Strauss, who one day exclaimed: 'Mahler, Mahler, and nothing but Mahler. . . . Everything is continually being compared to Mahler!'[81] Even Franz Schmidt, whose testimony is particularly significant in view of his general hostility to Mahler, recognized his tremendous influence on the interpretation of Mozart in Austria. Schmidt's biographer, Carl Nemeth, wrote:

In matters of interpretation, there was much to be learned from Mahler. Even the new manner of playing Mozart, which was unknown in Vienna before Mahler's era, left an impression, and it spurred on certain musicians to play Mozart sonatas in a similar manner. He introduced many novelties at the Vienna Opera—among them a reduction in tempo and the intensification of *piano* vocal cantilenas. The house on the Ring owes to him its worldwide reputation for Mozart. Schmidt, who had been trained in the style of Liszt on the basis of quite different and indeed opposing principles, completely changed his exuberant keyboard technique and performing style under Mahler's artistic influence. Obviously, this also influenced the way he played the cello.[82]

But these comments were written at a time when the Roller–Mahler productions had become part of musical history. As contemporary events, they shocked, or at least disturbed, most of the Viennese critics, even those who, like Julius Korngold, were well disposed towards Mahler. While recognizing that Roller was not the first to break with realism by relegating pure 'decoration' to the background,[83] he found his compromise solution to be a 'a still tentative experiment. . . . The stage spectacle derives its life, its poetry from the lighting.' 'A torch on the stage creates delights for the eye; a little lantern

laires' and the 'Grands oratorios de l'Église Saint-Eustache', he composed symphonies, quartets, and an opera, and wrote a number of pamphlets. In 1907, the French government awarded him a travel grant for a journey to Germany, Austria, and Italy. Harcourt could have attended either of the 7 Feb., 4 Mar., or 10 May 1906 performances.

[80]   ESM 296 ff.

[81]   Elsa Bienenfeld, 'Mahler, der Dirigent', *Moderne Welt*, Gustav Mahler Heft, 3 (1921–2): 7, 60.

[82]   Carl Nemeth, *Franz Schmidt* (Amalthea, Zurich), 74. On the same page Nemeth remarks that Schmidt disliked Mahler's emotionalism, which he considered to be artificial.

[83]   Korngold referred to Gordon Craig and others.

on the floor, an open door, letting in the gleam of the clear night sky, evokes a magical mood.' Furthermore, the leitmotivs of colour—red for pleasure and sensuality, black for death and mourning—illuminated the drama's meaning and gave it universal significance. 'The world is here presented with a first masterly attempt to solve the problem of combining music and dramatic action.' Stylization overcame certain obscure points in the libretto, especially the Sextet of the second act. At the same time, Korngold found the set of Elvira's room at the inn and the flames and smoke accompanying the death of Don Juan to be 'at odds with the rest of the mise-en-scène'. From a musical point of view, he praised Mahler for 'bringing out all the gold in the treasure casket of the Mozartian orchestra' and inspiring everything, including the recitatives, with naturalness and animation. Korngold regretted only the occasional excessive nuances, especially in the *piano* passages, and claimed that the principal weakness of the production was the cast, especially in the title role.[84] In the final analysis, the production was the 'first original solution' to the musical—dramatic problem of *Don Giovanni*, and thus the music and the drama appeared more indissolubly linked than ever before.

As we shall see, the differences of view among the critics were often startling, yet every Viennese newspaper published extensive reviews of the new production in the days following the première, sometimes on their front page. True to himself, Hirschfeld began his review with a few ironic comments about the change in the title. He then protested against the furious tempo of the overture. He approved 'the return to the original sequence of scenes, which Kalbeck's older version had unnecessarily changed'. However he found much to disapprove of elsewhere:

It was all colour and dynamics, as if we had before us a modern work devoid of ideas. All in all, Director Mahler—a truly brilliant conductor, and the finest interpreter of Mozart we know—has on this occasion unfortunately allowed himself to be misled into turning *Don Giovanni* into a music drama. Outflowing singing was avoided, the arias and ensembles were musically truncated and dramatically heightened by exaggerated mimicry. Everything, even the humour, was systematically sacrificed to the dramatic thrust so that the recitatives seemed only to be pushing their arias ahead of them as if one were ashamed of them.

Hirschfeld then proceeded to attack the cast even more violently than his colleagues. Kalbeck's new translation struck him as 'unsingable and often in bad taste'. Roller's towers may perhaps have facilitated the set changes, but they constituted 'a grey, prosaic presence in the middle of sumptuous scenes' and 'assassinated the Mozartian spirit'.[85] 'The attempted compromise [between

---

[84]   Korngold qualified his criticism by pointing out that the role of Don Giovanni had for a long time been 'spoken rather than sung' in Vienna, and that even celebrated singers such as Beck and Reichmann had had only one great moment, in the Commendatore's scene (see *Neue Freie Presse*, 22 Dec. 1905).

[85]   The last sentence comes from a long attack on Mahler's and Roller's productions published by Hirschfeld in the *Österreichische Rundschau*, 2 (1906): 2, 437 ff.

realism and stylization] could not be carried through; it kept putting us off and posing problems which, irritatingly, were only partly solved.'

Kalbeck refused to pass judgement on a production in which he was so closely involved, and handed his column in the *Neues Wiener Tagblatt* to Karpath, who, of course, lavished praise on the new translation. However, he admitted to being disconcerted by the towers. The scenery represented for him 'an abortive attempt which no doubt would soon be banished [from the stage of the Vienna Opera]'.[86] Karpath's main point was that the 'dazzling splendour' of the sets contradicted the intentions of the *Reformbühne* which had inspired them, and which 'stressed subdued settings and simplicity'. On the other hand, Ludwig Hevesi, the main spokesman for the Secession, wrote a one-and-a-half page essay on the new production in the *Fremden-Blatt*, which was later reproduced in his collection of essays, *Altkunst—Neu Kunst*.[87] He contrasted the *Don Giovanni* production with that of the Schiller cycle then being put on at the Burgtheater, using the old-fashioned painted wings, borders, and flats for settings, reflecting 'the primitive illusion so beloved of the Philistine of the 19th century' and praised the mood created by each one of the new sets. Later on, in the journal *Kunst und Kunsthandwerk*, he attacked Roller's opponents, who preferred 'old conventional form': 'Do they mean the form from 1787, which had its own authentic style?', he wrote. 'They mean the style which they were used to since their youth, that is to say nothing more than the conventional theatrical style of illusory illusion (*illusorische Illusion*), brought to its greatest flowering with the current style of the Schiller cycle.' In Hevesi's opinion, Roller had 'demonstrated the total bankruptcy of older conceptions'. The drama was not, as some had alleged, 'overwhelmed' by the sets, for they had been inspired by the music itself, right down to the smallest detail.[88]

Another habitué of Secession circles, Berta Zuckerkandl, wrote at length in the *Allgemeine Zeitung* mainly to justify Roller's aesthetics of the scenic art, which had met with so much hostility from the public and the press. She of course fully approved of the elimination of the scenic optical illusion in favour of settings intended 'to create mood and atmosphere within the performance space'.[89] However, in December 1905 the unreserved approval of critics such as Hevesi and Berta Zuckerkandl was very much a minority view. In *Die Zeit*, Richard Wallaschek called the mise-en-scène 'a comical experiment', and claimed that it resolved none of the real problems which the staging of *Don Giovanni* involved. He especially criticized Roller's sets for Elvira's aria and the champagne aria, and concluded that the whole effect was 'too stylized, too

---

[86] In fact, of all the décors that Roller designed for Mahler, the sets for *Don Giovanni* survived the longest. Karpath also wrote a long article on the preceding two years of Mahler's Hofoper activities in *Bühne und Welt*, 9 (1906): 793 ff.

[87] *Fremden-Blatt*, 22 Dec. 1905, and *Alt Kunst*, 259 ff.

[88] *Kunst und Kunsthandwerk*, 9 (1906): 2, 132 ff.

[89] *Wiener Allgemeine Zeitung*, 22 Dec. 1905, quoted by Baker, 'Roller', 198 ff.

painterly': only the ballroom,[90] the cemetery, and the final scenes relieved its 'general greyness'. The omission of the final Sextet rendered the opera 'more prosaic', and the reduction of the acting area on the stage produced an effect which was 'more oppressive than intimate'. However, in general he 'admired Roller's unusual artistry' and the economy with which he achieved his poetic effects. Wallaschek criticized the rapidity of several of Mahler's tempos,[91] and felt that Mozart remained 'unknown territory for the female singers of the Hofoper'.

In the *Deutsche Zeitung*, Maximilian Muntz emphatically stated that the evening of 21 December 1905 had been 'one of the saddest in the history of the Vienna Opera'. A 'resounding failure', and a 'sacrilege against Mozart's genius', the new production of *Don Giovanni* revealed nothing more than 'perverse impotence'. The performance 'totally lacked atmosphere' and, from beginning to end, everything 'miscarried': 'the conception, the cast, the interpretation of each role, the sets, the costumes, and the lighting'. It was in protest against these 'unbelievable blasphemies', Muntz believed, that 'murmuring filled the auditorium against the would-be "improvers of Mozart"'. In a longer article that appeared the following day, the same critic again inveighed against Roller's 'grey smokestacks', against his 'demented distortion' and 'sad caricature' of *Don Giovanni*. Roller obviously believed 'that a stage designer has claims on the music' and that 'Mozart's music needed colour'. The result was 'a series of tableaux vivants modelled on Mozart'. True, Mahler stood on the rostrum, but it was Roller, in fact, who 'conducted' the work, subordinating every aspect of the production to his personal views. And Roller's stylistic method, with its 'grey chimneys' and poverty of pictorial invention, was diametrically opposed to Mozart's richness of musical form. Furthermore, the orchestra was much too small, and the singers were obliged to move 'like marionettes' in order to preserve the mood of the 'tableau vivant'. Humour was banished altogether, for Roller the painter had no use for it. Mahler also bore a fair share of the blame for the failure; 'petty decorative excesses', and 'sensation at any price' merely hid the 'irresponsible artistic deficiency' of his directorship. It was all designed to cover up the fact that, in the Mozart year, the Hofoper did not have a single properly qualified Mozartian singer.

According to Max Graf, there were actually two *Don Juans*, Mozart's and Roller's, and they often had nothing to do with each other. Roller's sets would have been better suited to the spoken theatre, and his production suffered in general from 'the predominance of the drama at the expense of the music'. At the same time, Graf conceded that Mahler had surpassed himself during the performance. 'Action, movement, and the plot' came to the fore and the acting was on a par with that of the Burgtheater. However, Mozart's music was not given its due:

---

[90] However, even for the ballroom scene Wallaschek found fault with the way the characters ran away at the moment of Zerlina's scream.

[91] He singled out the Overture, the Elvira–Don Juan–Leporello trio, and the Serenade.

The orchestra is damped down and is only permitted to whisper, murmur, sigh. The orchestral drawing becomes a sketch in which a handful of lines hint at the original and a few pale colours express the mood. The orchestral accompaniment is only a shadow cast by the action: something insubstantial, fleeting and evanescent. A conversational tone reigns on stage: the most dramatic problems are handled in subdued voices, as in the antechambers of the aristocracy the parlando style even forces its way into the ensemble scenes. '*Don Juan*' is turned into a music drama, a realistic play, a conversational tragedy; the music becomes chamber music and the drama a French comedy. Is this the style of Mozart? No. It is the style of Gustav Mahler which filters Mozart through its acuity and restlessness until every measure is shot through with intellect and nervousness.

In Graf's opinion, Mahler had sought the dramatic element everywhere, except where it was really to be found: in the voices. Above all, *Don Giovanni* needed five beautiful, powerful voices. Unfortunately neither of the two existing casts could possibly do it justice. Roller's contribution could be described as 'the fantasies of a modern painter on *Don Giovanni*'. The scenery was 'part fervent fantasy, part sober experiment, without ever forming a whole'. While the towers were indeed a 'simple and ingenious' expedient for changing the size of the stage, for most of the time Mozart's *Don Giovanni* and Roller's had nothing in common. The painter had forgotten the music: in the champagne aria, for example, the 'poisonous green, dazzling red, and pale blue . . . irritated the nerves'. Obviously, as far as Roller was concerned, violent and clashing colours incarnated Mozart's hero. However, they had nothing to do with the aria in question and were at odds with the simple chords of the accompaniment.[92]

Two newspapers of lesser consequence also took part in the battle of words by attacking the new production, the *Sonn- und Montagszeitung* and the *Wiener Mittags-Zeitung*. In the first, Richard Robert complained that 'the work of the scenic designer was starting to take precedence over the intentions of the composer and the music',[93] while in the second, Emil Kohlberg called the new production 'a degeneration' of Mozart's masterpiece. Roller's towers were a 'monstrosity', and his 'gluttony of colours' revealed only a 'cheap showmanship'.[94]

Hans Liebstöckl, in the *Illustrirtes Wiener Extrablatt*, was inspired by the production of *Don Giovanni* to write a true piece of bravura, unsurpassed as yet in its sarcasms and its violence. He denounced 'the settings in all their forms, the towers, the colours, the drops, the lighting: Scenery! Scenery! Bring forth the high towers with holes! The Milky Ways! Glaring red trees! Mystifying

[92] *Neues Wiener Journal*, 22 Dec. 1905. The cast on the opening night on 21 Dec. 1905 included Forst (Zerlina), Gutheil-Schoder (Elvira), Mildenburg (Anna), Sembach (Ottavio), Reich (Masetto), Weidemann (Don Giovanni), Mayr (Leporello), and Haydter (Commendatore). Forst and Kiurina later alternated in the role of Zerlina, Sembach alternated with Maikl as Ottavio, and Moser with Reich as Masetto.

[93] *Sonn- und Montagszeitung* (25 Dec. 1905), quoted by Baker, 'Roller', 198 ff.

[94] *Wiener Mittags-Zeitung* (22 Dec. 1905).

courtyards! Dark chambers! Yellow castles! Lines, corners, contrasts, clashes of colour! Out with the discordant ingenousness!' These towers, he declared, had

a number of objectives. First they insult the eyes. Secondly, they are unacoustical, . . . and seventh, no one can explain what they mean! . . . Don Juan would, without a doubt, find them again in hell!:

Everything is extravagant, all is thought out as a surprise. Even the floor is stylized. A villa from a toy chest, scarlet red gardens right in front of it, violet changes in the horizon, red banquet halls in the style of a carnival stage, dilapidated walls, baffling flights of steps, a sheer and spectacular milky way. . . . Everywhere the expression of complete irritation. Something hateful, angular, uncouth, and terrible lurks beneath Professor Roller's splendour. He is a Professor who wants to dominate, crush, convince and impose a burlesque style upon us! The countless intentions, the brilliant ineptitude, the capriciousness of an illustrious provincial are everywhere in evidence. Someone ought to have said so honestly and confidentially to the Professor, between the first and second drink and in passing, as one might say 'Take bromide!' or 'Have a cold bath!' to a hypochondriac.

No single event was ever so hotly disputed during Mahler's directorship as this one. Yet it is interesting to note that a foreign observer, Eugène d'Harcourt, described this production, which was in so many ways experimental, as 'a masterpiece of [historical] reconstruction'. It gave him an overwhelming 'impression of youth and vitality': d'Harcourt was dazzled by the musical execution, 'marvellous for its precision and nuance, from beginning to end, under the bewitching baton of Monsieur Mahler'.

Some time later, the articles in the main musical journals also reflect the violence of the controversy. Max Vancsa, in the *Neue Musikalische Presse*, erstwhile champion of the young revolutionaries of the Vereinigung, claimed that Mahler and Roller were seeking to attract attention by outrageous innovations foreign to the spirit of the opera. Proof of this was the place the press accorded to these innovations, at the expense of the music. Vancsa believed that *Don Giovanni* had never before been performed in Vienna with such an inadequate cast. Demuth had never been the ideal choice for the principal role, and Weidemann's voice was inferior to his. As Elvira, Gutheil-Schoder 'bounced over the difficulties of the great aria with a careful dexterity worthy of a tightrope walker'. However, she failed to make a compelling impression. Sembach seemed like a mere beginner, and Haydter lacked 'the voice of thunder' expected of the Commendatore. Donna Anna had never been one of Mildenburg's best roles, and she was increasingly incapable of tackling the formidable vocal exploits which her second aria demanded. Mahler himself did not seem to be 'truly acquainted with the work's tragic grandeur', and as a result the performance lacked atmosphere. Max Vancsa predicted a short life for this 'historical restoration': he was certain that it would quickly be abandoned in favour of the earlier version, which the public would once again acclaim enthusiastically![95] Even Richard Specht, one of Mahler's first and most enthusiastic champions, expressed doubts. Obviously, Roller's painted drops deserved admiration for their 'real force of expression'. Yet the whole production had left him with 'an impression of confusion, or at least lack of resolution', because the 'continuously changing demands placed on the imagination' brought 'the audience to a state of bewildered unease'.[96]

Vienna's satirical and humorous journals could not afford to miss the occasion. Thus, *Wiener Caricaturen* carried a cartoon showing Mozart as the Commendatore in a suit of armour arriving for the final supper with Don Giovanni (pictured here as Mahler) and to carry him off to hell. The caption read 'He [Mozart] fetches Mahler, because he so violated his creation, Don Juan.' The viciously anti-Semitic *Kikeriki* lampooned the settings with a visual pun reflecting the grill-like groundcloth: 'If only one could at least throw Mahler, Kalbeck, and a pair of other "bunglers" of Mozart into jail!'[97]

Over a period of years Mahler had accustomed the public to his view of Mozart. However, the new production of *Don Giovanni*, with all its revolutionary innovations, was like a bombshell, abruptly breaking with established tradition, and many of his contemporaries were of course scandalized. Certain progressive Viennese commentators recognized that the character and myth of Don Juan were eternal, and that Mahler and Roller had only wished to achieve a kind of 'symbolic distance', to render the work's true character as a 'tragedy of pleasure, desire and vanity transfigured by the music and played for a romantic, post-Wagnerian audience'.[98] 'Everything has become tragedy: it was the *Don Juan* of E. T. A. Hoffmann', wrote another favourable commentator. 'The iron ring of fate closed in on the hero from the beginning. Singers of tragedy interpreted the main roles with a tragic conscience. Their talent brought the opera to life, but it was the life of German romanticism.'[99] To this it was possible to reply that Mozart's music was indissolubly bound to its time, and that its light, sparkling, and elegant character was difficult to ignore. Many people found the constant presence of the towers overbearing: their straight lines, neutral colours, and simple symmetrical shape introduced an element foreign to the work. Others considered the compromise between realism, stylization, and symbolism to be an imperfect one, and that the sets demanded either too much or too little imagination from the audience. But above all, the tragic rather than comic atmosphere of the production was sharply contested. After all, the opera was subtitled 'dramma gioccoso'.[100] Paul Stefan, however, was one of the first to note that

---

[95] Max Vancsa, *Neue Musikalische Presse*, 15 (1906): 2, 32.
[96] *Die Schaubühne*, 2 (1905): 7, 181 ff.
[97] *Wiener Caricaturen*, 24 (1905): 53, 9; *Kikeriki*, 46 (1906): 12, 9. See Baker 'Roller', 203 ff.
[98] PSG 68.
[99] Friedrich Rosenthal, 'Ein neuer Don Juan', *Die Musik*, 11 (1912): 17, 272.
[100] The importance of this subtitle, which also occurs in *Così fan tutte*, was surely overestimated.

if people were musicians (but it is not enough to have learned a few facts here and there), they would, they must realize that the spirit that animated these notes came from the heights and the depths. And perhaps it was the same with regard to the whole epoch. Perhaps the elegant forms were merely borrowed to serve as masks. Perhaps it sensed everything and was only too wise not to want to know it.[101]

In later years, speaking of Roller, Bruno Walter recognized that his talent was above all heroic and monumental, and that despite the miraculous success of his *Marriage of Figaro* the following year, he was at his best in drama, not in comedy. Yet despite all the criticism, his towers were often imitated in Germany and they continued to be used in Vienna for *Don Giovanni* until 1945, when bombs destroyed most of the Hofoper (which had in the meantime become the Staatsoper). When Strauss staged the opera in 1921, he conceived of it, as Mahler had done, as a 'romantic, tragi-comical play of masks'. After having toyed with the idea of highlighting the opera's 'buffo' aspect, and of restoring, among other things, the final ensemble,[102] Strauss limited himself to emphasizing Don Giovanni's libertinage, Zerlina's sensuality, and Leporello's craftiness. Unlike Mahler, he did not accord the same importance to the female characters and to the libretto's supernatural aspect. After giving the matter some serious thought, he retained Roller's towers, in the form of a vast portico.[103]

Much later, after the partisan furore and critical vindictiveness had subsided, Mahler admitted to Ludwig Karpath that he had never considered the towers perfectly suited to the atmosphere of Mozart's masterpiece and added that Roller himself had never been entirely satisfied with them. He wondered if perhaps he had really gone too far and whether, as his adversaries claimed, he had accorded excessive importance to the scenic element in the new productions.[104] It was in this context that Mahler is supposed to have said to Roller: 'A stage capable of suggesting everything should be absolutely empty',[105] thus giving the painter the idea for his forthcoming production of Gluck's *Iphigénie en Aulide*.[106] Mahler never publicly proclaimed his doubts about Roller's vision of *Don Giovanni*, but he did say to Karpath:

It was an experiment, nothing more. In the theatre, you must always experiment, otherwise you get stuck in routine. If it doesn't work, it's no great calamity. On the next occasion, you try something else. But keep what I said to yourself: many people were very

[101] PSG 69.

[102] According to Korngold, Strauss's major reform in his 1921 production concerned the musical execution, which he wanted to be as 'Mozartian' as possible. He sought to achieve a rendition which would be 'more sonorous', less 'shaded' and, as it were, 'less nervous'.

[103] Strauss chose not to use Roller's set for Elvira's room, and cut out her E flat aria 'Mi Tradi'. Julius Korngold (*Neue Freie Presse*, 22 May 1921) vehemently protested against this, and also Strauss's cutting of Don Ottavio's first aria ('Dalla sua pace'). He also criticized changes in the ballroom scene which made it appear as though the three orchestras were playing in one and the same room.

[104] BMG 123.

[105] Ibid. Roller used the expression in the article 'Bühnenreform?', *Der Merker*, 1 (1909): 5, 197, and added: 'All a painter can reply is "Let us experiment"'.   [106] BMG, ibid.

enthusiastic about it, and it would be an injustice to Roller and bad for the box office to deprive them of their enthusiasm.

However, Karpath's testimony is not entirely reliable, if only because, like Graf, he omits to mention in his memoirs the violence with which they had both attacked Mahler at the time. In any case, Mahler once again proved more far-sighted than his critics: it was certainly no accident that this production of *Don Giovanni* lasted longer than most of the others in which he collaborated with Roller.[107]

Indeed, the criticisms seem to have been of little consequence when we consider the dramatic force of the production, which revealed hitherto unknown depths and riches in Mozart. This was later stressed by the theatre critic Berthold Viertel, one of Karl Kraus's collaborators in *Die Fackel*. He considered Mahler to be 'the great modern example' of the 'producer as interpreter':

Mozart ... was dramatically enhanced, the great dramatist in him was revealed on stage. Far removed from the lame and sentimental rococo style and the precious mannerisms of previous productions, the glowing, revolutionary core of Mozartian humanity was revealed and found redemption. ... The sudden curtain swallowed up Don Giovanni like the jaws of hell, and with undramatic realism the harmonious conclusion of the work is simply cut. In Don Giovanni, the colours—red, black and white—resolutely accentuated the main lines of the action! The creativity of this producer-interpreter is also evident in audacious cuts and formal divisions, in arbitrarily selected tempos, and in the despotic attitude to the singers, who were treated as instruments that needed to be precisely adjusted. Mahler's imperious face was unforgettable when, before lifting the baton, he abruptly turned in profile to the audience, and thereby silenced it.[108]

At the end of 1905, when it began to be known that Mahler was preparing a Mozart festival to celebrate the composer's 150th birthday, and the press announced that in the summer the entire Hofoper company would be appearing in Salzburg, Graz, and Brünn, Angelo Neumann wrote to Mahler to ask him to add Prague to his itinerary. Mahler replied that performances were only planned for Salzburg, but added that if others were subsequently scheduled elsewhere, his request would certainly be considered.[109] Ultimately, the whole tour project was cancelled, with the exception of the Salzburg performance.

The preparations for the new Mozart productions absorbed all Mahler's time and energy towards the end of 1905 and at the beginning of 1906, and he refused many invitations to conduct his works. But they continued to be performed without him, especially the *Kindertotenlieder*, which Weidemann sang in Hamburg (again under Nikisch) and in Cologne (under Steinbach) in

---

[107] Franz Farga, *Die Wiener Oper* (Göth, Vienna, 1947), 291.
[108] Berthold Viertel, *Schriften zum Theater* (Kosel, Munich, 1970), 444.
[109] Letter to Neumann, 10 Nov. 1905 (HOA, Z. 1230/1905).

January.[110] According to the Cologne *Stadt Anzeiger*, the audience was impressed by Mahler's 'masterly orchestration' and 'striking economy of means'. Hermann Kipper, critic of the *Volkszeitung*, regretted that the songs, which were 'so heartfelt and profound', produced such a depressing effect.

At the beginning of January 1906 Mahler wrote to Fried from his sickbed (the night before, he had fallen out of bed in his sleep and cracked a rib) to tell him that the score of the Third Symphony was on its way, and to thank him for including his Lieder in forthcoming concerts. He also invited him to attend the first performance of the Sixth in Essen in May.[111] A few days later, he rehearsed the Sixth with the Vienna Philharmonic. Despite a few amusing incidents occasioned by the rectangular bass drum which Mahler had invented for the 'blows of fate' in the Finale,[112] the session proved to be a great success, and Mahler sent the following letter to the members of the orchestra:

I feel the need to express my heartfelt thanks to the members of the Hofoper orchestra for the joy they gave me by performing my new work so perfectly. I feel indebted to you all, individually and as a group. Permit me to say that I am proud to belong to your number, not only on account of the duties that derive from my position, but also on account of the bond of art, which unites all those with a vocation, irrespective of person or party.[113]

A month later Boston, Philadelphia, and New York witnessed the second series of performances of the Fifth Symphony in the United States under the Viennese conductor, Wilhelm Gericke.[114] Mahler had written to Gericke in November to thank him for planning to perform his symphony and to ask him to insert into the full score the final changes he had made after the Vienna

[110] The previous summer Mahler had written to Fritz Steinbach, advising him to perform the cycle rather than a group of Lieder and telling him the name of the publisher, C. F. Kahnt (undated letter to Fritz Steinbach, Library of Congress). The Gürzenich concert on 9 Jan., which Steinbach conducted, consisted of Beethoven's *Egmont* Overture and Violin Concerto (soloist Fritz Kreisler); Tartini's 'Devil's Trill Sonata' (with string accompaniment); Julius Weissmann's *Fingerhütchen* for baritone, women's chorus, and orchestra; Mahler's *Kindertotenlieder* (soloist Friedrich Weidemann); and Strauss's *Symphonia Domestica*.

[111] Postcard, dated 4 Jan. 1906, PML.

[112] See below, Chap. 6.

[113] HOA, G.Z. 87/1906, undated. This letter may possibly refer to the rehearsal of the Fifth Symphony on 7 Dec. 1905, and not the rehearsal of the Sixth. The original is in the archives of the Vienna Philharmonic.

[114] Wilhelm Gericke (1846–1925), a native of Styria, was a pupil of Felix Otto Dessoff and Julius Epstein at the Vienna Conservatory (1862–5). Ironically, it was he who obtained the Beethoven Prize in 1878, the year Mahler submitted his overture to *Die Argonauten*. Later, Gericke worked as Kapellmeister at the Linz Opera, and at the Hofoper under Jahn, before being appointed conductor of the Gesellschaftskonzerte (1880). Henry Lee Higginson, founder of the Boston Symphony Orchestra, heard him conduct at the Vienna Opera in *Aida*. Following a dispute with Jahn, Gericke accepted an offer from Higginson and succeeded the first conductor of the Boston Symphony, Georg Henschel (1850–1934). Within five years, he turned it into one of the best orchestras in the world, but bad health forced him into retirement. He was succeeded by Arthur Nikisch and Emil Paur. In 1898, he again gave in to Higginson and returned to head the Boston Symphony, where he remained until 1906, to be replaced by Karl Muck. He spent his last years in Vienna (cf. Elsa Bienenfeld, 'Gustav Mahler und Wilhelm Gericke', in the *Neues Wiener Journal*, 11 Apr. 1926). Mahler's letters cited here are now in the Houghton Library, Harvard University, Cambridge, Mass.

concert, which were too important and too numerous to be included in miniature score.[115] A few days before the concert, the *Boston Evening Transcript*
published a long article on Mahler's career and music.[116] After the concert, the
same newspaper reviewer described Mahler as 'a 20th century Berlioz'.
'Whether or not he realizes what he has conceived, he has filled his work with
such powerful moments, such transporting beauty, developing and transforming his themes into such dramatically interesting variations, instrumenting so
beautifully and powerfully, that he captivates and conquers his audience.' The
concert had had a resounding success and the press manifested an open-mindedness unknown in Europe. For the *Boston Sunday Globe*, the Fifth was

as fantastic, incoherent and overwhelmingly discordant in the main as any one of the
latter-day compositions heard at our concerts in recent years, not forgetting Richard
Strauss in his wildest flights of imagination. . . . Mahler evidently is a masterhand at
instrumentation. . . . Much of it sounds chaotic, yet the intervals in which the composer
shows comparative lucidity in the treatment of his themes are melodic and give brief
glimpses of a rich imagination that soon runs riot in dissonants and inharmonic utterances.
Out of this tumultuous composition may be selected for praise, and likewise enjoyment,
the scherzo, which, in the greater part, is beautifully written, especially for the strings.[117]

Three weeks later, after another two performances, Henry Taylor Parker
reported in the same paper that 'Mahler's hearers [had] listened as intently as
they had [at the first concert] and applauded music and performance heartily'.
According to Parker, Wilhem Gericke, who was approaching retirement,

was signaling it with the most remarkable achievement of his whole career here. . . .
The symphony could seem the fruit of insistent reflexion, untiring labor, and selfless
mastery of polyphony and instrumentation, often Mr. Gericke makes it sound like the
inevitable expression of deep thought and deeper feeling. The bigness and intensity of
idea and mood never escape him. . . . What, the curious hearer asks again, were the
ideas with which Mahler burned—no other word suits such intense music—as he
imagined and wrote and which he would awaken responsively in his listeners? It
becomes more and more impossible to take the symphony as music existing for its own
sake. . . . The form, the development, the treatment of the music breaks through such
limits.[118]

---

[115] Letters to Wilhelm Gericke of 11 Nov. and 20 Dec. 1905 (the dates were pencilled in, probably by
Gericke). Although it had apparently been announced that the performance would last an hour and a half,
it in fact lasted only 55 minutes, which suggests that Gericke's tempos were extraordinarily fast, or that he
made considerable cuts. The *New York Daily Tribune* reported that the New York performance lasted 59
minutes.

[116] It includes a long quotation from the famous 1897 letter to Arthur Seidl. According to the *Boston
Evening Transcript*, Mahler, when asked whether he would agree to conduct a festival of his works in the
United States, replied: 'Why should I? If I should absent myself from my post of duty during the season, my
singers would ask the same privilege, and that I cannot grant.' He added, 'without any apparent bitterness':
'Furthermore, whenever one of my symphonies is played before a new audience, failure is a foregone conclu-
sion.'

[117] Programme of the Boston Symphony Orchestra concerts on 2 and 3 Feb. 1906: Beethoven, *Egmont*
Overture; Schumann, Piano Concerto (soloist, Harold Bauer); Mahler, Symphony No. 5.

[118] *Boston Evening Transcript*, 24 Feb. 1906.

Mahler, Parker noted approvingly, took great liberties with 'sacrosanct form, modifying it, diversifying it and transforming it to express his ideas and feelings'. A few days after the first performance, the *Boston Evening Transcript* laconically announced that the symphony had 'made so sharp an impression' that it would be performed again on 23 and 24 February. Indeed, it had already been included in the orchestra's programme for one of its traditional visits to New York and Philadelphia. In Philadelphia, the *Inquirer* critic hesitated to pass judgement on the Fifth, but wondered 'whether the value of its contents is proportioned to the emphasis of its proclamation'. The rationale behind its 'explosive eruptions' escaped him. He deplored the absence of 'the kind of diagram with which it is customary to supplement compositions of this nature'. The article stressed the 'disproportion between the strenuosity of the effort made and the magnitude of the means employed on the one hand, and the importance of the result achieved on the other', and announced that the symphony would nonetheless be performed again by the Philadelphia Orchestra.[119]

Still in Philadelphia, the *Public Ledger* considered Mahler's thematic combinations to be superior to the melodies themselves, though it admired his 'formal mastery', 'profundity', and 'the continuous presence of a guiding line'. Rhythm, melody, and harmony all demonstrated Mahler's 'desire to rejuvenate music through counterpoint', while Strauss was satisfied with the triumph of harmony. Only the *Evening Bulletin* considered the work to be incomprehensible without a programme, and claimed that despite its unusual proportions, 'the rhythmic beauty of the Funeral March and poignant feeling of the Adagietto',[120] it had not made much of an impression in Philadelphia.

As in 1904, when the Fourth Symphony was premièred in New York, Richard Aldrich[121] published a long preview of the Fifth in the *New York Times* four days before the concert. He expressed his astonishment at the fact that Mahler was so little known in the United States, given his reputation in Europe, reviewed the programmes of his previous symphonies and discussed Mahler's change of heart on the subject. After a brief analysis of the Fifth, he summarized the programme published in the programme book of the Cincinnati concert: 'the plaint of one who has not realized his aspirations' (March); his despair (Allegro); the consolation of nature (Scherzo); his return to life (Adagietto) and his final triumph (Rondo).

After the 15 February concert at Carnegie Hall, Aldrich wrote: [122]

Mahler's symphony imposes by its length and breadth, the vast number and extent of its themes, the skilful handicraft with which they are put together, the bigness of the orchestral apparatus and the extraordinary skill with which it is managed. . . . This

---

[119] This performance does not seem to have materialized.

[120] Programme of the 12 Feb. 1906 concert in Philadelphia: Weber, Overture to *Der Freischütz*; Saint-Saëns, Cello Concerto No. 1 (soloist, Elsa Ruegger); Mahler, Symphony No. 5.

[121] See below, Vol. iiii, Chap. 1 for the biography of this critic.

[122] As we shall see (Vol. iiii, Chap. 1) the principal New York critics always reported on important events, but most of them did not sign their articles.

Fifth Symphony is a work that cannot be dismissed at one hearing as harsh, diffuse, lacking in distinction of theme and definiteness of purpose, although all these things appeared from time to time to be true of it, as it was unfolded before an uncommonly attentive and patient audience last evening. That it is deeply felt and tremendously sincere music is continuously borne in upon the listener, but that it is not the product of a strong and vigorous creative genius, an original force in music, is also evident. It seems that the composer is most strenuously seeking for self-expression, but though he is equipped with all that modern musical skill can give him in methods of treatment and resources of orchestration, his achievement seems continually to pant behind his ambition, rarely overtaking it.

The rest of the article describes each of the movements and concludes that the whole work arrested the attention of the listener despite the weakness of its musical inspiration, which was greatly inferior to that of Strauss.[123] The *Daily Tribune* reviewer expressed the same views: [124] Mahler was certainly more devoted to 'euphony' than most of his contemporaries, and possessed a greater 'command of more melodious polyphony'. The work contained 'moments of frank and simple utterance'. Nevertheless, he was 'obsessed by the prevalent conviction that when an ounce of inspiration cannot be commanded a pound of reflection and labor will serve as well'. Some time afterwards, Lawrence Gilman,[125] who wrote the music column in the magazine *Harper's Weekly*, also ranked Mahler below Strauss in every way. For him, as for many of his German colleagues, the Fifth was a 'prevailingly empty, prolix, and pretentious' work, 'a vast and tumultuous sea of commonplaces'. 'The melodic line lacks both beauty and saliency, the harmonic structure is banal when it is not laboriously ineffective . . .'

Out of politeness, Gericke sent only the most favourable reviews to Mahler who responded warmly:

My warmest thanks for your affection for my work. I am completely bowled over by the reviews. Not that they could add substantially to my delight. The fact that a musician like you became interested in my work and introduced it so lovingly to the public is more important to me than the most vociferous approval. How splendid the performance must have been which was able to make the listener understand such a complicated work and to introduce him to the innermost sense of such a forbidding and demanding piece of music![126]

In Europe, Mahler had agreed, during the first months of 1906, to conduct another series of performances of his Fifth Symphony first in Antwerp, and

---

[123] *New York Times*, 16 Feb. 1906. In the concert on the previous evening, Mahler's Fifth Symphony was preceded, as in Boston, by Beethoven's *Egmont* Overture and Schumann's Piano Concerto with the same soloist.

[124] The article was almost certainly written by Henry Edward Krehbiel (see below, Vol. iiii, Chap. 1).

[125] Lawrence Gilman (1878–1939), a self-taught music critic, became the chief editor of *Harper's Weekly* in 1911. In 1923 he began to work for the *New York Tribune* (which later became the *Herald Tribune*), where he stayed until his death. From 1929 to 1939 he wrote the programme notes for the New York Philharmonic and the Philadelphia Orchestra. His works include a dozen monographs, tributes, and opera analyses.

[126] Letter to Wilhelm Gericke of 12 Mar. 1906 (Houghton Library).

then in Amsterdam, where the Concertgebouw had also planned to perform the *Kindertotenlieder*, and *Das klagende Lied*. He and Mengelberg had corresponded on the subject since the previous summer,[127] primarily in order to agree on the date. Mahler had arranged to conduct a concert in Antwerp on 5 March and could not accept a date for Amsterdam which would oblige him to leave Vienna twice within the same brief period of time. Mengelberg seems to have misunderstood Mahler's motives, to judge by Mahler's letter to him:

With regard to the second half of your letter, permit me to say that I too was rather upset by this not particularly flattering conduct. Please believe me that it is not avarice which prompts me to ask you to go ahead without me. For your sake I would gladly conduct for nothing; Mammon is not all that important to me. But here I am confronted with an administration and I really have no choice but to decline the invitation definitively. But you must come to *Antwerp* to be with me for a few days or at least a few hours and also to hear my interpretation of the symphony. . . .[128]

These scheduling difficulties were overcome in early January 1906, when Mengelberg finally managed to fix the dates for the Amsterdam concerts for 8 and 10 March, immediately after the Antwerp concert.[129] A performance of the Second Symphony had originally been planned for Antwerp, Mahler's first stop. When he discovered that the concert hall used by 'les Nouveaux Concerts' did not have an organ, he asked the impresario Norbert Salter to suggest an arrangement for wind instruments of the organ part. In the end he decided to conduct the Fifth Symphony instead.[130]

Shortly before leaving for Belgium, Mahler dined at the home of his faithful friends Hugo and Ida Conrat. Josefine von Winter, the wife of Dr Josef von Winter,[131] recalled that several Viennese critics were present that evening, and that Richard Specht was one of them.[132]

[127]   In a letter of 1905, Mahler asked Mengelberg to return the score of the Fifth so that he could add the changes which had already been entered in the orchestral parts. He also asked him to return two scores of Mozart symphonies that he had lent him, for he 'needed them for the Mozart festival' (RMH 59). Mengelberg must have been forgetful, for Mahler wrote to him again towards the end of the year (MBR1, no. 305; MBR2, no. 346; RMH 61) to request the score of his symphony for the insertion of 'important and considerable alterations' (RMH 61). At this point, he still did not know the exact dates of the Amsterdam concert.

[128]   RMH 59. Mahler added that he had sent Mengelberg the scores of the first two Lieder (probably the *Wunderhorn-Lieder*) for inclusion in the programme, but that, with regard to the *Rückert-Lieder*, he would have to get in touch with the publisher, C. F. Kahnt (RMH 62).

[129]   As soloist, Mahler first suggested the Dutch baritone Johannes Messchaert, and then Friedrich Weidemann. He also added 'Ich bin der Welt', and two or three *Wunderhorn-Lieder*, to the *Kindertotenlieder* for the programme. Weidemann, he wrote, would perform without a fee if his travel expenses were paid. Sometime later, Mahler informed Mengelberg of Weidemann's cancellation, and advised him to 'give up the idea of performing the *Kindertotenlieder* if he could not find a good singer'. In an earlier, unpublished letter written in Feb. Mahler insisted upon conducting three rehearsals of his symphony, assuming that it would be 'carefully prepared before his arrival' by Mengelberg. Before the final rehearsal, he would also need to go over *Das klagende Lied* on the piano with the soloists (*Nachrichten zur Mahler-Forschung*, no. 29 (Mar. 1933), 9.

[130]   Undated letter to Norbert Salter, written in late 1905 (BSM, Munich).

[131]   See above, Vol. ii, Chap. 10.

[132]   Josefine von Winter also mentions 'Münz'. The presence of Maximilian Muntz, critic for the anti-Semitic newspaper *Deutsche Zeitung*, seems highly unlikely in the home of a rich Jewish family, particularly as he was an avowed adversary of Mahler. However, there is no other eminent Viennese critic with a similar name.

I sat next to Mahler who, of course, talked only with his neighbour Specht, with me he exchanged only a few words replying to questions; but I enjoyed listening to the clever, clear and serious way he treated each subject; he said he could not understand Max Reger, whose compositions seemed to contradict the laws not only of music but of all organic life, since he knew no change from calmness to movement, etc.; but he spoke with respect of that which he found incomprehensible. Of the new 'Don Giovanni' production and Roller's ideas he said that in Berlin it would have been acclaimed and celebrated (whereas here everyone felt called upon to condemn and attack). In this respect the Viennese could be compared to the ancient Athenians who, when roused, had never hesitated to condemn, ban, etc., whomever was not to their liking. It might have its advantages, was a possible incentive to the artist to do his best, while the Berlin enthusiasm might lead to stagnation. (This is a far cry from the notion that abuse has to be countered with abuse)—I was surprised at the importance he attached to the criticism of some obscure people in *Extrablatt* etc., by being annoyed and discussing it.[133]

Just before taking the train to Antwerp on the evening of 2 March, Mahler went for a walk in Vienna and made a few purchases. As usual, he wrote a note to Alma from the station describing his shopping activities.[134] The trip to Antwerp was less irksome than usual for he was alone in his compartment, and arrived on the morning of 3 March. He went straight to the Grand Hotel, where he settled in a large and comfortable room with two beds (an irony in itself, since Alma had not accompanied him) and a 'spacious and bright' bathroom, in which it sufficed to push a button to procure hot water, and where he spent an hour every day in the bath. The rehearsal, unfortunately, pleased him less than the hotel, and he felt like 'running away': 'It's going to be a hellish uproar. I would gladly do without my bath and go around dirty, if only the musicians would play a little more precisely.'[135] The warm welcome was a consolation: Mahler was bombarded with invitations and dined out every day: he found his Antwerp hosts 'very agreeable, rich, and yet simple people'. He was being generously hosted by the vice-president of the Société des Nouveaux Concerts, the Belgian tenor Ernest Van Dyck (or Van Dijck) who, on this occasion, proved himself particularly magnanimous since he had been a member of the Vienna Opera for nine years before Mahler was appointed, and had several times been

---

[133] Josefine also noted that Mahler had declared that he never attended violin recitals (which is what he had told Alma at the Zuckerkandl's in 1901) and that Specht talked disapprovingly of Huberman and approvingly of Ysaÿe (*Nachrichten zur Mahler-Forschung*, no. 11, (Mar. 1983)). Josefine von Winter (1873–1943) was the daughter of Rudolf Auspitz, a Member of Parliament. A painter and composer, she kept a diary of the concerts, operas, and exhibitions she attended. She died (date unknown) in the Theresienstadt concentration camp. Her memoirs, which were published in 1927, do not mention Mahler. In her diary she used abbreviations which are sometimes difficult to decipher.

[134] BGA, no. 159, undated (2 Mar. 1906).

[135] BGA, no. 160, undated (3 Mar. 1906). The score used by Mahler during the Antwerp rehearsals, which includes numerous alterations, was recently discovered in the library of the Royal Flemish Music Conservatory by the Dutch musicologist Robert Becqué. See above, Vol. ii, Appendix no. 2 on the Fifth Symphony, and Robert Becqué, 'Mahlers Antwerpener Partitur der Fünften', *Nachrichten zur Mahler-Forschung* no. 25 (1991), 8–10.

into dispute with him. In February 1898, for instance, at the time of the first performance of Leoncavallo's *La Bohème*, Van Dyck was feeling unwell and had tried to have the date of the première postponed. Mahler, however, had stood fast and the première had finally taken place on schedule, but without the star tenor.[136]

But Van Dyck had obviously chosen to forget about the past and to remember only the great conductor who had, nine years earlier, brought new life to the Vienna Opera. Mahler was touched by his kindness: 'He's a nice fellow', he wrote to Alma, 'if only he wouldn't sing!' What had displeased Mahler most of all in Van Dyck's performances was his old-fashioned, theatrical, style of acting, a characteristic which Cosima Wagner on the other hand had so much appreciated that she had engaged him many times to sing the title role of *Parsifal* at the Bayreuth Festival,[137] as well as the Bayreuth première of *Lohengrin*. Mahler's poor opinion of Van Dyck as an actor was to be confirmed two years later, when he and Alma heard him sing *Tristan* in Paris, and were so shocked by his histrionics that they left the official box in which they were sitting in the middle of the performance.[138]

The Antwerp concert included Liszt's transcription for piano and orchestra of Schubert's *Wanderer Fantasy*, in which the soloist was Eugen d'Albert, the pianist, composer and Liszt pupil, with whom Mahler spent some time discussing the coming Viennese première of his opera *Flauto Solo*, scheduled for November 1906.[139] On the eve of the final rehearsal, Clemenceau and Picquart arrived from Paris. They regretted Alma's absence, but the orchestra was so unruly that Mahler was relieved that she had stayed behind: 'I am glad that you will not be subjected to this hellish Breughel ... If Amsterdam isn't any better, I'll run away!' he wrote that evening.[140] Despite his love for Amsterdam, he feared that he could not face another disappointment, and asked his secretary Przistaupinsky to send a telegram summoning him back to

---

[136] See above, Vol. ii, 91 ff. and Erik Baeck, 'Die Beziehung zwischen Mahler und Ernest Van Dijk', in *Nachrichten zur Mahler-Forschung*, no. 33 (1995), 23 ff. Erik Baeck's research in the Ernest van Dyck Archive in Berlaar yielded several new documents concerning the 1898 conflicts which preceded the Vienna première of Leoncavallo's *La Bohème*, including the composer's letter to Van Dyck urging him to sing the première of his opera at all costs. In an article published in the *Neues Wiener Tagblatt* on 7 June 1904, Leoncavallo confessed that he had always regretted Van Dyck's replacement by Andreas Dippel for the première of his opera. Another hitherto unknown, and undated, letter from Mahler to Van Dyck answers the singer's request for a change in the Hofoper Spielplan: all of Mahler's efforts to rearrange it have failed and Van Dyck absolutely must sing the tenor lead in *Manon* on the following Monday. This letter could only have been written either in Feb. 1899 (before the performance of *Manon* on the 13th) or Nov. 1899 (before the *Manon* performance on the 27th). Van Dyck's farewell performance at the Hofoper took place in *Lohengrin* on 30 Sept. 1900.

[137] Between 1888 and 1901, and again in 1911 and 1912. The first Bayreuth *Lohengrin* took place in 1894. [138] See below, Chap. 10.

[139] Wilhelm Raupp, *Eugen d'Albert*, 199 and 201.

[140] BGA, no. 160, undated (4 Mar. 1906). In a recently discovered letter to Mengelberg, Mahler also complains of the Antwerp orchestra's lack of discipline. He asks his Dutch colleague to organize a piano rehearsal of *Das klagende Lied* in Amsterdam on the morning of his arrival (see Eduard Reeser, 'Gustav Mahler und Holland: Zwei Nachträge', in *Nachrichten zur Mahler Forschung*, no. 29, 1993).

Vienna 'on the Intendant's orders'. This would enable him to leave Amsterdam two days before he was due to conduct *Das klagende Lied*.[141]

On 5 March, the fourth concert of the Antwerp series of 'Nouveaux Concerts'[142] began with the Fifth Symphony and ended with the overture to Weber's *Der Freischütz*. Between the two, Mahler accompanied Eugen d'Albert in Schubert's *Wanderer Fantasy*, in the arrangement for piano and orchestra by Liszt.[143] At the end of the concert, Mahler received so much applause that he repeated the overture to *Freischütz*.

Antwerp was no doubt ill-prepared for a work that was as modern as the Fifth Symphony. *La Semaine* had warned its readers that it was 'the expression of a particular genre and spirit'. But the symphony was greeted with warm applause in the concert hall and for once the critical response was as cordial as that of the audience. Only the *Nouveau Précurseur* expressed reservations, describing the Fifth as a work so 'full of eccentricity' that Wagner, in comparison, seemed classical. Mahler was described as a musician who was 'always in pursuit of effects, always and only effects' whose music 'is always original, but full of eccentricities', and whose orchestration was 'perhaps not always technically ideal'.[144] 'All in all,' the critic concluded, 'there is much counterpoint; themes intertwine like fireworks, but the melodies are brief and quickly abandoned.'

On the other hand, Armand Timmermans,[145] the critic of the Antwerp newspaper *Le Matin*, in fact admired the length of the melodies and added:

In general they have distinction, but this is not always the case. For example, in the Scherzo there is a passage (in D) reminiscent of Viennese waltzes, despite the brilliance of the harmony and orchestration. But these are only details. The overall impression is that of a strong, original, dazzling work with violent contrasts and passionate accents pushed to the extreme, scarcely surprising from a composer with Czech blood in his veins.

Mahler 'wants to depict the pain and acute suffering of the soul in the wake of an irreparable loss'; then, in the Scherzo, 'the joy of life' and, in the Finale, the

---

[141] In fact Mahler conducted the first of the two performances, and Mengelberg the second.

[142] The Antwerp society 'Les Nouveaux Concerts' (Maatschappij der Nieuwe Concerten van Antwerpen) had been founded on 31 Oct. 1903 by eminent members of the city's community, with Ernest Van Dyck as vice-president. It had invited a number of famous conductors such as Hans Richter, Siegfried Wagner, Richard Strauss, Felix Weingartner, Arthur Nikisch, and others. It was no doubt the permanent conductor of the Society, Lodewijk Mortelmans, who had decided to engage Mahler (see Robert Becqué, 'Antwerpener Partitur').

[143] In the same programme, Eugen d'Albert performed Chopin's Nocturne in B, Op. 62, no. 1, and his own Scherzo, Op. 16. In a letter on 27 Nov. 1905 (HOA, no. 1233/05), d'Albert expressed the hope that Mahler would conduct the entire Antwerp concert, including Liszt's First Piano Concerto, which he was at that point expecting to play. But he added: 'I realize that after your great symphony, which I am anxious to hear again, the effort might be too much, and I shall well understand if you leave the concerto to be conducted by someone else.' Mahler in the event, did accompany d'Albert.

[144] The *Nouveau Précurseur* claimed that the local trumpet player had been unable to meet Mahler's demands and that the performance left much to be desired.

[145] Armand Timmermans (1860–1939), a native of Antwerp, studied at the Flemish Conservatory. Music critic of the *Matin* until 1914, he was also the composer of choral works, and three operas, including *Margarita* (1923) and *Vae Victis* (1924).

'struggle for the ideal'. In technical terms the score was 'of the first order': 'the harmonization, polyphonic elaboration, and orchestration are most interesting and extraordinarily powerful. Nothing is predictable, everything is liable to be surprising: the harmonic development, the phrasing, even the thematic elaboration.'

La Métropole described the Fifth Symphony as 'trenchant music of great originality . . . sometimes disconcerting . . . bestrewn with marvellous and surprising effects', but at the same time 'of vigorous inspiration and staying power'. Finally, *La Semaine* considered Mahler's music to be 'original without being eccentric', a display of 'exuberant, varied and distinguished colours', and added: 'His symphony is full of new rhythms and novel combinations, of an overtly fertile imagination; it is a cross between a czardas and a langorous Viennese romance, sometimes like a wild rhapsody, and sometimes like a Strauss waltz.'

More reserved than its French counterparts, the Flemish newspaper *Gazet van Antwerpen* called Mahler a 'controversial composer': 'Some people cannot come to terms with a Mahler Symphony after a first performance, and draw attention to its lack of structure. Others admire the effect of his orchestration, which is obtained mainly thanks to the brass instruments, and praise the strangeness of his conception.' The *Nieuwe Gazet* was prepared to admit that Mahler was one of the great modern composers. However, it criticized his lack of 'restraint with regard to the means at his disposal', his 'deliberate tearing to bits, shattering of the pleasant melodies which flow so easily from his pen' by the violence of the orchestra, which 'smothered them with all the devious devices and Gordian knots at a composer's disposal'.[146] A few days later, the Flemish review *Lucifer* nevertheless considered that the concert had been 'the main event of the season' and that the audience 'had understood and appreciated' the symphony. In Paris, the Antwerp concert was mentioned in the *Guide Musical*. It spoke of the work's 'undoubted originality' and 'orchestral mastery', and added: 'Yet ideas do not abound in this symphony, and the attraction exerted by an extremely masterful technique does not always make up for its excesses.' Early in the morning on the day after the concert, Mahler left for Amsterdam where, upon arrival, he wrote to Alma: 'I achieved a definite "succès" in Antwerp. Splendid press.'

Since his last visit to Holland eighteen months previously Mahler's music had continued to occupy an important place in Dutch musical life. The previous summer, the first performance of the Fifth Symphony had been given at the Scheveningen Festival, the summer home of the Berlin Philharmonic. The conductor was August Scharrer.[147] Thus, despite the failure of the Berlin

---

[146] For this reason the critic preferred the Adagietto to the other movements. He was enthusiastic about Eugen d'Albert's playing and noted that Mahler's tempos for the Overture to *Der Freischütz* were exceptionally slow, especially in the Introduction.

[147] August Scharrer (1866–1936), born in Strasbourg, was Korrepetitor at the Karlsruhe Opera (1897–8), Kapellmeister in Regensburg (1898–1900), and assistant conductor of the Munich Kaim concerts (1900–4) before becoming conductor of the Berlin Philharmonic (1904–7). He was principal conductor in Baden-Baden from 1914 to 1925, and then director of the Nuremberg Lehrergesangverein. He composed numerous orchestral and choral works and an opera, *Die Erlösung*, Op. 12.

performance conducted by Nikisch the preceding February, the work had remained in the orchestra's repertoire. Scheveningen was a small seaside resort, and the hall was half empty. However, those present applauded vigorously after each movement. Willem Landré, critic of *De Nieuwe Courant*, found 'the first movement imposing; the second infernally ugly, trenchant and grotesque; the third a cacophony, . . . the fourth intimate, beautiful and simple, . . . and the fifth, commencing simply, soon became so noisy that we had to laugh when a joker whispered to us that the symphony had no doubt been put together expressly for a deaf and dumb institution.'[148] The other critics were more moderate. The anonymous correspondent of the *Nieuwe Rotterdamsche Courant* wrote that a composer capable of writing such a Funeral March, and such an Adagietto, had the right to expect that what was less accessible and intelligible should not immediately be condemned to 'la mort, sans phrase'.[149] He felt unable to pronounce judgement on a work of such scope after one hearing. After the two performances of the Fourth conducted by Mengelberg in Amsterdam and The Hague in February 1905, Henri Viotta had also added it to the repertoire of the Residentie Orkest. Here again most of the reviews had been rather harsh, deploring a lack of 'original coherence' or 'inner motivation'. Henri Völlmar, correspondent of the *Nieuwe Rotterdamsche Courant*,[150] compared the second movement to Saint-Saëns's *Danse macabre*, and concluded that Mahler's music lacked character. The critic of the *Residentiebode*, who had heard the Fifth six months before in Scheveningen, made the grotesque mistake of confusing it with the Fourth, and informed his readers that the 'colossal work' had pleased him more on this allegedly 'second' hearing!

Mahler had great expectations with regard to the performance of the Fifth he was to conduct at the Concertgebouw. On the morning of his arrival, he went directly from the station to the Concertgebouw, and, as before in 1903 and 1904, found the orchestra 'admirably prepared' by Mengelberg. As early as this first rehearsal, he realized that the 'performance (would be) unsurpassable, even in Vienna'. Rehearsing *Das klagende Lied* for his second concert, he found the chorus 'marvellously disciplined', and prepared with the same care as the orchestra. Mengelberg, he wrote, was 'the only conductor to whom (he could entrust his works) with utter peace of mind'.[151] The Dutch conductor's enthusiasm for Mahler's work had not waned, and he seemed resolved to maintain the symphonies in the orchestra's repertoire. He even mentioned

---

[148] *Die Nieuwe Courant*, 1 July 1905, quoted by Eduard Reeser, 'Die Mahler-Rezeption in Holland 1903–1911', in Rudolf Stephan (ed.), *Mahler-Interpretation* (Schott, Mainz, 1985), 90.

[149] The expression 'La mort, sans phrases' is usually attributed to Abbé Emmanuel-Joseph Siéyès, when he voted in favour of King Louis XVI's execution in 1793.

[150] Born in The Hague where he later taught at the Conservatory, Henri F. Völlmar (1880?–1935?), composer and critic, had studied the piano under Charles van der Does and Carl Tausig. He accompanied Henryk Wieniawski on several European tours.

[151] BGA, no. 162, undated (6 Mar. 1906).

plans to conduct the Fifth in Rotterdam, The Hague, Haarlem, Utrecht, and Arnhem, and also two further performances in Amsterdam.[152]

Mahler wrote to Alma the evening of his arrival, mentioning the 'simplicity' and 'cordiality' of the Mengelbergs' welcome. He felt that he could count on them for anything, and was delighted that he had again accepted their hospitality. Elisabeth Diepenbrock's diary once again describes Mahler's daily life between rehearsals. On the day of his arrival, as soon as he was free to do so, he went to the Diepenbrocks' home, and was disappointed to find that Alphons was out. The following day he lunched at the Mengelbergs' with all his Dutch friends, including the Diepenbrocks and Henryk de Booy and his wife. Elisabeth noted that the guests were too dissimilar for serious conversation, but that the subject of Japan suddenly awakened Mahler's interest. Japanese art and thought had no doubt been introduced to him by his Secessionist friends, and he exclaimed: 'Everything (in Japan) is beauty, while in the West you have to hold your nose as soon as you go out on the street.' Japanese philosophy, he continued, was 'the highest form of religion'. Elisabeth Diepenbrock's husband protested, claiming that it was only a cult of the will, but Mahler persisted in his admiration of the absolute self-control the Japanese sought to achieve and declared that it was not incompatible with feeling. Later, to the delight of the assembled company, he described his childhood and the piano concerts he had given in Iglau at the age of 8. His father, he claimed, had had enough good sense to stop him reading the flattering reviews, rewarding him merely with a piece of cake.[153]

Just before the first concert, Mengelberg had been informed by Mahler that Weidemann had fallen ill with tonsilitis. So he engaged to replace him Gerard Zalsman, a Dutch baritone from Haarlem. Mahler had then wondered whether 'Zasman' would be able to learn 'in such a short time these difficult things'.[154] Unfortunately, only one rehearsal materialized and Mahler found the Dutchman's interpretation 'too superficial'. The rendition of the Fifth Symphony, on the other hand, filled him with joy. Yet despite the friendly welcome, the fidelity of his Dutch admirers, and the continued support of the press, Mahler felt out of his element and longed to return to Vienna. The 'very unpleasant' news of the conflict which, since his departure, had pitted the chorus of the Opera against Roller probably contributed to his desire to

---

[152] These performances took place in Mar., in Rotterdam on the 12th, in The Hague on the 14th, in Arnhem on the 19th, in Haarlem on the 20th, and in Amsterdam on the 21st and 22nd.

[153] RMH 21. Elisabeth Diepenbrock also noted that Mahler spoke with her husband about the latter's Lieder, no doubt after examining the scores. In this context it is of interest that Diepenbrock had just finished the *Hymnus de Spiritu Sancto* based on the text of 'Veni, Creator Spiritus'. It began with a descending fourth on the word 'Veni'. Did the memory of this work, in Maiernigg in June, have an influence on the first movement of the Eighth Symphony? This might explain why Mahler, although he knew the text, had forgotten some of it. See Eveline Nikkels, Alphons Diepenbrock, *Mahler-Freund und Mahler-Forscher der ersten Stunden*, in: Matthias Theodor Vogt (ed.), *Das Gustav-Mahler-Fest Hamburg 1989* (Bärenreiter, Kassel, 193).

[154] Letter to Mengelberg, in *Nachrichten zur Mahler-Forschung*, no. 29 (1993), 9.

go home, for he realized that it 'could have consequences for my own posi-tion'.[155]

Mahler's disappointment probably had something to do with the relative failure of his first concert. Since Gerard Zalsman had not had enough time to learn the two *Wunderhorn-Lieder* originally included in the programme,[156] the order had been reversed: the Fifth Symhony opened the concert, and was followed by the *Kindertotenlieder*.[157] The concert ended with 'Ich bin der Welt abhanden gekommen'. Even with this shortened programme, the last day was exhausting, beginning with morning and afternoon rehearsals, and concluding with the concert in the evening. Fortunately the news from Alma was excellent: she was having a very good time in Vienna and Mahler hoped that he might join in the fun when he returned.[158] The day after the first concert, when she sent him a 'biting' letter, Mahler's reply does not reveal the reason for her bad temper. Despite a 'splendid' performance of the Fifth Symphony and the *Kindertotenlieder*, the audience's response, though 'respectful', was noticeably not as warm as in earlier years. Elisabeth Diepenbrock's journal even labels it a 'fiasco', adding that for her and her husband the evening had been 'dreadful'. They found the Fifth 'strange' and 'whimsical', and had been 'unable to un-derstand it'.[159] Many of the audience left the hall after each of the *Kindertotenlieder*. Mahler was deeply depressed by the end of the concert, but during supper at the Diepenbrocks' he calmed down and began to regain his composure. Diepenbrock cheered him up by saying: 'I envy you your enemies!' Diepenbrock was soon to change his mind about the Fifth after hearing it under Mengelberg shortly after Mahler's departure.[160]

The account of the concert which Mahler sent to Alma concealed his disap-pointment and ill-humour. 'The young people went wild, . . . and the press was quite enthusiastic', he told her. And indeed, for once the attitude of the crit-ics made up, to a certain extent, for the audience's lukewarm reaction. Averkamp[161] considered that the Fifth towered above Mahler's other works. He was impressed by the 'noble cantilena' of the first movement and the abun-dance and 'uninterrupted flow' of Mahler's melodies, which, 'almost without repetition, variation, or transposition', held the listener's attention and took the place of classical development. He pointed out that 'two or three melodies'

[155] See below.

[156] 'Der Schildwache Nachtlied' and 'Des Antonius von Padua Fischpredigt'.

[157] According to the journal *Caecilia*, the *Kindertotenlieder* had a better reception a few days later, when they were sung by the same baritone.

[158] Postcard to Alma, dated 8 Mar. 1906, BGA, no. 163.   [159] RMH 22.

[160] Here is the passage from Elisabeth Diepenbrock's diary relating to the Fifth Symphony: 'Yesterday and the day before yesterday, Mahler's symphony (the Fifth) again. A great and glorious impression this time. Sitting downstairs, where everything sounds awful, ruined it for us the first time. Fons now finds it so magnif-icent, so excellent, and he calls Mahler "the only poet" of our time. At first he felt the Fifth was a step back after the Fourth, but now no longer. The Funeral March is wonderful and yesterday the Adagietto also made a deep impression on us . . .' (RMH 22).

[161] He published a brief account of Mahler's two concerts in the *Nieuws van der Tag* and a more exten-sive article in the *Weekblad*.

often occurred simultaneously. At the same time, Mahler strove for clarity and simplicity, but avoided 'the danger of banality'. Sometimes the fertility of his imagination was excessive, providing sufficient material for several works. In the Scherzo, in particular, 'spicy and graceful melodies alternated with emotional ones'. And yet the work lacked 'the unity created by the kind of compositional technique in which a theme passes through several variations', However, Mahler always managed to hold his audience's attention by his 'prodigious variety of sounds'. Mahler's 'calm and sure arm movements', his avoidance of histrionics and his prodigious mastery impressed Sibmacher Zijnen, who also stated that, in each of his symphonies, 'he casts his art into a new form determined by the musical contents'.[162] The Fifth, in his opinion, had more unity than its predecessors. After hearing it a second time two days later,[163] Zijnen was roused to indignation by the relative indifference of an audience which could not forgive Mahler for not giving it what it expected. But despite everything, he claimed that Mahler had 'swayed all listeners of good will', thanks to the 'irresistible fascination' of his 'masterful technique', the 'overwhelming power of his music' and the 'nobility of his poetic nature'.[164] Finally, the anonymous review in the magazine *Caecilia*[165] praised Mahler as a composer 'who has something to say, and knows how to captivate and convince his audience by the force of his personality'. Contrary to the earlier symphonies, the Fifth was not a 'puzzle'. 'All of a piece', it sustained the audience's interest until the end, and despite its 'exceptional wealth of colour', it 'obeyed the rules of form far more than was immediately apparent'. All in all, Mahler 'had something to say and knew how to lead his listeners along'. However, the anonymous author acknowledged that the public's response to the concert had lacked warmth.[166]

Strange as it may seem, given the warm reception of the *Kindertotenlieder* elsewhere, the Dutch audience and the press did not take to these songs. Gerard Zalsman had obviously not had time to study them properly. Yet Sibmacher Zijnen praised them as 'beautifully composed', with such a 'powerful atmosphere', and indignantly related the noisy departure of listeners between the songs. Because of the orchestral interludes, Averkamp called the *Kindertotenlieder* 'little symphonic poems', and claimed that the texts 'required a musical setting that paid more attention to the meaning of the words'. Mahler 'described too much with the orchestra and . . . sacrificed the declamation of the words in the process'.

However such reservations remained exceptional in the press. As usual,

---

[162]   In his 7 Mar. column in the *Handelsblad*, followed on 9 Mar. by a lengthier article.

[163]   Conducted by Mengelberg.

[164]   According to Zijnen, the trumpet player missed the first triplet of the theme and skipped to the following half-note.

[165]   According to Eduard Reeser ('Mahler-Rezeption', 92), the author of the article was Simon van Milligen.   [166]   *Caecilia Maanblad voor Muziek*, 63 (1906), Apr. issue.

Otto Knaap, Mahler's persistent enemy in the Dutch press, lambasted the Fifth Symphony as a 'hypermodern' work, far removed from absolute music, filled with 'brutal dissonances', 'deafening timpani and brass' and 'unbalanced masses of sound'. The Adagietto, which barely lasted half a minute (*sic*), was 'more bearable for normal ears', and Mahler's Lieder, though 'less modern', sounded dreary and monotonous.[167]

Between the two concerts, on 9 March, Mahler went for a walk with Diepenbrock through the old parts of Amsterdam, but he seemed troubled and preoccupied and 'scarcely looked around him'. One of his letters to Alma[168] shows that the news from Vienna worried him because the looming crisis could have 'unpredictable consequences'. The following morning, a brilliant day, he went on an excursion with Mengelberg and Diepenbrock to the Zuijder Zee near Laren. This was when Henryk de Booy took the famous series of photographs of Mahler and his Dutch friends on a track in the dunes at Valkenveen.[169]

By conducting two performances of *Das klagende Lied* in Amsterdam, Mahler had undoubtedly intended to show his faithful Dutch admirers, as he had previously done in Vienna, the originality of the music he had written at the age of 20. The decision proved to be a wise one, for the first performance was greeted with much applause.[170] The same programme also included two other contemporary works which were conducted by Mengelberg: Max von Schillings's *Dem Verklärten* and Richard Strauss's *Taillefer*.[171] Hugo Nolthenius, the critic of the *Weekblad voor Muziek*, travelled from Utrecht especially for this concert, but he was mainly interested in *Taillefer*. Thus it is not surprising that he admired in Strauss 'a spontaneity to the point of genius, with which he easily eclipses Mahler', at least in this early work. Nolthenius found evidence, in *Das klagende Lied*, of the young Mahler's intelligence and understanding rather than of his feeling or natural gift.[172]

Of the other Dutch critics, only Alexander Rappard, of *Nieuws van der Dag* preferred Schillings's *Dem Verklärten* to the other two works on the programme. He found the style of *Das klagende Lied* 'old fashioned', at times a little 'mannered', and too Wagnerian; and he agreed with the author of the programme notes, who had said that it contained 'a great spiritual force that

---

[167] According to Knaap, the tessitura of *Kindertotenlieder* was often too high for Gerard Zalsman.

[168] In BGA, no. 164, Mahler mentions Roller's conflict with the Opera chorus, and fears that it might have 'wide-ranging consequences'.

[169] RHM 22 and RBM, nos. 37–42. Postcard to Alma, 10 Mar. 1906 (BGA, no. 165). Mahler told her he was enjoying the fresh air after the exhausting rehearsals, during which he had had to be on his feet for long periods.

[170] According to the critic of *Caecilia*, the audience's enthusiasm made up for the cool reception given to the Fifth.

[171] Max von Schillings's *Dem Verklärten*, Op. 21 is a cantata for baritone solo, chorus, and orchestra. Strauss's *Taillefer* requires three soloists, as well as chorus and orchestra. The soloists for *Das klagende Lied* on 10 and 11 Mar. 1906 were Dina Mahlendorff and Lucie Coenen, sopranos; Maria Philippi, alto; Albert Jungblutt, tenor. The Toonkunst chorus and the backstage orchestra were conducted by Martin Heukeroth.

[172] RMH 93.

needed to be used sparingly'. The Dutch musical magazine *Caecilia* praised 'the expressive and appropriate atmosphere' of the work, though it criticized the 'inexplicable manner' in which Mahler treated the text, separating syllables and dividing the narrative between two soloists, all to the benefit of the 'orchestral illustration'. It recognized that 'his [Mahler's] style was already entirely there' and that the orchestration, for a 20-year-old composer, was astonishing. Zijnen[173] too marvelled at the young Mahler's orchestral mastery, his 'natural and correct understanding of the poetic content', and the striking contrast between the 'anxious and fantastic forebodings' on the one hand, and the 'poetry of the forest' on the other. Everything in *Das klagende Lied* seemed to prefigure the 'lyrical tone' of the later works. Although Mahler's third visit to Amsterdam had not been quite as successful as the earlier ones, he nevertheless left Holland in the sure knowledge that he had done much for his reputation.

Immediately after Mahler's departure, Mengelberg took the Fifth on tour in Holland. On 12 March he performed it for the members of the *Sociëteit Harmonie* of Rotterdam (an association of complacent middle-class Liberals who excluded Jews from membership). Willem Landré, now writing for the *Nieuwe Rotterdamsche Courant*, did not change the opinion he had formed in The Hague: 'The naive and the exalted, the beautiful and the ugly, the natural and the artificial are so strangely mixed in this symphony that after an hour and a quarter the serious listener finds himself in a state of mental intoxication. This symphony is magnificent, execrable, sublime, banal, clear, murky, . . . now this, now that.' Landré mainly admired Mahler's sense of form and lavished praise on the performance of the orchestra under Mengelberg.

Two days later, in The Hague, respect and admiration predominated, but reservations persisted about the symphony's second and third movements. For Eduard Bondam, the critic of *De Avondpost*, Mahler was an artist who, in this immense musical poem, had expressed his despair and his joy with the intensity of a superman and had himself lived through the terrible dichotomy between ideal and reality. Once again it was the Adagietto that most pleased both the press and the audience. At the concert in Arnhem, on 19 March, reactions in the hall were once again rather hostile, while the reviews on the other hand were becoming more and more favourable. Thus, the anonymous critic of the *Arnhemsche Courant* saw the Fifth as a balanced work of art in which not a 'bar was out of place'. To end his 'tour' of the Netherlands, Mengelberg performed the symphony twice in Amsterdam. The public remained lukewarm, to the great regret of Sibmacher Zijnen among others, since 'the playing on its own . . . merited a much more marked and cordial response . . . This performance by Mengelberg and his orchestra was a grand exploit that compelled respect!'[174]

---

[173] See above.   [174] RMH 94.

When Mahler returned to Vienna, the Mozart year and the Mozart cycle were well under way. The new production of *Don Giovanni*, and particularly Roller's 'towers', had divided the Austrian capital into two camps. Yet Mahler decided to retain them for the third major event in the cycle, *Die Entführung aus dem Serail*, which had been missing from the repertory since 1885.[175] To rediscover and restage the young Mozart's delightful masterpiece filled Mahler with joy during the rehearsals. A few days after the première he went on a sleigh ride with Alma on the snowy slopes of the Semmering where he had gone to recuperate. He kept singing the melody of the final quartet, and spoke again and again of Mozart, whom he 'loved more as a human being than all the others', and of the wretched life he had had. He could never forgive Constanze for remarrying so soon after Mozart's death.[176]

As in the case of *Così fan tutte*, Roller had to observe strict economy in devising sets for *Die Entführung*. As a result, his work was criticized with arguments diametrically opposed to those hitherto employed against him. Mahler made up two acts and five scenes out of the original three and placed Konstanze's great aria, 'Martern aller Arten', at the end of the first act. In the 1872 revival Johann Herbeck had added the Rondo 'alla Turca' from the A major Piano Sonata, and had orchestrated it for the occasion, as a prelude to the second act.[177] Mahler kept it in the same place and, like his predecessor, deleted two arias in the second act.

A report of a comic incident during the rehearsals of *Die Entführung* appeared in the contemporary press. It concerns Leo Slezak, whose repertory included both Wagnerian and Mozartian roles, and whose imposing presence and vocal stamina brought to such parts as Belmonte and Tamino an unusual and refreshing vigour:

Because Slezak-Belmonte had almost suffered an accident as he climbed the ladder to Konstanze's window, Mahler himself checked to see that the tower was secured in a firm position so that it posed no danger. . . . As Slezak began to climb, . . . it [the tower] began to slide back causing the tenor to do a [balancing] dance.[178]

---

[175] Except for one performance in 1891.   [176] AMM1, 123; AMM2, 124.

[177] The reviews show that Mahler received an ovation at the opening for his spirited conducting of the 'alla Turca' Finale of the Piano Sonata K. 331. In 1872, Herbeck's version did not include either Konstanze's great aria, 'Martern aller Arten' or Belmonte's third aria, 'Ich baue ganz' (no. 17), which was replaced by 'Un aura amorosa' from *Così fan tutte*, while the love duet was considerably abridged. Mahler did not restore Belmonte's last aria, replacing it with the second, 'Wenn der Freude Tränen', no. 15. He also cut Pedrillo's battle aria, 'Frisch zum Kampfe' (no. 13). For Selma Kurz's convenience, Konstanze's first aria ('Ach, ich liebte'), was transposed down a semitone. Blonde's arias were also lowered by a tone, whereas Pedrillo's Romance was transposed a tone higher (Robert Werba, 'Mahlers Mozart-Bild, am Beispiel der "Entführung aus dem Serail" ', *Wiener Figaro, Mitteilungsblatt der Mozart Gemeinde Wien*, Jan. 1976).

[178] Baker, 'Alfred Roller', 214, quoting the *Fremden-Blatt* of 28 Jan. 1906. It was also noticed, on the evening of the première, that Belmonte-Slezak had entered the palace through a window for the elopement scene, and had come out with the freed Konstanze through the main doorway of the palace. Roller, it seems, was very happy with his *Entführung* sets and felt that 'many people are now on my side', which is confirmed by the reviews of the production (Roller's letter to his wife, Milewa, see Liselotte Kitzwegerer, 'Alfred Roller', 100).

Slezak's near fall must have alerted the technical staff of the Hofoper to the possible dangers of Roller's towers which were used once again in this production, and for the last time, no doubt because of the *furore* they had created. But in this instance, the need for economy had taken precedence over artistic considerations.[179] Initially, the stage-right tower functioned as Osmin's house and the one on stage-left was part of the Pasha's palace. Lattices, rugs, and oriental decorations adorned the windows. Osmin was first seen picking figs from a tall fig-tree protruding from a stone well on stage-right of the esplanade. Several borders of painted foliage for the branches were hung, both downstage and upstage of the trunk. Small trees with bright red flowers were placed in tubs by the tower walls. Two tall cypresses and a few shrubs were visible in the Pasha's garden. The vegetation was deliberately kept to a minimum for the setting was meant to suggest the isolation and sadness of the three imprisoned Europeans, rather than the Pasha's summer abode. Beyond a simple balustrade, the backdrop represented the sea in parallel bands of blue and grey under a whitish sky which changed colour under the lights. A small ship was constructed for the entrance of the Pasha and Konstanze. Several drops were rehabilitated from former productions of other operas no longer in the repertory.[180]

The interior of the palace, in Act II, was characterized by the same austerity: a few oriental chandeliers hung from the rafters, and carpets were draped over great candelabras. The stage curtain went down behind the two front towers, and Roller was criticized for the narrowness of the set, which forced the chorus to 'push into the wings so as not to encumber the stage with its compact mass'. The bare quality of the décor brought out the vivid hues of the costumes. When the curtain rose for the final scene the sea was again visible, this time with a ship on it.

Although the austerity and simplicity of the design surprised and shocked many of critics, the cast was considered by everyone to be far superior to that of *Don Giovanni*. Konstanze was one of the finest roles of Selma Kurz's repertoire. Albert Kauders wrote in the *Fremden-Blatt* that 'with one powerful thrust, she climbed several rungs up the ladder of fame' and had 'entranced' the audience with her 'dazzling' interpretation, and the 'dash and bravura' of her coloratura. While the gentleness of her personality probably detracted from Konstanze's heroism, which was derived from opera seria, Kalbeck wrote that whatever the role lacked by way of bravura was 'made up for' by musical beauty. That she 'softened' certain passages in *Martern aller Arten* was justified by the role: 'the contradiction disappears together with the violence'. Thus, when Kurz sang the Allegro, she 'expressed a heroic impulse arising

---

[179] The budget estimate for the production was approved by the Intendant on 15 Jan. 1906. Its total was 2,200 kronen. The costumes were to be taken from the general wardrobe inventory at hand.

[180] The sea drop came from Smareglia's *Vasall von Szegeth* and the sky drop from Goldmark's *Merlin*. They had been sewn together into a single drop cloth. A design for the first set has survived as a copy by Anton Brioschi (Baker, 'Roller', 213 ff.).

from the situation, which any girl in love and in despair might have uttered'. Slezak's heroic voice was unusual for Belmonte but did not do disservice to the role. In the second and third casts, Georg Maikl and Johannes Sembach imparted to it a more traditional and elegiac lyricism. Although the role was apparently too high for her, Grete Forst earned much praise as Blonde, while the role of Pedrillo seemed to have been made to measure for Arthur Preuss, and Wilhelm Hesch carried off the honours of the evening as Osmin. He brought his velvety timbre, stage presence, and comic talents to bear on the role, although his voice never attained the cavernous fullness in the low register which Osmin ideally demands.[181]

Thus, unlike in the case of *Don Giovanni*, the critics had nothing but praise for the cast of *Die Entführung*. Even Mahler's enemies conceded that he had surpassed himself, 'as always when his genius is not sidetracked'. Korngold warmly praised the whole interpretation which, he thought, brought out all the marvels of the work, and approved of the new division of the opera into two acts. He noted that no one had on this occasion attacked Roller's towers.

Even Hirschfeld applauded this performance, which he found 'dazzling and worthy of a festival' thanks to Mahler's 'useful and assiduous' efforts. The whole evening had been illuminated by his 'nervous and refined [conducting] which made the sparks fly' and inspired his singers with 'joy and vitality'. In the *Wiener Zeitung*, he went so far as to condone the towers which he had so violently condemned in the production of *Don Giovanni*. But later, in the *Österreichische Rundschau*, he returned to his original position:

Only aesthetic inexperience or unusual obstinacy could place oriental-style window bars in the apertures of these grey towers. The realistic detail destroys the idealistic concept, and nothing is more distressing to the aesthetic sense than half-measures and mixtures. At once a seraglio and not a seraglio, the towers create an impression of pervading dissonance. Mozart's noble, pure spirit should be preserved from such childish experiments. Is it ugly or old-fashioned or inartistic or impractical to portray a seraglio when the set, which does not change, requires it? In a Mozart celebration, must we be incessantly bewildered and irritated by the transformation of what is natural into what is not? When we want to hear Mozart, must we be subjected to fads and novelties? Is a whim—building towers and painting them grey—really art?

In taking such diametrically opposed positions in two different publications, Hirschfeld doubtless failed to foresee that someday they might be compared, allowing posterity to draw unflattering conclusions as to his intellectual honesty. David Joseph Bach, on the other hand, found Roller's décors 'enchanting' and added: 'The towers, which by now have become so famous, are present once more; they serve their purpose marvellously by reducing the playing

---

[181] Starting with the fourth performance on 14 Feb., Gutheil-Schoder sang the role of Blonde, and Wissiak that of Osmin. Later, Breuer sang Pedrillo, while Seebock and Elizza sang Konstanze. Over half the opera (19 numbers) was sound-recorded with the original cast on the fairly primitive recording machines of the time (see below, Vol. iiii, Appendix).

space and without creating any side effects. This should prove itself even to the eyes of the stupidest viewer.' Schönaich and Kalbeck also lauded the towers as a judicious and harmonious solution to the problems of the work. Muntz was glad to see that Mahler had taken the criticisms of *Don Giovanni* to heart, but felt nevertheless that a work as naive as *Die Entführung* was eminently ill suited to such stark décors. Avowedly, Roller had 'sterilized' his 'monstrous towers', but he had been 'much too chary of his ways and means', 'merely suggesting' the location of the action, and inventing a 'poverty-stricken' architecture of 'dubious pictorial quality' whose lack of imagination was scarcely made up for by 'gimmicks and tricks'. After the 'unfortunate failure' of *Don Giovanni* Mahler was trying to 'demote' decoration, as well as limiting the movements and stylizing the gestures of his actors. Forever incapable of 'bowing before another mind, even that of Mozart', he had to 'comment on everything and interpret it in his own way', and never ceased to try out new tempos, nuances, and accents.[182]

Wallaschek also found the contrast between the bare stage of *Die Entführung* and the lavish décors of *Don Giovanni* ridiculous. The new sets were conspicuous by their absence, demanded too much from the audience, and weighed down the whole work with their inexpressive greyness. The critic of *Die Zeit* felt that the towers excessively reduced the playing space for the singers; its small size was incompatible with a score so rich in colour and 'oriental exuberance'. Only Mahler's conducting found favour in his eyes, with one exception: the 'Turkish March', which, he thought, was ruined by its rapid tempo. The error was all the more surprising in view of the fact that Mahler's approach to Mozart was in all other respects 'infallible'.[183]

Turning to *The Marriage of Figaro*, Mahler must have breathed a sign of relief since no financial restraints had been imposed and he was now able to start from scratch. In this new production his first step was to replace the spoken dialogues with Mozart's recitatives, which Kalbeck had translated into German several years before. Furthermore, da Ponte's trial scene had always appeared to him weak in comparison with Beaumarchais's original, which he used as a basis for an amplified version of the episode, including new, string accompanied, recitatives.[184] He offered the result for publication to Hinrichsen, the director of the Peters firm:

---

[182] Muntz conceded that Kurz had done justice to the music, though, as always, she had failed to bring the part to life.

[183] Cast for the first performance on 29 Jan. 1906: Kurz (Konstanze); Forst (Blonde); Slezak (Belmonte); Preuss (Pedrillo); Hesch (Osmin); Stehmann (Pascha Selim). Two days earlier a new production of *The Marriage of Figaro* had been presented at the Kaiserjubiläumstheater. On 28 Jan., Ferdinand Löwe celebrated Mozart's birthday with a performance of the *Requiem* at the Konzertverein. It was preceded by the Symphony in G minor, no. 25, K. 183.

[184] Mahler's version also included two recitativo-secco passages, a new exchange between Bartolo, Marcellina, and Figaro in the third scene of Act I which shed light on their earlier relationship, and another in Act II between the Countess and Cherubino.

The purpose of my revision is to replace da Ponte's rather nondescript recitatives and his wholly farcical prose with Beaumarchais's original dialogues and where this is impossible, at least to suggest their spirit. To this end, it was necessary to rework certain scenes, for example the flirtation between the countess and the page in Act II, the big court scene in Act III, and important details concerning the motivation of the characters in Act I. I think I have done it with the greatest possible discretion; the connoisseur will notice a foreign hand at work only in the court scene. These remarks apply only to the secco recitatives in this version. Of course, not a jot has been altered in the musical numbers, which Kalbeck has re-translated. . . . The revision of the vocal score as it now stands can be used in the theatre. The conductor has to accompany the recitatives and, where the bass is figured, he must include the cellos and the basses (two desks). Only in the court scene is it desirable, for dramatic reasons, to use the whole string orchestra. These long chords modulate in the manner of the secco recitative, and are uncommonly effective. If a theatre requests them, they could be added on a single sheet . . .[185]

This letter demonstrates the care and love with which Mahler prepared the new version of *Figaro* that Peters published shortly thereafter.[186]

Once again Mahler collaborated closely with Max Kalbeck in preparing a new translation of da Ponte's libretto. Kalbeck acknowledged this in the following inscription he wrote on the score:

Your name, esteemed Director, ought to have appeared on the first page of this book, for you have been more than an untiring collaborator and zealous supporter. The idea of bringing da Ponte's libretto closer to Beaumarchais's comedy came from you, and you have actively helped to carry it out. Since your modesty is greater than the merit you have shown, both in restoring the poet to his rightful place and in reviving Mozart's masterpiece, you have sought to avoid acclaim on this occasion. Forgive me if, with the gentle force of my affection, I draw you into the open: [it is] more honest than the deceptive glow of the footlights![187]

---

[185] The vocal score of the new version by Kalbeck and Mahler was published by Peters in 1907 (publisher's number 3168) with the subtitle 'Version of the Vienna Opera'. Initially the opera had been given in Vienna in two acts, with a single interval between the second and third acts of Mozart's original. Later Mahler realized that the two acts were too long, and returned to Mozart's original four acts. Both of Max Kalbeck's texts are included in the edition, one above the other, in the arias and ensembles. The five arias normally omitted are in the appendix: Bartolo's aria (no. 4: 'La Vendetta'); Marcellina's aria (no. 25: 'Il capro e la capretto'); Basilio's (no. 26: 'In quegl'anni'); and Suzanna's 'Al desio di chi t'adora', no. 28a, K. 577, composed for the Vienna revival of 1789 to replace 'Deh vieni non tardar'. In the Peters score, this aria is incorrectly assigned to the Countess.

[186] Letter to Henri Hinrichsen of 13 June 1906. Only the signature is Mahler's. In a subsequent post-card, Mahler added that the publication interested him only 'for artistic reasons', indicating that he had not demanded a fee. Mahler's version of *The Marriage of Figaro* was used in many German opera houses, Mannheim being the first to do so. Around the same time, Mahler thanked Hinrichsen for sending him the new score of Lortzing's *Undine*, edited by Pfitzner. Hinrichsen had asked for Mahler's advice on the version presented at the Vienna Opera, and he received a negative response. Mahler advised him to publish an orchestral score at the same time as the new vocal score, adding: 'it is high time to pay homage to Lortzing's principal work. It is very refreshing and effective, despite its weaknesses.'

[187] HOA Z. 412/1906. As in the case of *Don Giovanni*, Mahler asked Kalbeck to retain his earlier text for certain arias and ensembles, in particular Cherubino's two arias, the trio in the first act, the duet at the beginning of the third and the finale of the last act.

Roller and Mahler's approach to *Figaro* was diametrically opposed to the stylization of *Don Giovanni* and the abstract simplicity of *Die Entführung*. Conceiving it as a comedy of manners rooted in its own time, that dealt with real rather than symbolic characters, the décors and the mise-en-scène aimed at the realistic representation of a specific historical and social milieu. The critics realized that on this occasion Roller had not broken with tradition but, as stipulated by Beaumarchais, had merely mingled aristocratic and bourgeois elements. Some of the critics protested against the realism of the first set, a sort of 'lumber-room for saddles, harnesses, hunting equipment'. This disorder and the scraps of red wallpaper hanging from the walls suggested the 'dissolute neglect of the castle', its 'sumptuous superficiality masking profound depravity'.

In stark contrast, the Countess's room in the second act was furnished in perfect and purely aristocratic taste, with simple lines and light colours (white, gold, blue, and yellow). The atmosphere of luxury was tinged with a certain melancholy. Sunlight streamed through the shutters from a large window on stage-right. In the background, between the door and the window, two stools were placed under a large painting. The Countess's bed was on stage-left and beside it a stool for Cherubino.

The trial scene in Act III, modelled on Beaumarchais's original, took place in one of the castle's reception rooms. A red canopy covered part of the rococo architecture. At the end of the scene, after Figaro had been recognized by Marcellina and Bartolo, the curtain fell and rose again to reveal a vast antechamber, framed by two high marble columns and opening onto a park, visible in the twilight beyond a balustrade adorned with brightly coloured shrubs. Susanna leaned against a column to write the billet-doux with the pen, ink bottle, and paper which the Countess had taken from her bag: an inkblot on the white page provided a charmingly realistic detail. Later, after night had fallen, the back of the stage opened up, and backstage-right the light of a distant bonfire mingled with that of torches and candles. It imbued the celebration with 'a kind of mystical character'. 'Like a brightly hued ribbon, the little wedding procession wound around and between them [the columns] and the colourful crowd, excited by intrigues and amorous longings, huddled like children beneath their majestically bare masses.'[188] During the March and the Fandango (which, according to Specht, Mahler interpreted with almost 'painful' accents), a silent crowd slowly assembled around the blazing fires behind the palace gates, a suggestion of the coming revolution. According to George Sebastian, who was at one point Bruno Walter's assistant, Mahler particularly wished to suggest the imminent revolution during the wedding march in the third act of *Figaro*, whose accents 'could be construed as a kind of early guillotine'.[189]

---

[188]   Gustav Schönaich, *Wiener Allgemeine Zeitung* (1 Apr. 1905), 4.

[189]   See unpublished memoirs of George Sebastian, 115 (copy in BMG, Paris). Yet Beaumarchais's indication in the play only mentions 'Fireworks under the great chestnut-trees'. In the production by Giorgo Strehler which inaugurated the Liebermann era at the Paris Opéra in 1973, the pre-revolutionary crowd stormed the castle at the end of the third act.

The final set showed a terrace slightly higher than the park framed by two pavilions decorated with flowering bushes and inspired by those at Schönbrunn (by Fischer von Erlach). The silhouette of the castle with its lighted windows was seen in the distance under a starry sky in the middle of a vast French park with large trees. During the final ensemble, a number of braziers emitted a red glow, once again hinting at the imminent revolution.

Of Mahler's musical interpretation, Erwin Stein left the following description:

Perhaps the most extraordinary feature of Mahler's *Figaro* production was its character of improvisation. The precision of the ensemble had reached such a degree that the singers could relax. The musical shape of the phrases had become so sure that freedom of delivery did not distort them. The ensemble sang and moved freely on the stage, preserving the comedy's lightness of touch, yet perfect timing kept the musical as well as the dramatic form together. This production was miles away from a conception of comic opera that believes gay means rattling speeds. It was the leisure of even the quickest *tempi* that brought the points of music and play across. And the *tempi* of the *secco* recitatives changed freely according to the dramatic situation. . . . The main thing was the ensemble with the interplay of music and action. Mahler himself produced and did not allow any extra nuances which might divert attention from the music—no incidental laughter on the stage. The musical highlights were the finales of the second and fourth acts. The last finale, in particular, was built up as a great Nocturne, beginning in an atmosphere of curious suspense. Susanna's and Figaro's *allegro molto* duet (in 3/4) was very fast indeed but not without flexibility, the speed being dictated by the voices, not by the orchestra's figurations. And the *andante* ensemble, before the final *stretta*, was a climax of beautiful vocal sonority.[190]

Mahler made a considerable effort to achieve a perfect balance between the orchestra and the stage. For example, he added dynamic nuances in the score at the beginning of the last Finale, together with the following indication: 'Everything must be whispered, even when *forte*.'[191] In the mise-en-scène he carefully avoided all excess in comic effects. Given the overwhelming vivacity of the tempo and the action, Mahler dealt with the problem of contrast by creating moments of immobility during which attention was focused entirely on the music, 'which he considered to be unalterable, and which remained the determining factor'.[192]

The new cast found favour even with the severest critics. After having portrayed the page Cherubino 'with delightful high spirits and naive, childish humour' as a character veering between 'modesty and bliss' and overcome with mysterious torments and adolescent desire',[193] Gutheil-Schoder now triumphed as Susanna. Albert Kauders described her as a sort of 'hobgoblin'

---

[190] ESM 308.   [191] Otto Strasser, *Und dafür*, 33.

[192] Marie Gutheil-Schoder, BSP 36. Mahler once again agreed to transpose the keys of certain arias. Hilgermann sang the aria of Act III in B major instead of C, and Mayr his last act aria in D instead of E flat.

[193] Felix Salten, 'Die Gutheil-Schoder', *Schauen und Spielen, Studien zur Kritik des modernen Theaters* (Wiener Literarische Anstalt, Vienna, 1921), 283.

in command of all that happened. Her mastery of *mezza voce*, and the tenderness with which she sang the garden Aria swayed her many enemies among the critics in her favour and entranced the audience. Her performance elicited the following descriptions from three of Vienna's leading critics:

She 'does' a lot of things, though her taste in the choice of dramatic means is consummate. She alone is capable of tenderly adapting herself to the inexpressibly graceful contours of the work. She always 'fits in' with the ensemble, the music, the text and the set. Never monotonous, she has her own discreet shadings for the dreamy, capricious, enamoured and mischievous moments of the role. Even when merely listening, she is never of negligible importance on stage.[194]

Even the usually caustic Liebstöckl waxed lyrical about the new Susanna:

And the gentleness and tenderness of her capricious voice is quite remarkable! She never loses the plot and the action for an instant. Her face and entire being, and all impulses of her heart lend colour and interest to her acting. Even when at rest, she is in motion within. Despite all the commotion she gives Mozart his due. How admirably she sang in the ensembles yesterday and, in the last scene, finally cast aside her whims and high spirits to indulge her feelings to the full!

As for Richard Specht, he noted that Gutheil-Schoder's voice, which had been 'light, silvery and supple the whole evening', suddenly became 'hoarse and strained as she undressed the page for the fancy-dress ball and touched his young, masculine body. Despite the ingenuousness of the acting, it suddenly became hot and self-conscious—a delightful moment.'[195]

In *Figaro* Gutheil-Schoder thus scored one of the greatest triumphs of her entire career. Even Hirschfeld admitted that she had dazzled the audience, although, true to form, he lauded mainly the skill with which she used 'the faded remains of her voice'.[196] By choosing Mayr as Figaro,[197] Mahler took a risk, for Vienna was used to hearing a baritone in this part. Many critics claimed that Mayr lacked humour and vivacity and that his Figaro was far too jovial and good-humoured, mischievous rather than crafty. Kauders derided his 'elephantine grace'; inspired by Bavarian beer rather than by Spanish wine, but no one denied the radiant beauty of his singing. His success in this production influenced his career for many years to come.

Berta Förster-Lauterer's portrayal of Cherubino also represented a milestone in her career. Although the critics agreed that she lacked the boyish charm that the role demanded, they liked her 'sweet and gentle voice'.[198] Hilgermann's 'noble and classical' depiction of the Countess was already well

---

[194] Gustav Schönaich, in *Allgemeine Zeitung*.

[195] Richard Specht, 'Marie Gutheil-Schoder', *Die Schaubühne*, Berlin, 2 (1906): 49, 568.

[196] Korngold and Karpath also praised Gutheil-Schoder's performance. Muntz and Graf were alone in proclaiming that she had amply demonstrated 'the poverty of her artistic sensitivity and lack of soul'.

[197] Hirschfeld and Kauders considered that both his voice and his personality were unsuited to the part, while Wallaschek believed that his Figaro did not match the character created by Beaumarchais.

[198] Ludwig Karpath, in the *Neues Wiener Tagblatt*.

known in Vienna. While Hirschfeld and Graf criticized her for lacking grace and poetry, both Korngold and Karpath praised the purity of her singing and refinement of her phrasing. Weidemann's seigneurial bearing as the Count was also praised: he coupled aristocratic duplicity with noble sensual desire and a disdain for the feelings of others. According to Specht, he was smooth and cajoling, and displayed fiery energy in the scenes of jealousy and fits of authoritarianism.[199] Some however criticized his 'heaviness' and lack of polish. He gave the impression that he was a man divided against himself who had never really stopped loving his wife, and who courted Susanna more out of seigneurial habit than for reasons of genuine licentiousness. Whatever the inevitable reservations, the brilliant cast had rarely been surpassed in Vienna.

Mahler's staging of *Figaro* was soon considered to have been one of his highest theatrical achievements as director of the Vienna Opera. For once, Hirschfeld, Kauders, and Wallaschek joined the general praise and attacked only the restored *secco* recitative to which they much preferred the former spoken dialogues. Korngold, on the other hand, congratulated Mahler for 'loosening the tongues' of German-speaking singers and pointed out the great effectiveness of the recitatives. The influence of Beaumarchais's original text was everywhere felt, in Mahler's staging as well as in Roller's set. Figaro raised his clenched fist to the heavens on the F sharp of his first aria ('Se vuol ballare'), while the great bonfires lit in the third act and the last Finale clearly suggested the menacing, pre-revolutionary era. The costumes were inspired by eighteenth-century Spain: Susanna wore a flowery dress and apron, a white bolero bedecked with orange ribbons, and a black hairnet. The Countess was dressed in the style of Marie-Antoinette and wore a white and light blue dress decorated with flowers and partly covered by a large mantilla. In the first act, Cherubino wore a white and royal blue uniform with gold facings, grey boots, and a three-cornered velvet hat embroidered with pearls. He later changed into white jacket with a wide blue belt, feathered three-cornered hat and large lace collar. During the first act the Count wore a riding dress, a striped white and green flowery vest, a pink jacket lined with navy blue, and dark trousers and boots. Roller's sketches show Marcellina with a hint of a moustache, a flowery, red-checked jacket, a black dress, and a black mantilla with a large yellow knot. For the court scene, she changed into a yellow and green dress with lace collar and cuffs, with a bunch of flowers pinned on her bodice. The peasant women of the chorus wore dark skirts, flowery aprons, yellow scarves, and straw hats over red hairnets.

'Over-refinement' was the leitmotiv of Hirschfeld's various reviews of performances conducted by Mahler during the whole of the Mozart year. In his opinion, the thirty rehearsals for *Figaro* again resulted in 'a performance of indescribable tenderness and delicacy: the orchestra flowed easily and in an

[199] Richard Specht, 'Friedrich Weidemann', *Die Schaubühne* (1906–7), 597 and 599.

effervescent manner and was kept to a *mezzo-forte* throughout, even in the louder parts. . . . Mahler's Mozart is the Mozart of the twilight.' However a 'freer and healthier' interpretation would have been preferable: less attention to detail, less 'anxious care in every measure', in a word a performance such as Mahler had conducted earlier, before he was entirely master of the Vienna Philharmonic.[200] Roller came in for much the same treatment in Hirschfeld's column. The set for the first act was nothing but a 'painter's whim' that seemed ludicrous in conjunction with Mozart's divine music.[201] Mahler himself often changed his mind, but unfortunately his passing fancies remained on stage. Little in the performance pleased the carping critic besides the staging, neither Mahler's tempos[202] nor the cast.[203]

As usual, Maximilian Muntz considered the new production to be a failure, a worthless result of Mahler's and Roller's 'impotent and sterile' theories, which did nothing to overcome the 'weakness of the libretto' and deliberately sterilized the work's original dramatic effect. Only a 'modern', 'decadent' spirit could foist such sets on Mozart, and turn the characters into marionettes devoid of individuality. The unimaginative character of the sets,[204] the inadequate cast, Mahler's virtuoso conducting, and his 'weakening' of dramatic accents were all the result of 'modern decadence'.

The other critics maintained a greater measure of objectivity. According to Schönaich, the performance had plunged every spectator of good will into 'ecstasy'. But even more unexpected was Hans Liebstöckl's praise for a performance of 'unprecedented purity and beauty:'

Rarely on this and certainly on no other stage has Mozart's music presented such a radiant face, such divine goodness and serenity as yesterday; measure for measure, on the stage and in the orchestra, it shone in the sunset of a better, and unfortunately long lost epoch. Without further ado, it must be said that this *Figaro* is a brilliant achievement of Gustav Mahler, the singers, and the orchestra. Yesterday was a true Mozart festival. . . . Once again I am happy to report on an artistic event at our Hofoper. Gratitude obliges me to say that only Gustav Mahler's providential genius could have accomplished this. He disarms both 'objective' and 'subjective' critics, even if they are completely in the right. What is the use of criticizing him today, if he is conducting *Figaro* tomorrow? It is an unequal battle.

---

[200] Hirschfeld also protested against Kalbeck's 'romantic' translation and the 'prolix, pretentious, and bombastic' style of the recitatives. He claimed that the old text had been more singable and that thirty lines at most had needed to be revised.

[201] Hirschfeld approved of the sets for the second and fourth acts, but found the new staging of the letter duet 'contrary to the spirit of Mozart'.

[202] In particular the speed of the Overture and the slowness of Susanna's garden aria.

[203] Once again, Hirschfeld's rancour increased with the passage of time. In his first article he had treated Gutheil-Schoder well, though later, in the *Rundschau*, he compared her to 'a wild cat' and criticized her 'predictable exaggerations'.

[204] Muntz compared the columns of the antechamber of the Count's palace to the 'porticos of our large suburban railway stations' and criticized the garden of the last act for its 'unbroken symmetry, which is quite foreign to Mozart'.

1. Mahler by Moritz Nähr, 30/31 August 1907

(a)

(b)

2. Mahler walking
behind the Vienna
Opera (contempo-
rary postcard
c.1903)

(a)

(b)

3. Mahler annotating scores in Rome, March 1907

4. Signed portrait sent to William Ritter in 1906

Life at Maiernigg,
summer 1906

(a)

5. Mahler in front of the
Mahler villa

(b)

6. (*Above, left*). En famille at
Maiernigg, summer 1906

7. (*Above, right*). Mahler with
his daughter, Maria (Putzi)

8. (*Right*). Mahler with Maria

9. Mahler in Fischleinboden (Dolomites), 10 August 1907

10. Mahler at the seaside in Holland, March 1906, with Alphons Diepenbrock and Willem Mengelberg (Gemeentarchief Amsterdam)

DILETANTENZEICHNUNG   1904

11. Mahler listening to a rehearsal conducted by Mengelberg (anonymous drawing)

12. Mahler at the seaside in Holland, March 1906 (© Hans de Booy, private collection)

13. With Oscar Fried in Berlin, 8 November 1905

14. With Richard Strauss at the theatre entrance, Salzburg, August 1906

15. With Max Reinhardt, Carl Moll, and Hans Pfitzner in Moll's garden on the Hohe Warte, 1905

16. Conducting Beethoven's Ninth Symphony, Strasbourg, May 1905

17. (*Above, left*) Richard
Specht, critic of *Die Zeit* and
one of Mahler's first biographers (Bildarchiv des
Österreichischen Nationalbibliothek)

18. (*Above, right*) Paul
Stefan, another of Mahler's
biographers (Bildarchiv des
Österreichischen Nationalbibliothek)

19. William Ritter with
Janko Cádra in Munich-
Schwabing, 1907 or 1908
(Bibliothèque de la Ville,
La Chaux-de-Fonds, Suisse)

20. Julius and Josefine Korngold with their son Erich Wolfgang, 1911 (Helen Korngold, USA, private collection)

21. (*Below, left*) David Josef Bach, *Arbeiter-Zeitung* (Bildarchiv des Österreichischen Nationalbibliothek)

22. (*Below, right*) Max Graf, *Neues Wiener Journal* (Bildarchiv des Österreichischen Nationalbibliothek)

Dr. Richard Strauss und Familie

23. Richard and Pauline Strauss with their son Franz, about 1907

24. Bruno Walter

26. Klaus Pringsheim (Thomas Mann's brother in law), one of Mahler's assistants at the Vienna Opera (Bildarchiv des Österreichischen Nationalbibliothek)

25. Arnold Schoenberg with Alexander Zemlinsky in Prag, c.1917

27. Willem Mengelberg

28. Alfred Roller, photo by
Mme D'Ora Benda, 1909
(Bildarchiv des Österreich-
ischen Nationalbibliothek)

29. Gerhart Hauptmann by
Emil Orlik, 1909

30. Alma and her daughters, 1906

Kauders also expressed amazement at this 'divine performance', for Mahler's 'noble, beautiful, and convincing' spirit had brought Mozart to life 'as never before'. While admitting that new productions demanded a great deal of time, effort and money, and that they tended to deteriorate after only a few performances, he pointed out that no effort was too great to create such a 'paradise of sound'. 'The divine music flows freely, unimpeded and unclouded, with grace, gaiety and mischief from magical springs of sound. And Mahler was Moses with his staff, who brought this water from the rock.' While admitting that it would be difficult to change the slightest detail of the performance without jeopardizing it as a whole, Kauders questioned the wisdom of restoring the recitatives and replacing the piano with a harpsichord. He considered the ensembles of the second act exemplary with regard to shaping, musical colour, and nuances, a perfect harmony of sound, word, expression, gesture, and figure. This alone, he concluded, deserved our 'total gratitude'.

In the *Neues Wiener Journal* Max Graf confined himself to questions of detail, criticizing especially Gutheil-Schoder's interpretation. He nevertheless conceded that, after the mistakes made in *Don Giovanni*, this revival was a festive occasion at the Hofoper: the orchestra had played in the 'most beautiful chamber music style', and the transparency of the execution, the interpretation, and absolute fidelity to Mozart's score were exemplary. Korngold congratulated Mahler for teaching his singers the 'normal tempo' of dialogue in the recitatives, thereby giving the comedy its due. In his opinion Mahler had not distorted Mozart by reverting to Beaumarchais for the court scene, and his avoidance of stylization was perfectly correct. Despite the beauty of the sets, the critic for the *Neue Freie Presse* wondered whether Roller's emphasis on the comedy's 'romantic and picturesque' side was not detrimental to the gaiety and liveliness of the action.

Having criticized the production of *Die Entführung* down to the slightest detail, Wallaschek now claimed that the 'heavenly music' of *Figaro* had been sung 'so wonderfully' that one forgot any reservations one had about Roller's sets. Karpath regretted that so many contemporary singers should now be out of touch with Mozart's style. Schönaich, while sharing this opinion, admitted that Mahler had 'brought out all the grace, perfume and magic of this most exquisite work of art'. While it was possible to imagine a lighter, more sparkling production, this one was worth 'greeting ecstatically by all music lovers with a true feeling for art'.[205]

The virulence of most critical reactions to his famous towers could lead one to believe that Roller's achievement went unrecognized by the establishment

---

[205] Cast for the 30 Mar. 1906 production: Gutheil-Schoder (Susanna); Förster-Lauterer (Cherubino); Hilgermann (Countess); Kiurina (Barberina); Petru (Marcellina); Breuer (Basilio); Preuss (Curzio); Felix (Antonio); Weidemann (Count); Mayr (Figaro); Haydter (Bartolo). In the second cast, Gutheil-Schoder was replaced by Forst, Förster-Lauterer by Kiurina, Hilgermann by Weidt, Kiurina (in the role of Barbarina) by Pohlner (and sometimes Michalek), Petru by Kittel, and Weidemann by Demuth.

of the time. But the Archives of the Opera set the record straight. In 1906, his contract, which had been signed on a yearly basis since 1903, was renewed for a period of several years, and his annual salary of 10,000 kronen was raised to 16,000. He was given an office inside the Opera and granted disability pension rights which now allowed him to resign from the Ministry of Education. Whereas he had up to now only been only on an extended leave, he was able to give up teaching and devote all his energies to the Opera.[206]

To complete the 1906 festival, only the *Magic Flute* remained to be restaged. As with *Così fan tutte*, the grants were again insufficient for a complete overhaul, and Roller had to content himself with revamping Josef Hoffmann's forty-year-old sets.[207] Only a few of them were totally replaced,[208] but Roller, with Mahler's permission, nonetheless made some significant changes. The Queen of the Night no longer entered from the wings with her attendants, but rose up from behind the rocks in the foreground, which divided before her. Standing in front of her majestic throne, which was framed by two high rocky walls hitherto hidden by the curtains, she was surrounded by her ladies-in-waiting dressed in phosphorescent, steel-spangled gowns. Her imposing silhouette stood out against a gigantic moon, a star-studded sky of the kind Mahler had long envisaged.[209]

At the beginning of the first act, a huge sphinx dominated the stage. In Kalbeck's words, it was a 'symbol of the eternal and unchanging power of nature; a silent enigma responding to the questions of life with the silence of death'. It stood on a massive pedestal set against a cloudy sky. In the fore-ground were rocks covered with plants, rhododendrons, and giant azaleas that suggested the subterranean presence of Queen of the Night. For the first Finale, Roller built three imposing temples. The silhouette of the Speaker was seen against the bright light that emanated from the central edifice. As in 1897, Mahler arranged for Tamino's flute to summon up all sorts of animals, but after the première Roller omitted the lions and the elephant, which were incompatible with the scale of his architecture.

In Act II, Scene ii, Pamina was seen lying in a Nile landscape under a styl-ized arbour of roses in a paradise garden of palm trees, azaleas, and rhodo-dendrons—a sort of homage to the nineteenth-century painter Moritz von Schwind. Once again an almost absurdly large yellow moon shone through the trees 'like an enormous consecrated wafer that as it were neutralized the

---

[206] HOA, Z. 1045/1906. Letters and petitions of Roller, 14 and 15 Mar. 1906.

[207] As we have seen, Josef Hoffmann (1831–1906), a Viennese landscape painter and namesake of the famous Secession architect, designed the sets for the first *Ring* cycle at Bayreuth in 1876. In 1866, his sets for the *Magic Flute* were such a success in Vienna that three years later Franz von Dingelstedt appointed him Chief Stage Designer (*Leiter des Ausstattungswesens*) at the Hofoper.

[208] This cost 20,000 kronen. On 28 Apr. Mahler asked the Intendant for an extra 3,394 kronen for the costumes (G.Z. X. 15/1906). At the same time, he ordered a new *jeu de timbres* from the Paris firm Couesnon to replace the old glockenspiel (G.Z. X. 14/1906 no. 1473, letter of 18 Apr.), and applied for money with which to buy a second celesta from the firm of Mustel & Cie, which was also given the task of modernizing the first one (G.Z. X. 4/1906, no. 707, letter of 19 Feb.). [209] See above, Vol. ii, Chap. 3.

attributes of the Queen of the Night'. The sphinx and stormy sky reappeared, this time accompanied by lightning. For the initiation scene, Roller revived the eighteenth-century movable set: seen through a partially broken trellis, the bamboo forest shifted to the left, revealing a pile of rocks which gradually disclosed the initiation path.[210] The mountain then appeared, and Tamina and Tamino made their way towards it escorted by the two men in armour. They crossed rocks, a fiery abyss, and a stormy sea before triumphantly reaching their goal beneath a vast and starry sky. And once again, during the final apotheosis, the rocks parted before them, allowing them to enter the temple of the sun.

Here Roller designed a set in the manner of Appia, with high, stylized walls, platforms, staircases, and a large rear door, all on rigorously architectural lines. Palm trees and other kinds of tropical vegetation appeared above the wall on stage right. During the final apotheosis the set became totally abstract: Pamina, Tamino, Sarastro and the priests were seen in silhouette against a sky lined with golden rays and yellow, green, pink, and blue concentric circles. The triumphant party celebrated its victory on both sides of the stage, while the vanquished stood in the shadow. On stage-right, in the foreground, the group formed by the Queen of the Night and her three prostrate attendants could have been painted by Ferdinand Hodler.[211] At the end, the Queen was swallowed up by the rocks, while 'the champions of wisdom climbed hand in hand towards the circle of light where, as a symbol of immortality, the gleaming triangles of the pyramid pointed heavenward.'[212]

Mahler had always had a special affection for *The Magic Flute*, as witness his early *Neueinstudierung* in October 1897. He had subsequently conducted almost all the performances himself, and in Korngold's words, each and every performance had been 'a festive occasion'. David Josef Bach emphasized the natural quality of the revised production, and the fact that Mahler managed to 'preserve the popular simplicity of the score by adopting even tempos and avoiding exaggeration'. Erwin Stein also commented on the 1906 production:

The Magic Flute excelled by the sweeping fashion in which its diverse elements were combined, each being given its proper due. This was the true style of the opera, for the contrasting characters complement each other if each is presented in such full stature as Mozart's music suggests. Pamina was, in Mahler's own words, one of Schoder's most precious parts. He allowed her the full expressive range of Mozart's melodies. Her aria,

---

[210] One of David Josef Bach's reservations concerned this scene: he believed that the mobile set failed to create 'the illusion of movement' that was required at this juncture.

[211] See above, Vol. ii, Chap. 15. The painting in question is probably *Die Nacht* (1890).

[212] Max Kalbeck, *Neues Wiener Tagblatt*, 2 June 1906. In the second act, Mahler restored the dialogue in which the three slaves relate Pamina's flight and the Moor's perverse plans. He jettisoned the boys' chariots, which had caught fire the year before. Once again, he accepted a number of transpositions. Elizza sang her second aria in C minor, instead of D minor, Gutheil-Schoder Pamina's aria in F sharp minor instead of G minor, and Moser Papageno's 'Ein Mädchen' a tone higher, in G major. On the opening night, Maikl sang Tamino's first aria in the original key whereas Slezak, whom he replaced at the last moment, usually took it a semitone lower.

the duet with Papageno, the trio with Tamino and Sarastro were thrown into dramatic relief. The Allegro (3/4 time) after her mad scene remained flexible—could Mozart, who was sparing with expression marks, more clearly indicate his intention than by the highly expressive indication '*piano, crescendo, forte*' during the melody suggestive of Pamina's returning happiness? Mahler kept the musical atmosphere tense in most scenes of the finale, even in Papageno's *rondo*. His *scena*, the counterpart to Pamina's, is by no means just funny. The music is more elaborate than any previously connected with Papageno; he too must go through his ordeal. Anton Moser, a light baritone and good musician, sang splendidly and represented a most sympathetic figure. He was not more than a Papageno, gay, careless and very comic, but this Papageno was quite a personality. Hesch was a full-scale Sarastro, Kurz a brilliant Queen of the Night; Breuer, the famous Mime of Bayreuth, sang Monostatos. Georg Maikl as Tamino was not quite a match for the rest of the cast. If my memory serves me right, Slezak sang in a few performances, but his voice was too unwieldy for the part; at that stage at least of his career he was not a Mozart singer. Maikl, on the other hand, was a very capable, sure and musical artist, who adapted himself to any ensemble and took over at short notice any but the heaviest tenor parts. He was the type conductors like to work with. Maikl on the stage was never unpleasant or disturbing, but rarely inspiring.[213]

Other commentators placed greater emphasis on the extraordinary achievement of Wilhelm Hesch, who scored a resounding success in the role of Sarastro. Stein fails to mention the absence of Selma Kurz on the opening night and her replacement as Queen of the Night, Elise Elizza, who was brilliant and self-confident in the role, albeit uninspired. The role was later taken over by Charlotte Seebock.

The main criticisms of this production of *The Magic Flute* were that it lacked the naivety of a fairy tale, and that it failed to bring out the contrast between the forces of day and those of night. Nevertheless, the majority of the critics waxed lyrical in their praise. Even Hirschfeld, in the *Wiener Zeitung*, conceded that 'this time, the new is not merely new, but excellent', and that '[the staging] and the music constituted a harmonious whole'. Of course, in his opinion, Roller's simplified aesthetics were due not 'to the noisy applause of tasteless critics who approve everything on principle, but to objective opposition'. Mahler's principal adversary even recognized that his conducting was as 'masterful' as it had been ten years before, and concluded: 'After suffering this year from too many new translations and too much exaggeration, Mozart was celebrated yesterday in a joyfully reassuring manner'. While regretting that Roller did not have greater means at his disposal, the *Mittags-Zeitung* stated that he had 'done everything he could'. He had unfolded 'a wreath of colour', especially in the last scene. Mahler had attained perfection with singers who, with the exception of Hesch, were not Mozart performers of the first order.

The overall impression was of 'a perfect, eminently artistic Gesamtkunstwerk

---

[213] ESM 307.

of the kind we now tend to take for granted at our Opera', noted the anonymous reviewer of the *Wiener Allgemeine Zeitung*,[214] and added:

At some point we must mention the artistic achievement quietly accomplished in a devoted and unselfish manner by Mahler and Roller. The total energy and effort invested is on a par with the fullness and loftiness of their vision. . . . The Viennese, who carp and quibble and are perpetually concerned with personality cults, will perhaps realize in later years what glorious flowering it let slip by unnoticed.

Wallaschek also expressed deep admiration especially for the lighting effects. Max Kalbeck's article was more specific:

The art of the painter would be lifeless without the musical inspiration it receives from Mozart via Mahler. His [Roller's] 'sets'—sets in the metaphorical sense of the word, for Roller is the sworn enemy of all conventional screens and flats—are permeated with music: the sounds of his atmosphere, the dynamic marks of his light, and the chords of his colours can be played, and one hears them as the inner voices of the score. But however much they may surprise and startle us, or even disturb and shock, their supposed claims recede into the background, clinging more intimately and more inseparably to the music until they transform the entranced spectator into an uplifted and enriched listener. . . . Soloists and orchestra vied with each other in a performance characterized by subtle nuances and refinement.

Thus *The Magic Flute* had brought to a triumphal conclusion the whole Mozart cycle, which shows how effective Mahler's collaboration with Roller could be despite the financial limitations imposed on them. However, the account would be incomplete if it failed to mention the attacks of their perennial antagonists. Once again, the *Fremden-Blatt* singled out Gutheil-Schoder for criticism: 'one notices . . . her agonizing attempt to adapt her voice and character to the so-called chaste style of singing Mozart. Rumour had it that singers were selected for certain roles because they fitted into Roller's costumes, not because they could sing well.' Although the anonymous critic of the *Wiener Abendpost* (probably Hirschfeld once again) claimed that objective criticism had brought Mahler back to earth, and that his conducting was as masterful as in 1897, Paul Stauber, who was fast becoming one of Mahler's most vociferous enemies, claimed in the *Illustrirtes Wiener Extrablatt* that his conducting was becoming increasingly 'pointed, agitated and nervous', and was vastly inferior to his earlier achievements on account of his intransigent 'musical asceticism'. In the *Deutsche Zeitung*, Muntz went even further, deploring the 'nondescript' performance and the fact that Mahler 'deprived the singers of their individuality'. He claimed that, despite its superficial precision and over-refined style, the opera had been given a cool reception. As usual, Roller was accused of suffering from 'a lack of painterly imagination' and a predilection for 'the inevitable straight lines'.[215]

---

[214] Gustav Schönaich had died on 8 Apr., two months before the première of *The Magic Flute*.

[215] Cast for the 1 June 1906 première: Elizza (Queen of the Night); Michalek (Papagena); Gutheil-Schoder (Pamina); Weidt, Pohlner, and Petru (the Three Ladies); Forst, Kiurina, and Kittel (the Three Boys); Maikl (Tamino); Breuer (Monostatos); Moser (Papageno); Haydter (Speaker); Hesch (Sarastro).

Although Mozart's 150th birthday had absorbed most of the energies of the Hofoper in early 1906, Mahler and Roller, as seen above, had put *Lohengrin* into the programme as the only non-Mozartian production of the second half of the season. The previous production was particularly old-fashioned, and the first act of the new one had already been presented three months earlier on the occasion of the official visit of the King Alfonso XIII of Spain.[216] The complete première occurred on 27 February, a month before the first performance of the new *Marriage of Figaro*, under Franz Schalk. Although he seldom conducted it himself, Mahler kept a prominent place for *Lohengrin* in the repertory. It had always been very popular in Vienna and Mahler had a special admiration for its libretto. In his presence Schoenberg once attacked it as outdated and romantic, with its 'bewitchments, magic potions, and metamorphoses'. Despite the 'summons to patriotism' implied by the Grail legend, he went so far as to claim that 'it was hard to blame Elsa for wanting to know Lohengrin's origin'. But Mahler disagreed: 'It is the difference between man and woman,' 'Elsa is the sceptical woman. She is incapable of having the same degree of confidence in the man that he showed when he fought for her, believing her without questioning her guilt or innocence. The capacity for trust is masculine, suspicion is feminine.'[217]

Schoenberg later came to understand Mahler's view of the matter. 'Certainly, suspicion originates in the fear of the one who needs protection, while trust results from the sense of power of her protector.' Thus the subject was eternal, at least for Mahler, still influenced by the romantic tradition. However his view of *Lohengrin* was historical rather than legendary. Both he and Roller decided to respect its pre-Romanesque setting and, as in *Figaro*, to abandon the stylization which had characterized some of their previous productions. Some of the critics even thought that their concern for realism had been taken to a ridiculous extreme and that the production constituted 'a gesture of farewell to the former stage designers of the Hofoper'.

Preparations for the première of *Lohengrin* took place in an exceptionally tense atmosphere. For the 200 members of the chorus and the extras, Roller had designed costumes that were said to weigh 20 to 25 kilos (the anti-Semitic newspapers claimed that some of them weighed as much as 40 kilos). He demanded a considerable number of exceptionally long rehearsals in costume, and tension gradually mounted among the rank-and-file of the chorus. On the morning of the première, Roller made some very cutting remarks about the corpulence of the women in the chorus, in the presence of representatives of the company which had made the costumes. Such was the tone of his voice that one of the singers burst into tears. Shortly thereafter, the chorus sent a delegation to Roller, who declared that their complaints were groundless and refused

---

[216] See above, Chap. 4.

[217] Arnold Schoenberg, 'Gustav Mahler', 'Stil und Gedanke', in Ivan Vojtěch (ed.), *Gesammelte Schriften*, 20 ff. See above, Vol. i, Chap. 16, for an earlier version of this passage.

to let them into his office. On the following morning, the chorus sent Mahler a typed letter signed by all the members. They accused Roller of having deliberately humiliated the most corpulent women in the hope of eliminating them from the chorus, and of having supplied costumes which were far too heavy and cumbersome, especially in view of the fact that the stage was invariably overheated when Mildenburg sang: a young singer had fainted, and it had been impossible to carry him out before the end of the act.[218] Furthermore, the belts of the costumes were placed above the waist, which had prevented the chorus from singing properly. Finally the stage had only one exit in Acts I and III, which was potentially dangerous in the event of fire or panic. If Mahler refused to remedy this state of affairs, the chorus intended to take its case to the Intendant.

Mahler left Vienna for Amsterdam two days after the première of *Lohengrin*, and a solution to the conflict could not be found until he returned. In the meantime, an 'Imperial commission' had been set up and sent to inquire about the chorus's complaints. The choristers were requested to parade in their costumes, and the armoured costumes were weighed on a pair of scales. Roller's supporters insisted that Hans Makart's costumes for the procession in *Der Waffenschmied* were even heavier, so they were also fetched from the storeroom and weighed. Once again, all this fuss came to nothing; it merely increased the tension backstage and reinforced the general impression that Mahler always took Roller's side. The strike threatened for the evening of the première failed to materialize, and the 27 February performance was greeted with tremendous enthusiasm.

All the reviews mention the superb effect of the forest of spears against the blue sky of Act I of *Lohengrin*.[219] The shaking of the spears and the shifting groups seen, for example, when Elsa and Lohengrin make their entrance, brought the entire set to life. The King sat on a rock under a big tree on stage-right, from which he dominated the action on the grassy area in the centre of the stage. A number of his vassals stood behind him, though the vast majority, holding their tall and narrow shields, were grouped in front of him on a small eminence on stage-left. Later, during the prayer, the King came down from his throne to pray with his vassals, a psychological detail which conferred a human dimension upon him. The river flowed along gently in the distance, and the arrival of the swan was practically hidden by the chorus grouped to welcome the hero at the rear of the stage, with their backs to the audience. The brown skiff was criticized by some on account of its prosaic simplicity and also because it arrived directly, for experience had taught Roller that a gradual

---

[218] Otto Kunz, the biographer of Richard Mayr, confirms that one of the extras had fainted during a rehearsal of *Lohengrin*. At the end of the act Mahler is said to have declared that he was probably in a drunken stupor and deserved to be dismissed. Mayr, who sang the King, angrily replied that the man was starving to death, and that, with his wages of one crown per evening, this was only to be expected. The Opera physician later confirmed Mayr's diagnosis.

[219] Some of the critics complained that the backdrop representing the sky was slightly wrinkled.

approach along the meanders of the river, as Wagner wished, could not be achieved on stage. Thus, only the head and neck of the big white swan were visible from the orchestra seats. Eugène d'Harcourt among others complained about the swan's sudden appearance, and disapproved of the papier-mâché trees, which failed to blend with those that were painted. He considered both as symbolizing the unfortunate taste for realism that reigned on the German operatic stage.[220]

For the second act Roller had designed a vast, wholly practicable and complex set which was generally considered to be one of his highest achievements. A large Romanesque palace, or rather a Romantic vision of one, occupied the whole stage with terraces, a hall with columns and arcades, and several flights of stairs, with levels which made it possible for the bridal procession to descend slowly from the back to the front of the stage in several stages, though always in sight of the audience. The small cathedral door to stage-left was reached by a flight of steps which made the conflicts leading up to the entry of Ortrud and Telramund wholly visible. At the beginning of the act, Elsa appeared on stage-right and sang her first aria on the balcony of the Kemenate, which was supported by a single column. Crouching on three steps in the shadows below her were the two 'birds of ill-omen', Ortrud and Telramund. The moon shone through a gap in the ramparts. With the same skill that he had shown in *Tristan* and *Fidelio*, Roller achieved a gradual transition from the blue of the night to the grey of the morning and the dazzling gold of the day. This setting, both handsome and theatrically effective, aroused great admiration. However, some critics pointed out that the stage, as in the Valhalla scene in *Das Rheingold*, was cluttered up, and that the singers, especially the chorus and the extras, were short of space.

For the first scene of the third act, draperies considerably reduced the size of the stage. In the background, the four-poster bed, adorned with garlands of flowers, was brightly lit from within and partly hidden by heavy curtains. On stage-left, a Romanesque window with two stone arches and multicoloured panes opened to the Spring night; on stage-right, next to an arched door with heavy hinges, a wood fire was burning in a tall hooded fireplace. A massive beam decorated with large circles supported the ceiling. The characters were dimly illuminated by the ruddy glow of the fire and by the bluish light of the moon coming through the window. Wallaschek seized on these details to accuse Roller of having depicted 'spring in the heart; spring in nature, but winter in the room'. With regard to the costumes, the major change was Lohengrin's long, pearly grey woollen tunic, which replaced the traditional armour. He appeared bare-headed, like the Archangel Michael. Most of the vassals had large white cloaks and the kind of primitive armour used in the early Middle Ages. The noblemen wore tunics of heavy cloth trimmed with bands of stitching, breast-plates with buckles of steel, and pointed helmets.

---

[220] *Musique actuelle*, 154. Roller's original designs are reproduced in RSM2, 31–3.

The weight of these costumes, as we have seen, was the cause of the violent quarrel which had broken out between Roller and the chorus.

The former cast had only been slightly altered. Schmedes sang the part of Lohengrin as before, and the general feeling was that his voice had grown more supple and his phrasing more expressive. His imposing stature and fair hair were ideally suited to the role of messenger from heaven and a saviour of the oppressed, in contrast with the frail and slender Berta Förster-Lauterer, a tender and poetic Elsa. Throughout the opera, her voice retained its marvellous freshness and youth. Some reviews criticized Demuth (Telramund) on account of his uneven diction and his bourgeois rather than heroic personality. However, Anna von Mildenburg's wily and sinister Ortrud was unanimously acclaimed. Schönaich compared her to Klimt's 'Judith', and praised her acting for its unparalleled presence and grandeur. In Act I she 'sensed the enemy' in Lohengrin, silently summoned up all her energy, and started planning for her revenge. In Act II, she appeared truly daemonic: 'Like a black and monstrous bird she descends on the happiness of her enemy, and, having charmed her, she slinks into the palace like the personification of evil.' In her subtle and powerful portrayal of a 'female Alberich', the moments of calm and sinister immobility were even more disquieting than threatening gestures.

Although Schalk was on the podium, the critics discerned 'Mahler's spirit' at work during the whole evening, although Roller's hand was detected in the crowd scenes, the visual beauty of the groups on stage and the subtle poetry of the lighting. In Kalbeck's opinion, 'this ought to have been enough to disarm Roller's critics'. Mahler achieved extraordinary effects of immobility and simplicity, for example at the death of Telramund. He also restored all the cuts that had been made in the music, and paid particular attention to the choral dynamics.[221] With regard to Franz Schalk's conducting, Alma tells the following story:

He [Mahler] was to relinquish *Lohengrin*, [for] which he had previously conducted,[222] to Schalk. But Mahler did not want this glorious production to become a victim of Schalk's boring routine, and thus devised a devilish plan. He scheduled a rehearsal and sat on stage facing Schalk, who was to conduct the orchestra. Schalk was told to imitate slavishly every nuance and every movement of Mahler's baton. It is difficult to imagine anything more offensive to a man's pride. Schalk obeyed unwillingly. The orchestra grinned secretly. They all took pleasure in his humiliation. Mahler had not meant it that way, but the result, to quote the 'Fischpredigt', was that 'they all remained the same' (i.e. Schalk's tempos), and Mahler now had one more effective enemy at the Hofoper, which was already swarming with enough of those.[223]

---

[221] In the 'prayer' in Act I, Mahler omitted the wind accompaniment that was often added to make things easier for the chorus (see Paul Lorenz, 'Gustav Mahler, ein Unvergessener', *Österreichische Musikzeitschrift*, 12 (1957): 405 ff.

[222] Actually, Mahler had stopped conducting *Lohengrin* several years earlier.

[223] AMM1, 144; AMM2, 114. Alma states that Mahler conducted the first performances of the new production while he had only conducted Act I in Nov. 1905 during a gala performance for the King of Spain. Cast of *Lohengrin* on 27 Feb. 1906: Förster-Lauterer (Elsa); Mildenburg (Ortrud); Schmedes (Lohengrin); Demuth (Friedrich); Haydter (Herald); and Mayr (King).

That Mahler could have inflicted such a humiliation upon one of his assistants, to whom he had entrusted a significant part of the Opera's repertory, seems hardly conceivable. Yet Julius Korngold confirms it at least in part in his memoirs:

Whether one can call Schalk a pupil of Mahler's? Hardly; at best one against his will. He had to bow, like every other member of the Opera staff, to the suggestions of the brilliant director, dramaturge and conductor, but all the same he never adopted Mahler's pedantically strict study system. Besides which Mahler was not the kind of man who spared other people's feelings. He treated his subordinate conductors like beginners who had to learn how to do things, and he rarely entrusted them with new productions. And when he did he would always be there, checking and correcting. Once, Schalk had been given the job of conducting *Lohengrin*. I was by chance at a rehearsal a witness of how ruthlessly Mahler could interfere and give counter-orders. He snatched the score from the conducting Kapellmeister's desk, jumped up onto the stage and pointed out with violent gestures things that had been overlooked. He ironically hinted to the mens' chorus that they should behave like male choruses competing with each other for a choral contest. Small wonder that an ambitious musician like Schalk chafed at the bit and, since he had to bow before the superior genius even more than to his superior's authority, clenched his fist in his pocket. Mahler knew very well that Schalk was no friend of his. So I was somewhat surprised, when Schalk himself became Director, and his supporters were seeking to justify his appointment to his new position, to find that they were proclaiming him to be a pupil of Mahler.[224]

To be sure, Mahler never had a high regard for Schalk as a conductor, and much preferred Bruno Walter.[225] However the episode described by Alma and Korngold can only have caused great damage to the younger conductor's authority.[226] Be that as it may, Mahler's relationship to Schalk remained cordial, outwardly at least, until the end of his life.[227]

Every year Lilli Lehmann gave a number of performances at the Hofoper, and 1906 was no exception. Besides two of her most famous Italian roles, *Norma* and *Traviata*, she appeared as Leonore in the new production of *Fidelio*, but sang only one Mozart role, probably because Mahler insisted that 'guest artists' should take some time in order to fit in with the new productions. Thus Lehmann did not have the opportunity to sing one of her most famous

---

[224] KIW 225.

[225] Ibid. According to Richard Specht, Schalk's conducting 'lacked neither warmth nor liveliness'. Specht felt that although he had many admirers in Vienna, 'he lacked something and that his hand was not in touch with his heart' (RSM2, 120).

[226] When Mahler came to Vienna in 1897, many critics had noted the difference between his interpretation of *Lohengrin* and that of Richter. Kauders, in the *Neues Wiener Journal*, had commented on the 'muffled' sonority of the chorus in Act I, 'which only took part in action with whispers'; the rapid tempo of the Elsa–Ortrud scene in Act II; and finally, in Act III, the heightened melodic phrases of the love duet. He also thought that the first Prelude was more restrained and that of Act III 'faster and more enthusiastic' than when Richter conducted it.

[227] Schalk played an important part in the preparation of the première of the Eighth Symphony in 1910 (see below, Vol. iiii, Chap. 7).

roles, Konstanze in *Die Entführung* (which she sang the following year). For that of Donna Anna, she had agreed to learn Kalbeck's new translation, and that already represented a considerable effort for a single performance.[228]

No important new contract had been signed at the Hofoper since the beginning of 1906, because for the moment Mahler probably considered his ensemble sufficiently well endowed. He even accepted the resignation of Frieda Felser, a lyric soprano he had engaged at the beginning of the season and who felt she was not singing as often as she wished. She was undoubtedly the singer of whom he spoke one evening at a dinner given by the banker Paul Hammerschlag: some months before, he had hired her and placed great hopes in her, both vocally and theatrically. Unfortunately, she had been a great disappointment—not only to the public, but also to him. He had told her the truth that very morning and had been deeply depressed about it all day long.[229]

A few days after the première of *The Marriage of Figaro*, the Hofoper closed for Easter, and Mahler left Vienna for a holiday in Abbazia.[230] Alma provides no information at all about this trip, which was doubtless a brief one, and only a letter to Mengelberg[231] confirms that they spent the week as usual on the Adriatic. Mahler may well have spent his free time working on the orchestration of the Seventh Symphony, though its first performance was given only two years later. On 18 April, back in Vienna, Mahler and Alma read in the newspapers about two tragic events:

Gustav Mahler and I were badly shaken by the terrible San Francisco earthquake, but on the same day Professor Curie, the great discoverer of radium, was run over and killed by a carriage in Paris. Mahler and I knew of his hermit-like existence and his life, which was wholly dedicated to science. We unanimously agreed that this misfortune was the greater one. The discoverer and great benefactor of mankind, who sought and found this substance—versus the nameless mass of people swallowed up like a large question mark.[232]

Although he was busier than ever on account of all the Mozart premières in 1906, Mahler did not conduct more performances than usual.[233] Thus his assistants, Spetrino and Schalk, must have been overwhelmed with work, for since December Bruno Walter had been suffering from chronic pain and a cramp in his right arm. The trouble had started at the end of 1903, when, during a performance of *Tannhäuser*, he had felt the first symptoms, and had had to be replaced by Schalk.[234] After this, the pain had never left him, and

---

[228] Lilli Lehmann's performances were on 17 Apr. (*Traviata*), 20 Apr. (*Norma*), 23 Apr. (*Fidelio*), 26 Apr. (*Traviata*), and 28 Apr. (*Don Giovanni*). As in the previous year, she received a fee of 1,000 kronen per evening, free of deductions (HOA, Z. 36/1906, letter of 1 Jan.).

[229] Communication from Elisabeth Duschnitz-Hammerschlag. Mahler asked the Intendant to cancel Frieda Felser's contract on 31 Jan. (HOA, Z. 195/1906). On 13 June she was informed that her contract had been terminated (Z. 779/1906).

[230] Easter was on 15 Apr. in 1906, and the Hofoper was closed from Tue. 10 Apr. to Sat. 14 Apr.
[231] RMH 68.   [232] AML 46.
[233] Six performances in Jan., nine in Feb., and five in Mar.   [234] See above, Vol. ii, Chap. 15.

sometimes became so severe that he could no longer use his arm for conducting or playing the piano, as he recalls in his autobiography: 'Medical science
called it a professional cramp, but it looked deucedly like incipient paralysis.
. . . I went from one prominent doctor to another. Each one confirmed the presence of psychogenic elements in my malady. I submitted to any number of
treatments, from mudbaths to magnetism.' Walter finally decided to consult
Sigmund Freud, the most famous neurologist in Vienna, whose theories, writings, and methods were by now being widely discussed.

The consultation took a course that I had not foreseen. Instead of questioning me about
sexual aberrations in infancy, as my layman's ignorance had led me to expect, Freud
examined my arm briefly. . . . He asked me if I had ever been to Sicily. When I replied
that I had not, he said that it was very beautiful and interesting, and more Greek than
Greece itself. In short, I was to leave that very evening, forget all about my arm and
the Opera, and do nothing for a few weeks but use my eyes.[235]

It was due to Mahler's intervention that Walter obtained a special grant from
the Intendant to cover his expenses in Sicily.[236] The following postcard from
Mahler to Frau Elsa Walter was probably written at this time:

Dear Madam, Your husband shouldn't worry too much. With Schalk and Spetrino the
Opera is sufficiently provided for, and he should take this opportunity to have a really
good rest. (For people like us, this is only possible when we are ill: I have often had
this experience). So be brave and stay as long as you have to![237]

Mahler had often sympathized with a colleague's predicament.[238] Yet
compassion did not blind him to the necessity of maintaining strict discipline
at the Hofoper. He had attempted to prohibit the claque with only partial
success, as seen above[239] and to prevent the admission of latecomers to their

---

[235] BWT 164. Bruno Walter also recalled having read Ernst von Feuchtersleben's (1806–49) *Zur Diätetik der Seele* which helped him to recover his physical and mental health. A recent article attempts to explain why Freud decided to ignore the possible 'psycho-neurotic' nature of Walter's arm paralysis, and decided to treat it as an 'actual neurosis' (see Nicolas Gougoulis and Vassilis Kapsambelis, 'Recherches sur le concept freudian de la névrose actuelle: de la théorie aux maniements techniques', in *VIème Rencontre de l'Association internationale d'histoire de la psychanalyse* (Dunod, Paris, 1996), 493 ff.).

[236] Walter first received 400 kronen, and, two weeks later, a supplementary payment that enabled him to prolong his stay (HOA, G.Z. 111/1906 and Z. 251/I, letter from Mahler of 16 Jan., G.Z. 251/I, Z. 208, letter from Mahler of 3 Feb.). Bruno Walter thanked the Intendant for the second payment in a letter from Syracuse dated 8 Feb. (Z. 251/II).

[237] Undated postcard to Walter's wife (Library of the Performing Arts, Lincoln Center, New York). Bruno Walter conducted *Die Fledermaus* on 31 Dec. 1905 and did not return to the Hofoper until 9 Mar. 1906, when he conducted *Pique Dame*. Though his journey to Sicily had in fact enabled him to rest, his arm remained incapacitated for some time. However, Freud ordered him to take up conducting again, no matter what. After four more consultations, Walter eventually 'learned to forget' his arm while conducting. 'I finally succeeded in finding my way back to my profession. Only then did I become aware that in my thoughts I had already abandoned it during the preceding weeks' (see BWT 168, and George H. Pollock, 'On Freud's Psychotherapy of Bruno Walter', *Annual of Psychoanalysis*, 3 (1975), 291 ff.).

[238] See below, Chap. 6.

[239] According to Graf the leader of the claque, an upholsterer called Freudenberger, was replaced by someone called Schostal, whose 'skill' as a claqueur took him as far as New York. This of course confirms that Mahler never really succeeded in getting rid of the claque.

seats once the curtain had risen; he had refused to pay singers their full salary if they sang on more than three occasionss at another theatre; he had drawn up new regulations against the wearing of incorrect dress by members of the orchestra, and against their habit of noisily turning the pages of their parts. Recently, he had installed an American clocking-in system[240] for the extras and technical personnel, and ordered the stage-hands to wear felt slippers during scenery changes. He had created a system of fines and penalties involving deductions in salary, of which a list was sent to the Intendant every month. It generally included the names of members of the chorus, dancers, stage-hands, and sometimes even singers.[241] More recently, faced with some impossible demands made by the stage-hands, Mahler had obtained the dismissal of the ringleaders, conscious that the slightest hitch in the smooth functioning of the Opera could be disastrous.[242] The lesson he had learned to his cost in Kassel was applied to the letter at the Hofoper.

Mahler often recalled what had happened during one of the first Wagner performances he conducted in Vienna, when a percussionist[243] missed his entry and Mahler only then realized that he was absent. He always concluded this tale with a description of the musician's surprise when he received a threatening telegram and found Mahler waiting in person for him in his office at 5 a.m., and added:

When I punish someone, I always punish myself along with him. '*Justitia fundamentum regnorum*'—this principle, in my opinion, is nowhere more applicable than at the Opera: one step from the strictest path of justice—especially where the ladies are concerned—and you are irretrievably lost in the theatre. 'I have never done anything for personal reasons. I went over dead bodies, but everyone knew that it was all in a good cause. There were never any other reasons.'[244]

The man who could go to such trouble to improve the welfare of his collaborators, the man who imposed such strict discipline upon them, Mahler the tactful diplomat, Mahler the incorrigible idealist, all these different—even

---

[240] HOA, Z. 540/1905 and Z. 540/I. The Rochester time-clock cost 900 kronen, plus 250 kronen for the installation and for the punch cards.

[241] In Dec. 1903 the list sent to the Intendant on 3 Jan. included a fine of 100 kronen inflicted on the tenor Franz Pacal for some unspecified misdemeanour. Johann Strasky, an oboist in the Vienna Philharmonic, remembered that he often found himself on the list for rising from his seat during ballets to look at the legs of dancer Irene Sironi (Johann Strasky, 'So war Gustav Mahler', *Neues Wiener Journal* (28 July 1936)).

[242] See above, Vol. ii, Chap. 15.

[243] See above, Vol i, Chap. 2. According to Edgar Istel, the percussionist Mahler summoned to his office the following morning was none other than Johann Schnellar. Subsequently, Schnellar and Mahler were on good terms. See 'Erinnerungen an Gustav Mahler', *Neue Musik-Zeitung*, Stuttgart-Leipzig, 38 (1917): 6, 88. Between 1906 and 1910, Mahler often engaged him for performances of his symphonies outside Vienna (see below, Chaps. 7 and 8). In 1910 Schnellar participated in the première of the Eighth Symphony in Munich. In his memoirs (typescript, Akademie Library, Vienna), Karl Moll provides a more detailed version of this well-known incident. It seems that the percussionist lived outside Vienna and had arranged for a substitute during the last part of the performance in order to catch a suburban train home. The terrified substitute missed his cue. Mahler obliged the musician to move closer to Vienna and thereafter prohibited the use of substitutes. Nevertheless, he realized that the musicians were underpaid, and shortly afterwards obtained a salary increase for them.

[244] Edgar Istel, 'Erinnerungen'.

contradictory—facets of his character have been portrayed countless times by contemporary witnesses. Innumerable and mostly reliable descriptions, sketches, stories, essays, anecdotes, reports have come down to us of the man who for ten years reigned over the Vienna Opera. They paint a vivid and comprehensive picture of Mahler at work in and outside the Opera, of the tyrannical, but sometimes friendly Mahler, of the conductor, stage-director, educator, administrator, civil servant, member of the Court hierarchy, who became a legend immediately after his death.

As we have seen, Mahler's conflicts with Opera musicians were largely the result of his rehearsal demands. There is a famous anecdote of an ageing musician, exhausted and exasperated by an interminable rehearsal at the start of Mahler's tenure in Vienna, who stood up and took the new conductor to task: 'Herr Direktor, I have been in the orchestra for nearly forty years and have outlived many a conductor. None of them demanded such gigantic rehearsals! How am I supposed to find the time to give my private lessons?' Mahler stared at the man through his gleaming spectacles and quietly replied: 'Yes, yes, my dear fellow, I understand. But console yourself—you will soon have the opportunity to develop your teaching talents to the full!'[245]

And indeed,

he [Mahler] turned the lives of his collaborators into hell! Within a week he was the most hated man in the house. For years the orchestra had included many worthy old men, professors at the Conservatory, who were not inclined to obey the peremptory and rather unceremonious and strict orders of the director. Every gesture of opposition was rewarded by early retirement, and the vacant places were filled by talented and compliant young musicians. During the rehearsals, which were seemingly endless, Mahler obliged the old professors to repeat their parts over and over again until they complained. It sealed their fate: they had to go into early retirement for refusing to fulfil their contractual obligations. This put so much pressure on the pension fund that it ran out of money, and was only saved by the munificence of His Majesty, who made up the deficit out of his own pocket.[246]

Even allowing for a certain degree of exaggeration, there are so many anecdotes of this kind from so many different sources that there must have been some truth in the allegations. The records of early retirements and new appointments in the Opera archives confirm this. As seen above, the major conflicts which had broken out in 1902 with the Philharmonic occurred because the orchestra, which was organized as an independent republic, refused to accept in its ranks the new musicians which the Opera had engaged.[247] In the face of this constant opposition, Mahler had created the post

---

[245] Alexander Witeschnik, *Musizieren geht übers probieren: Die Geschichte der Wiener Philharmoniker* (Paul Neff, Vienna), 1967, 46.

[246] Ibid. 45.

[247] See above, Vol. ii, Chap. 13. Mahler engaged 14 new musicians in 1898 alone. Before his arrival the rate had been three per year. The last musician to be appointed by Mahler, Wilhelm Sonnenberg, died in the 1970s at the age of 93. He had joined the orchestra in 1901.

of 'orchestral inspector' for his brother-in-law Arnold Rosé, a move which ended up by bringing out the worst in Rosé's character and creating more tensions in Mahler's relationship with the orchestra.[248]

In 1906, one of Mahler's most active enemies, the Czech cellist Theobald Kretschmann, reached retirement age. A colourful representative of the Viennese 'old guard' and a legendary figure in musical circles on account of his Czech accent and bad German, Kretschmann gave an annual recital in the Ehrbarsaal, 'so that people wouldn't forget him'. And it is said that each time he included one of his own compositions in the programme; always the same one. However, in order to attract more attention, he regularly changed the title: the piece was variously described as 'Ave Maria', 'For You', and finally, 'The Battle of Solferino'.[249] This was the kind of musician the Viennese liked; for him tradition was far from being an empty word. He was one of those Mahler was determined not to tolerate any longer than was necessary, especially in view of his headstrong resistance to every order. In his memoirs Kretschmann himself later acknowledged his own obstinacy, admitting that that was the reason why he was always banished to the last row of the cellos.[250]

Kretschmann was far from being Mahler's only enemy in the orchestra. Mahler's rehearsal demands, and the kind of rigorous precision that he aimed to achieve, made many others. And yet this precision was not an end in itself. It was not even puritanical rigour or pedantry. It was primarily a conscious reaction against Viennese slovenliness and negligence. In this way he obtained

the extremely subtle rendering of all the important melodic lines, the surprisingly clear precision of the entrances, excitement, the fascinating sharpness of all the rhythmic and dynamic accents, the eloquent sign language of the left hand, the vibrant expressive power, whereby the left hand, loosely interpreting the phrase, became completely free of what the right hand, the master of the rhythm, was accomplishing.[251]

More than anyone, Mahler was well aware of the fact that 'the essence of music is not to be found in the notes', and often his untiring efforts and fanatical obstinacy were intended to have a psychological effect.

Mahler, the conductor, who belonged to no school or movement, had his own highly personal method of rehearsing, and got on the nerves of every musician. And yet every orchestra he rehearsed did so with passionate interest. This is because everyone immediately recognized and felt that he was the born educator. It was not great admiration and thrilling passion which distinguished Mahler's conducting, nor the craving for

[248] See above, Chap. 2, the story of the conflict between Franz Schmidt and Arnold Rosé.

[249] Alexander Witeschnik, *Musizieren*, 52.

[250] See Theobald Kretschmann, *Tempi Passati: Aus den Erinnerungen eines Musikanten* (Prohaska, Vienna, 1910), ii. 161. In a letter to the Intendant dated 22 Dec. 1905, Mahler stated that, 'according to the orchestral committee, Theobald Kretschmann no longer meets the necessary artistic requirements' (HOA, Z. 1387/1905).

[251] Bernhard Paumgartner, 'Erinnerungen an Gustav Mahler', *Österreichische Musikzeitschrift*, 23 (1968): 6/7, 313.

powerful effect (he often held back in crescendos where others accelerated).[252] Rather, it was the painstaking, almost pedantic way in which he trained his people to concentrate with the utmost attention on certain small and often quite simple passages. In Leipzig he went through numerous difficult parts of his symphony [the Third] fairly rapidly and then suddenly, as the rehearsal was about to come to an end, concentrated doggedly on the relatively easy beginning of the fourth movement. The passage was played quite faultlessly. Any other conductor would have contented himself with saying: 'Very softly and tenderly, gentlemen!' Not Mahler. He had the passage played a dozen times, trying to obtain the best legato and pianissimo that was humanly possible. The musicians sweated profusely. None the less, the forty bars were played again and again. Mahler seemed to be following the principle of a military parade with this precision which verged on torture. With this drill he wanted to achieve the greatest degree of concentration from the orchestra. And he achieved it! Anyone who has played under Mahler will testify that he was terrified by his acute ear and the sharp way he looked at one. The rehearsal hall became a parade ground. Few men would have dared use the rehearsal methods employed by this fanatically zealous conductor. Yet the musicians followed him; they grumbled, but were full of secret admiration.[253]

According to Zschorlich, Mahler's habit of concentrating on a certain passage was his way of 'testing the capabilities of an orchestra' since, in his opinion,

there was no pianissimo nor legato which could not be made a little more pianissimo or legato. Insisting on this unmeasurable, imperceptible difference, which was none the less imaginable, he proceeded to torment his men with his impossible demands. ... These oddities and indeed his stubbornness were construed as the expression of his abrasive, rough and austere personality. This man, who was not charming, and who did not wish to ingratiate himself, who by nature was abrupt, ironical and aloof, this unattractive, reserved and reticent person none the less aroused much secret affection.[254]

It is not difficult to imagine the effect such methods had on orchestral musicians, especially those of the Vienna Philharmonic, with their predilection for the easy way out and their unshakeable belief in their own unrivalled excellence. Mahler often acknowledged that he gave musicians a hard time. In Munich, after a rehearsal of the Fourth Symphony in 1901 during which he had mercilessly tormented a young cellist, a local musician said: 'Well, Herr

---

[252] Many critics stressed Mahler's strange penchant for slow tempos and subdued dynamics. In an article which appeared in the *Wiener Allgemeine Zeitung* on the day after his death on 19 May 1911, Karl Lafite noted that, when Mahler conducted it, the overture to *Die lustigen Weiber von Windsor* 'lost much of its meaning because of the greatly restrained tempo and the subdued dynamics of the *Strette*'; so did that of *Der Freischütz* with its 'foreign emotional manners'. However, in the same article, 'Mahler, der Romantiker', Lafite praised other Mahlerian performances such as operas by Mozart, Auber, and Boïeldieu, or overtures to *The Flying Dutchman, Euryanthe*, and *Eugene Onegin*.

[253] Paul Zschorlich, 'Gustav Mahler als Dirigent', *Strassburger Post* (25 May 1911). These observations were made during the rehearsals and the performance of the Third Symphony in Leipzig on 28 Nov. 1904 (see above, Chap. 1). Elsa Bienenfeld also stressed the way in which Mahler sometimes insisted on a certain detail, repeating a phrase or crescendo as much as forty times (*Moderne Welt*, 3 (1922–3): 7, 7).

[254] Paul Zschorlich, 'Gustav Mahler', *Die Hilfe*, Berlin (25 May 1911).

Direktor, I wouldn't like to play when you're conducting,' to which Mahler replied icily: 'Neither would I!'[255]

Yet even an inveterate adversary like Kretschmann praised Mahler's conducting.

His whole being, his rhythm, his will and creativity seemed to consist of cleverly calculated nervousness. His piercing glances often made the members of the orchestra feel uneasy. The emphasis on certain passages was aesthetically unpleasant; his strange behaviour towards the public was rather disagreeable. Yet despite the occasional imprecision of his conducting technique, his musicality was none the less most inspiring . . .[256]

To a certain extent Mahler seems to have deliberately fostered this state of anxiety among the musicians, for he believed that concentrated attention to the music was a precondition for a good performance. One of the problems which his very personal technique posed for the musicians was his insistence upon 'a continual elimination of the barline which, like the weave of a Gobelin tapestry beneath the lines of the drawing, has to retreat behind the melodic and rhythmic content'. In the hands of a bad conductor the barline became a hurdle, and 'the beats are scanned without making a distinction, like poetry declaimed by a bad actor'. When Mahler conducted, he brought out only what was essential, and it was often impossible to tell how many beats there were in a bar. 'Thus he often passes over the first beat in order to emphasize the second or the third, or whatever he wishes to emphasize.' This kind of conducting inevitably demanded far greater attention from the musicians. 'They must involve themselves in the performance, instead of thoughtlessly following and relying on someone else; those who are inattentive are hopelessly lost', said Mahler.[257]

Mahler's 'tyranny', which was one of the principal subjects of conversation backstage at the Opera and in the Viennese salons for ten years, has been discussed above. Arthur Seidl, one of the first (and only) critics to support Mahler at the time of the disastrous concerts in Berlin in 1895, described it thus in 1902 in *Moderne Dirigenten*:

Yet with the strong artistic force which imparts *verum gaudium* (true joy) to *res severa* (severity), there is in him a severe and domineering 'will to power'. This 'Director' Mahler is the born 'dictator' among our 'conductors', and this leads all the more naturally to friction in view of the fact that his innately imperious nature and mission lead him *nolens volens* to tyrannize those around him and reduce them to 'willing' slaves. They then react with the resentment of chained dogs, which sometimes bark vociferously, and sometimes merely growl in a rather audible manner. Vienna, that happy-go-lucky 'Capua of the wits',[258] provides an especially 'critical' ground for such delicate

[255] *Neues Budapester Abendblatt* (19 May 1911).
[256] Theobald Kretschmann, *Tempi Passati*, ii. 233.   [257] NBL1, 95; NBL2, 108.
[258] Franz Grillparzer called Vienna 'Capua der Geister' because the city of Capua was notorious for its luxury.

experiments. Observers began to take a conspicuous interest in the ruler's health, and, shortly after he had taken over the direction of the Vienna Opera, a more than obliging press speculated that this explosive, nervous and mercurial nature would quickly be exhausted by the dual position of conductor and director. More perceptive minds should have realized that it was precisely this 'personal union' that was capable of preserving a personality such as Mahler's from destruction, for it guaranteed the unity of the artistic will without the presence of any great obstacles, and in a beneficial and encouraging manner. And heaven knows that those who were closely acquainted with the shoddy theatrical magic of Pollini in Hamburg can only marvel at the fact that someone like Mahler could work with a Pollini and his theatrical set-up without being totally worn down or ruining his mental and bodily health! And those who know what it used to be like in Vienna can only welcome this successful 'combination' in the person of Mahler as being the best of all possible solutions, indeed as 'salvation' from the earlier sad state of affairs at the Opera.[259]

When Seidl asked Mahler how he could reconcile so many different functions, especially conductor and administrator, Mahler replied: 'It is the only way I can solve all the problems which arise.'[260] In the course of an interview with the critic Bernard Scharlitt he later stated: 'The separation of the artistic and administrative direction is unthinkable. This kind of "division of labour" is possible anywhere except at the Opera. Here—to borrow an example from daily life—the "cook" not only has to "prepare the meals", but also to "go and do the shopping himself"'.[261] And a year later, speaking to Eugène d'Harcourt, he added, 'You can't accomplish anything on the stage if it is not in perfect harmony with what is happening in the orchestra: therefore it must be the same person!'[262]

Thus Mahler insisted upon having total control over all artistic matters. He also made a point of being present almost every day in his office and available to his subordinates. Anyone who wanted a quick answer or a word of advice had access to him, even when he had an outside visitor with him. With regard to his successor Weingartner, who shut his door as soon as someone came to see him, he said in 1908: 'When Weingartner has visitors in the Director's office, the whole of the Opera comes to a standstill and valuable time is wasted for some conductors and producers, who have but a few urgent words to say to the Director. When I was there, my doors were always open for my most important people; never mind who happened to be visiting me. In this way I saved those who needed it a lot of time.' Edgar Istel, the Munich critic to whom he said this, remarked that Weingartner was only being polite to his visitors by closing his door. In Mahler's time, a warlike, 'Napoleonic atmosphere' emanated from the Director's office. Mahler remained sceptical: 'Yet does he,

---

[259]　Arthur Seidl, *Moderne Dirigenten* (Schuster und Leoffler, Berlin, 1902), 44–5.

[260]　Ibid. and 'Zu Gustav Mahlers Gedächtnis, eine nichtgehaltene Rede', *Der Merker*, 3 (1912): 5, 192 (see also by the same author, *Aufsätze, Studien und Skizzen* (Bosse, Regensburg, 1926), 303).

[261]　Bernard Scharlitt, 'Aus einem Gespräche mit Gustav Mahler', *Neue Freie Presse* (25 May 1911), 11.

[262]　D'Harcourt, *Musique actuelle*, 149.

on account of his politeness, have fewer enemies than I did? No, he merely has other enemies! And then his hands are tied out of deference to a thousand people. I had just as many enemies, but at least I could do what I wanted.'[263]

Mahler's office was on the corner of the Opera looking out on the Ring, next to a rehearsal hall in which he was liable to appear at any moment.[264] It contained a piano, a huge desk with a keyboard of pushbuttons and a telephone connected to the principal services. This office has often been described.[265] Mahler was to be found there during the whole day, except during lunch, during rehearsals and when he was conducting, or when he rested for half an hour or took a walk to the Belvedere or the Prater. Many anecdotes describe the feverish atmosphere of the waiting room, where visitors could spend hours when the Director was especially busy. Once a young Hungarian bass called Erdös, a student at the Conservatory, who had come to apply for a scholarship, finally expressed his impatience in a loud, deep voice. Mahler ran out of his office and slapped him vigorously. A few minutes later, when he finally admitted him to his office, he granted the young singer the scholarship with a mixture of irony and warmth for having so amply demonstrated the power of his voice.[266]

Many contemporaries have described Mahler sitting at his desk in front of a pile of mail and files, with sweat on his brow, groaning as he read his rehearsal notes, and complaining aloud: 'Let the devil be director! Am I an artist or a civil servant?' And to the answer: 'Don't be so hard on yourself Herr Direktor, and take things easy!' he replied with a bitter laugh such as only he could laugh, and shouted: 'Take things easy? I'm sure they'd like to take me out of it altogether!'[267] One of Mahler's most frequently quoted sayings was: 'Others take care of themselves and destroy the Opera. I take care of the Opera and destroy myself!' However, he felt that every day spent at the Hofoper demonstrated why this attitude was essential for him if he was to keep the immense apparatus under control. For ten years, Mahler's triumph was that of a man who was always ready to quit his job if need be, and who kept his letter of resignation ready in a drawer, convinced that 'he who is afraid to lose has already lost everything'. It was also the attitude of someone who 'could sometimes make certain concessions as a man, but never as an artist', who never lost sight of his ultimate goal, and who knew that the success of the whole depended upon the quality of the smallest detail. Why, otherwise, would he have been so concerned to maintain and reinforce the Opera's disciplinary regulations? The case of the prompter Max Blau can be added to those already cited: he was fired in January 1906 for having given a cue so loudly during a

---

[263] Edgar Istel, 'Erinnerungen'.

[264] See in Appendix 3A the plan of the first floor of the Vienna Opera in Mahler's time.

[265] Among others, by Hermann Behn, 'Gustav Mahler', *Die Musikwelt*, Hamburg, 8 (1928): 5.

[266] *Berliner Börsen-Courier* (16 June 1912).

[267] Siegfried Loewy, *Deutsche Theaterkunst von Goethe bis Reinhardt* (Knepler, Vienna, n.d. [1923]), 107.

performance of *Così fan tutte* that he was heard throughout the entire auditorium.[268]

At times, Mahler's perfectionism, his desire to control everything and to leave nothing to chance, worried the court authorities. 'Herr Direktor,' Prince Montenuovo would say, 'you shouldn't move the scenery yourself!'[269] But Mahler stood fast, because he felt that the results he obtained were due largely to his ubiquitous presence. A striking example of his artistic inflexibility is provided in the following incident, which occurred soon after his arrival in Vienna. For a new production of *Mignon*, he wanted real orange and lemon trees and sent August Stoll, the Hofoper's resident producer, to the orangery in Schönbrunn to fetch them. However, the palace's head gardener refused to let him have them. When Mahler heard about this, he left his rehearsal, leapt into a cab, and proceeded at top speed to Schönbrunn, where he threatened to resign if his request was refused. He then returned to the Opera at a gallop and took up the rehearsal where he had left off. The following day the palace gardener, who was taken aback by Mahler's behaviour, called on Prince Montenuovo to explain the danger to which the imperial trees would be exposed as a result of the change of temperature and the transportation.

Prince Montenuovo summoned Mahler at once, and in the mildest possible manner asked him to explain what it was all about. 'First,' he added, 'you really have no authority over the head gardener at Schönbrunn, and secondly, he is quite right to refuse your request.' Mahler bowed politely: 'In that case, your Highness, I have the honour to ask you to accept my resignation.'

'What?'

'Yes, I am going.'

'But dear Director, surely not for a couple of trees?'

'If I cannot fully accomplish my artistic aims,' Mahler replied, 'then the direction of the Opera is no longer of any interest to me.' And with that he went out.

For several days Mahler stuck to his decision and resisted all attempts at reconciliation. The Prince now began to take the matter seriously—not because he considered Mahler irreplaceable (in 1898 he had not yet really proved himself), but because his resignation for such a reason threatened to make the authorities look ridiculous. A bureaucrat of his acquaintance finally found the solution: Mahler's good friend, the civil servant Siegfried Lipiner, was asked to intervene. Lipiner ultimately convinced Mahler to give way. He did so only on the condition that the trees made by the Opera workshops should be better than the real ones at Schönbrunn.[270]

---

[268] HOA, G.Z. 67 and G.Z. 343/1906. Letters of 8 Jan. and 12 Mar. In the second letter, Mahler requested that Blau should be given an ex gratia payment to tide him over until he found another job.

[269] Hilde Spiel, *Du*, 266 (Apr. 1963), 52.

[270] Leo Feld, 'Die wunderlichen Geschichten des Kapellmeisters Gustav Mahler', *Neues Wiener Journal* (1 Apr. 1923). Leo Feld was the brother of Viktor Léon, who wrote the libretto for *The Merry Widow*. Feld wrote the librettos of Zemlinsky's *Der Traumgörge* (see below, Chap. 7) and *Kleider machen Leute*. This incident is

Another anecdote was often told to demonstrate Mahler's independent attitude vis-à-vis the Court and the Lord Chamberlain's Office, who were his immediate superiors. The story dates from the start of his time in Vienna and concerns his old acquaintance Bela Zichy, the one-armed pianist and Liszt pupil who had caused him to leave the Budapest Opera seven years earlier. Administrator of the Hungarian National Opera from 1891 to 1894, Zichy was also something of a composer. In 1899, after writing an opera entitled *Meister Roland*, he tried to use his influence with the Viennese court and the Emperor to have it performed at the Hofoper. Thus, one fine day the Prince gave Mahler the vocal score of the opera and added: 'His Majesty has displayed an interest in the composer.'

A few weeks later, having waited in vain for Mahler's reply, the Prince finally asked:

'What's happened to the opera?' 'What opera?' Mahler replied innocently. 'The Hungarian one, which I recommended to your attention.' Mahler suddenly seemed to know what he meant. 'Oh, that? Nothing doing, your Highness—It's rubbish!' The Prince looked extremely surprised. 'But I told you that His Majesty . . .' 'Ah, excuse me,' interrupted Mahler, adopting an official expression. 'If it is His Majesty's express command, the opera will be put on immediately, and "Imperial Command Performance" will be printed on the programme.' The Prince became rather impatient. 'But surely you understand that His Majesty does not wish to play such a prominent part?'—'Ah . . . And so I'm supposed to take the blame? Never! It is out of the question.' The Prince was thoroughly dismayed. 'So that means—?' 'It means that this opera will never be performed at the Hofoper as long as I am its Director.' 'And this is your final word?' 'My very last, Your Highness!' The Prince was at a loss. 'Then let me ask you for one favour, dear director, give it to me in writing. Send me a report that I can pass along . . . I really don't dare do it personally . . .' 'The Prince never had a letter more quickly,' Mahler told his friends the next day, and laughed.[271]

Other versions of the anecdote end in a more striking way with the Prince evidently insinuating that Mahler had not examined the score properly. To this Mahler replied that it would be perfectly useless, for Zichy 'had no talent!' 'But perhaps someday he might write a masterpiece like Beethoven', said the Prince. Mahler retorted: 'Nothing is impossible, but it is about as unlikely as oranges suddenly growing on a horse chestnut tree!'[272]

difficult to date: Mahler never 'restaged' *Mignon*, which was performed twice in 1898, on 13 Jan. and 27 Mar. According to Hermann Behn ('Mahler', *Musikwelt*, Hamburg, 1928), when the authorities refused to grant the money needed for some particular acquisition, Mahler often paid for it out of his own pocket. This was the case with a stage curtain opening in the middle 'in the Bayreuth manner', which he presented to the Hofoper.

[271] See Feld, 'Geschichten'. Mahler also told the story to Edgar Istel in 1908 ('Wie Mahler eine Productionsoper ablehnte', *Münchner Neueste Nachrichten* (23 May 1911), repr. in *Neues Wiener Journal* (24 May 1911)). NBL1, 103 and BMG 63 mention Prince Liechtenstein instead of Prince Montenuovo but it is possible that the Obersthofmeister himself might have stepped in, instead of his subordinate, whenever an important matter was at at stake. Max Graf tells another anecdote, similar to this one; it concerns an opera composed by the young Archduke Peter Ferdinand (LEM 143).

[272] NBL1, 103; NBL2, 117. To Karpath, Mahler apparently provided the following explanation for his refusal. 'I am not really motivated by a desire for revenge. Believe me, I played through Zichy's opera with

The letter Mahler claims to have written to the Prince is apparently no longer extant. However, the refusal he sent to the composer survives, and deserves to be quoted here:

Your Excellency! Honoured Count! I was under the misapprehension that Count Wilczek had undertaken to inform you that, regretfully, I cannot accept *Meister Roland* for performance at the Hofoper. I admit that there is a certain freshness and carefree quality about your undeniable talent. However, I must say that both the subject and its treatment point the work towards the operetta stage, where one is more inclined to overlook the rather exaggerated contrasts in the plot and the lack of musical original-ity. This at least is my humble opinion, and I am looking forward to the Berlin première, at which I plan to be present, with interest and with the greatest willingness to allow myself to be persuaded of the opposite.[273]

The least one can say is that Mahler did not beat about the bush, even when writing to a protégé of the Emperor! Nor did he hesitate to remind high officials that they were not competent to judge artistic matters. One day, for instance, after conducting Beethoven's Ninth Symphony in Vienna, Prince Montenuovo congratulated him on the performance, and added: 'I will only say that I have heard different tempos on previous occasions.' Aware that this opinion reflected the views of certain critics, Mahler replied in a friendly manner and with an innocent smile: 'Oh, really, Your Highness! So you have already heard this work?'[274]

When the opportunity presented itself, Mahler openly stated that his refusal to bow to any kind of pressure from the court was one of the main principles of his directorship. Otto Brahm, the Berlin theatre director, once told Arthur Schnitzler of an occasion at the home of Theodor Gomperz, the author of *Griechische Denker* (Greek Thinkers), at which Max Burckhard, the former director of the Burgtheater, Paul Schlenther, its new director, and Mahler were present.

In the most candid manner, Mahler rebuked his colleague Schlenther: ... With the Court authorities one had to behave in an entirely different way, for it was never too soon to make them realize that they were not permitted to interfere in artistic matters. As soon as they saw you giving in, there was no end to their intrigues. But in the end they stop short of infringing upon one's department. As dutiful Austrian bureaucrats, they had respect for this. One must never let them overstep their bounds. No one dared do so with him; even Prince Montenuovo had stopped shrouding himself in mystery. Mahler was able to see him immediately, for the Prince knew that at the slightest hint of difficulty he would offer his resignation. By obeying and submitting to every aristo-cratic whim or even orders from above one could never accomplish what one had in mind or defend one's opinion. He had recently been rebuked for his rudeness and

the greatest care and was determined to put it on if it had been at all possible. But it is not ... If His Majesty desires the performance, let him order me to put it on and I will have it called an "Imperial Command Performance".' Karpath also mentions Countess Stáray, a lady-in-waiting of the late Empress Elisabeth, who intrigued on Zichy's behalf (BMG 63).

[273] HOA, Z. VI. 23/1898, letter of 13 Apr.   [274] GWO 96.

reminded that in the court theatre the members of the court were entitled to a certain amount of respect. To this Mahler had merely replied: 'That may be so, but if it is, then this is not the place for me'.[275]

Vienna abounded with stories of singers who came to Mahler with letters of recommendation from high court personalities, and who were firmly turned away. The operetta singer Mizzi Günther, for example, arrived with a personal note from Archduke Franz Ferdinand, the heir to the throne. Mahler took the note, tore it up and said: 'So much for that. And now show me what you can do.'[276] Alma also related what happened when Prince Montenuovo urged Mahler to re-engage the soprano Ellen Brandt-Forster, who had had a short affair with the Emperor some years earlier:

However, she had lost her voice, and Mahler said 'All right, but I won't let her perform.' Prince Montenuovo replied that the whole point was that she should perform: the Emperor had made her this promise and in any case he was paying her out of his own pocket. Mahler replied: 'In that case she shall perform, but the programme will state "By command of His Majesty the Emperor".'

And once again Mahler had his way.[277]

The letter of resignation which Mahler kept ready in his drawer seems to have been written during the second year of his tenure at the Opera, after an archduke had demanded that he engage a mediocre singer. Mahler immediately went to see the Prince and tendered his resignation: 'As an official,' he stated, 'I am obliged to carry out this order. But as Director, I cannot agree to the engagement of a co-director, even by order of the Emperor. I am therefore forced to tender my resignation.' The Prince backed down, but thereafter Mahler kept the letter ready in a drawer. On another occasion, a male singer used his aristocratic connections to obtain an audition with Mahler. After a few brief measures, Mahler interrupted him and closed the keyboard. 'What about my letter of recommendation?' protested the singer. 'That's precisely why I stopped you,' replied Mahler, 'I am not interested in a man who needs a letter of recommendation!'[278]

And once, after repeated complaints from 'maltreated' singers, the Archduke Franz Ferdinand finally summoned Prince Montenuovo, his sworn enemy, and declared: 'I want an end to these scandals at the Opera!'[279] But his influence appears to have been limited, for his orders were ignored and

[275] Olga Schnitzler, *Spiegelbild der Freundschaft* (Residenz Verlag, Salzburg, 1962), 42.

[276] Leo Feld, 'Geschichten' and Hilde Spiel, *Du*, 266 (Apr. 1963). Mizzi Günther (1879–1961) began her career in Prague, and then sang at the open-air cabaret Venedig in Vienna and at the Carltheater. In his biography of Lehár, Stan Czech suggests that Mahler made her a 'fabulous offer' on condition that she let herself be coached by him (Stan Czech, *Schön ist die Welt: Franz Lehars Leben und Werk* (Argon, Berlin, 1935), 118). Shortly afterwards, Mizzi Günther achieved international fame as the first 'Merry Widow', on 30 Dec. 1905.

[277] AMM1, 144; AMM2, 142. Ellen Brandt-Forster's last contract terminated on 30 Apr. 1906. Alma only gives her initials, 'die Sängerin E.B.-F.', though this leaves us in no doubt as to who was meant.

[278] *Königsberger Zeitung* (19 May 1911).   [279] Leo Feld, 'Geschichten'.

scandals, an integral part of daily life in Vienna, continued to crop up until
the end of Mahler's tenure, and beyond. 'His friends remained loyal to him,
though his enemies were aided by the fact that he never replied to attacks and
intrigues. . . . No one is more at the mercy of the dead weight of convention
and "the cussedness of things"[280] than the performing artist', wrote Bruno
Walter in 1907,[281] just as Mahler was leaving Vienna. 'Indeed, Mahler always
treated the attacks and insults of the Viennese press with contempt: "Never
reply to anything" was his basic rule.' To Edgar Istel, he explained his
reasons:

'The problem only gets worse if you reply to it. The average reader usually skims the
news, and he can hardly ever remember it. It catches his attention when it is repeated
or refuted, and it sticks in his mind. My friends do not believe slander, and thus my
reply is of no importance to them. For my enemies, denials are equally unconvincing,
and thus they are of no use whatsoever.'[282]

On one occasion, however, he was on the point of breaking his own rule.
This was when, shortly after his marriage, the yellow press claimed that he and
a singer had been caught red-handed in a rehearsal hall at the Opera. The lady
in question was also married, and Mahler considered issuing a denial. But
when he showed the article to Prince Montenuovo, the latter threw it into the
wastepaper basket with a contemptuous gesture, and with the consent of the
singer and her husband the matter was left at that.[283]

To get out of difficult situations, Mahler acquired in the course of his career
a veritable arsenal of witticisms. They permitted him to say enough without
saying too much and, in an entertaining manner, earned him respect. Some of
them even reached the ears of the press, and journalists often asked Mahler to
confirm them. 'He told me,' writes Bruno Walter, 'that such pithy phrases came
to him instinctively, for experience had taught him that in this way he made
himself understood quickly and in the most comprehensive manner. . . . Their
practical usefulness was more important to him than their logicality.'[284]

Some of his sayings undoubtedly became distorted with the passage of time,
and of others there are as many versions as there are writers on Mahler. As
seen above, this is the case with 'Tradition ist Schlamperei'[285] And while it is
often asserted that Mahler once said: 'It is true that I batter my head against

---

[280]   The expression 'die Tücke des Objekts' ('the cussedness of things') was often used by Mahler.
[281]   BWT 244.   [282]   Edgar Istel, 'Erinnerungen', 89.
[283]   Ibid. The singer in question was probably Marie Gutheil-Schoder. Indeed, it is quite possible that
the Viennese journalists who criticized the 'shrillness' of her voice and failed to appreciate her acting talent
tried to find personal reasons for Mahler's faithful admiration. Mahler might have been in love with her in
1900, when she was first engaged at the Opera, but, after his marriage to Alma, it is extremely unlikely that
he ever had a liaison. Ludwig Karpath relates that Karl Moll visited him to complain about a newspaper article which suggested that Mahler was the real father of a child to which a singer at the Opera had just given
birth. Moll wanted to find out who was responsible for this absurd slander and reminded Karpath that, two
years earlier, at the time of Mahler's marriage, the same newspaper had clearly implied that Mahler should
refrain from marrying because he was impotent (BMG 117).   [284]   BWM 31–2.
[285]   See above, Chap. 1.

brick walls, but the walls finally cave in,' Bruno Walter quotes him in context, replying more simply to an official who asked him why he kept beating his head against the wall: 'Why not? I'll end up by making a hole in it.' Mahler's pithy aphorisms always had a precise purpose. Yet another cited by Bruno Walter must have slipped out in a moment of lucid pessimism: 'Often, what a man learns by experience is the best part of him.'[286] On another occasion, Mahler sent Bruno Walter to hear a new opera, and later wanted to know what he thought of it. When Walter said the work was interesting, Mahler replied spontaneously: 'Interesting is easy; beautiful is difficult.'[287] Other sayings were probably made up by journalists, for example the one—too good to be true— which was often cited by the press during the weeks after his death. To a singer who once complained that he was no longer interested in her 'moving on' or making progress (*Fortkommen*) in her career, Mahler is said to have replied, playing on the other meaning of the *Fortkommen*—moving out or away: 'I am taking good care that you do move on' (*Ich sorge eben für Ihr Fortkommen*).[288]

In January 1907, Korngold claimed in one of his reviews that 'the tyrant is softening', and that 'the practice of adhering strictly to the letter of the law is giving way to a more even-handed approach'.[289] Nevertheless, art always remained for Mahler a deeply serious matter which took precedence over everything else. Once when Eric Schmedes appeared before him at the behest of Princess Pauline Metternich to ask for permission to miss a few Hofoper performances because he had been invited to participate in the Paris première of *Götterdämmerung*,[290] Mahler replied: 'Even if ten princesses asked me to grant you leave of absence, you would not get it, because I need you here.' Franz Naval later recalled that when he was a member of the Hofoper Mahler insisted that he put the interests of the Opera and the wishes of its Director before his own career: 'I can do without you for two or three days,' Mahler told him when he asked for leave of absence, 'but not for three weeks! Have you taken leave of your senses. There's no point in talking about it, it's quite out of the question under any circumstances.'[291]

Mahler's efficiency and objectivity (*Sachlichkeit*) as administrator, director, and producer have often been commented upon, and in that connection he was often criticized for neglecting the human factor. Leo Feld related a typical example of this. Towards the end of a lengthy rehearsal, a singer pleaded fatigue. 'If I can hold out,' Mahler exclaimed, 'then so can you.' On another occasion, in April 1899, in the middle of the rehearsals for a new production

[286] BWM 103.   [287] BWM 99.

[288] *Österreichisches Volksblatt* (1 June 1911); *Leipziger Tageblatt* (25 May 1911); *Die Musik* (15 June 1911), etc.   [289] *Neue Freie Presse* (26 Jan. 1907).

[290] This première was conducted by Alfred Cortot at the Théâtre du Château d'Eau on 16 May 1902. The French ambassador had personally requested Princess Metternich to use her influence with Mahler (Erik Schmedes, 'Die Dinge der Vergangenheit', ed. H. Hergerth, No. 5, *Neues Wiener Tagblatt*, Sunday suppl. (21 June 1931)).

[291] Karl Marilaun, 'Gespräch mit Franz Naval', *Neues Wiener Journal* (30 Oct. 1924).

of Maillart's *Les Dragons de Villars*, the tenors in the chorus began to sing flat. Mahler tried several times to get them to raise their pitch, but his efforts were of no avail. Finally, one of the tenors stepped forward and told him that after singing *Lohengrin* the night before, they were all tired out and 'couldn't sing any better'. After a moment's silence Mahler exploded: 'One more word like that and it will be the last time you ever sing on this stage!' The whole chorus sided with their spokesman, and Mahler was obliged to cut the rehearsal short. However, it was henceforth understood that fatigue was not a good enough excuse for shortcomings at the Opera.[292] As far as Mahler was concerned, only one thing mattered, and that was the quality of the performance. Thus lack of interest and carelessness were his greatest enemies. To a percussionist playing the triangle who complained about the way he was being treated, he once shouted: 'And on top of everything else, you're trying to be insolent?! Be glad that you're learning something for a change! You don't even know how to hold your instrument properly!'[293]

More than twenty-five years after the first performance of *Die Rose vom Liebesgarten*, Hans Pfitzner recalled that Mahler had once said that 'it was never his ambition to give the first performance of a new opera, but to give the best'.[294] Leo Feld, a former Korrepetitor at the Opera, commented on Mahler's famous 'Sachlichkeit':

He was only interested in the thing itself. This total objectivity, or, to put it another way, enthusiasm for the object, was bound to bring him into conflict—in a world based upon total and touchy subjectivity. He was capable of taking a role away from a singer after the public dress rehearsal—for the good of the work and to the detriment of the singer, who quite understandably became his enemy. But he was enchanting and charming when he sensed artistic readiness; when he saw his aims understood and accomplished, in fact whenever he sensed somewhere a kindred spirit. Whether this was in rehearsal or in conversation—in the latter he was exactly as in the theatre: warm, decisive, and full of the kind of fascinating vitality that springs from a rich and lively spirit—he was thankful when he made progress toward his objective, and exasperated when he was held back . . .[295]

As early as 1902, Mahler declared in an interview published in the *Neue Freie Presse* that he was against public dress rehearsals, for the final changes to the staging and music could only awaken ill-feeling if made in the presence of witnesses:

During these public rehearsals, I never manage to get rid of a certain feeling of embarrassment. The dress rehearsal performance is never really perfect, and the presence of

[292]   Karl Weis, 'Eine Erinnerung an Gustav Mahler', *Prager Tagblatt* (21 May 1911).

[293]   Edgar Istel, 'Erinnerungen'. Istel adds that Mahler's interest in percussion led him to finance experiments carried out by Johann Schnellar, the first percussionist at the Opera, who was trying to perfect a new kind of rapidly tunable kettledrum.

[294]   Letter from Pfitzner to Fritz Busch, 27 Feb. 1931, see Pfitzner, *Briefe* (Schneider, Tutzing, 1991), nos. 511, 535.   [295]   Feld, 'Geschichten'.

the public only makes sense if everything is ready. The machinery of the Opera is so complicated that nothing is ever finished before the last moment. If I have still something to say to the artists, the presence of strangers bothers me. Furthermore, I do not understand why I should have to do without this final rehearsal, which is so important, and the final day of preparation. At the same time, it seems natural to invite the critics, for it is impossible to judge a work of art after just one hearing. Unfortunately, the critics form their opinions after the rehearsal, and only attend the première to report on completely superficial matters . . .[296]

Mahler always worked at such a feverish pitch of intensity that those who delayed or held him back exasperated him. It could lead him to utter the ultimate insult: *Dienstboten* (lackeys!).[297] In 1901, in the course of telling Natalie why a Hamburg orchestral musician whom he had hoped to engage had turned the offer down, he said angrily:

If an old man does not wish to leave the place where he has lived for many years, giving up his friends and uprooting himself to go elsewhere, it is understandable and pardonable. But if a young man doesn't do everything in his power to learn, grow and develop when he is given the opportunity to do so, indeed if he is not prepared to go to the ends of the earth for this reason, he should in truth be treated as the ancient Jews treated bondsmen who refused to be free after their serfdom had ended: as a sign of eternal and self-inflicted bondage, wooden pegs were driven through their earlobes, indicating symbolically that they were nailed to the posts of the house.[298]

It is easy to understand that people sometimes followed his orders unwillingly, objecting to his demands, his fanaticism, his 'arbitrary' ideas, the dry and wounding nature of his criticism, his 'tyranny' and, often enough, his inconsistency. For he was neither a theorist nor a thinker. As a born man of the theatre, he addressed himself to reality, and worked with a *Sachlichkeit* which was equalled only by his devotion to art. He also had a gift for improvisation and a taste for the spontaneous that easily led him to change his mind, as Egon Wellesz often witnessed:

In every new production and performance of new works, Mahler showed that he was a theatrical improviser. He sought to mould the staging from the score of the work, without reference to a particular theory of the stage. The richness and the limitless strength of his vision permitted him to take this liberty. He despised the facility of routine, which dried up the vital source of invention.[299]

Alfred Roller has more to say on the same subject:

As a full-blooded man of the theatre, Mahler was an improviser in regard to theatrical matters. Shortly after I arrived at the Opera, I complained that the frenzied activity of a repertory theatre made the scrupulous realization of the sets impossible. In a manner

---

[296] *Neue Freie Presse*, 17 May 1902.
[297] Alfred Roller, 'Mahler und die Inszenierung', *Moderne Welt*, 3 (1921–2): 7, 4.
[298] NBL1, 175, Nov. 1901; NBL2, 201.
[299] Egon Wellesz, 'Gustav Mahler und die Wiener Oper', *Neue Deutsche Rundschau*, 71 (1960): 2, 260.

that was both pertinent and to the point, Mahler explained the situation as follows: 'Everything that you can accomplish here will always have the transitory character of improvisation, but also—and don't underestimate this—its freshness.' With every new production he as it were rediscovered the language of the stage, and, making prodigal use of his immense strength, was as young, creative, enterprising, and bold as on the first day. He scoffed at comfortable patterns and abominated the Ariadne thread of routine . . .[300]

Mahler and Roller were in complete agreement on one essential point: the staging of a work can easily be based on the work itself, not on any preconceived theory. Kitzwegerer wrote: 'His designs never derived from a system. Each new theatrical task posed a new problem in regard to staging.' Mahler wholly shared these views: when asked to describe his 'methods', he replied that [German] opera-staging was on the whole very bad, but that as 'a man of action' words were not his business, for the artist should, like Goethe, not 'talk', but 'create', should like Wagner, set an 'example'.[301]

The French writer Eugène d'Harcourt obtained at firsthand from Mahler the following description of his methods. After the singers had rehearsed singly,

they all went on stage, and no longer concentrated on music. The acting now became all-important. Mr Mahler supervised the staging and tried out various solutions; an assistant made a note of his indications and decisions; then the artists were left to their own devices and the Director encouraged them to improvise as they saw fit.[302]

One of Mahler's favourite singers, Marie Gutheil-Schoder, describes her own experiences at the Hofoper:

He never came to a rehearsal with the production completely worked out in his mind. He probably had in his mind a certain image of an important scene as the climax of an entire act, but at the same time he always left room for individual expression: 'Just get on with it!'. . . Very nice, I like it . . . I'd like to keep that mood . . .' And thus everything grew out of the inspiration provided by himself and by others. When necessary, he personally demonstrated every step—not in order to be slavishly imitated, but to create a harmony of style and to maintain the general mood.[303]

How did Mahler start work on a *Neueinstudierung* or a *Neuinszenierung*? In 1907 he told Eugène d'Harcourt that when a production needed to be restaged, he set it aside for a while in order to be able to start from scratch. Then he began by working individually with each of the singers. During these piano rehearsals he did more than point out the nuances and correct the rhythm and intonation. He revealed to them his own interpretation in the orchestra and his view of the relationship between the psychology, the gestures of the characters, and the score. He never discussed the music without reference to the acting,

[300]   Alfred Roller, 'Mahler und die Inszenierung', 273.
[301]   Letter written in 1903 to the musicologist Carl Hagemann on the subject of operatic staging (*Die Musik*, 2 (1903): 9, 165).   [302]   D'Harcourt, *Musique actuelle*, 149.
[303]   Marie Gutheil-Schoder, 'Mahlers Opernregie', BSP 34.

or the acting without reference to the music.[304] The key to both lay in the score, not in a particular theory. His goal while staging a work was the perfect execution of the slightest detail, right down to the slightest movement on stage, and he strove for an inner unity. 'His heart was on stage while he sat on the podium . . .' wrote Bruno Walter. 'He lived in and with the characters, participated in their feelings and conducted or rather made music on the basis of the drama.'[305] Thus to every opera, and even the oldest, he applied the Wagnerian ideal of the *Gesamtkunstwerk*, distinguishing between moments of dramatic tension and those where the music had to reign supreme and where nothing was permitted to distract the listener's attention.[306] The architecture of the whole rested on such moments, which were the source of 'the inner life, the mood and the spirit' of an opera.

According to Roller,[307] Mahler strove to unify the diverse elements of a work. He would often base the staging on a feeling, part of the plot, or even on a character. In *Don Giovanni*, for example, it was Donna Elvira and her great E flat aria 'Mi Tradi', which was shifted to give it greater importance,[308] and in *Der Waffenschmied* it was old Stadinger and his song. Before and after these pivotal moments, everything had to be perfectly clear, and sometimes this unexpected emphasis on an apparently insignificant passage shed new light on the work as a whole. However much he may have wished to create a homogeneous whole, Mahler never neglected to develop the personality of each character. He rehearsed every singer and instrumental group separately 'so that each of the participants would feel that their part was the essential one, and that they need not worry about the others'.[309] Even in the most complicated ensembles he insisted upon the perfect realization of each part.

Mahler's ear was legendary in German-speaking countries. Tales on the subject abound, including an anecdote about a rehearsal of Smetana's *Dalibor* in which he requested one of the second violins sitting some distance away from him to play the same note on a different string. Similarly, during a rehearsal of Lorenzo Perosi's *La Resurrezione di Lazaro*, he once asked one singer in a chorus of 200 to stop singing an octave above the others. In yet another rehearsal, he stopped the orchestra to inform the fourth horn that he was slightly out of tune, although in fact it was due to the acoustics of the hall. And once—or so the story or the legend goes—when a pin dropped from a musician's jacket during a pianissimo, Mahler was horrified and exclaimed: 'But gentlemen, I did not write a piano note for cymbals at this point!'[310]

---

[304] Franz Ludwig Hörth, 'Der Wendepunkt der Opernregie', *25 Jahre Neue Musik, Jahrbuch der Universal Edition*, 119.   [305] BWM 53

[306] Examples of this were the aria of the Countess in the second act of *Figaro*, and the quartet in *Fidelio*.
[307] Roller, 'Mahler und die Inszenierung', 272.   [308] BSP 34.

[309] According to Emil Gutmann, when Mahler gave him the list of parts for the Eighth Symphony in 1910, he specified the qualities necessary for each instrument. See 'Gustav Mahler als Organisator', *Die Musik*, 10 (1911): 18, 366. His scores at this time suggest that what he really had in mind was an orchestra of soloists (see below, Vol. iiii, Chap. 7).

[310] Paul Zschorlich, 'Gustav Mahler als Dirigent', *Strassburger Post* (25 May 1911).

As seen above, Mahler's first step was always to 'elucidate the musical essence of the work' to his collaborators. He explained to each of them and in detail how to express the slightest gesture, movement, or attitude. But once they had entered into the spirit of the work, he often allowed them to do as they wished. And when, in this manner, they arrived at what he had in mind, he was 'as happy as a sandboy'.

He had eyes and ears everywhere. . . . He was indefatigable in insisting on repeats, climbed out of the pit onto the stage and back again, put singers, extras and props where they belonged; he alone directed all of the staging and music. Tense, tired, and grumbling about this new rehearsal style, the staff went home while he [the Director] proceeded to the wardrobe to look at the costumes and to make alterations, and then talked to the painter about the sets and to the fitters about the wings . . .

Although this strikes us as a faithful description of Mahler at work at the Hofoper, it was in fact written many years earlier about Carl Maria von Weber by his biographer. Julius Korngold quoted the passage in 1907 in order to demonstrate that great opera directors were in fact very similar.[311] Yet, during these days of intense work, one single purpose had to be kept in mind, as Mahler made clear during an interview:

I want to attempt to put into practice at the Opera what has been aimed at and partially achieved in the spoken theatre over the last few years. Everything that is personal should be of secondary importance; it is above all the work which should be at the centre of attention. That is why I wish as far as possible to avoid showcase operas where someone or other can shine in a star role. The Opera . . . possesses an excellent company. However, its members should not be working for their own personal success, but for the work, for the whole, for art. And just as all the performers should be devoted only to the service of art, I want to accustom a certain part of the public—even if it means departing from familiar paths—to appreciating opera not as a means of diversion, but as art. When a Wagner opera is performed, the doors are opened only at the end of each act. No latecomer is permitted to enter while an act is in progress; in this way the public is literally compelled to appreciate art and the work of art, and its mood should on no account be disrupted by a latecomer.[312]

Anna von Mildenburg left an interesting account of an incident which took place during one of the rehearsals of the new production of *Die Walküre* in January 1907.

In the second act, Roller had placed on the stage a rock against which I was supposed to lean during the *Todesverkündigung* (annunciation of death). I stated straightaway that this was incompatible with my view of the matter and that I would not use the rock. At this juncture Mahler cheerfully joined us: he had his hands in his pockets and was in the best of moods—friendly as a child, joyous and full of humour, as he always was when things were going his way, as was the case with *Die Walküre*. 'Yes, Mildenburg, you're going to lean, it will look terrific.' I took up his merry tone and protested,

[311] *Neue Freie Presse* (26 Jan. 1907).   [312] *Illustrirtes Wiener Extrablatt* (19 Mar. 1904).

because . . . But he impatiently interrupted me, stamped his foot and yelled something about dashed odd ideas. I was equally headstrong and refused to yield, thinking that I would indeed have to start having some odd ideas, for it had hitherto been clear to me, without giving the matter much thought, that the Valkyrie must stand before Siegmund in a calm, and even rigid posture if she is to have the strength and firmness necessary to execute Wotan's command, without allowing her own wishes to become apparent— just as in real life, when one forces oneself to be outwardly calm if one wants to hide one's inner agitation. The Valkyrie must stand there solemnly and depersonalized, the mere expression of Wotan's will. Wagner's music points in this direction: before Brünnhilde calls 'Siegmund, sieh auf mich' we hear the solemn, great, and mighty Valhalla motif. And here I was supposed to lean against a rock? How could I effect the transition to a light, relaxed manner after descending in such a serious way? Mahler and Roller referred me to Wagner's stage direction, which stated that Brünnhilde has to lean her head against the neck of her horse. Ah yes, but that was an entirely differ- ent matter, I replied. Brünnhilde was intimately bound up with Grane; he belongs to her and it is one thing to lean one's head against a horse and another to make oneself comfortable on a rock. It was all in vain . . . Mahler wouldn't hear of it, didn't listen, kept on contradicting me, and it was decided that I had to 'lean'. I said no more and clambered up to my rocky eminence to wait for the *Todesverkündigung*. I then descended slowly in step with the music, until the solemn Valhalla motif brought me to a standstill. At this point I stopped. Very calmly and with an innocent look I asked Mahler to act out the scene for me, and with the music of course. With the music, that was it; here we would have to meet and agree; its laws were the same for both of us, and here we would surely come to some agreement. He clambered up out of the pit and I gave him my shield and spear. He told the orchestra to play a few measures of the Valkyrie's descent. The Valhalla motif appeared, he inclined slightly towards the rock, and, as might have been expected, the shield and spear fell down on both sides! 'It's impossible, Roller! Mildenburg, you were absolutely right, leaning is out of question!' Laughing, he rushed back to the pit, and called back: 'No leaning!' The rehearsal continued. I knew that we would reach agreement in this way, for Mahler's method had become my own: to absorb as much music as one can, and then to let it flow out as gesture and movement; let oneself be driven and carried along by it, never parting from it, never resisting it . . .[313]

As seen above, changes of mind were far from unusual for Mahler, but he disliked having them pointed out to him almost as much as he disliked being told that his intentions could not be put into practice. When someone said to him: 'But yesterday you asked me to do *this*, and now you want me to do some- thing else?', he replied: 'You are right, but I am now convinced that it can only be done in this way. You must do as I say!' Thus part of the staging was real- ized at the last minute, sometimes even in the presence of the orchestra. As an example of how Mahler's ideas for the staging were often directly inspired by

---

[313] Anna von Mildenburg, 'Gustav Mahler' (1946 lecture, LPA, copy in BGM, Paris). Mildenburg's diary givs the date of this rehearsal: 4 Jan. 1907. In an article about Mildenburg published in 1948, Leonie Gombrich-Hock refers to the singer's 'monumental calm' and gestural economy during the *Todesverkündigung*.

the music, the baritone Gerhard Stehmann related the following incident, which took place during a rehearsal of *Così fan tutte*:

suddenly, with everything ready on stage, he told the oboe and clarinet to play together on their own. He continued to provide dynamic indications, toned them down, seemed impossible to satisfy and conducted as if he were oblivious to the world. Then he suddenly sprang up from the conductor's seat, leapt onto the stage and gave new directions which completely altered the staging. It was as though he had drawn a secret inspiration from the playing of the two instruments. . . . On another occasion he suddenly interrupted the orchestra during a rehearsal of *Tristan*, climbed nimbly onto the stage and stalked to and fro in an absent-minded manner, though in a great state of excitement. He asked the prompter to hand him the vocal score, but gave it back almost immediately, shaking his head. After hesitating for a few minutes, he then rearranged the staging in accordance with an inner image that was, as it were, magically compelling. Despite his seemingly disconnected and abrupt character, there was always, strangely enough, some inner motivation and unity that he wished to express. A moment later he was back on the podium in order to try out how the new feature fitted into the context of the whole.[314]

Mahler never considered any detail unworthy of his attention. Yet in this regard his stubbornness and readiness to contradict were often more apparent than real. Gerhard Stehmann remembered that Mahler one day noticed that he wore light grey gloves during Act II of *La Traviata*, and that he was not particularly happy with them. Asked for the reason for this small change in his costume, Stehmann faltered and did not know what to reply, yet Mahler did not pursue the point. Be that as it may, at this juncture stark simplicity was more than ever one of Mahler's guiding principles. Everything had to be the 'visible expression' of the music: nothing more, and nothing less.

Because Mahler was dealing with musical works, he had of course staged the music, not the libretto. Not in the sense of translating it, measure by measure, into images, gestures and movement, but in seeking to express the musical essence of the work in question through the totality of the visual presentation, and thus to achieve an astonishingly powerful overall impression, which was brought about by the smooth and purposeful conjunction of the various elements. Mahler spared no effort to communicate this musical essence to his collaborators on the stage. Images, examples, contrasts: all were pressed into service to show them the goal. Each warm-hearted explanation ended with a plea to listen closely to the orchestra: 'Everything is in the score.' When he finally felt that his collaborators were moving in the right direction, he gave them the freedom to choose their own way of reaching the desired goal.[315]

More than ever, he tried to banish from the stage superficial and conventional elements, preferring immobility to 'theatrical' or 'mechanical' gestures

---

[314] *Moderne Welt*, 3 (1921–2): 7, 18 ff. In 1950 Bruno Walter told Eleonore Vondenhoff that Mahler's authority was such that none of the orchestral musicians dared to speak or move while he was on stage giving instructions (personal reminiscence related to the author by Frau Vondenhoff).

[315] Roller, 'Mahler und die Inszenierung', 274.

performed in time to the music, something he considered only 'worthy of a puppet theatre'. Thus during a rehearsal of *Carmen* he told Gerhard Stehmann, the Morales, to sing his part 'lolling in his chair' instead of walking up and down. Stehmann did as he was told during the rehearsal, but on the opening night the trousers of his new costume were so tight that he feared they would split if he sat down and he decided to risk the inevitable reprimand and sing standing up.

The first act was scarcely over when Mahler appeared on the stage: 'Why didn't you remain seated?' Because, I replied hesitantly, for the real reason, the trousers, seemed so ludicrous to me—because I can't hit the high F sharp when I am sitting down; in any case not nearly so well as when I am standing up. 'Well', retorted Mahler, 'try to do it nonetheless'.

During the next performance, Stehmann still did not dare sit down. This time, however, he confessed why he had not done so and Mahler told him to have a new pair of trousers made. Stehmann wore them in the next performance, but at the last moment, genuinely concerned about hitting his high note, he found it impossible to sit still and stood up.

What happened at the end of the first act defies description. Mahler was up there like a shot, eyes blazing. 'Miserable fellow, why did you stand up again?' I really did not know what to say, so I asked ingenuously: 'But, Herr Direktor, were you in your box again?' 'Of course!,' he answered. I replied: 'How was I supposed to know?' He retorted: 'Do you sing for me or for the audience?' I replied: 'For you, of course, Herr Direktor!' And with an incredulous and indescribable look, which was nonetheless anything but angry, Mahler turned around, shook his head, and disappeared.[316]

A very similar story is told by Slezak. Mahler was in the director's box during a performance of *Die Meistersinger* conducted by Franz Schalk. In the *Werbelied*, in Act I, Slezak's memory failed him.

Max Blau in his box, normally so helpful and kind, was busy blowing his nose.[317] I whispered 'Samiel, help!'[318]—In vain. Agonizing seconds elapsed, while I heard a large part of my 'prize song' only in my mind. At last, thanks to Max, who roared loud enough to send the vocal chords into spasm, I picked up the thread and the act carried on to the end like a dream. Mahler came bounding on to the stage, shouting: 'What's happening to you?' At the end of my tether, I shouted back at him in the same tone: 'Why?'—He: 'Are you ill?'—Me: 'No!'—He: 'I thought it was going to stop.'—Me: 'Did you?'—Mahler, dumbstruck, looked at me in astonishment and then, because I had spoken to him in the same agitated tone that he had used himself, turned to Professor Wondra and observed gravely: 'Slezak is mad'.[319]

---

[316] Gerhard Stehmann, 'Kleine Erinnerungen an Mahler', *Blätter des Operntheaters* (Knepler, Vienna, n.d.), 1, 3.

[317] This was the prompter who, as we have seen, was sacked shortly afterwards for prompting too loudly at another performance.   [318] Allusion to one of Kaspar's lines in Weber's *Freischütz*.

[319] See Leo Slezak, *Meine sämtlichen Werke* (Rowohlt, Hamburg, 1959), 145.

Such stories show that Mahler was not always as 'despotic' as he was said to be, and prove that he was not a proponent of movement at all costs on the stage, where everything had to be the 'visible expression' of the music. 'These ladies and gentlemen always want to "act" ', he once complained to Ernst Decsey. 'They go in for grand gestures. Starting in the first act they swing their arms and bring out their entire arsenal—and nothing is left for the third act when the climax comes. Stand still! I always say to Tristan. Stop gesticulating and flinging your arms around, just sing three in a bar—one—two—three! And to give his words emphasis he stamped [his feet] on the floor: one—two—three! In brief, his ideal was a certain economy of gesture. He sought to obtain a desired effect with a minimum of mimicry, since even the slightest movement on stage had impact. The grand gestures had to be saved for the few climaxes. Grand gestures were only effective in a general context of small ones, or none at all.'[320]

The Tristan of whom Mahler was thinking here was Erik Schmedes. With Mahler's help he became not only a great Wagnerian singer, but one of the great singing actors of his time. Schmedes remembered that once, during the second act of *Lohengrin*, he unintentionally made a gesture of denial. Mahler immediately interrupted the rehearsal to say: 'You are supposed to do absolutely nothing at this point. You should look entranced, completely lost in thought, outwardly supported by your gleaming golden costume.'[321] Marie Gutheil-Schoder recalled that when she first arrived in Vienna, her acting tended to be realistic.[322] Mahler was the first to convince her of the necessity of stylization in opera. He did not hesitate to make her repeat the same episode twenty times over, sometimes in front of the orchestra. Above all, he wanted to make the most of the artist's own 'inner wealth'. If it was non-existent or of no interest to the audience, he preferred immobility.

As a producer, Mahler was most in his element in tragedy and drama. Yet he did not disdain comedy and always tried to bring out the comic aspect of situations by accentuating little details which 'clarify certain passages while fitting perfectly into the whole'. Sometimes he would add something at the last moment, but this never had anything in common with the run-of-the-mill traditional, senseless gags which are usually inserted to enliven comedies. Mahler believed that such details were only justified when they corresponded to an inner necessity and when they served to enhance the characterization.

On the first day of the rehearsals for a new production Mahler would assemble all his collaborators, including the stage designer, and get them to speak in turn about their ideas on the work. As they spoke, he took note of the opinions expressed, even though in most cases he ig nored what they said later on.[323]

---

[320] EDS2 and *Die Spieldose* (Tal, Leipzig, 1922), 74.
[321] Personal recollection of Dagmar Schmedes.   [322] BSP 34.
[323] Bernhard Paumgartner related this important detail of Mahler's working methods on Bavarian Radio in 1971. The remark is not included in his memoirs. (Communication from Anna Mahler, who participated in this broadcast).

He proceeded to make the singers act out their scenes as they imagined them in the course of studying the part; these preliminaries served to stimulate his imagination. Later on, an element of collective improvisation continued to contribute variety, interest, and freshness, and this overcame routine. Little by little, the production took shape in his mind and he began to make certain changes. At this stage, he made no notes and did not even look at the score. Yet according to Marie Gutheil-Schoder he already exercised an unbelievable influence on the dramatic development of the roles. He accompanied the singers in their 'work groups', giving each of them his complete attention. Slezak, who did not always appreciate Mahler's rigour, recognized that he brought out the best in everyone and that no one ever dreamt of walking out of these collective rehearsals, even during scenes in which they did not appear.[324] August Stoll, the Ober-Regisseur, wrote down Mahler's directions in a large book, but only during the final rehearsals. Even when Mahler was satisfied with the result, a new idea would sometimes occur to him at the last moment, and with a 'demonic tenacity' he would change the staging of a whole scene to bring it into line with a new detail. In the ensemble rehearsals, on stage, and in front of the orchestra, he displayed an unflagging energy. Like Weber, he ran between the orchestra and the stage with incredible energy, reducing the musicians to hypnotized silence.

He never balked at going over the same crescendo forty times if necessary. His demands were feared, and remained consistently high. 'The smallest shall be the greatest', he would often say, 'that's the case in music as it is in the Bible. If attention is not paid to the dots, a musical presentation is not possible.'[325] To which he added on another occasion: 'Strict adherence to the beat in singing [is indispensable] since the musical expression desired by the composer can only be achieved by exact observance of the note values.'[326] To Natalie he had also said as early as 1896:

It takes a long time, and much experience and maturity is necessary, before one learns to do everything as simply and exactly as it is, neither adding anything nor wishing to add anything that it does not already contain, for more can only be less. As a young conductor, my interpretations of great works were too artificial and affected. I added too much of my own, even if it was with understanding and in the spirit of the work. Only much later did I attain full truth, simplicity, and clarity, recognizing that true art is only to be found in what is wholly unaffected.[327]

With regard to Mahler's scrupulous concern for detail, Schoenberg made an enlightening comment about conducting and interpretation:

But, for example, among other things I once heard one of his 'colleagues' say that there is no special trick in bringing off good performances when one has so many rehearsals.

---

[324] Leo Slezak, *Meine sämtlichen Werke*, 142.

[325] Paul Bekker, in *Allgemeine Musik-Zeitung* (9 June 1905).   [326] EDS2, 151.

[327] NBL1, 30; NBL2, 55 ff. Conversation jotted down after a bicycle ride along the Attersee, 22 June 1896.

Certainly there is no trick in it, for the oftener one plays a thing through, the better it goes, and even the poorest conductors profit from this. But there is a trick for feeling the need for a tenth rehearsal during the ninth rehearsal because one still hears many things that can be improved, *because one still knows there is something to be said in the tenth rehearsal*. This is exactly the difference: a poor conductor often does not know what to do after the third rehearsal, he has nothing more to say, he is easily satisfied, because he does not have the capacity for deeper discrimination, and because nothing in him imposes higher requirements. And this is the cause: the productive man conceives within himself a complete image of what he wishes to reproduce; the performance, like everything else that he brings forth, must not be less perfect than the image. Such re-creation is only slightly different from creation; virtually, only the approach is different. Only when one has clarified this point to oneself does one comprehend how much is meant by the modest words with which Mahler himself characterized his highest aim as a conductor: 'I consider it my greatest service that I force the musicians to play exactly what is in the notes.' That sounds almost too simple, too slight to us; and indeed it is so, for we could attribute the effects which we experienced to far more profound causes. But if one imagines how precise must be the image engendered by the notes in one who is creative, and what sensitivity is necessary in order to distinguish whether the reality and the image correspond to one another; if one thinks of what is necessary in order to express these fine distinctions so understandably that the performing musician, while merely playing the right notes, now suddenly participates in the spirit of the music as well—then one understands that with these modest words everything has been said.[328]

Even though he recognized the importance of improvisation, Mahler flew into a rage when a singer would get tired of repeating the same phrase, and would say that 'the expression would come of its own accord on the evening of the performance'. In order to explain what he meant, Mahler avoided sweeping philosophical statements and preferred to make himself understood through brief and pertinent comments. There are many examples of this. For instance, to explain to Schmedes the transformation he was supposed to undergo upon drinking the potion during the first act of *Tristan*, Mahler told Bruno Walter to describe to him the symbolism of day and night as defined by Schopenhauer. But Schmedes was not an intellectual, and during the following rehearsal Mahler realized that he had understood none of it. Suddenly he had an idea. Stopping the orchestra he said: 'My dear Schmedes! Don't forget that before you drank the potion, you were a baritone; afterwards you are a tenor!' It was an immediate success.[329] In 1910, during a rehearsal of the Eighth Symphony in Munich, when the sopranos had to sing of the roses of the penitent ('Jene Rosen, aus den Händen'), he admonished them with the words: 'Redder, ladies, redder!'[330]

The more he simplified and stylized the staging, the less Mahler was concerned with the 'logic' and 'accuracy' of the details. 'Be glad you have the

---

[328] Arnold Schoenberg, 'Mahler', 'Stil und Gedanke', 7 ff.   [329] BWM 31.
[330] Bienenfeld, 'Dirigent', *Moderne Welt*.

logic of your voice!' he once told Schmedes in the presence of Gutheil-Schoder. Certain specific details, such as the blond hair of Michaela, seemed of secondary importance to him: the essential thing was that the audience should be captivated by the composer's imagination. And since by its very nature opera, in which the characters sing rather than speak, ran counter to realism, the symbolism of a scene was obviously of greater importance than mere accuracy. At the beginning of the *Todesverkündigung*, in *Die Walküre* for instance, Brünnhilde (Mildenburg) appears to Siegmund high up on the rocks like a supernatural being. At the end of the episode, when human feelings begin to stir in her, the aura of unreality suddenly vanishes, and she seems to recover a human dimension. 'Only a profound understanding can reveal what is incomprehensible in a work', Mahler was given to saying. Thus he was always prepared to alter his conception of a work and he never consciously tried to impose his own personality upon it. In fact, he humbled himself before the composers of the operas he conducted. Rethinking the work from beginning to end, adding nothing foreign to it, and yet jettisoning accrued habits and sacrosanct 'tradition': that was his constant aim.

In the presence of both Ludwig Schiedemair and Richard Specht, he insisted that 'tradition' had scarcely touched him and that 'prejudice', the cause of so much harm, had not left its imprint:

I still vividly remember Mahler's striking words about young musicians being inoculated with certain fixed ideas and the harm it does. Thus, if Mahler's interpretation of certain works occasionally resembles that of another conductor, it is not because they belong to the same school or because they share the same background; it is merely an accidental similarity of musical logic, possibly an inner necessity brought about by the spirit of the work.[331]

To this clear statement by Schiedemair, Richard Specht adds:

During his student days, for economic reasons, he had little opportunity to hear operas and to go to concerts. The inestimable advantage to him as a composer and conductor is apparent: neither his compositions nor his interpretations were encumbered with influences of any kind. In particular the fact that, as conductor, he did not feel the constraints of tradition (he later voiced the significant phrase 'Tradition is sloppiness') and was able to mould his own interpretations. This gave him the reputation of being an innovator, an irreverent smart aleck in places were easy-going habits were the rule . . .[332]

To Otto Klemperer Mahler's conducting always seemed 'absolutely natural', even when his interpretation disregarded so-called 'tradition'.

I still remember the opening of the second movement of Beethoven's Seventh Symphony: it sounded quite different, but I could absolutely say 'yes' to it. When he conducted you felt it couldn't be better and it couldn't be otherwise. That isn't the case

---

[331] LSM 34.   [332] RSM1, 14 ff.

with other conductors: with one you have this reservation, with another that, but you don't feel completely comfortable. With Mahler never.[333]

Mahler's own statements clearly explain why he was so suspicious of the concept of 'tradition' and why he became such an innovator and a reformer in the field of interpretation. According to Bruno Walter, his 'intuitive' understanding of musical works and their style protected him from arbitrary interpretative choices.[334] No one knew better than he the duties of the interpreter, to bring the works of a composer to life, to awaken and retain the interest of the listener and even more, to move him. Josef Reitler once asked him how he managed to conduct with such untiring freshness, even after a hundred performances. 'For me,' replied Mahler, 'there is no hundredth time. I conduct for that young man in the balcony who has never heard *Lohengrin* and who must go home with an impression which will last all his life.'[335] Long experience had taught Mahler the mysteries of audience psychology, and he was well aware that 'only temperament' had an effect[336] upon the listener, who was primarily impressed by the warmth of the performance and only rarely understood the beauty of the details.

In his description of a performance of *Tristan* at the Vienna Opera in December 1906, Ernst Decsey eloquently described the effect of Mahler's personality on both the performers and the audience.

I sat diagonally behind Mahler in the second row of the stalls, and could follow his every movement. The opera had just been newly staged by Roller, and I must say that I have never seen a staging that elucidated the work in such a 'dramatic' manner. . . . But let me return to Mahler. I had never heard such a deeply-felt performance, so much liberty combined with so much rigour: he complied with Wagner's wishes by proceeding from the letter of the notes and interpreting it in the spirit of the work. The lighting changed in accordance with the staging and so did the expression. Mahler— I think I may say this, because I have the distinct impression that it is true—re-orchestrated the work while conducting it. He altered the balance within the orchestra, and he improvised, for example, reducing the number of the first violins in order to bring out the second violins, and then bringing them back; or he toned down the violas by half, and then permitted them to play more loudly. In short, it was a nervous kind of music-making: the acute sensitivity of a modern soul sought to capture every shading of emotion, while a superior intelligence never lost sight of the main outline. With Hans Richter and his broad brushstrokes one felt that the big outline consisted of lines, with Mahler it consisted of dots. His body was completely caught up in movement, and in the semi-darkness he gave the impression of being a dwarf-like, fairy-tale character working away in a mystical manner. In the dazzling light of the conductor's podium, his attractively ugly face and dishevelled hair

[333] Peter Heyworth, *Conversations with Klemperer*, 31.

[334] Ernst Decsey was of the opinion that Mahler's conducting often gave one the impression that he had changed the instrumentation. However, this was simply due to the fact that he paid special attention to questions of balance.   [335] JRM (Josef Reitler, 'Gustav Mahler', 62, copy in BMG, Paris).

[336] NBL1, 129; NBL2, 146.

appeared ghostly pale. Every fleeting event in the orchestra was reflected in his sensitive face. At one moment he objected to a detail, whereby he turned up his nose and the skin around his eyes became fiercely wrinkled; the next moment his smile concurred with the euphony of the orchestra, which he enjoyed approvingly. In short, both angels and devils passed over his countenance: when he jerked back his head, lightning flashed from his glasses, behind which his eyes scrutinized, summoned, and stimulated—his entire being was both instrument and expression. In a sketch in the farce 'Er und seine Schwester', in which Girardi portrayed a conductor of this kind, who elicits waves of sound from the musicians with outstretched hand, or makes a stab at the kettledrum, there was an element of truth, as in every caricature. Later, it is true, Mahler calmed down noticeably, but no one could escape the overpowering nature of his presence.

The Hofoper orchestra grew with Brangäne's solo, swelling up with sound and colour. I thought at the time that it was a sort of 'choral breathing'. Like breaths emanating from a passionate breast, mighty suspended chords streamed out of the orchestra. Mahler and the musicians were so absorbed in their own playing that they almost seemed like priests officiating at a church service . . .

With this *Tristan*, Mahler demonstrated what he meant by the 'conductor as a producer'. Mastering everything with his eyes, he seemed to be more in command of the stage than of the orchestra. He lifted his head repeatedly, signalling to the singers, leading them and keeping them in time by looking at them. It is hard to understand how he could do all this with two eyes! At the end of the second act I heard him prompting the singer who was Tristan: *O König, das kann ich dir nicht sagen* (Oh King, this I cannot tell you). Opening his jaws and enunciating each syllable, he literally placed the words in the singer's mouth, and thus the singer was forced to repeat clearly and distinctly: *O König, das kann ich dir nicht sagen*. Mahler's prompting—he repeated it in every important passage—was worthy of the term 'conducting'. Wagnerian 'conducting' in the highest sense of the word. One sensed the importance of the word and saw what effect it had. And thus he was in total control of the total work of art.

On paper, the advantages and disadvantages of this mode of conducting are debatable, but the listener became ecstatic, even though the voices of the singers, which were often too low, were far from perfect. During the intermission I encountered Hermann Bahr, who was walking around in a state of excitement, and I could only utter the word 'Wonderful . . .' I began to love Mahler; Vienna became my Bayreuth.[337]

Many of his contemporaries confirm that 'Mahler's heart was on the stage'[338] during performances, and most of the singers felt encouraged by the intensity of his involvement. Even Slezak later admitted that his high C seemed easier to reach when Mahler was at the podium.[339] Gutheil-Schoder remembered that once, during a performance of *The Marriage of Figaro*, she lost her place and was obliged to start again. At the end of the act, she asked Mahler why he had observed her discomfiture with amusement rather than with anger. 'Well, it was

[337] EDS2, 147 ff.   [338] BWM 153, see above.

[339] Hans Müller-Einigen, 'Begegnung mit Gustav Mahler', *Weltpresse*, Vienna (10 Nov. 1948).

because I took my mind off you for a moment and had to laugh, because I saw that you also at the same moment had lost your place!'[340]

Mahler's conducting, according to Karl Krebs, the author of a book about contemporary conductors, resembled that of Berlioz in many respects. He had the same taste for 'violent and sudden contrasts', the same 'rapier thrusts' that threatened or cajoled a particular musician; the same scrupulousness, the same 'noble, marvellous' ear, the same magical sonority, and the same 'brilliant and supernatural energy which exerted an unforgettable effect on everyone who played under him'. The similarity is striking, and even extends to the 'demonic' faces they are said to have had.[341] Some of the musicians who played under Mahler in New York described their impressions fifty years after the event to William Malloch, who interviewed them many years later.[342] The violinist Hermann Martonne said that the most memorable thing was Mahler's way of 'breathing' between phrases. 'Not always just one, you know, one into the other, but he'd... breathe in between, stop off, see?... He'd always breathe, just like you sing.' When Malloch asked: 'Would he *tell* them to breathe?', Martonne replied 'Oh yes!... That was one of his main points.' In Vienna he had often been accused of *Cäsurenwahnsinn* (caesura-mania),[343] and he kept telling the orchestra: 'The rests are more important than the notes.'[344] Malloch's interview also reveals other striking, little-known aspects of Mahler's conducting: 'See? (breathing) That's almost... almost insensible,' continued Martonne. 'it's just enough to... to make it sound <u>natural</u>; just because it isn't quite natural, I would say. Makes it sound natural... altogether. Something Mahler could never stand was an . . . indifferent tone, indifferent music... No. He said, for instance: "Where Music is, the Demon must be!" '

Once in New York he went so far as to reproach a musician for the way he was seated, and insisted that he should sit on the edge of his chair, tense and attentive.

And he'd say to one of the instruments, 'Have you... have you <u>forte</u>? Have you *forte* there?' You'd think, you know, that... he approves it. The man says, 'Yes, forte.'—'Well

[340]   Marie Gutheil-Schoder, 'In Memoriam Gustav Mahler ', *Musikalischer Kurier*, Vienna, 2 (1920), 19.

[341]   Karl Krebs, *Meister des Taktstocks*, 106. Reference is often made to the famous silhouettes by Otto Böhler, which must surely have been made at an opera rehearsal or performance (and not, as Wilhelm Kienzl suggested, at a concert): Mahler is seated; certain characteristic gestures are directed towards the stage; the building is dark, with a spotlight catching his glasses.

[342]   The interviews were collected and broadcast by William Malloch in 1974 in a programme entitled *Mahlerthon* (see below, Vol. iiii, Chap. 5). William Fuller Malloch (1927–96), né Chester I. Williams, Jr., was born in Grand Rapids, Michigan, and studied music at the University of California. He made extensive research on the subject of tempo in eighteenth-century music, and wrote a great number of articles for various journals and magazines. However, he is best remembered for the two invaluable series of interviews he made in the 1960s with the last surviving eye-witnesses of Mahler's and Dvorak's American epochs (*I remember Mahler*, 1962, and *I remember Dvorak*, 1967), and for his broadcasts on KPFK, Los Angeles, particularly his 7-hour long *Mahlerthon*.

[343]   A pun on the word *Cäsarenwahnsinn* (megalomania). See A. F. Seligmann, 'Silhouetten aus der Mahlerzeit', *Moderne Welt*, 3 (1921–2): 7, 12, and Gerhard Stehmann, 'Gustav Mahlers Proben', ibid. 19, etc.   [344]   Fritz Egon Pamer, *Gustav Mahlers Lieder*, 108.

why do you play <u>fortissimo</u>?' . . . I remember a clarinet player, a very wonderful player—he was very fine, and Mahler always thought the world of him... and yet—one day, for instance... well, he says '*Piano, piano*'. 'But yesterday you said it was too *piano*.' And so Mahler explains, 'Well, well, you know, it all depends on our mood. Mood—it's all mood. Yesterday I probably thought it was too much. Today, I think it's too little.' You know, he—in that respect he was *human*, you know. He didn't say, 'Well, what I say goes,' you know. He just explained that it's all mood. I remember... the Brahms Third Symphony, in F major, and... about the last movement... he says, 'Now gentlemen, you see, that's like a cloudy day, not sunshine, cloudy, a little bit.' He always had pictures. That's one thing that was probably his really strong point... he never let music be just something mechanical. Even if it's <u>forte</u>, it's not always so <u>forte</u>; or *piano*, not always so *piano*... that's one thing that Toscanini never had. You can praise him to the sky, but that inner sensitiveness he lacked completely, I think . . .

When Malloch suggested that 'Mahler terrorized his orchestra too,' Martonne replied:

Oh, but you know, that was something different. If you do your duty and do it well and do it with your heart—he had nothing, nothing against you. He terrorizes when he sees something that is... shouldn't be... he'd never fuss around about things that are immaterial—that didn't matter. But when something counted, was important, meant something, why then he'd insist on it, you know, whether it was the spirit or whether the sound or whether the ensemble or anything. He'd just get what he wants, what he feels it should be. And he'd impart that to his musicians; his musicians should feel that too. Not only demand louder or softer, but demand the *spirit* of it. No, that atmosphere, that's something that... that's what made the man outstanding. My God, he didn't make any show; . . . he always had his hands right next to his body and that's *all*. And if he wanted something to come out, he'd just kind of make a little movement, that's all. Nothing for show. It was just inner. And that's why... rehearsals were never long. They didn't seem long because there was always that atmosphere: we're making music and we want to make better music and we want to make lovely music; we want to do justice to what's being said in music. I was shocked sometimes at how he jumped at people and how he fixed up scores and parts, but... that part of him, you know, as a musician... gigantic.[345]

Mahler was often criticized at the Opera for his predilection for 'actor-singers'—a preference which, without being exclusive, he certainly had. Nevertheless, for him the most important thing always remained the ensemble as a whole, and never a single individual performance. Reacting in all probability against the atmosphere which had prevailed at the Hofoper before his arrival, he had nothing but disdain for 'vocal prowess', demanded that singing be more than 'inexpressive cooing', and insisted that 'dramatic phrasing should not be treated like a solfeggio'.[346] With his annual invitations to Lilli Lehmann, and Caruso's two performances at the Hofoper in 1906 and 1907, he wanted to demonstrate that total vocal mastery was wholly compatible with dramatic

---

[345] *Mahlerthon*, 16 and 20.   [346] RSM2, 123.

temperament. Technical perfection was extremely important to him (as long as it was not at the expense of musical and dramatic expression), and thus he never scorned fine singing. He even engaged a professor of singing, officially known as 'Professor of Diction'. During the rehearsals, a harsh or impure sound made him suffer just as much as incorrect breathing or an inaccurate slur. However, on the stage the musician yielded to the man of the theatre: for Mahler, an opera was always something more than a concert in costume.

Experience taught Mahler that even the most gifted singers could not transcend the limitations of their personalities, and for this reason he sometimes altered his conception of a role to bring it within the range of a particular performer. Gutheil-Schoder, who spent a long time with him studying the role of Cherubino, once described her astonishment at Selma Kurz's gentle, dreamy interpretation of the role. Believing that Mahler had actually changed his conception of the character, she confessed to him that she was rather surprised. Mahler explained that he had merely taken into consideration Kurz's personality, which was unsuited to heady outbursts, and was trying to bring out the versatility and purity of her voice without making impossible dramatic demands.

In 1906 Mahler wrote the following to a singer from Saxony named Alois Hadwiger, whom he had considered engaging: 'Above all I must point out that no artist is engaged for a specific character type. Rather, each singer is employed on the basis of his individual character and is assigned only those roles to which he is suited.'[347] In this respect, Mahler was probably one of the first opera directors whose casting took personality and physical appearance into account along with voice.

To this day the most gifted opera directors suffer—and so did I during my long years at the opera—from the dictatorial demand for singers who are primarily suited to their roles vocally. Whereas acting talent and artistic personality are decisive in casting in the theatre, in the opera vocal considerations outweigh all the others. On untold occasions I was forced to assign a part to a singer for vocal reasons who was dramatically unfit for it! Because of this unavoidable primacy of the voice, opera producers are still faced with serious obstacles when it comes to dramatically satisfying performances. Furthermore, lively facial expression can make it difficult to produce technically faultless sound, and temperamental acting can pose problems for a singer's breathing.[348]

Bruno Walter, Mahler's closest disciple, was more aware than anyone else of the importance of drama and the scenic element in opera, and he had not forgotten the virulent criticism that had been levelled at Mahler for certain daring experiments such as assigning a dramatic role to a lyric tenor (or vice

---

[347] HOA, Z. 1093/1906, letter from Mahler of 29 Oct. In the end, Alois Hadwiger, Kammersänger of the Dresden Opera, was neither engaged nor 'invited' to make a guest appearance in Vienna. However, in 1907 Mahler wrote a letter stating that, as of 1 Sept., he was engaged to sing at the Hofoper. This enabled Hadwiger to avoid four weeks of compulsory military service in the Saxon army at a time when he was learning a number of new roles (HOA, Z. 199/1907, 16 Feb. 1907).

[348] Bruno Walter, *Von der Musik und vom Musizieren* (Fischer, Frankfurt, 1976), 185.

versa), bass parts to baritones, or even Sieglinde to a coloratura soprano like
Selma Kurz. He gave the role of Donna Anna to Vienna's greatest tragedienne,
Anna von Mildenburg, whose singing of Wagnerian roles unfortunately ruined
her vocal agility. He considered the most impossible castings: Mildenburg, for
example, as Queen of the Night,[349] or Schmedes as Don Ottavio,[350] but always,
for sound dramatic reasons. Marie Gutheil-Schoder explains why he was so
often attacked for his unorthodox castings:

Mahler's respect for the individuality of the artist was almost boundless. It is the key
to all the peculiarities which the outraged believers in orthodox tradition held against
him. It was the source of his keen interest in original interpretations and the nuances
of a role which otherwise, perhaps out of indifference, would have been treated in a
perfunctory or a stereotyped manner.[351]

Mahler was not only criticized for having disregarded the most elementary
rules concerning vocal types; he was also accused of having 'ruined' voices—
such as those of Weidemann and Gutheil-Schoder. With greater justice, he was
reproached for being prejudiced against bel canto virtuosos and for prefering
'actor-singers'. Indeed, despite his mania for precision, this born musician,
this lover of perfection and beautiful and unusual sounds, never forgot that
opera was theatre and that a drama must, after all, come to life on stage.

Such was the importance of the dramatic element to Mahler that he never
hesitated, as we have seen, to transpose an aria to a key suited to a particular
singer's vocal range. In these cases, his strict artistic sense and rigid faithfulness to the score gave way to the demands of the drama, and to the singer's
personality and physical capabilities. Similarly, he never opposed interruptions for applause as a matter of principle, and on occasion even expressed his
irritation with those who tried to stop the applause by hissing—for example
after Leonore's great aria in the first act of *Fidelio*. 'During an aria of this kind,'
he said, 'time stands still and the drama is suspended. Applause, therefore, is
entirely justified. It provides relief from the tension, liberation, and produces
new receptivity. These hissers are insincere snobs.'[352] At other times, however,
notably at the beginning of Scene ii in the second act of *Fidelio* when he had
reached the end of *Leonore* Overture No. 3, he would keep his arms raised so
that there would be no applause before the beginning of the Finale.

Much has been written on the subject of Mahler's tyranny but his happiness
and gratitude whenever his collaborators performed to his satisfaction are not
often mentioned. On such occasions, he introduced the custom which Pollini
had instituted in Hamburg: the presentation of a symbolic coin in the wings

---

[349] See above, Vol. ii, Chap. 3.

[350] Gotthard Böhm, 'Der Kammersänger: Vor hundert Jahren wurde Erik von Schmedes geboren', *Die Presse*, Vienna (1968).

[351] A typical example of this was his revaluation of the role of Elvira in *Don Giovanni* (see above and Marie Gutheil-Schoder, 'Mahleriana', in *Moderne Welt*, 3: 7, 15).   [352] BMG 128.

after the performance (in Vienna it was generally a silver crown).[353] Dagmar
Schmedes, daughter of the Hofoper's Heldentenor, remembered that Mahler
sometimes invited her father to dine with him in a restaurant to reward him for
his achievements. Once, after a performance of *Pique Dame* in which
Schmedes had really surpassed himself, Mahler smiled and remarked:
'Schmedes! If you ever lose your voice because of your deplorable drinking
habits, you can look forward to a long career at the Burgtheater!'[354] And when,
after a particularly long Wagnerian act, the tenor retired exhausted to his
dressing room, convinced that he would never be able to emit another sound,
Mahler always dropped in to boost his morale: 'Schmedes, you're nothing but
a coward! You know that you have nothing to worry about when I'm at the
podium!' Indeed Schmedes had acquired such confidence in his director that
once, after a night spent drinking heavily, he simply lay down during a
rehearsal of the first act of *Die Walküre* and passed out, only coming round
when he heard Mahler's voice saying: 'Hey, Schmedes! Are you asleep?'[355]

Schmedes' daughter traces this affectionate, almost father–son relationship
back to the first conflict which broke out between them shortly after Schmedes'
arrival in Vienna, when Mahler refused to give him leave of absence to sing
abroad. Mahler called him into his office and said bluntly: 'I hear that you have
been complaining about me to anyone who cares to listen. If you think that I'm
going to have you sing less often, you are mistaken. On the contrary, you are
going to be twice as busy!' Schmedes was taken aback, but from this moment
on his relationship with Mahler became extremely cordial. He even permitted
himself liberties which no other singer dared to take. Once, for example, while
rehearsing the second act of *Fidelio*, he persistently put his hand in the back
pocket of his trousers every time he sang the words 'Gott, welch' Dunkel hier!'
(God, what darkness here!) When Mahler asked him why he kept feeling for
his wallet, Schmedes replied that he desperately needed money to buy a piano.
Mahler immediately applied for a special grant from the Intendant to cover this
expense.

Another incident took place in 1902, during a rehearsal of *Das Rheingold*
without costume, one of the few works in which both of the two principal tenors
of the Hofoper ever appeared at the same time.[356] Schmedes, who always
prided himself on his appearance, was wearing a pair of white gaiters which
attracted the attention of his rival Leo Slezak. Slezak, who was notorious at the
Opera for his practical jokes, exclaimed: 'Erik, watch out, you're losing your
underpants!' To which Schmedes naively replied, 'Leave me alone, they're not
underpants, they're my gaiters!' Slezak nonetheless continued to stare fixedly

[353]   Dagmar Schmedes, 'Lohengrin in Person, Persönliches von Erik Schmedes', *Volkszeitung*, Vienna
(24 June 1924); Karl Marilaun, 'Gespräch mit Erik Schmedes', *Neues Wiener Journal* (11 Nov. 1917); Desi
Halban, 'My Mother, Selma Kurz', *British Institute of Recorded Sound*, no. 49 (Jan. 1973), 128.
[354]   Dagmar Schmedes, 'Lohengrin'.
[355]   Communication from Dagmar Schmedes to the author.
[356]   Slezak sang the role of Froh and Schmedes that of Loge.

at him until Schmedes became exasperated and made a mistake. Mahler wanted to know what was going on. 'Herr Director, Slezak is teasing me!' was the reply, and Mahler and the entire orchestra burst out laughing.[357]

Selma Kurz respected and admired Slezak as an artist but she got very angry at him when he made her laugh on stage during a performance. On several occasions, she threatened to complain about this to Mahler. One day, when the two of them were singing in *La Bohème* in Budapest to a packed house, Selma came on stage at the beginning of the last act to lie on Mimi's death bed. No sooner had she stretched out on it than she heard a crack from the wood of the bed. As she lay back on the bed its wooden joists creaked ominously and she felt the straw mattress giving way beneath her. She had only one thought: what would happen when Slezak, who weighed almost 100 kilos, sat down on the bed? The minutes passed in an agony of anticipation. The tenor arrived, sat down on the corner of the bed and immediately sized up the situation. In the middle of their deeply moving death scene he whispered: 'Oi weh, Selmale, es kracht' (Oh dear, Selmie, it's creaking)! She only just managed to finish the scene.[358]

Slezak's wit and good humour were also displayed on the Hofoper stage, most of the time without incurring Mahler's displeasure. Once, however, he went too far. While Mahler was busy with the soloists in a rehearsal, Slezak was as usual exchanging banter with some of the members of the chorus. Mahler turned angrily to him with the words: 'My dear Slezak, you are taking matters too lightly. You are always disrupting rehearsals with all sorts of merry pranks instead of settling down to business with the necessary respect! That's very sad! I'm breaking off this rehearsal in the hope that next time you will arrive in the right mood.'

At the next rehearsal, Slezak appeared with a deadly serious face. Entirely dressed in black, with black cuffs and collar, and a top hat lined with mourning crape, he held the vocal score under his arm. He wore a band of mourning. Mahler was astonished and called out: 'Why are you dressed like that?' To which Slezak replied: 'Herr Direktor, last time you said it was very sad and that I should come in the right mood'. Mahler took the matter in good part and laughed heartily.[359]

Schmedes was easily taken in by Slezak, and this often made him a target for his wit. Once, in the middle of the night, he was woken up by a telephone call in which a voice with a strong American accent (it was Slezak) asked him if he were singing *Lohengrin* the following day. Schmedes was extremely flattered and replied that he was, whereupon the anonymous caller, before hanging up, said: 'What a pity! If it were Slezak, I would certainly come!' The following day, Schmedes complained to Slezak about the rudeness of his American admirer. Slezak pretended to be scandalized at the uncouth lout who had awakened his

---

[357] Dagmar Schmedes, 'Lohengrin'.   [358] See Desi Halban, 'My Mother Selma Kurz', 137.
[359] Edgar Callé, 'Ernste und heitere Geschichten aus dem Theaterleben' (typescript), Vienna Stadtbibliothek. The author heard the anecdote from Ludwig Kaiser, a répétiteur at the Opera.

friend, and then broke into the song: 'Nie sollst du mich befragen . . .' (Never should'st thou ask me . . .)[360] When the penny finally dropped, Schmedes burst out laughing.[361] Sometimes, Mahler's quips revealed his exasperation only too well. During a preliminary rehearsal for *Die Meistersinger*, one of the singers was walking to and fro, betraying his impatience. Mahler, who was sitting at the piano, turned around and said: 'What is happening to you, Herr Kammersinger. Are you perhaps taking a cure at Karlsbad?'[362]

Even with the singers he did not particularly admire, Mahler could be exceptionally cordial, especially if they had made an effort or had done him a favour. Thus he once went backstage after the first act of *Siegfried* to congratulate Gerhard Stehmann, who had stood in for Theodor Bertram at the last moment to sing Wotan,[363] and exclaimed with great warmth: 'He never looked at my baton once and yet he never made a single mistake!' On another occasion, after Stehmann had saved a performance of *Figaro* by 'going over' a role in two hours, Mahler again went backstage specially to congratulate him.[364] On such occasions, Mahler always arranged for the Intendant to pay a special bonus to the singer in question.[365] When Mahler was pleased with the entire cast and distributed twenty-heller coins to everyone, those singers who wanted to obtain leave of absence jumped at the opportunity to make their request. Among them was Slezak, who then used to describe his financial situation in the worst possible colours, insisting that he had to earn some extra money by singing in Brno or Prague. 'All right!' Mahler would reply. 'Go ahead, but for heaven's sake, get some rest when you return!'[366]

The baritone Hans Melms, who came to the Hofoper in 1902, had several similar experiences. In 1903 he agreed to learn the role of the father in *Louise* within three days, without a rehearsal before the première. Two days later, Mahler called him into his office. 'What can I do for you?' he asked. 'Do you need anything?' It so happened that Melms was in dire financial straits, and he requested an advance of 4,000 kronen, which Mahler arranged to obtain from the Obersthofmeisteramt. Later, after earning Mahler's gratitude for his performance in another role,[367] Melms realized that his debt repayments had not

[360] Lohengrin's words to Elsa in Act I, the forbidden question.

[361] Edgar Callé, 'Geschichten'. As seen above (Vol. ii, Chap. 10), Schmedes was extremely jealous of Slezak's success. Lohengrin, in fact, was the only role they both sang.

[362] Gerhard Stehmann, 'Erinnerungen', *Moderne Welt*, 18.

[363] This was on 20 Dec. 1905. Bertram had been invited to Vienna for the complete cycle, but only sang in the 17 Dec. performance of *Die Walküre*.

[364] In *Blätter des Operntheaters*. The role which Stehmann 'went over' was probably that of Antonio, the gardener. He sang this only once, on 8 May 1907.

[365] This happened when Stehmann stood in for Bertram and also later, when he learned the role of the Nachtwandler in a few days for a performance of *Die Rose vom Liebesgarten* (HOA, Z. 5176/1905, letter of 22 Dec.).   [366] Leo Slezak, *Meine sämtlichen Werke*.

[367] Melms claims that this was after the new production of *Tristan*, in which he sang Kurwenal on 21 Feb. 1903. However, as seen above, this performance preceded that of *Louise*. The names of the two singers who sang the roles of the Father and the Mother in the Viennese première of *Louise* on 24 Mar. 1903 were omitted by mistake in Vol. ii, Chap. 14. They were Leopold Demuth and Laura Hilgermann.

been deducted from his salary. He then discovered that Mahler had managed to have the repayments waived, but had forgotten to tell him. With regard to leave to sing abroad, which he was always reluctant to grant, Mahler was infinitely more willing to co-operate when the singer in question had put himself out for the Hofoper. Examples abound of singers like Willi Hesch or Fritz Schrödter whom he supported financially because they were ill and unable to continue in their profession.

When he felt that it was necessary, Mahler could move heaven and earth to flatter the vanity or reward the zeal of members of the Opera. The title of Kammersänger, for example, the supreme reward for a singer in Vienna, was awarded by the Court only after the most careful deliberation. In 1900, the Emperor had bestowed it upon Nellie Melba on the day of her much-publicized command performance at the Hofoper. Sometime later, according to Ludwig Karpath, after a singer Mahler disliked had finally tendered her resignation,[368] the Court decided to award her the title of Kammersängerin by way compensation. Believing that his best singers had been slighted, Mahler demanded the same privilege for Mildenburg, Saville, Naval, Schmedes, Demuth, and Hesch. Karpath claims that his request was granted, although the singer in question had been at the Opera for ten years and the others a much shorter time.

Hans Melms, like so many others before him, recalled that Mahler was exasperated with singers who tried to ingratiate themselves with him by flattery, or who were capricious, or, having a high opinion of themselves, complacent. Those who refused to be corrected by a répétiteur at the Hofoper were quickly called to order. Appointed to the post in 1906 at the age of 21, the fourth répétiteur, Klaus Pringsheim (Thomas Mann's future brother-in-law) once came into conflict with a tenor who habitually sang the role of Mime[369] and resented taking orders from such a young man. Pringsheim complained to Mahler, who explained that it would be an error for him to summon the tenor immediately. Pringsheim should continue to work with him until he once again refused to follow his instructions. At that point, he should stop the rehearsal and summon Wondra, who was in charge of the preparatory work. Wondra would then pass the matter to Mahler by the official channels and he would then take appropriate action. According to Pringsheim, no young répétiteur had ever dared interrupt a celebrated Kammersänger in Vienna. But Mahler supported him.[370] Whenever he was preparing a new production and came up against the resistance of a singer, he often compelled him or her to practise for hours on end, until he achieved the desired result. In the words of Hans Melms, 'he didn't "plague" them for the fun of it. Mahler wasn't that petty—but because he disliked underachievement, delighted in good singing and acting, and had the utmost respect for art. . . . He disliked flattery, and appreciated sincerity and

[368] It could have been Marie Renard, or Edyth Walker, or Luise von Ehrenstein.
[369] The tenor was probably Hans Breuer. See below, Chap. 6, for the biography of Klaus Pringsheim.
[370] Klaus Pringsheim, 'Erinnerungen an Gustav Mahler', *Neue Zürcher Zeitung* (7 July 1960).

even bluntness, provided they went together with a true reverence for the great masterpieces.'[371] He could also be pleasant, even charming, to singers or musicians he respected, even if they did not always come up to his expectations, as can be perceived from the end of a letter Theodor Reichmann wrote him in answer to his admonishments: 'Dear Herr Direktor, I cannot end this letter without expressing my heartfelt admiration for your composure during the performance of *Siegfried* and for your humanity, friendliness, calm, and lucidity when we last met. I was touched and bowled over, and I promise to improve greatly.'[372]

When a singer or musician made a serious mistake during a performance, the last thing to do, if one wished to appease Mahler's wrath, was to make light of it. Chorus master Karl Luze, who was thoroughly acquainted with Mahler's character and could predict his reactions, described the following episode. Once, during a performance, one of the choristers made a wrong entry and Mahler appeared backstage at the end of the act with an angry look on his face. Anticipating what was about to happen, Luze ran up to him and said indignantly:

'Herr Direktor! What a scandal! What has happened is intolerable and there is only one solution: she must be fired immediately! If she stays at the Opera a day longer the same thing will happen all over again! She simply ruined the performance, didn't she?'

Mahler's anger was immediately assuaged, and he replied:

'My dear fellow, you take matters much too seriously! Do you think that the audience really noticed anything? She has a pretty voice and such things are bound to happen. It's not all that important!'

Luze believed that he had saved the unfortunate singer from being fired on the spot.[373]

When Mahler appeared in the first row of box No. 13 and the first flash of light shone from his glasses, negligence, routine and boredom, disappeared instantly. The telephone connecting his box to the stage rang unceasingly, reminding everyone of his vigilant presence. Often, it was only to make the supervisor mark the place in the vocal score so that he would remember later to distribute reproaches among the singers involved in the performance. It is not surprising that during his ten years in Vienna he was often accused of treating his collaborators inconsiderately, without warmth or understanding, indeed as mere instruments.[374]

It is certainly true that he quickly turned against people who disappointed him. In such cases, he was capable of becoming most inconsiderate. He was prepared to take a role away from a singer, however famous, a day or two before the première, wholly oblivious to the pain he inflicted. He always tended to

[371] Hans Melms, 'Erinnerungen an Gustav Mahler', *Neues Wiener Journal* (14 Nov. 1915).
[372] Letter from Theodor Reichmann to Mahler, 22 Dec. 1900 (HOA, 1900).
[373] Communication from Karin Sperr, who heard the anecdote from a lifelong friend of Chordirektor Karl Luze. [374] Max Kalbeck, 'Der Abschied Mahlers', *Neues Wiener Tagblatt* (7 June 1907).

overestimate those of his collaborators who acted in accordance with his wishes and to underestimate those who failed to understand him.[375] According to Roller, he invariably made a strong impact on those around him, an impression, and this came not from what he said, but from the example he set. He never asked anyone to do something he would have been unwilling to do himself. Confronted with the complaint that his demands were unrealistic, he usually replied: 'Why then are we artists?'[376]

Countless contemporary stories illustrate the almost uncanny fascination which Mahler exerted in Vienna. Ernst Decsey witnessed a characteristic scene during the period when hostility against Mahler would break out for the slightest of reasons—hostility that was personal and had no basis in fact. That was in 1905–6, at the time when Hirschfeld had labelled him the 'Meyerbeer of the symphony'. In the coffee houses Mahler was referred to contemptuously as 'that fellow'. Decsey sat in the Café Parsifal, a favourite meeting-place for Viennese musicians and music-lovers, listening to hostile criticism of Mahler at the tables around him.

Suddenly someone cried out: 'There he goes!' Everyone got up and ran to the window and stared out. Mahler and his wife were walking along on the other side of the Walfischgasse. He swung his hat in his right hand and stamped his left foot as though he wanted to tell the earth to obey him. His laughter was both childishly trusting and devilishly gay as he continued to gesticulate with his hat. Everyone stared at the bare-headed little man. After he had disappeared, they awoke from their trance, as it were, and looked at each other. They wanted to laugh to cover up the fact that the 'bungler', that 'fellow' whom they had been taking to task over tea and toast, could make such an impression, and that he might even be greater than they. Each of them took a piece of his personality back to his table with him, so to speak, and either kept quiet or turned to other subjects as the impression continued to work within him: Mahler... That is the way it always was. Behind his back, clenched fists; to his face, a shudder of awe.[377]

The Viennese writer Felix Salten left a striking description of how Mahler was regarded in Vienna, both inside the Opera and outside.

The intensity of his being seemed to fill the entire city. People who had never been in the Opera talked and quarrelled about him. . . . Others, who had hitherto scarcely known what an opera director is and indeed ought to be, started to ask about that nasty man Mahler. Everyone recognized him. The sharp contours of his unusual face soon became unforgettable. . . . Every movement of this slim and boyish man was still full of youthful passion. . . . When he was on the podium, . . . he completely forgot the audience, and indeed the very existence of other people. Beseeching, entreating, and cursing, plunging with laughter and tears from the highest bliss to the most bitter pain, furious and in a rage, he struggled with the diversity of reality for the work of the

---

[375] Ibid.

[376] During a rehearsal, a horn player once asked Mahler to be patient with him, and explained that he was suffering from a temporary indisposition. Mahler replied: 'Who can guarantee it will be over tonight? If you don't play properly now, how can I count on you during the performance?' (from an unidentified and undated newspaper clipping in the Vondenhoff collection).   [377] EDS2.

spirit. . . . It became apparent that someone who was able to immerse himself in his work with such intensity, someone who reached out to the stars in such an exuberant way at every creative moment, lived forever far above the vale of sobriety . . .[378]

Three different witnesses have described the exciting moment when Mahler entered the pit and climbed onto the podium:

The tension in the audience before the performance began was unbelievable! Everyone waited in silence; the only sound was the orchestra tuning their instruments. The lights went out, and only the orchestra, now also silent, was illuminated. Everyone wondered—'Who is conducting tonight?'—for it was not yet the custom to put the name of the conductor on the programme. Suddenly a small figure with flowing black hair approached the podium with rapid steps. The audience heaved a sigh of relief. Mahler tapped briefly with his baton on his music stand, cutting short the applause, and then the performance began.[379]

The small and only partly visible door on the right of the orchestra opens. There is a short pause and the audience holds its breath. Admitted by Wimpassinger, the venerable orchestral attendant, Mahler, who is still invisible, continues to 'govern', whispering at the very last moment: 'Schedule a rehearsal for tomorrow afternoon at 5! Frau Renard must go through Tatiana with me.' Then, flinging his left foot forward, he darts to the podium: a small, radiant, black and white combination of glasses and evening dress, like a dragon. He smiles, greets the concert master, nods to the orchestra, stretches out his right arm, the palm of his hand facing upwards, with a gesture of command, and takes possession, yes, that is the word for it, takes possession—leaning back like a beast of prey—of both the musicians and the audience with economy of gesture and calm determination. From this moment on, they are captive. Enchanted. Upstairs, downstairs, in the gallery, in the orchestra, on the stage.[380]

I would need the imagination and descriptive ability of E. T. A. Hoffmann to depict what used to happen when Mahler entered the orchestra pit at the Vienna Opera. The chattering audience, still full of everyday matters from the street, café or the office; the somewhat reluctant orchestra; the singers preoccupied with their make-up or costumes, puffed up with vanity and megalomania—they all fell silent the moment the lights went out and Gustav Mahler appeared in the door on the right. This of course was quite normal in theatres and concert halls. Yet what happened during the two or three seconds Mahler needed to reach the podium was something quite unusual and inexplicable. It is legitimate to talk of Mahler's 'suggestive power'. All at once, the business deals, make-up, quarrels and megalomania were forgotten. Was it a sudden purification? In these seconds one had the feeling that the whole world was holding its breath.[381]

Fritz Stiedry, who worked as singing coach in the Hofoper for some time, has also described how Mahler plunged the audience into a state of trance as soon as he started conducting:

---

[378] Felix Salten, *Geister der Zeit* (Zsolnay, Berlin, 1924), 125–7.

[379] Egon Wellesz, 'Erinnerungen an Gustav Mahler und Arnold Schoenberg', *Urbis Musicae: Studies in Musicology*, Tel Aviv, 1 (1971): 1, 77.

[380] Hans Müller-Einigen, 'Begegnung mit Gustav Mahler', *Weltpresse*, Vienna (10 Nov. 1948).

[381] JRM 56.

The unity of orchestra and audience was attained after a few measures. Both with regard to tempo and rhythm and dynamics he often went as far as he could go. Indeed, he made a point of doing so and passionately loved such contrasts. His adversaries contended that 'a healthy forte was unknown to him'. This was not entirely unjustified. In general, however, his success as a conductor was undisputed and even triumphal. His ecstasies had a hypnotic effect. Vienna was in a state of Mahlerian delirium.[382]

Although Mahler never thought of himself as a 'star', his Vienna public had come to consider him most of the time as the star of the performances he conducted. For this reason, his policy at the Opera was never to divulge the name of the conductor beforehand, and he made a point of never revealing his conducting plans to anyone but the staff of the Opera and his most intimate friends, to whom he explained:

Who would rank the contribution of the conductor and director lower than that of the singers, or deny his enormous responsibilities? But the public, which judges a performance in advance on the basis of the cast, might well be frightened away if the name of the conductor were known. And I must also think of the box office![383]

Hans Richter had undoubtedly upgraded the role of the conductor before Mahler arrived in Vienna, yet Vienna had still not come to fully understand the essential role of the man on the podium as the architect of the drama, and the mind that determined every word, gesture, accent, tempo, or change in tempo. When Mahler thought that he could intensify the dramatic effect or enhance the musical impact, he did not hesitate to change details in a score. To improve the overall sound in *Tristan*, he increased the number of double basses in the Prelude, and occasionally entrusted some choral parts to soloists placed in the orchestra or in the wings. To increase the volume of sound and give it greater colour, he often asked musicians to point the bell of their instrument above the music stand. They usually complained of the awkwardness of the position, which made it difficult to read their parts. To the wind players of the Berlin orchestra who declared that such a position was impossible, Mahler replied: 'It had better be possible! They said the same thing in Vienna, but changed their minds! In twenty years time, this will be the normal position!'[384]

Mahler's famous 'retouches', or 'alterations' to classical scores have always been misunderstood. Fritz Busch explains that Mahler 'never considered them

---

[382] Fritz Stiedry, 'Der Operndirektor Mahler', in *Melos*, 1 (1920): 6, 135. Fritz Stiedry (1883–1968) was born in Vienna, where he read law and studied music under Eusebius Mandyczewski. When he left the Austrian capital, Mahler recommended him to Ernst von Schuch, whose assistant Stiedry became in Dresden (1907–8). He was subsequently active as an opera conductor in Prague, Berlin (1916–23), and Vienna (at the Volksoper, 1923–5). After several years spent as a guest conductor, he returned to Berlin (Städtische Oper, 1929–33) and, like Fried, emigrated to Russia at the beginning of the Nazi epoch (1934–7). He ended his life in the United States, as conductor of the New Friends of Music orchestra in New York and the Metropolitan Opera. He was a close friend of Schoenberg and conducted several first performances of his works.   [383] JRM 62.

[384] In this respect Mahler was wrong. Often in his scores, especially in the climaxes, he requires the wind instruments to play with *Schalltrichter auf*, yet very few orchestras and conductors respect that indication.

a definitive solution to the problem of the musical realization of a work'. Rather, they were improvisations conceived for a specific acoustic context, and he applied the same procedure to his own symphonies after hearing them in concert halls that were unfamiliar to him.[385] Otto Klemperer also recalled that Mahler considered those alterations valid only for himself, and he only assumed responsibility for them when he was on the podium.[386] Nonetheless, he considered it indispensable to make changes in most classical scores. With regard to Beethoven's 'Pastoral' Symphony, he once said to Klemperer: 'Naturally, you will begin by conducting the work as it is written, but later you will realize that the instrumentation needs to be altered.'[387] In this respect, Hermann Behn considered Mahler to be the spiritual heir of Hans von Bülow, who was the first to place the trumpet backstage for the *Leonora* Overture No. 3, and to do the same with the horn in the overture to *Der Freischütz*, a practice later followed by many others. He also recalled Mahler's plan for a performance of Bach's *St Matthew Passion* in which several orchestral and choral groups would be placed well apart from each other.[388]

When Mahler chose a tempo which at first sight seemed arbitrary and surprising, it was always with the human voice in mind rather than the orchestra. In this respect, he was inspired by Wagner, who had written in *Über das Dirigieren*: 'Because they understand nothing of singing, our conductors fail to find the right tempos.' In Mahler's view, 'A tempo is correct when <u>everything</u> can still be heard. When a figure can no longer be perceived because the notes begin to overlap, the tempo is <u>too fast</u>. In a Presto the limit of <u>distinctness</u> is the right tempo: beyond that, the effect is lost,' to which he added that 'when the audience seemed unmoved by an Adagio, he <u>slowed down</u> the tempo instead of increasing it, as is usually the case.'[389]

Earlier in his career, he had stated:

What makes things difficult for those playing under me and what makes them complain is my frequent inability to repeat the same tempo. It would be extremely boring to perform a work in the same well-trodden way. This has a good effect on the singers and musicians: they cannot become lazy and indolent, and must always be on the alert.[390]

Otto Klemperer who had heard Mahler rehearse and conduct quite frequently, found it difficult to describe his manner on the podium because his 'art was so closely bound up with his personality'. 'The main thing seemed to me to be the simplicity of the way in which he made music. His tempos were absolutely self-evident and thus convincing. The same was true of his gestures.'[391] Another conductor, Siegfried Ochs, observed that

---

[385] Fritz Busch, *Der Dirigent* (Atlantis, Zurich, 1971), 138.
[386] Yet, a few weeks before his death, Mahler spoke to Alma and Ernst Jokl about publishing his modified scores of Beethoven, Schubert, Schumann, etc., (see below, Vol. iiii, Chap. 7).
[387] OKM 13.   [388] Hermann Behn, 'Gustav Mahler', in *Musikwelt*, Hamburg, 8 (1928): 5.
[389] AMM1, 69; AMM2, 78.   [390] NBL1, 96 (1897); NBL2, 108.
[391] I am thankful to Lotte Klemperer for sending me a copy of this letter from Otto Klemperer to an unknown addressee of 29 Apr. 1972.

his way of using the baton was diametrically opposed to that of Nikisch. Nikisch often hardly moved, and when he did give precise indications with the baton, his movements were so soft and elegant that ignorant people accused him of having rehearsed before a mirror. Mahler, who reminded one of Bülow at times, conducted with beats that were sharp and fast as lightning, though he did not lunge out very far.[392]

Hans Joachim Moser, the famous German musicologist, who heard Mahler conduct only once in Rome in 1907, described him briefly as 'a small ecstatic man, thin, driven by a powerful, tightly sprung will, a sovereign technician of conducting, acutely responsive to the sound being made'.[393] Known in his youth for his large and flamboyant gestures, Mahler had now developed a conducting technique of Olympian calm which amazed those who saw him on the podium for the first time. He was able to achieve what he wanted with the smallest gestures, as Arnold Schoenberg notes after hearing him conduct many times, in concerts and at the Opera:

This modesty was so characteristic of Mahler. Never a movement which was not exactly consistent with its cause! It was just as large as it had to be; it was executed with temperament, with life, energetically, powerfully, for temperament is the executive of conviction, and it will never be inactive. But there were no outbreaks without cause— none of that false temperament which today brings such great success to those who imitate Mahler's earlier manner of conducting. When he conducted thus, turning with violent movements to individual instrumental groups, really acting out for them the power and the force which they were to express, he had arrived at the frontier of manly maturity which still permits that sort of thing. When he had crossed that frontier, the change set in, and he conducted the orchestra with unexampled composure. All exertion took place in the rehearsals, and the violent gestures disappeared, ever greater clarity of the power of verbal expression replaced them. Here a young man had passed into maturity, and did not strive to retain gestures of youth, because he never deceived, but always did what was fitting to his situation. But he would never have conducted quietly while he was young; the rubato corresponded to his youth, the steadiness to his maturity.[394]

According to Hans Müller-Einigen, writing much later, Mahler had many imitators:

For decades, they studied the way he cleared his throat and the way he spat: dozens of minor conductors throughout the world. Some earned a good living by selling the umbrellas he kept losing. The Mahler cult prevailed in every opera house: in Mannheim, Barcelona, New York, and Stockholm. Everywhere Mahler's ambitious,

---

[392] Siegfried Ochs, *Geschehenes, Gesehenes* (Grethlein, Leipzig, 1922), 354.

[393] Moser, *Musikgeschichte in hundert Lebensbildern* (Löwit, Wiesbaden, 1958), 824. Hans Joachim Moser (1889–1967), musicologist and singer, was born in Berlin and studied musicology, philology, and history at the Universities of Berlin, Marburg, and Leipzig. He taught later at the Universities of Heidelberg and Berlin, and wrote a great number of books, particularly about early music. The most famous of them is *Geschichte der deutschen Musik* (1920–4).

[394] Arnold Schoenberg, 'Mahler' in 'Stil und Gedanken'. Franz Ludwig Hörth also stressed the acting talent which permitted Mahler to convey the expression he sought to achieve. See Hörth, 'Der Wendepunkt der Opernregie', *25 Jahre Neue Musik, Jahrbuch der Universal Edition* (Universal, Vienna, 1926), 120.

bespectacled little offspring kicked the podium briskly with their left foot and beck-
oned the violas with the outstretched palm of their left hand.

For this was one of his characteristically compelling, precise, and yet eminently
Austrian gestures: come hither, violins; come, cellos; come, come to me, bassoons, I
won't hurt you, closer, don't be afraid! Another was the lightning thrust from above at
the percussion, the surgical, razor-sharp movement indicating the entrance of a group
on stage. There was also the tender, almost conciliatory, graphic accompaniment of a
melody with neck, shoulders, and chin, and the impatient negation of an obtrusive
accompaniment by pulling back the left side of his body. Then there was the volcanic,
almost satanic way he leapt up at rhythmic and dramatic climaxes, for example when
Escamillo rushes onto the stage in *Carmen*, and finally (long before Toscanini!), the
rapturous and vibrating three fingertips, almost as moving as those of a bridegroom,
when it was a question of bringing out the joy or distress of humanity at the end of a
musical idea.[395]

Fritz Stiedry also left a striking portrait of Mahler on the podium:

Very calm and sparing of gesture, even modest, I still see him: elbows at his sides, torso
immobile like a statue, head held high, chin pointing upwards, careless movements, no
upbeat, downbeat down to the left, left hand practically motionless. Neither the stage nor
the orchestra ever got used to this style of conducting which, self-confident and haughty,
disdained the use of visual aids. Hence the endless rehearsals lasting for months, a torture
for everyone. For Mahler experimented, improved, and started over again incessantly. He
was never satisfied. Which is why he was always at his best with homogeneous works
(which, as is well known, are richest in meaning). Nevertheless, operas such as *Don
Giovanni* and *Meistersinger*, which are of a more heterogeneous nature, never quite suited
him. He stylized, doctored, and distorted them. They seemed to be in disguise. . . .

The revolutionary denial of all accepted standards lent his performances an artistic
magic without equal. His power of suggestion was enthralling, and could be recognized
right from the second bar. His sharp staccatos (attained after endless rehearsals),
remarkably restrained tempos (especially in Mozart's allegrettos, in contrast to the
operetta allegro customary in this country, which is deemed appropriate for comic
operas), unusually sharp accents, austere nuances, avoidance of everything smooth
and sweet, rigorous tempos, preference for pointedly punctuated rhythms and chords
cut off sharply, explosive allegros—all this was characteristic of him.[396]

Like many others before him, Hermann Behn remarked upon Mahler's
gestural economy:

Only in the last years of his life did I begin to perceive a considerable softening of
contrasts in his use of the baton. . . . Impetuous slashes were as foreign to him as
pedantically two or three in a bar; his gestures were precise, though restrained. He
achieved far greater effects with his free hand, his eyes, his lips. Under his baton, it
was absolutely necessary to play together correctly.[397]

[395]   Hans Müller-Einigen, 'Begegnung'.
[396]   Fritz Stiedry, 'Mahler und Schuch', Adolf Weissmann (ed.), *Sang und Klang Almanach*, 1920
(Weisfeld und Henius, Berlin, 1921).
[397]   Hermann Behn, 'Gustav Mahler'. According to Otto Klemperer, this gestural economy increased
after Mahler discovered that he had a cardiac complaint (OKM 21).

Such sobriety was all the more astonishing in an age in which one went to hear conductors such as Weingartner or Nikisch, just as one would go to see Isadora Duncan dance.[398] After laying all the necessary groundwork in rehearsal, Mahler no longer needed to convey his concepts through sweeping or brusque gestures. His 'hypnotic calm' and 'petrified immobility' were particularly in evidence in Vienna, where his long acquaintance with the musicians rendered such gestures superfluous. To Paul Clemenceau, he once said: 'My arms are not absolutely necessary when I conduct!' 'If I weren't obliged to wear glasses, I would only conduct with my eyes.'[399] To this, Fritz Stiedry adds: 'Yet this calm was the calm of a slumbering volcano. For mysterious reasons, you always had to be prepared to see it burst out into flame. It did so on occasion, though very rarely, and immediately afterwards the old immobility returned.'[400] With the Philharmonic, Mahler conducted to a considerable extent with his eyes, and held the baton lightly in his left hand or rested it against his hip. He rarely handled it like a whip, except in the great tutti.

Richard Strauss's remarks on Mahler's conducting are of particular interest because of the notorious severity with which he judged his colleagues. 'He was an excellent conductor, but extremely analytical and exacting. His wilful way of pulling apart his phrasing and paragraphs earned him the enmity of professional musicians; it cast a shadow on his great merit and his great earnestness in the practice of an art celebrated with great fanaticism.'[401] For Bruno Walter, 'the contrast between the frenzy of the orchestra and the immobility of the man who unchained it was almost eerie'.[402] Such was the intensity of his conducting that it sometimes concealed the weaknesses of the music itself. Audiences were literally entranced by performances that transcended technical considerations, that soared above routine and convention to attain celestial heights where 'the soul blossomed at the touch of beauty'.

Much has been said in the foregoing pages on Mahler the conductor, the interpreter, the stage director, the educator of singers and orchestral musicians, on his ideas, his methods, the qualities, and even his faults as an opera manager. A new note has crept in which sheds an important new light on his state of mind and his activity. Mahler was to spend only one more year in Vienna. He approached what turned out to be his final season in a somewhat cynical, even disillusioned frame of mind. He was beginning to weary of Vienna, the affairs, the spitefulness of journalists, and even the fragility of the great Hofoper machine. The ideal which had sustained him for so many years

---

[398] Paul Bekker, *Allgemeine Musik-Zeitung* (9 June 1905).

[399] Berta Zuckerkandl, 'Paul Clemenceau spricht über Gustav Mahler', *Deutsche La Plata Zeitung* (13 July 1929) and Paul Clemenceau, 'Gustav Mahler und Rodin', *Die Kunstauktion*, Berlin (13 July 1930).

[400] Fritz Stiedry, 'Operndirektor Mahler', *Melos*, 1 (1920): 6, 1.

[401] Richard Strauss, *Diaries*, quoted by Franz Grasberger in 'Gustav Mahler und Richard Strauss', *Österreichische Musikzeitschrift*, 21 (1966): 5/6, 283.

[402] BWM 78. Walter refers to the memorable performance of the *Symphonia Domestica* in Nov. 1904.

of enthusiastic labour began to seem chimerical, as so many exemplary productions, prepared with love and care, degenerated before his eyes:

After exerting myself to the utmost to achieve a perfect performance, I could not help noticing how even the best part of it gradually crumbled away when the work was repeated. The third, fourth, and fifth performances deteriorated visibly and I was unable, in the context of the repertory, to hold enough rehearsals to maintain the desired standards.[403]

Mahler expressed his disappointment as early as 1906 to the music critic Bernard Scharlitt,[404] and revealed that his dream had always been a sort of permanent festival of opera, in which all the performances reached the same level of perfection. But, he now realized that his ambitions were unattainable, and this thought became an obsession during his last years in Vienna.

In the course of time, I have become convinced that 'repertory opera' is an institution entirely opposed to our modern artistic principles. That is only too comprehensible. It comes from a time in which the concept of art was completely different to ours. In the era of the 'old operatic routine', putting on several hundred performances a year was a simple matter, for they were all on the same artistic—or unartistic—level. A modern opera director, even if he is a genius like Wagner, can hardly deal with such enormous quantities if he wishes to comply with contemporary standards of artistic perfection. However, 'model performances' have the major disadvantage that all other performances leave much to be desired. . . .[405] And, by the way, everything becomes old-fashioned with time, including me and my achievements. For Vienna, I am no longer 'new'. I wish to leave at a time when the Viennese will be able, at a later date, to honour what I have accomplished. I now intend quietly to devote myself to composing. I am well aware of the fact that as a composer I will gain no recognition during my lifetime. This will become my due only over my grave. The 'distance of the beyond' is the *sine qua non* for the proper judgement of someone like myself. As long as I am the Mahler down here on the earth, 'a man among men', I must resign myself to 'an all too human' treatment as a composer. Only when I have shaken off this earthly dust will I receive my due. To use Nietzsche's term, I am just an 'Unzeitgemässer' (a man not of his time). This is primarily due to the nature of my work. The true 'Zeitgemässer' (man of his time) is Richard Strauss. That is why he already enjoys immortality down here on earth . . .[406]

Scharlitt deserves posterity's gratitude for having induced Mahler to disclose his disillusioned state of mind in the autumn of 1906. His disappointment was only too well founded. Vienna, with its usual inconstancy,

---

[403] Edgar Istel, 'Erinnerungen'. This conversation took place in 1908.

[404] Bernard Scharlitt (1877–19?), pseudonym of Karl Litthardt, was a journalist and playwright, correspondent for the *Neue Freie Presse* in Warsaw. He published the first complete German edition of Chopin's letters in 1911 and a biography of Chopin (1919), and wrote a long article about Mahler in the *Neue Zeitschrift für Musik* of 2 May 1907, on the occasion of his tenth year as director (see below, Chap. 9).

[405] For Mahler, the only conceivable solution lay in the construction of a small theatre for summer festivals devoted to Mozart and Wagner.

[406] The interview with Bernard Scharlitt probably took place during the Salzburg Festival in the summer of 1906, for *Die Musik* published his review of the festival (Bernard Scharlitt, 'Aus einem Gespräche mit Gustav Mahler', *Neue Freie Presse* (25 May 1911), 11).

continued to reward his efforts with ingratitude. In the middle of the Mozart festival, which most of the critics ranked among his most outstanding achievements, even Korngold regretted that Mahler 'was not presenting more new works', citing the example of Paris, where composers like Saint-Saëns, Massenet, and Bruneau 'can have their works performed immediately, at least at the Opéra Comique'. Why had Mahler not yet put on the latest works by Eugen d'Albert and Humperdinck, or Massenet's *Jongleur de Notre-Dame*, or Debussy's *Pelléas et Mélisande*,[407] an 'experimental but captivating work', that was arousing the curiosity of musicians everywhere. And why had he not presented new Italian works like Puccini's *Madame Butterfly*, Giordano's *Siberia*, and Cilea's *Adriana Lecouvreur* to the Viennese audiences?

In *Signale für die musikalische Welt*,[408] Otto Keller exhorted Mahler to awaken the Opera out of its 'long hibernation'. He had been appointed as its administrator, not to 'promote his own works here and abroad'. He also complained of Mahler's 'military' manner in dealing with his colleagues, and his 'unpredictable nervousness', and declared that the artistic level at the Hofoper had never been so low nor the ensemble so mediocre. 'Nowadays people leap directly from the classroom onto the stage of the Hofoper. . . . Gustav Mahler has transformed our Opera, once an admirable and model institution, into a testing ground for the other theatres of the civilized world.' Tired of being constantly offended, insulted, and having their efforts rewarded by rudeness, many singers had resigned. 'The man whose undeniable brilliance should have been entirely suited to the leadership of our Hofoper has fallen victim to his own conceit and neuroses. The direction of our Opera should belong to a mentally sound artist, not to a presumptuous, sickly talent . . .'[409]

In the *Österreichische Rundschau*,[410] Hirschfeld claimed to be presenting an 'objective' picture of the 'decline' of the Opera, of the 'sickly spectacle of excessive nervous tension', and of a 'series of aimless and pointless innovations and experiments'. According to him, 'the fine arts were locked in battle against the music in a costly war', and the music was being overwhelmed by a 'collection of paintings' that had nothing to do with it.

The more the music is demoted, the more lavish and seductive the staging becomes. . . . This unbridled taste for luxury coupled with a tyrannical despotism is reminiscent of the last days of the Roman Empire. Its culture was characterized by mindless prodigality, the stimulation of the senses through an unending series of new and ever more fantastic exhibitions, and the dulling of emotions.

---

[407] By this time, Mahler had already heard of Debussy's work, and in Apr. 1907 he sent Schalk to the German première in Frankfurt (HOA, 1533/1907). Before leaving Vienna, he included Debussy's opera in the *Spielplan* for the following season.

[408] *Wiener Signale für die musikalische Welt*, 1 (1905/6): 7, 1 (22 Mar).

[409] Of the singers Mahler engaged immediately after they left the Conservatory, at least two—Lucie Weidt and Richard Mayr—later had great careers at the Hofoper. Furthermore, the Hofoper archives show that not one important singer resigned from the Opera during Mahler's final years.

[410] *Österreichische Rundschau*, 2 (1906): 6, 433 ff.

The tone of the article was as familiar as the accusations it contained. The only new feature was Mahler's weariness. He was not mistaken when he said he was 'no longer in fashion'. How else could he be accused of neglecting modern opera composers, after he had struggled so assiduously to defend *Salome* against the narrow-mindedness of the Viennese censorship? And how else could he have been reproached both for an exclusive interest in stage design and for devoting too much time to the musical preparation of new productions? Denigrating Mahler was obviously considered to be good form, and it is not difficult to understand that he was thinking of turning his back on this city where polemics triumphed over art, where genius, sacrifice, and genuine effort only met with scorn and incomprehension. With regard to the problems he encountered during these last seasons, he once confided mournfully to a journalist: 'There was the court, there was the press, there was the audience, there was my family, and finally the enemy in my own breast... Often, it was terrible!'[411]

[411]   Edgar Istel, 'Erinnerungen'.

6

Mahler in Vienna (XXII)—*Salome* in Graz—Première of the Sixth Composition of the Eighth—Salzburg Festival—Mahler in his maturity

(May–August 1906)

Veni creator

ALTHOUGH his main preoccupation for several months had been the restaging of the Mozart operas, Mahler had not forgotten *Salome*, the first modern theatrical masterpiece to have come his way since he had arrived in Vienna. But time was passing, and the Habsburg censorship had still not given way. The première had taken place in Dresden on 9 December 1905, and had been followed by performances in Prague and Breslau, and Strauss now wrote to Mahler to ask him if he had any objections to the Breslau production being brought to Vienna. Mahler replied in mid-March:

Dear friend! I have neither the right nor the desire to stand in the way of the Breslau project. Under certain circumstances it would perhaps be the best way of making my opponents in the matter see reason. You would scarcely believe the vexation this affair has already caused me, and, between ourselves, the consequences it might have for me in certain circumstances. For you have my word that I will not give in, even if it has to be dealt with at highest ministerial level. If our colleagues in Breslau have the courage for it, then in God's name let them go ahead! In that case, should Herr Löwe need our musicians or anything else, I am at his disposal; Roller, likewise, is ready to help in word and deed with the staging.[1]

Strauss thanked Mahler by return, but hoped

---

[1] MSB 116. In the same letter, Mahler writes that he has just heard Strauss's *Taillefer* in Amsterdam, and enjoyed it 'very much indeed'.

that the matter would not be counter-productive, i.e. that, instead of paving the way to the Hofoper for *Salome*, it would obstruct it even more. For God's sake don't make it into an affair of state! We have too much need in positions like yours of artists of your energy, brilliance and cast of mind for you to take any risks for the sake of *Salome*. Things will come right in the end, anyway![2]

In the meantime Ernst Decsey, no doubt on Mahler's advice, had persuaded Alfred Cavar, Director of the Graz Opera, that staging the Austrian première of *Salome* in Graz would be an enormous boost for the reputation of his opera house. Reviews of the Dresden première confirmed the sensational character of the work and Cavar set about solving one by the very considerable problems of staging it in a theatre of such modest dimensions. He would have to hire singers of international stature and to double the size of the orchestra, which normally consisted of forty-five musicians. This meant sacrificing some seats to the pit, but Cavar was determined to go the whole hog. He even invited the composer himself to conduct the first three performances. Since Strauss had conducted neither the Dresden opening nor the Prague and Breslau performances, his presence on the podium was bound to create a sensation.

The date of the première was fixed for 16 May. Mahler, although well aware that the Vienna censor was sticking to his objections, wrote to the Intendant on 11 May that he would be attending the dress rehearsal in Graz on the 14th as well as the première, for 'it was of the highest importance that the Director see this opera performed'. The following day the Intendant was further informed that Roller would accompany Mahler.[3] In Graz, Ernst Decsey took an active part in the preparations:

I went to the rehearsals. The music was taking clearer shape. Singers came off the stage humming their hitherto 'unsingable' parts. I felt I had become the altar-boy of the new music, I whetted the appetite of the citizens, I sent wafts of melodic incense around their noses, I opened their eyes to the purplish blue of the Syrian night and and gave them a foretaste of heathenish languor and Christian asceticism. I had them falling over each other to hear this 'Scherzo that goes tragically wrong'.[4]

The provincial capital of Styria certainly experienced the 'sensation' Decsey and Cavar had hoped to create. Decsey and Friedrich Weigemann,[5] the conductor who had done all the prepatory work, went to meet Strauss at the station before the final rehearsals. He greeted them with a typical Strauss sally: 'So, children, what does the jeweller's shop sound like? (*Na, Kinder, wie klingt denn der Juwelenladen?*)'. He was alluding to a line by Herod in the text.[6] Schoenberg and

---

[2] Letter of 14 Mar., AMS and MSB 117–18.

[3] HOA, G.Z. no. 1882, letters of 11 and 12 May 1906. On 18 May, Mahler's secretary submitted a bill of 160.70 kronen to cover Mahler's travelling expenses.

[4] Ernst Decsey, *Musik war sein Leben* (Hans Deutsch, Vienna, 1962), 72.

[5] See below, Chap. 7.

[6] 'Ich habe Juwelen': the words occur in Herod's final monologue, just before the Dance of the Seven Veils.

Zemlinsky arrived with their pupils, one of whom was Alban Berg.[7] The first three performances were already sold out: Johann Strauss's widow was going to attend the first performance and Puccini was coming from Budapest for the second.[8] Mahler and Alma arrived in Graz the day of the dress rehearsal and found Strauss ensconced in the Hotel Elefant, all ready with a surprise proposal: an automobile excursion that very afternoon to a neighbouring beauty spot.[9] According to Alma's record, they left immediately after lunch, although it had just rained and the roads were dangerously slippery. The car skidded terribly but Strauss would not turn back. When they arrived at their destination, they ordered a lavish tea at the local inn before setting off on foot for the beauty spot, which so impressed them that they could hardly tear themselves away.

Back at the inn, they took further refreshment and enjoyed themselves so much that Strauss was reluctant to leave. 'What the devil', he grumbled. 'They can't start without me, anyway. Let them wait.' It was beginning to get dark when Mahler suddenly stood up and said: 'All right! If you're not coming, I'll go and conduct for you.' Strauss finally agreed to go, but on the way back while Mahler was attempting to speed up the driver, Strauss tried to slow him down. Later, looking back on Strauss's curious behaviour, Mahler and Alma concluded that he had been hiding his concern about the coming performance behind a smoke-screen of frivolity.

Despite fears that the Christian Democrats in Graz would create an incident, the première of *Salome* was a triumph. The applause seemed never-ending as laurel wreaths were bestowed upon the singers, the orchestra and stage staff, and the composer. Jenny Korb, who sang the title role, took over twenty curtain calls. In a letter to his wife Strauss wrote that he himself had been tremendously moved by the performance, and that the applause had continued ten minutes after the iron curtain had come down.[10] Before and after this memorable première there were animated discussions at the Hotel Elefant among the musicians who had come for the performance. One of them remarked that if someone had asked him to learn the title role by heart he would have shot himself, to which Strauss replied, to everyone's surprise and delight, 'So would I!'[11] The following morning Mahler and Alma were having

---

[7] On the day of the première, Schoenberg and Zemlinsky sent a postcard to Hermann Watznauer which Berg also signed (PML).

[8] In a letter to his wife of 17 May 1906, Strauss mentions that Puccini was there, and also 'several young men who have come from Vienna with only the score as hand luggage'. See *Die Welt um Richard Strauss in Briefen*, ed. Franz Grasberger (Schneider, Tutzing, 1967), 169. Puccini wrote to one of his friends: 'la Salomé è la cosa più straordinaria cacofonica terribilmente' (Giorgio Magri, *L'Uomo Puccini* (Mursia, Milano, 1992), 7).

[9] Alma claims that it was the Golling waterfall, which, however, is situated 30 km. south of Salzburg, and could not have been reached from Graz. This error is already to be found in AMS.

[10] *Die Welt um Richard Strauss*, ibid.

[11] WKL 149. Alma only mentions one performance in Graz, but according to the Vienna Opera Archives (Z. 614/1906), Mahler attended the dress rehearsal on 14 May and the première on the 16th. The cast for the Austrian première of *Salome* was: Korb (Salome); Anderson (Herodiade); Günther-Braun (Herod); Jessen (Jochanaan); Kaitan (Narraboth).

breakfast before taking the train back to Vienna. Strauss came over to their table, Alma recalls, and told Mahler once again not to take things so seriously. 'The Hofoper, for example, what a pigsty! No one will give you any credit for getting so worked up about it. They just don't want to put on *Salome*! No, it's not worth it.' Alma adds: 'Basically, he was right. That was always my opinion. Every note Mahler wrote was precious to me, but his activity at the Opera, outstanding though it was, left me cold. I knew already then that all reproduction was ephemeral, whereas production [his composing] would last for ever.'[12]

Arthur Seidl gives an account of what was almost certainly the same conversation between Strauss and Mahler at Graz, but adds a reply by Mahler and comments of his own which differ considerably from Alma's. In Seidl's version Strauss rebuked Mahler for his excessive conscientiousness: 'You take everything too much to heart', he chided. 'The Opera, that stable, for example! If you wear yourself to the ground, no one will thank you for it! A pigsty which wouldn't even put on *Salome*!' When Strauss made disparaging remarks of this kind about the Opera, Mahler replied with the authority of simple common sense:

My dear Strauss! That someone can cease to derive any pleasure from opera and even finally abandon all hope in that institution, that is something that I can sympathize with and in some cases well understand. But what I cannot understand at all is how, in that case, he can go on having anything to do with opera and indeed in practice still put his heart and soul into it.[13]

Seidl comments that he cannot vouch personally for the accuracy of this report, but 'si non é Verdi, é ben Trovatore', and he was quite convinced that the views expressed in that conversation were thoroughly characteristic of both speakers.

Most of the critics present at Graz realized that they had been present at the birth of a masterpiece, and defended Strauss against his detractors. Ernst Decsey in the *Neue Musikalische Presse*, wrote: 'My only concern here is with art, and true art, like nature, is never immoral. Art's job is not to preach morality but to create. It has to be as the artist sees it. And so it is with *Salome*.' Whereupon he received an avalanche of insulting letters accusing him, among other things, of having been bribed to defend a 'fraud' (*Schwindeloper*). In the Vienna newspaper *Die Reichswehr*, Hans Liebstöckl also defended Strauss's masterpiece but emphasized its complexity in words that inadvertently echoed Bülow's famous remark after Mahler's performance on the piano of the Second Symphony in Hamburg: 'Compared to *Salome*, *Tristan* seems as friendly and naive as *The Magic Flute*'.

In the train bringing them back to Vienna, Mahler and Alma continued to discuss *Salome* while standing in the corridor contemplating the countryside 'fresh after a long rain'. A 'friendly, nice, old man, very even-tempered, almost the exact opposite of Mahler, the *worrier*'[14] introduced himself. It was the

[12]   AMM1, 124; AMM2, 125.
[13]   Arthur Seidl, 'Eine nicht gehaltene Rede als Nachruf', in *Aufsätze und Skizzen* (Bosse, Regensburg, 1926), i. 306. Seidl says that he himself was not present at this conversation, but that he was told of it by a third person.   [14]   AMM1, 125; AMM2, 126.

Styrian writer Peter Rosegger.[15] He joined in the conversation, which turned, wrote Alma, into a discussion on the meaning of the word 'success'.

We were talking about the notion of 'success' and its fallaciousness, Mahler thought any kind of success a poor yardstick. After all, we had just been to the première of *Salome*. There had been round after round of applause, and yet we were convinced that perhaps only one out of a hundred had really understood the music. All the others had followed their lead like sheep. And what about us? Throughout the performance hadn't we been full of doubts about the subject matter? Hadn't we found the music for the dance offensive? So much, in spite of all the virtuosity, seemed dubious. Then, suddenly, the audience decided that it was a success. <u>Who</u> had decided, and with what right? Rosegger said: 'Vox populi, vox Dei'.[16] We replied with the question: 'The people <u>over</u> time or <u>at</u> the time?'[17]

Four years later, Peter Rosegger was to recall his train conversation with Mahler in the following letter:

I well remember our conversation in the train on the value of applause. But I cannot recall your talking about a 'paradox'. We would agree, I think, that the applause of the public does not mean very much but that it is essential particularly in the theatre, to give fresh stimulus to the performers. And that it is also useful for the audience itself, and incites them to further receptivity.[18]

Clearly the triumph of *Salome*, a work in which Strauss seemed deliberately to run counter the spirit of the times, and which was nevertheless to win him more laurels than any of his other works, posed something of a problem for Mahler. As seen above, shortly after the Graz opening, Mahler, in an interview with Bernard Scharlitt, expressed his conviction that he would not be understood in his lifetime, that he was a man 'not of his time' (*Unzeitgemässer*), to use Nietzsche's expression,[19] while Strauss was a true 'Zeitgemässer' ('man of his time'), already enjoying his immortality here below. He added that he considered Strauss's operas to be superior to his symphonic works.[20] In a letter

---

[15]   Peter (Petri Kettenfeler) Rosegger (1843–1918), son of a farmer, was a well-known Styrian writer of novels and short stories, some written in dialect, which are still very popular in Austria. His principal works were *Waldheimat* (1877) and *Die Schriften des Waldschulmeisters* (1875). In his memoirs Wilhelm Kienzl describes inviting Strauss and Rosegger together to his home. They proved to be utterly incompatible despite their common Bavarian origin (WKL 149). According to Ernst Decsey, Mahler had once called Rosegger 'the greatest living poet'. '"With all the others you more or less feel the labour pains... cum grano salis natürlich, cum grano salis... (with a grain of salt, naturally, with a grain of salt)," he added, to assuage his conscience' (EDS1, 355).

[16]   The adage is not surprising coming from a populist writer like Rosegger, but it will be recalled that Mahler himself pronounced it both in Decsey's presence during the summer of 1905, and on the subject of Hugo Wolf (see above, Chap. 4).   [17]   AMM1, 125; AMM2, 126.

[18]   Letter from Peter Rosegger to Mahler dated 4 July 1910, AMM1, 473.

[19]   See above, Chap. 5, for the meaning of this, invented by Nietzsche. Cf. Bernard Scharlitt, 'Gespräch mit Mahler', *Neue Freie Presse* (25 May 1911).

[20]   Mahler talked to Scharlitt that day particularly about the 'completely different' way in which he and Strauss had set Nietzsche to music although they had both sensed the 'latent music' in his work. Mahler considered Nietzsche to be a far better composer than was generally acknowledged.

he wrote to Alma a short time later, he again returned to the subject of Strauss and *Salome*.

Your remarks about <u>Salome</u> interested me greatly. I told you all that in advance. But now you are underestimating the work, which remains outstanding in spite of everything, and even though, as you rightly feel, it is 'virtuoso' in the bad sense of the word. I predicted all that. Wagner, in this respect, was a different sort of fellow. The further you develop in life as a human being, the more you will sense the difference between the few great, <u>genuine</u> ones and the mere 'virtuosos'. I am delighted to see how <u>quickly</u> this is becoming clear to you. You sense Strauss's 'coldness', which lies not in his talent but in his <u>human side</u> (*Menschentum*), and it repels you.[21]

A few days after the Austrian première of *Salome*, Mahler was once again to measure the difference which set him apart from Strauss, both as man and musician. Both of them were to participate, for the fifth time, in the festival of the Allgemeiner Deutscher Musikverein, which in 1906 was to be held in Essen. After returning from Graz, he stayed in Vienna for three days only, just long enough to conduct *The Marriage of Figaro* and attend the very successful revival of Verdi's *Ballo in Maschera*, conducted by Bruno Walter.[22] For the first time the press accounts were favourable to Walter. Liebstöckl wrote that the performance had been 'masterly'. 'Every chorus was a feat; each ensemble a moment of happiness and exaltation. Herr Walter officiated in the orchestra pit, and this unforgettable evening was due to his efforts. He was as his best.' No theatre in Europe could rival the vocal ensemble of Kurz, Bland, Slezak, and Demuth.

In the *Neue Freie Presse*, Korngold suggested that Walter had perhaps 'burrowed too deeply into Verdi's music', but conceded that 'marvellous beauty had been revealed to the audience, and the dramatic element came through perfectly'. He also noted the exceptional show of public enthusiasm for the singers, all of whom had surpassed themselves. Max Kalbeck warmly praised the singers, but also congratulated Walter on having conducted 'the performance with such verve that the opera made an enchanting impression, and the audience positively revelled in the lovely melodies'. Wallaschek, in *Die Zeit*, thought that the role of Riccardo seemed made to measure for Slezak, while Demuth's performance as Renato proved that the art of bel canto was not dead.

[21]   BGA 169, undated (22 May 1906).

[22]   On 12 May, a *Neuinszenierung* of *Werther*, with Ernst Van Dyck as guest artist in the title role, opened at the Hofoper. Curiously, the revival of *Un Ballo in Maschera*, conducted by Walter, and described by him in his memoirs as his first great success in Vienna, is not mentioned in any of the archival records of the premières and new mises-en-scène during Mahler's tenure, probably because it was only a *Neueinstudierung*. This perhaps explains why Walter mistakes the date of this revival, situating it in the context of 1902: 'Mahler had entrusted to me the revival of Verdi's *Un Ballo in Maschera*, to which the Opera assigned its finest young voices. On that evening I made a conquest of the Opera, and even my enemies succumbed to an attack of nervous aphonia.' This success was probably of great help to the young conductor in overcoming the paralysis of his right arm under Sigmund Freud's treatment (cf. George H. Pollock, 'On Freud's Psychotherapy of Bruno Walter', *Annual of Psychoanalysis*, New York, 3 (1975): 291; and above, Chap. 5). The opera had not been put on since 1902, but was performed twelve times during the year 1906. Cast for the 19 May 1906 performance: Kurz (Oscar); Bland (Amelia); Petru (Ulrica); Slezak (Riccardo); Demuth (Renato); Reich (Samuele); Haydter (Tomaso) (cf. BWT 227).

The performance gave 'reason to rejoice', and was a 'worthy addition' to the repertory of the Hofoper. For Max Graf, it had been a well-inspired decision to revive one of Verdi's greatest operas. 'After a period of intellectual music people long to get back to a music which pleases the senses through sound. The exuberant melody works. Gustav Mahler cleverly responds to the mood of the time, by giving full rein to Slezak, Demuth, Kurz and Fräulein Bland in the Verdi opera', wrote Max Graf in the *Neues Wiener Journal*. 'The public loves it! They storm the box office and applaud until their hands hurt. A composer of eccentric symphonies and a clever opera director have rarely coexisted so successfully as they do in Gustav Mahler!'

Walter himself later underlined the dramatic character of his interpretation in his memoirs: 'Over and above the vocal and orchestral *appassionato* and the generally moderate and sometimes luxurious *rubato* in the melodic lines, I tried throughout to emphasize the dramatic intention as the most essential element in the performance, which accordingly reached its climax in the mocking chorus, with the contrasting voices of Amelia and Renato.'[23] Since the anti-Semitic *Deutsches Volksblatt* could not wholeheartedly approve of the young conductor's performance, it added a single discordant note in the chorus of praise: 'He [Walter] directed the performance with inordinate temperament, and would in his excess of zeal have got into real trouble with the *canzona* of the Page Oscar (last Act). But the orchestra with its admirable imperturbability covered up the momentary aberration of its conductor with prompt corrective action.'

Despite the limited success of the Fifth Symphony, Mahler had received several proposals for the première of his Sixth. As several letters already quoted have shown, he knew that it 'would pose enigmas that only a generation that has absorbed and digested my first five can tackle'.[24] Since his 'first five', and particularly the Fifth, had certainly not been well digested by the critics, Mahler knew that he could expect the worst with his new work. That was certainly why he turned down Busoni's offer in September 1905:

I need not emphasize that both your enterprise and you yourself are very much to my liking in every respect. It is even more 'obvious' that I would conduct a work of mine in your concert series with the greatest pleasure. But I do not know how I can help you at present. So far I have published five symphonies. All of them were failures in Berlin, with the exception of the Third, which I shall be happy to place at your disposal, if you can let me have an entire concert and a sufficient number of rehearsals (at least five). Is a big choral work [*Das klagende Lied*] entirely out of the question? Otherwise I do not know what I might suggest. My Sixth Symphony is at the printer's and will come out in the course of the year; it is very difficult and complicated. For all these, I need numerous rehearsals. In this respect my friendship for you won't make any difference! Once again, I am at your service. But everything must be just right![25]

---

[23] Ibid.   [24] MBR1, no. 238; MBR2, no. 336.

[25] 'Briefe Gustav Mahlers an Ferrucio Busoni', ed. Jutta Theurich, *Beiträge zur Musikwissenschaft*, 1 (1977): 3. Undated letter (postmarked 13 Sept. 1905).

Mahler no doubt hoped that the public of the Allgemeiner Deutscher Musikverein Festival was better equipped to understand his new work than any other, and he had thus accepted Strauss's invitation to participate. As the venue for the next festival, the committee had chosen Essen, in the Ruhr— Essen, with its coal mines and famous Krupp steel mills and arms industry, Essen, the 'gigantic industrial village with a population of several hundred thousand. General effect: gloomy, utilitarian, but powerful! One gets the impression of something unique in Germany . . .', as the Berlin theatre critic Alfred Kerr wrote in 1928.[26]

Essen possessed a good symphony orchestra, generously subsidized by Arthur Krupp. The festival was to last five days, and two orchestras were to take part: the local one, which would play in the first and third symphonic concerts, and the Utrecht orchestra, under its conductor Wouters Hutschenruyter. In December 1905, Mahler had asked his friend Mengelberg if, in his opinion, the Utrecht musicians would be capable, together with the Essen orchestra, of performing the Sixth. 'Can I agree to this?' he asked. 'Is it possible that these two groups (which I do not know) can, with sufficient rehearsals, give the first performance of a work of mine with some measure of success!'[27] Mengelberg probably reassured him, for Mahler finally consented.

In preparation for the première, Mahler had asked the Philharmonic in April to play through his new work at three reading rehearsals, and the orchestra had agreed unanimously to do so.[28] After these rehearsals, which evidently went well, he wrote the musicians the letter of thanks quoted above.[29]

The programme of the Essen Festival of Contemporary Music—the last one in which Mahler was to take part—was as follows:

24 May, at 6 p.m. (opening concert): Essen Orchestra, with Georg Hendryk Witte, conductor
Rudolf Siegel: *Heroische Tondichtung*, Op. 3
Otto Neitzel: *Das Leben ein Traum*, Fantasy, Op. 33
    (Alexander Kosman, violin solo;
    Otto Neitzel, cond.)
Richard Mors: *Dem Scherz sein Recht*, Symphonic poem
    (Richard Mors, cond.)
Frederick Delius: *Im Meerestreiben* (Sea drift), mixed chorus and orchestra
    (Heinrich Spiess, baritone solo)
Hermann Bischoff: Symphony in E major
Walter Braunfels: *Szene aus dem Märchenspiel* 'Falada'
    (Walter Braunfels, cond.)

---

[26] *Frankfurter Zeitung*, 'Reiseblatt' (24 Apr. 1997), R4.
[27] Undated letter (postmarked 29 Dec. 1905), RMH 65. Mahler asked his Dutch colleague to reply immediately, and assured him that his response would remain confidential.
[28] Minutes of the Philharmonic, HOA, G.Z. 75/906. The Orchestra had shown the same cooperative attitude at the readings of the Fifth two years before. Cf. above, Chap. 1.   [29] See Chap. 5.

Engelbert Humperdinck: *Festgesang zur Feier der silbernen Hochzeit des Kaiserpaares* (Eva Lessmann, soprano; Reinhold Batz, tenor; Essener Musikverein Chorus).

25 May, at 11.30 a.m. Chamber music concert in the Kruppsaal
Heinrich Zöllner: Quartet in C minor
Henri Marteau: Eight Lieder, Op. 10, for voice and string quartet (Eva Lessmann, soprano; Essen Quartet)
Paul Juon: Quintet for piano and strings, Op. 33
(Otto Neitzel, piano; Essen Quartet).

25 May, at 6 p.m. Concert at the Essen Theatre (outside the framework of the Festival): Utrecht Orchestra, with Wouters Hutschenruyter, cond.
Johan Wagenaar: *Overture to Cyrano de Bergerac*, Op. 23
Charles Smulders: *Morgengrauen, Tag und Abenddämmerung*, Symphonic poem
Max von Schillings: *Symphonic Prologue for Oedipus at Colonnus*
Hans Pfitzner: Prelude to *Käthchen von Heilbronn*.

26 May, at 10 a.m. Committee meeting of the Allgemeiner Deutscher Musikverein. At 7.30 p.m. Chamber music concert:
Bruno Walter: Quintet for piano and strings in F sharp minor (Bruno Walter, piano; Munich Quartet)
Hugo Kaun: Quartet No. 2 in D major, Op. 40
Hans Sommer: *Letztes Blühen*, Lieder cycle
(Josef Loritz, baritone; Otto Neitzel, piano)
Hans Pfitzner: Trio in F major, Op. 8
(August Schmid-Lindner, piano, and members of the Munich Quartet).

27 May, at 5.30 p.m. Concert at the Städtische Saalbau: Essen Orchestra
Mozart: *Maurische Trauermusik*
(Richard Strauss, cond.)
Mahler: Sixth Symphony
(Gustav Mahler, cond., Ludwig Riemann, celesta).

28 May, at 7.30 p.m., at the Cologne Theatre:
Jaques-Dalcroze: *L'Oncle Jadis*
Eugen d'Albert: *Flauto Solo.*

Once again, of the contemporary compositions included in this programme there were few that have withstood the test of time, apart from Mahler's Symphony, Pfitzner's Prelude, and Delius's *Sea Drift*.

Alma having had to remain in Vienna for a few days to take care of the children, Mahler made the long trip by rail to Essen alone. He arrived over a week before the concert, for which he had demanded seven full rehearsals.[30] Mahler

---

[30] The *Neue Musik-Zeitung* criticized the fact that the seven other orchestral pieces scheduled in the programme were 'packed' (*zusammengepfercht*) into the opening concert, which would last five hours in

wrote to Georg Hendryk Witte, conductor of the Essen Symphony Orchestra, to fix the number of rehearsals and ask him to obtain a celesta from Mustel in Paris,[31] and added that the drum section of the Sixth would 'probably require the participation of five musicians, not including the kettledrums'.[32] A short letter written by Mahler to Max von Schillings, vice-president of the Verein, is the only presently known document concerning the inclusion of the Sixth in the programme of the festival. Schillings had obviously written to Mahler asking him for a new composition, and this is Mahler's reply:

For the moment there only remains my Sixth Symphony waiting for a première but it will require an extremely large orchestra and a whole concert to itself. Of course, I do not know whether in Essen you are able to provide an orchestra which would meet my needs and the large number of rehearsals required. I am thinking of seven with the whole orchestra and possibly two or three with individual groups. For myself, with grateful memories of Krefeld and Basle, I would gladly agree to do it, but I do not wish to be immodest and would rather not go ahead at all with so unusual a project if it is likely to cause you insuperable problems. In any case, my heartfelt thanks for your kind offer.[33]

Arriving in Essen at 7 p.m. on 19 May, Mahler installed himself in his room on the first floor of the 'excellent' Imperial Hotel and worked away at his orchestra scores until 11.00 at night, and again the next morning from 7 to 9 o'clock. Contrary to what had happened two years earlier with the Fifth,[34] the orchestra 'did extremely well'[35] and Mahler wrote to Alma after the morning rehearsal that 'everything sounds exactly as I could wish. This time I think I will succeed.' He added that he intended to take an hour's nap before beginning the tiring afternoon session at 4.30.

On 21 May, Mahler sent Alma a telegram apologizing for not having been able to write to her during the day. His letter on the 22nd explained why. He

all. 'Why not have cancelled the final rehearsal, spreading the seven [composers] through a matinee and an evening? A single hearing [of the Sixth] would have presented fewer problems than this long-drawn-out, concentrated, multicoloured musical profusion.' (cf. Peter Andraschke, 'Gustav Mahlers Retuschen im Finale seiner 6. Symphonie', in Rudolf Stephan (ed.), *Mahler-Interpretation* (Schott, Mainz, 1985), 63).

[31] He assured Witte that he would 'often have occasion to use it, for it is employed by many modern composers, Charpentier and Strauss for example'.

[32] This letter has changed hands many times, passing from one autograph dealer to another and figuring in the following catalogues: Stargardt (1955); Nicholas Rauch, Geneva (1959); and Stargardt (1960).

[33] Undated letter (probably end of Oct. 1905), Bibliothek der Stadt Düren. Schillings in turn wrote to Strauss on 10 Nov., explaining Mahler's conditions. 'I am in favour of accepting the work, and I propose, now and in writing, to seek the opinion of the members of the musical committee.' Schillings goes on to suggest to Strauss other works suitable for inclusion in the festival. Cf. *Richard Strauss–Max von Schillings: Ein Briefwechsel*, ed. Roswitha Schlötterer (Ludwig, Pfaffenhofen 1987), 127. The *Neue Musikalische Presse* article implies that it was at the request of the Verein that Mahler authorized this première, other organizations having already asked for it.

[34] According to articles in the contemporary press, the Essen orchestra included many musicians who had participated two years earlier in the première of the Fifth as members of the Cologne Orchestra.

[35] Eighteen months later the concertmaster of the Essen orchestra, Alex Kosman, wrote to Mahler to remind him that he had been so pleased with his contribution that he had offered him a job in Vienna. Kosman thereupon asked him for a letter of recommendation to the Intendant of the Dresden Orchestra (HOA, Z.1 1100/1907, letter of 14 Nov.).

had spent seven hours at his table correcting the orchestra parts and five at the podium in rehearsal. He felt well despite his strenuous schedule, and was anxious to get on with the remaining rehearsals, for he had as yet rehearsed only the first three movements. A group of young musicians, all fervent admirers, had gathered around him in Essen and attended all the rehearsals, scores in hand. Among them was Ossip Gabrilowitsch,[36] a young Russian pianist who had travelled all the way from St Petersburg, probably because he had heard the Second Symphony there in January. Mahler was delighted by his vivacity and enthusiasm, and invited him to his table at mealtimes. Also in attendance were Julius Buths,[37] Oskar Fried, who followed Mahler 'like a shadow', and Alban Berg—Schoenberg's most brilliant pupil.[38] Another recent, enthusiastic disciple of Mahler was present: this was Klaus Pringsheim, whom Mahler had recently engaged as voluntary Korrepetitor at the Vienna Opera.

Pringsheim was the son of Alfred Pringsheim, a mathematics professor, and the grandson of a Munich businessman who had made a huge fortune at the end of the eighteenth century with the monopoly for coal transport from Upper Silesia, and in the nineteenth with a private railway he built for the same purpose. Pringsheim's twin sister Katia had married Thomas Mann, already a famous author,[39] the year before. At the age of 13, Pringsheim had heard Mahler conduct the Kaim Orchestra in Munich, and never forgot his interpretations of Berlioz's *Symphonie fantastique* and the triumphant coda of the Finale of Beethoven's Fifth Symphony.[40] This made a profound impression on him and without quite admitting it to himself he dreamed of working under this man 'who radiated magic power when in front of an orchestra'. Pringsheim studied all the scores of his symphonies and attended his concerts whenever possible. His teacher, Bernard Stavenhagen, continued to express his admiration for Mahler in spite of the rebuff he had suffered at Mahler's hands the previous year.[41] In February 1906, the dream seemed to come true when Pringsheim applied for the job of Korrepetitor at the Hofoper, and received a telegram from Mahler summoning him to his office the following Friday between four and five o'clock.

---

[36] Ossip Gabrilowitsch (1878–1936), born in St Petersburg and student at the Conservatory there, had studied piano under Anton Rubinstein and Navratil, and composition under Liadov and Glazunov. After being awarded the Rubinstein prize in 1894, he moved to Vienna for two years to study with Theodor Leschetizky. He made his debut in Berlin in 1896, and from 1900 onwards he made many concert tours (especially in the United States). From 1910 to 1914 he conducted the Munich Konzertverein. Settling in the United States in 1918, he conducted the Detroit Orchestra for a few years. Among his initiatives was a concert series which illustrated the history of the piano concerto and other musical forms. In 1906 Gabrilowitsch married Clara Clemens, the daughter of Mark Twain, a soprano whom he sometimes accompanied in recitals (see below, Vol. iiii, Chap. 6). His compositions were mainly for piano and for orchestra.

[37] Julius Buths (1851–1920), conductor, composer, and director of the Düsseldorf Conservatory, had conducted Mahler's works several times in the context of the Niederrheinische Musikfeste, among others the Second Symphony on 3 Apr. 1903 (see above, Vol. ii, Chap. 15).

[38] Cf. Hans Ferdinand Redlich, *Alban Berg* (Universal, Vienna, 1957), 294.

[39] *Buddenbrooks* was published in 1901 and *Tonio Kröger* in 1903.

[40] At the 24 Mar. 1897 concert (see above, Vol. i, Chap. 24).

[41] Mahler had refused Stavenhagen permission to conduct the Fifth Symphony (see above, Chap. 1).

At the interview Mahler asked Pringsheim about the musical scene in Munich, and particularly about Felix Mottl and his Wagner festival at the Prinzregententheater,[42] and about Max Reger, whom everyone was talking about as an important figure of the contemporary musical scene. After being appointed fourth Korrepetitor (singing coach),[43] Pringsheim enjoyed the privilege of seeing Mahler every day and working under his direction. Mahler had taken a liking to the young man, inviting him occasionally to the Auenbruggergasse. He had suggested as a matter of course that he should come with him to Essen.

Pringsheim has left a splendid description of one of the rehearsals of the Finale of the Sixth in Essen:

a prolonged roar of trombones and trumpets, wind instruments in the highest register, interspersed with cannonades of kettledrums, and the crashing of cymbals and drums like thunder and lightning—a chaos of sound in the empty hall—so deafening that the few listeners sitting down below were dumbfounded and, shaking their heads, smiling in disbelief, stared now at their scores and now at the conductor, for whom it was still not loud enough, and who, with those indescribable gestures which had such boundless power of command, was driving the orchestra to ever greater exertions. Then finally Mahler tapped for silence. Now, surely, he's going to calm things down. But no—he called over to the trumpets: 'Can't you play any louder?' Had we heard aright? A few times more he interrupted, and asked now this group, now that: 'Can't you play that louder?' And lo! the miracle happened: the chaotic masses of sound fell into place, peaks rose out of the waves, he built them up, piled peak on peak, and so emerged, overwhelming and gigantic, in masses that Mahler never before and truth to tell never again dared to attempt, the last movement.[44]

The orchestration of the Sixth posed serious problems for the orchestral musicians and the percussion had a particular hard time.[45] Several months earlier, Mahler had had a special instrument constructed to replace the bass drum, which he considered not to be loud enough for the climaxes of the Finale. At the first of the three readings that took place in Vienna in April, the enormous drum was installed for the first time amid a breathless hush. Mahler asked the percussionist[46] to try it out, but the result was weak and muffled.

---

[42]   Mahler had known Mottl since his youth, when they were both students at the Vienna Conservatory and Mottl was the head of the Wagner-Verein.

[43]   HOA, Z. 1016/1906. Ferdinand Foll (1867–1929) engaged by Mahler in 1897, Julius Lehnert, and Karl Weigl occupied the first three posts. As we have already seen (Chap. 5), Mahler took the side of his youngest singing coach against a tenor who refused to follow orders during a rehearsal (see Klaus Pringsheim, 'Erinnerungen an Gustav Mahler', *Neue Zürcher Zeitung* (7 July 1960); 'My Recollections of Gustav Mahler', *Chord and Discord* (1958), 114; 'Erinnerungen an die Uraufführung von Gustav Mahlers Sechster Symphonie', *Neues Wiener Journal* (15 Sept. 1923); and 'Zur Uraufführung von Mahlers Sechster Symphonie', *Musikblätter des Anbruch*, 2 (1920): 14, 496 ff.). As mentioned above, Pringsheim was present at the Auenbruggergasse apartment the evening Schoenberg and Zemlinsky were there, together with Theodor Streicher (see above, Chap. 3). His twin sister Katia Mann adds that Mahler took him on as an unpaid assistant (*volontär*), a detail confirmed by the Opera Archives. (HOA, Z. 1016, Aug. 1906).

[44]   Pringsheim, 'Uraufführung', *Neues Wiener Journal*, repr. in *Musikblätter des Anbruch*, 2 (1920), 14.

[45]   In his review for the *Münchner Neueste Nachrichten*, Rudolf Louis mentions Mahler's difficulty with the percussion during rehearsals.

[46]   The percussionist was probably Johann Schnellar (see above, Chap. 5).

Despite Mahler's insistence, the musician failed to produce a louder tone and Mahler angrily rushed over and struck the instrument with all his force. The inadequacy of the result compared with the effort required to produce it provoked general hilarity among the musicians.[47] Mahler stubbornly refused to acknowledge defeat, and the huge instrument was transported to Essen at enormous cost. There a final attempt convinced him to abandon the idea but the big wooden case, placed at the back of the stage, on the highest tier, attracted much attention, even though it was not used during the performance.[48]

During these days of hard work, the enthusiasm, affection, and admiration of Mahler's young disciples were a great comfort to him, but he was once again perplexed by Strauss's behaviour: not the slightest word of encouragement about the Sixth, merely a remark that the Finale was 'over-orchestrated'. Mahler rarely allowed himself to be depressed by his critics but this time he was really upset. His relationship with Strauss occupied a considerable place in the conversations which Pringsheim recorded:

As always he spoke simply, with touching humanity, and everyone hearkened to his words as to those of a sage. For Mahler taught like Socrates, conversationally, imparting infinitely much, but without the gestures of a teacher. He spoke not of himself, but of the other, whom he had never underestimated, wondering without envy or bitterness, almost resignedly humble, why everything which came easily to Strauss came with such difficulty to him, and his listeners felt the everlasting contrast between the blond-haired conquering heroes and the dark doom-laden sufferers. At this point one of us politely intervened to remind him of the 'masterly certainty of his orchestration'. Certainty (masterly into the bargain)? That was news to him. We learned, if we still had to learn it, that Mahler's 'craftsmanship', his incredible command of the orchestral apparatus, was not something he could take for granted. It was not a secure capital he could comfortably draw on which enabled him to compose symphonies without effort (how often his detractors have reproached him with it, trying to get at the master through his craftsmanship!). No—his craftsmanship was a highly laborious thing, won anew every day and with every bar, a truly creative process since his artistic will was constantly re-creating it. We learned that his last task, before writing down a score, was to decide on the instrumentation; that he himself, when the musical image had come into focus, often still had no idea what sound resources he would have to use for its realization, and what the score would ultimately look like. Even when the score

---

[47] AMM1, 125; AMM2, 126. The story is told differently in a text signed J.B. in the *Neues Wiener Tagblatt* of 24 Apr. 1925, and in *Fünfundzwanzig Jahre Dienstbarer Geist im Reiche der Frau Musika*, by Rudolf Effenberger, (Effenberger, Vienna, n.d.), the Philharmonic orchestra attendant. Effenberger describes a 'rehearsal before the [Viennese] première of the Sixth', but he is mistaken, for it took place in Vienna with the Konzertverein orchestra. The bass drum was allegedly 'brought over from the Opera' and the slightest blow created 'a deafening noise'. According to him, a trombonist seated in front of it leapt into the air at the first hammerblow and ended up sitting on the floor. When Mahler asked him what had happened, he replied: 'If this bass drum isn't removed, I won't play another note!'

[48] See Otto Neitzel's article in *Signale für die Musikalische Welt*. According to E. S. Moll ('Gustav Mahlers Persönlichkeit', in *Münchner Neueste Nachrichten*, 14 July 1910), Viennese instrument makers refused to build the drum and Mahler had it constructed to his own specification. He abandoned it after the trial run with the Vienna Philharmonic and the Essen première, but not before sending the instrument to several conductors in the hope that the particular acoustics of each concert hall would enable it to be played.

was at last complete, even after it was in print, he worked on it day and night. He worked, or rather, it kept on working within him all the time, during rehearsals, on walks, at table—moving toward the unattainable, highest perfection. Facile solutions were certainly not for him. And what about his 'certainty'? Was he not bound, instinctively and unconsciously, to reject it, just as he had openly rejected tradition and routine? Yet his was the uncertainty of one who forever strove and explored, for whom no standard of measurement, no yardstick existed—and who nevertheless, even in the deepest moments of his life, had never felt fully convinced that he was on the right path.

Those close to him were well aware of Mahler's 'uncertainty'. Even after the final rehearsal he was still not sure whether or not he had found the right tempo for the Scherzo, and he wondered whether he should invert the order of the second and third movements (which he subsequently did). He kept on making changes and improvements. After each rehearsal he asked everyone around him, musicians and friends, for their impressions, trying to determine down to the smallest technical detail, to what extent, in their impact on the listener, he had achieved what he intended. He listened carefully not only to favourable comments, but also to critical suggestions. Even the young Korrepetitor who had come with him from Vienna was asked for his opinion. He gave it, first boyishly shy, then growing bolder as his judgement and his advice were listened to—even though he could hardly believe in what was happening. Honestly, if I could not identify today, as if it had occurred yesterday, those passages to which I, the pupil, pointed with my finger, suggesting that they might be changed in this way or that, I would not believe it myself. They were minute details in the orchestration, but the passages were changed and remained changed.

What an experience for a twenty-two-year-old! To feel myself Mahler's friend, and to be esteemed as such was a profoundly blissful experience at the time, giving rise to boundless gratitude. And it was an experience of such lasting importance that it enriched my entire life, decisively affecting my path as a musician and my fate as an artist. And yet it was only the personal experience of him to whom it was given.[49]

In another article, Klaus Pringsheim stresses the fact that the 'details' he proposed for correction concerned only the balance between different sonorities, which was always more important to Mahler than their individual attractiveness or colour. He also recalls that while Mahler considerably 'thinned out' the score of the Fifth after the Cologne performance, he did nothing of the sort for the Sixth—the symphony which Strauss (the Strauss of *Salome*!) called 'over-orchestrated'. Bruno Walter also testifies that Mahler was 'almost reduced to tears' by Strauss's cutting remark. '"Isn't it remarkable,"' Pringsheim reports him as saying, '"how Strauss manages to get by with one or two rehearsals, and it always 'sounds right'? I wear myself out in countless rehearsals to bring everything out as I want it. But when, after a performance, have I ever been able to say that I was completely satisfied?"'[50]

Mahler's modesty and 'insecurity' seemed to increase with age. The following

---

[49] Klaus Pringsheim, 'Uraufführung', *Neues Wiener Tagblatt* and *Musikblätter des Anbruch*.

[50] 'Erinnerungen', *Neue Zürcher Zeitung* (7 July 1960). Pringsheim also relates that he was responsible for 'conducting' the backstage cowbells.

description of rehearsals for the Seventh Symphony in Prague in 1908 confirms this impression:

Nothing was ever unimportant to him. His extremely acute ear distinguished the most concealed middle voices even in a fortissimo of the entire orchestra. With his own works, he never wearied of touching up the orchestration. 'I got that bit wrong!' (*Das habe ich hier schlecht gemacht!*) he admitted without embarrassment before the orchestra, and experimented until the result pleased him ... The utmost concentration which was so characteristic of him was something he also demanded from others. His relationship with the orchestra was a mixture of touching amability and frightening despotism ...[51]

When he had finished the Sixth Symphony two years before, Mahler well knew that, once again, it would not be understood. But human nature is such that later he began to hope that its tragic character would make it more accessible than the 'humour' of some of his other symphonies.

From experience, I would say that the Fourth is the least suitable as an introduction to my work if one is not completely familiar with my compositions. So far it has only succeeded in surprising the audience. The Sixth Symphony would be the most suitable. It has more chance of being understood by the general public because of its altogether moving character. In most of the others, humour plays an important part, which is always difficult for an audience to grasp.[52]

In early May, C. F. Kahnt, the publisher of the Sixth, sent a press release to German newspapers and reviews to arouse interest in the Essen première.

Before Mahler gives his work to the printer, he always arranges for a sight reading. For his latest symphony, the Vienna Philharmonic once again placed itself gratis at his disposal, and it is from this source that first reports about this work have now reached the public. From what we have heard, Mahler's audacity in this symphony seems to surpass everything he has hitherto accomplished in composition. This time Gustav Mahler has not provided a programme for his symphony, not even an indication about the work's content.[53] The orchestral distribution, as explained in the pocket version of the score already available, is all the more significant. Especially the percussion! Nothing like it has ever been seen before.

A list of the percussion instruments followed, including of course the enormous square bass drum, struck with a heavy wooden mallet instead of a normal drumstick. The publicity-minded publishing firm also presented as a novelty the use of birch rods as drumsticks, to be struck sometimes forcefully, sometimes lightly, but Mahler had already employed them several times before.[54]

---

[51]   Edgar Istel, 'Erinnerungen', *Neue Musik-Zeitung*, 38 (1917): 6, 88.

[52]   Undated letter (about 1906) in an anonymous dealer's catalogue of autographs. To illustrate his idea of musical 'humour', Mahler explained to Natalie in 1901 that Beethoven was the father of humour, particularly in his First and Sixth Symphonies, which was the reason for their relative unpopularity. Beethoven's humour was understood less than the wit and cheerfulness of Haydn and Mozart (NBL1, 173; NBL2, 199).

[53]   On the night of the first performance, however, the audience was provided with a 48-page thematic guide, compiled by Richard Specht (see Peter Andraschke, 'Retuschen', 64).

[54]   In the Second and Third Symphonies.

The day before the Essen Festival opened (on 23 May), the *Neue Zeitschrift für Musik* carried an analysis of the Sixth Symphony by Ernst Otto Nodnagel, written in the enthusiastic eulogistic tone which was so characteristic of him and which often annoyed Mahler.[55]

On 22 May, Mahler sent another telegram to Alma, thanking her for her 'very sweet' letter, and explaining that once again he had spent so much time correcting the orchestra parts that he had not had time to write. On 24 May, again by telegram, he wished her a good trip and expressed his impatience for her arrival.[56] When she arrived at Essen on Friday 25 May, Alma found Mahler 'sad and worried', almost ill with anxiety. Two days later, a painful incident occurred backstage.

After the rehearsal, Mahler paced up and down in the dressing room sobbing and wringing his hands, completely beside himself. Fried, Gabrilowitsch, Buths and I stood there petrified, not even daring to look at one another. Suddenly Strauss came barging in through the door. He sensed nothing of what was happening. 'Mahler, tomorrow you have to conduct a funeral march or something of the sort before the Sixth. The mayor here just died[57] and it is the custom—but what is the matter with you? What is wrong? Ah well—' and he stumped callously off, leaving us worried stiff.

According to Alfred Roller, whose scrupulous honesty, rare objectivity, and boundless admiration for Mahler, always make his testimony particularly reliable, Mahler asked one of his friends (Roller does not identify him, but merely says that he was not a musician), whether his symphony had made any impression on him on first hearing. 'He [the friend] was still so deeply affected that he could only stammer through his tears, "How can a man of your goodness express so much harshness and cruelty?" To which Mahler replied seriously and firmly: "It is the cruelty which has been inflicted on me, and the pain I have had to suffer!"'[58]

Ferdinand Pfohl, Mahler's old Hamburg friend turned enemy, was present at the dress rehearsal and, listening to the major-minor motto of the Sixth, he recalled a walk he had once taken with Mahler around the harbour in Hamburg. They had both been fascinated by the distant sounds of three tug-boats and the common chords struck by their horns with irregular rhythms. 'Look at that!' said Pfohl, pointing to the activity in the harbour, 'That could be a symphony . . . of the rhythm of work.' Pfohl remembered this incident, when he was in Essen and heard not only the same common chord but a composition based on the sharp, determined rhythms of that smoky town with its steam hammers and huge forges and furnaces. This reminiscence did not, however, prevent Pfohl, true to his antipathy of former times, from snubbing Mahler in

---

[55] Cf. Helmut Kirchmeyer, 'Mahler-Berichterstattung der "Neue Zeitschrift für Musik" zwischen 1889 und 1911', in Mathias Theodor Vogt (ed.), *Das Gustav-Mahler-Fest Hamburg 1989* (Bärenreiter, Kassel, 1991), 199 ff.   [56] BGA, no. 170, dated 24 May 1906.

[57] The mayor of Essen, named Zweigert, had died that morning. He had been responsible for the recent construction of the Städtische Saalbau.   [58] RBM 24.

the hotel where they were both staying. When Otto Neitzel tried to introduce them, saying 'No doubt you know Gustav Mahler?' Pfohl turned away with the remark, 'Only too well, unfortunately'. He did admit later that he regretted his behaviour.[59]

Wouter Hutschenruyter, who himself conducted a fringe concert given on 25 May by the Orchestra of Utrecht, attended all the rehearsals of Mahler's symphony. Thirty years later he published his memories of this encounter in a Dutch newspaper,[60] praising Mahler's unique qualities as a musician and conductor.

Gustav Mahler had been described to me as impossibly difficult, rude, hot-tempered, and all the other dislikeable qualities one could think of. To my astonishment all that turned out to be absolute nonsense. They said he was difficult; I noticed that he only did what my father used to drill into me as a boy: 'good' means 'there's nothing missing', and that's what Mahler did his level best to do. Rude? During the many rehearsals I attended I never heard him say anything offensive to anyone. And hot-tempered? Well, now and then he could become aggressive, but never without justification, and the only peple who can't understand that are those who do not realise that a composer-conductor of genius such as he was becomes very tensed up during a performance of his work. Mahler was forthright in his behaviour with members of the orchestra and in the demands he made; he was grateful (and showed it) when they played his music well, and—the main thing—he was (then in Essen) never insulting.

Of Mahler as a conductor one can only speak in superlatives. He was a perfect master (naturally) of the technique, he had a relaxed, flexible, clear beat, avoided any superfluous movements—in his youth apparently he was supposed to have conducted rather 'wildly' —and kept his comments short and clear and to the point. His musical ear was a marvel of sharpness and exactitude; it was not only perfectly 'absolute', but also extremely sensitive to the finest possible tone differentiation. And precisely because Mahler's hearing was so reliable, so impeccable, I have always found it strange that the incident I will now relate could have happened at all.

The Sixth Symphony contains a part for celesta. Mahler wanted two celestas for it, and I was asked to play one of them. An organist from Essen had been engaged for the other. In the first movement there is a passage in which the celesta part is very important. Mahler wanted this passage to be played in a special way and urged us to take great care to get it right. The rehearsal begins: the particular passage approaches: the organist and I exchange glances and begin to play, following as exactly as possible the instructions of the composer. When we subsequently come to the place when we have to count a couple of pause-bars we notice... that we had started off one beat too soon! Naturally we were horrified! But the strange thing was that Mahler had not noticed the mistake at all! Again an example of how the mind can concentrate so much on one point that it completely fails to notice something else.

The incident, I need hardly say, didn't shake our belief in the infallibility of

---

[59] FPM 18 and 43. Pfohl, it will be remembered, could not forgive Mahler for his refusal to interview personally a young soprano he had sent to see him (see above, Vol. i, Chap. 9).

[60] Wouter Hutschenruyter, 'Mijn herinneringen aan Gustav Mahler', *Algemeen Handelsblad* (18 May 1936).

Mahler's hearing in the least little bit. It did one good to see the thankful pleasure with which Mahler enjoyed the success of his symphony, and how grateful he said he was for the devotion with which the work had been played.[61]

At the end of the final rehearsal, on Sunday morning at 11 a.m., a few catcalls could be heard amid the applause. Nonetheless, the success of the concert seemed assured, for the audience consisted mostly of musicians and informed music lovers.[62] Schillings opened the concert with a short tribute to the late mayor, who had been the festival's sponsor, after which Strauss conducted Mozart's *Masonic Funeral Music*. Mahler then appeared to conduct the Sixth Symphony. Until the last moment, he had had no doubts over the details of the score and even the order of the second and third movements, which was hastily reversed between the final rehearsal and the première.[63] Alma claims that he conducted the performance itself 'almost badly, ashamed of his own agitation and afraid that he might break down while conducting. He did not want to betray in advance the truth behind this most dreadful *antizipando* last movement!' It must of course be recalled here that Alma later considered the Sixth Symphony's three hammer blows as foreboding of the three reversals of fate which Mahler was to suffer the following year.[64]

Disconcerted by the obstinate rhythm and violence of the first movement, the audience of the première 'almost forgot to applaud' according to Alma.[65] But at the end of the performance, Mahler took six curtain calls and the musicians of the orchestra joined in the standing ovation. The ritual bestowing of the laurel wreath was even accompanied by a brass fanfare. But clearly it was a *succès d'estime*, with the majority of the audience bewildered by the length and expressionist outburst of the Finale. Once again, at a time when a large number of well-intentioned listeners thought they had come to terms with Mahler's music, they were genuinely puzzled by the new course it had taken. After the concert, he was in such a state of agitation that Mengelberg, whom Alma was meeting for the first time,[66] was really concerned for him and Alma hesitated at first to take him to the official banquet given at the end of the festival. Luckily, he seemed to calm down as soon as he found himself among the other guests.

The reviews of the première published in the German musical journals

---

[61] Cf. Eduard Reeser, 'Eine Erinnerung an die Uraufführung der 6. Symphonie', in *Nachrichten zur Mahler-Forschung*, no. 26 (1991), 6–10. Eduard Reeser sets out to find the passage in question: probably bars 199 to 202 of the first movement, followed by six bars of rest up to 209.

[62] One of Mahler's French friends, Guillaume de Lallemand, a captain at this time, seems to have attended the concert. 'To the "grosser Appell" of the 26th in Essen, I can joyfully reply "present",' wrote Lallemand to Mahler on 11 May 1906, asking him to set aside a ticket for him and explaining that because of the military authorities he would have to come to Essen incognito.

[63] For the première, the Oct. performance in Berlin and the Nov. performance in Munich, the Andante followed the Scherzo. In Vienna in Jan. 1907 Mahler apparently reverted to the original order of the movements (see below, Chap. 7).   [64] See below, Chap. 9.

[65] According to the correspondent of the *Musikalisches Wochenblatt*.

[66] He reminded her, at first sight, of Loge (in *Rheingold*).

reflected the embarrassment or indignation of the leading music critics. Otto Lessmann in the *Allgemeine Musik-Zeitung*, showed untypical moderation, probably because he was writing for the Verein's mouthpiece. Already well acquainted with Mahler's music, he had expected him to 'follow his (usual) path': contrasting movements of 'repulsive ugliness' with movements of 'noble beauty', and polishing details rather than working on 'the main lines of true symphonic composition'. He did recognize signs of a 'great spirit' in the 'virile force' of the first movement, the 'marvellous depth' and 'nobility of feeling' in the Andante, and the 'sunny, Schubert-like gaiety' of the Scherzo (*sic!*); but he thought that the Finale, certainly the richest and most interesting movement, went astray in 'the cacophony of a polyphonic labyrinth'—so much so that the listener eventually lost track, no matter how attentively he followed the score. But despite all the ugliness in his work, Mahler remained, for Lessmann, an 'imposing phenomenon'. For the *Musikalisches Wochenblatt*, on the other hand, the 'two-hammer-blow Symphony' was 'the grotesque product of a degenerate imagination'. Whatever acclaim it received in Essen, it would be a 'museum piece' for future generations. Despite Mahler's 'incredible sophistication in the use of ultra-modern means', the 'inner content of the Sixth is not commensurate with the enormous force deployed'.[67]

Otto Neitzel, the Cologne critic who also wrote for *Signale für die Musikalische Welt*, opened his account by observing that the work premièred on 27 May, had

by some external aspects of its orchestration, caused several cubic metres of ink to be spilled before the first note sounded. . . . This time, too, we had the casing of the bass drum being scratched with switches, producing the impression of a sheeted ghost turning somersaults in one's bedroom. . . . And the hammer blow! Since the most audacious modern means of orchestration were not sufficient to realize it, and pistol shots, not being permitted in concerts, could not be envisaged, Herr Mahler had the hide of a fully grown cow stretched on a frame a metre and a half square, added a depth of half a metre to provide the necessary resonance and placed this apparatus, hailed by many as the symbol (*Wahrzeichen*) of his newest work, on the highest tier at the back of the stage. Why this apparatus did not function remains unclear to me. It was said that no man strong enough to inflict a devastating blow on the cowhide could be found in Essen or its environs.[68]

The critic's tone then becomes more serious:

Cow bells and a celesta! Paradise on earth and Elysian fields above! It would all be so simple if Mahler's symphony were content to remain between these two poles. But in the meantime an enormous abyss has opened up, an unappeased longing, a despair, and a struggle on the part of the entire orchestra, especially in the final movement,

[67] According to this correspondent, the Allegro lasted 20 minutes; the Andante, 15; the Scherzo, also 15, and the Finale, 40 minutes.

[68] Otto Neitzel, 'Das 42. Tonkünstlerfest des Allgemeinen Deutschen Musikvereins in Essen', *Signale für die musikalische Welt*, 64 (1906): 41, 690.

where the brass section is given virtually no respite, with a groan, a moan, a cry and a roar which gives the symphony its tragic character. Superficial critics would deny this tragic aspect, but upon close listening it does possess it, and even more so than Mahler's earlier creations.

The dichotomy between lighthearted, even comic account, and comprehensive, sometimes profound judgement, is characteristic of most of the articles published about the première, in which scepticism and admiration are strangely mixed.[69] According to the *Neue Zeitschrift für Musik*, the Sixth had stimulated intense curiosity.[70] It showed the composer 'with all his good and bad qualities: his fantastic instrumental technique and his sometimes unfortunate thematic inventiveness alike'. Above all, the symphony was 'a strong will personified'.

Some composers burst into song (*singen aus*) because they cannot do otherwise. Mahler gives the impression that he turns to music to find in it his redemption. He seems to express his feelings above all in 'elementary colours' in which he shows undoubted originality. His thematic invention, on the other hand, has never been considered original. It becomes Mahlerian only through the way he arranges and develops it.

Mahler's music, the critic thought, lacked feeling, displaying instead 'tremendous will and indescribable technique'. 'If his art were not so terribly serious and sincere, if it were not so profoundly tragic, fewer people would be pondering on the Gustav Mahler enigma.' However the same critic, perhaps remembering that the review he was writing for belonged to C. F. Kahnt, the publisher of the symphony, added:

The Sixth Symphony is simpler, both in its themes and in the construction of its movements, than the Second, Third and Fifth, and despite the exceptional demands it makes it will perhaps make its way faster than some of its predecessors, precisely because of the simpler character of its content. A fortunate by-product will be increased interest in the percussion, that step-child of the orchestra. Richard Strauss was not mistaken when he jokingly suggested, with reference to Mahler's symphonies, that professorships in percussion should be set up in our conservatories.

In the *Münchner Neueste Nachrichten*, Rudolf Louis, anti-Semitic apostle of 'German nationalism', was true to form and had not a good word to say. 'Mahler's Sixth Symphony' he wrote 'was not as interesting as his Third, which had been the climax of the Krefeld Festival.' Noisy applause and 'careful staging' notwithstanding, the audience's reaction had lacked enthusiasm. Mahler's individuality, although striking at first, had lost the charm of novelty. 'Effects without cause, after the manner of Meyerbeer', 'little orchestral jokes'—everything

<hr />

[69]   Andraschke, 'Retuschen', 65.

[70]   The article is signed by Max Hehemann (1873–1933). Hehemann was born in Krefeld and studied there. Editor and musical critic of the *Essener Allgemeine Zeitung*, he founded in 1904 the Essen Musikalische Gesellschaft. He was a fervent admirer of Max Reger and organized the first festival of his work in 1905. Author of the German version of George Grove's book on Beethoven's symphonies, he also wrote a monograph on Reger (Munich 1911 and 1917).

which had seemed surprising in Krefeld had degenerated into 'mannerism'. Mahler was merely repeating himself; the Sixth was the weakest of his symphonies along with the Fourth. In the first movement—the best of the four—he demonstrated that he could create something out of nothing. But unfortunately, when he tried to create 'feeling, he offends the listener who is able to distinguish between true and false'. The Scherzo was more interesting in that it revealed the true Mahler, the 'bizarre caricaturist', the 'master of distorted lines and droll timbres'. The Finale, however, was quite literally painful, a 'lamentable failure', 'pretentious, overblown, and noisily insignificant'. It showed a 'compulsive striving for grandeur but impotently piled mass upon mass of sounds'. A few details here and there and the masterly orchestration might perhaps interest professional musicians, but the work as a whole could offer neither musical satisfaction nor aesthetic pleasure.[71]

The anonymous correspondent of the *Frankfurter Zeitung* definitely preferred, 'despite all its oddness', Mahler's Sixth Symphony to Strauss's recent *Symphonia Domestica*, because Mahler 'never lost sight of the dignity of his art'. Even if his musical ideas 'lacked originality' his musical style was 'strong and healthy' it never wallowed in 'flabby sentimentality'. In the first movement the 'clear striving' which the principal ideas displayed, compensated by the breadth of their overall structure for what they perhaps lacked in the way of concentrated expression. Nevertheless, 'the gigantic theme of the first movement is made up of numerous stages and subdivisions; now one, now the other appears, sometimes in its original form, sometimes as a variation, or again in polyphony.' Even if such procedures revealed 'reflection' rather than 'creative ingenuity', the way Mahler developed his themes ensured that there was never a moment's boredom. Furthermore 'the extraordinary clarity of this very diatonic music is strikingly revealed by the matchless orchestration.' Mahler's preference for brass instruments and his frequent use of percussion were immediately obvious, but were always used to serve 'an idealistic, superior point of view'. The anonymous critic found however that the Finale contained numerous 'abstruse, incomprehensible' passages, and preferred the heroic first Allegro, with its 'lapidary' first theme, its 'generous, melodious second subject, and the two middle movements, full of genuine feeling and charm'. All in all, the work 'captivates and stimulates' and would obviously 'cause a stir in the "neo-German" circles in Munich and Berlin'. 'As Bruckner's symphonies have shown, this Sixth will provide for future generations a faithful image of the highest level of the technique of symphonic composition of our day.' It would be interesting to discover the identity of this anonymous reviewer whose views were so much more enlightened that those of his colleagues.

True to his attitude in the past, Leopold Schmidt[72] drew up in the *Signale für die Musikalische Welt* after the Berlin performance, a catalogue of the

---

[71] *Münchner Neueste Nachrichten*, no. 265 (8 June 1906).
[72] See above, Chap. 4, for Schmidt's biography.

'innovations' which added nothing to the symphony, in particular the 'battery of percussion instruments' and the famous rectangular drum which Mahler had had built for the 'hammer blows' in the Finale, and which was not used despite its prominent position at the back of the stage. According to Schmidt, the Finale suffered from a 'hypertrophy of instrumentation': its 'indescribably grieving, longing struggle' was tragic because the 'struggle remained unresolved, the longing without fulfilment. Altogether, the whole symphony was utterly Mahlerian.' The 'reminders of Schubert', the 'moving Meyerbeer-like phrases', the 'harsh discords' could in no way serve as a 'core of artistic creation'. Schmidt found the first movement outstanding, and the two middle movements agreeable. Mahler in any case deserved to be heard, if only for his 'compositional skill' and innovatory orchestration.[73]

In *Die Musik*, the Strasbourg critic Gustav Altmann was utterly dismissive of the Sixth.

Fundamentally, ever since his Second Symphony,[74] Mahler has been saying the same thing though the way he says it has become more and more unbearable; he screams and raves at us for no apparent reason; and his 40–60 bar long themes are without form or significance, and the structure of his movements without logic. His music is a clever adaptation of elements borrowed from other composers: *Kapellmeistermusik*, but with an extravagance of means which might be described as 'Amerikanismus—the art of limitless opportunities'. Mahler could have written charming and original operetta music, but his obsessive striving for the grandiose (*Grössenteufel*) drives him to become grandiloquent and at times to lapse into sugary sentimentality.

The *Neue Musikalische Presse* published not only a general account of the Essen Festival by one H. Hammer, but also a long article by Eduard Reuss[75] exclusively devoted to Mahler's Symphony. Hammer merely observed in passing that 'if only Mahler had a rich and original melodic imagination', he would be 'one of the greatest men of all time'. Unfortunately, 'the muses had refused him that gift'. Time alone would decide if objective audiences of the future would be as easily convinced and 'stirred' as the audience of the première. Although Mahler obstinately 'refused to provide his listeners with the slightest extra-musical reference', 'every measure, every sound' belonged to the domain of illustrative music. Rather than a symphony in four movements, he had created four 'symphonic paintings'. Even the size of the orchestra was more suited to a symphonic poem. The Scherzo smacked of the grotesque dances of peasants in Dutch paintings. As for the Finale, its purpose remained unclear:

[73] *Signale für die Musikalische Welt*, 64 (1906): 60/61, 1070 ff.

[74] Gustav Altmann was the music critic of the *Strassburger Post* (see above, Chap. 3).

[75] Eduard Reuss (1851–1911), born in New York, was a pupil of Liszt and later of Marie Gabriel Augustin Savard in Paris. Professor of Music at Karlsruhe, he settled in Wiesbaden in 1896, and was appointed Director of the Conservatory in that town in 1899. After conducting for two years in the United States (1901–2), he became Professor at the Dresden Conservatory. Married to the singer and teacher Luise Reuss-Belce, he was the author of various transcriptions and publications, especially on Liszt.

It is a quest for an intangible something, the desperate thrashing about of a tortured soul finally torn to pieces by its pursuing demons. It is darkness not illuminated by any ray of pity: hell without purgatory! . . . The Director of the Vienna Opera should take care, or one day he might find himself on the heights, only to be buried alive under the avalanche of his own [sound] masses! All those before him who overstepped their limits have come to grief.

Such was the verdict of one of the important German critics. Articles in the local Essen press expressed virtually the same point of view, albeit with more moderation. Like Max Hehemann, author of an unsigned article in the *General Anzeiger*[76] suspected that Mahler 'first imagined the sonorities, and only later looked for the melodies'. The Sixth too closely resembled its five predecessors: 'the schema is already too well known: a march, a rustic movement, a *Volkslied*'. Despite its polyphonic and orchestral clarity, this music was 'born of the will instead of from the heart', forcing the attention without awakening feeling. The audience's applause was only for the composer's magisterial conducting.[77]

The *Essener Volkszeitung* review was more nuanced, withholding judgement and describing the symphony as 'classical in form', and 'accessible to the culti-vated listener who follows the composer's train of thought'. The critic had noth-ing but praise for the first movement and defended even the Finale, 'constructed with the greatest logical rigour, despite the crushing force of its waves of sound, . . . its profound emotion, grandeur, clarity and the trans-parency of the polyphonic fabric.' The *Rheinisch-Westfälische Zeitung* joined those who judged that the end result was incommensurate with the means used to achieve it. Consequently, one was 'astonished but not always carried away, or overwhelmed'. But the same critic admired the 'unusual thematic ideas', their earnestness and nobility, the power and rigorous logic of each movement, the harmonic originality, and the beauty and novelty of the orchestral colour. Whoever still doubted Mahler's greatness would be converted by the Andante, with its 'deeply moving themes and orchestration of unprecedented dexterity' .

Such indulgence was, on the whole, exceptional; the verdict of the critics was on the whole negative, their arguments being more or less the same. Once again, they convinced Mahler that his time had not yet come. In a letter to Ludwig Karpath accompanying the pocket score of the Sixth, Mahler wrote: 'After reading one critic (Leopold Schmidt), I left off. These little people are always the same. Suddenly they like my first five symphonies. The VIth will have to wait until the VIIth comes out.'[78]

---

[76] Perhaps Hehemann himself, for the opinions are identical to those expressed in the *Neue Zeitschrift*.

[77] This critic claimed that Mahler reduced the strength of the percussion section during rehearsals. He noted the contrast between Mahler's frenetic gestures during rehearsals and the sobriety of his conducting the evening of the première.

[78] MBR1, no. 229; MBR2, no. 352. The date first assigned to this letter, 1904, is certainly false. The final two sentences prove that it was written after the première of the Sixth in 1906. The pocket score of the Fifth, furthermore, was in print at the end of Sept. 1904, *before* the première (Eberhardt Klemm, 'Zur Geschichte der Fünften Sinfonie von Gustav Mahler', note concerning document no. 124).

Thus astonishment, and disapproval were the rule after the première of the Sixth, at least in the press. None of the reviews reveals the slightest understanding of this particularly difficult symphony. This time, however, condemnation by the critics, nothing new to Mahler after all, affected him less than Richard Strauss's attitude. Seated next to Alma that evening at the official banquet given by the Verein, Strauss commented on the Finale and its hammerblows: 'I don't understand why Mahler ruins the effect by starting out with his greatest strength and then steadily diminishing it.' As with the Finale of the First Symphony twelve years earlier, one of the keys to the work escaped him.[79] For Mahler, who later discussed the matter with Alma, the blow which strikes the hero down must be the weakest of the three. 'It is clear to anyone who understands the symphony at all,' writes Alma, 'that the first blow must be the strongest, the second weaker, and the third the weakest of all. Perhaps the immediate effect would have been stronger with the dynamic in reverse order. But that was not what mattered to Mahler.'[80]

Alma and Mahler concluded that Strauss was too much a 'man of the theatre' to understand him. It is obvious that, by an irony of fate Strauss, Mahler's close colleague and comrade-in-arms who had launched and generously promoted his career, who seemed better equipped to understand him than most of his contemporaries, was in fact incapable of understanding him, and even preferred mediocre composers such as Hermann Bischoff. Every year, according to Alma, Strauss programmed one of Bischoff's symphonies at the festival, each more or less identical to the preceding one. '"You'll see," he exclaimed each time, "this year it'll turn out well!"[81] And yet toward Mahler as a composer he was scornful and sarcastic at this time.'

But despite their differences overt or beneath the surface, Mahler continued to keep in touch with Strauss, if only because of *Salome*. It was probably at Essen that he asked Strauss for an orchestral score 'for his private library'. Strauss replied that Fürstner had agreed to this 'on condition that you promise in writing that your heirs will return it in the event of your death'. Mahler accepted, and asked Strauss to make haste: 'I am longing to lose myself in the mysterious labyrinth.' Back in Vienna, he was once again campaigning for *Salome*: 'I have not yet obtained acceptance, but I do notice a promising 'wavering' (I expected nothing more as yet). I have mentioned your willingness to wait until 1 November, which was accepted with revealing alacrity. All in all, I believe I can say with certainty that we will put on Salome next year. A definitive answer in the autumn, if that is alright with you.'[82]

Upon returning to Vienna, Mahler was confronted with a veritable mountain of work. He also had to face up to the fact that his Sixth Symphony was as little

---

[79] See above, Vol. i, Chap. 19.

[80] AMM1, 128; AMM2, 128. In the final version of the Sixth, Mahler of course suppressed the third hammer blow.

[81] AMM1, 128; AMM2, 129. As is often the case, Alma is exaggerating, for Bischoff in fact wrote only two symphonies.   [82] AMS and Strauss Archives, Garmisch, MSB 118, undated (7 June 1906).

understood as its predecessors. He was used to not being understood, and was not unduly affected by a phenomenon which repeated itself after every première. Nevertheless, he soon realized that Kahnt, his new publisher, was discouraged, especially since he, like Peters, had taken the trouble to publish a pocket edition of the score. In December, Mahler signed a new contract for 'Liebst du um Schönheit' with Kahnt. Later on, in a version orchestrated by a member of the Kahnt firm,[83] it was included along with the six Lieder with orchestra which had already been published.

In the meantime, Mahler's prospects for finding a new publisher in Vienna were improving, for the recently founded Universal Edition had bought all the rights to his earlier symphonies and entrusted the printing of the pocket scores to Waldheim Eberle. On 5 January Josef Stritzko, director of Waldheim Eberle, sent Mahler the new miniature score of the Fourth Symphony: 'I hope that this pocket score will meet with your approval', he wrote in the accompanying note. 'As you can see on the list, we have now succeeded in incorporating in this edition all the symphonies by you we have published, in both full score and piano versions, which will certainly result in a significant improvement in sales.'[84] And indeed, the first edition of the pocket scores of Mahler's first four symphonies bear the name of Universal Edition and the date 1906.

At the Hofoper, Mahler still had an important task to accomplish before leaving for Maiernigg. On 1 June, he was due to conduct the first performance of the new production of *The Magic Flute*. Two days before, the tenor Hermann Winkelmann, who had created the title role of *Parsifal* at Bayreuth in 1882, gave his farewell performance at the Hofoper as Tannhäuser, one of his finest roles. More than twenty-five years had passed since his debut at the Vienna Opera;[85] he had since appeared 1,308 times, according to contemporary newspaper reports. Of course, the anti-Semitic press hastened to clamour that Mahler had 'kicked him out', although he was 'still useful and even indispensable'. As soon as he appeared on-stage during the Bacchanal of Act I he was noisily acclaimed, and at the end of the performance endless ovations accompanied the presentation of laurel wreaths and white roses. The *Deutsche Zeitung* criticized Mahler, who was present in his box until the end of the

[83] The author was Max Puttmann. Alfred Hoffmann, who was then director of Kahnt, informed me many years ago that Puttmann at the time was under contract to the firm and remained so until his death. Probably at the editor's instigation, Puttmann published a six-column article (with photograph) entitled *Gustav Mahler* in the 1 Feb. 1906 issue of *Blätter für Haus- und Kirchen-Musik*. The article consisted of a succinct biography and list of Mahler's principal compositions. Puttmann's information was not always accurate, for he claims that the Finale of the Fourth Symphony was entitled *Das himmlische Licht* (The Celestial Light). The contract for 'Liebst du um Schönheit' is dated 8 Dec. 1906. The composer received 600 marks for the publication. The work is described as a song 'for voice with piano accompaniment'.

[84] Letter from Josef Stritzko dated 5 Jan. 1906. Mahler wrote, probably in Dec. 1905, to Otto Singer, transcriber for Peters, asking him to send documents relating to the Fourth Symphony (orchestral material). He informed Singer that he was meeting Stritzko 'at the end of the month' and that he would tell him about their discussion 'in the New Year' (undated letter to Singer, BGM, Paris).

[85] This debut had taken place on 7 Dec. 1880, in *Lohengrin*.

second act, for not appearing on stage to bid Winkelmann farewell, and also for assigning the direction of the performance 'to the youngest conductor of the institution, Herr Schlesinger [Bruno Walter]'.[86]

After the fall of the curtain a ceremony took place in the wings, with Winkelmann seated on a throne under a canopy bearing 'the insignia of his principal roles'. The chorus sang *Wachet auf* from *Die Meistersinger*, Marie Gutheil-Schoder recited a poem, four sopranos recited a 'quodlibet' in humorous verse, and members of the ballet gave him a silver laurel wreath. Bruno Walter bade him farewell in the name of the orchestra and Opera authorities. Overwhelmed with emotion, the tenor thanked them in a trembling voice and added: 'The dream of my life is now over!'[87]

Two weeks later, a similar farewell ceremony took place for Wilhelm Hesch after he had declined to renew the contract which he had signed ten years before, just before Mahler arrived at the Opera. This time, the reason was again apparently Mahler's refusal to allow him to accept 'invitations' outside Vienna. Furthermore, Hesch demanded a salary of 19,000 kronen. 16,000 had been proposed, and Mahler hesitated to offer better terms, largely because of Hesch's long illness with intestinal cancer.[88] The evening of his 'farewell performance' he sang the role of the high priest in Goldmark's *Die Königin von Saba*.[89] After the enthusiastic public had called him back on stage a dozen times and showered him with white roses, he improvised a speech in which he excused himself for his 'difficulty in speaking without a prompter' and concluded: 'Perhaps I will be back.' Outside the Opera a group of young admirers was waiting for him; as soon as he appeared he was applauded and carried off triumphantly to the Hartmann restaurant.

Mahler was not present that evening, having already left Vienna for Maiernigg, but he had left a letter for Hesch in which he said that he 'could not believe that you would leave us'. Four days earlier he had already written to ask him under what conditions he would consent to sign a new contract.[90] By August the conflict was resolved. Hesch obtained exceptional terms (especially for a bass, as Mahler wrote), probably by appealing directly to Prince Montenuovo: a six-year contract with an annual salary of 19,000 florins, but without a winter vacation. In a handwritten note to the Grand Chamberlain Mahler pointed out that six years was a long time in view of the singer's poor

---

[86]   The *Deutsche Zeitung* also reproached Mahler for choosing this farewell performance for the debut of a new bass, Lorenz Corvinius, who went unnoticed in the role of Landgraf.

[87]   According to the *Illustrirtes Wiener Extrablatt* of 18 Dec., Winkelmann had received the 'Salvator Gold Medal' from the mayor, Karl Lueger at the Town Hall the day before. In his speech, Lueger declared that 'everyone had hoped he would remain' at the Opera—a scarcely veiled criticism of Mahler.

[88]   Detail provided by Mrs Friedrich Zuckerkandl, who also indicated that the surgeon Otto Zuckerkandl (her uncle and Berta Zuckerkandl's brother-in-law) operated on Hesch.

[89]   Cast for the 150th performance of *Die Königin von Saba*, conducted by Bruno Walter on 13 June 1906: Elizza (Sulamith); Bland (the Queen); Forst (Astaroth); Slezak (Assad); Moser (Salomon); Hesch (High Priest).   [90]   HOA, G.Z. 680, Z. 497, letter of 9 June 1906.

state of health.[91] In the event, Hesch sang at the Hofoper only until the end of 1907: he died on 4 January 1908.

Leo Slezak, the principal 'star tenor' of the Opera with Schmedes, also created tremendous difficulties about the renewal of his contract, apparently for the same reasons. As we have seen on previous occasions, Slezak deeply resented being forbidden to accept 'invitations' to sing in other theatres. He considered these guest appearances indispensable to 'earning his livelihood', and the conflict remained unresolved for at least a year, when Mahler left, leaving the signing of Slezak's contract to his successor, Felix von Weingartner.[92] One of Mahler's handwritten agreements gave Slezak an unprecedented privilege: an annual leave of four months (15 May–15 September) with full salary.[93] Protests from other members of the Opera were not long in coming. At the end of 1907, Schmedes wrote to the Lord Chamberlain reminding him that he and Slezak shared the tenor roles, that he too was 'very dear' to the Vienna public, and that consequently he was entitled to at least as privileged a position as his colleague. The Prince would understand how bad the present situation was for his morale![94] At such times, Mahler realized how right he had been never to grant special privileges to any of his singers.

No doubt in anticipation of Slezak's possible departure, or perhaps to prevent him from thinking himself indispensable, Mahler engaged a new tenor, Karl Kurz-Stolzenberg, for the following season. Two years earlier he had been invited for a guest performance,[95] but was probably not particularly successful since his engagement at the Hofoper had been continually put off. His debut there seems to have been equally disappointing, for he wrote to Mahler on 27 November 1906, asking him to accept the cancellation of his contract at the end of the year:

I regret only one thing, namely that you did not even bother to take some interest in me. Two and a half years ago I signed the contract and agreed to such a low starting salary only because I was sure that you were going to work with me. But you let me perform without any stage rehearsal in the most unprepared way![96]

[91] HOA, Z. 937/1906. Letters and telegrams dated late Aug. Wilhelm Hesch (1860–1908), born in Elbe-Teinitz in Bohemia, had been engaged in Vienna after outstanding success in a Czech performance of *The Bartered Bride* during the International Fair of 1892. His principal roles were comic: Osmin, Leporello, and Van Bett (in *Der Wildschütz*) but he also sang Rocco in *Fidelio* and Benesch in *Dalibor*, and only two Wagnerian roles: Pogner and Daland.

[92] On 14 June 1906, the *Illustrirtes Wiener Extrablatt* declared that Mahler 'acted in an unfriendly manner towards Germany's most celebrated tenor', for when Slezak pleaded that in the interest of his family and his future he had to seek better conditions elsewhere, Mahler had allegedly replied: 'You can always try'. On 16 Mar. 1907, the *Neue Freie Presse* again mentioned the problems with Slezak's new contract. Several drafts, in Mahler's handwriting, are in HOA. They reveal that he was offered a five-year contract with a yearly salary of 32,000 florins (12,000 florins for his 'salary', 12,000 for 'Spielhonorar' (activity fee) and 8,000 as 'retainer') for a minimum of 60 performances per year. It also provided for a paid winter vacation once a year, and another, longer leave of absence so that he could sing in the United States.

[93] It seems doubtful that Mahler would ever have proposed such conditions if he had not been about to leave the Opera. Nevertheless Slezak's new contract, containing this clause, was signed by Weingartner.

[94] HOA, Z. 5357/1907, typewritten letter of 7 Dec.

[95] Kurz-Stolzenberg sang *Lohengrin* on 1 June 1904, *The Prophet* on 5 June, and in *Aida* on the 9th.

[96] HOA, Z. 1232/1906. Kurz-Stolzenberg finally left the Opera, but only at the end of the 1907–8 season.

At the end of 1906, another tenor, the Czech Franz Pacal wrote to Mahler asking him to forgive and forget the 'vexations and offence' which he had caused by leaving the Hofoper in 1905. Slander had played a big part in the aggravation of their mutual difficulties, he claimed, and yet he had always given proof of 'willingness and zeal in the service of art'. 'The enclosed reviews,' he added, 'will show you . . . that I am not totally without talent. You could still put me to good use, especially given the present lack of qualified tenors at the Opera.'[97] Mahler's response has disappeared, but it was undoubtedly negative, for after he left Vienna Pacal wrote to the Intendant claiming that the only cause of his departure had been his differences with Mahler, 'who had broken all his promises' and had even later denied making them. When Pacal (in his version of the story) had taken Mahler to task about it, Mahler had replied: 'If you start on that sort of thing, we're finished!' 'And from then on I *was* finished!' Pacal added. 'Mahler <u>destroyed</u> my entire career; he called me <u>talentless</u>, humiliating me in front of all the Opera personnel; said of me I was no actor and that I ought to be sent packing!'[98] Ultimately, however, the Opera authorities seem to have shared Mahler's opinion (if not his brutal frankness), for Pacal was never re-engaged.

Despite the troubled atmosphere and accumulated grievances of many singers at the Opera during the final months of 1906, there were still some who were ready to try anything to rejoin the Hofoper. On 18 November 1906, the tenor Franz Naval, who had left the Opera in 1902 and sung there as a guest artist in November 1906,[99] sent Mahler an unsigned letter in which he offered to pay him 20,000 kronen in exchange for a new contract for several years. Mahler would only have to place an advertisement in the 'confidential' column of the *Neues Wiener Tagblatt* and the sum would be put into his bank account by an anonymous donor. Mahler's reaction to the proposal can well be imagined, and the fact that he had the letter placed in the official archives of the Hofoper speaks for itself.[100]

As to the artistic level of the performances at the Hofoper during the 1905–6 season, the reviews which appeared in the daily papers and periodicals were mostly favourable. In the *Musikalisches Wochenblatt*, Helm, in spite of certain reservations about Roller's sets, maintained that Mahler's direction continued to be unsurpassable, even though the orchestra was too small in his opinion, for Mozart operas. In an article entitled *Zwei Jahre Wiener Hofoper*,[101] Karpath examined in detail the repertory and artistic resources of the Opera.

---

[97]   HOA, Z. 1367/1906.   [98]   HOA, Z. 521/1907, letter of 8 June.

[99]   On 11 Nov. he sang in *Un Ballo in Maschera* and on the 15th in *Les Huguenots*. On 11 Nov., the *Neue Freie Presse* indicated that Naval's re-engagement had been considered, but was ultimately rejected (HOA, Z. 1148/1906).

[100]   HOA, Z. 1264/1906, letter of 18 Nov. 1906. Much later, in an interview published in 1924, Naval describes the quarrel with Mahler which resulted in his resignation. He refrained, of course, from describing the methods by which he sought to obtain a new contract (see Vol. ii, Chap. 13, and Karl Marilaun, 'Gespräch mit Franz Naval', *Neues Wiener Journal* (30 Oct. 1924)).

[101]   'Zwei Jahre Wiener Hofoper', *Bühne und Welt*, 8 (1906): 19, 793 ff.

He pointed out that Prince Montenuovo's waiting room was no longer filled with Mahler's adversaries, for those who had grievances against him had finally realized that he was 'all-powerful', and that there was little chance that he would be replaced. In any case, almost all the present singers had been engaged by Mahler. As for the female singers, since the departure of the soprano Ellen Forster-Brandt and the contralto Luise Kaulich-Lazarich, only Elise Elizza remained from the Jahn era. Among the men, only the tenor Fritz Schrödter, the baritone Benedikt Felix, and the bass Wilhelm Hesch had served under Jahn. Karpath expressed satisfaction that the Opera now had great voices like Slezak or Selma Kurz, a soprano whose voice was fuller, more reliable, and more powerful than the usual coloratura, as her performance as Konstanze in *Die Entführung* had proved. Lucy Weidt continued to stand out in the ranks of the dramatic sopranos together with Elsa Bland, whose voice 'possessed astounding power even in the highest notes'.

Among the lyric sopranos Karpath singled out Gertrud Förstel, who had recently joined Rita Michalek, Grete Forst, and Charlotte von Seeböck.[102] During her 'guest appearances' she had conquered the Vienna public with 'the tender sincerity (*Innigkeit*) of her singing and acting'. He considered the alto group comparatively incomplete, for Laura Hilgerman increasingly sang soprano roles like Sieglinde and the Countess in *Figaro*, and Josie Petru was only suitable for comic roles, which left Hermine Kittel as the sole dramatic alto. Fortunately Theo Drill-Orridge, hitherto known mainly as a concert singer, was shortly to be engaged, but she was not a 'true alto' either. Karpath said relatively little about the male voices. He merely expressed the hope that Hesch would be re-engaged, and observed that the tenor Johannes Sembach's sick leave, which began shortly after the opening of *Don Giovanni*, had been prolonged beyond normal limits.[103] For the time being, he was being replaced by Georg Maikl, who had, in Karpath's opinion, been too rapidly promoted to first lyric tenor.

One of Mahler's assistant conductors, Francesco Spetrino, was leaving[104] and was to be replaced by Alexander Zemlinsky, whose latest opera, *Der Traumgörge*, Mahler had included in the repertoire for the following season.[105] Mahler requested and obtained a special bonus of 500 kronen[106] for Schalk, who conducted many more performances than usual (ninety-one) during this season while Bruno Walter was on sick leave (Walter had conducted only forty-two).

The Opera orchestra, in its role of Philharmonic concert orchestra, was about to leave on tour under Schalk's direction, for the second time since 1900.

---

[102] For mysterious reasons, Karpath did not mention Berta Kiurina.

[103] Sembach left the Opera at the end of the 1906–7 season.

[104] Spetrino ultimately remained at the Hofoper until 30 Sept. 1908, and conducted the Viennese opening of Puccini's *Madame Butterfly* on 31 Oct. 1907.

[105] HOA, Z. 815, letters of 9 and 24 Aug. 1906. Mahler himself conducted ten times during the month of Apr. On *Der Traumgörge*, see below, Chap. 7.　　　　[106] HOA, Z. 815, note of 9 Aug.

Its destination was the London International Exhibition, where it was to give concerts at the Queen's Hall and the Albert Hall in late June. This time, the lesson of the disastrous 1900 tour had been learned, and the steel magnate Arthur Krupp had volunteered to pay the expenses (£5,000 or 120,000 kronen), so that all the receipts could go to charity.

The 1905–6 Hofoper record showed above all a big increase in Mozart performances, and no premières apart from that of *Die neugierigen Frauen*. There were seventy-one performances of Wagner operas (including seventeen of *Lohengrin*), compared to sixty-two the previous year. The difference in the number of Mozart evenings—forty-five in 1905–6 compared to ten in 1904–5—was due to Mahler's decision to let certain operas 'sleep' before restaging them.[107] As regards finances, the 1905 deficit of 428,530 kronen was considered too high, and the High Chamberlain requested Mahler to reduce the 1906 deficit from 234,600 to 200,000 kronen. This seems to have been the main reason for the cancellation of the production of Max von Schillings's opera *Der Pfeifertag*. Despite the cost of the Mozart productions, expenditure was down compared to the preceding year (3,200,730 kronen instead of 3,286,024), quite an accomplishment in view of the number of new producions, and box-office receipts were up (2,991,496 kronen instead of 2,857,493 kronen). Thus the projected and approved deficit of 200,000 kronen was only slightly exceeded (by 9,234 kronen instead of 258,430 the preceding year).[108] Clearly, the economies prescribed by the Intendant had been carried out, and despite the outstanding artistic successes of the year and the expenses of the Mozart Festival, Mahler and Roller had almost succeeded in keeping within the budget.

During the final days of this Vienna season, Mahler received the visit, at the Auenbruggergasse, of Julius Korngold,[109] the music critic of the *Neue Freie*

[107]   The Wagner performances included four *Ring* cycles, and a complete chronological cycle of Wagner's other operas, with the exception of *Parsifal*. The complete list of works performed was as follows: *Lohengrin* (17); *Die Entführung aus dem Serail*, *The Marriage of Figaro*, *Carmen*, and *Die neugierigen Frauen* (12); *Tannhäuser*, *Cavalleria Rusticana*, and *Pagliacci* (11); *La Bohème* (10); *Don Giovanni*, *Les Contes d'Hoffmann*, and *Mignon* (9); *Aida*, *Die Meistersinger*, and *Die Fledermaus* (8); *Der fliegende Holländer* and *Die Walküre* (7); *Fidelio*, *Così fan tutte*, *The Magic Flute*, and *Lucia* (6); *Tristan*, *Die Rose*, *Il Trovatore*, and *Les Huguenots* (5); *Rienzi*, *Rheingold*, *Siegfried*, *Götterdämmerung*, *Freischütz*, *The Bartered Bride*, *The Queen of Spades*, *Norma*, *Rigoletto*, *Guillaume Tell*, *Faust*, *Un Ballo in Maschera* and *Lakmé* (4); *Hänsel*, *Evangelimann*, and *La Juive* (3); *La Traviata*, *Werther*, and *Die lustigen Weiber* (2); *Falstaff*, *Zar und Zimmermann*, *Les Dragons de Villars*, *Saint Elisabeth*, and *Die Abreise* (1).

[108]   WMW1, 219 and 286; WMW2, 184 and 240.

[109]   The following details should be added to Julius Korngold's biography (see above, Vol. ii, Chap. 14). He was the son of Simon Korngold, a Brno liquor merchant, and was married to Josefine Witrofsky, daughter of a Brno distiller. Gifted with a tenor voice and a genuine talent for the piano, he began his career as a critic in his native city. By chance, Hanslick read the excellent articles he had written for the *Brünner Tagesbote* and got him a job with the *Neue Freie Presse* in 1902. Korngold named his two sons after his favourite musicians: Hans Robert, born in 1892, after Schumann, and Erich Wolfgang, after Mozart. At the age of 5, Erich Wolfgang (1897–1957) began playing tunes on his father's piano, and started studying the piano and musical theory with Erich Lamm as teacher. The boy quickly showed astounding melodic imagination, which his father sought to develop through solid technical training. Later in life, Erich complained that he had 'never wanted to compose', and had done so 'only to please his father' (Luzi Korngold, *Erich Wolfgang Korngold* (Lafite, Vienna, 1967), 9). See also *The Last Prodigy: A Biography of Erich Wolfgang Korngold*, by Brendan G. Carroll (Amadeus, Portland, Ore., 1997).

Presse, accompanied by his 9-year-old son, Erich Wolfgang,[110] a musical prodigy, all the more astonishing since he had hitherto received hardly any musical training. Erich Wolfgang had shocked Robert Fuchs, one of Mahler's former professors at the Conservatory, by the audacity of a 'Sonatina Movement' composed at the age of 8. Nevertheless, Fuchs had agreed to teach the child counterpoint. Scarcely two weeks after he had begun he told the boy's father that his son knew more than most of his 20-year-old students. Unsure as to the direction his son's musical studies ought to take, Julius had decided to seek the advice of 'a great composer who was also a great performer, and whose intransigent objectivity in artistic matters guaranteed a sure, frank, and unbiased opinion'.

According to his memoirs, Julius Korngold's relationship with Mahler had been cordial ever since his *Neue Freie Presse* article following the Vienna première of the Fifth Symphony in December 1905. The open-minded, or at least moderate position which he, unlike his colleagues, had adopted with regard to the Sixth, strengthened their growing friendship, and Mahler began to meet him in cafés or at their respective homes. In one of his articles, Korngold dubbed the Sixth the 'Hammerblow Symphony'[111] and the appellation 'pleased Mahler, who was amused at the idea of being a demonic Haydn'. 'Thus I explicitly diagnosed the satanic character of this annihilating music', wrote Korngold. And Mahler responded in a postcard: 'What sort of "satanic" thoughts might one have while listening to my new symphony?! If you can attract these demons to Essen, I will greet them with joy.'[112] It was therefore only natural that Korngold should turn to Mahler for advice about his son's musical education.

And so one fine morning in June 1906[113] I made the pilgrimage to Mahler's apartment in the Auenbruggergasse with my little composer, who was practically invisible underneath

---

[110] Korngold, who died in Hollywood, was born in Brno. Artur Schnabel greatly admired Erich Wolfgang's Second Piano Sonata (1908) and played it all over Europe. Erich's Pantomime, *Der Schneemann*, was put on at the Hofoper in 1910. In 1912, the prodigious maturity of his first two orchestral works, the *Schauspiel Ouverture* (Op. 4, 1911) and the *Sinfonietta*, Op. 5, won the enthusiasm of Richard Strauss. Puccini later publically praised Korngold's first opera, *Violanta*, Op. 8 (1916). In 1920 he composed his masterpiece *Die Tote Stadt*, Op. 12, which opened simultaneously in Hamburg and Cologne but subsequently, never again achieved the same degree of success. After teaching at the Vienna Staatsakademie, Erich Wolfgang emigrated in 1934 to Hollywood where he wrote a number of Lieder, instrumental and orchestral works, but devoted himself mainly to writing film music.

[111] Korngold was referring to Haydn's 'Drumroll' Symphony. Obviously the article in question was published before the Essen première, and Korngold either attended the Philharmonic's sight-reading or Mahler played him the symphony on the piano.

[112] KIW 107. Julius Korngold's grandson informed me that Mahler's letters to Korngold had disappeared during the war.

[113] There is an element of doubt about this date, given that it has been changed to '1907' (by whom?) in the only existing partial edition of Julius Korngold's memoirs (in English). Erich Wolfgang says himself, in an article published for Zemlinsky's fiftieth anniversary, that he was 11 years old (i.e. 1908) at the time of his first lessons, which argues in favour of the corrected date. Nonetheless 1906, the date in Julius Korngold's manuscript, appears slightly more probable for two reasons. Erich Wolfgang began working with Zemlinsky one year after the interview with Mahler, and this work continued for two years, that is to say, until 1909, when Zemlinsky effectively left Vienna for Mannheim (before moving to Prague in 1910). Besides which, in 1907,

his straw hat. Erich played his cantata.[114] He played from memory, as he would always do, even with his most complicated scores. Mahler stood by the piano, manuscript in hand, and followed the score. But not for long: soon he began striding up and down in the room, with the hobbling rhythm he fell into when he was excited. 'A genius!' he exclaimed from time to time. The melody, power, and revolutionary sense of harmony had so strongly affected him. 'Take the lad to Zemlinsky', he urged. 'Above all, no conservatory, no drill! In private lessons with Zemlinsky he will learn everything he needs.'

Mahler's advice was soon followed and Erich Wolfgang became Zemlinsky's pupil. Some years later he visited Mahler again, and played to him several of his new compositions.[115]

After conducting two performances of the new production of *The Magic Flute* and one last performance of *The Marriage of Figaro*, Mahler left for Maiernigg. He had obtained an early leave of absence from the Opera, starting on 13 June, eight days before the official end of the season, which enabled him to travel with Alma. According to her account, the annual departure plunged him into a state of extreme nervousness. He was taking along the drafts and score of the Seventh Symphony and insisted on placing them at the bottom of a large and heavy suitcase. But even before leaving the apartment, as the porters were waiting in front of the door, he demanded that the suitcase be opened and the manuscripts placed on top. In the lobby of the building, after descending the staircase with Arnold Berliner, he changed his mind and had the suitcase opened once again. He and Alma finally carried the precious manuscripts to Maiernigg in their hands.[116]

Mahler intended to begin his vacation by reworking the orchestration of the Seventh. Things turned out differently, however:

On the first morning of vacation I went up to my Häuschen in Maiernigg firmly resolved to be really lazy (I needed it so badly) and gather my strength. As soon as I

Mahler, preparing to resign from the Opera, would have been in less of a frame of mind to receive a child prodigy composer (cf. Ernest Wolfgang Korngold, 'Das Vorbild meiner jungen Jahre', *Der Auftakt*, Prague, 14 Oct. 1921). The date of June 1906 is confirmed by Brendan G. Carroll in his biography of Erich Wolfgang (see above).

[114] This cantata, for solos, chorus, and piano, which Erich Wolfgang had composed in his father's absence, was entitled *Gold* and based on a text written by a schoolmate.

[115] KIW 122 ff. Luzi Korngold (*Erich Wolfgang Korngold*, 11) describes Erich Wolfgang attending the dress rehearsal of the new production of *The Magic Flute* with his father in June 1906. Mahler at the podium made such an impression on him that for the rest of his life he remembered details of the rehearsal, including the tempos and the instructions Mahler gave the singers. In an article published in the *Österreichische Musikzeitschrift* in 1967, on the occasion of Korngold's seventieth birthday, Bruno Walter relates that he knew 'only too well' the pianistic and compositional talents of the boy—living, as he did, in the same building as, and directly above, the Korngolds, he had had ample opportunity to hear Erich Wolfgang practise and play 'for hours on end'.

[116] AMM1, 151; AMM2, 147. This passage is inserted in her account of 1907, but the date of the incident is not indicated. Alma emphasizes Mahler's nervousness that year, and the disappearance of baggage during the trip to Rome could have justified his uneasiness (see below, Chap. 9). But as we shall see, in 1907 he left for the Semmering a few days before Alma, and then went straight on to Maiernigg to join her and the children. In 1905, Alma also arrived in Maiernigg before Mahler, whose Seventh had remained incomplete since the previous summer.

entered my old, familiar workroom, the *Spiritus creator* took hold of me, shaking me and scourging me for eight weeks, until the main part was finished.[117]

Here Mahler flatly contradicts Alma's memoirs, which claim that Mahler remained in a state of anxiety for two weeks, waiting for inspiration.[118] But it is also clear that his appeal to the 'Spiritus creator' sprang from the more or less unconscious fear of having to relive the torment he had experienced the previous year, when he had been quite unable to 'wash off the dust of the theatre' and begin composing.

Given this powerful initial impetus, this mother-cell, as it were, Mahler began to reflect on the other elements which the new work would contain and which would grow out of and complete this immense polyphonic, neo-baroque chorus in which he proclaimed his unshakeable faith in eternal values and the transcendental, after the doubts and anxieties which had played such an important part in his earlier works. A new vision was now taking possession of him, not merely that of a new work, out of a new genre, a symphony <u>for</u> chorus and orchestra, as one of his first draft 'programmes'[119] shows:

I. *Veni creator*
II. *Caritas*
III. *Weinachtsspiele mit dem Kindlein*
IV. *Schöpfung durch Eros, Hymne.*

It seems that such an idea had already taken possession of him at some earlier date, when he had envisioned a new kind of religious music, or rather had dreamt 'of putting the old church modes into the framework of modern music (*alte Kirchentöne im Rahmen moderner Musik*)'. At least he had spoken on those lines to the critic Arthur Seidl one day at the Munich station, and with such passion that he nearly missed the train.[120] With Alfred Roller, he had also discussed the possibility of composing a mass, but had realized that setting the Credo to music would have been impossible for him.[121] On the back of the first draft quoted above, he wrote the main theme of the 'Veni creator' movement.[122] Specht later reported him as saying: 'After the first theme, there will be no objectors left in the hall. It is bound to bowl everybody over.'[123]

Mahler's conception of the movement evolved rapidly, but one essential feature remained to the end: the chorus was to play a vital role, expounding and developing the themes of what appeared at first to be a massive Cantata, but was in fact a symphonic Allegro. Carried away by the flood of inspiration, Mahler put the entire hymn, or what he thought was the entire hymn, to music. He was more and more determined to give the chorus the central role, something he had

---

[117] BGA, no. 303, undated (8 June 1910), 423 ff.   [118] AMM1, 129; AMM2, 129.

[119] See below, Appendix 2 on the Eighth Symphony. A musical sketch of the first bars of the 'Veni Creator' is notated on the back of this preliminary programme.

[120] Arthur Seidl, 'Neuzeitliche Tondichter und Zeitgenössische', *Aufsätze und Skizzen* (Bosse, Regensburg, 1926), i, 310.   [121] See below and RBM 26.

[122] See below, Appendix 2.   [123] RSM2, 1st edn. (1913), 262.

never done except in *Das klagende Lied*, but at the same time he felt compelled
to compose an orchestral interlude which pursued the symphonic development.
Yet he was uneasy about it: something, he felt, was missing, and the orchestral
episode did not fit into the whole as well as he had hoped. On 21 June he wrote
to his old friend Fritz Löhr[124] asking him to translate the four lines beginning at
'Qui paraclitus diceris', indicating the scansion, as well as that of 'Hostem
repellas'. He asked Löhr to answer by return: he needed the information
urgently, both as 'creator' and 'creatus'.[125]

Later, he also asked him for a complete text of 'Veni creator', along with the
translation of the passage 'Firmans perpeti' and the two lines which began at 'Per
te sciamus', 'as that accursed old churchbook (*verfluchte Kirchenschmöker*) does
not seem reliable'.[126] And indeed, upon receiving the text, he realized that the
version in his hymnal lacked a long passage, precisely at the point where he had
composed the symphonic interlude. Quite miraculously, though, the words of the
new verses fitted it exactly. This strange coincidence strengthened Mahler's
conviction that when composing he somehow became the instrument of higher
forces. According to Alma, Mahler received the text by telegram[127] but he had
previously composed the entire 'Veni creator' from memory. It seems surprising,
however, that a new convert like Mahler should have known the whole of this
relatively little-known hymn by heart. Was the 'accursed old church book' from
which Mahler took the text of 'Veni creator' already in his possession when he
first began composing?[128] In any case, he felt so elated, so moved about this that
he told the story to Alma, Bruno Walter, and later to Ernst Decsey,[129] and spoke
of his 'ecstatic joy' at the 'miracle', the 'mystery' which made the 'words of the
text coincide exactly with the bars already composed, and with the spirit and
content of the composition'. Bruno Walter tells the story as follows:

No change was necessary. And the famous passage in the Eighth, on which Mahler
had always placed the greatest emphasis, *Accende lumen sensibus—Infunde amorem*

---

[124]   See above, Vol. i, Chap. 7, Löhr's biography. It will be recalled that he gave private lessons in Latin
and Greek at a girls' school. In 1907 he was named Secretary of the Vienna Archeological Institute and head
of the Department of Ancient Art at the University.

[125]   MBR1, no. 269; MBR2, no. 364. In the same note, Mahler asked Löhr if he knew of a verse translation of 'Veni creator'. Thus he had forgotten Goethe's, or at least had no conscious recollection of it (see
below, Appendix no. 2 on Symphony No. 8).

[126]   MBR1, no. 270; MBR2, no. 356. In this letter, Mahler incorrectly attributed the hymn to Saint
Francis. He also indicated that he was enclosing '100 Spiessen' (gulden or florins, that is 200 kronen) for
his old friend Heinrich Krzyzanowski, Löhr's brother-in-law.

[127]   AMM1, 130; AMM2, 131.

[128]   There is a third version of this famous episode which was certainly told to Bruno Walter by Mahler
himself and quoted in an interview published in the *Fremden-Blatt* on 18 Feb. 1912, just before the first
Vienna performance of the Eighth. According to Walter, Mahler composed the first verses of 'Veni creator'
from memory before trying, in vain, to find a missal in the Maiernigg library. Thus he certainly got hold of
the *Kirchenschmöker* as he calls it in his letter to Löhr, either in a neighbouring parish, or in Klagenfurt.

[129]   See below, Appendix 2 on Symphony No. 8. With the exception of a few details, the narratives of
Alma and Decsey are practically identical. Decsey claims that Mahler received the complete text from Karl
Luze, Chordirektor at the Opera (EDS1, 354) to whom he might also have written in case Löhr was not in
Vienna.

cordibus (these words he naturally knew by heart) could be left in its place! This fortuitous concordance of imagination and reality, not only in the technical but also in the intellectual sense, made a deep impression upon Mahler. Inclined to mysticism, indeed under its spell—like many a great mind, who is greater as a thinker than as a creator—he believed he saw in this concordance the working of a power which reigned over all art and over all life. He did not want to call it a divine power—he was too modest and too profoundly religious for that . . . Mahler told this story to all his close friends, and each time the experience moved him anew—indeed he was quite shattered when he thought again about it.[130]

Mahler continued to work with boundless energy. After the ardent invocation of the first movement, the choice of a text to complete a work of such cosmic conception was no easy matter. It is possible that from the outset, from the day he had first jotted down the words 'Schöpfung durch Eros, Hymne', Mahler was already thinking of Goethe, who had concluded his second *Faust*, the work which had occupied the poet all his life and which summed up his entire philosophy, with a final scene which was in fact an 'oratorio without music'. It had already inspired both Liszt and Schumann for it seemed to demand a musical setting. It takes place on lonely mountain tops at the approaches to Heaven. The prayers and meditations of the saints, church fathers, and anchorites are heard. Choirs of angels arrive carrying Faust's immortal soul. A choir of penitents (Gretchen among them) greet the arrival of the Mater gloriosa. Gretchen pleads for Faust. The Mater gloriosa tells Gretchen to come up to Heaven, assuring her that Faust will understand and follow her example. The closing hymn entitled 'Chorus mysticus' ends with a song of praise to 'Das Ewig-Weibliche', the 'eternal feminine'.

When Mahler met the critic Richard Specht, his biographer to be, in Salzburg in August 1906, he told him the whole story of the composition of the Eighth in the following terms:

Just think: within the last three weeks I have completed the sketch of a completely new symphony, something that makes all my other works seem like preliminary stages. I have never composed anything like this. In content and style it is altogether different from all my other works, and it is surely the greatest thing I have ever composed. I have probably never worked under such compulsion; it was a vision that struck me like lightning the whole immediately stood before my eyes; I had only to write it down, as if it had been dictated to me . . . This Eighth Symphony is already remarkable in that it brings together two works of poetry in different languages. The first part is a Latin hymn and the second nothing less than the final scene of Part II of *Faust*. Are you not amazed? I had longed to set to music the hermit scene and the Finale with the Mater

---

[130] According to Walter, Mahler had continued to compose without it (*Fremden-Blatt*, 'Aus der Theaterwelt', 18 Feb. 1912 and 'Bruno Walter erzählt von Mahler', *Neue Freie Presse*, 16 Nov. 1935). Mahler later gave Walter the manuscript of the text which he had certainly used while composing. It consists of eighteen lines, plus ten more noted in different handwriting and certainly later on: 'Infirma nostri corporis' (2 lines), 'Tu septiformis' (4 lines), and 'Per te sciamus' (4 lines). The lines bear the numbers 4, 3, and 6 (Bruno Walter Legacy, Library of the Performing Arts, Lincoln Center, New York).

gloriosa in a manner that would be different from all the sugary, weak ways it has so far been done, but then thought no more about it. Then the other day I came across an old book. I opened it to the hymn *Veni Creator Spiritus*, and immediately the whole thing was there: not only the first theme, but the entire first movement. In response to this I could not possibly find anything more beautiful than Goethe's words in the hermit scene! Even in form it is also something quite new. Can you imagine a symphony that is sung throughout, from beginning to end? So far I have employed words and the human voice merely to suggest, to sum up, to establish a mood. I resorted to them to express something concisely and specifically, which is possible only with words—something that could have been expressed symphonically only with immense breadth. But here the voice is also an instrument. The whole of the first movement is strictly symphonic in form yet it is completely sung. It is the egg of Columbus, 'die Symphonie an sich', in which the most beautiful instrument of all is given the role it was destined for, and yet not only as sound, since in it the human voice is the bearer of the poet's thoughts.[131]

Three years later, in a letter to Alma,[132] Mahler wrote a long comment on Goethe's text, contrasting the 'eternal masculine'—desire, effort, the driving force, the striving towards a goal—to the 'eternal feminine', the Mater gloriosa, incarnation of peacefulness, the supreme goal. His philosophical interpreta-tion explains his apparently surprising juxtaposition of two texts separated by a millenium in time, in different languages, and of different character.[133]

Bruno Walter describes the work's rapid progress:

With incomparable, elemental fervour Mahler threw himself into the setting to music of these words. What could concern him more than that mankind must call, beseech, demand in this way. Nothing was nearer to his heart than this appeal, entreaty, and challenge by humanity, and what a joy it was for him that there was an answer such as Goethe's promise. He could not tell me enough about the happiness he had experi-enced in surrendering himself so entirely to Goethe's words, and in being able so profoundly to identify himself with them. And yet this is his most 'objective' work. It is not Mahler, but all mankind which sings this hymn, and receives the consolation of the second movement.[134]

---

[131] Richard Specht, 'Zu Mahlers Achte Symphonie' (*Tagespost*, Graz, no. 150), 14 June 1914.

[132] BGA, no. 276, undated (22? June 1909). A letter which Siegfried Lipiner wrote to Alma on 12 Mar. 1906 (AMS) indicates that she and Mahler had spoken recently about *Faust*, and that Mahler had mentioned the commentary which Lipiner had written in his youth. It seems clear that in writing to Lipiner, Alma, no doubt influenced by her husband, wanted to erase to a certain extent the disastrous impression which the notorious dinner in 1902 had made on Mahler's old friends. Lipiner replied: 'In my opinion, the most impor-tant and meaningful thing in *Faust*, its only real greatness perhaps, has not been understood, and thus "my" commentary is of no help, for when I wrote it, I had not understood it myself.'

[133] Goethe himself admired 'Veni creator', and translated it into German in 1820. According to the psychoanalyst Theodor Reik, Mahler's strange combination of texts was perhaps inspired by an unconscious recollection of Goethe's versified translation, which he could well have read in the complete works. It may thus have been the result of a sudden inspiration rather than the result of lengthy meditation. Reik consid-ers Mahler's idea of the Virgin and the eternal feminine to have been consciously and unconsciously deter-mined by the conflict between his creative instinct and sexual desire which made him idealize woman as the Heavenly Mother, distant and unapproachable, because he no longer experienced effective sexual desire for his young wife (RHM 330).

[134] Bruno Walter, 'Mahlers Weg, ein Erinnerungsblatt', *Der Merker*, 3 (1911): 5, 170.

The building of this huge cathedral in sound, with all its polyphonic richness, took only eight weeks.[135] Mahler was under the impression that the music had been 'as it were' dictated to him.[136] The result of this intense burst of activity is and will remain a composition unique in the history of music: neo-baroque in the first part, intensely romantic in the second. Both in its conceptual power and the enormous breadth of its orchestral resources it represents the summit of Mahler's achievement. With understandable pride he wrote to Wilhelm Mengelberg in the middle of August: 'I have just finished my Eighth—it is the greatest thing I have done so far. And so strange in its form and content that it is impossible to write about it. Imagine that the universe begins to ring and resound (*zu tönen und zu klingen*). No longer with human voices but with revolving planets and suns.'[137] Sometime later he said to Richard Specht that this symphony was 'a gift to the nation. All my earlier symphonies are but preludes to this one. In my other works, everything is still subjectively tragic—this one is a great giver of joy.'[138] As in the Finale of the Second, but with greater richness of substance and a more disciplined style of writing, he had meant to and succeeded in delivering a message of cosmic peace and love. For the first time, pain and distress are absent, and if only for this reason the symphony is different from all others. In the final 'Chorus mysticus', the certainty of ultimate redemption is expressed in music of unsurpassable grandeur.

While the *Spiritus creator* was thus 'shaking and scourging' him for three weeks, Mahler almost gave up all other activity. He took just a few days in mid-July for a brief walking and cycling trip, first of all to Toblach.[139] On his way back, he stopped at Dölsach, near Lienz in the eastern Tyrol, and did a two-hour climb to Winklern north of there. Coming down again at breakneck speed, he took a carriage to Heiligenblut, near the Grossglockner, and the next day in Bleiberg did another three-hour climb, up the Dobratsch in the Villach Alps, from which he could enjoy the splendid view of the Karawanken, the Carinthian lakes, the Julian Alps, and the Tauern. The same evening he took the train back to Krumpendorf, where he had asked Alma to have his factotum Anton meet him with the boat.[140] The messages he sent his wife overflow with good humour and well-being, and contain all the usual details about his health and digestion.

From Toblach, Mahler had climbed as usual to his favourite spot in the

---

[135] Alma and Richard Specht both claim that it took only three weeks, but Mahler himself speaks of eight. Perhaps it was the first draft that took only three weeks to write.

[136] RSM2, 306.

[137] MBR1, no. 306; MBR2, 360, and RMH 69. According to the postmark this letter, which arrived in Amsterdam on 18 Aug. 1906, indicating that Mahler wrote it before leaving Maiernigg for Salzburg. Another passage from this letter is quoted below (Chap. 7).

[138] RSM2, 304. Wagner had called the *Ring des Nibelungen* a 'gift to the nation' in 1856.

[139] The card which he sent to Alma, most likely from Toblach, has vanished (see BGA 280 ff.).

[140] Cards of 18 and 19 July (BGA, nos. 171 and 172). The summit of the Dobratsch, 2,167 m., dominates one of the most panoramic views in Carinthia.

Sextener Dolomiten, Lake Misurina. But whereas in previous years he had left for Misurina in the hope of finding the inspiration to complete the Sixth and Seventh, this time he simply wanted a few days of rest in one of the few landscapes he knew which possessed something of the overwhelming grandeur of the first movement and final 'Chorus mysticus'.[141] In a short note to Fritz Löhr, written in Misurina, Mahler expresses his disappointment at having to abandon his work on the Eighth Symphony: 'Unfortunately, I have to go to Salzburg in mid-August, which this year I find particularly annoying.'[142] The entire Opera had been invited to participate in the festival celebrating Mozart's 150th birthday with a performance of *Figaro* conducted by Mahler, a truly imperial present the Emperor made to the birthplace of Austria's greatest musical genius. Although in all likelihood the Eighth was already finished at this date, Mahler resented interrupting his work, knowing that after Salzburg he would have little time left before returning to Vienna. And the prospect of having to immerse himself in the agitation of the little town with its crowds of music-lovers and musicians was far from welcome to him.

At the beginning of July, in Maiernigg, he had learned of the death of his old friend Henriette Mankiewicz, one of the few friends from old times to whom he had remained attached despite his marriage, as shown in the following letter, written sometime earlier, in which he reprimands her for coming after a concert to his dressing room, a place so ill-suited to friendly exchange:

But my dearest Henriette! 'Tu quoque?' I was certainly not unfriendly! At least not knowingly. But utterly exhausted . . . Surely friends like you should not come to a dressing room, where 300 well-wishers are treading on each others' toes! Obliged to wait for Alma and my sister, I was touchy and angry . . . And so—never again in a dressing room! Instead, come to my house afterwards, or invite me to yours![143]

The tone is that of a frank exchange between old friends, and Mahler was certainly affected by the death of someone who had witnessed his early battles in Vienna, even if his marriage had somewhat loosened their former friendship.[144]

At the turn of the century, the Salzburg Festival took place at irregular intervals since 1877.[145] But the 1906 festival, commemorating Mozart's 150th

---

[141]   MBR1, no. 271; MBR2, no. 359. This card to Fritz Löhr was perhaps written before those to Alma since Mahler usually climbed to Misurina from Toblach. Mahler thanks his friend for his philosophical help.

[142]   MBR1, no. 271; MBR2, no. 359. Undated letter to Fritz Löhr (July–Aug. 1906).

[143]   Undated letter, probably written after the Vienna première of one of Mahler's symphonies (Library of Congress).

[144]   Mahler's letters to Henriette Mankiewicz (Library of Congress) include a note in Alma's handwriting thanking her for flowers or sweets. Henriette Tauber Mankiewicz (1853–1906; see Vol. ii. Chap. 8) lived in Vienna at Strohgasse no. 35. She died on 30 June 1906 at Vöslau. Her daughter Grete married an army officer named Ernst von Schuch, son of the Dresden conductor and opera director.

[145]   Strictly speaking, the festival (*Festspiele*) was only created in 1920. Before, there had been periodic *Mozart-Feste*, which succeeded the 'Mozart Days' (*Gedenktage*) of 1856: 1877 (creation of the International Foundation which became the Mozarteum), 1880 (the opening of the Mozart Museum), 1887 (centenary of *Don Giovanni*), 1891 (centenary of Mozart's death), and 1901.

birthday, was to be a major event. Various grandiose projects like guest performances of the Munich, Dresden, and Berlin opera companies had fallen
through for lack of funds. Lilli Lehmann, who spent her summers in a house
she had bought near Salzburg, was artistic adviser to the festival. She thus
participated in the decision to abandon the unrealistic idea of these *Gastspiele*
and limited the festival to two productions: *The Marriage of Figaro*[146]
performed by the Vienna Opera under Mahler, and *Don Giovanni*, performed
in Italian and staged by the prima donna herself.

Programme of the Salzburg Festival, 14 to 20 August 1906.

14 August, at 7.15 p.m. (and 16 August):

Mozart, *Don Giovanni* (in Italian), Vienna Opera Orchestra, Reynaldo Hahn,
   conductor, Lilli Lehmann, stage director.

Geraldine Farrar (Zerlina); Johanna Gadsky Tauscher (Elvira); Lilli
   Lehmann (Anna); Georg Maikl (Ottavio); Anton Moser (Masetto);
   Francisco d'Andrade (Don Giovanni); Hermann Brag (Leporello);
   Gerhard Stehmann (Commendatore).

15 August, at 11 a.m. (opening concert) in the Hall of the Aula Academica
   (where all the concerts took place).

Vienna Philharmonic Orchestra, Felix Mottl, conductor.

Mozart, Symphony no. 34 in C major, K. 338; Variations on the Andante
   from the Divertimento No. 17, K. 334; Concerto in E flat, No. 22, K.482
   (Camille Saint-Saëns, piano).

Beethoven, Symphony No. 5.

17 August, at 11 a.m. (second orchestral concert).

Vienna Philharmonic Orchestra, Richard Strauss, conductor.[147]

Mozart: *The Magic Flute*, Overture,

Mozart: *Sinfonia concertante* in E flat for violin and alto, K. 362 (Alexander
   and Lili Petschnikoff, soloists).

Bruckner: Symphony No. 9.[148]

18 August: at 11 a.m.

Fitzner Quartet (Vienna); Franz Bartholomey, clarinet; Geraldine Farrar,
   soprano; Guido Peters, piano.

Mozart: Quartet No. 2 in E flat, K. 433 for piano and strings.

Mozart: Aria: *Non temer, amato bene* K. 490, with piano and violin obligato
   (Reynaldo Hahn, piano, and Rudolf Fitzner, violin).

---

[146]   Emperor Franz-Joseph had promised to pay the company's travelling expenses. It was only in Apr.
that Mahler finally selected his new production of *The Marriage of Figaro* for Salzburg.

[147]   This was the first time that Strauss had ever conducted the Vienna Philharmonic. As seen above, he
was replacing Karl Muck.

[148]   Assia Spiro-Rombro remarked in the *Musikalisches Wochenblatt* that the last-named work was 'ill-
suited' for a commemoration of Mozart. She castigated Strauss for being either 'sleepy or in a bad mood' and
said that he had turned the Allegro of the *Sinfonia Concertante* into an Andante, and the Presto into an
Allegretto. 'Famous men,' she commented, 'can have their off-days.'

Bach, Prelude and Fugue in A minor for organ (tr. Franz Liszt).

Beethoven, Variations in F major, Op. 34.

Mozart, Fantasy in C major, K. 475 and Sonata No. 14 in C minor, K. 457.

Mozart: Quintet in A major, K. 581 for clarinet and strings.

18 August, at 7.15 p.m. at the Salzburg Theatre.

Mozart, *The Marriage of Figaro.*

Vienna Opera production, Gustav Mahler, conductor; Rita Michalek (Barberina); Marie Gutheil-Schoder (Susanna); Berta Kiurina (Cherubino); Laura Hilgermann (Rosina); Josie Petru (Marcellina); Hans Breuer (Basilio); Arthur Preuss (Curzio); Friedrich Weidemann (Count); Benedikt Felix (Antonio); Richard Mayr (Figaro).

19 August: at 11 a.m.

Final Concert of Salzburg Church Music.

Liedertafel, Salzburg and Salzburg Theatre Orchestra; Josef Friedrich Hummel, conductor.

Michael Haydn, Motet, *Tenebrae factae sunt.*

Mozart, *Coronation Mass* in C major, K. 317.

Mozart, 'Te Deum' in C major, K. 141.

Mozart, 'Ave Verum' for a cappella chorus, K. 618.

20 August at 7.15 p.m.

The Mariage of Figaro (second performance).

Vienna Opera ensemble and orchestra, Gustav Mahler conductor.

Although the production of *Figaro* was recent and eight performances had already taken place in Vienna, Mahler insisted upon four full days of rehearsal to adapt it to the small Salzburg theatre.[149] On 10 May 1906, Mahler sent Count Kuenburg, President of the Mozarteum, a list of things to be done in preparation for the summer festival. In particular, he requested the removal of the first few rows of seats in the audience to permit the enlargement of the orchestra pit.[150] Mahler's extensive rehearsal schedule for *Figaro* left only two days, 12 and 13 August, for Lilli Lehmann to rehearse her *Don Giovanni.* In her memoirs, she criticizes Mahler's inflexibility and expresses her astonishment at his attitude (proving how little she knew him), for 'until then he had always given proof of sentiments of faithful friendship'. And indeed, although she had held 'many rehearsals' in her summer home, her production of *Don Giovanni* was judged by the press as being 'unworthy of a festival',[151] especially in

---

[149] Mahler considered that 'everything had to be adapted from the visual and acoustic points of view' to the much smaller stage (see below, and JRM, copy in BGM, Paris). Reitler mentions 'four rehearsals lasting from 10 o'clock in the morning until late at night, with short breaks'.

[150] Mozarteum Archives. These archives contain a telegram dated 21 Aug., in which Mahler thanks the director for his kindness and hospitality, and a *Neues Wiener Tagblatt* article dated 22 Sept. reporting that Prince Montenuovo had addressed his written thanks to all the Opera personnel for acquitting their duties 'so perfectly in unusual conditions'.

[151] In *Die Musik*, Bernard Scharlitt went so far as to say that the performance had taken place under an unlucky star.

comparison with the 'miraculous' *Figaro* performances in which Mahler and his Viennese company surpassed themselves.[152]

Later on that summer Mahler explained to his friend Ernst Decsey why he had spent so much time rehearsing a recent production which had already been so carefully prepared for its Vienna première and given a number of times in Vienna with the same cast:

Are we not playing in an entirely different house? Was not our *Figaro* conceived for the big opera house in Vienna? Isn't my first task the adaptation of the filigree of *Figaro* to this theatre, making the necessary acoustic and visual alterations? The figures of the singers appear much larger on this small stage, and so probably they should sing much more softly.[153]

It is obvious that Mahler spent most of his first days in Salzburg rehearsing assiduously, yet his letters to Alma never allude to his work and show a boyish lack of reverence for the festival and its many visitors:

The din is awful! I'm quite worn out. Yesterday, on arrival, was greeted by Roller, Stoll, Hassinger,[154] a Treasury official and a Privy Councillor from the Festival Committee (no virgins all in white). Got rid of them all except for Roller, who accompanied me to the hotel and remained there with me. Misurina, I mean Kiurina, no, Milewa,[155] was visiting Burckhard. We strolled through the town. Soon Strauss turned up and joined us.[156] I went back to the hotel[157] with him to sup, while Roller went to the station to fetch Schluderbach, or rather Misurina. At 8: 30, Strauss left for the festival reception (which I immediately got out of); in the meantime Roller returned with Toblach, I mean Schluderbach, and we were together for a little while. Tre Croci went off to bed and Strauss, together with a journalist, came back from the festival in high spirits. We talked about fees and percentages for an hour, then I left to go to bed. Couldn't get to sleep, the devil knows why.[158]

The following morning, before the 10 o'clock rehearsal, Mahler was scheduled to discuss the forthcoming performance of the Sixth in Munich with the

[152] Lilli Lehmann, *Mein Weg* (Hirzel, Leipzig, 1920), 433. The singer also complained that Mahler had brought a double cast to Salzburg for *Figaro*, while she had to be satisfied with one, and that Mahler had altered the seating of certain musicians in the orchestra in order to improve the theatre's acoustics. As a result, when Reynaldo Hahn began to conduct, he suddenly realized that certain players were not where he expected them to be. The surprise was so great that he was almost 'unable to go on conducting'.

[153] Ernst Decsey, 'Stimmungen vom Salzburger Musikfest', *Österreichische Rundschau*', 2 (1906–7): 98/99, 250 ff.

[154] Stoll was the principal stage director of the Opera, and Hassinger the Director's factotum.

[155] Milewa Stoisavljevic Roller (1886–1949) was born in Innsbruck, the daughter of an army officer of Croatian origin. An artist and ivory painter, she had studied under Alfred Roller before marrying him on 21 July 1906 in Graz. Mahler sent her a letter of congratulations (undated) at the beginning of his stay in Maiernigg (MBR1, no. 300; MBR 2, no. 355). He pretended not to remember her first name, hence his facetious attributions of various others which more or less resembled it, in this case that of his favourite lake in the Dolomites, of a singer at the Opera, and later of several other places in the neighbourhoods of Toblach and Cortina.

[156] Strauss had agreed to replace Karl Muck who had fallen ill and had cancelled his date with the Vienna Philharmonic for the opening symphony concert of the festival.

[157] According to a Salzburg newspaper, Mahler was staying at the Savoy-Nelböck hotel.

[158] BGA, no. 173, undated (16 Aug. 1906).

impresario Emil Gutmann. He had already had enough of these meetings and discussions:

The devil take these damned people! Strauss has already composed a few scenes from *Electra* (Hofmannsthal). He won't let it go for less than 10% per evening and 100,000 marks (mind you, this is only a guess on my part). Since he didn't ask me, I told him nothing about my antiquated (*antiquierten*) existence this summer. I don't think he would be very impressed to learn about the old-fashioned stuff (*veraltetem Kram*) I spent my summer working on.[159] Blessed, oh blessed, to be modern! . . . Tonight I will return to my room at about ten o'clock—20 letters, 50 invitations are already waiting. Friday at 4.30 a party given by Archduke Eugene.[160] The whole troupe of artists (1000 people) is invited. Frock coat is obligatory. I have no idea what I am going to do about it!

In his letter to Alma the following day, Mahler added: 'Strauss is with me constantly, and altogether very nice, as always when he is alone with me. But his nature will always be foreign to me. His way of thinking and feeling is worlds away from my own. I wonder whether one day we will meet again on the same star?' Fortunately, Roller's company was a real joy and they took all walks and meals together. When Milewa was present, 'they are very sweet with each other, but go on being as independent as before they were married'. He again mentioned the 'party' (*rout*) he was going to have to attend, and told his wife: 'Just imagine: [Marie Gutheil-] Schoder is reported to be pregnant. Although this is going to be very inconvenient for my repertory, I am rather pleased about it; at least she will disappear from our vicinity for a few months.'[161]

After a stroll with Strauss and the Viennese banker Paul Hammerschlag,[162] Mahler and Strauss went to the performance of *Don Giovanni*. Lilli Lehmann, responsible for the staging of the production, had insisted that the opera be sung in Italian, as it had at the Metropolitan Opera in New York where she had

[159] Mahler here is obviously alluding to his Eighth Symphony which, with its Latin hymn and polyphonic style, is 'antiquated' compared to the 'modern' drama *Elektra*.

[160] Archduke Eugene (1863–1954), a second-cousin of the emperor and a great lover of Mozart, protector of the Mozarteum, played an important role in the organization of the festival. He was one of the only genuine music-lovers in the imperial family.

[161] BGA, no. 174, undated (17 Aug. 1906). The news of Marie Gutheil-Schoder's pregnancy was false unless she miscarried early on, for her name continued to appear on the programme of the Opera throughout the following autumn and winter. Mahler's comments here confirm the existence of malicious rumours about her relationship with Mahler. Some even ascribed the paternity of the child to him (BMG 117; see above, Chap. 5, and Brendan G. Carroll, *Prodigy*, 80).

[162] Born on the same day as Mahler into a modest but cultured family, Paul Hammerschlag (1860–1934) studied and practised law before being appointed to an important post in the Giro und Kassenverein Bank. In 1909, he became Director of the Vienna Kreditanstalt, which he left in 1930, and in 1918 he was made Vice-President of the Chamber of Commerce. He was one of the founder members of the Konzertverein, and had met Mahler just before the inaugural concert (30 Oct. 1900). The Verein's first horn had been taken ill, and Hammerschlag went to the Opera to ask Mahler's permission to engage the first horn of the Opera to replace him. Mahler immediately consented. After passing the summer of 1905 in Sekirn, near Maiernigg, Hammerschlag rented a small castle on the Mönchberg, near Salzburg, for the following summer (information provided by Frau Elisabeth Duschnitz, Paul Hammerschlag's daughter).

sung the role of Donna Anna several times. 'The performance was so awful,' Mahler wrote to Alma, 'that after the second scene Strauss and I escaped horrified, and supped alone at the hotel.' In her reply Alma expressed the fear that Mahler had 'not been tactful', and had offended Lehmann with his speedy exit. 'Your remarks about Lehmann come too late,' Mahler answered, 'I have already reviled her in public. I have not done so with Strauss, so far, because he was always present. So I will control myself. I have already stepped on the toes of the Intendant in person; can therefore express myself with brevity in that direction.'[163]

In her memoirs, Alma quotes Mahler's wounding comment on Lilli Lehmann. It consisted of a misquotation from *The Magic Flute*—

> *Ein Mann muss eure Herzen leiten*
> *Denn ohne ihn pflegt jedes Weib*
> *Aus seinem Wirkungskreis zu schreiten*[164]

—in which Mahler replaced the word 'woman' (*Weib*) with 'cow' (*Kuh*). But Alma's account must be taken with a pinch of salt, for it would have been impossible for Lilli Lehmann, then on-stage singing Donna Anna, to have overheard any remark by Mahler. He probably made it during a rehearsal within hearing distance of a friend of the singer's. In her memoirs, Lehmann recalls:

While still in the theatre, Mahler expressed so unfavourable a view that all those who had been astonished by the excellence of the performance no longer trusted their own judgement and didn't dare to admit it . . . It was the only time he was ever unfriendly and, above all, unjust to me. But I did not hold it against him for I knew of his eccentric behaviour towards others.[165]

Rosa Papier's son, Bernhard Paumgartner, described the production of *Don Giovanni* in the following unequivocal terms which support Mahler's harsh judgement:

After somewhat hurried, on-the-spot rehearsals, an international group of stars sang and acted in the old style interlarded with lively, sweeping gestures . . . I had never seen Mahler behave quite so strangely as during the one complete rehearsal the opera had. I was sitting next to him in a dark corner of the auditorium. He accompanied the on-stage proceedings with a comical mixture of indignation and infectious hilarity, soft grunts and whispers, despair at the 'old rubbish' up on the stage, and bitter irony over the 'inappropriate; dreadful naturalism of obsessive opera maniacs' as when the actor

---

[163] BGA, no. 176, undated (18 Aug. 1906). In no other known letter of Mahler's does he admit so openly 'this terrible habit he has of offending and hurting people he has to deal with'.

[164] *The Magic Flute*, Act I, Finale: 'A man must guide your heart | For otherwise every woman tends | To go beyond her proper role.'

[165] Lilli Lehmann, *Mein Weg*, 436. Frau Lehmann's bad temper was almost as notorious as Mahler's in operatic circles, and gave rise to various anecdotes, including one in which she laughed aloud at Marianne Brandt's interpretation of the title role in *Fidelio*. It is also said that in Bayreuth in 1890 Lilian Nordica, the young American diva, approached her with the greatest deference, whereupon she turned away and said: 'I'm not taking any pupils this season!' (Irving Kolodin, *The Metropolitan Opera* (Knopf, New York, 1966), 97).

singing Don Giovanni (Francisco d'Andrade), killed the Commander with the elegance of a toreador, and then in the same pose wiped the sword clean on his cloak.[166]

The press also confirmed Mahler's poor opinion of the production. As a conductor Lehmann had recruited the young French composer Reynaldo Hahn, whom she had met in Paris. Hahn's memoirs contain a detailed description of the preparations for the production, together with summaries of the many letters he exchanged with Lehmann. First, a Don Juan had to be found who would be equal to the occasion. Lehmann had considered Franz Egenieff,[167] who unfortunately was not free, then Maurice Renaud,[168] proposed by Geraldine Ferrar (Zerline in the cast), who refused, after a period of reflection, and finally Mattia Battistini,[169] warmly recommended by Spetrino. Francisco d'Andrade only got the role after Battistini refused it. Lilli Lehmann well knew that he was 'no longer vocally up to it'. She also considered him 'somewhat mannered', but found him 'elegant, and still an excellent artist'. Her first meeting with him had been less than satisfactory:

I have heard Andrade[170] and spoken with him. He is a clown who sticks to his old pranks and stupid 'theatrical shock effects' . . . We have discussed the role and staging; he wants to do everything according to his old habits—things impossible for contemporary taste, which is more natural and simple. He insists upon having applause and told me so very clearly . . . He is terribly nervous and I am sure that within two or three days I will have to tell him that I cannot accept such nonsense, and he will refuse to sing.[171]

But since none of the other candidates for the role were free, and no other Don Juan could be found in Germany, Lilli Lehmann had to make do with Andrade, despite his 'impossible pantaloonery', which she describes in consternation in a letter addressed to Hahn: [172]

After his duo with Zerlina he wants the applause to end before Elvira's entrance. He also wants to sing the champagne aria three times, in different languages! For the final scene, he wants a curtain that closes and a burning rock. He performs the balcony trio like a puppet (*Hampelmann*)! It is awful, impossible in the performance as I conceived it.

---

[166] Bernhard Paumgartner, *Erinnerungen*, 65.

[167] Franz Egenieff (1874–1949), born in Gmund am Tegernsee, was the son of Prince Emil zu Sayn-Wittgenstein and his morganatic wife.

[168] Maurice Renaud (1861–1933) was born in Bordeaux. After studying at the Paris Conservatory, he made his debut at the Monnaie in Brussels before joining the Opéra Comique in 1890. In 1902 and 1905, he sang in Monte Carlo in the premières of two works of Massenet, *Le Jongleur de Notre-Dame* and *Chérubin*. He was later engaged by the New York Metropolitan Opera, and spent his last years in Paris as a teacher.

[169] Mattia Battistini (1856–1928), who came from the Rome region, is today considered to have been one of the greatest singers of all time.

[170] Francisco d'Andrade (1859–1921), born in Lisbon, brother of tenor Antonio d'Andrade. He made his debut in *Aida*, in 1882 in San Remo, and rapidly achieved international fame, but that was more than thirty years earlier. Don Giovanni was his most famous role.

[171] Letter of Lilli Lehmann to Reynaldo Hahn, quoted from his memoirs, *Thèmes variés* (Janin, Paris, 1946), 34   [172] Hahn, *Thèmes*, 34.

Lehmann's letter, summarized by Reynaldo Hahn in his memoirs, speaks volumes about the behaviour of star singers at the beginning of the century. The young conductor-composer had heard that Andrade prided himself on 'singing the Champagne Aria faster than all the other baritones in the world' and always insisted on 'doing his number'. Lilli Lehmann managed to wring a few promises out of him, made only on condition that he would not be 'deprived of his personality', but he was 'aggrieved and annoyed' by her insistence. He nonetheless consented to rehearse once or twice before the dress rehearsal, and to sing the Champagne Aria 'presto instead of prestissimo'. Hahn found his interpretation 'a little slick', but 'respectful nevertheless under the severe eye of the great Lilli'. At the first rehearsal, Hahn conducted the orchestral introduction to the Aria presto, as agreed, but Andrade burst in 'like a madman'. Hahn interrupted him and asked him to slow down. 'Slow down?' shouted the baritone. 'Not on your life! That's the way I have always sung it, with the greatest conductors in the world, even Hermann Levi!' 'That would surprise me', retorted Lilli Lehmann from the audience. 'I've known Hermann Levi all my life, and he would be incapable of conducting this aria in such a frenzy!' Andrade thundered angrily that he 'wouldn't be lectured', and declared that his portrayal of the role was a 'world-wide success'. Furthermore, he invariably 'brought the house down' with the Champagne Aria. At the end of her tether, Lilli Lehmann cut the discussion short: 'Let's get on! We'll take this up again later on!' She then left the hall, the image of wounded dignity.

At the following rehearsal the conflict broke out again. This time, Andrade had finally agreed to sing the Champagne Aria at a slower pace, but with manifest ill-will. Reynaldo Hahn concludes: 'At the performance (in which I must admit that he was very interesting, showing great assurance, impertinent swagger, and in the Finale of Act One and at the end of the opera, really great style), he sang his aria slower than he wanted to, but faster than during rehearsals.'

It is not difficult to imagine that a performance prepared in such a fashion was not up to Mahler's standards and that he did not hesitate to scoff about it in the presence of Lilli Lehmann or her friends. In any case, both the local press and German periodicals agreed with him, labelling Andrade an 'ageing' Don Juan, 'whose only real success with the audience was with the Champagne Aria'. According to the *Neue Musik-Zeitung* all the acclaim went to Geraldine Farrar, the brilliant young American singer from Lehmann's 'stable', who earned high praise with her 'actress's temperament' and the 'freshness and liveliness' of her stage performance. The *Salzburger Volksblatt* found the production much inferior to the one Richter had conducted in 1901. Among other things, it deplored the 'completely traditional, in other words conventional' character of Lilli Lehmann's staging.

Lehmann was making her debut as stage director. Having reached the ripe age of 58, she was then nearing the end of her amazing operatic career, which was unique, not only because of her vocal longevity, but also because of the variety of roles she had sung.[173] Born in 1848 of parents who were both singers, she was brought up in a musical environment and could already play the piano as a small child. Her mother had been her one and only singing teacher and she had made her concert debut at the age of 15 (1863), and her opera debut at 17 (1865), thus beginning a stage career that was to last almost sixty years. In 1870, after a triumphant guest performance at the Berlin Hofoper, she had become a full member of the company. Under Wagner's aegis, she had sung three small roles in the first Bayreuth performances of the *Ring* and had become a frequent and much acclaimed guest at Covent Garden, and also at the New York Metropolitan Opera, where she had been the first Isolde, the first Venus in *Tannhäuser*, and the first Brünnhilde in *Siegfried* and *Götterdämmerung*.

In 1880, at the request of the Steinways, she had undertaken a concert tour throughout the length and breadth of the United States. The prestige she gained on this tour and the successes of two of her American pupils, Geraldine Farrar and Olive Fremstad, made her a major influence in the development of singing, not only in Europe but in America, where she became known as 'the first lady of opera'.[174] She had sung an impressive number of world premières and her stupendous repertory had included 170 different roles in 120 works. As late as 1896, she sang the three Brünnhildes in Bayreuth. Although lacking the vocal power of a Brandt or Materna, she always managed to be heard above the fullest orchestral tutti thanks to the 'crystalline clarity' of her voice. Furthermore, contrary to the general rule, the singing of dramatic roles in no way diminished her agility in coloratura which enabled her to sing, as seen above, during a single yearly guest appearance at the Hofoper, such roles as Violetta in *La Traviata*, Norma, Konstanze (in *Die Entführung*), Fidelio, Brünnhilde, and even Isolde.[175] According to her pupils, at the age of 60 she could still sing the big Aria of the Queen of the Night without effort. Her technical mastery was such that she consistently resisted any suggestion of transposition from the original key.[176]

Although an adept of the 'realist' school of acting, which Mahler so emphatically rejected, Lehmann the actress was not without talent. She had been acclaimed for her stage presence, her graceful gestures, and also for her fiery temperament. However, although her versatility had become legendary, when once she had decided upon an interpretation, it remained fixed for all time. 'I have sung Isolde for twenty-seven years,' she once boasted, 'without

[173]   See Paula Breisky, 'Gedenken an Lilli Lehmann, zur hundertsten Wiederkehr ihres Geburtstages am 24. Nov. 1948', *Österreichische Musikzeitschrift*, 3 (1948): 11, 308 ff. See also above, Vol. i, Chap. 15.

[174]   Lilli Lehmann, who died in 1933, made her last appearance in 1913 but went on singing in concerts until she was over 70. From 1926 on, she gave singing courses at the Mozarteum. Most of her recordings were made between 1905 and 1907, that is around the time of the 1906 Salzburg Festival.

[175]   At least on one occasion, and for one act, under Mahler (see below, Chap. 9).

[176]   In the *Allgemeine Musik-Zeitung*, August Spanuth asserted that, in the Salzburg *Don Giovanni*, Lehmann had forced her voice in moments of passion and that her middle register had lost some of its 'earlier resonance'.

ever straying an inch from the interpretation which I thought right the first time I sang it!'[177] Mahler had long admired Lehmann as a singer, but his appraisal of her reactionary aesthetics in stage directing could only be harsh. The press at large was very unkind to her *Don Giovanni*, and some critics bluntly asserted that her stage-direction had been amateurish and even that her singing career had lasted too long. Josef Reitler[178] was particularly cruel to her in the *Neue Musikalische Presse*:

The singing was in Italian, so only highly cultured people could understand anything, although you heard the text twice over, thanks to the zeal of the prompter. The staging could not have been more mediocre, even in a smaller provincial theatre. Only Fräulein Geraldine Farrar stood out: never have I seen or heard such an enchanting Zerlina. . . . Frau Lehmann's Donna Anna is well known. In the F major aria she still touches the listener's heart. But despite all her theoretical ability she cannot disguise her considerable age. She moves with difficulty, her voice has become shrill and thin in the high register and you can distinctly hear her breathing. But Frau Lehmann is a great artist, and one cannot demand that she should be self-critical and draw the appropriate conclusions... Andrade was also once a great singer. Today he is only a speaker... half-closing his eyes and affecting the blasé epicurean. His costumes are, indeed, worth seeing, as is the gracefulness of his movements. And he only knows two tempos: Presto and Prestissimo. Voice is the least important thing for him, and he reels off Mozart *parlando*. Where he doesn't sweep the audience along by sheer speed, as in the Champagne Aria, he is a very mediocre Don Giovanni, with many an equal in Germany. Herr Brag from New York sang Leporello. His heavy-handed humour scarcely creates any gaiety, and since he can neither stand, walk, or sing, one wonders why the man became a singer... At the end, the jaws of hell, in which we would have so liked to see not only Don Juan, but also the little time-beater, and several others disappear, did not open. Instead, the public thanked Frau Lehmann for a 'successful' evening with stormy applause.

The same Josef Reitler, in the *Neue Musikalische Presse*, denied Reynaldo Hahn any talent whatsoever for conducting:

Already in the Overture Mr Hahn from Paris showed us what he could not do, namely conduct. He continued to demonstrate this without a single let-up the entire evening. Not one tempo that one would not have wished different, not one gesture of this elegant young man that had not obviously been studied before the mirror.[179]

---

[177] Paula Breisky, 'Gedenken' (see above).

[178] Josef Reitler (1883–1949) was born in Vienna, and completed his secondary education there. While studying music history with Max Friedländer at the University of Berlin, he wrote reviews of Philharmonic concerts for the *Frankfurter Neueste Nachrichten*. In 1905 he settled in Paris, where he became the pupil of the philosopher and sociologist Max Nordau, and correspondent for the Berlin *Vossische Zeitung* and Vienna *Neue Freie Presse*. It was at this juncture that he discovered Mahler's music and became an active supporter. In 1907 he returned to Vienna, where he was engaged by the *Neue Freie Presse*, signing his articles with the initial 'R'. Founder of the Neues Wiener Konservatorium in 1915, he remained its director until 1938, when the Anschluss forced him to leave Austria. After a year in France he left for the United States and founded the 'Opera Department' of the New York College of Music and the Opera Workshop of Hunter College, where he also taught music history. Reitler had written to Mahler from Paris in June about a project to perform one of his symphonies in France (MBR1, nos. 386–8; MBR2, nos. 353, 357, and 358). See below, Chap. 7).

[179] Josef Reitler, in *Neue Musikalische Presse*, 15 (1906): 17, 353 ff.

Without attaining the same degree of ferocity, many other critics were also severe. According to Julius Korngold, Reynaldo Hahn arrived from Paris at the last moment and had thus been unable to 'go beyond the merely decorative' in his conducting.[180] The *Salzburger Volksblatt* claimed that he had 'not succeeded in mastering the ensembles'. In the *Illustrirtes Wiener Extrablatt*, Paul Stauber found his conducting 'deficient in every respect', characterized by 'heavy affected gestures'. 'Reynaldo Hahn appears', wrote Assia Spiro-Rombro[181] in the *Musikalisches Wochenblatt*. 'Would that he had never done so! Would that the Commander, before taking hold of Don Juan, had thrown him into Hell! Perhaps he would have burst into flames, even if only stage flames. What an Overture: mannered, coiffured, sleek and flat beyond imagination! . . .' 'Heavens above, it is not as easy as Mr Hahn thinks to beat time!', wrote August Spanuth of the *Allgemeine Musik-Zeitung*, and added: 'Reynaldo Hahn was not even capable of following, and if the musicians in the orchestra and most of the performers on-stage had not been so sure of themselves, the whole thing could well have broken down completely.'

Mahler was thus not the only exasperated spectator, although he was probably the only one who had displayed his feelings by leaving the hall in the middle of the first act. In fact, as the days went by, his exasperation with Salzburg and the artificial excitement of the festival increased. He bitterly regretted having abandoned his composing and the peace and quiet of his Carinthian retreat. Furthermore, his digestion began to rebel against the local cuisine:

Yesterday was a day with driving rain. I spent the morning at a concert (conducted by Richard Strauss). In honour of Mozart, Bruckner's IXth was performed (the day before it was Beethoven's Vth). This work is the height of <u>nonsense</u> (*Unsinn*).[182] Salzburg quivered with enthusiasm. It was a sort of musical 'morning beer' with radishes and salty pretzels. Afterwards, in any case, a lot of Stigel beer was drunk. I lunched afterwards with Strauss and Roller. Specht arrived at dessert, pale and slightly unsteady.[183] Strauss took his leave and I spent an hour in quiet conversation with Specht,[184] then donned my rented frock-coat and got ready for the party. Favoured with a personal address by his Imperial Highness, I staggered excitedly over to the buffet, drank something, devoured some bread and butter and slipped out to be at the theatre for the 6 o'clock dress rehearsal of *Figaro* (behind closed doors), which came off excellently.

---

[180]	KIW 85 ff.					[181]	See below, Chap. 9.

[182]	For obvious reasons Alma deleted this sentence from the published version of this letter of 18 Aug. (BGA, no. 175, undated). Mahler's harsh verdict on Bruckner's Ninth is tempered by the fact that the Finale of his own Ninth clearly bears the mark of the lasting impression that Bruckner's final Adagio had made on him (cf. Rudolf Stephan, 'Zum Thema Bruckner und Mahler', in *Vom musikalischen Denken* (Schott, Mainz, 1985), 92).

[183]	Richard Specht, one of the earliest and most fervent Mahlerians, was well known for his drinking and drug-taking.

[184]	It was probably on this occasion that he spoke to Specht with such pride about his Eighth Symphony (see above). Korngold describes Mahler during the Salzburg Festival as 'imbued with the work and its triumphal atmosphere'.

Supped afterwards at the hotel with H. (Hammerschlag), Dr B. (Botstieber),[185] Roller and Specht . . . Strauss (quite rightly) continues to insist that I ought to write an opera; he thinks I would be good at it. This morning I shall go for a proper walk with Roller. This evening the performance. Sleep and digestion very inadequate. Tuesday evening—hurrah—I'll be with you. Would that I had never left![186]

Amidst all this commotion, Mahler was still able from time to time to elevate his thoughts to the transcendental realms of the 'Chorus mysticus' of the Eighth Symphony. Both Korngold[187] and Paul Hammerschlag[188] describe him strolling 'joyously, almost arrogantly' through Salzburg with a book sticking out of his pocket, 'a well-worn copy of *Faust*' in the Reclam edition. One day, glimpsing Korngold sitting next to Roller at an open window of the Hotel Bristol Café,

Mahler, who was passing by, gave a cry of joy and leapt, literally swinging through the window and landing at our table. Just at that moment a high Salzburg official passed the spot where the famous Director of the Vienna Opera was giving a display of high spirited, school-boy antics. He condescendingly praised the performance of *Figaro* the day before. Mahler's ironic smile as he received the official marks of recognition was indescribable. But his good mood had disappeared.[189]

In his review of the Salzburg Festival, Korngold called the performance of *Figaro* 'exemplary', 'adapted with great sensitivity' to the little Salzburg theatre. With its 'magic grace', it alone sufficed to make the festival unforgettable.[190] The local press expressed the same delight and amazement. The *Salzburger Volksblatt* claimed that it would be impossible with German singers to surpass this performance,[191] and praised the 'ensemble' in which 'ease, grace, and gaiety' reigned from beginning to end, inner life and expression animating every measure, and perfect harmony prevailing between the music and the action. In the *Neue Musik-Zeitung* Reitler mentioned the reservations of those who disapproved of the 'evil' influence of Roller and the Secession, but added that their catcalls had been drowned by the thunderous applause. Mahler had 'renewed Mozart' by reconciling him with the contemporary spirit, and the performance was a 'triumph in all respects'.

In the *Illustrirtes Wiener Extrablatt* Paul Stauber, declared enemy of Mahler, wrote: 'The secret of [Mozart's] style was revealed, all the hidden paths of his melody brought to light and illuminated unto the furthest corners of the score. . . . Chorus and orchestra formed an incomparable, indeed unique ensemble.'

---

[185] Hugo Botstieber (1875–1941) was a well-known Viennese musicologist, author of a 3-volume biography of Haydn (1927), as well as secretary-general of the Konzertverein from 1913 to 1937. He emigrated to England in 1938.   [186] BGA, no. 175, undated (18 Aug.).

[187] *Neue Freie Presse*, summer 1926 (quoted in AMM1, 130; AMM2, 130).

[188] Information provided to the author by Elisabeth Hammerschlag-Duschnitz.

[189] Julius Korngold, *Neue Freie Presse*, 1926.   [190] *Neue Freie Presse* (28 Aug. 1906).

[191] It praised Mahler for reinstating the recitatives, and for cutting short the applause after the Overture and at the end of each aria.

Assia Spiro-Rombro, in the *Musikalisches Wochenblatt*, criticized the slow tempo at which Mahler took the overture.

But everything else was in the spirit of Mozart. How the March resounded! Then the choruses: finally, finally all the tempos were rightly judged and the dynamics suited to the spirit [of the music]. Even if, here and there, one might wish some things different, namely stronger accents, on the whole, both in the orchestra and the ensembles, the ideal was almost attained. Mahler has captured the atmosphere, Mozart's meaningful, enveloping, other-worldly, imperishable atmosphere.

In the *Allgemeine Musik-Zeitung*, August Spanuth also asserted that 'every gesture and every accent was dictated by the spirit of the work. . . . The orchestra created wonders of nuance and colour under Mahler's magnetic direction. There were nuances within the nuances.'[192]

Josef Reitler was equally enthusiastic:

Since Gustav Mahler was conducting the performance, it was a foregone conclusion that this would be the high point of the music festival. And it was. It went far beyond the highest expectations. It was the ideal Mozart performance, which many have dreamed of but which no one had yet seen realized. The Viennese in the audience were, to be sure, a little blasé, but even they had to admit that it was considerably more effective in the smaller theatre than in the big Vienna Opera. Those who had not seen the new *Figaro* in Vienna—foreigners who had come from all over the world—watched the marvel unfolding before their eyes with astonishment, and many must have reverently sensed the prodigious greatness of the man who had produced it.

Lucky Vienna! You can call a Gustav Mahler your own. Do you realize what you possess in him? Something every other city in the world envies you for: the greatest director, producer and conductor, and above all a great human being. Were this performance of Mozart the only thing he had ever accomplished, this immense feat alone would assure him a place in music history.[193]

According to Josef Reitler,[194] Mahler 'had needed four rehearsals lasting from 10 o'clock in the morning until late at night, with short breaks, to adapt the Viennese production to the acoustics and scenic dimensions of the small hall'.

Several accounts, written much later, testify to the unique quality of the Salzburg *Figaro*. For Fritz Stiedry, it represented 'the unquestionable summit of Mahler's achievement as director and conductor'.[195] Karl Lafite, who had replaced Schönaich at the *Wiener Allgemeine Zeitung* after his death in April 1906, was of the same opinion,[196] and Angelo Neumann, a professional, if ever

[192] At the same time, Spanuth expressed reservations about the cast. Gutheil-Schoder's technique and voice were open to criticism; Mayr, in the role of Figaro, was 'too round and comfortable'; Kiurina needed 'practice in legato' before 'composing romances'. But he also wrote that in his view the cast 'brilliantly proved the soundness of Mahler's principle of making the ensemble his priority consideration'.

[193] *Neue Musikalische Presse*, art. quoted above.

[194] Josef's nephew Frederick Reitler kindly sent me copies of two essays entitled 'Ein jugendlicher Mahler-Enthusiast' and 'Gustav Mahler' (identified above and below under the initials JRM). The passages cited here are from the first document, 18.

[195] Fritz Stiedry, 'Der Operndirektor Mahler', *Melos*, 1 (1920): 6, 134.

[196] 'Mahler der Romantiker', *Wiener Allgemeine Zeitung* (19 May 1911).

there was one, of the operatic stage, claimed that it was quite simply 'the most perfect operatic performance (he had) ever seen in almost fifty years of experience'.[197]

The very idea of a festival of this type and the level of perfection reached with this *Figaro* gave Mahler cause for reflection during those few days in Salzburg. It had given him an opportunity, he told Bernhard Paumgartner, to go to the roots of Mozartian drama and explore it with all the possibilities offered in Salzburg without the drudgery of the daily repertory routine he so detested.[198] He expressed the same idea to Bernard Scharlitt during the interview quoted several times above.[199] To Fritz Stiedry he said that he would like to 'conclude and crown' his activity at the Hofoper with a 'festival year', a 'festival of gigantic dimensions, an "uncompromising" ["his favourite expression", Stiedry noted] presentation of all the worthwhile opera literature'.[200]

Before he left Salzburg, Mahler made the acquaintance of Josef Reitler, the young critic whose lively reviews have been quoted above, and who described their meeting in one of two unpublished essays.[201] Reitler had come to Salzburg mainly to meet Mahler and talk to him about the possibility of having one of his symphonies performed in Paris.[202] The young man's first encounter with Mahler had occurred seven years earlier, in 1899, when, as a 16-year-old, he had heard the Vienna première of the First Symphony which Mahler had conducted at the Vienna Philharmonic.[203] This event had been an inspiration for him when attending the Philharmonic concert with his parents:

From where I sat in the organ gallery I could see the eyes of the artist down below as he fought in vain against a recalcitrant orchestra and a generally hostile audience. The audience was already restless during the opening bars, and at the first high blast of the trumpets they laughed aloud. . . . The way he fought fired my imagination and left an indelible impression. How could I ever forget the noble, tortured face, the twitching mouth, the visibly superhuman tension and concentration with which the conducting composer compelled the orchestra, at least, to respect his intentions! During this performance the realization hit me like lightning that the task of a lifetime, my lifetime must be to champion Mahler and his work.

Needless to say, Reitler had been for a long time looking forward to his first meeting with Mahler and he went directly to the theatre to find out where he was staying.

The porter informed me that the dress rehearsal was in progress, and that a break would occur within an hour. When I explained that I wanted to speak with the director during the break, he shouted: 'The Director is not available for anyone, so he is not available for you!'

[197] Richard Batka, 'In Bezug auf den Artikel von Julius Steinberg im Wiener Fremden-Blatt vom 25. Mai 1911, "Aus Gustav Mahlers Prager Kapellmeisterzeit" ', *Fremden-Blatt*, Vienna (27 May 1911).

[198] Bernhard Paumgartner, 'Erinnerungen', 67.

[199] See above, Chap. 5, and below, Chap. 7.   [200] Fritz Stiedry, 'Operndirektor'.

[201] JRM (copy in BGM, Paris).   [202] See below, Chap. 7.   [203] JRM 5.

'But I have come from Paris—'

'I don't care where you come from! Today is a rehearsal day, and even a gentleman from Paris has no business here.'

This noisy altercation had aroused curiosity—theatre officials and singers awaiting their turn—and soon the whole thing was like a public meeting. In friendly and sometimes less friendly terms, people tried to tell me what every child in Austria knew: that the director was not to be disturbed, even during the intervals. The person that dared speak to him had not yet been born.

I replied that I couldn't believe it: I had come on purpose from Paris to see the director on an important matter. That only provoked new shrieks of protest.

Suddenly, however, a powerful voice was heard over the uproar: 'I'll try!' As I later learned, it was stage-manager Skofitz.[204] Everyone looked at him. At that very moment, Mahler came down the dark corridor which led from the orchestra to the street via the porter's lodge. He was dressed in a cycling outfit. He was visibly nervous and from time to time jerked and stamped rather than walked through the lane formed by the bystanders. I held my breath. What would Skofitz do? Would he keep his promise? He did! Boldly, he stepped into the path of the jerking, stamping director, whispered a couple of words and pointed at me.

Mahler looked me over from head to foot, and then said as he passed me by: 'Tell your father that I can see him tomorrow afternoon.' I was so young in appearance and behaviour at the time that Mahler could only take me for the son of his Parisian correspondent and promoter. The mistake was quickly corrected, and Mahler smilingly took me along outside with him before the goggling eyes of the onlookers.

It was not always easy for ordinary mortals to follow Mahler in his soaring flights of artistic fancy. But to keep pace with him on foot was equally hard, if not impossible, for his frequent stamping introduced a sort of irregular syncopation into his fast and nervous walking rhythm. He was silent as we walked, apparently still preoccupied with his *Figaro*, and I didn't dare disturb him. Suddenly he stopped and seized my arm. 'Have you seen the performance of *Don Juan*?' I hadn't, but before I could answer, he went on: 'Of course Lilli Lehmann is a good artist, a tolerable Donna Anna (following which, as if foreseeing Mildenburg's Donna Anna, he spoke of the dramatic essence of the role which Lehmann could never attain)—a splendid singer! But for her directing and the conductor she brought with her, she deserves...' Here Mahler employed a forceful expression which I was often to hear him use in heated debates which usually turned into grandiose Mahler-monologues . . .[205]

Mahler looked at his watch. 'Excuse me, but I must return to my rehearsal. I'll see you tomorrow at 3 o'clock—you, not your father!' He laughed heartily, and his laughter had something youthful and unburdened about it, like so much else about him. That [quality] always struck me, for it was in such sharp contrast to the truly Faustian struggle which weighed down the most important phases of his creations and interpretations.

Not every idol lives up to its promises at close range. But my first personal encounter with Gustav Mahler was no disappointment. The star which had lit my path

---

[204] Franz Skofitz was in fact one of the two 'Inszipienten'.
[205] Reitler here recalls Mahler's gratitude when Lilli Lehmann replaced Mildenburg in the last act of *Tristan* the following year (see below, Chap. 8).

only shone more brightly the closer I got to it. And I can say without exaggeration that every remark on general matters Mahler made enriched my knowledge, and my vision of the world and of art.

The following day, during his discussion with Mahler, Reitler suggested performing the First Symphony in Paris. Mahler, insisting that the First was the most difficult of all his symphonies to understand, was against the idea. Their negotiations continued by mail, and they next saw each other the following year when Reitler returned to Vienna and joined the staff of the *Neue Freie Presse*.[206]

Besides the *Figaro* performances Mahler had plenty to occupy him during his stay at Salzburg. For 18 August, he had planned an outing to Berchtesgaden with Roller and Hammerschlag, but this was called off because of heavy rain. An Austrian journalist, Otto Frischauer,[207] living in Paris at the time, paid him a visit. 'He made a strong impression of intellectual perversity on me', wrote Mahler to Alma. 'Perhaps Strauss will compose him someday. At present he is working on *Electra*.'[208] In his letters to Alma, Mahler had in all honesty to admit that the performance of *Figaro* had been 'really marvellous. Audience very attentive and quiet as a mouse. No interruptions for applause. I dined at the hotel afterwards with Roller, the Hammerschlags, and Dr Botstieber.'[209] He was also going to see their friends the Redlichs,[210] and was getting ready to leave the morning after the second performance to return to Vienna, and then on to Maiernigg, where he planned to spend two more weeks.[211] Alma had sent him a few staves of music in which she had noted, from memory, a passage from the Finale of the Eighth Symphony,[212] which proves that he had played them to her before his departure. In one of his letters from Salzburg, Mahler congratulated her on her excellent musical memory.[213]

When Mahler was leaving to come to the Salzburg, Alma had asked him to bring her back some marzipan sweets and biscuits, Salzburg specialities. She was amazed to see him get off the train at Klagenfurt with a huge case of these sweetmeats, the greatest part of which she passed on to their Wörthersee neighbours.[214] Immediately on his return, Mahler plunged into the Eighth

---

[206] See below, Chaps. 7 and 9.

[207] Berthold Frischauer (born in 1851 in Brno) was Paris correspondent of the *Neue Freie Presse* in 1899, when he was expelled from France, no doubt because of his pro-Dreyfus articles. His brother Otto (born in 1863) was also a journalist and Paris correspondent of the *Neues Wiener Tagblatt*.

[208] BGA, no. 176 (18 Aug. 1906).   [209] BGA, no. 177 (19 Aug. 1906).

[210] See above, Chap. 4.

[211] Mahler was unable to travel directly from Salzburg to the Wörthersee because the Tauernbahn railway line only opened in July 1909.

[212] BGA, no. 176 (see also illustrations 187 and 190) and AMM2, 131 (BGM, Paris). The passage was 'Der Frühgeliebte, nicht mehr Getrübte, er kehrt zurück'. Mahler corrected a few notes, including a harmonic progression. He was unable to recall the end of the passage, and scrawled: 'It develops in every possible way, but not this one. The harmonic progression would be utterly banal. Damn it—I can't find it myself. In the raucous tumult (*Juchhe Stübel*) of Salzburg, I lost sight of Eros.'

[213] BGA, no. 177 (19 Aug.).   [214] AMM1, 131; AMM2, 131.

Symphony[215] for the last two weeks of his vacation during which he entertained three guests, Alexander Zemlinsky,[216] Ernst Decsey,[217] and Julius Korngold. Korngold was on his way back from the Dolomites, he was staying in Pörtschach, and Mahler had surely invited him to visit him at Maiernigg:

there, in an hour of confidentiality, this man of genius revealed to me the tortures he experienced both in the composition and performance of his work. After my annual holiday in the Dolomites when staying in the warmer, lower-lying Pörtschach, I followed my irresistible impulse to visit Mahler in his Wörthersee villa. I missed the return boat, and I had no choice but to accept his warm invitation to spend the night. With great ceremony, he handed me a toothbrush, 'the most important, indispensable travel article,' he joked. For the first time, I saw him totally relaxed, natural, sociable, to the point of cordiality and simplicity (*Gemütlichkeit*), as if the demons which tortured him in his symphonies had been laid to rest. I became acquainted with the considerate husband, tender father, and friend, and I also discovered how much he respected the artists under him. He spoke of his own artistic destiny without bitterness, but admitted, with a pensive smile, that when his eyes fell on the bust of Wagner on his piano, he often thought: 'At least they can't murder you!'[218]

As usual, Alma is uninformative about their activities during this summer, the last one they spent entirely in Maiernigg. But Alfred Roller, who spent several days with them, has provided a detailed description of Mahler's daily life.[219] In the 'splendid isolation' of the Wörthersee, Mahler continued to devote a part of each day to outdoor exercise, and according to Roller he was 'not only a passionate walker, but also an excellent swimmer, a tireless rower, and an expert cyclist'.

He rose at 5.30 a.m., took his first swim by himself, and then hurried along hidden paths to his composing hut in the depths of the forest, where his first breakfast awaited him. Some seven hours of uninterrupted work followed. Before the midday meal he had another swim, usually made music on the piano, with Alma, and played with the children. After the meal he took a brief nap, something he never allowed himself in town, however much the morning rehearsals had tired him. If you tried to persuade him at such time to take a rest, he would explain that his exhaustion was only 'normal bodily fatigue'.[220]

After this short afternoon rest in the country, at around 4 o'clock came the daily long walk, on which he was usually accompanied by Frau Alma. It was often not easy for her. He could go at a very brisk pace without flagging. When he walked slowly he put one foot in front of the other almost daintily, straightening his legs at the knees, with each step. He was a 'narrow gauge walker'. But when he walked quickly, as on his long hikes, he leaned slightly forward, chin out, and put his feet down firmly, almost stamping. This type of walk had something stormy, something decidedly triumphant about it. Mahler was quite incapable of dawdling. His body always had poise, albeit

---

[215] HOA, Z. 937/1906. According to this document, Mahler returned to Vienna on 4 Sept.

[216] On 31 Aug. The day of Alma's birthday, she wrote a postcard to Arnold Schoenberg, which is a picture of the Mahler villa, with a rowboat leaving the shore. It is co-signed by Mahler and Zemlinsky (Library of Congress, Washington, and MBRS 183).

[217] Decsey described this visit to Mahler in EDS2, 143 ff.   [218] KIW 107 ff.

[219] RBM 16.

[220] Despite Roller's assertion, Mahler sometimes did take a short nap after lunch in Vienna.

not always a conventional one. He went much too fast uphill, I could barely keep up. His swim generally began with a powerful dive. He then swam for a long time underwater only reappearing far out in the lake, rolling happily around like a seal. Rowing together with Mahler was hard work. He had a very powerful stroke and much too rapid a rhythm. His strength enabled him to keep up this exertion for a long time.[221]

For his walks, Mahler

took great pleasure in wearing a grey walking suit. He liked to hang his jacket over his shoulder on a retaining loop, his cap he would pin to the front of his coarse linen shirt and his black plaited belt would be pushed well below his waist. He wore yellow lace-up boots and thin black knee-length socks. . . .[222] Mahler's fondness for walking came from his great love of the open air. This love was not concerned with particular or specially spectacular objects. Any place in field and meadow where he could linger undisturbed enchanted him and was for him 'the most beautiful' one. I remember resting with him on a little knoll in a forest one late summer afternoon. It was an abandoned clearing, sparsely dotted with slender red pines of no interest to the woodcutters. The ground was covered with moldering woodchips and dense bilberry scrub. Round about were other wooden knolls of a similar nature. Nowhere anything out of the ordinary, just peace and warm sunshine. But Mahler, lying on his back, dug his shoulders deep into the bilberry scrub as if he couldn't get close enough to the beloved earth. 'Isn't this a glorious spot! Isn't it wonderful here!' he kept saying again and again, until he was in such a glowing mood that he told me the plot of his defunct opera, *Rübezahl*.[223]

His evenings in the country he usually spent in the company of his wife. She often read aloud to him. Occasionally he read to her. She reports that during these summer months—the time when he did his real work—Mahler was always much more approachable, more human, more devoted than in the city. He even overcame his great reserve sufficiently to play his half-finished works to her.

At that time, Mahler gave the impression of being in perfect health. He slept soundly, relished a cigar, and enjoyed a glass of beer in the evening. He wouldn't touch spirits, however, and drank wine only on special occasions, preferring Moselle, Chianti, or Asti. One or two glasses sufficed to make him expansive and he would then indulge in puns which, to borrow Frau Alma's words, he himself enjoyed no end. But with all his capacity for sensual enjoyment—including the pleasures of the table—he always showed the greatest moderation and was never seen to indulge in excess. Drunkenness disgusted him as much as coarseness or indecency. The strict cleanliness he observed in regard to his body also extended, but without any prudishness, to his conversation and certainly also to his thoughts.[224]

---

[221] RBM 16–17. The postcard of 31 Aug. 1906, addressed to Schoenberg in Vienna (see above), shows Mahler's villa in Maiernigg, and the lake in the foreground with a rowboat leaving the shore, Mahler signs himself 'Gustav Mahler (two hands)', suggesting that he is the man at the oars.

[222] Ibid. 12. Roller says that Mahler slept in short nightshirts like riding shirts. He disliked long nightshirts and preferred to feel a little cold when in bed.

[223] Ibid. Their discussion on this occasion probably provided the inspiration for Roller's ballet *Rübezahl*, for which he himself wrote the story line (see below, Chap. 8).

[224] Ibid. 17–18. It must not be forgotten that this is Roller speaking, a rigorous, even puritanical man. It is likely that there is some exaggeration here, as also in his account of Frau Alma. Mahler's admiration for a play as brutally realistic as Wedekind's *Frühlingserwachen* which deals with an adolescents' sexual awakening, proves that he was surely less prudish than Alma usually maintained (see below, Chap. 8).

'"Unattractive, frail, ugly, a fidgeting bundle of nerves"—those are the expressions currently used to describe Mahler's outward appearance. They are wide of the mark, but he himself was partly responsible for them,' Roller wrote in his introduction to a book of pictures published after the Second World War. A benevolent but nevertheless scrupulously honest and careful observer, he has provided a detailed description of his friend and collaborator which in many respects differs radically from all others:

In his prime, Mahler possessed very good clothes but handled them carelessly. He fastened only the top button of his overcoats and stuck his fists deep into their pockets; his tie was slung together in three seconds into any old crooked knot, and by roughly grabbing the brim of his new hat with both his hands and pulling it down over his ears, he quickly made it look as shapeless as an old one. He listened to criticism on the subject with an indulgent smile, rather as if a small child was telling him a silly story. He might even correct the fault for a moment, just to be obliging—only to slip back into his habits a minute or so later. But by his indifference to the outward picture he gave of himself, he contributed to the impression of physical unfitness.

And yet he took great pleasure in seeing good-looking, well-dressed people. Often, as we strolled on the Kärntnerring after a morning's work at the Opera, he would draw my attention to an elegantly dressed, thoroughbred aristocrat in the crowd. His wife's beauty and her well-chosen attire had no more enchanted admirer than Mahler himself. But he felt no inner need to look elegant himself, and mere outward show bored him. So-called society was of little importance to him, and he never tried to show by his outward appearance that he belonged to any particular social group. It may also be that, since he always strenuously exercised his will in the course of his work, he felt he could permit himself a certain carelessness and relaxation in matters which he considered unimportant.

His neglect for his own clothing was not always innocent of another characteristic—a love of teasing. Now and then he took childish pleasure in the way his negligent apparel could embarrass people who attached great importance to external appearances. Once the silk lining of his coat had become torn. Far from bothering to remember such an unimportant detail, Mahler left it as it was, and the damage gradually acquired grotesque proportions. This became the source of a curious pleasure for him: 'It would be most instructive to know what goes on in the mind of the High Chamberlain's solemnly correct doorman when he helps me on and off with my torn coat. He wears his own tailcoat so solemnly and keeps a straight face—not a flicker. I assure you—when he helps me on with my coat, which really is badly torn. How can he imagine the order of things in the world, and what place in it would he attribute to me? Strange! Very strange!' I could not bring myself to disturb this long-standing idyll by drawing the torn lining to the attention of the responsible authority, that is to say Frau Alma. . . .[225]

Mahler's own tail-coat was always immaculate and new. Since he wore it for conducting he called it his 'working clothes'. Everything connected in any way with his work, he considered worthy of attention. At the podium, he was never other than elegant, straight-backed and full of explosive tension. Those who noticed the difference between this Mahler and his everyday incarnation helped themselves out of the difficulty with catchwords, like 'lives on his nerves', and conjured up for themselves, sometimes through auto-suggestion, an exaggerated picture of 'their' Mahler with modifications and nuances to suit all situations.

When most people observe a great man, the first thing they try and do is to discover in him their own faults and weaknesses. The best thing about Mahler's everyday attire, for example, was always his excellent shoes. The legend quickly arose that he was vain about his small feet! In fact, he simply loved walking, and like all walkers he knew the importance of good footwear.[226]

Among us southern Germans, Mahler was bound to be regarded as a short man. I never measured him, unfortunately. I estimate that his height was no more than 160 centimetres. His abundant hair, which he wore fairly long to please Alma's wishes, made his head seem somewhat too big. During the sunbathing sessions Mahler was so keen on, I could observe his naked body carefully. It was very well-shaped, with thoroughly manly proportions. His shoulders were broader than his clothed body suggested, and completely symmetrical. His pelvis was narrow. His legs, by no means particularly short, were straight and handsome and had hard, clearly developed muscles and little hair. The veins did not stand out at all. His feet were small with high insteps and short, regular, completely faultless toes. His chest was strongly voluted, had little hair and very clearly defined pectoral muscles. His stomach showed well-developed abdominal muscles, but absolutely free of superfluous fat—as was his entire body moreover—and showed the outlines as distinctly as on an artist's model. Because of my profession I have seen a great number of naked human bodies of all kinds, and I can affirm that the forty-year-old Mahler possessed a faultlessly beautiful, strong but slim man's body, although, of course, it could hardly have measured seven and a half times the length of his head.[227] The first time I saw him in the nude, I could not conceal my surprise at the splendid display of his muscles. Mahler laughed good-naturedly, realizing that I too had been influenced by the general gossip about his physical deficiency. The most beautifully developed muscles, really worth seeing for the clarity of their outline, were those of his back. I never saw his splendidly modelled bronzed back without being reminded of a racehorse in top form. His hands were those of a working man, short and broad, with the fingers ending abruptly, as if hacked off, instead of tapering. His fingernails—it must be admitted alas—were usually bitten short, often down to the quick and bleeding, and Frau Alma had a long struggle before she could cure him of this. His arms were slender, and yet surprisingly strong. For, contrary to the prevailing image, Mahler was very muscular. Many people saw him on occasions leap from the orchestra over the footlights onto the stage . . .[228]

Roller relates that the operation in 1901 had left Mahler with extensive internal lesions:

These obliged him to be especially vigilant about what he ate and to follow a strict diet. Nonetheless, he ate readily and with gusto: much fruit, especially apples and oranges, plenty of butter, light vegetables and desserts, little meat and then only from farm

---

[226] Ibid. 11.
[227] This is probably a discreet allusion to Mahler's short stature which, according to classical canons, would not have permitted him to serve as a model for a painter or sculptor.
[228] RBM 14–15.

animals. He refused to eat game or the meat of wild animals. Since every dietetic error might make him unfit for work, he was exceedingly cautious, even uneasy at table, especially if he was on the point of finishing a work and had only a few days of vacation left. In general he was extremely resistant to physical suffering. He sometimes appeared on the podium suffering an excruciating migraine . . . Only constant anxiety that he might be prevented from carrying out his work plan sometimes made him hypochondriac, and minor mishaps such as a wasp sting or a cut from a knife could throw him into despair. He was ridden by the secret fear of all artists who die young, that he might have to leave his work unfinished.[229]

In her *Erinnerungen*, Alma devotes considerable space to Mahler's constant fear of illness. He had a habit of trying all the different remedies and medicines friends recommended. Once, following Justi's advice, he took to eating a special wholemeal bread which she sent from Vienna to Maiernigg every two or three days. When Alma finally complained that she was having trouble digesting it, Mahler exclaimed with relief: 'You can't stand it *either*?! Thank God! I've been feeling rotten for the past week. We won't eat it any longer!'[230]

Max Graf has compared the 'deep, metallic sound' of Mahler's voice to that of a 'bronze bell': according to him, it contrasted with 'his small size and seemed to be the very expression of his will'. Roller observed that Mahler's voice had two distinct registers:

One, a very sonorous baritone, was for calm discourse, while a ringing tenor was used in his moments of inner excitement. His voice could become very powerful without leaving the lower register, and this was the tone in which he thundered during his famous outbursts in the Opera. 'Don't imagine I was really angry,' he once said to me after I had been caught for the first time in one of these thunderstorms and was feeling somewhat awed. 'Severity is the only means I have for maintaining the necessary order.' And thereafter I learned to tell by the sound of his voice whether he was merely 'putting it on' or really was excited. When he got really excited—no matter whether through pleasure or anger—or became interested in a subject of conversation, his voice immediately jumped with a sort of break into the higher register . . .[231] In any case, Mahler spoke in an uncommonly arresting and vivid manner, in clear, well-constructed sentences, without any bombast. His was a beautiful, pure German, entirely free from any foreign sound.[232] His speech was manly. The 'R' was rather strongly emphasized,[233] and very slightly rolled.[234]

Mahler's face has been described countless times: the sharp profile, the sombre countenance, the jet black hair, the features evoking an ascetic monk.

[229] RBM 18.   [230] AMM1, 91; AMM2, 96.

[231] Roller claims that after 1907, during the final years of his life, such abrupt changes in register became much less frequent.

[232] In his youth Mahler is said to have spoken with a slightly lilting accent which seemed to disappear with the years.

[233] According to Wilhelm Kienzl, Mahler's only trace of a Viennese accent was, like Karl Kraus's, in his pronunciation of the dipthongs *ei* and *au* (Wilhelm Kienzl, 'Rezensionen über Vorlesungen von Karl Kraus', *Grazer Tagespost*, Mar. 1911). Bruno Walter adds: 'Mahler spoke an everyday language—that of Grillparzer, Schnitzler, Hofmannsthal, and even Karl Kraus—but often mixed Bohemian with Viennese German' (information provided by Frederick Dorian, brother of the Schoenberg pupil Max Deutsch).

[234] RBM 20.

As they were constantly in motion he could look young one instant and aged the next. Schoenberg compares the evolution of his face to that of his music: the 'gentle, dreamy, illuminated quality, frequent among Bohemian Jews', had taken on a 'healthy ruggedness'.[235] Strength and ardour as well as struggle and suffering had modelled it. Roller describes the gradual transformation of his face with same terms:

Mahler was no free thinker, but a truly free spirit. His countenance bore witness to the price he paid to reach such heights. Examination of the photos in chronological order[236] shows how, at the end of his life, everyday insignificance had been transformed into sublime beauty. Here if ever, mind had created matter.[237]

Describing a series of photographs of Mahler, Schoenberg writes:

Mahler at 18 does not look one of like those young artists to whom it is more important to look like a great man than really to be one. He looks like someone who is waiting for something that is going to happen, though what it will be he does not yet know. A second picture shows him about twenty-five years old. Here something has already taken place. Curiously, the forehead has become higher; the brain obviously takes up more room. And the facial features! Formerly, in spite of all their striking seriousness, they were almost those of one who wants to acquire a little more strength before he sets to work. Now the features are tense. They show that he already knows that the world is capable of good and evil, but they are almost arrogant; he will soon make the world eat humble pie. But now let's turn straight to his head at the age of 50. How extraordinary that he could grow into that! Almost no resemblance to the pictures of him as a young man. The development from within has shaped it into something which has, as it were, swallowed up all the earlier stages. Certainly they too are there in the final stage. And of course anyone with eyes to see can already detect the grown man in the photos of his youth. But, when one looks at them one by one in reverse order, it is as difficult to see in them—however expressive they may be—the expression of the mature man as it is to see alongside a very bright light the beams of a lesser one. One must avert one's eyes from the certainties of the older face for a long time before discerning the potentialities in the younger one. Here it is the thoughts and feelings that have moved this man, that have shaped his features. This is not what happens to the young geniuses who look their best when they are young, and who turn into Philistines, even outwardly and visibly, when they grow older. One cannot learn one's appearance. And what one has learned does not remain, but goes away. But what is inborn goes from one climax to the next, develops itself to ever higher forms of expression. It makes leaps which become more enigmatic to the observer the more urgently he desires to understand them.[238]

Yet the most precious portrait again comes from the pen of Roller, Mahler's painter-friend. He starts by stressing the unusual shape of Mahler's skull, which was

---

[235] Arnold Schoenberg, 'Mahler', 'Stil und Gedanke', in *Gesammelte Schriften*, ed. Ivan Vojtěch (Fischer, Frankfurt, 1976), 22.

[236] Roller's text appears in an introduction to a collection of photos of Mahler.

[237] RBM 27.   [238] Arnold Schoenberg, 'Stil', 22.

unusually short, the back of the head being almost flat. The impetuosity of his nature showed itself in the powerful dome-like bulge of his forehead, which dominated his features increasingly with advancing age. This skull structure, together with his forceful lower jaw and the snake-like strands of naturally curly hair, dark to the end of his life, thrusting up from his forehead, gave his head that characteristic resemblance to an ancient tragic mask.[239]

Mahler sometimes grew a moustache during the summer months to avoid shaving. Once, perhaps during the summer of 1906, Roller saw him with a 'mighty, iron-coloured, stiff, full beard, traversed by two light-grey flames running down . . .

His teeth . . . were strong, white and regular. It was only in the last years of his life that he had any need for dental care, and even then not very much. On either side of his face between the strong chewing muscles and the mouth were three lines. A zigzag with a rounded outer edge at the corners of his mouth. A second running down from the wings of his nose and ending above the corners of his mouth—the line of suffering. And a third running from the cheekbone extension of the upper jaw, down to the horizontal branch of the lower jaw: it is characteristic of all men with uncommon will power. It was sharp and deep in Mahler's case, as if it had been cut by a knife into hard stone. Next to this line, directly over his eyeteeth, was another shallow hollow.[240]

His ears were small, close to the head, and had freestanding lobes and fine, intricately modelled auricles. His lips were nobly moulded. . . . They were thin and usually pressed together with an expression of firmness, opening slightly only when he was listening attentively. When he was in a bad mood, angry, or inwardly disgusted, he pulled his mouth sideways, took half his lower lip between his teeth, knitted his brow and wrinkled up his nose. It was a grotesque grimace, and when he wore it he really became the 'ugly Mahler' (*der hässliche Mahler*) of legend. It was not entirely his fault if some people were only shown that face and never saw him as other than the 'ugly Mahler'. Mahler was near-sighted and from his youth on wore glasses—sometimes spectacles, sometimes a pince-nez. At the end of his life he wore rimless oval spectacles with a gold bridge-piece, so that the surrounds made more of an impression than the eyes themselves. His irises were speckled, mainly dark brown. His eye-sockets stood out clearly all round. The tear glands were small and flat. Since manhood his habit of opening wide his upper eyelids gave him an expression of lucid wakefulness. When they drooped slightly, it meant that he was beginning to feel tired . . . He had a clever, candid pair of eyes which could face things squarely.

This lean face faithfully reflected every inner emotion of its bearer, and that is why it has been described in very different ways by many people, reflecting their different relationships to Mahler. The mask-like quality is mentioned by almost everyone. But while some talk of seriousness, sternness, or ascetic stubbornness as the predominant expression, others mention vivacity, nervousness, impatience, changeableness, and yet others of hardness, coldness, inaccessibility and arrogance. Those closest to Mahler could see well enough that all the feelings of a great, passionate human soul could be mirrored in his features, but that the basic temperament of this strong personality was a combination of suffering overcome and manly benevolence. Mahler must have

[239] RBM 21.   [240] Ibid. 22 ff.

endured many inner struggles and endless suffering. His music expresses what his lips kept silent.[241]

Mahler's kindness and generosity, so often overlooked or deliberately ignored in contemporary accounts of him, have been described by Roller with rare eloquence:

On that subject, people usually have little to say. But the occasions when, like any man in a responsible position, he could not avoid hurting people, those are described in faithful detail.

How excellent he was with children, and how quickly they learned to love him! His deep respect for the mystery of life was extended to the lowliest insect. But one of his favourite sayings was: 'Being tender doesn't mean being weak, and being sweet doesn't mean being sugary.' One day in his large Vienna drawing-room, he was pacing up and down preoccupied with expressing a difficult train of thought. An unfortunate fly disturbed him in his discourse, and several times Mahler waved it away with his hand. Finally he hit it so hard that it fell to the floor, where it lay fluttering and dying before him. To end its suffering, he stepped on it. But the way he lifted his foot unnecessarily high and held it hanging in the air, showed how difficult it was for him to take the dreadful decision. Disturbed, he stared at the shapeless little corpse at his feet, and waving his hand as if to calm and comfort it, he murmured: 'Quiet now, quiet now! You too are immortal!' He turned away, wandered disconsolately about the room and didn't go on with the conversation. Besides me someone else had watched this brief but remarkable scene, a renowned musician of Jewish origin.[242] 'Why get so worked up over having to kill a fly?!' he asked. No answer was forthcoming. But the questioner would have agreed with those who maintain that to understand Mahler you must yourself be Jewish.[243]

Anna von Mildenburg's impressions of Mahler confirm Roller's description. In an article written ten years after Mahler's death, she remarks that Mahler's respect for animals and his smile whenever he saw an insect or heard a bird sing reflected his personal religion. His pantheistic beliefs made him see the manifestations of God's will everywhere, and sensed its 'miracles and secrets . . . and contemplated them with the deep respect and touching astonishment of a child'.[244]

As to what Mahler felt about being a Jew, Roller had this to say:

Mahler never hid the fact that he was of Jewish origin. But for him that was not something to be pleased about, it was a challenge, a spur to even higher and purer achievement. 'It's like someone who comes into the world with one arm too short: the other arm must then learn to accomplish more, and ultimately perhaps it does things that two healthy arms would not have managed to do.'[245] That was how he once explained to me

---

[241] Ibid. 23 ff.

[242] The musician in question was probably Bruno Walter, and the conversation no doubt concerned the Opera.   [243] RBM 24 ff.

[244] Anna von Mildenburg, 'Aus Briefen Mahlers', *Moderne Welt*, 3 (1921–2): 7, 13 ff.

[245] Mahler seems to have used this image more than once, for Otto Klemperer also quotes it in an unpublished text written in 1965 (made available to the author by Lotte Klemperer).

the effect of his origins upon his work. Often, people who wanted to be agreeable to him would tell him that in view of the way he had developed he was no longer a Jew. That depressed him. 'People should listen to my work and see how it affects them, and then accept it or reject it. Their favourable or unfavourable prejudices with regard to the work of a Jew they should leave at home. That I demand as my right.' The main thing that bound him to other Jews was compassion. The reasons for this were based on his own frequent experiences, although he rarely spoke about them, and when he did, as a calm statement of fact, without bitterness or sentimentality: 'Among the poorest of men there is always one who is still poorer, and who happens to be a Jew.'

In his eyes, however, to be of Jewish origin should never be used to excuse depravity, meanness, or even bad manners. He refused to be partisan in questions involving Jews, and sometimes had more hard knocks to bear from that quarter than from the other side. 'It's a funny thing; the anti-Semitic newspapers seem to be the only ones who still have a certain respect for me', he would often say, laughing, during his last year as Director of the Vienna Opera. In the end, he succeeded in becoming completely indifferent to public praise or censure: 'We haven't the right to be pleased at praise from a reviewer whose criticisms we believe we can despise'. That was how he put it. But he made a distinction between the profession as a whole and individual members of it. Still, 'our superiors' (*die Herren Vorgesetzten*) was what he ironically called critics in general, even those friendly towards him, and there were never very many of them. On the whole, as far as critical judgements of him were concerned, his Jewish origin did him more harm than good. In any case, he never made an issue of his Jewishness. His sense of being chosen by God came from personal, not racial roots.[246]

Clearly, with all his objectivity and intellectual honesty, Roller tends to make of Mahler a sort of 'honorary Aryan' because he was his friend and a great artist. And this is after all not so surprising in a country and a society in which Jews played a pre-eminent role, but where anti-Semitism was practically endemic. Even as late as in 1974, an opinion poll taken by an Austrian magazine showed that 70 per cent of the population held anti-Semitic opinions.[247]

Alfred Roller's scrupulous portrayal of Mahler corrects many errors, exaggerations, and legends—in particular that of the suffering, sickly, anxiety-ridden husband described in certain passages of Alma's memoirs. In an interview with Dieter Kerner the author of 'The Illnesses of Great Musicians', Alma even claimed that 'Mahler was always ill. I never knew him otherwise. He overloaded his fragile constitution with a frantic amount of work and a constantly active ambition—he never rested.'[248] The reasons why Alma sought

---

[246]   RBM 25 ff.

[247]   According to the Austrian magazine *Profil*, quoted on 3 Jan. 1974 by the French newspaper *Le Monde*, 24% of Austrians possessed 'very marked' anti-Semitic tendencies; 45% believed that 'when a Jew performs a good action, it is out of self-interest'; 35% would not marry a person of Jewish origin; and 21% wished there were no Jews in Austria. *Profil* recalled that 80% of the bureaucrats in Eichmann's office were Austrian and concluded: 'Anti-semitism is such a matter of course in Austria and such a part of daily life that there is practically no obstacle to its expression. Anti-semitism is part of the national character.'

[248]   Dieter Kerner, 'Gustav Mahler', article published on the fiftieth anniversary of Mahler's death in the Baden-Baden review *Cesrasäule* (5 June 1961), and 'Gustav Mahlers Ende. Zu einem 50. Todestag am 18. Mai 1961', *Neue Zeitschrift für Musik*, 122 (1961), 7/8, 367. Cf. also Dieter Kerner, *Krankheiten grosser Musiker* (Schattauer, Stuttgart, 1967), 179.

to create this image have already been explained. At the same time, it is obvious that for Mahler his professional life came first. He considered it to be a mission rather than a job, and at the age of 46 he was still the same man who had once said to Natalie: 'Everything you do, do it as well as you possibly can. For me, everywhere and at every moment, it's *"hic Rhodos, hic salta"*!'[249] He also often said to Alma: 'I can't stand people who <u>under</u>do things. I only like those who <u>over</u>do things.'[250]

In always aiming for the highest and the best, and hence the most difficult, Mahler deliberately closed his eyes to everyday things. He only believed in the effort needed to surpass himself, while Alma always remained closer to mundane reality and found him 'inhuman' in this respect. Falling in love and marrying a wife for whom such a life of self-denial was unnatural had been his mistake and he was to bear its consequences until the end of his short life; and it must be conceded that his refusal to attach importance to material things and sacrificing so many earthly pleasures to his art would have made life difficult for any wife.

The sacrifice of his personal life to his music was an essential part of Mahler's ethic. Inevitably, he despised the conventions of a society to which he considered he did not really belong, and at times neglected the conventions of friendship, passing his closest friends in the street without noticing them, or, on one occasion, in the midst of a conversation with a musician, leaping from the street into a tram without even finishing his sentence.[251] Examples of this kind abound in the stories told of him at the time. Once during a heat wave he happened to enter a rehearsal room at the Opera where a composer was playing his opera to Bruno Walter. The sight of the composer pounding away at the piano in his shirt sleeves left Mahler so bored and disgusted that at the end he did not say a word, and let the man take his leave in a deadly silence, without even saying goodbye.[252] Yet he was usually courteous, and in public always behaved with perfect dignity. Being one of his friends, however, was never an easy matter. As many times above, especially during the Hamburg period, he often tired of his closest friends, for whom the only choice was then to wait until he came back of his own volition. The critic Gustav Schönaich was one of the few members of his profession who knew Mahler well in Vienna. When a professor of medicine, who had counted himself among Mahler's intimate

---

[249] *Hic Rhodos, hic salta* (Here is Rhodes, now jump!) Two explanations have been put forward for this Latin expression, of Greek origin. When the sea was rough, ships could not enter the harbour of Rhodes and people had to jump directly on shore from the ship. The other explanation refers to the famous Colossus of Rhodes which stood astride the entrance to the port, and inspired some people to try and jump from one side to the other. Figuratively, this expression means: 'You must seize the opportunity when it presents itself', or else 'You must continually strive to surpass yourself'. In Mahler's times this proverb figured in the elementary Latin manuals.

[250] AMM1, 147; AMM2, 144. In German 'to exaggerate' is *übertreiben* (literally 'overdrive'). In replacing the prefix *über* (over) with *unter* (under), Mahler created a neologism for which, for better or for worse, 'underdo' is a rough equivalent. [251] BWM 40.

[252] Ibid.

friends, asked Schönaich why Mahler no longer liked him, Schönaich replied: 'Because you like him too much.'[253]

Bruno Walter in his autobiography talks about the Viennese friends of his youth and first Vienna years and adds:

It may be asked why I do not place Mahler's friendship, to which I owe so infinitely much, in the same category with that of those people. It is because his was the objective, egocentric temperament of the great creator whose creative task makes him lose sight of his fellow-men, and whose absorption in music often blocks out his feelings for other humans. Of course Mahler knew pity, could share joy, espouse causes and be caring, give help and feel affection. He knew the meaning of friendship and he was a friend in his own way. But his way was not to deliver a steady flow of warmth, but to flare up and then go out, and though he remained attached to his friends to the end of his days, I used even then to define his relationship to them as 'intermittent loyalty'. We could rely on him, but the authentic meaning of friendship was revealed to us by those faithful people who proved as staunchly true to him as they did to us.[254]

Even with his close friends, Mahler at times showed distrust and sometimes hurtful irony, generally in moments when he had not been immediately understood. One August evening, after hearing a portly baritone sing Wolfram's Aria in *Tannhäuser* in audition, Mahler stated firmly, 'You have a very fine voice, but unfortunately I cannot engage you.' Irritated by the singer's insistent questioning, he finally put him before a mirror, saying, 'Just look at yourself and you will find the answer.'[255] As Klaus Pringsheim recalls, Mahler could be offensive at any moment. 'If Mahler were capable of hatred, he would not squander his hatred on those who harmed him. But, he could be utterly contemptuous: of the conceit of ignoramuses, of inflated incompetence, of the self-satisfaction and complacency of the eternally mediocre; he looked down upon all careerists and opportunists . . .'[256] Often, when criticized for his explosive temper, he tried to excuse himself on the grounds that his outbursts were short-lived and that he had finally given way, forgetting too easily that certain scars never heal. One of his favourite maxims, as remembered by his friend Emil Freund, was 'Anger and irritation don't improve a man.'[257]

All those who knew Mahler emphasized his abrupt changes of mood, his 'whims', his sometimes caricatural sense of humour. Some of his more perceptive contemporaries realized that his surly, aggressive behaviour was a way of hiding his timidity, and that his apparently 'theatrical' attitudes actually had nothing affected about them. In an age when, as Stefan Zweig writes, solemn formality was expected of the members of the establishment, Mahler insisted

[253] BMG 89.

[254] BWT 212. Whether intentionally or not, Bruno Walter evokes in this passage the point of view of the friends of Mahler's youth whom he had all but dropped after his marriage with Alma. Later, after 1909, he renewed his links with several of them.   [255] BMG 180.

[256] Pringsheim, 'Erinnerungen' in *Neue Zürcher Zeitung*.

[257] A saying of Mahler's, passed on by Emil Freund, Mahler's lawyer and childhood friend, to one Dr Kornfeld.

on being simple and direct. Klaus Pringsheim and Oskar Fried, who both knew him at the Vienna Opera, emphasize this aspect of his personality. It was not only a question of habit, but of ethics. Weary of the ceremonies of the Opera and the etiquette imposed by the Court, he often dreamed of a small town where life would be simpler, less conventional.[258]

The best moments in Mahler's life in Vienna always occurred after a performance or a concert when he relaxed with his friends at the Spatenbräu Restaurant in the Philipphof on the Lobkowitzplatz or at Leidinger's in the Kärntnerstrasse.[259] Often when he was pleased with a performance, he was full of good humour and would joke about incidents that had taken place during the evening. Yet when he spoke of music, he was always serious, even if he expressed his opinions in paradoxical and intransigent ways. On this subject, Hermann Behn, his old Hamburg friend, made some interesting remarks:

For those whose affection and understanding were beyond any doubt, he was immediately accessible, and a deep look into his childishly gullible eyes sufficed to obliterate the impression of harshness and recalcitrance [he sometimes gave]. His restless, desultory tendencies in conversation were easily curbed, simply by bringing up a subject close to his heart. Real and apparent paradox came naturally to him, and he enjoyed contradicting in the second sentence what he had affirmed in the first. The first words I heard from his mouth were: 'So you too have sold yourself to the devil?'— referring to music, the goddess of his soul, and before whose throne all his activity was but one single prayer.[260]

During Mahler's mature—Viennese—years crises of depression and melancholy such as he had known earlier in life, were practically a thing of the past. At the same time, philosophical questions about the origin and purpose of man continued to haunt him: 'Locked within himself as in a prison, unable to understand and accept human pain, cruelty, and malice, he could only forget his relentless questionings by means of the most intense activity', wrote Bruno Walter.[261] Mahler justified his notorious changes of mood, so unsettling for those who knew him and so striking in his music, by claiming that they were an integral part of his creativity: 'Believe me, all artistic creation is intimately bound up with irritability!'[262] Natalie had been astounded by his sudden changes, 'leaping abruptly from the most passionate "pro" to the most vehement "contre", and capable of overwhelming you with the partiality of his love and the injustice of his hate.' Since then, his temper had grown calmer, as Schoenberg later noted:

---

[258] As an example of Mahler's 'hysteria', Hans Gregor, Weingartner's successor at the Hofoper, cites Mahler's desire to be Kapellmeister in Schwerin. He then remarks upon the irony of fate that would ultimately take him to New York. (Hans Gregor, 'Erinnerungen an Mahler', *Die Zeit* (Vienna, 19 May 1911)).

[259] BMG 176 ff. Karpath recalls that Mahler continued to frequent this restaurant, owned by a certain Franz Hartmann, after it moved to the Kärntnerring. During the period when discreet moves were being made to ensure his appointment at the Hofoper, he frequented the same restaurant—then called the Kührer—in the company of Rosa Papier and Karpath.

[260] Hermann Behn, 'Gustav Mahler', *Die Musikwelt*, 8 (1928): no. 5.

[261] Bruno Walter, 'Mahlers Weg. Ein Erinnerungsblatt', *Der Merker*, 3 (1911): 5, 166 ff.

[262] NBL1, 35; NBL2, 50.

A man racked by passion who had gone through all the storms of life and 'was used to taking hard knocks from all sides', who had himself raised up and overthrown gods, at the climax of his life he possessed the composure, moderation, and perspective which is the result of a certain detachment. This enabled him always to grasp the essential in the works of the great.[263]

In his years of maturity, reading had remained an essential activity for Mahler whenever he could find time. He continued to seek aid and enrichment not only in philosophy, literature, and poetry but also in natural science. His interest in science was common knowledge in Vienna, and the physicist Ludwig Boltzmann, the author of the kinetic theory of gases, once wrote to him that it seemed to him literally 'monstrous' that two such men could live in the same city without ever having met.[264] Unfortunately, the scientist died shortly after writing this letter, and Mahler never did meet him.

Mahler's interest in physics was not new; already in his Hamburg years it had been one of the main subjects in his discussions with his engineer-friend, Arnold Berliner. Berliner spoke admiringly to Bruno Walter of the intuitive understanding Mahler brought to recent theories of physics, and the logical acuteness of his conclusions as well as the arguments he brought against them. Scientific conceptions of matter and electro-magnetism had undergone a major crisis since 1903, which was soon to be defused by the astonishing discoveries of the quantum theory and the theory of relativity. Einstein published his basic research on these two theories in 1905, but it seems unlikely that Mahler could have become aware of it. Much later, Mahler's daughter, Anna, recalled only that his books included the complete works of another great turn-of-the-century physicist, Hermann von Helmholtz.[265]

But despite the apparent diversity of his interests, the desire to thrust deep never varied, as confirmed by Bruno Walter to whom he would confide his moods and his reactions to his current reading. During the final years of his life, he hoped to use the increased amount of free time he now enjoyed to read and reread his favourite authors.

In his essay on Mahler, Arnold Schoenberg writes:

Talent is the capacity to learn, genius the capacity to develop oneself. Talent grows by acquiring capacities which exist outside itself; it assimilates them, and finally possesses them. Genius already possesses all its future faculties from the very beginning. It only develops them; it simply unwinds, unrolls, unfolds them. While talent, which has to master precise and already existing material, very soon reaches its apex and then usually declines; the development of genius, which seeks new paths into the

---

[263] Arnold Schoenberg, 'Stil', 21.

[264] AMM1, 151; AMM2, 148. Ludwig Boltzmann (1844–1906) also proved the exactitude of Stefan's law on black body radiation. Hans Müller-Einigen ('Begegnung mit Gustav Mahler', *Weltpresse* (10 Nov. 1948)) also emphasizes Mahler's more-than-ordinary interest in natural science and history.

[265] Mahler alludes to Helmholtz in the aforementioned letter to Richard Horn (see above, Vol. ii, Chap. 15). On this whole area, see also Herta Blaukopf, 'Frankfurt, eine Fehldatierung und die Physik', *Nachrichten zur Mahler-Forschung*, 20 (1988), 3–6.

infinite, extends throughout a lifetime. And thus it happens that no one single moment in this development is like another. Each stage is simultaneously a preparation for the next stage. It is an eternal metamorphosis, an uninterrupted growth of new shoots from a single kernel. It then becomes clear why two widely separated points in this development are so strangely different from each other that at first one does not recognize how much they belong together. Only on closer study does one perceive in the potentialities of the earlier period the certainties of the later one.[266]

Thus Mahler's efforts, impulses, struggles, constantly changing concepts all seemed to be part of his search for the essential. In fact, this searching consolidated and broadened a personality which nothing could deflect from its goal. Schoenberg once said, more in earnest than in jest, to a student: 'You only had to see how Mahler knotted his tie in order to learn something from him about the meaning of art.'[267] A statement he repeated in his writings: 'I would rather have seen how Mahler knotted his tie, and would have found it more interesting and instructive than learning how one of our musical bigwigs (*Musikhofräte*) composes on a "sacred subject".'[268]

Summing up Mahler's life, career, and development, Max Brod used the simile of a 'mountain torrent slowly digging its bed, ignoring obstacles, and flowing straight towards its goal without letting itself be deviated'. Bruno Walter, who witnessed Mahler's development at close range, discusses both the meaning of the Sixth Symphony and his endless search for transcendence in the following terms:

It inexorably portrays a terrifying, hopeless darkness, without a human sound. They are, so to speak, cosmic sounds, the dark powers themselves ring out and no soul sings of the suffering it experiences through them. And the man who had drawn this fearful musical picture of a godless world began to seek God in books. He had lost Him in the world, which seemed to him ever more dark and mysterious. Where was God, whose gaze had erstwhile, at least occasionally, met his own, and once even gloriously. He sought Him in Spinoza, Plotinus, and other philosophers and mystics. From the philosophers he turned to the natural sciences, scoured works of biology to see whether He who had disappeared from the cosmos might not perhaps reappear in the cell.[269]

Roller too noticed the frequent recurrence of God, of faith, and divine love in Mahler's conversation during this period.

Ernst Bloch called Mahler, among other things, a 'hymnic man' and 'hymnic' is perhaps the best word to designate the primary colour (*Grundfarbe*) of his nature. He was deeply religious. His faith was that of a child. God is love and love is God. This

---

[266] Arnold Schoenberg, 'Stil', 22.

[267] Hans Heinz Stuckenschmidt, *Schönberg: Leben, Umwelt, Werk* (Atlantis, Zurich, 1974), 102.

[268] Arnold Schoenberg, 'Stil', 19.

[269] Bruno Walter, 'Mahlers Weg'. Among Mahler's reading at this time, Alma mentions Dehmel, Wolfram von Eschenbach's *Parsifal*, Gottfried von Strassburg's *Tristan*, Giordano Bruno, Galileo Galilei, Friedrich Albert Lange's *History of Materialism* (see below, Chap. 7). She adds that Erica Contrat-Tietze's husband once said to her: 'Alma, you have an abstraction for a husband, not a human being!' (AMM1, 152; AMM2, 148).

idea was forever cropping up in his conversation. I once asked him why he didn't write a mass. He seemed perplexed: 'Do you think I could? After all, why not? Yet no, I couldn't—because of the Credo.' He began to recite the Credo in Latin. 'No—that I couldn't do.'[270]

Yet his faith was perpetually shaken by the spectacle of pain, evil, the cruelty of man to man and animal to animal, and by illness: he could never reconcile these realities with divine omnipotence. As seen above, he confided to Bruno Walter after the psychological shock of his brush with death in 1901: 'I possessed certainty, but I have lost it; and tomorrow I will possess it and lose it the day after.'[271] He only achieved true serenity when he became aware of being one of the 'chosen' ones, in whom the Creator chose to dwell, and he could speak to him 'face to face', in other words, when he was in the process of creating. At those moments the feeling was so powerful, so profound, that he no longer felt the need to place intermediaries between himself and God. Roller and Schoenberg both emphasize the price he had to pay to get to this point. Both read the traces which this struggle and this spiritual maturing had left in his face. And yet Schoenberg also claims that his inner richness was too great for him ever to be 'unhappy' in the banal sense of the term, for everything he experienced was transformed into music. Fortunately, he rarely doubted his own genius and never stopped seeking new reasons to believe, to fight, and persevere.[272]

Ten years after Mahler's death, Richard Specht wrote the following description of Mahler:

We must in any case guard against the danger of putting him up on a pillar as a medieval saint or demon, forgetting that these works were not created by an apocalyptical, legendary being but by a passionate, hot-blooded man reaching greedily for the greatest things, prone to sudden bursts of excessive intellectuality, and hungry for love and companionship, and then suddenly overcome with feelings of disgust and once more desperately alone. He was one who did not wait for life to come to him but seized hold of it, inebriated himself with music, gorged himself with books, plundered the souls of men, only to throw them away, drunk with power or suddenly weary with disappointment; in all circumstances, he was paradox personified. For next to the Gustav Mahler who was roaring with life, shouting with ecstasy, and raging with enthusiasm or fury, there stood another: kind, animated by the purest ethos, silent, relentless with himself, of childlike devotion—a lofty example of an uncompromisingly pure life and artistic accomplishment. And then once again he could be capricious and unreliable, on his bad days, deeply wounding, offensive in uncontrolled irritability, and, like a wayward goblin, gloomy, erratic, jerky, chiding, mocking—until he himself grew ill and hurt from secret shame. Until eventually all these contradictions were resolved into a moving stillness, a resigned but never weakly mildness and maturity.[273]

---

[270] RBM 26.   [271] Bruno Walter, 'Mahlers Weg'.   [272] RSM2, 27 and 76.

[273] Richard Specht, 'Gustav Mahlers Gegenwart', *Moderne Welt*, 3 (1921–2): 7, 1.

In fact, none of Mahler's contemporaries could ever say that they knew him thoroughly, for he only revealed fragments of his personality to each of them. In the last analysis, he belonged more to his work of creating and re-creating than to men.

Mahler's naivety and simplicity rarely escaped his contemporaries. Even those who understood and loved him least, even those who had every reason to feel antagonistic, were aware of these qualities. For instance, Wilhelm Kienzl, the German nationalist and hence anti-Semitic composer from Graz who resented Mahler's manifest lack of interest in his work, acknowledged and respected his 'complex' nature and 'unbelievably refined and sensitive nervous system':

Basically, he was as kind and obliging as a child, but also often brutally insulting, even terroristic . . . Everyone, even the most inveterate anti-Semites, considered him a whole-hearted idealist. And they were absolutely right. He practised his art, in both its product-ive and reproductive aspects, with wholehearted love and devotion almost to the point of self-destruction. The tragedy of his creativity destroyed him. His feverish urge to compose left him always unsatisfied, for under a thousand tortures, he was conscious of his musical eclecticism, but still would not abandon his struggle for the highest, a condi-tion which produced works which, in spite of many unoriginal details in the melodic invention, when taken as a whole bore the stamp of a significant personality of Promethean greatness and were therefore bound to create deep impressions upon recep-tive spirits. But how can a Jew be an idealist it will be objected? Of course, Semites in general have a materialistic approach to life. But when for once, it does happen that a Semite is an idealist, then he far outstrips most Christians in the way he lets that deter-mine his life . . . Mahler almost always acted against his own personal interest and always for the—for him—sacred cause of art. And that merits the highest esteem, whether one considers his symphonies to be revelations of the highest art or musical monstrosities.[274]

What prejudices underlie this apparent attack on the racial prejudice of the time! And how many years would it take before people ceased to accuse Mahler of the eclecticism which they attributed to his Jewish origins? But despite his prejudices, Kienzl at least understood Mahler's naivety, one of the most fundamental aspects of his character. It was the source of his love for children, and the reason why he often sought refuge in the world of childhood, as Behn reports:

He could discuss a folksong or one of Grimm's fairy tales with the same seriousness and affection with which he could hold forth on Kant's theory of reason or Schopenhauer's theory of the will. Jean Paul appealed to his sentimental side while E. T. A. Hoffmann corresponded to his penchant for the bizarre. But since it is the naive which appeals to the calm understanding of artistic intuition, Mahler's greatest affection was for popular poems and stories: Grimm's Fairy Tales, Bechstein's Book of Fairy Tales and *Des Knaben Wunderhorn* were his favourite books. This went hand in

---

[274] Wilhelm Kienzl, *Meine Lebenswanderungen* (1926, 151). In a footnote, Kienzl added that Strauss composed for his time while Mahler composed against it.

hand with his great and pure love for nature, and the interactions between them were the principal source of his inspiration . . .

'I shan't let anyone deprive me of the right to sing, like a child, naturally, just as it comes', he once said to me. 'I want to make sure that simple Nature has her place in music.' With his naive delight in song, he felt close to Schubert.[275]

Although he dreamt of an ideal friend in whom he could confide, Mahler never found one. He spoke little of himself, and assessed his own value only in relation to music. For this reason, he sometimes failed to understand the amour-propre of those around him. He could be enthusiastic over the success of some enterprise or converse endlessly on the meaning of existence, but he knew nothing of the little satisfactions of the ego. Certain people, like the critic Gustav Schönaich, called him the 'eternal soliloquist' and accused him of being too absorbed by his own opinions to think about those of others. However, unlike many great men, he knew how to listen as well as talk. And, thanks to the power of his intellect, the depth of his emotions, his sureness of judgement and liveliness of expression, his monologues never turned into lectures. 'Everything is all right now! We have solved the seven riddles of the Universe!', he would often say at the end of an evening of intellectual exchange. Such conversations would always fascinate the people he was with. They all became 'richer in ideas', 'more brilliant', as many of his friends would relate, in particular one who was friendly with him during his last years in New York.

He stimulated others as few people have ever done. Yet there was nothing in him of that superiority which refuses to consider any opinion other than his own. When he was able to believe in the honesty and conviction of a counter-opinion, then he valued it much more than the rather woolly plaudits which had all too often made his life difficult. Sensitive to the highest degree, he had an almost pathological aversion to anything not genuine. Sententiousness caused him physical pain. At such times, he would look round seeking help from his intimate friends, and, wringing his hands, would make signs to them, which only too often however would also be understood by those whom they concerned. That is why Mahler was considered by many to be arrogant and temperamental.[276]

Nonetheless, Klaus Pringsheim asserts that the distance Mahler created between himself and others stemmed neither from the feeling of superiority of a highly-placed official nor from the sort of coldness which characterized Adrian Leverkühn, hero of Thomas Mann's *Doktor Faustus*. On the contrary, he never ceased to be interested in all that was human. Among other examples, Pringsheim relates how a few lines in a newspaper about a suicide once threw Mahler into deep consternation. He constantly returned to the subject several days running, wondering what reasons could have pushed the unhappy man to

[275] Hermann Behn, 'Mahler', in *Musikwelt*.
[276] Maurice Baumfeld, 'Erinnerungen an Gustav Mahler', *New Yorker Staats-Zeitung* (21 May 1911).

go, at nightfall, to his chosen spot, and wait hours for the train which would run him over. He urged Pringsheim to read Dostoevsky, and told him that 'the greatest psychologist in world literature' could teach him more on the subject than any technical treatise. For 'abstract theory did not interest him. For him, the most convincing argument was always a comparison.'[277]

On Mahler's culture, his kindness, and his Dostoevskian love of humanity, William Ritter had this to say:

I have never met a more perfect example of universal culture than Mahler. Hearing him speak we no longer wanted to read Suarès or Nietzsche, Plato or Aquinas. When he described something, we felt that his conception of the world was as poetic and beautiful as Maeterlinck's or d'Annunzio's. And seeing him with his friend Richard Strauss, several of us immediately felt that the greater of the two was not the more insolent one. Anyone who did not know Mahler cannot imagine the extent of his goodness. Now when great knowledge leaves goodness and childlike candour intact, we are dealing with more than just an artist. The poet and the saint are not far off, nor are prophet and apostle if genius is added to the mixture. Mahler's art was not purposeless. His music sought to spread the word, to evangelize beyond all religions and cults. He loved mankind and he was perpetually thoughtful, preoccupied by human distress. [He was] of the race of Moses and Spinoza, both in his suffering and his genius.[278]

No one could approach Mahler without sensing his disquieting genius, ever ready to move into action, like a force of nature:

In this lean, taut, vibrating, quick-silver body, everything was life, movement, energy, and restlessness. His slight, ascetic figure seemed literally charged with nervous tensions striving to escape. He was an accumulator of unpredictable forces, filled with the fluid of enthusiasm which inevitably overflowed into all those who came within his sphere.[279]

Mahler himself was fully conscious of the force within him. Yet he hated obsequiousness and flattery, which he never considered appropriate, and often ill-treated his most faithful admirers. Nodnagel's dithyrambic articles often infuriated him as much as a brief, well-chosen word of praise could please him.

Loving mankind, Mahler sometimes forgot people. For this reason, as we have seen, his friendships were often intermittent. He could be as hard, as caustic, aggressive, icy as earlier he had been warm. Rarely insincere, he detested bourgeois convention, and his egocentricity meant that others had to adapt to his personality. He could cause offence without realizing it. As for instance, during a performance of *William Tell* when, after the first act, he

went backstage biting his lips. One of the singers who had just sung stood in his path, hoping for a word of encouragement from his director, but Mahler seemed to avoid him deliberately. Suddenly he turned around: 'Why do you force your voice so terribly? Sing the way you can, not the way you would like to!' The singer, thoroughly non-plussed at

---

[277] Klaus Pringsheim, 'Erinnerungen' in *Neue Zürcher Zeitung*.   [278] Ibid.

[279] William Ritter, 'Gustav Mahler', *Revue musicale de Lyon*, 3 (1911): 28, 857.

this unexpected outburst, first sought an excuse, found none, and finally said, faltering: 'Herr Direktor, when you have something like that to say to me, please do so after the performance, but not now, it's too depressing!' Mahler was simply struck dumb. That someone could take well-meaning advice as a personal insult was completely incomprehensible to him. 'All right,' replied Mahler brusquely, with a look of utter disgust, 'Get depressed!' He then turned around and left the stage.[280]

Sometimes Mahler's reflections were merely disconcerting. On one occasion, following a guest appearance by a singer from outside the Opera, Mahler happened to run across the singer who customarily sang the same role, in the corridors of the Opera. 'How did you find X yesterday?' he asked. 'Fine, Herr Direktor', was the answer. 'Excellent, wasn't it?' continued Mahler with a touch of impatience, 'The voice, the rhythm?' 'Certainly, Herr Direktor,' replied the singer, 'Absolutely magnificent!' 'What?' exploded Mahler, 'Magnificent? From very first note I was appalled!' And with a satisfied laugh he turned on his heel and walked away.[281]

Mahler was often amusingly naive about the offence his behaviour might have given. Richard Specht recounts an illuminating incident concerning Richard Wallaschek, the critic of the socialist newspaper *Die Zeit*,[282] who grew increasingly hostile towards Mahler during his last years at the Opera. Discussing Wallaschek's antagonism to him, Mahler

suddenly said thoughtfully: 'Could I perhaps have insulted him? As a matter of fact, two years ago someone from the Arbeiterverband (Workers' Association), whom I always supplied with Opera tickets came to request 60 tickets for *La traviata*. Naturally, I got angry and said that *Fidelio* or *Die Meistersinger* were better choices for workers than the trashy tale of a cocotte. The confused fellow stammered: "But Dr X [Wallaschek],[283] our musical director, specifically suggested *La traviata*." I yelled back: "Then tell that ass to keep his nose out of things!" Do you think that he could have taken it all that badly?' For a moment Frau Alma and I remained speechless. Then, as we burst out laughing, Mahler shaking his head said in a plaintive tone: 'If he is that petty, it was disgusting of the other man to tell him what I said!'[284]

Yet, as seen above, he could often be extremely tactful, especially when the interests of the Opera were at stake. With his enemies he was generally more than courteous. The cellist Theobald Kretschmann, the musician in the orchestra who perhaps hated him most, tells how upon his retirement, he went to say goodbye to Mahler. Mahler, shaking hands with him, expressed the hope that the clouds between them would dissipate, and that Kretschmann would not hesitate to solicit his help in any matter. His cordiality was such that Kretschmann concluded that Mahler had perhaps been criticized unjustly, and

[280] Gerhard Stehmann, *Gustav Mahlers Proben*, *Moderne Welt*, 3 (1921–2): 7, 18.
[281] Ibid.
[282] See above, Vol. ii, Chap. 14, for the biography of this critic.
[283] Wallaschek is not referred to by name in RSM2 but Specht mentions elsewhere that it was he.
[284] RSM2, 27, note.

had after all been nothing more than 'a willing tool in the hands of those who sought to strengthen his position by claiming him to be the sole saviour of Viennese art. They only did him harm!'[285] But Kretschmann also relates that when they ran into each other on the street in Munich in 1910, Mahler turned on his heel and ran off as if stung by a wasp. But Richard Specht claims that Mahler never held a grudge and completely forgot any hurt done to him.[286] On the other hand, the enmities he had provoked during his years of tenure as director of the Opera finally began to weigh heavily upon him, and made him feel tired, sad, even bitter. As we have seen, as early as 1898 he had begun to suffer from a veritable persecution complex.[287] This intensified during the final years of his life, as did his feelings of guilt towards those he had involuntarily hurt in the exercise of his functions. Remorse pursued him 'like a procession of ghosts'.[288] Specht emphasizes the feelings of disgust and sadness which his own violence and paradoxical behaviour finally created in him, even when, and perhaps particularly when, his opponents had finally given in to him.

Mahler's attitude towards criticism, no matter how violent and hostile, was complex. Irritation, boredom, irony, exasperation, and resignation all played a part. Those who knew him claim that he usually read every review of performances of his own works and those at the Opera. He showed a certain respect for the written word, whether or not in his favour, but had nothing but contempt for gossip. 'It is not the Vienna music critics that frighten me,' he once said, 'but the Vienna theatre reporters.'[289] These, indeed, were the mischief makers who poisoned the atmosphere and made scandals out of the slightest disputes. Many were those who, the day after a première, watched Mahler poring over a stack of newspapers at the Café Imperial.[290] 'The funny thing was that he automatically rejected every criticism made, and tried to explain to his friends why it was unjust. He could admit a thousand other shortcomings in the performance, but never the one with which he was reproached.'[291]

On one occasion, however, Richard Specht saw Mahler wounded to the quick. After the performance of one of his symphonies, a Berlin critic had written: 'The director of the Vienna Opera is a swindler.'[292]

I cannot forget Mahler's total bewilderment, and the pained incredulity with which he repeated this crude and excessively critical utterance . . . He refused to be calmed, not even when the insignificance and unimportance of the perpetrator of the enormity was pointed out to him. He put his head in his hands and repeated incessantly: 'I, a swindler? What have I done to deserve an insult for which the humblest citizen would obtain satisfaction in the courts? What made this man utter such a monstrosity; how could he have had the nerve? If he called me a bungler (*Stümper*) I would have to

[285] Theobald Kretschmann, *Tempi passati*, ii. 161. [286] RSM2, 82.
[287] See above, Vol. ii, Chap. 4. [288] RSM2, 27. [289] GWO 92.
[290] GWO 79 and 80.
[291] *Berliner Börsencourier* (21 May 1911).
[292] Mahler was not the only one to suffer this insult. Strauss's critics, it will be remembered, labelled *Salome* a 'Schwindeloper'.

accept it! But a swindler! I, a swindler!' He was as white as a sheet as he spat all this out, the insult rankled so much. Oskar Fried can bear witness to the bewildered bitterness of Mahler's first reaction to this insult.[293]

Mahler's stubbornness and his impatience when contradicted have also been the subject of much comment. Only the most solid arguments could convince him that he had been mistaken about something. But once convinced, Specht recalls, it was 'as if he had come out of a fog into purer, fresher air'. But when he lost his temper he would often say things he really did not mean. He would fiercely defend his heroes and idols, not permitting the slightest criticism of them. Even Wagner, whose personality was less than exemplary, as Mahler well knew but would not admit, was excused and pardoned because he was a man of genius totally devoted to his creative work.[294]

Mahler irritated or wounded many of his acquaintances by his vehemence. Others, like Schoenberg (himself renowned for his outrageous and paradoxical statements), were struck by the respect he showed at all times for those he considered great. Schoenberg's comment on this is worth quoting.

This lesson [Mahler's insistence on his respect for Wagner] was subsequently of great importance for me, for I realized that only people capable of showing respect are those who themselves merit respect. And the converse is also true: someone who cannot pay respect is himself not worthy of respect. And this is particular important today when ambitious people try to demolish the reputation of someone greater than they are in order to appear greater themselves.[295]

If Mahler was often unfair towards Brahms or Bruckner, his injustice stopped short when conducting their works. In human relationships he was much more attentive than people thought, and therefore more aware of the qualities of his interlocutors. His first question about people he did not know was generally: 'Is he a serious man?'[296] He manifested a touching, almost comic naivety towards those who liked his music, as the joke Schmedes was able to play on him in Graz shows.[297] Richard Specht relates that when Mahler was told that the writer Arthur Schnitzler had been quite overwhelmed by the Finale of the Sixth Symphony, he exclaimed: 'This Schnitzler must really be a splendid fellow.'[298] His pride as a composer made it impossible for him to consider as inferior anyone who liked and understood his music. One of the best ways to make his acquaintance continued to be to walk in front of him in the street whistling a theme from one of his works: Mahler never failed to fall

[293] Richard Specht, 'Mahler und die Kritik der Gegenwart', *Musikwelt*, Hamburg, 1 (1921): 8. Three different Berlin performances could have provided the occasion for this critical attack: the Second Symphony, conducted by Fried in Mahler's presence in Nov. 1905 (but the critics proved moderate on the whole); the Sixth, conducted by Fried on 8 Oct., or the Third, conducted by Mahler himself on 14 Jan. 1907.

[294] BWM 12. The young Mahler's interest in Wagner the man is shown by a brief biographical text relating to Wagner's stay in Magdeburg and the composition of *Liebesverbot*. The manuscript probably belonged to the impresario Norbert Salter (like Mahler's letters to Salter, it bears a number and the mention BSM, Munich).   [295] Arnold Schoenberg, 'Stil', 21.   [296] EDS2, 152.

[297] See above, Chap. 4.   [298] RSM2, 25.

into the trap. Yet at the same time Mahler detested obsequious behaviour and servile admiration: his fury with the tenor Franz Pacal, who ordered his son to kiss Mahler's hand in public, has often been recalled. But while himself displaying perfectly natural, instinctive modesty in public, he mistrusted certain forms of modesty. For instance, to someone who once recommended a young musician to him, adding that the person in question was 'a very modest beginner', Mahler replied suspiciously: 'What has he got to be modest about?' According to his interlocutor, Mahler 'considered modesty a quality to be displayed only by perfect professionals'.[299]

At the opera or elsewhere, Mahler never forgot services rendered to him and always showed his gratitude even if he did not express it in so many words. Moreover, the spectacle of misfortune remained intolerable for him.[300] He often insisted on bonuses or salary increases for those who worked with him at the Opera.[301] His constant concern was to free artists from all material worries so that they could concentrate on their work.

Mahler's sensitivity to the pain of others led him far beyond conventional expressions of sympathy, as is shown by the following letter to the bass Wilhelm Hesch, whose wife had just died:

My poor, dear Hesch, I can't find words to express my sympathy. We are all stunned. No words of consolation can help in such an affliction; at least I don't know of any. I only know one thing that might help you in this great trial: the knowledge that a friend's sympathy is genuine and heartfelt. And you know, my dear Hesch, that in me you have a friend who feels for you like a brother! How I wish I were at your side to help you ... I am asking myself all sorts of questions. How are the children, and how are you going to manage everything? And above all, how are you yourself? My dear friend, this affliction is a great trial from God and you will overcome it—for you are a man and an artist! ... Promise me, my dear Hesch, that you will be sensible—if not for God's sake, then for the sake of your children and friends. If only I were with you. Where will you go? Who is going to look after you? Write to me often please, and tell me everything that is happening ...[302]

These lines go well beyond conventional expressions of sympathy and show how deeply Mahler was touched by other people's misfortunes.

His concern for others sometimes took a disconcerting form. Emil Freund knew Mahler as a fellow-student in Vienna. He recalled an occasion when Mahler had been confined to his bed with a throat infection, and his roommate had looked after him, Mahler thanked him by saying, 'After all you've done for me, I can only hope that you will soon be ill, so that I can get my own back.'[303]

---

[299] EDS2, 146.

[300] Specht wrote that the spectacle of a starving unemployed man could reduce Mahler to tears. Lesser misfortunes of others could also move him to action. Specht relates that Mahler once decided to put on *Der Freischutz* 'because a student had written to him to complain that he had never seen it performed'.

[301] BMG 142. His intervention on behalf of several singers, including Schmedes, to obtain for them the title of *Kammersänger*, was made with such discretion that the artists in question never knew about it.

[302] MBR1, no. 239; MBR2, no. 262.

[303] Told by Emil Freund to Dr Kronfeld (see above).

The following, hand-written testimony, sent from Vienna to a musician at the Hamburg Opera, provides another example of his readiness to come to help of an old acquaintance:

Herr Otto Guth, whose bad luck it has been at a certain moment of his life to forget the moral code, remains in my memory not only as an excellent musician and dutiful member of my Hamburg Orchestra, but I have also become convinced in my personal dealings with him that he deserves the kindness of not being refused access to society and to life. I gave proof of my conviction at the time by keeping his position open for him in my orchestra at the Hamburg Stadttheater until he had finished his sentence and then reinstating him. With a good conscience, I hereby join my request to his, hoping that the esteemed authorities make it possible for him to earn his living again by allowing him to reside in the place where he is presently working. He is, let me repeat, in the highest degree worthy of such an act of kindness.[304]

Mahler's sensitivity to written insult, especially when it was a question of his compositions, has already been discussed. Modesty and pride entered into his attitude in equal parts. It was a remarkably balanced, indeed admirable attitude since few composers have been so little understood and appreciated in their lifetime. Yet he never, or almost never, fell prey to professional jealousy. The success of others did not affect him as long as it was merited. At most, he occasionally expressed indignation at the triumph of unworthy artists, quoting Schiller: 'I saw the sacred crown of fame profaned upon a lowly brow (*Ich sah des Ruhmes heil'ge Kränze auf der gemeinen Stirn entweiht*).'[305]

From 1902 onwards, when he was beginning to be taken seriously as a composer and his works were being played throughout Europe, he started to have grave doubts about the nature of his 'success'. Since he had decided to conduct the first performances of his works himself and was well aware of the magnetism of his presence at the podium, he always wondered whom the applause was intended for—the composer, the conductor, or the Director of the Vienna Opera.[306] Already in 1900, after signing the contract with Weinberger for the publication of the *Lieder eines fahrenden Gesellen*, he took the publisher's arm, looked him in the eye and asked him, smiling: 'On your honour! would you be publishing these Lieder if I weren't Director of the Hofoper?'[307]

In order not to take advantage of his position, Mahler consistently refused to conduct the world première of his works in Vienna, with the exception of his *Rückert-Lieder* in 1905. Natalie's chronicle and many other contemporary descriptions reveal the pride and self-confidence, arrogance almost, that went along with this humility. In his *Legende einer Musikstadt* Max Graf relates that he asked Mahler why, apart from his Lieder, he only composed symphonies.

---

[304] HOA, Z. 530/1897. Undated draft of a letter which was no doubt later copied by a secretary and sent to the local authorities. [305] BWM 100. [306] RSM2, (2nd edn.), 135.

[307] Siegfried Loewy, *Deutsche Theaterkunst von Goethe bis Reinhardt* (Paul Knepler, Vienna, undated (1923)).

Mahler replied: 'Every year, I have only two months of summer vacation in which I can compose. I must write great works if I want to be known to posterity.'[308] Graf then goes on to attribute a statement to Mahler which it is hard to imagine his ever having made: 'In thirty or forty years, Beethoven's symphonies will no longer be played in concerts. My symphonies will take their place.'[309] Mahler's respect and admiration for Beethoven is of course beyond question and, since Graf despised Mahler's music[310] he can easily be suspected of having voluntarily exaggerated or distorted his words. It is also significant that, in another book written after the Second World War, the same Graf quotes Mahler as saying something rather different: 'In thirty or forty years, my symphonies will be played at concerts as often as Beethoven's are played today.'[311] Mahler seems to have been in a very special mood during this interview with Max Graf, for he also spoke about his work at the Vienna Opera in the following terms: 'Believe me, people only know what I am after I have left. Then it is as though a simoom had blown through the theatre.'[312]

Lilli Lehmann reports another comment which seems more likely to be true. Struck by the contrast between the simplicity of the melodies and the complexity of orchestration in Mahler's work, it occurred to her that he might be the very man to guide the orchestra back to simpler ways as well. She put the question to him. He replied, with a scornful laugh: 'What can you be thinking of? In a hundred years my symphonies will be performed in gigantic halls seating 20,000–30,000 people, and will become great popular music festivals.'[313]

He detested applause, for 'politeness demands that the audience be thanked, which can only be done through bowing and making a display of oneself'. In that respect, his timidity was 'like a young girl's'. Taking bows, in his opinion, was for actors, singers, and virtuosos, but not for conductors or composers, and he consistently avoided appearing on stage during his tenure at the Vienna Opera. Outbursts of enthusiasm by the audience made him uneasy and even irritated him: 'I envy Renard and Kurz their lack of embarrassment when people stare at them through opera glasses', he remarked during an interview in 1906. 'I can't bear it. Of course I am not as pretty as the ladies!'[314]

Thus he often cut short applause or kept his arms raised between symphony

---

[308] Max Graf, 'Erlebnisse mit Gustav Mahler', *Neues Wiener Journal*, 1 and 2, 19, and 26 June 1921 and also GWO 83. If ever Mahler did, in fact, make this astonishing claim, it must have been before 1902, when Mahler's relationship with Graf finally came to an end (see above, Vol. ii, Chap. 13).

[309] LEM 320. As we well know, Mahler often expressed himself in paradoxes which could become outrageous if his relations with the interlocutor in question were strained. This was true in the case of Graf who, in 1902, made a point of telling Mahler of the poor opinion he had of the Fourth Symphony (see above, Vol. ii, Chap. 13).

[310] See below, Chap. 10, the article Graf wrote immediately after Mahler's departure for America.

[311] LEM 320.   [312] GWO 83.

[313] Lilli Lehmann, *Mein Weg*, 369. Emil Freund relates that when, one day, he advised Mahler to take out life insurance to protect his family, he replied: 'My family is taken care of by my works (*Meine Familie ist versorgt—durch meine Werke*)', further evidence of his confidence in the ultimate success of his works.

[314] *Fremden-Blatt* (6 Jan. 1907), 15.

movements or opera scenes.[315] For the same reason he was always very reluctant to agree to allow the public to be present at final rehearsals. Once, when conducting the Third in a city in Southern Germany, Mahler learned at the last minute that seats had been sold for the final rehearsal though he was not yet satisfied with the quality of the performance. Only the fact that the sale benefited the musicians' pension fund kept him from demanding the reimbursement of these tickets.[316] The audience clapped between the movements but observed a respectful silence while he spoke to the musicians. What in fact Mahler was saying to the orchestra was: 'It seems that our honoured audience wants a theatrical performance for the pittance they paid for their tickets. I am supposed to perform as a conductor-lecturer! But that is a service I am not prepared to render!' He then conducted right to the end and waited for the audience to leave before going over the passages in question with the orchestra.[317]

Mahler also hated to receive congratulations from his friends in the dressing room and generally requested them not to come.[318] He assiduously avoided autograph hunters and on one occasion spoke harshly to a young girl who asked for his autograph in the wings of the Musikvereinsaal: 'You're young enough to learn not to do this!'[319] But when he realized that he had frightened the child, he relaxed into a friendly smile and duly scribbled his name. But he never got used to his own celebrity, and continued to snap at people who gaped at him in the street with remarks like: 'Am I a wild animal that people stop and gape at me as if I were in a zoo?'[320]

Firmly convinced of the quality of his own works, Mahler saw no reason to be jealous of his fellow-composers, and could be ungrudging in his praise on occasion. He never doubted for one moment that posterity would one day do him justice and make up for all the injustices he had suffered at the hands of his contemporaries. If he sought also a measure of recognition by the public of his time it was only because he believed that without such encouragement 'the artist cannot complete his work and is doomed to disappear'. He constantly struggled to win the public's understanding. But he knew that true success and recognition would only come to his works after his death. That is one of the reasons why he finally decided never to be in a hurry to have his works heard for the first time.

[315] *Fremden-Blatt* (6 Jan. 1907), 15.
[316] Ibid. The performance in question probably took place in Dec. 1906 in Graz (see below, Chap. 7).
[317] Ibid.
[318] See above, Mahler's letter to Henriette Mankiewicz.
[319] Maria Komorn, 'Gustav Mahler und die Jugend', *Neues Wiener Journal* (31 Aug. 1930).
[320] Ibid. She often tipped the porter at the Auenbruggergasse in the hope of obtaining information about Mahler's life, as well as more autographs.

7

Mahler in Vienna (XXIII)—Caruso in Vienna—
*Le Juif polonais—The Barber of Seville—The Taming
of the Shrew*—The Sixth in Berlin, Munich, and
Vienna—The Third in Breslau and Graz

(September 1906–January 1907)

> My 6th seems to be another hard nut which the critics will be unable to
> get their puny teeth into.

THERE is a passage in Alma's *Erinnerungen* which describes a quite
unusual event in Mahler's life:

One evening, Mahler and I attended a performance of *The Merry Widow*, and enjoyed
it very much. Afterwards, at home, we danced and so to speak reconstructed Lehár's
waltzes from memory. Then something funny happened. We couldn't remember how
the tune went at one particular point, try how we might. In those days we were both too
snobbish to consider buying a copy of the waltz. So the two of us went to Doblinger's
music shop. Mahler engaged the manager in a discussion about the sale of his works,
while I leafed apparently aimlessly through the numerous piano selections and potpourris of *The Merry Widow* until I came to the waltz and the bars I was looking for. I
then went up to Mahler, he quickly took his leave, and once we were out in the street
I sang him the passage so as not to forget it again.[1]

Mahler at an operetta? Mahler humming a waltz? Such an incident in the
life of this 'martyr to music' is exceptional enough to prompt us to take a closer
look at the remarkable operetta which opened in Vienna on 30 December 1905
at the Theater an der Wien. Franz Lehár was not unknown to Mahler. Born in
the town of Komaron in Hungary in 1870, military bandmaster of the 3rd
Imperial and Royal Regiment of Budapest, he composed his first opera,

---

[1] AMM1, 152; AMM2, 148. On 3 Oct. 1906, the *Neue Freie Presse* announced that Mahler had
commissioned a full-length ballet from Lehár for the 1906–7 season.

Kukuschka, at the age of 26. This feat was unusual enough to attract the Emperor's personal attention and, two years later, in 1898, to persuade the director of the Budapest Opera to stage the work. But the ambitious young military bandmaster dreamed of seeing his work performed in Vienna, and sent the following telegram to Mahler: 'Urgently request Your Honour's presence at the performance of my opera, which I shall conduct myself. In Your Honour's hand lies the fate of my work, whose future Your Honour alone will decide. Franz Lehár.'[2]

Shortly thereafter Lehár, who had meanwhile taken up residence in Vienna, had occasion to board the train to Baden. He was dressed in full regimental bandmaster's uniform. Here is his description of what happened next:

Just when the train was about to start I got into a carriage in which a gentleman was sitting deeply engrossed in his newspaper. Hardly had I sat down opposite him when the train left the station and the gentleman reluctantly lowered his newspaper. Perhaps he had just finished reading the theatre news . . . Through sharp spectacle lenses the eyes of Gustav Mahler, Direktor of the Hofoper, were staring searchingly at me. For months I had been waiting daily, hourly, for a decision about my *Kukuschka*. Attempts to speak to him personally had failed. My telegram frantically beseeching him to come to the performance of the opera in Budapest had remained unanswered. And now suddenly I was sitting opposite the man who held my fate in his hands. A piece of luck that would never happen a second time!

That was one way of looking at it . . . On the other hand people told me the most hair-raising stories about Mahler. He was always on the defensive against his numerous enemies, flew off the handle at the slightest excuse, was a fanatic. Just recently a military band had marched past the Opera building playing a brisk March containing snatches from the *Nibelungen*. It was alleged that Mahler had flown into a rage at this blasphemy against Wagner, and had sworn never to allow a military bandmaster to set foot in the Opera. And at that moment there I was—in uniform! The golden lyre on my collar must have told him that a military bandsman was sitting opposite him. The penetrating look to which he subjected me went on and on, and was—or so it seemed—mocking, hostile, challenging. I thought: should I introduce myself, and make a few harmless remarks about this and that? I knew only too well what would happen. Since I was still full of ardent desire to see my opera performed in Vienna, I wouldn't have gone beyond a couple of sentences before mentioning my opera. Or should I tackle him head on and ask him what the verdict was going to be? What if he gave me one of those well-known sarcastic replies of his that his enemies—probably exaggerating—were always quoting? And at that time I did not have the self-control I have today.—So I was wavering between making an approach and keeping quiet, and Mahler would not have been the shrewd judge of people that he undoubtedly was if he had not sensed what a struggle the modest military bandmaster sitting opposite him was having with himself. His hard, mistrustful features began to soften somewhat. I had finally decided to introduce myself at least, and leave what happened next to my musician's lucky star. I was just beginning to say: 'Please allow me . . .' when there was a screeching of

2 Franz Lehár, 'Mein interessantestes Reiseabenteuer', unpublished manuscript written in 1930, quoted in Otto Schneiderheit, *Franz Lehár: Eine Biographie in Zitaten* (Lied der Zeit, Berlin, 1984), 51 ff.

brakes. Baden! I sprang to my feet, saluted as if in a dream, and stumbled confusedly into the corridor—without having spoken to Mahler. Missed opportunity, I thought afterwards, reproaching myself, for my opera was never accepted. Mahler probably gave my score, among a hundred others, no more than a fleeting glance.

Today I am glad that I didn't speak to him. What would he have found to say to me, an unknown military bandmaster? A few commonplace remarks such as one always keeps ready for awkward questioners? Or at best a few embarrassed phrases if I had said something about my opera? Either would have robbed this chance meeting of its charm, and destroyed the picture of the inspired thoroughbred musician which I have kept of him to the present day.[3]

In fact, Mahler must have remembered *Kukuschka* very clearly indeed. At the Imperial Café a few days after he had received Lehár's telegram, he had spotted the critic Ludwig Karpath, who he knew was of Hungarian origin, and asked him if he had heard of the young composer who had sent him his score. He had read the libretto, and 'if the music is as good as the libretto I shall put the Opera on'. But the score did not impress him, and Karpath, who had promised the Lehár family he would use his influence with Mahler, was unable to persuade him to stage the work.[4]

Finally *Kukuschka*, retitled *Tatjana* and revised by Max Kalbeck, one of the best specialists in this field, was produced at the Volksoper. In the meantime Lehár had composed for one of Princess Metternich-Sandor's charity balls a waltz, *Gold und Silber*, which became immensely popular throughout Europe. A long series of operetta's followed: *Fräulein Lieutenant*, *Arabella*, *Die Kubanerin*, *Das Club Baby* (1901); *Wiener Frauen*, *Der Rastelbinder* (The Travelling Tinker) (1902); *Der Göttergatte* (The Husband of the Gods), *Die Juxheirat* (The Spoof Marriage) (1904). They were all performed in Vienna at the Volkstheater, the Carlstheater, or the Theater an der Wien and were all well received. Offenbach's influence was revealed in the frequent irreverent allusions to classical antiquity (in *Der Göttergatte*, for example), but the music was unmistakably Slav in flavour and gave full rein to Lehár's inexhaustible melodic imagination. From *Das Club Baby* onwards Lehár had a collaborator in Victor Léon, Vienna's most celebrated operetta librettist and author of the libretto of *Wiener Blut*, a medley of tunes taken from Johann Strauss's music and put together after his death. Unfortunately, the operetta as a genre was then in full decline: 'About 1904, self-respecting music lovers no longer frequented operetta theatres which were left to women and their hangers-on.'[5]

A year later, however, on 30 December 1905, came the revelation. Not immediately, for during its first three months at the Theater an der Wien, *The Merry Widow* ran at a loss. But as soon as it transferred to the Raimund Theater, it became a sell-out. As Stefan Czech, Lehár's biographer, rightly points out:

[3] Ibid.   [4] BMG 352.
[5] Stefan Czech, *Schön ist der Welt: Franz Lehars Leben und Werk* (Argon, Berlin, 1957), 126.

The Merry Widow was much more than a stage success—it was a revolution; with it, a new type of operetta was born. The genre acquired that same naturalistic and artistic charm which Richard Strauss had given to opera. In the libretto already, the romantic puppets of yester-year were swept away, people of flesh and blood appeared, and the music expressed their inner qualities. . . . Above all, it was a revolution in musical inspiration: not music interpreting and accompanying, but music standing on its own two feet. As in Puccini a glittering tremolo tissue hovers over the melodic invention. The harmonic fabric, with its rich nuances, has impressionistic luminosity. The music develops out of itself, without any 'action' since nobody could or would want to keep it to himself. Even to the unmusical, it gives the feeling of melody. . . . The music had lightness and clarity, and at the same time provided a series of numbing little electric shocks. It was healthy with a touch of languor! *Die Fledermaus* 1906 . . . The music keeps renewing itself dramatically from the action. Unbelievable electricity crackles around every situation. Even the misunderstandings which follow in close succession are not the usual operetta devices, but arise naturally out of the characters. That is why their expression in song and orchestra sounds so right.[6]

Alma's story quoted earlier gains credibility from an article published in the Vienna *Volkszeitung* in 1924 by Julius Stern. According to him, Mahler seriously considered commissioning Lehár to write a ballet for the Hofoper because 'the present-day operetta and the dance are so intimately related to each other'. He thought that Lehár would also make opera more attractive, especially if he offered more refined music and original rhythm.[7] But Lehár had by then become such a successful composer that the Opera's ballet master, Josef Hassreiter pointed out the realities of the situation to Mahler:

Lehár would be foolish to let the good ideas which came to him for the Finale of an operetta be used for a ballet at the Hofoper. How many performances a year could he hope for at the Hofoper? At the most a couple. His royalties would be absurdly small, whereas an operetta with hundreds of performances on stages all over the world would earn him millions! Did they expect Lehár to give up good money for the sake of prestige?[8]

Lehár's technical ability and general culture were much superior to those of his contemporary rivals. Bernard Grün, another of his biographers, emphasizes the subtle mixture of Slav and Viennese influences to be found in him, and his use of modern instrumental colours similar to those of Strauss, Mahler, and Debussy, with divided violins, low-pitched wind instruments, and rhythmic and contrapuntal refinements all hitherto unknown in operetta.[9]

---

[6] *Schön ist der Welt*, 121 and 126. See also Bernard Grün, *Gold und Silber: Franz Lehár und seine Welt* (Langen-Müller, Vienna, 1970).   [7] Schneiderheit, *Lehár*, 53

[8] Ibid.

[9] None of Lehár's subsequent operettas (including *Ein Herbstmanöver* (An Autumn Manœuvre), *Graf von Luxemburg*, *Die Gelbe Jacke* (1909), *Zigeunerliebe* (1911), *Eva* (1911), *Frasquita* (1922)) ever attained the international popularity of *The Merry Widow*, nor did his opera *Giuditta* (1934). Only *Das Land des Lächelns* (1929) was a success of comparable magnitude. On 11 Jan. 1907, *The Merry Widow*, back again at the Theater an der Wien, celebrated its 300th performance, and on 24 Apr. its 400th. In the meantime its fame was beginning to spread world-wide.

Although Wilhelm Kienzl mentions hearing Mahler play waltzes on the piano,[10] his taste for light music was obviously rarely indulged and indeed played as small a part in his life as the social occasions with which it was associated. The only moment of the day when Mahler lived like a true Viennese was when he went to the café of the Hotel Imperial, a hundred yards from the Opera on the other side of the Kärntnerring. The Imperial, with its gold-framed mirrors, and elegant interior decoration, was rather like the Café Florian in Venice. Unlike the Griensteidl, it was not a predominantly 'literary' café. Intellectuals could be found there, but so could financiers, journalists, musicians, and diplomats, scientists, and even elegant idlers, particularly horse-racing enthusiasts. Frau Katharina Schratt, the Emperor's official mistress, went there from time to time, attracting those who sought to present their case discreetly to Franz Joseph. Among critics Gustav Schönaich frequented the Imperial until his death, as did Robert Hirschfeld, Bruckner's pupil Friedrich Eckstein, the tenor Fritz Schrödter, the conductor Franz Schalk, the pianist Moriz Rosenthal, and the socialist deputy and friend of Mahler, Viktor Adler. The critic Max Graf, another Imperial habitué, describes once seeing Mahler get up hurriedly from his table to listen to a military band passing by on the Ring.[11]

Others report seeing Mahler in the Seidel and Kremser cafés, but he only went there on special occasions. After an evening at the Opera, he almost always supped at the modest Spatenbräu restaurant in the Philipphof on the Lobkowitzplatz, or at Leidinger's in the Kärntnerstrasse.[12] His daily life as Director of the Opera had hardly changed since his arrival in Vienna. He invariably awoke at 7 a.m. and called for his coffee and newspapers. After dressing and a quick breakfast, he usually spent at least an hour at his desk. During the winter of 1905–6, he revised and copied the score of the Seventh Symphony during this moment of morning calm. 'Composition is my game of *Skat*,' he would sometimes say to Bruno Walter, alluding to Richard Strauss's favourite pastime.[13]

Just before 9 a.m., he would go and say good morning to Alma and the children, and then rush off to the Hofoper to look over his mail before his collaborators arrived. Alma tells us that in the evening after dinner, if he was not at the Opera, he would often lie back on the blue sofa in the living room while she read to him from such works as Dehmel's long poem, *Zwei Menschen*, Wolfram von Eschenbach's *Parsifal*, or Gottfried von Strassburg's *Tristan*. At that time she was attending a series of lectures at the University of Vienna on 'Pictures of Heaven and of the heavens' from Aristotle to Kant,[14] and went over her notes with Mahler in the evening.

---

[10] WKL 151.

[11] GWO 77.

[12] Zdenko von Kraft, *Wiens berühmte Zaungäste* (Stocker, Graz and Stuttgart, 1978), 177, and BMG 176. The proprietor of Leidinger's was Franz Hartmann.

[13] Bruno Walter, 'Erinnerungen an Gustav Mahler', *Neue Freie Presse* (16 Nov. 1935).

[14] In AMS, Alma notes that Professor Siegel's course was entitled 'Himmelsbild und Himmelsgewölbe' (Pictures of Heaven and the Heavenly from Aristotle to Kant).

he was touchingly sweet in his eagerness to explain everything I didn't understand, and in the process he often had to consult his philosophers. In this way we came upon Giordano Bruno[15] and Galileo.[16] I read aloud from 'The Triumphant Beast', 'The Ash Wednesday Banquet', Lange's 'History of Materialism',[17] etc. Tietze once said to me: 'Alma, you have an abstraction for a husband, not a human being!'[18] That was true.[19]

Then, as if to excuse herself, Alma adds: 'Yet I would not want to have missed a single day of my life at that time.'[20]

Another passage in Alma's memoirs reveals how some aspects of Mahler's music remained a closed book to her. Speaking of the way in which Mahler enjoyed turning beautiful melodies into 'diabolic grimaces' and of his 'mischievous pleasure in the caustic leaps of his imagination', she shows that she was quite unable to appreciate what might be termed the 'Hoffmannesque' side of his creative personality. Consequently, like the most reactionary critics of her era, she considered that the 'tunes' (*Weisen*) in the *Wunderhorn-Lieder* bore little relation to Mahler's real nature. 'He liked to draw my attention to those [caustic leap] passages which thrilled him with their originality. He called them "the Dolomites dancing with each other".' She found him much more 'authentic' in his 'uncanny scenes': 'In his strongest moments Gustav Mahler was prophetic, as were Beethoven, and Wagner, and indeed all musicians who have a message (*aussagende Musiker*).'[21]

Another remark from Alma's memoirs also shows how little she was able, sometimes, to understand his genius. She claims that Mahler had no musical imagination because he was 'unable to improvise two bars on the piano, something I had been capable of doing without the slightest effort since I was ten years old'.[22] Given Mahler's rigour and his dislike of the casual and the facile, his scorn for improvisation on the piano can well be imagined—even if tact forbade him to say so to his young, gifted, and vain wife, who was so proud of her instinctive musicality.

That summer Alma stayed in Maiernigg at least one week longer than her

---

[15] Giordano Bruno (1548–1600), Italian Neoplatonic philosopher, was born in Nola in the province of Naples, and burned at the stake in Rome, a victim of the Inquisition. Alma mentions both *The Expulsion of the Triumphant Beast* (*Spaccio de la bestia trionfante*), 1584, a mythological comedy, and *The Ash Wednesday Banquet* (*La Cena de le Ceneri*), 1595. Considered to be one of the first philosophers of doubt and a precursor of Descartes, Bruno's critique of Aristotelian physics and cosmology led him to a naturalist conception of the universe as 'universal unity'. 'All things in nature merge and are reborn in a vital impulse.' It is not difficult to understand Mahler's affinity for this form of thought, which was condemned as heresy by the church in the sixteenth century.

[16] The astronomer Galileo Galilei (1564–1642), born in Pisa, son of the composer Vincenzo Galilei, laid the foundations of modern astronomy and caused a veritable revolution in religious and scientific thought with his definition of the limits of science and faith *Letter to Christine de Lorraine*, 1636. His two principal works are the *Dialogue on the Chief World Systems* (*Dialogo dei Massimi Sistemi*), 1632 and *Dialogue on Two New Sciences* (*Discorsi e Dimostrazioni Matematiche intorno a due nuove scienze*), 1638. Condemned by the Roman Inquisition for having 'held and taught' the doctrine of Copernicus, he was forced to recant.   [17] See above, Vol. i, Chap. 7.

[18] Hans Tietze was an art historian and critic, and Erica Conrat's husband. His full name is quoted only in AMS.   [19] AMM1, 153; AMM2, 149.   [20] Ibid.
[21] AML 47.   [22] AML 259.

husband. Apart from the telegram and postcard he sent her before boarding the train in Klagenfurt, three letters and a card he sent from Vienna have survived, and a letter to Anna Moll. In the first letter he mentions that he had to make the trip in a sleeper, there being no 'free compartment' available, and he asks Alma to write immediately to Freiherr von Bahnhaus[23] to make sure that she and the family could travel in greater comfort. He also mentions that Emil Freund, his childhood friend and lawyer, had been waiting for him at the station in Vienna to discuss questions relating to Mahler's taxes. Alma once in her memoirs called Freund 'dumm und aufdringlich' (stupid and importunate). However, he was Mahler's lawyer and had told him on this occasion that the income he declared for taxes was insufficient because of the increased income he was receiving from concert tours and performances of his works. 'If I had not proposed an increase myself, I would have been in a terrible mess.'[24]

Mahler also informed Alma that the Conrat family had invited him to Dornbach, and he had been pleased to accept for the weather was superb. Frau Ida had already telephoned him, and he would go there as soon as he had locked up his manuscripts in the metal strongbox installed for the purpose in the Auenbruggergasse apartment. Another piece of news was that he had on his arrival found an article published in *Die Musik* concerning the success of his Fifth Symphony in Boston and a telegram from the Impresario Luise Wolff inviting him to conduct his Third Symphony in Berlin. Several days later he received another invitation from the St Petersburg impresario C. N. Schröder; however his programme for future trips outside Vienna was already fully booked and he had therefore been obliged to decline.[25] He also told Alma that Hans Kössler, the old friend from Budapest whom he 'used to be very fond of', was in Vienna and he was 'just the same as before. He seems gradually to forget his resentment.'[26]

Klaus Pringsheim, Mahler's new assistant at the Opera, later recalled his meetings with him during the last months of 1906:

One day when I came in [to his office] after the rehearsal, he was standing with his coat on. 'Come with me,' he said, 'I am going home.' He did not have a car waiting for him as he lived just a comfortable walking distance from the Opera. When we said good-bye in front of his house, he suggested that I fetch him again the next day at the same time. And the following day as well. And so it became a habit, and for me a daily event. He would talk about music, and I would walk beside him, an eager pupil open to all he said, yet I was also encouraged to ask questions. There was no question that he did not answer, no problem I raised which he did not discuss with me in detail. Quite often our walks would turn into unexpectedly long wanderings, and he sometimes would stop and stand still to make a point, gesturing with his hands—perhaps not in the

---

[23] Freiherr Karl von Banhans (1863–1942) was one of the high officials in the Austrian Railways, and was thus a colleague of Theobald Pollak. [24] BGA, no. 179 (undated, 3 Sept.)

[25] BGA, no. 182, dated 7 Sept.

[26] See above, Vol. i, Chap. 13 and BGA, no. 182. Mahler had just turned down Kössler's opera, *Der Münzenfranz* (first performed in Strasbourg in 1902) for the Hofoper.

Ringstrasse but in the Belvedere Park where he liked to go, or wherever there were few people about. I did not take notes of our countless conversations, but I know that I have retained within me more than could ever have been jotted down. It was not 'teaching', nor 'lessons' by a teacher, it was much, much more; a never-ending flow of spontaneous, personal statements by the musician Gustav Mahler. It was thanks to him that I was able to acquire, in addition to technical abilities and professional knowledge, a higher understanding and deeper insight into music as an inner foundation for my work. In the relaxed intimacy of our improvised walks, Mahler revealed the most likeable and gentle side of his character—utterly unpretentious, and therefore all the more moving. Once, as we were going up the Kärntnerstrasse at midday, he decided he would take home for his wife some tea-cakes or a special kind of sweet which would please her. He went into a shop and made his purchase. When he came out again, I wanted to take the packet from him but he would not allow me to do so. 'Why?' he explained, 'if I let it drop out of my hand and it falls in the muck'—he used in good Viennese the word 'Dreck' and pointed to the street, which was in a state the Viennese know only too well—'that would be no great tragedy. But if it happened to you, then you would feel dreadfully embarrassed.'[27]

Thus during his final Vienna season, Mahler still enjoyed moments of relaxation, despite the large number of major events planned at the Hofoper and his ever more frequent trips abroad to conduct his own works. As he had done the two previous years, he began the season by conducting *Tristan* the day after his return, on 5 September.

The need to find new singers was being felt at the Opera since several members of the existing ensemble had left or were about to leave. Sophie Sedlmair, who had been a member when Mahler arrived but had been used mainly as a stand-in for Mildenburg; had decided to pursue her career elsewhere.[28] Charlotte von Seebock sang Konstanze twice but failed to give satisfaction,[29] and Josie Petru died at the end of the summer of 1907. On 4 September, Gertrude Förstel,[30] a new lyric soprano, made her debut as Philine in *Mignon*.[31] She was to remain a member of the company for six years but sang mainly small roles during her first season at the Hofoper.[32] Mahler also auditioned Irene von Fladung, a young soprano who delighted him with 'her exceptional voice', her technical ease, and 'attractive appearance', as he wrote in his official letter recommending her engagement.[33] Unfortunately, her performance of a few small parts must have been inadequate, for her contract was cancelled and she left the Opera at the end of March 1907. Mahler was no doubt accused once again of having yielded to a passing fancy for an inexperienced beginner. Some of the season's new engagements proved luckier.

---

[27] *Neue Zürcher Zeitung* (7 July 1960). Concerning Klaus Pringsheim, see above, Chap. 6.
[28] She was to leave the Hofoper on 30 Dec. 1907.
[29] On 5 May and 14 Oct. 1906.
[30] Gertrude Förstel sang at the Vienna Opera from 1906 to 1912.   [31] See above, Chap. 3.
[32] First Genie in *The Magic Flute*, but also Annette in Erlanger's *Le Juif polonais*, and Peppina in d'Albert's *Flauto Solo*.   [33] HOA, G.Z. 1122/1906, letter of 17 Oct.

Three altos were added to the company (Sarah Charles Cahier,[34] who had made her debut as a guest singer in March and was immediately engaged, Bella Paalen,[35] and Theo Drill-Orridge.[36]

A new tenor, Philip Brozel,[37] also joined the Vienna Opera in 1907, but only for two seasons. He was mainly engaged as a stand in for Slezak and Schmedes when neither was available for dramatic roles, which had happened at the end of 1906. At this time Mahler had had several times to engage at the last minute from the Kaiserjubiläumstheater the ageing tenor Adolf Wallnöfer, an old friend from his time in Prague.[38] Further difficulties with singers arose in December. With Mayr and Hesch taken up with rehearsals for *The Barber*, Mahler was obliged to send for Max Gillman of the Munich Opera to sing Hagen in *Götterdämmerung* on 23 December. Two days later it was Willy Hesch's turn to fall ill, and he was replaced for the première of *The Barber of Seville* by Alexander Haydter. Needless to say, all these cancellations and guest appearances were greeted as a sign of the Opera's decline and Mahler's loss of interest. To replace Francesco Spetrino, who was about to leave the Opera, he decided to engage Alexander Zemlinsky as assistant conductor.[39] Zemlinsky had acquired solid experience with opera at the Kaiserjubiläumstheater, where he had been conducting since 1904 and had won considerable praise for his conducting of *The Magic Flute* the previous October. When he heard of his brother-in-law's engagement, Schoenberg wrote to Mahler from the Tegernsee, where he was spending his vacation:

I still can't exactly decide whether it is I or Zemlinsky who has been engaged at the Hofoper. But I couldn't care less anyway, and actually that isn't at all what I wanted to say. But really, how wonderful, how splendid that was of you today! I must tell you this, only one man on earth is capable of doing that, and that is Mahler. I have always liked you very, very much, perhaps you don't know it. But today I know why! Kissing your hands a thousand times—Your Arnold Schoenberg.[40]

[34] See below, Chap. 8. Sarah Charles Cahier sang in three guest appearances in Mar. and was given a contract on 1 Apr. 1907.

[35] Bella Paalen was a soloist in the performance of the Third Symphony in Graz on 3 Dec. 1906 (which Mahler conducted himself—see below). On 15 Apr. 1907 she sang as a guest artist in *Der Evangelimann* and was engaged as from 1 Sept. 1907.

[36] Theo Drill-Orridge was engaged on 30 June 1907 and remained at the Hofoper until 1916.

[37] Philip Brozel made a guest appearance in *Cavalleria Rusticana* and *Pagliacci* on 24 Apr. 1907. He left the Hofoper on 31 Aug. 1908.

[38] See above, Vol. i, Chap. 10. Wallnöfer sang on 7 Nov. 1906 in *Die Walküre*, on 30 Jan. 1907 in *La Juive*, on 2 Feb. in *Aida*, and 23 Feb. in *Tristan* (under Schalk's direction). He interpreted the title role in the revival of *Otello* on 3, 9, and 18 May (Zemlinsky conducting), as well as that of *Samson and Dalila* on 24 May.

[39] The contract was signed on 9 Oct. 1906. The engagement dated from 1 Nov. 1907 and ran for two years (HOA, Z. 1014/1906). An addendum dated 23 Dec. (accepted by the Intendant on 9 Jan.) changed the effective date to 1 May (HOA, Z. 1420/1906). When Weingartner decided to cancel his Hofoper contract in 1908, Zemlinsky returned to the Kaiserjubiläumstheater, where his performance of Dukas's *Ariane et Barbe Bleue* was hailed as a triumph on 4 Apr. 1908.

[40] AMM1, 371. At the end of 1906, Zemlinsky transcribed Mahler's Sixth Symphony for piano four hands (MBR1, no. 318; MBR2, no. 349). The meeting Mahler arranged with him in the following letter was probably to discuss either his engagement or *Der Traumgörge* (see below). The performance of *La Traviata* which is mentioned was that of 17 Apr. 1906, the first of Lilli Lehmann's guest appearances that year.

Zemlinsky himself also sent Mahler a thank-you letter:

Even at the risk of boring you once more, you must permit me to tell you how infinitely grateful I am to you. Not only because of the fact that through you, dear Herr Direktor, I attain that position which it has always been my greatest wish to hold, [but also because] your interest in my abilities has bolstered my at times rather shaky self-confidence, and of all living musicians only you, dear Herr Director, only you were capable of doing this in so full a measure. Excuse me if I grow tiresome, but today I really had to get it off my chest at all costs. Be assured that I will ever be conscious of the enormous gratitude I owe you for the happiness you have bestowed on me today.[41]

As seen above, Mahler had several months earlier decided to add Zemlinsky's new opera, *Der Traumgörge*, to the Hofoper repertoire.[42] Zemlinsky's career in the theatre had not progressed much since the Munich première of *Sarema*.[43] His next opera, *Es war einmal* (Once upon a time), had been premièred by Mahler at the Hofoper with Selma Kurz in the principal role, but it had lived through only twelve performances and was never revived until the 1990s.[44] Zemlinsky's next major work was the Hofmannsthal ballet, *Der Triumph der Zeit*,[45] which Mahler had refused to perform in 1901.[46] The frustrated composer was so distressed by his refusal that he orchestrated only the second act, which has survived under the title: '*Die Stunden*, ein Tanzpoem in einem Auszug, nach Hugo von Hofmannsthal.'[47] When he and Mahler started to see each other again with the founding of the Vereinigung der Schaffender Künstler in 1904, Zemlinsky was already busy composing *Der Traumgörge* with a new librettist, Leo Feld,[48] to whom Schoenberg had introduced him.

---

[41]   Undated letter (Oct. 1906), UPL.

[42]   The opera was officially accepted in June 1906 (HOA, Z. 734/1906).

[43]   See above, Vol. ii, Chap. 7. This first opera has been recently recorded (1997).

[44]   See above, ibid.

[45]   See Vol. ii, Chaps. 11 and 16. *Der Triumph der Zeit*, or rather its first act entitled 'Das gläserne Herz', had been the subject of Mahler and Alma's lively exchange during their first meeting in Nov. 1901 (see above, Vol. ii, Chap. 12). Zemlinsky had composed most of it while he was involved in his stormy passion for Alma and he virtually dedicated the work to her.

[46]   After *Der Triumph*, Zemlinsky composed another 'drama in mime', *Ein Lichtstrahl*, of which only a piano version has survived. The manuscript, dated 10 or 17 May 1901, belongs to the Library of Congress in Washington. A short list of Zemlinsky's early compositions includes three works for chorus and orchestra, 6 collections of Lieder (Op. 2, 5, 6, 7, 8, 10); five orchestra works, *Lustspiel-ouvertüre* (1895); Symphony in D minor (1892); *Orchester-Suite* (1895); Symphony in B flat major (1897); *Die Seejungfrau, Fantasy for Orchestra* (1905); eight chamber music scores, including the first String Quartet and four piano works. (See the programme of the world première of *Der Traumgörge* in Nuremberg on 11 Oct. 1980, and articles therein by Paul Stefan and Horst Weber, *Zur Dramaturgie des Traumgörge*. Weber quotes a letter written by Webern to Zemlinsky in 1919, expressing unqualified admiration for *Traumgörge* and his hope to see it on stage.)

[47]   See above, Vol. ii, Chaps. 11 and 16. *Die Stunden* was performed at the Zurich opera in 1992 in a choreography by Bertrand d'At. A suite from the ballet had been recorded two years earlier. Zemlinsky had heard the work performed once, in a concert conducted by Ferdinand Löwe at the Vienna Konzertverein on 8 Feb. 1903 (cf. Horst Weber, 'Stil, Allegorie und Secession, Zu Zemlinskys Balletmusik nach Hofmannsthals "Der Triumph der Zeit" ', in *Art Nouveau, Jugendstil und Musik* (Atlantis, Zurich, 1980)).

[48]   Leo Feld (whose real name was Hirschfeld) (1869–1924), born in Vienna, was the brother of Viktor Léon, the librettist of *The Merry Widow*. He was a member of the literary circle around Hermann Bahr and wrote a comedy, *Die Lumpen* which was a great success at the turn of the century, a witty caricature of the

The original idea for *Der Traumgörge* came from Heine's poem *Der Arme Peter*, set to music by Schumann, which tells the sad and romantic story of a young boy betrayed by his beloved.[49] Subsequently a fairy tale by Richard Leander,[50] *Vom unsichtbaren Königreich* provided additional material to enrich and fill out the plot. By 1903, Zemlinsky was writing periodically to his brother-in-law Schoenberg, then in Berlin at the Überbrettl cabaret, to inform him of his progress. As the project gradually took shape he was, consciously or unconsciously, drawing on his ill-fated love-affair with Alma Schindler.

Leo Feld's hero, Görge, is a young orphan living in a small village. To escape from this narrow-minded environment, he withdraws into the realm of his books and makes up his mind that someday his dreams will come true. His hopes are shattered by his fiancée's betrayal and he leaves his village for the city to follow the call of a fairy-tale princess. However, the cruel world of the big city once again shatters his illusions. He becomes involved in a proletarian revolution, only to discover that the rebels are murderers and plunderers. His only true friend is his new girlfriend, Gertraud who is accused by the workers of witchcraft. Totally disillusioned, he returns with her to his village and settles down to a peaceful life as a husband and father. Eventually, he realizes that Gertraud and the fairy-tale princess are the same person and that his dreams have indeed come true. Thus the opera is a series of confrontations between dream and reality, subjectivity and objectivity, naivety and knowledge, nature and civilization, all in the late romantic tradition.

Zemlinsky began to work on the piano score of *Der Traumgörge* in the autumn of 1904, and completed it within a few months. The orchestra score bears the date of 26 October 1906.[51] Many of Zemlinsky's letters to Alma during that year are concerned with his new opera, and with his piano-duet transcription of Mahler's Sixth Symphony,[52] which he brought to Maiernigg during the summer. It was no doubt at the beginning of that summer that he wrote to Alma:

I have the feeling that our visits—I mean Schoenberg's and mine—to your house can now take place in a much warmer and more cordial atmosphere, as we have always

milieu of the literary Café Griensteidl. Despite a measure of success in the Viennese theatre with some 15 plays, he left Vienna for Berlin where he was engaged at the Überbrettl cabaret by Ernst von Wolzogen and made the acquaintance of Schoenberg. He subsequently composed some 15 comedies in verse and prose. Feld also wrote the libretto for Zemlinsky's next opera, *Kleider machen Leute*, which opened on 2 Dec. 1910, at the Kaiserjubiläumstheater.

[49] Mahler had given their names, Hans und Grete, to one of his very first Lieder.

[50] Richard Leander was the author of the first poems set to music by Mahler (after his own), 'Erinnerung' and 'Frühlingsmorgen'. *Von unsichtbaren Königsreich* is part of a collection entitled *Träumereien an französischen Kaminen*.

[51] See Wulf Konold, 'Reality and Dream', introductory note to *Der Traumgörge*, CD recording (Capriccio, 1988).

[52] Zemlinsky played his transcription with Mahler, in Schoenberg's presence (see MBR2, nos. 349 and 350, undated (17 Apr. 1906) and: Evelinde Trenkner, 'Notate zu Gustav Mahler 6. und 7. Symphonie', *Keyboard Classics* (Sept.–Oct. 1989), 6.

hoped would be the case. I therefore hope that Herr Direktor Mahler is aware of our boundless respect and admiration for him, and accepts it with pleasure (please—this last sentence is meant for you only). Don't you also think that everything is going much better?[53]

Why did Mahler agree to perform an opera which promised to be even more static than Zemlinsky's earlier works? Certainly the subject, and the fairy-tale genre (to which *Es war einmal* already belonged) were of the sort that appealed to him. Also, even if Zemlinsky never confessed to him that the work was partly based on his own experience, Mahler would no doubt have guessed that this was the case, and may therefore have sought to provide his unhappy rival with a sort of compensation by producing his work. Mahler originally intended to schedule the première before the end of the 1906–7 season and had already consulted Roller for the décor. But the opening was postponed and rehearsals only began at the end of the following autumn. Weingartner attended them as soon as he arrived in Vienna. He was highly critical of the opera and demanded a large number of changes which Zemlinsky refused to make. This was certainly what caused Zemlinsky to resign from the Hofoper in February 1908.[54]

Strauss's *Salome* was still very much on Mahler's mind at the beginning of the new season. On 11 October, the *Illustrirtes Wiener Extrablatt* reported that all difficulties were now out of the way, since neither the Berlin nor Dresden censorships had judged the work 'offensive to religious sensibilities', but its prediction that 'Direktor Mahler would soon be rejoicing' proved premature. A few days earlier, Mahler had expressed his frustration in a letter to Strauss and recommended his encouraging another production of his opera as a means of overcoming the Viennese censorship's obstinate resistance:

I am reluctant to say so, but must inform you as soon as possible: <u>it is still not accepted</u>! My objection that I must know for certain before 1 November was answered with a shrug of the shoulders. What would be most welcome now is that <u>Löwe</u> should come straight out with a performance here as soon as possible. That would open a breach.[55]

---

[53] UPL. Many of Zemlinsky's letters to Alma concern his engagement at the Hofoper. He also intended to visit Mahler in Maiernigg in 1907 to play to him the finished score of *Der Traumgörge*, but was undoubtedly prevented from doing so by the tragic events of that summer.

[54] Zemlinsky himself never seems to have been completely satisfied with this opera. Indeed, he did not put it on in Prague, where he was musical director of the German Opera 1911–27, and where in 1912 he conducted the first Prague performance of Mahler's Eighth Symphony, as well as the première of Schoenberg's monodrama, *Erwartung*. Much later, the score and orchestral parts of *Der Traumgörge* were rediscovered in the archives of the Vienna Opera and the work finally opened on 11 Oct. 1980 at the Nuremberg Opera. From New York, Mahler wrote to Zemlinsky in early 1908: 'Unfortunately the news about your adventures with the new regime was not unexpected. Nonetheless I didn't imagine that W. [Weingartner] would so unceremoniously break his promise to put on your opera before anything else. I can well imagine how catastrophic this is for you' (MBR1, no. 401; MBR2; no. 394).

[55] MSB 120, undated (late Sept.–early Oct. 1906), MSB 120. Theodor Löwe was the director of the Breslau Theatre.

On 16 November, in a telegram sent from Breslau, Mahler confirmed the ill tidings: 'All efforts so far to no avail. Must accept that for the time being, but am certainly not giving up Salome.'[56]

In the meantime, Mahler had considered producing several other works. After refusing Max von Schillings's *Der Moloch*,[57] he had thought of Moniuszko's *Halka*, before turning to Debussy's *Pelléas et Mélisande*, the revolutionary work of which his Parisian friends had certainly spoken to him. After reading the score he had decided to put it on at the Hofoper, without even waiting for the results of the German première in Frankfurt on 19 April 1907.[58] But Weingartner, who succeeded him as director of the Hofoper, obviously disliked Debussy's opera, which was only produced five years later, on 23 May 1911, under the baton of Bruno Walter.

Mahler's next première was meant to celebrate the Emperor's name-day, on 4 October, but the choice of the work was not a happy one, to say the least. The French composer Camille Erlanger had borrowed the plot of *Le Juif polonais* from a novel by Erckmann–Chatrian.[59] Alma's claim that Erlanger's use of sleigh-bells[60] in a scene of the opera reminded Mahler of the Fourth Symphony, and that it had determined his choice, is more than doubtful. In fact Mahler had seen *Le Juif polonais* at the Opéra Comique in 1900,[61] and the composer enjoyed a solid reputation in France.[62] Mahler invited him to attend the final rehearsals and the opening of his opera, to which as usual he devoted much time, although he had entrusted Bruno Walter with the task of conducting the première.

Erckmann–Chatrian's novel had been adapted for the stage by the two authors themselves,[63] but the plot was much too thin to fill the three acts of a full-length opera. It tells the story of an innkeeper, Mathias, who fifteen years earlier robbed and killed a Polish Jew. In the last act, he dreams that he is being tried in court and condemned, and dies in his sleep of a heart attack. Despite the excellence of the mise-en-scène and the cast, only the second act was applauded, because of the folk dances with which it concludes. The audience 'sometimes showed

---

[56] Strauss Archives, Garmisch. A letter of Sept. 1906 from Mahler to Raoul Mader, then director of the Budapest Opera, indicates that he had taken up his campaign for *Salome* again as soon as the season began. In the letter he alludes to 'secret talks' with Prince Liechtenstein (HOA, Z. 1010/1906).

[57] See above, Vol. ii, Chap. 1. Mahler had also refused to put on Schillings's *Der Pfeifertag* for financial (and probably also artistic) reasons.

[58] The project was announced in the *Neue Freie Presse* on 16 Nov. 1906. On 3 June 1906 the *Fremden-Blatt* included *Halka* in its list of projects at the Opera, and announced that the productions of Schillings's two operas were 'merely delayed'.

[59] Émile Erckmann (1822–99) and Alexandre Chatrian (1826–90), both from Lorraine, wrote in collaboration a great number of novels which were very popular with the French bourgeoisie.

[60] The bells were those of the sledge of the murdered Jew.

[61] See above, Vol. ii, Chap. 8.

[62] Erlanger had been the pupil of Léo Delibes. Both *Kermaria* (1897) and *Le Juif polonais* had been performed at the Opéra Comique, and *Le Fils de l'étoile* (1904) at the Opéra. His *Aphrodite*, which had just opened at the Opéra Comique, had created a sensation and been acclaimed as a 'French *Salome*'.

[63] The play had opened in Paris in 1865 and played in several boulevard theatres before entering the repertory of the Comédie-Française. The libretto of the opera is by Henri Cain and P. B. Cheusi.

interest, but never enthusiasm'. The following days *Le Juif polonais* was violently attacked by the critics, who proclaimed Erlanger's opera to be inferior to that of Karl Weis[64] on the same subject, which had been performed at the Theater an der Wien in 1902. According to them, Erlanger's music played only an 'illustrative', 'decorative' role, since by its very nature it could not suggest remorse. Kauders, the most charitable reviewer, considered Erlanger's principal gift to be his flair for dramatic effect. Despite the poverty of melodic invention, he skilfully 'represented terrifying events by gripping realistic combinations of timbre and harmony'. Wallaschek condemned the scantiness of the plot, especially in the second act, the monotonous vocal writing in 'parlando', and the lack of originality of the music with its quotations from folk songs.[65] Only the orchestra had an interesting role. According to the *Sonn- und Montagszeitung*, the opera was a 'mosaic without design, in gaudy colours', with a primitive use of the leitmotiv-technique. Richard Robert, in the *Illustrirtes Wiener Extrablatt*,[66] attacked Erlanger's 'perverse harmonies and modulations' and his 'haphazard cacophony'. At the same time, all the critics recognized at least two moments of theatrical effectiveness in the work: the entrance of another Polish Jew who unwittingly reminds the murderer of his crime, and the judgement scene. Liebstöckl, however, with his customary wit claimed that these two moments did not sustain the audience's interest in 'a very ordinary murder and robbery by an utterly uninteresting murderer'. 'We live in miserable times', he concluded: 'music is becoming impoverished and too ashamed to sing out. Half-tones and muffled nuances reign throughout. People compose nothing but pangs of conscience!' Robert wondered why Mahler had selected the work, but professed to ignore rumours to the effect that there was a connection between this otherwise inexplicable choice and the fact that the Paris conductor Charles Lamoureux, Erlanger's close friend, intended to perform Mahler's symphonies in Paris. Maximilian Muntz also hinted that the choice of *Le Juif polonais* had been dictated 'by considerations foreign to the music'. By refusing to conduct it himself, Mahler had expressed his opinion of this 'concoction (*Machwerk*) . . . which prostitutes our Opera, . . . the work of a dilettante devoid of any artistic value'. A director who had struggled so arduously for the acceptance of *Salome* could not be deaf to the nullity of *Le Juif polonais*.[67]

[64] Karl Weis (1862–1944), composer and conductor from Prague, wrote seven operas and a great number of other compositions.

[65] Among others, 'Du, du liegst mir im Herzen', in the love duet, and 'O du lieber Augustin' and 'Z'Lauterbach, hab'ich mein Strumpf verloren'.

[66] Richard Robert (1861–1924), was until 1920 the pseudonym of Robert Spitzer, a pupil of Julius Epstein and Franz Krenn at the Vienna Conservatory. He began his career as a Theater Kapellmeister and pianist, worked as editor of the *Neue Musikalische Rundschau* (1885–91), and later wrote criticisms for several Viennese newspapers. From 1909 on, he was active as a pedagogue, first at the Neues Konservatorium, and later privately. A composer himself, he taught a great number of instrumentalists, composers, and conductors such as Rudolf Serkin, Clara Haskil, and Hans Gal.

[67] Cast for the 4 Oct. 1906 performance: Förstel (Annette); Kittel (Katharina); Maikl (Sergeant); Preuss (Doctor); Demuth (Mathias); Mayr (Forester). Camille Erlanger attended the Vienna première and, according to Muntz, he took a bow at the end of the performance despite 'energetic rejection' by part of the audi-

The *Mittags-Zeitung* detected multiple influences in Erlanger's music: those of Puccini, Massenet, and Charpentier. He was credited at most with a certain 'technical elegance' and a feeling for 'musical decoration'. Korngold regretted the lack of psychological development in the characters, and claimed that the music played a subordinate role in the opera, even, at times, slowing down the action. Hirschfeld derided the crashing boredom and musical 'eclecticism' of the new opera, while Kalbeck waxed ironic about the 'brand-new orchestra[tion], presenting in turn inside-out Wagner, dyed Mascagni, and starched Massenet, as if to call attention to the rag and pedlar trade'. Clearly, this time Mahler had made a mistake. Erlanger's opera was performed only three times, and this ill-inspired choice was surely a symptom of his discouragement over *Salome*, which he had hoped would be the centrepiece of the season.

Two days after the resounding failure of *Le Juif polonais*, the attention of the whole community of Vienna opera-lovers was directed towards a sensational event which was also used against Mahler by his many enemies. The legendary Italian tenor Enrico Caruso[68] was scheduled to make his Hofoper debut in a special performance of *Rigoletto* in the original Italian. Caruso was then 33. He had at first made a name for himself in his native Italy, particularly with historic first performances of such works as Giordano's *Fedora*, *L'Arlesiana*, Cilea's *Adriana Lecouvreur*, and Puccini's *La Fanciulla del West*. He had settled in the United States in 1903, and was now, thanks to the recent invention of the gramophone, famous on both sides of the Atlantic as 'the greatest singer in the world'. For his exceptional performance in Vienna, a benefit night for the Opera's pension fund, all the tickets were sold as soon as the box-office opened, despite the fact that the prices were three and even four times higher than usual. Caruso, who was no doubt anxious to conquer Vienna, had accepted an exceptionally modest fee of 2,000 kronen (in New York, he demanded $2,000—10,000 Austrian kronen—per evening). In fact, he had been won over by the promise of the title of Kammersänger, together with an Austrian medal for himself and his impresario.

Heinrich Conried, general manager of the Metropolitan Opera, had become Caruso's sole agent, and it was he who had supervised all the details of the Viennese *Gastspiel* with Mahler. On 10 January 1906, Mahler had accepted his offer of engaging Antonio Scotti for the title role of *Rigoletto*, if he would agree

---

ence. On his return to Paris, he wrote to Mahler to thank him for the 'great artistic joy' and 'honour' the production had given him. Mahler's reply on 15 Oct. acknowledged the fact that, despite all his efforts, the work had not been a success. He nonetheless expressed his 'lively interest' in Erlanger's future work. The three performances of *Le Juif polonais* were the only ones ever given at the Vienna Opera.

[68] Caruso had acquired international fame overnight when singing with Melba in Monte-Carlo (1902) and London. He had been engaged by Maurice Grau at the New York Metropolitan Opera in 1903 and had sung there for the first time in Nov., after Heinrich Conried had become manager. He remained a member of the Metropolitan Opera until his death in 1921, interpreting no less than thirty-six different roles. In 1906 he undertook a tour of European opera houses, and sang in many performances at the Berlin Opera.

to sing without fee.[69] Eventually, Scotti refused, but Caruso's first appearance in Vienna must have aroused a lot of attention in Italy because another famous baritone, Mattia Battistini,[70] proposed his services for the same evening. His agent wrote to Mahler that he had 'repeatedly expressed a keen desire to appear in your institution some time or other, if possible under your direction'.[71]

Caruso's Gastspiel had originally been planned for the spring, but it was finally postponed until October. Mahler wrote to Conried again on 5 September asking for a prompt reply concerning Scotti because Demuth could not sing Italian and the whole performance was thus endangered. Marcella Sembrich's participation[72] had also been discussed but eventually, none of these projects came to anything, and a young Italian baritone named Titta Ruffo was engaged for the title role of *Rigoletto*, while the coloratura star of the Hofoper, Selma Kurz, sang Gilda.[73] Caruso reached Vienna on 3 October, and rehearsed the same morning from eleven to twelve o'clock. The press reported solemnly that he had obeyed all August Stoll's instructions, and had sung the whole time with full voice.[74]

On 6 October, long queues began to form in front of the various entrances to the Opera as early as 7.30 a.m. on the morning of the performance. The box office opened at 6.30 p.m., and those refused tickets even for standing room demonstrated their displeasure with violence. Later on, the police had to intervene several times to clear a path for ticket holders. When at 6.00 p.m. Caruso arrived from Hotel Sacher in a closed car,[75] accompanied by his impresario,[76] the eager crowd awaiting him only let him pass after having a good look at him. After the performance, his admirers lay in wait for him at the exit, intending to carry him back to the Sacher on their shoulders in triumph, and it was not easy to convince them to let him return on foot, according to the *Neues Wiener Tagblatt*. It seems however that some of the audience had been disappointed by Caruso's physical appearance and modest bearing.[77] Yet everyone was dazzled by the splendour of his voice in all registers and his technique, which was 'hidden rather than shown off' and 'had become second nature' to him. Also admired were the naturalness of his diction, the elegance of his phrasing,

---

[69]   Letter of 10 Jan. 1906, HOA. 1906/59.   [70]   See above, Chap. 6.

[71]   HOA, 1906/878. Battistini made his debut at the Hofoper in 1910.

[72]   See below, Vol. iiii, Chap. 1.

[73]   Clemens Höslinger, 'Die Gastspiele Enrico Carusos an der Wiener Hofoper', *Österreichische Musikzeitschrift* 26 (1971): 11, 642 ff.   [74]   Ibid.

[75]   The Hotel Sacher is situated just behind the Opera, but Caruso made the trip by car, no doubt to avoid the enthusiasm of his admirers.

[76]   This was probably Emil Ledner who was the authorized representative of the Metropolitan Opera and was solely responsible for Caruso's tours. In his talks with Peter Heyworth, Otto Klemperer recounts that the accompanying impresario was even more feared than Caruso himself. When Caruso arrived at rehearsals, his impresario insisted upon the work in progress being interrupted immediately so that the tenor would not lose a second of his precious time (Peter Heyworth, *Conversations with Klemperer* (Gollancz, London, 1973)). Ledner had also been promised a medal by the imperial Court officials.

[77]   According to Max Kalbeck's review, in the *Neues Wiener Tagblatt*.

the timbre of his voice 'pure as a bell, effortless, with delicately expressed feeling', the beauty and refinement of his *mezza voce*, the great nobility and ease of his acting, the violence and passion of his outbursts.[78]

In his own account, Caruso admits that he was surprised and disconcerted by the reserve the audience showed at the start of the performance, but relieved, little by little, when it grew more enthusiastic. In the third act, Caruso delighted his audience by distractedly playing cards while waiting for Magdalena. And just when he reached the high C, he threw the pack up into the air 'and held the note triumphantly'. His aria 'La Donna è mobile' brought the house down and he had to repeat it. After the final A-sharp of the Quartet, Caruso inserted a cadence which he sang without taking a breath before hitting a triumphant high B. This too brought the house down. After the performance, countless wreaths and endless bouquets were brought onto the stage. Hofrat Viktor von Horsetzky von Hornthal, who had replaced Wlassack as Kanzlei-Direktor of the General Intendanz, presented Caruso with his Kammersänger title. The ecstatic audience summoned him back over twenty times, together with Titta Ruffo[79] and Selma Kurz.[80] The public's hysterical demonstrations finally brought tears to Caruso's eyes with a quivering voice he managed an awkward 'Auf Wiedersehen', followed by a louder, more confident 'A riverderci'. A troop of autograph hunters, singers, ballerinas, and music-lovers waited for him in the wings to ask for autographs on picture postcards carrying his portrait.

The *Deutsche Zeitung* tried to minimize Caruso's triumph by claiming that it had been shared equally by the three principal singers, and the *Allgemeine Zeitung* described it somewhat condescendingly, emphasizing the snobbish 'non-musical' character of the event, which showed that Vienna was about to become a 'modest provincial town'.[81] Mahler himself seems to have had some reservations about Caruso's interpretation of the first aria, but was completely won over by his performance by the end of the evening.[82] The following year he invited Caruso back to Vienna for four performances.

On 9 October, three days after this gala evening, the *Deutsche Zeitung*

---

[78] The *Neue Freie Presse* reported that the Duke's second air, traditionally deleted from the second act, had been reinstated and sung by Caruso with 'consummate artistry'.

[79] Korngold describes Ruffo as a 'very young man' whose chest voice was still inadequate, and whose voice in the treble 'strained and squeaked (*gequetschten*)'. Nevertheless, his F, F sharp, and A flat reportedly brought the house down.

[80] According to Selma Kurz's daughter, Desi Halban, Kurz sang several times with Caruso and always brought down the house as the page in *Ballo in Maschera*, especially with her famous trill. Caruso took umbrage at her success, and then stipulated in all his Vienna contracts that she should never sing with him again (Desi Halban, 'My Mother, Selma Kurz', *Recorded Sound*, London, 49 (Jan. 1973), 137). Caruso sang again at the Hofoper in 1907, 1911, 1912, and 1913.

[81] Cast for the 6 Oct. performance, conducted by Francesco Spetrino: Kurz (Gilda); Kittel (Magdalena); Caruso (Duke); Ruffo (Rigoletto); Hesch (Sparafucile).

[82] It seems surprising that Mahler should have heard the whole of the performance, for he took the train to Berlin that evening to attend the final rehearsals of his Sixth Symphony, conducted by Oskar Fried, but he might have heard several rehearsals.

published an article entitled 'The Caruso Scandal', which described the Gastspiel as 'a shameful Jewish affair'. It expressed outrage at the decoration awarded to Caruso and Emil Lindner, and at elevating Caruso to the rank of Kammersänger, a title the most illustrious Viennese singers only obtained after many years of service. The article also protested against the disgraceful increase in ticket prices, an action unworthy of a royal and imperial institution. and 'caused by Jewish touts'.[83] All the best seats had been snapped up by the 'Jewish plutocracy', to the detriment of the Vienna nobility and 'respectable' people who had chosen to stay at home and donate the value of their tickets to charitable causes. Even the brief appearance of one of the century's greatest singers was being used against Mahler, but luckily the attacks were in this case too violent and too unfair to be taken seriously.

During the summer of 1906, Mahler's French friends, the so-called Dreyfus-quartet, had organized with the help of Berta Zuckerkandl a ten-day stay in Vienna, Mahler having promised to put on for them the best of the new productions at the Hofoper. For these 'true music-lovers', Paul Painlevé and his friend Madame Romazotti, Georges Picquart,[84] Guillaume de Lallemand, and Paul and Sophie Clemenceau, a 'secret festival week'[85] was organized at the beginning of October and included *Fidelio, The Marriage of Figaro, Die Entführung, The Magic Flute,* and *Tristan und Isolde,* all conducted by Mahler himself.[86] Berta Zuckerkandl wrote about it later:

Unforgettable days of exceptional spiritual union between French and Austrians. Every performance was a masterpiece . . . We were sitting under the nut-tree [in the Zuckerkandl garden]. And Picquart told us that as he sat in prison, dishonoured and martyred, he thought of one thing: if ever he should return to life, he would make a sort of pilgrimage to the spots where Beethoven, whom he idolized, had lived. And his second most fervent wish was to hear *Tristan* conducted by Gustav Mahler.

The first wish had come true; and on that very evening the second was to be fulfilled, for Gustav Mahler was putting on *Tristan* for his friends, himself conducting. Picquart was as happy as a child and was so impatient that he left for the Opera an hour ahead of time. Since I wasn't going with him, we arranged to meet on the main staircase. My sister, L'Allemand, Painlevé and Picquart were scarcely out of the door

---

[83] According to the *Deutsche Zeitung,* even the balcony seats, which ordinarily went on sale only an hour before the performance, had been sold beforehand, for as much as ten or twelve kronen.

[84] On 13 July of that year Picquart and Dreyfus had been reinstated in the army, twelve years after Dreyfus's arrest and seven years after the Rennes trial.

[85] Berta Zuckerkandl, *Ich erlebte fünfzig Jahre Weltgeschichte* (Bermann, Stockholm, 1939), 186.

[86] *Fidelio* was performed on 9 Oct., *Figaro* on 12 Oct., *Die Entführung* on 14 Oct., *The Magic Flute* on 18 Oct., *Tristan* on 19 Oct. Cast for the performance of *Tristan:* Schmedes (Tristan); Mildenburg (Isolde); Kittel (Brangäne); Mayr (King Mark); Weidemann (Kurwenal); Breuer (Melot); Preuss (Shepherd); Stehmann (Steuermann). Mahler's French friends could also have heard *Le Juif polonais* on the 10th; *Werther* on the 11th, conducted by Schalk, with Franz Naval in the title role; *Ballo in Maschera* conducted by Walter, on the 13th; *Hänsel und Gretel,* a matinée on the 14th; *Manon,* conducted by Schalk, with Naval, on the 15th; *Tannhäuser,* conducted by Walter on the 16th; and *Trovatore,* conducted by Spetrino, on the 17th. For the ten days of the 'secret festival'. Mahler sent Arnold Berliner a preliminary 'programme' which was only slightly altered, with one performance held back and another moved forward a day (MBR1, no. 282, MBR2, no. 365).

when a telegram arrived. It was from Georges Clemenceau, then President of the Council, and stated: 'Please inform General Picquart that I have appointed him Minister of War. He must return today.'

An indescribable scene [followed] on the staircase of the Opera, where Picquart was waiting for me. As he read the telegram he grew pale, not from pleasure but from anger. Utterly beside himself at being thus deprived of *Tristan*, he angrily reproached me: 'You should have kept this telegram from me. Tomorrow would have been time enough.'[87]

But Mahler's chief preoccupation during the autumn of 1906 was neither *Le Juif polonais* nor the 'secret festival' for his Paris friends, but the revival of two repertory works which were to replace the sensational event he had originally planned for the autumn, the Vienna première of *Salome*. Rossini's *Barber of Seville* was one of his favourite Italian operas, but funds were lacking for a *Neuinszenierung*, thus he had to be content with a *Neueinstudierung*,[88] with Selma Kurz as the star. On the other hand, Hermann Götz's *Der Widerspenstigen Zähmung* (The Taming of the Shrew), a minor masterpiece which he loved since he had conducted it in Hamburg in 1892, was going to be revived with new sets and costumes by Roller.[89] Unfortunately, the première of *The Barber*, which had been planned for October, had to be postponed until later in the season because of the illness of Wilhelm Hesch, whose delightful Bartolo was much loved by the Viennese public.

The leading roles in *Der Widerspenstigen Zähmung*[90] had been assigned to two of Mahler's favourite singers, Marie Gutheil-Schoder and Friedrich Weidemann. For the sets and costumes, Roller chose colours which symbolized the different characters: bright red for the Shrew, white for gentle Bianca, brown for the coat of old Antonio. According to the *Allgemeine Zeitung*, 'these tints in themselves expressed the dramatic conflict'. Every costume was 'a variation on a given theme', and the production as a whole 'always tender, always beautiful, and always full of meaning'. For Liebstöckl, who was for once in good mood, the stage had 'atmosphere, colour, perfume, and humour. Herr Roller is a genius for interiors, backgrounds, and falling shafts of light which

---

[87] Ibid. AMM contains a shorter version of this incident. Alma claims that Picquart received the telegram in Mahler's box during the performance, at the moment when Tristan comes down the ship's stairway to meet Isolde, to the strains of the leitmotiv of Destiny. Picquart left the box immediately to catch the train for Paris, leaving a hastily scrawled card for Mahler: 'My deepest thanks for your friendly reception and the magnificent artistic welcome you prepared for me' (AMM1, 133; AMM2, 132). The composition of Clemenceau's cabinet was announced to the press on 25 Oct. 1906.

[88] See Vol. ii, Chap. 4, p. 127.

[89] According to the HOA, Roller's preliminary estimate for *Der Widerspenstigen Zähmung* was 25,000 kronen. His estimates for earlier productions had been 24,000 for *Lohengrin*, 27,500 for *Figaro*, 20,000 for *The Magic Flute*, 17,000 for *Le Juif polonais* (HOA, Z. 3725/1906, 12 Oct.). On 13 Dec., Roller informed the Intendant that the final cost of *Figaro* had only been 26,000 kronen, *The Magic Flute* 19,300 kronen, and *Le Juif polonais* 15,800 kronen (G.Z. X–46, Z. 5083/1906), thus demonstrating his concern for economy. An estimate of 20,000 kronen figures in the Oct. documents for *Der Moloch*. The cost of the coming *Neuinszenierung* of *Die Walküre* was estimated at 42,000 kronen, but with the opening postponed until the following year, only 23,000 kronen were included under this heading in the budget for 1906.

[90] *Der Widerspenstigen Zähmung* had been absent from the Spielplan for seventeen years.

idealize everything. The eye feasted on it all, leaving the ear to enjoy the orchestra which, under Mahler, has found again its bewitching sonority.'[91]

Erwin Stein left a description of one of the last rehearsals of *Der Widerspenstigen Zähmung*, with Mahler at the podium and Stoll, his ex-officio producer sitting behind him, taking notes which Mahler, leaning backwards, dictated:

Suddenly he would turn to the orchestra and call: 'Second clarinet! No accent on the G!' or up to the stage: 'Herr Felix! Stop moving when the chord strikes!' His eyes and ears were everywhere. To Schoder: 'Gnädige Frau, the gesture is too violent and won't come off!' To Lucentio: 'Lieber Leuer, when you declare your love you must look at Fräulein Kiurina. First you read from Virgil, thus' (he folded his hands like a book), 'and then you turn to her, singing your faked translation, thus . . .' And again: 'First fiddles! Hold your bows still between the phrases!' Weidemann had to push the joint from the dinner table at least a dozen times and the tailor's scene was repeated until it went with a bang. Without pause Mahler was talking, correcting, and 'mending', while at the same time acutely listening and watching.[92]

After much hesitation, Mahler decided to cut the final scene in which the two lovers speak to their parents, and the opera closes with their love duet. Mahler had originally intended to add a brief postlude, but he abandoned the idea during one of the last rehearsals.[93] Later, in 1908, the operetta composer Oskar Straus wrote to Mahler that he had discovered a score of Götz's opera dedicated by the composer to the conductor of the Mannheim première,[94] in which several deletions including that of the final scene had been made by the composer himself.

The role of Kätchen was ideally suited to Gutheil-Schoder's extraordinary talent as a singing actress, as Richard Specht later recalled:

When, in the second act, soft sounds suddenly crept into the shrill, commanding utterances of the authoritarian Kätchen, as she sensed, for the first time, the power of the

---

[91]   According to the 13 Dec. estimate, the whole production cost 21,336 kronen (Z. 5083 s/1906).

[92]   EWS 313.

[93]   Klaus Pringsheim ('Erinnerungen an Gustav Mahler', *Neue Zürcher Zeitung* 2322 (7 July 1960)) states that Mahler had asked him to compose the postlude. But Mahler found the first version, about three pages of orchestra score, unsatisfactory, and he asked Pringsheim to shorten it. The second attempt, which was only to accompany the slowly dropping curtain, also failed to satisfy him, although the orchestra parts had already been copied and played, and the opera finally ended without a *Nachspiel*. 'All the same,' Mahler said jokingly to Pringsheim, 'you can say that you were performed at the Vienna Opera!'

[94]   Letter of 10 Sept. 1908, AMM1, 433. Oskar Straus promised Mahler that he would give him the score 'as a modest token of my boundless admiration'. Nonetheless, at least according to Richard Specht, Mahler was never completely satisfied with his version of *Der Widerspenstigen Zähmung* (RSM2, 146 n.). Oskar Straus (1870–1954) was the son of a Mannheim bank clerk. Pupil of Max Bruch in Berlin and Hermann Grädener in Vienna, he worked as singing coach and conductor in many theatres before becoming pianist-composer at the Überbrettl in Berlin. After composing a number of popular operettas (*Die lustigen Nibelungen*, 1904; *Hugdietrichs-Brautfahrt*, 1906; and especially *Ein Walzertraum*, 1907; and *Der tapfere Soldat*, an adaption of Bernard Shaw's *Arms and the Man*), 1908, he emigrated to the United States at the beginning of the 1930s and composed music for the cinema. His later operettas were mostly performed in England, notably *Riquette*, 1925; *Mariette*, 1929; *Liebelei* (adapted from Schnitzler), 1934; and *The Three Waltzes*, 1937. *Mariette* utilized music by Johann Strauss senior, and *Liebelei* waltzes by Johann Strauss junior.

man who was going to master her, [all these were] things which no singer had ever done before her, even though a sustained note, or some other purely vocal detail, might suffer in consequence.[95]

The soprano herself recollected the following details of Mahler's stage direction:

An excellent way of making himself immediately understood by everybody was to give striking, often startling pieces of advice—as when he said to Petrucchio: 'Kiss Kätchen as though she were a sacrificial lamb. Treat her (after the betrothal) as though she were a suitcase.' Position (upstage, downstage, left or right) never mattered to him; what did matter was mental grasp of essentials and constant harmony with the music. Gesturing with the hands was only rarely allowed, and then only when what was going on in the mind could not otherwise be expressed. Dead time in the performance was banished. Once the mood was set, it had to be preserved by all available means. Nothing could destroy Mahler's equanimity more than when the audience interrupted with noisy applause a scene that was supposed to die away softly. It occasionally happened that he turned sharply round on the podium and ordered silence.

In my opinion, *The Shrew* was perhaps Mahler's greatest achievement as a director of opera. To him, Katharina was no obstinate wench, but a very clever, temperamental creature driven to such fury by her tiresome relatives, foolish father, and [other] intellectual inferiors that she ultimately turned into a shrew. Petrucchio, usually portrayed as the really rebellious one, was, for Mahler, a lovable, humorous cavalier who, through profound understanding of her feminine character, set things right by his firmness and severity (which however never lacked charm). Free from theatrics and exaggeration, the whole performance was constructed around the inner beauty of these two people.[96]

This time, even Hirschfeld welcomed the return of *Der Widerspenstigen Zähmung* who despite its seventeen years' absence from the Vienna stage, had 'lost none of its seduction'. Roller had 'faithfully illustrated [the opera's] colourful charm on stage', and Mahler had brought out both the tender and comic sides of the music. The ensemble was 'lively, witty, and gay', with every voice, character, and chorus member closely involved in the action. Even Wallaschek and Kauders, Gutheil-Schoder's traditional detractors, conceded that the astonishing performance which resulted from the impetuosity of her acting temperament more than made up for the limits of her voice.[97] For Kauders, Weidemann was the real hero of the evening, his vigorous voice expressing both boorishness and, where appropriate, tenderness and humour. For Korngold it was Mahler 'whose heart set the tempo'. For a work he considered more 'joyful than comic', the anonymous critic of the *Allgemeine Zeitung* declared that 'no other opera stage is capable of creating an artistic ensemble with beauty, nobility, and harmony comparable to this one, a veritable masterpiece of operatic culture'.

---

[95] Richard Specht, 'Marie Gutheil-Schoder', in *Die Schaubühne* (1906), 569.

[96] Marie Gutheil-Schoder, 'Mahlers Opernregie', BSP 34.

[97] Wallaschek expressed the hope that Mahler would not relinquish the conducting to one of his collaborators, for 'the level of the performance then inevitably dropped'.

The anonymous reviewer of the *Mittags-Zeitung* claimed that Mahler found it easier to attract the public with the masterpieces of the past than with contemporary works. He congratulated him on the incomparable production of *Der Widerspenstigen Zähmung*, in which he showed the Opera at its most perfect. Yet Liebstöckl noted that the house had not been sold out the evening of the première, and bewailed the fact that once again a work appreciated by the critics had been snubbed by the public. He thought the opera had never fully recovered from having had its première seven years after the *Meistersinger*, in which Wagner had 'monumentalized' German humour once and for all. Wagner himself had said that the basic motivation for his creation had been irony, and that the pain-relieving humorous element had only come later. Götz had added a smaller but worthy stone to the monument. But in his opera, as in the *Meistersinger*, the laughter was short-lived. That was unfortunate for comic opera, which ought not to have a serious message behind it. So Götz's little masterpiece of heavy-handed, ironic gaiety, had disputable features and highly dramatic serious elements. It was 'an opera for orchestra', since the vocal parts were not the best feature of the music. In the new production the acting and the scenery took the honours. Liebestöckl criticized Weidemann for either whispering or blurting things out, but not singing; Gutheil-Schoder's interpretation, however, he praised as a 'model of refinement and wit, both in acting and in singing'. Maximilian Muntz alone expressed reservations concerning certain 'decadent, anti-musical' traits which Mahler had added to Götz's work, and as usual he attacked Gutheil-Schoder for her 'lack of vocal naturalness and charm'. She succeeded in portraying the psychological evolution of the character, but at the end she seemed simply to 'lure the hero into her trap rather than undergo a transformation herself'. Roller's décors were mainly 'wallpaper fantasies', though the sets of the first act showed shabby sobriety. The orchestra's performance was ideal.[98] Finally Max Vancsa praised the production with warmth in the *Neue Musikalische Presse*, and approved Mahler's decision to lower the curtain after the lovers' duet. He stressed the exceptional quality of the vocal and dramatic performances of the two principal protagonists, and thought that Mahler's conducting 'united nobility and lightness'. The public 'seemed to want to give proof of its lack of discernment by shunning the première' despite the work's long absence from the Opera's *Spielplau*. Those present, however, had tried to compensate for their small number by the enthusiasm of their applause.

Mahler entrusted to Franz Schalk the direction of the following Hofoper première, Eugen d'Albert's *Flauto Solo*. This was a neo-classical opera in one act which the composer had played for Mahler personally in November 1905,

---

[98] Cast for the 3 Nov. 1906 revival: Kiurina (Bianca); Gutheil-Schoder (Katharina); Pohlner (Housekeeper); Leuer (Lucentio); Sembach (Schneider); Breuer (House tutor); Weidemann (Petrucchio); Reich (Hortensio); Haydter (Baptista); Felix (Grumio). *Der Widerspenstigen Zähmung* was performed five times at the end of 1906 and three times in 1907. It was probably in the context of this revival that Mottl conducted Götz's Symphony on 2 Dec., during the third Philharmonic concert.

in the course of a concert tour which had taken him to Vienna.[99] Anticipating Hofmannsthal's neo-classical librettos, and Strauss's late opera *Capriccio*, the text by Hans von Wolzogen (the librettist of *Feuersnot*) was set in an eighteenth-century German court. The plot centred upon two princely music-lovers, father and son (more or less modelled upon Frederick II and Frederick-Wilhelm of Prussia): the one favouring German music and the other Italian. In the end, the Italian soprano (ultimately revealed to be a Tyrolese) marries the German music teacher to the strains of a canon for seven bassoons, the 'pig song' composed by the bridegroom for the soldier-prince. Everyone is reconciled at the last moment as a part for flute, played by the prince, joins the round, and an Italian aria is sung by the prima donna. This charming libretto served d'Albert as a pretext for displaying his gifts for pastiche of military marches and minuets in the style of the eighteenth century, terminating in a particularly attractive grand finale.[100] Since another one-act opera by d'Albert, *Die Abreise*, was already in the Hofoper repertory, Mahler put the two one-acters on together, and rounded off a full evening's performance with a ballet.

The time for neo-classical stylistic games had not yet come, and Hirschfeld castigated *Flauto Solo* as endless, pointless conversations put to music by a composer lacking imagination, inventiveness, and feeling for drama. Muntz, on the other hand, praised both Wolzogen's libretto and d'Albert's instrumentation and skilful stylization of baroque music, although he criticized the length of the work and its 'overload'. For the *Mittags-Zeitung*, d'Albert was merely a 'witty and clever composer who knew how to bring out the best in voices'.[101] Kauders praised the 'complexity of the thematic fabric and development of leitmotivs' in the score, along with its 'richness of colour', but Wallaschek saw nothing in it but 'occasional music', 'vigorous but laborious efforts', a 'collage of disparate styles', 'musical expression' devoid of taste and authenticity. D'Albert himself ascribed the failure of the Vienna première to the inadequacy of the production, and put the blame on Mahler. In a letter to Gutheil-Schoder, he criticized him for not inviting him to the rehearsals and the première, which had originally been planned for 14 February.[102] Fortunately, he was just then aglow with the triumphant success of *Tiefland*[103] in Frankfurt. *Flauto Solo* met

---

[99] See above, Chaps. 1, and 3, and Wilhelm Raupp, *Eugen d'Albert* (Roehler und Amelang, Leipzig, 1930) 199. As seen above (Chap. 3), d'Albert's *Die Abreise* had been premièred at the Hofoper on 28 Feb. 1905, together with Leo Blech's *Das war ich*.

[100] Instead of creating new sets, Roller used those of Tchaikovsky's *Queen of Spades* with minor alterations. The cost of the sets was therefore merely 500 kronen, according to the estimate he sent to the Intendant on 18 Nov., while the costumes cost 5,500. Forty-three of the seventy-six costumes required by the opera were borrowed from the wardrobes of other productions.

[101] The newspaper reported that many cuts had been made which had made the action difficult to follow.

[102] Letter from Eugen d'Albert to Marie Gutheil-Schoder, Stargardt catalogue (sale of 29–30 Nov. 1966), no. 577.

[103] Mahler accepted *Tiefland* before leaving the Hofoper, and it opened in Vienna under Weingartner on 25 Feb. 1908. Its success was such that it was performed sixteen times during that year alone, and sixty-one times between 1908 and 1918.

the usual fate of one-act operas: after four performances, it disappeared for ever from the Vienna repertory.[104]

The *Neueinstudierung* of Rossini's *Barber of Seville* was now planned for December. Mahler had long conceived it as a vehicle for Selma Kurz's vocal agility and physical charm,[105] and personally took charge of the rehearsals and conducting. Hesch had still not recovered, and in the end the role of Bartolo had to be given to someone else. The Rossini masterpiece had not been performed since 1900 and Kalbeck had been commissioned to translate the recitatives, customarily replaced by spoken dialogues, into German.[106] As with Mozart's operas, Mahler accompanied them himself on the harpsichord, an innovation which Korngold praised in a long article in the *Neue Freie Presse*.[107] The harpsichord 'acted on the singers like a whip', Korngold wrote, adding that since the previous year they had made considerable progress in their speed of enunciation.[108] He also remarked that the fierce controversy over the restoration of the recitatives in *Così fan tutte*, *Don Giovanni*, and *Figaro* had finally subsided. In his opinion, a return to the old spoken dialogues, which always slowed down the rhythm of the action, was no longer conceivable.

The *Mittags-Zeitung* disagreed, protesting that the recitatives 'created too much distance between musical numbers'. Nonetheless, the anonymous critic declared that Mahler's direction was admirable: he was of course rather above that kind of opera and seemed 'almost' to play with all these pretty pieces and melting melodies, but he 'controlled, commanded and ordered everything on stage according to the laws of beauty and form, enhanced the contents by intelligently emphasizing the most subtle refinements'. As a 'songbird' and prima donna assoluta, Kurz merited comparison with Patti. After her great scene in the second act, she had been acclaimed 'with a fervour usually reserved for singers making their farewell appearance'.

Kalbeck also praised Kurz's performance as 'a feast for the eyes and ears', her virtuosity far outweighing her occasional shortcomings. Korngold joined him in admiring the speed with which she had left behind the *jugendlich-dramatisch* roles of the beginning of her career and mastered the coloratura

---

[104]   The first performance, on 28 Nov. 1906, was conducted by Franz Schalk and preceded by a short pantomime by Franz Skofitz composed after a libretto by Joseph Hassreiter, *Atelier Brüder Japonet*. The cast for *Flauto Solo* consisted of Förstel (Peppina); Sembach (Prince Ferdinand); Moser (Emanuele); Demuth (Pepusch); Mayr (Prince Eberhard). The evening concluded with *Die Abreise*.

[105]   Korngold drew attention to her considerable progress over the past few years, while Kalbeck claimed Mahler had waited too long for Kurz to 'be in full possession of her resources' before reviving *The Barber of Seville*.   [106]   The recitatives were not even included in the German scores.

[107]   In *Die Musik*, Korngold reported that in the first act, Mahler restored for Count Almaviva a second serenade, in a minor key, to follow the first.

[108]   At the same time, Korngold questioned the soundness of the customary practice of giving the role of Rosina to a soprano. He agreed with Kalbeck that Moser's voice was too young and weak for Figaro. Hesch, apparently unsurpassed as Bartolo, had been replaced by Alexander Haydter on opening night. The press commented upon the unusual slowness of Mahler's tempo in the overture, and also reported that latecomers had been refused admittance to the hall while it was being played.

repertory.[109] But while granting that she possessed exceptional vocal talent, Korngold considered that she lacked the requisite vivacity and gaiety required for soubrettes or sly young girls such as Rosina. He nevertheless praised her performance of 'Una voce poco fa'[110]—her scales, staccatos and trills in crescendo on the A and B flats,—which she had sung sitting at a table rather than standing near the footlights, like Italian sopranos.

The *Allgemeine Zeitung* also praised Selma Kurz, but did not altogether share Korngold's enthusiasm. German singers were probably unable to bring out Rossini's sparkling humour and incapable of singing with the high-spirited agility the music demanded. 'It was the orchestra prepared with infinite care by Mahler, which provided the chief source of delight, and gave free rein to all the joyful magic of Rossini's music.' Maximilian Muntz conceded that Selma Kurz had made progress in her acting, but he would have preferred 'an Italian performance of lesser refinement'. For Wallaschek, the theatrical success of *The Barber* depended upon the personalities of its principal interpreters—and in the ranks of the Vienna Opera, there were no singers at present ideally suited to the roles. Even the perfection of the ensembles and Selma Kurz's sparkling virtuosity could not make up for this basic deficiency.

However, other critics expressed their unreserved approval. In the *Montags-Revue*, Hedwig von Friedländer-Abel relished the gaiety and brilliance of the performance:

it was a truly comic *Barber* from start to finish, no aestheticism or refinement, an utterly genuine Rossini, realistic, swirling and sweeping. The exuberance of the orchestra was breathtaking. The crescendos went off like popping champagne corks. The famous 'storm' music with its parodies of thunder and lightning was particularly delightful. Mahler himself seems to possess something of this disappearing *buffo* spirit which, with its colourful arabesques, enlivens the drabnesss of everyday life.

Viktor Joss, in the *Signale für die Musikalische Welt*, referred to 'the sureness of style of this incomparable conductor, who again provided us with a model performance. Rossini's captivating, brilliant music, unhampered by problems of interpretation, worked its old magic in its new attire.' The Vienna public was evidently of the same mind, for this new production of *The Barber of Seville* was performed twice in December 1906, and ten times the following year, and remained in the Hofoper repertory for many years to come.[111]

---

[109] Nevertheless, Kurz had already sung the Queen of the Night in *The Magic Flute* twice (2 Nov. 1904 and 29 Nov. 1906), and twice that of Konstanze in *Die Entführung aus dem Serail*. Furthermore, Mahler had produced *Lakmé* for her in 1904.

[110] Following contemporary tradition, Kurz inserted after this aria the nightingale aria from Handel's *Allegro ed il Pensieroso*, and the final Rondo from Bellini's *La Sonnambula* (Korngold, in *Neue Freie Presse*).

[111] Cast for the 25 Dec. 1906 performance: Kurz (Rosina); Kittel (Marcellina); Maikl (Almaviva); Breuer (Ambrosio); Moser (Figaro); Mayr (Basilio); Haydter (Bartolo). Later on, Gertrud Forst occasionally replaced Kurz in the role of Rosina. According to Roller's estimate dated 13 Dec., 23 costumes were taken from the Opera wardrobe and seventeen new ones, including eleven uniforms, were made especially for this *Neueinstudierung*. The entire production, in which one set was taken from *Die neugierige Frauen* and another from *Der Corregidor*, cost only 6,000 kronen.

Mahler had made it quite clear in 1901 that he would never again conduct the Philharmonic concerts. No permanent conductor had been engaged since Hellmesberger's resignation before the 1903–4 season. Franz Schalk, Felix Mottl, and Richard Strauss were the three guest conductors[112] while Bruno Walter was to conduct the Nicolai Konzert of 27 January. The new season opened on 21 October with a Nicolai Konzert in which Schalk conducted Bruckner's Eighth Symphony. Mahler, conducting in Breslau at the time, did not attend. But he did attend the following concert on 28 October, in which Felix Mottl conducted the overture to Weber's *Euryanthe*, Schumann's Second Symphony, and Pfitzner's incidental music for Kleist's *Käthchen von Heilbronn*. A week later, in a letter to Pfitzner, Bruno Walter informed him:

I couldn't hear *Käthchen*—I was ill and recuperating on the Semmering. Mahler was tremendously taken with it; I know the Overture and find it splendid. The audience for the *Rose* was enchanted, but the attendance was poor; you have a public here, but only a small one.[113] Mahler says that in any case he will keep it in the repertory . . .[114]

Mahler's refusal to conduct subscription concerts in Vienna stemmed at least in part from the fact that the numerous invitations he received from engagements he accepted abroad no longer left him the leisure to do so. In Paris, Madame Ménard-Dorian's project for a Mahler concert visit in 1905 had failed[115] but the journalist and critic Josef Reitler went on trying to organize a performance of one of Mahler's symphonies.[116] In June 1906, Mahler thanked him for trying and added:

For the present, I must be satisfied that here and there a small circle of connoisseurs realizes that my works mean something and may even be of value. The first obstacle to a performance anywhere is the large size of the orchestra required. But the real difficulty is the utterly unconventional forms of expression [I use], and which only very few people today can recognize as coming from the composer's nature, and not from his arbitrariness and caprice.

I really doubt whether Paris at the present time is a good place for my music. Frankly, the thought of going to Paris to thrust it upon people there, when people in my own home country still find it so off-putting, had not yet occurred to me, and I do not know whether or not I should advise you, dear Herr Reitler, to undertake the thankless task of preparing the ground for me.[117]

Nevertheless, as we have seen, Mahler had consented to meet Reitler in Salzburg about the project. In Paris, the young critic had contacted impresario Gabriel Astruc on the subject of Mahler (whose name Astruc insisted upon spelling 'Mal-her'). Astruc advised him to see Edouard Colonne, who proved to

---

[112] As seen above, Karl Muck had cancelled in Aug. both his Salzburg concert and his participation in the Philharmonic concerts.
[113] Walter is referring to the 12 Nov. performance which he conducted. After Mahler's departure, *Die Rose* did indeed remain in the Hofoper repertory, with one performance in 1908 and two in 1910.
[114] BWB 88.   [115] See above, Chap. 3.   [116] See above, Chap. 6.
[117] MBR1, no. 326; MBR2, no. 353.

be equally ignorant of Mahler's work[118] but asked Reitler to lend him scores of the symphonies, as the young journalist later recalled:

Colonne took the material (along with a letter from Mahler explaining the conditions necessary for his consent). About a week later, he summoned me back to his home. He said that he had studied the six symphonies and had decided for the Fifth. But the large number of wind instruments the composer demanded was out of the question. He could afford an orchestra of such costly dimensions only for Berlioz's *Damnation de Faust*. I ventured to differ. In the first place, the Fifth was not an auspicious choice for an audience totally unfamiliar with Mahler's work. And secondly, as his letter inferred, Mahler would insist that the orchestra should be at full strength. I suggested the Second Symphony (C-minor). The idea was ill received. 'Are you crazy, Sir?!' shouted Colonne. 'A symphony with organ, chorus, soprano, and contralto solo! I already told you that we can only permit ourselves such extravagance for *La Damnation!*' One can imagine how painful it was for me to haggle over every single instrument. For the sake of the cause, I tried to keep the bargaining within reasonable bounds. Finally we agreed that I would contact Mahler once more.[119]

After the meeting between Mahler and Reitler in Salzburg,[120] the idea of performing the Third Symphony in Paris was considered. Mahler demanded a minimum of five rehearsals and insisted that his symphony open the concert.[121] The project finally came to nothing when Mahler refused to agree to the reduction in the numbers of instruments demanded by Colonne and Astruc, his impresario. Later on, a performance of the Sixth Symphony was considered, but Mahler soon realized how much this later work would confuse both audiences and professionals, as he wrote to Reitler:

Please let Colonne go his own way. Should he approach you again, it just occurs to me that my Fifth, which requires a comparatively normal number of instrumentalists, would correspond more to his intentions. And it would serve better as an introduction than the Sixth. Both of them will be hard for the Parisians to get their teeth into.[122]

Apparently, Mahler was not disappointed by the failure of these various plans:

For me to get away from here involves such difficulties that only under quite exceptional circumstances—and above all, only if I am guaranteed a full realization of my artistic intentions—could I make up my mind to come to Paris. And—believe me, the situation is not yet ripe! Let another year or two go by![123]

Thus Mahler had to wait for several more years before making his debut as a symphony composer in Paris. At the end of October 1906, on the other hand,

---

[118] Such ignorance is eloquent testimony to the lack of curiosity of French musicians at that time. The *Lieder eines fahrenden Gesellen* had already been performed in a Concert Lamoureux in 1904, and the success of Mahler's 1905 Strasbourg concerts had been well publicized in France.

[119] JRM 18.   [120] See above, Chap. 6.

[121] He also suggests bringing with him from Vienna the bells, the first trombone and the Flügelhorn (see MBR1, nos. 329 and 330; MBR2, nos. 361, 362, and 313 n.).

[122] LPA, New York, Bruno Walter Legacy.   [123] MBR1, no. 330; MBR2, no. 362.

he caused quite a stir when Oskar Fried premièred his Second Symphony in St Petersburg. In the journal *Oko* (The Eye), Victor Pavlovitch Kolomitsov[124] described Mahler as an 'astonishing personality, both fascinating and original'. After praising the conductor who had understood and conducted 'both Beethoven and Tchaikovsky', he recalled Mahler's 1902 interpretation of Siegfried's Funeral March, with its 'powerful crescendo and menacing force'—an accomplishment 'surpassing even Richter, Nikisch, and Mottl'. The Second Symphony, according to Kolomitsov, had created a sensation in the Russian capital, provoking discussions in which enthusiasm and indignation were expressed with equal passion. Nobody in the audience could be bored by this symphony, which at first sight seemed 'chaotic and absurd', because of the apparently arbitrary succession of 'monstrous roars' and 'gentle splashing'. 'True, this symphony shows little craftsmanship, application or architecture, and even less orthodoxy in its techniques. But what vast breadth, what spontaneity in the powerful creative outburst, what daring imagination in the coloration, and what passion!' In Kolomitsov's eyes the principal faults of the work were its length, dissonances, and abrupt changes in style, but he felt that it offered 'an undeniable and precious beauty' for those who could free themselves from the 'the magic circle of narrow prejudices'.

Such 'narrow prejudices' seem to have been widespread in St Petersburg, even in the highest spheres of Russian music, for one of Rimsky-Korsakov's intimate friends later wrote in his memoirs that 'in his [Rimsky's] house, it was said that Mahler's symphony was very bad, and contained absolutely nothing of genius, whatever Mr Kolomitsov might think'. The leading figure in the new Russian school pronounced the Second Symphony to be 'ungifted and tasteless' and its orchestration 'extremely coarse and cumbersome'.[125] 'You simply cannot imagine', he continued, 'what kind of a work it is. It's a sort of pretentious improvisation on paper in which the composer himself doesn't know what his next measure will be. It's a pity, really, for him as a musician. In truth he is a house painter.[126] Far worse than Richard Strauss.' For the *Russian Musical Gazette*, the work suffered principally from the lack of any psychological linkage between movements. Its anonymous critic preferred the second and third movements to the others, and claimed that the crashing din of the Finale went further than anything by Berlioz. The symphony as a whole 'astonished and stunned the audience rather than arousing pleasure and enthusiasm'. While Kolomitsov had called the execution 'perfect', the *Gazette* critic had some reservations about it. His opinion of the work as a whole was nevertheless favourable. It was a 'powerful, exceptional creation'.

---

[124] Victor Pavlovitch Kolomitsov (1868–1936), critic and translator of opera librettos, pedagogue, and concert organizer, was born into a family of St Petersburg lawyers. Like Korngold, he studied both law and music and practised the two professions simultaneously. He began writing music criticism in 1904, in the journal 'Russie', and continued until 1927.

[125] Vassilii Vasilevitch Yastrebtsev, *Reminiscences of Rimski-Korsakov* (Columbia University Press, New York, 1985), 418.   [126] *Maliar* in Russian means house painter.

The correspondent of the Berlin journal *Die Musik* simply noted that this première had been the main event of the season, and that the Second Symphony had made 'a profound impression in spite of its length'.[127] In the periodical *Teatr i Iskusstvo* (Theatre and Art) another anonymous critic[128] wrote of the symphony's 'great philosophical pretentions' and its 'confused programme'. He thought the work contained too many 'doubtful passages' and had

a large number of serious faults: in the first place, the lack of style, and despite the originality of the design and procedures, the lack of musical personality. . . . The remarkable technical procedures become an end in themselves. . . . The orchestration . . . is really exceptional, but, at the same time, its monstrous musical content, this sonorous column of pure delirium, this alternation of exaltation and absurd platitude, the absence of artistic logic, consistency, and perhaps even sincerity, all this pretentiousness, this affectation, useless emphasis and crushing power of the sonority, without a defined musical physiognomy, all this simply exhausts and overwhelms without offering one single genuinely artistic moment. Of course, this symphony is, in every sense of the word, an exceptional work, but . . . is everything exceptional good?

The same critic ended his account with a severe comment on Oskar Fried, 'an artist full of temperament' but guilty of 'mannerisms and agitation'.[129]

In the same year 1906 an event took place in Austria which proved decisive for Mahler's career and the diffusion of his work. This was the signing of a new contract with a relatively new Viennese publishing company, Universal Edition, which thereby became Mahler's principal if not exclusive publisher. Universal Edition had been founded in 1901 on the initiative of Johann Strauss's brother-in-law, the banker Josef Simon. One of the aims of the new firm was to produce the most handsome scores available: 'Insofar as presentation, printing, engraving, paper, and typography are concerned, the new editions will surpass in quality all the classical editions presently available.' An enterprise functioning under collective management and subsidized by the Austrian government,[130] it had soon announced the publication of 400 volumes

---

[127] The 10 Nov. concert (28 Oct. in the Russian calendar) took place in the concert hall of the Conservatory, under the direction of Oskar Fried and with the orchestra of Count Cheremetyev 'augmented' by the chorus of the Opera and the contralto Ottilie Metzger-Froitzheim. She also sang some Lieder on the same programme, which began with the overture to Weber's *Euryanthe* and ended with Fried's Cantata, *Verklärte Nacht* (see above, Chap. 4). The performance was organized by the piano firm C. N. Schroder, which later organized Mahler's 1907 concerts.

[128] The critic signed his article Alexander Ch-r. However, Isaïe Knorozovski writing for the same magazine, was a fervent admirer of Mahler, and wrote the reviews of his concerts the following year (see below, Chap. 10).   [129] *Teatr i Iskusstvo* (Théâtre et Art), no. 46, 12 Nov. 1906 (Russian calendar).

[130] The firm was founded by decision of a general meeting on 15 June 1901. This was announced by the *Neues Wiener Tagblatt* amongst others on 9 Aug., and in Dec. by Eduard Hanslick in a long article in the *Neue Freie Presse*. The list of collaborators included Anton Door, Julius Epstein, Robert Fischhof, Joseph Hellmesberger, David Popper, Carl Klindworth, Charles de Beriot, Arnold Rosé, and Raoul Pugno, all of whom were responsible for preparing new editions of classical works, some of them with commentaries in three languages. The founding members were, in addition to Josef Simon, the editors Bernhard Herzmannsky (Doblinger), Adolf Robitschek, and Joseph Weinberger. Initially conceived as serving the Austrian classical

of classical scores.[131] Later on, Universal Edition bought the rights of several of Bruckner's symphonies from Waldheim Eberle and Doblinger,[132] and of some works by Max Reger and Richard Strauss formerly published by Joseph Aibl.[133] By virtue of the 1906 contract, Universal acquired Mahler's first four symphonies (hitherto in the catalogues of Doblinger and Weinberger). This purchase greatly facilitated their diffusion. Furthermore, the piano transcriptions for four hands and the pocket scores were published simultaneously.[134]

In backing Mahler in this way, Universal was making a brave decision. Mahler's record as a composer was anything but brilliant. By 1906 every one of his symphonies except the Third had had unsuccessful premières. Yet none of his previous works had been so unsuccessful as the Sixth Symphony. Oskar Fried had included it in the programme of a concert given 'with the assistance of the Berlin Philharmonic' (not *by* the Berlin Philharmonic) on 8 October 1906. During the summer Fried had sent Mahler the schedule of rehearsals. Mahler replied from Maiernigg on his return from Salzburg that the number planned was insufficient: 'I would draw your attention especially to the Trio in the Scherzo: it can't be played often enough. The musicians must, so-to-speak, know it by heart.' Mahler advised Fried to begin rehearsing in Scheveningen, Holland, the summer home of the Berlin Philharmonic. Even though the orchestra's size was reduced during that time, at least the first winds, first strings, and percussionists would be able to learn their parts.[135]

Fried had just suffered a major setback when he had not been appointed director of the Frankfurt Museumkonzerte, a position he had been very keen to have. Mahler advised him not to be discouraged by this setback, which he himself had expected:

music market and making it more independent of the German houses, the firm soon came to base its reputation on new music, especially from 1907, under the directorship of Emil Hertzka. For over ten years the offices were located at no. 9, Reichsratstrasse (the present Mahlerstrasse). It was only in 1914 that the company moved to its present location on the Karlsplatz. In 1903 it published a piano score of *Fidelio* revised by Alexander von Zemlinsky.

[131] *Neue Freie Presse* (20 Oct. 1901). The first volume was devoted to Haydn's Piano Sonatas.

[132] As early as 1901, Universal published piano scores for four hands (by Joseph Schalk and Ferdinand Löwe) of Bruckner's Symphonies nos. 1, 2, 3, 5, and 6. After acquiring the rights to the Ninth from Doblinger in 1904, it published a pocket edition (edited by Ferdinand Löwe). The archives of the Peters Company reveal that in 1906 Universal offered Hinrichsen the rights to all of Bruckner's symphonies and Mahler's first four for a total sum of 160,000 marks (*Daten zur Geschichte des Musikverlages Peters*, ed. Bernd Paschnicke (Peters, Leipzig, 1975), 38, and Eberhardt Klemm, *Geschichte der Fünften Symphonie*, 93, n. 35). Hinrichsen did not accept, and it was only in 1910 that Universal acquired the rights to Bruckner's Eighth Symphony and the 'Te Deum'.

[133] In 1904, Universal Edition bought the Leipzig and Munich publishing house of Joseph Aibl, whose catalogue included most of Strauss's early symphonic poems (notably *Don Juan, Aus Italien, Till Eulenspiegel*, and *Tod und Verklärung*) and works by Reger and Suppé. Later contracts with Bartók (1908), Casella, Webern, and Zemlinsky (1910), Szymanowski (1912), Janáček (1917) and Krenek (1921), Kodály (1920), Milhaud (1922) and Martinů (1926), and many others, made the firm the leading publisher of 20th-century music; a position it took up again after 1945. Universal has also published the *Denkmäler der Tonkust in Österreich* (1919–42) and the complete works of Monteverdi and Gabrieli.

[134] According to the book *75 Jahre Wien*, published by Universal in 1976, Mahler was not even informed of the negotiations which led to the inclusion of his first four symphonies in the Universal catalogue. [135] Undated letter to Oskar Fried (early Sept., 1906), MBRS 55.

Such posts are for the race (*die Rasse*) of the Kogels[136] and Hauseggers[137]—ability is beside the point! But my dear Fried, <u>chin up</u>! Take comfort from my example—for most of my life I have gone through that sort of thing. You must go on looking—eventually a place you can slip into will turn up. I too shall keep my eyes open. You must remain in <u>Berlin</u> and—my dear Fried—be a little nicer to those who cannot be expected to understand your way of thinking and acting. Again, just think of me, who knows all this only too well. I, too, have been obliged, by the everlasting misunderstandings I encounter and the resulting accumulation of obstacles these cause, to find a *modus vivendi* with the little beasts. And don't forget our principal fault, our race (*die Rasse*): we can do nothing about it. The least we can do is try to attenuate those outward signs of our inborn nature which people find objectionable. By doing this we have to make fewer concessions in our work. I am hoping for the best, only you mustn't lose heart![138]

Because the letter he had written to him in Frankfurt on the subject had apparently gone astray, Mahler wrote to Fried again, a few days before the concert, to tell him that he would bring with him to Berlin the cowbells and gong for the Sixth. 'But since it will be necessary to make a lot of experiments to get the sound effect right, I would strongly advise you to call a general rehearsal on the <u>Monday morning</u> [the day of the concert], which would be most useful.' Mahler himself planned to arrive at the crack of dawn one day earlier, to be able to rehearse the bells and gongs with the percussionist.[139]

A few months earlier, Fried had included in the programme of another 'New Concert' three of Mahler's Lieder, 'Um Mitternacht', 'Ich bin der Welt', and 'Revelge', hoping to reap the benefits from the recent success of the Second. This time the singer was the tenor Ludwig Hess, who had sung at Mahler's Beethoven concert in Strasbourg.[140] He was warmly applauded, especially after the last song. The Berlin correspondent of the *Musikalisches Wochenblatt* praised 'the interesting sound picture' of 'Revelge', and the critic of the *Neue Zeitschrift* found it 'a piece full of warmth and humour, but nevertheless sad and full of special sound effects'.[141]

Mahler arrived in Berlin on 7 October 1906, just in time for the final rehearsal, which he found 'astonishingly good'. 'Fried is a splendid fellow', he wrote to Alma. 'A <u>shame</u> you aren't here. It sounds wonderful. The retouchings

---

[136] Gustav Friedrich Kogel (1849–1921), son of a trombonist in the Leipzig Gewandhaus, became head of the Berlin Philharmonic in 1887 and of the Frankfurt Museumkonzerte in 1903. He was succeeded in Frankfurt in 1903 by Siegmund von Hausegger. According to Hélène de Bary (*Museum, Geschichte der Museumsgesellschaft* (Brönner, Frankfurt, 1937), 109), several candidacies had been considered besides Kogel when Karl Müller (1818–94) had retired in 1891: Wilhelm Kienzl, Ludwig Rottenberg, Felix Weingartner, Hermann Kretzschmar, Raphaël Maszkowsky, and Mahler himself.

[137] See above, Vol. ii, Chap. 1 for biography of Siegmund von Hausegger.

[138] Undated card to Fried (early Oct. 1906), coll. Notar Hertz, Hamburg.

[139] Ibid.   [140] See above, Chap. 3.

[141] Programme for the concert on 19 Dec. 1905, conducted by Oskar Fried: Schubert, Symphony No. 8 (Unfinished); Bach, Violin Concerto No. 1 in E major (soloist: Willi Burmester); Mahler, 'Um Mitternacht', 'Ich bin der Welt abhanden gekommen', 'Revelge' (Ludwig Hess, tenor); Oskar Fried: Duo for Contralto and Tenor, 'Verklärte Nacht' (Ottilie Metzger-Froitzheim, contralto; Ludwig Hess tenor); Strauss, *Tod und Verklärung*.

are excellent ... The <u>Neissers</u> have both come for the symphony.'[142] The Berlin correspondent of the *Neue Freie Presse* reported that although the concert had been a success, the symphony had been less favourably received than the Fifth the year before. According to the *Berliner Zeitung* the middle movements had been applauded but the first and last had been received in icy silence. The *Vossische Zeitung* reported that the audience's response had been very mixed: 'some left the concert hall expressing their anger in fanatical terms, others crowded around the podium applauding and calling Mahler back with such genuine enthusiasm that he was obliged to take several bows'.

But as usual the Berlin press was virtually unanimous in its condemnation, with hardly a glimmer of comprehension. In the *Berliner Tageblatt*, Leopold Schmidt[143] declared himself unable to change his earlier opinion, formed after the première in Essen. The Sixth was not on the same level as Mahler's earlier symphonies. The first movement, by far the best, was not without a certain grandeur; the form was transparent and compact, and the effect imposing since for once Mahler had abstained from inserting 'incoherent ideas'. Such superficial effects as the cowbells and the celesta did not seem disturbing, and Schmidt had enjoyed the Andante, 'full of atmosphere and beautiful sonorities'. The Scherzo, on the other hand, was long-winded, affected, and at times pretentious. The Finale, however, despite one magnificent passage, 'put the patience of the audience to a severe test'. It revealed all the composer's usual weaknesses: his 'extravagance of form and means out of all proportion to his inventiveness'. His ideas, more than ever, betrayed their sources;[144] 'his titanic will outstripped his creative power and this incongruity could not be concealed by sophisticated technical means'. Mahler had let himself go in this Finale, which was full of 'bizarre' ideas.

He may be thinking: 'perhaps, in 150 years time, my music will sound as simple as Schubert's music seems to us today'. Possibly. But the adaptability of the ear so often quoted in defence of all eccentricities is too indiscriminate to be used as a reliable argument. There must be some limit if we are not to get lost in barbarism.[145]

However, Schmidt ended his article on a less negative note: even if Mahler did not point the way to the music of the future, this symphony could not be ignored. The composer's brilliant gifts and fertile imagination, which rose 'above the average level of studious mediocrity', deserved recognition. They helped, 'at least indirectly, to prepare us for the future'.[146]

Otto Taubmann, the critic of the *Börsen Courier*, also judged the Sixth

---

[142]   BGA, no. 183 (postmarked 7 Oct.).

[143]   See above, Chap. 4, for the biography of Leopold Schmidt.

[144]   Mozart, Schubert, Liszt, Brahms, and Wagner were, according to Schmidt, the composers from whom Mahler borrowed his themes.

[145]   As seen above, it was after reading Leopold Schmidt's article on the Essen première that Mahler decided to forego reading the others (MBR1, no. 229; MBR2, no. 352, to Ludwig Karpath).

[146]   Schmidt's article was reprinted in a slightly abridged form in *Aus dem Musikleben der Gegenwart*, (Hofmann, Berlin, 1909), 283.

Symphony to be inferior to its predecessors. 'In his handling of the orchestra, Mahler gives what almost amounts to a collection of sound pictures which could be used to illustrate a "practical guide to orchestration". In so doing, incidentally, he commits assaults on the eardrum which come close to the limit of what the normal ear can bear.' In the rich, over-rich polyphony of the work Mahler repeatedly combined themes that were incompatible with each other, and the result sounded dreadful. Taubmann was prepared to admit that use of this technique could be justified in *Salome* by the drama of the work, but was difficult to explain or justify in a symphony not intended as 'programme' music. He had not found one sustained musical idea in this composition, and while part of the audience had applauded, the majority had left shaking their heads in justifiable doubt.

According to the *Börsenzeitung*,[147] this long-awaited musical event amounted to a 'supreme expression of musical impotence'. 'It was impossible for anybody to express less, or anything so insignificant with such a display of pathos and bombast.' If you stripped the symphony of its 'superficial effect-making, its grease-paint of exotic harmonies, and its instrumental affectations' there was pitifully little left. 'How can so important a musician as Herr Mahler continues to be go against his own musical conscience and assault his listeners' ears with such crazy cacophony? It is beyond one's normal powers of comprehension.'[148] As to the *Berliner Zeitung*, it found nothing favourable to say except that Mahler had shown some of the characteristics of bohemian *Musikanten*, that is to say a preference for rich sonorities. The critic went on to accuse him of formlessness and long-windedness, of having borrowed almost all his melodic material from other composers, particularly in the Finale. The Andante he called 'one long jumble and gasping for breath', demonstrating Mahler's 'inability to invent original themes and develop them logically'. As to the cowbells, they 'left a taste of milk—but pasteurized milk'.[149]

Only the critic of the *Vossische Zeitung*, in the article already quoted above, made a serious attempt at greater understanding. He reminded his listeners that he had analysed the work in detail after its première in Essen. At the time he thought it might represent man, his exaltations, struggles, and joys, defying and yet defeated by fate, 'a song of destiny of vast dimensions'. Mahler, with his complicated inner life, his strange inclination towards both sentimental

---

[147] The critic was, in all likelihood, Otto Taubmann (1859–1929). Born in Hamburg, he was already launched upon a business career when he began to study music at the Dresden Conservatory. After working as a Kapellmeister, he moved to Wiesbaden before settling in Berlin (1889), where he taught composition at the Staatliche Hochschule. His work as a composer includes several long works for chorus and orchestra, an opera, and some chamber music.

[148] The critic discovered a 'great similarity' between a motif in the first movement and the first theme of Liszt's Concerto in E flat (a thematic reminiscence which has often been noted since then) and between the Finale and a theme of Schubert's Unfinished Symphony.

[149] At this time, the Sixth Symphony's percussion section consisted of five kettledrums, two military drums, one bass drum, cymbals, a xylophone, Glockenspiel, bells, birch rod and cowbells, and hammer. According to the *Berliner Zeitung*, it had been scaled down for this performance.

folk melodies and bizarreries, would continue to be an enigma for a long time yet. At its first performance in Berlin, his Second Symphony had been a fiasco, and yet ten years later the same work, in the same place, had gained a 'splendid victory'. How would the Sixth be received in ten years' time? Bruckner was still a subject of controversy and the same would certainly apply to Mahler for many years. In one respect both friend and foe were bound to agree: Mahler used independent, original forms of expression and spoke a language which was his own. Like Strauss, he was certainly one of 'the most interesting phenomena of our time, which is unfortunately poor in interesting phenomena'.

Such objectivity was exceptional in Berlin, where the *Allgemeine Musik-Zeitung's* correspondent was just as horrified by the 'truly infernal orgy' of the Finale as his colleagues in the daily press. Once again, it was 'physical torture, . . . an outrage for the ears' and 'not worthy of serious discussion'. This 'satanic symphony' also highlighted Mahler's weakness of borrowing from other composers, and did not contain anything essentially new. Emil Taubert, correspondent of *Die Musik*, no doubt because the general tendency of that journal had always been to praise Mahler, limited himself to a few comments on the behaviour of the audience, the 'young ladies' who seemed to understand what it was all about, and those 'serious people shaking their heads' because they found the orchestra far too large and the symphony far too long.[150]

A month later, the Sixth was no better received in Munich. This time, Mahler himself conducted the Kaim Orchestra[151] in a benefit concert organized by the impresario Emil Gutmann for the 'Austro-Hungarian Assistance Fund' and the 'Munich Poor'. The programme was unusually long: after the Sixth Symphony, the second half of the concert featured the Dutch contralto Tilly Koehnen[152] and the Hungarian pianist Ernst (Ernö) von Dohnányi,[153]

[150] The concert life of Munich was extremely lively at this time. The concert of 8 Oct. 1906 began at 8 p.m. It took place in the Philharmonie Hall, as one of Fried's 'Konzerte mit dem Philharmonischen Orchester'.

[151] The Kaim Orchestra consisted of seventy-five musicians with yearly contracts, supplemented by extras on occasion. Its programmes still tended to be more modern than those of the Opera orchestra, whose ten concerts per year were conducted by Felix Mottl. Around 1906, the twelve annual 'Kaim Concerts' took place on Monday evenings from Nov. to Mar., under the direction of the Finnish conductor Georg Schnéevoigt (1872–1947). Besides the Kaim concerts, twenty Volkssymphoniekonzerte were conducted with the same orchestra by Bernard Stavenhagen, who was also the chief conductor of concerts of the Musikalischen Akademie, on Wednesday evenings. The orchestra also went on tour in Germany and abroad, with the Kaimchor. The orchestra's rules required the audience not to clap between pieces on the programme, but this was ignored in the case of Mahler's Sixth. The Kaimsaal, renamed Tonhalle, had been built by Kaim in 1893 (see above, Vol. i, Chap. 24).

[152] Shortly after this concert Tilly Koehnen (1873–1941) wrote to Mahler asking him to accompany her in a recital at the piano. Fearing he would receive other requests of this kind, Mahler immediately gave up the idea of accompanying the Vienna recital of Johannes Messchaert, although he later agreed to accompany him in a concert in Berlin on 14 Feb. 1907 (AMM1, 379; AMM2, 326).

[153] Ernst von Dohnányi (1877–1960), pianist, conductor, and composer, was born in Pressburg, then in Hungary, and studied music with his father before entering the Franz Liszt Academy in Budapest. From 1897 to 1899 he studied the piano with Eugen d'Albert, to whom he dedicated his First Piano Concerto. In 1899, in Berlin, he began a brilliant career as a soloist, with tours of Europe and the United States. He taught the piano at the Berlin Hochschule from 1905 on, and returned to Budapest in 1916 to teach at the

both renowned artists. Mahler had written to the Munich impresario Emil Gutmann in advance warning him that he would be unable to conduct the second half of the concert, and would have to use, for the Sixth, all four scheduled rehearsals which 'were scarcely sufficient for the preparation of a work of such size and complexity'.[154] Ultimately, however, he gave in and accompanied Tilly Koehnen, probably out of courtesy, for she had recently begun interpreting his Lieder and symphonic movements.

On the evening of 5 November, before boarding the train for Munich, Mahler wrote an affectionate note to Alma, whom he had probably not seen before leaving for the station directly from the Opera.[155] On his arrival in Munich the following morning, he also sent her a humorous telegram in mock verse:

Im besten Wolsein eingetroffen—dann munter ins Hotel geloffen,—gebadet, und Kaffee gesoffen.—Poetisch ist mein heut'ges Kabel—wie man in München nur capabel,—denn Kunst erfüllt hier Mann und Wabel.—Man fühlt sich hier beinahe griechisch,—darüber freue ich mich viechisch.[156]

(A translation might read: 'In best of spirits, arrived today,—on foot to the hotel made my way,—took a bath and slurped café.—In rhyme I send you this my cable,—as only in Munich is one able,—for Art here is most respectable.—Here one could think one's almost Greek,—I find it great fun so to speak.')

This was the first performance of a Mahler symphony conducted by himself in Munich since the world première of the Fourth in 1901, which had failed miserably. The anti-Semites were even more plentiful here than in Vienna, but luckily the concert was to be a benefit and thus the success of the evening was more or less assured.

From 10.30 a.m. to 1.30 p.m. Mahler conducted the first rehearsal of his Sixth after which he lunched with Emil Gutmann and Bernard Stavenhagen, who had prepared the orchestra for him and was going to conduct a second performance a week after the première. Despite all his artistic reservations concerning Stavenhagen's interpretations of his works, Mahler considered him personally 'a very nice chap', as he wrote to Alma.[157] After distributing tickets

Academy of Music, of which he was appointed director in 1934. He was also appointed director of the Hungarian Philharmonic Society in 1919. After the Second World War, he emigrated to the United States for political reasons and ended his life as a professor at the Music Academy of Florida. As a composer, Dohnányi was a staunch opponent of the new school of Bartók and Kodály, and remained faithful to an academic style derived from Brahms. He left a large number of works in all genres, including three operas.

[154] Undated card to Emil Gutmann (autumn 1906), Stargardt sale of 11 Nov. 1965, no. 268. Mahler demanded six percussionists (not including the timpanist). Two other short notes from Mahler to Gutmann probably also date from this period. In the first, Mahler replied that he was not free on either of the two dates Gutmann proposed, and that it was 'impossible for him to leave Vienna during the month of March'. He suggested putting the concert off until the following season, and added: 'In any case, that would probably be better. "Play hard to get, and you will be all the more appreciated." ' In a second letter, he estimated his travelling expenses (probably for Munich) at 300 kronen: 'Yesterday evening was superb: you accomplished your task perfectly. All my best wishes for the continued prosperity of your enterprise!' (PML, New York).

[155] BGA, no. 188.   [156] BGA, no. 189.   [157] BGA, no. 190, undated (7 Nov. 1906)

for the concert to various Munich celebrities, he began rehearsing again at four o'clock. The zeal displayed by Klaus Pringsheim,[158] who had accompanied him from Vienna, released a vein of sarcastic humour rarely found to such an extent in Mahler's correspondence. Pringsheim, he writes,

again conducted the cow bells in the most virtuoso manner.[159] As a special embellishment one particularly big cow bell has been borrowed from the Hoftheater, and Pringsheim strikes it with his own hand. It obviously symbolizes the yodel. This gives the symphony, and Pringsheim, a very odd look which you, had you been there, would probably have greeted with that sorrowful shake of your head. I must consistently refuse all programmatic explanations. After the rehearsal, Pringsheim insisted on taking me to see his parents. They live in a splendid palace, where I drank tea and felt much at ease amidst these kind and cultivated people.[160]

Afterwards I went (alone) to the Residenztheater and saw a very funny play by Wilde[161] and felt very vexed that you were not there. You would have enjoyed it enormously. Today, at 10.00 a.m., the third rehearsal. The (orchestra) people are making a great effort. Since it is a benefit concert, the most distinguished people will be there (even Archduchess Gisela is expected).[162] The concert management insists that the cowbells shall not be behind the stage but on the podium, and struck in mime.[163] The big one is to be hung round Pringsheim's neck. He will have to run up and down with it, that being the only way to produce the natural sound. This will provide the hit of the evening, and is sure to be a resounding, even a striking success among the female section of the audience. I imagine Stavenhagen will repeat the cowbell passages at a popular concert.[164]

Since 1901 Mahler had been corresponding at irregular intervals with the Swiss writer William Ritter. It is time to say a few words about this young man who was henceforth to play an important and pioneering role as one of Mahler's most eloquent and enthusiastic advocates. A great deal about Ritter has been made available thanks to recent research by the Swiss scholar Claude Meylan, to whom all Mahlerians owe a debt of gratitude. Under the spell of Mahler's personality and works, Ritter had written to Mahler shortly after the Munich première of the Fourth Symphony, which Ritter and his friends had 'heartily booed'.[165] As we have seen, this 'scandalous' composition none the less worked its magic upon him, and he gradually realized that he was increasingly fascinated by it. On 26 December 1901,[166] he wrote a brief note to Mahler, who replied five days later:

---

[158]   Alma substituted the initial 'P' in AMM.

[159]   According to the diary of Janko Cádra (see below), Pringsheim had placed the cowbells under the organ and behind a partly opened door for which Mahler himself carefully gave instructions after consulting William Ritter and his friend who were sitting in the balcony.

[160]   It will be recalled here that the parents of Klaus Pringsheim were also Thomas Mann's in-laws. Mann had married Katia, the twin sister of Klaus.   [161]   *The Importance of Being Earnest.*

[162]   Archduchess Gisela was the daughter of Emperor Franz Joseph and the wife of Prince Regent Leopold (see above, Vol. i, Chap. 2).

[163]   Actually the cowbells were placed under the organ (see below).

[164]   AMM1, 368; AMM2, 319–20.   [165]   See above, Vol. ii, Chap. 11.

[166]   Claude Meylan has discovered among Ritter's papers a copybook in which he wrote his letters on carbon paper, thus preserving copies. Unfortunately he started using it only in 1902, thus it does not include a copy of his first letter to Mahler.

I am delighted by the great interest you show in my works, and am sending you by post, as requested, the score of my Fourth Symphony together with the piano reductions of my other works, insofar as they are available. . . . I would be personally most interested to know what you think of them, and I would be therefore very grateful to you if at some stage you could send me copies of your reviews.[167]

William Ritter was born in Neuchâtel, Switzerland, on 31 May 1867, the oldest of the eleven children of Guillaume Ritter, an engineer and architect of Alsatian origin who was also an amateur violinist and collector of paintings. As a boy William was interested mainly in history, geography, literature, and drawing, but his tastes soon turned to writing and music. He developed these talents more through private study than formal education, although he did for some time attend courses at the University of Neuchâtel and undertook serious musical studies in his native city. Wagner's music was a major discovery for the young man, who attended the Bayreuth Festival in 1886. The next twenty years set the pattern of a life characterized by unquenchable curiosity, ceaseless travel around Europe (to Bohemia, Slovakia, and Romania as well as France, Italy, Hungary, Albania, etc.), a passion for nature, expressed each year by long walking tours during the summer. He was also a tireless practitioner of the visual arts (several thousand drawings and watercolours), and a prolific writer. He met and made friends with many of the literary figures of his time (Barbey d'Aurevilly, Pierre Loti, Léon Bloy, Henry Bordeaux, Judith Gauthier, Willy, Colette, Stefan George, etc.) and also knew, admired, wrote about, and defended many leading painters and artists (Giovanni Segantini, Nicolae Grigoresco, Ferdinand Hodler, Arnold Böcklin, Le Corbusier). Finally, as an amateur musician, he met not only Mahler, but also Anton Bruckner (whose courses he attended for a short time at the Vienna University), the pianist Emil Sauer, Siegfried Wagner, Johann Strauss, Leoš Janáček, and later Igor Stravinsky and Ernest Ansermet.

Thus Ritter became a thorough connoisseur in modern art, in the cultures of several different countries and a witness and commentator of the music of his time. He wrote innumerable articles on literature, painting, and music for newspapers and journals. At a time when most cultured Europeans understood and spoke French, Ritter never took the trouble to master German, but many of his articles were translated into Czech and published by his friend Janko Cádra. He also wrote the first biography in French of Smetana and a great number of novels, few of which were ever published.

In his private life he displayed a complete disregard for all the conventions of the time. At the age of 25 he fell madly in love with Marcel Montandon, a youth of 16, the son of a French couple of Swiss origin who never seemed to have raised the slightest objection to their son's preceptor becoming young

---

[167] MBRS 145. The letters are now in the Schweizerische Landbibliothek in Berne. This letter was dated 31 Dec. 1901 (Vienna), but was only posted on 2 Jan. The postmark indicates that Ritter received it in Monruz (Neuchâtel) on 4 Jan.

Marcel's friend, lover, and companion. The two of them travelled widely around Europe and settled first in Vienna, and then in Switzerland. Marcel became William's secretary, a post he continued to hold until 1900, when he got married. Nevertheless Ritter's relationship with the young couple remained close. He even settled with them in Munich where Marcel and he attended the première of Mahler's Fourth Symphony in 1901. Also with them on that occasion was the young Gottardo, the son of the painter Giovanni Segantini, with whom Ritter was enamoured at the time, a love he soon transferred to his younger brother, Mario.[168] However, the main event in Ritter's private life occurred in 1903, in Prague, when he met Janko Cádra, a handsome Slovak student, fifteen years younger than him.[169] For the next twenty-four years, Cádra was to be William's friend and companion, always present at his side whenever they met Mahler and listened to one of his symphonies. Mahler was undoubtedly aware of the nature and closeness of their relationship, since several of his letters contain greetings to 'you and your friend' or 'to both of you'.

In 1906, the Paris firm Le Mercure de France issued a collection of essays by Ritter, which he immediately sent to Mahler because it contained a long essay about his music, together with the following letter:[170]

I am sending you herewith my book *Études d'art étranger* in which you will find the whole story of my conversion to your works, and also the first study on you published in French. . . . Now Sir I am somewhat perplexed. Who is going to translate all that for you? It is in quite difficult French, and one needs a good knowledge of our modern prose in order to appreciate the sincere admiration which inspires my writing. In a word, in order to write about Mahler I use a style which is itself that of Mahler... if that is possible! In any case these pages will give you the exquisite pleasure of being praised by a perfect anti-Semite!![171] They are based on the knowledge, as you will see, of three of your symphonies. But I intend not to stop there, but to publish my impressions of your works as and when I shall get to know you better. If the person who translates my work for you or tells you what it says is of abolute good faith, it will be impossible for him not to do justice to my own good faith. If you like I am even willing that we arrange to have a literal German translation of my work made under my supervision.

[168] This passage corrects the error I committed in Vol. ii, Chap. 12, where I stated that Ritter was accompanied by Cádra for this première. Actually the two friends only met in 1903. Giovanni Segantini had died in 1899. Mario, the youngest of his two sons, later on abducted William Ritter's younger sister, and the outraged parents forced her to marry him. As a consequence of this, William's other sister took the veil and died young in a convent. Later on, Mario abandoned wife and child and died in an airplane crash.

[169] Janko Cádra was born in Myjava (Slovakia) on 6 Dec. 1882. He died in Bissone (Switzerland) on 7 Oct. 1927.

[170] After the world première of the Fourth Symphony (see above Vol. ii, Chap. 11), Ritter had heard two other Symphonies in Prague: the Third under Mahler (25 Feb. 1904) and the Fifth under Leo Blech (2 Mar. 1905). To publish his first (and only) collection of essays, a thick volume of 471 pages, Ritter had borrowed some money from his family. It contains essays about the writers Camille Mauclair and Blasco Ibanez; the painters Edvard Munch, Josef Mehoffer, Nicolae Grigoresco, Hermann Urban, Nikolas Gysis, Albert Welti, and Arnold Böcklin; and the composers Nicolai Rimsky-Korsakov, Karel Kovařovic, Gustav Mahler, Edgar Tinel, and Johann Strauss, as well as an essay on a painting exhibition held at Munich in 1901, *Feux de la Saint-Jean*.　　　　　　　[171] Concerning Ritter's anti-Semitism, see below.

Ritter asked Mahler to acknowledge receipt of his book and asked him for a signed photograph of himself. He requested four-hand transcriptions of his Fifth and Sixth Symphonies, told him that he read, but did not write German, and finally assured him that he would go to hear his Sixth Symphony as soon as it was performed anywhere within reasonable reach.

This was Mahler's reply:

Dear Mr. Ritter

I have received your book and your kind letter and hasten to send you my hearty thanks, and also the photograph you asked for.[172] Taken a few weeks ago by an amateur photographer, it shows me in my present 'rejuvenated' state. I am afraid it is difficult for me to read your book as I am incapable of following all your brilliant, indeed re-creative, paraphrasing of the music. I would be very grateful for an adequate transla-tion, but do not dare ask you to go to such trouble. However, despite my amateurish knowledge of the French language, I could not resist from browsing a little, and have already received a wealth of stimulating insights. However I find myself much less complicated than your image of me, which could almost throw me into a state of panic. Maybe that one day I shall appear 'simpler' to you. There is one fact on which I should like to take issue with you since, if I understand you correctly, it does me injustice.

You quote a statement of mine: 'Beethoven only wrote one Ninth, but my symphonies are all Ninths.' Am I really supposed ever to have made this remark, which is not only outrageously tasteless—but also so utterly contrary to my true feel-ings? Believe me, my spiritual relationship to Beethoven would not permit me to utter such arrogant nonsense, even in a state of drunkenness, and my pride will be completely satisfied if one day I am considered a legitimate settler in the new territory which Beethoven has discovered for us.

Also, I am altogether averse to any comparisons, I believe that we are all only the rays of a primordial light (*Urlicht*) split up as it pushes refracted through the earthly medium. And that red, yellow, etc., right up to the 'ultra', all together, without order of precedence, 'praise the heavenly glory'.

The première of my 6th will take place in Essen on 27 May; I would be very happy to be able to shake hands with you on one such occasion.[173]

According to Bruno Vondenhoff, who edited the first edition of Mahler's letters to Ritter,[174] the phrase which had so shocked Mahler in Ritter's text was in fact a quote from a Czech review published in Prague after the performance of the Fifth Symphony conducted by Leo Blech in March 1905. Montandon was entrusted by Ritter with the task of thanking Mahler, of assuring him that no French reader would take the sentence about Beethoven's Ninth literally and that he would do his best to dissipate the misunderstanding in a further art-icle. By return mail, Montandon received a signed score of the Second Symphony and these two reassuring sentences:

[172] Now in BGM, Paris.
[173] MBRS 145, undated letter, postmarked upon arrival in Munich on 11 May 1906.
[174] MBRS 146

As to the 'misunderstanding', please assure Mr Ritter that there is no need whatsoever for him to worry. It is not my habit to react other than in a matter-of-fact way to views frankly expressed—and in this case certainly not, since they only reflect the honesty and unerring aesthetic judgement of the author. . . . Rest assured that reading these proofs of being understood from a totally unexpected source—'*legor et legar*',[175] I feel a profound joy.[176]

Ritter was not able to attend the Essen première of the Sixth, nor did he manage to visit Mahler in late August in Vienna as he intended.[177] In mid-October he sent Mahler an apology from Munich, explaining that he had only spent a few hours in Vienna on 2 October, had felt 'an ardent longing for his music', and had 'nearly gone mad with joy' upon returning to Munich, when he saw that the coming performance of the Sixth Symphony was announced there in capital letters on every wall in the city. He had immediately purchased tickets[178] and asked permission to attend the rehearsals, a permission which Mahler granted right away:

It would give me great satisfaction to welcome my 'little clan' (as you are kind enough to call yourself and your friend) at my rehearsals (in Munich). All the more so because my 6th Symphony especially poses dark puzzles to its listeners, and I would like to think that I have been understood by you both in particular... I will certainly not fail to call on you in the Biedersteinerstrasse so as to meet you at last personally, and I would like today already to ask you to give me an hour or two of your company during my 3-day stay. The best thing would be perhaps to have a meal together in a quiet restaurant.[179]

Ritter was of course overjoyed:

I am so looking forward to those days in November, just as twenty years ago I looked forward to going to Bayreuth, and I am infinitely grateful to you for your kindness to me. Since you agree we shall attend every rehearsal, and shall make a real celebration of the hours you will spend with us. You must not waste your time coming all the way out to Schwabing, we will come and report to you as soon as you give us the signal.[180]

---

[175] 'I am read and I will be read.'

[176] Claude Meylan found a copy of this letter, dated 13 May 1906, between two pages (of 11 May 1906) of Ritter's private diary.

[177] Ritter's note was sent to Mahler from Miava (or Myjava), Slovakia (then Hungary). Mahler answered promptly from Salzburg (MBRS 146, card postmarked 17 Aug.) and expressed the hope that 'my French and your German would permit us to understand each other'.

[178] According to Janko Cádra's diary, which was discovered by Milan Palák in the National Slovak Archive (Matice Slovenská), Ritter had worried lest he would not be able to find tickets for the benefit evening. For several days, he spoke and wrote to his friends only about Mahler and his concert.

[179] MBRS 147, postmarked 15 Oct. 1906. Two weeks later (3 Nov.) Mahler wrote to Ritter to confirm the rehearsal schedule which he had already set out in his previous letter, and suggested that he might prefer not to come until the afternoon rehearsal of 6 Nov., when the whole symphony would be rehearsed, whereas the morning rehearsal would begin with the third movement. Letter from Mahler to Ritter, undated (postmarked, 3 Nov. 1906, MBRS 148).

[180] Letter from Ritter to Mahler, dated 20 Oct. 1906, copy found by Claude Meylan among Ritter's papers.

So the Munich rehearsals of the Sixth Symphony were the occasion of Ritter's first meeting with the composer. Luckily for posterity, the prolific writer left a detailed record of them in his private diary:[181]

Thursday 15 November 1906

... I must put down something at least about our first meeting with the master. ... So, it's Tuesday, 6 November, ten o'clock in the Kaim-Saal ... A mighty orchestra is milling around on the stage. The celesta arouses curiosity, it's being looked after by a tender youth, very thoughtful, who later on in the passages where he has nothing to do will listen to the music with a kind of devotion. Let's go out and go up to the gallery. Through the first door on the left of the stage, which opens on to the corridor . . .; and from there we open the door to the stairway, and there is Mahler, very short, very dark, in a great hurry, and right next to us. Just time to say to Marcel 'That's him!' . . ., Marcel introduces himself as agreed, since he talks German. He will introduce us afterwards. But the name Montandon means nothing to him. 'And I am William Ritter.' At that he raises his head sharply and takes a good hard look at me. It's as if the light had suddenly dawned on him and his spectacles had cleared... Never have I been looked at so decisively, once and for all, with such a keen clairvoyance which weighs up and judges . . . A Jewish look, but at the same time full of kindness. I believe that from that moment onwards we have understood each other. But the problem is, what to say now. 'And this is my Slav colleague, Monsieur Janko Cádra!' He turns sharply towards Janko, who bows low, Austrian style, and for a moment he looks even more bewildered than before, but then shakes me vigorously by the hand and mutters some conventional formula about 'the pleasure of having met at last'. But he is terribly hurried and tired. Face sallow from a sleepless night, legs twitching nervously, and so small, so short, my God!... What's the best place for us to be? Does he advise the hall or the gallery? He doesn't really know, and since he is rather distracted we decide to leave him in peace, and go upstairs. We take our seats in our usual corner of the gallery, more or less in the same place from where on a former occasion we heard the Fourth with Gottardo Segantini.[182] The rehearsal begins with the extraordinary Scherzo, bar after bar, then fragment after fragment . . .[183] It's the same Mahler as five years ago, but much more nervous, his legs never stay still. He keeps prancing around. But with his musicians he has, unfailingly, the patience of an angel. The same tics as formerly. He 'leads with his chin', that is to say he repeatedly thrusts his chin forward and pushes the whole orchestra forward with it... At the sudden pianissimos the same way of crouching down and disappearing suddenly knees bent behind his desk, his two arms instinctively stretched wide like some poor devil falling into the water. In 1901 he was in a frock-coat, today he is in a rather threadbare black cheviot suit. No pretention to style, more-over. Low collar à la Casimir Périer into which descends the withered flesh of the neck of an old man. His brown eyes are very kind. He is completely clean-shaven, and thin-lipped. One would take him for a priest, a priest in spectacles, very learned and very

---

[181]   The two first rehearsals were scheduled for Tuesday, 6 Mar., at 10 in the morning and 4 in the after-noon. They were followed by a final (public) rehearsal, on the 7th, again at 10 o'clock.

[182]   The painter's eldest son, with whom Ritter was infatuated at the time.

[183]   According to Janko Cádra's diary, Mahler spent a great deal of time rehearsing two sections of the Trio at no. 78 (p. 92 of the score) and no. 87 (p. 105). The musicians showed signs of impatience but they refrained from displaying it because of 'the power of Mahler's glance' (*une force dans son regard, gentil, non brutal, qui sait désarmer l'ennemi*).

kind: an ascetic professor at some seminary or other. I get the impression that women, the senses, reputation don't matter any more for him, that he only enjoys music, and only lives for his music. He listens to it with delight. When he insists on having a passage played over again, it is at least as much for his own pleasure as it is to get it absolutely right. Perhaps since Essen he hasn't heard it again, this enormous, this entrancing symphony.[184] The bells are not as they should be; deeper, more resonant ones are required... They must be found at all costs, if necessary at the Hoftheater. Gutmann and Pringsheim promise to see to it. The Scherzo, having been taken to bits, is now played over again in its entirety to get an overall impression. It's extraordinary, incredible... typical Mahler music in other words: both grotesque and epic, and often epic in the grotesque or grotesque in the epic. But all the oddities of the orchestration don't in any way harm the musical grandeur, the closeness of the texture or the perfection of the composition. It's hardly over but Mahler jumps down off the podium and collapses like someone whose legs have given way under him into the nearest green and white seat in the first row of the stalls. . . . The gentlemen surround him, standing up and leaning forward. The orchestra spills out into the corridors and outside, feverishly excited... The atmosphere is sensational. . . . Mahler suddenly gets up and with arms dangling behind him, head thrust forward and something ataxic in his gait, disappears—and comes back with a sandwich in his hand. He collapses again on to one of the seats to wolf it hungrily down—the beast feeding itself while the mind is completely elsewhere. One of the Kaim-Saal waiters brings him a glass of water which he downs in one go. . . . And now the monstrous Finale in which the blows of destiny seem to rain down on a great passionate soul whose energies and despairs only grow quiet to listen to the great musical silence of the sounds of nature palpitating around them.

An heroic, an Alpine symphony was what I called it from the start, and having now heard it in full five times that's what I still say, only more so.[185] And conquering and stirring, climbing, always on the move, carried away by an aggressive impetus which goes on and on without stopping... except for a pause, for a rest in the Andante. But we don't know that yet. At one o'clock Mahler relinquishes his orchestra almost as exhausted as he is.[186] It's the percussion which is having everything flung at it and from which he demands things which it seems reluctant to perform. We dash downstairs, and again in the corner of the restaurant between the same two doors . . . we bump into the Master just coming out. . . . Mahler looks completely haggard and we feel sorry for him. He has not yet fully come down from the imaginary world of his creation, more alive for him than the realities of ourselves. He looks at us without recognizing us and reminds me of Grigoresco[187] in his moments of bewilderment. He

---

[184] In fact Mahler had heard his Sixth Symphony conducted by Oskar Fried in Berlin one month earlier.

[185] Ritter is thinking of the four rehearsals, the concert, and the second performance under Stavenhagen one week later, on 14 Nov.

[186] Cádra claims that the rehearsal lasted until 1.30 p.m. and that Mahler also rehearsed the Finale of the Sixth in the morning. According to him, the first, third (Scherzo in this version), and fourth movements of the Symphony were rehearsed in the afternoon. The two Mahler worshippers were apparently depressed by the poor quality of performance at these rehearsals, but this was by no means unusual with Mahler, with whom everything fell into place only at the very last moment.

[187] Nicolae Grigoresco (Grigurescu) (1838–1907) was a famous Romanian painter who liberated the art of his native country from the academic conventions of the nineteenth century. Ritter stayed with him several times in Romania and wrote several articles about his work.

is wearing a thick black overcoat, a shabby student's felt hat jammed flat on his head, and looking more than ever like a priest in civvies... From time to time he absent-mindedly tramples the ground with his feet and jerks with an arm... And I think of Jewish epilepsy. A tall, burly individual tries to accost him. He answers brusquely: 'Not the right time to talk to me about that; I can only think about my symphony.' And since we are still standing in front of him he holds out his hand with an 'Ah!' which proves that up to now he has been looking at us without seeing us. He says he is sorry, he is so tired; and we take our leave. . . .

. . . At three o'clock . . . we return on foot to the Kaim Saal and take up our position in the left-hand gallery. . . . If Mahler wants to talk to us, he will know where to give us the wink. This time he has arranged to have a high platform and a chair from which he will be able to conduct sitting down. He's king of the castle, as it were. First part: it's working comparatively well... It's always the same movement—brisk but measured—which he beats with both arms, and he looks just like a seagull sailing effortlessly over the waves. He turns round in our direction and shows by his look that he knows we are there. Before tackling the Andante, he explains that it has to be full of nuances, of great masses of sound. And the enchantment begins... Many more problems at that point... And just as light is being thrown on the fearsomely difficult score, lights have gone up in the hall. When he looked at us just now, his spectacles shone with the same gleam that one sees in the Böhler caricature. . . . Janko is particularly struck by the Jewishness of Mahler's gestures, his long pointed and hysterical hands, his way of clutching at his hair and his gesture of tearing off his ears...[188]

Wednesday, 7 November. . . .

This morning we are going to hear the whole symphony. Scherzo first, then the Finale, then the Andante. [And the opening Allegro last.] Mahler is again sitting on the top of his tower and beating his wings. . . . And the Scherzo is still causing difficulties. At one moment there is a little revolt even. The great tall fellow who runs around throughout the score, now to the bells, now to the special mallett which beats the bass-drum,[189] now to the cowbells, now to the cymbals and the gong... Suddenly Mahler gets worried about his comings and goings... 'But where are you then?—On the drum,—Then who's on the cymbals?—Me.—And on the cowbells?—Me.—But if you're on the cowbells, you can't be on the drum.—It's me nevertheless.—Then you're a prodigy of nature. ' A general round of laughter. And from then on the worthy fellow is prepared to carry out Mahler's slightest wish. He will clash the cymbals furiously above his head and spread the din over the whole orchestra.[190] But the minute after the 'prodigy of nature' incident, the three triangles are in trouble. Yesterday afternoon Mahler had insisted that they should stand up and strike nearer the base of the triangle. Impossible to get them to do it this morning... The idiots think they make themselves ridiculous by standing up, two of them at least. . . . Suddenly that snooty gawk of a kettledrum-mer who has nothing to do with the problem anyway . . . stupidly mutters: 'They're

---

[188]   Concerning Ritter's anti-Semitisim, see below.

[189]   In his article about the Sixth, published later in *La Semaine littéraire* in Geneva, Ritter explains that this mallet was used to hit the wood of the bass drum. In a letter to Gutmann (see above), Mahler had asked for six percussionists (not including the timpani) but he had obviously not succeeded in getting them.

[190]   At first sight it seems as though Ritter had written 'timpani' instead of 'cymbal'. However, the autograph manuscripts clearly has 'timpani'. What he is no doubt describing is the kettledrum player raising his arms and sticks as high as possible to beat his timpani.

making us do things we don't have to do! Never before have we been made to stand up
to beat the triangle!' We admired Mahler! With a tremor of anger in his voice, he immediately controlled himself, and with a dignity full of sadness replied: 'I don't enter into
that sort of discussion. You are here to carry out what I ask of you, and my job is to
teach you how to do it. You will never have to regret having obeyed me... After all I
know better than you what has to be done...' And they gave in. For the time being...
But the strength of routine or the ill-will was such that, while the next day in the
general rehearsal they made a good pretence of standing up, at the actual performance
in the evening no one moved... That grown men can be so stupidly stubborn over such
a little detail! The complete opposite of the ham actor! Afraid of being caught showing
off, afraid of looking silly by standing up like schoolboys giving answers in an examination...

Forgot to say that having decided—Janko and I—to stay in the hall, when Mahler
came in . . . I got up and went over to him. He was much steadier on his feet, less
sallow, looked a bit rested... After having enquired how he was and told him how
utterly thrilled I had been, I asked him how his composing was getting on: the Seventh
Symphony is finished, the Eighth too, the most colossal one with an immense chorus
at the end. And this news makes me mad with joy. Seeing him yesterday so weak, so
exhausted, the thought had occurred to me that he, like Beethoven, would not get
beyond the ill-starred 9th. Now we can hope again... The next morning, there will be
another rehearsal. He says of course we can come to it... And when I return from this
little chat, I am quite astonished to learn from Janko that Mahler when talking to me
had his hand on my shoulder like an old friend... And I hadn't even noticed it, being
much too occupied watching the expression in his kind eyes. . . .

Saturday 17 November 1906

. . . Must try to finish these interminable Mahler days. . . . So! Thursday 8
November, the great day! We are as usual in the Kaim Saal at ten in the morning. . . .
Janko and I are walking about in the foyer. . . . when who should come up to us but
Mahler. He apologizes for not having been able to find a moment to get together with
us for a chat. . . . Then, suddenly: 'Well, do you still find my music so <u>satanical</u>?
<u>Demoniac</u> I wouldn't mind. There's a big difference between <u>satanical</u> and <u>demoniac</u>...
Are the structure and proportions of the work beginning to become clear for you? Isn't
the line (or the curve [*Bogen*]) of the last part beautiful?' And while chatting with him,
I remind him that the idea of 'satanical' came to me especially after the brutal revelation of the strange Fourth, for which I was completely unprepared.[191] And he invites
me to Berlin for the Third on 15 January. He also tells us that he will not be conducting [himself that evening the rest of the programme], he will be leaving at once . . . by
motorcar. He has to be in Vienna tomorrow morning. He seems to be even better than
yesterday, in fine fettle; he has had his conductor's tower taken away, and will conduct
standing up today. . . .

Evening. We are among the first to be there, of course. . . . In our seats five minutes
before time. . . . From down below Marcel shows us the programme he has just been to
get autographed. Mahler was alone in the foyer, adjusting his tie in front of the mirror...,
he suddenly sees Marcel's reflection coming up urgently behind him. He kindly does
what he asks and also tells him to 'convey my greetings to Mr Ritter'. I was very moved

[191] See above, Vol. ii, chap. 11.

to learn that he could still think of me at such a moment. . . . And up in front the symphony is going ahead. At the unusual sounds, the satanic rumblings, the switches, and the strings being struck by the wood of the bows, I can see La Paz,[192] superstitious like any Spanish woman, showing signs of concern, leaning forward and looking between the chairs and the legs of the members of the orchestra... She's obviously searching to find where those utterly unmusical scratching sounds can be coming from... She finally leans over to her fat numskull of a husband, and I can see him giving her the explanation of an ignorant man who doesn't want to admit that he doesn't know. The poor princess thinks he's given her the answer. But at the end, when Mahler is introduced to her, she makes a couple of short, dry remarks to him, turns and goes off primly towards another group, and I can see . . . from the way she behaves the bad temper of the lady who disapproves: 'I couldn't after all tell him that his music has pleased me!' . . . Mahler's behaviour too is quite amusing: he wears a smile that is both happy and ironical, head thrust forward, eyes and spectacles shining. Evening dress makes him much more Jewish looking, seeing him thus I rediscover my Mahler of earlier days...; his posture moreover is deplorable, with his thumbs in his pockets and the other fingers hanging down the seams of his trousers... I've seen Mahler for the last time this year... and when . . . the pearls of the Liszt Concerto spill out over the piano keyboard... we are already picturing to ourselves Mahler fleeing through the dark night as fast as the motorcar can take him. I have finished my story.

In the article of reminiscences published by his adopted son on the occasion of Mahler's centenary, Ritter recalls once again the moment when he fell finally and totally under Mahler's spell:

It was only a quick glance, but a decisive one, by a man of authority, who took my measure—and established his mastery over me. From that moment onwards I no longer even tried to struggle against the fascination which this prodigious, in certain respects absolutely fantastic being exerted on me.[193]

Another article, published just after Mahler's death, briefly summarizes Ritter's impressions gathered during the Munich rehearsals:

It was with these rehearsals that my friendship with the master started, my admiration having begun with the Fourth Symphony. Mahler, with whom I had exchanged a few letters, now seemed to me not just a genius but a rare, god-like being, predestined to suffer and to triumph over death. From the day I met him in person, I trembled for his life. The unbelievable energy he so recklessly expended could only destroy such a fragile machine, in such bad condition! When questioned about his work this veritable fount of inspiration reassured me: the Vth and VIIth Symphonies were completed. The VIIIth was one immense chorus... he himself 'would never hear it, and [was quite] resigned [to that], since at that time there was not even a concert hall large enough to hold it, nor a man capable of organizing it'.[194]

---

[192] A Spanish Infanta, she had married Prince Ludwig-Ferdinand of Bavaria, the cousin of King Ludwig II (see below).   [193] *Revue musicale suisse*, 101 (1961): 1/2, 33.
[194] 'Le Chant de la Terre de Gustav Mahler', *Gazette de Lausanne*, 26 Nov. 1911. In reply to Mahler's last sentence concerning the Eighth Symphony, Ritter added: 'He counted without Emil Gutmann and the city of Munich.' Curiously enough this article contains information which Ritter never published elsewhere, particularly concerning *Das Lied von der Erde* and the Ninth Symphony.

Shortly after the Munich concert, Ritter wrote Mahler a letter of thanks:

Allow me to call you Master and Friend from now on, without any more of those official titles which are so worthless when it comes to expressing an admiration as
absolute as that which I have come to have, and an affection as profound as that which
I now feel after those magnificent hours I owe you during which you were so kind, so
indulgent to me and my friends. . . . I hope that what I write about the VIth symphony
will be better than the previous essay.[195] Now heaven and earth may pass away, but
nothing shall keep me away from your work. I intend to study it, get to know it to the
core, and write a book about it which shall be a model musical monograph in
French.[196]

In the same letter, Ritter promised to come to Berlin in January to attend all
the rehearsals and the performance of the Third Symphony. Mahler replied:

I shall very much look forward to reading your article on me! But I shall certainly need
a German translation, for I fear that the subtleties and nuances of your style will be
lost on me. I really cannot recommend to you any of the rubbishy articles that have
been written about me—they are usually characterized by misunderstandings or
complete lack of understanding. Even well-meaning and educated writers get hopelessly stuck in the outward form of my works—precisely because they do not take the
trouble to listen and listen again. Instead, they arrive at their conclusions after a single
performance.[197]

The fact that Mahler replied the very next day and sent Ritter the complete
schedule of his Berlin rehearsals shows how seriously he took the Swiss
writer's perception of his music and his talent as a writer, even if he could not
fully appreciate it, so superficial was his knowledge of French. He was obviously convinced of having at last found someone who was not only willing but
eager to listen and listen again to his music, and to make the effort of fully
understanding everything that appeared strange or suspect, or 'banal', or derivative, in his symphonies.

In the event Ritter was not able to travel to Berlin for the performance of
the Third Symphony,[198] probably because he could not afford the expense.
Throughout his entire life he was short of money, for he never earned a steady
income, except from 1908 to 1912, when he was appointed reader in French
to the Crown Prince and Princess of Bavaria. In the lengthy article he
published four months later about Mahler in the Geneva weekly journal *La*

---

[195] Ritter is alluding to the essay he had published in *Études d'art étranger*. His first newspaper article
on Mahler appeared in two instalments of the Geneva weekly, *La Semaine littéraire*, on 9 and 16 Mar. 1907
(see below).

[196] Letter from Ritter to Mahler dated in Ritter's copybook 12 Nov. 1906.

[197] MBRS 148, undated letter (postmarked 13 Nov. 1906).

[198] He informed Mahler of this in a letter dated on 29 Dec. (Ritter's copybook discovered by Claude
Meylan). Once again, he assured Mahler of his complete devotion to him and his works: 'Je sens bien que
rien jamais ne s'est emparé de moi et ne m'a bouleversé comme votre musique. Elle m'a fait vôtre absolu-
ment.' The correspondence between him and Mahler was interrupted after this letter until Sept. 1907 (see
below, Chap. 10). Ritter appears not to have been informed of the unhappy chain of events of that most
unhappy year of Mahler's life. He even believed for a time that he had 'fallen from grace' (see MBRS 149).

Semaine musicale, he attempted to 'define more precisely the features of Gustav Mahler's artistic physionomy'. He emphasized the major role played in his music by childhood memories, and in particular by military music and Bohemian folk music (from which he borrowed instruments like the E flat clarinet). Contrary to what he had written after hearing the Fourth Symphony, he no longer discerned any direct influence of Bruckner in Mahler's music, merely a few 'affinities in technique and composition':

For the past six or seven years, in the cities of Germany, the name of a strange and controversial composer has been appearing on the programmes of the major festivals, a composer of incredible audacity and dangerous, exquisite fascination, and who above all is feared. No one denies his inexhaustible poetic vein, nor his formidable creative power, or prodigious technique, but all speak about him with embarrassment and unease. He is everything his great predecessors were, but that does not prevent him from being himself, an explosion of individuality. But one doesn't trust him; one even boos him heroically; one turns away in horror. And then suddenly one bows down, subjugated. For his musical antics both astonish and shock with their basic unclassifiable originality, and their incidental originalities which in any other composer would appear charlatanesque. With him they fit perfectly. The originalities of detail form an integral part of the other main originality, and we should be no more irritated by them then by seeing orange and green calyxes, multicoloured tulips on the branches of a tree when the tree itself is a magnolia. Blackbirds, finches and nightingales perch on trees in our latitudes but what is abnormal about cockatoos perching on trees elsewhere? Mahler's symphony is an equatorial tree full of instrumental cockatoos.

Mahler is a personality of the first order who is at home in the company of the greatest composers. At the present time he is putting them all in the shade. Mahler is unbelievably complete and diverse: he is a great, an immense poet . . . He uses all the means handed down to him by the masters, and adds something more... The orchestra that he will leave behind him is no longer the one handed down to him by his predecessors, and he has invented new ways of making sounds which before him seemed impossible or ridiculous or which one left to tzigane orchestras: striking the strings with the wood of the bow, hitting with a mallet the frame rather than the head of the bass-drum; switches, large bells, cowbells, sleigh-bells . . . He makes muted trumpets produce sounds no one had ever dared to use before. But above and beyond his ingenuity in producing new sounds there is his musical soul, which can be compared with the greatest, whether in proud or in smiling mood . . . He knows Apollonian splendour as he knows Dionysian urge: he knows so poignantly the thousand voices of pain and the clamour of triumph. He is not afraid of the comic and the grotesque, he allies passion with humour. He is a philosopher who has reflected deeply upon all he has suffered. Read his work:[199] if it is soul and thought, it is also flesh and blood. And it is the only music which we feel to be modern, modern as of today, so much so that we cannot imagine anything beyond it. His analytical polyphony may well be obeying broad preconceived plans executed in the most perfect order, but it is crushing and

[199]   In a footnote appended to his article, Ritter informs his readers that four-hand versions of every one of Mahler's symphonies are available and that they can be played on the piano 'sans rien perdre de leur musicalité'. He also names the conductors other than Mahler who have successfully conducted his symphonies.

overwhelming: it never spreads out in a chain of fine lakes. There is always an unexpected jolt, or surprising instrumental flourish. These gargoyles-on-balusters and grimaces-on-cathedral-capitals are insignificant details in the general nobility and marvellous dignity of the whole. And it is the whole which must be considered if one wishes to be fair.

Ritter's comments about the Sixth Symphony are closely modelled on the notes he had made during the rehearsals. Its most marked characteristic was, he thought:

a martial, conquering demeanour, clearly delineated, [où soufflent toutes les travates[200] d'une énergie forcenée] with all its features heightened by a frenzied energy. Another kind of passion animates it, the passion for struggle, the passion for victory, the passion for joy even in the midst of suffering, the passion even for making suffering serve as a means to joy. Need I say that such are not the attitudes towards life and the game of the world of people like us? To that humanity something else is added, a commanding tone, the authoritarian and imperial air of a head of state, a great general, an ideal and prophetic leader of men. Along with the forging ahead, the other constant impressions are of climbing and dominating...

For the magical coda of the Scherzo, Ritter finds a striking literary image: 'What one might call the withering away of the orchestra, which suddenly seems like a body reduced to the state of skeleton, or a tree bereft of all its leaves.' He defends Mahler against the criticism often levelled against his symphonies, that of being too clever, since this 'cleverness' is no 'hindrance to inspiration'. 'These giant works never give the impression of stuffiness, of having been written indoors, so suffocating for me in Brahms', Mahler 'has let more fresh air into the symphony than it has ever had before, . . . he has pushed back its horizons to infinity.' Besides pointing out the 'modernity' of Mahler's music, Ritter, the biographer of Smetana, also emphasized its Slav and Central European roots:

These giant works . . . avoid being purely German . . . by employing a whole system of analogies which the lovers of Slav and Hungarian music . . . understand much more easily than the average listener in Munich or Berlin. An acquaintance with Dvořák and Smetana is much more useful than a knowledge of Brahms in getting to know Mahler. And the music of the Tziganes! It is not for nothing, I hope, that someone like Mahler, with all his intelligence, love and energy, has lived in cities like Prague, Vienna and Budapest; nor that he has conducted all the ancient and modern works of all nationalities in the Operas of these capitals and some others. Mahler has nothing to learn from anyone. . . . And if it pleased him one day to introduce the Magyar *tzimbalon*, the *cobza*, the Rumanian *pipes of Pan* into his orchestra, not only should I not be surprised, but I should be grateful to him for doing so, . . . he uses to advantage everything he sees, hears, and has to think about in such places. That being so, no wonder that we have in him a symphonist such as there has never yet been, a genuine symphonist of the new millenium.

[200] A thorough research of dictionaries and encyclopedias of the French language has not revealed the exact meaning of this neologism.

It is painful to have to remind oneself that the writer who thus extols the multiplicity of other than German influences which he can recognize in Mahler's music should have been and remained throughout his life a self-declared and unashamed anti-Semite. When he first threw himself at Mahler's feet and paid homage to his supremacy as a modern composer, he described himself—almost boastingly—as a 'perfect anti-Semite'. And in his autobiography[201] and his correspondence we find comments like: 'after having seen the Jew at work in Romania, Hungary, Slovakia, Moravia and Bohemia', or 'obsequious to the mighty, oppressor of the weak, swindling the peasant, poisoning him with adulterated liquor'. How could Ritter reconcile his brand of rabid anti-Semitism with his idolatry of Mahler? Perhaps—subconsciously—he was according Mahler 'honorary Aryan' status. And his frequent references to the Jewishness of Mahler's physical appearance and behaviour were only his way of enjoying the paradox he himself had created.

What is so remarkable about Ritter's article is that it was written at a time when he was the only one, or almost the only one, really to understand Mahler's genius, to perceive his importance as a composer, and to penetrate the absurdity of the criticisms levelled at him by most of his contemporaries. Even people like Schoenberg, Webern, Hauptmann, Dehmel, all of whom at one point or another fell under his spell, even they did not, perhaps, realize to the same extent as Ritter the dimension of this personality, the power of his imagination, the authenticity of his emotions, the novelty of his orchestration, the originality of his heterogeneous style, of his sudden breaks and changes of 'tone', despite or even because of the famous 'borrowings' which caused so much ink to flow. In this climate of critical incomprehension, it is not surprising, therefore, that two weeks after the publication of the second half of the article in Geneva, an unsigned article entitled *Ein Mahler-Enthusiast* appeared in the *Neues Wiener Journal*, allegedly written by a correspondent in Zurich. Ritter's article was described as 'a panegyric overestimation of a talent already recognized in Germany as bluff'. Ritter is accused of belittling other composers to magnify his idol, and the anonymous writer was especially indignant at the reference to Brahms as a 'chubby little barrel': 'What would Ritter say if, rendering like for like, we used Mahler's simian jaw and slovenly stance as a reflection on his demigod's music?' Mahler himself had described how a church choir singing Klopstock's poem 'Auferstehh'n, ja Aufersteh'n' had inspired the Finale of his Second Symphony, and this amply demonstrated his 'superficiality'.[202] The general feeling about Mahler's music in the German world of music was, the writer claimed, one of disappointment at the way he had developed.[203]

---

[201] Ritter's autobiography was allegedly written by his adopted son, Josef Tcherv, but he himself dictated and edited many passages. The original manuscript is preserved among Ritter's papers at the Bern National Library.

[202] The author is referring to Mahler's description of Bülow's burial in a letter to Arthur Seidl (MBR1, no. 209; MBR2, no. 216), which he permitted the latter to reprint in an article (see above, Vol. i, Chap. 23).

[203] *Neues Wiener Journal* (21 Mar. 1907).

Despite the inevitable and polite enthusiasm which characterizes official occasions, particularly benefit concerts, the Sixth Symphony was no better understood by the critics in Munich than it was in Berlin. The Bavarian capital loved above all Wagner and Richard Strauss. It was definitely prejudiced against Mahler, and the Sixth was not the type of music likely to change anyone's mind.[204] Before leaving the last numbers on the programme to Stavenhagen and returning to Vienna, Mahler conducted the Prelude to *Die Meistersinger*[205] and accompanied Tilly Koehnen in three Lieder with orchestra.[206] According to the Vienna *Neue Freie Presse*, he took ten curtain calls after his symphony, and was presented with a laurel wreath decorated with the colours of the Austrian Empire and the city of Munich. Prince Ludwig-Ferdinand of Bavaria[207] and Archduchess Gisela went backstage to congratulate him at length during the intermission. When his work was conducted a week later by Stavenhagen,[208] the Munich press, as in Berlin, once again gave full rein to its hostility, which had already been amply displayed after the first concert. The *Allgemeine Zeitung* considered the choice of some of the instruments employed, such as cowbells, xylophone, rods, hammer, etc., as 'nonsensical' from a purely musical point of view, even more so in the absence of an explanatory 'programme'. Mahler's art attempted, by a slavish and superficial 'imitation of nature' to give dead material the 'deceptive appearance of having life and soul, but it was only empty superficiality'. Nevertheless, although strongly influenced by Wagner and Bruckner, Mahler was an 'authentic' creator, as was borne out by the beautiful Andante, 'full of atmosphere'. The other movements were superficial, 'illustrative theatre music'.

Hugo Daffner,[209] the author of the above report, further developed his criticism in a long article in the *Neue Zeitschrift für Musik*. Once again, he savagely

---

[204]   Adolf Chybinski, 'Erinnerungen an Reger, Strauss, Mahler und Grieg, Blätter aus den Memoiren', in *Ruch Muzyczny*, Cracow, 1 (1957): 9, 20.

[205]   Most of the Munich critics hailed his interpretation with enthusiasm. The *Münchner Post* described it as 'thoroughly convincing despite the rapidity of the tempo and unusual dynamic nuances'.

[206]   They were Richard Strauss's *Hymnus*, Op. 33, No. 3; Weingartner's 'Frühlingsgespenster'; and Hugo Wolf's 'Er ist's', from the *Mörike Lieder*. The singer was Tilly Koehnen. After Mahler had left Bernard Stavenhagen conducted Liszt's Concerto No. 1 in E flat, with Ernst von Dohnányi as soloist—see above.

[207]   Princess Gisela was an Austrian Archduchess (see above Vol. i, Chap. 2). Prinz Ludwig-Ferdinand of Bavaria was the husband of the Spanish princess who had so disapproved of the sound of the rods (see above). A letter which Mahler addressed to him in 1906 was sold by Stargardt, in Marburg, in 1962. It accompanied a package containing the piano and orchestra scores of the Sixth Symphony. For politeness's sake, the prince had no doubt tried to soften the effect of his wife's brusque behaviour by asking Mahler to send him a score of his new work.

[208]   According to Janko Cádra's diary, it had been announced that Mahler would conduct the concert himself but he later cancelled his participation by telegram.

[209]   Hugo Daffner (1882–1936), composer and critic, doctor in musicology (Leipzig, 1904), had been a pupil of Thuille and Reger at the Akademie der Tonkunst in Munich. After publishing a number of compositions (including about thirty Lieder), he began his career as critic at the *Allgemeine Zeitung* and became the Munich correspondent for the *Neue Zeitschrift für Musik*, the *Königsberger Allgemeine Zeitung* (1907–8), and the *Dresdner Nachrichten* (after 1909). Later, he studied and practised medicine in Berlin during the 1920s. Author of a thesis, 'The Piano Concerto before Mozart' (1906), a monograph on Nietzsche's marginal notes to the score of *Carmen*, and another on the Salome theme in art history, Daffner died in Dachau, one of the first victims of Nazism.

criticized Mahler for 'profaning art with superficial, heavy-handed naturalism, . . . both photographic and phonographic', since cowbells, hammers, and birch rods had no place in a work which claimed to have no 'programme'. Mahler's themes gave an impression of 'wanting to but being unable to'. Even the Andante was rejected as belonging to an outmoded genre, inspired by, and watering down, the Romanticism of a Mendelssohn. Only the orchestration was 'worthy of the highest interest', with its 'combinations of hitherto unknown timbres' and the wonderful clarity of its smallest details. Daffner could not recommend anyone to listen to this symphony or read its score except as 'a manual of modern techniques of orchestration'.

The *Münchner Zeitung* likewise reproduced many of the clichés of contemporary criticism about Mahler, stressing his 'bizarreries', his 'quest for originality at any price', and 'penchant for refinement and sound effects'.[210] Mahler had regressed ever since the Second Symphony, and his present style, a pale reflection of his earlier manner, was characterized by rhythmic monotony and remarkably dull coloration. The verdict of the *Münchner Post* was equally emphatic: the Sixth must be rejected as a 'monstrous' work, in which Mahler's thematic banality, absence of inspiration, and lack of symphonic thought 'with organic strength' attained new depths. The critic regretted that 'the creator of the marvellous C minor Symphony and profound Fourth' had strayed into the labyrinth, already foreshadowed in the Fifth, made of 'gratuitous noisy sound experimentation, barbarisms, monstrosities, excesses, abominable ugliness'. Altogether it was musical grotesqueness with a strong emphasis on 'irony and self-parody', a 'Shaw translated into music'. A 'cold shower of rationalist mockery', with no attempt to escape from these 'destructive and negating spheres', it left the listener 'disconsolate and unsatisfied'. In the *Neue Musikalische Presse* the same criticisms and comparisons, couched in identical terms under the signature of Wilhelm Mauke,[211] showed that he was clearly the author of both articles. This time he stated in his conclusion that studying the shape of Mahler's mouth in Orlik's famous drawing had confirmed him in his conviction that Mahler was making fun of his audience, by 'parodying in his work the whole of modern music'. Some of the audience, quite rightly, had shown their lively opposition to 'Shavianism in the sacred art of music'.

For the critic of the *Bayrischer Kurier*, Mahler's symphony was a sensational event in the negative sense. By means of his technical brilliance the composer had tried in vain to make 'musical impotence clothed in tawdry finery, into the goddess of music'. Strauss, in comparison, seemed a tame classic. The only

---

[210] According to the *Münchner Zeitung*, Mahler finally abandoned the (rectangular) drum which he had had made to order, and the three 'hammerblows' of the Finale were struck upon a kettledrum with a wooden mallet.

[211] Wilhelm Mauke (1867–1930), composer and critic, was born in Hamburg. After studying with Hans Huber in Basle and the Akademie der Tonkunst in Munich he became the principal music critic for the *Münchner Zeitung* until 1919, and then again after 1924. He was a prolific composer, and wrote several operas, an oratorio, symphonic poems, a piano concerto, and chamber music.

things missing in the Sixth were 'the rattle of musketry, the boom of the cannon, the roaring of lions and the noises of tropical animals'. As for Rudolph Louis, the unrepentant anti-Semitic critic of the *Neueste Nachrichten*, he maintained the opinions he had expressed after the Essen première. The Sixth Symphony 'is not one of Mahler's strongest creations', 'it does not bring anything essentially new which one did not already know from the earlier symphonies. But it should be said that this Symphony is one of those works which can very well stand being heard more often, and which on closer acquaintance gains rather than loses.' Mahler's music was 'interesting throughout'. One could enjoy 'the charm of the details' 'once one had overcome what I felt to be the general impression of rejection and unfriendliness'. According to Louis, Mahler had 'greatly altered his instrumentation' since the première, had 'cut down on the use of percussion' and 'here and there touched up the melody and the voice-leading'. 'Here, as in Essen, the audience was most impressed by the Andante moderato. . . . It sounds absolutely lovely, although it has a sweetly cloying sentimental quality which is not everyone's cup of tea.' As for the Finale, it 'aspired to monumental grandeur, but failed to achieve it. . . . Nevertheless the Finale, in spite of all the crudeness and brutality which tried to make up for its lack of strength, it displayed an enormous amount of technical and structural skill which compels the highest admiration.'[212]

Mahler refused to give way to discouragement and chose to consider these outbursts as a mere prolongation of past experience: no first performance of his symphonies had ever been successful and 'the Sixth will have to wait until my Seventh comes out'.[213] In a letter written to Mengelberg after the Berlin concert, he added: 'My Sixth seems to be another hard nut which the critics will be unable to get their puny teeth into. In the meanwhile, it keeps muddling through as best it can in the concert halls. I am looking forward to the Amsterdam performance.'[214]

At the end of 1906 Mahler undertook three more trips abroad, two of them to conduct the Third Symphony, which continued to arouse interest in Germany. At the instigation of his friend Albert Neisser, the eminent dermatologist,[215] he had again been invited to Breslau at the end of October, where

---

[212] The 8 Nov. concert took place at 7.30 p.m. in the Kaimsaal (renamed Tonhalle).

[213] MBR1, no. 229; MBR2, no. 352, undated, to Ludwig Karpath.

[214] MBR, no. 308, MBR2, no. 366, undated letter (postmarked 15 Oct. 1906). See also RMH 72. Mengelberg had invited Mahler to conduct the Dutch première of the Sixth Symphony in Jan. 1907 (see below).

[215] See above, Vol. ii, Chaps. 11 and 13 and Vol. iii, Chap. 4. Albert Neisser was the first cousin of Siegfried Berliner, the father of Arnold, Mahler's close friend from Hamburg days. According to Doda Conrad, son of the soprano Marya Freund (née Mimi Henschel in 1876), Albert Neisser on that occasion introduced the soprano to Mahler, who declined to audition her in Neisser's salon, but asked her to sing an air from *Carmen* on the stage of the Breslau Opera, and thereafter sought to discourage her from singing opera, warning that 'there, it is fresco painting, while you prefer miniatures!' He steered her toward his own Lieder, which she was soon singing throughout Germany. She sang the *Kindertotenlieder* for their Paris première in 1912, and her success was such that she repeated them again during the same season at a Lamoureux concert. In 1914, Marya Freund sang the same cycle under Pierre Monteux in a programme at the Casino de Paris which also featured *Le Sacre du printemps*.

the local conductors Georg Dohrn and Hermann Behr had been entrusted with the rehearsals prior to his arrival.[216] Friedrich Weidemann and three musicians from the Vienna Hofoper (the first trumpet, first horn, and first trombone) accompanied Mahler to Breslau. Weidemann was to sing four *Wunderhorn-Lieder* and one *Rückert-Lied* in the same programme.

After two rehearsals in a row on his first day in Breslau, Mahler admitted that he was beginning to weary of conducting the Third. 'Unfortunately,' he added, 'the others are incapable [of conducting it].'[217] Magnificent weather in Breslau permitted him to take long walks between rehearsals and recuperate from the Vienna visit of the 'Dreyfus Quartet' which for ten days had taken up so much of his time. Just before the final rehearsal at 5.30 p.m. on the day before the concert, he wrote to Alma that everything was going well, but the rehearsals had exhausted him. He was going to take the night train back to Vienna immediately after the concert.

During the performance, the first movement, as so often in the past, was greeted with both boos and applause; the second and third with hearty applause, but the final ovation was, as usual, overwhelming. The press, however, who had shown such understanding for the Fifth the year before, expressed many reservations. The principal critics deplored the deletion of titles for the different movements. In the *Breslauer Zeitung*, Emil Bohn[218] thought that despite the beauty of many details, the first movement could not be considered to be a 'complete whole'. The second and third found greater favour with him, though in the fourth, with its earnest alto solo, he found the orchestra sombre, the effect 'depressing and even pessimistic' and the [following *Wunderhorn*] chorus 'contrived'. The length and uniformity of the Finale, despite many beautiful passages, were 'tiring'. Although he disliked certain features in Mahler's music, he would definitely follow his development with interest. The same comments—praise for the middle movements and criticism for the first and last—were forthcoming from the *Schlesische Volkszeitung*, which deplored the 'reminiscences' in Mahler's symphony and the lack of a programme. Nonetheless, 'the audience followed the performance from beginning to end, with real interest, and without tiring, thereby testifying to the importance of the work and the quality of the interpretation'.

Only Ernst Flügel[219] came out in favour of the Third Symphony in the *Schlesiche Zeitung*. The impression it produced on him was 'powerful, magnificent, at times overwhelming'. Even if one disliked certain details, 'the work as

---

[216] For the Breslau concert, Mahler was only absent from Vienna for four days. Apart from the note which he sent Alma, as usual, from the station in Vienna, and the telegram announcing his arrival at his destination, he sent only two brief notes from Breslau, see BGA nos. 186 and 187 (22 and 23 Oct. 1906). George Dohrn (1867–1942) was the chief conductor of the Breslau Orchesterverein and the Singakademie. Mahler wrote to him after coming back to Vienna: 'I would like to take the opportunity to tell you once again . . . what a pleasant memory I have of the Breslau days. . . . About the reviews, . . . I was quite astounded, and—I will readily admit—delighted.' (Undated card, Stargardt catalogue, sale no. 659, 16/17 Mar. 1995).

[217] BGA, no. 186.   [218] See above, Chap. 4, for Emil Bohn's biography.

[219] See above, Chap. 4, for Ernst Flügel's biography.

a whole was uplifting'. Everything, except for the first movement, could be easily understood, and anybody capable of producing such a Scherzo has 'something worthwhile to say to the world'. With his work, filled with 'passages of outstanding beauty' and 'instrumental wonders', Mahler had 'won the hearts of Breslau music lovers' as a 'relatively naive creative artist, who could claim his "goddess" to be imagination, that provider of life and diversity of form'.[220] But Johannes Fink, correspondent for the magazine *Die Musik*, thought that Mahler's success in Breslau was to be attributed to the conductor rather than his compositions, in which the 'brutality of contrasts' was almost intolerable, while the 'quotations' kept people wondering whether they were intended or unintended.

While Mahler, after returning to Vienna, was busy with the final rehearsals for *Der Widerspenstigen Zähmung*, his music was heard for the first time in the august precincts of the Leipzig Gewandhaus[221] with a performance of the Second Symphony. The concert, the fourth in the subscription series that year, took place on 1 November and was conducted by Nikisch. It was warmly received by the public at the dress rehearsal and at the concert, both of which were sold out. As in Breslau, however, the critics held aloof. Paul Merkel in the *Leipziger Neueste Nachrichten* castigated Mahler for his tendency to 'borrow dramatic passages from our great composers' and for deploying 'a host of musical ideas which however lacks the power of conviction'. Almost throughout, Mahler's language was 'cold and sober', devoid of personality, and by the time he had finished, it had 'fallen on deaf ears'. Where, on the other hand, he 'forces pathos into his language', it becomes hollow and verbose. Many words and long symphonies amount to nothing where the ideas do not spring from the mind or the feelings of the composer.

In the *Leipziger Zeitung* Arthur Smolian[222] described Mahler as one of several modern 'orchestral magicians, sound-hypnotists, and vocal and instrumental mass murderers. Despite all its brutality, ugliness, and reminiscences,'[223] Smolian found the first movement 'captivating', and preferred the 'folkloric amiability' of the Andante to the 'banality of the Scherzo', the 'tortuous, exhausting' length of the Finale, and the 'sought rather than found' 'Urlicht'. Mahler was not as skilled an orchestrator as Richard Strauss. 'If only Mahler were melodically and thematically creative', Smolian wrote, 'he could indeed be called the Meyerbeer of the symphony' in view of his technical bril-

---

[220] The Breslau concert took place on 24 Oct. with the participation of the Breslauer Orchesterverein, the contralto soloist Toni Daeglau, the Singakademie women's chorus and the Magdalena Gymnasium children's chorus. To begin with, Weidemann sang three *Wunderhorn-Lieder*: 'Der Schildwache Nachtlied', 'Des Antonius von Padua Fischpredigt', 'Das irdische Leben', and one *Rückert-Lied*, 'Ich bin der Welt abhanden gekommen'. A month later, Georg Dohrn engaged Weidemann to sing the same Lieder on 22 and 23 Jan. 1907, and asked Mahler to release him for those dates (letter dated 20 Nov., HOA, Z. VIII, 247/1906).

[221] Mahler had conducted the first two movements of the Second at the Lisztverein in Leipzig in 1896, and in 1904 the Third in its entirety with the Winderstein Orchestra.

[222] See above, Chap. 1, for the biography of Arthur Smolian.

[223] He even discovered traces of *Carmen* (!) and Beethoven's Violin Concerto in the symphony.

liance, good ear for effects, and superficial contrivances. But for this very reason he failed to rise to 'the true, spiritual essence of the absolute symphony'. The individual movements were 'spun out far beyond their actual ending', and 'the solemn singing sets in at a time when the audience has already been tormented by all sorts of stopgap music' to the point of becoming impatient.

In the *Leipziger Tageblatt*, Heinrich Zöllner[224] wrote that at first he had wondered whether Mahler was making fun of him, but concluded that he was laughing at himself. At the same time, the work showed true depth of feeling and contained moments of great beauty. He admired Mahler's mastery of counterpoint, even though the themes were sometimes 'not clearly stated' and therefore difficult to follow in their various transformations. Despite the 'hellish music' with which it began, the last movement, with its 'strangely touching' 'Urlicht' and the 'brilliantly conceived' chorus, probably made the deepest impression on the audience. Zöllner concluded that the Gewandhaus had made the right choice in performing Mahler's symphony. Indeed, it should not confine itself to this one symphony, as it was the responsibility of a top-ranking concert institution to acquaint the public with the works of outstanding contemporary composers. It was true that Mahler's music was sometimes strongly influenced by other composers, but this was of no importance since much of what he had to say was his own. Moreover, the symphony, particularly the second and the last movements, had received a great deal of applause from the Gewandhaus public, which normally showed little enthusiasm for novel forms of music.[225]

Die Musik wrote off the Leipzig concert with a very brief article which claimed that the symphony had produced 'neither joy nor enthusiasm' but certainly a 'sensation'. Mahler lacked 'creative force' and only his faith in his own originality, in the great ideas he got from others and the small ones which were his own, enabled him to write such symphonies of unheard-of length and undiscoverable depth.

Thus at a time when Mahler's early works were beginning to be accepted in some quarters, in others they remained as bitterly contested as ever. Perhaps the performance in Leipzig would have met with a different reception if Mahler had conducted it himself, for Nikisch's understanding of his music, as we

---

[224] Heinrich Zöllner (1854–1941), son of composer and chorus leader Carl Friedrich Zöllner, was a student at the Leipzig Conservatory, then taught at the Cologne Conservatory and conducted the Deutsches Liederkranz of New York from 1890 to 1898. Universitätsmusikdirektor in Leipzig from 1898 onwards, and professor of composition at the Conservatory from 1902, he was also the music critic for the *Leipziger Tageblatt*. From 1907 to 1912 he conducted at the Antwerp Opera. He composed a great number of works, mostly operas.

[225] Programme of the fourth Gewandhaus subscription concert, conducted by Arthur Nikisch on 1 Nov. 1906: Wagner, Prelude to *Die Meistersinger* and *Siegfried Idyll*; Mahler, Second Symphony. The two soloists, Frida Schreiber, contralto, and Jane Hannah-Osborne, soprano, were both members of the Leipzig Opera and the chorus was that of the Gewandhaus.

already saw in Berlin, was limited.[226] In any case, it was going to take a long time before the Sixth and Seventh Symphonies would achieve public recognition, a prospect which would have discouraged anyone but Mahler.

Shortly after his return from Munich, Mahler left Vienna with Alma for his native province of Moravia, where the Brünn (Brno) Philharmonic Society had invited him to conduct his First Symphony. As usual, he had accepted on the condition that he could take with him a group of musicians from the Vienna Philharmonic, including his brother-in-law Arnold Rosé.[227] The orchestra had been carefully prepared by August Veit, the local conductor, and Mahler's arrival created a sensation in the city, famous today for being the birthplace of Leoš Janáček.[228] Local music-lovers had clearly been perplexed by Mahler's First, but at least they gave the Director of the Vienna Opera a welcome worthy of him. According to Alma, Mahler followed her advice on this occasion by suppressing one of the last minute alterations he had made to the Finale,[229] lowering the volume of the first climax in order to give greater weight to the second. Now he went back to his original version, and during the last rehearsal he went through the entire movement to make certain that it sounded as he wanted it to.[230]

The evening of the concert, according to the local press, the hall was sold out and there was thunderous applause after every movement, and also when, at the final curtain call, Mahler was presented with a laurel wreath. The *Tagesbote aus Mähren und Schlesien* gave a long description of Mahler's conducting, his 'almost imperceptible' movements and the rigorous discipline which reigned throughout the orchestra. As a composer, it claimed, 'alone among his contemporaries he has the courage to follow the straight line of melody and not disdain folklore'. Indeed, he had often been criticized for using material borrowed from folk music in an artificial way and for 'emphasizing and ornamenting the most ordinary ditty in caricatural manner'. His art was certainly 'more lucid than Bruckner's'. But it is obvious that the critic was being chary of revealing his own personal impressions. In the *Brünner Zeitung*

---

[226]   In his biography of Arthur Nikisch, Heinrich Chevalley (Bote und Bock, Berlin, 1922) considers that this performance of the Second Symphony was a success and calls this concert a 'milestone' in the musical history of Leipzig. Chevalley adds that Mahler's other works (especially *Das Lied von der Erde*) were only performed at the Gewandhaus after his death.

[227]   The following musicians are listed in the *Mährisch-Schlesischer Korrespondent*: Arnold Rosé (violin); Karl Stiegler (horn); Adolf Wunderer (trumpet); Franz Dreyer (trombone); Otto Stix (double-bass); Anton Powolny (clarinet); and Heinrich Knauer (timpani).

[228]   The première of *Její Pastorkyňa (Jenůfa)* took place in Brno in 1904 (see above, Chap. 1), where Janáček's preceding work, *Počátek románu*, had opened in 1894. Mahler had shown interest in *Jenůfa* for Vienna, but he had asked for a German translation which did not yet exist. Real success for the opera only came with the first performance in Prague in 1916 of Janáček's new version.

[229]   See above, Vol. i, Chap. 19.

[230]   AMM1, 135; AMM2, 134. As mentioned earlier (Vol. i, Appendix 1 on Symphony 1), Strauss wrote to Mahler in 1894 saying that the Finale, in his opinion, should conclude with the first major triumph, but there is no written confirmation of this assertion of Alma Mahler's. The final version of the First Symphony is dated 1906 and it seems highly unlikely that Mahler could have altered the score simply in order to please his wife.

Mahler was congratulated for 'following his own path, unfettered programme music'. His thematic inventiveness was perhaps not the main strength of his work, but it had immediacy and was free from eclecticism. From the almost happy mood of the first movement the music became more and more powerful, and in the Finale it grew into a raging flood which swept one along. Altogether a highly interesting work whose impact it was impossible to resist. But in the *Mährischer-Schlesicher Korrespondent* the author confessed his bewilderment and uncertainty as to what exactly Mahler was trying to express, especially in the last two movements. He concluded that the First Symphony was 'programme music', close to, but not 'imitating', that of Richard Strauss, and could be admired in particular for its clever orchestration, 'thematic invention' and 'sound combinations'. Finally the correspondent of the Vienna *Neue Musikzeitung* reported that the First Symphony had enjoyed a 'striking, merited success' in Brünn, for the 'musical qualities which it displays in such astonishing abundance are seriously meant and of great significance'.[231]

Towards the end of this hectic year Mahler made two more trips to Graz. The success of the Lieder concert the previous year had persuaded Wilhelm Kienzl, the director of the Orchesterverein, to invite him to conduct one of his own symphonies. The Second had originally been considered, but was ruled out because there was no organ in the Stadttheater, and Mahler wrote to Kienzl: 'Since you were able to stage *Salome*, the Sixth should not create any insurmountable difficulties. But I must request that Herr Kapellmeister [Karl Friedrich] Weigmann prepare it with an appropriate number of rehearsals, to enable me to make do with just two complete rehearsals.'[232]

Judging that a symphony with chorus would be more impressive and appropriate for a benefit concert than a work for orchestra alone, Kienzl and his committee eventually selected Mahler's Third Symphony, and managed to round up the 94 orchestra musicians and 300 choristers it required. Once again, Mahler brought the first trumpet, first trombone, and first timpanist with him from the Vienna Philharmonic.[233] On his arrival in Graz on 1 December 1906, Mahler found the orchestra well prepared by Friedrich Weigmann and he wrote to Alma from the Steirerhof Hotel.

I didn't sleep much. When I arrived at 5.30 a.m. poor Weigmann was standing on the station platform. So he does not seem to have got much sleep either. We went to the

---

[231] This first Brünn Philharmonic Society concert of the season took place on 11 Nov. 1906 at 7.30 p.m. in the main hall of the Deutsches Haus. The programme, conducted by Mahler and August Veit, consisted of Mahler's First Symphony, Wolf's *Italian Serenade* (Max Reger's version for small orchestra), and Weber's Overture to *Euryanthe*. The Brünn writer Leopold Schwarz probably attended this concert and was introduced to Mahler, since shortly afterwards he suggested that he set his scenic poem *Daniel* to music. Mahler replied: 'I feel I should inform you that I do not write operas and that therefore, to my great regret, I cannot consider your esteemed offer' (letter from Mahler to Leopold Schwarz, 18 Nov. 1906, BGM, Paris. See below, Appendix to Vol. iiii: 'Why Mahler did not write an opera.'

[232] Undated letter to Wilhelm Kienzl (12 June 1906), Stadtbibliothek, Vienna, I.N. 178.622.

[233] Adolf Wunderer (horn); Franz Dreyer (trombone); and probably Johann Schnellar or Heinrich Knauer (percussion).

hotel on foot. I sent Weigmann home, took my time changing, and then had some excellent coffee and bread and butter . . . Now I am waiting for Weigmann to come and pick me up for the rehearsal. At the hotel, I am being marvellously well taken care of . . .[234]

In his memoirs, the Austrian composer Joseph Marx, a native of Graz, but already living in Vienna, recalls that he came to his native city with a small group of young musicians who listened to all the rehearsals, score in hand. He relates that Mahler entered the rehearsal hall as he often did, with a cigarette in his mouth. One of the ushers called out after him: 'Hey! You there! Smoking is not allowed in here!' Mahler, with devastating dignity, 'Ich bin Mahler'. The usher: 'Painter (*Maler*) or not, you can't smoke in here!'[235] Marx also notes that Mahler was delighted with the enthusiastic reception given his work,[236] although many conservative listeners left the concert hall shaking their heads. Ernst Decsey, who of course was also present, reports an important remark which Mahler made during one of the rehearsals:

he was surprised that the strings never managed to maintain the long notes in the Adagio at even strength. He broke off and said to the musicians: 'That comes from the fact that you play academically, but you should never play music academically! To hold a long *ff* note, just keep bowing back and forth, the more often the bow goes over the strings, the better it will sound. Of course, you have been taught differently—push full stroke, pull full stroke! But then the tip of the bow runs out of strength. You will do it right if you stop listening to your teachers and follow what life and experience teaches you!'

While going over the fifth movement, he turned to the women's chorus and said in his usual insistent manner:

Take a lesson from children! They always speak clearly, for they put all the emphasis on the word, on the consonants! The singer, naturally, is more concerned with tone; he doesn't so much want to say things to people, he wants to sing to them. The child simply wants to express himself, and doesn't yet know about showing off with the voice.

Decsey adds that, like a true musician, Mahler persuaded his listeners most effectively by the tone of his voice. It had the desired effect, for the women's chorus not only sounded beautiful but its words could actually be understood—a rare occurrence.[237]

---

[234] BGA, no. 192, undated (postmarked 1 Dec. 1906). During his next trip to Graz on 23 Dec., for the second performance of the Third, he again sent Alma a letter by pneumatic tube from the Vienna railway station (BGA, no. 193).

[235] Joseph Marx, *Betrachtungen* (Gerlach und Wiedling, Vienna, 1947). Composer, critic, teacher, and autodidact, Marx (1882–1964) was born in Graz and completed his university studies there in 1909, by which time his Lieder had already acquired a certain renown in Vienna. Professor at the Musikakademie of Vienna 1914–52 and its director as from 1922, he was also rector of the Hochschule für Musik (1924–7). He was hired as a critic by the *Neues Wiener Journal* from 1931–8 and by the *Wiener Zeitung* after 1946. Johann Nepomuk David was one of his pupils. Marx was a prolific composer of chamber and orchestral music, but is especially remembered for his hundred or so Lieder. He is usually considered to have been the leader of Austrian impressionism.

[236] Marx claims that Alma attended the Graz concert, and sat in a box seat, but he is certainly mistaken, as Mahler's cards to Alma, quoted above, prove.　　　　　　　　　　　[237] EDS2, 355.

The *Grazer Montagszeitung* reports that for the final rehearsal, Mahler conducted only the first and the last three movements. Since the concert was a benefit for the musicians' pension fund, a number of tickets had been sold for this rehearsal. Mahler therefore refused to rework those passages with which he was dissatisfied until the audience had left the hall. Only then did he make the necessary corrections.[238] If the *Montagszeitung* is to be believed, Mahler publicly provided explanations of the 'programme' of the Third which seem surprising and unusual, to say the least. The first movement, for example, depicts 'the approach of the warriors, the uproar of the battle, victory, and the retreat of the vanquished'. The nameless critic judged the music to be 'a marvellous illustration' of these events, and concluded that Mahler was 'a great personality'—despite the fact that 'his technique [was] superior to his creative power'.[239]

Before the concert, Ernst Decsey wrote a long commentary on the Third Symphony for the *Tages Post*, in which he recalled the original 'programme' of the work[240] and defended Mahler's taste for folk music, which he deemed 'in no way incompatible with technical refinement'. 'Why shouldn't a sincere, authentic work be born out of a sincere, authentic feeling?' he added. On the following day he described the performance itself, which took place before a fashionable audience in a hall filled to capacity. Mahler's podium was strewn with laurel leaves, the orchestra strings were placed in front of the main curtain, and the whole depth of the stage was taken up— apart from the wind instruments—by the women's chorus in long white robes and the children in dark costumes.[241] Mahler refused to allow a welcoming brass fanfare on the grounds that it might affect his frame of mind (he did the same at the end of the concert). According to the *Grazer Tagblatt* the applause was only 'respectful' after the first and third movements, but 'friendly and sincere' after the second, and at the end, 'unanimous and powerful, . . . swelling to great enthusiasm'. Mahler returned to take a bow a

---

[238] See above, Chap. 6, and the *Fremden-Blatt* account previously quoted (6 Jan. 1907). Graz is not mentioned by name in the article, which refers to 'a city in southern Germany'. The allusion is obvious, however, for Mahler never conducted the Third in Munich or any other south German city, and in any case never in the context of a benefit concert.

[239] The *Montagszeitung* also reports that Mahler warmly congratulated the orchestra after the rehearsal.

[240] EDS1, 356. Decsey describes an article he had written on the Third Symphony in which he related the posthorn solo in the Scherzo to a poem by Lenau, 'Lieblich war die Maiennacht' (Lovely was the night of May), in which the poet hears the same 'sound of solitude' in the middle of a forest. (This poem is reproduced under the title 'Der Postillion' in Albert Hiller, *Das grosse Buch vom Posthorn* (Heinrichshofen, Wilhelmshaven, 1985), 69. The postillion stops along his way at a cemetery, to pay a tribute to his former comrade buried there.) Mahler afterwards asked to see Decsey and told him that, when composing the episode, he had indeed thought of this very poem and of its atmosphere and he asked Decsey how *he* too had come to think of it. 'From that moment on,' concludes Decsey, 'I was considered a companion in misfortune (*socius malorum*)' (Ibid. 356). Decsey's pre-concert article (quoted at the end of Vol. ii, Chap. 16) mentions, in fact, neither Lenau nor the poem in question, but calls the Trio in the Scherzo a 'nocturne' in which 'this voice of man [the Posthorn] can be heard only because of its sheer beauty'.

[241] According to Decsey, the performers numbered 550. Other newspapers mention 94 musicians and a chorus of 300.

dozen times, and the triumph was such that he had to promise to return and conduct the work three weeks later.

Shortly after Mahler's death a member of the chorus who sang at this performance published a short article recalling the Graz concert:

Mahler's composing has been a subject of heated controversy, but in Graz we were all of one mind. Conducting his Third Symphony before a breathless audience in the packed Stadttheater, the slight, dapper conductor created an unforgettable impression. We who sang and felt the power of his eyes, the indescribable expressiveness of his small, elegant gestures, and were swept along by the fire blazing in the little man—for us, there was no doubt about him. What depth lay in the melancholy 'Mitternachtslied' (Midnight Song); what high spirit in the buoyant catchy folk tunes, what pure jubilation in the resplendent boys' chorus! 'Lord, I'd like to take you home with me, you golden boys (*Goldbuben*)!' he called out to the jubilant boys, and with his impulsive warmth of heart he shook the hands of whomever he could reach. And anyone with ears and instinct for orchestral music could only boundlessly admire his subtle, brilliant technique of instrumentation. Graz did its musical best, and with a single look or a slight encouraging gesture the nervous, restless little man brought out the best the musicians had to offer.[242]

The music critic of the *Grazer Tagblatt* was Wilhelm Kienzl,[243] one of the most prominent personalities in contemporary Austrian music. Although his aesthetic convictions were diametrically opposed to Mahler's, his opinion of the Third Symphony displays exceptional objectivity:

No one today, should pronounce final judgement upon a phenomenon like Mahler, as his life's work is not yet complete. And one work alone is certainly not sufficient to classify a master as belonging to a particular trend. . . . It is better therefore, to concentrate on immediate impressions. . . . Evaluations are always relative and incomplete, and usually only possible after a certain lapse of time.

About one thing there was no doubt, however: Mahler was

a very complicated, perhaps not yet fully crystallized personality whose hyper-subjectivity sometimes transgressed—not always with impunity—the invisible limits imposed on all works of art. The personal side of this undoubtedly excellent musician seems to me generally artistic rather than specifically musical. That puts him into the category of an eclectic. Indeed, in view of his extraordinary ability to exploit emotions he has not himself experienced, I would seriously put him forward as a perfect example of an eclectic who, although exploring steep and bold paths of his own choosing is nevertheless unable to direct art into new channels.

The symphony, though it seemed to demand a programme, was anything but programme, i.e. descriptive, music. It was 'solely the expression of the psyche of its composer, . . . thus achieving the highest degree of subjectivity ever attempted so far in great musical art.'

---

[242] *Grazer Volksblatt, Abendblatt*, 19 May 1911.
[243] See above, Chap. 4. The *Grazer Tagblatt* article appears in a collection of articles by Kienzl entitled *Im Konzert* (51 ff.).

For Kienzl, the 'extravagant first movement', a series of abrupt juxtapositions of 'muffled mourning sounds, military marches, cries of pain, glittering trills, the din of battle, and popular street songs', could only suggest to the puzzled audience that a reincarnated Kapellmeister Kreisler[244] was up on the podium making music at them. But then in the Finale,

the composer opens the most secret doors of his heart, and leads us into the purest, most authentic kingdom of musical art. . . . Here the listener indignantly rejected the constantly recurring temptation to identify the frequently obtruding musical reminiscences . . . The fevered sweat that moistens the listener's brow during the horrors of the first movement gives way to tears of emotion at the truly noble tones of the last movement.

It seemed almost as if 'the whole symphony had been written for the sake of this Adagio', in which

every voice sings in praise of love . . . and we feel a great vast breath sweeping over us from it. Life on this earth is mirrored in the loving eye of the eternal Father. Anyone who can write such an Adagio is really someone! The listener, deeply moved, recalls with astonishment the banalities of the first movement, which in retrospect no longer seem to have been the accidental products of a banal mind, but the result of a deliberate (no matter whether right or wrong) choice. In the building up towards climaxes, the economy of colours, and utilization of contrasting effects, Mahler is a master as he is in his unlimited mastery of orchestral means. . . . He knows how to keep the listener always in suspense, so that he never has time to feel tired. . . . The unique mixture of breath-taking temperament and meticulous mastery, combined with great outward calm, make Mahler a truly impressive conductor. Despite the hairline precision of his rhythm, his conducting had none of the 'tyranny of the beat', but only the highest artistic freedom.[245]

At the beginning of 1907, one of the most decisive years in his life and career, Mahler faced the redoubtable task of presenting his Sixth Symphony to a Vienna audience for the first time—redoubtable indeed because Vienna had proved particularly indifferent, if not hostile, to his work. Mahler, at this juncture, probably despaired of ever re-establishing normal relations with the Philharmonic, and in the absence of any proposal on their part he had accepted the invitation of the Konzertverein, who organized the event as an 'exceptional Novitätenkonzert' on 4 January 1907.[246] Its musicians were not up to the high standard of the Philharmonic, and rehearsals proved difficult. Yet even the gossip column 'Aus der Theaterwelt' of the *Fremden-Blatt*, always anxious to report conflicts or friction, recognized that harmony prevailed

[244] E. T. A. Hoffmann's most famous character (see above Vol. i, Chap. 7).

[245] The concert took place on 3 Dec. at the Stadttheater, and the proceedings went to the Graz musicians' pension fund. Bella Paalen, who was hired the following year at the Vienna Opera, was the contralto solo. The same concert was repeated under Mahler's direction on 23 Dec., again to a full house.

[246] The first Vienna performance of the Seventh Symphony also took place with the Konzertverein Orchestra this time under its permanent conductor, Ferdinand Löwe, on 7 Nov. 1909.

between orchestra and conductor, the only note of discord coming from a member of the wind section. Reprimanded by Mahler, he 'suddenly fell ill' just before the concert, and stated that he would remain so 'for all performances of Mahler symphonies'. Mahler brushed off the incident with a remark to the rest of the musicians in the Konzertverein orchestra: 'Gentlemen, that's the way I will always handle things! I have never achieved anything in my life through compliments, but only through criticism.'[247] Egon Wellesz, who attended the rehearsals, reports that on one occasion Mahler repeated a certain crescendo in the Finale twenty times before achieving the particular balance of sound he was looking for. He leaned over his desk in order to get nearer to the wind section, beating time with short and clear movements and creating 'a sort of frightening, almost demonic hypnosis which reduced the orchestra to submission'. Afterwards, the sonority of the passage was 'completely transformed' and the 'effect captivating'.[248] 'No other conductor,' adds Wellesz in his memoirs, 'ever achieved such a relentless, driving rhythm from the very first measure, with the accent on the upward beat, on the fourth quarter of the march tempo. It was as if one heard the footsteps of fate: inexorable.'[249]

Henceforth, Mahler could count on a sufficient number of admirers and disciples to give all his premières in Vienna an aura of triumph.[250] After the première of the Sixth on 4 November 1907, however, as the orchestra joined the audience in applause, the catcalls and boos from the balcony redoubled. A child's trumpet blared, and the battle between supporters and opponents continued until the lights went out.[251] Among the critics, only Korngold and to a certain extent Kauders tried to observe a measure of objectivity. The others attained new degrees of malevolence, and two articles deserve, in this respect, to be quoted in their entirety. This was what Hans Liebstöckl wrote in the *Illustrirtes Wiener Extrablatt*:

Yesterday, amidst the customary ovations for composer-conductors, Gustav Mahler's Sixth Symphony was performed, The Sixth! . . . Krupp makes only cannons, Mahler only symphonies. He is still composing as he always has. The only new elements are

---

[247] *Fremden-Blatt*, 6 Jan. 1907.

[248] Wellesz identifies this passage as no. 149 in the orchestra score. Here (bar 598), the trumpets, trombones, and tuba have a *molto crescendo* marking, swelling from pianissimo to fortissimo. (See Egon Wellesz, 'Mahlers Instrumentation', *Musikblätter des Anbruch*, 12 (1930): 3, 108, and EWL 46. In Dec. 1981 the Stargardt firm of Marburg sold a card from Mahler to Anna Moll, co-signed by Alma, Justi, and Arnold Rosé. It was written on the eve of the Vienna performance of the Sixth. Frau Moll is congratulated 'with admiration for her heroic courage'. She had probably undergone an operation.

[249] EWL 45. Wellesz also mentions the impression which the celesta made on him during rehearsals, especially during the first movement when celesta and violin chords contrast with the 'softly strange' harmonies of the trombones (no doubt bars 209 to 215): 'To my knowledge, this was the first time in an orchestral work that two different groups of chords were combined in contrapuntal fashion, without regard for harmony.'

[250] As we shall see below, Albert Kauders considered this première of the Sixth Mahler's greatest success in Vienna as a composer. On 12 Jan. 1907 Baron Heinrich Tucher von Himmelsdorf, Bavarian minister plenipotentiary and member of the Konzertverein committee, telegraphed Mahler in Berlin to ask him to conduct another performance of the work on 16 Feb. for the Deutscher Hilfsverein, 'given its enormous success'. (AMS. See below, Chap. 8.)   [251] *Fremden-Blatt* (6 Jan. 1907).

the celesta and the cowbells in the orchestra. Everything else is familiar stuff, was already there, has fooled us, but in other mixtures. But in the interim, the belief has grown that we must understand this composer. Richard Specht, who has written a thematic guide to the Sixth Symphony, states it explicitly: the thematic structure must be grasped. I do not know why there is all this pretence of ceremony, of occult sciences, of importance, as though Herr Mahler was treating his listeners to divine revelations. For despite the splendour and terrific noise of the orchestra, he is a very modest musician. He has little to give, nothing—superficialities aside—to take the breath away.

The whole art of composition is on the wrong path today. It is concerned in the first place with dimension, surface and big outlines, senses the power of technique, and lets go. Composition becomes a function of chance and good luck. This Sixth is a perfect example of this process. It springs from an overheated theatrical imagination. Throughout, it resembles a man showing off his artistry, who keeps on calling out: 'Now just listen to this!' The surprise does not come from genuine inspiration but from the consistent use of mannerisms. A musician who does not make music solely to meet some theatrical requirements must at once be aware that here we have a completely superficial, arbitrary way of writing music, in reality an unmusical, unworthy colloquial language with poetic and descriptive illusions. Mahler's orchestra has no fine, no generous ring. Shrillness, abruptness, whip lashes predominate and they appeal to the superficial, the crowd. His world lies between the march and the Ländler. But what a march, and what a Ländler! What brutality, what melancholy, what unbearable, dank piety! What genuflecting ecstasy! It all lies in the themes, all of them having a constructed face, and behind it, a machinery. They have no life of their own and fall apart as soon as they are taken out of their orchestral context. And can a discerning ear fail to hear the countless banalities which here and there stand out above the loquacious, billowing mass—those insipid ideas fluttering almost operetta-like above vast profundity. It sometimes seems as though the great examples out of the past had been forgotten and as though knowledge of what makes a piece of music eternal had entirely disappeared. As though the highest wisdom had been repudiated: that all music is born out of a need, out of an overflowing heart. And not out of the impulses of a nervous temperament! I know the objections of the enthusiasts. We haven't got the right ears for Mahler, we still have to acquire them. Wrong! In Vienna, there are hundreds of ears for him. Just look at the young people in the standing-room area, delighted, happy and applauding! But in spite of all the progress in the technique of sound and colour, I sense a shameful impoverishment of sensibility, an impotence of invention of the truly musical moment. The right mood isn't there, nor the tenderness, the happy introspection, the calm inherent in creation. All these things were alive and shining for the last time in Johannes Brahms, to be remembered for ever as it were. After him comes the circus of the moderns. The colossal symphony, billboard music, the obtrusiveness of the means: the legacy of Liszt, Berlioz and Bruckner, the makers of great occasions. The conflict goes deep, it has to do with the way we look at the world. Mahler is a mystic, he loves bells of all kinds, celestas, sudden chorales. He is forever on a pilgrimage, has always got something to atone for and put right. He composes original sin. The pure fools (*Die reinen Thoren*)[252] have always made the

---

[252] Liebstöckl is alluding to Wagner's *Parsifal*.

loudest noise. So yesterday, I went away troubled and depressed, even more troubled than usual when a Mahler symphony was on the programme. The Sixth has the faults of the whole system, and above all, its emptiness. *So sah ich Walvater noch nie...* (I have never yet seen Walvater thus).[253] But what is to be done? There is now such a thing as politics in music, and Herr Mahler too has a strong party, furiously applauding and religiously intolerant. Cults and fanatical priests are everywhere nowadays. It is just that here the evil is reproducing itself in a sphere where the zeal of dilettantes becomes most dangerous because it engenders idolatry.

Clearly Liebstöckl's culture and ear might well have permitted him to appreciate Mahler, but his taste—as he himself admitted—stopped at Brahms. He was incapable of going any further. Could the disappointment this must have caused him be the reason for his rancour?

Heinrich Reinhardt, one of the ringleaders in the campaign which was soon to break out against Mahler,[254] described the Sixth as follows in the *Neues Wiener Journal*: 'Brass, lots of brass, incredibly much brass! Even more brass, nothing but brass!—that was the first movement.' And after a few other ironic comments on the inversion of movements before the Essen première, Reinhardt continued:

None the less, the fourth movement is positively the last, and with it Mahler's symphony ends, for all symphonies must end sometime, even if they are as endlessly long as Mahler's Sixth, entitled 'tragic'. And now, heedless of the shrieks of rage of the Mahlerites, a loud, clear and energetic protest must be made against the corruption of healthy musical sense and taste by performances of this kind in the city where Beethoven, Schubert, Mozart, and Haydn lived and produced their most sublime works. Mahler is doubtless a musician and conductor of outstanding quality and quite unusual intelligence. His artistic grasp, too, is quite unusual. In a surprisingly short time he has succeeded in surpassing the most exalted music-makers of our time. He has 'overmahlered' Richard Strauss and would also like to 'overmahler' the whole of musical Vienna (*Er übermahlert Richard Strauss und möchte wohl auch das musikalische Wien übermahlern*).[255] But it shall not happen without a determined protest . . .

Then follows a virulent attack upon the Director of the Hofoper, who, instead of devoting himself to that institution:

produces, with rabbit-like fertility, a larger-than-life symphony every year, and sometimes even two. Theatre people used to maintain that Mahler was a fine symphonist.

[253]   Quotation from *Die Walküre*, Act III.

[254]   Heinrich Reinhardt (1865–1922), son of a Pressburg jeweller, studied under Bruckner at Vienna University. Pianist and organist, he composed before 1900 numerous Lieder, works for piano, and an opera (*Die Minnekönigin*). His operetta *Das süsse Mädel* (1901) was considered a landmark in the genre, but his subsequent works never achieved similar success. After writing occasionally for the *Neue Freie Presse*, Reinhardt took Max Graf's place at the *Neues Wiener Journal*. A comic opera by him, *Der Gast des Königs* (based on a work by Dickens) was produced at the Volksoper in 1916. Reinhardt started opposing Mahler in 1902, with the publication in the *Wiener Morgenzeitung* of a clever parody of the poem in the Finale of the Fourth Symphony, two days after its Vienna première. See Willi Reich, 'Kritik aus "Des Knaben Wunderhorn" ', *Österreichische Musikzeitschrift*, 23 (1968): 2, 93.

[255]   Play on words based on the name of Mahler and of the German word for painter (Maler).

Knowledgeable music lovers can now prove that he is not a good symphonist. So what, in fact, *is* he really? Some third thing, in any case—but nothing of the first order! Either Mahler the musician enjoys the role of the hypermodern orchestrator and affects a composer's exaltation, or he is the sort of symphonist he ought not to be... His melodic invention is minimal, his contrapuntal and thematic elaboration is nil, and many things which look imposing on his scores produce no effect because you don't hear them. The harps with their glissandos and the thrice-divided violas labour in vain to be heard during the assault of the gigantic army of brass, and the insistent and continuous ringing of cow and sheep bells cannot conceal the hopeless emptiness of the Sixth Symphony. The sheep with their bells have something very important to say in Mahler's 'tragic' symphony, and it is by no means impossible that he becomes the bell-wether.—You must be prepared for anything.

Heinrich Reinhardt's review does not only deride Mahler's melodic material and orchestral effects, it also ridicules his changes of mind concerning the order of movements in such a way that one might be tempted to believe that, for the Vienna performance, his last, he had switched back between the last public rehearsal and the concert to his original plan, i.e. Scherzo 2 and Andante 3:

The second movement? There isn't one really, since the third movement is actually the second, because the second is the third. In the score the second movement is described as an *Andante moderato*, and the third a *Scherzo*. But Mahler had the *Scherzo* played as second movement and the *Andante* as the third? Why? Nobody knows. The Scherzo begins almost melodiously. One begins to listen with interest. The theme breaks off abruptly. Another failure to make the grade apparently. Unexplained ecstasies and paroxysms follow. The Last Judgement seems about to fall on us. Brass, an enormous amount of brass, bass-drum, switches, kettledrum rolls—a sudden bang—the Scherzo is over. A joke (*Scherz*), which produces a vague melancholy. Now comes the third movement, which is really the second, as already explained, since the second is the third. That is clear, obvious, convincing, and requires no further justification. The third movement, which is therefore really the second, has the same effect as the second, which is *de facto* the third.

However, Reinhardt's joke is so involved, so elaborate, that it cannot be considered conclusive evidence of a new, last minute, change of order, if only because all the other critics (except Carl Lafite's *Wiener Allgemeine Zeitung* articles) review the various movements in the revised order chosen by Mahler for the Essen première, i.e. Andante 2 and Scherzo 3.

Of all Mahler's Viennese premières, this, the last he conducted, is the one which brought the Vienna critics closest to unanimity against him. Hirschfeld would have been untrue to himself had he not inveighed against Mahler's 'new effects'—the cowbells, hammerblows, switches—which had only one purpose—to conceal his lack of inspiration.

If he were capable of expressing tragic feelings through the power of music, he would gladly do without the hammer and its fateful blows. But he does not possess the true inner creative power. Thus, at the moment of greatest agitation in the 'Tragic Symphony' he resorts to the hammer. He cannot do otherwise. When sound no longer suffices, he strikes a blow. That is entirely natural. Speakers who at the decisive moment cannot find the right words beat their fists on the table. Mahler's example may one day revolutionize symphonic creation. In order to arouse feelings of anguish (hitherto evoked by a sorrowful melody), the score will simply direct an orchestra musician to break an expensive vase or smash a water pitcher. That will distress those who have long wondered whether the ironic parodies of funeral marches in the Mahler symphonies are supposed to evoke sorrow or laughter. The eternally recurring march and Ländler melodies and rhythms are also not to be considered symphonic whim or fancy: they too are rooted deep in Mahler the symphonist, for if he could think of other themes he would use them . . . The theme [of the Andante] could be attributed to a piece of salon music, or a Sonatina by Fritz Spindler (Op. 389 or some other mass production number), with just a couple of notes changed in an attempt to make it more interesting.[256]

Everything connected with sound effects in this movement was technically perfect and up to the level of modern *Kapellmeisterkultur*. But whenever Mahler did contribute a theme of his own, he failed to develop it and immediately modified timbres and shifted the rhythm, like 'jerky lighting changes' in a poor theatre production. The woodwind section in this symphony had been quadrupled in number and 'even great thoughts would be crushed by such masses of sound'. There was a lack of balance between the 'insipid, thin, often disjointed motifs and the torrents of colour that have been poured over them'. Then, suddenly, for some moments, the score would become simple, innocent, but this artificial pretence of calm was like the 'smile on the face of a ghost, biting, sneering, cold'.

Wallaschek in *Die Zeit* also deplored the disproportion between the effect achieved and the complexity of the means employed. He too condemned the insignificance of the motifs and their development,[257] waxed indignant at the use of new instruments, and claimed that the audience would never have guessed that the symphony was 'tragic' if the epithet had not figured on the programme.[258] The ringing of the bells destroyed whatever charm, atmosphere, and interest were to be found in the Andante. As to the first and last movements, nothing could conceal their lack of architecture and their 'harmonic padding', nobody was any longer interested in brilliant orchestration since this required no special talent. The only merit of this symphony, wrote Wallaschek, was that it contained fewer borrowings than its predecessors.

---

[256] Fritz Spindler (1817–1905), pianist and composer, author of numerous pieces of salon music and others for teaching purposes.

[257] Wallaschek compared the Sixth to the children's symphonies of Romberg and Haydn or to 'gigantesque potpourris of military bands'. The sight of percussionists, 'rising one after another to strike but a single blow' on their instruments, seemed to him ridiculous.

[258] The adjective (*Tragisch*) was indeed for the first time added to the title Sixth Symphony on the programme and posters.

No less violent was the article in the *Montags-Revue*. Hedwig von Friedländer-Abel considered that Mahler, this time,

has reached the highest peak which the modern orchestral music can climb. From there one can already see into the frightening abysses of delusion and self-derision, the mockery of all musical reason and tradition; yet the composer still has the strength to stand laughing on those giddy heights and contemplate the well-tended fields of the honest music makers far below. Like Wagner in his time, Mahler follows the thorny path of his ingeniously contrived system, the system of never-ending delirium, of deliberate intoxication. His music is conscious over-stimulation and intentional accumulation which, with their blinding nerve-racking combinations, make considered judgement impossible. Who can pronounce a judgement when he is about to be submerged in a stream of incandescent lava! Mahler stands more or less everything on its head, even those things which to a certain extent Strauss still respects. His eclecticism almost amounts to mania, mania above all in the way in which he borrows from others, the ecstatic fervour with which he allows the simplest melodic flower, picked by the wayside to be gobbled up and transfigured in the hellfire of his counterpoint. Seldom does he let his melodic flowers blossom in purity. Typical for Mahler, and also hyper-modern, is the way in which he disdains everything obvious[259] and straightforward in order to go by the most devious detours for the unusual, the preposterous, the breathtaking.

In this sense, Friedländer-Abel went on, every new Mahler symphony contained the same old stuff. He showed no development, only more brilliant and extensive variations of the same basic form. The 'great revolution' in his Sixth was his move 'from the less than beautiful to the deliberately ugly'. His themes were never 'simple or noble'; their development never natural or organic.[260] 'Again and again every little motif particle is dripped in, emerges and disappears, forms harmonies and helps to weave intricate new counterpoints, resulting in a deluge of restlessness.' After a further catalogue of complaints—the harshness of certain sonorities produced by the use of the upper register of the wind instruments, the lack of originality of the themes and the deliberate audacity of the counterpoint—the critic made some brief, but comparatively favourable references to the 'delicate, dream-like' Andante, and its magnificent orchestration. The best part of the symphony, however, was to her mind the Scherzo. 'Truly outstanding', 'vigorous, often gentle', but genuine symphonic music, with 'reminiscences of Schumann'. But no words were strong enough to express her distaste for the Finale, in which 'not a single note belonged to Mahler'. 'Utterly superficial' in style, it was 'the most monstrous symphonic movement ever composed', though artistically the most honest, since in it Mahler gave free rein to his 'contrapuntal and coloristic fantasies'. But Hedwig von Friedländer-Abel wondered whether the public would have the strength and courage required to follow him 'on his pathological paths'?

---

[259] What about the 'simplest melodic flower, picked by the wayside' mentioned above?

[260] Friedländler-Abel was one of the first people to notice the close resemblance between a theme of the first movement and another from Liszt's First Piano Concerto (see below, Appendix 2, on the Sixth Symphony).

Theodor Helm, the elderly and impartial Viennese music critic[261] who had never wholeheartedly endorsed the *Deutsche Zeitung*'s anti-Semitic bias, had been replaced on the staff of that newspaper by Maximilian Muntz, whose bitter and ceaseless attacks on Mahler as a conductor, composer, and Opera director, have often been quoted above. Helm's report on the Viennese première of the Sixth was published in the oldest German music journal, the *Neue Zeitschift für Musik*.[262] It describes the 'lively applause' and 'tumultuous ovations' with which Mahler's supporters greeted each movement of the new symphony, and the disapproval expressed by his opponents (the shrill sound of a children's trumpet was heard in the gallery during the final ovation). Concerning the work itself, Helm endorsed the scathing review written after the Munich performance by Hugo Daffner, the local correspondent of the same *Neue Zeitschrift*.[263] Daffner had called Mahler's melodic imagination 'eclectic', more 'willed' than spontaneous, and had accused him of 'profaning art with superficial, heavy-handed naturalism'. Helm praised Mahler's 'grandiose orchestral technique' but discerned in the Sixth innumerable 'reminiscences' of earlier music, Bruckner mainly, but also Wagner, Liszt, Beethoven, Mendelssohn, Goldmark, Grieg, Sinding, Massenet, and even Allegri's *Miserere*, ever popular in Vienna's churches.[264]

Maximilian Muntz thought that Mahler's Sixth was 'tragic indeed, but not in the positive or active sense because of its content, but passively because of its character and value as a work of art'. It was 'a catastrophe in a drama of our art and culture, the tragic element being the blatant disproportion between the enormous means employed and the decadent creative impotence of anti-music, inarticulate noise and ugliness of sound—which was proof of the paroxysm of an intense inner struggle caused by self-doubt'. Despite its four movements it was anything but classical, with its reminiscences, pastiches, and tragicomic themes. The slow movement was 'modernized Diabelli' with a few Tyrolian accents—a 'sandbank in the shallow waters of invention', a 'musical winter garden filled with artificial flowers and ill-defined perfumes'. The Scherzo displayed 'perverse wit and noise instead of musical humour', and the 'intolerable distortions' of an old-fashioned dance tune, while the Finale was 'a monument to the presumptuous weakness of decadence', 'ugly chaos', 'empty, cacophonous noise', 'endless theatrical agitation in the orchestra, . . . brutal strength of sound which violates the ear'. The applause of Mahler's 'adolescent' supporters did not dismay Muntz, who was certain that later on the work would be recognized as a 'transient artistic imposture'. He strongly condemned the members of the orchestra who had joined in the ovation.

More measured and courteous in his choice of words, Kalbeck nonetheless

---

[261] See above, Vol. ii, Chap. 1.
[262] In 1906, the *Neue Zeitschrift* had merged with another periodical, the *Musikalisches Wochenblatt*.
[263] See above, Daffner's report of the Munich première of the Sixth.
[264] *Neue Zeitschrift für Musik*, 17 (1907): 1, 56.

expressed similar condemnation: Mahler, in his orchestration, had overstepped the limits of the possible and become a 'prosaic noise-maker'. After the gong and hammer, he should, if he were consistent, resort to bombs and cannons. Despite its melodious Andante and humorous Scherzo with its romantic undertones, the symphony, once deprived of the purple of its puffed-up orchestration, reflected the woes of a man torn by inner conflicts, not those of a hero symbolizing the suffering and struggling of humanity. It was 'too intimate, too personal, too exclusive, too strange to be that'. 'Its extravagant melodies belong to the domain of the boundless and the supernatural . . . The battles fought are those of the mind, and unfold on the fields of fantasy, and the shapes emerging out of the mist gather like silhouettes who do not wish to be asked questions as to their real origin.' 'We love this symphony', wrote Kalbeck somewhat surprisingly, 'precisely because of these uncertainties, and would love it even more without all those fanfares, spasms, explosions . . .' On the other hand, if Mahler insisted on the tragic nature of this work without producing a programme, then he could not object to a listener interpreting the hero as being, for instance, the raving Ajax. Kalbeck then humorously describes an appropriate scene from the Iliad to which he, however, would not dare to subscribe, so as not to be taken for one of those Philistines whom Mahler covers with derision in the Trio of the Scherzo.

Greater moderation was displayed by Carl Lafite,[265] recently appointed as music critic of the *Allgemeine Zeitung*. For him, Mahler's latest symphony was 'above all the expression of a will'. However, it did include 'melodic and idyllic passages' which were not mere parodies. Indeed, Mahler sought to 'render homage to the healthy, naive assurance of our predecessors'. Even though the subtleties of orchestration frequently passed unnoticed and the opening theme lacked 'specific character', the bold harmonization and crescendo 'elevated it to a superior level'. The Scherzo and its 'delightful details', the Andante and its 'calm nobility', were unfortunately crushed by the frightening length and deafening developments of the Finale. Stunned by the brass, the listener could no longer discern the subtle elaborations of theme and counterpoint. 'A spectacle, but alas, nothing but a spectacle!' concluded Lafite.

Surprisingly, Albert Kauders, known for his conservative opinions rather than for his intelligence or literary gifts, was almost the only critic to appreciate Mahler's Sixth:

Among all the musical Hotspurs of our time, Gustav Mahler appeals to me most. He is one of the boldest challengers. His cult of ugliness, demonic inclination towards all that is exorbitant, excessive, immoderate and superhuman have repeatedly proved to

---

[265] A student of the Vienna Conservatory, Carl Lafite (1872–1947) directed the Wiener Singakademie 1900–5 and was appointed secretary general of the Gesellschaft der Musikfreunde in 1911. In addition to three operas and numerous works for solo voice or chorus, he composed two operettas based on themes from Schubert (*Hannerl*) and from Mozart and Beethoven (*Der Kongress tanzt*). He was also the author of *Das Schubertlied und seine Sänger* (1928). His son, Peter Lafite (1908–61) was the founder of the *Österreichische Musikzeitschrift* (1956).

be the characteristic features of his works. Yet, unlike other modern, exalted composers, he remains rooted in music! In this sense, he is the true child, or if he prefers, continuation, of Anton Bruckner.

Like Liebstöckl, Kauders compared Mahler's symphony to a

singular, wondrous tree, branching out and ramifying in novel ways into the blue infinity, laden with splendid foliage and tender fruit, but also with poisonous blossoms, knots, and thorns. And the tree is rooted in the nourishing soil of classical art, from which again and again it sucks up healthy sap, even as the maggots and parasites of modern reflection and hypertrophy eat away at its marrow. . . . In no other work has Mahler shown such comforting conservatism in the preservation of form and logical articulation.

The Andante, albeit overdeveloped, 'breathes peaceful happiness' with its 'masterly themes and magical mixtures of colour', while the Scherzo was a 'delightful, yokelish dance, a masterpiece of counterpoint and sparkling with truly Olympian humour'. The Finale alone, with its 'cacophonic inspiration and bizarre apparitions', aroused doubts in his mind because of its 'hollow verbosity', something usually absent from Mahler's work. The 'splendour of the sonority', and the 'magic combinations of colour' were beyond dispute, but in his eagerness 'to say everything' Mahler failed to confine himself to aesthetically acceptable limits and 'lost himself in the void, in nothingness'.[266]

Even Julius Korngold and David Joseph Bach, Mahler's two 'allies' among the critics, made no secret of their confusion and disarray. Bach deplored the absence of 'the language of the heart' in the new symphony, and recognized 'the true Mahler' only in the first and final movements. Yet he defended the introduction of new instruments, and the use of traditional instruments in hitherto unused registers, for 'the artist alone knows what means he needs to express himself'. 'Just as a poet does not write for German grammarians—a class of men devoid, by their profession, of literary understanding—so a composer does not write for music teachers, whose professional knowledge is worse than the ignorance of the naive listener.'

Like Bach, Korngold considered the Sixth Symphony to be inferior to its predecessors though it surpassed them in its unity of form and, unfortunately, in 'realism and nervous tension'. 'Melody' was abandoned in favour of 'theme', but at the same time, despite the symphony's general unity of atmosphere, the 'cleverly constructed' Finale, 'brimming with energy', suffered from an overabundance of counterpoint. Its garish colours, violent contrasts, and insistent brass instruments made it inferior to the Andante and above all, to the Scherzo, 'a veritable model of musical wit'. But whatever the Sixth's unevenness, Korngold concluded that Mahler possessed 'the temperament of a revolutionary

---

[266] Kauders called the Vienna première of the Sixth an unprecedented success for Mahler: the 'thunderous ovation' at the end of the performance echoed the Finale's most powerful tutti. The same critic reports that a metal hammer was used for the final chord.

and the nature of an artist, disdaining all limits and civilities in the relentless pursuit of his ideal, even as he remained a modern "man of nerves" with all the impulses and inhibitions of his time.' Korngold may not have understood Mahler's Sixth, but at least he recognized clearly the essential nature of the composer. But one lone voice of reason among such a chorus of protest and invective was small consolation.

Never before had the public's enthusiasm so utterly contradicted the critics' disparagement. No surviving documents reveal Mahler's reaction to this unprecedented barrage of criticism. But it is likely that the universal incomprehension he had previously encountered with his Sixth, even more so than with his previous symphonies, played a part in his decision to cancel the performance scheduled for January in Amsterdam. Yet, in August, he had written to Mengelberg thanking him for his praise after the première. 'Your intimate understanding and profound comprehension, amidst so much awful nonsense (coming even from those places where one might have expected a reasonable word about the essence of the work and not merely superficial technical comments) have been of great value and heartfelt consolation to me.'[267]

At that time, Mahler was still looking forward to his forthcoming trip to Holland, where he planned to go directly after the Frankfurt concert to conduct the Sixth on 24 January. In September, he asked Mengelberg to return scores in which he had noted certain changes so that he could transfer them on to his own copies.[268] In October Mahler wrote to his Dutch colleagues again describing the chilly reception of the Sixth in Berlin.[269] Yet he continued to look forward to the Amsterdam performance and offered to bring the cowbells along with him.[270]

It was only on 26 December, a month before the concert, that Mahler told Mengelberg he would have to return to Vienna immediately after the Frankfurt concert on 18 January, and would consequently have to cancel the Amsterdam performances.[271] He proposed rescheduling the concert for late April or early May, but Mengelberg replied that those dates were too late for his audience,[272] and suggested mid-February or early April. When Mahler declined,

---

[267] MBR1, no. 306; MBR2, no. 360, and RMH 69. In this undated letter (postmarked 18 Aug. 1906), Mahler thanks Mengelberg for what he had said about the use of the hammer in the Finale. He 'completely agreed' and said that he would follow his advice for the Amsterdam performance, and even try to have the score modified. Unfortunately, no information has survived concerning Mengelberg's suggestion.

[268] Undated letter (postmarked 12 Sept. 1906), RMH 71. Mengelberg had just lost his assistant, Martin Heuckeroth (1853–1936), who had left his job, and was looking for a new one. In a letter written on 22 Sept., Mahler suggested Kalman Feld to him, a young conductor who had conducted the Third Symphony in Budapest two years earlier, on 14 Apr. 1905 with Therese Behr as soloist. However, Mengelberg finally engaged Cornelius Dopper (1870–1939).

[269] Letter referred to above (postmarked 15 Oct. 1906), MBR1, no. 308, MBR2, no. 366, and RMH 72.

[270] In a card dated 10 Nov. 1906 (RMH 73), he gave Mengelberg the address of the Paris firm (Mustel) which could supply him with a celesta.

[271] Undated card (postmarked 26 Dec. 1906). Mahler conducted *Fidelio* on 25 Jan. and remained in Vienna for rehearsals of *Die Walküre*, which opened on 4 Feb.

[272] See Mengelberg's letter of 12 Jan. 1907 (RMH 79).

Mengelberg abandoned the idea of performing the Sixth, which he did not wish to rehearse and perform in the absence of the composer, and gave a performance of the First instead in the concert on 24 January 1907.[273]

Thus Mahler's Sixth, his 'tragic' symphony, had proved even less accessible to the Viennese Establishment than any of its predecessors, and he may well have felt it was an 'accursed' work in the light of the damning verdict of the 'infernal judges'. Mahler put it aside for the time being, and died a few years later without ever having conducted it again. Of all Mahler's works, it turned out to be the one that took the longest time to overcome the reluctance of conductors and impresarios, although its popularity has recently (1998) risen to new heights.

So far we have hardly ever seen Mahler yield to weariness or discouragement or bow to the negative verdict of critics. This time, however, he was deeply affected. Moreover, the Vienna debacle occurred at the very moment when the attacks on him as Director of the Opera were developing into a veritable campaign. One day, in the presence of Josef Bohuslav Förster, he gave free rein to a pessimism which was quite uncharacteristic of him:

If I didn't have children it would never occur to me to bother about the publication of my compositions. How long does such a work survive? Fifty years. Then come other composers, other times, other tastes, other works. What of it? I need a big apparatus, and who is going to give himself the trouble of rehearsing it properly? And even if someone finds the time and the enthusiasm, can I be sure that he can grasp what I had in mind? Better no performance at all than a bad one.[274]

Obviously the trials Mahler had experienced had shaken the confidence he had expressed in his triumphalist prophecies a year earlier.[275] An artist may be convinced that he is right, but he can never be certain of being understood. Creativity often goes in cycles, and Mahler's faith in himself was for the moment at a low ebb. But he was soon to recover under the pressure of other energies and as a reaction to the further blows which life held in store for him.

---

[273] RMH 23. By this time, all hell had broken loose in Vienna and Mahler had to reduce the number of his guest appearances. He wrote to Mengelberg from Frankfurt on 17 Jan., again expressing his regrets and advising him not to count on him during the current year. His next trip to Holland was scheduled for Jan. 1908 (when Mengelberg again hoped that he would conduct the première of the Sixth at the Hague on the 4th and in Amsterdam on the 9th (RMH 86, letter of 10 June 1907), but this trip was also cancelled because of his departure for the United States. The Dutch première of the Sixth eventually took place ten years later, on 14 Sept. 1916, with Mengelberg on the podium (RMH 23). [274] JFP 703.

[275] See above, Chap. 6, Mahler's declarations to Lilli Lehmann and Max Graf.

8

Mahler in Vienna (XXIV)—The Third
in Berlin—Encounters with Strauss
The Fourth in Frankfurt—The First in Linz—
The press campaign against Mahler
Die Walküre and *Iphigénie en Aulide*—Messchaert's
recitals—Schoenberg premières

(January–March 1907)

People are wholly unaware of the inaccessible kind of fortress a man lives
in if he is truly dedicated to himself and to his cause . . .

M AHLER'S brief but frequent absences from the Vienna Opera to conduct
his works were now increasingly held against him. In 1907 the first
attack came on 1 January, when Hans Puchstein published a thoroughly negative summary of his recent activities in the *Deutsches Volksblatt*. His
complaints were not new. He began by listing the composers absent from the
repertory (Lortzing, Marschner, Gluck, Weber, Berlioz, Donizetti, Tchaikovsky,
Smetana, Boieldieu, Flotow, Hérold, and Kreuzer); emphasized the shortcomings of some of Mahler's assistants at the Opera, particularly Bruno Walter; and
deplored the Director's 'moody character' and 'changes of taste' with regard to
his protégés. Puchstein believed that all this made him unfit to direct the
Vienna Opera, and voiced the opinion that the time 'was ripe for a change'. He
also criticized some of the singers. For example, he described Selma Kurz as
a 'singing doll devoid of temperament' and Marie Gutheil-Schoder as a singer
'with an imperfect voice'. And to make matters worse, Mahler had parted
company with both Winkelmann and Sophie Sedlmair,[1] whose plight was the

---

[1] Hans Puchstein, 'Unsere Oper im Jahre 1906', *Deutsches Volksblatt* (1 Jan. 1907).

subject of a long article in the *Fremden-Blatt* praising her reliability and her willingness to step in for a colleague at a moment's notice:

On countless evenings she had to come in from Hietzing merely to sit from seven o'clock until nearly midnight in the wings of the Hofoper in order to wait and see whether or not von Mildenburg would break down before the end. If she did, Sedlmair had of course to sing the role to the end. She performed her humiliating task with equanimity, for it was her duty to do so. But she was hurt nonetheless. Once, during a performance of *Götterdämmerung* conducted by Mahler, the Director had sent her a cup of tea onto the stage, for he had noticed that she was sitting in the wings in her fur coat looking rather 'shivery'. As so often before, she was not singing, and was merely waiting to see whether she might be required to step in. At this point the artist summoned up all her pent-up anger and let it be known to the Director that she could not accept the tea. Mahler was piqued. 'There is not enough sugar in the whole wide world,' Sedlmair told the Director, 'which could sweeten a cup of tea while I am waiting and sitting on a chair listening to someone else singing Brünnhilde.'[2]

From then on, according to the *Fremden-Blatt*, the singer confided to her diary that Mahler no longer addressed her as 'Dear Sedlmair', but as 'Madam'. The same 'Aus der Theaterwelt' chronicle has been quoted many times in the preceding pages despite the fact that it was unsigned and based on hearsay and backstage gossip.[3] This time it added that Sedlmair's Viennese admirers and colleagues had been forced to send the wreath and the presents that they had intended to give her at her farewell performance to Hanover. She had already left the Hofoper to take up her new position.[4]

Admittedly, Mahler did not have a very high opinion of Sedlmair's talents, and believed that her greatest asset was her ability to sing any dramatic soprano role at a moment's notice. A note he sent to Mildenburg at the beginning of November 1906 shows this quite clearly: '*Walküre* [on 7 November] is not a subscription performance[5] and it is impossible to give people Sedlmair. I really must ask you to stay here if it is at all possible. . . . Please don't cancel *Walküre*. It would be very damaging and most annoying for the audience.'[6] Thus Mildenburg's fragile voice never ceased to create severe difficulties for Mahler, both in practical and in psychological terms. Lucy Weidt, the young Austrian dramatic soprano whom Mahler had engaged five years earlier, and to whom he had assigned the role of Leonore in the première of the new production of *Fidelio* in 1904, also suffered greatly from the preferential treatment

[2]   *Fremden-Blatt*, 'Aus der Theaterwelt' (6 Jan. 1907).
[3]   See above, Chaps. 5, 6, and 7.
[4]   In fact, the contract of Sophie Sedlmair (née Offeney) was extended until 1 Dec. 1907.
[5]   The tickets for most of the performances at the Hofoper were sold on a subscription basis, but this one was obviously to be a special one, for which Mahler wanted to have the best possible cast.
[6]   Letter to Mildenburg, undated (4 or 5 Nov. 1906). The date can be determined fairly precisely, for Mahler announces his imminent departure for Munich and alludes to the performance of *Die Rose vom Liebesgarten* which Bruno Walter was to conduct on the 13th (ÖTM).

continually accorded to her rival, who was often ailing, and for whom she frequently had to step in at a moment's notice. As we shall see, she found it even harder to bear the star treatment of Elsa Bland in the revival of Verdi's *Otello*.[7]

As if to assist the press campaign soon to be unleashed against Mahler, last-minute cancellations and illness among the singers abounded at the end of 1906 and the beginning of 1907. As we have seen, Slezak was ill on several occasions. On 30 January he had to be replaced in *La Juive*, and on 2 February in *Les Huguenots*.[8] For the latter the only possible replacement in the Hofoper was Carl Kurz-Stolzenberg, who had just been engaged. Unfortunately he had unhappy memories of having failed in the role, and thus refused to try it again. Telegrams were sent to all the theatres that might have been able to help, though in the end *Aida* had to be performed instead, again with Wallnöfer. As we have seen, it was only in April that Mahler discovered in Philip Brozel a new tenor capable of replacing Slezak at a moment's notice.

At the end of January Selma Kurz was forced to stop singing for some time on account of an injury to her arm, which she was not allowed to move. For this reason the performance of *Die Entführung* on 28 January was sung by Elise Elizza. After Mahler left for Berlin on 6 January, his enemies declared that, in view of his own absences, he was no longer in a position to refuse singers leave when they requested it. Kurz, for example, was permitted to spend three weeks with the Monaco Opera, and she took advantage of her accident to leave Vienna a day early. 'I hope that the warm climate will do me good', she told Mahler.[9] At the beginning of February Gertrud Förstel, who was on holiday up on the Semmering, fell and twisted her foot while out walking, with the result that she had to stay in bed for a week. Mahler was now without either of his two coloratura sopranos.[10]

At this time a voice from the distant past, Arabella Szilagyi, the Brünnhilde in the Hungarian performances of *Die Walküre*, wrote to Mahler in the hope of being invited to sing in Vienna. She reminded him both of his former promise and the fact that in 1901 and 1902 he had invited two other old Budapest colleagues, Ilalie Vasquez and Wilhelm Beck.[11]

---

[7] See below, Chap. 9. On 4 Feb. 1907 Mahler asked the Intendant to grant Bland an ex-gratia payment of 90 kronen for having sung two performances only twenty-four hours apart, *Cavalleria Rusticana* on 1 Feb. and *Aida* on 2 Feb. In the same letter he suggested some kind of recompense for Hermine Kittel, who had sung three different roles in *Götterdämmerung*, a Rhinemaiden, a Norn, and Waltraute, as a result of Josie Petru's cancellation (HOA, Z. 528/1907).

[8] Letters dated 30 Jan. and 1 Feb. (HOA, Z. 470/1907). In both instances he was replaced by Adolf Wallnöfer, who was brought in from the Kaiserjubiläumstheater.

[9] Letter from Selma Kurz to Mahler dated 30 Jan. 1907 (HOA).

[10] Telegram dated 3 Feb. and letter dated 5 Feb. from Gertrud Förstel (HOA, Z. 145/1907).

[11] Wilhelm Beck made two guest appearances at the Hofoper on 10 Sept. and 11 Oct. 1901, at which point Mahler wanted to engage him for the ensemble. However, the negotiations came to nothing on account of 'financial differences', and the contract was never signed. See undated letter from Mahler to Karpath, probably written in the spring or summer of 1901, and the attestation signed by Mahler, probably in Oct. 1901, BGM, Paris.

If he remembers me only a little, the Director will know that it is very hard for me, after what has happened, to write this letter! But never mind! Once before you lifted me out of the void, for which I am eternally grateful—and now I approach you once again, asking you to take note of me as an artist! I still want to sing! I often see women who are older than myself—with much less voice and less ability—still making a fortune singing. I have a voice. I am an artist, and I should like to be an active artist for some time to come! Unfortunately I am very free now, so there is nothing to stop me! . . . Please allow me to come and sing to you.[12]

Mahler's reply was no doubt the same as on the occasion when Countess Wydenbruck asked him to take an opera into the repertory solely in order to please its composer. He had surely been informed of Szilagyi's vocal decline and the Hofoper, he will have pointed out, was not a charitable institution, and he was accountable to his superiors and to the public for any decision he made.

On 3 October the baritone Erich Hunold, a guest at the Hofoper, was a failure in *Walküre*. According to the *Neue Freie Presse*, 'Wotan's spear had once before—in *Das Rheingold*—proved too heavy for the guest singer's arm, and today he actually let it drop.'[13] In the spring of 1907 a guest appearance by the bass Felix von Kraus[14] and his wife, Adrienne von Kraus-Osborne,[15] whose participation in the Strasbourg Festival had led to an outburst of rage on the part of Richard Strauss,[16] failed to lead on to an engagement, as Mahler had hoped. In fact the couple were thinking of giving up concert tours, which often meant working 'with bad orchestras, incompetent conductors and miserable accompanists' in order to 'take up a permanent position' at a theatre, and thus suggested that they would stay in Vienna between 1 October and 1 April each year. The success of their guest appearance would have been sufficient to justify their engagement. However, Mahler considered their demands unacceptable. In addition to the post of 'elocution coach', Kraus was asking for 40,000 kronen a year for himself and 20,000 for his wife, and thus, on 6 May, Mahler sent him a telegram to tell him: 'No one regrets more than I do that as a result any lasting link between you and the Opera has become impossible.'[17]

It so happened that the two most important singers engaged by Mahler in 1907 were both contraltos. Sarah Charles-Cahier, who made guest appearances in March, was a great success.[18] On 13 March Mahler recommended that she should be engaged on the grounds that she had shown herself to be 'a very

---

[12] Letter from Arabella Szilagyi to Mahler, 17 May 1907 (HOA, Z. 806/1907).

[13] On 14 Mar. 1901 Erich Hunold had sung Mahler's *Lieder eines fahrenden Gesellen* at a concert in Prague conducted by Richard Strauss.

[14] For the biography of Felix von Kraus (1870–1937), see above, Chap. 3.

[15] Concerning Adrienne Osborne (Eisbein), see above, Chap. 3.

[16] See above, Chap. 3.

[17] Letter from Felix von Kraus to Mahler dated 23 Feb. 1907; telegrams from Mahler to Felix von Kraus dated 4 and 6 May (HOA, Z. 312/1907). Kraus suggested doing up to 50 to 60 performances, besides acting as *Vortragmeister* (elocution coach). In the end, he sang three roles as a guest: Mephisto, King Mark, and Sarastro (on 1, 21, and 27 Apr.). His wife sang the title role in *Carmen* on 20 Apr.

[18] On 5, 9, and 15 Mar. in *Le Prophète*, and as Carmen and Amneris.

experienced singer with exceptional artistic qualities which, in conjunction with her beautiful voice, suggested that she could sing a variety of roles'.[19] Two days later he recommended that her six-year contract should come into effect on 1 April, and not on 1 September, as envisaged. This would enable her to sing Dalila in a production of Saint-Saëns's opera that was to be mounted specially for her. The other contralto was Bella Paalen, who had sung the solos in the Third Symphony in Graz the previous December.[20] These two engagements were particularly significant, for Mahler was soon to show his predilection for this type of voice when composing *Das Lied von der Erde*, which includes his longest symphonic solo.

It was inevitable that all these departures and last-minute replacements would adversely affect the artistic level of the Hofoper. Mahler's adversaries took advantage of the fact in order to fire another broadside at him, especially since seat prices had just been raised at the two imperial theatres. When the increase was announced on 1 October 1906, the reason given was 'the change in the overall economic situation'. The rate of inflation between 1901 and 1911 is estimated to have been 2.3 per cent per annum, or 23 per cent for a period of ten years.[21] Franz Willnauer, who made a detailed study of the finances of the Hofoper in Mahler's time, also draws attention to the fact that the high ticket prices excluded all but the privileged classes: the upper middle class, the aristocracy, and the civil service.[22]

As for the equipment of the auditorium, no important improvement or change had been made since the level of the pit had been lowered in 1904. In September 1906 Roller sent a report to the Director to tell him that, as a result of the drop in voltage which had occurred during a rehearsal of Camille Erlanger's *Le Juif polonais*, the preparatory work on the lighting had been in vain, and it had been necessary to improvise during the dress rehearsal. He reminded Mahler of the fact that the same thing had happened during the

---

[19] Letter dated 13 Mar. 1907 (HOA, G.Z. 303/1907). Sarah Charles-Cahier remained at the Hofoper until 1911. A few months after Mahler's death, she was to sing the first performance (in Munich) of *Das Lied von der Erde*.

[20] See above, Chap. 7. Bella Paalen remained at the Vienna Opera until 1 Sept. 1937. She sang in Mahler's farewell concert, the performance of the Second Symphony which he conducted in Vienna in Oct.

[21] WMW 205.

[22] The increased ticket prices were as follows: orchestra stalls, 9 to 14 kronen (and up to 10 kronen for a matinee); front boxes, 12 kronen; gallery, from 2 to 5.50 Kronen; fourth to sixth row of the upper gallery, 2 kronen; standing room in the stalls, 2 kronen; in the third gallery, 1.60 kronen; and in the upper gallery, 1.20 kronen. However, subscriptions provided good value for money. Eugène d'Harcourt (*La Musique actuelle en Allemagne et en Autriche-Hongrie*, 143) reported that a full season ticket for 200 performances between 1 Oct. and 15 May cost 3,600 kronen. It was also possible to purchase half- or quarter-subscriptions that provided access to the theatre on certain days of the week. For example, a half-subscription cost 1,800. D'Harcourt also mentions a *Stammsitz* (reserved seat) system. By making an advance payment of 350 to 700 kronen, the subscriber was able to secure the same seat at each performance as long as he confirmed his reservation before 11 a.m. the day before. The number of *Stammsitze* was of course limited. In order to give some idea of the cost of living in 1903, Franz Willnauer quotes the following data: average workman's wages, 100 kronen a month; white-collar salary, 500 kronen; annual rent for a small flat in the suburbs of Vienna, comprising bedroom, sitting room and kitchen, about 400 kronen (WMW 205).

rehearsals for the new production of *The Magic Flute* in June, and that it had led to a considerable loss of time, energy, and money.[23] Two months later, Roller and Bennier pressed for urgent action to modify and improve the stage machinery, which was inconvenient and posed a danger for the Opera personnel. A few days later, Mahler obtained the necessary grants from the Intendant.[24]

After the dismissal of the prompter Max Blau on the grounds that he had once spoken too loudly.[25] Mahler added fuel to the flames, in the eyes of the yellow press, by appointing Augusta Koller to the post. She was the first female prompter in the history of the Hofoper, and carried out her duties more tactfully. According to the *Extrablatt*, Heinrich Fröhlich, the chief prompter, soon began to imitate her discretion,[26] perhaps because he wanted to keep his job.

But the chief complaint against Mahler in the Viennese newspaper was that he was so frequently absent from Vienna in order to conduct one or other of his own works. And there was substance in the complaint, for at the end of 1906 he went to Breslau, Munich, Brünn, and Graz (twice). At the beginning of the new year he asked the Intendant for leave between 6 and 23 January, in order to conduct his works in Berlin and Frankfurt, and on the way back in Linz.[27] At the end of December he had cancelled his fourth visit to Holland, where he had planned to conduct the local première of the Sixth Symphony, and he later cancelled another guest appearance in Strasbourg.[28] His last stop on the return journey was to be Linz, in Upper Austria.

According to Otto Klemperer, the performance of Mahler's Third Symphony in Berlin was originally to have been conducted by Arthur Nikisch, the chief conductor of the Philharmonic Concerts.[29] Having decided to conduct a series of concerts in London, Nikisch in the end agreed to allow the composer to conduct the work. This arrangement was made as early as 3 September 1906, the date on which Hermann Fernow, director of the Wolff Concert Agency,

---

[23]   The report is dated 28 Sept., and was passed on to the Intendant by Mahler two days later (HOA, Z. 1067/1906).

[24]   The report submitted by Roller and Bennier is dated 14 Nov., whereas Mahler's letter to the Intendant was written on 23 Nov. (HOA, Z.X. 41 and Z.X. 41/4584s/1906).

[25]   See above, Chap. 5. The incident filled several paragraphs in the 'Theater und Kunst' column of the *Neues Wiener Journal* on 20 Jan. 1906. According to the unsigned article, one of the singers had missed her cue. The prompter was very anxious to help her and prompted so loudly that Mahler began to gesture from where he was sitting. At the end of the act he rushed on stage to give him his notice.

[26]   *Illustrirtes Wiener Extrablatt* (11 Jan. 1907). The name of the new female prompter is not specified in the article but it is given in Wilhelm Beetz's study, which reproduces the list of Opera personnel compiled by Alois Przistaupinsky in *150 Jahre Wiener Operntheater: Eine Chronik des Hauses und seiner Künstler im Wort und Bild der aufgeführten Werke, Komponisten und Autoren vom 25 Mai 1869 bis 30 Mai 1919* (Hermes, Vienna, 1919), 24.

[27]   Letter dated 19 Dec. (HOA, Z. 5240s/1906).

[28]   See below. In a letter to Norbert Salter written in the autumn of 1906, Mahler gave details of the programme he intended to conduct in Strasbourg on 21 Jan. 1907: Beethoven, unspecified overture; Mahler, First Symphony; Beethoven, unspecified symphony. A single rehearsal was planned for 19 Jan. before the final rehearsal on the morning of 21 Jan. Mahler no doubt gave up this project at the same time as the Amsterdam one, though it may well have been that he thought that the number of rehearsals was insufficient (undated letter to Norbert Salter, BSM, Munich).   [29]   OKM 6.

issued the invitation to Mahler.[30] This concert must have seemed exceptionally important to Mahler, for it was an opportunity to make up for the disastrous incomplete first performance of 1897.[31] For this reason he decided to rehearse the choruses and the orchestra for almost a week.

Mahler arrived in Berlin on the morning of 7 January,[32] and was reasonably satisfied with the first rehearsals: 'The orchestra is certainly not first-rate—very competent, very attentive (though, as I am told, they are making an exception in my case), but one notices the slovenliness of the local celebrities (tout comme chez nous). I'm hoping for a reasonably good performance.'[33] Mahler thought he could detect a certain coldness in the attitude of the manager of the Philharmonic Concerts, Frau Luise Wolff, but it did not bother him.

Fried sat open-mouthed from start to finish, devouring and swallowing me whole, so that in the end he was sitting there like a boa constrictor incapable of movement. In the evening, at the restaurant with Berliner, he was rather melancholy. Finally he confessed that his eyes had been opened by the totally effective manner in which I did things, and that he himself could do nothing (though, as he added rather confidently, others could do even less!).[34]

Mahler had probably grown tired of Fried's devout admiration. At any rate, he kept away from him for the next two days, and spent most of his free time with Arnold Berliner. Unfortunately it was pouring with rain, which made it virtually impossible to go out for walks. On 9 January, having taken leave of his friends, Mahler decided that, since the weather ruled out outdoor activities, he would go and visit Richard Strauss. Since he was afraid that he might not find the house, Otto Klemperer, Fried's young assistant and disciple, whom Mahler had met in 1905 when the Second was performed, and who this time had the job of playing the off-stage side drum,[35] offered to accompany him to the Augsburgerstrasse:

We had to take the suburban railway, which was quite new then, though it did not interest Mahler much. Suddenly he said to me, 'You compose, don't you.' I did not regard my student works as compositions, and denied it. 'No, no,' he said and laughed, 'you are a composer, I can see it in your face!'[36]

In one of his letters to Alma, Mahler described the visit in some detail.

---

[30] AMS. Mahler jotted down the times of the trains at the bottom of the telegram: Berlin departure 9.40 p.m., arrival 8 a.m.; Frankfurt departure 8 a.m., arrival 4.30 p.m. One of the letters Mahler sent to Johannes Messchaert in Dec. 1906 proves that at that point Mahler had not given up the plans for the Strasbourg concert, and that he was subsequently intending to be in Amsterdam on 22 Jan. (RMH 77). A letter to Fried written at the end of 1906 shows that at one point Mahler was also planning to conduct the First Symphony in Reichenberg (now Liberec) in northern Bohemia, and that he hoped the young conductor would join him there (undated letter, PML).   [31] See above, Vol. i, Chap. 18.

[32] Mahler's correspondence indicates that he moved to a different hotel on 12 Jan. The first letters to Alma (BGA, nos. 194, 195, 196) are on the letterhead of Hotel Bristol, Unter den Linden 5 and 6, whereas those from 13 Jan. onwards (BGA, nos. 197, 198) are on that of the Grand Hôtel de Rome et du Nord, Unter den Linden 39.   [33] BGA, no. 194.   [34] Ibid.

[35] See above, Chap. 7.   [36] OKM 7.

Yesterday afternoon I visited Strauss. <u>She</u> welcomed me at the door and said 'Sh! Sh! Richard's asleep', and carried me off into her (very untidy) boudoir, where her old mother was sitting and drinking '*Káffe*' (not 'coffee'). She inundated me with a torrent of gossip about the financial and sexual events of the last couple of years, hastily fired off questions about 'a whole multitude' of things without waiting for an answer, would on no account allow me to leave, told me that Richard had had an exhausting rehearsal the previous morning in Leipzig, had then come back to Berlin to conduct *Götterdämmerung* in the evening, so that today he was very tired. He was taking an afternoon nap, and she was making sure that he could sleep undisturbed. I was quite touched. Suddenly, up she jumped and said, 'It's time to wake the rascal up'. Before I could stop her she dragged me with both hands into his room and roused him with a stentorian voice 'Get up, Gustav is here!' (I was 'Gustav' for an hour, and then suddenly it was back to Herr Direktor). Strauss got up with a patient smile, and then all three of us began to gossip with renewed vigour. We had some tea, and they drove me back to the hotel after we had agreed that I should come to lunch on Saturday.[37]

In this first account of Pauline's behaviour to her husband, Mahler finds her no more than disconcerting. But his subsequent reactions are of downright shock and dismay—and sympathy for Strauss, the principal victim in Mahler's eye, as the following account by Alma of what Gustav told her shows.

He [Mahler] was alone with Strauss in his study when Pauline, who was in a rage, burst in and threw a bottle of ink at her husband. Fortunately it missed its target. She exploded: 'We're using far too much paper in the lavatories, what do you think you're doing?' She then asked Mahler to tell her husband how much a normal man should use in the course of a day. Mahler was so disgusted that he found it difficult to recover his poise. He kept saying: 'Poor Strauss! Poor Strauss!' over and over again.[38]

Under these circumstances it is easy to understand that, as a postscript to his letter of 12 January, he wrote to Alma: 'Thank God that you aren't a general's daughter [like Pauline]!'[39]

Both Strauss and his wife were very much on Mahler's mind during his time in Berlin. On the day of his first visit to them he went with Berliner to a performance of *Salome*, conducted by Leo Blech:

The performance (orchestra and singers excellent—staging nothing but kitsch and Stoll)[40] again made an extraordinary impression on me! It is a work of genius, very powerful, definitely one of the most important of our time. Under all that rubble there is an active volcano, a subterranean fire—not just a firework! It is probably just the same with Strauss's whole personality! That is why it is so difficult in his case to separate the wheat from the chaff. But I have an immense respect for the phenomenon taken as a whole, and it has been confirmed afresh. It makes me very happy. I can go along with him <u>wholeheartedly</u>! Yesterday Blech conducted (excellently). Strauss is to

[37]   BGA, no. 195, undated (10 Jan. 1907).
[38]   AMS, handwriten annotation by Alma after Mahler's letter of 7 Nov. 1905.
[39]   BGA, no. 197.
[40]   August Stoll was the producer at the Vienna Opera. However, Mahler never allowed him to take any initiatives in the preparation of new productions.

conduct on Saturday and I shall be going a second time! Destinn was magnificent! The Jokanaan (Berger) not bad! The others tolerable. Superb orchestra! . . .[41]

Mahler's week in Berlin was crowded with events—a dinner party given by Frau Wolff for Mahler, Berliner, and the critic Oscar Bie; a meeting backstage at the Opera with the famous Dutch baritone Johannes Messchaert, with whom Mahler had been exchanging letters for several weeks about a recital of his Lieder; the enthusiasm of the choral conductor Siegfried Ochs, who wanted to give the first Berlin performance of the Eighth Symphony, and that of Oskar Fried; the daily conversations with Gerhart Hauptmann and Max Reinhardt; and the two evenings in the theatre. But nothing seems have made as much of an impression on him as his visits to Strauss and his wife. He went back to have lunch with them on 12 January: 'The Blechs were also being fed. I was the first to arrive. Soon Frau Strauss came in and struck up a lively conversation, which swiftly sank lower and lower until she was moved to say: "Good god, only a million—well, that isn't enough—5 million! And then Richard will give up music altogether".'[42]

As he was writing this account of the meal at the Strauss's in a letter to Alma, Mahler was briefly interrupted by Gerhart Hauptmann,

whose dear face lightened a little the terrible desolation into which I had been plunged by the hour spent with Strauss. A detailed description of the Strauss luncheon sticks in my throat. All I can say is that I have conceived a real loathing for 'Ahna',[43] and the absent-minded and conventional manner in which Strauss distributed the blessing of his attention (*die Sonne seiner Gnade*) between Blech and me. My friendly and respectful solicitude for him on such occasions evoked no response and was probably wasted on him, since it went unnoticed.—Repeated experiences of this kind make me begin to have doubts about myself and the world at large. Are other men made of other material than I? Damn it all, it's enough to make one retreat into a thicket and have nothing more to do with the world.[44]

That same evening, during the second performance of *Salome*, Mahler's attitude changed yet again!

The impression it made was stronger than ever and I am firmly convinced that it is one of the greatest masterpieces of our time.—I cannot understand it, and only suspect that from within the genius there resounds the voice of the 'earth spirit', which builds its abode not according to human taste (*sondern nach seinen 'Gehäuse' noch besser verstehen*),[45] but on the basis of its own unfathomable needs. Perhaps time will teach me to understand this 'dwelling' better. By the way, I met Strauss at the Opera before the

[41] BGA, no. 195

[42] BGA, no. 197, undated (12 Jan. 1907).

[43] Pauline Strauss's maiden name was de Ahna.

[44] BGA, no. 197, undated (12 Jan. 1907)

[45] See BGA, no. 198, p. 308. Alma lengthened Mahler's original text: *Ich kann es mir nicht zusammenreimen und nur ahnen, dass aus den Innern des Genie die Stimme des 'Erdgeistes' tönt, der sich eben seine Wohnung nicht nach menschlichem Geschmack, sondern nach seinen 'Gehäuse' noch besser verstehen*, in the following way: *sondern nach seinen unergründlichen Bedürfnissen baut. Vielleicht lehrt mich die Zeit, dieses 'Gehäuse' noch besser verstehen.*

performance, and (being alone) he was again very pleasant and insisted on meeting me afterwards. We met, he, his wife and mother-in-law, I with Berliner, in a restaurant and talked about all sorts of things at length and very pleasantly. It was thoroughly enjoyable, despite the fiery 'intermezzi'[46] supplied by the Eternal Feminine. However, she was in a good mood, and was on 'Gustav' terms with me . . .[47]

Two days later, there was a fresh disappointment. Strauss was unable to come to the performance of the Third Symphony. He left his card at Mahler's hotel and wrote:

Dear friend, I have to conduct concerts out of town every night next week, including Sunday, and, as I desperately need some rest, I shall unfortunately have to miss the opportunity to hear your wonderful work again this evening. The first movements, which I heard yesterday, once again made a tremendous impression on me on account of their distinctive strength and blossoming invention, and it gave me sincere pleasure to see that the audience is also gradually beginning to love and understand your art. Today I have once more written to Fürstner, and hope that the score of *Salome* will soon be yours . . . Please do not ascribe my absence this evening to a lack of interest or admiration. I have done too much work in the last few weeks, so please accept my apologies. Give my regards to your dear wife. With warmest wishes from my wife and from your true and admiring friend, Dr Richard Strauss.[48]

Mahler expressed his disappointment in two different letters to Alma:

Frau Pauline probably wouldn't allow him to come. 'Today you're going to stay home, play *Skat* and then it's off to bed.'[49] . . . I don't know what to make of Strauss. How is one to explain such unevenness, such mingling of good and bad? But my judgement on *Salome* is unshakeable. (Think of people like Titian, or the philosopher Bacon).[50]

At this point the long and meandering story of the meetings and exchanges of letters, the understandings and misunderstandings between Mahler and his most famous colleague draws to a close. The two composers were to see each other again only on two occasions, once in Toblach three years later, when the subject of their conversations is unknown, and then in Munich in 1910, during the rehearsals and première of the Eighth Symphony, where there is no record of any significant exchange of views. This is therefore a good moment to reconsider their relationship and to comment on a few of the statements made by Herta Blaukopf, the editor of the Mahler–Strauss correspondence, and Walter Thomas in his book *Richard Strauss und seine Zeitgenossen*.

46 Significantly, Mahler uses the very word that Strauss was later to employ in *Intermezzo*, whose principal character is none other than his wife Pauline.

47 BGA, no. 198, undated (13 Jan. 1907).

48 Letter from Strauss to Mahler dated 14 Jan. 1907, AMS and MSB 121. Herta Blaukopf notes that Mahler had been hurt by Strauss's last-minute cancellation, but that he himself had failed to attend the première of *Salome* in Dresden on 9 Dec. 1905 and quite obviously had not written beforehand to explain why he would not attend (Herta Blaukopf, 'Rivalität und Freundschaft', in MSB 189 ff.).

49 BGA, no. 200, undated (15 Jan. 1907).

50 BGA, no. 201, undated (16 Jan. 1907). Neither of the two great men referred to by Mahler had in their time enviable reputations as human beings.

Herta Blaukopf first of all underlines the traits which they had in common: both were dedicated Wagnerians, both were active as conductors and composers, both considered their theatrical work merely as a way of earning money, although, as we have seen, Mahler took his responsibilities at the Hofoper far more seriously than did his colleague at the Berlin Opera. Finally both believed in 'moral self-purification, liberation through work, and the worship of eternal nature'.[51]

With regard to Pauline Strauss, Mahler's and Alma's accounts might be suspected of exaggeration. No one, it might be thought, could be capable of such brutal and unpredictable outbursts of rudeness. However, *Intermezzo*, the autobiographical opera based on a true incident which Strauss composed (to his own libretto) between 1919 and 1923, suggests that their descriptions of Pauline's character were not at all wide of the mark. In the opera, she is depicted as a headstrong, jealous, passionate, and impulsive woman, always ready to explode with a torrent of words or abuse. Blaukopf comments that her 'unpredictable temperament and totally uninhibited manner' were the most striking aspects of her personality. Given all that we know about Mahler's character (and given also that Alma bore little resemblance to the picture of an ideal wife he had painted in Hamburg),[52] he was bound to feel as he did when confronted by someone such as Pauline. Furthermore, his attitude was widely shared by everyone who knew her at the time. Even Walter Thomas admits that her 'brutal frankness' frequently put her husband in an extremely embarrassing position,[53] although he makes up for this by crediting her with something that neither Mahler nor Alma seem to have been aware of, namely that she performed Strauss's Lieder 'as if she had written them'.[54]

As for Strauss, the reasons why Mahler could never really understand him, or, for that matter, why he could not understand Mahler, have already been discussed above.[55] The differences between their two personalities were never more apparent than during the Berlin encounters of January 1907. Mahler was all the more perturbed because he now perceived *Salome* to be a work of genius. Yet Strauss's character was disconcerting. It combined the naivety, the tenacity, and the practical cast of mind of a Bavarian peasant[56] with the refinement and indeed the sophistication of the artist who was soon to come under the spell of Hofmannsthal's[57] witty evocations of the past, and who for the rest of his life would favour a somewhat complacent kind of neo-classicism[58] which

---

[51] Blaukopf, 'Rivalität', essay published in MSB 133 and 213.

[52] See above, Vol. i, Chap. 20.

[53] Walter Thomas, *Richard Strauss und seine Zeitgenossen*, 26.

[54] Ibid. The author states that Pauline had sung hundreds of performances of his Lieder 'on both sides of the Atlantic', that she had been an 'ideal interpreter' of the part of Freihild in *Guntram*, and that an American critic had written: 'one would believe that she had composed them, while he sat at the piano, looking rather bored'.   [55] See above, Vol. ii, Chap. 14, and Vol. iii, Chaps. 2, 3, and 6.

[56] Communication from Willi Schuh, Strauss's biographer and friend.

[57] In *Der Rosenkavalier* (1910), *Ariadne auf Naxos* (1912), and *Der Bürger als Edelmann* (1917).

[58] In *Daphne* (1937), *Die Liebe der Danae* (1940), and *Capriccio* (1941).

was a far cry from the volcanic temperament of *Salome* and *Elektra*. Mahler, if he had lived, would probably have been saddened by and disappointed with *Der Rosenkavalier*,[59] as much by a clever libretto which was designed to please all audiences, and particularly Viennese ones, as by the pseudo-Viennese dance-music. He would perhaps have regarded it as a regressive step on the part of Strauss, and might perhaps have ascribed this to the negative influence of Hofmannsthal. He would have been even more upset by the spectacle of the two collaborators trying to repeat their success in the later *Arabella*, in which, so to speak, they unashamedly used most of the same ingredients in another clever but this time highly implausible libretto.

Blaukopf rightly emphasizes Mahler's conservative tastes in literature, his lack of interest in the Jung-Wien movement and the fact that he kept writers such as Hermann Bahr, Arthur Schnitzler, and Hugo von Hofmannsthal at a distance.[60] She illustrates this with a comment Mahler made in one of the letters to Alma which refered to Otto Frischauer, an Austrian journalist living in Paris: 'He made such a perversely sophisticated impression on me. Perhaps Strauss will compose something around him one day.'[61] Obviously he disapproved of Strauss's 'decadent' literary leanings. In fact, in Salzburg in August 1906, he did not tell him about the Eighth Symphony which he was on the point of completing, because he was afraid he might consider it to be 'old-fashioned rubbish'.[62] As it happened, Strauss was present at the première of Mahler's Eighth in Munich in 1910. However, he does not appear to have commented on the work. And Mahler, for that matter, does not seem to have been much impressed by *Elektra*, which Strauss apparently played for him on the piano at the end of 1906.[63]

People have often contrasted Strauss's 'pragmatism' with Mahler's 'idealism' (too often, according to Walter Thomas). It is certainly possible to argue that Strauss's practical cast of mind and the success he had enjoyed since his earliest youth prevented him from being sufficiently self-critical, and that this had an adverse effect on his development as a composer. Blaukopf surely exaggerates when she suggests that Strauss had also fought hard for recognition, and rejects the commonly held view that he 'hastened from one victory to the next', while Mahler's life was 'a history of self-denial and failure'.[64] True, Mahler had been tremendously successful as a conductor and opera director. However,

---

[59] As we shall see, Bruno Walter considered it unworthy of its composer, and described it at length, and with much irony, in a letter Mahler received a few days before his death.

[60] See above, Chap. 3, BGA 127 ff., and Blaukopf, 'Rivalität', MSB 198.

[61] See BGA, no. 176, undated (Salzburg, 18 Aug. 1906). Otto Frischauer was then Paris correspondent of the *Neues Wiener Tagblatt*.   [62] BGA, no. 173, undated (16 Aug. 1906)

[63] This probably happened when Strauss came to Vienna to conduct a Philharmonic Concert on 16 Dec. 1906 and was invited to lunch by Mahler at the Auenbruggergasse. See Blaukopf, 'Rivalität', in MSB 198 and 200, and Strauss's 'Blaues Tagebuch', 5: 5, communication from Alice Strauss to Herta Blaukopf (MSB 224 n. 99). It is of course possible that Mahler disliked the text of *Elektra*, for he had earlier turned down Hofmannsthal's ballet libretto for *Der Triumph der Zeit*, which Zemlinsky had sent him (see above, Vol. ii, Chap. 16).   [64] Blaukopf, 'Rivalität', MSB 134.

composing meant far more to him than conducting and he had had to strive continuously to be taken seriously as a composer. This had never been the case with Strauss, who had been hailed as a genius at an early age.

Yet Strauss had contributed more than anyone else to Mahler's career as a composer. Thus, he was deeply hurt when, in 1945, he read Alma's book, and discovered that Mahler, in his letters, had not displayed any gratitude for and little awareness of the role he had played in helping him to make a name for himself. In this respect, one can only sympathize with him. However, Mahler no doubt believed that he had waited long enough for recognition from his contemporaries, and that, since he deserved it, he could conveniently forget how it had come about. Furthermore, in Mahler's eyes, Strauss did not appreciate his recent works. Deep down, Mahler was probably fully aware of Strauss's true opinion of him, which the latter once voiced to Fritz Busch after Mahler's death: 'Look, he's certainly not a great composer. He's just a very great conductor. . . .'[65]

In fact, whereas Mahler certainly admired Strauss, and proclaimed *Salome* to be 'extremely powerful, a work of genius which is definitely one of the most important works written in our time',[66] Strauss never really appreciated the true extent of Mahler's creative gift. And whereas Haydn understood the greatness of Mozart, and Schumann that of Chopin, Berlioz, and Brahms, Strauss never succeeded in rising above the prejudices of the age of which he was the true embodiment. Although he conducted the First and Fourth Symphonies in Berlin during Mahler's lifetime, and in South America after his death,[67]Blaukopf suggests that they were 'his favourite symphonies' and asserts that the Fourth Symphony was a work, 'which Strauss liked so very much'.[68] Yet the fact that he conducted these works on occasion does not mean that he loved them, and there is no evidence that he conducted other performances of Mahler later on in his long life. His view of Mahler most likely remained the same as that of his librettist Hofmannsthal, who, 'when in the company of zealots and sycophants', was 'unable to understand the fragmentary, hybrid, more longed-for than properly finished quality of Mahler's music'.[69] There is nothing to suggest that Strauss ever paid more than passing attention to such towering masterpieces as the Ninth Symphony and *Das Lied von der Erde.*

Strauss appears to have been suspicious not only of Mahler's later works, but of every powerful new trend and progressive tendency in music. Although

---

[65] Fritz Busch, *Aus dem Leben eines Musikers* (Rascher, Zürich, 1949), 69. See above, Chap. 4.

[66] BGA, no. 195, undated (10 Jan. 1907).

[67] The Fourth on 19 Jan. 1909 and the First on 3 Dec. of the same year. He conducted the same two symphonies on tour with the Vienna Philharmonic in South America in 1923. According to Franzpeter Messmer (see Richard Strauss, *Biographie eines Klangzauberers* (M&T, Zurich, 1994), 128), Strauss played a transcription for piano duet of Mahler's First Symphony with the Munich conductor, Hermann Levi.

[68] Blaukopf, 'Rivalität', in MSB 212 and 214.

[69] Letter from Hugo von Hofmannstahl to Strauss dated 26 July 1928 quoted by Thomas, *Richard Strauss*, 166.

he had included Schoenberg's *Verklärte Nacht* and First Quartet in the programme of two Allgemeiner Deutscher Musikverein festivals, he later wrote to Alma Mahler that the composer of *Erwartung* and *Pierrot Lunaire* 'would do better to shovel snow than to scribble on music paper'.[70] Stravinsky's music does not seem to have particularly impressed him either. In his autobiography the Russian composer recalled one conversation in which Strauss reproached him for starting *L'Oiseau de feu* in a pianissimo manner and gave him the following piece of advice on how to dazzle an audience: 'You first have to surprise people with a big bang. After that they will follow you and you can do whatever you please.'[71]

However, early in his career, and especially in 1901, at the time when he was elected president of the Allgemeiner Deutscher Musikverein, Strauss had taken a great deal of interest in the music of his contemporaries. In the same year he moved to Berlin and founded a series of 'Novitätenkonzerte' in which he performed works by Bruckner, Pfitzner, Tchaikovsky, Paderewski, Elgar, Charpentier, as well Mahler's Fourth Symphony. In the programmes of the Verein festivals, he was always careful to include music of all kinds and Mahler was often flabbergasted by his admiration for mediocre composers such as Hermann Bischoff, which paralleled his inability to appreciate his own mature symphonies.[72]

One of Strauss's biographers, Walter Thomas, points out that his undistinguished physique was against him, whereas Mahler's ascetic, 'Franciscan' face, which Rodin described as 'similar to the faces of Mozart and Frederick the Great',[73] contributed much to people's interest in his music. There is no doubt an element of truth in what he says, though we now judge both Mahler and Strauss solely by their works. However, it was customary at the time to emphasize the contrast between the two composers' physiques. In 1903 Thomas Mann had employed this kind of contrast as one of the basic themes of his novella *Tonio Kröger*. This work is echoed in an article on Mahler by Mann's brother-in-law, Klaus Pringsheim already quoted above:

He kept coming back to the subject and spoke at length about his relationship with Strauss. . . . On that occasion he did not speak about himself, but of the other, whom he had never underestimated, wondering without envy or bitterness, almost resignedly humble, why everything which came easily to Strauss came with such difficulty to him,

[70] Letter to Alma Mahler, 1913, quoted by Willi Reich in *Schoenberg oder der Konservative Revolutionär* (Molden, Vienna, 1968), 116. The jury of the Gustav Mahler Foundation was made up of Ferrucio Busoni, Bruno Walter, and Richard Strauss. Busoni and Walter recommended that the award should continue for a second year.

[71] Igor Stravinsky, *Chronique de ma Vie* (Denoël, Paris, 1935), 95. This comment is rather surprising, given that few works by Strauss begin like this. He may of course have been thinking of *Also sprach Zarathustra*.

[72] AMM1, 128; AMM2, 128. According to Alma, Strauss performed every year at the Allgemeine Musikverein more or less the same 'Symphony', and when Mahler reproached him for his ill-considered fidelity to this obscure composer, Strauss answered: 'You'll see, this year he got it right!'

[73] AMM1, 187; AMM2, 178.

and his listeners felt the everlasting contrast between the blond-haired, conquering heroes and the dark doom-laden sufferers.[74]

Blaukopf stresses that, in addition to being an astute businessman who kept talking about his royalties, Strauss was also a deeply serious composer who, while conducting at the Berlin Opera, spent two whole years composing *Elektra*. Furthermore, he did much to change the nature of copyright, and incurred serious losses for refusing to compromise on this important issue.[75] Blaukopf also emphasizes Strauss's modesty. In a letter to Ernst von Schuch, who had conducted the premières of most of his operas, he wrote: 'Unfortunately I am one of those people who, when it is a question of what is in the best the interests of art, never for a moment imagines that these might clash with private interests. . . . Similarly, I am still willing to learn like a schoolboy from you, from Mahler, and from anyone who can actually do something, without thinking about the possibility that my pedestal might thereby be pushed aside.'[76]

Robert Hirschfeld, the Viennese critic who was Mahler's most bitter enemy, once wrote that all the 'fuss' people made about Mahler would never have happened if he had been 'a fat man with a reddish, two-day-old beard'.[77] Schoenberg remarks about Mahler's face and the way his life had modelled and transformed it are wholly pertinent.[78] It reflects an intensity and loftiness which that of Strauss does not, and this is also true of the music. Thus *Die Frau ohne Schatten*, the only work after *Ariadne auf Naxos* and *Der Rosenkavalier* in which the composer of *Salome* attempted to surpass himself, suffers from a pretentious, wordy, and obscure libretto that is obviously ill-suited to Strauss's nature. The opera is only partly successful, although Strauss's genius is apparent in many scenes.

Strauss acknowledged that Mahler's 'idealism' frightened him, as did his 'new Christianity'. According to Klemperer, he was 'certainly not a philo-Semite, despite his particular affection for his Jewish daughter-in-law, whose life he saved during the Nazi period. Although he often claimed that 'he had liked Jews such as Mahler', he found it difficult to understand Mahler's preoccupation with redemption. 'I don't know from what I am to be redeemed. When I sit down at my desk in the morning and I get an idea, I don't need redemption. What did Mahler mean by it?'[79] This illustrates perfectly the difference between Strauss's and Mahler's characters. Walter Thomas deplores the fact that comparisons between the two

[74] Klaus Pringsheim, 'Zur Uraufführung von Mahlers Sechster Symphonie', *Musikblätter des Anbruch*, 2 (1920): 14, 497. See also Blaukopf, 'Rivalität', in MSB 192.
[75] See above Vol. ii, Chap. 14.
[76] Letter to Ernst von Schuch, in Friedrich von Schuch, *Ernst von Schuch und Dresdens Oper* (Dresden, n.d. [1955]), 95.   [77] Thomas, *Richard Strauss*, 166.
[78] Schoenberg, 'Mahler' in 'Stil und Gedanke', *Aufsätze zur Musik*, ed. Ivan Vojtěch (Fischer, Frankfurt, 1976).
[79] OKM 21. Strauss said this to Otto Klemperer a few weeks after Mahler's death.

have resulted in a series of clichés, 'Jewish Christianity' being contrasted with 'Christian atheism', 'untimely man' (*Unzeitgemässe*) with 'man of the hour' (*Zeitgemässe*), seer with pragmatist, ascetic with sybarite, sacrificial victim with survivor, idealist with realist, 'hymnic' being with psychologist, tragic outcast with rich bourgeois in princely lodgings.[80] But is it possible to avoid such comparisons? It is certainly gratifying that, after so many years of neglect and disparagement, Mahler's music has taken precedence over that of Strauss in the concert hall, perhaps because from the very beginning he took more risks and had much loftier ambitions. As far back as 1902 Mahler had predicted: 'My time will come when his is past.'[81] By aiming as high as he did, Mahler was highly unpopular with the audiences of his time. He was looking forward towards the future, whereas Strauss thought mainly of his own epoch, and even more perhaps of his own well-being. Witness the statements he made immediately after the Second World War in the presence of Thomas Mann's son Klaus to a journalist who had asked him whether he had ever considered leaving Nazi Germany: 'Emigrate? Yes, when the food starts to deteriorate. In the Third Reich the food was very good, especially when one was raking in royalties from at least eighty opera houses. Apart from a couple of stupid incidents, I had nothing to complain about.' Strauss had been caught unawares by the two men, who had introduced themselves merely as Americans, deliberately concealing Klaus Mann's identity. Strauss repeated the astounding number of theatres from which he derived his income and then went on: 'Of course, if food supplies here were to get even worse, I would perhaps have to emigrate after all, to Switzerland, for example. But so far we've always managed to muddle through somehow or other.' In a letter to his parents that he later included in his book, *Der Wendepunkt*, Klaus Mann commented: 'Yes, he's the sort of person who "muddles through" all right, no matter what the regime happens to be. What if the Nazis were guilty of a meaningless and murderous war? What if millions of innocent people went to their deaths in gas chambers? What if Germany has been reduced to a heap of rubble. What is that to Richard Strauss?'[82] However, Strauss was already 81 when this conversation took place, and, like many old people, he was preoccupied with his own discomforts, and paid little or no attention to those of other people. 'The problem with Strauss', as Anna Mahler used to say, 'is that he came after Romanticism, and he refused to suffer.'[83] In old age Strauss was just as much concerned with material things as he had been in youth. It was something that Mahler often referred to rather disparagingly in his letters to Alma.

The two men could hardly have been more different. However, it is precisely

---

[80] The word *Unzeitgemässe* was used by Nietzsche in the title of his book of Essays: *Unzeitgemässe Betrachtungen* (1876). See Thomas, *Richard Strauss*, 168.

[81] BGA, no. 18, undated (31 Jan. 1902).

[82] Letter from Klaus Mann to his family, 16 May 1945, quoted in *Der Wendepunkt: Ein Lebensbericht* (Spangenberg, Munich, 1981).

[83] A statement Anna Mahler made several times in the presence of the author of this book.

the differences, contrasts, and contradictions which make the story of their numerous encounters so fascinating for the biographer. As Alma put it, 'Mahler and Strauss liked to talk to each other, perhaps because they were never of the same opinion.' She knew, and so did Mahler, what Strauss had done to further Mahler's career as a composer, and she clearly resented his refusal, in 1924 and 1939, to allow her to publish any of the letters he had written to Mahler.[84] Admittedly, Alma's *Erinnerungen* contain some incorrect statements, such as the claim that Mahler never conducted *Feuersnot* 'because he thought it was a repulsive work'.[85] In fact Mahler did conduct a number of performances of Strauss's second opera. Although he never considered it to be a masterpiece, there is no evidence for such an aversion.

Walter Thomas has interpreted Alma's remarks and the severity of Mahler's comments as an act of revenge, almost as if they resented the fact that Strauss was so famous.[86] In doing so he displays a certain ignorance of Mahler's character, for he was never guilty of even the slightest rancour when he believed that one of his colleagues was deservedly successful.[87] In this context Walter Thomas draws attention to the fact that in *Mein Leben*, which was written long after her book on Mahler, Alma modified her position, recognizing that the composer of *Die Frau ohne Schatten* was a master 'whose genius was often greater than his frivolity'. Mahler, on the other hand, 'strove every hour to reach the heavens—and I do not know whether he was always successful'.[88] The influence Max Burckard had on Alma, and the anti-Semitic sentiments which remained an undercurrent for the rest of her life, despite her two marriages to Jews, have already been noted. It is most likely that Alma was never fully convinced by the totality of Mahler's music. Like many of her contemporaries she may even have entertained the then widespread doubts as to the creative ability in music of Jews. This in itself should make us wary of her pronouncements about art and music. Yet one of the most original and surprising traits of her character was that she often spoke disparagingly of Jews (and Jewishness) and yet she could not live without them. How sad that none of her biographers has ever attempted to decipher this aspect of her complex and disconcerting personality.

As Thomas points out, no contemporary composer, not even Schoenberg or Pfitzner, ever fascinated Mahler as much as did Strauss. Blaukopf also makes a number of similar comments. However she overemphasizes the feeling of

---

[84] See Blaukopf, 'Rivalität', MSB 129 ff.

[85] AMM1, 39 ff.; AMM2, 52; see Blaukopf, 'Rivalität', 173.

[86] A view shared by Herta Blaukopf, who claims, rather unfairly, that Alma's book was bound to be 'anti-Straussian' (MSB 217). In my opinion, Mahler's letters are at least as critical of Strauss as Alma's remarks.

[87] There was at least one exception to this statement. When he was second Kapellmeister at the Opera in Leipzig, Arthur Nikisch, who was a few years older than Mahler, was naturally able to choose which operas he wished to conduct. When Nikisch fell gravely ill before the première of *Die Walküre*, Mahler openly rejoiced, boasting in a letter to his parents of his 'physical superiority' (see above, Vol. i, Chap. 14).

[88] AML 138.

rivalry—let alone of jealousy—that Strauss's successes aroused in Mahler. Admittedly, she only speaks of jealousy when she comments on Mahler's account of his lunch with Strauss, how 'he so absent-mindedly and conventionally bestowed the blessing of his attention indifferently between Blech and me'.[89] Yet even here it is hard to agree with her. Mahler merely disliked Strauss's distracted and superficial bonhomie, and his lack of genuine warmth.[90] He can hardly have objected to having been invited to lunch together with Blech.[91] Once, in Hamburg, many years earlier, Mahler had resented Strauss's behaviour when he had entered into secret negotiations with Pollini, the director of the Stadt-Theater, in an apparent attempt to oust him.[92] The Hamburg incident had been highly unpleasant and had caused Mahler to doubt Strauss's sincerity. However, this had happened many years earlier and, ever since 1900 Strauss had ceaselessly encouraged and supported Mahler as a composer. Furthermore, *Salome* had dramatically altered Mahler's estimation of Strauss. He was now the only German musician of his generation whom he genuinely admired. As Alma remarked, 'The only composer Mahler always cared about was Strauss. Next to him all the others were more or less unimportant.' His protracted battle with the authorities of the Hofoper about *Salome* suggests that he no longer harboured any conscious or unconscious feelings of rivalry. In any case, the two men were now active in two very different fields.[93] Quite apart from the fact that he was motivated by a sense of fair play, and that he admired the work, Mahler was convinced that *Salome* would be a success. And as director he badly needed a success of this kind after the failure of his recent premières. A less generous colleague might perhaps have gloated over the ban imposed by the censor.

Mahler's bitter remarks about Strauss and his wife were not due to the fact that he bore a grudge against them. Rather, they mirror his sadness at being misunderstood. It was the disappointment of a great artist in the presence of another who all too often seemed to consider art to be a commodity to be bought, and not a cause to be served. And finally, it was the disappointment of a man confronted with a character so different from his own, who was so oblivious of his efforts to understand him or to show his admiration. The French musicologist Dominique Jameux sees the two composers as heirs to two fundamentally opposed traditions in the history of music: Mahler as a follower of the nineteenth-century (Beethovenian) model of the promethean composer, the high priest of his art, whereas Strauss—in his maturity—was basically an

[89]   BGA, no. 197, undated (12 Jan. 1907). See above.

[90]   However 'warmth' is a comparative notion. In the long letter Siegfried Lipiner, who had known Mahler since his youth, wrote to him at the time of his engagement, he accused him of behaving 'coldly' to some of his best friends (see below, Appendix 4).   [91]   Blaukopf, 'Rivalität', in MSB 201.

[92]   See above, Vol. i, Chap. 19.

[93]   Walter Thomas discerns an element of pride in the letter in which Mahler relates that Strauss had told him that he should write an opera, and that he had 'plenty of talent' for such an undertaking. However, the remark is obviously ironic (BGA, no. 175, undated, but written on 18 Aug. 1906; see above, Chap. 6).

eighteenth-century master, 'composing for the most part to order, and delivering to a deadline he found no difficulty in complying with, naturally disposed to write music for entertainment, composing prolifically, every day, in all fields, not subject to moods, with a perfect knowledge of tastes and audiences, liked by instrumentalists and singers, looked on with favour by those in power, covered with honours: i.e. a Court musician—without a Court, except for the public.'[94] As Franzpeter Messmer wrote in his biography of Strauss, 'writing music was for Strauss a craft like any other. This was a typical Munich approach, almost medieval, as Thomas Mann wrote, but also modern, and far from any Romantic sentimentality.'[95] According to Messmer, Strauss today is often condemned for the 'banality' of his music, yet Mahler uses quite as many trivial motives and melodies. The difference of course is—as Adorno has pointed out—that Mahler's 'banalities' are deliberate borrowings or intrusions from the 'other' or 'lower' sphere of music, while Strauss's have every appearance of being spontaneous, and thus unconscious. The following lines in Messmer's biography present the Mahler–Strauss musical antinomy as seen through the eyes of a convinced Strauss supporter: 'Mahler's music gives the impression of being frequently interrupted, in bits and pieces, fragmented, suffering, tortured, while Strauss's music goes with a swing, sparkles, resounds, and possesses—just like the music of classical composers—a convincing degree of unity in each of his works . . .'

Herta Blaukopf has pertinently suggested another underlying reason for Mahler's obsession with Strauss during 1906–7: the difficulties he had experienced with the instrumentation of his Fifth Symphony, and with important decisions such as the order of movements of the Sixth. His indecision made him long more than ever for some kind of encouragement from his colleague:

The feeling of uncertainty and being at a disadvantage which he felt when composing the three purely instrumental symphonies may explain why in precisely those years Strauss played such an important role in Mahler's thoughts and feelings, why he registered and commented on Strauss's every word and gesture, and continually complained about his lack of warmth. Mahler envied him, although—like Tonio Krüger[96]—he certainly never felt he wanted to be like him, but simply wanted encouragement and admiration. The absence of any literary text in the music obviously caused him to rely more on the orchestra to express meaning and clarity. It may well be that his constant struggle for comprehensibility—his 'lack of self-confidence', as Pringsheim called it—was the reason why his inner dependence on Strauss's judgement was greater than it had ever been.[97]

Blaukopf uses the word jealousy only on one occasion, yet it is implied elsewhere in her essay. However, to suggest that Mahler was 'jealous' of Strauss is implausible. That on occasion he was unable to repress a feeling of envy is

---

[94] Personal communication to the author.
[96] The 'dark-haired' hero of Thomas Mann's famous novella.
[97] Blaukopf, 'Rivalität', in MSB 193 ff.

[95] Messmer, *Strauss*, 303.

understandable, especially when he considered how things had always come easily to Strauss, how structured and prosperous his life was compared to his own, and how happy Strauss was with Pauline despite her tantrums and volcanic temperament, whilst his own relationship with Alma was problematical, to say the least. Even Strauss's ability to secure good orchestral performances after a minimum number of rehearsals occasionally made him envious, as Pringsheim reports: 'It was strange . . . that Strauss was able to make do with a couple of rehearsals, and it always "sounded good". He, on the other hand, went to a lot of trouble in endless rehearsals to get everything to sound exactly as he wanted it to sound, but when had he been able to say after a performance that it had been faultless?'[98] Yet Mahler knew that he would never change, and that his numerous and endless rehearsals led to performances which were on a much higher level than those of Strauss. It would have been simply against his nature ever to be satisfied with what he had achieved.

In 1945, whilst reading in Alma's *Erinnerungen* one of Mahler's letters of 1907, Strauss came across the sentence: 'Are human beings made of a different stuff than I?'[99] He wrote a single word in the margin: 'Yes'... And indeed, 'Gustav Mahler was. . . . of quite different stuff. He could only look on the dark side, search his soul and take things to heart!' (this is Strauss again, but speaking through the mouth of his biographer, Franzpeter Messmer).[100] And Strauss was right: Mahler 'could only. . . . take things to heart' and that was indeed one of his greatest strengths. For few human beings have longed and striven for perfection as much as he did. Strauss, who had a more prosaic cast of mind, and knew how to turn everything to his advantage, must have had one of the greatest shocks of his life when he read these letters by Mahler and saw the unflattering picture they gave of him. He may well have found their changes of tone particularly disconcerting, veering as they did 'between respect and disdain, and between affection and antipathy',[101] especially since he had always displayed the greatest possible generosity towards Mahler. Yet Mahler was not really guilty of ingratitude. In fact, the two men were simply different. Strauss's 'healthy naturalness' and his grasp of reality[102] are certainly far more common than Mahler's perpetual striving for truth and profound insights, the virtues which led to masterpieces such as the Ninth Symphony and *Das Lied von der Erde*. Blaukopf surmises that Alma's book presented 'a picture that was meant to hurt, and evidently did![103] However, I believe that it was not Alma's reminiscences which hurt Strauss most, it was the tone and the content of Mahler's letters. This was compounded by the fact that Mahler was not trying to be offensive, but merely telling his wife in a candid manner about a colleague he respected and admired, even though he frequently found it impossible to understand him.

---

[98] Klaus Pringsheim, 'Erinnerungen an Gustav Mahler', *Neue Zürcher Zeitung* (7 July 1960), quoted by Herta Blaukopf in 'Rivalität', MSB 193 ff.   [99] Blaukopf, 'Rivalität', MSB 220.

[100] Messmer, *Strauss*, 308.

[101] BGA, no. 197, undated (12 Jan. 1907) and Herta Blaukopf, 'Rivalität', in MSB 202.

[102] Ibid. 219 ff.   [103] Ibid. 217.

During his visit to Berlin in January 1907 to rehearse and conduct the Third Symphony, Mahler went twice to the theatre. Max Reinhardt was then at the height of his fame as director of the Deutsches Theater (a post he had occupied since 1894 and was to hold until the Nazis forced him to leave in 1932).[104] Although he had installed a revolving stage and new, modern machinery—which implies that illusion was of importance to him—Reinhardt was always a determined opponent of naturalism. His speciality was grandiose productions in which he exploited a unique talent for crowd scenes, and combined declamation and pantomime with music and dance. Mahler had met him in Vienna in 1905, when his brilliant production of Shakespeare's *Midsummer Night's Dream*, which had made his international reputation, was touring the main cities of Germany and Austria.[105] But there was more than one aspect to his genius: he had also founded the Berlin Kleines Theater and, in November 1906, the Kammerspiele, in which he put on intimate plays by Ibsen and Hauptmann.[106] His current production was a controversial play by Frank Wedekind, *Frühlingserwachen*. The audacity of the subject matter, which deals in an explicit manner with the awakening of adolescent sexuality, frequently caused it to be banned. Everything in the play was calculated to shock: its criticism of a society which refused to admit the realities of sex, its description of the anguish of adolescence, its defence of the rights of youth, its mixture of lyricism, burlesque, satire, and expressionism. All this was so new and original that Mahler's friends talked of nothing else. 'I'll simply have to take this bull by the horns', he wrote to Alma. 'Fried raves about it—Berliner shakes his head in disgust.'[107]

Mahler describes the *Kammerspiele* to Alma as 'a delightful, small, and extremely elegant theatre, like nothing else in the world'. The next day he communicated his impressions of Wedekind's play to Alma: 'The play is his opus I, and is already 15 years old! Well, it stunned me. Tremendously strong and gifted and full of poetry. What a pity! He really should have achieved great things! But look at the company he keeps, and what's happened to him.' Even if the virulence and bitter quality of Wedekind's play struck Mahler as excessive, he was shocked neither by its brutal realism nor by its subject matter,

---

[104] See above, Vol. ii, Chap. 14, for biographical information about Max Reinhardt's early career. From 1894 to 1903 he had been a member of the naturalist Freie Bühne in Berlin, where he also made a successful debut as actor and stage director.

[105] Some famous snapshots were then taken in the Moll's garden. They show Carl Moll, Reinhardt, Pfitzner, and Mahler engaged in conversation (see above, Chap. 3, and KMA, nos. 55–7).

[106] The Kammerspiele had opened on 8 Nov. 1906. In Jan. 1907 Gerhart Hauptmann's *Das Friedensfest* alternated with Wedekind's *Frühlingserwachen*, which was performed 117 times in the 1906–7 season. Ibsen's *Ghosts* was performed from 14 Jan. onwards. Some of Reinhardt's most famous productions were Sophocles' *Oedipus* (Berlin, 1910); *The Miracle* (London, 1911); the *Oresteia* and *Julius Caesar* (Berlin); Hofmannsthal's *Jedermann* and Goethe's *Faust* (Salzburg, 1920 and 1933). He also directed a number of operas and operettas. Strauss dedicated *Ariadne auf Naxos* to him to thank him for having agreed to participate in the Dresden première of *Der Rosenkavalier* in 1911. Reinhardt first worked in New York in 1927. He left Germany in 1933 and subsequently emigrated to the United States. He died in New York in 1943.

[107] BGA, no. 196, undated (11 Jan. 1907).

which was extraordinarily provocative at the time, and continues to be disturbing. Thus Mahler the puritan who was 'eternally celibate', the man frightened by the realities of sex, existed only in the mind of his wife.[108]

Having accompanied Mahler to *Frühlingserwachen*, Gerhart Hauptmann, who was in Berlin because Reinhardt was producing one of his plays, invited him two days later to dine with the painter Walter Leistikow[109] before going to a performance of his play. *Das Friedensfest*[110] again at the Kammerspiele:

(Hauptmann was very anxious that I should see it, otherwise I would have preferred to stay in.) A frightful, realistic affair. If one likes this kind of art, one will of course get something out of it. I totally adopted the author's point of view so as to do him justice. Hauptmann asked if I could come up to him the next morning to talk about it. After the play Reinhardt came to meet me and we went to a bar and talked about everything, performance and play. He is an extremely astute man of the theatre with whom it is a pleasure to talk shop. Later Wedekind (having been invited by Reinhardt) joined us. I was in fine form and let myself go for once. However, they were very attentive and sympathetic. Perhaps I was even of some use to them. I did not find Wedekind unpleasant. Early this morning, straight after breakfast, Hauptmann walked in. 'I've come to hear what marks you're giving me' (*Ich hole mich meine Censur*). So I told him what I thought and we chatted rather pleasantly. After he had left his (delightful) little boy arrived in my room with the Englishwoman. She told me he could bear it no longer and wanted to say <u>good morning</u> to me. Sweet, don't you think? From the child I could tell how I stood with the parents.[111]

At the same time the rehearsals for the Third Symphony continued in a pleasant atmosphere, but to a strenuous schedule. To avoid over-exertion, Mahler slept until ten each morning, and for a further hour each afternoon. Siegfried Ochs,[112] a gifted choral conductor and a reliable and likeable musician, had prepared the chorus so well that Mahler considered accepting his proposal to give the première of the Eighth Symphony: 'In Vienna, judging by the stupidity of the critics, it is still not possible to think of a "world première" [there].'[113] The Third's simplicity struck its composer forcibly during the rehearsals: 'My Third seems like a Haydn symphony. For this reason people

[108] BGA, no. 197, undated (12 Jan. 1907).

[109] Walter Leistikow (1865–1908) was a painter, an ethnologist, and co-founder of the Berlin Secession.

[110] The full title of *Das Friedensfest*, which dates from 1890 like *Frühlingserwachen*, is 'A Family Catastrophe in Three Acts'. In it Hauptmann returns to the problem of heredity, which he had already examined in *Vor Sonnenaufgang*. In this naturalist drama the influence of Ibsen is obvious. The play, which takes place on a Christmas evening, depicts a reunion of a family of neurotics and alcoholics. There is a series of quarrels and violent outbursts. The father of the family has a heart attack and dies after one of these altercations. The second son, Wilhelm, falls in love with a healthy young girl, who, he hopes, will alleviate his sufferings and cure his neurosis. The play ends by asking whether the hero can manage to escape from the family curse.   [111] BGA, no. 199, undated (14 Jan. 1907).

[112] Siegfried Ochs (1858–1929) was born in Frankfurt. He studied in Darmstadt and Heidelberg and at the Berlin Hochschule, and in 1882, with Bülow's help, founded the Berlin Philharmonic Chorus. As its director he performed many neglected choral works, conducted complete performances of Bach's Passions, and first performances of works by Bruckner, Reger, and Wolf. He also composed a number choral works and wrote a book on *Der Deutsche Gesangverein*.   [113] BGA, no. 196, undated (11 Jan. 1907).

will probably think I'm crazy. I feel as though I couldn't care less about the whole thing.'[114] The letters Mahler sent Alma from Berlin indicate that for the moment he was on good terms with her and that for once she was writing as often as he did, that is to say, every day. On 10 January, he wrote:

My darling, I promise that I won't fall in love. She [Frau Wolff] is not the young girl you dreamt of, my Traumgörgl.[115] By the way, I dreamt of you today. You had your hair done the way you used to have it before we were married, and I liked you very much! Almschili, can't you get your hair done like that again. I like it far better than your current all-too-Jewish hairstyle.[116]

Mahler had received a telegram from Baron Heinrich Tucher von Simmelsdorf, Bavarian plenipotentiary minister in Vienna, and a member of the Konzertverein committee, asking him to conduct a second performance of his Sixth Symphony as a benefit for the Deutscher Hilfsverein. Because the preceding performance had not been a success with the critics and he was afraid the hall might turn out to be empty, he awaited the advice of Alma and her parents before replying.[117] In Berlin, everything went well at the final (public) rehearsal of the Third at noon on 13 January: 'I was greeted by an ovation, and received a great deal of applause both at the end and after the individual movements. Then I went to a meal given by Wolff in my honour, and after that visited as planned the painter Leistikow for an hour with Hauptmann. I still do not know why he thought that this was so important.'[118]

At last the day of the concert dawned. In the morning of the concert Mahler visited the National Gallery with Berliner, and later met Karl Osthaus, an art historian who had founded the Folkwang Museum, one of the first museums of contemporary art in Germany.[119] In the evening the audience reacted with 'unexpected warmth and understanding' to the Berlin première of the complete Third Symphony.[120] Mahler was happy with his

---

[114] BGA, no. 198, undated (13 Jan. 1907).

[115] This allusion to Zemlinsky's opera, which Mahler had recently accepted for the Hofoper, is missing from the version Alma published in AMM. See BGA, no. 195, undated (10 Jan. 1907). Other parts of the same letter were deleted by her, among others a sentence in which Mahler reproaches her for underestimating *Salome*.

[116] Alfred Clayton, who translated this chapter into English, compares this passage with another, from the memoirs of Claire Goll (née Clarisse Liliane Aischmann, 1891–1977) (*Traumtänzerin: Jahre der Jugend* (List, Munich, 1971), 228), in which Goll's mother, who is Jewish, urges her to change her hairstyle, particularly the ringlets at the side of her face, in the manner of orthodox Jews, with the following words: 'Only devout Polacks have ringlets, so get your hair done properly.' Mahler's use of this word is suggestive of the kind of Jewish anti-Semitism that was quite common at the time as a result of the influx into Vienna of the persecuted Jews from Russia.

[117] See above, Chap. 7. The unpublished passage summarized here is part of BGA, no. 197, undated (12 Jan. 1907). [118] BGA, no. 199, undated (14 Jan. 1907).

[119] Ibid. The Folkwang Museum had an important collection of expressionistic paintings. It had opened in Hagen, but moved to Essen after the First World War.

[120] The programme note by Paul Bekker was a long analysis of the Third in which he quoted the original titles of the movements. Mahler must certainly have authorized him to publish it, which proves that he had not yet reached a final decision concerning programmes, at least for the Third Symphony.

'splendid' performance.[121] However, this was not enough to make the Berlin critics change their mind. Just as he was about to get on the train for Frankfurt on 15 January, Mahler bought the *Börsencourier*, which, he told Alma, was entirely unfavourable. Recalling the performance of the work he had heard in Krefeld, Otto Taubmann[122] wrote that on this occasion he had been 'very much disappointed'. He had found the 'endless' first movement, more unsatisfactory than ever. It 'suffers from a chronic poverty of ideas', and, 'whenever the composer wishes to show that he can write "melodies", is replete with the most obvious reminiscences, and sometimes sinks to the level of vulgarity'. The Finale, on the other hand, was 'a fairly average piece of work', and toyed rather cleverly with 'the normal instincts of the "crowd"'. However, Taubmann liked the Minuet and Scherzo, with the exception of the famous posthorn solo, which he found 'hypersentimental' and sounded like a 'park band'. Finally, he considered Mahler's attempt to be 'profound' in the 'Mitternachtlied', 'a total failure'[123] on account of its scraps of disconnected declamation and its lack of ideas.

For Leopold Schmidt,[124] the critic of the *Berliner Tageblatt*, Mahler was in some respects 'more reactionary than most contemporary composers', and eschewed facile chromaticism. He was a 'teller of tales, or rather, a reteller of tales'. His borrowings and failure to create a style of his own made it necessary to take pleasure in the finer points of detail, for the work as a whole made a 'disheartening impression'. 'They [Mahler's works] reflect most clearly the tendency, which verges on the ridiculous, to employ the most minute and intricate presentation of ideas, and to espouse a cult of expressive means for their own sake. Everything is sacrificed to this: invention, structure and coherence.' However, Schmidt acknowledged that 'the genius who is in control of the Hofoper has slowly but surely won a place as a composer, so that the appearance of each new work constitutes a notable event in musical circles'.[125]

On the other hand, the critic of the *Vossische Zeitung* professed astonishment that Berlin had had to wait ten years before hearing the Third Symphony in its entirety. The opening movement was 'rather disturbing on account of its length and the harshness of its uncompromising musical style'. However, the other movements had enthralled the audience, and a group of enthusiastic admirers had applauded 'the man to whom, with Richard Strauss, our contemporary

---

[121]   BGA, no. 200, undated (15 Jan.1907), written in Frankfurt, where Mahler was staying at Hotel Imperial.

[122]   See above, Chap. 7 for biographical information on Otto Taubmann. His review of the Third Symphony is indeed unfavourable, but it does not 'deny me . . . any talent'.

[123]   Writing in the *Allgemeine Musik-Zeitung*, Otto Lessmann noted that the effect of this solo was diminished by the singer's lack of expressivity.

[124]   See above, Chap. 4. Schmidt published a more critical article in *Signale für die musikalische Welt* in which he contrasted Mahler's 'minimal invention' with his 'titanic will' and 'sovereign mastery of orchestration', and at the same time underlining the 'triviality' of his themes.

[125]   The last sentence appears in Leopold Schmidt, *Aus dem Musikleben der Gegenwart* (Max Hesse, Berlin, 1922), 283.

music owes its most vigorous and profound impulses'. The *Berliner Zeitung am Mittag* referred to Mahler as a 'Viennese entertainer', and stated that during the first movement the audience was 'in stitches'. The reviewer included a long list of 'reminiscences',[126] and declared that the effect of the 'very beautiful and expressive' theme of the Finale was marred by incessant repetition. In contrast to this, the critic of the *Börsenzeitung* was exceptionally broad-minded. While deploring the length and thematic poverty of the first movement, he had found that Mahler was 'natural and indeed likeable' in those that followed. In the Finale, the 'noble and broad melodic character of the flowing principal theme' had brought the work to a successful conclusion.

In the *Allgemeine Musik-Zeitung* Otto Lessmann praised the grace of the Minuet, the wit of the Scherzo, and the thematic development in the Finale.[127] He believed that the work had been easier to understand than in Krefeld, possibly because Mahler had consented to the publication of a programme. As a result Lessmann had revised his opinion of the Third Symphony, though he continued to believe that the first movement lacked 'melodic originality' and was rather 'banal and popular'.

In its obituary on Mahler published four years later on 21 May 1911, the *Berliner Börsenzeitung* claimed that he had at least one important admirer in Berlin: the Crown Prince. For years Mahler had been his favourite contemporary composer. It was a predilection he shared with his wife, who 'admired the songs of Strauss and Mahler' and often performed them in private. On several occasions the Crown Princess had had the symphonies played to her (no doubt in the piano duet versions) 'so that she might familiarize herself with the spirit, the themes and the ideas of these highly original works'. The Crown Prince often had to listen to the regimental band of the 1st Regiment of the Guard, but afterwards he would 'turn for solace to the works of Mahler'. Mahler's songs were often heard in the officers' mess when the Crown Prince was present, and Count Hochberg,[128] who 'had rehearsed Mahler's music with the band, sometimes conducted the works himself'.[129]

After his week in Berlin, Mahler had originally intended to conduct further performances of his works, in Frankfurt, and elsewhere. As we have seen, by the middle of December he had changed his plans so as not to be away from Vienna for too long. Leaving Berlin at 8 a.m. the day after the concert, he reached Frankfurt at 4 p.m. He was met at the station by his old friend, the conductor Ludwig Rottenberg.[130] Alexander Siloti, a young

---

[126] They were said to include Schumann's 'Aufschwung', Nicolai's *Die lustigen Weiber*, Verdi's *Il Trovatore*, Wagner's *Die Walküre, Tristan, Parsifal*, and Sullivan's *The Mikado*, which Mahler had certainly never heard.

[127] Lessmann thought that the opening theme was 'slightly Brahmsian'. The sixth Philharmonic Concert was given on Monday, 14 Jan. 1907 at 7.30 p.m. The performers included the Anna Schultzen-Asten Chorus, the children's chorus of the Nikolai-Marienkirche, and the contralto Maria Seret.

[128] See above, Vol. i, Chap. 14.   [129] *Berliner Börsenzeitung*, morning edn. (21 May 1911).

[130] See above, Vol. i, Chap. 21.

Russian[131] who was in Frankfurt to conduct the next Museumkonzert, was also there. He had studied composition with Tchaikovsky and had been one of Liszt's last piano pupils in Weimar. Settling in St Petersburg in 1903, he had initiated a series of orchestral concerts which attempted to steer clear of the conservative policies of the Imperial Music Society. Thus his programmes were composed mostly of lesser-known classical works as well as new compositions.[132] He promptly invited Mahler to conduct two of his concerts, and suggested programmes including some music by Haydn, Beethoven's Ninth, some Wagner extracts, as well as one of his own symphonies. 'The people [in St Petersburg] cannot forget my rehearsals, [from which] they have learnt so much', Mahler wrote to Alma, reporting on his meeting with Siloti.[133] On the *Börsencourier* review of his Berlin concert, which he had read at the station on his way to Frankfurt, Mahler comments in the same letter: 'In so many words it denies that I have any talent. I can't even orchestrate, it seems.'[134] And he adds two days later:

All over the place people are beginning to be very unpleasant about me, I am like a wild animal, with the hounds in hot pursuit. But, thank God, I am not one of those who die by the wayside, and the blows I have to endure everywhere (the Berlin critics are again almost unanimously 'scornful') simply have the effect of a massage. I simply brush my suit if people throw mud at it. 'Preserving myself and all powers defying.' . . . I feel like calling off Messchaert in Berlin. Why should I let myself be pissed on all the time? These little creatures obviously think I'm a kerbstone.[135]

Mahler was also worried by the news from Austria. 'People in Vienna seem to have gone mad. The papers here keep printing telegrams from there, saying that I have resigned—and that I have run up an incredible deficit, that I have become impossible etc. etc.'[136] 'Some people are obviously wishing I would stay away longer.'[137] He added: 'It's just as well we have fifty thousand bucks (*Spiessen*) and an annual pension of five thousand!'[138]

To Mengelberg, Mahler wrote from Frankfurt, once again to apologize for cancelling his Amsterdam concerts:

I am truly sorry. It has already become a pleasant habit to spend a few days with you each year, and this year I shall miss it <u>very much</u>. But on Monday I have to be back in Vienna (orders from above). So this time it would be better *not* to count on me. You

131   Alexander Ilyitch Siloti (1863–1945) was born near Kharkov. After studying theory and composition with Tchaikovsky, and piano with Nicholas Rubinstein, he was one of Liszt's last pupils. Siloti taught at the Moscow Conservatory, and then spent several years in Germany. In 1901 and 1902 he conducted the Moscow Philharmonic Orchestra before founding his own series of concerts in St Petersburg, which lasted from 1903 until 1917. He emigrated at the time of the Russian revolution, living in Germany, England, and the United States, where he taught for many years at the Juilliard School in New York.

132   See below, Chap. 10, on musical life in St Petersburg and its various series of orchestral concerts.

133   BGA, no. 201, undated (Frankfurt, 16 Jan. 1907) In the event Mahler did go to St Petersburg before he left for New York, but his concerts were organized by C. N. Schröder (see below, Chap. 10).

134   BGA, no. 200, undated (15 Jan. 1907).   135   BGA, no. 202.

136   BGA, no. 201, undated (16 Jan. 1907).   137   BGA, no. 200, undated (15 Jan 1907).

138   BGA, no. 202, undated (17 Jan. 1907).

know that in your case I feel that I am in good hands, both personally and artistically, so I think the best thing this year would be for you to do the Sixth without me.[139]

In Frankfurt Mahler had agreed to conduct the seventh Museumkonzert, and his Fourth Symphony was the main work on the programme. He got off to a good start, and had a 'delightful and pleasant' room at the Hotel Imperial. The orchestra was excellent and he was completely satisfied with the work done before his arrival by Ludwig Rottenberg, 'who is still the same dear old friend'. The musicians were cooperative, though in the 'delightful' last move-ment of Schumann's First Symphony the violins 'were more scratchful than graceful (*Kratziös als Graziös*)'. 'This', he told Alma, "is where I praise the Vienna Philharmonic (*meine Philharmoniker*), which unfortunately wants to have nothing to do with me.'[140]

The concert, including Mahler's Fourth Symphony, which had caused a scandal in the same city five years before under Weingartner, was a tremen-dous success. The *Frankfurter Zeitung* attributed this to the composer's 'meticu-lously prepared and warmly felt interpretation', though it was prompted to ask a question which Mahler obviously asked himself sometimes: 'Would Mahler the composer have been so successful today if Mahler the even more gifted conductor had not come to his support?' However, the critic reported that, in addition to the applause, there had been some hissing. He thought the work was uneven and full of borrowed themes, though he praised Mahler's melodic writing, contrapuntal skill, and the subtlety of the orchestration. However, he considered the last movement to be a 'stylistic mistake' because it stood in the way of the overall symmetry.[141] 'A further drawback is Mahler's lack of creativ-ity. One has the impression that one has already heard most of the themes somewhere else, or at most in a slightly different form.' On the other hand, the review had nothing but praise for Mahler's conducting. 'The opening chords [of the *Coriolan* Overture] established the tragic character of the piece, which was then maintained relentlessly to the very end.' Concluding the concert, Schumann's First Symphony seemed 'much fresher' than that of Mahler. Having been prepared 'with great devotion', the performance revealed many 'hidden beauties', and this was due to Mahler's alterations in the orchestration. Hans Pfeilschmidt, writing in *Die Musik*, said much the same as the critic of the *Frankfurter Zeitung*. The success of the Fourth Symphony, which had been a failure in Frankfurt in 1901 under Weingartner, was largely due to Mahler's conducting. As in the *Coriolan* Overture, he had stressed originality at the

---

[139] MBR1, no. 310; MBR2, no. 368; and RMH 81. See above, Chap. 7. In the same letter Mahler announces that he is sending the cowbells to Amsterdam, and asks Mengelberg to send back the score of the Sixth in order to make 'an important alteration' in the Finale. As we have seen, Mengelberg first tried to postpone the performance until Feb. or Apr. before finally abandoning it. Mahler sent his reply to Alma together with BGA no. 202 (see also RMH 79).   [140] BGA, no. 202.

[141] Like so many other critics, he preferred the Adagio and the coda of the first movement. He dismissed the development section of the first movement as being 'more interesting on paper than in performance', and called the Scherzo 'a maudlin dance of death'.

expense of his undoubted qualities. However, his 'work was unmistakably dear to his heart', and thus the audience had been far more favourably disposed towards it.[142]

On his way back to Vienna Mahler stopped off in Linz to conduct his First Symphony. Linz was not far from the little town of Hall where he had begun his career twenty-seven years earlier, and St Florian, where Bruckner had spent his youth. He had accepted the engagement on condition that the management of the Musikvereinskonzerte had agreed to engage twenty musicians from the Vienna Philharmonic. He changed trains at Passau, from where he sent Alma a postcard with a report on his last day in Frankfurt, and details of the final rehearsal and the concert there: 'Here, as in Berlin, people have been utterly charming to me.' Conducting at concerts for several days had obviously been a welcome change from conducting operas in Vienna.[143]

In Linz Mahler stayed at the Erzherzog Karl Hotel. All the preliminary rehearsals had been in the hands of the local conductor, Leopold Materna.[144] As his train was late, Mahler went directly from the station to the Landestheater.[145] The Linz critic Franz Gräflinger left a colourful account of the work-sessions and the concert:

The two full rehearsals went quite smoothly. The one on Saturday was conducted by Kapellmeister Materna because Mahler's train from Frankfurt was delayed and he arrived too late. His distinctive head appeared towards the end of the third movement. People turned and craned their necks, for quite a few of those present had never seen Mahler in the flesh before. After the usual introduction of the conductor, Mahler had the music stand lowered and began to conduct. Things went rather well. In fact, they went very well. 'I congratulate you,' he said to Materna, who had rehearsed the symphony with dispassionate precision. Mahler merely had to hone a few details. At one point he thought that the decrescendo in a forte–piano was insufficient, and gave an immediate ilustration of this dynamic mark by striking the podium with his hand. Then he explained something to the brass, corrected the intonation of a trombone, asked for a more intimate pianissimo. He thought the percussion sounded muffled. Then there was 'a good exercise for the strings', as Mahler called it. The passage soon sounded quite different. In the concluding crescendo in the last movement, when he wanted more volume from the horns (*Hörnerverstärkung*), the four horn players of our orchestra suddenly stood up, whereas of course those from Vienna remained seated. Mahler was very surprised. He stopped the rehearsal. The explanation followed. 'It would look too theatrical', he said. (Incidentally, the Universal score states: 'From here on . . . all the horns stand up in order to achieve the loudest possible sound.') Mahler is a practical man. The Finale ends with two accentuated unison crotchets. Because he

    142 The seventh Frankfurt Museumskonzert, which was given in the large concert hall of the Saalbau on Friday, 18 Jan., at 7 p.m., included Beethoven's *Coriolan* Overture, Mahler's Fourth Symphony (with the soprano Elsa Gentner-Fischer), and Schumann's First Symphony.
    143 BGA, no. 203, undated (19 Jan. 1907).
    144 Leopold Materna (1872–1948) was born in Graz. The son of a post office official, he was the brother of Hedwig Materna, who was a singer, like her more famous aunt, Amalie Materna.
    145 Franz Gräflinger mistakenly writes 'Landschaftliches Theater'.

thought the second one was not loud enough, Mahler assigned an extra crotchet to the timpani in order to increase the effect. Mahler certainly has a liking for percussion. ... For the Linz concert he had to omit the most important triangle entries in the Finale, whether he liked it or not, because there were only four percussionists. Incidentally, in the concert one of the percussionists clearly delighted him by playing at least one important triangle passage. During the rehearsal of the first movement Mahler spoke to the woodwinds about the mood of the piece, with its references to nature, about the young cuckoo (flute), the old cuckoo (clarinet) and the jay (oboe). At the full rehearsal (20 January 1907) everything went well with the exception of a passage for the third clarinet. The handful of listeners was enraptured by the first three movements. To the orchestra Mahler said: 'I am delighted! One notices that one is in Austria!' At the start of the concert Mahler was given a warm welcome, and both his symphony and his songs were greeted with tumultuous applause.[146]

In addition to Mahler's First Symphony, the programme of the Linz concert on 20 January included three songs—'Um Mitternacht', 'Aus! Aus!', and 'Erinnerung'—sung by Gustav Kaitan,[147] a tenor from the Graz Opera, who was accompanied by Leopold Materna. It ended with the *Leonore* Overture no. 3 conducted by Materna. In a long article in the *Linzer Zeitung* Franz Gräfliger wondered whether Mahler's 'wit, irony and banter' was merely a function of his orchestration. But the bulk of the article was devoted to describing the work and giving the earlier titles of the movements. The critic of the *Tages-Post* admired the 'Olympian calm' of Mahler's conducting,[148] but again gave a description of the work and then stressed one of the composer's most important characteristics, his love of nature. According to this newspaper, the concert had been 'a great success'. However, Alois Königstorfer, in a review in *Die Musik*, stated that it 'had not aroused any great interest' and that the audience had given the symphony 'a cool reception' because of its lack of invention.

Only the Stuttgart journal, the *Neue Musik-Zeitung*, carried a substantial review, which was by Franz Gräflinger.

The absolute musician from head to toe perplexed our audience. Such beautiful singing passages, such blossoming orchestral melody, and then—ideas interwoven so ironically, the deliberate use of well-known folk songs and Bohemian peasant music! But anyone able to hear its unusual combination of sounds will find enough that is of interest in Mahler's First Symphony. In the Finale those who were unfamiliar with Mahler's other symphonies were given a taste of his most personal orchestral mode of expression. The sharpest dissonances collide, all the instruments storm and rage, the themes wallow and snarl in a grandiose and unruly manner. The music towers up, and then implodes. Ideas join and tear themselves away. Armed with cudgels, all the good

---

[146] Franz Gräflinger, 'Gustav Mahler in Linz', *Linzer Tagespost* (21 May 1911).

[147] The year before he had sung the role of Narraboth in the first Austrian performance of *Salome*.

[148] *Tagespost* (25 Jan. 1907). Like so many other witnesses, Gräflinger contrasted his calm during the concert with his liveliness in the rehearsals. The *Tagespost* of 18 Jan. 1907 listed some of the musicians from the Vienna Philharmonic who took part in the Linz performance. They included Arnold Rosé (violin); Otto Stix (double bass); Anton Powolny (clarinet); Karl Stiegler (horn); Adolf Wunderer (trumpet); Franz Dreyer (trombone); and Heinrich Knauer (timpani).

and evil spirits of the orchestra hurl them at each other, as it were. It is an orchestral deluge.[149]

By the time Franz Graefliger's review appeared Mahler had long since returned to Vienna, and the Linz concert was a distant memory, for on his return he had found the Austrian capital in an uproar initiated and then deliberately sustained by the critics, the 'theatre reporters' and 'music journalists'. Before resuming his normal activities he had to do his best to restore some kind of order. Two days before he returned, the illustrated Sunday supplement of *Die Zeit* had published a set of four cartoons entitled 'A Month in the Life of the Director of the Opera'. Underneath were the words: 'We were unable to interview the Director'. The first drawing was of Mahler with a baton in his hand, and the caption was: 'The first week, because he was conducting the combined orchestras of Kötzschenbroda, Langensalza and Apolda in a performance of his new symphony.' The next drawing showed him in the cab of a locomotive: 'The second week because he was looking for an instrument with a hitherto unknown sonority.' Next he was seen at his desk with an enormous score open in front of him: 'The third week, because he was completely taken up with the revision of the Ninth Symphony which he has just completed.' In the fourth cartoon the singers of the Hofoper were seen crowding around the door of his office, which they were unable to enter: 'The fourth week, because he was recovering in the director's office from the exertions of his holidays.'[150]

On 13 January *Die Zeit* had already published a vicious attack on Mahler, then in Berlin. The article was by Richard Wallaschek, who, as we have seen, had become one of Mahler's sworn enemies.[151] It began by pointing out the restricted range of the repertory at the Hofoper, which contained no operas by Gluck, Marschner, or Lortzing; no French comic operas, and not a single nineteenth-century Italian work. Furthermore, it claimed that sumptuous 'new productions' would not have been needed if the average standard of the performances had not been allowed to fall to the point it had now reached. Wallaschek cited the example of *Carmen*, the current production of which he considered to be just as mediocre and as superficial as that of the Kaiserjubiläumstheater.

Wallaschek also criticized Mahler for again making cuts in the works of Wagner. In the case of *Tristan* this meant that the performance now finished at a quarter past eleven.[152] In fact, Mahler had criticized his predecessors, Jahn and Richter, for making cuts. However, it was certainly true that in the last two years his choice of new works—*Die neugierigen Frauen, Flauto Solo*, and *Le*

---

[149] *Neue Musik-Zeitung*, 'Von der Wiener Hofoper, Gustav Mahler als Operndirektor', 28 (1907): 13, 310.

[150] *Die Sonntags-Zeit*, illustrated suppl. to *Die Zeit*, 6 (1907), 1554 (20 Jan. 1907).

[151] See above, Chap. 6.

[152] Such cuts were made only in exceptional cases, for example when a singer was indisposed, and Mahler continued to perform the major Wagnerian dramas uncut. His successor, Felix von Weingartner, was later to be severely criticized for making permanent cuts.

Juif polonais—had not been altogether happy. Wallaschek now turned to his main grievance, Mahler's absences, the effect of which he considered to be catastrophic. Only recently a composer who had wanted to play his opera to Mahler had been told that the director was completely immersed in rehearsals for his symphony and, because he had to go abroad to conduct his works, could not be seen until the end of the month. For years the very same Mahler had been preventing members of his ensemble from travelling to other countries for fear that they might become international celebrities. Furthermore, those who conducted in his stead were far from being adequate substitutes, especially since Richter had left the Hofoper, discouraged by all the changes that Mahler had made, changes which had put an end to the pleasure he had previously taken in his work.

Admittedly, Roller's first productions—*Tristan*, *Fidelio*, and even *The Marriage of Figaro*—had been a success, but this euphoric period had not lasted. On account of his absences, Mahler no longer had enough authority, and this was why he had not been able to perform *Salome*. His policy as a director had occasionally become extravagant. Austrian opera composers were despondent, for they knew in advance that they had no chance of getting their works performed. The standard of performances was hardly better than when Mahler had arrived. Mahler not only chose new colleagues unwisely. He was making more and more experiments, and increasing the number of guest performances. Certain members of the Hofoper were unemployed for months on end, while others had had their voices ruined by excessive work. The ballet was in complete decline, and Tchaikovsky's *Nutcracker* and *Sleeping Beauty* were not being performed. 'However,' the critic of *Die Zeit* concluded, 'we are not complaining in order to deny that Mahler has the ability to be director. We are trying to demonstrate that we have a director whose name may be Mahler, but who is failing to keep the promises he once made and used to keep.'

On 12 January, the 'Backstage' column in the *Neues Wiener Journal*, which specialized in scandalmongering, referred to 'the nightmare of a mammoth deficit'. The following day, the *Montags-Revue* printed an article entitled 'Come back Gustav, all is forgiven!' Here Mahler was accused of spending days at a time, even weeks, away from Vienna at the height of the season. This was a time, as he had frequently declared, when the Hofoper could not grant leave to members of the ensemble. In his absence, the repertory was 'becoming monotonous, and discipline weakening'. Unfortunately, two hearts were beating in the same breast, that of the composer and that of the conductor. The Viennese public looked askance at his absences. It was calling: 'Come back, Gustav, all is forgiven!' 'Even the Sixth Symphony', the journalist added.

But this article did not differ significantly from many others. The 'Theatre, Art and Literature' section of the same issue, on the other hand, began with the sensational announcement that Mahler was about to resign: 'In artistic circles it was being said today that Herr Gustav Mahler will soon ask to be relieved of his duties as Director of the Hofoper.' The next day several other newspapers carried the startling news, notably the *Neue Freie Presse*, the *Neues Wiener Tagblatt* and, of course, the *Neues Wiener Journal*. The latter, however, added that it was a rumour without foundation, and that it had been denied in high places.

The following day the *Deutsche Zeitung* and the *Neues Wiener Journal* announced that Prince Liechtenstein was about to resign, and predicted that Prince Montenuovo was not likely to take his place, for the Lord Chamberlain could only be a high-ranking military man. Having lost his principal supporter, there was little chance that Mahler would retain his position. He would no doubt leave the Opera to devote himself exclusively to conducting concerts, something that he had often expressed a desire to do. The article also referred in an insidious manner to the 'conflicts' that had arisen between Mahler and certain singers and to the 'enormous deficit of the Hofoper', which was estimated to be as much as 200,000 kronen.

On 17 January Hans Liebstöckl joined in the attack with an article in the *Illustrirtes Extrablatt*. It was particularly trenchant and, as usual, in impeccable style. Recalling Mahler's meteoric rise to the post he had now held for ten years, the article noted the public's current dissatisfaction, which it attributed to 'the system, to Gustav Mahler's regime, to his nervous character, to his "impressionism" ':

Mahler is a parvenu in the best sense of the word. He has been lucky, more than anyone else. Many musicians have failed to make much headway in Vienna, unable to succeed despite great and ample gifts on account of a lack of showmanship. Today one begins as a conductor, because orchestras are currently all-important. The conductor is a *neu deutsch* invention. Genius is nowhere more clearly visible than in this exposed position. Here the genius can advertise himself, can act, celebrate, strike poses, and impress us with his authority. But nowhere is he more certain to be overestimated. Earlier in the history of music the conductor as an institution, as an independent entity, was unknown. He is now the leader, and in point of fact he needs nothing more than the ability to impose his will on the orchestra and to gain its respect. Gustav Mahler has this ability, and thus Vienna came to know him as a conductor. Journalists who knew nothing about music seized on the topic. The subject of the great conductor was illuminated from every angle. But for Herr Mahler this was only a means to an end. He had set his sights on much higher things, had great symphonies within him and, soon after becoming director, set himself up as a composer. This development—and we have witnessed it in all its stages—this development occurred at the expense of the Hofoper, was detrimental to the Hofoper, divided his interests. The director conflicted with the composer, and the composer triumphed. It is the same as in the case of Richard Strauss. The Berlin Hofoper is feeling the full effect of Strauss, and ours of Gustav Mahler. However, it is far worse in our case, for this is an institution of world-wide renown. In the ten years that Mahler has been at the head of the Hofoper, all the hidden flaws of his character have become apparent. There is of course a political dimension to the post Mahler occupies, and he has inaugurated policies of his own. He is courteous to his superiors, and harsh, abrupt and inconsiderate to those below him. He is at the mercy of his moods, his interest comes and goes quite suddenly. He does not have a single real friend at the Hofoper, not a single person, objectively seen, who is on his side. On the other hand he has bitter enemies, some of whom are unjust to him. Admirers from the early days of his Viennese reign soon vanished into thin air. A handful of enthusiasts who admire his symphonies remain. This, said the journalists, is the result of his genius. A genius becomes lonely and isolated, and comes into conflict with others. This is all well and good. Let Herr Mahler withdraw and isolate himself. But not as Director of the Hofoper, which, apart from an artist, needs someone with a heart and a benevolent character if it is to thrive. Mahler lacks these qualities. True, his influence is everywhere to be seen, but it is better at destroying things than at constructive work. This saviour has dismantled and dissolved the Hofoper. All its various parts are going their own way . . .

Mahler had done a lot of good during his first two years of his time at the Hofoper, Liebstöckl admitted. After that, he claimed, it was his assistant Wondra who did the casting.

Nothing is as it was, the former brightness is fading away, the plaster is crumbling down. And then there is the incessant round of new engagements and of guests. For a moment there were ten tenors. We have just allowed one of them to go. Minor deities are assigned to major roles, and are driven beyond the limits of their endurance. I do not want to name any names, having no wish to hurt people who are not themselves to blame if Herr Mahler overestimates their abilities. The development of more talented people has been held back and has simply been spoiled. Others again have been disregarded and have suddenly fallen into disgrace. Banished from the presence of the Master.

Mahler's neurotic regime has brought disorder not only to the Hofoper as such, but also to the people working with and around him. Talents have been stunted, and run-of-the-mill artists have found preferment. Those who are in favour are exploited until they drop dead, usually in unsuitable roles. Incomprehensible 'casting' is the order of the day. Furthermore, when Mahler takes it upon himself to produce an opera, he personally intervenes in everything, taking over the singers and playing every part through them. Each step they make is conceded to them by the Herr Director, each gesture, every musical phrase. Herr Mahler does not like beautiful singing. He literally pulverizes Wagner.

To sum up: in this, the tenth year of Mahler's reign, the Hofoper is severely demoralized and in a ramshackle state. It gets by on two or three good evenings. However, there are numerous mediocre, slovenly and routine performances which occasionally enrage the audience. The reasons are obvious. Herr Mahler lacks leadership qualities, he is not benevolent and calm, lacks objectivity, has no clear idea of talent, and does not have a steadfast solicitude for every aspect of the Hofoper. The composer has supplanted the director. With the giant monsters in his bosom, which we are given to hear every year, he merely treats the Hofoper as a cow capable of supplying one with butter. And now the system is taking its revenge. In box office returns, in reputation of the Hofoper, and in internal demoralization.

This article constitutes good evidence of Viennese ingratitude, scandal-mongering and injustice taken to an extreme. Seeing how far Mahler's enemies were prepared to go, it is easy to imagine that he might be tempted to leave the Hofoper, all the more so since he was no doubt aware that he had already shown what he was capable of. In the face of their spiteful attacks, which were developing into a veritable press campaign, anyone undertaking to defend Mahler was swimming against the tide. Nevertheless David Josef Bach was to do so on 1 February 1907 in the Journal *Österreichische Rundschau*. In a long Feuilleton entitled 'Der Fall Mahler' (The Mahler Case) he attempts to paint an objective picture of the situation at the Hofoper, ten years after Mahler's appointment. First of all, Bach reviewed each of the singers in the Opera's ensemble and reminded his readers that most of them had been engaged by Mahler. Before he came to Vienna, opera performances attracted people who came only to hear beautiful voices, whereas now audiences looked for more rounded 'artistic performances'. Admittedly, many old productions badly needed improvements, as the recent and successful *Neueinstudierung* of *Un Ballo in maschera* had proved a few months earlier. Admittedly, standards often suffered when performances were conducted by Mahler's assistants, and Bach attempted to appraise their qualities and defects. He described Franz Schalk as follows:

a diligent, skilled conductor with a very wide practical experience. He conducts absolutely everything, but rarely anything in which one feels that his personal preference is lifting him above his habitual facility. Often after the second or third performance, Herr Schalk takes over from the Direktor a presentation which has been precisely worked out down to the smallest detail. He has other tempos, other shades of interpretation—the orchestra becomes nervous, irritable, and finally they arrive at a sort of mutual tolerance agreement based on the listlessness everyone feels. Result: the conductor couldn't care less (*heisst sie dann Gleichgültigkeit*), and the orchestra just muddles through (*beim Orchester Schlamperei*).

For Bruno Walter, Bach also had only qualified praise:

He is someone who as a musician deserves the highest esteem. The honesty and ardour he puts into his work make one admire him even while one becomes aware that there is a gap between his noble aims and the results he actually achieves. But as a conductor he very rarely gives satisfaction. In nervous agitation he is almost Mahler's equal. But whereas in the decisive moment of the performance Mahler can master his own feelings and those of the orchestra, Walter in the heat of the moment loses control over himself and over others.

Bach's appraisal of Francesco Spetrino's talents was downright unfavourable:

Under his hands performances lose their life and lustre. The public gets bored, and so do the singers and members of the orchestra. In performances like that of *Aida* everybody ends up doing their own thing, and the audience is just about polite enough not to join in the general free-for-all; it keeps well out of it, sometimes in the literal sense of the word.

To these less than wholly reliable assistants Bach considered that Mahler left too much responsibility,[153] and he adds to the list of necessary reforms the hiring of competent stage directors, particularly for the daily repertoire. That the repertoire had diminished in breadth in recent years was an undeniable fact, but this was because the public's interest had waned as the artistic level of performances deteriorated when Mahler gave them over to his assistants. However, Bach also detected a grave defect in the Opera's administration: to his mind, the artistic Director should also be responsible for the Opera's finances. The present authorities had made a fatal mistake by increasing the price of seats beyond reasonable limits. In the conclusion of his article, Bach conceded that many problems needed to be solved at the Opera, but that Vienna should also be grateful to Mahler for all he had done: 'Gustav Mahler has given his best to the Hofoper. Is it likely that for a passing mood or some worse reason he is going to turn his back on the work he himself has in part created?'[154]

When this article appeared, Mahler had not returned to Vienna and the possibility that he might be going was only a subject of gossip in Viennese salons and cafés. However the rumours had become so insistent that Bach wrote another article on 18 January, this time in the *Arbeiter-Zeitung*, which he entitled 'Direktor Mahler amstmüde (Is Director Mahler tired of his job)?'

In the Viennese yellow press gossip columns an edifying argument has broken out. Who was the first to invent the news that Mahler intends to resign? For the present that still happens to be an invention and the best reason one could find for such a resignation is that any self-respecting artist must be fed up with having to work in a city where everything is judged from the point of view of gossip, blown-up sensationalism, and in terms of personal vanity and the thirst for publicity. I am more than willing to bet that the director did not confide his most secret intentions to scribblers who have the effrontery to concern themselves with artistic policy in Vienna. And, in any case, he is not in Vienna at the moment. And it is precisely this circumstance that has set the busy pens going. For certain members of the Hofoper, whose affection for their director resembles that of all creatures who think they have been maltreated (and this despite the fact that it was Mahler who for the most part discovered them, and who is responsible for their rather over-inflated importance), have seized this welcome opportunity to gossip like unsupervised domestics about their grievances to any scandalmonger they happen to meet. Every singer at the Hofoper is of course a genius, every diva a star, whereas Mahler is a petty man of questionable talent who bullies everyone within reach.[155]

---

[153] Bach finds in particular that they were too often entrusted with the task of searching for and engaging new singers. However, he adds that no such disaster had ever been witnessed in Vienna as had occurred at the Berlin Court Opera, where a performance of *The Magic Flute* had recently taken place with four guest-singers in the leading parts.   [154] *Österreichische Rundschau*, 3 (1907): 3, 225.
[155] *Arbeiter-Zeitung* (18 Jan. 1907).

Bach claimed that guest appearances were less numerous in Vienna than elsewhere. Only recently, in Berlin, there had been no less than four guest-singers in a performance of *The Magic Flute*. In Vienna, last-minute changes of programming, so common in the past, no longer occurred. What the Hofoper lacked was a producer capable of maintaining the standard of productions when Mahler was absent. Furthermore, it was unjust to blame him for the poverty of contemporary operas, or for the actions of his superiors, who had refused to allow him to perform *Salome*. And how could he be made responsible for deficits when he had no control over the financial administration of the Hofoper? Attacks of this kind would ultimately wear him down and deprive him of all the pleasure he took in his work.

Liebstöckl's attack was not to be the only one. Two days later Heinrich Reinhardt, the operetta composer, published an article in the *Neues Wiener Journal* with the title 'Mahleriana: Eine künstleriche Bilanz (An artistic balance sheet)'. In this he claimed that Mahler had ruined the Hofoper, both in artistic and financial terms, with his 'orgies of guest appearances', the ill-conceived appointments he had made, and his incomprehensible dismissals. He had neglected the repertory, closed the doors of the Opera to many 'highly interesting' new works which had been successfully performed elsewhere, and produced second-rate ones. He had also lowered the standard of the orchestra by pensioning off too many of its former members. Reinhardt also found fault with the 'tawdry decorations' for the works of Wagner. He complained that 'composing and conducting his symphonies' was now Mahler's principal profession, though he conceded that he had done sterling work with regard to renewing productions of older, established operas. However, he ended on a thoroughly negative note: 'After ten years, Gustav Mahler's balance-sheet shows a considerable deficit.'

On 21 January the *Montags-Revue* had stated that rumours of Mahler's resignation had 'met with an enthusiastic response at the Hofoper'. However, this was rather premature, for he had been appointed for life, and could leave only if he so wished. 'The clamour we aroused with two lines about a rumour was considerable, but it was not even as musical as Mahler's worst symphony. When Mahler reappears on the podium at the Hofoper he will be acclaimed. And the clamourers will disown their part in the chorus of denigration. A new role—and they will praise Mahler to the skies.' On 25 January the *Illustrirtes Wiener Tagblatt* again claimed that there was a considerable deficit at both imperial theatres. However, David Josef Bach was not alone in defending Mahler. On 26 January Korngold, writing in the *Neue Freie Presse*, reviewed every stage of Mahler's time at the Hofoper, and drew up a list of his strengths and weaknesses. He recalled the difficulties encountered by Weber in Mannheim and Dresden, and by Bülow in Hanover, when, like Mahler, they had assumed responsibility for both the music and the production. But, Korngold wrote, this was how Mahler had succeeded in creating a true ensemble and a true harmony between music and design, and had ended up by influencing opera houses everywhere. The main difficulty with such a great man was that he dwarfed everyone else. Korngold recognized the limitations of the repertory and the inadequacy of certain singers for certain roles,[156] and admitted that there was a difference between the standard of ordinary performances and that of new productions, but he warned that a different director would have different weaknesses, and that it would in any case be impossible to find someone who was on a par with Mahler. He reminded his readers that foreign visitors to Vienna still cried 'Mahler' and then rushed to the Hofoper. Thus, he concluded, one ought to be proud to have such a director.

On 22 January, writing in the *Neue Musik-Zeitung*, L. Andro also attempted an evaluation of Mahler's achievement. After praising Mahler's early years at the Hofoper and the singers he had engaged, such as Mildenburg and Gutheil-Schoder, both of them 'great actresses', Andro suggested that Mahler had found an ideal collaborator in Alfred Roller. Nevertheless, 'the bitter disappointments started with *Fidelio*' and continued with *Don Giovanni*, with its 'indescribably clever and bizarre staging' where only 'the music' was missing. Only *Figaro* had been a success. But here the characters were subordinated to the general effect, and 'not a single aria was really well sung in the style of Mozart. . . . One step further and we shall have a theatre of marionettes. But Mahler, who has achieved the ideal of Gordon Craig, may already feel that people are saying: less refinement, less lavish productions—but greater artists!'

Andro then accused Mahler of being a poor teacher, and of allowing the standard of performances to fall by the third or fourth evening, that is to say, as soon as he no longer conducted the work in question. The situation had not improved since the time of Jahn. 'The Mahler of today is forever seeking new challenges, new tasks, new sensations—he is not particularly interested in what has already been achieved.' However, the article ended on a positive note:

For what is so good about him, what makes his manner of running a great theatre so valuable, even if it is accompanied by curious quirks, is that he is always stimulating, shaking the audience out of its lethargy, teaching it to think and criticize. It is of little consequence that this has been turned against him on this occasion. He stands there, firm and sharply drawn, quite alone, impossible to mistake for someone else. And even if such people go off on a strange tack now and then, one has to be grateful that they exist.[157]

In the *Münchner Allgemeine Zeitung* of 7 February, Ludwig Karpath stated that the 'avalanche' of hostile articles had been unleashed by one of Mahler's

---

[156] Korngold felt that the Hofoper not only lacked first-rate singers. There were also far too many mediocre ones who were of little use.

[157] See 'Operndirektor', *Neue Musik-Zeitung*, 28 (1907): 13, 169. The rest of the article consisted of a critical appraisal of the Hofoper's principal singers.

'friends',[158] a journalist who, the day after Mahler's departure for Berlin, had referred to a remark Mahler had made about relinquishing his post at the Hofoper in order to devote himself entirely to composition. Karpath pointed out that Mahler's wish was well known. The other papers had merely pounced on it on this occasion, and had turned the fact that he 'wished to leave' into a suggestion that he 'ought to leave'. But this was false and malicious. Mahler could not afford to leave the Hofoper, nor could he do without his salary. In any case, he could certainly not leave as long as his current superior, Prince Montenuovo, felt he needed him. Thus there was no 'crisis'. However, Karpath believed that the management of the Opera had been shaken. If reforms were not made, 'Mahler will stumble and come to grief'. However, if he had really wanted to leave, *Salome* would have provided the ideal opportunity, for it would have been a première which would have been a box office success and restored the Hofoper's tarnished image. After his plans had been thwarted by the censor, 'he should have done everything in his power to compensate somehow or other for this serious loss of income. Instead, he committed the unpardonable error of putting on *Le Juif polonais*, and took none of the steps necessary to do something about the Hofoper's ailing finances.'

Immediately after his return to Vienna, and after a long conversation with Prince Montenuovo, Mahler decided to return to work, and to respond with deeds to the recent torrent of words. Before his departure, everything had been done to ensure that the new production of *Die Walküre* would be a resounding success, and Roller had promised to surpass himself. This was going to be the production Mahler had been dreaming of ever since Prague and Budapest.[159] As in *Das Rheingold* in 1905, nature was to be omnipresent and to dominate the entire work. For this reason Roller once again eschewed visible stylization in favour of poetic realism. In Act I the presence of nature in Hunding's hut was emphasized by the immense trunk of the ash-tree, which now occupied the centre of the stage and, before it reached the roof, divided into two enormous branches. The tree both protected and supported the hut. The dimensions of the hut and of the set as a whole were considerably smaller than in earlier productions. The main doorway, which was fairly small, was on the side wall, on stage-right, and was reached by four steps. The fireplace, in the wall on stage-left, was across the stage from the door, far enough away for Siegmund, after his entry, to cross over to it in the time stipulated by the score. The main illumination came from the fire, while the darkness on stage-right was dimly lit by a torch fixed to the wall next to the door. Near the fireplace were some shelves with tools on them.

---

[158] The anonymous author of the paragraph in the *Montags-Revue* of 13 Jan. 1907 quoted above.

[159] The importance Mahler attached to this new production is demonstrated by a letter to Max Marschalk that was probably written in Jan. 1907. Mahler urged Marschalk, who had told him that he intended to come to Vienna for the première of Schoenberg's First Quartet on 5 Feb. (probably because he was the director of Drei Lilien Verlag, which had published some of Schoenberg's early works), to attend the first performance of the new production of *Die Walküre* the evening before (4 Feb.), and offered to provide him with a good seat. See Gustav Mahler, *Briefe* (Reclam, Leipzig, 1985), 504.

In the central scene of the act, the meal, the three characters sat at the slightly raised table in the very middle of the set, in front of the trunk of the ash-tree. The advantages of the new set were explained by Ludwig Hevesi:

The famous door at the back, which later springs open and lets the full moon shine in, has been moved from the right corner to the left corner . . . The moon shines in, and by its light the lovers sitting at the hearth see each other clearly for the first time. Siegmund and Sieglinde look at each other and recognize what they are, . . . although in the past the moonlight shone in from behind, and not from the front, and thus cast a shadow over their faces. This was utterly absurd, and has been remedied by moving the door to the left. Passing by the ash-tree, the light now falls on their faces, so that the idea of recognition suggested by the text at last acquires its proper meaning. Furthermore, the hearth is more of an organic part of the building, being built into the wall. It used to stand well clear of it, reminding one of a portable petroleum stove.[160]

In one of his famous literary snapshots the inimitable Peter Altenberg dwelt on the moment when spring awakens: 'How wonderfully Roller has painted this arrival, like a mysterious greeting from brighter worlds! Gates and fence are black, and out of the bluish moonlit mist rise three old mountain pines, gnarled and knotted and transfigured by blue moonlight.'[161]

Berta Zuckerkandl, in a collection of articles published the following year, noted that Roller had observed even the smallest details stipulated in the score, with a tree 'whose very prominent roots enter the ground over a wide area', and whose top seemed to spread out over the hut. Furthermore, the drama gained depth and cogency from the fact that the table was nearer to the fire. Thus throughout the act Siegmund enjoyed 'the hearth's protection'. The distance between the table and the entrance to the bedroom corresponded closely to the requirements of the score, being based on the way in which the music portrayed Sieglinde's 'hesitant departure, her longing backward glance at Siegmund'.[162]

To facilitate the scene changes, Roller retained the double revolving stage used in *Das Rheingold*, which meant that a set could be prepared backstage while the previous one was in use. In Act II his love of nature and desire for realism led him to create a stage design that was as vast as it was complicated, though entirely practicable. It depicted a rocky massif modelled on a well-known part of the Dolomites, the Sellajoch near Bozen, 'a splendid gorge, with a grey rock wall on either side, descending both to the front and back of the stage'.[163] There was not a single level space in this mass of rocks so that the characters, as if in chains, had to stand immobile at various points on little platforms, the arrangement of which had been carefully worked out with reference

---

[160] Ludwig Hevesi, *Altkunst, Neukunst*, 267.

[161] Peter Altenberg, 'Aufführung der "Walküre"', *Das grosse Peter Altenberg Buch* (Zsolnay, Vienna, 1967), 309. [162] Berta Zuckerkandl, *Zeitkunst, Wien 1901–7* (Heller, Vienna, 1908), 185–6.

[163] Roller filled several notebooks with sketches before arriving at this design. His definitive plans are dated 1903 and 1904 (ÖTM). Hevesi claimed that the painter had also been inspired by the Val de Mesdi, where he had been several times, making numerous sketches in charcoal and in colour.

to the action. For the *Todesverkündigung* episode, Brünnhilde stood motionless in the midst of immense rocks. From these heights she looked down at the brother and sister, whose tragic destiny she personified. Prior to this, and during his great narrative, Wotan appeared 'chained to the rocks' like a latter-day Prometheus. At the end of the act, the duel took place high up at the back of the stage, at the top of the pass. This was still near enough to allow the audience to see the silhouettes projected against the sky, which was illuminated by flashes of lightning.

As in *Das Rheingold*, the lighting effects had been prepared with meticulous care. They were described by Hevesi as follows:

At first, in brilliant sunlight. Later, during Wotan's monologue ('Ich unfreiester aller') it merges gradually into a fatalistic grey. Later still, when Brünnhilde tells Siegmund of his approaching death ('Ich bin's der bald du folgst'), everything is dark: a thunderstorm approaches. This mood is particularly gripping. During the duel, Siegmund and Hunding are dark silhouettes on the top of the pass, and there are flashes of lightning behind them. In the past the whole duel used to be buried in darkness.

In the last act,

there had originally been real horses ridden by stable-boys dressed as Valkyries. Then, as the result of an accident, papier-mâché horses were used instead, on which harmless young ballet dancers did their best to gather up the heroes. . . . Roller had a completely different and visually much more convincing idea of the ride of the Valkyries. He made them come from the back of the stage straight towards the audience. First one, still far away, illuminated in distant perspective by a flash of lightning; then a second, then a third, closer and larger, sweeping out of a wild mass of clouds, and then disappearing in the forest. This was done in the rehearsals. However, the more it succeeded, the more everyone became convinced that it did not suit the serious nature of the work. It was the same with Fricka's golden rams in the second act. In the past they were cut out of cardboard and covered with a golden fleece. And they had splendid moving heads and legs. In the solemn context of the work it looked rather childish. The better such things are done, the worse they seem. It is less apparent with poor designs than in the context of the artistic perfection of Roller's production. In the rehearsals Fricka also appeared rather briskly on her golden rams, preceded by clouds of steam, etc. But when someone in the audience sees this kind of thing, he merely thinks: 'How have they done that?' It destroys the mood. So now Fricka has to leave her chariot in the wings and walk on. But the mounted Valkyries are simply clouds in whose fantastic forms one can seek the images one desires.[164]

The design for Act III was more or less that of Appia, though in reverse, with the rocky peak on stage-left instead of stage-right, and the outline of the pine trees on the left. The sleeping Brünnhilde had in the past been surrounded by a fiery circle. However, one did not have to be 'a firefighter to see that these little flames are not particularly dangerous'. With Roller, Loge, the god of fire,

---

[164] Hevesi, 'Die Walküre', *Altkunst, Neukunst*, 268.

responded to Wotan's summons in the shape of several tall flames that shoot up out of the ground after it has been struck by the spear. 'Then the spear gives him the order "Weiter hinaus" and the fire lights up the distant horizon. It is now a circle of fire several kilometres in diameter, around the entire mountain on whose peak the sleeping Valkyrie lies secure. He who crosses this immense fire must indeed be a great hero.'[165] At the end of the work the storm died down to reveal one of Roller's favourite starry skies, as in Act II of *Tristan*.

Roller's innovations also included changes to the costumes. In the past Hunding had been construed as the brother, or double, of Hagen, the anti-hero of *Götterdämmerung*. The new Viennese production departed from the Bayreuth interpretation by depicting Hunding as 'a respectable burgher and husband suddenly cuckolded by a demigod'. Furthermore, Roller had given him reddish hair and a beard, as if he were 'an honest, down-to-earth Teuton'.[166] Siegmund, on the other hand, had brown hair, as was suggested by a line in the last act.[167] In previous productions Wotan had always worn a blue cloak, and Brünnhilde a cape of the same colour. Roller now decided that the Valkyrie's armour and cloak should be grey, and that the only ornament would be the large white wings on her helmet. In fact the blue cloak had been specified by Wagner, but only for the stricken god who is the Wanderer in *Siegfried*. Roller considered that red was the only colour suitable for the character in *Die Walküre*. Wotan was 'brightness, radiance, dazzling brilliance. The god of war and blood, wearing a golden helmet with sparkling jewels and gleaming copper armour, and wrapped in a cloak that shone like a flame in the flickering light.'[168]

The libretto stipulates that Brünnhilde has to leap from rock to rock in Act II. For this reason Roller did away with the trains which had previously adorned the costumes of the Valkyries and that of Fricka. Berta Zuckerkandl remarked that the production 'was characterized by great simplicity. Simplicity of musical diction, simplicity of gesture, simplicity in the representation of nature.'[169] Ilka Maria Kügler,[170] in her thesis about German stage-productions of Wagner's Ring, emphasizes that Roller was the first to eliminate painted backdrops and to design entirely practicable sets, of which Act II of *Die Walküre* was one of the most perfect examples. However, during the rehearsals the singers experienced difficulties because the set was so large and 'artificial'.

Anna von Mildenburg remarked that some of her 'colleagues had reservations because it was practically impossible to stand naturally on two feet anywhere. Every step was either up or down.'[171] Yet she was enthusiastic about the set. It was, she believed, the first to comply with Wagner's instructions, which specified that Brünnhilde was to 'leap from rock to rock'.

[165] Hevesi, 'Etwas Walküre', ibid. 269 ff. [166] Ibid. 273.
[167] Act III, Scene i, Gerhilde's reply, 'Bei dem braunen Wälsung weilt wohl noch Brünnhild'.
[168] Berta Zuckerkandl, *Zeitkunst*, 187. [169] Ibid. 184.
[170] Ilka Maria Kügler ' "Der Ring des Nibelungen": Studie zur Entwicklungsgeschichte seiner Wiedergabe auf der deutschsprachige Bühne'. Dissertation, Univ. of Bologna.
[171] Anna Bahr-Mildenburg, 'Musik und Gebärde', *Neue Freie Presse* (15 May 1921), 11.

However, this had been impossible in the previous set, in which Brünnhilde might just as well have sung sitting on a bicycle. But at the beginning of *Die Walküre* I had always imagined Brünnhilde, with her joyful, dashing and childlike exuberance, her divine, serene and untroubled high spirits, as continually leaping, more above than on the earth. In this Roller was fully of my opinion, and so were his Dolomites. At the first performance of the new production of *Die Walküre*, after I had uttered my '*Hojotoho*', and as I was making my exit, I suddenly noticed a rocky eminence which I had forgotten and previously avoided. In a flash I sized it up, and all at once I had the idea of jumping over it. Never in my life had I risked a jump of this kind. But I was Brünnhilde through and through, my body full of high spirits as the rejoicing daughter of Wotan, and eager both to sing and leap, and so I simply had to jump. And thus I jumped as Brünnhilde and landed successfully as Brünnhilde on the other side of the rocky chasm. Backstage, as Mildenburg once more, I was aghast at my leap into the unknown. It had not been accomplished by my feet, but by the thought and my 'enthusiasm'![172]

But in one respect Mildenburg did not agree with Roller. More than in his previous productions, he used light very sparingly in certain scenes, especially the hut in the first act and the rock in the last:

In the dialogue between Wotan and Brünnhilde, Weidemann and I were enveloped in such darkness that our facial expressions and all the finer points of the acting remained completely invisible, and we had the feeling that it made the scene drag. Wagner's instructions are based on the premiss that one can see the performer. He was against people reading the libretto during the performance and directed the audience's attention towards the events on stage. Mahler was completely of our opinion, but at a loss, because his timid suggestions made no impression on Roller. Before the second performance of *Die Walküre* I begged him once again to persuade Roller to let us have a little more light. But he was not there, and Mahler was unwilling to make an alteration on his own. I could see his point. However, at the end of the performance he rushed up, calling to us from a distance: 'You're quite right, it's impossible like that. More must be visible next time.' He said this with vigour, and was about to rush off. But then he turned round again, stamped his foot on the ground, and said rather meekly: 'Please tell him, will you, just tell him that I also thought it was too dark—and tell him in no uncertain terms!'—and away he went.[173]

As might have been expected, the darkness complained about by Mildenburg exasperated most of the Viennese critics. In the first act Roller wanted to give the impression that light came only from the fire burning in the hearth. Always ready to defend members of the Secession, Hevesi, in his

---

[172] Bahr-Mildenburg, *Neue Freie Presse*, 11–12.
[173] Anna von Mildenburg, lecture on Mahler, 1946 (LPA, copy in BGM, Paris). In this lecture Mildenburg also recalled the argument she had with Mahler during a rehearsal of the second act of *Die Walküre* (see above, Chap. 5). A few days after this altercation she noted in her diary: 'After the rehearsal Gustav was annoyed because I was eating sausages—or rather, I had them in my hand—I know that I have to show respect for his presence. He poured scorn on me, and scolded and raved about the smell of garlic and onions, though this existed only in his imagination' (Anna von Mildenburg, Diary, 30 Jan. 1907, Nachlass Bahr-Mildenburg, ÖTM).

second article, which was written three weeks after the première, noted that the lighting had already been increased, as had the magic fire in the third act, and that the darkness over which so much ink had been spilled was in fact only relative, since the lights in the orchestra had contributed to the impression that had been produced. 'Wagner's *Walküre* is now a very dark family drama,' Hans Liebstöckl remarked, 'a marital tragedy in some heavenly suburb, complete with incest and a duel. There is impenetrable darkness in Hunding's dwelling, over the rocks, and over these characters, who are in any case entangled in a dark web of intrigue.'[174]

In the more enlightened and progressive circles in Vienna one commentator, the writer Felix Salten, also protested against the lack of light. Although he shared the wish to 'create new settings for the great theatrical masterpieces of the past', primarily because 'we wish to see through our own eyes, and not through the eyes of the past', he took exception to the darkness in Hunding's hut. At first sight the shadowy effect was very striking. However, it ceased to be appropriate as soon as the action started: 'We look at the stage without being able to see what is happening, a stage whose darkness conceals that which it is supposed to show and represent.' Salten thought that the door of the hut, reduced to the dimensions of a prehistoric dwelling, suited neither the action (the arrival of spring) nor the music, whereas the design for Act II was both too wild and too complicated. The divine and superhuman dimension of the characters was lost because the gods no longer predominated, and were dominated by nature. In Act III the darkness once again made it impossible to discern the Valkyries or to see Brünnhilde's entrance, so that it was impossible to grasp either her fear and dilemma, or that of Wotan. And Salten added:

Seeing and hearing effortlessly are the very essence of theatrical effect. Is it really necessary to point this out? . . . The painter has become too much of a painter, and has used the drama as material for one of his pictures. However, he should have subordinated himself to it. Here the painter has imposed his requirements on the stage, whereas it is the stage that should have imposed its requirements on him . . . One saw nothing, or almost nothing, of Mildenburg's superb acting as Brünnhilde . . .[175]

This sentence seems to suggest that Mildenburg had in some way influenced the writer, and it is not impossible that she may have been behind this article and its criticism of Roller. Be that as it may, this production was one of the greatest triumphs of her career, despite the fact that her voice was beginning to show signs of strain. A close friend of hers, Leonie Gombrich-Koch, later recalled how much the great soprano suffered when faced with the tragic truth:

This was a terribly painful time for all who were close to her, all the more so because Anna, with the help of her extraordinary imagination, could hear the correct sound,

[174] Hans Liebstöckl, 'Die neue "Walküre" in der Hofoper', *Illustrirtes Wiener Extrablatt* (13 Feb. 1907).
[175] Felix Salten, *Schauen und Spielen, Studien zur kritik des modernen Theaters* (Wiener literarische Anstalt, Vienna, 1921), 35 ff., 45. See above, Chap. 5 for information concerning Salten.

and was simply unable to believe that she had sung in any other way. I particularly recall one tragic episode from those troubled times, when we went to the Getreidemarkt to a record company that had recorded Anna's *Walküre*. She was horrified by the high notes, claimed that she had never sung in this way and that the recording was inaccurate, and demanded that the records should not be put on sale. At this time her nervousness and irritability increased before each performance, and we all shared in her anguish.[176]

Like many great performers in decline, Mildenburg surpassed herself with regard to the way in which she acted the part. All who saw her agreed that her Brünnhilde was unforgettable, as was Weidemann's Wotan. According to Richard Specht:

Mildenburg wrote and told me that the greatest mistake made by modern actors is that they are continually 'heroic'. They want to make everything 'significant' and in the process they lose the natural, lifelike tone. 'I can count the moments in my roles, Isolde, for instance, or Brünnhilde, in which I become superhuman and heroic. With regard to all the rest, daily life provides us with all the material that we need.' This is true also of Weidemann, and in this way he obtains his most powerful effects. It is even true of his Wotan, and it is precisely in this way that the tragedy of the god who craves love and power, who is prey to angry self-deception and longs for release, and who first attains to inner freedom and understanding love through the pain and comfort of self-denial, becomes moving in human terms and stirringly comprehensible, more than ever before ... In the scenes with Wotan and Brünnhilde, ... one had a feeling of mystic rapture far removed from everything that is 'theatrical', and one sensed, through these two rare examples, an intimation of the summits of the phenomenon of 'humanity' that Schopenhauer sees as the finest reward of great acting.[177]

On the rest of the cast, Erwin Stein remarked that Schmedes also turned Siegmund into a tragic figure; that Förster-Lauterer, as Sieglinde, displayed all her vocal freshness; that Hilgermann, who had previously been a fine Sieglinde, was now a perfect Fricka; and that Mayr depicted Hunding as a solid and robust peasant, and not as the conventional traitor of previous productions. With regard to Mahler's interpretation, Stein considered that the 'discretion of the accompaniment was a model. I shall never forget the ravishing *pianissimo* of the heavy brass in the second act of *Die Walküre* when Brünnhilde asks Siegmund to follow her to Valhalla.[178] In general the musicians of the orchestra had to play as delicately as in chamber music. The range of colour and dynamic shading he obtained from his forces was astounding.'[179] Otto Klemperer, who only heard the second and third acts of this *Walküre*[180] because he had a concert on the same evening, could not forget the incredible force of Mahler's musical interpretation:

---

[176] In Leonie Gombrich-Hock, 'Einige persönliche Erinnerungen an Anna Bahr-Mildenburg', unpublished text (1948), copy in BGM, Paris.

[177] Richard Specht, 'Friedrich Weidemann', *Die Schaubühne*, Berlin, 2 (1906): 50, 598.

[178] This is of course the *Todesverkündigung* episode.   [179] ESM 198.

[180] The performance of 11 Feb. (see below).

It was indescribable. Mahler, who was also the producer, was in supreme command. I had never seen the ending of the second act so clearly on the stage. The woodwind trills at the beginning of the third act were of an intensity that I never believed possible. In the big C minor episode, 'Nach dem Tann lenkt sie das taumelnde Ross'[181] the orchestra almost vanished. At the end of the magic fire the conductor seemed to surpass himself.[182]

Some critics, especially Richard Wallaschek, took issue with the slow tempo of Wotan's monologue and with the relative acceleration of the tempo of the whole work.[183] Nevertheless, the ovations which greeted Mahler at the beginning and end of each act were exceptionally loud that evening, no doubt in answer to the attacks on him and the rumours of his resignation. At the end of the performance, the tension that had mounted throughout the third act led to what can only be described as an explosion. Large parts of the audience rose to their feet to applaud furiously, thus responding to a number of vigorous catcalls.

Favourable for once, Robert Hirschfeld's verdict on Mahler's musical interpretation is all the more striking in that it came from his most determined opponent.

The performance as a whole was like an inspired improvisation that seemed born out of a moment of rapture. One noticed nothing of the hard work that had preceded it. There was freedom in every bar, the tempo often moved arbitrarily between an inordinate accelerando and ritardando. Mahler adapted the dynamics of the incredibly obedient orchestra to each passing weakness or strength of the singer. The nature of the performance—at times gliding along indulgently, and sometimes pushing on ahead in an energetic manner—derives entirely from Mahler's baton. It was primarily passionate, and in such an individual way that any other conductor would have changed the picture immediately ... Never has the *Todesverkündigung* been more noble, more powerful, more tragic or more frightening. The whole of the last act possessed a hitherto unknown musical strength and purity.

Hirschfeld still accused Roller of 'wanting to change everything', of subordinating the human to the decorative element, of being 'a stranger to music', in which he 'lacked confidence'. He also criticized him for dehumanizing the characters and suffocating life with matter, and for appealing to the unmusical members of the public with his inappropriate lighting effects and 'orgies of darkness'. But he was enthusiastic about the design of the first act—the arrival of spring—and also that of the second act. Roller, he thought, had

---

[181] Miniature score, p. 107 (Schott, Mainz). [182] OKM 7.

[183] Paul Stauber, *Die wahre Erbe Mahlers* (Huber und Lahme, Vienna, 1909), 41. As Ilka Maria Kügler has pointed out (see above, n. 162), at the end of his life Wagner was of the opinion that, despite the numerous instructions he had personally given to Seidl and Richter, he knew of no conductor to whom he could safely entrust his works. Kügler also draws attention to the fact that Wagnerian conductors before Mahler tried primarily to emphasize details and motifs, and to bring out the most famous passages. When Mahler arrived in Vienna, he was determined to change this tendency, and sought to underline the architectural design instead. He was thus obliged to find tempos which would relate to each other.

'surpassed Bayreuth' with 'the enthralling beauty' of the Ride of the Valkyries.

On this occasion Heinrich Reinhardt, in the *Neues Wiener Journal*, who had inveighed repeatedly against Mahler's policy as director, was at a loss. The only criticism he was able to level at the new production was that it had taken such a long time to materialize: 'Let us be glad that *Die Walküre* has been rediscovered in Vienna. However, there is no reason why we should rejoice. Making amends for old misdemeanours is praiseworthy, but it does not alter the fact that for years they were shameful and scandalous.'[184]

As was his wont, Hans Liebstöckl gave a detailed description of the production, which he characterized as 'a feast for highland tourists, for lovers of eternal darkness, for costumiers, for Wagnerians, for the lighting technicians, and, last of all, for musicians'. He objected to Mahler's 'furious' interpretation, and the fact that he 'hurries the singers along . . . The last act is, so to speak, a catastrophe, and the magic fire an immense and destructive inferno. The singers save what they can, and first of all themselves.' Liebstöckl, who preferred the old Hoffmann costumes[185] to the new ones, voiced the opinion that the work suffered from two collaborators who 'have a passionate genius for detail'. Wotan had been transformed into 'a figure from an Offenbach operetta'; his costume seemed 'fit for a feast, as if he were a dancer or juggler'. However, Hilgermann at least retained Fricka's divine character and noble bearing. Liebstöckl then went on to criticize the fact that the pines remained motionless in the gale, and concluded by complaining that the prevailing spirit of the Hofoper was 'loveless turmoil, art divorced from living simplicity. The great and painful uncertainty of all that is human sings its love song in Wagner's *Walküre*. In the final analysis the theatre must recede into the background so that the blissful message can be heard.'[186]

As usual, David Josef Bach defended Mahler and Roller against those who criticized them. He considered it absurd to complain that the darkness made it impossible to tell one Valkyrie from the other since it was impossible in any case to hear their individual lines during the tumult of the Ride of the Valkyries: 'No, the staging conforms wholly to the requirements of the work, its creator and its audience.' In the *Deutsche Zeitung*[187] Muntz also praised Roller, though he criticized his 'painterly and subjective interpretation' because it constituted a one-sided approach to the ideal of the *Gesamtkunstwerk*, and because it 'made a disjointed impression on the listener instead of concentrating his attention on the essence of the drama'. Unimaginative designs that

[184] *Neues Wiener Journal* (6 Feb. 1907), cited by Désirée Schuschitz, 'Die Wiener Musikkritik in der Ära Gustav Mahler: 1897–1907. Eine historisch-kritische Standortbestimmung'. Dissertation, Univ. of Vienna, 1978, 141.

[185] Josef Hoffmann (1831–1904), of the same name as the Secession architect, was an academic painter who designed the first settings of Wagner's *Ring* in Bayreuth in 1876.

[186] Hans Liebstöckl, 'Die neue "Walküre" in der Hofoper', *Illustrirtes Wiener Extrablatt* (13 Feb. 1907).

[187] 'Zur Neustudierung der "Walküre" im Hofoperntheater', *Deutsche Zeitung* (6 Feb. 1907).

'conformed to the laws of nature and of beauty' would have sufficed, especially as the prevailing darkness often hid the pictorial beauty.[188] Muntz also questioned the excessive detail of the design of Act II, which merely proved 'distracting'. Roller's structure was so complicated that the heroine had to 'perform prodigious feats of mountaineering in order to climb up and down the immense pile of rubble'. However, he admired the staging of the duel, which was 'the most successful part of the new production', and the design of Act III, and expressed approval of Mahler's interpretation and the cast.[189] On the other hand, the other Viennese anti-Semitic paper, the *Deutsches Volksblatt*, carried an altogether favourable review by Hans Puchstein who disapproved only of several of the costumes[190] and of the 'absolute darkness' which Roller had imposed onstage for several scenes.

Richard Wallaschek noted that both the new designs for *Die Walküre* and the musical interpretation were almost universally admired, whereas Max Kalbeck considered the evening to be another artistic triumph for Mahler. He had surpassed most of his earlier successes, and, with 'the clarity and sureness of his penetrating intuition', had thus provided a reply to 'the complaints and attacks' against him. Korngold had nothing but praise for the designs, especially for that of Act II, which showed that Roller was increasingly concerned to reconcile artistic imagination with the requirements of the stage. However he too disapproved of the darkness of Act I, although he praised Mildenburg's 'good style' and Weidemann's wild sadness. The *Fremden-Blatt* also admired the way in which Roller had combined realism and stylization. In the *Allgemeine Zeitung*, Berta Zuckerkandl voiced the opinion that, as a result of developments in the fine arts, the things that Wagner had been unable to attain as part of his ideal of the *Gesamtkunstwerk* were possible now that the art of design had become 'spiritualized' and had brought the various elements together to form a new synthesis. The production bore the stamp of great simplicity. Even 'the singers have once more learnt the difference between what is essential and what is not. . . . Mahler's concentration on the essential in Wagner had led him to impart to certain passages a wholly unknown grandeur.'[191]

[188] Puchstein, the critic of the *Volksblatt*, also objected to the darkness, though he admired the designs.

[189] He drew attention to the outstanding nobility of Weidemann's performance, Schmedes' vocal brilliance, the intelligence and strength of Mayr's portrayal of Hunding, and the singing and acting of Anna von Mildenburg, who 'for a long time had not attained to such artistic heights'.

[190] Puchstein criticized in particular the 'prudish pants' worn by Wotan and Hunding, Fricka's 'garish gown', and Siegmund and Hunding's 'Struwwelpeter hair styles'. On the other hand, the Valkyries' shorter skirts made their movements easier. He praised Mildenburg's 'matchless expressivity' in the *Todesverkündigung* scene, 'which none of her contemporaries can portray so graphically'.

[191] Cast of the performance on 4 Feb.: Förster-Lauterer (Sieglinde); Mildenburg (Brünnhilde); Hilgermann (Fricka); Schmedes (Siegmund); Weidemann (Wotan); and Mayr (Hunding). At the end of Jan. the costume department was asked to supply a grass carpet to cover the rocks (HOA, ÖTM, Z. 94/452/1/1907, letter dated 30 Jan. 1907). The condition of some parts of the set subsequently deteriorated and they had to be repaired and repainted (Z. 452.II/1907, letter dated 30 Apr. 1907). The final cost of the designs for *Die Walküre* was 43,443 kronen, about half of which came from the 1906 budget. This was 3,000 kronen less than had been estimated (Z. 452/III/1907, letter dated 31 May 1907).

Otto Klemperer considered the last production which Mahler and Roller were now to stage together at the Vienna Opera to be their supreme masterpiece: 'There is little one can say about the performance. It was so perfect that words cannot describe it.'[192] Mahler himself declared on several occasions: 'I believe it is the best thing Roller and I have done!'[193] And this time they went back as far as they could, for Gluck was then considered to be the founder or inventor of opera and no earlier work had found its way into the repertory, at least of large opera houses. Mahler may have chosen *Iphigénie en Aulide* because Wagner was so fond of it. In Dresden in 1848 he had prepared and conducted a version with a new denouement.[194] The work had been absent from the Hofoper repertory for thirteen years, and in her memoirs Berta Zuckerkandl recalled the extent to which Mahler became involved in it during the rehearsals:

He lived in a kind of trance. On the day of the première Emil [Zuckerkandl] saw him standing on the Ringstrasse in front of an advertising pillar and staring with a smile of delight at the poster for *Iphigénie*. Emil asked him: 'What are you looking at with such reverence.' And Mahler answered quite naively, and indeed in a childlike manner: 'I simply cannot look at that poster long enough. I stop at every advertising pillar, I can hardly believe that it is coming true, that this evening these singers and this orchestra will follow my instructions. It means so much to me.'[195]

Mahler decided to use Wagner's version, although he commissioned a new translation, made some cuts, especially in the ballets,[196] and inserted new transitional passages between certain numbers. On this occasion the classical plot imposed a stark sobriety on the designs that exceeded anything seen in previous productions. The entire action took place behind a gauze curtain that conveyed an impression of distance and toned down the colours. The single set, revealed as soon as the curtain rose on the first act, Agamemnon's spacious pale yellow tent with its ample folds. A tapestry served as a backcloth for the more intimate scenes. When there were more characters on the stage, the backcloth opened to reveal the wall of the Achaean camp and the masts of the Greek ships. In the final scene the tent suddenly disappeared, and one saw the harbour, the open sea, the altar erected on a hill for the sacrifice of Iphigénie, and the multicoloured ships with their pointed bows, at last ready to sail for Troy.[197] When Artemis appeared to carry off her future priestess, her dazzling white robe resplendent against a background of bluish-grey clouds,

---

[192]	OKM 8.								[193]	MBR1, no. 333; MBR2, 370.

[194]	Gluck's orchestration was slightly altered, and the original denouement, the marriage of Achilles and Iphigénie, was replaced by that of Euripides' tragedy. Just as the sacrifice is about to take place, the heroine is carried off by the goddess, who takes her to Tauris, where she becomes her priestess. She reappears in the second of Gluck's works based on the tragedy of the Atridae, *Iphigénie en Tauride*.

[195]	Berta Zuckerkandl, *Österreich intim*, 71.

[196]	He also cut one of Achilles' arias, 'Der Priester wagt er, dir zu nah'n' (*Calchas d'un trait mortel blessé*) (Act III, no. 44, or no. 27 in Wagner's version), which originally contained nine top Bs and twenty top As, of which Wagner retained only two top As. Mahler also added a few transitional bars after Iphigénie's aria, 'Das Loos, das mir beschieden' (*Il faut de mon destin*), no. 40 in the original score, no. 26 in Wagner's.

[197]	LKR 104.

we also sense, with childish awe and pain, the presence of the merciful goddess and when the darkness lightens and a fresh wind parts the clouds, when the waves mount joyously and the pennants flutter on the masts, when the distant islands gleam in the light of dawn and the terrible cry 'To Troy!' is heard, we are strangely enraptured . . .[198]

Roller had paid particular attention to the posture of the characters and their grouping on the stage. One of the most striking moments showed Clytemnestra drawing her daughter towards her protectively in a manner that recalled a well-known antique bas-relief. Before designing the costumes Roller had carefully reread the descriptions supplied by Homer.[199] The choristers wore white tunics and black wigs,[200] and were arranged symmetrically, as on a Greek vase. As in the past, Roller had used colours to symbolize the various moods of the action, and also lighting effects. The bright yellow of the tent at the beginning was intended to suggest both the stifling heat of Aulis and the epidemic raging among the Greeks. The sky, which was implacably blue at the beginning, merged gradually into a yellowish darkness. Even the yellow of the tent was continually modified. It was contrasted with the light brown of the ground and with other colours taken from classical painting—delicate pink, pearly grey, and dark violet—and threw into relief the sober hues of the costumes.

At the same time Mahler sought to impart a sculptural and marble-like quality to the production. Even the ballets were made to adopt the style and postures of classical painting. Among the leading ballerinas there were two young sisters, Elsa and Grete Wiesenthal, whose presence and talent 'expressed the grace of Gluck's music in visual terms'.[201] Margarete Wiesenthal had already attracted attention in the non-speaking principal role of *La Muette de Portici*,[202] and 'Vienna was later indebted to them for the creation of a new style of dancing'.[203] 'Indeed, it is possible to say', Egon Wellesz later remarked, 'that on this day Gluck was restored to the operatic stage in Vienna, where his reforms had first begun.' The cast for the production brought together all the great singers of Mahler's period as Director. Mildenburg played Clytemnestra with a kind of fury and rage that 'prefigured the blood-curdling dreams of the same character in the work by Strauss', which

---

[198]   Max Kalbeck, in *Neues Wiener Tagblatt* (21 Mar. 1907).

[199]   Hirschfeld remarked that the shield of Achilles was exactly as Homer had described it.

[200]   According to the estimate that Roller submitted on 23 Feb., and which Mahler sent to the Intendant on 25 Feb., the sets, costumes, and props cost a total of 33,000 kronen. Roller pointed out that the sum was so large because it had been impossible to use any of the Hofoper's existing props and costumes. Mahler recommended that he should refrain from giving the latter an exclusively Greek character, so that they could be used for other productions as well, e.g. *Samson et Dalila*, which was to be performed in May. The production required a total of 317 costumes (HOA, Z. 836/1907). In June Mahler informed the Intendant that the total cost had only amounted to 28,352 kronen, which represented savings of almost 5,000 kronen (HOA, Z. 879/II/1907, letter of 21 June).

[201]   Egon Wellesz, 'Gustav Mahler und die Wiener Oper, Festrede, gehalten am 26. Juni 1960 in der Wiener Staatsoper', in *Neue Deutsche Rundschau*, 71 (1960): 2, 257.

[202]   See below, Chap. 9.   [203]   Egon Wellesz, 'Gustav Mahler', 255.

she was to sing two years later.[204] 'I well remember', wrote Erwin Stein, 'her keen delivery of the aria "Waffne dich mit zürnenden Muthe" (*Armez-vous d'un noble courage*)',[205] the introductory bars of which Mahler played in the most daring *rubato* style. As Iphigénie, Gutheil-Schoder captivated the audience with her 'touching chastity'[206] and the simplicity of her bearing. According to Stein, 'she sang with noble passion, admirably blending human dignity with intensity of emotion, and achieved a truly impressive pathos when accepting the sacrifice demanded of her.' With his golden weapons, Schmedes embodied Achilles in a manner that was simultaneously tragic, brilliant, and heroic.

His voice rang out mightily when he quarrelled with Agamemnon, but he phrased very finely his duet with Iphigenia *Zweifle nie an meiner Treue* (*Ne doutez jamais*).[207] If Demuth did not bear himself quite like a great king and his movements looked sometimes a bit awkward, he had the excuse that, as a matter of fact, Agamemnon finds himself in an awkward position of indecision. He sang the very high part well and his voice beautifully matched that of Mayr (Kalchas) in the duet *Grausame Götter! So wollt ihr* (*O Divinité redoutable*).[208]

In a manner reminiscent of Klemperer, Gertrude Förstel was later to write: 'I consider the performance of *Iphigénie* under his [Mahler's] direction to be the highest attainable and previously unattained operatic achievement. At such heights no role was insignificant.'[209]

Lilli Lehmann, whose theatrical tastes, as we have seen, were far from being modern, stated that

The greatest of all his productions was *Iphigenie in Aulis*. It was perfectly balanced in every respect, the most beautiful example of the spirit of harmony in classical art that I can imagine. This was the summit of his achievement, probably because the great tragedy took place only within the confines of a simple tent, so that nothing impaired the art of Mahler or the singers. It would have suffered and become ineffectual as a result of unnecessarily ornate or inept staging, for superficial bombast stifles and kills all subtle feelings.[210]

With regard to the orchestra and the conducting, Erwin Stein noted that 'not many musicians are capable of realising the expressive beauty of Gluck's melodies, whose simplicity is deceptive. Gluck's music is usually played in an unbearably dull fashion. With Mahler it sounded rich and full of vitality.'[211] Anna von Mildenburg later emphasized:

---

[204] RSM2, 147. In the first Viennese performance of *Elektra* she played the role created by Ernestine Schumann-Heink in Dresden on 25 Jan. 1909.

[205] Act I, no. 13 of the original version and no. 9 in that of Wagner.

[206] OKM 8. Like Stein, Klemperer always remembered how Mildenburg had sung Clytemnestra's aria.

[207] No. 17 in the original version and no. 11 in that of Wagner.

[208] No. 5 in both versions. ESM 313.

[209] Gertrude Förstel, 'Erinnerung an Gustav Mahler', *Neue Freie Presse* (20 May 1911).

[210] Lilli Lehmann, *Mein Weg*, 368.

[211] 'But this did not prevent the performance from lapsing into tedium once Schalk took over', adds Erwin Stein.

the way in which, with his impetuous, nervous and hasty liveliness, he [Mahler] tamed himself and us, attaining classical serenity to the rhythm of classical music. The principle of allowing the music to lead the way has always stood me in good stead, and in this way I became acquainted with certain intentions of the operatic work that had been expressed with insufficient clarity, and which singers thus ignored.[212]

The Viennese critics reacted favourably to the new *Iphigénie*, with the sole exception of Wallaschek, who believed that Mahler had chosen the work merely because he was trying to reply to recent criticisms. However, he pointed out that 'one can be ennobled overnight, but to attain to the nobility of Gluck is impossible even after six weeks of more than hasty rehearsals'. Wallaschek also objected to the conflation of three sets into one, and to the fact that Roller had as it were sought to project a static painted image on to the stage.[213] Mahler's two persistent critics, Heinrich Reinhardt and Robert Hirschfeld, were for once full of praise, although Hirschfeld, as usual, qualified his remarks with a dash of irony:

As a conductor Gustav Mahler casts an even brighter light on Wagner's dramatically enhanced version with its richer orchestral colours. As a result the shadows have become darker still. We experienced a rendering which, tautly compressed without a break or pause, goes against the style of Gluck. And yet the performance, spurred on by Wagner and by Mahler's conducting, soars boldly and with vital force above the conventional forms of Gluck's day, the overall design, and the numerous ballets, to reveal Gluck's genius in all its greatness.

Hirschfeld praised the sets and costumes. He was struck by their 'profoundly serious, and indeed sombre conception', and impressed by the details alluding to the fate of the Atridae, the general 'Homeric' quality, and 'the garments with their folds, which contributed to the dramatic expression'. Thus he was prepared to overlook both the exaggerated acting of the two heroines and 'forceful accents' in the orchestra. There had been tense anticipation in the Hofoper, though the audience was unfortunately rather small. 'Those who refuse to allow themselves to be uplifted by Gluck', he declared, 'deserve to be whipped. . . . But it is also the duty of the Hofoper to offer such moments of unusual pleasure several times a year to a small and select circle of art lovers.'

Never before, according to Max Kalbeck, had the art of a painter supported that of a musician in such an effective manner. The unity of place and the restrained use of colour suited the work admirably, especially since Roller had introduced numerous nuances. He and Mahler had created a 'perfect

---

[212] Anna von Mildenburg, 'Musik und Gebärde, ii', *Neue Freie Presse* (22 May 1921), 9.

[213] According to Wallaschek, Gutheil-Schoder was what one imagined 'a Greek looked like', 'at least with regard to her appearance', whereas Mildenburg, despite acting her part with 'touching expressiveness', had failed in her attempt to imitate classical postures. Furthermore, he thought that Schmedes' high notes lacked brilliance and that his voice was 'too coarse' for the role of Achilles.

harmony', and the work gave the impression of being 'a long and powerful crescendo that culminated in the indescribably splendid final scene'. And Kalbeck added:

We delight in the pleasure of a god who from a safe height looks down on the drama of the world, and, lost in what we see and hear, become blissfully oblivious of our own existence as mortals. This is music, the music of Gluck, and we first perceive the full voice of its unbroken and mighty dramatic power in the spiritualized resonance of this perfectly attuned background that has been specially made for it.

While expressing reservations about the work itself, Korngold congratulated Mahler and Roller on having revived 'the spirit of Greece'. In a harmonious manner they had captured 'Gluck's severe simplicity, sublime calm and noble pathos'. There was no sign of exaggeration, of the wrong tone, of studied effects. Roller had surpassed himself. And Mahler missed none of the beauties of the music:

The orchestra spoke the language of Gluck, though for a modern audience. The prominence of the basses suited Gluck's stark severity. Sharp rhythms and an energetic sound, making one think that these were pedestals for the statues on the stage. A calm and floating grace is imparted to all the lyrical passages, whereas strength is imparted to the dramatic parts, but not Romantic colour.

Even Max Puchstein, the critic of the anti-Semitic *Deutsche Volksblatt*, although objecting to the shrill colours of the costumes and the 'monotony' of Roller's sets, lauded Mahler for the 'great devotion and understanding' with which he had rehearsed the work, and commented on the 'pleasantly calm' manner in which he had conducted. Unfortunately this exemplary performance, which was to be Mahler's swan song as director and producer at the Vienna Opera, was applauded only by a limited number of connoisseurs, who did not even fill the house the evening of the première. Furthermore, as a result of the recent press campaign, the performance was marred by both applause and booing which filled the entire auditorium in the middle of the performance.[214]

After these two unchallenged artistic triumphs, which were contested only by a small minority, it seemed as if Mahler's position in Vienna would have again been unassailable, and had after all not been seriously threatened by the press campaign in January. Even though he was not held in high esteem by the Emperor's entourage, whom he had often defied, decisions were still taken by Prince Montenuovo, who had the Emperor's full support. To those who complained about Mahler he habitually replied: 'Gustav Mahler is *my* opera director. Is there anything else I can do for you?'[215] Mahler's frequent absences

---

[214] Cast for the performance of 18 Mar. 1907: Gutheil-Schoder (Iphigénie); Mildenburg (Clytemnestra); Weidt (Artemis); Schmedes (Achille); Demuth (Agamemnon); Hesch (Calchas); Haydter (Arkas); and Stehmann (Patrocle). Mahler conducted five performances of *Iphigénie* before handing the work over to Schalk. [215] BMG 191 ff. and KIW 108 ff.

certainly worried the Prince, not because they paralysed the life of the Hofoper, as Mahler's enemies claimed, but because they obliged the director to grant members of the company the leave of absence that he had previously refused them. At the time of Mahler's return, Felix Mottl, who was struck by the violence of the press attacks and by the rumours of resignation, started wondering whether the Vienna post might not soon become vacant, and he asked his friend Countess Marietta Coudenhove to bring the matter to the attention of Princess Hohenlohe, the widow of the former Obersthofmeister. Prince Montenuovo was questioned and his reply was categorical: 'the rumours of a Mahler crisis returned year after year and were currently quite unfounded. Mahler was very much a *persona grata* with him.' However, Montenuovo later admitted that the possibility that Mahler would leave had not been wholly without foundation.[216] In fact, when Mahler had suggested that he might hand in his resignation (no doubt hoping thus to reinforce his position by measuring popular support), the Prince had replied: 'For God's sake, don't say you want to resign! If the archdukes hear that, they'll be along here like a shot!'[217]

As we have seen, Mahler had gradually been overcome by weariness since the summer of 1906. He had begun to realize that he would never be able to complete the exemplary reforms that he had begun to introduce. The viciousness and partiality of journalists who even went so far as to praise the unpolished performances at the Kaiserjubiläumstheater, and its director, Rainer Simons,[218] at his expense, filled him with disgust, especially when the attack came from Hirschfeld, or from a mediocre composer like Reinhardt, or from a fool like Wallaschek. Though he knew that Gluck's operas at that time only attracted small audiences he was saddened by the the half-empty houses for *Iphigénie*, which he considered to be the most accomplished of his Viennese productions.[219] He felt he had been disowned by the Viennese public, which owed so much to him.[220] Furthermore, his friends and faithful admirers had not been able to prevent several troublemakers from gaining access to the promenade seats behind the orchestra, from where they regularly expressed their hostility to him by whistling and booing.

Mahler was also weary of the persistent hostility shown by most of the members of the orchestra. He told Korngold in 1907 that he would probably have felt obliged to pack his bags much earlier had he not found a letter in his papers which ruled in his favour against something the orchestra committee was pressing for.[221] Despite unfailing support from his superiors, he was exhausted by this state of permanent tension, all the more so since he admired the orchestra wholeheartedly and knew that its skill and ability were unique in

[216] BMG 193 ff., letter from Princess Hohenlohe to Countess Coudenhove dated 23 Jan. 1907.
[217] KIW 111.
[218] Bruno Walter, letter to Pfitzner dated 18 Mar. 1907, BWB 91.
[219] The same thing had happened when *Der Widerspenstigen Zähmung* had been revived the year before.   [220] KIW 111.   [221] Ibid.

the world. He was no doubt mortified at not having been invited by the Philharmonic to conduct the première of his Sixth Symphony. The new salary increases he was about to obtain for all the members of the Hofoper were not likely to diminish the hostility of the majority of the musicians.

The success of the *Walküre* production and the artistic triumph of *Iphigénie* had not disarmed the Viennese critics. Only Mahler himself was apparently impervious to their constant disparagement. As late as 4 June, Korngold was struck by his calm when he visited him at a time when he had practically made up his mind to leave Vienna and the Opera:

What is known as the 'Mahler crisis' seems in fact to exist for everyone except the person at the centre of it all. . . . [When going to see Mahler] one thought one was about to visit someone on his deathbed—in a room in which people with tender hands are engaged in smashing the windows on a daily basis—and instead one found a man sitting up straight and briskly at work. He was working like someone who would still be the director in fifty years' time. . . . And a short time ago a friend met him on a day when either the whole of *Die Walküre* production had been declared a failure because Siegmund's hair was not the right colour, or the director's resignation had been called for because he had failed to prevent a singer becoming ill. Mahler smiled happily, his face shone. 'I think I have found the solution to the *Oberon* problem,' he exclaimed joyfully. 'Just think, no additional recitatives!' He smiled, but not at what had been written about him! Mahler makes it rather difficult for those who hate him to gloat over their deeds. In the words of Goethe, 'people are wholly unaware of the inaccessible kind of fortress a man lives in if he is truly dedicated to himself and to his cause'.[222]

Having quoted this from his 1907 article, Korngold then continues in his memoirs:

On the occasion of the tenth anniversary of his arrival at the Hofoper I tried to size up the sum total of what this sorely harassed man had achieved. I tried to help him as best I could by weighing up his weaknesses against his strengths, though without giving the impression that I was a mere apologist. In Mahler's Sixth Symphony there is a characteristic recurring motif, a clear, resounding A major chord which, in the course of a decrescendo, merges into an A minor chord. I chose this as a symbol of Mahler's directorship. 'The radiant major of his virtues contains the minor of his failings', I wrote, 'the one simply emanates from the other.'[223] Mahler then sent me a postcard with nothing on it except an A minor chord for oboes which grew into a powerful A major chord for trumpets, trombones and timpani. Underneath this he wrote: 'Very much amused. Many thanks, Gustav Mahler.'[224]

But for the time being all was not lost. Mahler was still firmly in command. He had no desire to leave the Hofoper or strike out into the unknown, and he remained deeply attached to Vienna, the musical city *par excellence*, where he had studied music and discovered the glories of a musical tradition without

---

[222] *Neue Freie Presse* (4 June 1907). Excerpts from this article are quoted in Korngold's memoirs.
[223] Korngold is referring to the conclusion of one of his articles, published in *Neue Freie Presse* on 26 Jan. 1907.   [224] KIW 112.

equal. As we shall see,[225] a quarrel had broken out on 16 February during the rehearsals for Auber's *La Muette de Portici* between Alfred Roller and the ballet master of the Hofoper, Josef Hassreiter. To the delight of the journalists, this had once again clouded the atmosphere. However, Hassreiter had no desire to leave the Opera, and thus the quarrel soon subsided, as did the new spate of rumours.

In order not to give his enemies further cause for complaint, Mahler decided that he would accept no invitations to conduct his symphonies until the summer (with the exception of a few excerpts that he intended to perform in Rome during the Easter vacation). His letters to the Dutch baritone Johannes Messchaert[226] show that he had been planning to conduct a concert in Berlin devoted entirely to orchestral songs on the lines of the one he had given in Vienna in 1905.[227] Messchaert was famous throughout Europe for his interpretion of Lieder and oratorios. Born in Hoorn, Holland, he had studied with Julius Stockhausen at the Cologne Rheinische Musikschule, had been active as a choral conductor, and had taught at the Conservatory in Amsterdam. In 1890 he had moved to Wiesbaden and started teaching at the Frankfurt Conservatory. Since then, he had toured Europe, had given highly acclaimed Lieder recitals in all major cities, and had also earned particular fame with parts in oratorios such as Christ in Bach's *St Matthew Passion*. Messchaert was now approaching 50 and his reputation could now only be compared with that of his former teacher, Julius Stockhausen.

If singing is simply the transformation of breathing into sound . . . then Messchaert is a singer by God's grace, for he possesses this ability to a high degree . . . Endowed from birth with one of the loveliest voices, his gift of freely and nobly projecting it in all circumstances is the result of study, insight and the development of taste . . .; with him word and sound are intimately merged, they permeate each other, each gives the other colour, life and mood.

Thus wrote the Berlin critic Leopold Schmidt in 1917, in celebration of Messchaert's 60th birthday.[228] Such high praise was by no means unusual in contemporary reviews of Messchaert recitals. Thus it is not surprising that Mahler should have agreed to undertake the interminable train journey from Vienna to Berlin, solely to accompany Messchaert's recital of his Lieder. One year earlier, the baritone had given three Lieder recitals[229] in Vienna at the Bösendorfersaal, and the programme of the third, on 18 January 1906,

---

[225] See below, Chap. 9.

[226] Johannes Messchaert (1857–1922) initially planned to become a violinist. He studied singing at the Cologne Conservatory and then in Frankfurt and Munich. After leaving Frankfurt in 1911, he taught at the Hochschule für Musik in Berlin until 1920. He later moved to Zurich, where he taught at the Conservatory until he died. Some of Mahler's letters to Messchaert were published by Eduard Reeser in RMH (pp. 74–83), others by Rudolph Stephan in Ernst Herttrich and Hans Schneider (eds.), *Festschrift Rudolf Elvers zum 60. Geburtstag* (Schneider, Tutzing, 1985), 491 ff.   [227] RMH 74.

[228] Leopold Schmidt, article dated 20 Sept. 1917, in *Musikleben der Gegenwart* 170 ff.

[229] The first recital had a Schubert programme and the second was an all-Brahms evening.

consisted of Schumann's *Dichterliebe*, two Loewe Ballads, and five of Mahler's second collection of *Wunderhorn-Lieder*.[230] The whole recital had been accompanied on the piano by one Richard Pahlen. The reviews had been brief and insignificant, but the unsigned article in the *Neue Musikalische Presse* called Messchaert's art 'unsurpassed and unsurpassable'.

The initiator of the Berlin project was Herwarth Walden,[231] the founder of the 'Verein für Kunst' (Society for Art), a private institution whose aim was to 'further the cause of modern art'. Most of the evenings—concerts, lectures, and literary readings—took place in the salon of the art dealer Paul Cassirer, but Messchaert's recital, which seemed bound to attract a larger public than usual, was to be given in the larger Künstlerhaus. Walden was a prolific writer, critic, and champion of the expressionistic cause. He had also composed several operas and a number of Lieder and promptly sent Mahler one of his larger scores, together with a letter to which Mahler replied with his usual frankness:

After rapid perusal of your work I can't quite make up my mind about it. I find it has a certain originality which I like, but I am also put off by an unmistakable imprint of the 'self-made man' in it (I hesitate to use the harsher term 'Dilettantism', since I myself am not yet clear about it). The best thing will be for you to play the work over to me in February when I shall be in Berlin for the Lieder recital (during the three days of my stay which will be taken up with the rehearsals with Messchaert, I will keep one afternon free for you). After that we can discuss further.[232]

Walden had originally promised Messchaert and Mahler that the Lieder recital would be given with orchestral accompaniment, which explains both artists' enthusiasm for the project. Mahler at first wanted to have the Berlin recital take place in the middle of January, immediately after the first performance there of the Third Symphony.[233] There should be 'two or three orchestral rehearsals' before it. In one of his first letters to Walden, Messchaert informs him that he will in any case sing the *Kindertotenlieder*, which he 'likes very much', but will perhaps also include some early *Wunderhorn-Lieder* with piano accompaniment which he has not yet seen or heard.[234] However, Walden must have let Mahler know sometime in December that the cost of hiring an orchestra would probably be too high, a piece of news which elicited the following reply:

You must arrange somehow that I have an orchestra at my disposal for the Messchaert concert. My compositions would loose their character without an orchestra, since they are intended for orchestra, and the treatment of the instruments in combination with

---

[230] The Loewe Ballads were 'Der Nöck' and 'Hochzeitslied'. Among Mahler's *Wunderhorn-Lieder*, Messchaert had chosen 'Der Schildwache Nachtlied', 'Wer hat dies Liedlein erdacht', 'Wo die schönen Trompeten blasen', 'Rheinlegendchen', and 'Lob des hohen Verstandes'.

[231] Herwarth Walden (born Georg Lewin) (1878–1941?) later founded the magazine *Der Sturm*. A pupil of Conrad Ansorge, he was also a composer, with a number of Lieder and several operas to his name.

[232] Letter from Mahler to Walden, in *Festschrift Rudolf Elvers* (see above), 494.

[233] Letters of 8 and 12 Sept., ibid. 492 (see above).

[234] Letter from Messchaert to Walden, ibid. 493.

the singing voice is what gives the thing its style. It would be a big mistake to employ substitute means when trying to win understanding for something new.[235]

But Mahler's admiration for Messchaert and enthusiasm for the Berlin project prevailed, since he eventually accepted to travel to Berin in the middle of February, especially for the concert, and to accompany the singer on the piano.[236] He was obviously delighted to have aroused the enthusiasm of such a well-known, respected, and admired artist. He allowed him to make any transpositions he desired, and suggested a programme consisting of five early *Wunderhorn-Lieder*, the *Kindertotenlieder* cycle, and a third group consisting of late *Wunderhorn-Lieder*[237] and the *Rückert-Lieder*.

In January in another letter Mahler outlines the definitive programme. In the event there was one minor difference: it contained sixteen songs, whereas Messchaert in fact sang eighteen, for he could not bring himself to perform only the first and third of the *Lieder eines fahrenden Gesellen*, as Mahler had suggested, and thus sang the whole cycle.[238] Later on Mahler wrote again to call off a planned meeting with Messchaert in Vienna on 26 January, for at that point he was still intending to go on from Frankfurt to Strasbourg. He added that Bruno Walter, 'who is completely at home in my music, and knows all my wishes, will be at your disposal'. Mahler was confident that he and Messchaert would reach agreement with regard to rehearsals in Berlin on 12 and 13 February before the recital of the 14th: 'Apart from this I shall be happy to comply with whatever special artistic requirements you feel you need. As I shall be at the piano, I can adapt the accompaniment to suit your wishes and disposition.'[239] The next letter shows how much Mahler was looking forward to hearing and accompanying Messchaert, for he suggested a rehearsal in Vienna, assuming that he would not have to be at the Opera on the evening in question. For his third recital in Vienna Messchaert had chosen to sing works by Schumann and Mahler that included the *Kindertotenlieder*.[240]

Mahler was already in Berlin in January and about to conduct his Third Symphony when he received a letter from the Dutch contralto Tilly Koenen, who had sung under him in Amsterdam in March 1906, and whom he had

---

[235] Letter of Mahler to Walden, 29 Nov. 1906, ibid. 494.

[236] Mahler requested a Steinway piano 'with the lightest possible action' (ibid. 497).

[237] RMH 74, undated letter, probably Dec. 1906. The programme suggested in this letter included four early *Wunderhorn* songs, 'Um schlimme Kinder', 'Ich ging mit Lust', 'Starke Einbildungskraft', and 'Zu Strassburg auf der Schanz'. It is most likely for this occasion that Mahler started to orchestrate the last-named song (BMG, see below, 'Catalogue of works'). Four late *Wunderhorn-Lieder* are also included: 'Des Antonius', 'Rheinlegendchen', 'Irdische Leben', and 'Wo die schönen Trompeten'. A later version of the programme (letter of 28 Jan. 1907, see *Festschrift Rudolf Elvers*, 497) included five early *Wunderhorn-Lieder* with piano: 'Um schlimme Kinder', 'Ablösung im Sommer', 'Starke Einbildungskraft', 'Nicht wiedersehen', and 'Selbstgefühl', as well as the *Kindertotenlieder*, the first and third of the *Gesellen-Lieder*, and the four published *Rückert-Lieder*.   [238] RMH 76, undated letter probably written in Dec. 1906.

[239] RMH 77.

[240] Ibid. In the reply that he drafted on Mahler's letter to him Messchaert invited him to dinner after the Vienna concert, and asked if he objected to the inclusion at the beginning of the programme of three songs by Karl Weigl. In the event these were not included in the recital.

accompanied in a Kaim concert the following November. She now asked him to accompany the *Kindertotenlieder* in a recital she was due to give in Vienna.[241] He replied at once. 'It would be very tempting to hear you sing my songs and to accompany you. However, I simply cannot do this in Vienna, and in the nine years I have lived there I have had to make a point of not doing it in order not to offend sensibilities of numerous kinds. If you need me for this purpose <u>somewhere else</u> I will gladly accede to your request. But it would give me great pleasure to see you when you are in Vienna, and perhaps we could run through one or other of my Lieder . . .'[242]

Mahler suddenly realized that, if he carried out his promise and acted as accompanist for Johannes Messchaert at a concert in Vienna, he might trigger off a series of further requests of that kind. He wrote to him at once:

I very much regret that I must ask you to do without me <u>in Vienna</u>. When you are there I shall explain to you in person the trivial though important reasons that oblige me on this occasion (and only in Vienna) to forgo the great pleasure of accompanying you. I will say only this. If I were to appear with you in public, it would involve me (!) in a host of personal difficulties, and would offend numerous people (who of course couldn't hold a candle to you) very much indeed. As you can imagine, I receive many such requests in Vienna, and I have always refused them on principle. I thought I could make an exception for a unique singer like yourself. However, it has now become clear that by doing so I would make quite a lot of petty little people very angry indeed. And in order to cut this Gordian knot I must ask you to allow me to retract my promise.[243]

On the day he returned to Vienna, on 21 January Mahler again wrote to Messchaert and offered to arrange a rehearsal with him a few days later. The day after Messchaert's recital, which he was unable to attend because he had to conduct *Die Entführung*,[244] Mahler, who had heard the rehearsal in the afternoon, once more expressed his admiration for him.[245]

In Vienna, as elsewhere, Messchaert enjoyed considerable prestige, and most of the principal critics attended his recital. Some of them even praised the *Kindertotenlieder*. Ludwig Karpath, in the *Neues Wiener Abendblatt*, stated that the cycle was 'one of the best products of Mahler's muse', even though 'the piano accompaniment is only a pale reflection of the very characteristic orchestral colour in which Mahler has clothed the gloomy subject'. In the *Fremden-Blatt* Albert Kauders remarked that the composer had wished to 'move, touch, and overwhelm with the means provided by modern expressive art', and that he had

---

[241] Tilly Koenen, letter to Mahler dated 9 Jan. 1907. BGM, Paris. The dates of her three Vienna recitals were 7, 5, and 25 Feb. 1907. It is obvious in the letter that Mahler had wanted to engage her as soloist for his Berlin performance of his Third Symphony, but that she had been unable to accept.

[242] RMH 80. Undated letter to Tilly Koenen (mid-Jan. 1907). See also AMM1, 379; AMM2, 326. Accompanied by Coenraad V. Bos, Tilly Koenen sang the *Kindertotenlieder* in Berlin in her third recital on 21 Feb. 1907.   [243] RMH 80. Undated letter (mid-Jan. 1907).

[244] Alma went to Messchaert's concert in his stead.

[245] RMH 82. Undated letters (21 and 29 Jan.). At the end of Feb. Mahler wrote to Tilly Koenen to thank her, in terms reminiscent of those he had used in the case of Messchaert, for 'the interest you take in my spiritual children' (RMH 84).

been wholly successful because his songs had been sung by 'a conjurer of the soul, a master of expression and of mood'. The cycle had exercised an irresistible fascination, and the listeners were so enthralled that they automatically obeyed the injunction not to applaud between the various numbers. But they applauded vigorously at the end of the cycle, which had been both 'profound' and 'painful'. Neither Wallaschek nor Hirschfeld were prepared to change their minds however. Wallaschek stated that the *Kindertotenlieder* were merely 'artificial flowers when compared with the fresh, real flowers of Schumann', whereas Hirschfeld thought they were a symptom of the decline of the Lied,[246] especially when compared with the songs that Wolf had written at about the same time.[247]

In the meantime the final plans for Messchaert's Berlin recital were being made. In a letter to Walden,[248] the baritone shows himself to be an astute—if over-cautious—businessman, since he asks Walden to pay him his fee, not as usual after the concert, but at the beginning or after the first group of songs! Later on, Mahler insisted on inserting a printed notice in the programme, requiring that there be no applause between the *Kindertotenlieder*.[249] The programme for the Messchaert Berlin recital, on 14 February 1907, at 8 o'clock in the evening, included five early *Wunderhorn-Lieder*, the five *Kindertotenlieder*, the four *Lieder eines fahrenden Gesellen*, and four *Rückert-Lieder*.[250] Otto Klemperer recalled that there were 'perhaps about a hundred listeners' at the Künstlerhaus in Bellevuestrasse that evening.[251] And yet, he wrote later, 'it was wonderfully compelling. I had never seen such modesty. It was quite unbelievable.'[252] 'Messchaert didn't have a large voice, but it was extraordinarily expressive. He was really the Josef Joachim of the voice—nothing less. His singing in Bach cantatas was indescribable.'[253] 'It made one feel rather sorry that the audience was so small.'[254] However, an unsigned article

---

[246] In particular, he discerned numerous 'faults in the handling of words'.

[247] The first *Kindertotenlieder* (1901) and Wolf's last songs, the *Michelangelo Lieder* (1897), were in fact four years apart. Messchaert gave three recitals at the Bösendorfer Saal. The first was devoted to Schubert, the second to Brahms, Wolf, and Richard Strauss, and the third to Schumann and Mahler. The programme of the third recital on 28 Jan. was as follows: Schumann, six Lieder from Op. 35 (no. 2, 'Stirb', Lied' und Freud' ', no. 6, 'Auf das Trinkglas'; no. 1, 'Lust der Sturmnacht', no. 10, 'Stille Tränen', no. 11, 'Wer machte dich so krank', no. 12, 'Alte Laute'). Mahler, *Kindertotenlieder*. Schumann, seven Lieder from Op. 39 (no. 1, 'In der Fremde', no. 2, 'Intermezzo', no. 3, 'Waldgespräch', no. 5, 'Mondnacht', no. 6, 'Schöne Fremde', no. 7, 'Auf einer Burg', no. 12, 'Frühlingsnacht'). Messchaert was accompanied by Richard Pahlen.

[248] Letter from Messchaert to Walden, 28 Jan. 1907. See *Festschrift Rudolf Elvers*, 497 ff. Later on the singer required that the paper on which the programme and the texts of the songs was to be printed should be of the 'noiseless' type, so as to avoid the sound of pages being turned during the concert (leter of 6 Feb. 1907, ibid.). However, as it happened, the texts of the songs were not published in the programme.

[249] Letter from Mahler to Walden, *Festschrift Rudolf Elvers*, 498.

[250] The programme of the Berlin concert included five *Wunderhorn-Lieder* with piano accompaniment ('Um schlimme Kinder', 'Ablösung im Sommer', 'Nicht Wiedersehen', 'Selbstgefühl', and 'Starke Einbildungskraft'), the *Kindertotenlieder*, the *Lieder eines fahrenden Gesellen*, and four *Rückert-Lieder* ('Blicke mir nicht', 'Ich atmet' einen Linden Duft', 'Um Mitternacht', 'Ich bin der Welt abhanden gekommen').

[251] OKM 17.

[252] Also see Otto Klemperer, undated letter to Alma Mahler (1911 or 1912) written after the première of *Das Lied von der Erde*.   [253] Peter Heyworth, *Conversations with Klemperer*, 27.

[254] OKM 17.

in the *Vossische Zeitung*, possibly out of politeness to Messchaert, stated that there had been a sizeable audience and 'a first-night atmosphere'. He alluded to the Graz concert, regretted the absence of the orchestra, which Mahler 'treats in such a personal manner', and stated that the *Rückert-Lieder* were 'certainly among the best songs that Mahler has composed'. To judge by his review in the *Allgemeine Musik-Zeitung*, Paul Bekker,[255] who was soon to publish the first important study of Mahler's symphonies, does not seem to have been convinced by his Lieder, to say the least:

Mahler's naivety does not stem from an ignorance of the world or from a lack of experience. On the contrary, he has ascended through every level of knowledge and has struggled fiercely to assimilate what he has learnt. And now he yearns for and longs to return to the magic of nature . . . Now and then he becomes slightly sentimental: 'Ich bin der Welt abhanden gekommen'. And thereby, without meaning to do so, he reveals the extent to which popular feeling and expression are part of his artistic mentality, and the fact that his symphonic works are merely mannered and inflated constructs that are artificial and the result of intellectual effort, works whose extended forms he was no longer able to fill with material of his own. . . . But, in everything that Mahler says as a composer of songs we hear a very special voice whose individuality is unmistakable. . . . Mahler at the piano is just the same as Mahler the conductor. He is extremely precise, and avoids any kind of personality cult. And for this reason he is exciting and stimulating.[256]

Leopold Schmidt, who had come more or less to the conclusion that Mahler's latest symphonies were a sign of his 'creative impotence', was more favourably disposed towards his Lieder:

On Thursday an enthusiastic and attentive audience gathered in the Künstlerhaus for a Mahler concert organized by the Verein für Kunst. Gustav Mahler had come from Vienna to accompany Johannes Messchaert, who sang many of his Lieder. Mahler's songs are always interesting and sometimes rather beautiful. He has a penchant for popular texts such as those from *Des Knaben Wunderhorn*, for they enable him to dwell on humour and intimate emotions, and to achieve an unusual mixture of slightly antiquated and modern styles. But Rückert's profoundly serious *Kindertotenlieder* have

---

[255] Paul Bekker (1882–1937) was born in Berlin. He studied the piano and the violin, and for a time played the violin in the Berlin Philharmonic. In 1906 he embarked on a career as a critic, writing in turn for the *Berliner Neueste Nachrichten* (1906–9), the *Berliner Allgemeine Zeitung* (from 1909 onwards), and the *Frankfurter Zeitung* (1911–25). In the course of his career he championed Mahler, Schoenberg, Krenek, and Schreker. In 1925 he became Intendant of the theatre in Kassel, and from 1927 to 1932 held a similar post in Wiesbaden. In 1933 Bekker left Germany and settled in the United States. His publications include *Oskar Fried* (1907), *Offenbach* (1909), *Das Musikdrama der Gegenwart* (1909), *Beethoven* (1911), *Das deutsche Musikleben* (1916), *Kunst und Revolution* (1919), *Franz Schreker* (1919), *Die Weltgeltung der deutschen Musik* (1920), *Gustav Mahlers Sinfonien* (1921), *Kritische Zeitbilder* (1921), *Die Sinfonie von Beethoven bis Mahler* (1922), *Klang und Eros* (1922), *Neue Musik* (1923), *Richard Wagner: Das Leben im Werke* (1924), *Musikgeschichte als Geschichte der musikalischen Formwandlungen* (1926), *Materiale Grundlagen der Musik* (1927), *Organische und mechanische Musik* (1927), *Das Operntheater* (1930), *Briefe an zeitgenössische Musiker* (1927), *Wandlungen der Oper* (1934), and *The Story of the Orchestra* (1936).

[256] *Allgemeine Musik-Zeitung*, Berlin (22 Feb. 1907).

also proved to be an inspiration. The masterly rendering of the piano version of the orchestral accompaniments united with Messchaert's perfect singing to produce an unusually powerful and lasting impression.[257]

Among those who attended Messchaert's Berlin recital was Otto Klemperer, whose help Fried had enlisted for performances of the Second Symphony (in 1905, when he had conducted the off-stage instruments),[258] the Sixth Symphony (in 1906, when he played the celesta), and the Third Symphony (in 1907, when Mahler entrusted him with the backstage snare-drum part). At that time Klemperer was not quite 22. He was already eager to make his mark, and he was a fervent admirer of Mahler. As we have seen, when he accompanied the latter on a visit to Strauss, he had declared that he intended to become an operatic conductor. However, he had still not found a vacancy.

Oscar Fried intimated to his young disciple that, in order to attract Mahler's attention, he should talk to him about his music, or, better still, he should make a piano arrangement of some of it. And that is what Klemperer did. It so happened that early in the year he went on a concert tour with the cellist Jacques van Lier,[259] in the course of which he was in Vienna on three occasions. He visited Mahler in February and March and was given tickets for *Die Walküre* (as we have seen, he only heard the last two acts because he had played at a concert that evening)[260] and for *Iphigénie*.[261] In April, on his third visit to Vienna, he managed to arrange a meeting with Mahler, during which he played for him the Scherzo of the Second Symphony from memory. Mahler then asked him: 'But why do you want to become a conductor? You are an excellent pianist.' Klemperer replied that it was his dearest wish, and asked him for a reference. Klemperer added:

He refused, saying 'A reference can be forged. But go and see Rainer Simons tomorrow at the Volksoper, and tell him that I sent you.'[262] I did as I was told, but it was to no avail. So I went back to Mahler and said: 'It is no good without a recommendation.' Thereupon he took a visiting card out of his pocket and wrote a recommendation that I have to this day. It opened every door. It says: 'Gustav Mahler recommends Herr Klemperer as an excellent and, despite his youth, very experienced musician, who is predestined for a career as a conductor. I can vouch for a successful trial period as Kapellmeister, and will be happy personally to furnish further information about him.'[263] This really was my *Creator Spiritus*. I sent a photostat of the recommendation to all the larger theatres in Germany. However, most of them did not reply, and others

---

[257] *Signale für die musikalische Welt*, 65 (1907): 15/16, 258.   [258] See above, Chap. 4.

[259] Jacques van Lier (1875–1951) was a Dutch cellist who played in the Berlin Philharmonic and taught at the Klindworth-Scharwenka Conservatory from 1899 to 1915.   [260] 11 Feb. 1907.

[261] Mahler heard the performance of *Iphigénie en Aulide* on 18 Mar. 1907 (see Peter Heyworth, *Otto Klemperer: His Life and Times*, i. 27).

[262] As we have seen, Rainer Simons was about to lose his principal conductor, Alexander Zemlinsky, whom Mahler had engaged at the Hofoper.

[263] Lotte Klemperer gave this card to BGM, Paris, together with her father's conducting score of the Ninth Symphony. Mahler had handed it to Klemperer on 22 Apr. on the occasion of his second Viennese concert.

wrote back to offer me unpaid positions which, for obvious reasons, I could not accept.
I would only have accepted it in Vienna with Mahler, under any circumstances, but the
Hofoper had no unpaid positions of this kind.[264] In the end Mahler's recommendation
did in fact help me to obtain my first engagement, and from 1907 to 1910 I worked
under Angelo Neumann in Prague as chorus master and Kapellmeister.[265]

On 16 October, no doubt at Mahler's behest, Klemperer was engaged to accompany Johannes Messchaert in his recital in Prague. The programme included
the *Kindertotenlieder*.[266]

In January Mahler had declared that he could tell from Klemperer's face
that he was a composer. However, Klemperer did not take himself very seriously as a creative artist, and it would never have entered his head to play his
works to the director of the Vienna Opera, though Mahler no doubt suggested
that he should do so. Bruno Walter, Mahler's favourite disciple, was not so
modest. In 1905 Mahler had been forced to listen to one of his latest works,
and Alma recalled his dilemma:

I only saw him 'making a conscious effort' once. On this occasion Bruno Walter played
to him his symphonic tone poem *Peer Gynt*, whose anaemic sterility horrified him from
the very first bar. But he spoke words of encouragement to Walter. On a later occasion,
when Rosé played a quartet by Walter, Mahler sat with him for a long time in the green-
room discussing aspects of the work, giving him advice, etc. He told me afterwards that

---

[264]   However, Klaus Pringsheim had been engaged on an unpaid basis the year before. This may have
been the reason why Mahler was unable to engage another korrepetitor

[265]   OKM 8 and Peter Heyworth, *Klemperer*, i. 38. In the latter Klemperer stated that Mahler had added:
'It's always the first engagement that is so difficult. Later on it comes of itself.' He also related that in the
summer of 1907 he attended the festival of the Allgemeiner Deutscher Musikverein in Dresden, where he
heard Schoenberg's First Quartet. Sitting in a café, he overheard a conversation between two musicians
concerning a vacancy in Prague. When he discovered that one of them was none other than the critic
Richard Batka, Klemperer set off in pursuit and finally caught up with him at the station. He showed him
Mahler's card, whereupon Batka advised him to go at once to Marienbad to see Neumann. He found the
director of the Deutsches Landestheater ill in bed. Neumann read Mahler's card and engaged him for five
years on the spot. He arranged to meet him in Prague, where Klemperer arrived on 15 Aug. He conducted
Der Freischütz a fortnight later.

[266]   Otto Klemperer (1885–1973) was born in Hamburg. He enrolled at the Hoch Conservatory in
Frankfurt at the age of 16, and later continued his studies at the Stern and Klindworth-Scharwenka
Conservatories in Berlin, where he was a pupil of James Kwast (piano), Xaver Scharwenka, and Hans
Pfitzner (composition). After leaving Prague he was principal conductor at the Stadt-Theater in Hamburg
(1910–14), at the Strasbourg Opera (1914–17), where he was also head of the Conservatory for a year, and
finally at Cologne (1917–24). His activities in Cologne and his first orchestral concerts in Berlin turned him
into an international figure. Nonetheless he accepted the post of musical director at the Wiesbaden Opera
(1924), and, in 1927, at the Krolloper in Berlin, which put on a number of new works every year. Here
Klemperer conducted the German premieres of Janáček's *From the House of the Dead*, Schoenberg's *Die
glückliche Hand*, Krenek's *Das Leben des Orest*, Stravinsky's *Oedipus Rex* and *L'Histoire du Soldat*, and
Hindemith's *Cardillac* and *Neues vom Tage*. The Nazis' influence in Berlin finally secured the closure of the
Krolloper in 1931. Klemperer was then employed at the Staatsoper. In 1929 he had become conductor of the
Philharmonic chorus, a post previously held by Siegfried Ochs. In 1933 his contract with the Staatsoper was
abruptly terminated, and he emigrated to the United States. Here he became conductor of the Los Angeles
Orchestra, and made guest appearances with the New York Philharmonic and in various cities in Europe
and South America. After having reorganized the Pittsburgh Orchestra, Klemperer returned to Europe in
1947 to become conductor of the Budapest Opera. He finally moved to London, where he made a series of
historic recordings with the Philharmonia Orchestra. They include Mahler's Second, Fourth, Seventh, and
Ninth Symphonies, and *Das Lied von der Erde*.

he found it exceptionally difficult to encourage Walter, for he was unable to see that he had a future as a composer, but at the same time did not wish to offend his loyal friend.[267]

On 8 January 1907 Arnold Rosé, the cellist Friedrich Buxbaum,[268] who was a member of his quartet, and Walter gave the first performance of the latter's Trio. Mahler was in Berlin on the day of the concert, but he had attended a rehearsal before he went and had nearly fallen asleep. Thus he was perfectly aware of what he was saying when, in a letter to Alma, who had commented in an entirely negative manner on the work, he remarked: 'After hearing his Trio I am afraid I have to agree with your opinion of Walter. Your "review" is pitiless, but unfortunately it is the truth. It is sad to see such ardent and pointless labour. So you can see why I had trouble staying awake.'[269] It is easy to imagine what went through Mahler 's mind when, in the course of one of their evening walks, Walter declared that he considered the second theme of the first movement of the Sixth Symphony to be too weak and sentimental, and that it did not come up to the level of the powerful opening. Mahler's reaction was eloquent. He said nothing, and they continued to walk through the darkness in silence.[270]

The day after the première of the new production of *Die Walküre* Arnold Rosé and his quartet gave the first performance of Arnold Schoenberg's First Quartet Op. 7[271] in the Bösendorfersaal. A week earlier there had been a concert of Schoenberg's songs at the Ansorge Verein. On this occasion the singers[272] were accompanied by Alexander Zemlinsky. Egon Wellesz recalled that Schoenberg himself arranged to have cards printed which specified that

---

[267] AMS.

[268] The programme included Mozart: Quartet in G major, K. 387; Bruno Walter: Trio in F major; Brahms, Clarinet Quintet (with Franz Bartholomey).

[269] BGA, no. 195, undated (10 Jan. 1907). Alma noted that during the rehearsal Mahler was seized by an uncontrollable fit of yawning, and that he only managed to stay awake on account of his professional ability to listen.

[270] Wolfgang Stresemann, 'Bruno Walter', in *Grosse deutsche Dirigenten* (Severin und Siedler, Berlin, 1982), 133. Stresemann suggests that this was one of the reasons why Walter never performed the Sixth Symphony. Alfred Clayton, a Zemlinsky scholar, says that Walter never forgave Zemlinsky for having been commissioned in his stead to do the piano reduction of this Symphony. His hatred of Zemlinsky continued until the 1920s.

[271] After finishing the First Quartet Op. 7 in the summer of 1905, Schoenberg began two works which were to remain unfinished, a choral piece, *Georg von Frundsberg*, and a string quintet. During the summer of 1906 he composed the first of the *Two Ballades* Op. 12 (the second was composed in 1907) for a competition organized by *Die Woche* (see above, Chap. 2) and began work on an opera based on a play by Gerhart Hauptmann, *Und Pippa tanzt*, which was also destined to remain unfinished. In the autumn he completed the *Eight Lieder* Op. 6, and wrote part of a quintet for piano, clarinet, oboe, violin, and cello based on a poem by Dehmel, *Ein Stelldichein*, a kind of preliminary sketch for the *Kammersymphonie* Op. 9, which absorbed all his energies for several months. The work was completed in summer 1906 on the Tegernsee in Bavaria. It was followed by the chorus *Friede auf Erden* Op. 13, which was composed in Feb.– Mar. 1907. Thereafter Schoenberg began work on the Second Quartet (Mar. 1907–Apr. 1908).

[272] Elsa Parzeller (soprano), Theo Drill-Orridge (alto), Arthur Preuss (tenor), and Anton Moser (baritone). The programme included a total of twenty songs to poems by Richard Dehmel, Gottfried Keller, Friedrich Nietzsche and others. Besides 'Mädchenlied' Op. 6 No. 3 and 'Der Wanderer' Op. 6 No. 8, which are specifically mentioned, the number of songs on the programme suggests that it also comprised the *Two Lieder* for baritone Op. 1, the *Four Lieder* Op. 2, the *Six Lieder* Op. 3, and the *Eight Lieder* Op. 8.

the audience simply 'had the right to listen in silence' (and not to make a noisy display of its disapproval).[273] The listeners obeyed these instructions and the songs were reasonably well received. But that did not prevent some critics from subsequently accusing Schoenberg of being mad. Korngold considered that he was now concerned merely to emphasize 'the abstruse aspect of his theories', and employed 'painful altered chords' in conjunction with 'the most tortuous intervals'. Wallaschek considered these 'arid studies, devoid of invention, energy, passion, or the slightest feeling', to be nothing more than a 'parody of modern art'. Despite his 'personal liking' for Schoenberg, Karpath thought that the songs belonged to 'the realm of madness', whereas Kauders considered that they displayed both 'a great deal of atmosphere and expressive excitement' and a total absence of musical thought.

   Performed in a small concert hall, the songs were applauded by the majority of the listeners, most of whom were friends and disciples. It was a different story a week later, when the Rosé Quartet gave the first performance of Schoenberg's First Quartet in D minor in the Bösendorfersaal as part of its subscription series; and even more so three days later at the première of the *Kammersymphonie* Op. 9 given by the same ensemble (with eleven wind players from the Bläservereinigung) in the Musikvereinsaal. Alma described the first of these two concerts as follows:[274]

Towards the end of his life Mahler tried to provide help and succour for all those who were striving for higher things, especially for Schoenberg, whom he wanted to protect from the brutality of the mob. On two occasions he became personally involved in disputes at concerts. The first of these incidents occurred during the first performance of the Quartet Op. 7. The whole audience was listening with quiet and dutiful amusement when the critic Karpath[275] shouted 'Stop!' in the direction of the stage (an unpardonable transgression), whereupon everyone started to whistle and shout in a way I have never heard before or since. One wretch stood in front of the first row of seats and whistled at Schoenberg (who kept on coming forward, making excuses this way and that with his Jewish Bruckner-like head, and at the same time bowing in an embarrassed and peremptory manner).[276] Mahler jumped up and accosted the fellow, saying very loudly, 'I must get a good look at a wretch who can whistle like that!' Thereupon the man lunged out to hit him. Moll saw what was happening and shot through the squabbling audience to separate the irate pair, much to their great surprise. He then chased the stout burgher, who was intimidated by Moll's superior strength, out of the Bösendorfersaal. But at the door he recovered his poise and shouted: 'Calm down! I whistle at Mahler too!'[277]

---

[273]   Egon Wellesz, *Arnold Schoenberg: The Formative Years* (Dent, London, 1921), 23–4.

[274]   According to Egon Wellesz, Arnold Rosé rehearsed the Quartet over forty times (ibid. 23).

[275]   AMM only gives an initial, K. As we shall see, although Karpath did in fact voice his disapproval in this way, it was at the first performance of the Second Quartet on 22 Dec. 1909. Alma obviously confused the première of the First Quartet with that of the Second, which Mahler did not attend.

[276]   Alma, recalling that she had first met Schoenberg through her teacher Zemlinsky, remarked: 'He [Zemlinsky] said at the time, when I expressed my dislike for Schoenberg (he was very ugly and unappetizing in those days, although he later changed), "Take a good look at him, for the world will talk a lot about him one day!"' (AMS and AMM1, 100).   [277]   AMM1, 142; AMM2, 140.

A number of witnesses have described this extraordinary scene, which shows how numerous and determined Mahler's (and Schoenberg's) enemies in Vienna had now become. According to Richard Specht, the man stood next to Mahler deliberately, in order to demonstrate that he was dissatisfied, and Mahler shouted at him: 'How can you dare to whistle when I'm applauding?' To which the man retorted: 'I also whistled at your filthy symphony!' Specht adds that the altercation would have degenerated into fisticuffs if the two of them had not been separated.[278] Bruno Walter later recalled that Mahler then snapped back at him: 'Coming from you, that doesn't surprise me!'[279]

The account of the incident given by Egon Wellesz differs with regard to certain details, though it may well be the most accurate one, for the young composer no doubt noticed everything that happened at the first performance of a work by his revered teacher. Furthermore, Schoenberg's pupils shared an almost mystical admiration for Mahler:

At the end of the Quartet an older man in a dinner jacket who was sitting at the end of the third row on the right stood up and began to whistle on a key. Mahler and his wife were sitting behind him. I sat two rows further back, also at the end of a row, so I could see what happened quite clearly. Mahler shouted furiously: 'I'm going to risk five gulden and box your ears.' The man recognized Mahler, turned round and said: 'You're not in the Opera here. You can't tell me what to do.' Mahler wanted to go for the man, but was held back by his wife. In the meantime two of Schoenberg's young pupils had rushed up and, despite his protests, led the man out of the hall. Schoenberg's supporters then gave him and the Rosé Quartet a rousing ovation.[280]

Wellesz makes the point that the listeners' difficulties were compounded by the fact that Schoenberg had not supplied a programme, as he had done for *Verklärte Nacht*, and that the quartet, which was in one movement, constituted a daring amplification of the formal pattern established by Beethoven which had been enriched with the kind of 'psychological' thematic transformation found in the symphonic poems of Liszt and Richard Strauss.

Two years later, when the Viennese première of Schoenberg's Second Quartet caused an even greater scandal in which three of the leading music critics in Vienna were said to have been involved, the *Neue Musik-Zeitung* marked the occasion by publishing a controversial article on Schoenberg. It recalled the première of his First Quartet, and pointed out that Mahler's support for the young composer had contributed to the passions that had been

[278] RSM2, 29.

[279] Bruno Walter, 'Erinnerungen an Gustav Mahler', *Neue Freie Presse* (16 Nov. 1935). An almost identical account of the incident appears in 'Mahler und der Zischer', *Deutsche Warte* (Berlin, 6 June 1919), and in PSG 77. In New York the *Musical Courier* (31 May 1911), claimed that Mahler had said: 'It is scandalous not to let a composer have his say without these appalling interruptions. This man has something to tell us and he deserves a respectful hearing.' Otto Klemperer's version of the incident in the Bösendorfersaal is virtually the same as that of Richard Specht and Bruno Walter, but he claims, wrongly, that it took place at the premiere of the *Kammersymphonie* on 8 Feb. and that the police had to intervene (OKM 17). See also BWT 169.   [280] EWL 54.

unleashed, for in Vienna he had had 'a small band of fervent supporters and a great number of implacable enemies'.[281]

At the Musikvereinsaal three days later tempers were already beginning to fray at the start of the concert, which began with Ermanno Wolf-Ferrari's innocuous *Kammersymphonie* for piano, strings, and woodwind. The work was just as eclectic as his operas. However, it was of considerable importance to Klaus Pringsheim, who played the piano part, for this was his first appearance in public. Bruno Walter had originally intended to take part in the performance, but was unable to do so because he had received orders at short notice to conduct *Lohengrin* at the Opera a few days earlier. Zemlinsky was then asked to deputize for him, but declined the offer because he did not have enough time to prepare for the concert. At this juncture Mahler suggested that the task should be assigned to the young Korrepetitor, who was determined to justify the trust placed in him and learned the work in less than a week. After the decision had been taken, Mahler met him at the Opera and sent him home immediately, relieving him of all his duties until after the concert. Pringsheim later thought that the performance must have been a success, for not a single critic commented on his youth or inexperience.[282]

The fact is that no one in Vienna was in the least interested in the music of Wolf-Ferrari, whereas everyone was waiting rather impatiently for the première of Schoenberg's *Kammersymphonie* Op. 9, even those who were firmly intent on demonstrating against the 'insanity' of the young composer of what was jokingly referred to as the *Folterkammersymphonie* (Torture Chamber Symphony). The young composer himself had awaited this première with much anticipation.

I had so much pleasure composing it, everything had gone so easily and seemed so convincing that I was sure that the public would spontaneously react to the melodies and moods and would find this music as beautiful as I did. I expected much from the sound of the unusual combination of 15 solo instruments—that is, five strings, eight woodwinds and two horns.

How mistaken Schoenberg was! 'In the middle of the performance,' Alma recalled, 'people started to move their chairs loudly and to leave in an ostentatious manner. Mahler got up rather angrily and asked them to be quiet, and they complied with his request. At the end he stood at the front of the box and applauded until the agitators had all left.'[283]

Egon Wellesz, in his book on Schoenberg, also mentioned the departure of scandalized listeners, and added in his memoirs:

Never before nor since has a performance ended in such uproar. Schoenberg's supporters applauded with as much fervour as his enemies whistled. The principal cause of all

---

[281] *Neue Musik-Zeitung*, 30 (1909): 261. The concert given by the Rosé Quartet on 5 Feb. finished with Schubert's C major Quintet.

[282] Klaus Pringsheim, 'Erinnerungen an Gustav Mahler', *Neue Zürcher Zeitung* (7 July 1960).

[283] AMM1, 142; AMM2, 140.

the uproar was surely the use of the instruments and not the musical substance of the work. It was very daring on Schoenberg's part to combine ten wind and five solo string instruments in a chamber work. The uproar began in the Scherzo, where Schoenberg exchanges the flute with the piccolo[284] and the clarinet in D, which is rather piercing at the best of times, with an E flat clarinet.[285] But matters really came to a head towards the end, when the piccolo, oboe, English horn and clarinet in D are required to play very high-pitched triplets *fortissimo* against the horns and strings.[286] People already began to leave the hall rather noisily in the middle of the one-movement work. Later some of the audience began to bang their seats up and down, to slam shut the doors of the hall, and to whistle continuously on their keys. A number of very young pupils of Heinrich Schenker, the great opponent of all post-Brahmsian music, were particularly conspicuous in the concert of whistlers. During the final minutes of the performance there was such an uproar that it drowned out the music. Rosé, altogether master of the situation, played the first violin and conducted. It was an extraordinary achievement.[287]

It is legitimate to ask to what extent Mahler in fact appreciated and understood Schoenberg's music. The following passage, which comes after Alma's account of the premiere of the *Kammersymphonie*, has led to a great deal of controversy: 'we went home and spent the whole evening talking about the Schoenberg problem. Mahler said: "I do not understand his music, but he is young. Perhaps he is right. I am old, and perhaps I no longer have the ability to understand his music".'[288] He certainly found it difficult to come to grips with Schoenberg's scores and told him so with the utmost frankness after examining that of the First Quartet: 'I have conducted the most difficult scores of Wagner; I have written complicated music myself in scores of up to thirty staves or more; yet here is a score of not more than four staves, and I am unable to read them.'[289] In 1909 he made a similar admission to Ernst Decsey concerning a Schoenberg work. This time it was the Second Quartet.[290] At times, he felt discouraged, and would ask Richard Specht: 'Why am I still writing symphonies if that is supposed to be the music of the future.'[291] Max Graf, not the most reliable of sources, claims that he was in the habit of saying: 'There is something in this music, but I simply cannot understand it.' However, Schoenberg himself concludes: 'But he had the courage to blame this deficiency on his own ear, not on the unfamiliar sonorities.'[292]

However Specht, who often talked to Mahler at this time, adds that, even when he did not understand his music, he had 'far more respect for the struggle' of someone like Schoenberg than 'for those who ruminated on the eternal yesteryears or for those who worshipped the cult of the eternal here and now'.[293] Klaus Pringsheim gives a fuller account of Mahler's answer when he

[284] Rehearsal no. 40.   [285] Rehearsal no. 38.   [286] Two bars after rehearsal no. 112.
[287] Egon Wellesz, *Arnold Schoenberg*, 23 and EWL 57. In 1925 Schoenberg published a version for string orchestra, and in 1935 one for full orchestra.   [288] AMM1, 142; AMM2,140.
[289] Arnold Schoenberg, *Aufsätze*, 348.
[290] EDS1, 354. Richard Specht confirms that when Mahler received the score of this work, he complained that he found it difficult to read (RSM2, 28).   [291] RSM2, 29.
[292] GWO 351.   [293] RSM2, 29 ff.

questioned him after the première of the *Kammersymphonie*: 'He was personally unable to follow in the path of the younger composer, who was thirty-two
at the time. But the very fact that it was a new path was an added reason to
support the man who pursued it, and from whom—this was something he had
said to me on previous occasions—unusual things were be expected in the
direction that he had decided to pursue.'[294]

Mahler's difficulties increased after Schoenberg had shown him the score of
the Second Quartet and, while discussing the *Five Pieces for Orchestra* Op. 16,
had explained to him his new concept of *Klangfarbenmelodie*.[295] However, the
problems Schoenberg encountered when trying to make himself understood
reminded Mahler of what he had gone through at the same stage in his own life,
and henceforth he displayed a genuine affection for him. That the feeling was
mutual is demonstrated by the fact that Schoenberg dedicated the
Harmonielehre to Mahler, and also by Schoenberg's famous Prague lecture of
1912, which was later expanded and turned into an article.[296]

After the first performances of the First Quartet and the *Kammersymphonie*,
the only Viennese critic to come to Schoenberg's defence was Elsa Bienenfeld,
the musicologist and friend who had once engaged him to teach at the
Schwarzwald Academy.[297] On 12 February, in a long article in the *Neues
Wiener Journal*, she attempted to show by means of detailed analysis that
Schoenberg was not a madman, and that the 'confusion' that the listeners at the
première had ostensibly heard was merely an illusion. It stemmed from the
abundance of the material, the complexity of its elaboration, and its wealth of
polyphony, all qualities that Schoenberg had inherited from his great predecessors. All the other critics were full of indignation, scorn, horror, or simply
nonplussed. If even a moderate and open-minded person such as Korngold
could write: 'When an artist, immersed and infatuated with his fantasies,
however honest we believe him to be, commits such things to paper—so be it.
But one ought not to perform them!',[298] it is not difficult to imagine the verbal
excesses indulged in by others. Thus Richard Wallaschek, in *Die Zeit*,
professed that he was amazed at the calm and patience of the audience, when
confronted by 'the mental illness of the century . . . with its anguish, its inner
uncertainty and its eternal doubts . . . The art of making such things was not
as difficult as the art of performing them.' Albert Kauders saw in the Quartet
nothing but 'the cult of ugliness', 'a triumph of cacophony' and 'a musical
Tartarus' reminiscent of Dante. Its 'infernal confusion' tormented 'the senses
and feelings of normal listeners' and caused 'actual physical pain'. After the
Kammersymphonie, he felt, anything could happen:

---

[294]   Pringsheim, 'Erinnerungen'. Josef Bohuslav Förster recalled that, during a rehearsal of the
Kammersymphonie, Mahler asked the musicians to play a C major chord, thanked them, and left the hall
(JFP 681).
[295]   AMM1, 228; AMM2, 210. See also RSM2, 28. See below, Vol. iiii, Chap. 5.
[296]   See RWM 11 and Arnold Schoenberg, 'Stil und Gedanke'.
[297]   See above, Vol. ii, Chap. 16.   [298]   *Neue Freie Presse* (10 Feb. 1907).

If one has spent three decades participating in word and deed in the development of music, one has seen things come into existence, ripen and flourish that in their infancy were regarded with scorn and disdain. I now consider that nothing is impossible, not even that, in the foreseeable future, music will be abolished and that non-music will take its place. The principle of ugliness in music has already acquired the status of a system. It is in fact rather surprising that Schoenberg still refers to his latest work as a 'symphony'. 'Antiphony' would be the better word. The language is dominated not by consonance, but by dissonance. The motifs writhe in a chaotic tangle and tumble over each other in a haphazard fashion, submerging and obscuring each other. As soon as a comprehensible idea, the elaboration of which one would like to follow, appears, two others arrive yapping at its heels and harry it to death.[299]

Writing for the *Wiener Allgemeine Zeitung* Carl Lafite belonged to the small minority of critics who regarded Schoenberg as 'a serious and honest person', and thought that his Quartet deserved to be taken seriously, even though it was easier to understand his intentions when reading the score than when listening to it for the first time. On the whole members of the audience as well as critics agreed with the views expressed by Paul Stauber:

Schoenberg's *Kammersymphonie*, in which fifteen instruments were given the task of producing the most horrible and arbitrary dissonances in the loudest possible *fortissimo*, and of engaging in a loathsome and inartistic racket, represented the zenith, or should I say, the nadir, of this kind of 'art'. I call on all musicians, and not on Bahr, Moll, Berta Zuckerkandl, and least of all on Schoenberg and the miniature dervishes prancing around him, I call on all reasonable people to bear witness that this 'music', if it is not just a huge joke, is designed to injure ears and feelings in the most brutal fashion imaginable. Mahler, who attended the rehearsal of this 'work', is said, I am told by reliable witnesses, to have declared that he no longer understood this music. Yet the next day he applauded after the performance for all he was worth. There was no turning back for him. And he had to bear the full consequences of his abrupt change of mind.[300]

Alma recalled that on the night of the first performance of the *Kammersymphonie* 'Guido Adler, the senile (*verkalkte*) Professor of Musicology',[301] telephoned to voice his concern: 'Gustav really went out on a limb today... It could cost him his job... You should stop him from doing this kind of thing! I went home and wept at the way music is going! Yes, I wept....' Anyone reading this passage in ignorance of the past or of Guido Adler's role in 1904, when he drew Mahler's attention to Schoenberg and persuaded him to accept the honorary presidency of the Vereinigung, would think that he was a sworn enemy of modernism. No doubt he was, in Alma's eyes, if only because he had never really liked her, for reasons we shall examine below. At any rate, in view of his role in introducing Schoenberg to Mahler three years earlier, it was natural that

---

[299] *Fremden-Blatt* (11 Feb. 1907).

[300] SWE 40. The *Kammersymphonie* was followed by *Chanson et Danses*, two pieces for wind sextet by Vincent d'Indy.

[301] The word *verkalkte* (senile) only occurs in AMS. Guido Aldler was only five years older than Mahler.

he should feel some responsibility for the dangerous position that the director of the Hofoper had chosen to adopt.

Unfortunately, Adler was right. Mahler was taking a serious risk in providing support for Schoenberg's audacity at a time when he himself was already the object of attacks. We merely have to read the article by Paul Stauber quoted above, or Hans Liebstöckl's comment that the score of the Quartet had 'ruined two of my evenings. It is almost worse for one's eyes than for one's ears'. He then described what another journalist in Berlin had written about him:

I am said to have attacked not only Schoenberg, but also Gustav Mahler, who has repeatedly shown himself to be friend and adviser of the Schoenbergian muse. The composer had been introduced by Mahler's brother-in-law, Rosé, and Mahler had only joined the coterie at a later stage. This is well known in Vienna, and does not alter the fact that the director of the Hofoper shields Schoenberg's musical excesses, and that in an incident at a Schoenberg première in the Bösendorfersaal he came close to expressing his convictions with the help of fisticuffs. I fail to understand why one should not be allowed to rebuke 'one of the greatest living musicians' when he makes a mistake and takes part in a hoax that bears little or no relation to his usual standards. I certainly do not think it 'desirable' to 'moderate my words' or to 'give a more balanced opinion' when we are dealing with a blatant example of histrionic propaganda for publicly manifested decadence (*Entartung*).[302]

The reaction of Mahler's enemies had come sooner than expected. The worst of it was that, by openly supporting Schoenberg, he gave credence to the idea that he was now at the head of a clique that encouraged the most demented flights of fancy of its members and thus constituted a grave threat to the established musical institutions. Schoenberg certainly reciprocated Mahler's friendship, as witness the following letter he had written him the preceding summer:

Your letter gave me extraordinary pleasure. Nothing could have pleased me more than the fact that you say we have come closer to each other. It gives me more pleasure and fills me with greater pride than if you had praised one of my works—though of course I have the greatest respect for your judgement. I consider personal affection to be the most important aspect of human relations, and I believe that nothing else could fully develop without it. As I have already said, I am extremely pleased and proud; and— ever conscious of what separates us—I hope to be not entirely unworthy of your friendly feelings. . . . Please convey my very best wishes to your wife and tell her that I am glad she has finally discovered that I am a 'decent fellow'—I have always maintained that I am, though unfortunately very few people are willing to believe me.[303]

The published correspondence between Schoenberg and Karl Kraus contains the following letter, which was written in May 1906:

[302] *Illustrirtes Wiener Extrablatt* (1 Mar. 1907).

[303] Letter to Mahler dated 18 July 1906, AMM1, 371. Schoenberg also mentioned the possibility of attending the Salzburg Festival, no doubt to hear Mahler's performance of *The Marriage of Figaro*, and announced that he was putting the finishing touches to the *Kammersymphonie*, offering to send Mahler the score and a piano duet transcription. He declined Mahler's invitation to visit him at Maiernigg on account of his wife's pregnancy, which ruled out a fourteen-hour train journey from the Tegernsee in Bavaria, where they were spending the summer vacation.

Dear Mr Kraus, For some time now I have been meaning to draw your attention to what has been happening with regard to Mahler. In particular I hope to convince you that he is an extraordinary man, someone who is quite unlike anyone else past or living. Hence the quite unheard-of manner in which he has been treated by the press.[304]

The suggested meeting with Kraus no doubt took place, but it was not until May 1907 that *Die Fackel* thought fit to defend Mahler, and then only in a single sentence which derided one of his principal detractors, Heinrich Reinhardt, for placing 'the musical culture of Gustav Mahler far below the musical culture of the composer Reinhardt'.[305] On 12 May Kraus wrote to Schoenberg asking him to take up Mahler's defence in *Die Fackel* himself. This was Schoenberg's answer:

Dear Mr Kraus, I cannot carry out my intention of writing an article about Mahler for *Die Fackel*. First, at the moment I am so depressed by numerous disappointments and other unfortunate matters that I do not feel like doing anything. But then there is so much I have to do, some things which are unavoidable, and some things to which I have committed myself, that, even if I were in the right mood, I would not get round to doing it. Furthermore, it is terribly difficult to write a short article about Mahler. A book, yes—as you say, a book would be so much easier—but I don't know where I would begin to stop. I cannot organize the material and do not know how to keep it within a certain length. But I hope one day to get round to writing it. And perhaps you will then be kind enough to remember me.[306]

Thus Schoenberg declined to defend Mahler publicly against the attacks that were levelled at him. In any case, no one would have taken him seriously. He had acquired the reputation of being insane, and in addition to this was widely considered to be a member of the Mahlerian 'clique'. However, there can be no doubt about Mahler's admiration for him. This is demonstrated in a letter to Richard Strauss written in the same year 1907:

Yesterday I heard the new Schoenberg Quartet, and it made such a powerful and indeed overwhelming impression on me that I cannot help recommending it most strongly for the Tonkünstler meeting in Dresden. I am sending you the score by the same post, and hope you will be able to find the time to have a look at it. The Rosé Quartet is prepared to play the piece if its travel expenses are reimbursed. Please forgive me for troubling you, harassed as you are, but I think you will also be pleased with it.[307]

Thus Mahler was not nearly as baffled by the First Quartet as has sometimes been claimed. His solicitous interest in Schoenberg was boundless. Remembering the difficulties that he himself had encountered at that time in

---

[304] Friedrich Pfäfflin, *Karl Kraus und Arnold Schoenberg: Fragmente einer Beziehung*, ed. Heinz Ludwig Arnold, *Text und Kritik* (Sonderband Karl Kraus, Munich, 1975), 130 ff.

[305] *Die Fackel* (22 May 1907), 17. See below, Chap. 9. Heinrich Reinhardt was a composer of operettas which included the immensely successful *Das süße Mädel*.

[306] Arnold Schoenberg, undated letter to Karl Kraus (13 or 14 May 1907), Stadtbibliothek, Vienna.

[307] MSB 122. The Quartet was in fact performed in Dresden, where Otto Klemperer heard it for the first time.

life, he wanted Schoenberg to be able to devote himself entirely to composition. Thus he not only attempted to enlist the support of Baron Rothschild, but also, as early as February 1906, tried to secure Schoenberg's appointment as conductor of the Singverein.[308] And in 1908 Mahler 'warmly' recommended Schoenberg's Second Quartet to Strauss.

However, it may well be that this obstinate and unflinching support for an artist who was rejected so decisively by Viennese society was an indirect reply to the opposition that Mahler himself had encountered. He was tired of having to justify himself, and wanted to show that his thirst for adventure could make him take risks that were not associated with conducting, producing operas, or composing monumental symphonies. He had been accused of flaunting tradition and of tyrannizing both works of art and the people under him. He had been unceasingly reminded that, although he was a conductor of genius and an incomparable producer, he was also a mediocre administrator and someone who composed miserable symphonies. A powerful cabal had sworn to bring about his downfall, and was willing to resort to any means to make him resign. Hence the virulence and frequency of the attacks made on him were breaking all records.

On the surface, at least, nothing had changed in Mahler's life. As an official appointed by the Emperor, his engagement could only be terminated if he agreed to it. For the moment at any rate he did not intend to resign. The zeal with which he had revived *Die Walküre* and *Iphigénie en Aulide* proved that, as far as his work was concerned, he still possessed the same enthusiasm and ardour as in the past, and his weariness, which resulted from the ill-tempered and unfair nature of the criticisms levelled at him, was counterbalanced by the pride that came from the knowledge of his own genius. He knew he was irreplaceable, and he wanted the imperial authorities to appreciate his true worth instead of continually criticizing him for being absent. He also wanted them to take a greater interest in making his task easier, and hoped that they would sanction the necessary improvements. In the months that followed they were faced with a dilemma. Were they sufficiently interested in him to do what was necessary to keep him?

Mahler was no more worried than he had ever been about losing his post. As always, he undoubtedly believed that being afraid is tantamount to having lost the battle. Admittedly, he continued to keep his letter of resignation in his drawer. This is one of the reasons why he did not hesitate to provoke the conservative Viennese by vigorously applauding the young iconoclast, Schoenberg. By pointing so forcefully to new horizons he was in effect saying that his vision was not restricted to the small world of Vienna, its fashions, its gossip, its intrigues, and its smiling cruelty. And by adopting this position he was, perhaps unconsciously, getting ready and inwardly preparing to take his leave.

---

[308] In a letter to the composer Oscar Posa (HOA, Z. 304/1906) Mahler stated that he was unable to recommend him for this position because he had put forward Schoenberg's name, and had heard nothing since.

9

Mahler in Vienna (XXV)—Grete Wiesenthal and
La Muette de Portici
Roller and the ballet—Journey to Rome—
Final opera productions
Mahler's departure from the Opera—Putzi's death—
Diagnosis of heart ailment

(March–August 1907)

In ten years at the Vienna Opera, I have come full circle . . .

MAHLER'S dislike for ballet was an open secret at the Vienna Opera. When asked about it in private, he usually replied that he considered it impossible to reform such a purely decorative art form. It was probably a project for a ballet submitted to him in 1901 by Hofmannsthal and Zemlinsky[1] which prompted him at that time to define his views on this subject to Natalie and Lipiner. Lipiner thought that a revival of the art of dancing was possible, provided that the element of mime predominated and that the music was 'nobler and more meaningful'. 'Nothing can be done for it in its present form,' Mahler replied. 'All one's efforts would be in vain!'[2] To explain what he meant he described the terrifying stories he had once found himself inventing for a boy suffering from scarlet fever. He had started by picturing 'dreadful giants and monsters, with two heads and four arms' and then with more arms than an octopus and with 'ten, twenty, a hundred heads', until ultimately he found himself obliged to invent something with no monstrous attributes at all. As far as he was concerned, 'all those involved with the ballet, be they artists or spectators, have unbridled and depraved

---

[1] See above, Vol. ii, Chap. 16.   [2] NBL1, 156; NBL2, 181.

imaginations, and it is absolutely impossible to improve and raise them to a higher level.'

But from the start the aim of the Secession had been to work for the revival of all the visual arts. It was inevitable therefore that it would one day direct its efforts towards the dance. In late 1906 it had put on a programme of Javanese dances by a very talented young dancer who was visiting Vienna. 'It was a highly poetic and artistic performance,' wrote Hevesi,

pushing back the frontiers of the permissible way beyond the strict conventions which have to be observed in daily life. Which is another way of saying that the dancer was rather scantily clad. She imitated, successfully it would seem, the postures of statues in Indian temples, being helped by a similarity in physical attributes, a nose, a heavy mass of black hair, enormous dark eyes and generously over-painted lips. With her long well-developed limbs, ('perfectly proportioned' according to Hevesi), she was possessed of an elemental beauty, not of a conventional type, but unique to her alone. The designers of the Secession had provided a tent shaped like a temple, with carpet-covered floor and a little altar with an enthroned Buddha placed between 'tall vases and flowering cherry trees'.

This pseudo-oriental décor pleased an audience hungry for anything exotic, but still with little idea of the genuinely oriental. No one found it strange that these 'Hindu' dances should have taken place in front of a statue of the Buddha rather than of one of the gods from the Ramayana, and in front of Japanese cherry trees at that. The dancer wore a crown of flowers, a simple skirt, and a brassière. She flourished her veil in a restless manner and brought to the god ritual offerings of water, dust, flowers, and small candles. The audience felt that it had been transported to the Orient:

Mata Hari appeared and danced in the garden until she espied the flower of love and shuddered as she recognized it. Urged on by the wild cries of the throng, she whirled around with ever greater abandon and discarded her garments one by one. The veils, the girdle, the pearls and flowers were all cast off, until only one last thin wisp of cloth remained on her naked body as she sank to the ground. A female attendant entered and spread a white silk cloak over the beautiful woman. To what extent this rhythmic activity was dance, and to what extent it was Hindu hardly worried the spectators. They were indulging their eyes to the full.[3]

It is clear that Mata Hari (the Eye of the Sun), whose later notoriety was due more to her tragic condemnation to death as a spy than to her career as a dancer, had profoundly impressed the Secessionists and their guests on that December evening in 1906, for their spokesman, Ludwig Hevesi, waxed so lyrical that he imagined maddened oriental crowds watching the dancer and uttering savage cries. The *Illustrirtes Extrablatt* accused Mata Hari of having sunk to the level of variety theatre. Two other exotic dancers appeared in Vienna in the same month: Maud Allen, who danced 'The Vision of Salome' in

---

[3] Ludwig Hevesi, *Altkunst, Neukunst*, 280 (16 Dec. 1906).

the presence of Mahler, Prince Montenuovo, and Josef Hassreiter, the ballet master at the Opera; and Madame She, the 'Golden Venus', who was covered with bronze paint and adopted 'sculptural poses'. But Mata Hari's oriental striptease made a much deeper impression on account of 'this line, that movement, the wonderful gestures of her hands, there a beautiful bow, here an enchanting curl'.[4]

Mata Hari was born in Holland as Margarita Gertruida Zelle. Her father was a hatmaker by profession. As the wife of an officer in the Dutch colonial army, she had become acquainted with Indian dancing in Indonesia. In 1903 she had left her husband and daughter and gone to Paris. There she led the life of a *demi-mondaine* with an exotic and entirely fictitious past: a sadistic husband, Indian parents, and a childhood spent in a temple in the south of India. In 1905 she was introduced to the Parisian public by Émile Guimet, who transformed a room of his museum into an Indian temple for the occasion. She soon became famous, commanded enormous fees, and was idolized by a circle of right-wing intellectuals, and especially by Léon Daudet. She put on a show at the Olympia Theatre and became a protégée of the impresario Gabriel Astruc. However, when André Antoine engaged her to play Cleopatra in Shakespeare's play, she was dropped before it opened on account of her lack of talent. In 1906 she sang a short aria in Massenet's *Le Roi de Lahore* at the Monaco Opera, met Puccini, and conceived the idea of creating the title role in Strauss's *Salome*. She had acquired her real name, Lady MacLeod, from the husband she had recently abandoned, and her success at the Secession had aroused in her mind hopes of a Viennese career. Six weeks after her performance for the Secession, which Mahler may have attended, she wrote to him in rather imperfect French:

You will remember me from when I was presented to you by Maître Massenet after I had interpreted the Hindu Air in his work *Le Roi de Lahore*. I would be very pleased to interpret character airs for you or, better still, to be your principal actress. I have had costumes and authentic jewels sent from India. I could do 'Melusine', 'la Muette', the 'Gott des Lichts' in Excelsior. I am sure you will remember everything we talked about. I could dance authentic dances in every oriental work. I shall send you some photographs to remind you of me. Yours sincerely, Lady MacLeod (Matà-Hàri).[5]

---

[4] Ibid.

[5] HOA Z. 134/1907, letter dated 29 Jan., and sent to Mahler from Berlin. In addition to Maud Allen and Madame She, Ruth Saint Denis made her Viennese debut with a programme of Indian dances at the Ronacher Cabaret (Ludwig Hevesi, *Altkunst, Neukunst*, 282). Mata Hari (1876–1917) later tried in vain to ingratiate herself with Diaghilev. Before the First World War she bought a house in Neuilly, where she led the life of a high-class 'demi-mondaine', and subsequently appeared in music-hall revues at the Folies-Bergères and the Gaumont Cinema. Her last stage appearance was at The Hague in 1915. During the war, many of her lovers were members in the armed forces. Initially in the pay of an American colonel, she later offered her services to the French counter-espionage service which sent her to Spain. Here she was on intimate terms with the German naval attaché. A victim of the spy fever which swept across France in 1916–17, she was arrested on 15 Jan. 1917 after returning from Madrid, tried in camera, defended by an ineffectual barrister who was in love with her, and, despite a complete lack of evidence, condemned to death and shot on 15 Oct. of the same year.

To judge from the above letter the young dancer had added singing to her artistic accomplishments and was longing to display her many gifts on the Hofoper stage. However, her talents obviously failed to meet Mahler's require- ments; he was more exacting in this respect than Massenet, who was always a devoted admirer of the fair sex. As far as the position of 'principal actress' or mime was concerned, Mata Hari's suggestions had little chance of arousing Mahler's interest, for he had just discovered a first-rate candidate in the Opera's corps de ballet. Unfortunately this was under the control of the ballet master, Josef Hassreiter, who was always very jealous of his rights, as Mahler was soon to learn to his cost.

The Hofoper was in the process of preparing a new production of Auber's opera *La Muette de Portici* for the end of February. For the title role Mahler first thought of an artist who was also an accomplished actress and whom, moreover, he had trained himself: Marie Gutheil-Schoder. However, when they came to discuss the possibility it was soon obvious to both of them that, given the negative attitude of certain critics towards the singer and the reservations they had expressed about the quality of her voice, her assignment to a silent role would give her enemies the opportunity to make even more sarcastic remarks. There was only one other solution and that was to find a performer with a gift for acting in the corps de ballet. Roller then remembered a young dancer who had made an impression in a minor role in the ballet *Excelsior*. Although Grete Wiesenthal had been with the Hofoper since 1901, she had never made a solo appearance because of Hassreiter's violent antipathy to her. Many years later she told the story of the events which gave rise to a true Viennese 'Affär':

One day, Alfred Roller sent for me and gave me a vocal score of Auber's *La Muette de Portici* with the request to study the part of Fenella (La Muette) and work out an interpretation of it. He also asked me not to tell anyone about this experiment for the time being. Astonished and delighted, I agreed, and, burning with zeal I set about studying the part.

Bruno Walter was to be in charge of the new production and also to conduct it. When I had finished studying 'Fenella' I was referred to him, and he rehearsed the role with me at the piano before I presented it to Gustav Mahler for critical scrutiny.

Straight after the first scene Bruno Walter made some encouraging remarks which transformed my doubts about the quality of my work on 'Fenella' into joy and confi- dence.

Now, however, came the rehearsal in the presence of Gustav Mahler, who alone was to decide whether I should perform 'Fenella'. I went into Mahler's office with Bruno Walter, in a state of fearful expectancy. There I was standing in front of the man I admired so much and respected so deeply, to whom I wanted to show that the corps de ballet did not merely contain marionettes, as he liked to call us, but thinking and creative dancers.

Alfred Roller's presence helped me to overcome Gustav Mahler's nervous and decidedly discouraging manner, and with a deep sigh I cast aside my anxieties and doubts and performed the first scene. When I had finished, I scarcely heard Mahler's words of praise, but observed all the more intensely what he criticized. I left without knowing whether I had won or lost. But I was so tired and exhausted after such great exertion that I hardly cared.

Only a few days later I was called back to Alfred Roller, who gave me the good news that Gustav Mahler had chosen me for 'Fenella'. At the same time he told me not to tell anyone about the Director's decision, giving as his reason that in the Lord Chamberlain's office the ballet master would probably oppose my selection for the role, claiming that a principal actress suggested by him would perform the role far better than I, someone who did not even have the rank of soloist. Since Gustav Mahler did not wish to allow his ballet master to dictate the casting of 'La Muette', he sought to counter such dreary intrigues with an accomplished fact; so my first rehearsals with the singer were shrouded in secrecy.

No one up in the ballet studio knew about these rehearsals, least of all the ballet master, who included me in the dances he was rehearsing for *La Muette de Portici*, I had to dance in them in order not to give anything away.

There was a lot of speculation about who would play 'La Muette', and in the end everyone thought that the part had been assigned to Frau Gutheil-Schoder, whose great acting skill would probably have done justice to the part, which involved mime and nothing else.

The ballet master said nothing on the subject, but nonetheless seemed indignant, for as yet no one had requested him to rehearse a 'Fenella' selected from the corps de ballet.

The secret ensemble rehearsals with the soloist and myself were supervised by August Stoll, who must have thought I was very fragile, for he kept saying to Leo Slezak, who was singing the part of Masaniello: 'Please, be careful you don't squash her, she is just a wisp of girl!'

Slezak, who was a giant, laughed. He did his very best, and hardly dared to touch me.

Then the day of the first stage rehearsal arrived. We had already had a dance rehearsal in the ballet studio, and now we were told: 'all ballet soloists down to the stage!'

Everyone was standing on the stage waiting for the rehearsal to begin and chatting in an informal manner. The question of who was going to play 'La Muette' was now being asked openly, and my colleagues were also discussing it among themselves.

I stood waiting in the wings.

August Stoll, the director, appeared, explained the placing of all the participants, and then the rehearsal began.

All at once a loud voice rang out over the stage: 'The mute girl "Fenella", Grete Wiesenthal!' And there I was in the middle of the stage. Taken all of a sudden from the circle of my colleagues, I was only dimly aware of their amazement, jealousy and indignation, for as far as they were concerned I had no right to this important part.

I was too absorbed in my work on 'La Muette', and in the responsibility I felt was required to justify the extraordinary fact of my selection, to feel any pleasure about my victory over jealous colleagues, or the sensation. A sensation which reached a climax when the ballet master immediately tendered his resignation on account of the insult he had suffered. Nor did I become aware of the full meaning of this. For the time being

I had too much work to do, and was too excited about perfecting my role, and too young and tender to be able to grasp or enjoy so much at once.

The Lord Chamberlain's office naturally refused to accept the ballet master's resignation and decided to appease the artist, who had served the institution for so long, by allowing him to nominate his own 'Fenella', who in fact alternated with me in the performances that followed.

When I awoke the next morning, everyone in Vienna had heard of me. The ballet master's resignation was in all the papers, which mentioned Mahler's 'brusque' treatment of this 'deserving man' and of the outstanding career that awaited me.

And I? I went solemnly, and almost anxiously to the rehearsals, trying repeatedly to show Mahler, Roller and Bruno Walter that I was suited to the part of 'Fenella', one of the most taxing of miming roles.

I was full of enthusiasm and no effort was too great. At one of the final rehearsals they were trying out the height of the rock from which I was to jump into the sea, and while Roller was still asking me whether I thought the structure was too high, I had already jumped. I think I was so enthralled and enthusiastic at the time that I would have hurled myself into a real abyss.[6]

The young dancer, for whom this typically Viennese scandal marked the start of a brilliant career,[7] related that she had only understood how successful she had been when, backstage, she saw the enthusiasm of those of her colleagues who were her friends. In the heat of the moment the gigantic Slezak, who had taken so much care to be gentle with her during rehearsals, hugged her so vigorously that she almost fainted. Later, in the fifth act, when he was about to sing the Lullaby aria,[8] he asked her in a whisper to wish him luck.

The press reports differ slightly from Grete Wiesenthal's account, claiming that the girl had arrived late at the rehearsal of the corps de ballet on Saturday 16 February and had merely smiled when Hassreiter demanded to know the reason for her lack of punctuality. Ten minutes later, on the stage, he finally found out, and then had an altercation with Roller, who apparently retorted: 'But you're completely ignorant.'[9] It is easy to understand why Hassreiter, after

---

[6]   Grete Wiesenthal, *Der Aufstieg: Aus dem Leben einer Tänzerin* (Rowohlt, Berlin, 1919), 190 ff. and *Die ersten Schritte* (Agathon, Berlin, 1947), 181. Margarethe Wiesenthal (1885–1969), was born in Vienna, and with her sister Else, first engaged by the Hofoper at the age of 10. She left it after the *Muette* affair, and began to organize dance events at the Secessionist cabaret *Fledermaus*, using music by Beethoven, Schumann, etc. She was soon touring Europe and even the United States. She subsequently worked with Max Reinhardt and danced the role of the scullion in *Le Bourgeois Gentilhomme* by Hofmannsthal and Strauss (1912). After this she took part in two more Reinhardt productions and appeared regularly at the Salzburg Festival, where she danced in *Iphigénie en Aulide*, with Bruno Walter conducting, in 1930. She was also a noted choreographer, and taught at the Staatsakademie in Vienna. Between 1945 and 1956 a company named after her toured the world.

[7]   After 1908 Grete Wiesenthal became very popular with young painters, poets, and musicians on account of performances with her sisters Elsa and Berta, notably *Frühlingsstimmen* to music by Johann Strauss. Hugo von Hofmannsthal wrote for her the ballet scenarios of *Die Biene* and *Amor und Psyche*, which were produced at the Munich Opera, and *Das Fremde Mädchen* which was performed in Berlin. In 1908 Franz Schreker composed the pantomime *Der Geburtstag der Infantin* and the ballet *Der Wind* for her (EWL 61).

[8]   Act IV, no. 13 in the Branders vocal score: 'Du pauvre ami fidèle, descends à ma voix qui t'appelle.'

[9]   *Deutsche Zeitung* (19 Feb. 1907).

thirty-seven years at the Opera, twenty of them as head of the ballet, thought that he deserved more respect and immediately tendered his resignation, not to the director, but to the Lord Chamberlain. In general the press held Roller primarily responsible for this unfortunate affair, claiming that he wanted to direct all of the Opera's choreography, as in the case of the ballet *Rübezahl* of which he had written the scenario and hoped to produce the work himself at the end of the season.[10]

Leo Slezak tried to ease the tension by declaring backstage that a male actor would be perfect for the role of Fenella and that, since his doctors had ordered him to rest his voice,[11] he could make a very good job of it himself.[12] But the quarrel was too bitter to be assuaged by a joke. Each day Hassreiter spoke to the press, which was only too happy to be able to exploit a new 'scandal' so soon after the one provoked by Mahler's absences. Everything the ballet master said was at once reported, with the obvious intention of aggravating the situation. Hassreiter declared that he refused to be 'made ridiculous in front of the corps de ballet'.[13] Having been ballet master for the last twenty years,[14] he had suffered long enough from Mahler's contempt for his art. This was the last straw. The Prince immediately summoned the director and rebuked him rather sharply. Mahler did his best to defend Roller, but the Prince refused to give way: 'This is the first time you have defended a breach of the rules. My conscience as a civil servant will not allow me to support you in that.'[15] To appease Hassreiter, whom he could not allow to leave, the Prince persuaded him to agree to a compromise solution in which the Opera's principal actress, Kamilla Weigang played the role of Fenella alternately with Wiesenthal.[16]

The revival of *La Muette de Portici* at the end of February 1907 was only moderately successful. Wallaschek wrote that the singers at the Vienna Opera had 'lost the feeling for the vocal style of Auber's time', and that Bruno Walter's conducting was 'inadequate'. The performance as a whole aroused only 'slight

---

[10] See below.   [11] See above, Chaps. 7 and 8.   [12] *Fremden-Blatt* (17 Feb. 1907).

[13] *Die Zeit* (15 Feb. 1907).

[14] For seventeen years prior to this Hassreiter had been principal dancer. His resignation was announced in the *Neue Freie Presse* and *Die Zeit* on 18 Feb. 1907 and in the *Deutsche Zeitung* the following day. On 19 Feb. the *Illustrirtes Extrablatt* announced that he had been replaced by the deputy ballet master, Karl Godlevsky. Alma Mahler gives a largely inaccurate account of the incident, stating that Mahler had given Roller the right to produce a ballet (this clearly refers to *Rübezahl*) and that the latter had often summoned the corps de ballet to his office for rehearsals. Thus on one occasion Hassreiter 'found himself in an empty hall' (AMM1, 148; AMM2, 145). In AML, Alma also cites the quarrel with Hassreiter as the principal reason for Mahler's departure (AML 141).

[15] AMM1, 148; AMM2, 145.

[16] HOA, Z. 1041s/1907, letter dated 11 Mar. This stipulates that in addition to her salary every dancer is to receive a supplement of 50 kronen for each performance. Mahler had already clashed with Hassreiter in 1902 over the renewal of his contract, offering him a two-year one instead of the promised six-year one. Moreover he had asked him, without increasing his salary, to undertake the training of solo dancers and ballerinas, and in fact proposed to reduce his annual salary from 6,000 to 5,000 gulden in view of the fact that he could easily earn at least of 1,000 gulden (2,000 kronen) from private lessons. Hassreiter took the view that the lessons did not concern the Opera, and that he deserved the 1,000 gulden if he was to assume responsibility for training the dancers. It seems that he had his way. (Letter from Hassreiter to Mahler, 15 June 1902, HOA, Z. 399/1902.)

interest' despite the excellent staging.[17] Alfred Kauders, in the *Fremden-Blatt*, was less critical concerning Bruno Walter's conducting, 'which was marked by vigour and meticulous care',[18] but Hirschfeld once again pointed out the inadequacy of the Viennese singers and what he considered to be the excessive importance accorded to the decorative element. Hedwig von Friedländer-Abel, in the *Montags-Revue*, seems to have been totally overwhelmed by Grete Wiesenthal.

Her movements never reminded one of the ballet school. Each time we see a really talented mime performance it stirs in us a longing for a kind of ballet which is not absurd and which offers genuine talents an opportunity to unfold. Miss Wiesenthal is certainly not the only one whose abilities have been concealed.[19]

La Muette de Portici was performed only five times in 1907. However, Hassreiter's outburst, his quarrel with Roller, and Grete Wiesenthal's undoubted talent attracted enough attention to make her a star overnight. However grave the breach of professional etiquette, Mahler and his stage designer had spotted a winner. According to Kauders, she immediately convinced the spectators.

that she would overcome every disadvantage, that she would succeed despite her insignificant appearance, her youth, her diminutive stature and her slender figure. She was a success; and she enthralled the audience. And the most disturbing thing, her slender figure proved to be of help. For one saw the most delicate muscles at work in her face, her hands, her fingers. Miss Wiesenthal struck poses that may have been conceived as stylized, but in fact looked natural.

Bruno Walter conducted the performance. Many years later he recalled:

In Auber's *La Muette de Portici* the actress playing Fenella has the difficult task of coordinating her movements precisely with the music while appearing continually to act in a very lively and emotional manner. I can confirm from personal experience that a very sensitive artist with a gift for music and drama, the dancer Grete Wiesenthal, succeeded, in the performance of the work which I conducted at the Vienna Opera, in coordinating the musical and rhythmic requirements of the role with its dramatic and emotional content, which she expressed in a very touching way. However, she could only achieve this because, while acting very precisely, she treated the dramatic aspect as the most important part of her task.[20]

Once again Mahler and Roller had achieved an artistic triumph and also revealed the hidden talent of a rare artist. Yet both were to pay dearly for this

---

[17]   Wallaschek noted that Mahler had restored a scene with Elvire and Alfonso at the beginning of Act III. He found Slezak's voice much 'too lyrical' for the role of Masaniello, a surprising statement in view of the fact that he was singing heroic roles more frequently, and that Eugène d'Harcourt writes the exact opposite in his book (see below). Hirschfeld criticized Slezak's 'lack of style'.

[18]   Kauders was full of praise for Grete Wiesenthal's 'captivating and prodigious' performance.

[19]   Hedwig von Friedländer-Abel (see above, Chap. 7) also praised the chorus and Bruno Walter, who conducted 'with fire and a precision that did justice to every detail'.

[20]   Bruno Walter, *Von der Musik und vom Musizieren* (Fischer, Frankfurt, 1957, 1976 edn.), 195. See also BMG 129.

achievement. In her memoirs Grete Wiesenthal states that Prince Montenuovo shared Mahler's earlier view, considering that any 'intellectualization' of the dance was doomed to failure. Thus he was quite satisfied with Hassreiter's traditional style and recalled that one day the ballet master had told the assembled dancers that the director planned to make as little use of the ballet as possible. 'Some of the company were indignant, and some listened with indifference, and some perhaps thought that it had an attractive and easy side.'[21]

If Mahler's contempt for the ballet had continued unabated, there would have been no conflict, and Hassreiter's antiquated performances would have continued to satisfy an audience made up of reactionary habitués. Unfortunately the influence of Roller and the Secession had indeed made him realize that artistic truths could be revealed through the medium of dance, and his first attempts at reform unleashed storms of protests and undermined his authority. In March, Mahler gave Grete Wiesenthal and her sister Elsa important roles in the 'Dance of the Priestesses' in Gluck's *Iphigénie en Aulide*. But for a dancer with character the disadvantages of belonging to the Opera's corps de ballet, especially after having incurred the wrath of its master, Hassreiter, were only too obvious. After five years she had merely secured a modest success in the small role of the black woman in the ballet *Excelsior*. As soon as *La Muette* disappeared from the repertoire she was once more 'neglected', and even demoted by Hassreiter, who wanted to show her that the Director's wishes were of no importance when it came to ballet. Thus she called on Mahler in mid-April, and, pointing out that she had received only a very modest fee for the performances of *La Muette* in which she had participated, asked to be promoted to soloist, if nothing else.[22] Mahler was surely unable to accede to her request and thus on 2 May she and her sister Elsa decided to terminate their contracts.[23] Hassreiter agreed with alacrity. On each of the two letters he wrote: 'The undersigned has not attended dancing lessons for the last eight and a half months and has very much neglected her career as a dancer, which is a great pity, for she is very talented.' However, Grete Wiesenthal owed her brilliant career and her later artistic achievements to this resignation.

Mahler told Eugène d'Harcourt, the French critic who was studying the state of music in Austria and Germany, not to regard this production of *La Muette de Portici* 'as typical of what we are doing at the Hofoper' for it was in fact an old production, and had been hastily revived:[24]

In general, the strings play Auber's music with only a few centimetres of bow, almost invariably '*saltato*', and the woodwinds are continually dying away. No doubt under the

[21] Grete Wiesenthal, *Der Aufstieg*, 139.

[22] HOA, G.Z. 431/1532/1907, letter dated 14 Apr. 1907.   [23] HOA, G.Z. 526/1907.

[24] The work had not been in the repertoire for nineteen years. In order to refurbish the sets and design the new costumes Roller merely asked for 6,000 kronen, which came out of the 20,000 kronen set aside for revivals (letter dated 16 Feb., HOA, Z. 698s/1907). Two days later he requested a supplement of 700 kronen for the stage-hands' overtime during the rehearsals (HOA, Z. 741s/1907, letter dated 18 Feb.).

pretext of lightness, the playing is jerky and abrupt. Furthermore, the superb crescendos of the overture are non-existent, whereas the 'vulgar' tone of the percussion section, Auber's weakness, is clearly exaggerated. The poor quality of the performance did not prevent the audience from applauding rather loudly.[25]

The critic singled out, among the 'pearls of the performance', the prayer in Act IV, which was sung by the chorus 'with a perfection and a moving tenderness impossible to surpass: it was remarkable on account of its sonority, its polish and its impeccable precision: and that superb final chord swelling, and then dying away, with its low E flat minor tonic.'[26] While the revival of *La Muette* was not the best that the Vienna Opera had to offer at the time, given the economies Mahler and Roller were forced to make, it was surely a far cry from the inadequate rendering which their enemies claimed it to be. However, the work disappeared from the repertoire after five performances.

According to Alma Mahler, the conflict between Hassreiter and Roller and the fact that Mahler insisted on supporting his designer persuaded Prince Montenuovo to part company with him. But the sequence of events which led to his resignation was in fact complex. As we have seen, for some time the Prince had disapproved of the Director's concert tours and absences. But there had been other things about which they disagreed. To begin with, Mahler could not resign himself to the censor's ban on *Salome*, which he considered to be a personal insult. Furthermore, when the time came to renew the contract of the tenor Fritz Schrödter, whose voice had lost most of its brilliance,[27] Mahler recommended that in the interests of the Opera his salary should be reduced. It seems that his relations with Schrödter had always been strained, and that this antagonism was a well-known fact, which is illustrated by the following anecdote related in the musical gossip column of the *Extrablatt*: 'Director Mahler sees Schrödter, and *rushes* up to him: "How are you? What have you been doing? I haven't seen you for a long time!" Schrödter: "You're making a mistake, Director, my name is Schrödter." '[28] The tenor put up a spirited defence, intriguing in every possible way to ensure that the conditions of his former contract remained unchanged, calling to his

---

[25] Eugène d'Harcourt, *La Musique actuelle en Allemagne et en Autriche-Hongrie* (Durdilly, Paris, 1908), 151. Like Wallaschek, Harcourt felt that the famous duet 'Amour sacré' had been sung without warmth, and he recalled the performance by Villaret and Lasalle thirty years before at the Paris Opera, when the audience had gone into raptures. He thought that the Barcarolle in Act II had been 'shouted rather than sung', and that the tempo was too slow. He also noted that Mahler refused to allow the famous duet to be sung near the prompt box, and stated that the role of Masaniello did not suit Slezak's 'natural resources'. However, he admitted that his performance of the 'Lullaby' aria was 'a triumph of skill and sleight-of-hand' and based on a 'mixture of head and chest voice'. 'The abundance of feeling and the exquisite nuances easily outweighed the artificiality of his interpretation.'

[26] Cast for the performance of 27 Feb. 1907: Elizza (Elvire); Wiesenthal (Fenella); Maikl (Alfonso); Slezak (Masaniello); and Mayr (Pietro).

[27] Mahler had nevertheless engaged Schrödter to sing 'Revelge' for the three concerts of his Lieder he had conducted: in Vienna on 29 Jan. and 3 Feb., and in Graz on 1 June 1905.

[28] *Illustrirtes Wiener Extrablatt* (1 Nov. 1907).

defence powerful advocates such as Katharina Schratt, the mistress of the Emperor,[29] and Princess Hohenlohe, the widow of the former High Chamberlain.[30] It was obvious that he would use Mahler's known dislike of him to depict himself as one of his victims.

However, Mahler decided not to drop the issue. He could not allow the budget of the Opera to incur unnecessary expenditure at a time when he had been refused the grants needed to stage the last two parts of the *Ring*.[31] After all, Schrödter was not only well past his prime, he was notoriously unmusical,[32] and had also been booed twice recently, in *Les Contes d'Hoffmann* and in *Die Königin von Saba*.[33] Furthermore, Mahler knew that Schrödter had been boasting about his influence behind the scenes, and that he had sworn that he would defeat the Director.[34]

The tension generated by this dispute, compounded by the conflict between Roller and Hassreiter, had already clouded the atmosphere at the Opera when a third incident occurred which Alma describes as follows:

Mahler was in the habit of noting his own appointments in the big ledger used for the Opera repertoire. Under the heading 'After Easter' he simply wrote: 'Rome, three concerts'. Yet he had only been granted leave for Easter week, and from Rome Mahler had intended to ask for a short extension (for the third concert).[35] However, malevolent officials arranged for the ledger to be seen by the Prince, who immediately sent for Mahler. He started by telling him that the Opera's takings deteriorated whenever he was away. Fortunately, Mahler was able to prove then and there that the opposite was the case. But their conversation became rather heated, and thus they agreed to think about Mahler's resignation.[36]

Alma Mahler's archives contain a letter from Prince Montenuovo written on 14 March,[37] which makes it possible to date this stormy interview. Montenuovo thanks the director of the Opera for letting him know his 'desiderata' in the event of resignation, and assures him that 'he will consider them favourably, when the time comes to submit them to the supreme authority [i.e. the Emperor]'. Thus the letter Alma included in her *Erinnerungen*[38] was obviously written by Mahler straight after this conversation, which took place on 10 March. It confirms that the end of Mahler's tenure was envisaged from that

---

[29] David Ewen, *Music Comes to America* (Allen, Towne & Heath, New York, 1947), 98, states that Schrödter had been a protégé of Katharina Schratt for some time.

[30] See above, Chap. 8.   [31] *Leipziger Neueste Nachrichten* (20 May 1911).

[32] WLE 195.   [33] *Montags-Revue* (9 June 1907).

[34] *Österreichische Volkszeitung* (14 June 1907). The article by Balduin Bricht mentioned the tenor's 'comings and goings' and his 'demands', and claimed that Mahler, who had resigned as a result of this incident, had suggested 'appointing a director more in accordance with the wishes of Schrödter'.

[35] In fact, the letters to the impresario Norbert Salter cited below prove that Mahler agreed to conduct only two concerts a week apart, and that he was planning to return to Vienna two days after Easter. As the theatre was always closed from Tuesday to Easter Saturday, he always left the capital at this time every year.

[36] AMM1, 148; AMM2, 145.

[37] AMS and UPL.

[38] AMM1, 405. There is a slightly different draft in Alma Mahler's archives (ibid.). The letter was undoubtedly written before the summer, for Mahler mentions his *two* children.

day on and that the Prince had also asked him to state the conditions under which he would agree to leave his post.

Mahler now enumerated these conditions, no doubt after having consulted his friend, the lawyer Emil Freund. They included an increase in the pension to which he was entitled after ten years' work (from 11,000 to 14,000 kronen, the latter being the amount that he could normally have claimed after thirteen years);[39] a grant of 20,000 kronen to cover removal expenses, for he would have to leave Vienna;[40] and, on his death, a pension for his family in accordance with the statutes of the Opera. He concluded by noting: 'I myself would not wish to justify my claims by adducing the support of arguments based on the nature of my work and the way in which I have carried out my duties for ten years (and these one could certainly call "war years").'[41]

Thus the possibility of Mahler's departure had not only been broached as early as March 1907, but examined in some detail. Yet it is true that at this time the two men could still have come to an agreement, having decided to keep the matter secret. Mahler left for Rome without saying a word to anyone about his conversation with the Prince. But the idea of leaving the Vienna Opera had begun to take root. He probably considered it while he was in Italy, and soon began to see the advantages involved. It would allow him to lead a quieter life, to compose in peace for several months of the year, and to earn more money for his family. However, for the time being it was only a vague plan; as the Emperor's employee, he could only be relieved of his post at the behest of the sovereign.

Leaving Schalk to conduct the second performance of *Iphigénie* on 23 March, Mahler left for Rome with Alma on 19 March the day after the première. Scarcely an hour after leaving Vienna the train stopped suddenly on the Semmering Pass in the middle of nowhere. Alma, like most of the other passengers, got out of bed. In the end the silence and the fact that the train was no longer moving also woke Mahler, though he soon fell asleep again despite the general commotion going on around him. Another breakdown, later on, further delayed the passengers, who missed their connection and the sleeping car for which they had made reservations. After this series of misadventures, they arrived in the Italian capital to find that all their luggage, which contained their clothes and the orchestral material for the concert, was missing. The combined efforts of the Austrian ambassador, Count Lützow, and Count San Martino, director of the Academy of Santa Cecilia, were of no avail, and Mahler

---

[39] Mahler stated that he had to provide for his family's future and 'build a house' in the country or enlarge the villa at Maiernigg.

[40] He pointed out that during his first six months in Vienna, Jahn had received his full salary whereas he, as a director, was earning only 5,000 kronen a month.

[41] The text of Mahler's letter to Prince Montenuovo was published in AMM1, 405 ff. It is undated, but in a handwritten note Prince Montenuovo (UPL) Mahler acknowledges receipt of the letter and promises 'dass ich dieselben [Mahler's desiderata] gewiss mit dem allergrössten Wohlwollen prüfen werde wenn der Moment gekommen sein wird dieselbe an Ah. [allerhöchsten] Stelle anzumelden.' The note is dated 14 Mar. 1907.

had to resign himself to using scores from the library and for several days to wearing clothes bought locally. Instead of the fine shirts he usually wore, he had to go around with stiff collared ones which made him look 'like a candidate for Confirmation'.[42]

Pope Sixtus V had founded the Congregation of Musicians of Rome under the order of Saint Cecilia in 1585. It had been granted the title of Accademia by Gregory XIV in 1839, and had become increasingly important during the nineteenth century. Count Enrico di San Martino, a rich aristocrat from Turin, was elected president in 1895. Although not himself a musician, he was a passionate music-lover and a talented administrator. For some years, Count San Martino had been searching for an adequate and permanent hall for the orchestral concerts of the Accademia, which had until then been held either in the small hall of the Accademia, or in the Teatro Argentina, or the Teatro Adriano. In 1907 he had decided to remodel the Teatro Corea into the 3,000-seat Angusteo, which was to be opened in 1908. Thus Mahler's 1907 concerts took place in the small hall of the Accademia itself.[43]

The principal aim of the journey was not to conduct in Rome, but to visit the Eternal City, whose monuments had been dear to the heart of every nineteenth-century German. Between rehearsals, Mahler methodically toured the sights, and had as his guide the German historian Friedrich Spiro,[44] whose wife, Assia Spiro-Rombro, was a correspondent for the *Musikalisches Wochenblatt*.[45] According to Alma, Spiro knew every stone in Rome and its history, especially in the Roman forum. Mahler took a particular fancy to the Via Appia, which he liked to visit between rehearsals: 'I noted,' Alma remarked, 'that Mahler saw everything more from the literary and historical point of view than as nature in all its truth.'[46]

Two letters which Mahler sent to the impresario Norbert Salter suggest that it took him a long time to make up his mind about his two programmes. Assia Spiro-Rombro's article for the *Musikalisches Wochenblatt* shows that he had considered the Third Symphony,[47] and had abandoned the idea because of the

---

[42]   On 19 Apr., the *Wiener Theatergeschichten* column of the *Illustrirtes Wiener Extrablatt* reported Mahler's difficulties and finished by asking what, if his scores had also been stolen, 'the thieves could possibly do with this music'.

[43]   *Il Messagero* (22 Sept. 1988), 14. Count San Martino remained a leading figure in Italian musical life until his death in 1947. A year after Mahler's visit he made a decisive contribution to the establishment of a permanent symphony orchestra and chorus, which gave concerts in the Augusteo (formerly Teatro Corea), a hall seating more than 3,000 listeners. Until then, the concerts had taken place in two different Roman theatres, Teatro Argentina and Teatro Adriano.

[44]   See Christa Maria Rock and Hans Brückner (eds.), *Judentum und Musik* (Hans Brückner, Munich, 1938). Born in Berlin in 1863, Friedrich Spiro was a professor of music, and his wife, Assia Spiro-Rombro, a violinist, born in Kagalnik near Rostov in the Ukraine in 1873. According to Professor Karl Spiro (University of Basle), Friedrich Spiro's grand-nephew, the latter went to live in Rome before the First World War, and continued to teach music there.

[45]   In 1906 Assia Spiro-Rombro wrote a review for the same journal of the Salzburg Festival (see above, Chap. 6).   [46]   AMM1, 150; AMM2, 146.

[47]   Mahler had written to Friedrich Spiro, probably at the beginning of the year, to ask what he thought about the possibility of performing the Third. 'I am sending you a miniature score, and I'm already very

lack of an adequate chorus and the difficulty of finding a soloist. Mahler finally drew up a programme of classical works, adding to each concert 'an excerpt from one of my symphonies that can be played in more easily by the orchestra and that will not make things too difficult for an audience unfamiliar with my style'.[48] For the first concert he chose two movements from the Second Symphony,[49] and for the second the two final movements of the Fifth, asking for the score and parts to be sent to him in Vienna so that he could make further changes before taking them to Rome. As *pièces de résistance* he envisaged Beethoven's 'Eroica' and Fifth for the first concert and Schumann's First for the second.[50]

Shortly afterwards Mahler wondered if it might not be better to give two wholly classical programmes dominated by Beethoven and Wagner,[51] and to perform one of his own compositions later during a second visit. He demanded a minimum of four rehearsals for the first concert, but for the time being the plans to perform his own music had been thwarted by the loss of his luggage, which contained the scores and the parts. For the classical works Mahler had surely brought along, as he always did, his own parts with his own markings, and he was forced rather reluctantly to use the parts belonging to the Santa Cecilia Orchestra. Naturally the programme he had now made up consisted of works that did not need a large number of changes.[52]

Five days after Mahler and Alma had arrived in Rome, the luggage was still missing and it now became necessary to find clothes for Mahler to conduct in:

For the first concert, which promised to be something of a sensation, Mahler had to borrow a tailcoat. Unfortunately it had been made for a tall man and Mahler looked like a little boy in his grandfather's dressing gown. The German proprietor of the boarding house in which we were staying because it was inexpensive offered to lend him his own tailcoat. Unfortunately an enormous star was sewn on the front. It was the badge of an athletics club of the kind worn by honest Germans from Cologne. However, it would have looked very odd on the podium. It was difficult to convince the man that the star made it impossible to use the tailcoat, and he went off in a huff. So I turned

curious to know how you will deal with the task—which seems to me extraordinarily difficult—of translating *Des Knaben Wunderhorn* into Italian! . . . Do they have valve trombones in Rome, or do they have slide trombones? In case of the latter I should have to bring along a trombonist from here for the big solo in the first movement!' (undated letter to Spiro, BGM, Paris).

[48]　Undated letter to Norbert Salter (*c.* Jan./Feb. 1906) numbered 6 by the addressee.

[49]　No doubt the second and third movements.

[50]　Undated letters to Norbert Salter (Jan.–Feb. 1907, BSM, Munich). The recipient wrote the number six on this letter.

[51]　In a second letter to Friedrich Spiro (probably written in Mar. 1907) Mahler stated that he had at first chosen 'ein "Parade" Program', replacing Beethoven's Fifth with the Seventh, and the *Leonore* Overture with *Coriolan*, preferring to play well-known and often performed works he knew in view of the short time and small number of rehearsals at his disposal (BGM, Paris).

[52]　The musical journal *Ars e Labor* (i, year 62, 15 May 1907) published five pictures taken on the occasion of Mahler's concert: three taken in the hall, Mahler rehearsing; the audience at the concert; the royal box with the queen Mother; Mahler in the secretary's office at the Accademia Santa Cecilia, probably marking the scores for the concerts; and Mahler asking his way in a Roman street. Only the photo of Mahler marking his score was reproduced in RBM no. 58.

my attention to the big tailcoat. I shortened the sleeves and the trouser legs, and intended to sew up the flies, which were completely open (I do not wish to say exactly where) but Mahler would have none of it. So I fastened the flies from the inside with a large gold pin, the only one I had at hand. I warned Mahler before the concert that he should not touch it. As usual he went ahead to see that everything was in order, i.e. the parts, the seating arrangements and so on. I arrived shortly before the concert, but just in time to prevent a catastrophe: the pin was no longer where it should have been, and had become very visible. I put it right, and Mahler laughed as he climbed on to the podium.[53]

In the end the programme for the concert on 15 March 1907 consisted of three classical works: Beethoven's 'Eroica' Symphony, the 'Prelude and Liebestod' from *Tristan* and the Prelude to *Die Meistersinger*. According to Count San Martino, the orchestra was exhausted as a result of overwork in municipal concerts, academic concerts, and theatrical productions. In fact, the Roman audience had been particularly conscious of this at a municipal concert the previous day. Thus the next day it was astonished to find the same orchestra galvanized by Mahler's baton, and playing 'with a rare perfection that took care of the smallest detail'. Like many others before him, Count San Martino was greatly impressed by Mahler's 'extraordinarily effective gestures'; made 'not only with his hands, but with his ten fingers, his eyes, and his whole body, turning to each instrument in order to encourage or tone it down'.[54] The concert was a tremendous success, although Mahler's interpretations were found unusual, causing animated discussion as the audience left after the concert.[55] During the interval Margherita, the Queen Mother, invited Mahler to her box in order to congratulate him. She talked about the disappearance of his trunk, and even offered to help him find it.[56] According to the *Messagero*, the audience was enthusiastic about Mahler's conducting technique and his 'sober, correct and effective movements', as well as 'the epic, grand, and intensely passionate spirit of the master of the symphony [Beethoven]' which he had evoked in the 'Eroica'. The reviews were for the most part unenlightened. Only Nicola d'Atri,[57] in *Giornale d'Italia*, made an effort to describe his impressions and to analyse the 'unexpected and unusual' aspects of these interpretations, which 'demonstrated the undeniable individuality of the artist'. He admired

---

[53] AMM1, 150; AMM2, 146.

[54] Accademia nazionale di Santa Cecilia, *I concerti dal 1895 al 1933*, 1. Ricordi del presidente (Manuzio, Rome, 1933), 70 ff. [55] According to Nicola d'Atri (see below).

[56] On 23 Mar. The Mahlers' luggage apparently had still not arrived, for Alma writes to Justine: 'Wir haben viel Missgeschick unser Gepäcke zu kriegen.' (Rosé collection, UWO, Shelfmark E12-Ajp-513.)

[57] Nicola d'Atri (1866–1955), was born in Lucera (Foggia). In 1901 he helped to found the *Giornale d'Italia*, and was its music critic for thirteen years. From 1914 to 1916 he was personal secretary to Antonio Salandra, the President of the Council (Prime Minister), who was also a close friend. Through him he was able to persuade the City of Rome to buy the Augusteo Hall and rebuild it for the orchestral concerts of which he was one of the principal initiators. In 1913 he became a member of the Accademia Santa Cecilia, and its concert committee, and in 1954 he succeeded Bernardino Molinari as its vice-president. D'Atri was a man of culture and great discernment, and until his death he never ceased to influence artistic life in Rome.

the simplicity, honesty, and sobriety of his conducting, as opposed to the kind of gesticulation favoured by most Italian and German conductors. Under his baton the Roman orchestra had become 'a vigorous and perfectly balanced organism', and from this emanated its innate power, and, where necessary, its vigour and energy. 'We have never heard more sustained *pianos* and *fortes*, or more extraordinary string sonorities,' he continued, 'we have never been more conscious of the consummate technique of an ultra-modern conductor, who can elicit an infinite number of different effects and use them solely as a means of expression, and always in the service of the work.'

D'Atri remarked that the interpretation of the 'Eroica' had caused some surprise, despite its effectiveness. Mahler seemed to be saying: 'This is the way I feel Beethoven, I have made him come alive for you, and now you can go and discuss traditions and everything else among yourselves.' After recalling that Wagner had advocated a much freer interpretation of Beethoven than his predecessors, the Roman critic added: 'The essential thing is that the artist's feeling is pure. Does Mahler go too far? Is he too excessive at times? Perhaps he is, but in fact Beethoven in his works revealed that he was a "monster of excess" with regard to sentiment and sensibility, and was defined as such by the divine Wagner, who proceeded to outdo him. It is a fault, but the happy fault of an interpreter who, by sinning thus, affirms his character as an artist.'

The other accounts were lacking in substance. *La Capitale* thought that 'Gustav Mahler is in truth everything an artist should be: an artist by temperament, by nature and by culture'; and that his interpretation was 'powerful and suggestive'. *Avanti*, the newspaper of the Italian socialist party, believed that Mahler knew how to 'extract surprising and unforgettable effects from the most secret recesses of the orchestra, with renewed vigour. *Il Popolo Romano* thought that Mahler was 'a musician of rare skill, who conducted in a clear, even obvious, energetic and assured manner, who dominated the orchestra and elicited striking effects and shadings. He fully justifies the fame he has achieved in his relatively short career.' And finally *Il Messagero* reported that the whole audience rose spontaneously and applauded at the end of the concert. 'Visibly moved', Mahler was called back to the stage a number of times.

Mahler's luggage finally arrived before the second concert, which took place a week after the first (again at four in the afternoon). He now made a last-minute change, substituting the Adagietto of his own Fifth Symphony for the Dance of the Sylphs from Berlioz's *La Damnation de Faust*.[58] This came after Tchaikovsky's *Romeo and Juliet* and Weber's *Euryanthe* overture, and was followed by Beethoven's Seventh Symphony. On this occasion the audience included several members of the royal family and high aristocracy who had not attended the first concert, not only the Queen Mother, but also the dowager

[58] The piece did not appear in early announcements of the programme, nor in the volume published by the Accademia Santa Cecilia in 1915.

Duchess of Genoa and the Princess of Montenegro. According to *La Tribuna*, the applause was not quite as loud as before—the audience was slightly less enthusiastic, despite 'the great expressive power and vivid colours' which characterized the performance of *Romeo and Juliet*. It also described the Adagietto as 'an elegant and melodious fragment, not particularly original in regard to form or content'. In Beethoven's Seventh Symphony the anonymous critic emphasized not only the 'expressive elasticity of the rhythm', the 'rich colouring', and the 'striking contrast' in the Allegretto, but also the nervousness of the orchestra, 'which followed the movements of Mahler's baton less faithfully' than the week before, so that the performance was less effective than that of the 'Eroica'.

Nicola d'Atri wrote only a rather lukewarm paragraph about the second concert in the conservative *Giornale d'Italia*, claiming that the programme was less interesting and the performances less precise than the week before. On the other hand, the socialist newspaper *Avanti* believed that 'the vibrant performance of Beethoven's Seventh saw the interpreter almost continually on the same sublime heights as its creator'. Although Alma does not say so, it is likely that the rehearsals with a tired and mediocre orchestra (Mahler was to become even more aware of this three years later) were difficult and that his fundamentally German sense of discipline caused a certain amount of friction. This was surely the reason why the performance was not on the same level as the one the previous week.

The most substantial account of the two concerts was written by Assia Spiro-Rombro[59] for the *Musikalisches Wochenblatt*:

Everything one would like to say, everything that one feels and experiences, is so different, so dissimilar, so divergent from everything encountered before that one cannot find words to describe it. Usually, in hearing this or that work, one is grateful simply if the performer does it justice and performs it faultlessly, as it is, but with Mahler things are quite different. He does not simply present the work to us, he draws and paints all the deepest and hidden aspects of the character of the composer whose work he is conducting. He permits us to share his impressions, experiences, joys and sufferings. He gives us his portrait, transports us to dionysian ecstasy, making us feel that we are experiencing these revelations for the first time.

Assia Spiro-Rombro went on to describe the characters of Weber and Tchaikovsky as Mahler had depicted them in his Roman concerts, and added: 'And then again the all-shattering, all-reconciling, all-embracing, tender, great, powerful, loving, all-seeing, all-commanding genius of Beethoven, we saw it with such clarity![60] All that one had imagined as ideal, all that one had

---

[59] Assia Spiro-Rombro later lived in Basle, travelling each summer to Lucerne for the master classes given by her friend, the pianist Edwin Fischer.

[60] *Musikalisches Wochenblatt*, 38 (1907): 28, 622. Since the preceding year, the *Wochenblatt* had merged with the *Neue Zeitschrift für Musik*. Assia Spiro-Rombro added that 'for the first time the construction of the finale of the *Eroica Symphony* became perfectly clear, the floating, dancing web of multicoloured variations that flutters and soars to the tragic crisis and finishes in a frenzy'.

wished, that one had suspected, even that which one had not suspected, was conjured up in front of one's eyes.'

The enthusiasm of this enlightened listener surely did little to dispel Mahler's feeling of frustration. He was certainly captivated by the art treasures of the Italian capital, although letters describing his impressions do not seem to have survived. But from a musical point of view, it is clear that the orchestra was not good enough to satisfy all his requirements. Furthermore he still had a long way to go to gain a footing in Italy as a composer. However, he does not seem to have been unduly disappointed, for three years later he accepted another engagement.

On the return journey Mahler had been invited by Enrico Schott to stop in Trieste where, on the evening of 4 April, he conducted, this time at the Teatro Comunale Giuseppe Verdi, built in 1801 and inspired by La Scala in Milan, a programme comprising of Wagner's Prelude to *Die Meistersinger*, his own First Symphony, and Beethoven's Fifth Symphony.

Curiously enough, the *Triester Zeitung* did not review the concert. It nevertheless published a report of Mahler's arrival from Rome on the evening of 2 April after a twenty-four-hour train ride and his starting to rehearse at the theatre less than one hour later. Like many previous reviewers, the author of the unsigned article comments on the rapid and totally fascinating way in which he taught the orchestra to execute every one of his intentions and the 'thousand subtleties' of his orchestration. He had apparently complimented the local conductor, Maestro Cantoni, on the preparatory work he had already carried out.

Most of the Italian newspapers carried reviews of the concert. The *Osservatore Triestino* remembered Mahler's December 1905 visit, when his Fifth Symphony had 'disconcerted' the public. After the First Symphony, its enthusiasm had been spontaneously expressed: 'The immediate impact is undoubtedly due to the rich melodic content which pleases, captivates and strikes emotive chords. . . . The "symphony" is a tone poem of great descriptive power, in which inventive genius goes hand in hand with a wise and knowledgeable development.' *L'Indipendente* suggested that Mahler's 'strange personality, harnessing such energies, evoking such passions and impressions as burst forth from a restless perception reflecting our agitated life', had been the subject of many debates in Trieste. The *Meistersinger* Prelude had been conducted 'with verve and *esprit*' and Beethoven's Fifth 'sculpted with vehement strokes, hammered out with fiery impetuosity, releasing a new life form from the Colossus's stone'.

According to *Il Gazzettino*, from the very first bars of the Wagner Prelude, 'a quiver of admiration ran through an audience enthralled by that impetuous momentum, by the energy with which the conductor infused into the orchestra all his soul, intellect and emotion'. A 'composer of genius, powerful, a daring representative of the modern school', the composer of the First Symphony was praised for 'his total mastery of orchestration, the technique—sometimes extravagant—the texture, the vibrant colouring'. The longest and most substantial, although unsigned, review was that carried by *Il Piccolo*. The First Symphony had been far more successful than the Fifth eighteen months earlier, but the public had been wrong—the Fifth was far superior to the First. The article praised the long initial pedal, 'insistent, immobile as a colour in the sky', and elsewhere the 'robust density of orchestral colouring', the 'bold and undisguised contrasts of colours and of instruments'. He found the popular nature of certain themes 'an all-too-bizarre surprise': 'within the eruptive work-ings of the orchestra, resembling an intensive and tormented labouring of the brain, the folk tunes seem to have an exaggeratedly naive spirit, too plain and rudimentary'. According to this critic, Mahler as a composer was a typical product of his epoch:

There remains this strange alchemist of ideas, who is not assuaged until the orchestra responds to the rhythm and tremor of his imagination; there remains the complex and tempestuous essence of the modern age, the vast vision, a whirlwind of activity, advancing fitfully, tracing its fragmented trail, storming the skies, but with breathless anxiety at times reaching the most bitter and heartbreaking despair.

In the interpretation of Beethoven's Fifth Symphony, the same critic noted 'a solemn and shining serenity'. Unfortunately, the moderate tempo of the Finale 'does not rise to . . . that overwhelming impression of being projected into the infinite which had on other occasions electrified the audience'.

According to the musical journal *L'Arte*, the Scherzo and Finale of Mahler's Symphony were more successful than the other movements. The critic rejected the negative judgements of his Viennese colleagues who discerned in his music only 'a morbid and corrupted spirit, the imbalance of a fevered brain'. In the First Symphony, he had heard instead 'the restlessness of a young spirit, yearning for everything, blinded by splendour, always inquisitive and ready to adapt'. Mahler's 'vigorous passages of beauty and originality', 'variety of acoustic colours', and 'brilliant orchestral inventions' were to his mind worthy of praise.[61]

When he returned to Vienna on 6 April, Mahler found the press more aggressive than ever. On 3 April the *Deutsche Zeitung* had cited his absence as a further instance of 'the current mismanagement at the Opera':

Having assured himself of a gigantic income, which might be called exorbitant in view of his pernicious activity, Mahler 'travels in symphonies' with his own brand name and in the meantime everything at the Opera is in complete disorder . . . Mr Mahler wanders around to Italy in search of laurels and even more money—one of these days we shall work out how many months' leave of absence he has taken recently for his own

---

[61] See *L'Arte*, 38 (1907): 7 (7 Apr. 1907). The translation of the Italian reviews of Mahler's concert in Trieste is by John and Noretta Leech. From the Hotel de la Ville there, Mahler wrote to Norbert Salter to tell him that he was sending 300 lire, undoubtedly his agent's commission. 'In Vienna I shall reply to your last letter in detail' (undated letter to Salter, in the possession of Alun Francis, London).

affairs. He is not in the least interested in how his deputy is faring with the Hofoper in Vienna.

Before Easter the same paper had already been talking of 'total bankruptcy' and 'the beginning of the end'. On 8 April it once again asserted that Mahler was 'leading the Opera to moral and artistic ruin', simply because the sudden illness of the baritone Anton Moser had necessitated the last-minute cancellation of a performance! As usual Mahler did not take these attacks very seriously. He was used to them. The only new development was that they occurred more frequently. In fact, as soon as he was back he devoted all his attention to the administration of the Opera. Before leaving for Rome he had sent the producer August Stoll to Germany in order to recruit new singers.[62] Slezak had refused to sign his new contract and insisted on unacceptable conditions. Fortunately Sarah Charles Cahier had scored a great success as a guest artist on 5 March in a hastily refurbished revival of *Le Prophète*, with Bruno Walter conducting, and then on 15 March in *Aida*. In *Die Zeit* Richard Wallaschek called her voice 'powerful though sometimes nasal, hollow and veiled in the lower register; scarcely good enough for one of the bigger provincial stages'.[63] But once again his views were largely inspired by political considerations. The *Montags-Revue* found that Cahier was worthy of being compared with 'the unforgettable Walker', and praised her 'powerful, dark, and organ-like voice' and her 'careful training'. Only her rather English intonation, noticeable in the syllables she stressed and in the vocalises, was singled out for criticism.[64] Everyone was looking forward to her return as a member under contract in April, and to her appearance in *Samson et Dalila* in May. In March two tenors, Karl Jörn and Walter Soomer, had to be invited at the last moment, the former for two and the latter for four performances, because neither Schmedes nor Slezak was available (Schmedes was immersed in the rehearsals for *Iphigénie en Aulide*, and Slezak in those for *La Muette de Portici*). As we have seen, Adrienne von Kraus-Osborne made her Vienna debut in April in the title-role of *Carmen*, while her husband performed three different roles, but these guest appearances did not lead to their being offered contracts because the terms they demanded were excessive.[65] At first sight the situation appeared more or less normal, though the exceptional number of guest appearances suggested that something was perhaps amiss.

On 17 April, a fortnight after Mahler had returned from Italy, several Viennese papers, including the *Neue Freie Presse*, announced that Fritz Schrödter had refused to accept Mahler's proposals for his new contract: a

---

[62]   Stoll visited Karlsruhe, Dortmund, Barmen, Düsseldorf, Bremen, Hamburg, Berlin, and Munich (letters dated 21 Mar. and 17 Apr., HOA, G.Z. 332/1183/1907).

[63]   The performance on 5 Mar. was conducted by Bruno Walter, with Slezak in the title role.

[64]   Cast for the performance of *Aida* on 15 Mar. 1907: Bland (Aida); Cahier (Amneris); Slezak (Radames); Weidemann (Amonasro); and Mayr (Pharaoh). Karl Jörn had made a number of guest appearances at the Hofoper in 1905–7. Mahler was to meet him again in New York (see below, Vol. iiii, Chap. 4).

[65]   See above, Chap. 8.

salary of 14,000 kronen a year for six years (instead of the previous 21,000), and a cancellation clause that would come into effect after three years.[66] Mahler must have explained to the Lord Chamberlain his reasons for refusing to accept Schrödter's conditions, which he considered incompatible with most elementary interests of the institution. In the meantime Schrödter had not been idle. He had even spread a false report that he had received an offer from the Berlin Opera of a salary of 60,000 marks a year (or 51,000 kronen!). On 29 April the *Neue Freie Presse* reported that he had approached the Intendant directly and had had succeeded in maintaining the level of his salary. The news was soon confirmed by the rest of the press, notably the *Illustrirtes Wiener Extrablatt* of 2 May.[67]

This was an overt slap in the face for Mahler, and his interview with Prince Montenuovo must have been even stormier than the previous ones. Alma recorded that ever since the *La Muette* affair in February, the Prince, hitherto Mahler's faithful supporter, had become 'disagreeable and irritable, waiting for a chance to get rid of him'.[68] The tension had increased since their altercation about the Rome concerts, and Mahler had also become 'nervous and irritable', no doubt because the idea of leaving the Hofoper 'affected him more than he was willing to admit'.[69] Furthermore he probably knew that Felix Mottl, who was very anxious to leave Munich, where he had been reviled by the libellous press and had had to take a journalist to court,[70] had visited the Prince to tell him that he would like to return to Vienna. They even discussed the conditions for a possible engagement at the Opera. The Prince seems to have promised him Mahler's post if the latter resigned, and Mottl had even begun preparations to leave Munich.[71]

Under these circumstances it was inevitable that Mahler finally tendered his resignation.[72] He had done so frequently in the past, but since their altercation in March he knew that the Prince would now accept it.[73] The press soon announced that Mahler had 'recommended engaging a new director more in line with Schrödter's requirements'.[74] It is certain that Mahler almost

---

[66] In August 1906 Mahler had advised the Lord Chamberlain not to sign a long-term contract with Willy Hesch and, in view of his health, to reduce his salary. At the end of Mar. 1907 he agreed to prolong the contract of Benedikt Felix on condition that his salary was reduced to 10,000 kronen a year (letter dated 29 Mar., HOA, G.Z. 350/1391/1907).

[67] Richard Specht (RSM2, 150) states that Schrödter's re-engagement was the principal reason for Mahler's departure. [68] AMM1, 148; AMM2, 145.

[69] AMM1, 151; AMM2, 145. [70] See below.

[71] According to a letter from Princess Hohenlohe to Countess Coudenhove cited by Ludwig Karpath, Mottl visited Prince Montenuovo on Maundy Thursday, 28 Mar. 1907. Montenuovo and Wetschl promised that he would immediately be called if Mahler confirmed his desire to leave the Hofoper (BMG 191).

[72] As we shall see later on, the term 'resignation' is wrong because Mahler had been appointed by the Emperor and could only be released by him. It was used here, as it was in the contemporary press, for convenience's sake.

[73] Ludwig Karpath and several other witnesses emphasized Mahler's amazement when Prince Montenuovo accepted his resignation without further ado (BMG 182).

[74] *Montags-Revue* (9 June 1907). The article, which referred to the singer Schrötter (*sic*), stated that Mottl 'had already been appointed', and that he would prove incapable of managing the Opera.

immediately regretted his decision, as did the Prince, for it was made in a moment of anger. Yet he no doubt thought that it was unworthy of him to acknowledge the fact. In any case, nothing had yet been decided upon, for Mahler and the Prince had once more parted after having promised each other to keep the matter secret.

On 21 April, just as Mahler was becoming embroiled in an argument with the Lord Chamberlain over Schrödter's re-engagement, there was an outburst of whistling at the Opera during a performance of *Tristan* in which Felix von Kraus was making a guest appearance as King Mark. Mahler was very upset: 'If even the public is abandoning me,' he said to one of his friends, 'my time is really over.'[75] Four days later, a performance of *Cavalleria Rusticana* and *I Pagliacci* gave Heinrich Reinhardt the opportunity to claim that 'Director Mahler has at last been able to furnish proof that it is possible to put on Italian operas with a small group of singers who clearly had no voices'. Hitherto the erstwhile leader of the Hofoper could always see to it that the singers with good voices could hold their own against those with poor voices. Yesterday there was no indication that such a humdrum precaution was being taken—poor voice quality, promoted to a first principle, dominated almost unhindered. 'Today it seems that only those who have demonstrated without a shadow of doubt that they do not have good voices can remain at the Opera, enjoying the director's favour and all the advantages that derive from this.'[76]

At the same time the papers were delighted to be able to focus on yet another 'affair'. Mahler had personally promised Lucy Weidt the role of Desdemona in the revival of *Otello* which was to open on 3 May. She took part in all the rehearsals, but was informed by Wondra on 25 April that she would be singing only at the dress rehearsal, for the première had been assigned to Elsa Bland, who had been engaged by the Hofoper three years after her. She complained to the Intendant:

I was quite literally paralysed by these instructions, and went straight to director Mahler to remind him of his promise that I would sing the youthful dramatic roles at the premières. The director replied: 'Now you certainly won't be singing!', whereupon I immediately declared that under these circumstances I would have to tender my resignation, which I am doing herewith.[77]

In support of her request Weidt recalled that she had appeared on stage only once in February, twice in March, and twice in April, mainly as Fricka in *Das*

---

[75] *Königsberger Zeitung* (19 May 1911). In *Die Zeit* Wallaschek praised Kraus's performance. However, he stated that the Opera's standards had been declining for four years, that the intonation of the two main characters had left much to be desired in the love duet, and that the darkness in Act II 'constituted a negation of the theory of the *Gesamtkunstwerk*'. He noted that a great deal of vocal opposition had mingled with the applause preceding each act.

[76] *Neues Wiener Journal* (25 Apr. 1907).

[77] Undated, unnumbered letter from Lucy Weidt to the Intendant (c.26 Apr.). The original is not in the singer's handwriting. She must have dictated it to a secretary at the Opera or in the Intendant's office. The letter is accompanied by a short note signed by Mahler, and dated 29 Apr., (G2. 490/1680/5/1907).

Rheingold. This role did not suit her at all, and had been imposed on her. She recalled that she had learnt and rehearsed the role of the Countess for the new production of *Figaro* the previous year, and that Hilgermann had sung the première. At the time Mahler had solemnly promised that she would sing Isolde and Desdemona, especially as he was also giving Hilgermann the role of Sieglinde in the new production of *Die Walküre*, which she had also been counting on. Having failed to receive from the director 'the encouragement to which I feel entitled as an artist', having signed her new contract only because she had been promised new roles,[78] and having turned down far more advantageous offers from theatres abroad, she now saw only one solution, which was to leave the Hofoper.

In a particularly curt letter to the Intendant (whom he in fact suspected of having encouraged Weidt to resign), Mahler advised against complying with the singer's wishes, because 'the reasons she cites do not justify this'. For a start, a decision had not yet been reached in the case of *Otello*. Furthermore, it was specified in the singers' contracts that they should never consider a role to be their personal property. If Weidt received permission to sing at the première, it might be necessary to accept the resignation of Elsa Bland, who would certainly tender it.[79] In a note sent the same day to one of Angelo Neumann's assistants at the German Theatre in Prague, Mahler pointed out that 'Frau Weidt has tendered her resignation on a very trivial pretext' and that, under these circumstances, he could not grant her leave of absence until his superiors had reached a decision.[80] The position Mahler adopted on this occasion was unusually harsh and unyielding, and it is quite conceivable that his bad temper reflected his psychological state at a time of tension and depression.

As might have been expected, the press quickly seized on the Weidt affair, and a whole column was devoted to it in the *Neues Wiener Journal* on 25 April. The following day it dwelt on a new 'scandal', for in the absence of a tenor, it had almost been necessary to cancel a performance of *Le Prophète*. The first guest appearance of Philip Brozel,[81] who was to have sung the title role, had

---

[78] The correspondence between Weidt and Mahler from 30 Jan. to 22 Feb. confirms that the singer was disappointed because she was not singing Sieglinde in the new production of *Die Walküre*, and that she had been asking for the role of Desdemona for three years. In order to placate her, Mahler granted Weidt a week's leave to sing in London. At the same time he agreed to increase her annual salary from 24,000 to 28,000 kronen (1908), to 30,000 (1909), and finally to 32,000 (1910 and 1911). Like her colleague Selma Kurz, her contract gave her the right to annual unpaid leave from 25 May to 22 June (see Lucy Weidt's letters of 30 Jan. and 7 Feb., and Mahler's letters of 9 and 22 Feb., HOA, G.Z. 24/1907). Weidt's new four-year contract only came into effect on 1 Nov. 1908.

[79] Letter from Mahler to the Intendant dated 29 Apr. (HOA, G.Z. 490/1680/I/1907).

[80] Letter dated 29 Apr., HOA, Z. 513/1907. (This letter was recently sold by an antiquarian dealer in New York.) Lucy Weidt sang Isolde in Vienna on 12 June in a performance conducted by Schalk. According to the *Illustrirtes Wiener Extrablatt*, it was a great success.

[81] On 24 Apr., in *Cavalleria Rusticana* and *I Pagliacci*. However, Brozel was engaged by the Vienna Opera from 1 Sept. 1907 to 31 Aug. 1908.

been so disastrous that he had departed immediately.[82] Slezak, who had been suffering for some time from chronic hoarseness, had gone to Italy to recuperate.[83] Schmedes was asked at the last moment to replace him, but as he was just leaving to make a guest appearance at the Frankfurt Opera, he refused, despite being threatened with disciplinary action. Wallnöfer was not available either, and thus it became necessary to ask Karl Kurz-Stolzenberg, a tenor who had previously been 'banned from the Opera'. Although suffering from stage fright, he finally saved the situation. The 'Pas des Patineurs' had to be omitted, and someone tripped in the 'Marche des Soldats' just as he was crossing a bridge, and was prodded in a sensitive part of his anatomy by the lance the leader of the following group was carrying. At the end of the work, when the torch failed to land in the powder-magazine, 'only the director, beside himself with rage, exploded'. The palace then collapsed for no apparent reason and the curtain had to be lowered rather hastily.

On 28 April the *Neues Wiener Journal* carried a long article entitled *Mahleriana* (although unsigned, it was in fact by Heinrich Reinhardt), which accused Prince Montenuovo of systematically protecting Mahler instead of dismissing him, and called for the creation of the post of a 'truly independent and competent general Intendant'[84] to serve as an intermediary between the director and the Lord Chamberlain. The article referred to all the 'scandals' that had occurred since Mahler's arrival, condemned many of the singers he had engaged, defended Fritz Schrödter 'who has proved himself and is entitled to respect' and attacked 'a certain singer almost totally lacking in vocal ability' who was given the best roles.[85] Reinhardt stressed the mediocrity of several recent performances and even claimed that the standard of the orchestra had declined. He attributed many of the ills at the Opera to Mahler's 'unpredictable nature', 'illogicality', 'nervousness', and indeed 'neurasthenia'. Furthermore, Mahler wanted nothing more than to leave, and no longer considered directing the Opera as anything but 'a troublesome sideline'.

Gustav Mahler has brought off a sorry exploit. It was not easy to achieve such a marked decline in the glittering reputation of the world's leading opera house. This took more than ten years. But now it has happened, and we speak for the overwhelming majority in demanding an immediate and radical reorganization of the Vienna Opera, and that this unavoidable act should commence with Gustav Mahler's retirement.

Such an article would not have mattered much if it had appeared a few years earlier, but at the end of April 1907, in the climate then prevailing, it joined

---

[82] Slezak was being particularly uncooperative with regard to the renewal of his contract because of frequent guest appearances by tenors from other cities. Accounts of these incidents appeared in *Neues Wiener Journal* (26 Apr.) and *Illustrirtes Wiener Extrablatt* (2 May).

[83] His absence made it necessary to defer the revival of *Otello* from 28 Apr. to 3 May.

[84] Since Plappart's departure the post of Intendant had remained vacant.

[85] This was a reference to Gutheil-Schoder. However, she had ceased to be the main target for the Viennese critics several years earlier.

many others in the dossier that the Lord Chamberlain was compiling against Mahler.[86]

On 30 April Wallaschek also condemned the low quality of the singers Mahler had engaged and his casting errors, and recalled both the excellent singers he had 'expelled' and those, all too numerous, he had invited. On 2 May the *Extrablatt* added to the list of grievances the problems in the repertoire caused by the absence of suitable singers, the dismissal of the tenor Johannes Sembach,[87] the notorious deficit,[88] and the 'tenor crisis'.

When Mahler announced his programme for the new season there was still no hint that he might be leaving the Hofoper. As we have seen the programme included Alexander Zemlinsky's *Der Traumgörge*, Julius Bittner's *Die rothe Gred*, Claude Debussy's *Pelléas et Mélisande*,[89] Carl Goldmark's *Ein Wintermärchen*,[90] Weber's *Oberon*, the last two parts of the *Ring*, Gluck's *Armide*, Cimarosa's *Il Matrimonio Segreto*, Boieldieu's *Jean de Paris* as well as Cherubini's *Les Deux Journées*, Méhul's *Joseph*, and Schumann's *Genoveva*. For this last work Mahler intended to use the best singers of the Opera in order to erase the memory of its failure under Herbeck.[91] It was a singularly ambitious programme, even if only half of it was destined to materialize, and it showed that for the moment Mahler was certainly not losing interest in the Opera.

On 6 May, in the *Wiener Montags-Journal* J. E. Mand returned to the attack on the subject of the deficit. Furthermore, he accused Mahler of 'wilfully changing his tempos so often that the orchestra is listless and dejected', of 'having bankrupted the Philharmonic's pension fund by retiring no less than seventy musicians', and of being preoccupied with his own immortality. According to Mand, his time was over, for he was no longer young enough to carry out all his duties at once. It was imperative that he should leave the Opera before it was 'tarnished by hatred, discontent and discord'. And Mand believed that he should not be replaced by a musician, but by an experienced man of the theatre.

Accusations that Mahler was losing interest in the Opera and thinking only of his work seem all the more unfair since he had just won the long battle he had fought on behalf of his staff. On 3 May the *Illustrirtes Extrablatt* announced that two days before, in the course of a lengthy meeting with Prince

---

[86] Most of these articles were preserved in the archives of the Opera.

[87] This took place in May, though in fact his dismissal had been decided upon at an earlier date.

[88] The *Extrablatt* of 3 May estimated that it amounted to 35,742 kronen on 20 Apr., and attributed it to the increase in ticket prices, the poverty of the repertory, Mahler's mismanagement, and the excessive cost of Roller's new designs. However, it was impossible to arrive at this figure before the end of the year, and in any case Roller never exceeded the financial limits that had been agreed upon. He was particularly economical in *Otello*, *Samson*, and *La Muette*, refurbishing the old scenery as best he could.

[89] Mahler sent Franz Schalk to Frankfurt to attend the German première of Debussy's work.

[90] The *Illustrirtes Wiener Extrablatt* of 8 Mar. published an interview with Goldmark about his new work, which Mahler had already accepted for the following season.

[91] *Illustrirtes Wiener Extrablatt* (1 May 1907). On 28 May Mahler wrote to Humperdinck that he was planning to perform *Heirat wider Willen* the following season (HOA, unnumbered document).

Montenuovo, he had at last obtained the long-awaited increase in the salaries of members of the orchestra,[92] the chorus, and the dancers.[93] The *Neues Wiener Journal* and the same issue of the *Illustrirtes Extrablatt* of 3 May referred to another long conversation between Mahler and the Prince the day before. It concerned 'the new contract for Schrödter, Weidt's letter of resignation, and presumably the departure of Johannes Sembach'. The paragraph ended rather ominously: 'During his ten years as director there have been many weighty conversations between Mahler and Prince Montenuovo, and it has often been said that Mahler was prepared to leave. Until now, however, this was only conjectural . . .'

On the other hand the leading German musical journal, the *Neue Zeitschrift für Musik*, published on 2 May a long article by Bernard Scharlitt entitled 'Gustav Mahler und das Wiener Hofoperntheater'. It gave a very positive account of Mahler's directorship and 'deliberately avoided' saying anything about him as a composer and conductor. Scharlitt, who was obviously a fervent Wagnerian, praised him for having 'carried out Bayreuth's aims' in Vienna; for having given 'ideal performances' of Wagner's works; for having achieved, thanks to Roller's contribution, a revalorization of the *Bühnenbild*; for having applied Wagner's 'artistic principles' to other composers, for instance to Mozart; for having enriched the general repertoire of the Opera, and especially that of its *Neueinstudierungen*. Consequently, Scharlitt concluded: 'If Mahler actually carried out the intention that he has often expressed, leaving his post as director at the end of his first decade, and devoting himself solely to his creative activity, the Hofoper and the Viennese public would suffer an irreparable loss.' On the same day Bruno Walter, in a letter to his parents, worried about his own future in Vienna, and commented: 'but unfortunately it is quite possible that Mahler will leave in the very near future. However, please treat this with great <u>discretion</u>. But then it would all be over once more, for a new director (Mottl, Schuch or another candidate) would appropriate all the new works and productions that Mahler has luckily assigned to me, and the old calamities might return, maybe only half as bad as before, but twice as painful because they are being repeated.'[94]

Yet in his heart of hearts Mahler had still not made up his mind to leave. On 4 May he said to Julius Korngold: 'They want to get rid of me, but they won't!'[95] However, most of the Viennese press now treated him as if he were about to step down: 'Great confusion reigns at the Opera on account of this Viennese impertinence,' Roller wrote to his wife on 29 April. 'I admire Mahler, who

---

[92] This amounted to 500 kronen annually on condition that new members were automatically admitted to the ranks of the Philharmonic. This at last settled the dispute which had arisen between Mahler and the orchestra's committee in 1902 (see above, Vol. ii, Chap. 13).

[93] Every member of the chorus was to be paid an extra 1 to 2 kronen per performance in addition to an attendance bonus of 55 kronen annually. Dancers were also to receive an 'attendance bonus' on a weekly basis. These increases entailed extra expenditure by the Opera of 100,000 kronen annually.

[94] BWB 92.   [95] *Neue Freie Presse* (18 May 1913).

refuses to allow himself to be thrown off-balance and goes on steadily, like the knight in the Swabian legend. It seems that a combined effort will be made to bring about his downfall. If only people knew how glad he is to be going.'[96] However, Mahler, hardened by years of criticism, slander, and the hostility of journalists, would probably not have resigned if his resolve had not been strengthened by an unexpected event. Since March, Prince Montenuovo had become increasingly conscious of the loss the Opera would suffer if he were to leave. Furthermore, he began to suspect that Mottl might not be able to leave Munich. Thus he tried to persuade Mahler that he should not allow a fit of temper to determine his actions.

On 17 May an unsigned article in the *Extrablatt* entitled 'Gustav Mahlers Sehnsucht' claimed that the director had told 'a prominent individual' that he was intending to leave the Opera and devote himself to creative work.[97]

Mahler has repeatedly expressed a desire to resign from his post, which prevents him from working as a composer. However, there have also been a number of unfortunate affairs which have contributed to his depression ... He is seriously contemplating resignation, and is doing so at a time when the Hofoper is artistically stable and when no outside pressures force him to do so ... It is said he will leave the post he has occupied for the last ten years after the première of Goldmark's new opera *Ein Wintermärchen*.

With all these details, the author clearly wished to give the impression that he knew everything that went on behind the scenes at the Opera, and wanted to push Mahler finally to make up his mind to resign. The following day, the *Extrablatt*, in another article with the same title, reported that Mahler, when tendering his resignation, had said: 'I can't take it any more!' And the journalist once more provided a long list of Mahler's 'sins': too many guest artists, uninspired engagements, excessive expenditure, the director's absences from Vienna. He took obvious pleasure in recalling Mahler's grievances against the Vienna Opera: the ban on *Salome*, the première of the ballet *Atelier Bruder Japonet*, which he had opposed, although in the end the Prince had forced it on him; and then his quarrel with a member of the audience at the first performance of Schoenberg's Quartet 'which people had tried to use against the director, though in vain'.

Despite the lies and exaggerations they contained, these articles came fairly close to the truth. During that same month, Mahler spoke to Bruno Walter in his office and, tipping forward the chair he was sitting in, said: 'If I wanted to stay in this position, I would only have to lean back firmly in my seat and I could stay where I am. But I am offering no resistance, and thus 'shall end up sliding off'.[98] A few days later, Walter received an urgent summons from Mahler brought to him by his factotum Hassinger. Once again, he found Mahler

[96] LKR 105.
[97] The article stated that Mahler had said that he would occasionally return to conduct concerts in Vienna.   [98] BWM.

in his office, ready to go home. They walked through the Stadtpark in the direction of the Auenbruggergasse, and Mahler then told him that his decision was irrevocable and that he was going to leave Vienna. With some emotion Walter said that this would be a terrible loss to the Opera and that there would be a void after he had left. Mahler simply replied: 'In ten years at the Vienna Opera, I have come full circle.'[99] This is probably when Mahler wrote the following note to Countess Wydenbruck: 'Thank you for your kind words and invitation. If I am still alive on the 27th (which, in view of the difficulties the director of the Opera is currently experiencing, is very doubtful) I shall be delighted to come . . . I am very much looking forward to meeting you.'[100]

Since Mahler had not refuted the first report, the Viennese papers began to print almost daily articles or paragraphs on 'The Crisis at the Opera'. On 20 May J. E. Mand, in the *Montags-Journal*, claimed that he had 'always known Mahler better than he knew himself', that Mahler had aspired to more than conducting operas, and was seeking immortality. Thus a new epoch was beginning for him. The impossibility of finding a director who was both a great artist and an astute businessman was clear for all to see. Obviously, it would be better to assign to an intendant the role of director, restricting the director's role to that of artistic director. On the same day the *Illustrirtes Wiener Extrablatt* announced that Mahler would remain only to the end of the current season, and would then be replaced by the director of the Budapest Opera, Raoul Mader. The same information appeared in the *Neues Wiener Journal*, which mentioned the 'large pension' Mahler would receive, and pointed out that he would now devote himself exclusively to appearances as a guest conductor: 'Mahler is already said to have arranged a tour for the coming season, in the course of which he will conduct a wide variety of orchestras.'

By now all the papers reported that Mahler's departure was a foregone conclusion, although it was still possible to delay it. Since a denial was not forthcoming, the journalists finally approached Mahler himself. Mistakenly believing, as indeed seemed probable, that the news had come from the Lord Chamberlain personally, he decided that he could not tell 'a lie', and admitted that he had asked for his release. This was immediately hailed as a triumph by all those who had repeatedly announced his departure since January. On 23 May the *Neues Wiener Journal* hastened to communicate the good news to its readers. Mahler was said to be tired of his job and no longer capable of running the Opera, even with the support of his superiors; and his 'system' had turned out to be a failure. The article named several possible candidates for his post: Raoul Mader,[101] Ernst von Schuch, who was the favourite of the *Neues Wiener Journal*, and Felix Mottl.

---

[99] BWT 245.

[100] Undated letter to Countess Wydenbruck, who wrote the number 15 on it (BMG, Paris).

[101] Formerly a Korrepetitor at the Vienna Opera, Mader was now director of the Budapest Opera. He happened to be visiting Vienna at this time.

Of course, there were many people in Vienna did not want Mahler to leave, but they did not always raise their voices above the din. On 22 May, an unsigned article in the *Allgemeine Zeitung* tried to put the record straight:

Almost ten years ago Gustav Mahler was appointed to the directorship of the Vienna Opera. For ten years Vienna has put up with the fact that within its walls a man of genius had found a sphere of action suited to his abilities which enabled him to create new, beautiful and unusual things. For ten years the guardians of the city's artistic life have allowed it to be influenced by someone as disturbing as Gustav Mahler, a rousing and restless troublemaker. For ten years, though angry and insulted, they have none the less watched how our leading operatic establishment has been jolted out of the 'comfortable rut of routine' and led along new paths to new goals. For ten years musical Vienna has languished under the sceptre of an autocrat, of someone who is shamelessly self-reliant, who trusts in his own strength, and obeys his intuition, who brusquely and proudly rejected all the cliques and their leaders when they tried to offer him a firmer and more solid foundation for his power, though not for his work.

Ten years—but now it seems that everyone is becoming impatient. They are no longer content to put a brave face upon it, but are blowing their bugles for the attack, albeit in wrong and unmusical manner. Conspirators are prowling around the Opera. No paper dagger is too dirty to be launched against the hated director. Industrious as ants, they assemble and pile up one snippet after another—in the newspaper columns directed against the arts and the theatre—with the object of 'smothering' the director. No tenor can suffer from hoarseness without them establishing a direct connection between the unfortunate inflammation of his mucous membranes and the detrimental quality of Gustav Mahler's directorship. If a ballerina slips in some clumsy kind of way we are immediately informed that she tripped over the Herr Direktor's nervous legs. Any incident, however stupid, that occurs at the Opera is attributed to the evil intentions of the director. And at the same time the director's great, successful, beautiful and artistic designs are simply attributed to chance. The director is held responsible for hare-brained ideas of the actors and for the rancorous escapades devised by an arrogant prima donna or the vanity of a tenor. But all the beautiful, good and great things that happened at the Opera under his directorship materialized 'without assistance'. The director had nothing to do with it. . . .

The newspapers! Yes, this of course is a weak spot in Gustav Mahler's character. He took no notice of the papers. He has never tried to establish a relationship with those who bestow or withhold immortality on a daily basis, he has never kowtowed to journalists. Indeed, he never even deigned to issue a denial when those at the Opera who considered themselves 'enslaved and humiliated' accused him of the most far-fetched crimes against their greatness and genius. Of course Gustav Mahler's belief that great deeds suffice to gain public support, and his adherence to the maxim: 'An artist should work and should not talk!' were out of place in a city where an artist's being is far more important than his ability. His way of immersing himself in his work and his activities, of letting the world do as it pleases, does not recommend itself to a crowd which expects its artists to grovel at its feet, to pander to its tastes, and to feed its curiosity with anecdotes about their private lives. If they do this, the Viennese public, through the press, bestows upon them the epithet 'darling'. And there's the rub, Gustav Mahler has never understood how to become a 'darling'. If he had kissed Herr Slezak on stage in front of the audience, if for some Christmas issue he had told stories of 'How I broke my first baton', he would no longer have been confined to the arts pages, and would have gone to the theatrical gossip columns, and his 'popularity' would be altogether different. But he has never sought 'to keep in touch with the press'. He may well have gone too far in this regard, in fact, further than was wise. Many a slander and libel might have been defused in time if Mahler had not declined to accept the help of the press, if he had not been so isolated and retiring. The director's aloofness from journalists was the reason why many lies and accusations levelled against his management had time to make their mark, and were difficult to refute.[102]

The article then listed lies that had recently appeared in the press: the deficit (which was invention pure and simple), the 'public was staying away from the Opera' (in fact the house was nearly always full); the 'intolerable' relationship between Mahler and the staff of the Opera (in fact in six years he had twice negotiated salary increases for them; and no one at the time had mentioned a possible 'deficit'); the numerous guest artists (in fact they were no more numerous than those engaged in Munich by Mottl, who, it was thought, would take over from Mahler).

There are more than enough people thirsting for revenge. The journalists to whom he was not nice enough; the tenors whom he cajoled with insufficient warmth; the ballet that he did not value and care for with sufficiently gentle passion, quite forgetting the esteem in which this genre is held in the most important circles in the palace; the designers, and costumiers and purveyors of stage props forced to flee to the lumber-room in the face of a new art of stage design. A high price has been paid for Roller.

The *Wiener Allgemeine Zeitung* concluded that Vienna did not deserve someone like Mahler.

A group of Viennese admirers of Mahler who were distressed by the news of his departure, reacted by drawing up a somewhat ill-inspired and clumsily written 'address', for which they collected seventy signatures in two days.

It is now ten years, almost to the day, since you first wielded the baton in our opera house and succeeded in making transparent in a wholly novel manner a work with which we were familiar. If one sums up the intervening ten years, one becomes aware, with gratitude and admiration, of the extent to which you have greatly enriched every one of us: by what you have done to recreate well-loved works in a wholly new and impressive manner, to reveal their essence in the shape of sound; by a splendid series of artistic deeds that attained the goal of a new style of representation; but above all, and perhaps even more than by the details of your work, by your shining example, which, sweeping away imprecise prejudices, and free of any kind of personality cult, fulfilled the inexorable demands of rigorous artistic practice. An example that taught unconditional respect for art and, through the personality that gave it, introduced new and living cultural values into our artistic life.

It was a foreordained consequence of the loftiness of your approach to art that those entrusted with the expression of public opinion would—with a few exceptions—sum

---

[102] *Wiener Allgemeine Zeitung* (22 May 1907).

things up quite differently and in a largely negative manner. Achievements such as the Wagner and Mozart cycles, together with the almost unbelievably perfect productions of *Fidelio*, *Iphigénie en Aulide*, *The Merry Wives*, *The Shrew*—a list that could easily be five times as long without being exhaustive—have been ignored as if they merely fulfilled a self-evident requirement, while attention has been drawn to the many unfortunate accidents and difficulties that are everyday occurrences in the running of a theatre and which can only too readily be used as weapons against a person who abhors such things. May these words serve to show that all these occasionally intolerable voices do not give a true impression of public opinion: the gratitude of a number of people who are very much in your debt, in whom those works have remained inextinguishable in the form given to them by your grandiose interpretative powers, who have received from you, as a lasting gift, crucial and unforgettable impressions, and who know what you mean to us now and in the future.

Those who put their signatures to this text, which was delivered to Mahler by hand, claimed that they had not approached anyone who had professional dealings with him, or who might have felt obliged to sign. They included some of the leading figures in the Viennese world of the arts; writers such as Hermann Bahr, Hugo von Hofmannsthal, Arthur Schnitzler, Stefan Zweig, Peter Altenberg, Alfred Polgar, and Felix Salten; musicians such as Lilli Lehmann, Oskar Nedbal, Julius Bittner, Gustav Gutheil, Arnold Schoenberg, Ludwig Bösendorfer, Josef Labor, Julius Epstein, Anton Door, Robert Gound, Heinrich Schenker, and Josef Venantius von Wöss; artists such as Gustav Klimt, Max Kurzweil, Kolo Moser, Josef Hoffmann; and men of the theatre such as Adolf von Sonnenthal, Josef Kainz, Max Burckhard, and Paul Schlenther. The aristocracy was represented by Countess Misa Wydenbruck.

The authors of this text meant well, but their initiative was not only clumsy, it was also misplaced, for Mahler, having made up his mind, wished to leave Vienna without a great deal of fuss. Some of his supporters, and David Josef Bach in particular, deplored the awkward literary manner of this 'address', which was symbolically dated 11 May, the tenth anniversary of the first performance Mahler had conducted at the Hofoper. Admittedly, those who appended their signatures included 'a number of serious and earnest men, who honestly wished to pay homage to Mahler as an artist'. But it was also true that many of them knew nothing about music; and it was not true that none of them had ever had any artistic or personal dealings with the Director.[103] Furthermore, there were some honourable people among his enemies, and 'not everyone who did not adore Mahler was necessarily a rogue or an idiot'. Mahler's adversaries replied forthwith. On 25 May, the day the 'address' appeared in print, the *Neues Wiener Journal* criticized its lack of clarity and faulty style, and pointed out that it failed to mention Mahler's management style, which had had 'a baneful influence' on the Opera and 'ruined its reputation'. It ran through the familiar list of his failures and 'mistakes': an unfortunate choice of new works,

---

[103] The list in fact included the names of two of Mahler's close friends, Emil and Berta Zuckerkandl.

the engagement of mediocre singers, and so on, and declared that it was not hostile to him personally or to his directorship, but to his 'system'.[104]

The next day, 26 May, the *Extrablatt*, in the absence of its regular critic, Hans Liebstöckl, published a venomous interview with Hirschfeld, who called the 'address' a 'toast' and an 'effusive speech given at a banquet' which could not be taken seriously. He also tried to discredit those who had put their names to the document by stating that some of them had never managed to understand what music was all about. One of them wrote 'articles about Viennese night-clubs',[105] another had 'publicly stated that he is incapable of uttering a word about the music of *The Merry Widow*'. Others would be 'at a loss for words if they were asked to explain the meaning of the word "art" ', and some had not set foot in a concert hall for thirty years. Furthermore, all these intellectuals only went to the Opera on gala nights; they overlooked Mahler's absences and the plethora of 'guest artists'. They were unaware of the disasters which occurred when his new productions were handed over to his assistants. Hirschfeld ended by recalling the warmth with which he had initially supported and defended Mahler. His attitude had changed at the same time as that of Wallaschek and Hans Liebstöckl, the critic of the *Extrablatt*, when Mahler 'had abandoned the Opera to devote himself to his own work and to promoting his own career'.[106] Furthermore, it was quite clear that he could no longer carry on as before. A document signed by the members of the Opera, by discerning Wagnerians, or by the musicians of the Philharmonic Orchestra might well have caused a greater stir than this miserable 'address'. However, if the address had been signed by members of the Opera, it would have doubtless been said that they had been forced to do so, but since it came from people who were not connected with the Opera, they were discounted as knowing nothing about music.

Countless unfounded rumours found their way into the columns of the newspapers. It had been reported that Roller and Rosé would also leave the Hofoper, which the *Extrablatt* denied. But, as a possible successor to Mahler the same paper mentioned the producer August Stoll, the Chordirektor Hubert Wondra, and even the ageing tenor Hermann Winkelmann. On 28 May it added to this list the director of the Kaiserjubiläumstheater, Rainer Simons. Mahler was exasperated by these foolish and misleading reports. In a letter to Julius Korngold that was probably written in the same week, he expressed his weariness and irritation in an ironic manner:

Mr. X's[107] burgeoning literary talent was bound to flourish under the warm sun of a 'Mahler crisis'. Now, thank God, interest will soon shift to my successor, and then, in

---

[104] The paper reported that Weingartner was visiting Vienna, and suggested that he would be an 'excellent replacement for Mahler'.

[105] A reference to Peter Altenberg, who was famous in Vienna for his Bohemian lifestyle as much as for his literary gifts.

[106] Hirschfeld in fact 'changed his mind' earlier, at a time when Mahler rarely conducted his own works.

[107] Korngold deliberately suppressed the critic's name when citing this extract from a letter in his memoirs.

the shade afforded by my emeritus status, I shall be able to sit in the corner of a pleasant café and enjoy the new plant life purveyed to the 'reader' by the arts columns on a daily basis. I am now beginning to discover that such 'news' is very interesting and that a reporter is very important![108]

A report by Josef Reitler, who had just moved from Paris to Vienna to join the *Neue Freie Presse*, shows that in these turbulent times Mahler was still very interested in artistic questions in general, and musical ones in particular. One of first things Reitler did was to telephone Mahler. 'He said, "Come over immediately. Would you like to go to the Opera this evening? We're doing *Fidelio*,[109] and the house will be half empty. It will be good to know that there's at least one person in the theatre who can really listen. So come through the Kärntnerstrasse entrance, the porter will know what to do.' After the difficulties he had encountered in Salzburg, Reitler thought that Mahler might forget, but he was wrong. He had no difficulty in coming through the artists' door, but then bumped into a giant who refused to let him pass: 'Are you a tenor?' he said. It was Slezak, trying his best to play a practical joke, even on a stranger. And then there was Hassinger, who guarded his master's room like Cerberus.

It was five in the afternoon. The performance of *Fidelio* began at seven. Yet Mahler was already wearing tails, and the Beethoven score lay open on a tall desk. I was rather surprised, but Mahler replied: 'Yes, I need these hours before the performance in order to get into the spirit of the work. Most conductors only do this when they take up the baton. But that is too late. And as for the score—well, by daylight there are just the familiar notes. But in the evening, in the theatre, these notes come alive in a mysterious kind of way. Flames and signs and wonders flash out of the score, and in these flames and signs I keep discovering new and unknown beauties. This happens no matter whether I am conducting Beethoven, Mozart or Wagner.'

These words, spoken quite dispassionately—and not, of course, in a polemical manner—by someone who certainly knew his Mozart, Beethoven and Wagner by heart as well as anyone, are still the most compelling argument against conducting without a score that I know,[110]

Reitler added. Later, before going home, the young journalist spoke to Mahler again, having been asked by the *Neue Freie Presse* to interview him.

In order to dispel these rumours Mahler gave Korngold a brief interview on 28 May, and his remarks were published in the *Neue Freie Presse* the same day:

I have not submitted a written resignation. I have taken those steps with the authorities which I felt constrained to do by the well-known circumstances that have given rise to so much comment, and I am now allowing things to take their course. The decision is out of my hands. Thus I am not in a position to answer questions about who my successor might be. No one knows less about it than I do. I continue, as is my duty as

---

[108] KIW 112.

[109] This was no doubt the performance on 13 May, the only one Mahler conducted before the summer.

[110] Reitler recalls that Wagner, Strauss, Pfitzner, Richter, Nikisch, Mottl, Schuch, and even Weingartner conducted from the score (JRM 56).

director of the Hofoper, to do what I have to do in a serious manner and . . . work harder than ever, if that is possible. There is always a great deal to do before the end of the season. I have already drawn up the repertoire to the end of the season on 22 June.

Mahler went on to speak of the Wagner cycle (which was to begin on 3 June with *Der fliegende Holländer* and finish on 21 June with *Götterdämmerung*) and the season's last important revival (Ignaz Brüll's *Das goldene Kreuz*) which was to run from 4 June together with the new ballet, *Rübezahl*.[111] He replied in a non-committal manner to a question about whether he would conduct again before the end of the season, and reiterated that he was continuing to work as if his directorship were to last for another fifty years. In fact, he had just been studying the score of a new opera. The article also revealed that he had had a long interview with Prince Montenuovo the day before, and that the name of the elderly tenor Wallnöfer had been added to the list of his possible successors. On 25 May the *Extrablatt* was still trying to fan the flames. In the article which announced Felix Weingartner's presence in Vienna it claimed that numerous members of the Philharmonic Orchestra wanted Mahler to return. On 2 June the *Deutsche Zeitung* claimed that this was merely a tactical ploy. It added that, 'despite the efforts and support of the Jewish press', the committee had almost unanimously rejected him, adding that 'the Philharmonic Orchestra did not wish to be misused in order to enable the director to keep his job'.[112]

The next day the *Neues Wiener Journal* stated that Mahler wished to retain his post, while on 26 May the *Reichspost* thought that his 'weariness' was only a ruse to enable him to obtain the best possible terms for his resignation, which was 'anything but voluntary'. According to the *Extrablatt* of 29 May, he had already sent emissaries to several German cities in search of a new post (which, as we shall see, was probably true). At the same time the papers continued to carry daily reports of 'scandals' at the Opera. Thus the *Extrablatt* of 28 May revealed that Schmedes, because of a sore throat, had withdrawn before the performance of *Die Walküre* on 26 May and that once again he had had to be replaced by Kurz-Stolzenberg; that, on the same evening, because Weidemann had also fallen ill, a baritone called Hermann Jessen had to be brought from Graz at the last moment; that the following day *Samson et Dalila* was given instead of *Carmen*; and that the young tenor Hans Ellensohn, a newcomer, had been such a failure that he would soon have to leave the

---

[111] Mahler also announced a revival of Bizet's *Djamileh* (which did not come about) and two visits by guest artists which also failed to materialize. One of them was a young tenor called Hans Schütz, and the other a Swiss singer, Modest Menzinsky. In fact, he sent the latter a cable on 22 May to say he was waiting for him in Vienna, and another two days later to ask him to prepare a list of roles, which were not all Wagnerian (HOA, unnumbered telegram). Six months later, in reply to a request by Weingartner, Mahler stated that Menzinsky had disappointed him: 'Uneven impression and useful vocal means but somewhat unusual, and not used in an interesting way.' He had rejected a guest appearance 'because his terms were too high' (see Weingartner's telegram of 28 Nov. and Mahler's handwritten draft reply, HOA, Z. 349/1907).

[112] According to the *Deutsche Zeitung* of 2 June and the *Extrablatt* of 1 June, 86 votes were cast for Mottl, only three for Mahler, and one for Bruno Walter.

Opera.[113] The *Neues Wiener Journal* of 2 June disclosed that two days earlier, during a performance of *Les Huguenots*, Leo Slezak had fallen on his right arm at the moment when he was supposed to have been killed by Catholic bullets. He had been taken to hospital, and it was feared that he had a fracture. Since Schmedes was already ill, difficulties loomed ahead with regard to the repertory. Besides, Mahler was never in his office. He had been refused the funds he had requested for new productions because the Opera's takings were still on the decrease. And a very high-ranking member of the Court had recently declared: 'These endless "scandals" are becoming rather tedious!'[114]

At the beginning of May the revival of Verdi's *Otello* conducted by Zemlinsky almost had to be postponed because Slezak, who was to have sung the title role, was recuperating in Italy. Schmedes withdrew on the eve of the opening night, and the ageing Wallnöfer, 'a singer trained in an unusual manner' (Korngold), who seemed rather miraculously to have kept his voice, had to be brought in from the Kaiserjubiläumstheater.[115] Mahler was immediately accused of having waited until Winkelmann had left before reviving a work in which Slezak had been a triumphant success. Demuth was accused of lacking the personality required for the role of Iago. Only Zemlinsky met with the approval of most of the critics, including Hirschfeld, who disliked every other aspect of the production. However in the *Extrablatt* Stauber criticized the new conductor for 'not being in touch with the orchestra' and for his inability to tone down his fortissimos. Kalbeck, on the other hand, thought that 'the performance surpassed earlier ones in that the overall impression was one of greater unity and consistency'.[116]

The anti-Semitic papers seized on Wallnöfer's weaknesses and on his 'lack of theatrical and musical expression'. They were also very critical of Elsa Bland who, in three years at the Hofoper, had invariably been 'quite uninspired and unbearably bad'. However, her principal fault may well have been that Mahler had preferred her to Lucy Weidt, for other critics, and Kauders in particular, found that she brought to her role the required breadth and emotional structure. Stauber thought that in the final passionate scenes she achieved 'an astonishing grandeur' and 'won the listeners' hearts with an overwhelming *Ave Maria*'. Yet the *Montags-Revue* thought that with this role she was 'venturing on unfamiliar territory', and that 'her powerful and full-bodied

---

[113] The engagement of this singer, who came from the theatre in Erfurt, lasted only from 10 Apr. to 31 Aug. (HOA, G.Z. 16/1462/1907).

[114] The article listed all of Mahler's possible successors, who now included Weingartner and Muck. Mottl, long regarded as the favourite, was 'now out of the running'.

[115] Wallnöfer was a member of the Volksoper. He was mentioned on several occasions as a candidate for the post of director. According to the *Neues Wiener Journal* of 26 Apr., the role of Otello was to have been sung by Philip Brozel. However, after the failure of his first guest appearance on 24 Apr., he had left the Opera. The opening night, which was to have been 28 Apr., had to be postponed.

[116] Max Kalbeck and Paul Stauber noted that, during the performance on 3 May, Demuth tripped on a step as he approached the Venetian ambassador. It seems that he had some difficulty in getting through the rest of the performance.

soprano voice had been forced to produce soft shadings, which were not always successful'. However, Hedwig von Friedländer-Abel praised Zemlinsky, who sought 'the hidden meaning of a mood', and when necessary 'was capable of passion and colour'. But she felt he still had much to learn. Muntz, on the other hand, was of the opinion that the evening had not been a success, primarily because Zemlinsky was 'a novice as far as dynamic nuances were concerned'. In his opinion, he could not have started his career at the Hofoper with a 'more thankless task'.[117] Zemlinsky was fortunate in that Muntz's ill-will was echoed by only a minority of reviewers. Korngold, on the other hand, praised the new conductor's 'sense of form and dramatic effect', and the *Allgemeine Zeitung* gave him the credit for a performance 'full of zest and life'.[118]

Mahler's latest discovery for the Vienna Opera was the American contralto Sarah Charles Cahier,[119] who had made her debut on 5 March as a guest singer in *Le Prophète*. The whole of Vienna soon realized that the young contralto's voice and talent were of the first rank. In order to demonstate this Mahler hit on the idea of staging Saint-Saëns' *Samson et Dalila*, which never had been performed in Vienna, although thirty years had passed since its première in Weimar.[120] The work was conducted by Bruno Walter, and costs were kept to a minimum by borrowing sets from Goldmark's *Die Königin von Saba* and Smetana's *Dalibor*.[121] Many years had passed since Saint-Saëns had been performed in Vienna, and the work's hollow nobility was considered to be lacking in warmth and old-fashioned. Kauders could not understand why it had taken so long to put it on, seeing that Saint-Saëns himself had often been acclaimed in Vienna.[122] He thought that the role of *Samson* suited Schmedes. However, the new contralto was the centre of attention, and the audience was captivated by her striking voice, her sublime diction, and the sensitive nature of her phrasing. Even if she was not flamboyant enough as a biblical temptress, her presence alone justified the choice of Saint-Saëns's work. Kalbeck also praised Cahier's 'singing, acting and vocal agility', whereas Hirschfeld appreciated her polished vocal technique but criticized her acting and the fact that her interpretation 'lacked inner energy'.

[117] Muntz thought that the behaviour of the audience in the gods, which applauded endlessly, was 'fit for a circus'.

[118] Cast for the performance on 3 May: Bland (Desdemona); Kittel (Emilia); Wallnöfer (Otello); Leuer (Cassio); Demuth (Iago); and Mayr (Ludovico).

[119] She had formerly sung under the name of Mrs Morris Black and was sometimes called Madame Charles Cahier.

[120] It was not entirely unknown in Vienna for the principal arias had been sung in various concerts. Plans for this première went back to 1903. In a letter to Camille Saint-Saëns Anna von Mildenburg wrote: 'A few days ago Director Mahler gave me the score of your famous opera *Samson et Dalilah* [*sic*], which, on condition that the role of Dalilah is sung by me, will be performed here at the start of the next season.' Mildenburg asked the composer to transpose the heroine's part up to a key more suited to her, and gave him Mahler's address in Maiernigg 'in case you should wish to contact him'. This project did not materialize (letter to Camille Saint-Saëns dated 1 July 1903, Musée du Château de Dieppe, Fonds Camille Saint-Saëns).

[121] An estimate presented by Roller on 17 Apr. put the cost of refurbishing the scenery at 2,370 kronen, whereas the cost of new costumes and props was not expected to exceed 17,000 kronen.

[122] He had appeared at the Opera on 3 Mar. 1879 as a composer, a conductor, and a virtuoso pianist.

However, Korngold was more impressed by the 'noble warmth' of her inter-pretation and the subtlety of her phrasing, than by her voice, which he consid-ered 'lyric rather than dramatic'. Unlike Muntz, who treated the performance as a new setback for Mahler, an unsigned review in the *Allgemeine Zeitung* (probably by Carl Lafite) called Bruno Walter's conducting 'excellent, and full of enthusiasm'; in fact it was even more convincing than Sarah Charles Cahier's 'intelligent' performance. On the other hand Hedwig von Friedländer-Abel thought that Cahier's French training was particularly helpful even if her voice was more suited to 'expressive cantilenas' than to passionate dialogue. Despite the reservations voiced by the press, the new contralto was a great success, and as a result *Samson* was performed three times before the end of the season, and nine times in the following season.[123]

At the beginning of May Lilli Lehmann came from Berlin for her annual guest appearances. In 1907, she sang on five occasions in four operas,[124] and then stayed in Vienna an extra day to attend a performance of *Tristan* conducted by Mahler, with Mildenburg as Isolde. Having shared the director's box with Alma and Justi she was initially reluctant to accompany them back-stage after Act II, and was somewhat surprised to find Mahler drinking tea and talking to 'about thirty people'. As she was admiring his ability to stay calm and concentrate in the middle of all the noise, Hassinger rushed in to say that Schmedes was hoarse and would not be able to finish the performance. It had already been necessary to cut part of the Love Duet to save his and Mildenburg's voice, for Mildenburg was looking rather tired. With a composure that astonished Lilli Lehmann, Mahler took the score of the last act and quietly made the necessary cuts, about which Schmedes was then informed. The deci-sion had scarcely been taken when Hassinger reappeared with more bad news: Mildenburg was exhausted and could not sing the rest of her role.[125] Hermann Bahr, who for some time had been having an affair with the singer, recorded in

[123] Cast for the performance on 11 May 1907: Cahier (Dalila); Schmedes (Samson); Moser (High Priest); Reich (Abimelech); Hesch (old Hebrew). In the *Montags-Revue* Hedwig von Friedländer-Abel singled out Roller's costumes and sets, the 'feeling for nature' and the 'cloud effects' in Act II and, in the last act, the way in which the Temple finally collapsed.

[124] *La traviata* (in Italian on 4 and 17 May); *Die Entführung* (7 May); *Don Giovanni* (10 May); *Fidelio* (13 May). After the first performance of *La traviata* Korngold praised Lehmann's interpretation, the preci-sion of her voice, the 'bravura of her trills', the 'nobility of her phrasing' and the emotional quality of the final scene. The cast included Maikl (Alfredo); and Moser (Germont). After *Die Entführung*, Korngold once again praised Lehmann's vocal mastery and the nobility of her style. The cast for the performance on 7 May conducted by Mahler included: Forst (Blondchen); Maikl (Belmont); Preuss (Pedrillo); Hesch (Osmin); and Stehmann (Pasha). After *Don Giovanni* Korngold stated that Lehmann was an 'ideal' Donna Anna, even 'when, as on this occasion, she is not at her best'. The cast for this performance, which Mahler also conducted included: Lehmann (Anna); Gutheil-Schoder (Elvira); Forst (Zerlina); Maikl (Ottavio); Demuth (Don Giovanni); and Mayr (Leporello). Lilli Lehmann had originally planned to sing Norma and Isolde on this visit. As on previous occasions, she was paid 1,000 kronen a night, without any deductions (letter from Mahler to the Intendant dated 29 Mar., HOA, G.Z. 351, 1392s/1907). At the behest of the Archduke Eugen, who lived in Salzburg (see above, Chap. 6) and often played music with the great singer, Lehmann had just been awarded a coveted Austrian decoration (*Illustrirtes Wiener Extrablatt*, 26 Apr.).

[125] As seen above, it had been the duty of Sophie Sedlmair, who had just left the Opera (see above, Chap. 8), to wait backstage in case Mildenburg could not finish a performance.

his diary that she had lost her temper with Schmedes on stage because he was so unpleasant that she found him 'devoid of tact and a bad partner'. Bahr indicated that the tenor's lack of sympathy—he was also indisposed—helped to make the excitable and sensitive soprano lose her voice.[126]

This time Mahler 'exploded as if someone had thrown a lighted match into a powder barrel'. 'Beside himself with rage and distress, and jumping up and down like a jack-in-the-box', he ran about in all directions. The interval was almost at an end. He decided on the only possible solution: to finish the work without the heroine, cut the 'lament', and have the *Liebestod* played by the orchestra on its own. The musicians were being informed of these new cuts when Lilli Lehmann, who was about to go back to her seat, had an idea. She said to Alma: 'If I had known what was going to happen, I could easily have sung a few bars of Isolde.' Alma ran to fetch her husband, who reappeared, beamed at her, and asked 'if she would really agree to do him this favour'. 'Even if they have to call me back from the grave,' he added, 'I'll conduct anything you want if you ever need me!'

The great singer rushed to the stage to examine the set, thinking that it was 'already quite a feat to get up (to Tristan)'. Then she went to Schmedes' dressing-room in order to find out how the characters were positioned on the stage. She then hurried to the wardrobe to put on her costume, while Mildenburg helped her with the wig, and finally spent the last few minutes in a rehearsal room, refreshing her memory with the help of a korrepetitor. She had not sung the role for quite some time, with the exception of the *Liebestod*, and requested that there should not be an announcement that she was singing. Since the last act had been considerably abridged, she was soon on the stage, and the work came to an end so quickly that she almost felt that it had been 'a dream'. She later claimed that she had drawn the long hair of her wig over her face 'to avoid being recognized' and that only her voice betrayed her identity. (However, the *Illustrirtes Wiener Extrablatt* stated that 'the blonde Lehmann replaced the brunette Mildenburg'). Be that as it may, Lehmann had never received a greater ovation.[127]

Lilli Lehmann later paid the following homage to Mahler in her memoirs:

I was probably the first person he told that he would be compelled to give up his post; and this on the very day I had intended to comply with his long-standing wish that I should spend a few months at the Vienna Opera, in order to sing Armide and the two Iphigenias. (It had also been a plan mounted by Wilhelm Jahn!) But our dream was not to come true.

The things which forced him to leave Vienna were rather complicated. Mahler did not have a talent for management or for figures. I had to promise him every year to give

---

[126] *Meister und Meisterbriefe um Hermann Bahr*, ed. Joseph Gregor (Bauer, Vienna, 1947), 216.

[127] At Mahler's suggestion the Intendant paid Lilli Lehmann an extra 1,000 kronen for having saved the performance on 19 May (HOA, G.Z. 596/1392/1907). Lehmann immediately wrote to thank Viktor von Horsetzky, at that time the acting Intendant, and expressed the hope that she would be able to return to Vienna, 'for I am very attached to the productions of the Hofoper'. After Mahler's departure she was invited to Vienna in 1909 and 1910.

my guest appearances, but he could never specify a time, so that for example what had been decided on for March would often be deferred to April or May, and then take place in February after all. He was always an idealist, granting himself and others neither time nor rest. It was only natural that he should have dismissed the claims of those who sought to promote private interests in the court theatre, and as a result he made enemies in high places. And who could hold it against him if, in his impulsive way of seeking beauty, he often believed he had found it with means forced upon him by others,[128] which he later recognized as mistaken, and never counted the cost in the process. He never sought to fill his own pockets, and never thought of himself. As a friend one had to give him practical advice about certain matters and make him aware of his rights and his future.[129] Mahler was a nervous artistic fanatic, looked like a devil, was as lovable as a child, and was a kind guardian and father to his sister, wife and children. He was immensely powerful and for many years had certainly been an inwardly sick man. He set about the tasks he wished to complete with enormous energy, an energy which, when it met a congenial force, could blend into the most beautiful and harmonious collaboration, and could even take a subordinate role. It was always a great pleasure to work with him. I was sorry that—seeing that he could not stay—he had to cross the ocean in order to achieve what so many people want, freedom from having to work in his later years, for his family and, last but not least, for his creative work. He had given Vienna a great deal, even though sometimes in an ugly manner, as, for example in *Don Giovanni* which he described to me as a total failure,[130] or in *Figaro*, which could have been a splendid production if the sets, and indeed some of the costumes, had not flown in the face of naturalness or elegance.[131]

The cordiality of Mahler's relationship with Lilli Lehmann is further illustrated by a passage in her memoirs in which she recalls having been asked by Mahler for advice about an offer he had received from the National Conservatory of Music of America. This letter has found its way only into an East German edition of his correspondence:

They've asked me to specify my fees! Please, dear friend, telegraph the sum you think I ought to name—not knowing America, I'm afraid of making a blunder.—I'm supposed to put it in Reichsmark.—I see from your letter that I owe this offer to you. It's so nice of you to have thought of me, and I feel such gratitude in my heart at this moment, that a letter isn't enough for me to express it. . . . Please don't mention this letter to my sister. Perhaps it would be better to ask the people in New York to suggest the fees?[132]

It is fascinating to realize that Mahler could have been tempted to accept an American offer only a few months after he had been appointed to the directorship of the Vienna Opera.

---

[128] Lehmann is obviously referring to Roller.

[129] Lehmann here tells the story of a proposal Mahler received from the National Conservatory of Music of America (see below).

[130] This passage may well have been motivated by the rather unkind remarks that Mahler had made in Salzburg the previous year during a rehearsal of Lilli Lehmann's own production of *Don Giovanni* (see above, Chap. 6).   [131] Lilli Lehmann, *Mein Weg*, 368.

[132] Gustav Mahler, *Briefe* (Reclam, Leipzig, 1985), no. 287. The letter could have been written only in spring 1898, as established by Zoltan Roman, *Gustav Mahler's American Years 1907–11. A Documentary History* (Pendragon, Stuyvesant, NY, 1988), 2–8.

However, the principal artistic event in Vienna during May was neither the revival of *Otello*, nor the première of *Samson et Dalila*, nor even Lilli Lehmann's guest appearances. Despite all Mahler's efforts it took place not at the Hofoper, but at the Deutsches Theater,[133] where the complete company of the Breslau Opera had come to perform the Viennese première of Richard Strauss's *Salome*. The performance was conducted by Julius Prüwer, and Fanchette Verhunck alternated in the title role with two other sopranos, Albine Nagel and Jenny Korb. The tickets were sold out long beforehand, and this showed that the Viennese were eager to get to know a work which was in the news whenever it was performed.

Josef Reitler took the opportunity to write an article for the *Vossische Zeitung* in Berlin in which he defended Mahler and his management of the Opera, and described the performance at the Deutsches Theater. He thought that it was 'a scandal' that the work had to be staged in an unsuitable theatre simply because the censor 'refused to sanction a work in which a saint is beheaded' at a court theatre. At the Café Imperial, he later met Mahler who told him: 'I no longer read reviews, but what you wrote about me is full of sense. Time will prove you right about *Salome*, too. It's an epoch-making work, even if people hiss and the critics are abusive.'[134]

In the *Neue Freie Presse* Julius Korngold attacked the censor's decision in a long feuilleton, and reminded his readers that the Hofoper was the only court theatre in Europe to have rejected *Salome*. As predicted, the ban had only served to whet the public's curiosity. The auditorium was completely full before the curtain went up, for theatregoers had been warned that nobody would be admitted once the performance had started. The audience included numerous artists, musicians, and members of the aristocracy: Marie Gutheil and her husband; Julius Epstein; Andreas Dippel, the tenor formerly at the Hofoper who had become joint director of the Metropolitan Opera;[135] Oskar Straus, the composer of operettas; Alfred Grünfeld, the famous pianist; Count Lanckoronski and Countess Wydenbruck, etc. Many members of the audience were busy reading the libretto while they waited and there was a great deal of tension in the auditorium. However, the staging did not disappoint the impatient audience, nor did the work's 'unprecedented realism' and its vivid combination of theatre and 'Straussian programme symphony'. Korngold thought that the performance occasionally left something to be desired, especially in regard to the 'differentiation between Salome's moods' and the playing of the orchestra which sometimes drowned out the voices in a theatre in which the acoustic's were poor. Not only was Fanchette Verhunck one of the few singers who dared to perform the Dance of the Seven Veils herself, she also overcame all the vocal difficulties of the title role. The audience had been so entranced that, when the curtain fell after Herod's famous line, 'Man töte dieses Weib!', there was time

---

[133] The orchestra pit was enlarged to include the central section of the front rows of the stalls.
[134] JRM 63.   [135] See below, Vol. iiii, Chaps. 1 to 3.

for a few protesters to hiss before the tumultuous applause of the vast majority broke out.

In the *Deutsches Volksblatt* Hans Puchstein stated that *Salome* contained 'much that is bizarre, much that is extravagant, but also much that is noble and overwhelmingly beautiful'. Before the curtain went up Wallaschek observed in the audience 'a slightly unhealthy excitement, a feverishness that clouded people's judgement'. A deathly silence prevailed for several seconds after the curtain fell and before the applause began. Heinrich Reinhardt, in the *Neues Wiener Tagblatt*, concentrated on the audience: the elegance of people's clothes, hairstyles, and carriages. He thought that Verhunck's performance of the principal role was 'almost ideal'. People listened to 'Salome's demonic song with feverish pulse and bated breath'. Maximilian Muntz reported that, as had been expected, this sensational work had been sensationally successful, and acknowledged that it made a far greater impression than the initial shock might have led one to suppose. In the *Extrablatt*, Paul Stauber, who was standing in for Hans Liebstöckl (who, like Karpath, was in the United States) thought that Strauss's music failed to touch 'heart and soul, though it assailed our nerves'; that it was 'produced by the energy of a genius, which extends the limits of music in an unforeseen way without infringing them'; and that it merited the greatest admiration. He believed that the orchestral technique, with its wealth of colour and expression surpassing that of Wagner or Berlioz, could almost be described as monstrous or diabolical. 'In the midst of the cascades of sound there were moments of absolute beauty, uncanny power and profound emotion.' Stauber recorded that the applause at the end was thunderous and had easily drowned out the whistling of the opposition. 'It emphasized the fact that the evening was a sensational artistic event.' Mahler was no doubt hurt by this triumph, having done all he could to perform the work at the Hofoper. Was he not right to leave a capital and a country in which, at the stroke of a pen, and in the name of a narrow and reactionary idea of public morality, it was possible to ban a dramatic masterpiece, and one that was subsequently recognized as such everywhere?[136]

The last event of the season at the Hofoper, and the one which marked the end of Mahler's directorship and his collaboration with Alfred Roller, was a modern ballet which attempted to infuse new life into the genre. In the course of a conversation with Roller in Maiernigg the previous year, Mahler had told him the story of *Rübezahl*, the youthful opera for which he had written a libretto and a few numbers. It was a legend about a misshapen and ridiculous spirit who comes down from the mountains, carries off a princess, and, in an attempt to make her happy, gives her the means to escape and return to the world of

[136] In fact, *Salome* had also been banned at the Metropolitan Opera in New York, at the request of J. P. Morgan (see below, Vol. iiii, Chap. 1). Cast of the first Viennese performance on 25 May, conducted by Julius Prüwer: Verhunck, who alternated with Nagel (Salome); Fellwock-Costa, who alternated with Neumann-Seebach (Herodias); Trostorff, who alternated with Briesemeister (Herod); Waschmann (Narraboth); and Beeg, who alternated with Schützendorff (Jochanaan).

mortals.[137] While it is easy to see what attracted the young Mahler to this romantic and Hoffmannesque subject with its mixture of comic, grotesque, and fairy-tale elements, it is difficult to understand what led Roller, who wished to win his spurs in the field of ballet, to find it interesting. As we have seen, Mahler probably felt an obscure need to reform the dance, at a time when the majority of contemporary dancers such as Isadora Duncan, Ruth Saint Denis, and Maud Allan were well known in Vienna, and when accounts of the young Russian school were beginning to circulate.

The previous November Josef Hassreiter had choreographed a new ballet entitled *Atelier Bruder Japonet* to music by Franz Skofitz, the Opera's head 'stage manager' (*Oberinspizient*).[138] In this old-fashioned and purely decorative divertissement the ballet master's only concern had been to pander to the tastes of the Viennese audience.[139] At the première on 28 November 1906, it was part of a double bill that also included a new one-act opera by Eugen d'Albert, *Flauto Solo*.[140] Mahler, who attended the dress rehearsal the day before, was so dismayed by the foolishness of the scenario and the poverty of the choreography that he thought about forbidding the performance. 'Herr Hassreiter went straight to the Lord Chamberlain, inviting him to come and see for himself whether or not the ballet should be jettisoned. The Prince supported him and the première went ahead as planned.'[141] All the Viennese critics with the exception of Mahler's two loyal supporters, Julius Korngold and David Josef Bach, found the work 'entertaining and agreeable', preferring it to 'psychological or dramatic' endeavours aimed at renewing the genre.[142]

But Roller had convinced Mahler that it was not only possible but in fact desirable to reform the dance. Their first attempt, which was a complete success, had been with the 'Greek' dances in *Iphigénie en Aulide*. No doubt this was why Roller was given permission to create in *Rübezahl* a thoroughly 'modern' ballet,[143] this time with the help of Karl Godlewsky, an actor and assistant ballet master, who also performed the title role.[144] The new work had three acts, and lasted an hour and ten minutes or half the evening. The scenario was almost certainly by Roller himself, although he did not put his name to it. Mahler had already decided to leave the Hofoper by the time of the première, so what the critics said was influenced by whether they were for or

---

[137]　See above, Vol. i, App. 1.

[138]　Franz Skofitz (1865– ?) was also the author of the other ballets produced at the Hofoper, *Künstlerlist*, *Pan*, and *Das Urteil des Paris*.　　　　　　　[139]　Robert Hirschfeld, *Wiener Abendpost* (29 Nov. 1906).

[140]　See above, Chap. 7.

[141]　*Neues Wiener Journal* (23 Feb. 1907), *Sturm in Wasserglas* (A Storm in a Teacup).

[142]　*Wiener Allgemeine Zeitung* (29 Nov. 1906).

[143]　Although he created the sets, the costumes and the lighting, his name did not appear on the posters.

[144]　Twelve years later, in 1919, Karl Godlewsky succeeded Hassreiter as head of the Vienna Opera ballet. On 2 June 1907, the evening began with *I Pagliacci*, with the following cast: Gutheil-Schoder (Nedda); Schrödter (Canio); Demuth (Tonio); and Stehmann (Silvio), and continued with a revival of Ignaz Brüll's *Das goldene Kreuz*. The sets and costumes for *Rübezahl* cost 44,000 kronen, and were largely paid for by the twelve performances given in 1907 and 1908.

against him. As in Mahler's early libretto,[145] the first scene of *Rübezahl* showed a princess and her companions at play in the forest. Rübezahl, having observed them, carried them off to his mountain kingdom. Act II was set in his cave, and Act III in which the princess recovered her freedom took place in the royal palace. Reports stated that the set for Act II consisted entirely of rocks and precious stones that symbolized Rübezahl's wealth. There was also a decorative waterfall, and the costumes were studded with gems.[146] The score included extracts from Delibes' *Naïla* (The Spring) and *Sylvia*, music by Léon Minkus, the last act of *Coppélia* (which had never been performed in Vienna), and *Petitionen*, a waltz by Josef Strauss. It had been prepared by Julius Lehnert,[147] who also conducted the performance. Some critics found Roller's 'compositions with light' incomparable. For most of them, the evening's chief attraction was the set for Act II, although Max Kalbeck's general impression was that the image was 'overladen and confused', 'devoid of imagination', with a 'plethora of colours and lighting effects which makes one feel rather giddy'.[148] Liebstöckl, on the other hand, was captivated by Roller's 'bacchanal of colour and lights'. Carl Lafite also described the visual display as 'harmonious' and 'intoxicating', but found the entire ballet boring and dull, and the choreography devoid of imagination: a painter had had the Opera at his disposal and had succeeded in creating a beautiful ballet, full of good humour and poetry. However, he had lacked 'a good writer and a choreographer with ideas of his own; and also someone like Delibes or a Minkus'. Albert Leitich, faithful to the party line of the *Deutsche Zeitung*, dismissed Roller's *Rübezahl* as worthless, and took exception to the 'flowery night-gowns' of the princess and her companions, and the pastel colours of the costumes, which were hardly 'worthy of an unimaginative schoolmaster'. Only the 'Dance of the Emeralds' in Act II[149] had found some favour with the audience. 'Soon,' he added, 'everything will be different, and one can only hope that Herr Roller will take the same path as Herr Mahler!'

As might have been expected, Hirschfeld was equally critical. Only Mahler's regular champions, Elsa Bienenfeld, Julius Korngold, and David Josef Bach, praised in their reviews the colours and nuances of the new ballet, and also the way in which Roller had grouped the characters on stage as 'stylized images'. Finally, the unsigned review in the *Neues Wiener Journal* raved about the authors of a ballet which had 'added new and splendid effects to an

---

[145] See above, Vol i, Chap. 5 and App. 1

[146] *Illustrirtes Wiener Extrablatt* (19 May 1911).

[147] Julius Lehnert conducted ballets at the Hofoper from 1 May 1907 to 30 Apr. 1913.

[148] However, in the *Montags-Revue*, Hedwig von Friedländer-Abel stated that the acting element in the show had been 'somewhat inadequate'. She was still waiting for a ballet which would unite dancing with acting in a convincing manner.

[149] The act included a series of dances for various precious stones: rubies, moonstones, topazes, amethysts, opals, sapphires, turquoises, diamonds, garnets, beryls, and emeralds. For the procession to the castle in the last act Roller used golden and silvery veils 'which lent an astonishing brilliance to this symphony [of colours]' (*Neue Freie Presse* (2 June 1907)).

antiquated genre, which as a result was lively and charming'. This first and rather timid attempt to renew the dance could hardly have been a complete success for too much remained to be done. We can only speculate about what might have happened if Roller and Diaghilev, for instance, had been able to collaborate. And this would not have been impossible if Mahler had stayed on at the Opera. At any rate, Roller had proved that there was an audience in Vienna for this kind of spectacle for, by the end of 1907, *Rübezahl* had been performed eleven times.

By 2 June, the date of the première of *Rübezahl*, Mahler had already lost interest in the Opera, and was preoccupied with his own future. According to the *Neues Wiener Journal*, on 31 May he had another interview with Prince Montenuovo, who confirmed that he had taken cognizance of Mahler's desire to be relieved of his duties at the Hofoper.[150] For several weeks he had been making discreet enquiries, and examining the various offers made to him without yet being able to reach a decision. From the very beginning he had hoped that Felix Mottl would succeed Mahler, but it was not clear whether Mottl would be allowed to leave Munich by the Bavarian authorities.

The most tempting offer Mahler had received at this time, and the most interesting from a financial point of view, was without doubt the one made by Heinrich Conried, director of the Metropolitan Opera in New York since 1903.[151] Conried was both well known and feared in German theatrical circles, where he had a reputation for offering enormous fees to German opera stars to entice them over to the United States. His two outstanding achievements had been to make an international star of the tenor Enrico Caruso, who had been engaged by his predecessor, Maurice Grau, and to have put on the first performance of *Parsifal* outside Bayreuth. As a result he was in disfavour with the Wagner family, but could comfort himself with the thought that he had made 100,000 dollars net profit on the production.

At the beginning of the 1906–7 season Conried had run into difficulties when Oscar Hammerstein, a cigar trader who had become a millionaire, decided to build a new opera house not far from the Metropolitan. Hammerstein, a businessman who was just as shrewd as Conried, managed to engage, at great expense, a galaxy of first-rate singers including two famous sopranos, Nellie Melba and Luisa Tetrazzini, the tenor Alessandro Bonci, and the baritone Maurice Renaud. He had also acquired the rights to a number of new French operas, such as Charpentier's *Louise*, Massenet's *Thaïs*, and Debussy's *Pelléas et Mélisande*. In order to counter such stiff competition, Conried was counting heavily on the sensation that would be caused by *Salome*, which, he hoped, would attract full houses for several months. Unfortunately the dress rehearsal, which was held before an invited audience,

---

[150] The same report mentioned Arthur Nikisch as one of his possible successors.

[151] See below the biography of Heinrich Conried (1848–1909) in Vol. iiii, Chap. 1. He had succeeded Maurice Grau as head of the Metropolitan Opera in 1903.

shocked New York society, and the work was immediately banned at the request of most of the board of directors.

During Conried's reign, the programmes at the Metropolitan were divided equally between the German and Italian repertoires and he knew very well that success of the German works depended largely on the quality of the conductor, especially since the great age of Wagnerian singers had come to an end. Thus he was determined to engage a great German conductor at any price, and he was among the first to hear the rumours about Mahler's decision to leave. He immediately telephoned him to offer 'the highest fee a musician has ever received', that is to say 125,000 kronen for a season of six months,[152] a contract for four years, and a free return trip across the Atlantic for two. To an intermediary, because Mahler did not want the Hofoper's staff to know of his negotiations, Conried sent the following telegram:

Artistic questions can certainly be resolved to your satisfaction. If America or the conditions there do not suit you, I am prepared to include a clause providing for the termination of the contract. I am prepared to organize concerts of your works. In any case, a personal interview would be of greatest importance and I am sure what the result will be. If you receive any other serious proposals, no matter from whom they come, I am prepared to demonstrate to you, that mine is the highest our society can offer. I would also be prepared to agree if Mahler were to prefer an 'invitation' for four to six weeks. The invitation should be repeated each year. Greetings. Heinrich Conried.[153]

However, Mahler hesitated for two reasons. First of all, he was not as yet sure that he would be able to leave Vienna and, second, he was unwilling to face six months a year in the United States without knowing the conditions under which he would be working. For this reason he made a counter-proposal and suggested a two-year contract for four months' work a year at a salary of 100,000 kronen (about 20,000 dollars),[154] or else for two months' work a year, in which case he was prepared to start immediately, even if it proved impossible to leave Vienna (in other words, he was asking for half the four months' fee, or 50,000 kronen). And if he succeeded in freeing himself, he was prepared to reconsider the original idea of six months. A meeting with Conried was soon arranged in Berlin at the beginning of June but Mahler had to keep his negociations secret until the problem of his successor had been resolved. A few days before leaving for Berlin Mahler had in principle agreed to spend a two-month period in New York, from 15 February to 15 April.

---

[152] It is not clear how Conried intended to exploit Mahler's talents during these six months, for the Metropolitan's New York season lasted less than five months. He probably hoped that Mahler would conduct on one of the tours the Opera undertook each spring, and he may also have toyed with the idea of becoming his exclusive agent in the United States and as he was already doing for Caruso finding concert engagements for him.

[153] Undated telegram from Conried (24 May 1907, AMS). The intermediary was most likely the one to whom later communications were sent, i.e. Rudolf Winternitz (see below), the manager of Atelier Blaschke which prepared costumes for the Opera, on the Mariahilferstrasse 33, in Vienna.

[154] In 1906 a krone was worth $0.2027.

Mahler took the train to Berlin on the evening of 4 June, and on 5 June went directly from the station to Hotel Kaiserhof, where Conried was staying, and where they intended to discuss his proposals. After their first conversation Mahler made up his mind to telephone Alma to keep her abreast of the negotiations, but after trying in vain for two hours to contact her on a very bad line, he finally decided to send her a letter and a telegram simultaneously.[155] Conried was full of enthusiasm about their project and offered him an exclusive contract (similar to that of Caruso) for eight months, and a salary of 180,000 kronen. They finally settled on a three-month contract and 25,000 kronen a month, with Conried agreeing to pay Mahler's travelling expenses and living quarters in a first-class hotel. The length of the contract had not yet been agreed upon, for Mahler preferred to commit himself only for one year. The agreement stipulated that Mahler was to conduct only Wagner and Mozart at the Metropolitan opera, but Conried also agreed to organize six concerts for him, one of them devoted to his Second Symphony.[156]

After writing this letter to Alma, Mahler had another meeting with Conried. He finished by comparing his earnings if he agreed to spend six months a year in the United States or accepted an engagement as guest conductor for six to eight weeks. For the first time in ten years he was beginning to realize that his Viennese salary was low, at least according to American standards, and the idea of earning enough money to be able to devote more time to composition suddenly became very attractive. However, to Emil Freund, his lawyer-friend who had no doubt teased him about the dramatic increase in his income, he said: 'I don't want to be a millionaire; if I wanted to be a millionaire, I'd go and speculate on the stock exchange.'[157] From now on his ambition was to achieve a level of financial security that would allow him to devote himself to his work, and at the same time to ensure his family's future.[158] Clearly, the monthly salary Conried was offering meant that his financial worries were over. In two months, he would now earn 50,000 kronen, a good deal more than his annual salary at the Hofoper (36,000 kronen and a performance fee each time he conducted).[159]

---

[155] The telegram appears only in AMS. The letter (BGA, no. 206) is written on note paper of Hotel Der Kaiserhof. It is undated (5 June 1907).

[156] BGA, no. 200, undated (5 June 1907), written on the notepaper of Hotel Der Kaiserhof, Berlin.

[157] Emil Freund to one of his friends, Dr Kornfeld, who transcribed onto a typewriter page a series of Mahler's sayings (BGM, Paris).

[158] In a letter no doubt written before his negotiations and meeting with Conried, Mahler told his sister Emma, who worried about the monthly payment of 50 kronen that she received from her brother (see above, Vol. ii, Chap. 13, 496) that he was not yet in a position to assess his financial prospects: 'I probably can't count on a fixed salary in future, so I must practise order into my affairs.' Card to Emma Rosé, undated (June 1907), Ernst Rosé collection, sold at Sotheby's, New York, Nov. 1984). The Rosé collection (RWO) also contains a letter to Justine, which is undated but was meant to accompany a sum of 1,000 kronen, 720 for her, and 280 for Emma. This was apparently Mahler's last payment to his sisters for he writes to Justi: '720K: Rest an dich.' The date is uncertain but the card can only have been written in 1907 or later because Mahler is staying with the Molls at the Hohe Warte (RWO, Shelfmark E6-MJ-300).

[159] See Vol. ii, Chap. 2. Mahler's annual salary, amounted to 24,000 kronen at the time of his appointment. It had risen to 36,000 kronen in 1901, at the time of his illness (see above, Vol. ii, Chap. 4). Mahler also received an additional fee for each performance he conducted.

Before leaving Berlin, Mahler wrote briefly to Oskar Fried:

I wanted to come to see you in a car, but had to leave at four instead of six thirty so that I could stop in Dresden for three hours to deal with an urgent matter. That's why I couldn't see you . . . But now that I am a free man, and will probably pass through Berlin quite often, I hope to see much more of you. I shall continue to live in Vienna. Of course I shall not be conducting any more. The uproar would be too much for me . . . I am getting a headache and need to get out into the fresh air.[160]

What the 'urgent matter' was that Mahler had to deal with in Dresden is not clear. Either Prince Montenuovo had asked him to talk to Ernst von Schuch about the latter's candidature for the directorship of the Vienna Opera, in view of the fact that Mottl had now withdrawn. Or Mahler may have wanted to talk with him about the truncated performance of the Sixth Symphony which had been given two months earlier, on 5 April, by the Königliche Kapelle, and to discuss the inclusion of another of his symphonies in the following year's programme. No doubt because he was alarmed by the length and overpowering tutti of the last movement, Schuch had suddenly found it impossible not to commemorate the tenth anniversary of Brahms's death, and had hastily added the latter's First Symphony to the programme, retaining only the two middle movements of Mahler's Sixth.[161]

The press had not seen through this last-minute change, especially since everyone in Dresden knew that the Sixth Symphony and particularly the last movement had elicited a very lukewarm response elsewhere. In the *Dresdener Zeitung* Heinrich Platzbecker[162] revealed that the orchestral committee had hesitated for a long time before deciding to play the work. However, he felt that it was absurd to cut the first and the last movements, for the audience knew what to expect from someone who was 'extremely modern'. Taken out of context, the two middle movements conveyed the impression of 'the colourful dress in the portrait of a lady whose face and hands are invisible.' In any case, if Schuch had conducted the last movement he would surely have toned down some of its harsher features. It was a well-known fact that in Vienna and Berlin the 'witches' sabbath' had been decried and greeted with laughter. However, a composer had the right to have his works played in their entirety. In the Andante, despite its 'learned bric-à-brac and grandiloquent formal patterns', his mastery was beyond dispute. The bizarre rhythms, the irony and parody in the Scherzo had baffled most of the listeners and only a few people had applauded Schuch, who had taken only three bows.

---

[160] Undated postcard, Leo Baeck Institute, New York. Mahler added that his wife and daughter, who had been ill, had recovered.

[161] The concert at the Dresden Opera was on 5 Apr., at 7 p.m. The programme consisted of: Brahms, First Symphony; Mahler, two movements from the Sixth Symphony (Andante moderato and Scherzo); Beethoven's *Leonore* Overture No. 3. Schuch redeemed himself the following year with a performance of Mahler's Fourth Symphony, which occurred on 17 March and was a great success.

[162] Heinrich Platzbecker (1860–1937), who was born in Merzenhausen, composed a number of successful operettas, humorous songs, and choral works.

In the *Signale für die Musikalische Welt*, Friedrich Brandes,[163] the critic of the *Anzeiger*, who had been present at the première in Essen, once again described the Sixth as 'programme music without a programme', and professed to admire its 'alchemy'. 'Mahler has his own recipe and a pantry full of ingredients which serve as a substitute for a lack of invention': the march, the Brucknerian chorale, old sentimental songs, little old-fashioned dances, and reminiscences of Beethoven, Schubert, and Mendelssohn. The only 'new' thing in this 'Krupp Symphony'[164] was the 'wobbly dance' in the Scherzo, with its subtle rhythmic devices.

Mahler writes the best and most modern *Kapellmeistermusik*. Except as regards originality, a concept which seems to be old and outdated, he surpasses all his rivals with his elaboration and structure, his instrumentation and combinations of timbres, his knowledge of the literature, and especially his length, which he is able to make one forget with all kinds of surprises, nostalgic reminiscences, stupendous hammering sounds, and even old-fashioned musical jokes. Finally one thing cannot be overlooked: Mahler is one of the most serious of contemporary musicians. This explains his relentless and challenging approach. The fact that his symphony is a great drama without any other actors springs from his character which makes him concentrate on making new discoveries and devising new combinations, and not on sudden inspirations.

Hermann Starcke, the critic of the *Dresdener Nachrichten*, congratulated Schuch on the 'tact' which had led him to commemorate Brahms's death by 'cutting off the head and tail' of Mahler's symphony, leaving only the 'fillet' in the middle. Written 'under the aegis of Bruckner', the Andante was

the music of an artist and a conductor who can do much, who has read and listened to a great deal of music, who really understands how to write a score. But this music never manages to enthral the listener or to arouse his interest. On the other hand, the Scherzo is a really nasty piece of work, a deliberate mockery. One strident effect follows another, the motifs are not living beings, or building blocks that could function as the basis of a symphony. They are simply artificial figures in burlesque costumes who follow each other in a grotesque manner. Polyphony turns into a tangled voice-leading, and the musical poverty verges on nudity. At the end of the piece the listeners' patience was exhausted. True, a handful of ardent Mahlerians attempted to save the situation with some ineffectual applause but they were drowned out by hefty protests and hissing by the whole of the audience (something that has never happened before). The rest was silence—icy silence.

The correspondent of the *Musikalisches Wochenblatt*, Paul Pfitzner, confessed that he was 'not among Mahler's admirers' and that he considered that his 'lack of invention' and his orchestral excesses were fatal weaknesses. Nonetheless Mahler was a serious musician who deserved that a work of his should be presented in full, not in truncated form. If Schuch disliked the outer

---

[163] *Signale für die musikalische Welt*, 65 (1907): 48/49, 832 ff. For the biography of Friedrich Brandes, see above, Vol. i, Chap. 23.   [164] Essen became famous on account of the steelworks.

movements he should have left the symphony out of the programme. In any case he had done Mahler an ill-turn, since out of context the Scherzo, in particular, had appeared incomprehensible.[165]

Thus, in Dresden as elsewhere, Mahler had been ill-served and misunderstood. One might have thought that the admiration aroused by his choral symphonies would encourage critics to be favourably disposed towards his 'new excesses', but exactly the opposite was the case. Once again the truncated Sixth had strengthened the general feeling that Mahler was merely an artisan, a professional of the orchestra who believed himself a creative genius. A month before Schuch's act of disloyalty to Mahler, Arthur Smolian[166] had made similar remarks in the *Signale für die Musikalische Welt* about a complete performance of the Sixth in Leipzig given by Hans Winderstein and his orchestra. On this occasion, however, the audience had demonstrated its enthusiasm in a noisy manner, which only served to embitter the critic of the *Leipziger Zeitung* even further. Like his colleagues in Dresden, he saw only 'a would-be greatness'; 'skill and technique' and 'unashamed arrogance', all of which deceived audiences which were 'only too easy to deceive'. 'There is no trace of intelligence or feeling in all this trash and commotion, with the exception of 'a few musical flowers plucked from other people's gardens.'[167]

Thus the last two performances of the Sixth Symphony during Mahler's lifetime, one complete, the other fragmentary, only helped to increase the lack of understanding that was to dog the work for years to come. There were no other performances that summer to make up for the setbacks suffered by the Sixth. Johannes Messchaert continued occasionally to perform Mahler's songs, and included two of the *Rückert-Lieder* in the final concert of the Niederrheinisches Musikfest in Cologne on 1 July. His refined and sensitive performances were a great success, as always.[168] But Mahler at this time no longer worried about whether his works were being performed or not. His main concern was to finalize the details of his new contract. In Berlin, he had told Conried that it would be impossible for him to conduct more than two performances a week in New York, but on returning to Vienna he began to worry that this stipulation might have been misunderstood. In a telegram he explained that he had not made it in order to claim extra payment for conducting more frequently, but because he feared that the long and numerous rehearsals required in the case of Wagner's operas would tire him to the point of not being up to a third performance.

[165] *Musikalisches Wochenblatt*, and *Neue Zeitschrift für Musik*, 38 (1907): 23 (6 June), 622.
[166] See above, Chaps. 1 and 7.
[167] On 11 Mar. Hans Winderstein conducted the eleventh Philharmonic concert (the third 'contemporary evening') given by the Winderstein Orchestra, which on this occasion comprised 110 musicians.
[168] The 84th Niederrheinisches Musikfest took place from 29 June and 1 July at the Gürzenich Hall and was conducted by Fritz Steinbach. The programme of the final concert included: Strauss, *Don Juan*; Tchaikovsky, Violin Concerto (with Mischa Elman as soloist); Mahler, 'Ich bin der Welt abhanden gekommen' and 'Ich atmet' einen linden Duft' (with Johannes Messchaert, baritone); Thomas, Ophelia's aria from *Hamlet* (with Amy Castle, soprano); Wagner, *Parsifal*, parts of Act II, and Act III, and the Prelude to *Die Meistersinger*.

Nevertheless, 'I shall prove to you in America that I am placing my ability and whole being at your disposal.' This time Conried refused to agree. He replied to their usual intermediary that Mahler would have to conduct three times a week: 'After our meeting he must be aware that he will not have to conduct three times if for any reason he is unable to. Mahler must feel that he is musically at the head of the whole venture and that I will take certain steps only after consulting him.'[169]

Although the terms of the contract had not yet been finalized, and although Conried had not been authorized by Mahler to make his appointment public, it was announced in the *New York Sun* on 8 June and in the *Telegraph* on 9 June. The Metropolitan Opera's general manager had visited Europe not only for the sake of his health, but also to recruit a Wagnerian conductor, and Mahler was 'Europe's most famous conductor'. The European press remained silent, for Prince Montenuovo had not yet found a suitable replacement for Mahler, who in any case was still hesitating and did not make up his mind until the end of the month. A letter from Mahler to the impresario Norbert Salter shows that an approach had been made by Oscar Hammerstein, Conried's rival. He should 'make me a precise offer', Mahler wrote.[170] In another letter to the same addressee, Mahler added:

I am submerged by such a flood of projects and proposals that I cannot make my mind up, especially since they have not yet found someone to replace me. Obviously I must first get a general idea of the whole situation. The best thing would be if you were to collect everything that is sent to you concerning me, so that we can discuss the whole thing when I am in Berlin <u>in the very near future</u>. It looks almost certain to be America (I have offers from several other people). In principle the Mannheim offer[171] and the others of the same kind would suit me perfectly. But I can only decide about this after I have considered the main options. However, I can confirm today that I am unlikely to be free from February to April. And in any case I have already accepted engagements for The Hague[172] and Russia.[173]

On his return from Berlin Mahler found that the excitement aroused by the Vienna Opera's 'directorship crisis' was greater than ever, even though it was now only a matter of choosing his successor. As we have seen, Schoenberg had rejected Karl Kraus's proposal to write a long article on 'The Mahler case'.

---

[169]   Undated telegram from Mahler to Conried (8 June?) and reply dated 10 June (AMS).

[170]   Undated letter (no. 8) to Norbert Salter (May–June 1907), BSM, Munich. Fortunately, the impresario numbered the many cards and letters he received from Mahler in 1907, some of which are dated.

[171]   In HOA there is a telegram which Mahler sent on 7 May to Wilhelm Bopp (1863–1931), the director of the Mannheim School of Music. He states that he 'will probably stay (in Vienna) and would be glad to be of help to him'. Bopp had just been appointed director of the Vienna Conservatory, which was about to become the 'Kaiserlich Königliche Akademie für Musik und Darstellende Kunst'. No doubt he was hoping that Mahler would agree to join his staff.

[172]   The Diligentia Orchestra in The Hague had engaged Mahler for 8 Jan. 1908 (see below, Chap. 10). He had accepted the invitation despite Mengelberg's reservations (letter from Mahler to Mengelberg, 15 Apr. 1907, RMH 85).

[173]   Undated letter to Norbert Salter, numbered 9 by the addressee (BSM, Munich).

Thus on 22 May, *Die Fackel* published only a short paragraph attacking Heinrich Reinhardt.[174] When Mahler's decision to leave the Opera was announced, Ludwig Karpath had been in the United States. As soon as he returned to Vienna he went to see him and then published 'A Conversation with Gustav Mahler', in the *Neues Wiener Tagblatt* of 5 June, the day Mahler left for Berlin to see Conried. Much later he published it once again in his memoirs, *Begegnung mit dem Genius*.

It was not originally my intention to comment in any detail on my forthcoming departure from the Vienna Opera. However, recently so much has been said about me which is untrue that I no longer have any reason to adhere to my earlier reticence, at least as regards the grossest lies. To begin with, it is completely untrue that I have been toppled by 'affairs' of any kind. I have not been toppled at all. I am going of my own freewill because I wish to become completely independent. Also, and this is of the utmost importance, because I have come to realize that the operatic stage is an institution which continues to be very problematical. If it is still possible to achieve anything anywhere, then it is in Vienna, where the conditions for working in an effective manner are far better than anywhere else. But even here one can also come to a dead-end and find it impossible to go any further. Of course, I cannot explain in a few words how all this comes about. However, a single aspect will suffice: for example, the dearth of new operas of good quality at the present time. That is all for today; I shall have more to say about it another time. I believe that I have done everything that could be done. Of course, it is not for me to say; it is not for me to evaluate the results of my directorship. However, I would like to stress one thing: in no theatre in the world can standards be maintained at a level where each performance is as good as the previous ones. But this is what I dislike about the theatre. For of course I would like every performance to be at the same high level, in other words, to attain to an ideal that is unattainable. No one before me has been able to do it, and no one after me will be able to do it either. And as I have finally come to understand this after ten years of hard work, I am leaving a post which, I can say this quite categorically, was still open to me until I had finally come to a decision.

It is simply not true to say that the deficit at the Hofoper has greatly increased and that this was the reason why I had to go. Please remember that the initial estimate is always based on the takings of the previous season. And the Hofoper's takings have increased from year to year, so of course the estimate for the last season was far greater than the estimate for my first season. Looking at it just from these increased estimates, two years ago we had a deficit of about fifty thousand kronen, but this was long ago covered by takings.[175] And despite the increased prices there is no deficit this season either. In the last few weeks, probably on account of the early onset of the warm

---

[174] See above, Chap. 8.

[175] The Opera's accounts were audited at the end of the year, and not at the end of the season. Later, in the spring, an estimate of forthcoming deficit was drawn up in order to determine the amount that had to be covered by a direct grant from the Emperor. In 1903 the estimated deficit was exceeded by 52,750 kronen; in 1905 by 258,430 kronen; in 1906 by a mere 9,234 kronen. In 1904 it was actually 36,943 kronen higher than the real deficit. The 1907 'crisis' affected the total at the end of the year, and the real deficit, which amounted to 247,333 kronen almost equalled that of 1905. But Weingartner failed to do much better, running up an extra deficit of 136,668 kronen by the end of his first year (WMW 286).

weather, takings have fallen by about twenty-five thousand kronen, but this is of absolutely no importance, for box offices are always subject to minor and temporary fluctuations of this kind. We only need rain for a fortnight and the small loss will be made good. Since the accounts are audited on 31 December, anyone who knows anything about these things will tell you that 1907 will end with a considerable surplus. The autumn, which is always the best theatrical season, will prove my point. So there is no deficit, and it follows that a deficit cannot have caused my 'downfall'.

I have never drawn the person of the monarch into my affairs and do not propose to do so now. I would have considered it too disrespectful, and I have no wish to be guilty of such a thing. But since there have been suggestions of this kind, I should like to make it clear that all such rumours are untrue.

And how often do I have to say that my contract[176] has not come to an end, for the simple reason that I have never had one. I am a civil servant appointed by the emperor, and, as you know, such appointments are for life; one can only be relieved of one's duties by going into retirement. I do not have the right to ask to be dismissed, and can ask [only] to go into retirement. And if this is refused, I will have to stay. I was also amused by the report that I am receiving a pension from the Budapest Opera.[177] This would of course be very agreeable but unfortunately it is not the case. However, it is true that from the beginning of next year I would have been entitled to a higher pension from the Hofoper, and that I relinquished this right of my own accord because I wanted to leave now. You can see that I am not particularly good at taking care of my financial interests. Admittedly, I applied for retirement several months earlier than I had originally intended to, but that was purely for family reasons—my wife and children were very ill recently—and for no other . . .[178]

I wanted to leave quietly, and to announce my departure to no one. I do not know how the news was made public before it should have been. What displeases me is the fact that people are still taking pot-shots at me even as I leave. I am leaving of my own free will, and that should be enough. I do not need to assure you that I am not responsible for 'addresses' and other statements of a similar kind. I wish to leave quietly, and for this reason I shall not be appearing on the podium again. I don't want people to stand up for me, but I do not wish to be slandered either. Without sounding boastful, I would like to point out that it is thanks to me that the salaries of the orchestra and the chorus were increased four weeks ago. Since this did not offer an opportunity to slander me, it was not reported. You know better than anyone that I never thought of becoming conductor of the Philharmonic. But some people seem to know more than I do, and so all of a sudden I was described as being a candidate for the Philharmonic post.[179] I cannot deny everything: I have neither the time nor the inclination. But in psychological terms it is interesting to see how everything is being dragged in that will harm me in the eyes of the public. All I can do is to point out quietly what I have achieved. No one can say that I have ever looked to the right or the left. I have always gone my own way and thus have had to put up with a great deal. I shall not take another

---

176 Weingartner was later the first director of the Vienna Opera to be given a contract.

177 The *Neues Wiener Journal* of 29 May had claimed that Mahler was entitled to a pension of 8,000 kronen from this institution, but that he had not been paid it since he was an Austrian civil servant.

178 Anna had had scarlet fever, and Alma had had an operation.

179 The *Extrablatt* of 1 June and the *Deutsche Zeitung* of 2 June had both suggested that Mahler was trying to retain his post by having himself elected conductor of the Philharmonic (see above).

permanent appointment but I have no intention whatsoever of giving up my conducting career in the concert hall or in the opera altogether. Naturally I have had many
offers, but we are not talking about that.[180]

To conclude, Mahler expressed the hope that Mottl would soon succeed him.
'I congratulate myself and the Vienna Opera on having such a successor. Mottl
will pick up where I have left off.' The dignity of this text and the information
it contained should have silenced Mahler's more virulent ennemies at least
temporarily. But polemics were the order of the day and in May and June the
daily papers demonstrated that Mahler was right to defend himself by speaking out. On 29 May the *Neues Wiener Journal* claimed that he had been 'forced'
to hand in his resignation, and that he still hoped that it would not be accepted.
However, the Lord Chamberlain had 'already sent emissaries all over Germany
to start negotiations with possible successors'. On 2 June the *Extrablatt*
reported that two singers, Anna von Mildenburg and Marie Gutheil-Schoder,
who owed their whole careers to the Hofoper,[181] had tried to draw up a new
petition signed by the members of the Opera. However, the meeting they had
organized before the performance on 29 May was a total failure,[182] and they
received so few signatures that they had had to abandon the idea. At the same
time an attempt was made to accuse Mahler of having something to do with the
fact that the baritone Josef Ritter, who had left the Opera in 1906, had gone
mad in Salzburg. After all, he had been dismissed without having been given
the title of *Kammersänger*.[183]

Of course Mahler still had a great number of admirers who did not hesitate
to write in his defence, even now, when he no longer needed their support. In
the *Musik-Literarische Blätter* on 26 May Viktor Lederer called into question
the way in which the Hofoper was run, and pointed out that the duties of the
director were too numerous and varied. He could not deal with everything—
psychological problems, the whims of singers, rehearsals, the planning of the
repertoire, the supervision of the productions—and he could not be everywhere at once, 'the spirit moving upon the face of the waters, the hydraulic
engineer and the ship's carpenter'. Lederer suggested that the director's duties
should be reduced in order to give him time, as was done in the case of university professors who wanted to travel or pursue research. There should be a
dramaturge who would be Mahler's assistant, have the time to travel on his
behalf to hear new works, and choose singers. He would also be responsible for
preparing the versions, transcriptions, and translations of the works being
performed, and act as an intermediary, 'a sort of literary adviser in times of
crisis . . . a professional with musical and literary training, sound judgement

---

[180] *Neues Wiener Tagblatt* (5 June 1907), and BMG 184 ff.
[181] *Deutsche Zeitung* (2 June).
[182] Bruno Walter was conducting *Carmen* that evening. The *Illustrirtes Wiener Extrablatt* claimed that
one of the singers who did not attend had said that 'one should not get involved in something the director
himself is extremely reticent about'.　　　　　　[183] *Deutsche Zeitung* (1 and 2 June).

and practical common sense'. Was Vienna really going to let Mahler go as easily as Weimar had once done with Liszt?[184] Such a creator of genius was worthy to be the director of the Vienna Opera, and no one else was capable of replacing him.

In the *Fremden-Blatt* of 30 May Albert Kauders had obviously wished to be objective. He had listed all the productions staged, refurbished, or revived by Mahler during the ten years of his tenure. He rejected the unfair allegations that had been made against him and, like Lederer, suggested that an assistant should be appointed in order to relieve him of some of his duties. Furthermore, the reduction in the number of outstanding premières was largely made up for, in the season now coming to an end, by the striking success of the new productions.[185] Mahler could not in fact be accused of anything except his well-known ruthlessness (*Rücksichtlosigkeit*) and his arbitrary attitude to certain singers. As a director he could not be surpassed, and thus, Kauders concluded, it would be better to change certain aspects of his management than allow him to leave.

On 3 June, Richard Robert, the critic of the *Extrablatt*, recalled in the *Montags-Zeitung* his earlier reservations about Mahler's management but also pointed out that he had made a unique contribution to Viennese musical life. 'He was often wrong, but the fact that he was there was very fortunate as far as the Opera was concerned.' Soon after arriving in Vienna, and at a time when he was at the height of his popularity, Mahler had said: 'I know very well that those who praise me to the skies today will be stoning me to death tomorrow ... In any case, no theatre director should stay in his post for more than five years.' He had been rather prescient. In fact, his greatest admirers had become his worst enemies. Those who once criticized nothing, not even his worst excesses, now vilified him, hopelessly and without respite, and for quite absurd reasons. The only real drawback about the 'system' was the 'democratic' tendency to favour minor singers at the expense of more famous ones. His enemies had taken to criticizing everything; they had conveniently forgotten the positive aspects of his directorship, and showed no sign of being grateful for what he had done in the course of ten years at the Hofoper.[186]

On 4 June the *Allgemeine Zeitung* carried an unsigned article that praised Mahler's refusal to compromise, his theatrical genius, and his 'vision'. It also recalled the anarchy which had reigned at the Opera when he arrived, his battle with Viennese vanity and the then prevailing 'cult of famous actors'. Julius Korngold and Max Kalbeck wrote similar farewell articles in their usual newspapers. Kalbeck recalled that he had felt uneasy about Mahler at the time

---

[184] The cause of his departure from Weimar in 1861 was the refusal of the authorities to stage *The Barber of Bagdad* by Cornelius.

[185] Kauders thought that the only worthwhile contemporary work Mahler had not put on was *Tosca*.

[186] Robert commented that 'there has never been an ideal opera director, and there never will be'. However the growing list of candidates for the director's post showed clearly what Vienna was about to lose.

of his arrival. However, this unease had soon given way to absolute confidence. Admittedly, Mahler, who had a natural penchant for the unusual, and hated routine of any kind, was not ideally suited to running a repertory theatre. Even his greatest triumphs and his most perfect performances had failed to satisfy him

because he could hardly ignore the fact that they were all without exception closely bound up with his own person. He was unable to take lasting pleasure in his creations because he had to repeat them day after day. . . . The discerning critic and penetrating interpreter of scores, the supreme master of the stage and the orchestra showed that he was anything but an easy man to get on with, or a good judge of human nature. A strong man himself, he judged the weak on the basis of his own character and the situation he was confronted with, without making any attempt to understand what they were like and what they were feeling. He was too willing to think too highly of them if they fell in willingly with his quickly changing plans, and to think too little of them if they didn't agree with what he was trying to do. But—and this was his most dangerous mistake—whether they were with him or against him he left them in no doubt at all as to how little they meant to him, with their petty and often ridiculous ambitions and sensibilities. 'Conscientiousness can do a lot, love infinitely more.' Without warmer feeling, affection that extends beyond the job they are doing to the individual persons who are doing it, it is impossible to establish good working relations. . . . The failures of his projects, the realization that even the most perfect things on earth are nothing but scrappy patchwork, are reminders to the artist that he too is a weak man, but do not discourage him. And if he sees his frail bark come to grief on the rocks, he should not put the blame solely on the wind and the waves, but ask himself whether he may not have set off on the wrong course, without due knowledge of the hostile seas he must cross, trusting blindly to his own genius. An experienced mariner can perhaps bring his ship safely to port, no matter what obstacles he encounters.

We are sorry to see Gustav Mahler leave his post. For with the Director of the Vienna Hofoper, who lent the prestige of his famous name to that institution, we are also losing the imaginative dramaturge, the incomparable conductor. He has ended his career prematurely, has proclaimed the promised day but not ushered it in. 'Thou art fallen, bright morning star!'[187]

Julius Korngold, in an article also published on 4 June in the *Neue Freie Presse* and which began with the question: 'Is it true that we are losing Mahler?', recalled other composers who had managed theatres, for example Wagner, Weber, and Marschner, and more recently, Weingartner and Strauss. They had not been accused of neglecting their theatre or of choosing the wrong works because they were jealous of other composers.[188] Since Mahler's management had always depended on his artistic qualities, how could people talk of a 'crisis' at the Opera, especially in the light of his recent successes? It

---

[187] 'Der Abschied Mahlers', *Neues Wiener Tagblatt* (7 June 1907).

[188] In this context Korngold gave as example Rainer Simon, director of the Volkstheater who, apart from *Tosca*, had also had a long string of failures. Korngold felt that Mahler had chosen for the coming season all the works which for the moment seemed viable.

was true that box office takings had fallen slightly, but this was due to the rise in ticket prices. If the Opera was really experiencing a 'crisis', then one could only hope that it would continue!

And then there were 'affairs' and scandals and difficulties in theatres everywhere. In German opera houses the ensembles had to be supplemented or renewed from time to time. For example, the *Süddeutsche Monatshefte* had recently pointed out that there were deficiencies in the repertoire and the staff of the Bavarian Opera. However, there had not been a reference to a 'crisis'. 'None of the candidates mentioned has the slightest hope of replacing Mahler. His faults should not make us forget his virtues.' People were quick to mention his nervous temperament, but they tended to forget 'his heroic courage, his unwavering sense of justice—which explains many of his actions—and his innate naivety'. 'Simple, frugal, without affectation, a child', he lacked wisdom and prudence, qualities which were banal and commonplace. Borne along by the torrent of new artistic ideas which poured out of him at all times, he had never hesitated. A critic in Rome had recently described it as unthinkable that Vienna could bear to lose an artist of whom it should be proud. 'The time is not far off when the importance of the Mahlerian epoch will be universally recognized, and looked upon as a wonderful legend, a glorious period at the Hofoper.'[189] This time was to arrive sooner than Mahler's friends imagined, for a series of failures a few months after Weingartner's arrival turned most of the Viennese critics and public against him.

On 7 June David Josef Bach pointed out that the main reason for Mahler's departure was the fact that it was impossible, anywhere and under any circumstances, to maintain the standards of operatic performances at a constant level, 'for no artist, no director, no conductor, and no singer can give his best three hundred times a year'. Even someone who worked as tirelessly as Mahler had been forced to come to this conclusion. 'No one could have been more acutely aware of the incompatibility between the daily routine of a theatre and the highest artistic principles.'[190] Bach also thought that the Intendant, and not the Director, 'should have the task of comforting singers whose rivals have obtained a coveted role or who have been refused leave in the middle of the season'. A director had other things on his mind, and it was not his task to be a 'father to all and sundry'.

Mahler's enemies among the critics did not disagree fundamentally with this diagnosis, but the news of his coming departure from the Hofoper gave the opportunity to twist the knife in the wound. Recently returned from America, their most eloquent spokesman, Hans Liebstöckl, wrote the following article in

---

[189]   An unsigned article in the *Allgemeine Zeitung* of 7 June drew a parallel between Vienna and Munich, which was refusing to allow Mottl to leave: 'What howls of rage there would have been, what a press campaign Vienna would have seen if Mahler had had to bring a court action like Mottl's; yet the latter had constantly received continual expressions of sympathy.' In the *Arbeiter-Zeitung* the same day, Bach emphasized how much more Germany supported and defended its artists than Austria.

[190]   *Arbeiter-Zeitung* (7 June 1907).

the *Illustrirtes Wiener Extrablatt* of 11 June. The leitmotiv of his January article[191] had been the word 'genius', too often applied to Mahler in his opinion.
His new leitmotiv was 'Feuergeist' (fiery spirit), a description of Mahler much
used by his supporters and friends:

So there is room at last for a new man at the Hofoper. Gustav Mahler is going. To
the many things at the Hofoper we have to thank him for he has now added something
very important—his resignation. The performing artists there, with few exceptions can
breathe again, the season-ticket holders can hope for better times. After all. But saying
goodbye softens the heart. Shall I repeat all the things I have said—nay, felt compelled
to say—in the ten years Mahler has been running the Opera? More amusing perhaps
to listen to the friends who are now publicly mourning him. The snobs are there, with
their agonized epilogues, elegies, open letters, telegrams of support from sanatoriums.
And from all sides regret at the passing of the 'fiery spirit of genius'. . . . How did one
define a 'fiery spirit of genius'? 'Fiery spirits', apparently, didn't have a 'Stammtisch'
[a regular table in a restaurant where one meets friends], shunned afternoon tea invitations, didn't like to meet people, avoided 'at homes' and took pleasure in disappointing high society ladies. And above all they couldn't stand the Viennese cult of
personalities in the arts. That was people's idea of a 'great man', a 'fiery spirit'. Their
idea of a genius was 'someone who was antisocial, arrogant and vulgar'. But the greatest German musicians liked visiting the homes of respectable middle-class and aristocratic families, and the most immortal of sonatas and quartets carry dedications to
aristocratic patrons. Johannes Brahms actually had a 'Stammtisch'. And Liszt a countess, and Wagner a king. In any case we can hardly expect our Mahler enthusiasts to
know how the really great actually lived. If they knew who Haydn was, they wouldn't
have needed to deceive themselves about Mahler! One thing is certain: none of
Mahler's predecessors has been so consistently, so inexpertly overestimated as he has
been. No other musician has had so much fuss made over him by idle non-musicians
and leisured onlookers. And yet he was only a great and temperamental conductor,
whose 'fire' often missed its target, who tried everything only to abandon it at once,
whose horizon didn't extend much further than the orchestra. I myself in moments of
grateful rapture have enthusiastically praised his qualities, and I have often enough
recognized that he could sometimes disarm all criticism. But he had, and that became
clear in the fourth year of his directorship, no ability to see things in the round, no
heartwarming, enduring love. His image became ever clearer for the objective
observer—the image of an artist with strange mannerisms and unsound opinions. His
own music stood up and testified against him. From symphony to symphony it became
more insubstantial, mediocre, took on unacceptable ways of behaving. This incessant
attempt, through noise and cheapjack devices, to acquire the nimbus of a fiery spirit
of genius aroused involuntary resentment. He succeeded alright, he won over those
without judgement and confused the waverers, but the fruits of dishonest practice soon
became apparent. The Hofoper was taken over by a destructive arbitrary spirit which
is paralysing it still today in all its limbs. Great talents were destroyed, small ones took
over, the quality of singing was ruined, the cold manner in which bel canto was stifled
upset even the most patient. The 29 new productions of the last ten years have disap-

[191] See above, Chap. 8.

peared again with two or three exceptions, and the new arrangements of the classics either lost their sparkle by the second or third performance or failed straight away at the first. The theatre painter made a name for himself. Still today Don Giovanni's castle terrifies me in my dreams. Still today, I can hear the eleven thousand guests who kept rushing in and out. The 'scandals' were just a side-show to all this: they came from the system; were the inevitable result of it. In the end the Hofoper was a pigeon roast, a training ground for mediocre talents, a nest of frustration. And from the first tenor down to the humblest theatre doorman there was nobody left who liked going to the Opera. Those who sensed this lost no time in getting out. A small secondary manage-ment, which has unfortunately still not resigned, took over the other business when the Director went on his frequent journeys. The Hofoper muddled along from one day to the next with 'Hoffmann's Erzählungen' and Puccini's 'Bohème', for ten whole years and under a 'fiery spirit of genius'!

The mistake of the Mahler regime was in the system. Conductors are as a rule bad directors. In my opinion no more conductors should be appointed to run the Hofoper. As a conductor Mahler could have done a lot for the Hofoper. But he was also régis-seur, took a personal interest in each singer only to drop him shortly thereafter. His aversion to any kind of fine singing led to the strangest experiences. I will mention only the *Barber*, the *Shrew*, the *Iphigénie* with Wagnerian trimmings, the *Euryanthe* which flopped, the over-studied *Walküre*. An arithmetician managed to count a total of 20 absolutely top-ranking performers at our Hofoper. And even then there are not enough to put on 3 decent performances a week. The whole Institute lost its sense of direction, the schedule of successive performances fell victim to arbitrary timing. On the face of it Wagner received special treatment. He was renovated from start to finish, but became obsolete again for lack of impressive soloists. The series of experiences came to an end with the *Figaro* and the *Entführung*. Also, besides Mahler there really was no one else who could inspire enough respect to maintain what had been achieved at the same level. Mahler possessed an infallible lack of taste in anything to do with singing. He chose the most ludicrous casts and stuck to them. I simply cannot see in him anything of the 'more deeply probing' orchestral conductors there has been so much talk of lately. They, like much of what has been written in the last few days about Mahler, are friendly imaginings. In the meantime Mahler himself has been talking and letting himself be interviewed, something which fiery spirits don't normally like to do. He has denied that the scandals were the cause of his resignation, and also played down the fall in receipts. A fortnight of wet weather would be enough to make up the deficit. What decided him to resign, he said, was the realization that no system could ensure that the productions are all of equal quality, that there comes a low point which no director can avoid. Unfortunately it has taken ten years of arbitrariness and moody behaviour to bring him to recognize this, whereas he should have realized it before five years were up.

Gustav Mahler does not leave a pleasant legacy behind him, he leaves a variegated collection of low points and his successor will have to work very hard to put the Hofoper on a sounder footing again and prevent it from having problems. What is surprising, and yet typical, is the general feeling of helplessness which is affecting everyone. I shall certainly not venture to propose candidates. But it would be ridicu-lous now to start combing the whole of Germany for a new 'fiery spirit'. The Hofoper has no need of one. Its artistic needs could be looked after by two or three conductors of high rank, and first-class, gifted stage-managers. And at their head all that is needed is a competent theatre man with taste and culture and a firm hand, and who above all 'understands something about good singing', to put it crudely. In times like these, when we have the 'Liebesgarten' and Herodias's dear little daughter, that kind of person rarely comes to the fore. But they exist all the same, and one need not look far to find them. A high standard was achieved under Jahn, and under Jauner, and also in the first five years of the Mahler era. Peaceful artistry and steady work will do the Hofoper good. It needs to recover from the spasmodic efforts of a fiery spirit, it needs a kindly respectable gentleman, someone who has as little as possible of 'the modern' about him. There are two commandments for the Hofoper: fine singing on the stage, fine playing in the orchestra. And the new head who can bring that about, and who can happily combine intelligence and passion, will win praise even from the most 'dissatisfied journalists'. He does not have to be a conductor, he can have his 'Stammtisch', and leave the 'deeper probing' to the professional probers. Let him fill the gaps in the ensemble and respect the tradition!

A cleverer defence of mediocrity, a more brilliant pleading for the wrong cause could hardly be imagined. But Liebstöckl was obviously summarizing the views of a great many Viennese conservative opera-goers, although few of them would have had the same talent for distorting facts and transforming virtues into defects.

On 9 June the *Deutsches Volksblatt* printed a sharp reply to Korngold's article of 4 June. It claimed that Mahler had 'neglected the Opera, by spending his time promoting his own music', that he had driven away the great singers and lowered the quality of the orchestra by replacing many of its musicians. After so many 'affairs', how could he claim to be leaving 'of his own free will'? What other reason could there be for the deficit (this myth died hard) than declining performance standards, which no longer satisfied the capital's 'fashionable audiences'?[192]

From now on, most of the articles were about the choice of Mahler's successor. Felix Mottl had long been considered the favourite, and on 4 June the Viennese press was still generally of the opinion that he would probably succeed Mahler and that Franz Schalk would succeed him in Munich. Ludwig Karpath once again played the role of confidential intermediary, and it is thanks to him that we know the details of Mottl's negotiations with the Vienna Opera and of his visit to Prince Montenuovo while Mahler was in Italy.

Since the beginning of spring Mottl's reputation had been threatened by two articles which had appeared on 21 and 26 March in the *Bayrischer Kurier*. The first bore the title 'The Decline of the Munich Opera' and the second 'The Munich Opera, Act II'. Written by a journalist called Paul Siebertz, they

[192] Among the recent scandals Hans Puchstein, who probably wrote this article (although it is signed R . . . r), singled out the 'tenor crisis' which, when Schmedes was ill, meant that *Rienzi* had to be dropped from the Wagner cycle at the end of the season. Similarly, other performances of the cycle, with Kurz-Stolzenberg in *Tannhäuser* and *Lohengrin*, had been mediocre, and in any case it had been necessary to borrow a baritone from the Volksoper for the latter. This was Josef Schwarz, who later became one of the most popular baritones in the history of the Vienna Opera.

attacked Mottl (the *Generalmusikdirektor*). Albert, Freiherr von Speidel, the Intendant, who had replaced Ernst von Possart the previous year, and Albert Heine, the principal producer. Heine was simply accused of adopting 'a coarse and impolite tone of command' in rehearsals. The accusations levelled against Speidel and against Mottl's wife, Henriette Standthartner-Mottl, were of a more serious nature. Speidel was criticized for showering favours on the pretty young singers he engaged for the Opera and for having as mistress one of the actresses at the Royal Theatre. And Mottl was attacked in revelations made by an impresario called Karl Schels, who had sworn to bring about his downfall. Schels stated that Frau Mottl, who was on the payroll of the Munich Opera but never sang in performances, had received bribes from the Nuremberg impresario Eugen Frankfurter in return for an assurance that he would receive a Bavarian decoration and that his artists would be given preference at the Munich Opera.[193] Schells accused Frau Mottl of having promised her pupils engagements at the Munich Opera, again in return for bribes.[194] Mottl was accused of having become 'autocratic', of having dismissed excellent singers and of having replaced them with his favourites (an accusation which, like those that preceded and followed it, was only too familiar); of being responsible for the 'decline' of the Opera; of having forced Bernard Stavenhagen to resign from the directorship of the Musikakademie in order to obtain his salary; and of giving private lessons, both at the Akademie and at the Opera.

The accusations were so serious that the three people involved instituted legal proceedings and sued Siebertz for libel. The case was tried between 16 and 19 May 1907. After hearing statements from numerous witnesses, it became clear that most of the accusations levelled at Frau Mottl were true. However, her husband could not be held responsible for her indiscretions. They had been separated for four years, and were soon to get divorced. It was shown that he had been completely unaware of her debts, and that the other slanderous accusations were simply due to the malevolence of Karl Schels. Ernst von Possart, a friend of Richard Strauss, and the previous Intendant of the Opera, testified in Mottl's favour in an impressive and eloquent manner. In the end Siebertz was required to pay the costs of the case.

Mottl, no matter how much he wanted to leave Munich, could not have resigned before the court had reached its decision because that would have given the impression that he was admitting his guilt. On 24 May he told Countess Coudenhove[195] that he had tendered his resignation and was waiting to hear from the Prince Regent of Bavaria. On 4 June he told Karpath that the decision was imminent. However, the Prince Regent's initial response on 6 June was negative, and this was reported in the Viennese press the next day.[196]

---

[193] It was demonstrated in court that the majority (65 per cent) of guest artists at the Munich Opera had come from his agency.   [194] This charge proved unfounded.   [195] See above, Chap. 8.

[196] It was also 'revealed' that Conried had engaged Mahler for a series of thirty concerts in the United States, for which he would be paid 240,000 marks (about 185,000 kronen).

On 8 June it was announced that Speidel, the Munich Intendant, had gone to Budapest to meet with Prince Montenuovo. The outcome of this interview was entirely negative, at least from the Viennese point of view: Mottl was not only required to stay in Munich for the length of time stipulated in his contract, i.e. until 1910, but he was also going to be offered a new contract that would be distinctly more advantageous than the existing one. On 9 June an open letter from the Prince Regent to Intendant Speidel appeared in the press, forbidding him to accede to Mottl's request on the grounds that 'the departure of a conductor of such exceptional importance . . . would constitute a severe, almost irreparable loss to the Bavarian capital'.[197]

Mottl's only hope of being released from his contract was now a private audience with the Prince Regent.[198] On 11 June, the *Illustrirtes Wiener Extrablatt* carried a full-length article about the 'Directorship crisis'. Since Mottl was not going to be released from his Munich contract, it suggested that the next Hofoperndirektor should be 'a practical man of the theatre' who would be advised by an artistic committee. The *Extrablatt's* candidate was Rainer Simons, who would thus combine the directorship of the Opera with that of the Volksoper. Other possible candidates—such as Karl Muck, Felix Weingartner (Berlin), and Ernst von Schuch (Dresden) might well find it as difficult as Mottl to terminate their contract. When it had been announced that Mottl was on the point of leaving, the Munich press had reacted so violently, that both Intendant Speidel and the Minister of Culture had feared that they might be dismissed. And the Prince Regent had given Mottl one of the Kingdom of Bavaria's most coveted medals, and added: 'So here's a beautiful medal, and now stop making such a fuss. So let's stop talking about your leaving! The good citizens of Munich would never forgive me. I don't want to hear any more about it!'[199]

Since Mottl had always assured Prince Montenuovo that he would have no difficulty in leaving Munich, the latter felt deeply offended when he heard the news. On 16 June, he issued a communiqué to the Viennese press stating that he had never made an offer to Mottl, or indeed to anyone else, but that Mottl had communicated his wishes in an indirect manner before taking steps to leave his present post. He had claimed that he was tied to the Munich Opera only by a normal theatrical contract, that could be terminated at any time, and that he wanted to leave 'at any price'. Furthermore, the Prince had recently discovered that since the beginning of the year Mottl had been in negotiations for another post,[200] 'which also led to a strengthening of his position'.

[197] *Illustrirtes Wiener Extrablatt* (9 June 1907).

[198] BMG 197. After the audience on 15 June, Mottl wrote to Countess Coudenhove: 'I am beside myself! My life's hopes are shattered. Nothing can be done. I have tried everything. I think my good humour has gone forever. It is the most unbelievable thing which has ever happened.'

[199] *Illustrirtes Wiener Extrablatt* (11 June 1907).

[200] Conried had offered Mottl a five-year contract at the Metropolitan Opera and an annual salary of 500,000 marks. Ludwig Karpath claims that the Austrian conductor could easily have been released from his contract if he had analysed its clauses correctly, and if he had permitted the Emperor Franz Joseph to intervene personally with his cousin the Prince Regent of Bavaria, as he was to do in the case of Weingartner

However, according to Ludwig Karpath, who continued to champion Mottl, the latter had not acted in this Machiavellian way. His only mistake had been that he had not shown Prince Montenuovo his contract when they first met in March. The Prince was now in a very awkward position, for he had been counting on Mottl and had not entered into any other negotiations.[201] At this stage, it seemed impossible to retain Mahler, who was angry and hurt, since he realized that his resignation had been accepted before a successor had been found. He might still have agreed to stay under certain conditions, especially if he had been granted two months' leave a year to conduct in New York. But he was much too proud to admit this. Thus the Prince's renewed efforts to retain Mahler were doomed to failure.

When he returned from Berlin after his meeting with Conried, Mahler found a letter from the Lord Chamberlain urgently summoning him to his office. The Prince had no doubt been informed confidentially that Mottl had withdrawn his candidacy. Alma later recalled waiting interminably in a Viennese tearoom while Mahler was in the Prince's office:

He finally came back in the best of moods, having rejected the Prince's offer to let him stay on as director of the Vienna Opera, and done it by quoting the Prince's words back at him. For, at the beginning of the year[202] Montenuovo had said that he 'had no use for a director who spent his time on concert tours, promoting his own music'. At the time Mahler had replied that if a director scored a personal success it added to the Opera's renown. The Prince now acknowledged that he had changed his mind and that Mahler had been right. Mahler replied: 'But look, Your Highness, I have now come to realize that an opera director should only be concerned with his official duties and that he ought to *be there!*'[203]

It is quite probable that, although the two men had come to know each other well in the course of ten years, the Prince failed to detect the irony in Mahler's reply. He probably knew very well that no artist with an international reputation would ever agree to devote himself entirely to the Opera. As we shall see, he had probably been expecting a very different response from Mahler, and his position was most awkward because there was no solution to the 'directorship crisis' in the foreseeable future and summer was approaching fast. For Mahler

---

with the German Emperor. Mottl's letters to Karpath confirm that he was genuinely convinced that it would be easy for him to leave Munich, especially after the articles published in the *Bayrischer Kurier* and he was not being duplicitous in negotiating with other theatres. His 'dearest wish' was to return to Vienna, his native city. However, Prince Montenuovo always remained convinced of the contrary (BMG 200 ff.). The *Extrablatt* (13 June) and the *Neues Wiener Tagblatt* (14 June) disclosed that Mottl had signed a new five-year contract in Munich, which guaranteed an annual income of at least 42,000 marks which was significantly higher than that of Mahler, and the promise of a pension of 15,000 marks annually.

[201] Karpath recorded that in 1910, when Weingartner left, Mottl was again one of the candidates for the directorship of the Vienna Opera. On this occasion, he asked for a formal offer but never received one because Prince Montenuovo remembered only too well his humiliation in 1907. Mottl had a heart attack during a performance of *Tristan* and died on 2 July 1911, less than two months after Mahler.

[202] See above, Chap. 8.

[203] AMM1, 157: AMM2, 153.

it was galling to see that the Bavarian Regent had done everything in his power to keep Mottl, thus acting as he himself might have wished the Austrian Emperor to behave. At this juncture, the Viennese papers, the majority of which remained hostile to Mahler, returned to the offensive, fearing that he might be tempted to change his mind and remain in Vienna. Names of other possible successors were suggested day after day: Karl Muck, Ernst von Schuch, Felix Weingartner, Rainer Simons, and also Richard Strauss and Franz Schalk. On 9 June the *Deutsches Volksblatt* even mentioned Richter, who was reported to be about to leave for New York to conduct a season at Hammerstein's Manhattan Opera. This false news must have seemed ironic to Richter, who had left Vienna seven years earlier in a mood similar to Mahler's, feeling he had 'experienced nothing but ingratitude' there. He now looked back 'on the time he spent in the Austrian capital with melancholy and bitterness'.[204] On 13 June the *Neues Wiener Journal* published the results of a poll of Viennese composers, conductors, and musicians,[205] which showed that the majority were in favour of keeping Mahler. Oscar Straus replied in a particularly striking way: 'Today no one could replace Mahler without making us aware of what we have lost. The city that permits Mahler to leave does not deserve him. In any case I believe it is wrong to consider only conductors for the post of director. No conductor is capable of running the Opera.' Angelo Neumann, who had discovered Mahler twenty years before, was interviewed by the *Prager Tagblatt*, and declared: 'The Vienna Hofoper should not be permitted to lose a man of such genius, in the full flower of his artistry.' He added, however, that an artist could grow weary of the arguments and disagreements that were part of the daily life of a theatre. He too thought that the qualities of a conductor and those of a director were seldom to be found in one and the same person. Furthermore, artistic cooperation became problematical between a conductor and members of his ensemble, there were hundreds of possible differences of the kind which could occur for administrative reasons between the members and the director of a large institution.[206]

The season at the Hofoper ended in a gloomy mood that reflected the Director's state of mind. Wagner had again dominated the repertoire with seventy-six performances (there had been seventy-one the previous year), and five complete *Ring* cycles. Mozart was performed only twenty-two times, compared with forty-five performances the year before (which had been the 150th anniversary of his birth). The repertoire comprised fifty-seven operas and

---

[204] Marie Richter's (the conductor's widow) words to Ludwig Bösendorfer, the piano manufacturer. See Christopher Fifield, *True Artist and True Friend: A biography of Hans Richter* (Clarendon, Oxford, 1993), 277.

[205] The replies published came from Julius Epstein (Mahler); Edmund Eysler (Mottl or Rainer Simons); Theodor Grädener (a dual artistic and administrative directorship); Karl Kapeller (Mottl); Eduard Kremser (Mahler or Simons); Karl Lafite (Mahler or Mottl); Richard von Perger (a director who would not be the subject of gossip . . .); Richard Robert (Mottl); Hans Wagner (Mottl, Schuch, Weingartner, Stavenhagen, Schalk, or Zemlinsky), etc.

[206] *Neues Wiener Tagblatt* (14 June 1907). The unsigned article also revealed that a journalist had interviewed Mottl in Munich. He was still pinning his hopes on an audience with the Prince Regent on 15 June.

one operetta (*Die Fledermaus*). This total exceeded that of the previous year (fifty) though a number of works were performed only once. Some of the singers were ill, and Mahler had had to grant them sick leave. This meant that he was obliged to bring in numerous guest artists, for whom it was sometimes necessary to revive old productions, inevitably of inferior quality. The small number of premières (*Le Juif polonais*, *Flauto Solo*, and *Samson*) reflected the fact that Mahler was discouraged by the 'sterility' of contemporary composers and by the ban on *Salome*. However, the success of four revivals, *Die Walküre*, *Der Widerspenstigen Zähmung*, *The Barber of Seville*, and *Un Ballo in Maschera*[207] made up for the relative failure of the two final productions, *Otello* and *Samson et Dalila*, both of which were given at the very end of the season.[208]

Box office takings fell short of the estimated sum by 72,500 kronen, whereas excess expenditure amounted to 200,000 kronen. Yet the deficit was still lower than in 1905, and this was probably due to increased ticket prices and to the singers' illnesses and the subsequent cancellations. Above all, this 'bad' year shows that Mahler was discouraged by the poor quality of the repertory performances and by the vicious attacks of the press. Some of the problems could of course have been resolved the following year if he had stayed on in Vienna and if he had regained the support which he felt he deserved after ten years of hard work.[209]

Shortly before the summer vacation, Prince Montenuovo found himself in a thoroughly embarrassing position. So did Mahler, who was unable to make any firm plans for the future. Weingartner was now the favourite candidate but as chief conductor of the Königliche Kapelle in Berlin he was running into the same problem as Mottl had experienced in Munich. Muck was about to leave for Boston and had just signed a new contract for the subsequent period with the Berlin Opera. Schuch was over 60. Nikisch would never consent to leave Leipzig, where he was treated much better than Mahler in Vienna. Strauss had declared that he would never accept the post of director (especially in a theatre which had refused to stage *Salome*). And Richter had already turned down the post ten years before.[210]

---

[207] The *Neueinstudierung* of *Un Ballo* was first performed on 18 May under Bruno Walter, with the following cast: Kurz (Oscar); Bland (Amelia); Petru (Ulrica); Slezak (Riccardo); Demuth (Renato). There were 12 performances in 1906, and 9 the following year.

[208] However, there were twelve performances of *Samson et Dalila* in 1907 and 1908, and six of *Otello*. Operas performed in the 1906–7 season: *Die Walküre* and *Der Widerspenstigen Zähmung* (14); *Un Ballo in Maschera*, *La Bohème*, and *Les Contes d'Hoffmann* (13); *Lohengrin* and *I Pagliacci* (12); *Carmen* (11); *The Barber of Seville* and *Cavalleria Rusticana* (10); *Der fliegende Holländer* and *Mignon* (9); *Tannhäuser* and *Aida* (8); *Tristan*, *Die Meistersinger*, *Faust*, and *Die Fledermaus* (7); *Das Rheingold*, *Entführung*, *Don Giovanni*, *Lakmé*, *Manon*, *Les Huguenots*, *Hänsel und Gretel*, *Fidelio*, and *Iphigénie* (5); *Figaro*, *Flauto Solo*, *Lucia*, and *La Muette* (4); *Rienzi*, *Il Trovatore*, *Otello*, *Le Juif polonais*, *Der Freischütz*, *Le Prophète*, *Samson*, and *Das goldene Kreuz* (3); *La traviata*, *The Bartered Bride*, and *Die Königin von Saba* (2); *Così fan tutte*, *Guillaume Tell*, *The Queen of Spades*, *La Juive*, *Der Evangelimann*, *Die Rose vom Liebesgarten*, *Die lustigen Weiber*, *Werther*, *Sainte Elisabeth*, *Die Abreise*, *La Dame blanche*, and *Le Postillon de Longjumeau* (1).

[209] WMW 222 and 286.

[210] On 14 June the *Neues Wiener Tagblatt* recalled his being offered the post in 1897, and having turned it down because he had discovered in Budapest that he was not suited to the post of director (see above, Vol. ii, Chap. 1).

Although many cards and letters passed between Mahler and the impresario Norbert Salter concerning professional matters, only one more substantial letter (probably written in May) from this troubled period seems to have survived. It was addressed to Richard Strauss and concerns Alfred Roller:

I am sure you know what is going on here. I'm leaving.—Unfortunately—and I can predict this very precisely—it seems that Roller will also go. He is an outstanding artist and a practical man of rare talent. This affects me a great deal for I consider it to be of the utmost importance to keep him in a theatre. There are unsuspected possibilities in him.

It occurs to me that perhaps in Berlin you might be able to employ him (above all in Berlin)! You would experience unusual things with him! I pass this idea on to you because something may come of it. But please treat it strictly in confidence, for it would be seriously misunderstood here. Could you drop me a line to let me know what you think of the idea (in an advisory capacity)![211]

This letter was not entirely without effect, for some months later Strauss talked to Roller at length 'about the possibility (or more precisely the impossibility) of obtaining an appointment in Berlin'.[212]

Some of Mahler's friends considered his departure from Vienna to be a tragedy, and desperately tried to find ways of keeping him. One of them was Guido Adler whose plan it was to make him head of the Vienna Conservatory. However Mahler's faithful friend underestimated two psychological factors: the sense of defeat he would feel if he moved from the Opera to the Conservatory, and the insurmountable difficulties he would encounter when adapting to a task so different from the one to which he had devoted all his energy and passion.[213] Another plan by the New York impresario Charles Löwenstein involved a new concert hall to be built in Berlin. Seating 3,000, it would have been suitable for concerts and opera performances, and Löwenstein asked Mahler to become its artistic director. However, the project was too vague to be of any interest to him in the foreseeable future.[214]

---

[211] Undated letter from Mahler to Strauss (MSB 123). On 25 Mar. Max Burckhard had written to Mahler in Rome to tell him that he had just heard from Milewa Roller that her husband's contract, which was due to end in the summer, had not been renewed. In fact he did not wish to remain at the Opera unless he received a ten-year contract or was given the status of 'civil servant' (AMM1, 402). Roller's contract was finally renewed in June. He stayed at the Opera for seventeen months under Weingartner (until 31 May 1909).

[212] Letter from Roller to Mahler, 13 Mar. 1908, AMM1, 427. Roller's contract was finally extended to May 1909 (HOA, Z. 2585/1907).

[213] RMA 49. Edward Reilly reproduces two cards to Guido Adler from Count Max Wickenburg who was then reorganizing the music department of the government on this subject. Mahler considered the project 'impossible to realize for the time being'. This telegram to Wilhelm Bopp (see above), who had just been appointed director of the Vienna Conservatory, no doubt refers to an appointment he might have accepted if he had stayed in Vienna.

[214] Letter from Charles Löwenstein to Mahler, dated 25 May 1907 (AMS). Löwenstein reminded Mahler that he had been in touch with him in 1898 via Lilli Lehmann on the subject of a series of subscription concerts that he wished him to conduct. Fuchs's illness had prevented Mahler from considering his offer seriously. He probably met Löwenstein in Berlin on 5 June.

On 14 June Balduin Bricht,[215] in the *Österreichische Volkszeitung*, wrote that Mahler's principal shortcoming was his character, and especially his lack of diplomacy. For this reason he had many admirers but 'only a few friends'. Most of his enemies were unable to explain the reason for their hostility and usually ended up by saying, 'I've had enough of Mahler!' Three days later J. E. Mand wrote that the best solution would be to keep him on as artistic director, but to engage an Intendant who would be responsible for the administration, as was the case in Dresden. On 19 June, the *Extrablatt* suggested that Schalk should be appointed acting director, and on 27 June disclosed that Hans Gregor, the director of the Komische Oper in Berlin, who had also been mentioned as Mahler's successor, was in Vienna.[216] However, he did not seem eager to leave his present post. It was becoming clear that no one had the slightest desire to succeed Mahler. In fact an article by Albert Kauders, in the *Fremden-Blatt* on 4 July said as much, and on 20 June the *Neue Musikalische Presse* asked whether Mahler might change his mind if his task were made easier.

Mahler must have asked himself this question many times. At any rate, it may explain why, before leaving Vienna for the Summer, he requested an interview with Moritz Benedikt, the editor-in-chief of the *Neue Freie Presse*.[217] In the course of a conversation which lasted for more than an hour, Mahler gave him a detailed account of his position and described the events which had led him to the present situation. Benedikt was deeply impressed and later remembered him as one of the most exceptional men he had ever met. At the end of their conversation, in the course of which he realized that Mahler had been treated rather shabbily, he promised to support him in his newspaper.[218] On 16 June (the day after Mahler had left for Maiernigg) the *Neue Freie Presse* carried two articles about him. One of them, although unsigned, was certainly by Benedikt ('Unmusical Remarks on the Mahler Affair'), while the other was by Max Burckhard, the friend of Alma's youth and former director of the Burgtheater ('The Mahler Affair as a Political Event').

In the first article, the author noted that Italy had a law to prevent the export of works of art, and wondered whether it would be possible to formulate a similar one to prevent the export of artists.

---

[215] According to Sandra McColl, Balduin Bricht was born in Verbò, Hungary, in 1852, and wrote only for the *Österreichische Volkszeitung*.

[216] Hans Gregor (1866–1945), who was born in Dresden, worked as an actor at the Deutsches Theater in Berlin, and then managed several theatres before moving to the Komische Oper in Berlin. In 1910 he was to succeed Weingartner as director of the Hofoper, a post he held until 1918. The Opera archives show that Gregor's candidacy was ruled out at the beginning of June (Z. 2.874/1907).

[217] Moritz Benedikt (1849–1920), born in Kwassitz (Moravia), studied law and economics in Vienna. After travelling extensively for several years, he was engaged by the *Neue Freie Presse* in 1872. He became assistant editor of the paper in 1881, and director in 1908. As such he exercised a powerful influence on Austrian politics, particularly in economic affairs.

[218] GWO 98. Max Graf, whose desk was apparently in the antechamber, claims to have spoken to Mahler for half an hour while he was waiting to be admitted into Benedikt's office.

Of course, such a law would be unthinkable. We may not even dream of it in private; for it would go against the most elementary notion of personal liberty. Only one thing can be done, and that is to ask those in high places, who so often have to decide the fate of an artist rather arbitrarily, not to approach such questions in a bureaucratic manner but to have some regard for the artistic reputation and welfare of the city.[219] We have just had a classic example of the aristocratic frivolity with which such things are handled here. The post of director of our Hofoper unexpectedly became free. Theatre director, Opera director, these are important pastoral offices in a big city! Both fruitful and debilitating ideas can emanate from this pulpit. A ruler of the theatre, a man of such standing and such influence, has it in his power to raise the standards of taste or to debase them to the lowest level; and one might be forgiven for thinking that such a vacancy should not arise without having found someone to fill it; that an opera director who has held the position for ten years, many of whose ideas must have become a part of the institution, cannot simply be dismissed without knowing that a worthy successor is ready to step into his shoes. Happy men, up there in their court offices! They do not seem to have given a moment's thought to this important question. The sun is hot enough as it is—why add to the day's burden with unnecessary cares? Plenty of names were put forward, the list of candidates was long and impressive: it still is. For the present, however, this is how the matter stands: the ones we can have we do not want; and the ones we want we cannot have.

So perhaps this resignation was accepted a little too hastily. We do not in any way intend to concern ourselves with the personal aspect of the matter; nor is it up to us to evaluate the artistic ability of the man who is about to leave. It is beyond dispute that he is a great conductor and director. His time in office bears witness to this. Anyone who has succeeded for a whole decade in keeping his feet on the ground between the Court and the audience, amid the whirl of contradictory influences, must be either a very pliable rubber doll or a man of iron and steel. Mahler seems to be the latter. Numerous people have complained of his reserve, his intractable nature, his lack of charm, without realizing what a compliment such criticism implied! '*Etranges animaux à conduire*' was Molière's rough description of his actors. To run a theatre one must be a master of the difficult art of saying no. A pleasant theatre director is a contradiction in terms, a wooden horseshoe, a wolf with the manners of a lamb. There are people who understand how to refuse graciously, how to be rude with the greatest politeness; Dingelstedt knew how to do this.[220] But it is not to be recommended, for it requires a very high degree of sophisticated deceit and is always slightly duplicitous. The same thing is true of directors as of the diplomat in Frederick the Great's day. It was a story Bismarck used to tell. The man was universally recommended to the king. They praised his fine manners, his social polish and above all the fact that he was exceptionally amusing at the dinner table. 'Amusing at the dinner table?', Frederick exclaimed, 'Out he goes!'

Affable directors and amusing diplomats are very similar. Mahler does not belong in this category, as we know. Let us make no mistake: his curt manner, his astounding ability to say no, have hitherto been his best support, the screw which kept him firmly on his pedestal. And let us not forget that he is also a creative artist. Again, we are not

[219] This is clearly an allusion to Prince Montenuovo who, without taking into account the artistic reasons for Mahler's behaviour at the time of the Hassreiter quarrel, had simply told him that he was 'countenancing irregularity'.

[220] Franz, Freiherr von Dingelstedt was director of the Vienna Opera from 1867 to 1870.

concerned with the value of his music, only with the fact that he is one of the few musicians whose names are known the world over. Whatever his significance as a composer, he is undoubtedly famous, world famous. If anyone doubts this, let him turn to America, which has long since stopped being satisfied with famous artists whom we no longer need, and now demands our newest talents, sampling these precious wares like a connoisseur, and aware of their true value. As soon as Mahler was free in the Old World, he was summoned to the New World. The well-known siren's song of a clever impresario accompanied on a golden lyre with golden strings sounds across the water, beckoning and calling, and it does not call in vain. But we let our man go. We let him go light-heartedly, as if to prove once again how carelessly we manage our intellectual capital. As if we did not know, from many an unfortunate experience, how difficult it is to acquire, and how much more difficult to defend! Whenever a post becomes vacant at our colleges we experience the greatest difficulty in finding a suitable candidate. We squander our fame and yet have discovered all too often that it can rarely be replaced. Since we allowed Hans Richter to go abroad, the Philharmonic has continued to look for a conductor, even though there is certainly no dearth of conductors. There is no shortage of batons wielded in an individual manner, yet there is no one of whom it could be said that he is the natural leader of this particular group of artists. If there were no express trains the symphony would be in a bad way in Vienna, which was once its cradle and its home. . . .[221] Stewards and chamberlains are available by the dozen, while artists are great rarities. But we are still so full of the medieval spirit of feudalism that we often hoard such common wares and throw away the solitaire with an aristocratic gesture. So of course we always lack the one man we really need, the only one nature forgot to duplicate.

We could learn from Munich how a city should guard and protect its living artistic heritage. The difference between us and them is striking. Both Mahler and Mottl resigned, but how utterly different was their way of handling the same situation! Here no one lifted a finger to stop him from going after he had resigned—one musician less, so what!—whereas there all those involved united to prevent him from leaving—since great artists are hard to find! The Intendant appealed to the minister, the minister appealed to the private secretary of the Prince Regent, the secretary appealed to the head of state in person: and all together threw their weight against the door through which the fugitive was attempting to escape. There on the Isar is the modern spirit of art, there they know its magic, the miraculous power of art, its patent ability to construct cities, they recognize it as a source of light that can spread its brilliance over a whole nation, there they understand that its ideal worth is also a very real one, which can increase the attractive qualities of a big city like nothing else; they know from long experience that this intellectual capital produces good returns. Here, too, we are beginning to think rather more wisely about artistic questions. But how long will it take before such views have become common property, how long, in particular, until they have come to the attention of those official circles which normally determine the fate of this Cinderella? Every Privy Councillor with responsibility for the arts thinks that he is more important than art or artists. Yet how many Privy Councillors are there compared to a single great painter or sculptor? A thousand would not be enough.

---

[221] Since Hellmesberger's departure, in the wake of the 1903 scandal, the Philharmonic had had only guest conductors.

Rooted in this barren bureaucratic soil is the fatal irresponsibility with which one elegantly evades important questions in artistic life. A Mahler crisis was to come to a head because one thought Mottl would come, and now it turns out that Munich does not intend to let Mottl go. So now we have neither Mahler nor Mottl . . .

It is hardly worth refuting the statement that Mahler was not dismissed, that he left of his own free will. We know what 'of his free will' means in such cases. It is a convenient way of putting it. When a minister is dismissed, one always says that he handed in his resignation; but who and what forced him to do this is never mentioned. Such voluntary constraints are sometimes forced on less highly placed individuals. The crisis could easily have been avoided if they had really wanted to do so. But it was more elegant to let events take their course. Vienna possessed an outstanding conductor, whose stature is acknowledged even by his opponents, and when one evening he threw down his baton in a temper, we smiled and waved goodbye. Able theatre directors are extremely difficult to find these days. Once, we had, working in this city at the same time, Laube, Dingelstedt, Herbeck: now a good theatre director is a tremendous rarity. Vienna possessed a man who could truly be said to be one of these rare birds, and no sooner did he show a touch of Wanderlust than with the utmost courtesy we opened wide both doors—please walk this way. If only he had been blue-blooded, or with some august title, or else some political muckraker! But just an artist . . .!

We have done our best not to refer to the personality of the man who is leaving us, and, if it had been possible, we would not even have mentioned his name. We are dealing with a certain state of affairs, a century-old way of doing things, one might say, a hallowed tradition of the Court. What is happening to someone today could happen to someone else tomorrow. . . . An opera director leaves us after ten years, and they do not even deign to tell the public why. Why should the public bother its head about the real reasons for this departure? Yet slightly more consideration would be advisable. The Opera has known times when it was the listener who was the rare bird, and such times could come again. The audience on strike—we should be on guard against such an event.

And there is something else. Vienna has grown; the number of theatre-goers has increased tenfold, whereas the number of theatres has barely doubled. In order to be able to hear a world famous work not permitted to be shown on the imperial stage we were obliged to call in an opera company from Breslau. This brings shame on Vienna, which used to be called the capital of German music. We need a second large opera house, independent and free, we need it urgently, and surely we have enough lovers of art who possess the courage and the means to bring this idea to fruition. It would be a good deal, and for Vienna and the arts it would be a stroke of good fortune.[222]

Benedikt's article accurately reflects Mahler's state of mind just before he left Vienna, and makes an eloquent plea for an artist who knew that he was unique, and felt as if he had nevertheless been given notice like a servant by narrow-minded officials. One can sense Mahler's bitterness about the behaviour of Prince Montenuovo and his half-hearted efforts to retain the man who had reformed and rejuvenated the Vienna Opera.

---

[222] Unsigned article, 'Unmusikalische Bemerkungen über den Fall Mahler' *Neue Freie Presse* (16 June 1907).

An article on the same subject by Max Burckhard was published in the same issue, and the imperial authorities no doubt imagined that the *Neue Freie Presse* was embarking on a campaign in support of Mahler. After having described the splendour of the capital as seen from the Kahlenberg, and Vienna's unique wealth, which derived from the confluence of so many ethnic and cultural groups, Burckhard went on to deplore the political decadence of a city and a country which were obliged to accept the supremacy of Germany in general, and Berlin in particular. He then stated that if Austria wished to retain some kind of supremacy, it would have to be in the realm of the arts. It so happened that the Burgtheater was in a thoroughly decadent state,[223] and that the Viennese public was interested only in plays imported from Berlin.[224]

And yet we still have something! We still have something which shows that we are really important. Something which draws visitors to Vienna and fills them with admiration, something that every Austrian can be proud of and that every German here can be proud of too, seeing that the fate of German culture in Austria is closely bound up with the fate and importance of Vienna.[225] We have our Opera. Our Opera, with an orchestra that its director, Mahler, has moulded into a unified and wonderful instrument. Our Opera, with its conductor who arouses the greatest interest and boundless admiration whenever he lifts his baton. Our Opera, with its series of productions whose outstanding, and often incomparable artistic quality has been acknowledged even by the opponents of the person who, through his intuition, his individuality and his perseverance, brought it into being.

Yes, this we possess. Even today. And soon we shall possess it no more. We should not deceive ourselves: our Opera is what it is on account of the personality, the tenacious strength, and the artistic integrity of the man who has been at its head for ten years. The things which have gone wrong are not his fault, but the result of chance, of circumstances and situations which are beyond his control. But the Vienna Opera is what it is because of him. And to allow the man who has created and maintained this artistic unity to leave Vienna not only means losing a man, a personality; it means destroying existing works of art and those in the process of being created; it means annihilating an artist's work; it means allowing the artistic institution which the Vienna Opera is today to descend from a secure and lofty position to uncertain depths.

And yet one is simply allowing this man to go. And many people are even glad. And it is only natural that they should be glad, because they are the people who caused all this to happen. And Germans are glad, Germans acting in the name of German culture. Those who should have kept him, and kept him at any price, are allowing him to leave. Not light-heartedly, of course. But they are letting him leave all the same. Because pressure is being brought to bear on them. Not only in the Jockey Club, but also among the 'German people'. Oh, unfortunate German people in Austria!

The fact that we are in the process of destroying the last public institution which is still pre-eminent, of losing the last thing which shows that we are a force to be reck-

---

[223] Max Burckhard had been the director of the Burgtheater, also a court theatre.

[224] In 1905, for example, Max Reinhardt and his company had given a performance of Shakespeare's *Midsummer Night's Dream* to Vienna.

[225] An allusion to Burckhard's German nationalist ideals.

oned with, makes the 'Mahler case' 'political' in the fullest sense of the word. And for this reason it is unforgivable that Mahler is being allowed to leave. Unforgivable despite the fact that his departure gratifies certain influential people. Unforgivable despite the possibility that a time would come when one could no longer persuade him to stay. Unforgivable despite the fact that he himself wishes to go. We should not allow him to leave.[226]

Max Graf, who claims to have been present when Mahler visited Moritz Benedikt, later wrote that the vigorous intervention of the *Neue Freie Presse* came too late to have any effect. Under certain conditions Mahler would no doubt have stayed in Vienna. Given the difficulty he was experiencing in finding a successor, Prince Montenuovo must have tried to persuade him to remain. However, both were too proud to admit that they had changed their mind. This was true of Mahler, whose pride forbade him to stay on simply because of Mottl's refusal. In any case, he thought that the whole affair had been handled in a scandalously casual way.[227]

The last-minute effort by Vienna's biggest daily paper was of no avail, but it must have come like balm to Mahler's wounded feelings. If it did, he had little time to savour the effect, for further misfortune awaited him in this unhappy year. Mahler's family had not been well since the beginning of the spring, Alma recalls in her *Erinnerungen*:

I returned from Rome ill and under the weather. In my absence the English nanny[228] had scalded three of the younger child's fingers. She seemed unwell, I did not like the way she looked, the scalding alone could not account for it. She became feverish, and was sick. It was scarlet fever. I stayed to witness the illness reaching a peak and her gradual recovery, and then went into hospital for an unavoidable operation. My heart was with my convalescent child. Her sister had been taken to my mother. When I had recovered, and the child was well again[229] we all met at the station and went to Maiernigg on holiday as we did every year.

Very few documents have survived concerning this troubled period. One of them is a letter written to Alma by Alexander Zemlinsky:

Dear friend, Whatever have you been up to! You're always ill and now you're having an operation? What's the matter? Poor thing, you are having quite a nasty Spring. But I hear that you are well again, and that your daughter is much better, and that

---

[226] Max Burckhard, 'Der Fall Mahler als Politicum', *Neue Freie Presse* (16 June 1907).

[227] In the *Deutsches Volksblatt* (25 June 1907), Hans Puchstein again described Mahler as the 'disorganizer' of the Opera, claiming that he had alienated the entire company, and was now 'clinging to his post. He had refused to resign, and was obviously waiting to be dismissed with gentle force'. The *Extrablatt* of 28 June 1907 suggested solving the crisis at the Opera by means of a dual directorship consisting of either Hans Gregor and Hans Richter, or Rainer Simon and Raoul Mader.

[228] Miss Turner.

[229] Anna Mahler told me that her premature return after her attack of scarlet fever was the result of family tensions. Later she was always seen as the cause of Putzi's illness and death. Karen Monson (*Alma Mahler, Muse to Genius* (Houghton Mifflin, Boston, 1983), 77), also states that Anna had felt in some kind of way that the adults around her considered her to be responsible for the death of her sister. She suffered for many years from semi-conscious remorse.

unfortunately the wish you have been expressing for years is at last to be fulfilled: Director Mahler is leaving the Opera! So now *my* suffering is about to begin. For the moment I cannot in the least imagine what is going to happen, especially in my case. For me it is simply a disaster! I know exactly what I shall be losing, whoever his successor is. I am in a dreadful situation.—But I do not want to trouble you with my problems on top of everything else. I hope I shall be able to talk to you about every-thing soon.[230]

A few days later, Zemlinsky added in another letter:

If the Director is leaving there is one thing about it that cheers me up: I hope to have the opportunity—and I will no longer find it difficult to prove to him how much I have always admired him and always will (although I know he never asks for anything) of that sort.[231]

Mahler's feelings about the decision he had just made to leave Vienna are expressed in two letters to Arnold Berliner, an old friend from his Hamburg days. One was a short note sent in the middle of June: 'Everything is true. I am going because I cannot stand the riff-raff any longer. I am not going to America until mid-January, and shall remain until mid-April . . .'[232] and the other was sent in early June after arriving in Maiernigg: 'I am only risking having to put up with three months of feeling uncomfortable per year, against which I shall have earned a net 300,000 kronen in four years.'[233]

When in fact did Mahler leave Vienna for Maiernigg? A letter dated 20 June in the Opera Archives states that he had been 'away from Vienna' since 15 June.[234] Mahler wrote three times to Alma from the Semmering on 23 (or 28?) and 29 June[235] whereas the *Neue Freie Presse* announced only on 22 June, the last day of the season, that Mahler had left Vienna. It is conceivable that he tired of reading the Viennese press commenting in one way or another about his departure, and was now acutely conscious of the fact that there was noth-ing more he could do at the Opera, where the sole concern of the authorities was to find someone to replace him. On 21 June he finally signed his contract with Henrich Conried and probably went to spend a few days with the Conrats, near Vienna, or with the Redlichs in Göding, until both Gucki and Alma had

---

[230]   Undated letter (June 1907), UPL. Another letter announces Zemlinsky's forthcoming visit to Maiernigg, to play his transcription of the Seventh Symphony to him and that of the 'new work' (undoubt-edly the Eighth. At this juncture, Mahler must have asked him to prepare the piano reduction of the Seventh Symphony, a task which he finally entrusted to Alfredo Casella.

[231]   This second unpublished letter was undoubtedly written after 10 June, for Zemlinsky referred to two performances he conducted at the Hofoper on 8 and 10 June.

[232]   MBR1, no. 337; MBR2, no. 371. Undated letter to Arnold Berliner (June? 1907).

[233]   Undated letter to Arnold Berliner (postmark 4 July 1907, MBR1, no. 336; MBR2, no. 372).

[234]   Letter to Mahler from Willy Scriba, dated 19 June. A reply drafted by a secretary refers to the fact that Mahler had 'left the Opera on Saturday'.

[235]   BGA, nos. 207 to 209. The first card was mailed from Puchberg, at the foot of the Semmering, on 23 June, just before Mahler boarded the train to the Schneeberg, but it must in fact have been written on 28 June. Unfortunately the original copies of the letters, presently in the Moldenhauer collection, are inacces-sible. The letter and card of 29 June (nos. 208 and 209) were written in the Hotel Hochschneeberg.

31. Silhouettes by Hans Boehler

(a)

(b)

32. Caricature by Oscar
Garvens

G. Mahler

33. Silhouettes by Troianski
(St Petersburg, 1907)

Моментъ 1.

Моментъ 2.

Моментъ 3.

Архи-дирижеръ г. Малеръ. Три момента дирижерства.

(Рис. П. Троянскаго).

34. *A month in the life of the Vienna Court Opera Director. Director Mahler is unavailable because:*

In the first week he is rehearsing his latest symphony with a combination of obscure provincial orchestras;

In the second week he is looking for an instrument with yet undiscovered sound characteristics;

In the third week he is too pre-occupied with revising his recently completed symphony;

In the fourth week he has to recuperate from the rigours of his holidays, in the Court Opera Management office

Die Zeit, 20 January 1907

Direktor Mahler ist nicht zu sprechen:

35. The untoward incident in the Court Opera Theatre. [Panic in the auditorium. Smoke above the procenium, due to a short circuit in the electric wiring.] Note the singer (Slezak) appealing for order from the stage. Note also the conductor's armchair in front of the orchestra pit, immediately below the stage

Illustrirtes Wiener Extrablatt, 5 May 1905

36. Box Office Takings.
Weingartner: ... and by the way, did the increase in ticket price at the Court Opera produce good results?
Mahler: Yes! Yes! ... in the takings at the Volksoper (the rival popular opera house in Vienna)
Der Floh, 1907

38. The Tragic Symphony. [The Sixth was ridiculed for the introduction of unusual percussion instruments.]
'Good Lord, I forgot the motor horn! Now I shall have to write another symphony'
Die Muskete, 10 January 1907

37. The Management of the Court Theatre intends to save money by dismissing all the singers, the chorus and orchestra, and replacing them by gramophones. Director Mahler will be replaced by an automaton
Der Floh, 1906

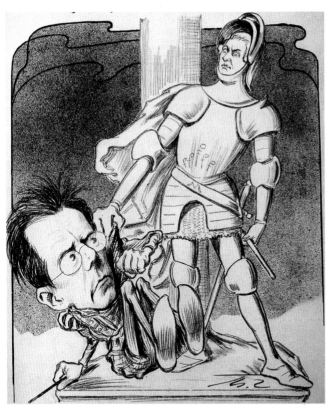

39. Mozart as the Commendatore's Statue comes to fetch Mahler because he has so disgracefully abused his child Don Giovanni

Wiener Caricaturen, XXIV (December 1905): 53, 9

40. *Mahler's Metamorphoses.* After the performance of his latest symphony, some critics remarked that Mahler could not free himself from reminiscences of his revered masters, and had also borrowed from folksong. Mahler is now considering whether, while conducting the future performances of his works, he should not also adopt the facial expressions and attitudes of each of the composers who have influenced him [Wagner, Liszt, Schubert, Beethoven, Meyerbeer and folksong instrumentation with a real Viennese flavour]

41. Roller's sketches for Beethoven's *Fidelio*, act I, scene 1 (Rocco's Stube), 1904 (Theater Museum, Bildarchiv, Wien)

42. Roller's sketches for Beethoven's *Fidelio*, act I, scene 2 (prison), 1904 (Theater Museum, Bildarchiv, Wien)

43. Roller's sketches for Mozart's *Le nozze di Figaro*, act IV (garden), 1906 (Theater Museum, Bildarchiv, Wien)

44. Roller's sketches for Mozart's *Don Giovanni*, act I, scene 1 (before the Commendatore's palace), 1905 (Theater Museum, Bildarchiv, Wien)

45. Roller's sketches for Mozart's *Don Giovanni*, act II, scene 3 (cemetery), 1905 (Theater Museum, Bildarchiv, Wien)

46. Roller's sketches for Wagner's *Das Rheingold*, scene 2, 1905 (Theater Museum, Bildarchiv, Wien)

47. Erik Schmedes with Friedrich Weidemann in *Tristan* (with Roller's costumes)

48. (*Below, left*) Erik Schmedes as Loge in *Rheingold* (with Roller's costume)

49. (*Below, right*) Leo Slezak as Walther in *Meistersinger* (Bildarchiv des Österreichischen National-bibliothek)

50. (*Above, left*) Richard Mayr

51. (*Above, right*) Friedrich Weidemann as Wotan in Roller's production of *Walküre*

52. Johannes Messchaert

53. Anna von Mildenburg as Ortrud in *Lohengrin*   54. Sarah Charles Cahier as Dalila

55. Lilli Lehmann   56. Selma Kurz as Elisabeth in *Tannhäuser*

57. Toblach and its neighbourhood, where Mahler made many excursions in the years 1897–1907

58. Postcard view of Schluderbach and the Hohe Gaisl (1906), where Mahler stayed in 1907

59. Postcard view of Lake Misurina (with the Drei Zinnen)

60. Postcard view of Landro (early 1900s), with Monte Cristallino

Mahler's four French friends
'The Dreyfus Quartet'

61. Paul Clemenceau

62. Paul Painlevé

63. Georges Picquart.

64. Guillaume de Lallemand

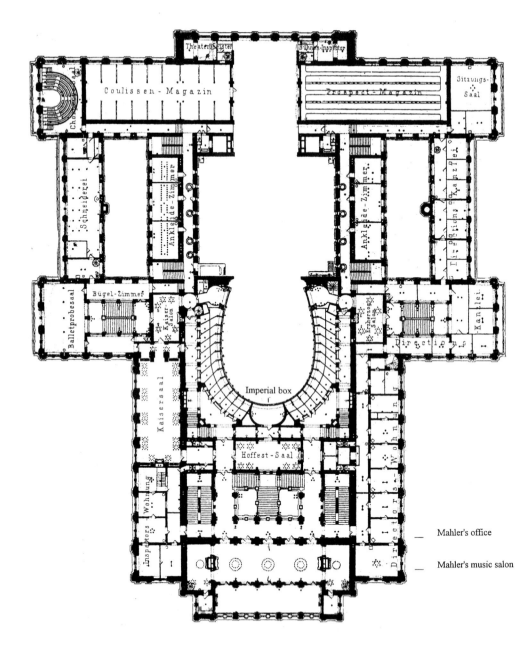

Chor-Zimmer

Coulissen - Magazin

Theater-Sorten

Bühnen-Inspektor

Prospect - Magazin

Sitzungs-Saal

Schneiderei

Anklede-Zimmer

Anklede-Zimmer

Theaterfond-Kanzlei

Balletprobesaal

Bügel-Zimmer

Kaiser-Salon

Erziehungs-Saal

Direction

Kanzlei

Kaisersaal

Imperial box

Theaterfond-Wohnung

Inspektors-Wohnung

Hoffest - Saal

Director's Wohnung

— Mahler's office

— Mahler's music salon

65. The Vienna Opera in Mahler's Time. First balcony level plan

completely recovered and until he believed the danger of scarlet fever to be passed. He then went to the Hochschneeberg, primarily it seems in order to reserve a room for Alma and the children for September. He had no doubt decided not to travel with them to Maiernigg and to arrive only once the house had been opened up. When he returned in September, he intended to spend his mornings in his office at the Opera, joining Alma in the afternoon. But things were to turn out differently.

As he left Vienna on 29 June, Mahler met Anna von Mildenburg and her fiancé, the writer Hermann Bahr, at the station on their way to a holiday on the Wörthersee:

We travelled together as far as Wiener Neustadt. It wasn't much fun.[236] I felt the first symptoms of the migraine which I have been having every afternoon for a week. In the evening it worsened, and I spent an hour walking around bareheaded in the fog. Afterwards I felt better and slept quite well. I hope the pain won't return while I'm here![237]

Mahler spent his day in the mountains alone, in foul weather and thick fog, reading a new work by Dimitri Merezhkovsky,[238] a book he found 'superb, very original, and welcome company here in my solitude. . . . It's one of those books I shall read again.' The following day he took the train to join Alma and the children in Maiernigg.[239]

Having reached the Wörthersee, Mahler was able to relax and enjoy the fresh air. This year the scenery proved to be more soothing than it had ever been, especially after the frustration, distress, uncertainty, and heartbreaks of the preceding weeks. But the period of relaxation was not to last: 'On the third day of our holiday,' Alma wrote, 'the older child was already beginning to show alarming symptoms. It was a combination of scarlet fever and diphtheria,[240]

---

[236] As seen above, Mahler did not like Bahr very much (see above, Vol. ii, Chap. 16).

[237] Undated letter to Alma (BGA, no. 208, postmarked 29 June 1907).

[238] The Russian essayist and novelist Dimitri Merezhkovsky (1866–1941) made his European reputation with *Christ and Antichrist* the trilogy (1892–1904), in which he argued the need for a synthesis between paganism and Christianity. Significantly, Russian Christian ideals triumphed over the pagan spirit of the west.

[239] From this letter it can be gathered that Mahler took a train on 30 June from Wiener Neustadt at noon, and arrived at Klagenfurt at about half past seven.

[240] Diphtheria is caused by the Klebs-Loeffler bacillus. Laryngeal diphtheria, or croup, which Putzi apparently contracted, is characterized by the development of 'false membranes' at the level of the vocal chords. These are liable to extend to the sub-glottal region, resulting in disturbed phonation, the obstruction of the respiratory tract, progressive difficulty in breathing and, finally, asphyxia. Treatments were developed from 1894 onwards. It was already known by 1907 that an early injection of serum could shorten the course of the disease and convalescence. Such a treatment would no doubt have been applied if the child had fallen ill in Vienna. This serotherapy would be accompanied by general treatment (milk, then milk and vegetable diet) and local applications (washing the throat, and a tube if the throat was obstructed). A preventive vaccine became available only in 1913. The exceptional seriousness of some varieties of diphtheria is sometimes attributed to the presence of another infection. Thus it is quite possible that Putzi had the misfortune to contract diphtheria and scarlet fever simultaneoulsy. I am grateful to Jacqueline Roskam, of Liège, for this information. She also pointed out a mistake in the French edition of this book (Fayard, Paris, 1984, Vol. iii. 81), in which I stated that scarlet fever and diphteria rarely broke out at the same time and wrongly identified Putzi's scarlet fever as 'faux croup' (laryngotracheobronchitis), an illness which is hardly ever fatal.

and she was doomed from the start. A fortnight of fear—decline—the danger of suffocation. A terrible time. Nature did what it could: storms and red skies.'

On 4 July hope was not yet lost, for when Mahler wrote to Berliner: 'Terrible misfortunes. I shall tell you everything when I see you. Now our eldest daughter has contracted scarlet fever and diphtheria!'; he did not mention the possibility of a fatal outcome.[241] Neither did he allude to such fears in a letter written to Emil Freund at the same time: 'Just imagine, our Putzi, after arriving sound and healthy, went down with scarlet fever. Unfortunately with diphtheria as a complication to an already difficult situation. And now there is nothing more we can do except to be frightfully careful.'[242]

But Putzi's condition worsened day by day, and Alma's harrowing recount continues:

Mahler loved this child so much that he retreated more and more often into her room, inwardly taking leave of his adored child. During the final night, when the tracheotomy was carried out, Mahler's servant [Anton] always stood outside his door, so that if he were awakened by the noise he could calm him down and bring him back to his bedroom. And so he slept the whole night. This terrible night, in which my English nanny and I set up an operating table and put the poor, poor child to sleep. During the operation I ran along the shore screaming loudly though no one could hear me. At five o'clock in the morning (the doctor had forbidden me to enter the room) my English girl came and said: 'It's all over'. And I saw the beautiful child lying with eyes wide open, gasping for breath, and so we suffered another day—until it was over.

Mahler ran back and forth weeping and sobbing outside her, or rather my, bedroom door, for with a sort of death wish I had put her in my bed. He fled so that he would not have to hear her. He could no longer bear it. We sent a telegram to my mother, who came immediately. All three of us slept in his room. We could not leave each other for as much as an hour. When one of us left the room we were afraid he or she would not come back. We were like birds in a storm, we dreaded the hours to come, and how right we were![243]

Until then, Mahler made no secret of the fact that he preferred his elder daughter Putzi (Maria Anna). He and Alma had a tacit understanding that this lively little girl with pitch-black hair, who was independent, stubborn, and capricious in a somewhat 'demonic' way, was 'his' daughter, whereas Gucki,[244] with her blond hair and light-blue eyes, resembled her mother. Mahler had 'an individual and special relationship' with each of the children. He liked to tell them 'grotesque tales, jokes, ghost stories and loved to read to Putzi Brentano's fairy tale *Gockel, Hinkel und Gackeleia*'.[245] When they were at Maiernigg, the

---

[241]   Unpublished letter to Arnold Berliner (BGM, Paris). Another letter, probably written on 5 to 6 July, was addressed to Emil Freund: 'Our Putzi, who arrived here strong and well, has caught scarlet fever. Unfortunately she also has diphtheria.' Mahler invited Freund to come and spend a few days in Maiernigg in Aug. 'when all will be in order here' (BGM, Paris).

[242]   Undated letter to Emil Freund, early July 1907 (BGM, Paris).

[243]   AMM1, 153; AMM2, 149. The parish register of Keutschach and the announcement in the *Neue Freie Presse*, state that Maria Anna Mahler died on the morning of 12 July.

[244]   Communication by Anna Mahler to the author.   [245]   AMM1, 91 (1904); AMM2, 96.

child would often walk to the *Häuschen* in the morning to look for him. 'They had long conversations there. No one knew what about. I never disturbed them.'

We had a prim and proper English girl who always brought the child to the door neat and clean. After some time Mahler came back holding the child's hand. And by that time she was usually 'splattered' with jam from head to foot, and then I had to placate the English girl. But they both came back so happy and pleased from their conversation that it secretly gave me a great deal of pleasure. She was every inch his child. Wonderfully beautiful and defiant, and unapproachable—things promised to become dangerous. Black curls, big blue eyes! Though she was not fated to live long, she was destined to be his pride and joy for a few years, and that in itself is a kind of eternity. He wanted to be buried with her, and we complied with his wish.[246]

Elsewhere Alma described Putzi's birth, which had caused terrible suffering for mother and child: 'She lay there as if she were dead, completely blue, and thus she set out on her short and dramatic existence, which finished as stormily and dramatically as it had begun.'[247] Alma's brief and moving account of her eldest daugher's death is of special importance because it is the only one: Mahler himself took refuge in a silent, and almost inhuman grief, as on all the other occasions when he had suffered a cruel blow of fate. But it is easy to imagine what went through his mind: the memory of the *Kindertotenlieder*, which he had begun before Putzi's birth and finished in the year his younger daughter was born; the memory, perhaps of the Sixth Symphony with its forebodings and the three 'blows' of fate; the panic that had seized him one day while composing the Sixth Symphony and then the intense human grief, which had been expressed in several of his works—an obsession which seemed so remote from his daily life as a busy artist and director, and which nonetheless was something he looked for in the faces of others:

He laughed a great deal; but if someone else laughed it got on his nerves.—He often said, as we were talking about people: 'Oh that's a beautiful face, someone who has really *suffered*!' On other occasions he commented: 'An empty face, it has no pain in it!' Those serene rays of sunshine, breaking with difficulty through the clouds, those only came from him in the last year, when too much suffering had taught him what joy is.[248]

1907 was not a happy year for Mahler. His ten glorious years at the Opera were a thing of the past; he was facing the uncertainty of life on a new continent; and to add to all he had now lost, under particularly tragic circumstances, the child who was his greatest joy, who had, it had seemed, been born for a long and happy life. But Mahler's chapter of woes was still not complete. An event occurred almost at once which had serious, long-reaching consequences for him. Alma recalled:

---

[246] AMM1, 134; AMM2, 133 (see below).   [247] AML 250.
[248] AMM1, 152; AMM2, 148.

A relative[249] took care of all the frightful things that death brings with it. On the second day after the child had died, Mahler asked my mother and me to go down to the shore. There, for no apparent reason, she had palpitations of the heart. I bent down to the lake in order to make a cold compress for her heart. Then Mahler came down the path, his face distorted with grief. My eyes wandered up and beyond him—and up above me on the road I saw them, lifting the coffin into the carriage.[250] I now understood the reason for her sudden heart attack and for the way he looked. Mahler and I were so distraught, so helpless that—with almost a feeling of happiness—I fainted and was unconscoius for a long time.

The doctor came, diagnosed a serious cardiac dysfunction and ordered complete rest; he failed to understand how I could still walk around with such a heart. Mahler wanted to cheer us up in our mournful room and said: 'Look here, doctor, don't you want to examine me as well? My wife is always worrying about my heart. She shall have some good news today. She needs it.' The doctor examined him. He stood up and looked very serious. Mahler was lying on the sofa, Dr Blumenthal[251] had knelt down beside him, and said, almost cheerfully (like most doctors when they diagnose a fatal illness): 'Well, your heart is certainly nothing to be proud of!' And this diagnosis was the beginning of the end for Mahler.[252]

The last dramatic line of Alma's narration has given rise to endless comments, and it is partly responsible for a widespread view, much romanticized and distorted, of Mahler's last years. His heart condition has nearly always been defined as a desperate illness while the truth of the matter is in fact very different, as will be seen later on. What is indeed certain is that Mahler, who loved the open air, sport, rowing, swimming, and walking, was shattered by Carl Blumenthal's diagnosis. After the initial shock wiser counsels prevailed. After all, Dr Blumenthal was only a country doctor and his fears may have been exaggerated. Thus it was decided that Mahler should go to Vienna to consult Professor Friedrich Kovacs, who had treated Alma.[253] An appointment was made, and Mahler left Maiernigg on 17 July, in the company of the neurologist Richard Nepalleck, who had come to Maiernigg to be of service to the bereaved couple. As usual, Mahler wrote a card to Alma from the station, and another one when he was on the train, to reassure her. He enjoyed a good meal in the buffet car, arrived in Vienna at six o'clock and booked in at the Hotel Imperial. It had been decided that he should not stay at the Hohe

---

[249] This was the neurologist Richard von Nepalleck (1864–1940), whom Alma had chosen, together with his brother Wilhelm (1862–1924), Master of Ceremonies at the Court, as her 'Wahl-Onkel'. Richard Nepalleck co-signed a letter which Mahler wrote to Alma in the train from Klagenfurt to Vienna (BGA, no. 210).

[250] Maria Anna was laid to rest in Keutschach cemetery near Maiernigg on 13 July. The coffin was moved to Vienna and re-interred in 1909 (I am indebted to Herta Blaukopf for this information).

[251] Dr Carl Viktor Blumenthal (1868–1947) was born and studied medicine in Graz. From 1894 until 1928, he was the district physician (Districtsarzt) of Viktring and its neighbourhood.

[252] AMM1, 154; AMM2, 150.

[253] Friedrich Kovacs (1861–1931) was born in Vienna and studied medicine there. Head physician at the Franz-Joseph-Spital from 1893, he held the same post at the Wiener Allgemeines Krankenhaus from 1900. A diagnostician and teacher of high repute, specializing in internal medicine, he published a great deal, notably on the pathology of the circulatory system.

Warte just in case his presence, so soon after little Putzi's death, might pass the infection on to Anna Moll's youngest daughter, Maria. No plans had been made for the future. If the diagnosis turned out to be correct, Mahler and Alma had decided to find somewhere else for the rest of the summer and to follow the advice of Kovacs. Neither of them could face the idea of staying in Maiernigg with its traumatic memories. And in any case they were already of the opinion that the climate of the Wörthersee was unhealthy.

When Mahler left Carinthia, Alma and Anna Moll were already preparing to move out, and he urged them, in a letter written on the train from Klagenfurt to Vienna, to let Miss Turner, the faithful Anton, and Kathi the chambermaid do the packing.[254] He also reminded them not to forget the score of Weber's *Oberon*, which he intended to work on that summer, and had left in his room.[255]

Having arrived in Vienna in the afternoon, Mahler sat in the Imperial Café, no doubt reading the newspapers, when he met Ludwig Karpath, who told him that he had heard from the best possible sources that Prince Liechtenstein, the Lord Chamberlain himself, had said: 'We will not let Mahler go, we shall not grant him permission to go.' Later on, he met Karl Moll, dined with Richard Nepalleck, and went for a short walk after dinner, after which he retired to bed at nine, and slept until half past seven the next morning:

I feel very well—if Blumenthal hadn't said anything I would already have been roaming about for a long time—and wouldn't have gone to bed before midnight yesterday. So you see, my love, everything has its good side.—From now on I shall make a point of not doing too much, and if I have to stay here (in Vienna) I shall live and do what Kovacs tells me to do.[256]

We do not know what the Viennese doctor told Mahler, for the telegram he sent Alma the next day is no longer to be found. According to her *Erinnerungen*, Kovacs diagnosed inborn 'contracted mitral valves on both sides, with compensatory movements'.[257] He ordered Mahler to give up sport altogether: no mountain climbing, no bicycle rides, no swimming, indeed, with incredible short-sightedness he recommended this man who had always practised the most strenuous sports to take a field course to accustom himself to 'walking', overlooking the inevitable psychological effect of all these prohibitions. For the next few days, Mahler obediently followed the doctor's instructions and taught himself how to walk. 'He practised walking slowly for the first time in his life. His diligence was touching. Looking at his watch, he walked for five minutes, for ten, and so on.'

---

[254] BGA, no. 210, dated 17 July written in the train to Vienna and co-signed by Richard Nepalleck.

[255] BGA, no. 211, dated 17 July 1907. Mahler hoped to stage his version of *Oberon* at the Hofoper before he left (see below, Vol. iiii, Appendix 1, and above, Chap. 8). It was published by Universal Edition after his death, and includes further 'melodramas', or orchestral passages that utilize the work's principal motifs to provide a musical backdrop for some of the dialogue. Mahler also asked Alma to bring a book by Mommsen (surely vol. i of his *Römische Geschichte*, see above, Vol. ii, Chap. 4), Beethoven's letters, and Rückert's poems, and to leave behind only the works of Goethe and Shakespeare.

[256] BGA, no. 212, undated (18 July 1907).   [257] AMM1, 155; AMM2, 151.

As seen above, many writers about Mahler have assumed that the diagnosis of 1907 was that of a fatal heart disease. But it was no such thing. Nowadays, the idea that Mahler's mitral incompetence was inborn has mostly been abandoned. It is now usually described as a rheumatism of the heart resulting from a streptococcal tonsilitis. A detailed description of the mechanism which often leads from tonsilitis to lesion of the cardiac valves is perhaps necessary here. Those who have the patience to read the following scientific explanations will perhaps better understand why the diagnosis made in 1907 for Mahler was not that of a fatal heart disease, contrary to what has been generally claimed.

The origin of the valvular dysfunction can be traced back to a tonsilitis caused by haemolytic streptococcus, an infection which can lead to complications of an inflammatory nature: the two main ones are post-rheumatic fever (which has no after effects) and rheumatism of the heart. This can have serious consequences on the three components of the heart: the pericardium (pericarditis), the myocardium (myocarditis) and the endocardium (endocarditis). The endocardium is a membrane which lines the cavities of the heart: its folds form the mitral valves (which separate the left atrium and ventricle), the tricuspids and valve (which separates the right atrium and ventricle), and the aortic sigmoid valve situated at the base of the aorta. When the endocardium is affected with inflammation, it can, as it heals, shrink, thus creating a gap where the valves close, since they no longer fit together. This leads to mitral or aortic incompetence. Another possible consequence is adhesion of the commissures of the valves, which leads to mitral or/and aortic stenosis. The size of the lesions determines the extent to which the heart no longer functions properly, and, in those years before heart-surgery, there was a real danger of heart failure if the lesion was a major one, which it was not in Mahler's case.[258]

Professor Kovacs's diagnosis, as seen above, was mitral incompetence and stenosis, a heart condition with which many people have led an active life and lived until a ripe old age. Apparently the damage to Mahler was for the moment mainly psychological: Alma was right[259] in describing Friedrich Kovacs's diagnosis and advice to Mahler as 'incredibly short-sighted' for it took him several months to realize that his forces were undiminished, and that he could without danger resume an active life. In fact, from 1909 on, he conducted close to fifty Philharmonic concerts a season, with the countless rehearsals they required, and realized at that time how unfounded his early fears had been.

Yet he had at first been weighed down with anxiety, sadness, and distress. 'We were afraid of everything', Alma recalled. 'When we were out for a walk, he kept stopping to take his pulse. During the day he would often ask me to listen to the noises made by his heart to find out whether they sounded normal, excited, or calm. For years I had been frightened by the whistling sound that

---

[258] Another possible complication can be caused by bacterial infections of the damaged endocardium. This is what is known as subacute bacterial endocarditis, the illness which was to kill Mahler four years later. (Personal communication from Dr Pierre Simon Perret, Paris, a cardiologist and musicologist who pointed out a number of inaccuracies in the description given in Vol. iii, Chap. 49 of the French edition of this book). See below Vol. iiii, Chap. 8.　　　[259] See above and AMM1, 155; AMM2, 151.

could be heard very loudly on the second beat, and had long suspected that his heart *could not* be healthy.'[260] Alma was surely exaggerating, for if she had really been worried about it, she would have earlier seen to it that Mahler was examined by a cardiologist. However, he now gave up his favourite sports for good. This in itself was enough to upset his inner equilibrium. He bought a pedometer to take with him when he went on walks, and 'his life became a torment'.[261] And yet, in the light of the doctors' concern at the time of his haemorrhage in 1901, it seems unlikely that they had failed to notice the symptoms of mitral stenosis.[262] They probably did not mention them, because they did not consider them to be particularly serious.[263] Natalie's manuscript quotes Mahler's words after the auscultation: 'They felt my pulse and my heart. Fortunately it is solidly anchored in my chest and shows no intention of giving up.'[264]

In 1907 medical science was probably still unable to provide a more accurate diagnosis, or to understand the cause of Mahler's valvular dysfunction, which was most likely a streptococcal infection from which he had suffered as a child or later. As early as 1963 Dieter Kerner, the author of *Krankheiten Grosser Musiker*, suggested this, claiming that a hereditary cardiac defect would surely have become apparent at an earlier stage and that the origin of Mahler's disease was probably a severe attack of rheumatic fever.[265] Today this is no longer in doubt, for tests carried out during Mahler's last illness in New York in 1911 revealed that he was suffering from subacute endocarditis caused by streptococcus viridans, an illness which often affects patients suffering from mitral incompetence or stenosis.[266]

Thus Bruno Walter and Alfred Roller were wrong in believing they had detected early signs of Mahler's heart 'disease'. Their accounts of an incident which took place on stage at the Opera during a rehearsal of *Lohengrin* are almost identical.

In order to emphasize the required commotion among the assembled 'nobles' as the knight appears with the swan, he had been pushing around as if they were feather weights the rather substantial bodies of some of the singers to put them in their correct places. As he left the stage at the end of the scene he suddenly stood still for a moment on the wooden stair that led down to the stalls, and pressed his hand to his

---

[260] AMM1, 179; AMM2, 171. This passage refers to the summer of 1908; by that time the doctors had modified their initial diagnosis. Alma was obviously thinking of the weeks after Putzi's death.

[261] Ibid.

[262] The condition may well have worsened with the passage of time.

[263] I am grateful to Stuart Feder, the author of 'Gustav Mahler Dying', *International Review of Psycho-Analysis*, 3 (1978), 123 ff., a psychological study of Mahler during his last illness, for pointing this out to me. [264] NBLS, Feb. 1901, and above, Vol. ii, Chap. 10.

[265] *Krankheiten Grosser Musiker* (Schattauer, Stuttgart, 1986), 178. In France it is said of the rheumatic fever resulting from streptococcal tonsilitis that it 'licks the joints and bites the heart'.

[266] Mahler's brother Ernst may also have died of subacute endocarditis. See below, Vol. iiii, Epilogue, and Nicholas P. Christy's article 'Gustav Mahler and his Illnesses', *Transactions of the Clinical and Climatological Association*, 82 (1970), 207.

heart. It was the first time I felt alarmed by the prospect of the impending catastrophe.[267]

Bruno Walter's report has Mahler stopping short just as he had taken two members of the chorus by the hand and was leading them 'enthusiastically' to King Heinrich. For a moment he stood 'pale as death, with his hand on his heart', and this prompted Walter to think of heart disease.[268]

Where did Mahler and his family spend the rest of the summer of 1907? Although no letters of Mahler with dates showing them to have been written between the end of July and his return to Vienna on 24 August have surfaced, recent evidence paints a different picture from that left by Alma in her *Erinnerungen*: 'I packed the barest necessities and we fled from Maiernigg, which was full of memories which tortured us, to Schluderbach in the Tyrol. Here, amid wonderful scenery, we revived somewhat, and tried to picture our future life.' Alfred Roller was the only visitor mentioned that summer.

Schluderbach (not to be confused with Alt-Schluderbach, in the neighbourbood of Toblach, where Mahler and Alma were to spend the next three summers) lies at 1,442 metres above sea level, on the road that leads from Toblach to Cortina d'Ampezzo. The hamlet used to include a few houses which were destroyed during the bitter battles of the First World War. Mahler and Alma probably stayed in one of the two hotels, both of which have survived until today.[269] Although Mahler had stayed there only once, in 1905, he had often passed by Schluderbach on his way to Lake Misurina (1,750 metres above the sea level), one of the most spectacular spots in the Dolomites, which he had visited several times in search of inspiration.

Despite its prevailing mood of sadness and depression the summer had apparently had some lighter moments. Mahler and Alma had settled for a night with Anna Moll in Misurina and they occupied three separate rooms:

My mother was in my room speaking very quietly (we had got into the habit of whispering because Mahler heard every noise no matter where it came from, and it disturbed him). All of a sudden my door was opened and slammed shut rather

[267]   RBM 16. 'And yet,' Roller added, unaware that the two illnesses were linked, 'Mahler did not die of a heart attack, but of a streptococcal infection of the blood after repeated attacks of tonsilitis.'

[268]   BWM 42. Roller assigns the incident to 1904, but it is far more likely that it occurred during rehearsals for the new production of *Lohengrin*, premièred on 27 Feb. 1906, or the previous Autumn, during rehearsals of Act I, which was performed for the King of Spain on 14 Nov. 1905. Alma reproduces Roller's account (AMM1, 156; AMM2, 151). Contemporary medicine no longer links this incident to mitral stenosis, which could have only led to a feeling of suffocation.

[269]   See above, Chap. 4. The two hotels at Schluderbach were at the time Hotel-Pension Schluderbach (Proprietor Hans Ploner) and Hotel Sigmundbrunn (Proprietor Alois Baumgartner). It seems surprising that the doctors, whose instructions had been so strict that summer, should have allowed Mahler to stay at such an altitude, although he had not been examined by a cardiologist. However, the fact that Mahler stayed in Schluderbach that summer is confirmed by an autograph *Albumblatt*, on two staves. It has the opening theme of the Sixth Symphony, and a dedication to an unknown person. It is dated 'Schluderbach, Aug. 1907', and signed by Mahler (Stuttgarter Antiquariats-Messe, 25 Jan. 1990). Marianna Trenker, (in the text quoted below in Vol. iiii, Chap. 2) also states that Mahler spent the summer of 1907 in Schluderbach, which she calls Neu-Schluderbach.

violently. Mahler confronted us, seething with rage: 'Some idiot slammed a door in the corridor! The scoundrel interrupted my train of thought. I shall go and complain!' We were startled but then we simply had to laugh: 'But Gustav, you've just done exactly the same!' He quickly understood the irony of the situation. He used to quote a phrase from the *World as Will and Representation*:[270] 'How many inspired thoughts have been reduced to nothing by the crack of a whip!'[271]

Mahler never spoke to anyone about his grief and about Putzi's death. Only one known letter refers to it. It was written to Hermann Behn on 9 October 1907:

Forgive me for not replying to your kind letter, which meant a great deal to me. Even now you must make do with this rather summary procedure—not only because I am not yet in a mental state to talk to you about what you wish to know. I also consider it to be impossible suddenly to resume our mutual exchange of news after such a long time.—We ought to meet again—it's something I should very much appreciate. Now that I can move around on my own, we should be able to manage it if we wish. This time I am not coming to Hamburg because I am taking the ship from Cherbourg.[272]

But Mahler's silent grieving was not unusual. He behaved in the same way after the deaths of his parents and Otto's suicide. The full measure of his feelings can be deduced from the reports from witnesses who encountered him after he returned to Vienna. Alma tells how he forbade her to wear mourning, refusing to let her 'play to the gallery'[273] and Bruno Walter wrote to his parents on 13 September:

Parting from Mahler will be very, very hard for me, whatever happens, because despite everything[274] I love him very much and always will. No doubt you have heard about his terrible misfortune: at the beginning of summer he lost his older child (4½ years old) from scarlet fever. A beautiful, gifted, exceptionally strong and healthy child. As a result he is a broken man: outwardly one notices nothing, but those who know him can tell that inwardly he is at the end of his tether. She seems to be taking it better, with tears and philosophy. I don't know how anyone can come to terms with something like that.[275]

Shortly after Putzi's death, and probably during Mahler's brief visit to Vienna in order to consult Professor Kovacs, the writer Arthur Schnitzler once saw him sitting on a bench in Schönbrunn and found him so depressed that he

---

[270] By Arthur Schopenhauer.

[271] AMM1, 63; AMM2, 73. The incident could only have taken place in 1907, for in previous summers Mahler had always gone to Toblach and Misurina alone.

[272] Letter to Hermann Behn, property of Notary Hertz, Hamburg. It was numbered 44 by the recipient.

[273] AML 73. Alma also claims that, in his will, Mahler advised her 'to see people, go to concerts and the theatre'.

[274] Bruno Walter was undoubtedly Mahler's favourite confidant and disciple. Yet it is obvious from this letter that there had been moments of tension between them. Walter had no doubt kept his parents informed of them, but the other letters in which he certainly alluded to them have vanished, or were deliberately not included in the volume of his letters. Walter might perhaps have resented Mahler's obvious lack of appreciation for his music. In the same letter of 1907, he told his parents that he had finished a cantata for soloists, chorus, and orchestra, *Das Siegesfest* (The Victory Festival).

[275] Letter dated 13 Sept., BWB 95.

'wondered how he was able to go on living'.[276] To the end of his life Schnitzler never forgot his solitary and silent affliction. Ludwig Karpath who, as we have seen, met Mahler in July on the terrace of the Café Imperial, later wrote: 'I saw before me a man overcome with sorrow and despair,' but the meeting must not have particularly pleased Mahler who, since his clash with Karpath over the *Wunderhorn-Lieder* in 1905,[277] and especially since the première of Schoenberg's First Quartet, had no use for him.[278] Max Graf, another critic for whom Mahler had no great liking, met him on the Ring at the end of the summer. Mahler, who had not replied to his letter of condolence, rushed up to shake his hand. He then hurried away as fast as he could. Graf was unable to decide 'whether he was suddenly overwhelmed by the memory of the sad event which had brought us together, or whether it was a feeling of pain or disappointment, the stirrings of anger after his initial affability'.[279]

Among the letters of condolence received by Alma, there was one from Gustav Klimt, dated 14 July:

Dear Madam, I am saddened by the fate of the dear and wonderful child and share your grief—there remains the wish and the hope that the passage of time will help to alleviate your sorrow—and bravely overcome the inevitable in these cheerless days. Yours very sincerely Gustav Klimt.[280]

In his usual awkward way, Pfitzner wrote in the autumn: 'My heart felt thanks for your letter. I heard of your cruel loss, but hesitated to write because I simply could not believe it. Forgive me for saying nothing; whatever I said would seem trite to you.'[281]

Mahler's distress was the more intense because his misfortunes had all come in the same short space of time. As regards his health, from the beginning of the summer 1908, when he returned from Toblach, he began to accept the new state of affairs. But those who knew him well noticed that he was no longer the same man. For example, Alfred Roller noticed that the sound of his voice had changed: 'when he was irritated his natural baritone would rise in an instant to a tenor. After 1907 he spoke only in the lower register.'[282]

Alfred Roller's description of the month spent near Toblach is of special interest:

---

[276] AML 165.   [277] See above, Chap. 2.

[278] BMG 188. Karpath adds that this was his last meeting with Mahler. Hearing that his old enemy Plappart, the former Intendant, had died, Mahler hastily scribbled a telegram which the journalist promised to send off. Karpath also states that Mahler later on resented the fact that, in an article in the *Münchner Allgemeine Zeitung*, the journalist had stated that he had taken leave of only one Viennese journalist, Moritz Benedikt. Mahler certainly did not want his visit to the *Neue Freie Presse* to become common knowledge, and wrote to his sister Justine from the United States to complain about Karpath.

[279] GWO 92.   [280] Alma Mahler Archives, UPL.

[281] Ibid., undated letter from Dresden, probably written in Sept. 1907. At the beginning of Oct., Pfitzner came to Vienna (where he conducted Beethoven's 'Pastoral' Symphony), and Mahler suggested he conduct a performance of *Die Rose vom Liebesgarten* at the Opera (letter dated 13 Oct. 1907 from Pfitzner to his publisher Max Brockhaus, *Hans Pfitzner Briefe*, i, no.101 (Schneider, Tutzing, 1991)).

[282] RBM 20.

The summer failed to bear artistic fruit. After little Maria-Anna's death he left Maiernigg for ever and took rooms in Schluderbach. His mood was one of silent resignation. The happy rambles of the past were replaced by careful walks. A friend of his youth succeeded in restoring his shattered confidence in his body.[283] Mahler once more dared to go on longer walks, and made angry remarks about the doctor who had intimidated him. But fast walks, climbing mountains, rowing and swimming were no longer possible. Henceforth I often saw him smoke only half of the single cigar the doctor allowed him at the end of a meal, before looking at it pensively and putting it away in silence.[284]

As in 1901, after his first near encounter with death, the psychological effects of which have only recently been appreciated,[285] it is above all Mahler's music that allows us to perceive and feel how his outlook on life had changed. According to Alma Mahler he composed virtually nothing during the summer of 1907. But she does say that one of the books he had taken with him to Schluderbach had given him much more than the mere pleasure of reading it. Alma tells the story in *Mein Leben* as if it were a fable with the moral: 'One good turn deserves another.' Many years before, when her father, Emil Jakob Schindler, was still alive, one of his close friends was a young Jew called Theobald Pollak, who suffered from tuberculosis, and held a minor post in a transport company. On Schindler's fiftieth birthday he invited all his friends to the castle of Plankenberg. Heinrich von Wittek, Minister of Transport at the time, was one of the guests, and during the meal it fell to him to propose a toast to mark the occasion. He concluded his speech, came round and embraced Schindler, and, as a birthday present, promised to do his best to grant his dearest wish. Schindler thought for a moment, and then asked him to find Pollak a senior post in his ministry. This request presented the minister with a dilemma, for he was a confirmed anti-Semite, and Pollak had never expressed the slightest wish to convert to Christianity. However, Wittek had given his word. Shortly afterwards he did in fact find a job for Pollak, who thereafter made a brilliant career in the civil service, and ended up with the coveted title of Hofrat (Privy Counsellor). Pollak never forgot his debt of gratitude to Schindler, and after Schindler's death, he remained on affectionate terms with the rest of the family. He was delighted when Alma married a Jew, and regularly sent her presents, flowers, small delicacies, scores and books.[286]

Coming back to the summer of 1907; Putzi had died, the doctor had made his diagnosis, and Mahler had left his beloved house on the Wörthersee, his

---

[283] The friend in question may have been Emil Freund, with whom Mahler still had both friendly and business dealings. With all his other friends such as Lipiner or the Spieglers, he had broken relations since his marriage, and those he had kept with Fritz Löhr were not close enough for him to be invited to Toblach, especially at such an unhappy time. [284] RBM 19.

[285] See above, Vol. ii, Chap. 10.

[286] AMM1, 156; AMM2, 151 ff. And AML 15; and personal communications from Alma Mahler. Mahler addressed Pollak as Baldi, and felt an endearing and almost tender affection for him. He refers to him frequently in his letters and was extremely worried when in 1910 he had a recurrence of pulmonary disease (cf. MBR1, no. 358; MBR2, no. 438).

summer work, and even his beloved Häuschen where he had composed for six successive summers in the midst of the forest. It was then that, almost by chance, he began to read a book of poems which struck responsive chords within him. It had come as a gift from Theobald Pollak,[287] who had suggested that he might set some of the poems to music. The book was *Die Chinesische Flöte* (The Chinese Flute) by Hans Bethge,[288] an anthology of poems based on translations of Chinese models.[289] They proved to be the unexpected source of inspiration for a new cycle of songs which gradually became a symphony of Lieder. According to Alma, Mahler made some early sketches for the music that summer during his walks in the woods around Schluderbach. The meditative texts were a perfect embodiment of his new perception of life and of the world, of his all-consuming melancholy and the pessimism which, in the last song, gives way to a sad, yet hopeful parting mood, bathed in an all-pervading light that is earthbound no longer.

[287] Knud Martner brought to my attention the fact that Bethge's anthology, although dated by the publisher 'Early July 1907', was not available in bookshops until the autumn, and that Mahler could only have read it in 1908. Yet it was reviewed in the *Börsenblatt der deutschen Buchhandel*, Leipzig, no. 156, on 8 July 1907, and it seems highly unlikely that Alma could have been mistaken in stating that Mahler read *Die Chinesesiche Flöte* in the summer of 1907, shortly after Putzi's death. However she does wrongly claim that Pollak had given the book to her some years earlier (AMM1, 156; AMM2, 152). Pollak might well have received an advance copy from the author or the publisher.

[288] Insel Verlag, Leipzig, 1907. For information on Hans Bethge (1876–1946) see Vol. iiii, Appendix 1. According to the late Dr Rudolf L. Ernst, founder of a Mahler Society in Sydney, Australia, Bethge's book had been given to Pollak in 1907 by one of his former pupils, Frau Rosanes, the wife of a Viennese doctor. In remembrance of this gift, Pollak, when he died, left Frau Rosanes a precious antique porcelain bowl. This later passed from her son, Dr Heinz Rosanes, into the collection of Mrs Collen Pick, Double Bay, Sydney.

[289] Rather than translations, Bethge's poems are improvisations on themes suggested by the poems of Li-Tai-Po and other great Chinese classical authors. Bethge could not read Chinese, and made use of French translations by Judith Gautier and the Marquis d'Hervey Saint-Denis (see below, Vol. iiii, Chap. 2, and Appendix no. 1).

10

Mahler in Vienna (XXVI)—Weingartner is appointed
The Vienna Opera after Mahler—Opening of
the new season
Journeys to Russia and Finland—Farewell to Vienna

(August–December 1907)

*Instead of something whole, rounded off, as I had dreamed, I am leaving behind
unfinished bits and pieces: such is the human lot.*

M AHLER was still in Fischleinboden in the Dolomites on 11 August 1907
when he finally learned that he could go ahead with his plans for the
future. A letter dated the 10th from Prince Montenuovo informed him there
that the Hofoper administration had received official notification the previous
day from the Berlin Opera to the effect that Weingartner was now free to take
over the post of director of the Vienna Opera. In his memoirs, Weingartner
gives a detailed account of his Vienna appointment. He explains, among other
things, that when he first received an offer from Montenuovo he was hesitant
because of all the unfortunate experiences he had undergone in opera houses
from the outset of his career, and in particular in Berlin. If in the end he
allowed himself to be convinced, it was on account of the Vienna Opera's reputation, and of the opportunities he would have to realize long-cherished plans,
including the production of his own operas, as he candidly admits. The Prince,
on receiving the new candidate's acceptance in principle, took care not to
repeat his previous mistakes, and asked him immediately for a copy of his
current contract in order to have it examined by a lawyer. A major difficulty
then arose in the shape of a clause in which Weingartner had undertaken that,
when leaving the Berlin Opera in 1898, he would continue to live in Germany.[1]

[1] WLE, ii. 146.

In June it had been decided, at a meeting between Weingartner, Montenuovo, and Freiherr Frantz von Wetschl, the acting Intendant since Plappart's departure, that the Austrian Emperor would make a direct appeal to the German Emperor to ensure that the conductor be definitively released from his obligations. Weingartner refused to commit himself for more than one year, but this proved easy to accept, since the Lord Chamberlain, too, had envisaged a release clause in favour of the Opera stipulating the same period of notice. All the negotiations were carried out in the greatest secrecy, the Mottl affair having taught prudence to all concerned. On 5 July Wetschl wrote to Weingartner, who was spending the summer at his villa at Bad Kreuth in Upper Bavaria, to announce the favourable outcome of the Austrian Emperor's intervention. All Weingartner now had to do was to address an official letter of resignation to Count Georg von Hülsen-Häseler, Intendant of the Berlin Opera. Hülsen in due course advised Weingartner, on 17 July, that the German Emperor had agreed in principle.[2] But it was not until 9 August that he officially notified the Prince of the successful outcome of his demarches. At the same time Montenuovo received a letter from Weingartner, confirming that he would take over the direction of the Hofoper,[3] whereupon the Prince wrote at once to Mahler: 'I hasten to inform you of this, for I was as impatient as I am sure you yourself have been, to learn when you will be free.' It had been agreed that Weingartner would come to Vienna at the beginning of September to finalize the details of his contract. And the Prince was pleased to report that the Emperor had graciously agreed to grant the various requests Mahler had made in March, namely a pension of 14,000 kronen; an allowance of 20,000 kronen for removal expenses; and after his death, a pension for his wife equivalent to that of a Privy Councillor's widow, amounting to 2,000 kronen a year.

Weingartner's reputation in the German-speaking countries and abroad was more than sufficient to justify his appointment to Mahler's post. Born in Zara, Dalmatia, in 1863, Paul Felix Weingartner, Edler von Münzberg, was of Austrian nationality. After studying composition in Graz under Wilhelm Mayer Remy, he had studied philosophy at the University of Leipzig while continuing his musical education at the Leipzig Conservatory. In 1883 he had studied for a time under Liszt, who put on his opera *Sakkuntala* at the Weimar Opera the following year. He then started on his career as orchestral conductor, occupying posts in Königsberg, Dantzig, Hamburg, and Mannheim. In 1891 he was appointed conductor at the Berlin Opera and director of the Orchestral Concerts of the Königliche Kapelle. In 1898, after enduring hostile criticism from conservatives in the Prussian capital, he abandoned conducting at the Opera, stating that he had developed a deep-rooted aversion to everything associated with opera. He then went to Munich, becoming director of the Kaim

Concerts, but continued to fulfil his duties as director of the Königliche Kapelle concerts in Berlin. It was as director of the Kaim Concerts that he arranged for the première of Mahler's Fourth Symphony in Munich in 1901.[4]

Like Mahler, Weingartner achieved recognition as a conductor through his attention to detail and his punctilious respect for the composers' score indications. The 'charm and temperament' he also displayed in his performances evoked universal admiration at the time.[5] Under him, the concerts of the Berlin Hofkapelle and the Kaim Orchestra attained a high standard. Unfortunately he was equally well known for his instability. From 1891, the date when he first signed a contract with the Berlin Opera, he handed in his resignation no less than ten times, that of 1907 being the eleventh. The motives behind the crises he thus provoked seem to have been either to increase his salary or to put himself in a position to accept more alluring offers from other cities. His pretexts—poor health, the need to rest, pathological nervous trouble, or the desire definitively to give up conducting—though not lacking in variety, always proved to be unfounded. But in Georg von Hülsen, Intendant of the Berlin Opera and son of the previous Intendant, whose differences with Hans von Bülow had caused such a stir,[6] Weingartner had a powerful opponent.[7]

In 1898, on leaving the Berlin Opera, Weingartner had to give a formal undertaking not to leave Germany, nor to accept any position as permanent conductor or as director of an opera house in Europe. This, then, was the principal difficulty that Prince Montenuovo and Baron Wetschl had to overcome through their Emperor's intervention with the German sovereign. At the beginning of September they called a further meeting with Weingartner and the Berlin Intendant in Munich. One of the clauses in the agreement reached on this occasion was that if Weingartner left Vienna he would remain bound to the Berlin Opera by his existing contract which was valid until 1921. A few days after very reluctantly accepting this solution, Weingartner went back on his

---

[4] See above, Vol. ii, Chap. 11. In the years that followed, Weingartner made many tours, notably to England and the United States. As a composer he had already tackled practically all genres, in particular three operas, *Sakuntala* (1884) mentioned above, *Genesius* (1892), and the *Orestes* trilogy (1902). He later wrote five more, *Kain und Abel* (1914), *Dame Kobold* (1916), *Die Dorfschule* (1920), *Meister Andrea* (1920), and *Der Apostat* (never performed). His music, forgotten today, seems to have belonged to the much-decried school of Kapellmeistermusik in that it possessed no personal style. His output also included seven symphonies and five string quartets. Weingartner's name in the history of music is most often associated with the series of recordings he made in the 1930s, particularly one of the first complete sets of Beethoven symphonies, his many performances of the works of Berlioz, which he often conducted in theatres and concert halls, and several books and essays he wrote about conducting. From 1927 to 1935 he gave master classes for young conductors at the Basle Conservatory.

[5] See the *Bilder-Atlas zur Musikgeschichte von Bach bis Strauss*, ed. Gustav Kahnt (Schuster & Löffler, Berlin, 1911).   [6] See above, Vol. i, Chap. 17.

[7] Weingartner's version of his interminable conflict with Georg von Hülsen is given at length in WLE. In 1912 Hülsen published a short work entitled *Der Fall Weingartner, eine aktenmässige Darstellung* (The Weingartner Case; The Documentary Evidence), which appeared over the signature of the lawyer Arthur Wolff (Österfeld and Co., Berlin, 1912). After various court cases Weingartner was condemned to pay a fine of 9,000 marks to the Berlin Opera. The book shows that while he was not solely to blame for the dispute, honesty and forthrightness were not his foremost qualities.

decision and launched a fresh attempt to gain his full freedom. This brought him up against the resolute opposition of Hülsen who, angry at this latest instance of bad faith, simply broke off negotiations.

At the beginning of October 1907 it was decided that Weingartner would in any case continue to conduct the concerts of the Berlin Königliche Kapelle which employed the Opera's orchestra. He was excused from this duty in January and February 1908 but was expected in Berlin for the performance of 9 March. But a few days before he was to conduct there for the first time since his Vienna appointment, again on a flimsy pretext, he abruptly declared that he was no longer bound by any obligation to the Berlin Opera. He thus gave Hülsen the perfect opportunity to accuse him of breach of contract and to bring a first court case. This was followed by several more, lasting until 1911, when Weingartner was called upon to make a public apology to Hülsen for a violent attack on him two years earlier in an 'open telegram' to the press. None of this concerns us much, except that it shows Weingartner's character in a rather unpleasant light that conforms with his behaviour during the early months of his Viennese activity, when he seemed determined to destroy everything that Mahler had left behind at the Vienna Opera.

Weingartner's appointment was officially announced in Vienna on 20 August. The press, listing his literary and musical works, called him a 'prolific composer', a 'conductor of genius', and a 'trenchant writer on music'.[8] Journalists predicted that Mahler would leave very soon and that there would be a brief 'interregnum' presided over by Schalk.[9] The première of Zemlinsky's *Der Traumgörge* was still planned for the 4 October celebration of the Emperor's name-day. It was to be followed by those of Goldmark's *Ein Wintermärchen* and Puccini's *Madama Butterfly*. Weingartner would not be conducting at the Opera before January 1908. According to the *Neue Freie Presse*, Mahler would continue to live in Vienna and would devote himself wholly to composing until his departure for the United States, which was still to take place in January. Some papers expressed surprise that Weingartner should have agreed to succeed him, because, as seen above, when leaving the Berlin Opera nine years earlier he had professed to hate the theatre and had even undertaken, in exchange for his freedom, never again to accept a post in a European theatre.[10]

As for Mahler, at the time when he received the letter from Prince Montenuovo announcing the good news of Weingartner's release from Berlin, he had moved with his family from Schluderbach to one of the most beautiful sites in the Sextener Dolomiten, Fischleinboden, a wooded valley nestling at

---

[8] *Illustrirtes Wiener Extrablatt* (20 Aug. 1907).   [9] *Neue Freie Presse* (20 Aug. 1907).

[10] On 20 Aug. the *Neues Wiener Journal* claimed that Mahler 'still knew nothing' of the engagement of his successor and that he did not even know whether 'contrary to what he has good reason to believe, there might not still be thoughts of keeping him on'. The same issue carried an article by a Berlin correspondent containing details of Weingartner's conflict with the Berlin Intendant and expressing doubts about his capabilities as a director because of his 'nerves'.

the base of towering Dolomitic peaks.[11] A picture postcard of the Drei Zinnen, the three well-known highest peaks in the Sextener Dolomiten, was addressed by Mahler and Alma to Justi from Fischleinboden. It bears the postmark of Innichen, five kilometres to the East of Toblach, the date 13 August, and the stamp of the Hotel Dolomitenhof.[12] Two photographs of Mahler were taken there that summer, not far from the hotel. They show him out walking in the mountains. He looks rather careworn, and is wearing a waistcoat and jacket, knee-breeches and walking boots. One hand is on his hip, the other, which is against his thigh, he holds a walking stick on which he is leaning. The photograph bears the signature of Alfred Liebig, whose identity remains unknown, and is dated 10 August 1907.[13] It suggests that Alma's descriptions were slightly exaggerated, and that, even though he was taking things easy, he still went for walks in the mountains.

After spending a last a week in Fischleinboden, Mahler travelled with Alma to Maiernigg where he no doubt wanted to put his most precious belongings in order. They had already decided to sell the Villa, convinced that they could never bear to live there again, but found to their surprise that they could still enjoy its charm: 'We returned yesterday from Fischleinboden,' Alma wrote to Roller, 'and we don't dislike being in our villa as much as we thought we would. We are now constantly discussing our future and since Gustav is more than ever disgusted with Vienna and wants more than ever to get away—we discuss the question of our future home from all angles.'[14] Later on, when Mahler was back in Vienna, Alma's cheerful letters from the Wörthersee proved that she enjoyed her last days there and Mahler joked about this in another letter: 'Reading them makes one want to drive straight away to Maiernigg and buy a villa there.'[15] On the 31st, Alma's birthday, he even felt nostalgic for Carinthia: 'It must be lovely in Maiernigg. I get wafts of that mild, pure air from your letters.'[16]

Early in the morning on 24 August, Mahler left for Vienna with Emil Freund who had joined him in Maiernigg. The train stopped at Marburg an der Drau (Maribor), where he posted the first of two reassuring postcards from the

[11] Fischleinboden (or Fischleintal) is situated near the village of Moos, a short distance from Sexten, and 15 km. from Toblach. See also letter from Alma to Roller mentioning Fischleinboden, undated (middle of August 1907, ÖTM, quoted BGA, p. 326. See below.).

[12] The address of the picture-postcard is written by Alma in Secession letters, and signed by her, together with Mahler, and Jenny Perrin (Rosé collection, RWO. Concerning Jenny Perrin, see above, Vol. i, Chap. 5, and Vol. ii, Chap 15. See also Vol. i, Appendix 2 on Symphony No. I and BGA 147 and 496.). The Dolomitenhof Hotel in Fischleinboden had been built in 1905 by a mountain guide named Innerkofler. It still belongs to the same family but the old hotel was destroyed after the Second World War and replaced by a modern one. Mahler announces that he will return to Vienna on 20 Aug.

[13] The photographs are now in the Manuscript Department of ÖNB, Vienna. However, Roller gives a different date (1909) for the same photograph (BDB, no. 225; RBM, no. 67; KMA 107 and 108).

[14] Otto Pausch, 'Mahlerisches in den Rollerbeständen', *Studia Musicologica*, Budapest, 31 (1989), 351, card to Alfred Roller, mentioned above (BGA 326).

[15] BGA, no. 222, undated (29 Aug. 1907).

[16] BGA, no. 226, undated (31 Aug. 1907).

station.[17] One of them reads: 'I am feeling fine—better than the whole time in Maiernigg. I see that I only need a change.'[18] Upon arriving in Vienna in the evening of the 24th, he was met at the station by Karl Moll and Hassinger, and went with Moll straight to Döbling, since he had arranged to stay with his in-laws in the Osterleitengasse 2a.[19] He spent the next morning at the Opera, where he was interviewed by a journalist sent by Julius Korngold from the *Neue Freie Presse*. Still in Maiernigg, Alma was beginning to worry about the smallpox epidemic which was gaining ground. 'Everyone is getting vaccin-ated', Mahler wrote to her, advising her to ask Dr Blumenthal to do the same without delay in Maiernigg.[20] The next day he sent, 'for your entertainment', an anonymous paragraph from the *Wiener Mittagszeitung* (26 August) headed 'Mahler's New Works'. Quoting from the *Berliner Tageblatt*, the article, unsigned,[21] asserted that the director of the Opera had already sold his house in Maiernigg and bought a 'new one, a small villa' in Mödling,[22] and that he had completed a 'Faust Symphony', the Eighth, based on 'the death of Faust', which would have its première in the United States. He had also completed 'a number of chamber works', and the score of his new version of Weber's *Oberon*. It was too late for this to have its première in Vienna, so probably he would conduct the first performance in the United States.[23]

In the *Neue Freie Presse* of the same day appeared the unsigned interview that Mahler had mentioned to his wife the day before:

What are your plans for the immediate future at the Hofoper?, was our interviewer's first question.—'I have promised to go on working at the Hofoper until my successor arrives', answered Director Mahler. 'I have just taken over the management again and must get myself organized. Naturally I shall carry out my full duties as before, and that includes conducting. My interest in this institution, which means so much to me, will never fade. What I myself am to perform at the Opera has not yet been decided.'—'And your further plans for the future?'—'I have various plans. But nothing is definite except my journey to America; I shall set off on that, health permitting, at the end of January of next year. After all, until a week ago I did not know how long I would have to remain at the disposal of my superiors. That is why no precise plans could be made.'—'What will your commitments in America be, Herr Direktor?'—'As far as

[17] BGA, nos. 214 and 215 (both postmarked 24 Aug.). Marburg, which is now called Maribor, is a Slovenian town situated on the river Drau, at the point where what was then the main railway from Klagenfurt to Vienna turned sharply north towards Graz.

[18] BGA, no. 214, postmarked 24 Aug.

[19] BGA, no. 216 (postmarked 25 Aug.). The Molls had rented a house with a big garden in Döbling (see BGA, no. 221), while awaiting completion of their new villa, designed by Josef Hoffmann, at Wollergasse 10, a short distance from their first house in the Steinfeldgasse. They only moved to this new house in Aug. 1908.

[20] BGA, no. 216 (postmarked 25 Aug.). Mahler recommends the same vaccination for Gucki and Miss Turner.

[21] In the accompanying letter, BGA, no. 218, undated (26 Aug. 1907), Mahler wrongly states that the article is by Max Kalbeck.

[22] Julius Korngold's memoirs reveal that Mahler did actually think of settling in Mödling (KIW 108).

[23] *Wiener Mittags-Zeitung* (26 Aug. 1907).

America is concerned I have undertaken to conduct some opera performances and several concerts between the end of January and mid-April.'—'Is it true that you will only conduct operas by Wagner and Mozart?'—'The only thing which has been agreed is that I shall not conduct *Parsifal*; but I shall be conducting works by other composers. I have stipulated that performances conducted by me must be prepared to an artistically satisfactory level; but I have committed myself only as a conductor.'— 'In the concerts, will you conduct only your own works?'—'I shall not just be conduct- ing my own symphonies, but works by others. I can assure you that I get more pleasure from conducting a symphony by Beethoven or Schumann than one by myself. Until now I have generally avoided conducting at concerts. I have only attended perfor- mances of my own works, or conducted them when my presence was essential. I never enjoyed it. My travels to conduct them were always undertaken "when circumstances demanded it".[24] Now it is different. Now I am free, I can do concerts again, and it is all the same to me whether it is my name which is on the programme, or that of some other contemporary composer.'

'Finally let me say again that until the end of December I have undertaken to remain at the Opera, which I shall continue to run in my usual manner. As I have said, my other plans are not yet firm.'[25]

The day after his return to Vienna, Mahler received the following letter from Weingartner:

Dear Sir and friend, What seemed impossible a relatively short time ago has now come to pass: I am really to be your successor in Vienna. Instead of all the things I could say to you, permit me to express just one wish. I learn from the newspapers that you will continue to live in Vienna. I therefore wish and hope that the friendly relations which existed between us and which seem to have lain dormant over the last few years will revive and henceforth continue without interruption. I shall be very happy indeed soon to see you again in Vienna and remain until then, with all best wishes, devotedly yours, Felix Weingartner.[26]

Mahler, in a letter to Alma, commented ironically on this 'love letter': 'He [Weingartner] seems to have acquired the conviction from reading the *Neue Freie Presse* that I might become either useful or dangerous to him according to the circumstances.' Indeed, as far back as the year 1901 Mahler had had occasion to doubt his colleague's sincerity. It will be recalled that during the Kaim Orchestra's tour the Fourth Symphony had frequently met with a hostile reception. In Karlsruhe, probably fearing the audience's reaction, Weingartner had been 'taken ill' during the first part of the concert. After an interval of forty minutes he performed only the Finale of Mahler's Fourth. Then, cured as if by magic, he had gone on to conduct Beethoven's First Symphony and the *Leonore* Overture No. 2. What was more, he had opted out of plans to conduct the second hearing of the work in Munich and its première in Berlin, giving less

---

[24] *'Der Not gehorchend, nicht dem eigenen Triebe'* ('when circumstances demanded it, not of my own volition)—Quotation from Schiller's *Die Braut von Messina*.

[25] *Neue Freie Presse* (26 Aug. 1907).

[26] Letter dated 22 Aug. 1907, written from Bad Kreuth.

than convincing reasons. The insincerity of the excuses in the letter he subsequently wrote to Mahler were only too obvious, and the protestations of friendship and admiration it contained certainly irritated him.[27] From that time he broke off relations with him. Here is the text of his reply to Weingartner's 1907 'love letter':

Dear Sir and friend, Please accept my warmest thanks for your kind letter, and rest assured that it is a true source of satisfaction to me to see you as my successor. I am handing over my post to you with relief and pleasure and feel sure that with you the Opera's future is secure.—It will be a pleasure to see you when you come to Vienna, and I beg you to consider me to be completely at your disposal should you find it appropriate to use my services. To our next meeting in Vienna then, dearest friend![28]

Mahler told Alma that Richard Nepalleck, 'whom I like more and more',[29] had come to see him at the Molls on the same day that he had received Weingartner's letter. Everybody had greeted him 'with affection and respect at the Opera' although Wondra and Przistaupinsky were 'the only ones who behave marvellously'. 'So everything is going better than we thought.' Mahler dined that evening with the Zuckerkandls in Purkersdorf.

They were delighted, and Emil cheered up visibly. His health has also improved over the last few days. Just think, they are following Dr Lahmann's diet to the letter and speak very highly of it;[30] they implore me to do the same. I thought the food excellent. I feel ever so much better here. At any rate my nervous condition is almost over . . .[31]

Mahler spent his afternoons in the Molls' garden in the Hohe Warte, and the following day he sent Alma a postcard from there. Emil Freund, who had come to keep him company, added his signature.[32]

On 27 August, the *Neue Freie Presse* published another interview with Mahler in which he explained the underlying reasons for his resignation. The interviewer was none other than Josef Reitler, who later explained that he had been sent because the reporter usually assigned to this sort of task, a certain Hirsch, had failed to obtain an appointment with the director:

I made my way to the Opera with a heavy heart. What would Mahler say when I confessed my reason for coming! Indeed, he was very much against giving an interview.

[27] This letter of 30 Nov. 1901 was given by Mahler to his younger sister Emma Rosé, who bequeathed it to her son Ernst (see above, Vol. ii, Chap. 11).

[28] Undated letter to Felix Weingartner, *c*.26 Aug. 1907 (BMG, Paris). Edgar Istel, who had a long conversation with Mahler in Prague in 1908, claims that he always spoke of his successor with 'the respect he felt was due to a great artist, a colleague and a distinguished man' and that he took no part whatever in the 'campaign' being waged against him in Vienna ('Erinnerungen an Gustav Mahler', *Neue Musik-Zeitung*, Stuttgart, 38 (1916): 6, 88). He always called him 'Herr *von* Weingartner', emphasizing the aristocratic *von* (see above, Chap. 5).

[29] BGA, no. 219, undated (27 Aug. 1907). Concerning Alma's relationship with the Nepallecks, see above, Chap. 8.

[30] The German physician Heinrich Lahmann (1860–1915) directed an establishment in Dresden where Bruno Walter went for a cure the following year (cf. MBR1, no. 377; MBR2, no. 394, to Bruno Walter). On 30 Aug. Emil Freund also gave Mahler a dinner prepared in conformity with Dr Lahmann's principles.

[31] BGA, no. 220, undated (27 Aug. 1907).   [32] BGA, no. 221, undated (28 Aug. 1907).

It was only when I explained to him how important it was for my career not to come back empty-handed that he started to talk. And as he talked he grew so heated that in the end it seemed as if he had been waiting just for this moment to speak out about all the things that had angered, saddened and embittered him. It was a volcanic eruption. I was so overcome by this outburst that I forgot that an interviewer is usually supposed to take notes.

Once outside in the street, still shaken from the experience, I realized to my horror that I had either failed to grasp or had forgotten the reasons for Mahler's resignation. I rushed back into the Opera, past the startled porter, up the spiral staircase. 'For God's sake, Hassinger, I must speak to the Direktor again.' 'Then you'll need to go after him,' Hassinger calmly replied. 'The Herr Direktor has just left by the Operngasse door. You'll have trouble catching him up.'

And indeed Mahler had been swallowed up in the usual evening crowds around the opera house. Perhaps I could reach him by telephone at home! But all at once I felt ashamed, both at troubling him further and at admitting my journalistic incompetence. Utterly distraught, I staggered home. Already I could hear Dr Sternberg's scornful laugh as I arrived without the commissioned article. My debut with the *Neue Freie Presse* was a total failure and would probably bring instant dismissal!

Nobody has yet been able to ascertain how the thing we call inspiration occurs in human beings. In the same way I am unable to say how it was that in those tortured moments I suddenly saw the light. As the mists cleared away there arose a memory in my feverishly working brain: had it not seemed to me, as I listened to Mahler's tirade, that I had read much of what he was saying somewhere? And now I remembered where: in Richard Wagner's essay on the Viennese Hofoper there was an exhaustive explanation of how an opera house that played every night must of necessity also have inadequately prepared performances, and how, therefore, in the long run it would be intolerable for the director of such a house to lend his name to such performances. The passages needed for a newspaper article were quickly found in Wagner's writings, and the whole thing appeared in the following day's issue of the *Neue Freie Presse* under the heading: 'Gustav Mahler on the Reasons for his Resignation'. A bad conscience kept me away from the coffee-house for many days. Then, when I met Mahler again, he simply said: 'You did your job very tactfully. That was exactly what I was wanting to say.' His resignation was of course not due exclusively to artistic considerations but nothing expresses his feelings in this connection so well as his constantly repeated remark: 'You can't produce good theatre without enthusiasm. And they have knocked every bit of enthusiasm out of me.'[33]

Here is the text of Reitler's famous interview:

The fact that people generally overlook the organic defects in the way theatre is run can probably be explained by the public being thoroughly inured to them. Just look at our opera calendar. Works in the most contradictory styles follow hard on each other's heels. And we must play every night. It goes without saying that performances cannot all be equally good. There is insufficient rehearsal time. This means not only that performances are inadequately prepared as a whole but also that individual singers are insecure. Some just go through the motions, others strive for applause for their own

[33] JRM 64 (copy in BGM, Paris).

particular performance by thrusting themselves forward out of the artistic context. Is it possible in these circumstances to have an artistically perfect performance? Ten years ago I boldly said yes to this question, believing with youthful optimism that I could change the world, but in the course of those ten years it has become increasingly clear to me that under the prevailing system it is quite impossible to come up with good performances only. The means are simply not there. Assuming that good performances are the goal of an artistic institution, there exists an incompatibility between means and ends that can only lie in that institution's defective organization. It is ludicrous to blame the director. But it is up to the director to decide whether he should surrender his higher artistic principles or treat the institution which he heads as a commercial enterprise. I chose the former course, and resigned my post when I could no longer reconcile it with my artistic conscience. Perhaps other circumstances hastened my decision. But I must make it clear that I left of my own free will.

Mahler continued to express these views up to the time he left Vienna. Two days after the interview he wrote to Alma and congratulated her for writing to him every day. Work on the Molls' villa was progressing:

It's coming out famously! Why shouldn't we do the same?[34] Forget the gossip you hear about the Theuers![35] Those people don't really expect one to take the nasty nor the good things they say too seriously. They don't know what to talk about, and criticize other people because it's the first thing that comes to mind. You can be sure that the Theuers will like you a lot when you are there. [Mahler continues] Today I'm going to be vaccinated. I feel really fine, subjectively. If I didn't know about the 'verdict' I would not know that anything was wrong with me. All the same, I'm taking *great care* and avoiding all exertion. My digestion is all right again.[36]

When he was vaccinated, Mahler also underwent a cardiac examination by Dr Franz Hamperl:[37]

He found a <u>slight</u> valve defect, fully compensated, and plays down the whole thing. He says that I can carry on with my job exactly as before and can live a completely normal life so long as I avoid <u>over-exertion</u>. It's funny, basically he said exactly the same thing as Blumenthal, but there was something reassuring in his way of saying it. And in fact I don't feel afraid of conducting any more.[38]

Mahler had a meeting with Zemlinsky and decided that 'marriage suits him'[39] because his face was more rounded; also with Roller, who was '*extraordinarily nice*'. The same evening, remembering that the following day, the 31st, was Alma's birthday, he sent her a further card: 'I'm afraid it's too late for a

---

[34] As we shall soon see, Mahler and Alma planned to build a house in the country to replace the one in Maiernigg. They first thought of the countryside around Vienna, in Mödling (see above) or Heiligenstadt, then of two summer resorts in the Salzkammergut, Ischl or Aussee.

[35] Theuer was the architect who had designed the Villa Mahler in Maiernigg.

[36] BGA, no. 222, undated (29 Aug. 1907).   [37] See above, Chap. 9.

[38] BGA, no. 223, undated (30 Aug. 1907).

[39] In 1906 Zemlinsky married Ida Guttmann, sister of his first love, Melanie Guttmann. In 1908 they had a daughter, Johanna. Ida died in Berlin in 1929, and a year later Zemlinsky married the Prague singer Luise Sachsel.

present—and with the best will in the world I can't think of anything suitable [to buy you]. Almschi, you know how hopeless I am about things like that!'[40]

The heat in Vienna was stifling, and Mahler longed for the cool air of the Semmering. But in those days vaccines were given in very strong doses, and he began to suffer from an inflammation of ganglions in his arm which made him feverish. The evening meal at Emil Freund's was a success and he went for a walk with Albine Adler, his childhood friend from Iglau. On Saturday evening, 31 August, he finally returned home to the Auenbruggergasse where the new chambermaid, Kathi, was there to take care of him. It was Alma's birthday and he promised her that as soon as she was back they would go on a shopping expedition, to buy her a present: 'With luck it's the last time we shall be separated on this day!' Pollak had come to visit him to tell him about his recent trip to England. 'In myself I feel *quite* excellent. Not even a *suspicion* of a certain ailment,[41] but I am continuing to live very carefully and quietly.'[42]

On the evening of the 31st, Mahler went for a walk with Bruno Walter and met Arnold Rosé for the first time since his return. He dined with his sister and brother-in-law in the Auenbruggergasse apartment, and they were joined by Emil Freund. Unfortunately there was noisy building work going on in the flat immediately below the Mahlers'. If he could he would spend several days of the coming week with the Redlichs in Göding, but was still troubled by the inflammation in his arm caused by the smallpox inoculation, especially at night. And his digestion was 'quite upset'. The banker Paul Hammerschlag became part of the group which had surrounded him since his return. On 30 and 31 August Mahler was photographed, at Roller's instigation, in the Opera foyer by Moriz Nähr, whose pictures of him are still the best that anyone ever made.[43] 'According to Roller the photographs are first-rate', he wrote to Alma on the 31st. Bruno Walter took advantage of Mahler's relatively freer timetable to play him his latest work, a symphony he had composed the previous year. 'Unfortunately it left me completely cold, and I plunged him into the deepest despair by frankly saying so.'[44]

These two cards are the last ones Mahler sent to Alma from Vienna to Maiernigg in 1907. So probably she was back in Vienna by the beginning of the following week, spending a few days on the Semmering as suggested by Mahler[45] before finally returning home. Mahler was still having trouble with his arm. However, the doctor's reassuring diagnosis had persuaded him to resume conducting, and he wanted to do so in *The Magic Flute* on 4 September. As this would be his first appearance on the podium since his

[40] BGA, no. 224, undated (postmarked 30 Aug.1907).
[41] Probably haemorrhoids, a trouble which Mahler never entirely managed to clear up.
[42] BGA, no. 226, undated (postmarked 31 Aug.).
[43] RBM, nos. 46 to 56; KMA, nos. 79 to 91.
[44] BGA, no. 227, undated (1 Sept. 1907). In the autograph Alma crossed out three lines at the end of the second card, rendering the text illegible.
[45] BGA, nos. 223 and 224, undated (both 30 Aug. 1907).

resignation, it was essential that no one should know about it. So Zemlinsky took charge of the rehearsals. That evening, however, one of the singers caught sight of Hassinger in the foyer, carrying the director's tail-coat, and rushed on to the stage calling: 'We're going to have to watch out, children! It's the Direktor conducting!' This happened a few minutes before the Overture. Some of the ladies and gentlemen on the stage rushed to peep through the curtains at the orchestra pit. 'At last a bell rang and the opening chord was heard. Sighs of relief escaped from a number of singers: "It wasn't true! It's Zemlinsky!"'[46] The decision was taken at the last moment, for Mahler's arm was still painful and he was worried that it would hamper his conducting.

The atmosphere at the Opera was exceptionally calm. 'Behind the Scenes Backstage', a regular column in the *Neues Wiener Journal*, commented that Mahler had never been so kind, friendly, and considerate. For the moment his principal concern seemed to be finding out about the best ways to combat sea-sickness.[47] Rehearsals for Puccini's *Madama Butterfly* were to begin early in October upon the return of Selma Kurz, who at the end of August had requested by telegram that her vacation be extended on the grounds that she was 'completely exhausted'.[48] The *Fremden-Blatt* of 8 September announced that 'in accordance with the wishes of the composer' (Zemlinsky), who had decided to make further changes to his score, the première of *Der Traumgörge* was being postponed. Meanwhile there were feverish preparations for Caruso's guest appearances, for which soloists and chorus were to sing in Italian. They were to start with a name-day gala performance for the Emperor on 4 October of *Aida*, conducted by Spetrino. The great tenor's second Gastspiel promised to be another sensation as this time he was singing not only in two performances of *Aida* but also in *La Bohème* and *Rigoletto*.

The Opera archives show that Mahler continued to take an active interest in administrative affairs that summer. One of the matters that concerned him was renewing the contract of Mildenburg, who requested new terms: an increase in salary, a minimum duration of seven years, exclusivity of stage costumes and wigs, etc. Mahler gave her satisfaction on all these points, and the contract was duly renewed.[49] As already mentioned, Slezak too was insisting on very stiff terms before agreeing to the renewal of his current contract, which would last only until September 1908. He had become aware of his status rating as a star

[46] *Fremden-Blatt*, 'Aus der Theaterwelt', 8 Sept. 1907. The same article, unsigned, reappeared in the *Münchner Zeitung* of the 12th. The reporter claimed that it was Mahler who had recommended Weingartner to Prince Montenuovo, after Mottl but in preference to Muck. He also reported that Hesch had jokingly suggested to Mahler that he should have done the same as the ballet dancers at the Opera, who were inoculated in the thigh rather than the arm.

[47] *Neues Wiener Journal* (14 Sept. 1907).

[48] HOA, Z. 873/1907, telegram of 27 Aug. 1907.

[49] HOA, Z. 720 and 725/1907. Letter to Mahler from the lawyer Gustav Harpner, dated 20 June. Letter from Viktor Horsetzky to Ferdinand Graf, 26 July. Letter to the Director from the Intendant's office, July. Handwritten, undated letter from Mahler to Ferdinand Graf, his assistant secretary (beginning of Aug. 1907).

and wanted to be able to accept the invitations he was receiving from all sides. Two handwritten drafts for the new contract exist, one of them in Mahler's hand. On condition that he sing at least sixty times a year in Vienna, Slezak was offered an annual salary of 32,000 florins (64,000 kronen).[50] By accepting a new contract for five years the tenor would obtain the right to make two visits a year to the United States, but these would have to be between 15 May and 1 September. He would also be entitled to an annual winter leave of two weeks and, for 1908, several months leave to enable him to perfect his technique in Italy. However, there are doubts about the total duration of the new contract, three years in Mahler's draft version and five in the other. It was obvious that a real bel canto star had emerged at the Hofoper, despite the director's strenuous resistance. Slezak was so popular with the public that they were prepared to move heaven and earth in order to keep him. The exceptional favours he was granted did not pass unnoticed, and certain of his colleagues, notably Erik Schmedes, were going to insist on similar treatment.[51]

In June, the Dutch cellist Wilhelm Willeke, the orchestra's cello soloist, had written to the Director requesting help in terminating his Viennese contract, which he had been trying to do for several months. He had given up hope of improving his financial or general circumstances in Vienna and had received an infinitely more advantageous offer from the Metropolitan Opera. Mahler acceded to his request and probably met this musician again at the Met.[52] He also negotiated the return to the Hofoper of the baritone Hans Melms, who had left for the Kaiserjubiläumstheater in 1904.[53]

It will be remembered that in May, at the time of the *Otello* première, Mahler had had to deal with an attempted resignation by Lucy Weidt, furious at finding her rival, Elsa Bland, chosen to sing the role of Desdemona, the leading female role, on the first night. At the time, he had pointed out to the Intendant that Bland could equally well have complained if her colleague had been given the role. This was exactly what happened at the beginning of the new season, this time in *Aida*. Bland reminded the director (whose departure she 'infinitely regretted') that she had always sung the title role, which had been given to another singer 'only four or five times'. It was terribly important to her and she begged the director 'not to wound me by taking this role away'.[54] So right to the end Mahler was encountering problems raised by the professional jealousies of singers, to whom he continued to reply as before: 'No one can have the exclusive right to a role at the Hofoper.'

---

[50]   The total included 12,000 florins salary, 12,000 'activity allowance' and 8,000 'fixed remuneration'.

[51]   See above, Chap. 3. Despite an announcement by Weingartner of the tenor's forthcoming departure, Slezak eventually signed a new contract, for a period of five years. Having regained his freedom for the following five years, he spent the rest of his singing career at the Vienna Opera, with the exception of the years 1912 to 1917.   [52]   HOA, Willeke's letters of 28 June and 9 July 1907.

[53]   Letters from the lawyer Günter Rodler to Mahler, 5 July 1907, HOA.

[54]   HOA, letter to Mahler from Elsa Bland, 31 Aug. Lucy Weidt sang the role in Oct., in the two performances with Caruso.

In the middle of August 1907 Mahler had received a heartbreaking letter from the alto Josie Petru, whom he had engaged in 1902. Addressing him as 'my kind benefactor', she thanked him for having so far spared her the necessity of resigning; she now realized, however, that she could no longer go on and asked him 'with tears in my eyes and a deadly despair in my heart, to be good enough to let me go . . . A thousand thanks, dearest maestro, for all your outstanding kindness. Please grant this last request that my departure be arranged in a way that is not dishonourable for me. I have loved and venerated my director like no other, and now say my last farewell.' This letter takes on its full import when it subsequently transpired that Josie Petru was soon to die of the painful illness from which she had been suffering for several months,[55] probably tuberculosis.

In September Mahler finally began conducting again; on the 11th *Tristan*, on the 12th *Don Giovanni*, on the 15th *Die Walküre* (as part of a complete *Ring* cycle), on the 22nd *The Marriage of Figaro* and on the 30th *Iphigénie en Aulide*. Although we know that he wanted at all costs to avoid any kind of publicity, it is still surprising to see how little space these last performances were given in the press. The *Neues Wiener Journal* of 13 September noted that he had unexpectedly appeared on the rostrum two days before, for *Tristan*, and had received public acclaim, 'as usual'. Same story in the *Illustrirtes Wiener Extrablatt*. Only Julius Korngold, in the *Neue Freie Presse*, added after *Figaro* that Mahler seemed to have decided, like a soldier, to 'remain at his post'. The result had been 'a fine Mozart evening'.[56] Korngold adds that there was a particularly loud ovation at the end of the second act. 'Mahler resists but he will have to accept that people shake his hand more warmly on departure.' The paragraph in *Die Zeit* also notes that he interrupted the applause at the end of each interval by immediately signalling the musicians to recommence. After *Die Walküre* of 15 September, the *Extrablatt* observed that 'Hoch Mahler' (Long live Mahler) had been heard from the 'gods' but that the house had been almost empty because 'the Wagner cycle no longer draws the public'.[57]

Despite all the dignity and reserve Mahler showed in the course of these final performances, the anti-Semitic press continued its attacks. In an article entitled 'Mahler scandals at the Hofoper' the *Deutsches Volksblatt* of 24 September waxed indignant over 'the serious excesses of the claque which Mahler is supposed to have abolished'. He had only announced that he would conduct no more in order to fuel curiosity. If the 'demonstration' coming from the corner where 'Mahler's admirers are always clustered together' was 'somewhat timid' at a *Don Giovanni* performance where his appearance had not been

---

[55] Letter to Mahler from Josie Petru, written in Davos on 13 Aug. 1907 (HOA, Z. 838/1907).

[56] Cast of the last *Don Giovanni* conducted by Mahler at the Hofoper on 12 Sept.: Forst (Zerlina); Gutheil-Schoder (Elvira); Weidt (Anna); Maikl (Ottavio); Demuth (Don Giovanni); Mayr (Commendatore).

[57] *Illustrirtes Wiener Extrablatt*, 16 Sept. 1907. The critic adds that in the last act 'the magic fire had been left too long backstage, and only one rocket lit up'.

announced, the one after *Walküre* had been 'better staged'. Mahler, embold-ened, had announced in advance that he was conducting *Figaro*, with the result that 'repulsive' scenes had preceded each act. 'Behaviour of this kind should be brought under control by the court authorities as soon as possible. The decree forbidding excessive demonstrations of approval or displeasure by audiences at the imperial theatres should also extend to the Director's claque, and thus avoid a scandal in the form of vociferous reaction which this Mahler-enthusiasm might very well provoke.' Right to the end, Mahler remained the target of the anti-Semitic press.

On 20 September Mahler went to Munich for a further meeting with Heinrich Conried to finalize the details of his contract.[58] In the course of this discussion it was decided that his repertoire in New York would include *Tristan, Der fliegende Holländer*, the *Ring, Fidelio*, and *Der Freischütz*, in other words German works only, although Alfred Hertz would continue to conduct *Parsifal*.[59] Mahler undertook to conduct during four months of each year for four consecutive years, and also to give concerts.[60] After his departure from Munich, however, new difficulties arose. Mahler proposed that he should arrive in New York a month earlier than agreed, leaving Vienna on 12 December, a fortnight before Weingartner's definitive arrival. In this way he would be able to rehearse the operas allocated to him much more carefully. He informed the director of the Metropolitan Opera that it was essential to have this month of extra rehearsals, for which he asked a very high fee, 50,000 kronen, on account of the loss of earnings he suffered as a result of the cancellation of a series of concerts in Russia, Holland, and Germany. Conried decided the sum was excessive and Mahler reduced it to Kr. 30,000. In the end Conried paid him only Kr. 25,000.[61]

Rudolf Winternitz, wardrobe director at the Opera, who had all along been serving as intermediary, sent a telegram advising Conried to accept this final figure and to reserve a cabin for Mahler and Alma on the German ship which was leaving Cherbourg for New York on 12 December. In a letter sent three days later to the director of the Metropolitan Opera, Winternitz informed him that Mahler had bitterly complained of his 'pettiness'. The concerts he had been obliged to cancel would have brought him in almost as much, besides opening up 'a valuable field of activity for the future'. Moreover he, as a direct-or himself, failed to understand how the 5,000 kronen Conried had deducted from the fee for this extra month could not be included in the budget of this

---

[58] *Neue Freie Presse*, 22 Sept., *Neues Wiener Tagblatt*, 23 Sept. and BGA, no. 228 (postmarked 20 Sept.), written and posted at the railway station in Vienna. In it Mahler asks Alma to read a telegram from Angelo Neumann 'left by mistake on the desk'.

[59] See below, Vol. iiii, Chap. 1. At the beginning of the summer the German press, in particular the *Neue Musik-Zeitung* of 23 July, had announced that Hertz would conduct both *Parsifal* and *Salome*.

[60] *Neue Freie Presse*, article quoted above of 22 Sept.

[61] UPL, telegram sent on 24 Sept. and letter on 27 Sept. by Rudolf Winternitz. The letter is addressed to a hotel in Bremen, whence Conried was probably about to embark for the United States.

huge institution. Conried also seems to have stipulated that Mahler should drink no wine or other alcohol during the whole period he was conducting. This, too, Mahler had found petty and irritating. Despite all this, 'he is embarking on your joint project with great enthusiasm. He is working on Isolde with Fremstad,[62] and Mildenburg was delighted with both of them this morning and wishes me to tell you that "*Tristan* will undoubtedly be a great success".' He was also working with the soprano Rita Fornia[63] (who was to sing Elvira for him in *Don Giovanni*) but he wanted to make his first appearance with *Tristan* before tackling *Fidelio*.

The supplement to the contract, which Mahler signed on 21 June, confirmed the terms of this letter. Mahler undertook to conduct twice a week and to cancel his prior engagements in Holland and Russia during December and January. The archives of the Metropolitan Opera confirm that, during a period of four years, he was engaged for three months a year, that his stays in New York and his travel expenses would be paid for by Conried,[64] and that an advance on his salary would be paid into Mahler's bank in Vienna during November.[65]

Once he had taken the decision to leave Vienna at the beginning of December, Mahler was obliged to cancel all the engagements he had accepted for the end of the year and the early weeks of 1908. He had for instance agreed the previous April to conduct the Diligentia Orchestra in The Hague on 8 January 1908,[66] not knowing that this organization was fiercely hostile to Mengelberg's. The latter had nevertheless invited him to conduct two concerts with the Concertgebouw, on 4 January in The Hague and 9 January in Amsterdam.[67] After his meeting with Conried and his decision to bring forward the date of his departure for the United States, Mahler wrote again to Mengelberg offering to come to Holland either after his Wiesbaden concert on 9 October (though he knew this date would not be convenient) or after his return, during May (too late for the Concertgebouw). Meanwhile he cancelled his concert with the Diligentia Orchestra 'because I found it very embarrassing to conduct for an organization which is a hostile competitor of yours'.[68]

---

[62] Olive Fremstad (1871–1951). See below, Vol. iiii, Chap. 1, the biography of this singer who first performed the role of Isolde under Mahler's direction on 1 Jan. 1908.

[63] Rita Fornia (1878–1922), an American soprano born in San Francisco, pupil of Jean de Reszke, began her career in Germany and was subsequently engaged by the Metropolitan Opera in 1906.

[64] The cost of the journey from Vienna to New York is quoted here as being 1,300 kronen, the return journey 1,000. As well as paying his New York hotel bill, the Metropolitan Opera was to give Mahler a lump sum of 700 kronen for expenses.

[65] The Giro und Kassenverein, care of Paul Hammerschlag.

[66] Undated letter to Willem Mengelberg, postmarked 15 Apr., RMH 85.

[67] Letter to Mahler from Mengelberg, 10 June, RMH 86. Mengelberg suggested the Sixth Symphony and offered Mahler a fee of 1,700 marks for the two concerts. The Diligentia Orchestra had offered him 1,000 for the single concert on the 8th.

[68] RMH 92. During the summer, Mengelberg went to Dresden with Schillings. He visited Marion von Weber and looked at the Mahler manuscripts in her library. He describes this visit in a letter to his wife written in Dresden on 19 July (RMH 88. See above, Vol. i, Appendix 2 on unfinished or lost works.).

The change of Mahler's plans for the next few months brought many further cancellations. As seen above he had asked the Berlin impresario Norbert Salter[69] to represent him and to negotiate with various organizations in Germany and abroad concerning possible engagements. Interesting details emerge from the copious correspondence Mahler exchanged with Salter between March (when he asked Prince Montenuovo for his release) and October (when he finalized the details of his Russian tour). It becomes clear that Mahler wanted to make the most of his newly acquired freedom by conducting as much as possible. Further, he wanted to earn fees comparable with those of other conductors of high repute, like Strauss and Nikisch. He did not mind whether he conducted his own symphonies or the classics. However, in his haste to make use of all the opportunities that presented themselves, he often committed himself too quickly, and was subsequently obliged to extricate himself by any means or pretext that came to hand. All this shows that he was still very much a novice in the career of guest conductor and that he needed the active assistance of an energetic and shrewd agent.

It is a great pity that Salter's replies have disappeared. They would have given us a better idea of his personality and of the year's negotiations. The first difficulty arose from the fact that Mahler's success in Russia in 1902 had been so great that there were several concert societies competing for the honour of engaging him. We have seen that in January 1907 he had met in Frankfurt the pianist-conductor Alexander Siloti, who straightaway asked him to conduct several concerts for him in Moscow and St Petersburg for a fee of 1,000 roubles per concert.[70] Originally Beethoven's Ninth Symphony and Mahler's own Second were proposed. Mahler accepted, but explained that his reply could not be definitive until August, when the date of his departure from the Vienna Opera would be finally agreed. He hesitated a long time before accepting Siloti's offer, principally because Fried had in strict confidence passed on to him a letter from the pianist showing that sincerity was not his strongest suit.[71] Besides, he was still not sure that he was going to be able to obtain his release from the Vienna Opera. 'Between ourselves,' he wrote to Salter, 'everything depends on <u>Vienna</u>! It could happen that in the end I might still have to <u>stay</u>. (But in this case I would demand at least 2 months leave, if not more, that we could use for concerts.) However, this would only happen if a peremptory order came from the highest authority. Otherwise I shall hold out for my resignation, which in principle has already been accepted.'

Mahler was also invited by Yuri Sachnovski,[72] Director of the Moscow Conservatory, and by the Warsaw Philharmonic. Having decided to undertake

---

[69] Several months earlier, Norbert Salter had moved his 'Konzert-Direktion' from Strasbourg to Berlin (24 Rankerstrasse, W.50).

[70] See above, Chap. 8. At that time a rouble was worth 2.53 kronen, or a little under 2 marks.

[71] Undated letter to Salter numbered 10 by the recipient (Apr.–May 1907), BSM, Munich. Mahler secretly sent on to Salter the letter Fried had received from Siloti.

[72] Yuri Sergevich Sachnovski (1866–1930) was a Moscow composer, conductor, and theatre critic.

the long journey, he wished to conduct at least four or five concerts, but he knew that he would nonetheless have to choose between Siloti and Sachnovski.[73] In the face of this dilemma he decided to ask Salter to carry on with the negotiations, but also continued to write to the various organizers himself. At the beginning of June he once more stipulated that the Warsaw concert take place before the Russian ones, so as not to have to do the interminable train journey twice. As far as the programmes were concerned, he preferred the organizers to submit suggestions from which he could choose, and he added: 'Please, I must make it a <u>condition</u> that wherever my works are played they must be <u>well prepared</u>! Please be so good as to see to this!'[74]

A few days later, Mahler sent Salter two letters from Siloti. To escape from his moral obligation to the latter he suggested that Salter make use of a clause in the contract that C. M. Schröder, the Petersburg impresario, had made him sign in 1902, giving Schröder first option for any concerts Mahler might decide to conduct in Russia. This clause was only valid for two years but it could, by mutual consent,[75] be discreetly extended. Mahler announced in his next letter that he had agreed to conduct in Berlin on 30 December and that from there he would go to Amsterdam, where his first concert was to take place on 4 January. He might also be prepared to conduct operas, so long as the casts were first-rate and the number of rehearsals was sufficient to guarantee the quality of the performance.[76]

Later there was talk of an engagement in Ostend, Belgium, suggested by Salter; but Mahler discovered that concerts there took place in a hall where drinks were also served. If the restaurant service was to persist through the performances, Mahler was determined to refuse. Also, the journey from Maiernigg to Ostend was so long that it would only be worthwile for at least two concerts. In this letter he revealed his real reason for wanting to rid himself of his moral obligation to Siloti: Siloti was 'a deceitful fellow (*ein falscher Kerl*)'. He had found this out thanks to Fried, whom he did not want to embarrass by using this information.[77] He later accepted Sachnovski's proposal, which involved one concert in Moscow and one in St Petersburg, but still without refusing Siloti's offer, so that the situation with regard to the various organizers became more and more complicated. Schröder had already offered him a concert in Helsingfors, in Finland (then under Russian rule) but he hesitated to undertake the extra journey. Meanwhile, Emil Gutmann was offering him an engagement with the Kaim Orchestra and Hans Gregor a performance at the

---

[73] Letter no. 11 (Apr.–May 1907), ibid.   [74] Letters nos. 12 and 13, ibid.
[75] Letter no. 14, ibid.   [76] Letters nos. 15 and 16, ibid.
[77] Letters nos. 17 and 18, ibid. As seen below, Mahler was probably right not to accept Siloti's offer. Like Walter Damrosch (see below; Vol. iiii, Chap. 4), Siloti was a mediocre conductor who kept the public's interest thanks to his imaginative programmes. Like Damrosch, he feared that guest appearances of great conductors like Mahler would show up his own technical and interpretative limitations (see below, Siloti's reaction to Mahler's St Petersburg concert).

Komische Oper in Berlin.[78] But for the moment he could not accept anything else (this was at the beginning of August) because he was to arrive in New York between 10 and 14 January, and was not yet certain of being free of his Viennese obligations.[79] Gregor's offer, with a fee of 1,000 marks per performance, was not high enough, since at least a fortnight's preliminary rehearsals were required. Perhaps this project could be postponed until the following summer? In any case after his return tour to Russia he would have to spend some days in Vienna, so as to hand over the reins.[80]

Other projects were taking shape parallel to these, in particular concerts in Leipzig and Dresden, which could precede the one in Berlin.[81] Warsaw was offering fees of 1,250 marks after an initial offer of 1,500, and Mahler found this haggling unseemly and wanted to withdraw. There was still a concert planned for Moscow, between the ones in St Petersburg, but on reflection Mahler preferred to give it up so as not to spend two consecutive nights on the train. However, he was beginning to worry because Schröder's project allowed for only one concert a week, and it seemed absurd to him to conduct only four concerts in a month.[82] The very thought of the tour was beginning to weigh on his mind and he would willingly have cancelled it! What was more, he had found out that Nikisch had been paid 1,000 roubles a concert in Warsaw, and he wanted his fee to be at least as much.[83] He was beginning to wonder if, from the legal point of view, it might still be possible to cancel both the Siloti and the Sachnovski projects without becoming involved in a lawsuit. Yet the following letter shows that he had still not given up the Siloti concerts, for which the fee offered was 2,500 roubles all told![84]

At this point Mahler learned to his amazement in a letter from Salter that a 'crisis' was brewing at the Metropolitan Opera and that Conried's departure was imminent.[85] Fortunately the four-year contract Mahler had signed could be terminated in the event of a change of director. However, Conried, whom he was about to meet once more (or whom he had already seen), had so far mentioned nothing to him. In the following letter, written a few days later, Mahler informed Salter that, in accordance with an agreement he had just concluded with Conried, he would leave for New York on 12 November (*sic*) in order to have three weeks' extra rehearsal. Given the turn that events had

---

[78]   The *Fremden-Blatt* of 26 Sept. announced that, according to an article published in Berlin the day before, Mahler had been engaged there to conduct several performances. The work chosen for this Gastspiel was *Carmen*. [79] Letters nos. 19 and 20 (early Aug. 1907), ibid.

[80]   Letters nos. 21 and 22 (Aug. 1907), ibid.

[81]   A letter from Norbert Salter to the mayor of Strasbourg, dated 16 Sept. 1907, shows that concerts there were also envisaged for Oct. and Nov. These did not materialize, as no date could be found to suit Mahler and the organizers (Archives municipales de Strasbourg).

[82]   Letters nos. 23 to 25. In letter no. 24, Mahler asks Salter to write to him henceforth at the Hotel Imperial, which indicates that he was already back in Vienna.

[83]   Letter no. 26 (end of Aug.), ibid.   [84] Letters nos. 27 and 28 (beginning of Sept.), ibid.

[85]   Letter no. 29. Conried did in fact leave the Metropolitan at the end of the 1907–8 season, but mainly because of ill-health.

taken (this time Conried must surely have told him that he would leave his post) he would return to the United States for the next season, and wanted to meet Salter to discuss the possibility of exclusive representation. Rather than go to Russia in haste before December, he would prefer to postpone the entire project until the following year.[86] As for the other projects—Berlin, Leipzig, and Dresden—for which the contracts had fortunately not been signed—they could simply be cancelled.[87]

Copies of a series of telegrams dating from the end of September have survived in the early manuscript of Alma Mahler's *Erinnerungen*. They throw light on the difficulties Mahler created for himself by changing the date of his departure for New York. Sachnovski asked for the programme of his concert in Moscow on 14 December 'New Style',[88] and informed him that he was to be paid a thousand roubles per concert, those in St Petersburg being organized by Schröder with the Orchestra of the Marinsky Theatre. Siloti, who was certainly very keen to have Mahler, then offered 500 roubles more than Schröder. But Mahler resisted the temptation. Then on 27 September he sent Schröder the following telegram: 'Profound apologies. Impossible to come December. If you wish, can postpone to next season.' Schröder's response was not long in coming. The next day he sent an angry telegram, to which Mahler replied:

Dear Sir, Despite your rather peremptory refusal, allow me now to renew my telegraphic effort of yesterday and to justify it by the following considerations. When I made the agreement with you I believed I would be free to leave as from the autumn. But now the requirements of the Lord Chamberlain are that I should remain in my post until 1 January.—I could easily fulfil my engagements with you between 15 October and 15 November. However, in December the long and difficult business of handing over control here will begin. If you insist that I conduct in December, I shall have to wind up all my work here during the second half of November. This inordinate effort will make it very difficult for me to carry out my obligations to you, in view of the heart condition which I was found to have last summer. In any case my doctor has forbidden me to undertake such exhausting tours. His prohibition will also very likely compel me to cancel my American contract, even though he considers the sea crossing much less dangerous for me than the long and repeated train journeys to and in Russia.

This is how things stand. If you agree to do me the favour of dispensing with me in December, I shall be glad to be at your disposal between 15 October and 15 November, or to conduct the two concerts, and more if you wish, at a later date. In this way we could continue a relationship which might be of interest to us both in the future.

[86] Letter no. 30, written after the meeting with Conried on 20 Sept. The year's final letter to Salter (no. 31) was written in Wiesbaden at the beginning of Oct. It was about programmes for the concerts in Russia. Meanwhile, Mahler continued his own correspondence with the various Russian organizers.

[87] On 16 Nov. Mahler wrote to the publisher Gustav Bock, president of the Berlin Philharmonic Chorus, apologizing for his inability to be present at the celebrations marking the twenty-fifth anniversary of the Philharmonic Orchestra because of his approaching departure for the United States (Universitätsbibliothek, Giessen, a letter where only the signature is handwritten).

[88] At this time the Russian calendar was thirteen days behind the Western one. Unfortunately it is difficult to be sure of the dates of the various telegrams in the typed copies of AMS.

Whereas if you insist, I shall naturally try to fulfil the obligations I have assumed. But it might well be that my doctor (whose advice prompted my telegram to you) orders me to cancel at the last moment. This would upset me very much and would also probably put you in a much more embarrassing situation than at present, where you have two and a half months ahead of you to find a replacement. (I believe that Fried, or Brecher etc., would be happy to swap dates with me.)

I should therefore be grateful for a favourable reply, if at all possible, to this renewed request. I feel certain that in the years to come I shall be able to convince you that I am not unreliable, but that this time I was forced by circumstances to cause you inconvenience.[89]

The least that can be said here is that Mahler is not entirely sincere, which explains his awkwardness. His real reason for wanting to change the dates of the St Petersburg concerts was that he had decided to leave early for the United States. One might also wonder why he decided to advance his departure, given the obvious difficulties to which he was exposing himself. The explanation is probably that for purely artistic reasons he wanted to allow himself more time to rehearse the performance which would mark his New York debut: and also, no doubt, that in this way he could earn slightly more without the strain of multiple train journeys and rehearsals with a number of new orchestras. However that may be, Schröder yielded, inviting him to conduct three concerts, two in St Petersburg (26 October and 9 November, Western calendar) and one in Helsingfors (now Helsinki) (1 November).

Before undertaking the long journey, Mahler went to Wiesbaden for one concert at the beginning of October. From now on his aim was probably to spend as little time in Vienna as possible, since all the necessary arrangements had been made, so as to escape from the sadness inherent in his situation as departing director. During this period he wrote little, not through lack of time, but probably because he did not have much to say to his friends. In the middle of July he had confessed his disappointment to Berliner over the attitude of his superiors at the Opera: 'It's all true. I'm leaving because I can't stand this rabble any more.'[90] At the end of September, Mahler again wrote to his old friend, who was proposing to visit him in Vienna: 'To me, to us, it goes without saying that you can never come at a wrong time. Though you will sometimes have to keep yourself amused without me, because I am, as I shall explain when we meet, no longer so "fit and active" as you remember me from earlier times. I shall be away from 5 until 11 October. Either before or after that we shall be delighted to see you.'[91]

---

[89] AMM1, 390. Letter of 1 Oct. 1907.

[90] MBR1, no. 337; MBR2, no. 371, BGM, Paris. The card is not dated, but the envelope is postmarked 17 July. In his previous letter (quoted above, Chap. 9) Mahler had spoken to Berliner about Putzi's illness and had reassured him about his contract with Conried which had been 'drawn up by a lawyer'.

[91] MBR1, no. 339; MBR2, 373. This card was part of the Wolfgang Rosé collection. It is wrongly dated in MBR (1908). The dates of Mahler's trip to Wiesbaden correspond exactly with those mentioned. It is a Korrespondenzkarte with the Vienna Opera heading and Mahler did not use these after he had left the Opera.

Now that the Maiernigg house was being sold, Mahler and Alma were thinking more and more of acquiring another house in the country. In one of his
letters to Alma he suggested building their future house at either Ischl[92] or
Aussee.[93] But a few days after his return from Schluderbach the Viennese
paper *Wiener Mittags-Zeitung* had announced on 26 August, as we have seen,
that he was thinking of settling in Mödling.[94] According to Julius Korngold's
memoirs 'there happened at that time something so incredible that the author
[Korngold] cannot let it pass unnoticed. Even his tragedy [Putzi's death] did
not disarm spite and hostility. A "humorous" article warned the inhabitants of
Mödling about the invasion that threatened them.'[95]

According to Bruno Walter Mahler was beginning to be accustomed to living
'in the shadow of death', and gradually returning to a normal rhythm of activity, while being very careful not to overdo it:

More important than the undoubtedly upsetting changes in his working habits was, it
seemed to me, the marked transformation in his attitude to life. The mystery of death,
to which his thoughts and feelings had so often flown, was now suddenly within sight—
casting its dark shadow over his world and his life. And although we conversed about
unsentimental, 'practical' things, I could sense unmistakably the darkness which had
descended over his whole being. 'I shall soon get used to it,' he would say.[96]

One evening when Bruno Walter was conducting *Un Ballo in Maschera* at
the Opera, the pianist Moriz Rosenthal, who had not seen Mahler for a long
time, caught sight of him on the terrace of the Café Imperial. Mahler, 'very
agitated and disturbed', rushed up to him and said, without any preliminaries:
'I have eaten something bad. Can you tell me what I should do now.' The
pianist was amazed:

Electrified by this display of confidence in my medical ability, I jumped up and took
him to a chemist's where, with the aid of the apothecary, I immediately initiated a carefully thought-out, strategic pill campaign. Mahler, now somewhat calmer, returned with
me to the café where we waited for Walter and his wife. . . . They arrived a quarter of
an hour later, and Mahler's first (ironic) question was: 'Colossal success for the singers,
of course?' Walter replied, without a trace of bitterness: 'Of course.' We spoke about
America and the material advantages for an artist of a tour of the United States, and I
gave him a favourable picture, I'm afraid. Half an hour later Mahler stood up and was
so friendly in saying goodbye, that I accompanied him on his way for a bit, never
suspecting that I would never see him again.[97]

Bruno Walter also relates that during this same waiting period Mahler showed

---

[92] BGA, no. 222, undated (postmarked 29 Aug. 1907).
[93] BGA, no. 240, undated (28 Oct. 1907).   [94] See above.
[95] KIW 108.   [96] BWM 42.
[97] Moriz Rosenthal, 'Mahleriana'. (See Hans and Rosalem Moldenhauer, 'Gustav Mahler und Moriz
Rosenthal', *Das Orchester*, Mainz, May 1982, 430.) Rosenthal's last encounter with Mahler undoubtedly took
place shortly before Mahler left for the United States. Bruno Walter conducted *Un Ballo* only once during
the autumn of 1907, on 3 Oct. See above, Vol. ii, Chap. 10, another anecdote from the memoirs of Moriz
Rosenthal, and his biography.

him the programmes he had drawn up for the concerts in St Petersburg. Walter respectfully drew his master's attention to their austere (*undankbar*) character.

He was quite surprised, and exclaimed: 'I hadn't actually thought of that!' And when he had worked out new programmes as a result of my criticism, he showed me one and asked: 'Now isn't that one a "cheer-jerker"?' (*applaustreibend*).[98] This comical expression clearly showed his disdain for applause and success. Personal vanity was the last thing he thought about when he conducted, and he utterly detested exaggerated praise. But he was quite confident of his own importance and powers, and remained unshaken in the face of hostile criticism.[99]

Before the Vienna première of *Madama Butterfly*, the most sensational event of the autumn at the Hofoper was the second series of 'guest appearances' by the famous tenor Enrico Caruso, the greatest international singer of his time (along with Feodor Chaliapin, whose star career had also been built on both sides of the Atlantic).[100] In the autumn of 1907, Caruso had carried all before him in Berlin. Later on, in Budapest where he had sung a single performance of *Aida*, Caruso had made a bad impression in his opening aria, 'Celeste Aida'.[101] He had not sung since his throat operation, two months earlier, felt unsure of himself and had not succeeded, as the performance went on, in regaining his composure. The Viennese *Fremden-Blatt* of 5 October also stated that the cost of tickets in Budapest (400 kronen) had been too high, which is not surprising because, for the first time in his career, Caruso was receiving for each appearance the largest sum he had yet earned anywhere, $2,000.[102]

Caruso arrived in Vienna on 3 October with his secretary, his accompanist, and his impresario (Emil Ledner, Conried's agent). This time it had been decided that he would take part in four performances. From among the list of works considered (which included *Lucia di Lammermoor*, *Il Trovatore*, and *La Traviata*) the final choice was *Aida* (this, with Brioschi's new designs which had for three years been one of the Hofoper's chief attractions), *La Bohème* and *Rigoletto*. Mahler, remembering painful multilingual performances in Budapest, had decided to have everyone singing in Italian, which required considerable effort, particularly on the part of the chorus.[103] As before, Caruso's fee was to be 12,000 kronen a night, a colossal sum for the period.[104]

---

[98] See below, Alma Mahler's account of the origin of this word.   [99] BWM 100.

[100] Mahler was soon to meet him again at the Metropolitan Opera. Chaliapin had given a series of performances at the Berlin Opera, in Apr. 1907.

[101] Michael Scott, *The Great Caruso* (Knopf, New York, 1988), 102 ff. The tenor himself acknowledged that 'he had never encountered such an attitude from the press' as he had in Budapest. The *Fremden-Blatt* article announced that the Viennese performance of *Aida* was to take place without even a stage rehearsal, while *La Bohème* would have a full rehearsal with orchestra.

[102] Michael Scott, *Caruso*, ibid.

[103] Letter from Alois Przistaupinsky to Viktor von Horsetzky, 21 July 1907. In honour of its famous guest, the Opera even had the programme notices (*Theaterzettel*) for the two performances of *Aida* printed in Italian.

[104] According to the article from *Die Zeit* already quoted, Caruso's four performances at the Hofoper would bring in a net total of 120,000 kronen, of which 48,000 would be paid to the tenor. Thus, despite Caruso's exceptionally high fee, the Opera's pension fund would receive the sum of 72,000 kronen.

In the days before his arrival the Viennese press carried a whole series of previews, interviews, and hyperbolic stories. As the year before, all this publicity exasperated Vienna's 'true friends of art'. As soon as he arrived, Emil Lindner organized a press conference[105] at the Hotel Bristol where Caruso was staying, and the tenor handed out signed caricatures to the journalists. Despite everything, most of the critics conceded that the star singer was also a great artist, and altogether worthy of his reputation.

Although there was not the same level of violence and hysteria as in the preceding year, unpleasant scenes took place at the box office, when the tenor's fans fought for the few remaining tickets, and also when some of them failed to obtain them. This time, however, Alois Przistaupinsky was posted with detectives near the box office to prevent professional touts from reselling tickets on the pavement outside the Opera. The touts, discouraged, eventually returned the tickets they had managed to acquire, which meant that sixty or seventy seats were once again at the disposal of spectators who had earlier been turned away.[106] As mentioned earlier, the first performance, on 4 October, was held in honour of the Emperor's name-day. On this occasion Caruso walked from the Hotel Bristol to the Opera, wearing a top hat. To escape the acclaim of his admirers, massed in front of the Opera to see and greet him, he slipped in quickly through the artists' entrance. At the end of the performance a crowd of onlookers and fans again awaited him at the stage-door. And once again they attempted to unharness his horses and to pull him in triumph to his hotel.

A few days later, the 'Aus der Theaterwelt' column in the *Fremden-Blatt* regaled its readers with stories of some of the tenor's antics. While captivating the public with the beauty of his singing and the intensity of his characterization he had, it seemed, also been entertaining his fellow-singers and stage personnel with practical jokes. In *Aida*, for example, during the Triumph Scene in the second act, he had stood with his back to the audience miming the orchestral highlights for the benefit of the chorus, moving his lips like the wind players, puffing out his cheeks for the trumpets, and drawing an imaginary bow across his knee as if playing a cello. In the second act of *La Bohème* he drew with charcoal on a tablecloth in the Café Momus a caricature of Richard Mayr, who was singing Colline that night. The act finished in the wildest gaiety because he had ordered a vintage champagne at his own expense for the 'bohemians' at all the tables. As in the previous year, there were innumerable curtain calls, and laurel crowns and sheaves of flowers were thrown on to the stage.

After the first performance of *Aida*, Julius Korngold reported in the *Neue Freie Presse* that the great tenor's success had been even more impressive and complete than the year before. It was not a case of expecting a trumpet and

---

[105] Caruso declared on this occasion that Mahler's engagement was a 'master stroke' on Conried's part and that he could not fail to be a sensation in the United States.

[106] *Illustrirtes Wiener Extrablatt* (5 Oct. 1907).

then being disappointed to hear a clarinet instead. His voice was a 'noble instrument nobly played': he was an artist who did not allow himself the slightest affectation, the slightest use of facile effect; his interpretation was 'full of beauty and profundity'. Kalbeck admired Caruso's unsurpassed mastery in breath control,[107] the perfect balance of registers and ease on top notes, now swelling to a fortissimo, now dying away to nothing.[108]

Albert Kauders noted after the second performance of the same work on 9 October that the great tenor, instead of trying to dazzle by means of exploits in sound alone, was intent on carrying through the melodic line, bringing to a rounded interpretation warmth and intense emotion rather than superficial brilliance. With masterly restraint, Caruso was able to give the impression of a literally unlimited crescendo. Just as one was ready definitively to classify him as a lyric tenor he would produce heroic notes 'like lightning out of a blue sky'.

Liebstöckl, in the *Extrablatt*, made some general remarks about modern publicity and 'the lost and dying art' of bel canto which earned large sums for Caruso, the theatres and the agents:

Herr Caruso is one of the most precious products of this retrospective and speculative business philosophy. On the whole, his vocal material is neither startlingly big nor especially brilliant, nor has it a fascinating charm . . . The cantilena is heard with its natural impulsion, its living soul, and technically perfect, even if certain things are slowly crumbling away, the top register for example, which now needs the whole throat in order to be heard. Herr Caruso knows this very well. I know of no singer with a clearer view of himself, or showing more caution, than this treasure of the declining art of singing. The A is delivered like a precious gift, prepared and produced with economy. The restraint one observes in him is less a virtue than a discreet necessity.

Further on, Liebstöckl observed that Caruso avoided heroic roles and that Radames was among the most dramatic in his repertoire. Thus he sang his first aria in mezza voce, conserving his strength for later. Consequently, he had shown signs of fatigue only at the very end. 'To sum up,' he continued, 'Caruso's art remains: the incomparable art of flow in the line, the art of building the cantilena, freely shaping it and using tone as if it were an instrument. Everything sounds smooth, all of a piece: beautiful, rounded, cared for: deficiencies almost become advantages.'[109]

Korngold, after hearing Caruso in *La Bohème* on 6 October, acclaimed him as the artist 'whose impact reaches the depth of soul and feelings', especially in comic scenes. His performances would be remembered as complete incarnations, conceived in perfect simplicity despite their abundance of detail.

---

[107] On the other hand Caruso's mastery of breathing annoyed Heinrich Reinhardt, who accused the tenor of nursing his voice for two whole acts of *Rigoletto*, using the full voice only for 'La donna e mobile'. He acknowledged, however, that the voice was one of the most beautiful and best schooled of its time but 'too fragile' for heroic roles.

[108] Cast for the performances of 4 and 9 Oct., conducted by Francisco Spetrino: Weidt (Aida); Cahier (Amneris); Caruso (Radames); Weidemann (Amonasro); Mayr (Ramfis); Hesch (King).

[109] *Illustrirtes Wiener Extrablatt* (5 Oct. 1907).

Kalbeck, the same night, saw in Caruso not only 'a powerful artistic personality' but 'balm for the ears and a feast for the eyes'.[110] After *Rigoletto*, Korngold again marvelled at 'the flood of warmth and beautiful sound' the great tenor produced, and at an art which enlightened and enriched everyone, singers and teachers of singing, public and critics.

Kalbeck pointed out, however, that on his farewell evening Caruso's voice occasionally 'faltered' and that he was guilty of some lapses of taste in trying to please the public, for instance in the last act, when, like the preceding year, he sang his aria while shuffling a pack of cards.[111] Far from reproaching him for his three successive encores of 'La donna e mobile' and that of the opening phrase of the quartet, Kauders considered that these had been insisted upon by the audience.

Only now can we fully abandon ourselves to the delight of his vocal mastery! Only now, when we have learned to see him as the apostle of bel canto, the supreme singer who, disdaining mere effects, brings to his devoted listeners the highest form of artistic enjoyment through the noble line of his cantilena. At the end, Caruso was called back before the curtains again and again. People stayed in their boxes and seats as if the performance were still going to continue, applauding and waving their handkerchiefs. Caruso, to whom laurel wreathes and bouquets were being presented, led Demuth to the footlights. Only later did he come alone—about twenty times—calling 'Grazie' and 'A reviderci' [*sic*] into the storms of applause.[112]

Caruso did not appear in Vienna again in Mahler's lifetime. In February 1910, Emil Ledner suggested Caruso nights for *Carmen*, *I Pagliacci*, *La Bohème*, or *Tosca* to Weingartner but the Hofoper director replied that he could not arrange for these works to be sung in Italian. 'As for putting on works that Herr Caruso has already sung, that would not seem advisable for practical reasons.'[113]

Mahler could have heard in full only Caruso's first performance on 4 October for the following evening he was on a train to Wiesbaden. He had agreed to conduct, for the first time in years, an exclusively classical programme in the sixth and last concert of a festival held at this large spa not far from Mainz. After changing trains at Frankfurt, where he had a hasty breakfast at the station with his friend, the conductor Ludwig Rottenberg,[114] he

[110] Kalbeck was particularly dazzled by the top C in the love duet, projected 'easily, like a rich cavalier tossing a gold piece'. Cast for the performance of 6 Oct., conducted by Francisco Spetrino: Kurz (Mimi); Forst (Musetta); Caruso (Rodolfo); Moser (Marcello); Stehmann (Colline); Mayr (Schaunard).

[111] Kalbeck described an incident that night which proved Caruso 'was human': he had gone flat in his second-act aria, following which he had sung louder than usual, particularly on the high notes. His voice, fatigued by this continuing strain, had 'almost cracked'. Kalbeck saw in this a characteristic instance of the public's pernicious influence on the tenor.

[112] Several critics noted how Caruso liked to share his applause with his colleagues. Cast for the performance of *Rigoletto* on 11 Oct., conducted by Francisco Spetrino: Kurz (Gilda); Kittel (Maddalena); Caruso (Duca); Demuth (Rigoletto); Hesch (Sparafucile).

[113] HOA, 1910/180. Not until Leoncavallo's *Pagliacci* on 20 Sept. 1911, under the direction of Hans Gregor, did Caruso appear again in Vienna.

[114] BGA, no. 230, telegram of 7 Oct. 1907. Concerning Ludwig Rottenberg, see above, Vol. ii, Chap. 6.

arrived at his destination and went straight to his hotel, the Victoria, only to discover that it was both shabby and noisy, and that he would probably have trouble sleeping there. Without even unpacking, he went on the Kurhotel and then to the Nassauerhof where at last he found a relatively comfortable room. He was already wondering, as he contemplated 'the idiotic hubbub of a "fashionable" watering crowd', 'What on earth am I doing in a place like this!'[115] And he remembered that, early in the preceding summer in Maiernigg, 'only the Theuers' indigestible Nockerl[116] and garlicky roast veal could have given me the absurd idea of accepting the telegraphic offer. Anyway, the programme is easy, very "cheer-jerking" (*applaustreibend*).[117] Let's hope it pays for my fur coat. At the moment I'm sitting undressed[118] in my room waiting for my luggage, which I left at the Victoria Hotel . . . . so as not to lose a minute.'[119]

Mahler's 'easy' programme included Beethoven's *Coriolan* Overture and Fifth Symphony, followed by the 'Prelude and Liebestod' from *Tristan*, and the Prelude to *Die Meistersinger*. It was an elegant occasion, for the concert on 9 October marked the close of a big orchestral festival, held unfortunately in the vast hall of the new Kurhaus, seating only 1,300 but blighted by dreadful acoustics. The audience displayed great elegance, gowns and jewels glittered under the bright lights, and the young Kaim orchestra lived up to the occasion, and brought the whole audience to its feet, roaring its applause, at the end of the 'Liebestod'. According to A. Heibel, critic of the *Wiesbadener Neueste Nachrichten*, Mahler that evening 'triumphed in the classical field' and delighted his public with an 'unadulterated' Beethoven that 'conscientiously followed the score'.[120] Hans Georg Gerhard,[121] in the *Wiesbadener Zeitung*, placed him among

the most interesting conductors, not in the outward sense of theatrical self-presentation on the rostrum, but because of his musical interpretation. One hardly notices that he is conducting, he uses the baton so discreetly. Yet his every glance penetrates into some far corner of the orchestra, his every measured and exact gesture has a precise goal, and achieves it. He merely recalls, as it were, everything that was decided in a clear and unambiguous fashion in rehearsal, and leads his flock calmly, with a confidence that underpins the orchestra's self-assurance and complete reliability. As a conductor, Mahler is more a draftsman than a painter [Maler]. Clarity of line and

---

[115] BGA, no. 231, dated 7 Oct. 1907. 'Wer hat mich gebracht in dieses Land?' As seen above, Mahler often used this phrase, apparently unconscious of its being a slightly corrupted version of Molière's *Les Fourberies de Scapin*: '*Que diable allait-il faire dans cette galère?*' And he used the English word for 'fashionable'.

[116] Nockerl is a typical Bavarian and Austrian dish, a kind of dumpling, sweet or salty. Theuer was the architect who had designed the Villa Mahler in Maiernigg, and was the Mahlers' neighbour.

[117] See above. According to Alma, this expression was invented by the Viennese critic Gustav Schönaich in connection with Hans Richter's beard (AMM1, 393; AMM2, 336).

[118] In the nude: the original manuscript uses the word '*ausgezogen*' (undressed), not '*angezogen*' (dressed) as in Alma's printed text in her *Erinnerungen*. [119] Ibid.

[120] Heibel noted that for the Beethoven symphony the wind instruments were doubled by those of the Wiesbaden Orchestra. He claimed that only once, in the Andante, were the strings drowned by the brass.

[121] Hans Georg Gerhard was the conductor of the Wiesbaden Beethoven Concerts.

balance is his guiding principle; he is not much concerned with feasts of tone or riots of colour; he keeps a tight rein on the orchestra, allowing for no deviation from his intention and no lapses above or below the line which he has drawn. His orchestral images are remarkably clear, gripping, luminous, one can accept them with a harmonious satisfaction even where one disagrees with Mahler's interpretation.[122]

The imperial decree releasing Mahler from his obligations from 31 December onwards and appointing Felix Weingartner as director of the Hofoper[123] bore the date of 5 October. All the requests made by Mahler in his March letter to Prince Montenuovo were granted. He would henceforth receive an annual pension of 14,000 kronen[124] 'on condition that he would never direct, or conduct, in a Viennese theatre'. Weingartner, formed in the tradition of Liszt rather than Wagner, was to give the Opera an orientation quite different from Mahler's. Despite his obvious gifts, revealed at a very early age, he made his reputation as a conductor more by the elegance and precision of his baton than by his passion. Moreover, he had himself always acknowledged a preference for concerts rather than theatre, and the Viennese critics, used to the exceptional intensity of Mahler's conducting, were soon struck by his lack of dramatic temperament. It is not surprising therefore that all former Mahler supporters soon turned against his successor, all the more so when Weingartner seemed determined to make his mark by undoing everything that Mahler had done, and often done very well. In particular he reduced the number of Wagner performances and made cuts in them, while allowing the lighter works a much larger place in the repertoire.

Thus in January he enraged half the music-lovers in Vienna by making his debut at the Opera with a fully 'renovated' *Fidelio*, stripped of the *Leonore* Overture No. 3, deprived of Roller's opening and closing sets, and in a production so much modified that many scandalized members of the audience demonstrated during the performance.[125] As seen above (Chapter 1), Weingartner had used the prison set for the whole of Act I and done away with the bastion set

---

[122] Among characteristic features of Mahler's interpretation Gerhard noted the tension he maintained in transition passages like the famous one that introduces the Finale in the Beethoven C minor Symphony; the woodwind passage in thirds in the Andante; the short pause which heightened the violence of the opening chords of the *Coriolan* Overture; the bite of the dotted rhythms; the tranquillity and breadth of lyrical passages; the vivid clarity of the polyphony in the *Meistersinger* Prelude. But Gerhard also reproached Mahler with 'excessively subduing' the colours, of being sometimes 'too doctrinaire, too calculating, too reserved', of being not sufficiently Dionysiac, of failing to attain 'paroxysm, ecstasy'. He also regretted the slowness of certain tempos, for example in the Scherzo and the Finale of the Fifth: and the speed of others, as in the Prelude to *Meistersinger*.

[123] HOA, Z. 1112. Weingartner's contract guaranteed him a total annual sum of 36,000 kronen (15,000 kronen salary; 13,000 performance fees; 8,000 fixed remuneration, with an additional sum for removal expenses). There was a mutual release clause operable at the end of each year. His pension was to increase by 1,000 kronen annually, rising to 15,000 kronen if invalidity rendered him unable to conduct. He was finally persuaded to promise that he would only exceptionally undertake tours to conduct his own works: which shows that this was the principal grievance against Mahler.

[124] HOA, no. 5514/1907. On 22 Feb. 1901, the Emperor had granted Mahler an increase in salary. It had been decided at that time that after six years he would be entitled to a retirement pension of 6,000 kronen, rising by 1,000 each year up to a maximum 14,000 (see above, Vol. ii, Chap. 10).

[125] Kalbeck criticized the absence of any *Leonore* overture and the casting of Demuth as Pizarro, who, according to him, seemed like a 'kindly uncle', not a scoundrel. Hirschfeld was alone in applauding the less-

in the last scene. He acknowledges in his memoirs that his new production was badly received and that Slezak was needed in the role of Florestan to draw the public.[126] Wellesz, and all pupils of Schoenberg later indignantly recalled this 'systematic destruction of Mahler's incomparable production'.[127] In an article published on 1 October 1908 Richard Specht, one of the leading members of what was now called the 'Mahler-clique', expressed the view that 'in half a year, ten years' creative work of the greatest and highest aspiration has been destroyed and dismantled' and claimed that Weingartner seemed to want to 'obliterate all traces of his predecessor' by deliberately reviving, with his own modifications, all the major works that Mahler put on.[128] The shadow of Mahler hung long and heavily over his successor's work. Weingartner arrived in Vienna in mid-November and immediately gave the *Fremden-Blatt* an interview which it published on the 22nd. After making routine compliments to his predecessor and to the Opera itself, he announced the departure of Slezak and Selma Kurz[129] and a reduction in the number of guest performances. We have seen that the new director had undertaken to keep the number and duration of his own absences from Vienna to a minimum. But on 16 October, Karl Kraus published the following article in *Die Fackel*:

I interest myself as little in operatic comings and goings as in the world where they happen. But it occurs to me in passing that in leaving his post, Herr Mahler's dignity is less impaired than is his successor's in assuming it. If an opera director were required to prove his competence by writing a satire, Herr Mahler, who apparently stumbled over old Princess Metternich's train, would perhaps be in a position to do it.[130] However, he does not write a satire; he conducts and beats time.[131] Meanwhile Herr von Weingartner makes his entrance in a kind of musical Walpurgisnacht, as if he felt obliged to display all the lack of humour needed by a director of the Vienna Opera to put up with the dressage imposed by the master of the imperial stables.[132]

ening of 'dramatic emphasis' in the new interpretation. Kauders, writing in the *Fremden-Blatt*, saw it as a 'triumph of the impersonal'. Schoenberg's pupils were shocked by the cuts made in Wagner scores (EWL 115). L. Andro, in an article she published in summer 1908 in the *Neue Musikalische Presse*, pointed out that Weingartner seemed determined to do the contrary of whatever his predecessor had done, notably by making cuts in *Die Walküre* while bringing back passages in *Les Huguenots* which Mahler had cut. Specht also observed that the auditorium was no longer kept dark during performances, with the result that there was now talking in the boxes again. Moreover, the 'distinguished conductor' hardly ever appeared on the rostrum (on Weingartner's Wagnerian 'counter-reformation' see also below, Vol. iiii, Chap. 2).

[126]   WLE, ii. 157 and 185.

[127]   EWL 115. See below, Vol. iiii, Chap. 2, and, in the same chapter, Roller's long letter describing Weingartner's misdeeds.

[128]   'Der Direktor Weingartner', in *Die Schaubühne*, Berlin, 4 (1908): 40, 189.

[129]   Both had received offers from the United States which they wanted to accept. But we have seen that Weingartner was soon able to persuade them to sign new contracts with the Vienna Opera.

[130]   This sentence makes it clear that Pauline Metternich participated in the plots and press campaigns that led Mahler to resign.

[131]   'Beats time' (in German 'hält Takt'). Probably a play on the word *Takt* which can also mean 'tact' (e.g. 'Takt zeigen'- to be tactful).

[132]   *Oberstallmeisterliche Dressur*. A play on words. *Obersthofmeisteramt* = the service of the Lord Chamberlain. The chief Oberhofmeister, Prince Liechtenstein, was in charge of the imperial stables. In fact, of course, the man responsible for the imperial theatres was the second Lord Chamberlain, Prince Montenuovo.

The worthy Herr von Weingartner, during his brief stay in Vienna 'was kind enough to receive a representative from this paper'. It seems that he will exercise this kindness more often but that, once he has taken up his directorship, he will be in Vienna less often. When asked about his intentions and plans as director of the Vienna Opera, Herr von Weingartner admitted that he was about to embark on a big concert tour through England and Scotland and that before the New Year he would direct a music festival in Kiel exclusively devoted to the performance of his own compositions. In February he would conduct an important concert in Warsaw, which would not prevent him from directing his newest piece, written for Goethe's *Faust*, in the Weimar Hoftheater at Easter. But we are not to suppose that he is completely given over to preparations for his tour. Herr von Weingartner is still up to his eyes in work to be done before he leaves Berlin, for he has five concerts to conduct for the Königliche Kapelle. So as not to have too many irons in the fire he has declined an invitation from the Vienna Philharmonic to conduct several concerts in the coming season... Of all the wholesale businesses that of selling music seems to me by far the most objectionable because of the enormous contrast between the nature of the commodity and the way it is commercialized. There are 'jobbers' in the stock market. This seems to be the way in which Herr von Weingartner runs concerts.

Ten days later the Viennese press announced that Weingartner had been invited to the Cologne Opera to conduct a performance of his work *Genesius*.[133] It was becoming clear that the idea of changing directors in order to get one who would spend the major part of his time in Vienna had misfired, and that henceforth no internationally known conductor would be prepared to devote the greater part of his time to the Vienna Opera. Announcements about concert tours and engagements accepted by Weingartner did nothing to reduce Mahler's bitterness as he saw how readily he had been released from his post, only for his successor to be granted all that he himself had been refused.

In an article published in *Signale für die musikalische Welt* in September, Karpath recalled that Mahler had left of his own free will, and chiefly because of criticism levelled at him for too often absenting himself to conduct his own symphonies. Despite shortcomings in his directorship he had brought incomparable prestige to the institution with his uncut performances of Wagner, his quite unprecedented standards of excellence in Mozart, and also by improving orchestral standards, engaging singers of international rank, closing the auditorium doors during acts, and, for the first time, according the visual arts their due role in the stage productions. Still, Weingartner's arrival awakened great hopes. Much could be expected of him, despite fears that over-frequent absence might prevent him, too, from devoting as much energy to the Hofoper as it needed. The *Neue Musik-Zeitung* of 26 November speculated as to whether Weingartner would put on his own works at the Hofoper. It observed that the new director had had nothing to do with the stage for a great many years. And it enumerated works dropped from the Viennese repertoire that

---

[133] See above, Vol. i, Chap 24.

should be revived, such as Gluck's *Orphée*, and *Der Freischütz*. Unfortunately the 'apathy' of the Viennese public was to blame for many of the mistakes and omissions. It was impossible to put on productions, however splendid, if they had to play to empty or only half-full houses.[134]

In the event, Weingartner held his post for only two and a half years and left Vienna even more discouraged and disgusted than his predecessor. His experiences at the Hofoper were described at great length in his memoirs, which he completed in 1928 and in which he tried to rebut the numerous accusations made against him. They reveal that even before he accepted the post, his friends were trying to dissuade him from 'taking on the hornets' nest' of the Hofoper; and that he was immediately confronted by the violent hostility of the critics favourable to Mahler, notably Julius Korngold.[135] According to Weingartner, Korngold was 'not an enemy to me but to Mahler's successor'. He acknowledges the competence and talent of the critic of the *Neue Freie Presse* but complains of the 'inaccurate and tendentious' way the Viennese press reported everything he said. In December the new director had a foretaste of the difficulties Mahler had experienced before him, when Mildenburg refused to sing in *Tristan* with Schmedes on the pretext that she had previously been booed in this work because of him. As for Mahler, Weingartner reproaches him with having received him in September,

in a very cool and formal way, with none of the old cordiality which had made our dealings so friendly in former times. What I found at the Opera only partially pleased me. A few outstanding artists. Others already showing signs of vocal decline, the ensemble often less than perfect. Had it always been so, or was it my heightened critical sense that prevented me from listening with the same delight as when I had first been in the house?—Only the wonderful orchestra shone with undiminished brilliance.[136]

Weingartner's comments on the epoch preceding his own are frequently severe:

Newspaper articles and pamphlets[137] eagerly affirmed, then and later, that under my predecessor there had been nothing but 'gala performances' (*Festvorstellungen*).— *Tristan*, at least, could hardly have been in this category—and this was equally true of other operas, as I quickly found out. . . . There is no doubt that at the beginning of his time in Vienna, and later as well, Gustav Mahler achieved extraordinary things. But his own compositions gradually met with success, which incited him to go on composing. One major work immediately followed another, thus leading to a dilemma whose conflicting influences he could not altogether reconcile within himself, perhaps partly because of his less than perfect health. Prince Montenuovo, who always spoke of Mahler with the greatest respect, told me repeatedly that it was this dilemma between composing and

---

[134] *Neue Musik-Zeitung*, 29 (1907): 4, 88.

[135] Yet Korngold's article in the *Neue Freie Presse* about the *Fidelio* of 24 Jan. is written with obvious admiration and respect. Weingartner emphasizes that Korngold's hostility was all the more to be feared because it was expressed with unfailing moderation and with a false air of objectivity.

[136] WLE, ii. 151.

[137] A clear reference to Paul Stefan's brochure, *Gustav Mahlers Erbe* (PSE, see below).

directing, and the eventual swing of the pendulum in favour of the former, that brought about Mahler's friendly parting with the Obersthofmeister's Office. As I gained more insight into the Hofoper, the quality of many of the performances and of the internal management convinced me that Mahler had not been devoting his full attention to the institution for some time. Productions of a remarkable standard, even if not pleasing to me in all particulars, included *Lohengrin, Die Walküre, Der Widerspenstigen Zähmung* and Mahler's last and finest new production, *Iphigenie in Aulis.* Unfortunately, the two last-named operas naturally appealed only to a small public: whereas the newly produced Wagner works were so often performed, or in theatrical language 'done to death', that they no longer exerted their proper pull. Alongside these were productions which through years of performance without rehearsal had come to look so tired that the public's continually dwindling interest did not surprise me. But what was positively disastrous was the small number of operas in the repertoire: there were gaps wherever one looked. Composers like Lortzing and Marschner were totally absent, along with the French *opéras comiques* and the earlier Italian works except the *Barber.* Of Weber only *Der Freischütz,* of Meyerbeer only *Le Prophète* could be given, both in lamentable productions. The more recent composers were represented only by *La Bohème, Madama Butterfly* and *Die Königin von Saba.* The schedule operated within very narrow limits, and the continual complaints I received about lack of variety were fully justified. It was fortunate that shortly before I took office *Madama Butterfly* had been so successful that it was possible to put it on two nights in the week; otherwise there would have been a real danger of having to keep the theatre dark many nights.[138]

Weingartner adds that Goldmark's *Ein Wintermärchen,* not a brilliant work, was a success because of its composer's popularity in his native city. (Unfortunately the work soon had to be withdrawn, as Mahler had prepared only one cast.)[139] He claims that Mildenburg and Schmedes were 'on the brink of vocal collapse'; that Weidemann was a 'singing actor' rather than a great singer; that ballets were not of sufficient number or quality to take a normal share of the repertoire; and that Mildenburg and Weidt, the two principal Wagnerian sopranos, had both been granted leave in May, precisely the time when the Opera every year performed a complete cycle of Wagner's works. His conclusion is: 'Of all the lies levelled at me in the course of my life, one of the most blatant is that of the "rich inheritance" I supposedly came into in Vienna.' In his opinion the hostility he encountered when he took the production of *Fidelio* to pieces was of a 'racist nature: he was accused of obeying a deep-rooted anti-Semitic reflex in destroying the work of his predecessor, and had heard that preparations were being made to unleash noisy protests if he made even the slightest change to 'Mahler's *Fidelio*':

[138] Stefan, *Gustav Mahlers Erbe,* 154. *Madama Butterfly* was performed fourteen times in 1907, twenty-seven in 1908, twenty-one in 1909, and fourteen in 1910. No other production of the Mahler era was so successful.
[139] The première of *Ein Wintermärchen* took place on 2 Jan. 1908, the day after Weingartner officially became director. Probably Mahler did not arrange for a double casting because the work seemed to him too weak to hold the stage for long. A letter from Mahler to Humperdinck, written on 28 May 1907, said that an opera by Humperdinck, *The Forced Marriage (Heirat wider Willen)* was to be included on the bill for the 1907–8 season; but it was never performed at the Vienna Opera.

Conscious that I was treading on dangerous ground, but confident that I had an obligation to be, not a sensation-seeker, but a faithful interpreter of Beethoven's mighty spirit, I made my debut at the Hofoper podium. The threatened protest scenes did not occur, but most of the reviews showed clearly that the agreed password was not Beethoven, but Gustav Mahler. The password would have remained the same, but used to different effect, if I had left everything just as it was, and had bowed to my predecessor in reverential admiration, for when on other occasions, I felt convinced I could safely follow in Mahler's footsteps, I was called a mere imitator with no personality of my own. 'Whatever you do, you'll be wrong!' That was the motto on the banner they brandished against my directorship.[140]

The fact remains that if Weingartner had not been determined to mark himself off from his predecessor at any price, he would not have made such systematic and arbitrary changes in a production which many people in Vienna had hailed as a magnificent success.

Weingartner complains that within the Opera itself he soon came up against the hostility of Roller, who was obviously far from delighted at seeing two of his finest sets for *Fidelio*[141] done away with at a stroke of the pen or at being obliged to forgo his famous 'orgies of darkness'; or, above all, at the appointment of an *Oberregisseur* (stage director), Wilhelm von Wymetal who was to take over many of the tasks previously assigned to him as *Leiter des Ausstattungswesens*.[142]

What was more, Roller was aware of the fact that the new director was by no means a wholehearted admirer of his work. Weingartner makes the following reservations about it in his memoirs:

His landscapes cluttered the stage with realist-three-dimensional structures which were very expensive, and almost impossible to fit into the Hofoper's inadequate warehouses, and which also hampered rehearsals on stage, as the mechanical equipment of the opera house was so outdated that it often took a whole day to put up sets of this kind and another day to take them down. Despite these considerations I was prepared to take into account his artistic personality which I fully acknowledged; but I had to take issue with the way he wished to put into practice his ideas on lighting. I had repeatedly drawn Roller's attention to the need for more light on the stage, which was plunged for long periods in the dreariest gloom, and had once received the reply that his eyes must be different from mine. This I did not doubt, but had to insist that I had to rely on my own eyes as well. . . . At the point in the second act of *Siegfried* where day was supposed to have broken and where the exiguous ray of light that fell on the stage suggested moonlit scenery at the most, I ordered an appropriate change in the lighting, regardless of objections.[143]

---

[140] WLE, ii. 160.

[141] Weingartner states that the *Oberregisseur* he was soon to engage, Wilhelm von Wymetal, found a way of putting back the set for the final scene without using the *Leonore* Overture No. 3 as an interlude.

[142] Chief designer. As seen above, the German word *Ausstattung* embraces the entire technical equipment of the theatre.

[143] WLE, ii. 183.

Roller's resignation had become inevitable, and he handed it in on 31 May 1909, nine months before Weingartner's, without being able to complete his designs for the four sections of the *Ring*.[144]

After Mahler's death Wilhelm von Wymetal,[145] Weingartner's *Oberregisseur* published in a Berlin magazine a still more negative account of the state of the Hofoper before his arrival.

In the period of struggle when Mahler, with Roller, was exploring new ideas of stage design, each new experiment unleashed violent battles between applauding admirers and hissing opponents of the tireless, restless researcher and experimenter. . . . For a time Mahler succeeded but in the end he fell victim to his own daring, pioneering iconoclasm. . . . Mahler's axe first fell on what was formerly an incomparable vocal ensemble. The darlings of the public, well aware of their position, and unwilling to be remoulded by him, were pushed into the background, pensioned off, driven away, and in their place appeared younger, more amenable talents. The fact that these young singers, few of them of the standard of the older ones, were cheaper, was also important for Mahler, who could now devote a much greater part of his budget to his production visions. The result was a slow but steady decline in the Opera. When Mahler himself was on the podium he could conjure extraordinary things from even minor performers by the magic of his baton. But Mahler hated repertory opera and wanted exceptional festival performances (*Ausnahmefestspiele*) twice a week. This lofty aspiration brought about a state of affairs where, towards the end, one could take pleasure only in works he had prepared himself and even then, often enough, only when he himself was conducting. Woe to anyone who strayed into the Opera on other occasions! It was through this unevenness of standards that the Opera lost its main body of regular supporters. The costly production experiments in Mahler's later years, led to a continuous deterioration in the Hofoper's finances.[146]

A somewhat hasty and prejudiced verdict on Mahler's work at the Vienna Opera! At this time, however, Wymetal was himself a member of the Opera and had been for four years the object of violent criticism on the part of the former director's many admirers, which obviously helps explain the polemic nature of his comments. When he speaks, for example, of the Opera's reduced box-office takings in Mahler's later years, he was either misinformed or deliberately lying. We have seen, in fact, that 1906, one of the years with the greatest number of new productions, had the smallest deficit ever. Most of the other criticisms of Mahler do not stand up to closer examination. In any case Wymetal, in an article published two years later, put forward a point of view that was almost the exact opposite.[147]

It is undeniable that Mahler's artistic success was based on one essential factor recognized by all, namely his genius; but that genius was not inexhaustible

[144] *Götterdämmerung*, with his designs, was not performed until the end of 1910.
[145] Wilhelm, Ritter von Wymetal began his career as an actor in Pressburg in 1889, then went to the Residenztheater in Berlin. After an engagement in Brno (1892–6) he played leading roles at the Prague Landestheater from 1897 onward. His career as a stage director was therefore a relatively recent development.
[146] Wilhelm von Wymetal, 'Vorgänge an der Wiener Oper', *Vössische Zeitung* (Berlin, 8 Mar. 1912).
[147] See below.

and could not transform *all* the Opera's performances. Mahler was himself a victim of an institution of his time, the 'repertory theatre'; and he understood this perfectly well. With a 'repertory' of fifty-three works (1905–6), or of fifty-eight (1906–7), the level of performances could not remain constant, for most of them were put on without any rehearsal. Mediocrity was an inevitable part of the routine, and Mahler's principal mistake was in believing that he would be able to reform all this. At the time of leaving Vienna he declared in Alma's presence: 'Repertory theatre is dead.'[148] Actually the old system lingered on for another fifty years, while—in parallel and as a consequence—festivals proliferated. Mahler had already glimpsed a possible solution for the future of the Opera: a limit to the number of performances of each work, which would enable the performers always to give of their best. In the 1920s an experiment by the Krolloper in Berlin showed the way forward: a few works were put on several times each year. The success of this experiment proved that Mahler had been right in claiming, at the time of his departure, that the 'repertory' system would come to an end in the not-too-distant future.

Controversy was rife during Weingartner's first year as director, and he was constantly compared unfavourably with his predecessor, often, it seems, with good reason. Paul Stefan,[149] one of Mahler's earliest, most passionate and eloquent admirers, had played an important role in the Ansorge Verein, and later dedicated himself to the cause of modern music in the daily *Die Stunde*, the weekly journal *Die Bühne*, and, after 1912, the journal *Der Ruf*. A born polemist, he deeply resented the way Mahler had been treated by the Viennese press and the Court authorities, and published in 1908 a booklet entitled *Gustav Mahlers Erbe* (Gustav Mahler's Legacy),[150] giving an entirely favourable account of the ten Mahler years. Paul Stauber, the *Illustrirtes Wiener Extrablatt* critic, immediately replied with a pamphlet entitled *Das wahre Erbe Gustav Mahlers*[151] (The Real Legacy of Gustav Mahler), contesting and contradicting Stefan on all points. Figures, facts, dates, and statistics were exchanged with

---

[148]   See below.

[149]   Paul Stefan (1879–1943) was born Stefan-Grünfeldt in Brno and had read law, philosophy, and history of art at the Vienna University, and then musical theory under Hermann Grädener and composition under Schoenberg. He wrote for some time for the *Neues Wiener Journal*. As we shall see, he was one of the Mahler admirers who organized the friendly farewell meeting on the platform of the Westbahnhof on 9 Dec. 1907.

[150]   *Gustav Mahler's Erbe: Ein Beitrag zur neuesten Geschichte der deutschen Bühne und des Herrn Felix von Weingartner* (PSE, 1908). This little monograph was later followed by a short biography of Mahler (1910, rev. 1921), a book of tributes to Mahler on the occasion of his 50th birthday, *Ein Bild seiner Persönlichkeit in Widmungen* (BSP, 1910), by *Das Grab in Wien* (PSG, 1913), and by *Mahler für Jedermann* (1922). In 1921, Stefan founded the journal *Musikblätter des Anbruch*, published by Universal Edition, gave many lectures, and became the Vienna correspondent for the *Neue Zürcher Zeitung* and *Musical America*. He was also one of the founding members of the ISCM and its vice-president for Austria. He left Vienna after the Anschluss and spent his last years in the United States. Besides his writings on Mahler, he left books and monographs on *Oskar Fried* (1911), *Max Reinhardt* (1923), *Anna Bahr-Mildenburg* (1922), *Arnold Schoenberg* (1924), *Franz Schubert* (1928), *Dvorak* (1934), *Arturo Toscanini* (1935), and *Bruno Walter* (1936). He also wrote two books on the Vienna Opera, *Neue Musik in Wien* (1921), and *Geschichte der Oper* (1932).

[151]   SWE.

surprising violence and passion. Mahler had after all left Vienna and now cared very little what was written about him. Weingartner, who had shown a decidedly mean streak in his various disputes with the Berlin Opera, almost certainly had a hand in the publication of the second brochure which, supreme irony, was eventually bound together with Stefan's and sold under the same cover with the title: 'Mahler: For and Against' (*Für und gegen Mahler*).

Paul Stefan's text is however not without its defects: it sets out to be a veritable panegyric on Mahler's years in Vienna, and throughout puts the blame for Mahler's difficulties and ultimate departure down to one man, Robert Hirschfeld, who in his articles had continually minimized Mahler's most admirable exploits and emphasized his failures. Voices were soon raised in defence of the *Wiener Abendpost*'s critic; Max Vancsa, for example, recalled in *Die Wage* that Hirschfeld had championed various causes, that he was not a philistine, that he had never nursed 'ignoble personal grievances', and that he had not been alone in criticizing Mahler.[152]

After Stauber's brochure had appeared, L. Andro reminded her readers in the *Allgemeine Musik-Zeitung* that it was thanks to Mahler alone that the Viennese had been shaken out of their apathy and had learned to 'have an opinion' and take up the cudgels for their Opera. She considered that the two brochures suffered from the same fault; they attacked or defended personalities rather than issues, and attributed far too much importance to Hirschfeld. Mahler had been bound to leave sooner or later. Andro also felt that too much weight had been put on Mahler's 'clique', his group of intimates, who in general took relatively little part in public life. 'Mahler had wanted to serve art, Weingartner only the public.' The new director had been wrong to inaugurate his reign by destroying his predecessor's productions of *Fidelio* and his *Der Widerspenstigen Zähmung*, and his choice of new works had been extremely unfortunate.[153]

Even after Weingartner's departure the arguments did not cease. Indeed much later, in 1920, Max Graf set about defending Robert Hirschfeld, who had been dead for six years, against Richard Specht's accusations.[154] Had not the critic of the *Wiener Abendpost* fought against Hanslick and defended Bruckner and Wolf, had he not been the first to argue in favour of Schnitzler and Wedekind, had he not been an admirer of Karl Kraus?[155] Had he not helped to get Schoenberg's

---

[152] *Die Wage, eine Wiener Wochenschrift*, 11 (1908): 51/52, 1185.

[153] L. Andro mentions in particular *Le Vagabond* by Xavier Leroux, as well as revivals of Lortzing's *Der Wildschütz*, Auber's *Fra Diavolo* and *Le Domino noir*, and Méhul's *Joseph*. See L. Andro, 'Opernkrieg, Zwei Wiener Kampfbroschüren', *Allgemeine Musik-Zeitung*, Berlin, 36 (1908–9): 9, 179.

[154] In the article 'Mahlers Feinde' (Mahler's Enemies) in the review *Der Anbruch*, 2 (1920): 7/8, 278).

[155] On 16 Oct. 1907, Karl Kraus in *Die Fackel* praised an essay by Hirschfeld on Wedekind. Schoenberg immediately wrote to him complaining that this 'repulsive philistine' had only written it so as not to 'be thrown on the scrap-heap'. For Schoenberg, it was impossible to 'have anything in common' with Hirschfeld because of 'all the journalistic offences committed by him, all his vengeful actions, all his attacks on contemporary art and artists' (cf. Friedrich Pfäfflin, *Karl Kraus und Arnold Schoenberg, Fragmente einer Beziehung: Sonderband K. Kraus* (Text und Kritik, 1975), 132). Kraus seems not to have been convinced, for on Hirschfeld's death he spoke of him, in his obituary, as 'a fine intelligent man, who hated impostors more than he could say'. See *Die Fackel*, 16 (1914): 16, 398.

Harmonielehre printed, and been a founder member of the Konzertverein Orchestra? Was it then fair to describe him, as Specht did, as 'a perpetual enemy of the new', an example of the 'jealous peevishness, morose irritability and sterile resentment of success which eradicated young blossoms as if they were weeds'?[156] Thus, thirteen years after Mahler's departure from the Opera and nine years after his death, the quarrel between his friends and enemies was still going on.

The cause of all these arguments was clearly Weingartner's determination to distance himself from his predecessor and manifest his own personality, to work 'not for the Opera but against Mahler',[157] not only in *Fidelio* but in the revivals of *Der Widerspenstigen Zähmung* and *Les Huguenots*, and of *Die Walküre* in June 1908.[158] Moreover, it soon became obvious, as mentioned earlier, that he was absenting himself from Vienna even more than Mahler, and that whereas Mahler had been bitterly criticized for the forty-two performances with guest artists given in his last year,[159] Weingartner had more than doubled this figure, with more than a hundred such guest performances in 1908 alone! There had also been objections to some of the new works chosen by Mahler, notably Erlanger's *Le Juif polonais*. But *Das süsse Gift* (The Sweet Poison) by Albert Gorter, a totally obscure composer,[160] a one-act opera first performed at the Hofoper on 28 October 1908, closed after only two nights. Indeed, the only indisputable successes put on by the new director in his first year were the new production of *Siegfried*, on which Roller collaborated, and Eugen d'Albert's *Tiefland*,[161] programmed by Mahler before he left.

The last important première of the Mahler era, at the end of October 1907, was *Madama Butterfly* which had received its world première at La Scala, in Milan, three years before. According to the diary column 'Aus der Theaterwelt' in the *Fremden-Blatt*, the English impresario who had put the work on in London in 1905 had at that time exchanged letters and telegrams with Selma Kurz in an attempt to persuade her to sing the title role. Scarcely had the contract been signed when the singer learned of the work's catastrophic première in Milan.[162] She then moved mountains to release herself from her engagement, and eventually succeeded... only to find two years later that Mahler was going to give her the same role in Vienna.[163]

---

[156] *Musikalische Kurier*, Vienna, 2 (1920): 22, 258. Graf's article was a reply to Richard Specht's article, 'Mahlers Feinde', *Musikblätter des Anbruch*, 2 (1920), 7/8, 278 ff.

[157] Joseph Reitler, 'Gustav Mahler ist tot', *Bühne und Welt*, Berlin, 13 (1911): 19, 299 ff.

[158] See below, Vol. iiii, Chap. 2.

[159] This refers to the number of performances given by 'guest' artists, not the number of artists invited.

[160] Albert Gorter (1862–1936), born in Nuremberg, was the principal Kapellmeister of the Strasbourg Theatre from 1903 to 1910 and conducted the performance of Mahler's Third Symphony in the Alsatian capital on 8 Nov. 1905 (see above, Chap. 4).

[161] The Viennese première took place on 25 Feb. 1908.

[162] The first version of the work, in two long acts, was badly received on 17 Feb. 1904, and it was the revised version, in three acts, which triumphed in Brescia the same year, and then at the Teatro d'Alverne in Milan.

[163] *Fremden-Blatt*, 8 Nov. 1907. According to this article, the publisher Ricordi was so furious over the failure at La Scala that for several months he forbade the theatre to perform Puccini's other works.

Rehearsals for *Butterfly* commenced on 1 October for a première date of 31 October, when the composer, invited by Mahler to Vienna,[164] would be present. The public gave the new opera a triumphant reception, but the critics in no way shared its enthusiasm. Elsa Bienenfeld, spokeswoman for the Viennese avant-garde, found Puccini's music 'thin rather than delicate' and lyric rather than dramatic. She criticized the poverty of his harmonization, orchestration, and polyphony, and the 'absence of firm bass lines and inner parts', though she acknowledged that the work had had an 'enormous' success and that Roller's sets were exceptionally beautiful. But Korngold, in the *Neue Freie Presse*, discerned in Puccini 'the most authentic melodic gift' of modern Italy. The score, despite its 'sentimental monotony', was full of taste and delicacy, 'eminently theatrical, lively, witty, showing off the voice, and in the best passages deeply felt'. Other papers stressed Selma Kurz's personal triumph. 'From the vocal point of view she is at the height of her powers. Her acting assumed with surprising ease the continual movements and gestures and the rapid footsteps proper to the role of the little Japanese girl,' wrote Maximilian Muntz, who also praised the 'wonderful details' that Roller brought into his 'authentic picture of Japanese life'. Hans Puchstein felt that the presence of the composer had contributed much to the success of the staging. According to him, Mahler's absence had enabled August Stoll, titular producer at the Opera, to emerge from 'the undeserved humiliation of his position'.

For Wallaschek, *Butterfly* was a richer work, musically speaking, than *Tosca*. He too was astonished that Selma Kurz could have adapted so well to the role of an 'agile, nimble and dainty doll', the more so since the vocal writing contained no ornamentation with which to display her coloratura agility. This critic's only exception to the staging was that it 'conformed to custom' by making the Japanese seem like 'clowns'. As for David Josef Bach, he saw in Puccini the makings of a 'true artist', close in sentiment to the German Romantics. The success of *Madama Butterfly* did not fade. Indeed, it grew as the months went by, so much so that the work was performed sixty-two times during the three years that followed. As we have seen above, this one opera enabled Weingartner to solve many of the problems with the repertory that arose during the early months of his directorship.[165] The day after the

---

[164]   Letter to Puccini from Mahler, 17 Oct., HOA Z. 1020. In a note dated 8 June, the official acting as Intendant, Hofrat Viktor Horsetzky, suggested that if Mahler believed the work would be successful, the particular conditions laid down by Ricordi, who wanted 6 per cent of the takings (as opposed to 5 per cent, the usual figure at the Vienna Opera), should be accepted.

[165]   Cast for the first performance on 31 Oct., conducted by Francisco Spetrino: Kurz (Cio-Cio-San); Kittel (Suzuki); Maikl (Pinkerton); Breuer (Goro); Weidemann (Sharpless). Alma Mahler wrongly gives the date of this première as 1902 (AMM1, 51; AMM2, 63). She confirms that Puccini attended the final rehearsals but wrongly asserts that Mahler was there too. According to her, Puccini asked him to be presented to the two arch-duchesses who watched the dress rehearsal from the imperial box, and Mahler had reluctantly agreed. Actually Mahler left Vienna ten days before the première of *Butterfly*. Alma might have been thought to be confusing the première with that of *La Bohème* in Nov. 1903, but we know that Puccini then declined an invitation to attend (see above, Vol. ii, Chap. 15).

première, before leaving Vienna, Puccini wrote to Mahler: '*Illustre Maestro*, Infinite thanks for all you did for my *Butterfly* at the Imperial Opera. I am indebted to you for having my opera performed in the leading theatre of this country. Please accept my gratitude and my respectful greetings, your much obliged Giacomo Puccini.'[166]

Before leaving for Russia, Mahler chose, for his farewell performance at the Vienna Opera his favourite work, *Fidelio*. All the arrangements for his future had now been made, and he was determined to avoid at any price the demonstrations customary at 'farewell performances'. He kept his planned public appearance a secret. 'I must report,' wrote Alma of this *Fidelio* and of the November farewell concert,[167] 'that these last performances were *empty*, so that Mahler had the additional mortification of being abandoned by the public.' This assertion is somewhat inaccurate in two respects. *Fidelio* was a work which had never been very popular in Vienna, and in any case the name of the conductor was never disclosed beforehand. As for the performance of the Second Symphony on 24 November, we shall see that there were full houses for both the public rehearsal and the concert.

One of Mahler's last letters to the Intendant's office dates from 15 October and concerns precisely this final performance of *Fidelio*, in which Georg Maikl sang Florestan because Schmedes was still unwell. Mahler explains that the young tenor had to pick up the role at the last minute, having sung it only once before, in 1906, and that because of it he had been obliged to sing on four successive nights without a break.[168] In his opinion such an exploit merited a special payment of 300 florins and an increase in salary. His salary, was in fact less than that of some of his colleagues, such as Leuer and Breuer. Yet not only did he sing more important roles: he was also a 'fine, conscientious member of the company'. If some sort of gesture was not made he was likely to be discouraged and leave.[169] This eloquent pleading by Mahler in favour of a young member of the Hofoper ensemble once again does much to belie the frequent criticism he had to endure concerning his 'lack of regard' and 'inhumanity' in dealing with his subordinates.

On 15 October 1907 Mahler left the podium of the Vienna Opera after having conducted 649 performances there, 62 of which he had rehearsed and prepared himself.[170] Four days later, on the evening of 19 October, he set off

---

[166] HOA Z. 1020/1907, letter of 1 Nov. 1907, on paper from Vienna's Hotel Bristol. Just as he was leaving for Russia, Mahler asked the Intendant's office to extend Francisco Spetrino's contract, which was about to come to an end. Spetrino had just conducted, and rehearsed in Italian, the three works for Caruso's *Gastspiel*, and was needed to carry on conducting *Butterfly*.   [167] See below.

[168] *Faust* on 12 Oct.; a rehearsal for *Butterfly* on the 13th; *Cavalleria Rusticana* on the 14th; and *Fidelio* on the 15th.

[169] In fact Maikl stayed at the Hofoper until his death, and was eventually awarded the rank of Kammersänger.

[170] See Franz Willnauer, 'Mahler und das Opernschaffen seiner Zeit', in Carmen Ottner (ed.), *Oper in Wien 1900–1925: Symposium 1989* (Doblinger, Vienna, 1991), 86. Willnauer adds that Mahler had taken the artistic responsibility for 191 premières, 62 of which he had conducted himself; 24 of them were either world or Viennese premières.

for Russia to conduct two concerts eleven days apart in St Petersburg, and a
third one in between in Helsingfors (now Helsinki).[171] He sent a first card to
his wife on the morning of the 20th, from the station in Warsaw, after an 'excellent' night. He was struck, as he had been five years earlier, by the dirtiness of
the station. Again he did not have time to look at the town,[172] although the
change of trains took two hours.

With great reluctance I ordered a cup of tea, which was served by a very churlish
waiter in a greasy coat and a filthy shirt. I could not bring myself to order anything else
from the fly-infested buffet (even at this time of the year Warsaw manages to produce
a wealth of blowflies). But I took my treasures out of the suitcase and kept myself
happy for an hour.[173] Then I walked up and down looking for our old Jew. I couldn't
find him, but quite a lot of young ones instead (I decided not to bring you one as a
souvenir). However, I had my money's worth of entertainment. There is something very
exotic about the sight of such totally foreign types. You want to ask every single one
who he is, what he does, dreams, hopes. Young and old rushed in all directions. I was
extremely interested by a company of women—three generations—two old ones, one
middle-aged (very nice) and three flappers like organ pipes,[174] the eldest with a charming, very tall young man—all Slav types; they kept on moving to various parts of the
station, engaged in conversation, yet they didn't take the train. What were they doing
there, I wonder?[175]

Arriving in St Petersburg on 21 October after a further twenty-four hours in
the train, during which he again worked on the Fifth Symphony, Mahler was
met at the station, as in 1902, by his cousin, the engraver Gustav Frank, who
took him to the Hotel d'Angleterre.[176] His room, overlooking the courtyard, was
next to the one he had shared with Alma five years before. Unfortunately it was
noisy, and he feared for his sleep. At five in the evening, after a long rest, he
went for a walk with Frank and was taken back to his home for a family dinner.
Although Frank's children got on his nerves, Mahler found his cousin 'still the
same sweet man, rather philistine'[177] and added: 'He is longing to get away and
can hardly bear it any more. He is probably going to forfeit his pension (by the
way, he is actually an Excellency) and move to Munich.'[178]

---

[171]   Mahler wrote to the Intendant's office on 5 Oct. explaining that he had tried to cancel his visit to
Russia, which was to have taken place in Dec. but that having failed in this he had had to bring the dates
forward. The number of concerts was thus reduced to three, on 26 Oct., and 2 and 6 Nov. (HOA Z. 995/1907,
letter signed by Wondra, 5 Nov.).

[172]   BGA no. 233, postmarked 20 Oct. 1907 (7 Oct. Russian style), Sotheby catalogue, 29 Nov. 1985,
no. 148; and Stargardt catalogue, 9 Mar. 1988, nos. 641, 915.

[173]   Probably the score and orchestral parts for the Fifth Symphony (possibly Alma's copy), which Mahler
was once again correcting before the St Petersburg concert. Later on, in the same letter, he tells of spending most of the day-hours in the train correcting the score and parts of the Fifth.

[174]   This current German expression means of decreasing (or increasing) size.

[175]   BGA, no. 236, undated (22 Oct. 1907).

[176]   Now the Hotel Astoria, on Isakievskaya Square.

[177]   This sentence was deleted by Alma in AMM.

[178]   In 1911 Frank fulfilled his intention of leaving Russia and settled from then on in Munich. See Ina
Barsova, 'Mahler und Russland', *Muziek & Wetenschap*, 5 (1995–6): 3, 289.

Gustav Frank had come to Russia in 1890 as a member of a group of engravers from Western Europe who had been invited there as part of a larger plan to improve the quality of Russian engravings. In 1899 he had become a member of the Imperial Russian Academy of Arts, and by 1907 his work had been rewarded with a title of 'Secretary without portfolio, fourth grade—State Counsellor'. The Russian musicologist Ina Barsova was able to draw up a list of his principal engravings and drawings, whose subjects include three Czars, several Grand-Dukes, as well as a number of writers and artists.[179] Thanks to Frank, Mahler had been introduced in 1902 to a few high personages of St Petersburg society such as Grand-Duke Konstantin, a music-lover and talented poet in his own right, and president of the Russian Imperial Music Society, and Duke George of Mecklenburg-Strelitz, a German nobleman who had made a fortune in Russia and financed his own string quartet.[180] Despite his successful career there, Gustav Frank was feeling less and less at home in Russia and, as Mahler wrote to Alma, he was now planning to return to Western Europe.

Musical life in St Petersburg was flourishing at that time, certainly as far as symphony concerts were concerned, but it suffered, until the second decade of the twentieth century, from two handicaps, the ultra-conservative tastes of Russian high society and the lack of first-rate conductors. The Imperial Russian Music Society had been founded in 1859 on the initiative of Anton Gregorievich Rubinstein. At the beginning of the twentieth century it was still the main artistic institution in Russia, had established branches and founded the first Russian conservatories in all the main cities. In St Petersburg, it gave ten orchestral concerts a year in the sumptuous Hall of the Assembly of Russian Nobility. However, its very conservative programmes deliberately avoided any works other than those in the general repertory. Consequently they appealed less and less to the general concert-going public of the capital and had finally closed down by the time Mahler returned to Russia in 1907.[181]

In the second half of the nineteenth century, the famous Russian industrialist, music publisher, and immensely wealthy Maecena Mitrophan Belayev (1836–1903) had started his own series of orchestral concerts in 1885, the Russian Public Symphony Concerts, whose self-appointed mission was mainly to perform new Russian music, especially that of the Five. They lasted until the Revolution. Unfortunately Belayev's concerts were often badly conducted by composers such as Rimsky-Korsakov, Lyadov, and Glazunov, whose podium technique was unprofessional. Thus the concerts were often poorly attended, and soon incurred large deficits, paid of course by the ever generous Belayev.

Another concert series had been initiated by a wealthy Russian nobleman,

---

[179] The list includes Emperors Alexander II, Alexander III, and Nicolas II, and the Grand-Duke Konstantin Romanov, as well as Leon Tolstoy, Eleonora Duse, etc.

[180] See Barsova, 'Mahler und Russland', and Aloys Mooser, *Souvenirs: Genève 1886–96, St. Pétersbourg 1896–1909* (Georg, Geneva, 1994), 133.

[181] *Russkaya Muzykalnaya Gazeta*, 42 (21 Oct. 1907), 938.

Count Alexander Dimitrievich Cheremetyev. In 1882 he had formed a sixty-musician orchestra of his own and later on, in 1898, organized a series of popular orchestral concerts. By 1906, Count Cheremetyev's orchestra had performed 100 concerts,[182] had given early performances of Wagnerian excerpts and important premières such as that of Sibelius's First Symphony, and Mahler's Second (under Oskar Fried) and classical and modern oratorios. Unfortunately Mikhail Vladimirov, the conductor of the series, was also second-rate, thus the artistic level of the concerts was low, and the public was attracted mainly by the low prices of the seats.

The situation was thus ripe for reform, and particularly for symphony concerts with more adventurous programmes on the one hand and first-rate foreign conductors on the other. The first requirement was fulfilled from 1903, by Alexander Ilyich Siloti's subscription concerts. Siloti had married the daughter of a wealthy benefactor of the arts, who provided financial support. His concerts appealed to the liberal intelligentsia of the capital, all the more so because they took place in the same hall as those of the Imperial Society, that of the Assembly of Russian Nobility, in which the acoustics were superior to those of the Conservatory Hall. During the 1903–4 season, the success of Siloti's first five concerts was such that their number was soon increased to six, and then to eight. Siloti was the first to give not only concert performances of the final scenes of *Tristan* and *Walküre*, but also premières of new compositions by Arensky, Liadov, Rachmaninov (Siloti's cousin), and even Tcherepnine. Of the French school, he performed works by Bruneau, Charpentier, d'Indy, Chausson, Dukas, Magnard, and Debussy, and of the German, Strauss, Schillings, Reger, and Humperdinck. As a conductor, Siloti was self-taught and his conducting technique was not that of a true professional but he did have a rare gift for transmitting his own enthusiasm to the musicians. Furthermore, he sometimes invited foreign conductors and, as we have seen, had tried hard to convince Mahler to accept his rather than Schröder's—invitation.

By 1907 the need was felt in St Petersburg for a new series of concerts which would regularly introduce foreign virtuoso conductors to the public of the capital. According to the *Muzykal'ny Truzhenik* (The Musical Worker), the concert series was at first to have been organized by the Marinsky Theatre's orchestra itself[183] but it was later decided to use the Marinsky orchestra, but enlist the help of a professional impresario, who was the head of the piano-firm C. M. Schröder.

The first contact between Mahler and the musicians, on the morning of 22 October, went off very well:

[182] One of them had included Mahler's Second Symphony in 1906, under Oskar Fried.

[183] The *Muzykal'ny Truzhenik* on 1 Aug. said that two concerts were planned, one conducted by Artur Nikisch, the other by Mahler. However, the 15 Oct. issue announced instead four Schröder concerts performed by the Imperial Marinsky Opera Orchestra to be conducted respectively by Gustav Brecher (from Hamburg), Hermann Westler (from New York), Oskar Fried (from Berlin), and Gustav Mahler (from Vienna).

The orchestra received me very warmly, rehearsed extremely well and at the end was full of enthusiasm. Afterwards I went back to the hotel and was about to sit down to lunch when old Madam Abaza[184] turned up: she very much wanted me to lunch with her. I declined, but promised to come another time. She looks very well, and seemed to need to talk with me. Although I was hungry and not very communicative, there was no getting rid of her. There was something peculiar about her conversation: she came to me as to a spiritual adviser; she seems very afraid of death and would like to know what happens afterwards. Something I said five years ago must have stayed with her. And it was as if she had been waiting impatiently for five years to take up where we had left off. She said of my Second Symphony that she had found it very extraordinary and that it had left such an impression on her. I asked if she remembered the text. She asked, 'Is there a text? The way the chorus sang, one couldn't make out the text.' I: 'Read it and you will find the answer to your questions.' She: 'I must have it.' And off she went straight away—no doubt to a music shop to get it.[185]

When she had gone, Mahler took lunch, finding that the food at the Hotel d'Angleterre was not as good as before, which made him consider changing to the Hotel de l'Europe on his return from Helsingfors. The pianist Ossip Gabrilovich, whom Mahler had met in Essen the year before, had become one of his most ardent new admirers, and had made him a present of a basket of apples. He had also sent him his younger brother Artur, a young lawyer who kept him company each day, alternating with Gustav Frank. 'Just like his brother in his incredible delicacy and his sweet way of attending to every detail.'[186] 'Do you remember,' he wrote to Alma on the 22nd, 'that peculiar smell that is everywhere in Russia, even on the train? A mixture of wood smoke and Russia leather? It reminds me all the time of when we were here together.' Even the room he had shared with Alma made Mahler nostalgic: 'I wander about the hotel. I feel positively angry if I see anyone come out of no. 28 on the second floor. Today, as I was going up to my third floor room, out came a woman in curlers! I was very nearly rude!'[187]

Mahler worried from afar about Alma's health. She had had a 'nervous attack' and had had to see her doctor, Friedrich Kovacs:

You are still young, you **must** shake it off! Good lord, when I think what I would do to get rid of my defects, and you give in after a fortnight. Rest while I am away, and use this time to improve your health![188] . . . Be **good** now, and don't do anything silly (*lumpe*

---

[184] See above, Vol. ii, Chap. 7.

[185] BGA, no. 236, undated (22 Oct. 1907). According to a letter written by Joseph Rubinstein to Wagner on 24 Feb. 1872, Cosima Wagner met Julia (or Yuliya) Fyodorovna Abaza, née Stube (?–1915), a singer and patron of German origin, who had been a friend of Tchaikovsky's. She is mentioned in his diary, and in Mar. 1879 there had been an avant-première performance, in costume, of *Eugene Onegin* at her house (see David Brown, *Tchaikovsky: The Crisis Years, 1874–1878* (Gollancz, London, 1983), 180). Julia Abbaza had obviously heard the first Russian performance of Mahler's Second Symphony under Fried in November 1906.

[186] See above, Chap. 6 and BGA, nos. 235 and 237, undated (21 and 24 Oct. 1907).

[187] BGA, no. 237.

[188] Ibid. In the same letter Mahler advises his wife to wait until he returns before taking a decision about a building site that appeals to her in Heiligenstadt (not far from the Hohe Warte).

nicht),[189] even if you start feeling better. You must be well for America. In any case I am confidently hoping that the sea trip, and our stay over there <u>sine cura</u>, will do you good.[190]

Mahler was anxious about Alma during most of his stay in Russia and Finland, for she had stopped writing letters, and merely sent telegrams saying 'All is well'. 'There must be a reason for your silence', he wrote on the 25th.[191] 'Please let me know through Mama or Justi what is wrong. Time drags terribly on this visit. Tomorrow it will only be a week since I left and it already seems like three.'

So far the rehearsal schedule, between nine and twelve o'clock each day, had prevented Mahler from visiting the Hermitage Museum, for after lunching with Gabrilovich he always rested, on the advice of his doctors, until five o'clock, when Frank came to fetch him for a walk in the town. 'The orchestra here is really charming and warm towards me', he wrote. 'You would be amazed at how nice people are.' The final rehearsal on 25 October went very well. That evening the members of the committee came and asked him if he would conduct a benefit concert for the orchestra the following year. Mahler was already contemplating a return to Russia in October 1908, before he left again for the United States, to conduct concerts and operas.[192]

The 26 October concert, held in the Conservatory hall,[193] was acknowledged by Mahler himself as a 'colossal success'. The programme, relatively short for those times, included Beethoven's Seventh Symphony, the *Carnaval romain* Overture by Berlioz and, to finish, the Prelude to *Die Meistersinger*. The programme Mahler had proposed to Norbert Salter at the beginning of October had also featured the 'Prelude and Liebestod' from *Tristan*, which he conducted in the second concert and in Helsingfors. It was customary for a soloist to appear at each concert. Mahler had suggested that the solo contribution be divided in two, before and after the overture which was in the middle of the programme, but Schröder inserted the solos after the symphony. They were sung on this occasion by Tilly Koehnen, the Dutch contralto who had participated in Mahler's last concert in Munich and who had also performed the *Kindertotenlieder* in her Berlin recital early in the year. She sang Beethoven's *Ah perfido!* followed by three orchestral Lieder.[194]

---

[189]　*Lumpen*, in Austria, means more or less 'to go out and have a good time', to live it up. One wonders what Mahler was referring to with his *lumpe nicht*. From the care Alma took to cross out various passages in his letters it seems certain that there was something concerning herself that she wanted to keep secret from posterity. Could it have been her budding fondness for alcohol?

[190]　BGA, no. 237.　　　　　　　　　　　　　[191]　BGA, no. 238, undated (24? Oct. 1907).

[192]　BGA, nos. 239 and 240, undated (25 and 28 Oct.).

[193]　*Russkaya Muzykalnaya Gazeta*, 42 (21 Oct. 1907), 938. The Schröder Concerts took place in the Conservatory hall, a vast theatre with 2,000 seats. The concert on 26 Oct. was the first of the season. The net takings of these concerts went to the 'Mutual Aid Society for Impoverished Conservatory Students'.

[194]　See above, Chap. 7. Two of Tilly Koehnen's solo numbers had been performed at the Munich concert in Nov. 1906 ('Hymnus' by Richard Strauss and 'Er ist's', from Hugo Wolf's *Mörike Lieder*). Only the third song was new. It was 'Die Musikantin' by Max Fiedler, a conductor Mahler had known well in

Of all the articles which appeared in the St Petersburg press, the one written by Alexander Ossovsky for the daily *Slovo* (The Word)[195] was the most substantial, and also the most important since its author was the most influential critic in the Russian capital:

An iron will. Powerful emotions. Mighty ideas. And above all, the stamp of majestic mastery. That is Mahler,

> A broad winged inspiration
> The eagle's daring flight.

The oval of his face and the line of his profile are reminiscent of ancient Egypt. Now we see Ramses III and now Sesostris the Great, and that same mercilessness so evident among Egypt's rulers. As if it were a huge vice, a giant's hand grips your soul, casts it down to Hell, reaches it up to Heaven, drives your feelings to breaking point, but to all your entreaties for mercy there is the one same response: 'Resign yourself to your fate, helpless creature! This is how I will it to be!'

Satan and God have taken up abode in this apparently fragile body and there they struggle for possession of its soul, but neither of them, it seems, can triumph. There stands behind them yet a third—the recalcitrant and proud human 'ego', which has experienced the whole range of crests and troughs, gazing the while upon the struggle, undaunted.

By and large, there is something overpowering and uncanny, something that cannot be confined to the limits of our present age. I should say that this is something 'Michelangelo-like', for which there are no words or paints, which only chiselled stone or a work in bronze can convey.

And this something is realized in sounds. Itself elemental, it is akin to that most elemental of arts—to music. Gustav Mahler directs the orchestra, and if the secret of holding sway over the masses lies in the power of suggestion, then Mahler is a mesmerist of genius. You seem to feel directly, yes almost see, the magical current emanating from the conductor to your soul.

This small man stands awkwardly on the podium, and makes magic incantations over your soul. His small eyes burn with a satanic fire, after throwing a predatory

Hamburg. Among the proposals Mahler sent to Salter in Oct., the programmes suggested for Moscow had been either this one (with the *Coriolan* Overture replacing the Berlioz) or the second St Petersburg programme (with the Prelude to *Meistersinger* instead of the *Tristan* excerpts). At that time Mahler envisaged conducting more or less the same programme in Warsaw around 12 Nov. (undated letter to Salter, written in Wiesbaden on 7 or 8 Oct., BSM, Munich).

[195]   Alexander Viasheslavovich Ossovsky (1871–1957), musicologist and historian, born in Kichiniov, son of a lawyer, studied law and music simultaneously in Moscow. He studied composition under Rimsky-Korsakov at the St Petersburg Conservatory (1896–8), and remained on friendly terms with him until his death. In 1894 he became a music critic for the newspaper *Slovo* and the journals *Artist* and *Russkaya Muzykalnaya Gazeta*. He wrote programme notes for Siloti Concerts between 1906 and 1917. Professor of the History of Music and Aesthetics at the St Petersburg Conservatory from 1916, he taught for two years after the Revolution at the Kiev and Odessa Conservatories (1919–21). An opera studio was set up and run by him at the Leningrad Conservatory, which he directed during Glazunov's illness. Director of the State Philharmonic from 1923 and the State Institute for Theatre and Music (1943), Ossovsky translated the memoirs of Berlioz and Gounod into Russian. He left a considerable number of books and articles, notably on *Bach* (1907); *Glazounov* (1907); *Historic Russian Concerts* (Paris, 1907); *Belayev and his Editions* (1910); *The World Role of Russian Classical Music* (1948); *Glinka, Research and Documents* (1950). An anthology of his articles was published in 1961 (see below).

glance, as an eagle does with his prey, upon the host of musicians under his command. An obstinate chin, stern and broad, juts forward. His jaws are convulsively clenched. He nervously grinds his teeth in a superhuman effort of will-power and feeling; his hands make abrupt and decisive motions to which the eye is not accustomed. There is an atmosphere of apprehension. Even the musicians follow their master with utmost attention, as though the new Ramses was threatening them with some kind of terrible punishment, and they expend so much nervous energy producing their sounds that they will later recall this performance as they would a nightmare in which it was not they who were playing, but rather some demon inhabiting them.

And the fullness of Mahler's orchestral sound is indeed marvellous, a fullness of emotion, of thought, of will-power, of expression—I cannot define it further, but Mahler simply knows no unsignificant sounds. In each and every one of them resides a part of Mahler's very soul. And the impression being experienced is so much deeper that one thing is clear: this man does not exhaust his soul before us, a soul in the midst of which terrible forces collide, hot blood boils in his veins, curbed only by a powerful will. It is the beauty of Vesuvius, beneath whose restraining crust the gurgling of the subterranean forces of Hell can be felt. We are gripped by the horror he arouses in us, and are reminded of Dostoevskian psychology.

Among contemporary European conductors there is undoubtedly no other whose personality could be considered so much in harmony with the inspirations of that other Titan of feeling, thought, and will-power, Beethoven:

> By the mighty efforts of his will-power
> He, like a god, created world upon world,
> Through agonising dreams despondent,
> Impatient, gloomy, utterly alone.[196]

And this was how Mahler was creative in his concert. How forceful and beautiful as well as deep and crushing was, for example, his performance of the Seventh Symphony, that most Hellenic of Beethoven's works because of the divine proportionality of its structure and the clarity of spirit imprinted on it. And yet, in Mahler's rendering, this laughing and sun-flooded ocean of sounds was austere and grand, for beneath a gentle surface bottomless depths and crushing power could be discerned. And under Mahler's baton, this more than a hundred-year-old work seemed young and fresh, as if born yesterday. It is the same force and the same freshness that rang out in Wagner's very familiar Overture to *Die Meistersinger*.

Mahler simply cannot be otherwise. He himself lives everything he is peforming. He makes everything his own and, thus transfigured by his personality, the work appears so vivid and full of individual features, as if it were a living organism. Mahler is a powerful artistic force, such as one rarely encounters in the history of the arts. He imposes his own individual and indelible seal on whatever he touches. No school, no tradition, no style can withstand the imprint of his leonine paw. All his ideas and conceptions, down to the smallest detail, are strictly his own; they belong to a stubborn and solitary character. Mahler refuses to change works of art into stylistic mummies. What of it? In his interpretation, each work is different from the other, each has a life

---

[196] The author of this poem remains to be identified.

of its own. For example, he contrasts Mozart with Beethoven, Weber with Tchaikovsky (I am using for this comparison works that Mahler performed on his first visit to St Petersburg five years ago). The secret behind this unity and diversity resides in the total fusion of the artist with the work he is performing. And for this reason Mahler seems to me so clear and uncomplicated, and so convincing. He does not rely on effect for the sake of effect, nor does he attempt to display more than is actually there. Even his gestures are sober and straightforward, as those of a figure in an Assyrian bas-relief. Even when receiving an ovation he bows reluctantly and somewhat angrily. It was not for applause that he has dedicated himself to art. He is a man of ideas, invested with a sacred mission.

This explains why, with the final chord of Mahler's last concert, we experienced a feeling of joy, of completeness, of spiritual exaltation. The sounds which had faded away had not only been heard, they had been understood and lived. A new precious treasure had enriched our mind and our soul, a new light had shone in the depths ... Therein lies all the joyful revelation of art.[197]

This long review, whose style and contents awaken memories of the great critics of the Romantic era, notably Schumann, reveals in its author a sensibility, culture, and perspicacity exceptional at the time. It shows that, far from Vienna and from the pettiness and prejudice of old Austria, Mahler's rejection of tradition and his determination as an interpreter to 're-create' the music to which he was devoting himself, could be understood and appreciated, and not taken as an affront to the past. Mahler's concerts remained very much alive in the memory of Ossovsky. Probably in the same year, on the occasion of Nikisch's visit to St Petersburg he wrote:

Not long ago we were lifted to these heights by other means. Through other vistas, our hearts filled with horror, we found ourselves staring at primeval chaos. And the man who brought this about was no less a genius than the great Artur.[198] But Nikisch is a proud Titan: Gustav Mahler, on the other hand, is a hero who bends everything to his will, and has the mentality of an eagle. Nikisch forces us to submit to his granite-like power, whereas we submit of our own volition to Mahler's power. Because he is profoundly human.[199]

Yet even in St Petersburg Mahler the conductor was not received by all with the same admiration. After Mahler's second concert, Alexander Siloti, who, as we have seen, had himself wanted to engage Mahler for three concerts at this time, wrote a letter to Ossovsky with the chief aim of upbraiding him for his enthusiasm:[200]

My dear Fifi, Yesterday I saw you at a distance and yet I so much needed to talk to you! . . . I want to pester you on the subject of Mahler the conductor, because I do not

[197] *Slovo* (The Word), 21 Oct. 1907 (3 Nov. in our calendar). I am particularly grateful to Colman W. Kraft for having translated this article for me at short notice.
[198] This refers to Nikisch.
[199] Alexander Ossovsky, *Selected articles and correspondence* (E. Bronfin, Leningrad 1968 edn.), 276.
[200] Siloti's concert, on 31 Oct. (Western style), had been a resounding failure.

care what K[olomitsov][201] will write but I do care what <u>you</u> have written. Put your hand on your heart and admit that Mahler's second debut should have been less satisfying to you [than the first]: *Coriolanus* was technically better than Siloti's, but <u>not Tristan</u>. However Siloti, the young conductor whose aspirations outstrip his performances, Siloti has conducted *Coriolanus* only once, *Tristan* twice, Mahler fifty to a hundred times. I bow to Mahler's musicianship, but his performances offer tremendous technique and no <u>spontaneous talent</u>, something which, despite his prima donna tendencies and his fondness for hackneyed pieces, obviously abounds in a man like N[ikisch]. On my way to hear Mahler I was preparing myself to think poorly of <u>Nikisch</u>. But on leaving the concert, I thought even more highly of Nikisch than before.

Since M[ahler] was using doubled winds, I was awaiting *Tristan* with pleasurable impatience. As a <u>man</u> I was happy [that he was no better than me], but as a <u>musician</u> I was sad. (You know me, and will trust the sincerity of my feelings.) M[ahler] and N[ikisch] both have established reputations. For me there is <u>hope</u> only in the <u>future</u>. (Only this hope gives me the strength to work—regardless of the press's barking.) With all my poverty, I would not change places with M[ahler]. With enormous <u>musical jealousy</u> I will revel as I listen to N[ikisch].

I shall remain forever grateful to Mahler for giving me a lesson in conducting technique, but as far as interpretation goes, that is to say <u>spontaneous creation</u>, its metal is silver, not gold.

To say that I did not understand *Tristan* is incorrect, since I was the one to say that *Coriolan* was better. And here is further proof: the crowd in itself does not understand anything, but feels things unconsciously as if by wireless telegraphy. It applauds <u>mindlessly</u> and this crowd which knew *Tristan* by heart applauded <u>differently</u>, even though *Tristan* is infinitely more brilliant than *Coriolanus*. You, too, you have often accused me of taking liberties with the tempos. Well! After yesterday's *Coriolanus* there should be no more such criticism of the insignificant pup I am as a conductor. Once again I repeat: the difference between M[ahler] and N[ikisch] is the same as between Rubinstein and Bülow. And I <u>bow</u> before Bülowism whereas I <u>melt</u> before Rubinsteinism (I mean Bülow as pianist, for his conducting is quite another matter).[202] Well, I've told you everything that was on my mind and I feel relieved. I'd so much like a talk with you, a long talk![203]

[201] Viktor Pavlovich Kolomitsov (1868–1936). Here Mahler's accusation, instigated by Fried, that Siloti was dishonest, finds support. Actually Siloti was the critic's close friend, and wrote him many letters thanking him for his articles. Unfortunately the author has been unable to find the article Kolomitsov wrote about Mahler on this occasion, probably in the paper *Oko* (The Eye). He made the following remarks in the paper *Novaya Russ'* (New Russia) on 25 Jan. 1910, after Mottl had conducted Beethoven's Seventh Symphony in St Petersburg: 'Mottl also showed that he is a remarkable artist in the symphonic domain. Admittedly, in the Seventh Symphony he was unable to make us forget Mahler, who only recently astounded us with his "demonic" interpretation of this same symphony. One can delight endlessly in the sensations Mottl evokes, but one can hardly be said to "learn" anything from him. He is not like Mahler, who backs up in rehearsals the views he has formulated with so much logic, strength and conviction. Mottl operates directly by the intuition that springs from his immense talent, an intuition which often cannot be articulated but which he succeeds in communicating both to the players and the audience.'

[202] In German in the text.

[203] Letter from Alexander Siloti to Alexander Ossovsky, 28 Oct. (10 Nov.) 1907: Alexander Siloti, *Letters and Recollections* (Leningrad, 1963), 235. Siloti adds that in the interval, Glazunov congratulated him for not having engaged Mahler. He also says that Schröder, when he asked him why Mahler, in his second concert, had not accompanied Pugno, had replied that 'Mahler is a mediocre accompanist; he admits it himself and it's a well-known fact'. We have seen that Hans Richter started the same rumour in Vienna, when

Thus even in a distant country the art of conducting as practised by Mahler roused controversies. But the fact that Mahler, after long hesitation, had refused Siloti's offer in favour of a rival, and the reservations expressed by Fried about Siloti's character, cast doubt on his objectivity. Ossovsky's review, on the other hand, is all the more valuable in that he had heard Mahler on two occasions only five years before, so that he was listening with a completely fresh ear. Other accounts in the Russian press were much briefer. The 'Discourse' (*Riech*) stressed the technical perfection of his performances: 'Mahler belongs to the objective and balanced school of conductors who believe in fidelity to the music. He dedicates to it all his care and all his technical mastery, serving the spirit of the composer without being drawn into the slightest subjectivity.' According to this critic, the Finale of Beethoven's Seventh was the high spot of the concert: it was 'entrancing in its joyous pathos', 'played with fire and yet with astonishing precision'. In his opinion, the Prelude to *Die Meistersinger* succeeded above all through the transparency of the orchestral texture. The *Novoye Vremia* (New Times) underlined Mahler's 'lack of affectation and false pathos' and his 'supreme clarity and exactitude' which did not exclude fire and ardour. The St Petersburg Gazette (*St-Petersburgskiye Viedomosti*) devoted more space to Tilly Koehnen's art than to Mahler's, which tells us much about the tastes of its critic, identified only by the initials A.K. For him, Mahler 'performed the Seventh Symphony particularly well, with its glorious Allegretto and its fiery Finale, sparkling with gaiety' in which he 'brought out wonderfully the grim humour and the Hungarian-style chord rhythms' (*sic*). As for the *Russkaya Muzykalnaya Gazeta*, whose article in 1902 had been the most substantial of all, it contented itself this time with reporting that Mahler had been just as successful as before and that his interpretations had had 'the same sharpness of outline', 'the same perfection, the same clarity and the same elegant simplicity' and above all 'the same wonderful graphic intensity and the same persistent, vital energy'. In particular he had rejuvenated the Berlioz Overture, giving it 'fresh colours and an honest musical soul'.

Isaiah Knorozovsky,[204] music critic of the magazine *Teatr i Iskusstvo* (Theatre and Art), recalled in his review of the concerts Mahler had given in St Petersburg in 1902. According to him these had not been successful with the mass public,

Mahler was conducting the Philharmonic Concerts (see above, Vol. ii, Chap. 5.) The source of it was probably Mahler's dislike of virtuosi and stars, and his reservations about the concerto genre itself (in particular see the comments Mahler made after hearing Joachim playing the Brahms Violin Concerto, Vol. i, Chap. 21). As it happened he did not much like Rachmaninov's music. However that may be, it is unlikely that a conductor accustomed to the infinitely more demanding discipline of the Opera would have the slightest difficulty in accompanying a concerto, something which he was to do many times in New York.

[204] Isaïe Moïsievich Knorozovsky (1858–1914), born in Grodno, died in Lausanne. After studying law at the University of St Petersburg he studied music theory and composition with L. Sacetti and Nicholas Soloviev. A lawyer and journalist, he worked on both the paper *Novosti* (The News) (1877–87) and the magazine *Teatr i Iskusstvo* (1879–1914). In 1904–5 he was also publisher and editor of *Teatral'naya Russia* (Theatrical Russia) and *Musykal'ny Mir* (Musical World).

which disliked his concentrated restraint and his tendency to slow down the tempos, which was taken for listlessness of temperament. . . . On this second visit, Gustav Mahler has displayed the same traits of his artistic nature: intense thoughtfulness, harsh sluggishness. Yet today these qualities conquered and mesmerized the public. His performances have pleased even though they went against established tradition. Take the example of Beethoven's Seventh Symphony. We know that conductors always try to perform it with grace and lightness, and playfulness. And when, right in the middle of a happy day, the silhouettes of melancholy clouds seem to loom in the Allegretto, most performers give this movement the character of a quiet elegy. Mr Mahler is quite obviously suggesting that one must be true to Beethoven's titanic nature in all its manifestations. If there is joy, it must be boundless and indomitable. If there is sadness, it must crush and overwhelm us. Touching sighs of pity are not in the character of a titan. He can only groan, and at those groans the universe shudders. The feelings of joy that a titan experiences burst forth from him like a wind-squall preceding a storm, impetuous and devastating. This view of the work leads Mahler to give the whole symphony a Dionysian face of frightening relentlessness and powerful grandeur. At the same time, because of this harshness and violence, it weighs heavily on one's soul.

Whether this interpretation pleases is a matter of subjective, individual taste. A lyrical person with a liking for softness will prefer light happiness and and quiet sadness. On the other hand, a person with a stormy nature will favour tragic accents. But the point here is no longer subjective taste or personal preference. The point is that the composition was presented to us in all its wholeness and radiance. From this point of view Mahler's conducting is beyond all praise. He captivates the listener. Listening to him, one begins to believe that only thus could the Titan Beethoven rejoice and repine. Any other interpretation seems unthinkable and against Beethoven's musical spirit.

In the Prelude to *Die Meistersinger*, the 'monumental structure was conveyed to us as if carved in a block of granite. Impossible to imagine sharper relief or greater clarity' nor, in the *Carnaval romain*, more 'brilliant expressivity or sumptuous sound'. On the other hand the same critic, in an article written at the same time about a concert given by Siloti on 20 October,[205] mocks the 'naivety' of the 'wonderful' pianist's questionable 'attempt to conduct', who need only go and listen to Mahler to understand his own insufficiency.

The day after the concert the weather was colder, and Mahler at last 'with pride and relish put on my fur coat'. 'I find the St Petersburg climate very pleasant', he wrote to Alma. 'Too bad that you're not with me!'[206] He was visited by the wife of the minister Sabouroff, whom he had met five years before, and was obliged to accept an invitation to dine with her on his return from Finland but there is no further mention of the lady in Mahler's last letters.

The following day, on arriving in Helsingfors, Mahler responded to a

[205] The programme had included Beethoven's First Symphony, Mozart's E flat Concerto, K. 482 (with a Ms Lavandowsky as soloist), Napravnik's *Folkdance Suite* Op. 20 (or Op. 23) and scenes from Mussorgsky's *Khovanshchina*, which Knorozovsky calls 'quite an untalented composition'.

[206] BGA, no. 240, undated (28 Oct. 1907).

further telegram, sent by Alma from the Semmering. He sent her his first impressions of the city: 'Helsingfors is superb because of the sea, which thrusts into the city all over the place and is visible everywhere. But I'm moping, because I can't spend much time walking: I have a long rest after rehearsals (and after meals).'[207] Before he left Vienna, Arnold Rosé had praised the hotel in the Finnish capital and its restaurant. Mahler saw in this a sign that Rosé's digestion was better than his own, as he wrote to Justi on his way back from Finland:

I have not been able to bear the heavy fatty food, and the noise in the hotel was terrible. Still, it is a beautiful city, with the sea cutting such a beautiful line into it. I like Petersburg enormously, I could easily live there, in the country. The Russians understand these things, as do the English. The Viennese, in comparison, are miserable plebeians. It's horrible to think back on our tenements, the endless smell of goulasch in the streets, the dreadful eternally blowing wind.[208]

From Helsingfors, Mahler wrote to Alma to describe his first day there:

It's pouring with rain here and I can't wear my beautiful fur coat. In the evening I went to a popular concert and got to know my orchestra. It is astonishingly good, and disciplined, which says a lot for Cajanus,[209] the conductor here, who in any case has a very good reputation in the musical world. He was here this afternoon and kept me company. A most likeable, serious, modest man. At the concert in the evening— complete with beer tables—Axel Galén[210] suddenly came and sat with me, and brought his wife. After the concert he stayed for a while talking to Cajanus and his wife

---

[207] BGA, no. 242, undated (31 Oct. 1907)

[208] Letter to Justi, undated, postmarked 27 Oct. 1907, Russian style, i.e. 7 Nov. (RWO).

[209] In the translations of Mahler's letters, I have deliberately retained the original spellings of Finnish names, for instance 'Cajanus' and 'Galén'. Robert Kajanus (1856–1933) was the initiator of modern music in Finland. A student of the Helsingfors Conservatory, he studied from 1877 to 1879 music theory and conducting in Leipzig with Hans Richter, Carl Reinecke, and Salomon Jadassohn. Between 1879 and 1880 he was in Paris, studying composition with Johan Svendsen. He made his conducting debut in Dresden in 1881–2, conducting his own works. In the same year, 1882, he founded the Philharmonic Society Orchestra of Helsingfors, which each year gave a season of symphonic concerts, popular concerts, and popular soirées, and three years later an orchestral school and a chorus. In 1900 Kajanus gave several concerts with his orchestra at the International Exhibition in Paris. In the 1920s he directed the Finnish Opera, and taught at the Royal Academy in Stockholm and at the University of Helsingfors. From his youth Kajanus was a friend of Sibelius whose chief interpreter he became, conducting his music virtually everywhere in the world. In the 1930s he was the first to record his works.

[210] Born in Björneborg (Porissa), Akseli Gallen-Kallela (1865–1931) (Mahler spells his name Galén in the letters he wrote to Alma) is still regarded as the greatest Finnish painter. He had studied mostly in Paris (1884–90), where he attended the Académie Jullian and the Atelier Cormon, and had exhibited some of his pictures at the Secession in Vienna in 1901 and 1904. In 1899–1900 Gallen had painted four frescoes on *Kalevala* subjects for the much admired Finnish pavilion of the International Exhibition in Paris, designed by three of his friends, Eliel Saarinen, Herman Gesellius, and Armas Lindgren (see below). Later on, Gallen travelled widely before and after the First World War, notably in East Africa (1923–6), the United States, and particularly in New Mexico. Like many of the Viennese Secessionists, Gallen was an artisan as well as an artist. He made and printed a great many woodcuts and designed carpets, furniture, and stained glass. He was a friend of Sibelius, Strindberg, Munch, Gorky, etc. (See the article by Anniki Toikka-Karvonen published in Gallen's centenary year, and the catalogue of the Gallen Museum, Tarvaspää, near Espoo, on the outskirts of Helsinki. The Museum's collections include many letters exchanged by Gallen between 1901 and 1904 with Karl Moll, Alfred Roller, and the other members of the Viennese Secession.)

and a pianist from Brussels.[211] Galén was in very good spirits and made a great impression on me. I made my excuses at 11 o'clock, however, and went to bed, which caused quite a stir, since people here seem to sit up half the night and even to the crack of dawn. On Saturday, the day after the concert, Galén is going to take me out on the water in his boat. Then in the evening I'll go back to St Petersburg.[212]

Akseli Gallen-Kallela was then the most famous painter in Finland. He was the first Finnish artist to break away from European influences, creating a vigorous and original style rooted in his love of nature and in national traditions. Mahler had met him in Vienna in January–February 1904, when a whole room in the Secession's nineteenth exhibition had been given over to Gallen's paintings.[213] Mahler had lent him his box at the Opera for one evening. Although Gallen had studied painting in Paris, he had returned to his native country in 1890 and, from then on, had taken his inspiration from the traditional legends of his country and drawn a series of illustrations from the *Kalevala*. In one of his most famous pictures, dating from 1894, *Symposium* (originally *The Problem*), he had portrayed himself sitting at a table with his friends Jan Sibelius and Robert Kajanus. The three artists, half-drunk, are sombrely gazing at a phantasm, a winged spectre in the foreground, probably an allegory of artistic creation.[214] Although Gallen was predominantly a symbolist, his paintings reveal at times either an expressionistic violence, or a deep, underlying melancholy which Mahler does not seem to have perceived in his personality. Gallen was a close friend of Jan Sibelius and, since two pieces of Sibelius were to be performed, it is not surprising that he should have been present that evening at the Hotel Societetshuset, where the noon and evening concerts of the Helsingfors Philharmonic took place during the autumn and winter months. Mahler wrote to Alma:

At the concert I also heard some pieces by Sibelius, the Finnish national composer they make a great fuss about, not only here but elsewhere in the musical world. One of the pieces was just ordinary 'Kitsch' spiced with certain 'Nordic' orchestral touches like a kind of national sauce. *Pui Kaki!*[215] They are the same everywhere, these national geniuses. You find them in Russia and Sweden—and in Italy the country is overrun by these whores and their ponces. Axel is made of altogether different stuff with his twelve schnapps before the soup, and his boat, and one feels that there is something genuine and robust about him and his kind.[216]

---

[211] Arthur de Greef (1862–1940), a student at the Brussels Conservatory, won a piano prize there in 1879 along with Isaac Albeniz. After working with Liszt and Saint-Saëns he became a professor at that Conservatory in 1887 and gave many concerts abroad, particularly in Paris. De Greef left compositions in various genres.   [212] BGA, no. 243, undated (2 Nov. 1907).

[213] The room exhibited five paintings and a whole series of engravings. Gallen returned to Vienna with his wife and children in 1908.

[214] See Alessandra Comini, 'By a Finnish Fireside. An evening with Mahler and Gallen-Kallela', *Muziek & Wetenschap*, Amsterdam, 5 (1995–6): 3, 327 ff.

[215] Alma explains that this was an expression of disgust used by little Gucki.

[216] BGA, no. 241, undated (30 Oct. 1907).

Despite the reservations Mahler had expressed about his music, he found Sibelius 'extremely sympathetic, like all Finns'. He had told Alma that the programme of the 'popular concert' of 19 October contained 'several pieces'. In fact only two Sibelius works were played that evening: the symphonic poem Op. 16, *Vårsång* (Spring Song),[217] composed in 1894, and the *Valse triste* from the music for the play *Küolema* Op. 44 (1903). So Mahler's verdict seems to have been based exclusively on these two fairly minor pieces. It is unfortunate that he did not hear more recent and more representative works like the Third Symphony or the Violin Concerto,[218] in which the Finnish composer was developing the more personal voice of his maturity.

The next day, Sibelius came to visit Mahler at his hotel. He later spoke of his various meetings with Mahler to his first biographer, Karl Ekman:

Mahler and I were together a great deal. His long-standing heart complaint obliged him to lead an ascetic existence, and he was not fond of ceremonial dinners and banquets. We grew close during a number of walks when we talked about all kinds of musical problems, of life and of death. When our conversation touched on the nature of the symphony, I said that I admired its style and severity of form, and the profound logic that created an inner connection between all the motives. This was my experience in the course of my creative work. Mahler's opinion was just the opposite. 'No!' he said, 'the symphony must be like the world. It must be all-embracing.'[219]

Mahler's way of life was wholly unpretentious. He was a highly interesting person: I respected him, as a human being and an artist, for his high ethical principles, even though his opinions about artistic matters differed from mine. I did not want him to think that I had come to see him merely to interest him in my compositions. When he said in his abrupt way: 'What would you like me to conduct of yours?' I answered simply 'Nothing'.[220]

---

[217] Information provided by the Finnish musicologist Nils-Eric Ringbom and the Sibelius biographer Erik Tawaststjerna (see Tawaststjerna, *Sibelius*, tr. Robert Layton (Faber, London, 1986), ii, 76).

[218] It is interesting to note that Sibelius went to St Petersburg around 10 Nov., in other words immediately after Mahler's departure, to conduct a complete programme of his works, including the first performance of his Third Symphony. In mid-Nov. 1907, a few days before performing Mahler's Second Symphony, the Konzertverein gave the first Viennese performance of Sibelius's First Symphony. It should be recalled that in 1909 Sibelius composed a big Funeral March for orchestra entitled *In Memoriam*, Op. 59, very similar in character to the opening Funeral March in Mahler's Fifth Symphony. According to Tawaststjerna, Sibelius had studied the score of this work during a visit to Berlin.

[219] Tawaststjerna, *Sibelius*, ii. 76 ff. In fact the two preoccupations coexisted in Mahler who, in Jan. 1905, declared in Webern's presence that it was possible to construct an entire work out of one motif (see above, Chap. 2). Sibelius's phrase gave birth to a whole book by Lionel Pike, *Beethoven, Sibelius and 'The Profound Logic'* (Athlone, London, 1978). In this study the author examines the 'profound logic' of the works of Sibelius in the light of the logic which governs the compositions of Beethoven. Erik Tawaststjerna observes that no symphony of Mahler's tried to be as 'all-embracing' as the Eighth, which he had just finished; and that the two composers had in common their love and awareness of nature, in whose presence they reacted very differently, since 'Mahler's music is centred on man even though his relationship with nature is an important ingredient in his make-up, whereas Sibelius's reflects an almost mystic sense of identification with nature' (Tawaststjerna, *Sibelius*, ii. 78)

[220] Karl Ekman, *Sibelius* (Kustannusosakeyhtiö, Helsinki, 1935), 185 (tr. Edward Birse (Knopf, New York, 1938), 190 ff.). See also Ernst Tanzberger, *Jean Sibelius* (Breitkopf, Wiesbaden, 1962). The programmes drawn up by Mahler and conducted during his illness between Feb. and Apr. 1911 by Theodor Spiering included the Violin Concerto Op. 47, the *Symphonic Fantasy* Op. 49, and *Pohjola's Daughter* by Sibelius in a programme entirely given over to the Slav and Scandinavian 'national' schools (together with Svendsen, Tchaikovsky, and Dvořák).

Sibelius's frame of mind during his meetings with Mahler has been explained by his modern biographer, Erik Tawaststjerna:

It is obvious from his account of their meeting that Sibelius was anxious to approach Mahler as one composer to another, rather than appear to be begging favours from an internationally celebrated conductor. There was no personal rivalry between them at this stage: others were taking care of that! Had not Sibelius's own teacher, Martin Wegelius, played off Mahler against him? And had not Busoni in all innocence spoken of the relative enthusiasm of the applause at a Berlin concert where works by Mahler and Sibelius shared the same programme? As yet, Sibelius had not been used as a stick with which to beat Mahler, but that was to come only a few weeks later, in St Petersburg.[221]

This was indeed what had happened in St Petersburg, where the première of Sibelius's Third Symphony had been a great success. The *Novoye Vremia* had much preferred it to Mahler's Fifth:

The orchestration is modern without striving for originality at all costs; if Herr Sibelius thinks that new sound combinations are appropriate to the musical material, he uses them, but if not, he refrains. In this respect he is very different indeed from a composer like Mahler, whose whole aim is to astonish us with everything he can think of. Herr Sibelius is a serious and sincere artist, without the newest Jewish composer's circus tricks nor the pretentiousness that one finds with Strauss and Mahler.[222]

According to Erik Tawaststjerna, Sibelius's words ('I did not want him to think that I had come to see him merely to interest him in my compositions')

prompt the thought that the very reverse was his intention, and that it was pride, rather than modesty and sensitivity, that caused him to answer Mahler's question with 'Nothing'.[223] Moreover, the word 'Nichts' undoubtedly sounded less modest and sensitive than he himself imagined. One could argue from the premiss that Mahler's question was a mere courtesy rather than a genuine inquiry. But the great conductor was always fascinated to hear from other composers their views on the interpretation of their own work, and no doubt looked forward to a serious and detailed discussion. In any event Sibelius's response must have seemed distinctly chilly.[224]

In his account Sibelius recalls having found Mahler occasionally brusque, even rude, when he was contradicted. 'One night Mahler wanted to eat in a restaurant called Gambrinus where the orchestra musicians went.' Sibelius advised him to choose a different, more elegant place, to which Mahler retorted: 'I shall go where I like!'[225] According to Sibelius, Mahler was in a sombre mood brought about by his heart condition, and the Helsingfors orchestra was not enthused by his presence or by his conducting. It seems that Anton Sitt, who had been Concertmaster of the orchestra for twenty-five years, even

---

[221] Tawaststjerna, *Sibelius*, ii. 77.   [222] Ibid. 80 ff.
[223] According to Tawaststjerna, a friend of the Finnish composer called Axel Carpelan had suggested he send Mahler the symphonic poem *En Saga* and the Third Symphony.   [224] Ibid. 78.
[225] Karl Ekman, *Sibelius*, 191.

said to Sibelius, with disappointment and surprise: 'And he is supposed to be the new Hans von Bülow!'[226] Nothing of this is reflected either in Mahler's letters or in press accounts. On the contrary, Evert Katila, in *Uusi Suomi* observed that 'a perfect understanding existed between the conductor and the musicians', who 'played with rare zeal and devotion'. 'There was no sign of slackness or fatigue as a result of the extra rehearsals. Everyone carried out his task with the greatest enthusiasm. The players were completely won over by the conductor, whose good nature and professionalism have left the most pleasant memories. The strings played particularly well.'[227]

All the critics were struck by the surprising economy of gesture that was henceforth to characterize Mahler's conducting, even though he had been given only two days to rehearse. During these sessions, he 'used thousands of inspired gestures. . . . Before the public, he withdraws into himself. Things decided in rehearsal become a sort of secret between the conductor and his players. In a concert he keeps his distance, and his professorial appearance only rarely gives way to flashes of lightning. He is aware that the orchestra knows its task.' The same critic, K. F. Wasenius,[228] emphasized that Mahler never tried to curry favour with 'elegant gestures'. His face expressed 'extreme tension. Few conductors are capable, as he is, of obtaining such powerful crescendos and accelerandos with such restricted means. With iron determination, he thinks only of what he is in the process of doing.'[229] Yet 'he is aware of each player, and collaborates with him in his efforts towards a harmonious ensemble.'[230]

In a letter to Alma, Mahler describes the audience for the concert on 1 November, and proudly adds that people had come to listen to him from all over Finland.[231] The press confirms his enthusiastic report and adds that he was greeted by a fanfare as well as the usual applause.[232] This he met, as usual, with more impatience than pleasure, and attacked straightaway the opening bars of Beethoven's Fifth Symphony. The rest of the programme was the same as in Wiesbaden the previous month. The *Coriolan* Overture was followed by the 'Prelude and Liebestod' from *Tristan* and the Prelude to *Die Meistersinger*. During the thunderous ovation at the end of the evening he was presented with two laurel crowns.[233] He said himself that these touched him less than 'the applause of the audience, which seemed to have understood his art perfectly'. As usual, he took only two or three bows after each item on the programme.

Reviews in the Finnish press indicate the amount of interest and curiosity Mahler's conducting and interpretations had aroused in Helsingfors. Karl

[226] Tawaststjerna, *Sibelius*, ii. 77.   [227] Evert Katila, in *Uusi Suomi*, 2 Nov.
[228] According to Harold Johnson (*Sibelius* (Faber, London, 1959), 79), K. F. Wasenius was both a critic and a seller of sheet music. Erik Tawaststjerna (op. cit., 170) says that his articles in *Hufvudstadsbladet* were signed 'Bis'.   [229] *Hufvudstadsbladet*, 2 Nov.   [230] Article quoted, from *Uusi Suomi*.
[231] BGA, no. 243, undated (2 Nov. 1907).   [232] *Uusi Suomi* and *Hufvudstadsbladet*.
[233] One came from Kajanus and the Philharmonic Society, the other from the famous Finnish singer Aïno Ackté, friend of Sibelius.

Flodin, critic on the *Nya Pressen*, the Swedish language newspaper in Helsinki,[234] wrote that this concert would leave an everlasting memory for those who had heard it, for they 'had encountered a personality and a character, sensed the world of feeling and thought inside that great head with the wild hair, the elongated face, the black eyes behind their gold-rimmed spectacles, the narrow mouth indicating the strength of character. His lips look scarcely capable of smiling.'

Flodin felt that this face well suited Mahler's conducting, which, despite his refinement of nuance and his attention to detail, was 'concerned above all with the great outline', which 'emphasized his conception of the pieces' and which would 'fix on certain details which he made his own through a new and striking approach'. Beethoven's and Wagner's scores were heard 're-formed, freshly painted, given a new accent, translated into Mahlerian, a musical language as valid as any other'. 'In the hands of the autocrat everything is severe, methodical, controlled. From among the moods of musical expression he emphasizes the masculine element, cruelly honest and characteristically robust.' Thanks to his moderate and very 'surprising' tempos, 'the structure of the movements seemed even richer and more interesting'. The opening four notes of Beethoven's Fifth Symphony were a surprise, being played 'weightlessly and without *portamento*: just an energetic statement' of these notes. The motif subsequently became 'more and more stern and threatening'. The Scherzo, taking on the character of an Allegretto, became something new and very rare, and the transitional passage preceding the Finale, 'full of new and personal ideas, of surges in the dynamics and of vivid nuances in the tempos'.[235] The Prelude to *Tristan* was played 'with unexpected restraint in the fortissimos' and that of *Die Meistersinger* was 'unforgettable'.

For K. F. Wasenius, critic on *Hufvudstadsbladet*, the other Swedish-language newspaper, Mahler was undoubtedly 'one of the great conductors in the world'. His conception of the Fifth Symphony was 'strong and calm', and unfailingly original. 'The first movement was played energetically and with extraordinary clarity, without exaggerated haste or ardour.' Mahler's way of handling this orchestra reminded the critic of 'the breathing exercises done by modern choruses'. The slow tempo of the *Coriolan* Overture gave an impression 'of profound tragedy: a magnificence, a kind of antique grandeur, that produced, through the power that emanated from the orchestra, a devastating effect'.

---

[234] Finland, with its half-Swedish, half-indigenous population, remains bilingual even today. Karl Flodin (1858–1925), a Finnish musicologist, critic, and composer, studied at the University of Helsingfors, and then in Leipzig. In 1901 he launched the journal *Euterpe* in support of avant-garde art and literature. Between 1908 and 1921 he lived in Buenos Aires, where he was music critic of the newspaper *La Plata*. Flodin left a number of compositions, for piano as well as solo voice and chorus.

[235] Flodin wrote that the orchestra's attack was often less than simultaneous and that the slow movement of the Fifth Symphony was marred by a false entry which produced an unexpected dissonance and brought a frown to Mahler's brow.

Evert Katila, critic of the Finnish-language paper *Uusi Suomi*, thought that Mahler's chief qualities were 'clarity, rhythmic firmness, and a direct conception, free of affectation'. He always presented a composer's works just as they were, without adding or omitting anything. 'It all seems so simple and natural that one wants to exclaim: "That's exactly how it should be." '[236] In the other Finnish-language daily paper, *Helsingin Sanomat*, an unsigned article emphasized the total domination that 'this conductor, undoubtedly the most famous in the world', exercised over his orchestra. In two days of rehearsal he had entirely transformed 'the spirit in which works are played' and the 'presentation of the theoretical content of each work'. The critic was struck above all by Mahler's 'sense of rhythm'. He described the concert overall as 'a triumph of preparation in every aspect, every sound, every phrase'.[237] Nevertheless, the Finnish-language critics seem to have been all the more surprised by his relatively restrained interpretation of the Prelude to *Tristan* in that it contrasted with a 'more passionate and perhaps more striking' version by the Finnish conductor Georg Schneevoigt who was in charge of the Kaim Orchestra in Munich at the time and who had recently conducted in Helsinki.[238]

The day after the concert, Akseli Gallen had promised Mahler that he would fetch him in his boat and take him out on the tidal lakes (*Schären*) around the capital. Mahler started a letter to Alma while he was waiting for him at the hotel Societetshuset and watching the quay outside the window for Gallen's boat.[239] Unfortunately it was raining 'which I fear will make it slightly less pleasant. But wait! What's this? Even as I write the sun's coming timidly out! So perhaps everything will turn out well after all.'[240] His account of the excursion is worth quoting in full:

My day with Galén turned out extremely well. He and a very famous architect whose name I have forgotten[241] fussed around me like two wet-nurses. They wrapped me in rugs and fed me on Finnish sandwiches until I felt quite sick. I was shivering like a greyhound (—but so were they). After a three-hour sea trip hugging the cliffs, with a great variety of views opening up, we reached our destination, where a carriage and

---

[236] According to Katila, the second theme in the *Coriolan* Overture was characterized by a slight accelerando combined with a sudden diminuendo 'that gave a sense of anguish', 'as if one's heart had stopped beating under the pressure of some terrible suspense'. In the Scherzo of the Fifth Symphony Mahler made 'humorous rallentandi' in the basses (this undoubtedly refers to the famous bass passage in the Trio), while he played the Finale 'vertiginously'.

[237] This critic drew particular attention to the extraordinary crescendo, from pianissimo to fortissimo, which gave momentum to the introduction to the Finale of Beethoven's Fifth Symphony. He noted that at the beginning of the opening Allegro the first pedal point, unlike Bülow's, was 'fairly short, while the second one was longer'.

[238] It will be recalled that Alexander Siloti in St Petersburg had also been taken aback by Mahler's interpretation of this Prelude.

[239] I am grateful to Alessandra Comini, art historian and musician, for finding out and letting me know that Mahler's hotel was situated on the water. It is today the Helsinki City Hall.

[240] BGA, no. 243, undated (2 Nov. 1907).

[241] This was Eliel Saarinen, one of the greatest figures in twentieth-century architecture (see below).

horse were waiting, and after a merry journey, we arrived at a charming house—very much à la Hoffmann[242]—more a castle really.

The architect lives there with a friend of his (whose name I took in; it is Gesellius)[243] winter and summer. Right by a lake, with a view to the sea from upstairs. Delightful rooms, like a Finnish Hohe Warte. These two architects, very sympathetic young men both of them, were married for about a year to two young women, all of them living very happily together (they are childhood friends); until a year ago it occurred to them that life without change is just 'mere existence'—what were they to do? Well, they exchanged wives, and for the past year have been living just as happily together, building more houses and peopling theirs. Good story, isn't it?—[244] In the evening, in the deepening twilight, we sat around the fireplace where huge logs hissed and crackled as if in a smithy. Galén, who had been staring strangely at me throughout the trip (like a hunter does with a hare) suddenly put up an easel and began to draw me. Very Rembrandt, with just the fireplace. After he had been at it for half an hour I started to fidget, so we got up and went out for a walk in the woods. I was very pleased to have escaped and took care not to remind him about the painting. An hour later it was time for me to go and I was actually saying goodbye when the master of the house brought the easel with, to everyone's amazement, the picture on it, fully completed. A wonderful picture and a good likeness.[245] You would be astonished! He's a marvellous chap! And it was a wonderful sight to see him at the helm of the boat, generally bolt upright, his glowing eyes staring into the distance—so straight and upright; like a Viking. I think women must be endlessly falling for him! I was very much warmed by all these kind people, who were so friendly yet never burdensome. I even, without a word to anyone, went into the next room and slept for a while on a couch, and there was not a sound to disturb me.[246]

Akseli Gallen's 'inspired portrait sketch' of Mahler has been described by Alessandra Comini:

Mahler glances downward at the fire, his slightly bent head supported by his right hand in a characteristic listening or resting gesture, with the forefinger pointing upwards along the length of his cheek, and the other fingers bent in at the first knuckle. The composer's usually pale face has taken on a roseate hue of glowing kindling wood, reflecting the flickering flames that illuminate it from below. A Rembrandtesque chiaroscuro throws his black hair and upper torso into inky shadow, while the gleaming cuff on his raised right arm flashes out with a yellow-white that is picked up in the lenses of Mahler's wire-rimmed glasses.[247]

---

[242]　The famous Secession architect.

[243]　Herman Gesellius (1874–1916) had been associated for some years with Saarinen and Lindgren (see below).

[244]　Akseli Gallen must have told Mahler this story, but there seems to have been a misunderstanding: Saarinen's first wife, Mathilde, had left him to marry Gesellius; and he had later married Gesellius' sister, Loja.

[245]　Akseli Gallen-Kallela's portrait of Mahler (dimensions: 38 × 57.5 cm.) was bought in 1937 by the painter's son Jorma Gallen and given to the Gösta Serlachius Fine Arts Foundation in Mäntta, Finland, where it remains. It has been exhibited at various times alongside other pictures by the same painter.

[246]　BGA, no. 244, undated (4 Nov. 1907).

[247]　Alessandra Comini stresses that 'the work was painted on the spur of the moment, and the canvas not primed', so that 'much of the initial coloristic vibrancy has been lost'. She also stresses the similarity between Mahler's pose in Gallen's picture (KMA 206) and that in a little-known Mahler photograph (BGM, Paris, KMA 70)

The property of Hvitträsk, 'White Lake' in old Swedish, where Mahler went that memorable day, is still regarded as one of the masterpieces of early twentieth-century architecture and interior decoration.[248] Built by the lake of the same name between 1902 and 1904 by Eliel Saarinen, with Armas Lindgren and Herman Gesellius (co-architects of Helsingfors Railway station, built between 1906 and 1914, and of the National Museum, completed in 1912),[249] then equipped and decorated up to 1906 by the three architects with the help of Akseli Gallen (carpets, decorative frescos, furniture, and stained glass), it remains 'a living witness to important developments', passing, 'with remarkable ease, from nationalist romanticism (with its references to fortresses, medieval churches and rustic farms) to a nationalist purity': 'a mixture of tradition, boldness and charm'. At Hvitträsk, each of the three partners built a house of his own. All the interior decoration, fireplace, tiles and bricks, ornamental copper-work, furniture, carpets and curtains, was specially conceived and created by chosen craftsmen. Built high on a cliff dominating the lake, 24 kilometres from Helsinki, Hvitträsk was planned as a 'house-workshop' where the three friends had decided to 'live and work in a community with artisans'— carpenters, smiths etc—and in close contact with nature. The influence of the Viennese *Jugendstil*, together with that of Charles Rennie Mackintosh and the English 'domestic revival', is everywhere visible, and above all there is 'a spirit of returning to sources, of archaism and rustic expressivity'. This is manifest in the logs and beams of the ceilings; in the great wooden crown-shaped chandelier lighting the entrance hall; in the huge fireplace in front of which Gallen painted Mahler, fortress-like and massive, with its flared copper canopy and its two round orange ceramic 'towers'; in the coarse wool carpets, with Gallen's designs, running from the walls over couches and thence to the floors. 'Handcarved furniture for the living-room had just been completed the year before Mahler's visit and included a suite of three armchairs, built of oak with intarsia and convoluted ornamentation, and we may imagine Mahler sitting in one of these handsome upholstered chairs facing the glowing "smithy" fire.'[250] The arrangement of space, and of forms in the spaces, was—and is—particularly fortunate, and it is easy to understand the deep impression made on Mahler, as much by the 'romantic forest-setting of Hvitträsk and its charming arts-and-crafts interior' as by the kindness and generous hospitality of the owners.[251]

[248] See *La Maison témoin du 1900 finlandais: Connaissance des Arts* (Paris, Dec. 1972), 108 and 'Trois amis au bord d'un lac de légende' by André Fermiger, *Le Monde*, Paris (19 Oct. 1978), 15.

[249] The plans for the museum date back to 1901.

[250] Comini, 'Finnish Fireside', 341 (see n. 245 above).

[251] Ibid. 344. Gesellius, Lindgren, and Saarinen had opened an architectural office in Helsinki in 1896, before completing their studies at the Polytechnic Institute. The famous Finnish pavilion at the Paris International Exhibition of 1900, 'a chapel-like edifice with a romantic tower', designed and hand-built by the trio of architects, was their first important work, and their whole reputation was based on it. In 1905 Armas Lindgren (1874–1929) left his companions and sold them his house. Gesellius died in 1916. Later on, in 1922, Eliel Saarinen emigrated to the United States, where he had a brilliant career which was carried on by his son Ero (the General Motors Technical Institute in Warren, Michigan, is a notable example of their

On the evening of his return from this memorable trip Mahler took the train back to St Petersburg,[252] where rehearsals for his final concert were due to start. These promised to be taxing, for the programme included his own Fifth Symphony,[253] and the orchestra did not know his music, except for the Second, which Fried had conducted the previous year. Despite his initial anxiety he soon realized with relief that all was going well. Two days before the concert he wrote to Justi: 'The orchestra here is really splendid. They remind me of the Vienna orchestra: even their mischief. But despite all that I have them well in hand. They want to invite me for two concerts of my own music.[254] I seem to mean more to them than I do to our dear "beast-harmonic" orchestra.'[255] To Alma he added:

The rehearsals for this concert have been very tiring. But I think I have survived them perfectly well. The public rehearsal today was completely sold out. Enormous success. I seem to have risen to become a sort of second Nikisch. In any case I've never seen so much serious interest, and so many nice enthusiastic young people. There are already a great many who can tell the difference between Mahler and Nikisch (who until now has been called the favourite conductor here). I've been to several performances at the theatre, very interesting.[256]

Mahler had decided, on his return to St Petersburg, not to change hotels after all for he had been told that the Hotel d'Europe would be far more expensive. Instead, he moved to the upper floor of the Hotel d'Angleterre, which was less noisy and had a superb view of the beautiful square 'with the beautiful church of St Isaac'. But he continued to complain of the 'insane' level of uncleanliness and the high price of his room, eight roubles a day, which in

work together). Settling in Cranbrook, Michigan, Saarinen and his son retained ownership of Hvitträsk until 1969. The whole estate was bought by the Finnish government in 1981. Today it is a museum. Only Saarinen's original house, the one where Mahler spent the afternoon and evening, has been preserved just as it was.

[252] His original intention, as we have seen was to take a night train on Saturday, but he may have delayed his departure until the next morning, as he arrived back from Hvitträsk at quite a late hour.

[253] On 4 Sept., Mahler telegraphed Peters to send him the orchestral material which he had taken to Rome with him but which had not arrived in time for the concert (Eberhard Klemm, 'Zur Geschichte der Fünften Sinfonie von Gustav Mahler', *Jahrbuch Peters, 1979 (Aufsätze zur Musik*, Peters, Leipzig, 1981)), 50. Hinrichsen's reply, the following day, was accompanied by the new edition of *The Marriage of Figaro*, which had just come out.

[254] 'Zwei eigene Konzerte'. This wording is slightly ambiguous, as it could also mean 'two of their own concerts'.

[255] In German, a pun on *Phil-* and *Viehharmoniker* (*Vieh* = cattle).

[256] BGA, no. 246, undated (8 Nov. 1907). In the original rehearsal schedule (Alma Mahler Archive, UPL, Philadelphia) there were only two rehearsals for this concert in addition to the general rehearsal, but all evidence suggests that Mahler obtained at least one additional rehearsal, without which it is highly unlikely that he would have agreed to conduct a symphony of his own. List of performances at the Marinsky Theatre between 3 and 9 Nov. 1907 (western calendar): on the 2nd, a Siloti Concert; the 3rd, a ballet; the 4th, *Eugene Onegin* (which Mahler saw); the 5th, *Tannhäuser*; the 6th, *Rigoletto*; the 7th, Rimsky-Korsakov's *Invisible City of Kitech*; the 8th, César Cui's A *Prisoner in the Caucasus*. There were also opera performances in the great hall of the Conservatory at this time, notably Mussorgsky's *Khovanshchina*, works by Puccini, and Wagner's *Der fliegende Holländer* with 'The Company of Mr Dracula'. During Mahler's earlier stay the Marinsky Theatre put on *Dubrovsky*, by Napravnik (24 Oct.); *Tannhäuser* (the 25th).

Germany would have been enough for a magnificent suite. In the evening he went to the Marinsky Theatre to a performance of *Eugene Onegin*: 'A wealth of means employed, but rough, and amateurishly used—as everywhere, and soon in Vienna too! You will all see soon!'[257] But Alma's silence worried Mahler as often before. She had given no sign of life apart from two telegrams stating 'all are well'. He found this new habit of hers both disturbing and irritating:

But Almschi, this is a new procedure, and I don't know at all what to make of it. Logic tells me that either: everything is not all right, and your telegram is meant to calm me down a bit without telling me anything; or else, everything is all right, in which case I don't understand why you haven't even had time to scribble a card to me.[258]

But he went on receiving telegrams from home. He would have liked Alma to make suggestions, as she usually did, as to what he might bring her from his trip. He spent his afternoons in his room, 'reading, sleeping, dreaming and looking out of the window'. An evening spent at the home of his devoted admirer Madame Abaza seems to have been his only social activity during this final week; obviously he was taking his doctors' recommendations very seriously. His letter to Justi contains the following paragraph:

I don't think for a moment that we shall be leaving Vienna for good. And even if we do leave, I'm convinced that we would be together perhaps much more often than we are at present. It's always the same: no visitor comes to Vienna without seeing the museums several times, yet there are perhaps a million Viennese who have never been to them. I haven't gone to them myself for years, yet here in Petersburg I've already been twice to the Hermitage.[259]

As soon as he got back from Finland, Mahler had to make further corrections to the orchestral parts of the Fifth Symphony. He spent almost two full days, 3 and 4 November, on this task: 'I've just finished, in agony. There is a large sore on the middle finger of my right hand.'[260] Mahler's music was no longer totally unknown to the public in the Russian capital, as the Second Symphony had had a great success there the year before, under Oskar Fried.[261] In the programme for 9 November the Fifth was followed by two movements from a Mozart concerto[262] and Rachmaninov's Second Concerto, played by the French pianist Raoul Pugno. Mahler then returned to the podium to wind up the evening with the *Coriolan* Overture and the 'Prelude and Liebestod' from *Tristan*. In the audience was a young Russian composer who was soon to make a name for himself, and who fifty years later recalled the concert in these words:

---

[257] BGA, no. 245, undated (5 Nov. 1907).   [258] Ibid.
[259] Letter to Justine Rosé of 7 Nov., quoted above (RWO).
[260] BGA, no. 244, undated (4 Nov. 1907).   [261] See above, Chap. 7.
[262] The movements Pugno played at this concert were probably the first two from the Concerto No. 22, K. 482 (since the key is given as E flat). The French pianist was accompanied by the Russian conductor Mihail Vladimirov (1870–1932) (see Siloti's letter to Ossovsky, quoted above). Pugno had originally intended to play *Les Djinns* by César Franck, but the *Musykalnaya Gazeta* reported that the score of the work had 'gone missing in the train where Madame Landowska's harpsichord was also damaged'.

I remember seeing Mahler in St. Petersburg, too. His concert there was a triumph. Rimsky was still alive, I believe, but he wouldn't have attended because a work by Tchaikovsky was on the programme (I think it was *Manfred*, the dullest piece imaginable).[263] Mahler also played some Wagner fragments and, if I remember correctly, a symphony of his own. Mahler impressed me greatly—he himself and his conducting.'[264]

It is a pity that Igor Stravinsky did not write down his impressions of Mahler's symphony, but he was then under the influence of the Russian establishment and his mentor, Rimsky-Korsakov, who hated and despised contemporary German and French music, as will be seen later on. Stravinsky had just then completed his own Symphony in E flat, which received a first, unrehearsed 'sight-reading' performance on 22 January 1908 during an 'orchestral gathering of Musical Novelties' by the Imperial Russian Court orchestra. Stravinsky probably reacted to Mahler's Fifth Symphony in 1907 in much the same way as Debussy when he listened to the Second in 1910. For the time being Strauss was the only Germanic composer really to have established himself beyond the frontiers of his own country. That evening in St Petersburg, the two first parts of Mahler's Symphony were received in complete silence and only the third, comprising the Adagietto and the Finale, was applauded, though politely rather than warmly.

The programme notes for the concert included an anonymous and quite lengthy text attempting to define the 'frames of mind' and the moods evoked in the Fifth but insisting from the start that this was 'pure' music, not 'programme' music. Rimsky-Korsakov, who had disliked Mahler's Beethoven interpretations in 1902, disapproved even more of his Fifth Symphony, as the memoirs of Vassily Vassilievitch Yastriebstsev show:

We talked of Mahler and his talentless, tasteless symphony with its excessively coarse, heavy orchestration. 'Obviously he's discovered new continents!' Rimsky-Korsakov joked. 'No,' he continued, turning to me (I had not heard the symphony in question), 'try to imagine it! A sort of pompous improvisation on paper by a man totally unaware of what will follow from one bar to the next. Really I pity him as a musician. A real scribbler. . . .'[265] Much worse even than Richard Strauss.'

Rimsky-Korsakov's rejection of Mahler as a composer is in no way surprising, for the proud and talented member of the young Russian school of The Five, the man who had done so much to put Russia on the map of European music, had in old age turned into an embittered reactionary, the head of a 'cloistered, sectarian, moribund musical world'.[266] Among contemporary

---

[263] Here Stravinsky is confusing the second programme Mahler conducted in 1902 with those of 1907.

[264] Igor Stravinsky and Robert Craft, *Conversations with Igor Stravinsky* (Doubleday, Garden City, New York, 1959) 38.

[265] Untranslatable pun. The Russian word *Maliar*, an adaptation of the German *Maler*, means a bad painter, a doodler. Vassily Vassiliévitch Yastriebstev, *Recollections of N. A. Rimsky-Korsakov* (Leningrad, 1960; Columbia University, New York), 439 (31 Oct. 1907, Russian calendar).

[266] See Richard Taruskin, *Stravinsky and the Russian Traditions: A Biography of the Works through Mavra* (Oxford University Press, Oxford, 1996), 55 ff.

composers Rimsky accepted and appreciated only the music of his own pupils, the most gifted of whom was Alexander Glazunov. 'A fear of disorder and unconventionality closed his mind to the music of the younger Europeans, like Debussy and Strauss, both of whom, but especially the latter, could arouse in him a righteous indignation that became proverbial among his contemporaries, and especially his pupils.'[267] Against Debussy's *Estampes*, Rimsky had 'fumed for three days', having discerned 'neither technique nor imagination' in any of them. Strauss's *Salome* had upset him considerably and he had called the composer an 'impudent decadent'.[268] The Swiss critic Aloys Mooser[269] also tells of Rimsky's complete rejection of—and contempt for—the new schools of German and French music. Of Strauss's *Zarathustra* he had written in 1898 that it was nothing but 'a bad joke and a mockery of contemporary art and of those people who pretend to understand a work so totally devoid of any kind of original meaning'.[270] The same year he had returned the score of Debussy's *Après-midi d'un faune* to Mooser with these scathing words: 'Take back this filth! Is it supposed to be music? It's musical prostitution!' For Rimsky, 'the only advances in music are taking place in Russia, and only with us!'[271] All the products of the new Western European schools were dismissed by him in the same intolerant manner, Charpentier, Dukas, D'Indy, Fauré, and Debussy as well as Strauss, Schillings, and Reger.

Rimsky-Korsakov's short-sightedness was shared by many professional musicians in Russia. The very serious *Russkaya Muzykalnaya Gazeta* (Russian musical Gazette) regrets that 'the length and complexity of this work make a clear and precise definition of its true characteristics very difficult'. Mahler was known to have conducted works of his own twice at the same concert,[272] the article continued: if he had done so on this occasion, the hall would have emptied for the second performance, and 'the patience of those who had applauded would have worn thin, despite all their courtesy'. The critic found

something unsympathetic about this straining after genius, something unhealthy, hysterical and irritating in the character, approach and development of this music. Sometimes one has the impression that the composer has lost control of his composition, as if he fell prey to his obsessions, as if he was tormented, abused and imprisoned by distressing pathological thoughts . . . The musical ideas with which he works lack originality and fail to reveal a creative personality. At best they are 'reminiscences from operas and concerts' whose melodic quality often shows less than good taste. His eager striving for novelty finds expression only in the development, the combination of

[267] Ibid.   [268] Ibid.

[269] Mooser, *Souvenirs*, 121 and 195. Aloys Mooser (1876–1969) was born and died in Geneva. His mother was Russian and his grandfather an organ and piano maker. He studied organ and theory in his native city, and later theory and composition with Balakirev and Rimsky-Korsakov in St Petersburg. After leaving Russia in 1909 he became music critic of the Geneva periodical *La Suisse*, a position he held until 1962. From 1923 to 1946, he directed, edited, and published the independent Swiss periodical *Dissonances*.

[270] Mooser dates this rash statement of Rimsky's 11 Feb. 1898, but does not mention its source (*Souvenirs*, 196, n. 2).   [271] Ibid.

[272] A reference to the double performance of the Fourth Symphony in Amsterdam in 1904.

themes, and the form of the composition which contains many effective passages. But this striving sometimes reaches such a degree of artificiality that the symphony becomes a sort of phantasmagoria where familiar faces are glimpsed in distortion. Only here and there does the listener's task become easier, as if the composer were 'restored to himself' and his work were suddenly starting to 'succeed'. This is true particularly of the Finale. The source of Mahler's art is a careful study of scores by Wagner, Bruckner and Strauss. But he possesses much less natural, individual talent than the last two composers (Wagner being above consideration). He is more or less a *self-made composer* [in English in the text.] No amount of cacophony dismays him. . . . He has retained the noisy style, the heaviness and the hysterical agitation of Strauss. . . . This symphony would be more at home in Paris, where there is general wonder at anything which is in the first place brilliantly chaotic and then difficult to understand, and where Strauss is admired even by those whose hearts still have a place for *Mignon* by Thomas. . . . The listener far from attaining any ideal, gained only utter nervous exhaustion.

Not until the second—classical—half of the concert, had the listener been rewarded for his patience. The interpretation of the *Coriolanus* Overture had been 'a strong and concise affirmation of the character of this work', 'masterfully conducted'. 'A raging lion was let loose in the orchestra, and this time the final appeasement seemed a real appeasement, a conquest of peace and not of the ideal which was absent in the symphony.'

Most of the Petersburg critics show the same lack of comprehension for Mahler's style of composition. Only Alexander Ossovsky, in the journal *Slovo* (The Word), displayed more moderation. In his opinion the ideological content of the work was easy to grasp, the form was interesting and new, and certain passages, notably the entire Finale, were 'magnificently successful' despite the 'length' and 'confusion' of the work as a whole. The *Novoye Vremia* wondered whether this 'nonsense', this 'pretentious racket' could possibly be taken seriously.[273] It claimed that Jews were rarely 'outstanding composers'. Thus Mahler 'fed on the ideas of others'; his music, 'both frenzied and decadent', was 'crude', and evoked only 'painful impressions'. Probably one needed to look no further than a work like this to find the reason why he had had to leave the Vienna Opera.

An unsigned article in the Discourse (*Riech*) ranked Mahler the composer far below the conductor. His work had

neither form, nor unity, nor defined atmosphere. It was a furious jumble of sounds that followed each other without rhyme or reason and which, in my opinion, have no meaning. It is true that here and there from this chaos there emerge beautiful themes, marvellous and interesting harmonies, surprising instrumental effects, but these are nothing more than oases, disappearing as fast as they appear . . . In short, this symphony makes a chaotic impression and, by its intolerable length, simply bores and exhausts the listener.

---

[273] It had asked the same question in connection with the previous work, the Second, here bizarrely referred to as the Eighth and compared with the Fifth at several points.

As for the *San-Peterburgskiye Viedomosti*, it too, saw in the Fifth Symphony only a 'mixture of sounds which do not harmonize with each other', 'abrupt, meaningless transitions from *piano* to *fortissimo*', 'superficial effects' with which the composer 'tries to hide his lack of invention'. On the other hand the 'crystal clarity' of the *Coriolanus* Overture had made 'a profound impression' on the listeners. The *Novoye Vremia* even suggested that the audience's enthusiasm after the Beethoven and Wagner works 'contrasting so strongly with the cool reception of the Fifth Symphony, must have wounded the composer's self-esteem to the quick'. Ossovsky expressed the same enthusiasm for Mahler the performer as he had after the first concert. In the excerpts from *Tristan* he admired

the precision and power of the orchestral chords and tutti, the intensity and elegance of the strings, the skilful and artistically proportioned balance of the counterpoint and of the various orchestral groups, the splendour of the crescendos and decrescendos, revealing in their perfect gradation his sovereign virtuosity and also his desire to realize down to the last detail the master's intentions.

Yet many critics that year seem to have been taken aback by Mahler's original treatment of the *Tristan* excerpts, 'lyrical', restrained, luminous, and spiritual, rather than vehement.[274] This was probably symptomatic of his state of mind at the time, the new view of the world he had gained through terrible suffering, soon to be translated in his music into an evolution of his conducting style.

Mahler's second concert gave Knorozovsky occasion to write at length in *Teatr i Iskusstvo*, chiefly about the Fifth Symphony. In 1902, his three concerts, which had been 'coldly received' because 'his tendencies to slow tempos and his reserved concentration did not appeal to the larger musical public'. This time he claimed that the conducting had been 'a fantastic success, especially in the *Coriolanus* Overture, which he interpreted, in the proper sense of the term, with genius'.

As a composer he made an impression that is more difficult to define. On the one hand the whole audience was bound to realize that it was in the presence of an exceptional artistic personality, striding ardently to embrace the grandest designs, and carrying people along in the spontaneity of its creative aspirations. On the other, everything the listeners were presented with was so unusual, so new, so crushing in the monumentality of its forms and the gigantic complexity of the problems it posed, that the public was as if lost in a labyrinth . . . Even the experts lost hold of the thread.

After writing at length about Wagner's inheritance and the genre of the symphonic poem, Knorozovsky suggested that in the history of music Mahler belonged to a 'later stage' than Strauss, for

he is leading us towards the edifice from which the symphony of the future will issue. . . . The classic symphonic forms do not satisfy him. They are too narrow for the broad

---

[274] See Siloti's remarks above.

intentions which are his. But he recognizes the necessity for <u>organic</u> forces, springing from the inner nature of the music itself. A striking example of <u>individualism</u>, he requires symphonic forms that will give the composer all the space he needs to express his own range of feelings, even if their juxtaposition seems born of pure caprice. Naturally the space is not without reasoned limits, beyond which lies 'formlessness'. It is not possible, to give a clear definition of these limits after just one single hearing of Mahler's gigantic work. However, that they exist and that they are conditioned by the organic necessities of the music itself is an obvious fact, underlined by the division of his symphonies into movements which in turn are grouped in 'parts'. Each movement impresses us by its colossal dimensions and by the Protean development of all its constituent material. At first sight one might easily mistake this for verbosity. But on closer examination of the work one realizes that it is the exhaustive comprehensiveness of a man who feels profoundly, and who tackles things from several angles at once. He is incapable of a superficial approach to the theme he has chosen. He will not leave it until he has said all that he has to say about it. The monumentalism of his architectonic structures and the extreme complexity of his interweavings in sound spring directly from his spiritual make-up, which always and everywhere tends toward the grand and the boundless. . . . Mahler's themes, if we fasten on their essence, are characterized by simplicity, naturalness and attractiveness. But what profusion there is in their subsequent development and in their multiple interlacings! What boundless inventivity the composer displays in carrying them out! Mahlerian polyphony is characterized, despite its extreme complexity, by an astonishing clarity and translucence. His harmony, strikingly bold in its procedures, nevertheless produces an impression of naturalness and ease. And the most remarkable thing of all is that the contrapuntal and harmonic styles blend into a homogeneous whole which reconciles these two such disparate and historically separate elements in a higher level of unity. Admittedly this marriage of harmonic and polyphonic styles is the most characteristic feature of all modern music, but no other composer (and this includes Richard Strauss) has brought their union to such a level of perfection and homogeneity . . .

And the orchestration! . . . In this area Mahler stands as an all-powerful master, whose reign over the enchanted realm of orchestral sound seems definitely assured. . . . He uses certain orchestral combinations only to the extent needed to produce a clear musical profile. . . . He blows up the traits to the limits of the possible. He builds up the instrumental groups, particularly the brass and woodwinds, to numbers undreamed of by other composers. He passes each mood through a prism of the most diverse nuances. In the Allegro furioso and the Rondo Finale he raises the atmosphere to a point of tremendous tension. It seems impossible to go any further. Wrong! Mahler demands still more. He intensifies the feeling of exaltation, reaching a climax in which any other composer would be seized with vertigo, and his music would plunge into indescribable chaos. Similarly, whether depicting deep inner sadness in the Funeral march, or evoking unclouded gaiety in the Scherzo, he gives free rein to his feelings with total spontaneity and absence of restraint. The funeral dirge, growing little by little, becomes a searing lamentation, beyond expression, while a folk dance, a 'Ländler', initially of great simplicity, gradually turns into an exalted hymn, almost Bacchic in its abandon. . . .

I am convinced that modern symphonic music possesses in Mahler one of its most innovative and brilliant exponents. If I compare Mahler with Richard Strauss I must unhesitatingly prefer the former, although his reputation as a composer is infinitely lower. . . . Mahler has to rely entirely on effect, for pure music offers the listener no point of reference beyond what is purely musical. Yet the effect is irresistible. It works on the listener in an almost unconscious manner. This is the mark of a very great talent.[275]

In conclusion, Knorozovsky remarked that Beethoven's *Coriolanus* suited Mahler the interpreter better than the *Tristan* excerpts. Knorozovsky here displays exceptional perspicacity in his appraisal of Mahler as a symphonist. Only William Ritter, in several passages quoted at length above, and Felipe Pedrell[276] showed themselves equally capable at the time of appreciating Mahler to the full. If the whole of Knorozovsky's article was translated for him to read—which is by no means certain—Mahler must have been relieved to have found at least one enlightened critic in the land of his idol Dostoevsky.

Returning to Vienna on the afternoon of Tuesday 12 November, Mahler found Felix Weingartner waiting for him and ready to take over the reins of office at the Hofoper. Their meeting had been arranged several weeks earlier, and Mahler had several sessions with him to put him in the picture and settle the most important matters. On 16 November he notified the Intendant's office that the handing-over process would be completed in a few more days, and asked permission to leave Vienna early in December in time to take the ship leaving Cherbourg on the 12th for the United States.[277]

Having taken leave of the Opera in the most discreet manner possible, Mahler wanted nevertheless to say farewell to the Viennese public, since he had committed himself not to conduct in the capital in the future. For this reason he accepted, after some hesitation, an invitation from Franz Schalk to conduct the Second Symphony at a Gesellschaftskonzert on 24 November 1907. It had originally been planned that Schalk himself would conduct the work. However a week before the concert, Josef Reitler met Mahler at the Café Imperial:

Franz Schalk was sitting in another corner, engrossed in reading the newspapers. 'Really it's a dreadful thought, having to face the public once more and having to work with the Philharmonic the majority of whose members are opposed to me' said Mahler. And he suddenly invited Schalk over to our table and asked him whether he thought he might be able to take over the forthcoming concert. Schalk gave one of his typical grunts, which could equally well mean yes or no. 'Thank you,' said Mahler, 'I'll think it over.' And after Schalk had left us he said, 'Did you see that face? Can such a man conduct my music? No, I'll have to do it myself!'[278]

Although the work normally needed only two soloists, the importance of the occasion led a number of singers at the Opera to offer their services, notably Anna von Mildenburg, who had already sung the *Kindertotenlieder* while

---

[275] *Teatr i Iskusstvo* (Theatre and Art), no. 44, 4 Nov. 1907 (Russian calendar).
[276] See below, Vol. iiii, Chap. 3.   [277] HOA, Z. 1105/1907.
[278] JRM 68 (copy in BGM, Paris).

Mahler was still in St Petersburg.[279] To enable the singers and the orchestral players from the Opera to take part in this concert, three ballets were scheduled at the theatre for the evening of the public rehearsal.[280] Mahler wrote to Mildenburg at the beginning of the week, describing 'the usual confusion' which reigned in the Gesellschaft's plans, the dates and times for rehearsals having been changed several times. Elise Elizza had already rehearsed the main soprano passages for the Finale. Actually Mildenburg was unlikely to be able to sing at the public rehearsal (and therefore at the concert) because she was supposed to be rehearsing for *Die Walküre* that night. She had probably wanted to sing the alto solos, for Mahler added: 'For *Urlicht* I always prefer an alto voice, as you know. So there is only the solo in the last movement.'[281] Mildenburg, who no doubt considered the soprano's brief appearance in the Finale to be beneath her dignity, finally withdrew, although her participation had been announced in the press. Eventually two sopranos, Elise Elizza and Gertrud Förstel, and two contraltos, Hermine Kittel, and Bella Paalen took part in the performance, which was exceptional in several ways. As in Basle in 1903, *Urlicht* was sung by Hermine Kittel. According to the *Fremden-Blatt* of 26 November, the soloists for the Finale stood in the first row of the chorus, rather than at the front of the stage.

Egon Wellesz, as Schoenberg's pupil, had always been allowed to attend all Mahler's rehearsals. This time, however, when he arrived with his young wife at the Musikvereinsaal, he found the doors closed. Just then Mahler arrived and explained that since Schalk was the official head of the Gesellschafts-konzerte, he could not take the responsibility of letting them in without first asking the players' consent. After a few minutes the orchestra's messenger boy arrived bearing the Herr Direktor's invitation to the young couple to come in. They were the only listeners present at this first rehearsal, but Mahler waited until they were seated before beginning the rehearsal.

Just before Figure 2 in the score he broke off and took out the trills in the violas and cellos parts.[282] Shortly afterwards, in a *fortissimo* for the whole orchestra, something troubled him. He tapped his baton and said: 'Something is wrong'. Just then the door to one of the boxes in the auditorium opened and Bruno Walter emerged, calling out as he did so: 'The first clarinet played B flat instead of B natural,' much to everybody's surprise, including Mahler.

---

[279] A concert of chamber music took place on Wednesday 6 Nov. at 7.30 p.m. in the Kleiner Musiksaal, conducted by Friedrich Karbach and with the following programme: Mozart: *Symphonie concertante* in E flat for oboe, clarinet, horn, and bassoon (K. 197b); Dvořák: *Nocturne* for strings, Op. 40; Mahler: *Kindertotenlieder* (Anna von Mildenburg, soprano; conductor Bruno Walter); Robert Gound: three movements from the *Suite in A*, for strings, Op. 20. According to Richard Specht, *Die Musik*, 8 (1907–8): 5, 319, Walter's accompaniment of Mahler's Lieder was 'fiery'.

[280] HOA, G.Z. VII. 76/4628s/1907. The letter from the management to the Intendant's office, dated 17 Nov., states that extra musicians are to be hired for the Opera on the evening of 23 Nov. so that the Philharmonic players can be free.

[281] Undated letter to Mildenburg (between 19 and 21 Nov. 1907), ÖTM.

[282] In the critical score the violins and violas still have a tremolo here.

Before the final movement something unusual happened. Mahler tried to explain the meaning of this movement to the Philharmonic in words; he had wanted to depict Jacob's wrestling with God. This is what he had in mind: 'I will not let you go unless you bless me'.[283] This explanation of the Finale, which has remained indelibly fixed in my mind, contains in a few words everything that in earlier years Mahler had written to his friends about this movement.[284] . . . Selma Kurz sang the last-movement soprano solo.[285] She had a clear, beautiful voice, but not very big. In the passage 'O Tod! Du Allbezwinger!'[286] the trombone chords have to be played *pianissimo*. Despite several repetitions of this passage, the melody, in the voice, was still too faint. Suddenly making up his mind, Mahler said: 'Let's leave the trombones out,' and then intoned in mock-solemn manner, 'Hail to the conductor who in the future will play my scores as the acoustic of the hall demand!'[287]

The concert of 24 November was to remain forever engraved on the memories of all those who understood and admired both Mahler's music and his personality.

I can remember clearly that when I heard Mahler's Second Symphony for the first time I was, especially at certain points, seized by an excitement that took physical expression in the rapid beating of my heart. But this did not prevent me, as I came out of the concert, from examining what I had just heard in the light of every criterion known to me as a musician and to which, as we believe, a work of art must unconditionally conform: . . . I weighed the value and originality of the themes, inspected details of counterpoint and harmonization, spied out possible formal weaknesses, and finally decided that the whole thing did not please me, that in fact it displeased me in every possible detail. But I had forgotten the most important thing, namely that the work had made an extraordinary impression on me, that it had caught hold of me and overpowered me against my will: that a work of art can have no loftier impact than when the emotion that raged in its creator is transferred to the listener, to rage and surge in him as well. For I had been moved; moved to the utmost.[288]

So Schoenberg, as in 1904 when he discovered the Third, was still reluctant to yield entirely to music that seemed to him to lack compositional discipline. But full and definitive acceptance was to come. Mahler's late works completed

---

[283] Genesis 32. Mahler had already used this image in connection with the composition of the Third Symphony (see NBL1, 60; NBL2, 76, and above, Vol. i, Chap. 23).

[284] Here Wellesz is probably alluding to the famous letter Mahler wrote to Arthur Seidl in 1897 (MBR1, no. 209: MBR2, no. 216). It had already been published several times.

[285] Egon Wellesz is mistaken, for Selma Kurz did not take part in this farewell concert.

[286] Bar 649 of the Finale.

[287] EWL 46 and Egon Wellesz, 'Mahlers Zehnte Symphonie', *Österreichische Musikzeitschrift*, 16 (1961): 4, 172. Here Wellesz adds that, at number 44, Mahler commenced the diminuendo in the third bar of the horns and dropped fifteen bars of trombone chords. See also Egon Wellesz, 'Erinnerungen an Gustav Mahler und Arnold Schoenberg', in *Urbis Musicae*, Studies in Musicology, Tel Aviv University, summer 1971, 72.

[288] Arnold Schoenberg ('Gustav Mahler', 'Stil und Gedanke', in *Gesammelte Schriften*, ed. Ivan Vojtěch, i. 20) does not mention the date of the concert to which he is referring. Later he was to mention as his first encounters with Mahler's music, totally negatively, only the First and Fourth Symphonies (8 Mar. 1899 and 20 Jan. 1902). So it seems unlikely that he heard the previous Viennese performance of the Second on 9 Apr. 1899, shortly after his violent reaction to the First.

the slow conquest. The famous 'Prague lecture' of 1912 was not only a glowing 'defence and exposition' of Mahler's music, but also in a sense a public reparation made for having failed for so long to appreciate its true worth. But strange as it may seem, Schoenberg's disciples were for their part already totally committed. To Heinrich Jalowetz, Webern's best friend at the time, the Second was 'elemental'. 'This is not a symphony,' he exclaimed, 'but a phenomenon of nature!'[289] Alban Berg, who was also present and who, sensing the emptiness and desolation there would be when Mahler left, was determined to attend all the events of the autumn, wrote:

I want to take full advantage of Mahler's last, beautiful days in Vienna, to let him then leave for America, mourned by the small flock of those bereft of him. I have heard that he will not conduct *Salome* there, but *Fidelio*, one of the most magnificent of his achievements, while we poor Viennese will be reduced to waiting for what 'Weingartner', the Opera's new director, has to say.[290]

Berg had been engaged for several months to the beautiful Helene Nakowski. She was away from Vienna the night Mahler conducted the Second Symphony. The following day Berg wrote to her:

Today, darling, I was unfaithful to you for the first time. I must tell you that by being faithful I mean something different from most people: I understand the faithfulness of a lover as being a sensation—a state, that never quits the lover for an instant—that follows him like his own shadow—that has become a part of his whole personality—a feeling of never being alone, always leaning or supporting—in a word, a feeling that without the loved person one cannot be a complete, autonomous human being!! It was in this sense that I was unfaithful to you today!! It happened in the Finale of Mahler's symphony, as I gradually slipped further and further away from the world—as if in the whole world there existed nothing but this music and myself, hearing it. And as, over-whelming and exalting it came to an end, I felt a sudden little pang, and heard a voice say: 'And Helene?' It was only then that I saw my unfaithfulness, and so I am humbly asking for your forgiveness![291]

Contrary to what Alma writes,[292] the hall was absolutely full, both for the public rehearsal on Saturday the 23rd and for the concert the following day, which took place, like all the Philharmonic Concerts, on a Sunday at half past twelve midday. 'A kind of madness greeted the conclusion of the work, so full of meaning and of special relevance. No one would move, and he, the enemy of applause, so unused to bowing, had to keep coming back. I can still see the impassive face of the man who was leaving us. He never conducted in Vienna again.'[293] 'The scene built up to a farewell in the concert hall, Korngold wrote

[289] Erwin Stein, *Orpheus in new Guises*, 8.
[290] Unpublished letter to Frida Semler, an American friend of Smaragda Berg (Stadtbibliothek, Vienna, unedited material). When he wrote this letter, at the beginning of the autumn of 1907, Berg still thought that Mahler was intending to conduct a series of new productions and performances in Vienna.
[291] Alban Berg, *Briefe an seine Frau* (Langen-Müller, Vienna, 1965), 21.   [292] See above.
[293] PSG 91.

in the *Neue Freie Presse*, 'expressed with a heartfelt enthusiasm that has rarely, if ever, been vouchsafed to any artist in Vienna who was not a stage performer. People were honouring the composer, the director, the conductor—the whole of Mahler's genius, now lost to Vienna.'[294] Everywhere in the Musikvereinsaal people were waving handkerchiefs and hats; it was a wild, endless storm of applause.

Kauders wrote:

Yesterday's concert marked the zenith of the comet's victorious ascent. With a calm reserve we had not previously known in him, Mahler marshalled with his baton the assembled army of voices and instruments. And he received the roaring storms of applause with steely stillness, as if the tribute were self-evident. After each movement, and especially after the Finale, which unleashes all the powers in the realm of sound, the applause and the shouting raged like an echo of stupefying polyphony. No doubt there was a strong personal note in all this ecstasy. For the musical world of Vienna, Mahler was a precious possession, whose worth many are only beginning to appreciate now that they are losing it. In this parting, people are thinking not of his faults or his mistakes, which sprang from his excitable individuality, but of his manifold artistic virtues, which brought forth from the depths of music so much that was sacred and noble.

Kauders also recalls that, eight years earlier, in the same hall, people had laughed, mocked and whistled, and for several days afterwards had made fun of the gigantism of the same work. 'But this exceptional man was not intimidated; with iron will and inexorable energy he continued on his tortuous, fissured paths. . . . Little by little Gustav Mahler compelled the admiration of the musical world, not by winning hearts but by enslaving the senses.' As for the work, it was, according to Kauders, 'the most human' of Mahler's symphonies, the document of 'a great terrorist genius who, striving for unattainable goals, meets the fate of Icarus'.

Carl Lafite, while recognizing that the enthusiasm of the audience had known no limits, still upbraided Mahler for his 'reminiscences' and 'orchestral jokes'. He noted, like most of his colleagues, that the public had been 'ravished' by the Viennese *Gemütlichkeit* of the second movement and had vainly tried to get it encored, being overruled by the steely determination of the composer. He had profited from this lesson and had made no break between the last sections.

Apart from a few Mahlerian idiosyncrasies, certain insistent bass figures, some ugly intervals which would have been better left out because they are meaningless, and some strange orchestral jokes, . . . I could not see what there was in the work that could have 'provoked' a listener, unless it were the countless borrowings from... well, from every possible predecessor. . . . Personally I did not like the work. Gustav Mahler, who conducted it brilliantly, possessed in the Philharmonic admiring and enthusiastic

---

[294] *Neue Freie Presse* (25 Nov. 1907).

cohorts. He was overwhelmed by the storms of applause which broke over him. Some naïvely held to an unalterable conviction that if they called him back often enough he would make a speech.[295]

Once again the majority of Viennese critics were determined to make Mahler pay for his success with the public, even on the eve of his departure from Vienna, and attempted to prove that those who had so enthusiastically applauded him were mistaken. Worst of all was the article Richard von Perger[296] wrote for the newspaper *Die Zeit*. To Perger it was obvious that Mahler's were not symphonies in the ordinary sense of the word, being virtually devoid of 'overall musical design', of strong themes and in-depth development. 'His muse,' he wrote, 'approaches us in the guise of a priestess with the torch of philosophy in her hand, speaking of earthly suffering, death and resurrection. But under her skirts is a very worldly little man, highly intelligent and eager to please.' Although Mahler was 'never boring', what he had to say was nonetheless 'commonplace, unoriginal' and even trite. 'What a pity,' concludes Perger, 'that a man of such imagination, aspiration and ability does not possess among all his gifts real creative power and naive invention! He would be among the very greatest.' It is easy to understand the reluctance of the paper's regular critic, Richard Wallaschek, to write about this farewell concert, given the unshakeable hostility to Mahler he had so often displayed; but it is extraordinary to think of the conductor of the Gesangverein and head of the Vienna Conservatory taking up his pen, the day after the farewell concert of the former director of the Opera, to deny Mahler all creative talent, even if he was perhaps expressing the opinion of a majority in Vienna?

Max Kalbeck wrote mainly about the audience at the concert: its 'attention did not lapse even for a moment, its interest was held from the first note to the last, it remained intent and rapt to the end'; it would not be 'deterred by the violent humours of this orchestral despot' from enjoying the wealth of 'his exquisite sound combinations'. In a long feuilleton published a few days later, Korngold emphasized Mahler's Viennese roots and in particular his affinities to Bruckner, as well as the influence that Berlioz had had on his compositions. On the one hand he stressed the originality of his language (putting himself at odds with most of his colleagues); on the other, his debt to his times, with their 'tensions and explosions'. He drew attention to the unity and quality of the 'symphonic substance' in the first movement, recalled how well Brahms had thought, and spoken, of the Scherzo,[297] and praised, in the Finale, the fine vocal writing and the authenticity of the religious feeling, 'its warmth, fervour and solemn grandeur' and its 'original treatment of orchestral colours'. After

---

[295] *Allgemeine Zeitung* (25 Nov. 1907).

[296] Richard von Perger (1854–1922), composer and pupil of Brahms, had been conductor of the Gesellschaftskonzerte from 1895 to 1900 (see above, Vol. ii, Chap. 8).

[297] Korngold quotes Brahm's verdict on this movement, 'Ein ans Geniale streifendes Stück' (a piece bordering on genius) (see above, Vol. i, Chap. 23).

the farewell concert, therefore, it was only Korngold who spoke of the Second Symphony as we might speak of it today, if we did not already know it by heart.

At the end of the concert the public itself performed a noisy symphony of farewell: a significant occurrence. An artist like Mahler cannot be kept down. Deprived of the glittering power of the theatre, he exerts his hold over the mind still more powerfully in the concert hall. All attempts at separation are useless: the bond between Mahler and the musical public of Vienna is not so easy to break . . .

But this was wishful thinking on Korngold's part. Vienna has always known how to treat its great men very well, but only after their death. Mahler was, for Vienna, dead already. He knew it well, and so did most of those who had unanimously applauded him in the concert-hall and at the theatre:

The great hurricane of applause which, after a magnificent performance by the Philharmonic, raged in the packed Musikvereinsaal for a full quarter of an hour, was the surest proof that the seed sown by Mahler in Vienna will not easily disappear, that the traces of his activity will remain indelibly engraved in the history of Viennese artistic life. The public would not move from their seats, and clapped until their hands were sore. Was it just profound emotion, or was there an uneasy conscience here and there? It seemed to me that many who had driven Mahler out of Vienna with their wagging tongues were now trying to bring him back again with their clapping hands, and hold on to him... Too late! His person is lost to us, and all that remains is the hope that the composer will see the words of his symphony's closing chorale come true: 'Arise, arise my soul, from your brief rest'. [298]

Even Mahler's enemies had to acknowledge that his last days at the Opera were marked by dignity, discretion, and silence. The first rehearsals for Goldmark's *Wintermärchen*, whose première, scheduled for the 2 January, had already commenced.[299] Those for *Der Traumgörge* were probably still going on, for it was only at the beginning of the new year that Weingartner cancelled its projected performance.[300] One year earlier Mahler had already voiced his disillusions about the Vienna Opera to Bernard Scharlitt who had interviewed him in Salzburg.[301] In his opinion, the sense of quality and the taste for perfection that characterized modern opera-lovers could not be satisfied by the old concept of 'repertory theatre'. He considered that there was only one solution: to set up summer theatres, which would not threaten the great houses already

---

[298] Viktor Lederer, 'Wotans Abschied' (Wotan's Farewell), *Prager Tagblatt* (27 Nov. 1907). The rest of the article emphasizes the dignity with which Mahler took his leave of Vienna. The concert of 24 Nov. took place in the big Musikvereinsaal, with the organist Rudolf Dietrich, the Singverein chorus, and the four solo singers named above. According to the *Fremden-Blatt* the Gesellschaft made a loss of 7,000 kronen because of the number of rehearsals Mahler stipulated, and this despite the fact that both the public rehearsal and the concert were sold out and the composer-conductor did not charge a fee.

[299] At the beginning of the summer Goldmark had written to Mahler to make sure that his work was going to be put on, as planned, in the autumn. The director's reply gave Nov. as the date for the première. For once Goldmark asked for a percentage of the takings (HOA, Z. 837/1907). On 21 Nov. Lucy Weidt wrote to Mahler requesting leave between 29 Nov. and 6 Dec., as she had already finished learning the 'short, easy' role of Hermione in the new Goldmark work.   [300] See MBR1, no. 401; MBR2, no. 389.

[301] See above, Vol. ii, Chaps. 5 and 7.

in existence and which would give 'definitive' performances of Mozart and Wagner. At that time (summer 1906) Mahler already felt that Vienna was tired of him because he was no longer a 'new phenomenon'. Egon Wellesz also observed that one fact alone would have sufficed to make 'repertory theatre' henceforth unworkable: the star opera singers were receiving from all sides, and particularly from the United States, offers which they could no longer be forced to reject, for by accepting them they would make far more money than if they remained in Vienna. Consequently directors could no longer count on being able to retain a stable and balanced company.[302]

'Repertory theatre,' wrote Alfred Roller in 1909, 'seems to me to be simply a misunderstanding. Admittedly Gustav Mahler was able to show that sacred festival performances (*Weihefestspiele*)[303] are possible in repertory theatre. But he imposed them thanks to his exceptional strength, quite against all the dispositions of his institution.'[304] The mistake of the responsible authorities in Vienna lay in their failure to perceive the need to reform and restructure their institution, while keeping Mahler at all costs and allowing him more free time. Weingartner's subsequent failure demonstrated not only that he was not essentially a man of the theatre, but also that henceforth no conductor with an established reputation would devote all his time to the Opera, because there were now star conductors just as there were star singers.[305]

A few days before his departure, in a moment of melancholy, Mahler said to a 'young artist':[306] 'It was all experiments; the real things were still to come.'[307] Among the unrealized projects he was always to regret, as seen above, were a Gluck cycle (with Lilli Lehmann);[308] a Weber cycle including the new version of *Oberon* he had been working on since the beginning of the year;[309] *The Barber of Bagdad* by Cornelius; the last operas of the *Ring*; and new productions of *Die Meistersinger* and *Tannhäuser*. But he told both Scharlitt and a reporter from the *Neue Freie Presse* who interviewed him in Vienna in

---

[302] EWL 116. [303] This was the subtitle Wagner gave to *Parsifal*.

[304] Alfred Roller, 'Bühnenreform', *Der Merker*, 1 (1909): 5, 194. See also LKR 48.

[305] Wilhelm Kienzl recalls in his memoirs that he was asked whether he would be prepared to accept the post of director of the Vienna Opera. He replied that he would accept, but only if the nature of the post was changed, with the director becoming 'a member like the others' and a 'spiritus rector' (WKL 166).

[306] Probably Schoenberg or one of his pupils, since the conversation was noted by Elsa Bienenfeld. According to Paul Stefan (PSG 132) Mahler said this during his leave-taking from Schoenberg's pupils at the Casino Zögernitz. But we shall see below that the gathering he describes took place two or three years later (see below, Vol. iiii, Chap. 4).

[307] 'Es waren alles nur Versuche, das Eigentliche wäre erst gekommen.' Cf. Elsa Bienenfeld, 'Gustav Mahler und die Wiener Oper', *Neues Wiener Journal* (19 May 1911), PSM 76 and PSG 132. In PSM the sentence is given as, 'It was all experiments, but going forward always involves feeling one's way!' Mahler's famous remark reported by Richard Specht (*Festschrift zur Wiener Musikfestwoche*, 1912) should also be recalled: 'An artist is like a marksman in the dark. He fires his arrows, but does not know whether he hits [the target] or what he hits.' [308] See above, Chap. 9.

[309] See above, Chap. 8, and below, in Vol. iiii, the Appendix. Mahler's version of *Oberon* received its première in Cologne in 1913, conducted by Gustav Brecher and with sets by Roller, who had discovered a means of rapidly changing the sets. The English text had been retranslated, and for a background to the spoken dialogue Mahler merely repeated certain passages from the score 'which produced a magical effect' (*Wiener Mittags-Zeitung*, 4 Aug. 1919).

August that, in leaving Vienna, he was deeply convinced that the system of repertory opera had had its day. To Alma, in the train to Paris, whence they would travel to Cherbourg and then New York, he again said: 'Repertory opera is finished (*ist hin*). I'm glad I don't have to stay to witness its decline. To the end I managed to keep from the public the fact that I was making silk purses out of sows' ears (*dass ich mit Wasser gekocht habe*).'[310] In ten years, largely thanks to him, things had changed with vertiginous speed. Court theatre in the manner of the eighteenth and nineteenth centuries, as practised by Jahn, was already just a distant memory. The door was wide open to the future and the twentieth century.

During this unhappy time Mahler's calm and silence showed, above all, the seriousness of his wounds, and also perhaps his expectation and inward preparation for a new life, a new continent, rather than a new state of mind or a new serenity. A consolation to the end was the loyalty of Prince Montenuovo. We shall soon see that when Weingartner left in 1910 the Prince again spoke with Mahler to try and bring him back to the Hofoper, at least as a guest conductor. Admittedly, at the time of their confrontation in March, and then when Mottl failed to get permission to leave his post, Mahler experienced some bitterness, and felt he was far from being valued at his true worth. At the end of 1912, when Bruno Walter was leaving the Vienna Opera where he had been Kapellmeister, for Munich, the prince told him that two years earlier Mahler himself had recommended him for the post of director, and Montenuovo in fact only released Walter on condition that one day he would accept this post.

The prevailing opinion in Vienna of the Opera's ten Mahler years soon started, predictably enough, to change. Max Graf's verdict, on 1 November 1907, was as follows:

In my opinion Gustav Mahler's activity as director of the Hofoper was, despite his natural artistic genius, altogether destructive. Despite his ten years in Vienna Gustav Mahler remained a stranger: whereas even Brahms, that truculent son of the north German heathland, was touched and changed by the beauty of the Viennese country-side and the stimulating warmth of Viennese social life, so that some of his prickles were blunted, and many sharp edges of his rough nature were smoothed, Mahler withdrew more and more into himself the longer he was here. He shared none of the inclinations of Viennese society, was not captivated by the magic of the city, and in none of his compositions is it possible to discern that the man who created them was working here on Viennese soil.[311] How little naturalness, sense of beauty or real sensuousness there is in these works which, propelled by a gigantic ambition, stubbornly pursues absurdities, and remind one of Goethe's saying that nothing is more dreadful than imagination without taste! Over the years Gustav Mahler shut himself more and more egotistically away from Viennese life, which has always stimulated and refreshed every

---

[310] AMM1, 160; AMM2, 156.

[311] Today we are in a position to grasp the full absurdity of this last remark. As for the preceding one, hindsight shows us that it was precisely because Mahler 'shared none of the inclinations of Viennese society' that he was able to carry out such exemplary reforms at the Opera.

lover of beauty, and which irresistibly attracted the great masters of music who came into the city, so that they never again wished to leave the enchanted mile. As director of the Opera Gustav Mahler set himself against all the traditions of Viennese artistic life—and tradition does not always mean 'sloppiness'.[312] Mahler, unable to appreciate independent artistic personalities, broke up the opera company. Instead of strong characters who could hold the public, there came for the most part mediocre talents that made an easy keyboard for Gustav Mahler to play upon, and the despised prima donnas were replaced by the prima donna on the podium. The comparative rareness of new works dulled the interest of a public that rightly demands novel sensations, and desires to be constantly interested and attracted afresh; while many a much-loved older opera lost all its effectiveness through the experiments of the new chief of design (*Don Giovanni*, for instance). The established opera audience became dissatisfied and ill-tempered. For a number of years this did not matter, as electric trains were bringing in from the suburbs a new public which previously had lived too far away to come to the Opera. But in the end this audience dwindled too, and there was a deficit despite the increase in ticket prices. The most important task of the new opera director will be to win back an established opera audience that feels at home, that on the basis of its experience is entitled to have an opinion, and that can expect to see its taste reflected on stage.[313]

This article so much embarrassed one of the editors of the *Österreichische Rundschau* that he sent an apology to Mahler. Mahler replied:

As I don't have much time these days for reading papers . . . I don't even know what you're talking about. But anyway I'm glad to be in touch with you again, and I take this opportunity to greet you warmly and assure you of my sympathy. It would in any case never occur to me to hold you responsible for an article by Herr <u>Graf</u>. Whatever it contains, I must bear it like all the rest. In a few weeks I'll be a thing of the past, and both sides will be able to reflect more calmly on all these matters.[314]

Much later the same Max Graf, in a book called *Die Wiener Oper* which appeared after the Second World War, was to come into line himself with prevailing opinion and acknowledge that the Mahler epoch had been not only a golden age for the Vienna Opera, but one of the great periods of operatic art worldwide. The book acknowledges that Mahler's successors, Weingartner and Hans Gregor, were both failures, and accuses the latter of turning the Opera into an 'enormous bazaar'.[315] In 1914 Wilhelm von Wymetal, the stage-director appointed by Weingartner mainly to demolish what Mahler had put together, wrote: 'In their collaboration Mahler and Roller raised the principle of the greatest possible stylization in production to historic heights, working not through realism and illusion, but through light and colour, suggestion and

---

[312] An allusion to the famous remark Mahler made at the Opera during rehearsals for *Fidelio*.

[313] Max Graf, 'Wandlungen in der musikalischen Gesellschaft Wiens', *Österreichische Rundschau*, 13 (1907): 3, 201 ff.

[314] Unpublished letter, probably to Alfred von Berger, one of the three co-editors of the *Österreichische Rundschau*; Nov. 1907. Cf. *Nachrichten zur Mahler-Forschung*, 26 (1991), 4–7.

[315] GWO 84; LEM 323.

atmosphere.'[316] This homage to the old regime is the more surprising since Wymetal, two years earlier, had been strongly critical of Roller's work in its entirety.[317] After the First World War Richard Strauss, when himself directing the Hofoper (under the new name of Staatsoper) recognized in his turn that the era of stable ensembles was over. In 1922 a critic by no means hostile to Strauss judged that 'artistic conditions at the Vienna Opera have galloped downhill. Even the most naive spectator becomes more and more aware that Mahler had reigned over the house like a shining archangel, and that since his departure inadequacy and unworthiness have occupied the throne. We had gradually to get used to this decline as best we could.'[318]

Franz Schalk, who was then co-director of the Vienna Opera, wrote in 1919: 'The post-Mahler years passed by, or rather lurched from wave to wave of chance and fashion, without higher guidelines, without concept or method.'[319] And yet Franz Schalk cannot be suspected of partiality towards Mahler. He neither liked nor understood him, as is shown in the following passage from a letter he wrote to Richard Strauss the same year (1919):

The catch-phrase about the sad fate and the warning example of Mahler is a completely Jewish idea. It is ridiculous to put a martyr's halo on him. I was there for seven years of his directorship. He behaved (quite rightly!) like an absolute autocrat, and was inordinately praised on one side—and almost more mindlessly attacked on the other. His ruthlessness extended not only to artists but to works, and he committed a number of artistic sacrileges that anyone else would have been pilloried for. The fact that he finally had to go (after ten years) was principally his own doing. In the last three years of his directorship he increasingly withdrew, both inwardly and outwardly, from the theatre—he had in a sense given all of himself, and could no longer think of ways to capture the public's interest. At the same time his symphonies began to gain ground, and this detached him completely. When at the very end in Vienna he quite openly displayed his grief at leaving the Opera, this was a certain kind of sentimentality that seizes hold of anyone who has had to give up a sphere of activity he has known for years.—He experienced true martyrdom only with his works, which in the beginning met with a resistance as extreme as the way in which they are now proclaimed as the zenith of the art of music, the highest peak of the holy mountain thrown up by Beethoven. But the world is like that, it exaggerates; only posterity is fair, and it has not yet pronounced its judgment on these matters.[320]

Today this version of events leading up to Mahler's departure today seems to be strongly prejudiced. It is coloured in any case by the personal opinion Schalk himself had of his former director, and by their numerous conflicts.

---

[316] Wilhelm von Wymetal, 'Parsifal in Wien', *Allgemeine Zeitung* (Berlin, 30 Jan. 1914).

[317] See above.

[318] Theodor Haas, 'Die Wiener Staatsoper unter Richard Strauss', *Neue Musik-Zeitung*, Stuttgart, 43 (1922): 24, 229, quoted by Franz Grasberger in *Richard Strauss und die Wiener Oper* (Schneider, Tutzing, 1969), 110.

[319] Franz Schalk, 'Zeitwende im Operntheater', *Wiener Mittag*, 'Festbeilage' (15 May 1919).

[320] Letter from Schalk to Strauss, 18 Apr. 1919, in *Richard Strauss und Franz Schalk: Ein Briefwechsel*, ed. Günter Brosche (Schneider, Tutzing, 1983), 119.

Indeed their two characters were utterly at odds, as frequently mentioned above, or at least far too different for Schalk to be able to understand Mahler the man and the artist, to fight by his side and share his triumphs and disappointments. One can hardly blame him for his incomprehension, given the humiliations and frustrations he endured at the hands of a director whom he could only half appreciate. At least he understood the artistic stature of this 'ruthless autocrat'. What was more, most Viennese had come to share this posthumous admiration. After the First World War, everyone in Vienna spoke of the Mahler epoch as a golden age of opera. In 1924 a deputy in the Austrian parliament, the honourable Dr Ellenbogen, put it as follows:

Under Mahler the concept of an outstanding production (*Glanzvorstellung*) implied the endeavour to bring out the most secret beauties of a work in its performance. In those days the essential idea was to raise the artistic level, to give a perfect performance, to choose the finest works and to attract performers utterly intent on giving their artistic best. Today, however, the work and its performance are secondary. Significantly, the high point is now the interval. Whereas in former times the public was systematically encouraged to view art with religious seriousness and to deepen its understanding of the works, the main thing nowadays is: flirting, preening and chatting in the intervals.[321]

As many of Mahler's enlightened contemporaries had predicted, he is today remembered not only as one of the great composers of this century, but also as its greatest opera-director. How right he had been when he prophesied: 'Now they mock me but then they will put up monuments to me.'[322]

After the Anschluss the latent or avowed anti-Semitism of many Austrians again coloured the judgement of posterity. In a work called *Musik aus Wien* (The Music of Vienna), published in 1943, Alexander Witeschnik wrote:

The genial pleasure-master Wilhelm Jahn was followed by the volatile demon Gustav Mahler. The evident nervous fanaticism of this cerebral Jewish musician (*jüdischer Gehirnmusiker*), unbelievably foreign to the Viennese atmosphere, fascinated his contemporaries. Through Mahler, the axe struck at the very roots of the splendid house . . . Mahler's overheated triumphs were the reckless flailings of a madman who was heedlessly undermining the artistic and financial foundations of the house.

And about Mahler as a composer Witeschnik added: 'Here before us stands Mahler the Jew complete: the born showman, the spirit bound to subvert even where it intends otherwise . . .'

Twelve years later, in a second edition published after the war, Witeschnik had slightly moderated his language, although his basic opinion remained much the same:

---

[321] *Neue Freie Presse* (27 Feb. 1924), report concerning the debate on the finances of the national theatres.

[322] From a typewritten-page of 'Mahler's proverbial sayings', which Emil Freund dictated to a friend of his, Dr Kornfeld (copy in BGM, Paris).

The musical pride of the Ringstrasse, the Vienna Hofoper, finished with Wilhelm Jahn. Time has grown weary. The bubbling spring ran dry. In 1896 Bruckner went to his fathers. A few months later, Brahms followed. Hugo Wolf lived in the twilight world of the madhouse. In 1899 Johann Strauss, too, was laid in his grave. A shadow fell over the world. Gustav Mahler moved into the Hofoper.[323]

However, there was at least one admiring observer of the Mahler epoch, someone whose destiny was to throw the most tragic and prolonged of shadows over the world. He was a young student from Linz, an unsuccessful artist who had heard Mahler conduct in Vienna in 1906 before moving there himself the following year:

Although he was frugal, did not smoke or drink, and had no vices, he was obviously having difficulty making ends meet. Much of his money went for the opera, the drug that kept him alive. He attended the opera at least once a week, sometimes twice. In this way he saw his favourite Wagnerian operas. . . . In his eyes Wagner reigned supreme above all other operatic composers. It was an opinion he had formed in Linz, and it was now confirmed by the superb performances at the Opera House, with Gustav Mahler conducting.[324] . . . He had a high regard for Jewish musicians and spoke enthusiastically about Gustav Mahler and the compositions of Felix Mendelssohn.[325]

This failed painter, opera lover, music addict, was Adolf Hitler, who became the most notorious and brutal anti-Semite in history, and even more strangely, the perpetrator of the most massive genocide humanity has known, although he himself may have been half-Jewish, as was perhaps Wagner who inspired him, perhaps more than any other, to his monstrous undertaking—Wagner, at least one of whose great works Hitler discovered brilliantly 're-created under the magnetic baton of the Jew Mahler . . .' Even in the unpublished part of his memoirs, commissioned by the Nazi party, August Kubizek, Hitler's friend from Linz days, recalled that Hitler had 'the greatest admiration' for Mahler. Although Jewish, he was 'nevertheless esteemed by Adolf Hitler, because Gustav Mahler championed Richard Wagner's music-dramas and produced them with a perfection which for those times was nothing short of dazzling'.[326]

---

[323] Alexander Witeschnik, *Musik aus Wien* (1943 and 1955 editions), 355, extracts quoted by Kurt Dieman in *Musik in Wien* (Molden, Vienna 1976), 18.

[324] During his first stay in Vienna, in May–June 1906, the young Hitler, who had just turned 17, went several times to the Opera, notably on 8 and 9 May. On the first of these evenings there was *Tristan* with Mahler conducting: on the second, *Der fliegende Holländer*, conducted by Schalk. We know these two precise dates thanks to postcards sent by Adolf Hitler to August Kubizek, with whom he was later to attempt to write an opera. Hitler also saw *Lohengrin*, his favourite work, probably on 22 May, again with Schalk conducting. When he finally settled in Vienna, in autumn 1907, he had with him a letter of introduction to Alfred Roller, given him by Frau Motlach, mother of his former landlady in Linz. But it seems he was too shy to use it. It is not impossible that he attended Mahler's farewell performance at the Hofoper, the *Fidelio* of 15 Oct. 1907.

[325] See Robert Payne, *The Life and Death of Adolf Hitler* (Prager, New York, 1973); Bradley Smith, *Adolf Hitler, his Family, Childhood and Youth* (Stanford University, Stanford, Calif., 1967); John Toland, *Adolf Hitler* (Doubleday, Garden City, NY, 1976;) William A. Jenks, *Vienna and the Young Hitler* (Columbia University Press, New York, 1960); and J. Sydney Jones, *Hitlers Weg begann in Wien, 1907–1913* (Limes, Wiesbaden, 1980). The latter work contains the most precise and up-to-date information about the weeks Hitler spent in Vienna in May 1907.

[326] Brigitte Haman, *Hitlers Wien: Lehrjahre eines Diktators* (Piper, Munich, 1966), 94 ff.

As Mahler was leaving Vienna, Hermann Bahr summed up what he had achieved as head of the Hofoper in one short sentence: 'It was the Vienna Opera's greatest period, an absolutely unique attempt to run an opera house on purely artistic principles.'[327] The last two things Mahler did before leaving his office at the Opera were one of them provocative and the other conciliatory. At the last minute, when reminded that all the decorations he had received from the Emperor of Austria and from foreign sovereigns were still in the drawer of his desk, he said off-handedly: 'I'll leave them. My successor can have them.'[328] He thus revealed not only his contempt for the honours but also his resentment towards the imperial Austria which had underestimated him and which was so ready to let him go. Also in the course of this final day spent in the office he had occupied for ten years he copied the following letter which he had written before the summer and now dated 7 December 1907 and had printed:

To the members of the Hofoper

The hour has come that puts an end to our work together. I am leaving the place of work that has meant so much to me, and I hereby say farewell.

Instead of something whole, rounded off, as I had dreamed, I am leaving behind unfinished bits and pieces: such is the human lot.

It is not for me to judge the effect of my work on those it was intended for. But at a moment like this I can say of myself that my intentions were honest, my goal was high. My efforts could not always be crowned with success. No one is so vulnerable to 'the inertia of matter'—'the cussedness of things'—as the practising artist. But I have always given everything I had, subordinating my own self to the task in hand, my own inclinations to my duty. I did not spare myself, and could therefore call upon others to do their utmost as well.

In the stress of battle, in the heat of the moment, there were bound to be wounds and mistakes both on my side and yours. But when a work succeeded, when a task was accomplished, we forgot our cares and trouble and felt we were richly rewarded—even without the outward trappings of success. We have all progressed, and with us the institution for which our efforts were made.

From my heart I thank all of you who encouraged me in a difficult and often thankless task, who helped and strove with me. Accept my most sincere good wishes for your future course in life and for the continued success of the Hofoper, whose fortunes I shall always follow with keen interest.

Alfred Roller's papers include an early version of this farewell letter, which Mahler left in the hands of his friend and principal collaborator at the Opera when he left for Maiernigg. Roller wrote on it in pencil the date when he had received it, 3 June 1907.[329] The most important difference between Mahler's

---

[327] Hermann Bahr, *Tagebuch*, quoted by Kurt Dieman, *Musik in Wien*, 18.

[328] 'Anekdotisches von Mahler', *Bohemia* (20 May 1911). The newspaper *Die Zeit* announced on 12 Sept. 1907 that both Mahler and Schlenther, director of the Burgtheater, were to be awarded the Commander's Cross of the Order of Franz-Joseph.

[329] See Evan Baker and Oskar Pausch, 'Gustav Mahlers und Alfred Rollers Briefentwürfe für den Abschied von der Wiener Oper 1907', *Das Archiv Alfred Roller* (Böhlau, Vienna, 1994), 214 ff.

original manuscript and the printed version is the presence of two opening paragraphs, later suppressed:

You will not take it amiss if I spare you the formalities, and myself the upset, of a personal leave-taking. This therefore is my way of bidding you 'farewell!' Now that our work together has come to an end, I naturally cast my mind back over the path we have followed, step by step, over rough and smooth.

It may often have seemed to our flagging spirits that we were going wrong, that we had lost our way in the confusion of short-term objectives. But neither faint-heartedness nor lack of understanding could divert us from our path, nor (*sic*) what keeps us together, our common [goal].

The time has now come for me to leave the place of work I have come to love.

The substance of these introductory remarks was effectively summarized into a new, three-line-long opening paragraph. Most of the former third paragraph, which Roller probably found too pathetic in tone, was quite simply erased. Curiously enough, Roller introduced into the third paragraph of the final version one of Mahler's favourite expressions, 'Die Tücke des Objekts' (The cussedness of things). The most unfortunate of Roller's alterations was undoubtedly his replacement of Mahler's original 'unser', alluding to the work accomplished by the opera-director and his collaborators, with a peremptory 'mein', by which the writer appeared to be distancing himself from the members of the Hofoper who had worked with him for ten years. Alma Mahler was no doubt right when she many times insisted on Roller's 'Rücksichtslosigkeit' and attributed to this unfortunate trait of his character some of the major problems Mahler encountered during the last years of his tenure. This was all the more regrettable since Mahler's aim in writing this message had been to disarm the ill-will which he knew to be festering within the Opera by recalling that he, the despot, the tyrant, had only ever been the instrument of a higher power, the servant of a cause. It was perhaps a clumsy effort, because it was now formulated as a personal justification instead of laying greater emphasis on collective responsibility. The letter, which Mahler had had printed and pinned up on the big notice board near the artists' entrance, was found on the ground the following day, torn into little pieces. Once again Mahler's humility towards music and its masters had been taken for arrogance and complacency. Once again, carried away by his own intensity, and by the emotions of parting, the man of genius failed to bear in mind the human frailty of others.

The last two European performances of a Mahler symphony before his departure for the United States took place in November and December 1907, not in Germany or Austria, but in England under Thomas Beecham, and at the Czech Philharmonic in Prague under its permanent conductor Vilém Zemánek.[330] Zdenek Nejedlý, a young Czech musicologist who was soon to

[330] Vilém Zemánek (1875–1922), was born in Prague, the son of a German rabbi. He was a medical doctor before studying music in Vienna, mainly under Guido Adler. A gifted entrepreneur and severe discip-

write one of the earliest books about Mahler,[331] published a lengthy review in the newspaper *Den* (The Day). He began by saying that the composer of the Fourth Symphony was for him one of the most interesting figures in contemporary music. He confessed that he experienced

a sort of malicious glee at seeing the odd expressions on the faces of concert enthusiasts as they listen to a performance of a Mahler symphony, or when I read reviews of his works in Vienna, in Berlin, or in this country. It is with Mahler that we can see most clearly the uneducated behaviour—or rather the defective education—of today's audiences and of modern 'musical circles'.

Nejedlý drew attention to the inconsistency between Mahler's complete rejection of all programmatic music, and the explicit programme which was displayed in the Fourth Symphony:

His attempts at expressing 'the joys of heaven' at times lead him into overt triviality of expression. Mahler introduced ' irony' (a purely programmatic element) into his music, and in the Third Symphony by parodying triviality he attains true irony. In the Fourth Symphony there is no parody, but plenty of triviality, and that triviality—although of the genuine Viennese type—comes across clearly. We might say that here Mahler has undertaken a courageous experiment that has not quite worked out. He wanted something new, but the experiment has bogged him down. Otherwise, the whole newness of Mahler's symphony, which constitutes something of a cornerstone in the most modern of music, works its magic here too. Here you will not doubt for a single moment that you are listening to music of the twentieth century, not only on account of the work's technical complexity but also due to its daring in the construction of simple melodies. In these, too, there is a good deal of sophisticated treatment, to such an extent that the result is a dangerous toying with triviality. To give a first performance of such a work at a popular concert is a move at first startling but also most pleasing.[332]

Unfortunately, Nejedlý thought that the performance 'was not—and could not have been—up to the highest standards' and that 'our Philharmonic played the notes, but it was not playing Mahler', although 'it did its best' and 'performed to a much higher standard than usual'. Although not frankly favourable, Nejedlý's assessment was undoubtedly exceptional at the time in

linarian, he succeeded in raising the level of the orchestra. He was a convinced Mahlerian and conducted a great number of Mahler performances between 1904 and 1918, when he was dismissed from his post as a German citizen. He played an important role in rehearsing the orchestra for the première of Mahler's Seventh Symphony in 1908 (see below, Vol. iiii, Chap. 2 and Jitka Ludvová, 'Mahler, Zemlinsky und die Tschechische Philharmonie', *Nachrichten zu Mahler-Forschung*, 36 (1997), 4).

[331] Zdeněk Nejedlý (1878–1962), the son of a music teacher and composer, received an all-round musical education in Prague. In 1908, he started teaching musicology at the University, and became a passionate champion of Smetana, whom he considered, together with Fibich, Foerster, and Ostrcil, the true representatives of Czech music, while he always remained opposed to such leading figures as Dvořák, Jánaček, Suk, and Novák. Nejedlý spent the war years in the USSR and became a convinced communist and a politician when he returned to his native country. Minister of Education from 1948 to 1953, he occupied many other official posts. He was a prolific writer, and left some 200 books, in particular, *Josef Bohuslav Foerster* (1910), *Mahler* (1913), *Wagner* (1916), *Novák* (1921), and four volumes of a *Smetana* which was to be his *magnum opus* but remained unfinished. [332] *Den*, 219 (7 Nov. 1907), 8.

that it attributed to Mahler's original and modern spirit much in the music that was disturbing and even shocking.

Dalibor, the Czech musical journal, felt that the Fourth Symphony was 'interesting and ingenious' rather than 'original and profound':

In the first two movements the work is made somewhat shallow by the choice of motivic material that at times borders on the banal, while its individuality of expression is weakened considerably by its evident openness to outside ideas, and to such a large extent that whilst listening to the work we can recognize various individual 'quotations' and marvel at the great number and variety of styles, artistic trends and composers from which they come.

Mahler's style and general conception were 'more lucid and simple' than in the Second Symphony (which had been heard in Prague four years earlier), his melodic writing was 'accessible, if at times also crude', and only the instrumentation gave the work 'at least from the outside a touch of modernity'. Both symphonies clearly displayed 'foreign elements—including to a large extent, Czech ones'.[333]

Smetana, the other Czech musical journal, discerned in the Fourth Symphony more 'sophisticated culture of today' than 'natural and unaffected naivety'. It revealed its author's 'desperate searching for new paths', with 'moments of harmonic naivety [which] alternate with true absurdities'. Jan Reichmann, the *Smetana* critic, imagined Mahler to be a 'confirmed ironist', practising 'dissimulation and affectation', 'making fun of the average, uncomprehending audience'. 'Mahler does not mean quite seriously the things he says. The Germans of course elevate such a "path-finder" (*pfadfinder*) to the status of a god, and the unthinking crowd of "cultural philistines" (*Bildungsphilister*), so despised by Nietzsche, crawls along in meekness and in silent, foolish wonderment after its idol.' How wrong the Czech critic was to believe that Mahler's paradoxes were well accepted and warmly admired in Germany! It seems that the Fourth Symphony was still being completely misunderstood.[334]

The second English performance of Mahler's Fourth Symphony took place on 3 December in the Queen's Hall in London, under a conductor whose name is rarely associated with Mahler and who, on this occasion, was experimenting with a then unfamiliar composer. In 1905, a body of sixty excellent musicians had been assembled under the aegis of the violinist John Saunders, who was their leader and chairman. It included several of the finest players in London, such as the hornist Aubrey Brain and the clarinettist Charles Draper. They had given a series of concerts which, despite the low price of seats, had failed. The

---

[333] *Dalibor*, 30 (1907): 5/6, 48.

[334] *Smetana*, 2 (1907): 20, 299. Programme of the 5th Concert of the Czech Philharmonic, conducted on 3 Nov. 1907 by Vilém Zemánek: Mahler, Symphony No. 4 (sop. solo Marie Musilová); Beethoven: Romance in F, Op. 50 (Antonio de Grassi, vl.); Piano Concerto No. 3, Op. 37 (Zdeněk David, pia.); Overture to *Prometheus*, Op. 43.

press had announced at that time that the young Thomas Beecham (then 28) wanted to give a series of concerts with a chamber orchestra. Draper contacted him and, during their first conversation, Beecham, in characteristic manner, spoke only of performing works practically unknown. Neverthelesss, an agreement was reached and a series of four 'Thomas Beecham concerts' was announced. They were to take place at the Bechstein Hall and to begin on 1 November 1906, at which time the orchestra had been rechristened the New Symphony Orchestra.

When its second season opened, on 14 October 1907, Beecham had reorganized the New Symphony Orchestra, brought it to full symphonic strength, and moved it to the 'ampler accommodation' of Queen's Hall.[335] The *pièce de résistance* of his third concert, on 3 December, was Mahler's Fourth Symphony. His choice of soloist for the symphony was very unusual, to say the least, since Blanche Marchesi, daughter and pupil of the more famous Mathilde, was a dramatic soprano who had already sung Isolde and Brünnhilde on the stage. All but one of the other works on the programme were in fact solo numbers for Mme Marchesi.[336]

As for the reviews, they were just as scathing as they had been two years earlier, after the previous performance of the same work under Henry Wood. According to the unsigned article in *The Times*, Mahler was 'a man who ought to be heard', but this symphony was 'never likely to become popular' because 'the character of the themes employed and the manner of working them out' were 'so entirely disproportionate':

Mahler makes tunes that are simple to the verge of being childish, and applies all the resources of modern orchestration and modern learning in the manipulation of them . . . Mahler treats a tune that is introduced first in a quasi-Haydnish manner with so many cacophonous distortions and so many frankly ugly effects that the result cannot help being inartistic as well as painful.[337]

The *Morning Post* devoted a good deal more space to Blanche Marchesi's solo numbers than to Mahler. The Fourth Symphony was described as 'entirely unconventional' and often 'quaint in effect'. 'The composer introduces his uncommon devices into his working-out sections, but his subject matter is always straightforward, melodious, and the Adagio charming.' The Scherzo was singled out for containing 'much curious device, some of it not always pleasing

[335] See Charles Reid, *Thomas Beecham: An Independent Biography* (Dutton, New York, 1962), 53 ff.

[336] Mathilde Marchesi (1821–1913) was one of the most famous and admired vocal teachers of all times. Her daughter, Blanche (1863–1940) made her debut in London in 1896, sang at Covent Garden in 1902, and also taught singing at the end of her career. Programme for the 3 Dec. concert conducted by Thomas Beecham: Méhul, *La Chasse du jeune Henri*, Overture; Wagner, *Der fliegende Holländer*, Senta's Ballad; Mahler, Symphony No. 4 (Blanche Marchesi, sop.); Handel, *Alcina*, Air, 'Ah, mio cor'; Schubert, *Der Hirt auf den Felsen* (Charles Draper, clar. solo); Cyril Scott: *Aubade* for orchestra; Marie Horne, *Songs of the Wind*; Holbrooke, *Varenka*, Gypsy Song; Johann Strauss, *Frühlingsstimmen*, Op. 410; Wagner, *Tristan und Isolde*, Liebestod.

[337] *The Times* (4 Dec. 1907). Heartfelt thanks are due to Richard Landau and Lewis Foreman for sending me this review upon very short notice.

in its effect owing to the excessive freedom of the contrapuntal treatment to be noticed at the beginning, in which there is a violin solo. . . . Under Thomas Beecham it was given a careful reading, but one of little distinction.'

Finally the *Sunday Times*, in a brief notice, found that the new work, 'despite its melodiousness and picturesque colouring', had 'a curious lack of real distinction', and that the Finale was 'naive to banality'. The opinions expressed by the musical journals were no more enlightened. The *Musical News* dismissed the Symphony as containing 'pleasing themes and passages, but on the whole the effect is discursive, and ultimately more than a little tedious.'[338] As for the *Musical Standard*, it criticized the symphony for:

a paucity of genuinely original matter . . . which renders it intolerably dull. It reminds one of the ponderous tomes which German professors add to their academic shelves at regular intervals, works which represent fabulous industry and correctness of detail, but which are of interest only to the academic clique. The first movement is spun out to a wearisome length and although it makes an attempt at lightness and gaiety, the whole thing is wearisome and common-place and 'weighs' as heavy as lead. The Scherzo is certainly better and more intesting in outline, and in the Adagio expectation of something exceptional is raised. But the last movement in which a German folk-song is introduced is an anti-climax and is not far removed from the bathetic.[339]

This first encounter with Mahler's music made little impression on Thomas Beecham himself. Mahler's name is not even mentioned in his memoirs and played practically no role in his life as a conductor. In fact, the important encounter for him of the year 1907 was that with Frederick Delius which had occurred at the end of the first concert of the series, on 19 October.

Some members of the Opera had already taken leave of Mahler in a way which must have touched his heart, that is to say by performing his works. As we have seen, Mildenburg sang the *Kindertotenlieder*, with Bruno Walter conducting, on 6 November. Two days before leaving for America Mahler wrote her a personal farewell:

Dear old friend, I have just written a formal letter to the 'honoured members', which will be put up on the noticeboard. But as I was writing it it seemed to me that you were not one of them and that for me you have always been separate from the rest. I kept hoping in these last few days to see you face to face. But now you are on the Semmering (where admittedly it is much nicer). So I can only send you, by way of farewell (from the theatre—not from Vienna, where I shall continue to live), these few heartfelt words, and press your hand in spirit. I shall always follow your progress with the old attachment and sympathy, and I hope that in calmer times we shall find ourselves together again.

---

[338] *Musical News* (14 Dec. 1907). This review is signed L.M., possibly the critic and composer Lionel Monckton. Heartfelt thanks are due to Tony Duggan for finding and sending me this review just before the MS of this volume was due to be sent to the publisher.

[339] *Musical Standard* (7 Dec. 1907), 352.

In any case you know that even far away I remain a friend on whom you can rely. I'm writing this amid terrific turmoil. Fondest farewells, and keep your chin up![340]

The day after Mahler's departure another member of the Opera, also chose to take leave of him by a performance of his works. Selma Kurz included three *Wunderhorn-Lieder* in the programme of an orchestral recital she gave on 10 December, again with Bruno Walter conducting.[341] Everything suggests that both singers went to Mahler to sing his Lieder to him and receive his advice on interpretation. During his last days in Vienna he again revised and corrected the score of the Fifth Symphony in the light of its recent performance in St Petersburg, further thinning out the scoring of the first and final movements.[342] On 5 December he wrote to the director of Peters:

Dear Mr Hinrichsen, I am thinking of publishing my Seventh Symphony. Before considering any other offer I should like to ask you whether in principle you are interested in my new work, and to request a reply by telegram as I have to leave on Monday to embark for America. To give you an idea of the work I should say that it is generally cheerful and humorous. There are no exceptional instrumental requirements (4 horns, 3 trumpets). Only in the fourth (the last but one) movement, a serenade, are a guitar and a mandolin required.

In the event of your being interested in the work I should like to ask for your consent to the possibility of the world première (so long as I find the artistic conditions favourable) taking place in America in the course of the coming season.[343] As for the European première, I have in mind the next festival of the Allgemeiner Deutscher Musikverein, either in Vienna or in Amsterdam-Frankfurt (with Mengelberg).[344]

But Hinrichsen felt he had already gone to enough trouble for the Fifth Symphony, uncompensated as a result of the small number of performances. Besides, the score had been substantially revised, and Mahler was now pressing him for a new edition, which would be very expensive. So he replied by telegram: 'Cordial thanks. Unfortunately no longer possible

---

[340] Undated letter to Mildenburg (7 Dec. 1907), ÖTM.

[341] The programme of this concert, at 19.30 in the Grosser Musikvereinsaal, conducted by Bruno Walter, was as follows: Weber: *Oberon* Overture; Thomas: *Hamlet*, Mad Song (soloist Selma Kurz); Mahler: 'Das irdische Leben', 'Wo die schönen Trompeten blasen', 'Wer hat dies Liedlein erdacht' (id.); Liszt: *Hungarian Fantasy* (soloist Vera Shapira); David: *La Perle du Brésil*, Mysoli's aria; Verdi: *Sicilian Vespers*, Bolero (soloist Selma Kurz). The singer also performed, as encores: Bellini: *La Sonnambula*, Rondo; and Verdi: *Un Ballo in Maschera*, the page's aria. Vera Shapira, soloist in the *Hungarian Fantasy*, was the wife of the critic Richard Specht.

[342] EWL 44. Egon Wellesz states that he saw the score 'as revised and approved for the indispensable new edition, Gustav Mahler. Dec. 1907.'

[343] The *New York Times* of 6 Oct. 1907, had announced that Mahler would conduct the première of his own Seventh Symphony in New York in the course of his first season there. The news was given as coming from Walter Damrosch, permanent conductor and programme planner of the New York Symphony Orchestra. The fact that nothing came of this was doubtless because Conried had contracted the right to organize Mahler concerts at the Metropolitan Opera and eventually dropped this project.

[344] Undated letter to Peters (dated 5 Dec. 1907 by the recipient). In his haste, Mahler forgot to sign it. He gave as his address the Hôtel Bellevue in Paris. See Eberhardt Klemm's previously quoted article, 'Zur Geschichte der Fünften Symphonie von Gustav Mahler', 50.

having concluded various important contracts. All best wishes for your success in America.'[345]

After another fruitless attempt with Breitkopf and Härtel,[346] Mahler entered negotiations the following year with a Berlin publisher, recommended by Fried, for publication of the Seventh Symphony.[347] A week before he was due to leave for America, Mahler met Strauss, who had come to Vienna to conduct a Philharmonic concert on 1 December.[348] After the public rehearsal the day before, Karl Moll fetched Mahler from the Opera for lunch at Hartmann's restaurant. They were joined by Strauss. Mahler, naturally anxious to know what kind of reception he might expect in America, asked Strauss who had already been several times across the Atlantic: 'Isn't it a nonsense for me to be going to work in New York, where none of the preconditions for understanding what I am trying to do are to be found?' To which Strauss simply replied: 'But Mahler, you are and remain a child. Over there you get up on the podium and do this—(he waved an imaginary baton)—and then you go to the cashier and—(a gesture of counting money).'[349] One wonders whether Strauss's down-to-earth businesslike approach did not reflect his secret irritation at Mahler's well-known 'idealism'. He wanted to provoke him, to remind him that an artist is also an artisan who needs to be free from material worries in order to create without making too great a sacrifice. Mahler no doubt did not take him seriously, but nonetheless took such cynical honesty as sadly indicative of Strauss's character.

Among the close friends Mahler wished to take leave of in person were the Zuckerkandls, who had exerted an important if unintentional influence on his life by introducing him to Alma. They now lived at 22 Nusswaldgasse in Oberdöbling,[350] not far from the Hohe Warte. On this farewell visit Mahler talked peacefully with Emil and Berta, who recalled some of his remarks in her memoirs:

How I love your garden, the gentle swaying of the walnut trees, this sacred reminder of Beethoven. He achieved what will never be bestowed on me: perfection... In the

---

[345] Eberhardt Klemm, 'Geschichte', 51.

[346] See below, Vol. iiii, Chap 2.

[347] The firm was Lauterbach and Kuhn (see below, Vol. iiii, Chap. 2 and Vol. iii, Appendix 2, on the Seventh Symphony).

[348] Programme of Vienna Philharmonic concert, conducted by Richard Strauss on 1 Dec. 1907: Spohr: Overture to *Jessonda*; Wagner: *Eine Faust Overture*; Debussy: *Prélude à l'après-midi d'un faune* (first Viennese performance); Strauss: *Symphonia Domestica* (first performance by the Philharmonic). This was probably Mahler's first hearing of a work by Debussy (he was soon to conduct the *Prélude* in New York). The Philharmonic concerts in the 1906–7 season were conducted by Franz Schalk, Richard Strauss, and Bruno Walter: those of the following season by Schalk, Weingartner, and Walter.

[349] Unpublished memoirs of Karl Moll, typescript, 61 (copy in BGM, Paris). Moll had a slip of memory in stating that Strauss was in Vienna to conduct rehearsals of *Feuersnot*. Actually the incident can only have taken place at the time of the Philharmonic concert mentioned above, which provided the only opportunity for Strauss and Mahler to meet between his resignation and his departure for the United States.

[350] The Zuckerkandls had moved there quite recently. The historic dinner party given by them, during which Mahler met Alma, had taken place in their former house, on Alserbackstrasse (KMI).

performance of a work of art perfection can be attained only for a flash, for perfection means fulfilment, and both are just one breath of eternity. I hope for perfection every time I rehearse and conduct an opera, but I achieve this blessing only as a flash of lightning which passes through my soul, flares up, and then is gone again.[351]

As mentioned earlier, Berta Zuckerkandl's memoirs are subject to errors and flights of fancy.[352] This time, however, the words quoted convincingly reflect what must have been Mahler's state of mind at that time. Berta also recalls the following exchange between Mahler and her husband:[353]

'I am aware (said Mahler sadly) that I am leaving behind only bits and pieces. I shall stress that in my letter to the Philharmonic.[354] Despite everything, they are first-rate artists (*künstlerische Potenz*). They will understand.'—'I doubt it,' (Emil replied). 'Dear friend! You are much too inclined to assume that others share your idea of the artist. And you are forgetting the barricades which that very orchestra has erected against your efforts. They will never understand that your severity is an artistic principle. You have achieved what no one else has. And that only by showing no mercy.'—'Anyway for me, as for you—and that is what binds me to you so closely—lying is pointless, incomprehensible. Science and art cannot exist without conscience. But I can't deny that I feel sad when I recall how, ten years ago, I firmly believed I could attain perfection'—'You have grasped what I learned to understand long ago. That everything temporal is but a likeness.[355] And to understand that is tragic.'[356]

Before leaving Vienna Mahler said two further things in confidence to Berta Zuckerkandl. The first reveals a fundamental optimism which is perhaps surprising in a composer generally reputed for his extreme pessimism. 'Even if it should fall on bare rock, no seed can ever, ever be lost. It will always grow in the end! One has only to wait.'[357] The second was more intimate in character:

I'm taking my homeland along with me. My Alma, my child. It's only now that the heavy burden of work has been lifted off my shoulders that I know what my most precious task will be. Alma has sacrificed ten years of her youth for me. No one knows,

[351]   Berta Zuckerkandl, *Österreich intim*, 71.

[352]   Concerning Rodin's visit to Vienna in 1902 for instance, the words which Berta quotes as his after a performance of *The Marriage of Figaro* almost certainly had their origin in her imagination (see above, Vol. ii, Chap. 13). In the same book, a letter supposed to have been sent by Berta to Sophie Clemenceau in Paris in 1907, after Mahler's departure from Vienna for New York, says that he has been replaced at the Philharmonic by 'the Opera's ballet conductor'. Now as we know, this replacement took place in 1901, and Hellmesberger left the Philharmonic two years later as the result of a scandal.

[353]   Emil Zuckerkandl died on 28 May 1910.

[354]   We have seen that the letter was in fact addressed to all the members of the Opera.

[355]   *Alles Irdische ist nur ein Gleichnis*, a paraphrase of the line in *Faust* Part II, which Mahler set to music at the end of the Eighth Symphony.

[356]   Unpublished passage from Berta Zuckerkandl's *Österreich intim*, put at my disposal in the 1960s by her daughter-in-law, Mrs Friedrich Zuckerkandl.

[357]   *Österreich intim*, 72. The final sentence, perhaps Berta's, appears only in the unpublished manuscript.

can ever know, with what absolute selflessness she has subordinated her own life to me and my work. It is with a light heart that I set off on my way with her.[358]

Mahler also took his leave of Josef Bohuslav Förster, the faithful friend who, since the Hamburg days, had shown continuous affection and loyalty. Förster said how sad he was, and Mahler tried to console him:

It's true that I'm going, but you know my contract provides for long holidays, and I shall always spend part of them in Vienna. I am keeping our flat, and there are some family members here, and a few friends. We shall now actually be able to spend time together again. We can revive our Hamburg days—you remember? Until now, I've been so busy that we couldn't see much of each other. Now it will be different, and I'm already looking forward to our meetings. Incidentally, have you read Giordano Bruno? . . . What a man, what a thinker! Have we made any progress at all? Didn't Bruno know everything we know today?[359]

And Förster comments:

That was just like him! In a single moment he had forgotten all that oppressed him, all the ingratitude, the bitter disappointments, the painful impressions of the last days and hours, the betrayal of those 'supporters and admirers' who had turned their backs on the outcast once his power and authority were gone. The hero, thrust by unclean hands from his throne, soared up on wings of the spirit to the land of happiness, where earthly things are all forgotten.[360]

We have seen that Karpath, in a report in the Munich *Allgemeine Zeitung*, was to reproach Mahler bitterly[361] for not having taken his leave of the Viennese critics, even those who had supported him. But ever since 1905[362] and the Viennese première of Mahler's Lieder, their relationship had deteriorated, so it was not to be expected that Mahler would feel any need to say goodbye. On the other hand, he wrote to Max Kalbeck, whose honesty and objectivity he had often appreciated, in spite of the lack of understanding he had shown for Mahler's works:

Your kind letter gave me great pleasure. I feel that what you wrote was dictated by personal feelings going beyond mere convention. Our relationship is unfortunately like an embryo with all its limbs, but which never developed for some reason or other. I firmly hope that the new pattern of my life will bring you within the circle of those dear and precious to me, for I have long thought of you as a friend, almost a relation.[363]

---

[358] AMM1, 411. This excerpt from Berta's diary was not included in AMM2. At first sight, Mahler seems to be alluding to both Alma and Gucki. However, since he is expressing his devotion to Alma and speaking of her youth, 'my child' is more likely to allude to her, particularly since Gucki did not accompany her parents to the USA until the following year.

[359] JFP 705. Förster recalls that at the time a new edition of Bruno's works was being issued in Jena.

[360] Ibid. The final sentence is a paraphrase of the text from the Finale of Mahler's Second Symphony,

[361] See above, Chap. 9, and below.   [362] See above, Chap. 2.

[363] MBR1, no. 278; MBR2, no. 375. The original of this letter was sold after the war by the Viennese antiquarian Ingo Nebehay.

In one of the cards he sent Korngold during the autumn,[364] Mahler made an effort once again to explain the basic reasons for his departure:

If I want to leave my post, it is not 1) the fault of 'the wicked journalists' (I truly would leave them, too, without rancour), nor 2) 'because I want to devote myself to composition' (I am always ready, when composition wants to devote itself to me), but solely because I have realized that the theatre (in its present form) is a non-artistic institution and that all the outer and inner conflicts that it causes for a man of my (our) sort flow from the essence of the thing. For that reason therefore I could not put the blame on anyone if I now feel I must desert the flag—not even myself![365]

Korngold goes on with the story:

For me, this painful loss included a personal gain. For now there was nothing to hinder friendship with this gifted and fascinating man. At one time there was a plan to create a post for Mahler that would give him overall supervision of Austria's state musical institutions.[366] There was also talk of restoring him to his post. But he was tired of Vienna, tired of Europe, and the call to America found him ready to take flight . . . We took leave of each other in a suburban café. Although the outcast could scarcely flee far enough, it was with reluctance that he crossed the wide sea. But his irregularly beating heart, which had suffered damage, reminded him that he, who had thought in his tireless work only of the future of art, must now think of the future of his family. And how brightly his matchless energy flared up for the new task! There, too, he was to shake up tradition, conjure an orchestra out of nothing, fight for Beethoven against the opera stars.[367]

Mahler sent Bruno Walter a note in reply to his farewell letter:

My dear friend, Thank you very much for your kind letter. Neither of us need waste words on what we mean to each other.—I know of no one who understands me as well as I feel you do, and I believe that for my part I have entered deep into the workings of your soul. Enclosed is the picture your wife asked for. Best wishes to both of you. Hoping to see you again in May.[368]

A few days later, the young conductor wrote to his parents:

It was very hard saying goodbye to Mahler. . . . Despite all I have suffered because of him[369] and may still suffer in the future—for he can be terribly difficult at times—he

---

[364] The cards and letters Mahler sent to the critic of the *Neue Freie Presse* have disappeared. Fortunately there are some extracts in his memoirs, now published in KIW.

[365] Korngold explains that the admiring articles he had written on the Second Symphony and Mahler's farewell concert had provoked a particularly vicious anonymous letter to the *Neue Freie Presse*.

[366] This undoubtedly refers to Guido Adler's proposal (see above, Chap. 9).   [367] KIW 113.

[368] MBR1, no. 259; MBR2, no. 378. The original of this letter is in the Library of the Performing Arts, Lincoln Center, New York. Bruno Walter owned a copy of the text of the 'Veni Creator' written in Mahler's hand (see below, Appendix 2, on the Eighth Symphony). Mahler probably gave it to him when he was leaving the Vienna Opera.

[369] What Bruno Walter was secretly reproaching Mahler with is unknown and was perhaps mentioned in the sentences which were omitted from the published version of this letter. Unfortunately the autographs of Mahler's letters of Bruno Walter are not presently accessible. The 'sufferings' Walter says he experienced at Mahler's hands could have been caused by Alma's sharp tongue and her jealousy towards anyone who had played an important part in Mahler's past (according to Anna Mahler, Spoleto, Sept. 1982). It is also likely that Walter had not forgiven Mahler for his lack of support when, after his unsuccessful Vienna debut, he had been bitterly attacked by the press.

remains one of the people dearest to me in the world. And despite all the pain, what I owe him is immeasurable.[370]

Alma Mahler's book contains an account of a 'farewell evening' Mahler allegedly organized in a restaurant in Grinzing to take leave of Schoenberg and his pupils. Actually this lively event took place later, in 1908 or 1909, as is proved by a short, recently discovered autobiographical text by Berg.[371] The group of young avant-garde musicians was by then effervescent with activity. On 7 November, when Mahler was still in Russia, they held a concert of chamber music works by Alban Berg, Karl Horwitz, Rudolph Weirich, O. de Ivanov, Heinrich Jalowetz, Erwin Stein, Wilma von Webenau, and Anton von Webern—in the Council Room of the Wiener Kaufmannschaft (Vienna Chamber of Commerce). Three Lieder by Berg were premièred (sung by Elsa Parzeller) together with his Variations for piano and his Double fugue for string quintet and piano, both with the composer at the piano, and also Webern's Quintet for strings and piano.[372] A week after Mahler's departure, on 17 December, Schoenberg composed his first deliberately atonal work, the first of his Two Lieder for voice and piano Op. 14 (a setting of Stefan George), embarking on his mature style and permanently alienating the European musical Establishment, Strauss for example. Alma Mahler attended the November concert with Zemlinsky, who was still regarded as mentor of the group. To him Mahler sent the following note a few days before he left:

We should like to say goodbye to you—couldn't you and Schoenberg drop in again? I'm afraid we have not got a free evening left, so it would have to be in the afternoon.— Preferably at 4 o'clock, when we are always in.—Please also bring my score [Seventh Symphony]. You can have it back on my return.[373]

At the last moment, unknown to Mahler, Paul Stefan and three Schoenberg pupils, Anton von Webern, Karl Horwitz, and Heinrich Jalowetz, hastily printed and sent to a group of friends and admirers of Mahler the following message:

Gustav Mahler's admirers will be gathering to say farewell to him on Monday 9 December, before half past eight in the morning, on the platform at the West-Bahnhof, and invite you to attend and to inform others of like mind. As this demonstration is intended as a surprise for Mahler, you are earnestly requested not to take people having connections with the Press into your confidence.[374]

---

[370] BWB 97. Letter to his parents of 10 Jan. 1908.

[371] Stargardt auction, Marburg, Nov. 1965, see below, Vol. iiii, Chap. 4. This page in Berg's handwriting, intended for his friend Hermann Matzenauer, who was planning to write his biography, now belongs to Erich Alban Berg. Richard Specht's book confirms that the gathering took place later (RSM2, 21). However it is possible that there was another, shorter, farewell evening in 1907.

[372] Cf. Willi Reich, *Alban Berg* (Atlantis, Zurich 1963), 23, and H. F. Redlich, *Alban Berg*, (UE, Vienna, 1957), 294, as well as H. H. Stuckenschmidt, *Schönberg: Leben, Umwelt, Werk* (Atlantis, Zurich, 1974), 97.

[373] MBR1, no. 320; MBR2, no. 374, undated (beginning of Dec. 1907). As seen above, Zemlinsky had previously made a four-hand piano reduction of the Sixth Symphony.

[374] PSG 92 and BDB 256.

So on the departure a group of about 200 people were standing on the station platform. They included notably Gutheil-Schoder and Schmedes from among the members of the Opera, Rosé and the members of his quartet with some of the other Philharmonic players, all of Schoenberg's pupils (a large group by now), and several painters such as Alfred Roller and Gustav Klimt. Mahler at last appeared, wearing a dark winter coat and a soft felt hat.[375] He was greeted by a friendly cheer and, very moved, exchanged a glance and a nod with all those waiting to say goodbye to him. Alban Berg was present with his fiancée, Helene Nahowski:

Helene was face to face with Mahler for the first time. She was profoundly moved, fascinated by his personality. As she reached out a bouquet to him, Mahler dropped his glove. Helene bent down to pick it up. Mahler thanked her and held her gaze for a long time. Helene said to me of this: 'I have never in my life been able to forget those eyes or that look'.[376]

Whoever saw how all those who came (and there were about two hundred people) greeted each other, anyone who saw how warmly, how emotionally every one of them shook Mahler's hand, and how affectionately and delightedly he submitted to it, how he, who had always been so sparing of his words, found so many kind words for his faithful friends, must have been delighted, and those who loved him could enjoy this last happy moment. It had all been organized at a few hours' notice, and no 'official' personalities had been notified. There was no artifice: simply an overpowering wish, among all of us, to see once more the man, to whom we owed so much... The train started to move. And Gustav Klimt said what we had all been feeling about the sad ending of a great epoch: 'It's over' (*Vorbei!*).[377]

Mahler wrote Schoenberg a card on the train, thanking him for having helped organize this farewell and asking him to thank and 'convey regards to all the young friends'.[378] The emotion aroused by the spontaneous demonstration shows clearly in Alma's account:

It was time to leave Vienna. Schoenberg and Zemlinsky had gathered their pupils and Mahler's friends on the station platform. Pollak[379] had arranged for them to get on to the platform secretly. When we arrived, there they all were, their hands full of flowers,

---

[375] According to the *Illustrirtes Wiener Extrablatt* of 9 Dec. The Viennese press also announced that Mahler's friends had given him as a farewell gift an autograph letter by Beethoven to the bass singer Friedrich Meyer, who was the first Pizarro in *Fidelio*, see *Le Guide musical*, Paris, 53 (1907): 51, 811. This allegedly 'unpublished' letter had in fact been included the year before in *Beethovens Sämtliche Briefe*, ed. Alfred Christian Kalischer (Schuster & Loeffler, Leipzig, 1906), i. 161.

[376] Eleonore Vondenhoff's account of a conversation with Helene Berg, placed at my disposal by the writer (copy in BGM, Paris). When she spoke with Helene Berg in 1972, a thoroughly unreliable book had been published, claiming that Berg had placed a Lied he had recently composed on Mahler's seat in the train (see Berndt Wessling, *Mahler: Ein prophetische Leben* (Hoffmann und Campe, Hamburg, 1974), 244). Helene Berg explained that her late husband would never have done such a thing; he had far too much respect for Mahler (see below, Vol. iiii, Appendix, 'Mahler Myths').

[377] PSG 92.

[378] Library of Congress, Washington, DC. The *Wiener Werkstätte* card was posted from the station at Almstetten, between Vienna and Salzburg. Alma wrote the address.

[379] The name of this faithful friend, an official at the Ministry of Transport, appears only in AMS.

eyes full of tears; they climbed into our compartment and garlanded seats, floor, every-thing. We pulled slowly out of the station, without regret or nostalgia. We had been too hard hit, we only wanted to get away, far away. We were indeed almost happy the further we got from Vienna. We did not even long for our child, which we had left with my mother. We knew that no amount of care and love can prevent the worst from happening. One is nowhere invulnerable. We had been hardened by fire. So we believed. But one thing, despite everything, filled our thoughts: the future.[380]

As the train moved off Mahler and Alma were still at the windows, exchanging a few last words with their closest friends. Those on the platform waved hats and handkerchiefs. Then husband and wife, after a last look upon the crowd of friends, closed the window and sat down facing each other, choked with emotion, in a compartment which looked like a greenhouse full of flowers.

Several newspapers the same evening published accounts of the former director's departure. David Josef Bach wrote in the *Arbeiter-Zeitung* of his farewell letter to the members of the Opera, which in his opinion 'did honour to Mahler the man and the artist', but violently criticized the farewell at the station and the 'childish' invitation issued by Schoenberg's pupils. He consid-ered that henceforth it would be necessary to 'protect him from his friends'. The text of the note had been 'as poorly inspired' as the famous 'address' of the previous spring, 'which had provoked as much derision among his enemies as it did shame and anger among the true friends of Mahler the artist'. Bach expressed a hope that calm would return after so many battles and that

the unedifying Mahler squabble can at last be stilled. Mahler truly has nothing to fear if peace and prudence reign once more in Vienna. The organizers wanted the press to remain unaware of their demonstration. That would only have been possible if the whole business had not taken place. These gentlemen, in any case, hardly distin-guished themselves by any absence of links with the press; they should really, it follows, have excluded themselves.[381] Then the whole thing would have collapsed—which would have been the best thing to happen.[382]

Ludwig Karpath, in an article published five days later in the Munich *Allgemeine Zeitung*, set out to avenge the honour of his profession, which Mahler had apparently offended by not making farewell visits to journalists:

Mahler left Vienna on Monday... It is striking that a man who, ten years ago, found his way to every office and every newspaper editor, who was not too proud to talk with even the most junior reporter, who was deified by the Viennese press as no other artist before him, should now have seen fit to leave our city without observing even the most elementary rules of politeness. His friends call it greatness, I say it is discourtesy and ingratitude. Why did Mahler not display this 'greatness' at a time when he still needed all those to whom he today denies the most basic social consideration? And if he is really so far above the conventions, why did he wait, a week ago, for over an hour

---

[380] AMM1, 160; AMM2, 155.
[381] Indeed Paul Stefan was himself a journalist and music critic.
[382] *Arbeiter-Zeitung* (9 Dec. 1907).

outside the office of the editor of one paper alone[383] whose wide circulation abroad might, he probably calculated, be useful to him later on? He is said to be bitter towards the Viennese papers, they had hurt his feelings. Precisely the opposite is true. Without the Viennese press, his rapid rise in Vienna would have been impossible. Without its support he would long since have ceased to be director of the Vienna Opera. This can be demonstrated with mathematical precision. Certainly there were some that often mauled him, but a solid majority swung the incense continually.

According to Karpath, it was untrue that Mahler had never spared his efforts (as he claimed in his farewell letter to the members of the Opera): there had even been times when he had 'spared more efforts than was in the interest of the house'. 'In recent years he has remained under the bad influence of a clique that tightly enclosed him and knew how to stifle his better impulses.' Karpath went on to quote in its entirety the article by Bach referred to above, observing that despite the request in the circular put out by Schoenberg's pupils, the leading papers had nonetheless sent reporters to the station. According to him, the numbers at the Westbahnhof were 'laughable'.[384] The article well demonstrates how much the Viennese press resented being robbed of its favourite target. It is easy to understand Mahler's reaction to this virulent column by his former supporter: he refused ever to see him again.[385]

An answer to Karpath's article is provided by Richard Specht, who, in the substantial book he published after Mahler's death, criticized the behaviour of the Viennese journalists:

In the last years of his career in Vienna Gustav Mahler was treated like a schoolboy, harried like a criminal delinquent, even libelled concerning his private life. And with the exception of a few who loyally supported him and objected to this vulgar manhunt, but whose voices were drowned in the din, people said nothing. Because people in these parts are so well-bred and refined. Except that there is another word for refinement of this kind.

'Nowhere else in the world,' writes Felix Salten[386] in his essay on Mahler, . . .

is aspiring youth so shamefully ill-treated by bankrupt old age as in Vienna. Nowhere does sterility so impudently masquerade as criticism and gloatingly jeer at budding

---

[383] Karpath is here alluding to Mahler's visit during June to Moritz Benedikt at the *Neue Freie Presse* (see above, Chap. 9).

[384] Ludwig Karpath, the column 'Aus dem Wiener Musikleben', *Allgemeine Zeitung*, Munich (14 Dec. 1907).

[385] BMG 189.

[386] *Geister der Zeit* (Zsolnay, Berlin, 1924), 59. Felix Salten (1869–1945) (Siegmund Salzmann), born in Budapest, began his studies in Vienna, which he had to interrupt at an early age in order to earn his living, first of all as theatre critic of the *Allgemeine Zeitung*. In 1902 he joined *Die Zeit*, and in 1906 he left for Berlin, writing for the *Morgenpost* and becoming theatre correspondent for the *Neue Freie Presse*. A prolific playwright, novelist, librettist, and essayist, Salten emigrated to Switzerland in 1938. A member of the literary group *Jung Wien*, he was for forty years a friend of Arthur Schnitzler, who admired him as a journalist, but considered that creatively he was an epigone. He is perhaps better remembered today for the attacks Karl Kraus made on him in several issues of *Die Fackel*. In one of them, Kraus wrote, 'He is always writing things on which his friends are already working.' After reading this, Salten slapped Kraus's face in public.

growth. Nowhere should a man be allowed to hide his fury at his own sterility behind the excuse that he is zealously guarding a venerable tradition, nowhere should he be allowed under cover of such an excuse to trample to the ground all new art, every new idea, every fresh stirring.[387] Nowhere are artists so completely and helplessly at the mercy of envious and intolerant criticism by people who have failed to make the grade. And all this amid complete indifference on the part of the public.—Now, of course, they are singing Mahler's praise. But they only do it because he is dead. When he was alive, in the fullness of his powers and his work, needing perhaps the comfort and encouragement of a good word, he was never more than a target for their insults. For, because he is alive, he must not be praised or encouraged. All their sympathy is only for the dead. For the dead they are full of admiration; the dead they defend passionately as if they were in need of protection. They are captivated by the dead. But they are not to be 'caught out' by the living. Well, Mahler is dead; but he was himself convinced that the extraordinary agitations of his time in Vienna had hastened the onset of his heart disease. He is dead; but those who reviled him and made his work a misery for him are still alive, and are not even ashamed.[388]

When the Orient Express arrived in Paris, Mahler and Alma were met by a number of French friends and the young Russian pianist Ossip Gabrilovich, who took them straight to the Hotel Bellevue. The next day, they went with the Clemenceaus and Paul Painlevé to the Opéra to see *Tristan*, conducted by Paul Vidal, with Van Dyck and Madame Grandjean in the title roles. Sung in French, the production was certainly mediocre. And there is no proof that Mahler stayed to the end. Alma's book indeed contains an account of another Paris performance of the same work, this time on a gala evening, when Van Dyck made Mahler furious by standing next to the prompter's box and loudly shouting the tender replies in the love scene.[389] Mahler was so indignant that he left his box, although it happened to belong to the Prefect of Police. After the performance, the five friends dined at Weber's, whence they jointly sent a card to Berta Zuckerkandl. Mahler wrote on it: 'I also thought of your husband, who would certainly have been furious!'[390] Their stay in the French capital was to be somewhat disturbed by an unexpected 'false note' of which, according to Alma, Mahler remained unaware. Ossip Gabrilovich, the young Russian musician who was still showering Mahler with demonstrations of friendship and respect, developed a passion for Alma. One evening, visiting them in their Paris hotel room, he took advantage of Mahler's temporary absence to declare: 'I have a terrible confession to make; I am falling madly in love with you. Help me to prevent this. I love Mahler; I must never hurt him.' 'I was embarrassed and could find nothing to say', writes Alma.

---

[387] This undoubtedly refers to Robert Hirschfeld.   [388] RSM2, 145.

[389] AMM1, 191; AMM2, 181. According to Alma, the incident took place in 1909.

[390] This unpublished card now belongs to Berta's grandson, Emil. It is dated 11 Dec. and was posted on the 12th. The address was written by Alma. The performance at the Paris Opéra on 11 Dec. was conducted by Paul Vidal, with the following cast: Grandjean (Isolde); Caro-Lucas (Brangäne); Van Dyck (Tristan); Bartet (Kurwenal); Cabillot (Melot); Gresse (Marke).

So I was still capable of inspiring love, not old, not ugly, as I saw myself at the time! He was reaching for my hand in the darkness when the light suddenly came on and there was Mahler in the doorway, full of love and kindness, and the spectre was gone. But this scene helped me for a while to survive the moments when I felt I didn't matter any more.[391]

As always in such cases, Alma's reaction was not free of ambiguity. On the one hand she was not displeased at being attractive and feeling her power over men, but each time she experienced this the balance she maintained with such difficulty, and her determination to sacrifice some of her strongest ambitions were shaken. It was then that she felt again deep within herself the desire for a different life, fuller and freer. For the moment Mahler had nothing to fear, for despite the blows of the previous few months he was still the greatest, most universally and justly admired man she had ever met. But heaven help him if he should weaken! What was more, Alma was much more pleased than Mahler to be leaving Europe for the country of wide open spaces, of youth and adventure. In Vienna she had always suffered from being merely the director's wife, and never being able to express her own personality. She was probably aware that, in America, home of liberty and democracy, women often played a capital role. It was likely that there she would be able to affirm her personality, far from the constraints of an ossified society living on its prejudices and on its cult of the past.

For several months Mahler had been living in half-acknowledged dread of the impending sea voyage. He had taken all sorts of advice concerning the most effective remedies against seasickness. 'A humorist among his friends had even given him a medical kit containing an arsenal of bottles with drops, essences and mixtures, and instructions for use . . .'[392]

Now came the journey from Paris to Cherbourg;[393] there we took a small tender—night—a choppy sea; at last, in the distance, a mass of lights, our ship [the *Kaiserin Augusta Viktoria*].[394] Mahler was afraid of the sea but would not show it. Then suddenly the huge, glittering liner was right beside us, we could hear the Marseillaise, and all was forgotten. Full of courage and good cheer we danced over to the big ship. Up on deck we were straight away received and conducted to our staterooms. A wonderful meal was served in the salon, and all at once I felt with delight that we were moving. Mahler was angry when I said so: he did not want to know, for now the music was gone and he was afraid again. Violent storms, seasickness which he tried to stave off by lying stiff and straight on his back across the bed—as if in a cardinal's sarcophagus—eating nothing, saying nothing, until the sickness subsided. Such, despite wonderful impressions of the sea, was the experience of that first crossing.[395]

---

[391] AMM1, 160; AMM2, 156.   [392] *Illustrirtes Wiener Extrablatt* (25 Oct. 1907).

[393] Just before boarding their train in Paris at the Gare de l'Est, Mahler and Alma wrote a card to the Rosés: 'Today we go on board the ship. Tell your beads and so on (*betet Rosenkränze und Ähnliches*).' (Postmark 12 Dec.1907, RWO.)

[394] Here Alma wrongly gives the name of the ship that she and Mahler were to take the following year, which was in fact the *Amerika*.   [395] AMM1, 161; AMM2, 156.

On the boat Mahler made the acquaintance of the Wagnerian tenor Alois Burgstaller, who was soon to be in his cast for *Die Walküre* at the Metropolitan Opera.[396] In the course of a spontaneously organized concert on board, a benefit for the sailors' pension fund, Mahler provided the piano accompaniment for the tenor in some Schubert songs and also for two little-known American lady singers.[397] When they arrived on the ship, Mahler and Alma found a telegram from Gerhart Hauptmann in their cabin: 'Dear friend, heartiest wishes for a happy crossing on the fine ship that brought me back from America some years ago. And a happy return to the beloved Europe which needs men like you more than its daily bread.'[398] But Mahler was thinking only of the immediate future, feeling that any return to Europe could only be a return to the past.

[396] Burgstaller was to have sung almost all the Wagner performances conducted by Mahler, but he suffered from a chronic sore throat and was replaced most of the time, first by Heinrich Knote and then by Karl Burian.

[397] They were Mesdames Holtzmann-Haymouth and J. H. Schary. See *New-Yorker Staats-Zeitung* (22 Dec. 1907); also Ludwig Karpath, 'Gustav Mahler in Amerika', *Moderne Welt*, 3 (1921): 7, 33.

[398] AMM1, 402.

APPENDIX 1

Catalogue of Mahler's Works

Autograph Sources (the source is undated if no date is mentioned)

APD   Autograph preliminary draft (for full movement or substantial part of one): orchestral works are mostly in *Particelli*; Lieder mostly v(oice) and p(iano)

AOD   Autograph orchestral draft

AFC   Autograph fair copies

CFC   Copyist's fair copy (included only when necessary)

Libraries

ACA	Amsterdam Concertgebouw Archive
ASI	Arnold Schoenberg Institute, Vienna, Austria
BBC	Biblioteca Bodmeriana, Cologny, Switzerland
BMG	Bibliothèque musicale Gustav Mahler, Paris
BLL	British Library, London
BSB	Berlin, Staatsbibliothek Preussischer Kulturbesitz
BSM	Bayerische Staatsbibliothek, Munich
CPA	Czech Philharmonic Archive, Prague
GMF	Gesellschaft der Musikfreunde Library, Vienna
HLH	Houghton Library, Harvard University, Cambridge
HMS	The Hague, Gemeente Museum, Mengelberg Stichting
HOA	Hofopern Archiv, see ÖTM
IMG	Internationale Gustav Mahler Gesellschaft, Vienna
JNJ	Jerusalem, Jewish National and University Library
LCW	Library of Congress, Washington, DC
LPA	Library of the Performing Arts, Lincoln Center, New York
MAS	Moldenhauer Archive, Spokane, Washington, DC
NLC	Newberry Library, Chicago
NUE	Northwestern University, Evanston, Ill., USA
ÖNB	Österreichische Nationalbibliothek, Vienna
ÖTM	Österreichisches Theatermuseum, Vienna
PML	Pierpont Morgan Library, New York City

RWO   University of Western Ontario, Rosé room, London, Canada

SAG   Straussarchiv, Garmisch

SBW   Stadts- und Landesbibliothek, Vienna

SOU   Southampton University Library, Great Britain

SSB   Paul Sacher Foundation, Basel, Switzerland

SUL   Stanford University Library, Stanford, Calif.

UEA   Universal Edition Archive, Vienna

UPL   Van Pelt Library, University of Pennsylvania, Philadelphia

VPA   Vienna Philharmonic Archive

YUL   Yale University Library, New Haven, Conn.

COMPLETED WORKS

0. **Piano Quartet movement in A minor**: *Nicht zu schnell. Entschlossen.* AFC (1876), PML (Rosé bequest). Published Sikorsky, Hamburg, 1973. 1st publ. critical edn. IGMG/UE 1997. 1st public perf. (?) New York, 12 Jan. 1964, Peter Serkin and Galimir Quartet.

1. **3 Lieder** for tenor and piano (1880), poems by Mahler, dedicated to Josephine Poisl. AFC, RWO. 1st perf. Radio Brno, 30 Sept. 1934: Zdeněk Knittl, tenor; Alfred Rosé, piano. AFC, RWO. 1st publ. critical edn. IGMG/UE 1990.

   (a) 'Im Lenz' (19 Feb. 1880).
   (b) 'Winterlied' (27 Feb. 1880).
   (c) 'Maitanz im Grünen' (5 Mar. 1880), cf. 3c.

2. **Das klagende Lied**, poem by Mahler. Original vers. (1880), in three parts, for soprano, alto, tenor, baritone, bass solos, chorus, and orchestra. 1st perf. Manchester 7 Oct. 1997/Nagano. CFC (with auto. corrections), YUL (Osborn coll.). 1st rev. (Dec. 1893). AFC, PML (Heineman coll.); 2nd rev. (May 1899) (without *a*), for soprano, alto, tenor solos. 1st perf. Vienna, 17 Feb. 1901. Publ. Sept. 1902, Weinberger. Critical edn. IGMG/UE 1978.

   (a) ['Waldmärchen' (omitted in 1899), for soprano, alto, tenor, bass solos. 1st perf. Radio Brno 26 Nov. 1934/Alfred Rosé. Publ. 1973, Belwin-Mills.]
   (b) 'Der Spielmann'. APD (21 Mar. 1880), SBW; AOD, SBW.
   (c) 'Hochzeitsstück' (Beg. of APD, Oct.–Nov. [1880], J. Bruck coll., NYC).

3. **5 Lieder** for voice and piano (1880–7), forming Part I of *Lieder und Gesänge*, entitled after Mahler's death: *Lieder aus der Jugendzeit*, poems by Richard Leander, Mahler, and Tirso de Molina; entitled, in the only known manuscript, '5 Gedichte komponiert von Gustav Mahler'. AFC, RWO. Publ. Feb. 1892, Schott. Critical edn. IGMG/Schott 1990.

(*a*) 'Frühlingsmorgen' (Richard Leander). 1st perf. Prague, 18 Apr. 1886.

(*b*) 'Erinnerung' (Leander). 1st perf. Budapest, 13 Nov. 1889.

(*c*) 'Hans und Grete' (Mahler), practically identical with 1*c*. 1st perf. Prague, 18 Apr. 1886.

(*d*) 'Serenade aus Don Juan' (Tirso da Molina) (1887).

(*e*) 'Phantasie aus Don Juan' (Tirso da Molina) (1887).

4. **4 Lieder eines fahrenden Gesellen** for voice and orchestra (1884–5), poems by Mahler. 1st surviving, AFC, v & p, RWO (1884–5?); 1st surviving AFC, v & o, (1893?) and 1896, SSB. 1st perf. Berlin, 16 Mar. 1896. Publ. Dec. 1897, v & p and v & o, Weinberger. Critical edn., v & p and v & o, IGMG/Weinberger 1982.

(*a*) 'Wenn mein Schatz Hochzeit macht'.

(*b*) 'Ging heut' morgens übers Feld'.

(*c*) 'Ich hab' ein glühend' Messer'.

(*d*) 'Die zwei blauen Augen'.

5. **First Symphony**, D major (1885–8) [sketched as 'Symphony I' (1885) (GAM 99)]. 1st perf. 'Symphonic poem in two parts', Budapest, 20 Nov. 1889. 1st rev. without (*b*) (Jan. 1893); 2nd rev. with (*b*) (16 Dec. 1893): 'Symphony (Titan) in 5 movements (2 parts)'. CFC of movements 1, 3, and 5 (of the 5 movement version of the work (RWO). AFC, YUL (Osborn coll.). 2nd perf. 'Titan, symphonic poem in the form of a symphony', Hamburg, 27 Oct. 1893: CFC, LPA (Walter coll.). 3rd perf. Weimar, 3 June 1894. Final rev. without (b) (1896). CFC, ÖNB. 4th perf. 'Symphony in D major', Berlin, 16 Mar. 1896. Publ. Dec. 1898, Weinberger; May 1906, UE. 1st critical edn. IGMG/UE 1967; 2nd critical edn. 1992.

(*a*) *Langsam, schleppend; Immer sehr gemächlich.*

[(*b*) *Andante alegretto [sic]. Blumine.* AFC (16 Aug. 1893 renovatum), subsequently omitted. Publ. 1968. Presser.]

(*b*) *Kräftig bewegt, doch nicht zu schnell.* AFC (27 Jan. 1893 renovatum).

(*c*) *Feierlich und gemessen, ohne zu schleppen.*

(*d*) *Stürmisch bewegt. Energisch.* AFC (19 Jan. 1893 umgearbeitet).

6. **9 Wunderhorn-Lieder** for voice and piano (1887–90), forming Parts II & III of *Lieder und Gesänge*, entitled after Mahler's death: *Lieder aus der Jugendzeit*. AFC, RWO. Publ. Feb. 1892, Schott. Critical edn. IGMG/Schott 1991.

(*a*) 'Um schlimme Kinder artig zu machen': 1st perf. Berlin, 14 Dec. 1907.

(*b*) 'Ich ging mit Lust'.

(*c*) 'Aus! Aus!': 1st perf. Hamburg, 29 Apr. 1892.

(*d*) 'Starke Einbildungskraft'.

(*e*) 'Zu Strassburg auf der Schanz': AOD, unfinished, BGM.

(*f*) 'Ablösung im Sommer': 1st perf. Berlin, 14 Dec. 1907.

(*g*) 'Scheiden und Meiden': 1st perf. Budapest 13 Nov. 1889.

(*h*) 'Nicht Wiedersehen!': 1st perf. Hamburg, 29 June 1892.

(*i*) 'Selbstgefühl': 1st perf. Vienna, 15 Feb. 1900.

7. **Second Symphony**, C minor (1888–94), with soprano, alto solos, and mixed chorus. AFC (18 Dec. 1894), PML (Kaplan dep.). 1st perf. (*a*), (*b*), and (*c*) Berlin, 4 Mar. 1895. 1st complete perf. Berlin, 13 Dec. 1895. Publ. 1895, 2 pianos (Hermann Behn), Hofmeister; orch., 1897, Hofmeister & Weinberger; April 1906, U.E. Critical edn. IGMG/UE 1970. FS edn. Kaplan Found., New York, 1986.

   (*a*) *Allegro maestoso (mit durchaus ernstem und feierlichem Ausdruck)*. 1st vers. AOD (8 July 1888), JNJ; AFC (as *Todtenfeier*: 10 Sept. 1888), SSB. Final vers. (29 June 1894 renovatum).

   (*b*) *Andante moderato (Sehr gemächlich)* (begun 1888). AOD (30 July 1893), location unknown.

   (*c*) *In ruhig fliessender Bewegung*. AOD (16 July 1893), PML (Lehman dep.).

   (*d*) *Urlicht (Sehr feierlich aber schlicht)*, alto solo, from *Des Knaben Wunderhorn* (*c*.1892). AFC (19 July 1893), BLL (Zweig coll.).

   (*e*) *Tempo des Scherzo. Wild herausfahrend; Kräftig; Langsam; Misterioso*, poem by Friedrich Klopstock and Mahler. AFC (18 Dec. 1894).

8. **Third Symphony**, D minor (1895–6), with alto solo, women and children's chorus. AFC (22 Nov. 1896), PML (Lehman dep.). 1st perf. (*b*), (*c*), (*f*) Berlin, 9 Mar. 1897. 1st complete perf. Krefeld, 9 June 1902. Rev. May 1899. Publ. 1899, Weinberger; Jan. 1906, UE. Critical edn. IGMG/UE 1974.

   (*a*) *Kräftig. Entschieden*. AOD (28 June 1896), AFC (17 Oct. 1896).

   (*b*) *Tempo di Menuetto (sehr mässig)*. AOD (June 1895), former Ernst Rosé collection; AFC (11 Apr. 1896). 1st perf.: Berlin, 9 Nov. 1896/Nikisch. 4th perf.: Budapest, 31 Feb. 1897.

   (*c*) *Comodo. Scherzando. Ohne Hast*. AOD (June 1895), PML (Cary coll.); AFC (25 [29?] June 1896).

   (*d*) *Sehr langsam. Misterioso*, alto solo 'O Mensch!', poem by Nietzsche (summer 1895). AOD, PML (Cary coll.); v & p (summer 1896), LCW.

   (*e*) *Lustig im Tempo und keck im Ausdruck*, alto solo, women and children's chorus: 'Es sungen drei Engel', from *Des Knaben Wunderhorn*. APD, v & o (Aug. 1895), PML (Cary coll.); AFC (8 May 1896), PML (Lehman dep.).

   (*f*) *Langsam. Ruhevoll. Empfunden*. AFC (11 Nov. 1896).

Analyses of the above works will be included in Volume i.

9. **10 Wunderhorn-Lieder** for voice and orchestra (1892–8) (*a*), (*b*), (*c*), (*d*) and (10*d*) entitled in 1892: *5 Humoresken*. Publ. 1899–1900, Weinberger.

   (*a*) 'Der Schildwache Nachtlied' (1888?): APD, LCW; AFC, v & p (28 Jan. 1892), BSB; AFC, v & p (26 Apr. 1892), GMF. 1st perf. Berlin, 12 Dec. 1892.

   (*b*) 'Verlorne Müh': AFC, v & p, MAS; AFC, v & p (1 Feb. 1892), BSB; AFC, v & o, GMF. 1st perf. Berlin, 12 Dec. 1892.

   (*c*) 'Trost im Unglück': ADP, v & p, MAS; AFC, v & p (22 Feb. [1892]), BSB; AFC, v & o (26 Apr. 1892), GMF. 1st perf. Hamburg, 27 Oct. 1893.

   (*d*) 'Wer hat dies Liedlein erdarcht?': AFC, v & p (6 Feb. 1892) BSB; AFC, v & o, GMF. 1st perf. Hamburg, 27 Oct. 1893.

(*e*) 'Das irdische Leben' (1893: NBL1, 10; NBL2, 27): APD, priv. coll. (Newlin), USA; AFC, v & o, PML (Cary coll.). 1st perf. 14 Jan. 1900, Vienna.

(*f*) 'Des Antonius von Padua Fischpredigt': AFC, v & p (8 July 1893), PML (Lehman dep.); AFC, v & o (1 Aug. 1893), HLH. 1st perf. Vienna, 29 Jan. 1905.

(*g*) 'Rheinlegendchen': AFC, v & p (9 Aug. 1893), BSB; AFC, v & o (10 Aug. 1893), PML (Lehman dep.). 1st perf. Hamburg, 27 Oct. 1893.

(*h*) 'Lied des Verfolgten im Turm': AFC, v & p (July 1898), PML (Lehman dep.). 1st perf. Vienna, 29 Jan. 1905.

(*i*) 'Wo die schönen Trompeten blasen': AFC, v & p (July 1898), PML (Lehman dep.). 1st perf. Vienna, 14 Jan. 1900.

(*j*) 'Lob des hohen Verstandes': APD in E, entitled 'Lob der Kritik' (bet. 11 & 16 June 1896); APD (21 June 1896), MAS. 1st perf. Vienna, 3 Feb. 1905.

[(*k*) 'Es sungen drei Engel' (summer 1895, cf. 8*e*): No known autograph of song version.

(*l*) 'Urlicht', AFC, v & o (19 July 1893); BLL (Zweig coll.). Cf. 7*d*.]

10. **Fourth Symphony**, G major (1899–1900), with soprano solo. AFC, GMF. Complete preliminary drafts and orchestral drafts of (*a*), (*b*), and (*c*) broken up and dispersed, now in ÖNB, PML, BGM, MAS, SUL. 1st perf. Munich, 25 Nov. 1901. Last rev. July 1910. Publ. Jan. 1902, Doblinger; Jan. 1906, UE. Critical edn. IGMG/UE 1963.

(*a*) *Bedächtig, nicht eilen* (1899–1900).

(*b*) *In gemächlicher Bewegung, ohne Hast.* AFC (5 Jan. 1901).

(*c*) *Ruhevoll (Poco Adagio).* Partial AOD (6 [5] Aug. 1900), MAS & BGM; AFC (5 Jan. 1901).

(*d*) *Sehr behaglich*, soprano solo: 'Wir geniessen die himmlischen Freunden', from *Des Knaben Wunderhorn*. AFC/orig. song, v & p (10 Feb. 1892), BSB; AFC/id., v & o (12 Mar. 1892), GMF. 1st separate perf. Hamburg, 27 Oct. 1893. Orch. rev. 1900.

11. **7 Lieder** entitled, after Mahler's death, *Aus letzter Zeit.*

(A) **2 Wunderhorn-Lieder** for voice and orchestra (1899–1901). Publ. Aug. 1905, Kahnt. Critical edn., v & p and v & o, IGMG/Kahnt, 1984.

(*a*) 'Revelge' (June/July 1899): CFC, v & o, LPA (Walter coll.) (NBL2, 135). 1st perf. Vienna, 29 Jan. 1905.

(*b*) 'Der Tamboursg'sell': APD, PML (Lehman dep.); AFC, v & p (12 July 1901) and AFC, v & o, MAS. Another AFC, v & o PML (Lehman dep.). 1st perf. Vienna, 29 Jan. 1905.

(B) **4 Rückert-Lieder** for voice and orchestra (1901). 1st perf. Vienna, 29 Jan. 1905. Publ. Aug. 1905, Kahnt. Critical edn., v & p and v & o, IGMG/Kahnt 1984.

(*a*) 'Blicke mir nicht in die Lieder!': ADP, v & p (14 June 1901), ÖNB; AFC, v & p, Vienna (priv. coll.).

(*b*) 'Ich atmet' einen linden Duft' (summer 1901) (NLB1, 166; NBL2, 193 ff.):
AFC, v & p, BSM; AFC, v & o, BSM.

(*c*) 'Ich bin der Welt abhanden gekommen': APD (3) (one: 16 Aug. 1901),
PML (Cary coll.); AFC, v & p, BGM.

(*d*) 'Um Mitternacht' (summer 1901): APD, SBW; AFC, v & p, BMG; AFC, v
& o, ASI.

(C) 1 **Rückert-Lied** for voice and piano (Aug. 1902) (AML 33).
'Liebst du um Schönheit'. AFC, BMG. Publ., p & o, 1905, Kahnt; orch. Max
Puttmann (1910?). Critical edn., v & p, IGMG/1984.

12. **Fifth Symphony** (1901–2). Orch. 1903. Rev. 1904, etc. Two APO of the third
movement, PML (Lehman dep.); FC by Alma Mahler, LPA. 1st perf. Cologne, 19
Oct. 1904. Publ. Sept. 1904, Peters. Rev. 1905, 1911. 1st critical edn.
IGMG/Peters, 1964; 2nd critical edn. 1988.

1st part
(*a*) *Trauermarch* (*In gemessenem Schritt. Streng. Wie ein Kondukt*) (prob. 1901).
(*b*) *Stürmisch bewegt mit grösster Vehemenz* (prob. 1901).

2nd part
(*c*) *Scherzo* (*Kräftig, nicht zu schnell*) (summer 1901).

3rd part
(*d*) *Adagietto* (*Sehr langsam*) (prob. 1902). FS edition, Kaplan Found., 1992.
(*e*) *Rondo–Finale* (*Allegro*) (1902).

13. **5 Kindertotenlieder** (1901–4), poems by Friedrich Rückert, AFC, v & p, songs
(*b*) to (*d*); and v & o, complete, PML (Lehman dep.). 1st perf. Vienna, 29 Jan.
1905. Publ. Aug. 1905, Kahnt. 1st critical edn. IGMG Kahnt, v & p and v & o,
1979; 2nd critical edn. 1992.

(*a*) 'Nun will die Sonn' so hell aufgeh'n' (summer 1901) (NBL1, 166; NBL2,
193). APD, v & p, GMF.
(*b*) 'Nun seh' ich wohl, warum so dunkle Flammen' (summer 1904) (AMM1, 91;
AMM2, 97).
(*c*) 'Wenn dein Mütterlein' (summer 1901). APD, v & p, auctioned, Paris, 1997.
(*d*) 'Oft denk' ich, sie sind nur ausgegangen' (summer 1901).
(*e*) 'In diesem Wetter' (summer 1904).

Analyses of the following works are included in Volume iii.

14. **Sixth Symphony**, A minor (1903–5). AFC (1 June 1905), GMF. 1st perf. Essen,
27 May 1906. Rev. 1906 and 1907. Publ. Mar. 1906, Kahnt. Critical edn. IGMG
Kahnt 1963. 1st edn. (*b*) Scherzo, (*c*) Andante; 2nd edn. (*b*) Andante, (*c*) Scherzo.

(*a*) *Allegro energico, ma non troppo* (summer 1903?).
(*b*) *Scherzo* (*Wuchtig*) (summer 1903).
(*c*) *Andante moderato* (summer 1903).
(*d*) *Finale* (*Allegro moderato*) (summer 1904).

15. **Seventh Symphony**, B minor (1904–5). AFC, ACA. 1st perf. Prague, 19 Sept. 1908. Publ. Dec. 1909, Bote & Bock. Critical edn. IGMG/Bote & Bock 1960.

    (*a*) *Langsam; Allegro risoluto ma non troppo.*
    (*b*) *Nachtmusik* (AFC: *Nachtstück*) (*Allegro moderato*) (summer 1904).
    (*c*) *Schattenhaft* (*Fliessend, aber nicht zu schnell*) (summer 1905). Incomplete APD (15 Aug. 1905), LPA (Walter coll.).
    (*d*) *Nachtmusik* (*Andante amoroso*) (summer 1904).
    (*e*) *Rondo–Finale* (*Allegro ordinario*) (summer 1905).

16. **Eighth Symphony**, E flat major (1906), with 3 sopranos, 2 altos, tenor, baritone, bass solos, children's chorus, and mixed double chorus. AFC, BSM. 1st perf. Munich, 12 Sept. 1910. Publ. Feb. 1911, UE. Critical edn. IGMG/UE 1977.

    (*a*) Hymnus: 'Veni Creator Spiritus' (Part I) (drafted: July/Aug. 1906).
    (*b*) Finale scene of Goethe's Faust (Part II) (drafted: July/Aug. 1906).

Analyses of the following works will be included in Volume iiii.

17. **Das Lied von der Erde** (1908), 'Symphony for tenor and alto (or baritone) and orchestra', poems adapted from the Chinese by Hans Bethge. AD, complete, v & p, priv. coll., Kallir, Scarsdale, NY. AFC, v & o, PML (Lehman dep.). 1st perf. Munich, 20 Nov. 1911/B. Walter. Publ. 1912, UE. Critical edn. v & p, IGMG/UE 1989; v & o, IGMG/UE 1964.

    (*a*) 'Das Trinklied vom Jammer der Erde': AOD, v & o (14 Aug. 1908), missing.
    (*b*) 'Der Einsame im Herbst': AD, v & p (July 1908), see above, Kallir coll.
    (*c*) 'Von der Jugend'. APD, v & p, and AOD (in folder dated 1 Aug. 1908), GMF.
    (*d*) 'Von der Schönheit': AD, v & p (21 Aug. 1908), see above Kallir coll.; APD, v & o, PML (Lehman dep.).
    (*e*) 'Der Trunkene im Frühling': AOD, SBW.
    (*f*) 'Der Abschied'. APD, v & p (1 Sept. 1908), HMS; AOD (1 Sept. 1908), HMS.

18. **Ninth Symphony**, D major (1909). AFC, PML (Lehman dep.) 1st perf. Vienna, 26 June 1912/B. Walter. Publ. July 1912, UE. Critical edn. IMG/UE 1969. FS edn. (*a*) to (*c*), UE, 1971.

    (*a*) *Andante comodo*: AOD, ÖNB.
    (*b*) *Im Tempo eines gemächlichen Ländlers*: AOD, ÖNB.
    (*c*) *Rondo–Burleske* (*Allegro assai. Sehr trotzig*): AOD, ÖNB.
    (*d*) *Adagio* (*Sehr langsam; molto adagio*): AOD (2 Sept. 1909), BGM.

19. **Tenth Symphony**, F sharp (1910), unfinished. Sketches, AOD and AFC, ÖNB. 1st perf. (*a*) and (*c*) Vienna, 12 Oct. 1924/F. Schalk. FS edn. 1924, Zsolnay. Publ. (*a*) and (*c*) 1951, AMP. 2nd FS edn. Ricke, Munich, 1967. Performing vers. by Deryck Cooke, 1963. 1st incomplete perf. BBC London, 19 Dec. 1960/Berthold Goldschmidt; 1st complete perf. BBC London, 13 Aug. 1964/Berthold Goldschmidt. Publ. Faber, 1976.

(*a*) Andante. Adagio.
(*b*) Scherzo (*Schnelle Viertel*).
(*c*) Purgatorio (*Allegretto moderato. Nicht zu schnell*).
(*d*) (*Scherzo II*) 'Der Teufel tanzt es mit mir'.
(*e*) Finale (*Einleitung; Allegro moderato*).

Fragmentary and unfinished works will be listed in Volume i.

UNFINISHED WORK, COMPLETED BY MAHLER

Weber, Die Drei Pintos, opera in three acts (libretto rev. by Karl von Weber and Mahler, 1887-8). 1st perf. Leipzig, 20 Jan. 1888. Publ. 1888 (?), Kahnt.

TRANSCRIPTIONS AND ARRANGEMENTS

Bruckner, Symphony No. 3 (Transcribed for piano duet, supposedly in collaboration with Rudolf Krzyzanowski, whose name, however, does not appear on the title-page (see Vol. i, Chap. 4). Publ. Bussjäger & Rättig, 1878.

J. S. Bach, Suite aus seinen Orchesterwerken (1909). Bach-Gesellschaft score with aut.   corrections sold at auction in 1992. Publ. Feb. 1911, Schirmer.

(*a*) Ouverture (from Suite No. 2).
(*b*) Rondeau (from Suite No. 2).
(*c*) Badinerie (from Suite No. 2).
(*d*) Air (from Suite No. 3).
(*e*) Gavottes 1 and 2 (from Suite No. 3).

WORKS REVISED BY MAHLER

1. Orchestration

Mahler left several different revised versions of many works. The location of the various scores is briefly listed here.

Bach, Cantatas Nos. 19, 65, 78: SOU
Beethoven, Quartet No. 11, in F minor, Op. 95 (version for string orchestra): VPA; publ. 1990, Weinberger
—— **Symphonies Nos. 1 and 2:** SOU
    No. 3: SOU, UEA
    No. 4: SOU

Nos. 5 and 6: UEA
No. 7: UEA, CPA
No. 8: UEA
No. 9: SOU, UEA
—— Overtures: Coriolan: SOU, UEA, CPA
Egmont: UEA, HMS
Die Weihe des Hauses: SOU, UEA, SBW
König Stephan: SOU
Leonore Nos. 2 and 3: UEA
—— Piano Concerto No. 5: SOU
Bruckner, Symphonies Nos. 4 and 5 (with substantial cuts): UEA
Mozart, Symphonies Nos. 40 and 41: UEA
Schubert, Quartet No. 14, in D minor, 'Der Tod und das Mädchen' (version for string
    orchestra): D. Mitchell coll.; publ. 1984, Weinberger.
—— Symphony No. 9, in C major: SOU, BSM, UEA
Schumann Symphonies No. 1: YUL, Osborn coll., UEA
    No. 2: UEA, SOU
    No. 3: Copyist's score, IGMG
    No. 4: YUL, Osborn coll., UEA
—— Overture to Manfred: UEA
Smetana, Overture to the Bartered Bride: UEA
Wagner, Prelude to Die Meistersinger: UEA
Weber, Overture to Oberon

2. Stage Versions

Mozart, Le nozze di Figaro (new accompanied recitative for the trial scene), publ.
    Peters, 1906
Weber, Euryanthe (changes to the libretto and several passages in the score), libretto
    publ. Künast, 1904?
—— Oberon 'Neue Bühneneinrichtung' (added 'melodramas'), publ. UE 1919.

APPENDIX 2

Detailed History and Analysis of Works Composed between 1904 and 1907

SIXTH SYMPHONY IN A MINOR (1903–1904)

Composition

As seen above,[1] Mahler completed the Sixth in the summer of 1904, shortly after he had added two new *Kindertotenlieder* to the cycle he had begun in 1901. Before settling down to work once more, he made a two-day 'lightning excursion' to escape from the blazing heat of Maiernigg to Toblach and Misurina,[2] as he often did when he felt he had reached a natural break in his creative activity. In this case, one can assume that the main object of this 'Blitzausflug' was to find the necessary inspiration to complete the huge Finale which he had probably planned and sketched out 'in his head' the preceding year.[3] The postcard he mailed to Alma from Schluderbach on 11 July contains the following passage: 'One thing above all: could you look in the <u>middle drawer</u> of my <u>writing table</u> (you have the key) and bring me the <u>manuscripts</u> that are there. I need above all the 2nd and 3rd movements of the Sixth, which I forgot to bring with me.' Since he does not ask for any sketches for the opening Allegro, it seems safe to assume that he had already brought that with him to Maiernigg, either in the form of sketches, or *Particell*. Admittedly, Alma claims in her *Erinnerungen* that during that first summer Mahler composed only two movements of the Sixth[4] but I find it hard to believe that he could have finished the middle movements without also having sketched, not only in his head, but on paper, the opening Allegro and had brought the sketch with him to Maiernigg.

Alma having arrived on 14 July with the manuscripts, Mahler, who had just returned from Toblach, promptly set to work. By the end of the summer he had completed not only the huge Finale, but also the two Nachtmusiken for the symphony that was to follow. It is almost certain, in fact, that the draft of the Finale was already complete on August 18, when he made another 'lightning excursion' to the Dolomites.[5] According to Alma, Mahler came looking for her as soon as the symphony was finished, so that he could play it to her as he had done with the Fifth two years earlier.

---

[1] See above, Chap. 10.

[2] BGA no. 100, dated 11 July and mailed in Schluderbach; no. 101, undated and written in Toblach (same date); and no. 102, mailed the same day in Villach.

[3] In AMM, Alma states that 'the idea for the other movements was already complete in his head'.

[4] AMM1, 79; AMM2, 87.

[5] See BGA, no. 103, card mailed from Dölsach, near Lienz, dated 19 Aug. 1904.

MANUSCRIPTS: DIFFERENT VERSIONS[6]

The Autographs

Only one single autograph sheet is presently known as evidence of Mahler's early composition process, a *Particell*-fragment of the first movement, containing four systems written on a 22-line page, and including bars 93 to 122, i.e. the end of the exposition including the double bar. Mahler did not make any further substantial changes in the composition: most of the voices are already notated, as well as many dynamics, tempo nuances, and details of instrumentation.

The complete autograph score of the Sixth Symphony is in the Library of the Gesellschaft der Musikfreunde in Vienna. It contains 129 double sheets, or 262 written pages counting the title-pages, and is dated 1 May 1905 at the end. Many autograph corrections made by Mahler in red, blue, and black pencil show that he carried out at least at least four different revisions. Not all of these corrections were retained in the first printed score. Mahler had considered using three 'extra' brass instruments in the Finale, but they do not appear in the first edition of the score.[7] A twenty-bar section of the same movement (750–70) is extensively corrected, requiring an inserted page (*Einlage*).[8] The idea of using a hammer did not occur to him until he had finished his copy of the score.[9] The three blows were added in blue pencil to the autograph score at bars 336, 479, and 783. Hans-Peter Jülg claims that Mahler's markings at these three crucial moments imply that he had also planned to use the hammer at bars 9 and 530.[10] Several important changes were also made in the Andante.[11] The original order of the movements has been changed, the Andante becoming the second (instead of the third) and the Scherzo the third (instead of the second).[12]

The Copyist's Manuscript

The next source available to modern editors of the score is a copyist's manuscript which bears many corrections in Mahler's hand. It was probably used for the reading rehearsal in Vienna and later by the engraver of the plates for the first edition.[13] The

---

[6] Bayerische Staatsbibliothek, Munich, Mus. Mss. 7661. See Peter Andraschke, 'Struktur und Gehalt im ersten Satz von Gustav Mahlers Sechste Symphonie', in Hermann Danuser (ed.), *Gustav Mahler* (Wissenschaftlicher Buchgesellschaft, Darmstadt, 1992), 206 ff.

[7] They are a 'tenorhorn', a 'tenortuba', and a bass tuba. The role of these instruments was mainly restricted to the sombre threnody which starts at bar 790 of the coda, but Mahler notes on p. 258 of the autograph score that when they are not available, the passage should be played by four trombones and a bass tuba, an option which he retained in his final version. See Hans-Peter Jülg, *Gustav Mahlers Sechste Symphonie* (Katzbichler, Munich, 1986), 28.   [8] Jülg, *Sechste*, 29.

[9] Constantin Floros suggests that Mahler's idea of using a hammer might perhaps have originated in the poem by Alexander Ritter which inspired Strauss's tone poem *Tod und Verklärung*, particularly since it is published in the score which Mahler certainly knew:

Da erdröhnt der letzte Schlag	Now booms the final blow
Von der Todes Eisenhammer,	By the iron hammer of death
Bricht den Erdenleib entzwei,	Breaking in two the earthly body
Deckt mit Todesnacht das Auge.	Covering the eye with the night of death.

See Floros, *Symphonien*, 182.

[10] Jülg, *Sechste*, 30 and 41. See below, the section concerning the Finale.

[11] Particularly in bars 96–101.   [12] Jülg, *Sechste*, 29.   [13] IGMG, Vienna.

order of the two middle movements is identical with that of the original version: Scherzo second and Andante third. There are many new changes in the last bars of the Finale (729–70).[14] The 'extra instruments' are no longer mentioned. The last hammer blow is now written in ink, but the others are added in pencil, as is the mention 'hammer' at the beginning of the movement. It is curious to note that the only blow written into the score by the copyist is the one that Mahler later decided to suppress.[15]

The First Edition

As we have seen,[16] Mahler decided just before the Graz Festival in 1905 to accept C. F. Kahnt's offer to publish the Sixth. A full score and a pocket were published before the first performance, and also a small 'thematic guide' by Richard Specht and Alexander Zemlinsky's piano four-hand reduction.[17] Mahler decided during the rehearsals[18] to change the order of the middle movements and Kahnt published soon after the première a new pocket score which differs from the former one only in this respect. Because of this, the numbers serving as reference points are altered, the Andante going from 46 to 62 and the Scherzo from 63 to 103.

The Second Edition

When Mahler received the first copies of the first edition in Maiernigg at the beginning of summer 1906, he set about revising the whole score again, correcting numerous printing errors and making the orchestration still lighter, especially in the Finale. These changes were made in the plates of the first edition in red, blue, brown, and black pencil.[19] Mahler's avowed aim was to further clarify with *Retuschen* the 'essence of the work'.[20] This he did in more than one way, not only by lightening the instrumentation, but also by clarifying the voice-leading, crossing out some doublings, making the rhythm more precise and the musical substance more immediately apprehensible.[21] These corrected proofs are now the only known source for the second version of the symphony. The most striking change in the orchestration occurs at the very beginning of the first movement, in bars 2 to 5, where Mahler cut out all the woodwind parts and decided to use only strings. Some of the tempo markings were altered

---

[14] Bars 746 to 759 are noted on a separate page as an insert (*Einlage*). See Rudolf Stephan, *Gustav Mahler: Werk und Interpretation* (Volk, Cologne, 1979), 54.

[15] Jülg, *Sechste*, 30; Stephan, ed., *Werk*, 43, and Peter Andraschke, 'Gustav Mahlers Retuschen im Finale seiner 6. Symphonie', in Rudolf Stephan, (ed.), *Mahler-Interpretation: Aspekte zum Werk und Wirken von Gustav Mahler* (Schott, Mainz, 1985), 79.

[16] See above, Chap. 4.

[17] In a letter addressed to Schoenberg in 1913, Alban Berg calls Zemlinsky's transcription of the Sixth 'easy to play'. See *The Berg–Schoenberg Correspondence*, ed. Juliane Brand, Christopher Hailey, and Donald Harris (Norton, New York, 1987), 198. Some sources had mentioned 1910 as date of publication of Zemlinsky's translation but the score is dated 1906 and Theodor Helm mentions having examined it in his review of the Vienna performance of 1907. See *Neue Zeitschrift für Musik*, 17 (1907): 3, 56.

[18] See below, Klaus Pringsheim's reminiscences of these rehearsals.

[19] IGMG, Vienna. See Stephan, *Werk*, 20, and coloured plate no. 2.

[20] Letter addressed to Willem Mengelberg on 18 Aug. 1906 (MBR1, no. 306; MBR2, no. 360).

[21] A typical example of this is quoted by Jülg (*Sechste*, 37). It occurs in the transition from development to recapitulation in the Finale (bars 554 ff.), where the horn takes up the second theme against a rich chordal background of strings, harp, celesta, and woodwind. Mahler now uses two horns instead of one, and adds a new marking to their part: '*etwas hervortretend*'.

in the Finale, for instance *Allegro moderato* replacing *Sostenuto* at the beginning of the Introduction. At bar 642 of the same movement, he also changed the tempo marking from *Tempo I (Allegro energico)* to *Molto pesante. Tempo sehr anhaltend.*

He also lightened the percussion in the section beginning at bar 625 of the Finale. He not only cut out the third hammer blow (in bar 783), but also modified the orchestration of the same bar, and that of the following one, doing away with the oboes, and breaking off half the horns and half the trumpets at 785. After completing this last revision, Mahler returned the proofs to Kahnt with his imprimatur, certainly before the end of the summer of 1906.[22] It is of course strange to imagine him revising the most tragic and 'negative' of all his works while in the process of composing what is surely the most optimistic of them all, the Eighth. The order of the movements for this second edition remains 2. Andante and 3. Scherzo. The new score was published by Kahnt in the same year as the preceding one, but in full score only, again with the same plate numbers. This has proved particularly confusing for those musicologists who have not had a chance to examine the corrected plates.

New written indications are added, such as that concerning the cowbells at bar 198 of the same movement, the hammer at bar 336 of the Finale, and the cymbals and tamtam at bar 479.[23] Mahler no doubt recorrected proofs of the new edition, yet again, for a few details of his recent corrections are not included in the new score.[24] On 17 January 1907, Mahler wrote to Mengelberg[25] asking him to send back his copy of the score because he had decided to make some further changes.[26]

THE CRITICAL EDITIONS

The first of these was published under the auspices of the Internationale Gustav Mahler Gesellschaft (IGMG) and its president Erwin Ratz, Vienna, in 1963. For musical reasons, which have since then prevailed, Ratz reinserted the order of the middle movements as Mahler had intended before the Essen rehearsals. All the alterations made by him in the corrected proofs of the first and second editions were inserted by Ratz, as well as those in Willem Mengelberg's score. In the revised miniature score which Hans Ferdinand Redlich published five years later,[27] he somewhat arbitrarily decided that Mahler himself would probably not have retained all the corrections, and inserted only the main ones.

---

[22] In the same letter, Mahler regrets that he has already sent back the corrected proofs with his imprimatur to Kahnt some weeks ago for he would have liked to follow his advice concerning the hammer. See Jülg, *Sechste*, 37.   [23] Ibid. 34 ff.

[24] Jülg enumerates a few of these differences (*Sechste*, 36). The orchestration of bar 782 (that preceding the suppressed third hammer blow), and of those that follow is modified. In bar 783, that in which Mahler cut out the third hammer blow, the flute did not originally play. They now have a *fortepiano* marking, the four horns too, but with mute (instead of without), the trumpets piano and fortepiano instead of fortissimo, etc. Rests are also added to underline the dotted rhythm in the string parts in bars 783 and 785.

[25] RMH 81.

[26] Two corrections introduced in Mengelberg's score are mentioned by Ratz and inserted in his 1963 critical edition: the strings play an octave higher in bars 407–14 of the Finale.

[27] Eulenburg, London, 1968. See Redlich's introduction, p. xxix.

GENERAL OUTLINE

At first glance the Sixth Symphony may seem like a step back, a return to the past and to the classical form of the four-movement symphony. But a closer look at the score reveals a work that is anything but classical. With its huge Finale, which alone lasts half an hour, its dark, bleak, tense, tragic character, its almost brutal energy, its ending in catastrophe, it is, in fact, an amazingly original and complex conception, a work that fully belongs to the twentieth century. It is certainly one of Mahler's most 'difficult' scores, and yet, strangely enough, it seems to be becoming one of his most popular symphonies. Its excesses, its length, its moments of extreme violence, its all-pervading pessimism have fascinated a great many writers, musicologists, and analysts right up to recent times. To quote only the most recent publications, one of the most detailed and profound studies is that of the Finale by Bernd Sponheuer,[28] which synthesizes all the writings of his predecessors, and appeared in 1978; that of Norman Del Mar, a whole book in itself, dates from 1980[29] a recent and substantial monograph by Hans-Peter Jülg[30] was published in 1986; and *Mahler's Sixth Symphony: A Study in Musical Semiotics* by Robert Samuels came out in 1995.[31]

Bernd Sponheuer points out that the first three movements of the Sixth establish a situation which is resolved, but in a negative sense, in the Finale, where the 'catastrophe' is achieved by using all the main melodic elements of the preceding movements (with the exception of the Andante). Likewise Paul Bekker wrote in 1920: 'He [Mahler] builds a Finale that carries within it the chaos of the whole work and only now brings it into order (*zur Ordnung formt*). And now that is achieved which in the early symphonies could only be brought about through the powerful intervention of outward means: the combining (*Zusammenfassung*) of all the conflicting elements into a whole in a grand unity of gesture (*Wurf*), an impeccable logic of structure which only a genius in architectural form (*architektonische Gestaltung*) could achieve.'[32] Thus, Bekker sees in the Sixth the true outcome of the enterprise Mahler had embarked upon in the First Symphony, the building of a powerful tragic Finale. Mahler also fully realizes in the new work his grand vision of a symphonic unity achieved in the midst of unending diversity. In the first and second movements,[33] he states a number of themes, all made up of short motifs. Using this wealth of motifs and the variant procedure so brilliantly described by Adorno, he creates the sinister world of the Finale. 'Negative' fragments are sometimes reused in 'positive' atmospheres or episodes, or vice versa. Thus the colossal musical architecture unfolds in a manner as logical as it is elaborate, with a complexity comparable only to that of Schoenberg's greatest works.

One of the most striking features of the work, of its sequence of moods and atmospheres, is undoubtedly its symmetry. The rising curve of the first movement, leading

[28] Sponheuer, *Zerfall*, see above.
[29] Norman Del Mar, *Mahler's Sixth Symphony: A Study* (Eulenburg, London, 1980).
[30] Jülg, *Sechste*, see above.
[31] Cambridge University Press, Cambridge, 1995.
[32] BMS 226.
[33] The Scherzo will be henceforth referred to as the second movement.

from darkness to light, is answered by the descending curve of the Finale, which ends in an abyss of pessimism. From the second page of the opening movement the tragic outcome is predicted by the famous leitmotiv (or 'motto') of the work, a major chord whose third drops by a semitone to become minor, reversing the traditional procedure of the 'Picardy third' (*grosse Terz* in German) where the last chord of a minor piece becomes major.

THE HAMMER BLOWS

The use—for the first time in musical literature—of a hammer as a musical instrument, as well as the number and placing of the hammer blows have given rise to much comment. Alma's *Erinnerungen* set the tone of the discussion, and in particular her statement concerning the 'subject' of the Finale, the fall of a 'Hero' who 'is dealt three blows, the third of which fells him like a tree'. These words she claims to have been Mahler's own.[34] The next paragraph of Alma's memoirs which concerns the Sixth has attracted even more attention. She calls the Sixth a 'prophetic' work, because Mahler had, as in the *Kindertotenlieder*, 'anticipando musiziert' (anticipated his whole future while composing), for he too was fated by destiny to receive three blows of which the third would kill him.

That Mahler did not at first invest the hammer blows with a symbolic meaning is a certainty because he had originally planned five instead of three blows,[35] which are written in blue pencil, and later crossed out two of them, the first in the Introduction to the first movement (bar 9); the second in the introduction to the recapitulation (bar 530). The third one, in the introduction to the coda (bar 783) was maintained in the first edition of the symphony. The blows that were crossed out were meant to underline important structural points in the movement and each one of them preceded a statement of the double—harmonic-rhythmic—leitmotiv.

On the other hand, the three blows which Mahler kept appear without warning at the beginning of the *Durchführung* and before its last section. Coming as they do after moments of relative optimism (bars 334 and 479), they acquire dramatic significance and are followed by agitated episodes which can be interpreted as the symphonic hero's response to them.[36] In the second edition, however, Mahler deliberately omitted, as mentioned above, another blow, the last, the 'death' blow, which figured in the manuscript, probably because he felt that its appearance, shortly before the last—funereal—section of the coda, was too obvious and might sound too theatrical. Or did he perhaps identify with his symphonic hero, and as an afterthought decide that he would be tempting fate if he thus dealt him a 'death' blow?

That Mahler was superstitious, like many men and artists then and now, is certain.

[34] AMM1, 92; AMM2, 97.

[35] They are inserted in blue pencil. See above the section concerning the autographs and Andraschke, 'Retuschen', 79.

[36] Redlich names these blows 'the cutting axe of destiny' (*Axthieb des Schicksalls*) (Eulenburg Introduction, note to bar 336), and Bekker 'the intervention (*Eingreifens*) from something from another world' (BMS 200).

He proved it later on by refusing to call *Das Lied von der Erde* 'Symphony No. 9'. The hammer blows that remain are inserted in the massive sound of an orchestral tutti, so they have to be heard above an already considerable volume of sound. The problem of producing an audible blow in performance—'a short, loud, but dully resounding blow of non-metallic character (like the stroke of an axe)', as Mahler puts it in his instructions—, has never been satisfactorily solved.[37] He himself failed in his first attempt, when he had a huge instrument constructed and brought to Essen for the première.[38] Reviews of the last Vienna performance only mention a not very conspicuous 'two-metre-long hammer'.[39] Some conductors today use elaborate, sometimes even theatrical devices to achieve the effect, but I doubt whether Mahler would have approved of them since they only succeed in giving the hammer blows an exaggerated symbolic and programmatic meaning which he probably did not mean them to have. As for Alma's statement that Mahler had 'set his own life to music', doubts must be raised. First of all, he was not dealt a fatal blow with the medical diagnosis made in July 1907.[40] His heart ailment was serious but 'compensated' and he soon learned to live with it and led a life that was just as active as before. The infectious illness he died of was only indirectly connected to the 1907 diagnosis. And the most cruel blow of all, perhaps, was the one Alma dealt to him, not in 1907 but in 1910, when she had to admit that she had been unfaithful to him.[41]

THE ORDER OF THE MIDDLE MOVEMENTS

As seen above,[42] the original order in the complete autograph manuscript, is Scherzo 2/Andante 3, but it was reversed later on, with a pencil marking, but probably <u>after</u> the première. In the copyist's manuscript used before the première by the engraver of the first edition,[43] the order remains: Scherzo 2/Andante 3. However, Mahler changed the order during the Essen rehearsals, and the second pocket score which appeared soon after the première is identical with the preceding one, except for the order (now Andante 2/Scherzo 3). Mahler's next performance, in Munich in November 1906, again occurred with the same order.[44]

After Mahler's last performance of the Sixth, in Vienna on 4 January 1907, most of the critics[45] reported and described the movements in the order in which they were performed, i.e. Andante 2 and Scherzo 3. Two others, Heinrich Reinhardt (*Neues Wiener Journal*) and Karl Lafite (*Wiener Allgemeine Zeitung*), nevertheless mentioned the Scherzo before the Andante. However their articles, on closer scrutiny, cannot be

---

[37]   Theodor Adorno suggests using an electronic sound. See TAM 165; TAMe 126.

[38]   See above, Chap. 6.

[39]   See Theodor Helm's review of the Vienna première of 4 Jan. 1907 in the *Neue Zeitschrift für Musik*, 74 (1907), 3, 56 ff.   [40]   See above, Chap. 8.   [41]   See above.

[42]   See below, Vol. iiii, Chap. 7.   [43]   See above, the section concerning the first edition.

[44]   This is the occasion on which Mahler gave the work the title *Tragische Symphonie*.

[45]   In alphabetical order, David Joseph Bach (*Arbeiter-Zeitung*), Hedwig von Friedländer-Abel (*Montags-Revue*), Robert Hirschfeld (*Wiener Abendpost*), Max Kalbeck (*Neues Wiener Tagblatt*), Alfred Kauders (*Neues Wiener Journal*), Julius Korngold (NFP), Hans Liebstöckl (*Illustrirtes Wiener Extrablatt*), Maximilian Muntz (*Deutsche Zeitung*), and Richard Wallaschek (*Die Zeit*).

taken as evidence of a last-minute change of order. The longest one, by Heinrich Reinhardt, is ironical and disparaging, and uses the change of order as a leitmotif, implying that no composer can be taken seriously who thus changes his mind on such an important matter. Nevertheless, his description of what may be the Scherzo is so vague that it is impossible to identify the movement he is referring to, in any case not clearly enough to make it contradict all the other existing evidence.

After Mahler's death, all the biographers and analysts who wrote about Mahler spoke of the Andante as the second movement of the symphony, including Ernst Decsey,[46] Richard Specht,[47] and Paul Stefan.[48] Even Paul Bekker, whose major work on the symphonies appeared in 1921, kept them in that order,[49] as did Willem Mengelberg, who, in his first Dutch performance in 1916 used a score in which Mahler had made alterations without inverting the middle movements.[50] Yet when Mahler's complete works were performed for the first time as a cycle, in Amsterdam in 1920, the order was Scherzo 2 and Andante 3, and Mengelberg had written on the first page of his score: 'Nach Mahlers Angabe II erst Scherzo dann III Andante' (According to Mahler's indications, first II Scherzo, then III Andante).

Mahler conducted his Seventh Symphony in Amsterdam in October 1909, and this was probably the occasion for further discussion of the Sixth and its performance with Mengelberg. The composer must once again have expressed doubts as to the order of the middle movements.[51] This most likely explains why Mengelberg contacted Alma in 1919, and requested her advice for his forthcoming performance. The reply soon came in the form of a telegram dated 1 October 1919: 'Erst Scherzo dann Andante herzlichst Alma' (First Scherzo, then Andante affectionately Alma).[52] Mengelberg's Mahler Festival was for Alma an all-important event. Much as I have sometimes felt compelled to cast doubt on her testimony, either because of her memory lapses or because at times she intentionally distorted the truth, I see every reason here to believe she was passing on Mahler's final decision to a conductor who had, more than any other, performed and defended Mahler's music.

However, given that Mahler himself changed his mind so many times, it is understandable that a conductor might nowadays wish to stand by the order in the second version, if he is deeply convinced that he can serve the work better by doing this. In the first and second American performances, on 11 December 1947 and 10 April 1955 in New York, with Dimitri Mitropoulos conducting, the Andante was the second movement. The same applies to F. Charles Adler's 1953 recording, the first in history, and in John Barbirolli's 1967 version.

To my mind, Mahler's change of mind in Essen can be attributed to his insecurity at the time, which was reported by many witnesses. As Klaus Pringsheim recollected:

---

[46] Decsey, 'Mahlers Sechste Sinfonie in Wien', *Grazer Tagespost*, 10 Jan. 1907.

[47] RSM2 (1912), 294 ff.   [48] PSM (1912), 124 ff.   [49] BMS 219 ff.

[50] Gemeente Museum, The Hague. Mahler's own score, which he revised in the last year of his life, has—for the time being perhaps—disappeared, but fortunately his alterations were copied by Willem Mengelberg into his conducting score, a quarto copy of the second edition with Andante 2/Scherzo 3.

[51] See Karel Philippus Berned-Kempers, 'Mahler und Willem Mengelberg', in *Bericht über den internationalen Kongress*, 1956 (Böhlaus, Graz, 1959), 45.

[52] This is of course surprising in view of the fact that, in her *Erinnerungen und Briefe*, written as mentioned above ten years after Mahler's death, i.e. about 1921, her reminiscences of the summer of 1904 speak of the Scherzo as the third movement (AMM1, 92; AMM2, 97).

'Even after the final rehearsal he was still not sure whether or not he had found the right tempo for the Scherzo and whether he should invert the order of the second and third movements (which he subsequently did). He kept making changes and improvements . . .'[53] The resemblance between the openings of the first and second movements (a repeated ostinato on A in the low strings) was probably called to Mahler's attention as a weakness by one of his friends and disciples who had not yet realized how convincing this similarity can sound in a work in which everything is exceptional. Furthermore, the sequence of keys (E flat–C minor), and the need for the moment of repose provided by the meditative Andante before the hurricanes of the Finale, seem to be all-powerful arguments in favour of placing the Andante next to the Finale. Moreover, the ironic and distorted Scherzo, which denies the exultant coda of the first movement of which it is a parody or caricature, loses its meaning altogether when it is not heard immediately after it.

In an article published in 1992 the Austrian composer Karl Heinz Füssl,[54] editor of several Mahler symphonies for the Critical Edition, has convincingly analysed and enumerated the 'hermeneutic and musical' reasons why the order of movements in the Ratz edition should not today be altered. In Füssl's view:

1. The Scherzo belongs after—and with—the opening Allegro because it varies and carries forward some of its thematic material and could be considered an example of 'developing variation', the device defined and used by Schoenberg. The order with Andante 2 would destroy the thematic and harmonic unity of the work.
2. The Scherzo uses the same keys as the first movement, A minor in the beginning and F major for the Trio.
3. The key of the Andante, E flat, is the furthest removed from that of the end of the Allegro, A major, whereas the C minor beginning of the Introduction to the Finale serves as transition from E flat major to A minor which is the main key of the last movement.
4. A slow movement precedes the Finale in five other of Mahler's Symphonies: 1, 2, 4, 5, and 7.

In conclusion, Füssl expresses admiration for Erwin Ratz who, at a time when the history of the various autographs and versions was still incompletely known, intuitively guessed the rightful and original order. An overwhelming majority of conductors in our time have adopted Ratz's order of movements. To my mind Mahler changed it in Essen because he was quite simply frightened by the audacity of his own original conception.

CYCLIC PROCEDURES

Unlike the thematic links in the preceding symphonies, which are easy to find and relatively few, those in the Sixth are almost innumerable. They result from a deliberate

---

[53] See above, Chap. 6 and Klaus Pringsheim 'Zur Uraufführung von Mahlers Sechsten Symphonie', *Musikblätter des Anbruch*, 2 (1920): 14, 496 ff.

[54] Karl Heinz Füssl, 'Zur Stellung des Mittelsätze in Mahlers Sechste Symphonie', in *Nachrichten zur Mahler Forschung*, 27 (Mar. 1992), IGMG, Vienna.

choice which is fundamental to the very conception of the work. The most obvious recurrence is that of the 'motto' mentioned above (the major chord becoming minor). It is accompanied, in the bass, by an obstinate rhythm, that, named by Redlich, of the 'cosmic catastrophe', and rightly compared with the rhythmic leitmotiv in the Ninth Symphony (bars 57 ff.):[55]

The Andante contains no thematic material in common with the other movements, with only one possible exception.[56] However, the Scherzo is linked both to the opening Allegro and to the Finale. Its principal links with the first movement are the opening bass ostinato, a repeated crotchet A (now in 3/8 instead of 4/4) and the falling chromatic motif, in characteristic—quaver/two semiquavers—rhythm, of the first theme (bars 16 and 17), which, clothed in trills and in the rattling sonority of the xylophone, takes on a frankly diabolical character in the development of the Allegro (bar 20, then 154 and 156). Another basic motif from the Scherzo (the rising arpeggio: bars 11 ff.) plays a leading role in the Finale from the introduction onwards (bar 19), sometimes in its original form, sometimes varied or inverted. It also becomes an integral part of theme A of the Finale (bars 115, 117, 118, etc. then 125, 127, etc).[57]

The list of parallels between the opening Allegro and the Finale is impossible to draw up exhaustively, for each theme is made up of numerous motifs, and a great many of them are common to both movements. The octave leap in theme A of the first movement plays a constant and fundamental role in all the 'fate' motifs of the Finale. It is present in two melodies of opposite character: the mournful and grandiose utterance beginning at bar 3 of the Introduction (where it is a leap upwards), and the tuba motif springing from the chaos at bar 16. In the first movement, the third bar of the A theme (in the form of a descending scale) reappears later in the first bar of theme B (transformed into an arpeggio but retaining its characteristic rhythm: bar 77). This same motif is to be found almost everywhere in the Finale where it becomes an integral part of the second theme (bars 194, 201, 203) and of the development.

Theodor Adorno observes that a basic (octave leap) motif of the Finale (bar 16, etc.: A–B–C–A) is in effect a recurrence of the beginning of the opening theme of the first Allegro (bar 6: A–C–B–A) and that, in the same movement, 'chorale-like wind stanzas in minims whose motifs do indeed differ radically from each other . . . are brought together by their use of the chorale.'[58] This list could be indefinitely prolonged, because, as usual, Mahler never ceases to use the same motifs, turning them into new figures which lose their identity as they become part of new moods and atmospheres. In this symphony, especially in the Finale, Mahler's structural genius, while not expressed with the same mathematical rigour that characterizes twelve-tone music,

---

[55] Symphony No. 9, first movement, bars 1–2, 4–5, 108–9, etc.

[56] This is the 'sighing' motif of bar 8, which plays an essential part in the movement. Such 'sighing' motifs exist also in the first movement (bars 11–12, 37, 362). Although the atmosphere and tempo are different, the design and rhythm are strikingly similar.

[57] Thematic links are not confined to the leading parts. Sponheuer notes, in bar 194 of the Finale, a countermelody derived from theme B of the first movement (bassoons and solo viola). Later it recurs in the melodic line of the B (bars 201, 203, and 207).

[58] TAFe 105.

attains to the same mastery of equally complex material and the same unity within diversity. It is therefore easy to understand why so many writers have attempted to analyse and catalogue the motifs and their transformations and to penetrate the mysteries of this huge structure, which is one of the richest, most complex, and most coherent that Mahler ever created. Subtler and deeper than simple thematic relationships, close correspondences have been pointed out between the various movements. The analogy between the second themes of the outer movements, with all that that implies for the developments to come, has been noted, along with the striking analogy between the meditative moments, with their cowbell sounds, that provide the only real link between the Andante and the other movements. In the outer movements, the march rhythm representing destiny recurs, 'heavy and obstinate in the opening movement, processional or belligerent in the Finale',[59] and there is another equally important rhythmic recurrence in the chorales, as seen above. But the list of more general links does not end there. Bernd Sponheuer has shown that key moments in the opening Allegro have counterparts in the Finale, where in a sense they find their fulfilment (*Erfüllungsfelder*) and play a double role, referring to the past while acting as functional elements of the last movement.[60] The same writer observes that in these repetitions, or allusions, the original expression of the episodes is intensified, so that 'the process exposed in the development of the first movement and brought to a merely provisory end, is developed in a more concentrated and richly conflicting way in the Finale. But this return to the process also means a critical revision of the first attempt at its solution: with pitiless exactitude each impulse—and every impulse in this movement tests the breaking strain of the area defined in the second theme and already formulated in the coda to the first movement—is followed by its own collapse (*Niedergang*).'[61]

ANALYSES

This list includes only analyses that deal with the symphony as a whole: those concerned only with one particular movement are quoted in the section concerning the relevant movement. Almost simultaneously with Richard Specht's analysis (48 pp.) brought out by Kahnt, publisher of the symphony, in 1906, there appeared two by Ernst Otto Nodnagel in the *Neue Zeitschrift für Musik*[62] and *Die Musik*.[59] To be mentioned are also those by Hermann Kretschmar (3 pp./1913),[64] Karl Weigl (22 pp./1913),[65] Richard Specht (6 pp./1913,) and Paul Bekker (25 pp./1921).[66] Among those of more

---

[59] Redlich, Introduction to Eulenburg pocket score, p. xiii.

[60] Sponheuer, *Zerfall*, 339. The cowbell episode in the development of the opening Allegro (bars 198 ff.), the major beginning of the recapitulation bars 286–9, and the design of the coda (bars 374 ff.), and the major apotheosis of the B theme (bars 444–81) being the decisive moments of the first movement; in the Finale, the bell episode in the Introduction (bars 29 ff.), the major beginning of the recapitulation, presenting the material in reverse order (theme B first), the two cantabile sections (bars 364–84 and 458–68) and the closing section of the recapitulation (728–72) which looks back to D major beginning of the development (288 ff.). [61] Sponheuer, *Zerfall*, 340. [62] 73 (1906): 21/22, 465.

[63] 5 (1906): 16, 233. [64] *Führer durch den Konzertsaal* (Breitkopf, Leipzig, 1913), 808 ff.

[65] *Mahlers Symphonien*, ed. Edgar Istel, 103. [66] RSM2, 292 ff.; BMS 207.

recent date the most important are by Erwin Ratz (8 pp./1957)[67] and Hans Ferdinand Redlich (7 pp./1963 and 30 pp./1968),[68] Constantin Floros (29 pp./1985),[69] and Christopher Hailey (23pp./1988).[70]

ORCHESTRATION

4 flutes and piccolo, 4 oboes and cors anglais, 5 clarinets and bass clarinet, 4 bassoons and contrabassoon, 8 horns, 6 trumpets, 3 trombones, bass trombone, tuba, timpani and percussion (big drum, side drum, glockenspiel, cowbells, deep-toned bells, cymbals, tamtam, triangle, sticks, hammer), xylophone, 2 harps, celesta (two or more if possible) and strings. Two instruments had never before been used by Mahler—the celesta, which as we have seen he discovered in 1903, and the xylophone, which he never used again. Redlich stresses the symbolic significance of some of these sound sources—the cowbells (nature, solitude), the hammer (fate), the xylophone[71] (the devil's laughter), and the deep bells (symbol of a religious credo).[72]

A TURNING POINT

Eberhardt Klemm calls the Sixth 'a turning point in Mahler's output' and his 'final farewell to the world of the *Wunderhorn-Lieder*'.[73] In the Fifth the trumpet signal and the 'military' signals can be seen as memories of his youth. In the Sixth, on the other hand, the band instruments—bass drum, cymbals, snare drum, E flat clarinet, and brass—are used in a way which is no longer military (military calls and fanfares are strikingly absent from this symphony). The marches have also grown more abstract, even though they are still accompanied by snare drum rolls and cymbal clashes. In the Fifth, the Ländler and waltzes in the Scherzo have not yet broken with their origins, rustic or Viennese, and become the grating symbols of the *Alltag* (of the daily run of the mill)[74] that are found in Mahler's last scores. In the Sixth, the Scherzo is in three-time but is

---

[67] Erwin Ratz, 'Gustav Mahler: Symphonie Nr. 6 in a-moll' (1957), in *Gesammelte Aufsätze* (Universal Edition, Vienna, 1975), 123 ff.

[68] 'Mahler's enigmatic Sixth', in *Festschrift Otto Erich Deutsch zum 80. Geburtstag* (Bärenreiter, Kassel, 1963), 250 ff., and Introduction, pp. iii ff.

[69] Gustav Mahler, Vol. iii, *Die Symphonien* (Breitkopf, Wiesbaden, 1985), 155 ff.

[70] 'Structure and Tonal Plan in Mahler's "Sixth Symphony" ', in Hermann Danuser (ed.), *Gustav Mahler* (Wissenschaftliche Buchgesellschaft, Darmstadt, 1992), 253 ff.

[71] Like Adorno, Redlich mentions a whip (*Holzklapper*). This appeared with a tambourine only in the first edition of the score from bar 179 of the Finale onwards.

[72] The large array of percussion instruments understandably caused concern and Mahler explained to the Opera orchestra before the first reading rehearsal in Vienna that his aim was not to 'make noise', but 'to achieve variety of timbre'. See Franz Gräflinger, '42. Tonkünstlerfest zu Essen', *Musikalische Rundschau*, Munich, 2 (1906): 13, 194 ff., quoted by Floros, *Mahler* (Breitkopf, Wiesbaden, 1985), iii, 160.

[73] Eberhardt Klemm, 'Notizen zu Mahler', *Festschrift Heinrich Besseler zum 60. Geburtstag* (Karl Marx Universität, Leipzig, VEB, 1961), 448.

[74] Georg Wilhelm Friedrich Hegel, *Phänomenologie des Geistes* (Ullstein, Frankfurt, 1970), 16.

no longer in any way a dance. Only some grotesque effects are reminiscent of the Hoffmanesque derision of the first symphonies. Otherwise, as Sponheuer so clearly shows, the Sixth carries straight on from the Fifth in that its 'inner negative coherence . . . signifies, in its negativity, the same as the futile, positive transcendence of the chorale in the second movement of the Fifth: the impossibility of a solution under the conditions that prevail. The critical intention of the breakthrough (*Durchbruch*), in which all truth resides, is by no means abandoned: but as for the utopian hope of a truly satisfactory world, the musical realization of that is abandoned, for it turns it to untruth by making claims for the fulfilment of this hope, allowing it to triumph in the work while the existing social order continues to deny it. The Sixth Symphony passes the harshest judgement on this kind of idealism: it neither presents inner unity in the traditional sense of a complete whole in which all contradictions harmoniously disappear, nor places a despairing hope in breaking, at a blow, through the circle of coherence, revealed for the first time in this symphony as being inescapable.'[75] In this respect, Sponheuer and Klemm regard the Sixth as more 'realistic' than all the preceding symphonies, Sponheuer claiming that 'the progress made in this symphony consists in the failure it consummates'. 'If the preceding symphonies find their particular poignancy in just those moments where the inner coherence of the composition is shattered—the moment of breakthrough (*Durchbruch*), the turning inside out of the smoothly rounded symphonic sphere—exactly the opposite happens in the Sixth: here there is no breakthrough, only an insistent concentration upon the immanent activity of musical characters fixed from the outset, here there is, in Hegel's words, the "cold ongoing necessity of the thing"[76] which finally brings about the fatal collapse of the immanent unity from within.'[77]

For the same reason Theodor Adorno believes, with regard to the Sixth, that it is no longer possible to speak of a 'symphonic hero' or even of a single individual destiny, but that one experiences in it 'the blind and violent march of the many'.[78] Redlich also stresses that the rhythms in the Sixth, march, procession, dance, chorale, are 'collective'.[79] Several writers have also noted that the chorales in the Sixth, far from expressing any hope in a *Durchbruch* of any kind, are moments of intense negativity, expressing a sort of petrified and desperate formalism that seems to symbolize one of the principal forces against which human beings are bound to fight, even if in vain. 'It may well be that the much vaunted tragic character of the Sixth Symphony is itself the expression of that imminent coherence to which Mahler's work increasingly tended', writes Adorno. 'This coherence allows for no escape, so that the life that pulsates in the great Finale of the Sixth is not destined for destruction by the hammerblows of fate but to an internal collapse: the *élan vital* stands revealed as the sickness unto death Kirkegard speaks of.'[80]

But it is time to examine each movement of this unique work more closely.

---

[75] Sponheuer, *Zerfall*, 289.
[76] Hegel, *Phänomenologie*, 16, quoted by Sponheuer, *Zerfall*, 289.
[77] Ibid.
[78] TAM 51; TAMe 35.
[79] Redlich, 'Enigmatic Sixth', 253.
[80] TAF 128 ff.; several words quoted here of the original text are missing in TAFe 91.

(*a*) Allegro energico, ma non troppo

Key: A minor. Transition in D minor. Second theme in F major. Recapitulation in A
major, with the second theme in D major.

Time signature: 4/4.

Rhythm: March.

Tempo: See above. Underneath the main marking there is: *Heftig, aber markig*
(vehement, but pithy). For the second theme: *Schwungvoll* (spirited).

Duration: According to Specht's thematic guide, published before the première
(this timing was certainly given to him by Mahler after the reading rehearsal
in Vienna); in the Vienna performance of January 1907: 22 minutes; and in the
Vienna performance of 1907:[81] 22 minutes; at the Essen première: 20 minutes;[82]
Mahler's own timing, in the corrected proofs of the second edition: 23
minutes.

Analysis: Peter Andraschke has made an extensive study of the first movement on
its own (21 pp./1978).[83]

In the five bars of introduction, the march rhythm, which is strongly marked by the
basses and the snare drum, symbolizes the determination of the 'hero' (or heroes).
Clarity and conciseness are the essential qualities of this movement, in which Mahler
respects far more than usual the classic rules of sonata form. Two characteristic
features of the first theme (bar 6: strings) will recur in later movements: the descending scale motif, with its characteristic rhythm (a dotted crotchet followed by two semiquavers) already mentioned above, and, immediately after the two successive
statements of theme A, the double leitmotiv or 'motto' of the work (rhythmic and
harmonic: see above). The opposition of the major and minor mode, from which
Schubert had already drawn so many magical effects, is now one of the basic elements
of the symphony as a whole, but it is the minor mode which here marks the real sense
of arrival rather than the radiance of the major, as in all baroque and classical musical literature. Another important motif (A′) is the one which bears a strong likeness, at
least in its second, diminished, form (bars 34–6) to a motif of the third movement of
Liszt's First Piano Concerto.[84]

The transition episode (or bridge) is an odd, expressionless chordal chorale in the
woodwinds (bars 61–76). It follows abruptly from the first theme and is accompanied by
a counter-subject, in pizzicato in the lower strings, that is a variant of A. 'As it takes the
form of a chorale,' writes Adorno, 'this bridge remains static, deprived of the transitional
force that the scheme would suggest; and dissonances disturb its colour. This has an
immediate consequence for the structure and progress of the music. The chorale in
effect leads nowhere. The second theme, which follows it with blinding suddenness, is
in no way prepared by it. Because the "bridge", although in its usual place, does not

---

[81] Theodor Helm gives this timing in his *Neue Zeitschrift für Musik* article. See 74 (1907): 3, 56.

[82] According to the *Musikalisches Wochenblatt*.

[83] 'Struktur und Gehalt im ersten Satz von Gustav Mahlers Sechster Symphonie', in Danuser, *Gustav Mahler*, 206 ff.

[84] Bars 34–6, and 29–30 (augmented). See Liszt's Concerto No. 1, in E flat, 3rd movement, bars 17 ff.,
trombones. This 'quotation' was noticed by the critics of the first Vienna performance. See Henry-Louis de
La Grange, 'Music about Music in Mahler: Reminiscences, Allusions, or Quotations?', in Stephen Hefling
(ed.), *Mahler Studies* (Cambridge University Press, Cambridge, 1997), 122 ff. See above, Cyclic Procedures.

really lead to it, this theme has an effect of brutal surprise, further enhanced by the fact that no modulation leads to it: the dominant chord of D minor which ends the chorale is followed, in an interrupted cadence, by the tonic of F major. The striking character of the second theme—surprise as character—does not result only from the theme itself, but from the formal organisation of the whole movement.'[85]

This second element (B), in F major (bars 76 ff.: strings), belongs to the rich family of Mahlerian themes which rise by conjunct intervals. Mahler described it to Alma in the following terms: 'I have tried to portray you in a theme. I don't know if I've succeeded, but you'll just have to put up with it!'[86] The rising profile represents an optimistic impulse within a movement which in other respects expresses far more determination than hope. Bruno Walter never conducted the Sixth Symphony because he found this theme 'not strong enough, too sentimental, and a let-down after the powerful, grim beginning'[87] to which Adorno replies: 'It is often noticeable that they [Mahler's themes] are there for the sake of their function, such as that of extreme contrast; the lyrical theme of the first movement of the Sixth Symphony is the familiar example of such necessity. Its necessity is incorrigible, arising from the objective problem of the form. The whole is to crystallise from the individual impulses without regard to preconceived types. . . . Whatever their genesis might be, the stigmata of contrivance in Mahler testify to the impossibility of reconciling general and particular in a form exempt from the compulsion of a system in them. Mahler's music atones for turning away from the frame that no longer supports it, yet which still, and for long, lays claim to unanimous meaning. That Mahler, nevertheless, does not more adroitly conceal such objectively founded incompatibility benefits the content of his music. Where it sounds contrived, fruitlessness itself speaks from it and nominalist art as such. . . . Mahler could not be defended against incomprehension by denying the contrivance and stylising him into a Schubert that he was not and did not wish to be. Rather, that element would have to be deduced from the content. The truth of Mahler's music is not to be abstractly opposed to the elements in which it falls short of its intention. It is the truth of the attainable. It is contrived both as a will to reach the unattainable, to go beyond the insufficiency of existence, and also as a sign of the unattainable itself.'[88]

Adorno's arguments in defence of this theme are virtually, then, the same as those he used to explain the problem of the major apotheosis in the Fifth. He sees this melody above all as a symbol and as construction material,[89] and Mahler proves him right to the extent that it is never restated, but that its many variants assume preponderance right to the end of the movement (as also happens in the Finale). A fragment of theme A, weightily declaimed by the trombones and the tuba, then *martellato* in the strings, serves as a transition between the two expositions of B. Particularly striking in

---

[85] TAF 152 ff.; TAFe 108 ff.   [86] AMM1, 92; AMM2, 97.

[87] Bruno Walter, *Grosse Dirigenten* (Severin & Siedler, Berlin, 1984), 133. Bruno Walter told Wolfgang Stresemann about an evening walk he took with Mahler, during which, 'with his usual frankness', he expressed his opinion of the 'Alma' theme to him.

[88] TAM 168 ff.; TAMe 128. Heinrich Schmidt mentions possible sources for Theme B of the Sixth, Schumann's *Abendlied*, no. 12 of the *Zwölf vierhändige Klavierstucke für kleine und grosse Kinder*, Op. 85, and the second theme of Chopin's B minor Sonata. See Schmidt, 'Formprobleme und Entwicklungslinien in Gustav Mahlers Symphonien', thesis, University of Vienna, 1929, 206.

[89] Adorno draws attention to the very original harmonization of the B themes of both the Sixth and the Seventh Symphonies, which 'becomes heartbreaking as it has been before only occasionally in Schubert' (TAM 146; TAMe 110).

the accompaniment to theme B is the presence of a long garland of semiquavers (cellos and woodwinds, then woodwinds alone) derived from the theme itself, and prefiguring the procedure of 'total thematism' which Mahler was to approach yet more closely in the first movement of the Ninth. Theme B, transformed and finally replaced by its own imitations, augmentations, and variants, concludes the exposition at the end of which, for the first time since the First Symphony, Mahler places a repeat sign.[90] This shows above all how closely linked to sonata form is the conception of this work where 'the intensification of expansive power in it needs to be complemented by a capacity for imposing order. In the consciousness of his complete technical mastery he dares to undertake a work of Beethovenian type.' [91]

The conciseness of the second theme is as striking as its links with the first, of which it is in a sense the major counterpart. In the recapitulation it reappears only fleetingly, in its original form at least. The opening rhythm, still strongly marked, introduces the development which, with the same conciseness, first exploits the various cells of theme A, the descending chromatic motif (this time with the addition of trills and the 'diabolical' xylophone—in bar 129, arising from bar 20), then its inversion. The two first bars of A are elaborated in a climax of dazzling power in E minor with the full weight of the brass section, after which there is a move back to the main key. The 'fate' rhythm, inexorably beaten out by the snare drum and the timpani, gives the passage that follows a half-military (triangle, cymbals) and half-sardonic character (xylophone). A new march theme springs up, typically Mahlerian, and based on fragments of theme A (bars 157 ff.). Soon motifs derived from B mingle with the new march which becomes increasingly triumphal, in D minor. But the rhythm eventually loses its vigour and insistence, and a reminiscence of B, in the basses, ushers in an extended lyric episode in slow tempo, recalling in its atmosphere and its effect, in the midst of the turmoil of the first movement, the 'nature' episodes in the parallel movement of the Second Symphony. Cowbells, chains of parallel tremolo chords, in the high strings and celesta, and later violin trills *sul ponticello*,[92] conjure up a pastoral setting, while the major–minor motto and the chorale are gently recalled by the brass, and the woodwinds play simple calls, ascending 'Mahlerian' fourths in dotted rhythm.

The second part (*Sehr ruhig. Grazioso:* bar 217) quietly elaborates a variant of B, which grows more and more tender with the solo violin rising to stratospheric heights, after which the chorale and the string tremolos reappear for the last time. This long meditative episode, centring around G and E flat major, is cut short (*Tempo I. subito. Sehr energisch!*), in a totally unexpected key (B major), by a brutal and curtailed variant of A (A', the 'Lisztian' motif). With some references to the chorale, it modulates gradually towards the main key and towards the recapitulation, which starts in the major (but only stays in it for four bars). The exposition is clearly recalled, but its various elements are modified, notably by richer orchestration and new modulations

---

[90] It should however be noted that Mahler had considered inserting one at the end of the A minor Allegro of the Fifth Symphony.   [91] TAM 131; TAMe 96 ff.

[92] Monika Lichtenfeld calls this passage a 'Klangfläche' (sound surface) and compares it with the fourth section of the Introduction to the Finale of the Second Symphony, and rightly speaks of chords 'without tonal function', of mere 'coloristic' character. When the reminiscences of B appear (bar 204, bass clarinet; 216, bassoon; 217 ff., woodwinds; and 234, bass clarinet), this Klangfläche serves as 'a foil to a vague memory of the past'. This is the section that Mahler several times recalls in the Introduction to the Finale. See Monika Lichtenfeld, 'Zur Klangflächetechnik bei Mahler', in Ruzicka, *Herausforderung*, 129.

(E minor, D minor).[93] The transition episode (bars 336 ff.) in particular takes on a new appearance, influenced by the 'nature' episode in the development (a new example of what Adorno calls 'the irreversibility of time'), with the chorale in crotchets in the woodwinds and the oscillation of parallel chords this time in quavers (pizzicato strings). Theme B (in D major) is only evoked in longer and longer note values, as an introduction to the concluding episode in march rhythm (bars 374 ff.), 'a dramatically abridged preparation of the coda'. It commences pianissimo, in *gemessener* (more measured) tempo, with the opening subject in the trombones over a low ostinato F sharp, but it is soon cut short, as at the end of the development, by an accelerated variant of the same theme played tutti, triple fortissimo *(più mosso: Wie wütend drein-fahren*: attack as if furious), ever more insistent and determined. Soon elements from B join in, with the scale motif from A, inverted and ascending. Throughout a brief episode in E flat minor the rhythm intensifies and the march grows more and more triumphal until it arrives in the key of A major. In a commotion of brass and percussion, (bars 441 ff.) the B theme, augmented and shortened,[94] reigns supreme as the tempo keeps getting faster while fragments of the chorale (trombones) and of A (horns and trumpets) enrich it. Sometimes it is augmented, sometimes in its original form. The same theme sings of triumph and victory to the end. But the triumph has been too swift to be final, as the return of the harmonic, major–minor, 'motto' reminds us (bars 473–4, *molto ritenuto*: trumpets and trombones). Redlich speaks of 'a triumphal epilogue . . . with the augmented "Alma" theme in A major blaring out in trumpets and trombones and seconded by the thematically simplified shouts in the eight horns. This premature glorification of a second subject at the expense of the sternly forbidding characteristics of theme group A and the bridge is the measure of the symphony's tragic content. Never again in this work will the sun "rise so bright"[95] as in this epilogue. . . .'[96]

(b) Scherzo

Key: A minor (Trio in F major).

Time signature: 3/8. In the passage that anticipates the Trio, and in the Trio itself, the metre continually alternates between 3/8, 4/8, and 3/4.

Rhythm: Ländler, but distorted by accentuation of the third beat of the bar and, in the Trio, by changes of metre.

Tempo: *Wuchtig* (heavy). In the Trio: *Altväterisch* (old-fashioned). *Grazioso*.

Duration: According to Richard Specht and Thedor Helm (see above): 11 minutes. According to the *Musikalisches Wochenblatt*, at the Essen première: 15 minutes. Mahler's own timing in the corrected proofs of first edition: 12 minutes; of the second edition: 15 minutes.[97]

---

[93] Berg's motif for violin and woodwinds at bars 110 ff. of 'Marsch', the third of his *Orchesterstücke* Op. 6, is a near quote of Mahler's bars 270 ff. (See Marco Devoto, 'Alban's Berg "Marche macabre"', in *Perspectives of New Music*, 22 (1983–4) 1/2, 443).

[94] This 'résumé' of B, comprising a rising, and then falling section (bars 444–8) is evoked at the very beginning of the Introduction to the Finale (bars 5–7).

[95] *Nun will die Sonn' so hell aufgeh'n*, a quotation from the Rückert poem set by Mahler in the first of the *Kindertotenlieder*. [96] Redlich, Introduction, p. xvi.

[97] Jülg explains this three-minute difference in timing by suggesting that Mahler, in one of the two scores, failed to alter the timings when he inverted the order of the middle movements (see the last quoted duration for the Andante, and Jülg, *Sechste*, 34).

Form: A B A¹ B¹ A² Coda.

Alma claimed that the starting point for this extraordinary movement lay in the 'unrythmical games' of little Putzi[98] and in 'doleful children's voices getting more and more tragic'. How could innocent play have inspired such odd and disturbing music? If, in 1903, Mahler genuinely perceived Putzi's cries as doleful, it is easy to understand how, three years later, he could have been under the impression that he had predicted her death in the two tragic works of that summer. For the Scherzo of the Sixth is at once a dance of death and a grotesque Hoffmann scene 'in the manner of Callot'.[99] The effect of caricature comes from the cross-rhythms, the changes of metre (in the Trio), the orchestration, notably the use of E flat clarinet and xylophone, and even the dynamics: 'There is something sinister about the Scherzo of the Sixth,' writes Adorno 'not least because, thanks to the put-on crescendi and chromatic *fauxbourdon* passages in the middle voices, the orchestra seems to swell like a body threatening to burst and caused untold damage.'[100] The same writer observes that here the 'the Sixth bracketed in terms of motifs and harmony between the outer movements, asks how, from a minimum of initial materials, a maximum of changing characters is to be distilled.'[101] Mahler was never more imaginative in his use of timbre and unusual orchestral effects than in this movement.[102] Never before had Mahler so distorted, not to say caricatured, a dance rhythm, which becomes virtually unrecognizable. Redlich speaks in this context of 'sinister artificiality',[103] Ratz of 'a demonic creature of grotesque appearance'. In the opening rhythmic ostinato are manifested the same 'laborious obstinacy', the same 'rigidity', the same 'deliberate refusal to move' as at the beginning of the symphony, and also the intentional monotony inherent in the whole work.[104] Here, as we have observed, man is prisoner of his own destiny and is forbidden escape by a *Durchbruch* of any kind. The principal theme is characterized by an ascending arpeggio motif (or fanfare), always on an upbeat, that will later play an essential role in the Finale.

The major–minor 'motto' reappears as early as bars 26–8, slightly disguised by an inner chord within a chain of tonics and dominants rendered peculiarly disquieting by the parallel motion of the upper voices and the persistent minor second in the top part. Before the Scherzo proper is even finished, the Trio theme,[105] with its changing metres, is announced, but closely combined with the chord motif (bars 51 ff.). As for the Trio itself, it contains no trace of the languid waltz rhythms which characterize those in the preceding symphonies. Instead, it intensifies the unease with its grotesque curtseying,

---

[98] AMM1, 92; AMM2, 97. As seen above (Vol. ii, Chap. 10), Alma wrongly wrote 'children'. The Scherzo was actually written in 1903, before Anna was born.

[99] The opening motif in the violins (bar 5) has been found reminiscent of the famous popular Viennese song, 'Ach du lieber Augustin', of which Mahler retained a traumatized childhood memory (see, Vol. iiii, Chap. 7), as he told Freud during their interview in Aug. 1910.

[100] TAF 142; TAFe 101.   [101] TAM 140; TAMe 103.

[102] For instance the thunderous low brass parallel chords in the second strain of the main Scherzo theme (bars 26 ff., 81 ff., 221 ff., etc.), which reaches the depths in the Fafner-like growls of 231 ff., the plaintive descending scales of the horns, adorned with grace notes (176 ff.), the four horns later playing the same motif in thirds (348 ff.), the sinister muted trumpets playing in unison (186–8), the many passages involving woodwinds alone, and in an unusual range (bars 273 ff. for instance), etc.

[103] Introduction, p. xvii. Redlich suggests the Mephisto movement of Liszt's *Faust Symphony* as model for Mahler's Scherzo.   [104] Ratz, 'Symphonie Nr. 6', *Aufsätze*, 123.

[105] Redlich observes that this is a variant of the ostinato opening motif (bars 4–5).

its changing accents, its unstable metre, its ceremonious counterpoints, and its cari-
caturing of old-fashioned 'gallant' style. An acid woodwind sonority accompanies this
wobbling dance for marionettes, whose faded tinsel and clumsy pirouettes are evoked
by parodied melodic formulae. Scherzo and Trio are to be successively and alternately
repeated, each time with numerous variants. Before the first repeat of the Scherzo, the
ostinato in the timpani (bars 172 ff.) is accompanied by a plaintive chromatic passage
from the eight horns, with characteristic grace notes, after which the principal theme
(woodwinds) is accompanied by the strings *col legno*[106] (in F minor: bars 183 ff.). This
passage is repeated in E flat minor, with changes in the orchestration, after the repeat
of the Trio.[107] The final Scherzo is then abbreviated, ending in one of those moments
of 'panic' that occurred several times in the preceding symphonies.[108] The oboes,[109]
over a seventh chord of ill-defined tonality in the context of the preceding D minor
tutti,[110] play a derisive descending arpeggio against the beat ('a painful distortion of
the Trio theme') and a chromatic scale rapidly covers four octaves from top to bottom.
The Coda ends with a final recall of the Trio (woodwinds and solo violin) beneath which
the muted trumpets reiterate the major–minor 'motto' with meaningful insistence. The
atmosphere is close to that of *Das irdische Leben* or of the later *Purgatorio* in the Tenth
Symphony. Grotesque neo-classical melodic figures lead gradually down to the bass
register, in a spectral diminuendo obtained through orchestration rather than dynamics, the 'motto' passing from muted trumpets to muted horns (with woodwinds doubling
the top part) and thence to muted trombones, while the principal motif fades on the
contrabassoon and dies away in pizzicato on the basses, and two pianissimo but
accented strokes on the solo timpani.

(*c*) **Andante moderato**

> *Key*: E flat major. The second theme is in G minor, episode B′ in the first develop-
> ment, in E minor then E major, the second episode in C major, etc. (see below).
> *Time signature*: 4/4.
> *Tempo*: Apart from a few rallentandos and accelerandos, this changes only in the
> 'etwas drängend' (somewhat urgent) episode in the second development. The C
> major episode (bar 116) carries the indication *Misterioso*.
> *Duration*: According to Richard Specht and Theodor Helm (see above): 14 minutes.
> According to the *Musikalisches Wochenblatt*, at the Essen première: 15 minutes.
> Mahler's own markings in the proofs of the first edition: 15 minutes; of the
> second: 12 minutes.
> *Analysis*: Luciano Berio contributed a detailed melodic analysis of the movement to

---

[106]   As in the ghostly episode of the *Wunderhorn-Lied* 'Revelge'.

[107]   Redlich speaks of 'a recapitulation resembling that of a sonata', with a slower episode in F, then in
E flat minor. Floros quotes, in relation to the second Trio, in D major (bars 273 ff.) of the Sixth the oboe
d'amore theme of the Scherzo of Strauss's *Symphonia Domestica*. Since the score of this work was published
in Mar. 1904, and Mahler's Scherzo was composed in 1903, this cannot have been an unconscious reminiscence (Floros, *Symphonien*, 171 ff.).

[108]   The most famous one is at the end of the Scherzo of the Third Symphony.

[109]   Bars 401 ff.

[110]   This is a clear anticipation of the beginning of the Finale, the chord being almost the same. It might
well be taken as another reason for placing this movement before the last.

the Colloque international Gustav Mahler held at the Musée d'Art Moderne in
Paris in 1985.[111]

Form: The following summary of the form is borrowed from Theodor Schmitt, who
has produced the most detailed analysis of a movement which, despite its apparent simplicity, is in fact quite complex:

BARS

1 to	20	Theme A (E flat): 1st phrase: 1–10; 2nd: 10–14; 3rd: 14–20.
20 to	27	Theme B (G minor).
28 to	55	Theme A' (E flat): 1st phrase: 28–36; 2nd: 36–42; 3rd: 42–53; Transition: 54–5.
56 to	65	Theme B' (E minor and A minor).
64 to	83	Development 1 (1st part: E minor: 64–71; 2nd: B and E minor: 72–7; 3rd: E minor: 78–83).
83 to	89	Episode 1: 1st part: 83–9; 2nd: 89–93: E major.
99 to	114	Theme A" (E flat): 1st period 99–108; 2nd: 108–11; 3rd: 112–14.
115 to	138	Episode 2: 1st part: C major: 115–23; 2nd: A major: 124–38.
139 to	145	Theme B": A minor.
146 to	190	Development 2 (1st part: 146–59—variant of B: C sharp minor and F sharp major; 2nd: 160–72—variant of A': B major; 3rd—variant of development 1st, 2nd, and 3rd parts: 173–84: E flat; 4th—Abgesang: 185–90).
191 to 201		Coda.[112]

Themes A and B alternate more or less regularly, but asymmetry comes in with the
variants and the two sections described here by Schmitt as 'episodes', where the elaboration of the themes takes on the character of free lyrical expansion. Because of its
expressive and formal peculiarities Schmitt compares this movement at once to an
orchestral Lied (element A), a symphonic intermezzo (element B), and an Adagio in the
Bruckner tradition (developments and episodes). This movement brings to the
symphony's dark and bleak world its only moment of true calm. It is also the only one
which does not share motifs with the others, the cowbells being one of the few common
features. It has been described by Specht as a 'song of solitude' with an 'Arcadian
atmosphere', by Redlich as a 'dream intermezzo', while Bekker speaks of a 'visionary
enchantment' while criticizing the 'banality' of the principal theme. Arnold Schoenberg
answered this criticism in advance in 1914 with the detailed analysis of the opening
theme that appeared in his famous Mahler lecture, later transformed into an article. He
shows, for instance, that the lengthening of certain values (especially in bars 4 and 7)
produces two asymmetrical periods of four and a half bars each, instead of the traditional eight bars. 'This shows a sense of form developed to the highest degree, as found
only in great masterpieces. It is not the artifice of a "technician"—a master could not
achieve it if he set out to. Such things are inspirations beyond the control of the
conscious mind, inspirations that only come to genius, which receives them unknow-
ingly and produces solutions without even being aware that there was a problem.'[113]

[111] 'Une Mélodie de Gustav Mahler', in *Colloque international Gustav Mahler* (Association Gustav
Mahler, Paris, n.d. [1986]), 108 ff.

[112] Theodor Schmitt, *Der langsame Symphoniesatz Gustav Mahlers* (Fink, Munich, 1983), 144.

[113] Arnold Schoenberg, 'Mahler', in 'Stil und Gedanke', *Gesammelte Schriften*, 17.

828 *Appendix 2: History and Analysis*

Indeed the 'sadly intimate tone' (*trübselig innige Ton*) of the melody derives a great deal of its charm from the 'ambivalences' occurring 'between the ends and beginnings of phrases', and from the 'metrical irregularity . . . which folksong-like melodies bring with them to symphonic prose'.[114] Several writers have noted that it still belongs to the world of the *Kindertotenlieder*.[115] On the basis of its very accompaniment, an Alberti bass, it has been called 'unsymphonisch'. Paul Bekker who, as we have seen, regarded it with favour, describes it as 'trying to get itself forgotten in the course of the movement',[116] Adorno discerns an 'inertly reified, derivative' (*dinghaftes, Abgeleitetes*), 'non-spontaneous' element in it,[117] while Redlich finds models for its 'disarming sentimentality' in Flotow, Kirschner, and Lassen.[118] In effect, its cells and motifs are developed at length during the movement, while the melody itself is recapitulated only with variants that transform it or break it up. The second theme (B), introduced by the English horn in an uncertain key, is distinguished from the first by its brevity (it is stated in one bar) and by the four imitative bars that complete it. Its ambivalence of key results from the leading note's absence from the dominant chord, which produces a modal impression.[119] Still more important is its close resemblance to the first bar of theme A (bar 1), of which it is a free inversion, a resemblance which is repeatedly confirmed in the developments that follow.[120] It is not limited to the theme, either, since the thirds in the accompaniment to B (described by Schmitt as 'pendular') were already part of theme A (bar 8). The necessary contrast is nevertheless obtained through the instrumentation, the first element being played by the strings and the second by solo woodwinds.

Although the movement begins simply as a song without words, in developing its various components Mahler soon uses techniques such as augmentation, diminution, transposition, and inversion, but in a way that is anything but academic. In section B', for example, the 'pendular' thirds (which have now become fourths; see bar 56, oboes) are linked with a fragment of A (bar 59) followed by B in the horn, and the material arising from one and the other continues to be closely entwined in the development that follows. The serene exaltation of Episode 1, in E major (bars 84 ff.), recalls the atmosphere of the opening of the gates of heaven at the end of the Adagio in the Fourth, perhaps because it is announced by the same key change (G to E major). With its triplets turning calmly on themselves, its trilling birdsong in the strings (bars 87–8) and its cowbells, it celebrates nature, whose voice takes on a solemn note (8 horns), again recalling the end of the Adagio of the Fourth in one of the few episodes of the work to 'open up a new sound space'.[121] 'The world is far removed, a presentiment of eternity opens the skies to the lone watcher.'[122] The peace and stillness of nature serve here as a counterpart to the passion and vitality of human striving,[123] like 'a vision, a phantasm, Utopia'. In the second episode (bars 115 ff.), in C major, once again a key

---

[114] TAM 142; TAMe 107. The words *trübselig, inniger Ton* are not included in the translation.

[115] Redlich notes the resemblance between bar 9 of the Andante and the first Lied of the cycle, which concludes with the same strain. See Redlich, Introduction, p. xix.

[116] BMS 220.   [117] TAM 120; TAMe 89.

[118] Redlich, Introduction, p. xii.

[119] Schmitt (*Symphoniesatz*, 148) suggests the Aeolian mode (minor with flattened leading note).

[120] Ibid. 146

[121] BMS 221 and Schmitt, *Symphoniesatz*, 158. Schmitt devotes 8 pages to an analysis of this episode alone.   [122] BMS 221.   [123] Schmitt, *Symphoniesatz*, 163.

arrived at without the slightest preparation, the flutes and clarinets superimpose upon the theme, whose various fragments have been taken up by the basses, an ethereal counter-melody like the one in the Adagio of the Fourth Symphony. Then come a series of modulations, as is customary in a development: A major, A minor, and C sharp minor. The 'moment of intensity' achieved with the arrival of this last key is at once the climax and the 'final phase' of the movement.[124] But a recapitulation of the principal complex would no longer be appropriate after this broad ebbing of the tide. It would seem academic and artificial. Thus it is left aside and the concluding episode assumes, almost imperceptibly and without the slightest break, the function of a coda. This ending has elicited the following comment from Adorno: 'This exemplifies the subtlety and delicacy with which Mahler's sense of the irreversibility of time announces itself in his mature symphonic work. His principle of the variant, the deviation (*Abweichung*), is applied to subverting the large-scale forms. In consequence the entire movement ends up in a different place from the one intended by the composer, or rather by the overall structural design.'[125] The principal theme, having reached its peak on the high notes, breaks up as it sinks down again to the low register of the strings[126] and dies, pianissimo, on a simple pizzicato in the basses.

(d) Finale

Key: C minor (Introduction), A minor (Allegro), etc. (see below).

Time signature: Alla breve and 4/4.

Rhythm: March (in the allegro passages).

Tempo: See Analytical Table below. It is, as can be seen, more than usually subject to changes, especially because of the repeated appearances of the slow introduction.

Duration: According to both Specht and Helm (see above): 30 minutes; according to the *Musikalisches Wochenblatt*, at the Essen première: 40 minutes. Mahler's own timing in the corrected proofs of the second edition: 32 minutes.

Analyses: Besides the complete analyses already listed, the following concern only the Finale: by Erwin Ratz (15 pp./1956),[127] Eberhardt Klemm (6 pp./1961),[128] Bernd Sponheuer (71 pp./1978)[129] and finally two, still more recent, by Mathias Hansen (11 pp./1982),[130] and Siegfried Oechsle (18 pp./1997).[131] Peter Andraschke has concentrated his attention only on Mahler's changes in the Finale in the various stages of the manuscript, plates, proofs, and versions[132] and Adorno's extensive analysis should also be mentioned.[133] The analyses of

---

[124] Schmitt devotes 11 pages to the analysis of this 'second development'.

[125] Adorno, TAF 144; TAFe 102.

[126] The role played in the final bars by the famous added sixth (here C) should be noted (bars 198–9). Donald Mitchell (DMM2, 323) observes that the recapitulation of A intervenes before the end of the big climax of the second development (tuba and low strings, then violas and cellos: bars 159 ff.), and before the return of the main key of E flat, while the violins, flutes, and oboes resume the countermelody mentioned above (bar 115).   [127] Erwin Ratz, 'Formproblem', in *Aufsätze*, 131 ff.

[128] *Notizen*, 447; and Ruzicka, *Herausforderung*, 67.   [129] *Zerfall*, 281 ff.

[130] 'Marsch und Formidee: Analytische Bermerkungen zu sinfonische Sätzen Schuberts und Mahlers', in *Beiträge zur Musikwissenschaft*, 22 (1980): 1, 3

[131] 'Strukturen der Katastrophe: Das Finale der VI. Symphonie Mahlers und die Endzeit der Gattung', *Musikforschung*, 50 (1997): 2, 162 ff.   [132] Andraschke, 'Retuschen', 63 ff.

[133] TAM 130 ff.; TAMe 96 ff.

Adorno, Klemm, and Ratz differ only in details, although Adorno has the development starting later than his colleagues.[134] Nevertheless, like Sponheuer, he divides the *Durchführung* into four parts, whereas Eberhardt Klemm finds in it five 'Felder' (fields) or 'Räume' (areas)[135] each with 'its specific structures and its own variation technique', with 'catastrophes' being produced between them, 'so complex is the event when a transition is made from one entity (*Gestalt*) to the next'. As for Erwin Ratz, he distinguishes in the 'principal section' of the *Durchführung* (bars 336–478) episodes that are 'positive' and others that are 'negative'.[136] Redlich[137] regards the structure of the movement as being more complex still, and divides the *Durchführung* into ante-recapitulations (bars 229 to 235), development properly speaking (129–43), and then post-recapitulations (520–641), principal recapitulations (642–772) and coda, which he describes as 'final recapitulation'. Mathias Hansen's[138] analysis increases the complexity even further, dividing the exposition into 'principal variants No 1 and 2' and treating the first sections of the *Durchführung* as reprises of the introduction (bars 229–65), of the second variant (265–336), of the first and second variant (336–457), and of the introduction (458–78), so that the true *Durchführung*, in his view, extends only from bar 479 to 519.

The thoroughness and detail with which all these analysts have undertaken their task, and the disagreement between them on several points (here just briefly summarized), gives some impression not only of the structural complexity of this Finale but also of its irresistible fascination for post-war generations. I reproduce below the analytical table prepared by Bernd Sponheuer, who made a more detailed study of the work than his predecessors and devised a personal and judicious synthesis. In his view, the four reappearances of the introduction divide the movement into distinct sections, and facilitate the analyst's task:[139]

Introduction: bars 1 to 113.

Bars		Keys
1–15	*Sostenuto*: 1st part (Theme I; Motto).	C minor
16–48	*Etwas schleppend*: 2nd part (Genesis of A and B; cyclic motifs).	A minor
49–64	*Schwer. Marcato* (Heavy. Marcato): 3rd part (Chorales; statement of bridge material [*Überleitung*]).	C minor
65–97	*Etwas fliessender*: 4th part (Genesis of A).	
98–113	*Allegro moderato*: 5th part (transition to A).	

---

[134] At bar 271. Sponheuer compares Adorno's, Klemm's, and Ratz's analyses of the development in a conspectus, where he notes the main differences between them (*Zerfall*, 314). Bekker also has the development starting later.

[135] No. 1: bars 229–89; 2: 288–335; 3: 336–84; 4: 385–478; 5: 479–519.

[136] Negative: bars 336–63; positive: 364–84; negative: 385–96; positive: 397–448; negative: 449–57; positive: 458–68; negative: 469–78.

[137] 'Enigmatic Sixth', 256 and Introduction, p. xxii.

[138] 'Marsch', 20.

[139] Sponheuer, *Zerfall*, 312 n. 56. Redlich considered on the other hand that these repeated appearances of the Introduction made the structure of the movement exceptionally complex.

BARS   KEYS

Exposition: bars 114 to 228.

114–38	*Allegro energico*: Main theme (A).	A minor
139–90	*Pesante*: Transition or bridge (chorales, octave leaps, I and motifs from A).	
191–216	*Fliessend*: Secondary theme (B) (*Abgesang*, bars 205 ff.).	D major
217–28	*Belebend*: Concluding theme (with motifs from B, octave leaps, and motifs from A).	

Development: bars 229 to 519.

229–87	Introduction 2 (abridged: I, motifs from B, connection with 1st movement, cowbells, motifs from A).	D and F sharp minor
288–335	*Sostenuto*: Devel./1st part (modelled on the *Abgesang* of B. I, chorales).	D major
336–96	*A tempo*: Devel./2nd part (octave leap motifs).	D minor
		A major
		F minor

Bar 336: 1st hammer blow.
Bar 364–84: cantabile 'enclave' (B, chorales, A in the bass).
Bar 385 *Etwas wuchtiger. Alle mit roher Kraft*
(Somewhat more weighty. All with robust strength).

397–478	*Kräftig, aber etwas gemessen* (Strongly, but still controlled): Devel./3rd (central) part in march time (model: A, with chorale).	
		C minor
		E flat major
		C major
		G major
		A major
	Bars 458–68 *Allmählich sich beruhigend*: cantabile 'enclave' (I, chorale and B).	A major
479–519	Devel./4th part (octave leap themes).	D minor
		C minor
		D minor

Bar 479 *Pesante*: 2nd hammer blow.

Recapitulation: bars 520 to 772.

520–74	*Wieder etwas zurückhaltend* (Once again somewhat slower): Introduction 3 and A.	C minor
575–641	*Grazioso*: Reprise of B (with motifs from A and increasingly preponderant chorales).	B flat major, A major
642–67	*Tempo I* (*Allegro energico*): Reprise of A.	A minor
668–727	Modified reprise of the bridge (with B, A, octave leaps, chorale).	

(cont.):

BARS		KEYS

728–72 *Bewegter (Halbe)*: Concluding theme, compressed (I, octave leap, chorale, B and A
transformed, rhythmic motto).   A major

Coda: bars 773 to 822.

773–89 Introduction 4 (motto, I).   A minor

790–822 *Bedeutend langsamer* (Considerably slower):
Epilogue (octave leaps, chorale).

This scheme shows both the strictness and the formal liberty of this extraordinary symphonic movement, the longest Mahler wrote except for the opening Allegro of the Third. Erwin Ratz emphasizes not only the logic and coherence of its 'architecture', but also the 'concentration', even 'conciseness' (*Knappheit*) of the thought, despite the exceptional length.[140] He observes that this logic is all the more admirable in that 'the more dramatic the content of a musical work, the more acute is the problem of the recapitulation'. Redlich gives as models for this vast structure, characterized in particular by the four reappearances of the introduction 'in the manner of a rondo',[141] the first movement of Beethoven's last Quartet, the Finale of Berlioz's *Fantastique* and the Finale of Brahms's First (not to mention the first movement of Mahler's own Third). However, in Adorno's view, 'its formal conception differs from that of the earlier work in that epic expansion attains tightest control of itself: in this sense the movement is the centre of Mahler's entire œuvre. The polyphony of the Fifth Symphony is adjourned; the temporal dimensions would have been incompatible with contrapuntal attention to the simultaneous. Its place is taken by a no less closely successive form of connection through the profuse elaboration of theme and motif. . . . In keeping with its emphatic basic character the movement is a sonata finale, not a rondo. The long introduction, beginning four times on different intervals, not only serves to articulate the whole, but is later integrated with the Allegro.'[142]

As seen above, Mahler made numerous changes to this work, those in the Finale alone being the object of a study by Peter Andraschke.[143] They consist essentially of a substantial reduction in the percussion part, both in the numbers of instruments used and in the dynamics, so that the transparency of the sound is enhanced. In addition, I should note the abandonment of mixed timbres in favour of a more intense individuality in the voices that determine the motivic structure. The changes that Mahler made to the dynamic markings bring out a sort of wave-motion dynamic that rises and falls around certain precise culminating points.

Sponheuer sums up the various functions of the Introduction in the following manner:

1. It is, in its key structure, an anticipation of the course of events (*Verlaufsgestalt*) in the movement as a whole.
2. It contains the constituent elements of the themes of the Finale and an essential first step towards its genesis.
3. It constitutes a link with the preceding movements.[144] The opening chord, the key of which is as uncertain as that of the melodic gesture that follows, is

---

[140] Ratz, 'Formproblem', *Ausätze*, 135.

[142] TAM 131 ff.; TAMe 155.

[144] Sponheuer, *Zerfall*, 299.

[141] Redlich, Introduction, p. xix.

[143] Andraschke, 'Retuschen', 63.

described by Redlich as 'the chord of chaos'.[145] Sponheuer observes that it is an altered ¾ chord[146] which resolves, again ambiguously, on the tonic of C (with an added third). As Adorno puts it, 'the curtain rises on something ineffable and invisible'.[147]

The broad musical 'gesture' of the opening (I: bars 3 ff.) reproduces horizontally the intervals of the chord, at least in its descending second section (bar 6).[148] From the high A flat that marks its apogee (bar 5) to the low A where it winds up (bar 16), it covers almost five octaves. The second part of the phrase (strings and horns) is accompanied by the double motto, rhythmic and harmonic, in A minor, a key that nothing had led one to expect (trumpets and trombones). One could hardly imagine a more eloquent, striking, and grandiose opening. The events that follow increase the tension even further. As seen above, the Introduction is in five parts. The second is one of the most anguish-ridden moments in symphonic literature. Over a tremolo chromatic descent in the basses, the dark voice of the tuba states a new motif, henceforth referred to as 'octave leap' motif, followed by three notes in dotted rhythm, B–C–A, repeated four times. Later these three notes will be incorporated in the principal theme of the movement. From the same frightening abyss will eventually emerge the stylized fanfares of the Scherzo (which will also form part of A).

Suddenly (bar 27) the darkness is dispelled by the sound of bells and by the oscillating parallel chords of the first movement. These accompany the genesis of theme B, the 'organic' consequence of the preceding motif whose rhythm it shares (bars 39 ff.: horn). Other elements appear, as if by chance, notably the extended octave leap of the concluding theme (bars 43/44: horn and bar 46: trumpet), after which the string tremolos descend towards the bass, finishing on the tonic of C minor.

Without any transition there now appears the sternest, most 'negative' and sinister chorale that Mahler ever wrote (low woodwinds, then woodwinds and horns, then strings and brass, bars 49 ff.). Strange as it may seem, given the optimistic role always played by chorales in symphonic music, notably that of Bruckner, this chorale is the most negative element in the whole Finale, with its obstinate rhythm, its solemn, 'learned' polyphony and its sinister monotony.[149] Whether it symbolizes 'the resistance of matter', the implacability of fate or perhaps simply death, this hostile, reactionary, and unyielding element unquestionably has a negative meaning and a negative role. In the section that follows (bars 65–97; G major), again introduced by the double 'motto', other elements of the main themes to come appear one after another,[150] before the chorale is resumed and developed, crescendo, with motifs from B and the octave leap motif.

---

[145] Siegfried Oechsle analyses this chord as 'doubly altered', a C minor chord with 'divided fifths', i.e. the note G simultaneously ascending to A flat and descending to F sharp ('Strukturen', 175).

[146] C–E flat–F sharp–A flat.   [147] TAM 201.

[148] Sponheuer observes that this 'gesture' sums up, in its ascending and then descending curve (*Aufrauschen und Niedergang*), the movement as a whole (*Zerfall*, 313), like the instrumental introduction to the Lied 'Ich bin der Welt abhanden gekommen'.

[149] Adorno speaks of a dark (*düster*) chorale and recalls in this context the 'heavily processional' tempo (*Wie ein schwerer Kondukt*) indicated by Mahler in the middle of the opening movement of the Ninth Symphony (bars 327 ff.).

[150] One of them is the motif common to both themes (bars 69–70 and 77–8). In the crescendo, Sponheuer notes the presence of elements common to all the themes of the Finale. He observes that this crescendo will be repeated almost note for note in the recapitulation (bars 469–78).

Thus is reached the transition (Allegro moderato, A minor: bar 98), which in fifteen bars modulates from C minor to A minor, and prepares for the first theme with a rhythmic ostinato and arpeggio motifs.[151] The Introduction, while depicting chaos, night, anguish, and all the 'negative' forces threatening man, has also given us witness of the birth of the themes to come, with a logic well concealed but so tight that each event has seemed to proceed naturally from the preceding one. Sponheuer observes that rhythm is a founding element in all the thematic material of the Finale, and that by modifying it without changing the intervals (or vice versa) Mahler sometimes obtains unexpected variants or parallels.[152] Once the main tempo, Allegro energico, is established, the initial theme (A, violins and woodwinds: bars 114 ff.), in the form of a march, is stated with the utmost conciseness. Its structure is complex, but it is made up of numerous fragments already encountered. Next, there is a transition episode (bars 139 ff.) combining the elements of A with an elaboration of the chorales from the Introduction. This transition episode (*Pesante*) is so long and so significant that some writers have considered it a thematic complex on its own.[153] It is in fact a development within the exposition. The brass plays the leading role in it and it is characterized by its long note values, its large melodic intervals, and its dense polyphony. It has long been considered a symbol of 'all that threatens man'.[154] Towards the end of this section, a short pause intervenes immediately after the first beat (bar 176), the importance of which commentators have frequently stressed, for it acts as punctuation before the final *stretto*, where the dactylic rhythm (a quaver and two semiquavers) appears for the first time, which will characterize the various climaxes of the Finale.

The second theme (B: horns, then woodwind: bars 191 ff.) now comes in after a sudden modulation to D major on an outburst of quavers (flutes and clarinets). As we have seen, several motifs are common to themes A and B (for instance in bars 194–201, already present in the first movement, and bar 197). Despite its optimistic posture and its major key, the character of B remains close to that of A, tension and defiance rather than real optimism. Adorno calls this 'probably the most novel-like constellation anywhere in Mahler, dancing like an imperiled boat in choppy water. Without being ashamed of the simple sequences of its consequent phrase, this asymmetrical theme, purified of continuous movement is unfathomable in its expressiveness. It changes iridescently between careless joy and surging intoxication. It is helped in this by its structure. Like prose, it strings together heterogeneous components, above all widely separated rhythmical values, which are nevertheless, by virtue of their harmonic links, organically intertwined. . . . At the same time the theme's complex form enables it to be utilised equally well as a unity, to be selected and spun out like an individual component, and, above all, allows all the subterranean connections between its motifs to be exploited.'[155] The brevity of the concluding theme (bars 217 and 228), derived from B, with motifs from A and from the chorale and the extended

---

[151] The rhythmic ostinato (bars 98 ff., then bars 116 ff. of A) is actually an accelerated form, in dotted rhythm of the motif A–B–C–A played by the tuba at the beginning of the Introduction (bars 16–19). As for the arpeggio motifs, in their two versions, rising and falling, they are to be found at the heart of theme A (bars 115, 117, 118, 121, etc.)

[152] *Zerfall*, 301 ff. The same author lists the three principal rhythms utilized in the various thematic elements.

[153] Oechsle, 'Strukturen', 171. Adorno names this section *Fortsetzungsthema* or *Bläserthema* (TAM 132 ff.; TAMe 98).   [154] Ratz, 'Formproblem', 162   [155] TAM 132; TAMe 98.

octave leap, is soon compensated by the return of the Introduction, where theme I appears inverted, and in imitations. The secondary theme B is now to have an even more important role than it did the first time.[156]

The beginning of the reprise, marked by an interrupted cadence (bar 229), briefly evokes the chord oscillation, then the fanfare of A, then the opening of B. At the moment when the obstinate bass figure seems to be preparing the return of the first theme, the second instead continues to dominate (horn, then trumpet), but is continually interrupted by the piercing arpeggio from A (bars 273, 275, etc). The first section of the *Durchführung* properly speaking (bars 288 ff.: *Sostenuto*) is a variation on theme B and its 'Abgesang'. According to Sponheuer, this episode is the true conclusion of the exposition, whose epilogue was abnormally short. The lyrical expansiveness of this passage is once more cut short, just as it approaches its climax, by an interrupted cadence and by the first hammer blow.

The second section (bars 288 ff.) uses mainly the chorales and their octave leap motif with, at the beginning, an agitated underlay of rapid scales and dotted rhythms in the strings. The episode here being developed is the transition passage of the exposition (bars 139–90). In the middle of this section is the first of the 'cantabile enclaves', thus designated by Redlich and Sponheuer (*In tempo etwas beruhigend*: In a slightly calmer tempo, bars 364 ff.). Erwin Ratz describes this lyrical flight as 'the moment of calm to which one forever aspires, but which must be left as soon as attained'. It develops theme B, the most 'positive' element in the Finale.[157] During a gradual descent from the heights, the quiet lyricism is brutally disrupted by elements from A,[158] and by a march rhythm that soon infects the whole orchestra with the 'barbaric violence' (Adorno) of its dactylic rhythm (already mentioned above). A general pause both precedes and reinforces the conclusion of this episode, and it also constitutes its climax.[159]

Now begins the central section of the *Durchführung*, another warlike march, in C minor, based on theme A and the chorales. It soon leaves its initial key to touch in passing, on a series of major keys (E flat, C, G, A). Just before the end of this section, a second 'cantabile enclave' (*Allmählich sich beruhigend*: Calmer little by little; bar 458) meditates on theme I, with, as always, elements of the chorale and of B. It leads to the last part of the *Durchführung*, announced by the second hammer blow (bar 479) and by an interrupted cadence. As in the Bridge, the brass (and then the woodwind) exchange octave leaps. The size of the 'leaps' continually grows, almost to the point of caricature. Theme I and the chorale are also present in this last episode: 'The great march is installed between the concrete piers of the wind theme. . . . However the correspondence between the second and fourth parts of the

---

[156] Sponheuer notes that the first chord (bar 229) has already lost its 'vague' character. Over a pedal of D, it becomes a chord of the seventh on the subdominant of D minor. This reprise will proceed to recall the development of the first movement, thematically through the falling arpeggio of B (bars 101 and 103); in terms of sonority through the cowbells and the celesta; and harmonically through the chain of parallel chords.

[157] Its optimistic character is underlined by two elements: the ascending scale in conjunct intervals, a true Mahlerian 'fingerprint' (bars 194 and 198, augmented in 366); and the arpeggios (bars 192 and 200).

[158] One of them is the rising arpeggio that is also part of B (bars 202 and 204).

[159] 'Before the third part of the development, this caesura gives breathing space in the otherwise over-dense mesh, the tension leads onto a colon, like that in a march introduction, so that the interruption only heightens the expectation which is fulfilled in the great March . . .' See TAM 134; TAMe 99.

development is not a mechanical one: the latter varies the former in intensified form.' [160]

This, then, is the huge *Durchführung*, which Theodor Adorno called 'the symphony proper' and which he claimed had 'to be constructed in such a way that it becomes neither incongruous with what has gone before, nor entangled in itself. For this, the improvising freedom that adopts the pattern of the development as a corrective is not enough. That freedom is only sanctioned in that each main section, which very precisely develops its models, soars expansively towards its end, as if its own progress had loosened the constraint; such a parallelism of disintegration-fields unifies the diversity of characters to exactly the same extent as it softens the matter restrained; the great rhythm of the development becomes itself one of necessity and freedom.'[161] Sponheuer also marvels at 'the way in which it [the *Durchführung*] succeeds in reconciling the immensely expansive character of the musical ideas, for instance those in the principal and secondary themes (in comparison with which the octave leap themes are somewhat rigid and static, despite the shattering power of the brass), and the very free (*losgelassene*) dynamic of the epic design, which truly moves between extremes, with the calculated severity of an organically symmetrical architecture, without curtailing the developmental possibilities of one or the other.'[162]

Following Adorno, Sponheuer also notes the tendency of the whole Finale towards recurrence, the first section of the development reworking theme B, the second the Bridge, and the third the various motifs of the principal theme. This tendency is again confirmed in the recapitulation which, like the other sections, begins with a reprise of the Introduction. At first glance this seems to be literal, with arpeggios on the harp and celesta, the C minor framework and the ¾ chord. However, the 'chord of chaos' no longer has the tonic C as its bass note, but the second degree, D, prolonged as a pedal for nine bars. Further, the second phrase (superimposed on the major–minor 'motto') now remains in the key of C minor, instead of ending in C major as at the beginning. The second section (bars 537–74) likewise draws 'consequences from preceding events' and from the well-known Adornian law of the 'irreversibility of time',[163] concerning itself exclusively with the second theme. As before, this springs from an episode of *Naturlaute* (tremolos on the violas, chords on the clarinets and celesta, basses and harps), but it is twice interrupted after four bars. Now the solo violin resumes, in inversion, theme I (the variant here being derived from that in Introduction 2). But our attention continues to be monopolized by the falling fragment (horn, then oboes) from B (bars 201 and 203 in the exposition).[164]

Thus it happens quite naturally that the oboe goes on to restate the whole second theme (*Grazioso*: bar 575) over an outburst of quavers from the clarinets (it will be recalled that B appeared in the horn in Introduction I). This episode is beginning to be perceived as simply a variant of the initial introduction, but this impression fades when the violins (then the brass) pick up, in exalted mood and augmented time values,

---

[160] TAM 135; TAMe 100.   [161] TAM 133; TAMe 98 ff.

[162] *Zerfall*, 316. The same writer notes that the *Durchführung* ends at bar 519 but that it is in fact pursued further in the recapitulation 'which is also a reprise of the critical episodes (*krisenhaften Konstellationen*) in the development' (*Zerfall*, 344).

[163] TAF 144; TAFe 102.

[164] As seen above, this fragment was already a part of the second theme in the opening Allegro (bar 77, end), and has already served as countermelody in the third bar of theme B in the Finale (bar 194).

the rising phrase from B (as in the cantabile enclave in bars 364–84). This reprise 'in the manner of a chorale' thus draws a new 'consequence' from the development. Still with the same rigorous logic, fragments of the chorale begin to mingle with the continuation of B, and then others appear, derived from A, bringing us to a passage (bar 642) that is a joy to all analysts: while the violins and woodwinds continue to declaim, in the same exalted tone, the Abgesang of B (see bars 201–2 of the exposition), the basses recapitulate, triple forte, the principal theme (A). Thus the sections have been positively telescoped, while at the same time there has been a 'recapitulation in reverse' (B having preceded A). As Adorno observes, the reprise now 'smoothens the sharp contours' of the exposition, assuming 'an expression of sketchy ghostliness reminiscent of "Revelge". The recapitulation becomes an apparition; the character legitimises the remaining symmetry.'[165]

This character of phantom-like evocation also justifies the brevity of the successive reminiscences, which proceed in reverse order. Although the leitmotiv is twice affirmed (bar 754), elements of B, of A, of the octave leaps and the chorale give rise to a new elaboration of the 'bridge' from the exposition, considerably varied, and soon followed by the return of the concluding theme,[166] a return which Bernd Sponheuer describes as 'living with the force of memory'. The brief moment (bar 765) where the low brass reiterate several times one of the most 'warlike' motifs from theme A (bar 118) has been magnificently characterized by Adorno: 'In the Finale of the Sixth, immediately before the last repeat of the introductory section, which already belongs to the coda, the brass once again intones one of the principal motifs of the movement, and treats it sequentially, four bars before the final strike-up. These bars contain the feeling of "despite everything!", of success in the face of a doom which the latter can do nothing to diminish. It is a feeling which is expressed with extreme directness; it is as unmistakably present as the spoken word can be, but devoid of every unmusical literariness or anything extraneous to form. What is said, is said wholly in the language of music . . .'[167]

In a tempo marked 'calmer', a descending scale (inversion of the rising scale in the second bar of I) gradually leads to the lowest register of the orchestra, which gives full voice to the moment at which 'driving force turns to catastrophe, where a strength that can still, as it is struck down, unfold all its glittering brilliance, seems to flare up simultaneously with the possibility of utopia and the reality of its fall'.[168] The coda supplies a negative response to this last lyrical outburst. First, on an A in the basses, the chord of 'chaos' reappears (celesta, woodwinds, low strings) and is joined by all the voices of the orchestra, gaining a new power. Then the violins declaim theme I, for the first time in the principal key of the symphony. The outcome is not far away, and the last spasms of violence freeze in the abyss of nothingness.

It was here, at the beginning of the second phrase of I, that previously the third hammer blow sounded, at the moment when the major–minor 'motto' (accompanied by

[165] TAM 126; TAMe 93.

[166] Bars 728 ff. Sponheuer notes that it is considerably expanded here, by comparison with its marginal role in the exposition. Adorno speaks in this respect of 'Erfüllung als Abgesang' (Completion as Abgesang), for it is 'a compressed recapitulation of all the episodes of completion and all the ecstatic moments of the movement, of all the cantabile enclaves of the *Durchführung*, which are called up as they are quoted'. See Sponheuer, *Zerfall*, 319.   [167] TAF 145; TAFe 103.

[168] Sponheuer, *Zerfall*, 350.

its rhythmic counterpart) was heard. The last low A, pizzicato, in the basses, is taken up by the mournful voice of the tuba, which is soon joined by the four trombones in a lugubrious dotted-rhythm threnody, a final echo of the octave leap motif. During this 'anti-apotheosis'[169] it slowly disintegrates over a long roll in the timpani, in twenty-five bars of 'the most despairing music ever written by man'.[170] Soon nothing remains but the melodic descending octave and the obstinate tuba motif, A–B–C–A, which is repeated in augmentation by the bass clarinet and the cellos before being violently cut short by a shattering minor chord on all the winds, whose effect is doubled by the fact that this time it is no longer preceded by the major chord. All is now at an end: this is despair, the night of the soul, defeat, embodied in the fateful, throbbing rhythm of the 'motto' in the timpani. 'The insatiably ecstatic intensification of the feeling of living consumes itself. The liftings up are those prior to the fall into that darkness which only entirely fills the musical space in the last bars. Through pure musical intensity what takes place in the movement becomes one with its own negation.'[171]

The more closely one examines this Finale, with its 822 bars, the clearer becomes the irresistible logic of its architecture. 'Think of the tautness and conciseness of form in the Sixth, where not a note is superfluous, where everything is such a necessary and far-reaching component, so organically enmeshed', wrote Schoenberg.[172] It is easy to understand the fascination it held for the three members of the Viennese school, and the celebrated performance it received under Anton Webern in Vienna in the 1930s, and Berg's reference to it in a letter to Webern: 'the only Sixth, despite the *Pastorale*'.[173] Through it, too, can be understood the third of Berg's *Pieces for Orchestra*, Op. 6: 'Opus 6 is Berg's creative reply to Gustav Mahler's conception of the symphony. It is the spiritual and technical influence of Mahler's world that unmistakably manifests itself in this, the young Berg's last early work; and it is never subsequently quite absent from Berg's world picture in maturity.'[174]

The freedom, vigour and originality of Mahler's conception, the incomparable mastery of its realization, the absolute coherence and unity between the whole and the parts, 'a unity between the epic and its construction, between the strictness of sonata form and the great novelesque (*romanhafter*) arch (*Verlaufskurve*)',[175] was bound to captivate Mahler's immediate successors. Previously the themes, angular and ungrateful as we have seen, the obstinate rhythms and the acute tension constantly present, had just as strongly repelled Mahler's contemporaries, who saw in all this only a further and obvious proof of his creative impotence. That, in this huge epic movement, he did violence to musical norms, seems to me to be obvious. Indeed this is the reason why the Sixth remains one of Mahler's most difficult works, not just to understand and analyse, but even to listen to.

Siegfried Oechsle rightly considers Mahler's 'Tragic' Symphony to be a *ne plus ultra* in symphonic composition, but it is at the same time a new beginning: 'its historical

[169] Sponheuer, *Zerfall*, 350.
[170] Klemm, sleeve-notes for the Eterna recording of Mahler's Sixth.
[171] TAM 136; TAMe 100. Oechsle compares the brass threnody which ends the Coda to an 'Aequale', a piece of music for 3 or 4 trombones played at funerals during the nineteenth century (see 'Strukturen', 180).
[172] 'Mahler', in *Aufsätze*, 23.   [173] Redlich, Introduction, p. vi.
[174] Redlich, *Alban Berg: Versuch einer Würdigung* (UE, Vienna, 1957), 88. In the same work, (pp. 87 and 101) and in Theodor Adorno's book (*Berg* (Lafite, Vienna, 1968), 81 ff.), there are comments on the relationship between Berg's 'Marsch' and the Finale of the Sixth.
[175] Sponheuer, *Zerfall*, 294.

finality is the result not of a preponderance of the negative (hammer blows, endings in minor, or melodic caricatures) but of going to the extreme limits of the symphonic process with the contrasts inherent to the form. . . . To have forced the extremes together again is a triumph of composition in the literal sense of this term, and Mahler has enjoyed it to the full. The overall form has held together, but it has been stretched to the limits of what it can hold and comes dangerously close to disintegration. And the internal complexity and outward extension have been pushed so far that one cannot but ask oneself whether any further development was possible.'[176] Knowledge of nineteenth-century repertory may perhaps be enough as an introduction to the earlier symphonies of Mahler, but a familiarity with his musical legacy, that is to say the great works of the Viennese school, is necessary if one is fully to accept as early features of twentieth-century music the asperities of the Sixth Symphony (and those of the Seventh). It is no accident that the most eloquent and perspicacious of Mahler's apologists, the first writer to 'lift from Mahler the curse of music history',[177] was Theodor Adorno, himself a serial composer and a disciple of Alban Berg.

For these two symphonies of Mahler's late maturity belong to the musical literature of the twentieth-century, and could only be assimilated by a generation that had already granted Schoenberg classic status. Perhaps, too, it was necessary to know the subsequent development of this great revolutionary despite himself, to have followed his full progress as a composer, inventor, thinker, and especially to understand that 'no detail has significance in itself: what counts is what it becomes within the whole'.[178] In this respect, the themes of the Sixth resemble Schoenbergian note-rows more than the symphonic themes of the nineteenth century, and this work is a considerable step forward from the previous symphonies: 'The Seventh, like the Eighth, shows what deep resistance he afterwards mobilized, a resistance that only lost its power in the late works. But with this Finale Mahler took his leave from two kinds of musical—and not only musical—misconception, from the affirmative immanence of the work of art closed in upon itself, and from the illusion of utopia reached by the breakthrough (*Durchbruch*).' [179]

According to Adorno, the Sixth well merits the 'grandiloquent' (*offiziel*),[180] nineteenth-century epithet of 'Tragic' that Mahler himself applied to it at the time of the first Viennese performance. Its message remains essentially pessimistic, since the conflict with the blind force of destiny ends in defeat and despair. For Sponheuer, the greatest success of this Finale is, paradoxically, this 'powerful failure', this ultimate ruin, for 'the intransigence of the development, the playing out of the epic, is identified with that of the form'.[181] However, Sponheuer refuses to give this dead-end an extra-musical significance, seeing in it only the 'concrete musical logic of the work' and a 'step forward in realism'.[182] As a faithful posthumous Adorno disciple, he will not accept any 'pathetic fate symbolism', and sees in the very concept of 'spirit' a word devoid of meaning, a 'rhetorical flourish' (*Floskel*). However this may be, all Mahler's works, at least until the Fifth, were deliberately endowed by the composer himself with

---

[176] Oechsle, 'Strukturen', 181 ff.
[177] Translators' preface in the French version of TAM (Éditions de Minuit, Paris, 1960, 10).
[178] TAF 141; TAFe 100.   [179] Sponheuer, *Zerfall*, 352.
[180] TAF 141; TAFe 100.   [181] Sponheuer, *Zerfall*, 295.
[182] Ibid. 293 and 352.

an extra-musical meaning, and one cannot avoid asking oneself what was the nature of the failure Mahler was thinking of. Several other writers have pondered the question, and that from the earliest performances. Paul Bekker wanted to limit its implications by seeing in it only a partial vision of things. He even claimed that the 'spirit' (the object of Sponheuer's sarcasm) was not destroyed at the end of the work.[183] Erwin Ratz subtly analysed the octave leap theme as simultaneously representing 'that which threatens man' and 'the forces that rise in him to resist and surmount it' (*Widerstand und Überwindung*)'. 'Thus,' he added, 'we arrive at the knowledge that what threatens us basically lies within us, is even almost desired by us so that we can grow through it, and that all outward seeming is just the visible manifestation of our inner development.'[184] It is difficult to follow Ratz when he claims that the suppression of the third hammer blow in the Finale indicates an inner change in Mahler, and that it modifies the meaning of the conclusion. Here the human personality is supposed to reach 'a higher stage of evolution' where 'nothing can be lost', [185] whereas the dropped third hammer blow would have reinforced the feeling of an 'absolute end'. Redlich, who embarked upon a long polemic attacking Ratz's ideas and decisions in editing the score, claimed on the contrary that Mahler, if he had lived, would without doubt have reinstated the third hammer blow, above all because it made clear the form of this last movement, which, as seen above, was never the aim of the three hammer blows retained by Mahler in the first edition.[186]

Eberhardt Klemm considered this 'death symbolism', so characteristic of Mahler, as being not 'a sign of morbidity or decadence', but 'new musical territory'.[187] Adorno before him saw in the 'negativity' of the Sixth both a 'difficulty' and a new source of richness. 'In flagrant contradiction to everything familiar from absolute, programme-less music, his symphonies do not exist in a simple positive sense, as something granted to the participants as a reward: on the contrary, whole complexes want to be taken negatively—one should listen, as it were, against them. "We see an alternation of positive and negative situations."[188] A stratum that was reserved to literature and painting is conquered by absolute music. The brutally intrusive passage in the coda of the first movement of the mature Sixth Symphony[189] is heard directly as an irruption of the horrible. To conventional thinking this seems literary and unmusical; no music ought to be able to say no to itself. But Mahler's music is receptive precisely through its stringent capacity to do so, which extends into its selectively indiscriminate material, a content that is both non-conceptual and yet incapable of being misunderstood. Negativity for him has become a purely compositional category: through the banal that declares itself banal; through a lacrimose sentimentality that tears the mask from its own wretchedness; through a hyperbolical expression in excess of the music's actual meaning.'[190]

Later on in the same text, Adorno, like Sponheuer, attacks the post-Romantic ideology of the symphony as an heroic epic. As we have seen above, he views it rather as 'the brutal and blind march of the multitude' and explains: 'How much Mahler's intrinsic

[183] BMS 208.   [184] Ratz, 'Formproblem', 140.   [185] Ibid. 146.
[186] Redlich, Introduction, pp. ix and xx. See also Sponheuer, *Zerfall*, 286.
[187] 'Notizen', *Herausforderung*, 449.
[188] Ratz, 'Formproblem', *Aufsätze*, 141.   [189] Bar 382 *(Piu mosso subito)*.
[190] TAM 163 ff.; TAMe 125.

musical negativity runs counter to the enthusiastic programme of Berlioz or Liszt is shown by the fact that Mahlerian novels have no heroes and honour none, unlike those noisily proclaimed in two titles of Strauss and countless ones of Liszt. Even in the Finale of the Sixth, despite the hammer blows which, in any case, have not been properly heard hitherto and no doubt await their electronic realisation, one will look in vain for the figure who is supposed to be smitten by fate. The music's abandonment to unbridled affect is its own death, the unabated vengeance of the world's course on Utopia. The dark and even despairing parts recede in that movement behind others of turbid brooding, of overflowing exuberance, of rising tumult; the only real exceptions are the bilious wind chorale in the introduction and the trombone passage in the coda. The catastrophes coincide with the climaxes. It sometimes sounds as if at the moment of the final conflagration humanity grew incandescent again, the dead came to life once more. Joy flares high at the edge of horror.'[191]

Despite the interest and novelty of such observations, which singularly enrich our understanding of Mahler's music, it is important once again to recall the passage in Alma's *Erinnerungen* concerning the Sixth: 'In the last movement he describes himself and his downfall, or, as he later said, the downfall of his hero, "the hero struck three times by fate, the third blow felling him like a tree". Mahler's words. No work came so directly from his heart as this one.'[192] Mahler undoubtedly attributed a meaning to the 'negative' end of the Sixth, even if he could probably never have put it into words. What, then, is this enemy confronting the 'pure', the demigods, the heroes? In Mahler's own life the most ferocious enemy had always been inertia, pettiness, mediocrity. He had learned a hundred times to his cost that boldness and determination could by no means always triumph against enemies such as these. To this public, professional battle against the *Alltag* (the everyday, the run of the mill), against the resistance of matter, can perhaps be added a long battle which he was fighting in private against Alma, or rather against the egotism, fickleness, frivolity, hard-heartedness of which he knew, and she knew, she was capable. And this was to be a losing battle. Mahler kept the secret well, but there can be no doubt that from 1904 he was aware of the seriousness of the problem (even if, in his first movement, he gave the 'Alma theme' an altogether positive role), nor that he had privately drawn his own conclusions about the inability of human beings to communicate with each other, something which even the most tender and devoted love could not overcome.

Among the other meanings Mahler might have included in this 'All's ill that ends ill'[193] or 'per aspera ad inferno'[194] is the idea of the inevitable death that awaits all heroes and all humans as the outcome of all their struggles; of the powerlessness of any being before the dark forces that control their destiny; or even perhaps the weakness of intellectual speculation before the brute strength of reality. But this dead end obliged him, in his following works, to invent, in the next symphony, other paths towards sunnier landscapes.

---

[191] TAM 165 ff.; TAMe 126.   [192] AMM1, 92; AMM2, 97.

[193] 'Erst der Schluss gewinnt die Autentizität eines Endes schlimm, alles schlimm' (TAM 140; TAMe 103 ff.).   [194] RSM2, 241.

SEVENTH SYMPHONY IN E MINOR (1904–1905)

Composition

Mahler's letter to Alma quoted above[1] leaves no doubt as to the date of composition of the two *Nachtmusiken* of the Seventh Symphony. They were written at the same time as the Finale of the Sixth, in the summer of 1904, while movements 1, 3, and 5 date from the following year. The draft orchestral score of the first movement, which was probably composed last, gives the date of the work's completion, written on the last page: '15 August 1905 Septima finita'. Thus, the writing of *Nachtmusiken* may have been a reaction, a sort of relaxation, after completing the Sixth Symphony,[2] an exceptional occurrence in the creative life of the mature Mahler, for he had hardly ever before worked on two symphonies at once, nor started a new work by composing the middle movements first.

In June 1905, when he decided to compose the three remaining movements, he suffered one of the worst creative blocks of his career as a 'summer composer'. Hans Ferdinand Redlich claims that it was because the two *Nachtstücke* were intermezzi that Mahler had so much trouble the following year trying to integrate them into a larger symphonic structure.[3] Yet Alma claims in her *Erinnerungen* that the *Bauskizzen* for the missing movements had been prepared in 1904.[4] As we shall see, Mahler's sketchbook reveals that he had not really planned anything at all for the first and last movements. Mahler found relief from his frustration in 1905 only by travelling once more to the Dolomites and walking around Lake Misurina, a physical and mental relaxation which had several times before played a key role in his creative life. This time, inspiration did not come to him there, but only when he returned to the Wörthersee and boarded a boat for home at Krumpendorf. 'At the first stroke of the oars, the idea of the opening theme . . . (or rather its rhythm and character) came to me. Four weeks later the first, the third and fifth movements were done and ready.'[5] Since the draft score is the only one to be dated at the end, it seems safe to surmise that it was completed after the Scherzo and Finale.

Alma's story about the 'sketches' of the Seventh, which she claims were brought to Rome in the spring of 1907,[6] seems to me open to doubt. Why should Mahler have been travelling with his old sketches at a time when a fair copy of the score had been completed eighteen months earlier? However, if he had indeed taken the fair copy with him to Italy, it is not surprising that he insisted on keeping it at hand during the whole return trip to Vienna because of what had occurred on the way to Italy, when all his luggage, including his revised scores for the Rome concerts, had been lost, and had been recovered only several days later.[7]

---

[1] See above, Chaps. 3 and 4, and BGA, no. 303, undated letter (8 June 1910). Mahler wrote: '*deren beide Andantes*' but Donald Mitchell points out that the tempo marking of Nachtmusik 1 is *Allegro moderato*, and that *Andante amoroso* replaced the original *Andante con moto* in Nachtmusik 2 (see the 'Chronology' included in the 'Commentary' of *Gustav Mahler: Facsimile edition of the Seventh Symphony* (Rosbeek, Amsterdam, 1995), 18, n. 7).

[2] Yet, as we shall see, the compositional mechanisms of Nachtmusik 2 are among the most elaborate and complex ever utilized by Mahler.

[3] Hans Ferdinand Redlich, Introduction to the Eulenburg pocket score of Symphony No. 7, p. vi.

[4] AMM1, 115; AMM2, 117. Once again this makes the Seventh a very special work in Mahler's production for he had nearly always conceived the outline of his symphonies before starting to compose.

[5] BGA, no. 303.

[6] See AMM1, 150; AMM2, 147.   [7] See above, Chap. 8.

MANUSCRIPTS

A considerable number of autograph sources are available for the Seventh, far more than for other Mahler symphonies. One of the rarest and most fascinating of these sources is the sketchbook which was presented by Karl Moll to Anna Bahr-Mildenburg in 1943, and which is now part of her Nachlass, in the ÖTM.[8] It is one of the very few such sketchbooks preserved, the others having belonged to Alma Mahler until her death.[9] The ÖTM sketchbook was inventoried, analysed, and described by Stephen Hefling, who believes it was chiefly (and perhaps exclusively) used during the summer of 1905. It contains material used in both the opening Allegro (mainly) and the Finale of the Seventh. The sketches range from very rough ideas of a few bars' duration to longer segments of 20 to 22 bars. Some of the more developed ideas may continue for two or three pages. Indications of instrumentation are rare. As Stephen Hefling has noted, in his detailed study of these sketches, Mahler rarely wrote more than a few bars without immediately making revisions, even in the shortest fragments. The bass and soprano parts are nearly always present, chord progressions are often notated in simple rhythms beneath the melodic material, and they are sometimes replaced by figured bass numerals.[10] The same notebook also includes several sketches of material used much later in the first and last movements of the Ninth Symphony.[11]

The theme of the first movement, with its characteristic rhythm, is noted on the first page inside the cover of the Bahr-Mildenberg sketchbook which bears the title 'Skizzen', a 'rudimentary but energetically sketched fragment', perhaps made on the boat.[12] After studying the contents of the sketchbook, Stephen Hefling thinks that 'extensive compositional sketching' for the outer movements of the symphony were most unlikely to have been made in 1904.[13] The sketchbook contains material for the Introduction, the main theme, the second idea, the secondary theme, and the recapitulatory climax. Hefling believes that Mahler could have proceeded 'directly from the rich yet fragmentary ideas scribbled in this one to full-page sketches and drafts' at his composing table in the Maiernigg *Häuschen*.[14] Yet Mahler himself compared these early sketches to 'building blocks' and usually determined 'their proper arrangement' in preliminary drafts and short scores (*Particell*).[15] The Bruno Walter Collection (LPA,

[8] It is an oblong booklet containing 30 leaves (originally 32), on each side of which 6 staves are printed (see Stephen E. Hefling, 'Mahler's Seventh Symphony Sketchbook' in Stephen Hefling, (ed.), *Mahler Studies* (Cambridge, Cambridge, 1997), 169 ff.). Hefling provides conclusive evidence that this was not Mahler's last sketchbook. It also contains sketches not used in any of his surviving works.

[9] According to Alma's memoirs (AML 366), she found, when she arrived in Vienna in 1947, that a bomb or a grenade had damaged the top-floor library in her house at the Hohe Warte, and destroyed Mahler's and Werfel's desks with all their precious contents, and she was able to save only these two sketch books. One of them was presented by Alma to the conductor F. Charles Adler and is now in the Musiksammlung of ÖNB (Mus. Hs. 41.634). The other, containing sketches for the middle movements of the Seventh, is in the Moldenhauer collection, but is not accessible to anyone.   [10] Hefling, 'Sketchbook', 184.

[11] Ibid. 191.

[12] Ibid. 187. This is to my mind doubtful because Mahler states in his letter to Alma quoted above that 'only the rhythm and atmosphere' of the Introduction occurred to him on the boat.

[13] Contrary to Donald Mitchell, in the essay included in the 'Commentary' of the *Facsimile Edition*.

[14] Hefling, 'Sketchbook', 212 ff.

[15] Ibid. 214. An additional sketch exists for the last movement. It appears to be an attempt to create a contrapuntal combination, not ultimately used, of several motifs from the Finale (BGM, Paris).

New York), also includes a *Particell* fragment of the Scherzo (on three or four staves, bars 86–131). It consists of one leaf and a half of another.[16] The recto side of the full leaf contains a draft of the main theme of the movement (bars 11 ff. of the final version) and the contrasting theme (bars 54 ff.).

Mahler's orchestral draft score of the first movement has been preserved, also in the Bruno Walter collection. The title-page reads: '7. Symphonie. I Satz. Partitur' (First movement. Score).[17] It is made up of eleven four-page quires written recto-verso (in large format, 20 and 22 staves). Quire 7 contains 8 pages, two of which have been covered over. The quires are numbered, and an extra blank page covers a former version of bars 227–37. To the second page of the fourth quire is joined a page in *Particell* format (bars 144–73 of the final version), so that altogether there are fifty written pages. Mahler went on to make many corrections in pencil and to change most of the tempo markings. It is particularly interesting to note, above bars 284 to 288 (Bote & Bock score, 42), the phrase *Steine pumpeln in's Wasser* (stones plop into the water). This is probably Mahler's attempt to define the special kind of sonority he was aiming for by indicating that the bass instruments were to play pizzicato and arco simultaneously.[18]

The fair copy of the orchestral score of the Seventh was given by Alma Mahler at the time of the Amsterdam Mahler Festival in 1920 to Willem Mengelberg[19] who bequeathed it to the Concertgebouw. It was published in facsimile at the time of the 1995 Mahler Festival and as usual incorporates many further changes and additions.[20] The manuscript is undated and has no title-page. Its musical substance is identical with that of the final version, but there are many differences in orchestration and dynamic markings. From the compositional point of view, the most important differences occur in the second movement (bars 48 to 61), where the triplet passage includes an imitation that was later eliminated. The mandolin part is added in pencil to the second *Nachtmusik*, and the first page of the Finale is replaced by another, stuck on over it.

ÖNB possesses a copyist's manuscript of the score (wrongly attributed to Alma's hand) with numerous corrections by Mahler.[21] It post-dates the Amsterdam score, because the above-mentioned passage in the second movement appears in its final form. It was undoubtedly used by the printer as *Stichvorlage*. Later changes were certainly made in the proofs, and additional markings were surely found in the original orchestral parts that Mahler corrected before and after his various performances of the work. Unfortunately, they have not been traced. The Amsterdam Concertgebouw also owns a copy of the printed Bote & Bock score with corrections made by Mahler at the time of the 1909 concerts. The publisher issued a printed list of typographical errors and alterations soon after the first performances.

---

[16] See Edward Reilly, 'The Manuscripts of the Seventh Symphony', in *Facsimile Edition*, 79. According to Reilly, the odd notations 'Wörth' and 'Belfast' were apparently used as keys or reminders of materials to be used or omitted.

[17] A second quire has '*I Satz. Entwurf*' (Sketch or *Particell*) written on it, but unfortunately it is blank inside.   [18] Reilly, 'Manuscripts', 80.

[19] AML 145 ff. Alma had already given some manuscripts of *Das Lied von der Erde* to Mengelberg in 1917, on the occasion of his debut in Vienna with the Vienna Philharmonic. See Mitchell, 'Chronology', in *Facsimile Edition*, 27 ff.   [20] Ibid. 82.

[21] Since the score of the Seventh was only published after the 1908 Prague première, Donald Mitchell points out that this score was probably the one which was circulated among Mahler's circle of Viennese admirers, and the one he mentioned in a note addressed to Zemlinsky written in the autumn of 1907 (MBR1, no. 320; MBR2, no. 374).

PUBLICATION

The full story of the publication of the Seventh Symphony is told in a later chapter.[22] After a number of unsuccessful initiatives, Mahler finally entrusted the score to the Berlin firm Lauterbach und Kühn, only to discover a short while later that its entire catalogue had been purchased by Bote & Bock. Unfortunately, the correspondence between Mahler and this latter publisher seems for the time being to have disappeared, except for a letter concerning the title-page, which Mahler had asked Roller to design. Thus the exact date of publication is at present not known. It was definitely written some time in 1909, before the Holland performances (2 October in The Hague, and the 3rd and 7th in Amsterdam).[23]

The critical edition of the Seventh which appeared in November 1960 was the first to appear in the series published under the auspices of the IGMG. It was the most needed, for Mahler did not correct the proofs with his usual care, and the original score contained, in addition to the many changes he made after Amsterdam, some 800 printing errors. In approaching the work, the 1959 editors had at their disposal the autograph fair copy, the copyist's score which served for publication, as well as Mengelberg's score corrected by Mahler himself.[24] As with the Sixth Symphony, Hans Ferdinand Redlich and Erwin Ratz are at odds. Redlich, takes the line that changes made by Mahler in Mengelberg's score were not entirely convincing and that Mahler, if he had lived, would have discarded at least some of them. So he does not include them in the Eulenburg pocket score, which is therefore simply a new corrected edition of the original version published in 1909.

GENERAL OUTLINE

This is symmetrical, with the two principal movements framing a sort of 'symphony within a symphony' formed by the three intermezzi (the two *Nachtmusiken* with the Scherzo between them). It has been noted that this overall structure resembles that of Bartok's Fifth Quartet. It has no parallel in Mahler's production except perhaps for *Das Lied von der Erde*[25] and the Tenth,[26] although there is a resemblance with the structure of the Fifth.[27] The inner three movements of the Seventh constitute a 'unity in itself',[28]

---

[22] See below, Vol. iiii, Chap. 1.

[23] See below, Vol. iiii, Chaps. 2 and 4.

[24] Numerous difficulties arose when the critical edition was being prepared because of differences discovered between the Amsterdam score and the instrumental parts. Indeed, it was not always possible to be sure if corrections had been made by Mahler during rehearsals or had been wrongly copied by the performers into their parts (see Erwin Ratz's Introduction to the 1959 critical edition).

[25] This also contains, after the 'Andante' (*Der Einsame im Herbst*), three shorter and lighter movements which might be considered 'intermezzi', *Von der Jugend*, *Von der Schönheit*, and *Der Trunkene im Frühling*.

[26] Between the first and the last movements are two Scherzos framing the 'Purgatorio'.

[27] According to Mahler himself, the real first movement is the second, the A minor Allegro (see Vol. ii, appendix on the Fifth). Like the more famous Adagietto, the second *Nachtmusik* might be regarded as an introduction to the Finale.

[28] Hans-Klaus Jungheinrich, 'Nach der Katastrophe: Anmerkungen zu einer aktuellen Rezeption der Siebten Symphonie', in Peter Ruzicka (ed.), *Mahler—eine Herausforderung: Ein Symposion* (Breitkopf, Wiesbaden, 1977), 188.

a 'dream island'.[29] Their length almost equals that of the two movements traditionally charged with conveying the 'message' of the work, the first and last. This throws light on one of its essential aspects, the need that Mahler felt to turn away from the pessimism of the Sixth, and the wild outbursts in the Allegro of the Fifth, towards a more poetic world, lit by romantic visions ('à la Eichendorff', stresses Alma),[30] a world of which 'night' is the 'theme' rather than the 'programme'. Recollecting times past appears to be the main 'theme' or 'mood' of the work, at least in the inner movements, yet, as we shall see, the manner in which these recollections are presented is far more complex than appears at first hearing. In the Seventh Mahler also returns to 'progressive tonality', a method he had abandoned in the preceding symphony: 'In the Seventh,' writes Adorno, 'the first movement, after an introduction with copious key changes, is in E minor. The three middle movements—all, including the Scherzo, night pieces—then descend to the subdominant region. The first Nachtmusik is at home in C major, the subdominant tonality of the relative major of E minor; the Scherzo falls further into D minor, the relative minor of the subdominant of C; the second Nachtmusik, finally, remains on the same harmonic level, but brightens it by replacing the D minor by its relative major, F. The Finale restores the balance between the first and the middle movements. These, however, exert a weight that the Finale cannot quite compensate. It must remain a dominant within the relative tonality of the first movement, and so be in the C major of the first Nachtmusik. The harmonic homeostasis of the whole symphony, the principal key, would, accordingly be centred on C major, making the Seventh a C major symphony.'[31]

If the key-structure of the work is easy to summarize, the atmosphere, the substance, the meaning of the Seventh are anything but easy to define. Peter Davison, in his thesis[32] and in two substantial articles,[33] has discerned a great number of ambiguities in the Seventh, particularly in the two Nachtmusiken. One of them is Nachtmusik 1's asymmetric key-scheme, its inability 'to establish a long-term dominant polarity', and its lack of 'a single arch' to direct it. Another is the arbitrary tonal structure of Nachtmusik 2: 'The problem lies in the dialectic between the narrative and the architectural analogies of form, for despite the narrative implications of tonal procedure, the architectural function of tonality has not been totally abandoned; it is a force reluctant to be denied.'[34] According to Davison, and this perhaps accounts for much of the uneasiness which this symphony has met through the years, 'the work is a series of unresolved dualisms, which operate at many levels, from polarisation in the schemic organisation to the tonal ambiguities of the smallest details of the musical language. . . . The *per aspera ad astra* model and the Seventh's failure to achieve it is the first layer of contradiction. . . . The unresolved dialectic between the Finale and the *Nachtmusiken* is most obvious, at an associative level, as the contrast between night and day. There can be no synthesis in human perception of the inevitable cycle of Nature and in this sense, the work is anti-dialectical.' In Davison's view, 'the work's non-realisation of its immanent implications is a calculated ambiguity which reflects the artist's attempt to find a coherent interpretation

[29] RSM2, 303.

[30] See below the section headed 'A Programme?'   [31] TAM 42 ff.; TAMe 27 ff.

[32] 'The Nachtmusiken from Mahler's Seventh Symphony: Analysis and Reappraisal', Dissertation, Jesus College, Cambridge, 1985.

[33] 'Nachtmusik I: Sound and Symbol' and 'Nachtmusik II: "Nothing but Love, Love, Love"?', both in James Zychowicz (ed.), *The Seventh Symphony of Gustav Mahler: A Symposium* (University of Cincinnati, Cincinnati, 1990).   [34] Davison, 'Nachtmusiken', 68.

of his subjective experience. Mahler does not begin to synthesise in the traditional symphonic way; that is a fallacious ambition. Here is an enigmatic, self-confessed failure, a work which sets out to be incomplete and unsettling.'[35] But this essential truth concerning the Seventh could, inevitably, only be discovered in retrospect: 'The Seventh's effect relies so much upon the failure of the work to fulfil its immanent aesthetic criteria. . . . The recognition of contrived "failure", music which seems to analyse its own shortcomings, can only be slowly realised in the course of a work's reception.'[36] This, I think, explains why so many analysts and commentators, in Mahler's time but also later, have failed to understand some of the problems inherent in the Seventh. Paul Bekker heard it mistakenly as 'a convincing solution of the symphonic dialectic',[37] Hans Ferdinand Redlich[38] held on to 'an abstract, 19th century criterion of symphonic completeness and originality' and was disturbed by the 'unbridgeable gulf of stylistic incompatibility' between the outer movements and the middle ones: 'the element of critique and irony in Mahler is wasted on him,' notes Davison. For Hans Swarowsky,[39] 'music builds up in a single arc, through a hierarchy of motif, phrase, theme, section, form and work. But a problem arises in a work like the Seventh Symphony, where that hierarchy is provocatively undermined.'[40] According to Davison, 'the Finale's ambiguous rôle emerges in that it is a contrast to, not a synthesis of its [the symphony's] middle movements.' But we shall come back to this later.

CYCLICAL PROCEDURES

Here, in contrast to the preceding symphony where thematic references between the movements are subtle and innumerable, Mahler seems not to have wanted to unify the movements in the same way, except for the two outer movements. The principal theme of the opening Allegro reappears at the end of the Rondo, and plays a decisive role in its Coda. The most interesting connection so far discovered between the Seventh and any previous work is the similarity pointed out by Donald Mitchell to exist between certain melodic turns in the Serenade (4th movement) and the second theme in the Finale of the Sixth (see below).

LANGUAGE

In this respect, the Seventh is without doubt Mahler's most 'advanced' work, with incessant dissonances and sudden modulations packed tightly together. Moreover, some of the themes are constructed around a double melodic fourth (especially in the first movement where this interval is never absent). Fourths are even to be found in the

[35] Ibid. 80.   [36] Ibid. 12.   [37] BMS 237.
[38] Introduction to Eulenburg pocket score.
[39] In *Wahrung der Gestalt, Schriften über Werk und Wiedergabe, Stil und Interpretation in der Musik* (Universal Edition, Vienna, 1979), 135 ff.   [40] Davison, 'Nachtmusiken', 8.

underlying harmony[41] and they have the well-documented effect of denying traditional tonal function (see especially bars 45 ff., then 81–2 and 85–6 in the first movement). However, Dominique Jameux, a specialist on Berg and the Viennese School, believes that Schoenberg and his disciples familiarized themselves with the Seventh only later on, in 1909, and that the Seventh's fourths could not have influenced the *Kammersymphonie* Op. 9.[42]

However that may be, some of the characteristic features of Mahler's 'late style' are already prefigured in this work. Its melodic harshness and bold, almost aggressive, dissonance, alongside an orchestral sophistication often seen as gratuitous, have long made it 'the most unpopular of Mahler's symphonies'. Christopher Alan Williams observes that, in the first movement, the interval of a fourth 'comes to pervade the texture progressively, through a kind of vegetative growth Schoenberg would later term "developing variation". . . . The movement's quartal harmony is more a product of the incremental proliferation and unfolding of the main theme's single descending fourth than an assertion of complex non-diatonic sonority *per se*. . . . Mahler's quartal harmonies are primarily motivic rather than harmonic in origin.'[43]

In a study of the Seventh's musical language, Serge Gut concludes that 'the essential harmonic structure (*l'ossature harmonique*) of Mahler's language is extremely simple, clear and classical' but that it is characterized by two different factors. First of all a 'nucleus (*noyau d'ancrage*)' made up in general of perfect chords, major or minor, simple or amplified,[44] less frequently by "classified" dissonant chords',[45] and 'a wrapping (*enrobement*) resulting from thematic development and from substantial and audacious contrapuntal procedures (*travail*) from which the most cruel dissonances arise'.[46] Gut observes that Mahler's procedures in this symphony are 'very exceptional in Germanic music of that time' and that amply anticipate Schoenberg's later procedures.[47] He underlines Mahler's method of 'superposing various layers, each one simple and with its own logic', which 'sometimes generate violent clashes', 'the frequent independence of the harmony from the thematic process' and the contrast between a 'static vertical harmonic language, simple and conservative and a horizontal contrapuntal language which is essentially dynamic and audacious'.[48]

[41] See notably the trumpet chords in bars 46 and 47 of the first movement.

[42] See Jameux, 'L'École de Vienne face à la VIIème Symphonie de Mahler', in Zychowicz, *Symposium*, 124 ff. Thus Schoenberg had probably not studied the score of the Seventh when he composed his *Kammersymphonie* Op. 9. See Schoenberg's letter to Mahler of 19 Dec. 1909, AMM1, 446.

[43] Christopher A. Williams, 'Mahler's Seventh Symphony and the Emergence of a Post-tonal Harmonic Vocabulary', unpublished paper quoted by Hefling, 'Sketchbook', 188, n. 26.

[44] The author explains in a footnote that he calls 'amplified' chords those that have been enriched by adding a second or a sixth to a perfect chord.

[45] Dominant chords which can be sounded without preparation.

[46] Serge Gut, 'Consonance et dissonance dans le premier mouvement de la Septième Symphonie de Mahler', in Zychowiz, *Symposium*, 47 ff.

[47] Gut points out, in bar 47 of the first movement, a melodic motif in the transition from the Introduction to theme A, which is harmonized by its own notes. As a result, three different, simultaneous fourths are sounded on the third beat of bar 47. Such interchangeable procedures between horizontal (polyphonic) and vertical (harmonic) writing are prophetic (Ibid. 62).   [48] Ibid. 64 ff.

A PROGRAMME?

Eichendorff

'While he [Mahler] was composing the Serenade,' Alma writes, 'Eichendorffian visions hovered before him, murmuring springs, German Romanticism.'[49] Who was this poet so dear to nineteenth-century German composers, and who, according to Alma, was Mahler's inspiration at least in one of the movements of the Seventh? Born (like Gerhard Hauptmann) in Silesia in the same year as Rückert, Josef von Eichendorff (1788–1857) spent a happy and privileged childhood in the country manor belonging to his family. From the Catholic high school in Breslau he went to study law in Halle and Heidelberg, where he met Schlegel, Arnim, and Brentano, and discovered the *Knaben Wunderhorn* which was later an important influence on his work. After travelling to Paris and Vienna to complete his education, he became passionately involved in resisting the French invader, enlisting in 1813. He spent two years in the army, and even entered Paris with the allied troops in 1815. It was then that he wrote the most famous war poem of the time, the *Song of the Soldiers*. Thus he was already well known as a poet when, in 1815, he published his first important novel, *Ahnung und Gegenwart* (Surmise and Reality). He continued to write both prose and verse and published the work for which he is best known, *Aus dem Leben eines Taugenichts* (Scenes from the Life of a Good-for-Nothing) in 1824. After holding various administrative posts in Breslau, Berlin, and Danzig, he moved to the Prussian capital in 1831, as a highly placed ministry official. He retired in 1844, travelled around Germany and finally settled in Silesia where he wrote his *History of German Poetic Literature*. He then devoted himself to writing in his native province until his death.

Eichendorff gave German poetry some of its most accomplished masterpieces. His poems were set to music by Schumann (notably in the *Liederkreis* Op. 39), Mendelssohn, Brahms, Robert Franz, Hugo Wolf, and, more recently, Othmar Schoeck. They are steeped in a 'healthy' and 'happy' romanticism, full of memories of a country childhood, passionate nostalgia, and visions of nature: 'horizons lost in mist, forests and mountains'. Guitars 'converse with nightingales in rococo or romantic gardens bathed in moonlight'.[50] It was no doubt an image like this that gave rise to Mahler's Serenade (Nachtmusik 2 or fourth movement), but Eichendorff's influence can also be discerned in the title itself,[51] borrowed from the eighteenth century, and in the march of the first Nachtmusik, expressing the *Wanderlust* of a nameless soldier. Horns call to each other across a natural landscape where birds sing, trees rustle, and the secret voices of nature murmur as in 'the night hours, when the senses, free of noisy demands, open themselves to promptings beyond the rational'. The visions conjured up in the two Nachtmusiken,

---

[49] AMM1, 115; AMM2, 117.

[50] Marcel Brion, *L'Allemagne romantique* (Albin Michel, Paris, 1963), 306. Many Eichendorff poems were inspired by twilight (notably *Zwielicht, Der Abend, Im Abendrot*) or night (*Nachts, Die Nacht, Nachtgruss, Mondnacht, Nachtlied, Stimmen der Nacht, Winternacht, Frühlingsnacht, Nachtzauber, Gute Nacht*). *Das Ständchen* could well have been Mahler's principal source of inspiration for the Serenade (see below).

[51] Mahler used the word once, in a letter to Henri Hinrichsen of 5 Dec. 1907 (*Jahrbuch Peters* 1979, ed. Eberhardt Klemm (Peters, Leipzig, 1980), 50 ff.).

like those of Eichendorff, belong to a long past idyllic world, although, once again, the idyll is rich in ambiguities as we shall see later. But it is obvious that Mahler is glancing backward at his own past and childhood recollections in Nachtmusik 1, which contains many recollections of the *Wunderhorn-Lieder*.

However, Peter Davison has shown that calling Eichendorff's poetry merely 'idyllic' is a gross over-simplification of its true nature: 'The relationship between Mahler and Eichendorff goes far deeper than one or two associative details in the instrumentation and form', if only because 'both artists use the idyll for ironic purposes.'[52] In both of their worlds and works, the Romantic idyll is endangered, if only by Nature which, as 'an uncontrollable force . . . intrudes upon the stylised restraint of the form'. There are several such intrusions in Mahler's Serenade or Nachtmusik 2 (see below). Davison picks out two poems which could have inspired Mahler for this movement— 'Ständchen' (Serenade) and 'Marmorbild'. One of them, *Das Ständchen*, 'captures the nostalgic and ironic disruption of the idyll with an allusion to human mortality'.[53] But Davison quotes another, longer, poem, included in Eichendorff's second novel, *Dichter und ihre Gesellen*, also a Ständchen,[54] in which 'the attempt to relive a past experience merely exaggerates its futility' and 'the poet is alienated from love and the conventions of love, now only observing its regret'. In the end, 'the destructive violence of the emotion . . . causes the collapse of the idyll', and the poet breaks his lyre. 'The final lines of the novella are a day-time celebration of a worldly triumph, but expressed in such a way as to be defiant against the natural order of things.'[55] Is that not what Mahler also does in the Finale of his Seventh, Mahler who uses 'Rationalism . . . as a weapon in its own demise' and transforms 'the naivety of Romanticism . . . into irony through a ruthless self-honesty'.

Peter Revers also defines Mahler's apparent desire to 'return to the idyll' as a 'longing for the good old days' which does nothing, in the last resort, but widen the distance 'between man and life and the unspoiled world of the "Golden Age"'.[56] He also points out the ambiguous nature of the second poem quoted below as a possible inspiration for Mahler's Serenade, 'Marmorbild'. It 'is about an aged man for whom the idyllic night atmosphere primarily evokes recollections of the past' and who is thus 'outside the idyllic world'. In the last stanza, 'it is the experience of death that produces the distance

---

[52] Davison, 'Nachtmusiken', 56.   [53] Ibid. 58.

[54] It is included in chap. 19 of *Dichter und ihre Gesellen*. See Davison, 'Nachtmusiken', 58.

[55] Ibid. 61. Here are the last lines of Eichendorff's *Dichter und ihre Gesellen*:

'So stand er noch lange in Gedanken oben—da ging die Sonne prächtig auf—die Morgenglocken klangen über Stille, und der Einsiedler sang:

"Wir ziehen treulich auf die Wacht
Wie bald kommt nicht die ew'ge Nacht
Und löscht aus der Länder Pracht,
Du schöne Welt, nimm dich in Acht!" '

('He stood there for a long time—thoughtfully looking down—the sun rose in its glory—the morning bells rang out through the silence, and the hermit sang:

"We faithfully mount our guard
For the eternal night comes soon, too soon,
To extinguish the splendour of field and forest.
Thou beautiful world, be on thy guard!" ')

[56] Peter Revers, 'Return to the Idyll?', in *Colloque International Gustav Mahler 1985* (Association Gustav Mahler, Paris, 1986), 40 ff.

between reality and experience of life and the untroubled idyllic atmosphere'.[57] In his two Nachtmusiken, Mahler 'seems to refer to a certain state of idyllic poetry in which the ideal becomes more and more a dreamlike state of being, gradually withdrawing from the immediate reality of life. . . . The dream of the ideal is increasingly manifested as mere nostalgia, and hence becomes more elegiac or satirical.' Elegiac or satirical, two moods between which Mahler seems to be constantly hesitating in the Nachtmusiken, as I will show later in the analysis of movements 2 to 5 of the Seventh.

Revers and Davison point out that both Nachtmusiken give prominence to man's relationship to Nature, symbolized in the first by cowbells, echoing horns, and 'bird voices' and in the second by the genre itself of the Serenade, which evokes the open air, fountains, and idyllic gardens. Mahler himself identified the presence of Nature in the tenorhorn theme at the beginning of the Seventh. He even suggested to Richard Specht a meaning for this theme: 'Hier röhrt die Natur.'[58] Nature is, as always, 'the crucial issue' of Mahler's art. He perceives man's relationship to Nature as 'volatile and ambivalent': Nature is infinity and man's perception of it encompasses the 'harmonious and happy', 'the painful and hostile'.[59] As Davison points out, it is 'an uncontrollable force which intrudes upon the stylised restraint of the form', it is 'perceived as a seductive and chaotic environment', as witness the first Nachtmusik, where 'the anti-artistic confusion of the birdsong and the jarring presence of the naturalistic device' are evidence of the conflict between Nature and civilization.[60]

Davison has looked for further answers to some of the paradoxes and ambiguities of the Seventh in the writings of Mahler's favourite philosopher, Gustav Theodor Fechner. Of interest to the Seventh is the title of one of Fechner's books, *Die Tagesangesichte gegenüber der Nachtangesichte* (The faces of the day as opposed to the faces of the night).[61] 'Night and day,' according to Fechner, are 'nothing but a symbol of man's subservience to nature.' They are 'part of the great unity of creation, even if the purpose of that unity is incomprehensible' to man because his 'subjectivity limits his understanding of creation'. In Fechner's view, 'the dialectic of night and day does not exist. Metaphorically it is always night, and Nature is permanently hostile. Day is deluding, exceptional in creation. Without this recognition, limited human minds perceive conflict.' The relevance to Mahler and the Night–Day dialectic of the Seventh is obvious. Yet 'Fechner and Mahler were anti-dialecticians and [only] deistic belief brought about the resolution of worldly contradictions. . . . The Seventh Symphony, because it constantly acknowledges the limitation of the subjective response, is not the product of the Romantic aesthetic paradox, but an analysis of it.'[62]

The Seventh stands out among Mahler's symphonies if only because it conveys no message and does not even seem to move forward in any particular direction. Adorno was surely the first author to understand and write that 'the Mahlerian concept of form is dynamic', which means that it is based on a narrative progression, not an architectural structure: 'The Mahlerian variant is the technical formula for the epic and novel-like element of the always different yet identical figure.'[63] Thus it is not surprising that

---

[57] Ibid. 42. [58] 'Röhren' is the German word for the roar of a stag.

[59] Davison, 'Nachtmusiken', 75.

[60] Mahler once told Natalie Bauer-Lechner that art should reflect, at least in part, the infinity (*Unendlichen*) of nature. (See 'Das Unfassbarre der Natur', NBL1, 140 ff.; NBL2, 150 ff.)

[61] Leipzig, 1879. [62] Davison, 'Nachtmusiken', 83. [63] TAM 116; TAMe 86.

the aim, the goal towards which the course of the Seventh is directed, should be impossible to define since there is no logical narrative thread in the work, no 'teleological process'.[64] This symphony seems to welcome intrusions with a strange passivity, to mirror the endless diversity of the twentieth-century man's experience, a diversity which has become impossible to synthesize, as if, for once Mahler surrendered himself without a struggle to the aggressions of the world or to memories of a long vanished past,[65] a past recalled as irretrievable in a disillusioned present which knows that all illusions will be destroyed, that nostalgia is fruitless, victories deceptive, and that ambiguities can never be solved. The various symbolic sounds—cowbells (pastoral), deep bells (religious), birdsong, military signals—are puzzling because they appear at random, out of context, and thus apparently devoid of any symbolic meaning. Even the main 'themes' of the work, nature, day, and night, are far more complex and ambiguous than they appear at first sight. Nature can be frightening as well as idyllic, chaotic as well as reassuring; the *Weltlauf* (daily bustle) can be seen either as good-humoured or pointless and grotesque. The most obvious literary leitmotiv is Night, but that too can have many shades of meaning. In the Seventh, it has little to do with the blissful night of Tristan and Isolde. In the Scherzo, it seems to be a metaphor for the unconscious, its terrors and visions, its surrender to the dark forces of the 'Ich'. Night in Mahler's Seventh is akin to the Night of Novalis's *Hymns*, in which shadows of the past appear, vague yearnings, and deceived hopes. It is perhaps even more akin to the Night 'older and deeper than the day' of Nietzsche's Zarathustra, of the 'Midnight Song' which Mahler set to music in the Third Symphony, a night of clairvoyance and heightened lucidity whose revelation is more essential than that of light. Theodor Fechner, Mahler's favourite philosopher whose writing he read in the last hours of his earthly existence, also believed that night allows man 'to see beyond experience'.

Finally night can also symbolize eternal sleep, an image for death, or the night which precedes and succeeds existence. Not only does it induce the appearance of recollections of the past, it also encourages an identification, a fusion of man with Nature. This was one of the basic concepts of Fechner's idealistic philosophy with which Mahler's last works are impregnated. At the time of the Seventh, such a fusion was still unattainable. Thus the whole Symphony illustrates first and foremost the ambiguity of Mahler's relationship with reality and the world at large.

These speculations about the meaning of the Seventh and its dialectic of Day and Night should not make us forget the few 'keys' which Mahler himself certainly suggested for the first two movements of his work to Willem Mengelberg, during his last trip to Holland in October 1909. Here they are, as written down by Mengelberg. At the start of the first movement: 'Elemental tragic force. Metaphysical death (war)'; at the start of the first theme in the second movement:[66] 'Strict march. "Night Watch" Rembrandt. Left, right, left, right. Suggest olden times'; then, at bar 83 (Trio): 'A sweet beloved on a soldier's arm, amorous looks and squeezes.'[67] Willem Mengelberg also left a complete 'programme' for the work as a whole, once again based on Mahler's

---

[64]	Davison, 'Nachtmusiken', 81.

[65]	See Henry-Louis de La Grange, 'L'Énigme de la Septième' in Zychowicz, *Symposium*, 13 ff.

[66]	Bar 30.

[67]	Karel Philippus Bernet-Kempers, 'Mahler und Willem Mengelberg', in *Bericht über den internationalen Musikwissenschaftlichen Kongress*, 1956 (Böhlaus, Graz, 1958).

remarks during the Amsterdam rehearsals which I have quoted below at the beginning of the various sections concerning each movement.[68] It must be conceded that the extremes of human suffering and joy described in Mengelberg's programme appear today very exaggerated, more Mengelberg, perhaps, than Mahler, especially as regards the first movement. For despite the similarity of the principal theme in the Allegro to the one in the Sixth, little is to be found in it of the pessimism of the Sixth. However, they are quoted below, if only because of the Dutch conductor's close association with Mahler, and particularly with this Symphony.

Alphons Diepenbrock, who attended the Amsterdam rehearsals and also discussed the work with Mahler, recalls the composer's reluctance to provide 'keys' or programmatic associations for his Nachtmusik 1: 'It is not true that he [Mahler] had tried to depict the "Night Watch". He mentioned this picture only as a point of comparison. It is a night walk, and he says himself that he was thinking of a patrol (*Scharwache*). Besides, he says something different each time. What is certain is that it is a march in a fantastic kind of chiaroscuro, hence the analogy with Rembrandt. The fantastic colours are enough in themselves to carry the imagination back into the past, suggesting a tableau of soldiers and mercenaries.'[69]

ANALYSES

Analyses of the Seventh are far less numerous and extensive than for previous works, for the reasons I have just mentioned. As usual, I mention here only analyses of the whole symphony. More or less contemporary are those of Karl Weigl (17 pp.),[70] Hermann Kretschmar (1 p.),[71] and Richard Specht (5 pp.).[72] That of Paul Bekker (30 pp./1921)[73] was followed, though not for another forty years, by that of Erwin Ratz (9 pp.),[74] whereas Hans Swarowsky devoted twenty-five closely packed pages (from which I shall quote frequently) to the five movements.[75] Rudolph Stephan published a 'bar group' analysis of the five movements, with a comparative chart of those of Hermann Scherchen and Hans Swarowsky.[76] The most recent analysis is that of Constantin Floros (25 pp./1985).[77]

ORCHESTRATION

The dimensions are relatively normal: 4 flutes and piccolo, 4 oboes and cor anglais, 4 clarinets and bass clarinet, 3 bassoons, 4 horns, 3 trumpets, 3 trombones, tuba, timpani, and percussion: bass drum, snare drum, tambourine, tamtam, triangle,

[68] Edna Richolson-Sollitt, 'Mengelberg spreekt', *De Muziek*, 5 (1934), 30.
[69] Alphons Diepenbrock, letter to Johanna Jongkindt, 17 Oct. 1909, quoted in RMH 31. See below, Vol. iiii, Chap. 5.   [70] In *Mahlers Symphonien*, ed. Edgar Istel, undated (1913 or 1914).
[71] In *Führer durch den Konzertsaal* (Breitkopf, Leipzig, 1913), 810.
[72] RSM2, edn. 1913, 299.   [73] BSM 237.
[74] 1960, in *Gesammelten Aufsätze* (Universal Edition, Vienna, 1975), 147.
[75] In *Wahrung der Gestalt: Schriften über Werk und Wiedergabe, Stil und Interpretation in der Musik* (Universal Edition, Vienna, 1979), 135.
[76] In Rüdiger Görner (ed.), *Logos Musicae: Festschrift für Albert Palm* (Steiner, Wiesbaden, 1982), 202 ff.   [77] Floros, *Gustav Mahler*, vol. iii, 'Die Symphonien', 184 ff.

cymbals, *rute* (brush), cowbells, deep bells (of indeterminate pitch), glockenspiel, 2 harps, guitar, mandolin, and strings. The Seventh also uses a rare brass instrument more usual in wind bands than in a symphony orchestra. This is the tenorhorn, an instrument played vertically like a tuba which, despite the mind-boggling confusion of names and categories in its instrumental family, is called 'baritone' (in B flat) in England and in France.[78] Obviously Mahler wanted a very special, penetrating sonority for this solo which dominates the whole of the Introduction, starting at bar 2. Another interesting innovation is the 'concertante' ensemble in dialogue with the rest of the orchestra in the second Nachtmusik, an ensemble containing not only two harps, but two instruments hitherto foreign to the symphony orchestra, the guitar and mandolin. After Mahler, Webern used them in his *Five Pieces for Orchestra*, Op. 10, Schoenberg in his *Serenade*, Op. 24 (1923), and Stravinsky made use of the guitar many years later, in the ballet *Agon* (1957).

(*a*) **Langsam; Allegro risoluto, ma non troppo**

Key: B minor (Introduction); E minor (Allegro), ending in the major. (See synoptic table below.)

Rhythm: Slow or fast march.

Tempo: There are many discrepancies between the tempos indicated in the Bote und Bock edition and the fair copy (Amsterdam Concertgebouw, here mentioned as 'OR'): *Langsam (Adagio)* (Slow); at bar 19: *Etwas weniger langsam, aber immer sehr gemessen* (A little less slow, but still very measured) (OR: *Più mosso poco*); at bar 32: *Tempo I (Adagio) Subito, aber fliessender als zu Anfang* (suddenly, but more flowing than before); at bar 50: *Allegro risoluto, ma non troppo* (OR: *Allegro energico—subito*); at bar 118: *A tempo sempre l'istesso* (OR: *Sempre l'istesso tempo. Nicht schleppen* (do not drag)); bar 134: *A tempo Allegro* (OR: *Etwas gemessener* (somewhat more measured)); at bar 174: *Molto pesante e misurato*; at bar 196: *Moderato* (OR: *Nicht eilen* (do not hurry)); at bar 212: *Wieder Tempo I; Subito Allegro I*; at bar 257; *Gemessener*; at bar 258: *Meno mosso*; at bar 266: *subito Allegro I Ziemlich ruhig* (fairly calm) (OR: *Ziemlich hastig* (fairly hasty)); at bar 317: *Sehr breit* (very broad) (OR: *Wieder a tempo. Gemässigt* (more measured)); etc.

Duration: 20 minutes[79] (according to William Ritter at the Munich performance, 16 minutes).[80]

Mengelberg's programme: 'This concerns night, a tragic night. No stars, no moonlight, no celebration, no happy people, no quiet sleep. It is the reign of the power of darkness, which Mahler expresses as a violent force, stubborn, brutal and

---

[78] John Williamson notes that the draft score assigns the part to an alto trombone, and adds that this instrument was originally used a few more times in the Allegro (see Zychowicz, *Symposium*, 37). Mahler had considered using the same instrument in the Coda of the Finale of the Sixth (see above). It is used in Pfitzner's opera *Die Rose vom Liebesgarten*, which Mahler had conducted at the Vienna Opera a few weeks before composing the first movement of the Seventh.

[79] At the Prague première, according to August Spanuth's review in the magazine *Signale für die musikalische Welt* (see above).

[80] William Ritter noted these durations at the first performance in Prague in 1908 (see 'La VIIè Symphonie de Gustav Mahler', *Revue de la Société Internationale de Musique*, Paris, 4 (1908): 11, 583 ff.).

tyrannical. There are moments where we hear the unshakeable hope of humanity, and its suffering. In these moments lies the tragedy of life, which ardently
longs for light and love, if only . . . ! The particular colours of the instrument
Mahler uses solo (the tenorhorn), the heavy, falling character of the intervals in
the principal theme, the angular rhythm, the mobility of the accompaniment, all
these express tyrannical rule. The solo declares: "I am the master here! I shall
impose my will!" Without this image, the music of this movement is incomprehensible.'

Analysis: John Williamson has appended seven Schenkerian graphs to his analysis
of this movement.[81] more recently he published an extended Schenkerian analysis of the Introduction alone.[82]

The first movement of the Seventh Symphony, like that of the Third, is preceded
by a slow Introduction which is later reiterated in the body of the movement. As with
the Finale of the Sixth, it allows us to witness the genesis of the various themes and
motifs later used. The wilful and dynamic character of the Allegro section has been
noted in all descriptions, but even more striking is the fact that the slow episodes
occupy more than half the duration of the movement.[83] Never before in a first movement has Mahler so abandoned himself to nostalgic reverie and sweet expansiveness:
the complete opposite of the implacable tension characterizing even the 'melodic'
theme in the first movement of the Sixth.[84] The synoptic table below follows that of
Hans Swarowsky,[85] but with certain modifications. Swarowsky calls the principal elements
of the Introduction A and B, and those of the Allegro C and D. Following my normal practice, I shall call the former I, I' , and I" and those in the exposition A, B, and C.

BARS		KEYS
Introduction: bars 1 to 49		
1ST SECTION		
1–19	Theme I, followed by a restatement of its opening bars.	B major and minor
19–26	Transition theme (I').	
2ND SECTION		
27–39	Theme I" (prefiguring A).	E flat minor
39–49	Transition (2nd phase of A and I").	B minor

[81]   See *Symposium*, 27 ff.

[82]   See Williamson, 'The Structural Premises of Mahler's Introductions: Prolegomena to an Analysis of
the First Movement of the Seventh Symphony', *Musical Analysis*, 5 (1986): 1, 29 ff.

[83]   The Finale of the Tenth Symphony has the same peculiarity (see Vol. iiii, Appendix 2).

[84]   Very few conductors today follow Mahler's tempo markings for the second theme: '*A tempo (sempre
l'istesso). Mit grossem Schwung*' (With great impetus). This of course increases the general feeling of a
predominantly slow first movement. See Nancy Miller, 'A matter of tempo', in *Opus*, New York (Apr. 1986)
20 ff.

[85]   *Wahrung*, 135. Swarowsky's analysis also contains a precise scheme of periodicity of musical
phrases by number of bars, which is of great interest to interpreters of the work, as well as a table of the
different tempos with specific metronome markings (ibid. 142). Rudolph Stephan devotes an entire article
(Überlegung zur Taktgruppen-analyse: Zur Interpretation der 7. Symphonie von Gustav Mahler', *Logos
Musicae, Festschrift für Alfred Palm* (Steiner, Wiesbaden, 1982), 202) to a comparison between analyses of
periodicity in the first movement by Swarowsky and by the conductor Hermann Scherchen.

(cont.):

Exposition: bars 50 to 144

50–75	Theme A.	
76–9	Transition (calls in fourths, rhythm and preparation for B).	E minor D major
80–98	Theme A′.	B major
99–117	Transition (A, A′).	E minor
118–33	Theme B.	C major
134–44	Concluding theme (C: see I′).	G major

Development: bars 145 to 372

1ST SECTION (modified reprise of the exposition)

145–73	(A).	E minor
174–85	(A′ + I).	B minor
186–95	Transition (A′ + I, inversion of A).	
196–211	(B and A″).	
212–27	Transition (A, A′, I′).	

2ND SECTION (combinations)

228–44	(I, A, B, I′).	C major
245–57	(I, I′, A′, B, fanfares).	G major
258–83	(I′, A, A′, B, fanfares).	E flat G major
284–97	(A, I′).	
298–316	(I, A′, I′, fanfares).	E flat minor, A major, B minor
317–27	(I, I′, A, A′, B).	B major
328–37	(I′, A′, B).	

3RD SECTION (reprise of the introduction as transition)

338–53	1st section (I, A, B).	B major
354–72	2nd part (B + I, I′, A + A′).	B minor and major

Recapitulation: bars 373 to 494

373–426	Theme A.	E minor and major
427–49	Theme A′.	B major
450–64	Transition (A, A′).	
465–86	Theme B.	G major
487–94	Theme C (I′).	E major

Coda: bars 495 to 547

495–511	(I″, A′).	E minor
512–22	(A).	
523–47	(A, A′).	E minor and major

Swarowsky underlines the evolving character of the thematic material in this symphony, which is constantly varied and altered in procedures of great subtlety and complexity. He notes in particular that the transition episode in the Introduction (I′) plays an essential role in the development, at the point where it is transformed into a chorale (bars 258, 262, 304, etc.). Adorno was therefore right in calling it

Durchführungsthema. More interesting still is the double role played by each section
in the whole, the Introduction, Exposition, and first part of the *Durchführung* consti-
tuting a unity in themselves, so that, in terms of tonal function, it could be maintained that this movement has three expositions. In the same way the third section
of the *Durchführung*, the Recapitulation and the Coda constitute another unity, and
the reprise of the Introduction (at the end of the 2nd section of the *Durchführung*)
could be considered as the first part of the Recapitulation, and the Coda as the third
section, creating a symmetry with the three expositions previously mentioned. The
three parts of the *Durchführung* also constitute a unity, with the first and the third
having double functions. Swarowsky therefore proposes an alternative scheme for
the seven parts of the first movement, taking into account these unusual structural
features:[86]

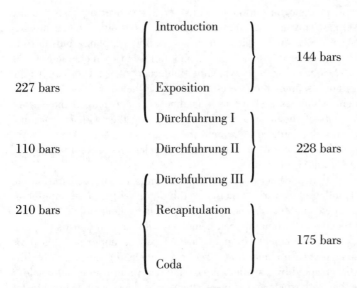

	Introduction	
		144 bars
227 bars	Exposition	
	Dürchfuhrung I	
110 bars	Dürchfuhrung II	228 bars
	Dürchfuhrung III	
210 bars	Recapitulation	
		175 bars
	Coda	

   The dactylic rhythm which was already present in the climaxes of the Finale of the
Sixth plays a determining role in the first movement of the Seventh, so do dotted
rhythms, but here it is intensified (as in the Miserere in Verdi's *Trovotore*) by the fact
of being a dotted quaver followed by two demisemiquavers. 'Here nature is calling like
a stag',[87] said Mahler himself of this opening tenorhorn solo (I) whose darkness, depth,
and almost funereal grandeur[88] recall the no less nocturnal music he had written on
the same 'theme'—Nature—in the Third Symphony. The theme moves to the woodwind, then to the trumpet, back to the woodwind and finally back to the tenorhorn but
the timbre of the low brass predominates as it did in the minor section of the first movement of the Third. Once again the opening chord includes the 'added sixth' which is
becoming a 'fingerprint' in Mahler's mature style. In the slightly quicker march that
serves as transition (I': winds accompanied by pizzicato) no one could predict the

---

[86] Swarowsky, *Wahrung*, 140.   [87] RSM2, 299.
   [88] Redlich even sees in the tenorhorn theme an echo of the trombone solos in the first movement of the
Third Symphony.

solemn and mysterious chorale transformation that is to appear later on in the development.[89]

The third element (bars 27 ff.: trombones), also in dotted rhythm, prefigures the main Allegro theme (A). With the return of the opening tempo, theme I appears transformed and broadened (I″). The initial descending fourth motif of I″ (tenorhorn), to which another descending fourth is added, fuels the transition towards the Allegro. Theme A appears not as if compounded of previous motifs (as in the Finale of the Sixth) but as their logical consequence. Its likeness to the opening theme of the previous symphony, which has the same tense, wilful, angular style, has often been noted. This character is further intensified by the superimposed fourths and by the large melodic intervals. However the energy of this first element is soon exhausted as an unexpected lyricism gradually takes hold of the first violins, which twice anticipate the ascending curve of the second theme (B: bar 118).[90]

Theme B is stated in dialogue between violins and horns over arpeggios in the cellos, the lyrical vein growing more and more abandoned. It has often been compared with the one that occupies a similar place in the preceding symphony but, despite having as its point of departure an ascending scale motif, it is closer in character to the world of the *Kindertotenlieder*[91] with its typically Mahlerian 'sighs'. The march from the Introduction (I′) now assumes the role of a concluding theme and leads in a few bars to a development, which, as we have seen, is almost twice as long as the exposition. The main elements of theme A are exploited first, together with its variant I (derived from the Introduction), after which the tempo broadens (bars 196 ff.: *Moderato*) and the violins, first solo and then tutti, develop the second subject by combining it with a variant of the first.

The second section (bar 228) consists of a new variant of theme A (featuring the triplets from bar 71) followed by various motifs from B and I′, either superimposed or closely intertwined. Then suddenly, in the context of this movement which belongs to Mahler's most 'advanced style', there appear, combined with calls in fourths (A′) and reminiscences of A and B, elements from his distant past, trumpet fanfares (bars 247 ff.) and birdsong (bars 255 and 256). The main thematic substance of this *Naturlaut* episode (interrupted by a swifter passage mixing A and B in a violin solo)[92] is a solemn chorale (bar 258: winds and strings) which, as we have seen, is but a metamorphosis of I′. The second part of this extended episode (bars 298 ff.) multiplies the fanfares, the calls in fourths and the birdsong, and spills into a moment of pure ecstasy. This is a voluptuous augmented form of the B melody, high in the violins (bars 317 ff.: *sehr breit*) over arpeggios in the harps and strings and trills in the woodwind. Soon motifs from the Introduction support the ecstatic violins (I′ and I″ in the horns, then I′

---

[89]   Alexander L. Ringer detects in this theme a possible reminiscence of the fourth of Schumann's *Nachtstücke* Op. 23. See ' "Ende gut alles gut" '. Bemerkungen zu zwei Finalsätzen von Johannes Brahms und Gustav Mahler', *Festschrift Rudolf Stephan* (Laaber, Laaber, 1990), 297 ff.

[90]   The motif constructed from two falling fourths (A′) which begins the second part of the first theme is accompanied by descending chromatic thirds in the horns, different only in rhythm from those which will serve as countermelody to theme B. Here Mahler discovers a new means of creating a unity within a symphonic movement.

[91]   See in particular bars 60, 61, and 62 of the first Lied, bars 40, 41, and 42 of the fourth and bars 119 and 120 of the Seventh Symphony. See also bar 121 of the Seventh and bar 3 of the Andante of the Sixth.

[92]   At bar 286, Mahler wrote, 'Stones plump into the water' on the first autograph score.

in the trombones, with the dactylic rhythm). It has been justly claimed that this is one of the rare episodes in Mahler's music to radiate the sensuality of Strauss. The ecstatic melody and sumptuous orchestral texture of its accompaniment are all the more effective in the context of a movement where the darkness and mystery of the beginning have been dispelled only by the harsh fourths and dotted rhythms of theme A.

This moment of intense lyricism gradually and naturally merges into a return of the slow Introduction (bar 338) with its dotted rhythm. The opening theme (I) is expanded into a new melody shared by the basses and trombones and pursued by the tenorhorn, which accelerates the ascending scale of B (bar 350). From then on, fragments of B intertwined with others from I and the *Durchführungsthema* in the trombones, display Mahler's unlimited ability for creating new melodies with materials already stated. Thanks to these variants, the return of the Introduction gives the feeling of a progression, not a return to the past. This time it is the triplet chains of theme A (from bar 71) that introduce the true recapitulation (*Allegro come prima*). From the fifth bar on, it takes a new and increasingly triumphal turn (bar 394: *Grandioso*), continually alternating between major and minor. Next the transition episode (A'), with its calls in fourths, is expanded in an atmosphere of proud conquest. The altered curve of theme B (C major, bars 465 ff.) pursues it into a seemingly inevitable consequence of its form in the development, with new note values and orchestration (the horns' counter melody is replaced by calls in fourths and imitations in the trumpets). A new climax of tranquil exaltation[93] leads into the march (I'), again used as a transition, this time to the Coda.

A grandiose and conclusive version of the main theme (A or I''), taken up from the trumpets by the violins, now dominates the texture with a repeated climactic *grupetto* (bars 505, 509, 5210, etc.).[94] As it approaches the end, this ultimate metamorphosis of A accelerates and turns towards the major (with triplets from bar 71, the fourth calls from A', etc.). The conclusion is swift and abrupt, with a series of discordant fourths which sound astonishingly modern for a work completed in 1905. 'The first movement of the Seventh is closely related to the outer movements of the Sixth', writes Adorno. 'But Mahler's capacity to renew symphonic types from within themselves is not confined to after-echoes. Through a changed illumination the whole movement becomes a variant. It translates the attainments of the preceding orchestral symphonies into the image-world of the early Mahler. . . . Despite the most emphatic construction the movement is sensuously more colourful than anything previously written by Mahler; his late style goes back to it. The major is resplendent with added notes, as a kind of super-major, as in the famous chord from the Adagio of Bruckner's Ninth. The contrasts, including those of timbre, are deepened, as is the perspective; even the wind chorus is toned down as compared to its previous appearance, for example, through opposing the althorn and solo trombones. Exploitation of the shared thirds allows chords originally located far apart to follow each other according to diatonic rules. All in all, harmonic resources are noticeably increased.'[95]

---

[93] The ornamental line in the first violins in bars 478–9 foreshadows strikingly similar passages in the first movement of the Ninth Symphony.

[94] This might be regarded as a foretaste of the famous gruppetti in the Finale of the Ninth, first appearing, like them, in short note values (semiquavers), then in longer ones (quavers).

[95] TAM 136; TAMe 100 ff.

'The shadow of the Sixth, in which the movement exists, then becomes the realm of shadows of the three middle movements. The tragic aspiration of the Sixth has disappeared. It has been banished probably less by that ominously positive element that, to be sure, ruins the Finale,[96] than by a half-consciousness that the category of the tragic cannot be reconciled with the epic ideal of a music open in time. Having mastered totality, the composition turns its thoughts to the opposite, a meaning that arises from fragments.'[97]

(b) Nachtmusik (Night music)

Key: C minor and major (First Trio in A flat major; second in F minor).

Time signature: 4/4.

Rhythm: Slow march.

Tempo: *Allegro moderato* (introduction); *Tempo subito, molto moderato* (*Andante*) (bar 30); *sempre l'istesso tempo* (bar 83: 1st Trio); *Gehalten* (held back) (bar 141); *Poco meno mosso* (bar 161: 2nd Trio).

Duration: 14 minutes (see above. William Ritter claims 21 minutes, but this is probably a mistake).

Analysis: Bernd Sponheuer (1989).[98]

Mengelberg's programme: 'The march is regular and rapid, whether loud or soft. Sometimes is it heard right up close, sometimes in the distance, where the plains stretch far away. When it sounds from afar, Mahler's music carries impressions of meadows and peace, of great open spaces, and of the calm produced in us by nature. When the marchers arrive in a village, the beloved of one of the soldiers is there. She sees him in the ranks and runs part of the way at his side, her arm in his.'

Form: ABA.C.ABA (with Introduction and Coda), in other words a symmetrical form which is virtually that of a military march with two trios. Hans Swarowsky observes that the reprise (ABA) is abridged. He sums up the whole as follows:

Introduction	29 bars
ABA	131 bars
C	51 bars
ABA	106 bars
Coda	26 bars

As expected, the first of the three 'intermezzi' has an infinitely simpler structure than the opening movement. In a more detailed synopsis, however, Swarowsky distinguishes two different sections in the Introduction, which are both recapitulated, but at different places in the movement (no. 1: bar 122; no. 2: bar 179), and notes that material from the second Introduction is sometimes combined in the development sections

---

[96] Adorno's condemnation of the Finale is not surprising considering his overall view of Mahler's music, but there are many more subtle ways of appraising this movement.

[97] TAM 137; TAMe 101.

[98] Sponheuer, ' "O alter Duft aus Märchenzeit!" Prozeduren der Erinnerung in der ersten Nachtmusik der Siebten Symphonie Gustav Mahlers', in Matthias Theodor Vogt (ed.), *Das Gustav-Mahler-Fest Hamburg 1989* (Bärenreiter, Kassel, 1989), 469 ff.

with elements A (for example in bars 62, 141, and 245). These are divided by the recapitulation of the second section of the Introduction, Groups A and B are always restated in the same key (C minor and A flat major) whereas C, in its second appearance, is transposed into C minor. It should also be noted that the end of this movement, on the dominant, suspends the activity rather than concluding it.

Peter Davison notes that the whole Introduction is based on a dominant pedal and thus prepares for the entry of the march-music, and sees the whole movement as opposing art and nature, the reality of *Alltag* (daily run of the mill) symbolized by the marches with chaotic nature represented by the bird voices. Thus he detects in the structure several episodes which he calls suspensions of immanent structural context, which create 'formal asymmetries and irregularities'.[99] He also emphasizes 'the ambiguity of the modality which pervades the key-structure and harmonic language of the movement', and 'creates an underlying restlessness'.[100]

Several features combine to recreate the atmosphere of Mahler's early *Wunderhorn-Lieder*:[101] military calls in the brass, the rhythm of the accompaniment borrowed from 'Revelge' (low violins *col legno*: bar 33, etc.), birdsong (recalling the Introduction of the First Symphony and the Finale of the Second), the slow march rhythm, and the altogether diatonic character of the melodic elements, particularly the deliberate 'popular' character of element B (bar 83), played by the cellos over triplet chords in the horns. Even in the final figure, in pizzicato triplets, in the violins (bars 337 ff.), irresistibly recalls the one which concludes the third song of the *Gesellen Lieder*. On the other hand the proliferating triplet motifs, derived from the fanfares and birdsong, which proceed without apparent reference to the themes proper, foreshadow the melodic embroideries and garlands so frequent in Mahler's late style, from the Eighth Symphony on. The three appearances of the major–minor 'motto' (bars 28–9; 187–8; 337–8) are, like the cowbells, a reminiscence from the preceding symphony.

As noted earlier, the abundance of symbolic elements—march rhythm, military fanfares, echoing horns, wind-band music, birdsong, cowbells—is bewildering. It would be too naive to imagine a military patrol or soldier protagonist walking through a variety of landscapes. Yet the obsessive presence, in the context of the good-natured march, of the characteristic rhythm of the tragic song 'Revelge' is hard to explain, as is the no less constant return of birdsong.[102] in what appears elsewhere to be an urban landscape, with the band music and the Rembrandt painting suggested as an inspiration for the piece. The oboe duet in the second Trio (bars 165–72) appears as the first moment of pure lyricism in Nachtmusik 1, yet it reverts to the military dotted rhythm in its seventh bar (bar 171). Once again, it seems as though Mahler were quoting at random from memories of the musical environment of his distant past—stylized fragments bound together in no way except that they are all recollections, presented as an interior monologue à la Schnitzler or in the manner of a Joycian 'stream of consciousness'.

---

[99] They are bars 1–29; 121–32; 161–4; 179–89; 211–22; and 318–43.

[100] Davison, 'Nachtmusiken', 31.

[101] Richard Specht (RSM2, 300) describes this march as 'one that might have been heard during the Thirty Years' War', and as 'a phantom night-watch in ancient market places'. In the first Trio he hears 'an old soldiers' song', and in the second 'the forgotten ditty of wives abandoned'.

[102] The descent in to the lowest register (cellos and basses) of the birdsong motif (bars 141–8) foreshadows the same occurrence in several passages of the 'Abschied' movement of *Das Lied* and the 'cadenza' of the first movement of the Ninth Symphony (bars 382–3 and 386 ff.).

The *rufend* (calling) and *antwortend* (answering) horn figures, like the beginning of Berlioz's *Scène aux champs* in the *Symphonie fantastique* set the scene in nature. Admittedly the second horn is not placed off-stage like the second oboe of Berlioz,[103] but the same effect of distance is obtained by the use of the mute. As Wolfgang Dömling[104] points out, Mahler gives himself up to the sheer pleasure of the sounds, and in no way seeks to evoke concrete events, as can be seen in the episode (bars 280 ff.) where the cowbells are superimposed on a 'military' horn theme.[105] The same author draws attention to the character of some of these episodes where time is, so to speak, suspended (beginning of the Introduction; bars 122 ff.; bars 211 ff.; beginning of the Coda).[106]

As always with Mahler, even the most apparently free improvisation announces or states a thematic element. Here it is the principal theme of the movement which, three times repeated, starts low, first played by the bassoon then twice by the tuba. The mood painting proceeds imperturbably until it reaches a rapid descending scale in the woodwinds and lower strings, accompanying the famous major–minor 'motto' from the previous symphony (bars 28 and 29). This marks the beginning of the movement proper (bars 30 ff.). Two march themes alternate, as seen above, A in the horns (imitated in the cellos), and A' in the basses with contrabassoon.[107] The return of the first is accompanied by new 'birdsong' episodes in triplets in the winds,[108] after which the first Trio (B) introduces a melody which, despite its outrageously 'band-music' flavour, is full of subtleties and asymmetries, with insolent accompanying triplets from three horns.

---

[103] The score of the *Fantastique* is marked simply 'lontano'.

[104] See Wolfgang Dömling, ' "En songeant au temps . . . à l'espace . . .", über einige Aspekte der Musik Hector Berlioz', in *Archiv der Musikwissenschaft*, 33 (1976): 4, 243.

[105] Dömling observes that the 'answer' of the third horn reproduces the 'question' only in its final fragment (see Wolfgang Dömling, 'Collage und Kontinuum, Bemerkungen zu Gustav Mahler und Richard Strauss', *Neue Zeitschrift für Musik*, 133 (1972): 3, 131). He concentrates on bars 122 to 131, where Mahler requires that 'the cowbells should always be discreet and intermittent' and should 'imitate in a realistic way the bells of a grazing flock'. These bells are not in the same plane (*Ebene*) as the horn calls, but are contrasted by their indistinct rhythm, their indeterminate pitch, their intermittent sound, and their remoteness (*In weiter Entfernung*). He compares Mahler's *Naturlaut* to Strauss's *Naturbild* (Nature scene), in *Aus Italien* and the *Alpensinfonie* for instance, and notes that Mahler alone gives instructions such as 'like a bird-call', and specifies distances for the placing of the instruments. In his reply to Dömling, Tibor Kneif (in 'Collage und Naturalismus, Anmerkungen zu Mahlers Nachtmusik I', *Neue Zeitschrift für Musik*, 134 (1973): 10, 623) points out that the cowbells are to reappear in the Rondo, that a 'collage' is not an 'allusion to reality' but an intrusion of 'reality itself', and that Mahler, clearly gives them the character of 'objets trouvés'. He recalls Mahler's use of cowbells in the Sixth and his very precise instructions about their location, either 'in the distance' or 'getting closer' or 'in the orchestra'. Here, in the first *Nachtmusik*, they are at first 'very distant' (bar 126) and then 'in the orchestra' (bar 260). See also Wolfgang Dömling's reply to Tibor Kneif, 'A propos Mahler und Collage', *Neue Zeitschrift für Musik*, 135 (1974): 2, 100.

[106] Hans-Klaus Jungheinrich (article quoted previously, 192) and Monika Lichtenfeld (same work, 129) treat the first *Naturlaut* episode (bar 20 ff.) as a *Klangfläche* (sound surface) comparable to those of Ligeti. Lichtenfeld remarks that the chords are empty of thirds and that the 'goal' is reached with the perfect major chord in bar 28, which becomes minor. The episode is repeated at bar 179.

[107] Peter Davison finds several convincing reminiscences of Bizet's *Carmen* in Mahler's Nachtmusik 1: the second march theme in the bass (bars 48 ff.) and the bass line of the opening of Act III of the opera (which also has a night scene with characters—the smugglers—marching in the dark); the opening flute theme and Mahler's bars 58 ff; and finally Bizet's 'fate' theme at the end of the overture and Mahler's bars 199–201 ('Nachtmusiken', 35 ff.). These thematic affinities are all the more convincing because *Carmen* was an opera Mahler admired and had often conducted in Hamburg.

[108] Echoing horns and birdsong are two typical Eichendorffian themes, like night and 'Wanderschaft' (see Davison, 'Nachtmusiken', 33).

Next, the horn dialogue, varied and amplified, and accompanied by the first appearance of the cowbells 'in the distance',[109] brings back the first march (and the bird motifs in triplets, now on low strings, surprisingly enough). Two passing allusions to the dactylic rhythm of 'Revelge' maintain the 'military' atmosphere, and the march finishes piano with imitative writing for low strings. The second Trio (C: bars 161 ff.) is again introduced by several bars of *Naturlaut* (sustained octaves and trills in the oboe and strings, then clarinet fanfares). The climate of nostalgic tenderness irresistibly recalls Mahler's first works (in particular *Das klagende Lied*), evoked as it is by oboes and distant horns. After a new intrusion of *Naturlaut*, during which the march theme tries, as before, to re-emerge (trumpet and solo violin, then solo violin, then trumpet and trombone, solo violin, and bass), element C is brought back by two cellos, doubled by oboe and cor anglais, as the 'Revelge' rhythm grows obstinate (horns and trumpets), with insistent fanfares in the clarinets (*quasi tromba*).

Particularly striking is the mysterious and magic transition which brings back the first March (bars 211 ff.). (Mahler wrote some of his greatest music in such transitional or conclusive passages.) Over the bass motif (A'), a solitary flute recalls (pianissimo and 'hastily') the previous birdsong, now interrupted by a hardly perceptible high tremor (harp tremolo and violin trills). The edifice is harmoniously completed by the return of the first two episodes, freely varied. The second repetition of episode B alters its original form, the horn triplets now pizzicato in the violas, and the 'Revelge' rhythm now taken up by the trumpets, with a new countermelody high in the woodwinds. Finally the coda, for solo woodwind and low strings, combines theme A', the *Naturlaut*, and the major–minor motif and ends with a long triplet figure derived from the birdsong, and moving from cellos to clarinets, and then to violins and again cellos. 'Nature, in the form of bird-voices', has the last word.[110] A particularly sophisticated instrumental effect is heard in the end, when the trumpets play the major–minor motif diminuendo, from fortissimo to piano, while the flutes play a crescendo-decrescendo, from piano to forte to piano again.

As Adorno has observed,[111] the debt to Mahler of Adrian Leverkühn, the imaginary composer in Thomas Mann's *Doktor Faustus*, is 'more . . . than the high G on the cellos from the end of the first *Nachtmusik*'. Leverkuhn finishes his final *Faust-Kantate* with a high G (in harmonics) on the cellos,[112] as Mahler finishes the second movement of his Seventh: 'One group of instruments after another retires, and what remains, as the work fades on the air, is the high G of a cello, the last word, the last fainting sound, slowly dying in a pianissimo-fermata. Then nothing more: silence, and night. But that tone which vibrates in the silence, which is no longer there, to which only the spirit harkens, and which was the voice of mourning, is so no more. It changes its meaning; it abides as a light in the night.'[113]

[109] They return, but this time 'in the orchestra' at bars 280 ff. Davison notes they are now exploited 'as a goal, a place for the march to go to', and that two other appearances of these bells had originally been planned by Mahler, at bars 62–7 and 239–44. Both were cut at some time between the completion of the fair copy of the score and the first edition. See Davison, 'Nachtmusiken', 43.

[110] Ibid. 45 ff.

[111] TAM 69; TAMe 48.

[112] Peter Davison has noted that the ending of the first Nachtmusik on G—Dominant of C minor—is only resolved in a tonic chord of C major in bar 7 of the Finale (Davison, 'Nachtmusiken', 23)

[113] Thomas Mann, *Doktor Faustus*, end of chap. 46. It is well known that Adorno collaborated with the author in the conception and writing of the novel. Thus, he, better than anyone, was in a position to know

(c) **Scherzo**

Key: D minor (second element and Trio in D major).
Time signature: 3/4.
Rhythm: Ländler and Waltz.
Tempo: *Schattenhaft*[114] (Ghostly). *Fliessend, aber nicht schnell*;[115] *in den Anfangstakten noch etwas zögernd* (Flowing, but not fast; slightly hesitant in the opening bars). *Etwas flotter* (a little more lively) (bar 54); *klagend* (plaintive) (bar 108); *Pesante* (bar 243), etc.
Duration: 11 minutes (see above. William Ritter says 10 minutes).
Analysis: Talia Pecker-Berio presented a thorough analysis of the movement at the 1989 Symposium held at the Sorbonne in Paris.[116]
Mengelberg's programme: 'This is a Dance of Death, as seen in old frescoes, for example the marvellous series on the famous bridge in Lucerne. Death plays the violin, inviting people to dance, as sooner or later all of them must. Mahler gives this music to a viola; a remarkable melody. The clattering of bones, baleful laughter, ghostly dancing, all can be recognized here. Mahler has painted a fragment of medieval legend with the colours of the modern orchestra. In this movement there is nothing real; it is a reflection of yesterday's world, peopled with ghosts.'
Form: Hans Swarowsky's detailed scheme is again reproduced here, once again adjusting his system of initials. The Scherzo sections are here designated by A, A', B, B', etc. and those of the Trio by T^1, T^2, T^3, etc.

Scherzo
BARS

1–12	Introduction	⎫
13–23	A	⎪
24–37	A'	⎪
38–53	B (with A)	⎬ 71 bars
54–65	B'	⎪
66–71	B + B'	⎭
72–85	Introduction	⎫
86–96	A	⎪
97–107	A'	⎪
108–15	B	⎬ 107 bars
116–27	B'	⎪
128–59	B + B'	⎪
160–78	Transition	⎭

the extent of Mann's debt to the Seventh Symphony. The high G (*arco*) in the cellos, is in fact supported by a pedal point. Elsewhere in the book, Leverkühn's imaginary Violin Concerto begins with an 'Andante amoroso of a dulcet tenderness bordering on mockery', a description perfectly suited to the second *Nachtmusik* (*Faustus*, chap. 38).

[114] Adorno observes that this marking reappears only once in Mahler's work, in the first movement of the Ninth. Floros observes that the passage in Strauss's tone poem *Till Eulenspiegel*, which follows Till's death sentence (muted violins, violas, and trombones) is marked *schnell und schattenhaft* (Floros, *Mahler*, iii, 199).   [115] The last three words are twice underlined in the score.
[116] See Zychowicz, *Symposium*, 74 ff.

Bars

Trio

179–88	T¹	
189–209	T²	
210–46	T³	82 bars
247–60	T⁴	
261–92	Transition	

Scherzo reprise

293–312	Introduction	
313–33	A	
334–44	A′	140 bars
345–60	B	
361–72	B′	
373–400	B + B′	
401–4	Introduction	
405–16	A	
417–27	B′ + T⁴	
428–43	T²	71 bars
444–63	T³	
464–71	T⁴	
472–504	Coda	33 bars

The structure is symmetrical, as befits a Scherzo. However, with its syncopations, its timpani strokes on the last beat, its pizzicato, its atmosphere at once plaintive and ghostly, and with the wild waltz episode, this movement is the one that most clearly foreshadows the style of the inner movements of the Ninth (and the Tenth). Mengelberg believed that the idea of a medieval *danse macabre*, led by death with his violin, was the basis of the Scherzo. This is the only movement in which openly derisive intentions can be detected. Despite Mengelberg's programme, fleeting forms, nightmarish visions, shadows, phantoms, seem to drift by, rather than the skeletons of a *danse macabre*. The viola solo mentioned by the Dutch conductor is the one in bars 112 ff. and 313 ff., but Mahler had already used the same image once before, in his 'programme' for the Scherzo of the Fourth, which is much less disquieting than this one. Its disturbing quality comes from the rapid triplet figure in the principal theme, evoking fleeting shapes barely glimpsed, from rhythmic oddities and from the dynamics themselves, which rarely rise above piano, with fortes and fortissimos that are really accents and that are principally marked for the softer instruments. Even though the Second, the Fourth, and the Sixth Symphonies also exploit the possibilities of the genre, nowhere else does Mahler succeed in creating such an atmosphere of anguish and fear. The first bars are particularly striking, with major sevenths divided between the timpani on the weak beat (on A) and pizzicato in the low strings on the strong beat (B flat). In Mahler's whole output there is nothing more 'experimental' (nor more successfully so) than this opening whose halting progress is for the moment governed by no tonality at all. In this macabre and freezing void, muted violins embark on a round that whirls in rapid triplets, ceaselessly flaring up and falling back on themselves. A piercing, plaintive motif (flute and oboe: B, bars 38 ff.) is soon superimposed, a motif that prompted the following remarks from Adorno: 'Similarly ambivalent is a melody of the woodwinds and later of the strings, a kind of *cantus firmus* to the hurrying main theme of the Scherzo of the Seventh Symphony, which no longer has any pretence of innocence. Marked *klagend* (lamenting) by Mahler, it combines, as only music can, the barrel-organ grinding of the world's course (*Weltlauf*)[117] with that which expressively mourns it.'[118]

The plaintive motif soon degenerates into a waltz caricature (B', in D major–minor, violins: bars 54 ff.), with the horns marking a coarse three-time. Its characteristic melodic leap of a sixth widens more and more towards the end,[119] with grotesque *portamenti*. This new 'witches' Sabbath ends with a veritable breakneck leap down two and a half octaves, into the previous sinister exchange of timpani and low strings presided over, more strongly than ever, by the Berliozian Angel of the Bizarre.

All the elements are now restated with numerous variants, after which a return to the opening motif heralds the Trio, whose theme is taken, as in the second contrasting episode of the Nachtmusik 1, by two oboes imitating distant horns.[120] It includes incidentally a reminiscence from the second Trio in the Scherzo of the Fifth (violin solo: bars 197–8).[121] Numerous parentheses (solo violin and flute, then flute and violin, etc.) punctuate and separate the different phrases of the Ländler with rapid quaver figures. The third element (solo viola: bars 210 ff.), recalling the fourth motif (A') in the first movement, is soon taken up by violins and horns in dialogue, then by a trumpet and trombone, while the weak beats continue to be heavily stressed (string pizzicato, then horns, then trumpets). The melodic distortion, and the oddness of the cross rhythms and the sonorities, make this Trio another high point of strangeness within Mahler's output.

In the reprise that follows, the various motifs alternate in the same order as before, but Mahler, as always, introduces innumerable changes (the plaintive motif, notably, reappears in E flat minor instead of D minor). The mobile triplet figures, fleeing like clouds across a stormy sky, again give rise to steadily growing anxiety. The waltz motif is savagely parodied by the trombones, and the lyrical theme of the Trio, now in the cellos, concludes the final intervention of this wild waltz. At the final reappearance of the 'void' of the opening bars, a quintuple fortissimo is marked for the cellos and basses (bar 401): like Bartók much later, in some of his quartets, Mahler asks for the strings to be plucked so violently that they hit against the wood of the instrument.[122]

---

[117] In Adorno's cosmogony, the idea of *Weltlauf* is the opposite of *Durchbruch* (see TAM 18, TAMe 9, etc.). [118] Ibid.

[119] Redlich observes that the big leaps in the waltz melody (B') served as Berg's model for the second of his Orchestral Pieces, Op. 6, *Reigen*.

[120] Redlich recognizes in this oboe duet (bars 179 ff.) the 'naivety' and 'harmonic poignancy' of the *Wunderhorn*, but this view is contradicted by the melodic and rhythmic distortions and by the sudden changes in tempo that maintain the eerie atmosphere of the Scherzo. Erwin Stein (*Orpheus in New Guises*, 12) is closer to the truth when speaking of the music's feverish 'haste', of its seeming to 'seek protection against an unknown danger', of its 'thrills of terror' which remind him of 'a child afraid of the dark'.

[121] Swarowsky observes that Mahler does not indicate a slowing down of the tempo for the Trio, but that it has to broaden to accommodate the rapid intrusions (*più mosso subito*). In his opinion, this slowing down is not marked because it seemed in those days obvious for the Trio of a Scherzo (op. cit., 147). The fact that Mahler writes *Wieder wie zu Angang* for the Scherzo's recapitulation suggests that the tempo of the Trio has not been the same.

[122] Dika Newlin observes that this marking heralds the tendency, frequent in Schoenberg, to ask players to surpass themselves or even to attempt the impossible. Just before this pizzicato, the woodwinds are required to play in a 'screaming' (*kreischend*) manner, prompting the following remarks by Adorno: 'The

The Scherzo ends with a reprise of the Trio, ever more richly orchestrated and ever more abandoned. The climax arrives (bar 417: *Wild*) when the trombone and the tuba play the last element from the Trio (T⁴) while the violins repeat the savage waltz from the Scherzo (B'): 'The Trio, only lightly sketched and interrupted, speaking with a voice almost more touching than anything else in Mahler, literally becomes the victims of symphonic development, brutally distorted as was once Berlioz's *idée fixe* of the beloved in the desolate Finale [of the *Symphonie fantastique*], only to recover its beauty in a consequent phrase of dignified composure (bar 428).'[123]

In the Coda the orchestral palette gradually thins and lightens as the themes break up. The end comes with cross-rhythms on the timpani and pizzicato chords in the violas. Pizzicatos, submediant-dominant, followed by a tenuto tonic in the basses appear to conclude, but, in a last thematic flicker, two brief fragments persist (bass clarinet, then bassoon), followed by a fermata in an ominous void. A single tonic note on the timpani followed by a pizzicato viola chord in the major puts an end to the spectral dance.

(d) Nachtmusik (Night Music)

Key: F major (with many modulations in the second edition).

Time signature: 2/4.

Rhythm: The 2/4 rhythm of Serenades.

Tempo: *Andante amoroso. Mit Aufschwung* (With impetus): *Graziosissimo* (bar 56); *Sehr fliessend* (Very flowing) (bar 142), etc.

Duration: 11 minutes (see above. William Ritter gives the same duration).

Mengelberg's programme: 'What a huge contrast between this movement and everything that has preceded it! It is a true serenade. A man sings beneath a window. It is dark, and this darkness has something disturbing in it. The song must not be too loud yet it must be heard! In playing this movement, care must be taken with the secondary voices and with all the sonorities. No sleeping dog must be woken! Nevertheless, the man proceeds, fully serious. He believes what he is singing. Truly in love, he forgets the circumstances and sings: "Come, come! Without you, I can't live!" '

Analysis: Dieter de la Motte has published a brilliant and detailed 'Tendenz-Analyse' of this extraordinary movement, fascinating if only because it has no parallel anywhere in Mahler's production, or in the orchestral repertoire.[124]

Orchestration: Its main characteristic is the extensive use of instruments with plucked strings: guitar, mandolin, and harp. The mandolin part was added by Mahler in pencil in the Amsterdam manuscript, and the guitar part consequently reduced drastically. As Peter Davison notes, the instruments of accompaniment assume 'an unaccustomed importance in the colouring of the movement, which contradicts their traditional functional role'.[125] This is one of the many original

forced tone itself becomes expressive. Tonality, the great category of musical mediation, had interposed itself as a conventional lubricant between the subjective intention and the aesthetic phenomenon. Mahler heats it up from within, from an expressive need, to the point that it again becomes incandescent, speaks, as if it were immediate. Exploding, it accomplishes what was later taken over by the emancipated dissonance of Expressionism.' (TAM 32; TAMe 20).

[123] TAM 140; TAMe 104.

[124] See de la Motte, *Musikalische Analyse* (Bärenreiter, Kassel, 1990), 107 ff.

[125] Davison, 'Nachtmusiken', 49.

traits of this most original of movements. The woodwind also plays an important role, mostly as soloists, as do the first and second horns (often stopped). Most of the scoring is of chamber-music lightness.

Form: ABACA.DE.ABACA. Hans Swarowsky's scheme, quoted below, cannot suggest any of the subtleties of the composition, nor any of its many formal ambiguities, complexities, asymmetries, disruptions, and the frequent unbalancing of the periodic structure thanks to elisions and overlaps:[126]

BARS		KEYS
1ST SECTION		
1–4	Refrain.	F major
4–7	Accompanying figures (re-used later as thematic elements).	
8–16	Theme A.	
17–22	A (varied repeat).	
23–5	Refrain (concluding).	
26–7	Accompaniment.	
28–34	Theme B.	
35–7	Refrain.	
38–51	A.	
51–3	Refrain.	
54–5	Accompaniment.	
56–75	Theme C: *Graziosissimo*.	
76–84	A (+ C).	
85–92	A (varied repeat) + C.	
93–8	Accompaniment (concluding).	
2ND SECTION (development, with new material).		
99–113	Theme D.	
114–25	A, developed.	
126–49	(A + C).	A flat major
150–7	(A + C).	F minor
158–65	(C).	A flat major
166–9	(A).	G flat major
170–5	Accompaniment (concluding form).	
176–86	Theme D.	
187–94	E¹ (or Trio).	B flat major
195–210	E².	B minor
211–27	E³.	G flat major
228–35	E¹.	F major
236–43	E³.	
244–51	E².	
252–8	Preparation for reprise.	
259-63	Refrain.	

---

[126] In the last pages of his article ('Idyll', *Colloque*, 48 ff.), Peter Revers gives several examples of these startling irregularities, and elsewhere speaks of the extreme 'contrast of the antecedent and consequent' phrases.

Bars   Keys

3RD SECTION (reprise)

264–72	A.
273–8	A (varied repeat).
279–81	Refrain.
282–3	Accompaniment.
284–91	B.
292–4	Refrain.
295–306	A (inversion).
307–10	Refrain (varied, fuller).
311–31	C (varied, crescendo).
332–40	A.
341–53	A (varied, inverted + C).
354–62	A (concluding form).

Although the concluding theme remains in the opening key and the development introduces new thematic elements, the structure remains closely akin to sonata form, even if the frequent recurrences of the refrain can also suggest rondo form. The movement is not entitled Serenade, but the presence of a guitar and a mandolin, the marking *Andante amoroso* (instead of the *Andante con moto* in the fair copy of the manuscript), and the chamber music orchestration show that Mahler is referring to the genre of the eighteenth-century 'nocturne' or 'Nachtmusik'.[127] None of the main features of the movement have been encountered in Mahler's works before. Bruno Walter speaks of a 'sweet and tender eroticism' but the preponderant impression is of delicate and subtle stylization, of a language and style that are 'distanced', alienated,

---

[127] Florio, hero of Eichendorff's *Das Marmorbild* (The Marble Statue), sings from the top of a hill a nocturnal poem:

> What Silence in the forest! Only the wandering moon
> Crosses through the high hall of the beech trees [. . .]
> Often the nightingales wake in soft accents
> As from a dream.
> Everywhere stirs in the trees
> The sweet thrill of memory.

(Eichendorff, *Das Marmorbild*.) Another poem, entitled Serenade (*Das Ständchen*) (and set to music by Hugo Wolf) must have been known to Mahler:

> Between pale clouds
> The moon peers on the rooftops;
> A student down in the street
> Sings before his sweetheart's door.
>
> And again the fountains are splashing
> Through the silent solitude,
> Again the trees rustle from the wooded mountains
> As in former, happier times.
>
> Just so in my young days
> (On many a summer night)
> I plucked my strings here
> And worked out many a joyful song.
> But from a silent threshold
> My love has been borne to her rest.
> And you, my gay friend,
> Sing on, sing ever on!

as it were, as in the first Nachtmusik, its aim being in no way to revive times past.[128] It is in this respect a brilliant anticipation of the neo-classical style that was then soon to appear everywhere in Europe. From the point of view of composition, form, and use of timbre, Mahler never wrote anything more subtle and refined, which explains why Schoenberg and his disciples particularly admired this movement.

Although the idyllic surface is always present as a reference, Peter Revers notes 'the extreme contrast between passages of light-hearted serenade-like character, and others which are inserted as irritating interjections'. He even suggests as an example the various interruptions of Beckmesser's Serenade in *Die Meistersinger*.[129] De la Motte[130] makes several important points in his analysis of the movement: what, in this deceptive music, sounds at first 'agreeable and clear' to an unprepared ear becomes in fact, 'mysterious and unclear for a more penetrating ear'; furthermore, 'what seems so transparent and disposed in good order proves opaque and closely interwoven'. He feels that 'the whole terminology on which the hearer bases his feeling of order, all the way down to the terminology of "melody" and "accompaniment", turns out to be questionable.'[131] The same author then proceeds to unravel the highly intricate mechanisms at play in each phrase and each bar, easily proving that no distinction can in fact be made between melody and accompaniment because identical melodic cells are used in both.

Never before was Mahler closer to the ideal he formulated in 1905 in the presence of Anton Webern, that of constructing a whole movement (if not a symphony) from one or several melodic cells.[132] De la Motte shows for instance that the opening 'Refrain' is in many ways a closing section, that passages seemingly introduced as reprises (for instance bars 38 ff.) are in fact 'consequences' of what precedes, and thus should be heard as 'development'; and calls 'the whole 390-bar movement a miracle of the art of the developing variation'.[133] After unravelling a great number of Mahler's clockwork mechanisms, he describes the intricate texture of this movement as the work of a 'Webern in 19th century clothing'.[134]

Several musical models have been suggested for the opening refrain, for instance Schumann's fourth *Nachtstück*, Op. 23,[135] and *Träumerei* from his *Kinderszenen*[136] but neither link seems very convincing. Hans Heinrich Eggebrecht suggests, as an inspiration for the chamber music group with solo violin of the refrain, the small groups of strings which play in Viennese cafes and restaurants.[137] Although Mahler's 'ironic naivety' has little in common with the emotional intensity of *Tristan*, Davison establishes a parallel between the opening measures of Wagner's opera, and the dissonant chord in bar 2 of Nachtmusik 2. But, more important still, he quotes *Siegfried Idyll*, another Serenade, as one of Mahler's models.[138]

---

[128] Redlich claims to find a certain 'humour' in the refrain. In his view, the whole movement suffers from 'a need to re-create the vanished world of mediaeval romanticism' and from 'involuntary resemblances to other compositions' (HFR 203).   [129] Revers, 'Idyll', in *Colloque 1985*, 46.

[130] See above.   [131] De la Motte, *Analyse*, 107.   [132] See above, Chap. 2.

[133] De la Motte, *Analyse*, 112.   [134] Ibid. 113.

[135] HFR 203. The resemblance is not convincing, although the key is F major and the arpeggio chords may suggest a guitar.   [136] DNM 187.

[137] Hans Heinrich Eggebrecht, *Die Musik Gustav Mahlers* (Piper, Munich, 1982), 50.

[138] Davison, 'Nachtmusik II: "Nothing but Love, Love, Love"?', See Zychowicz, *Symposium*, 89 ff. On p. 91, Davison compares the sectional analysis of each of the two works and draws striking parallels.

It is hard to detect in Nachtmusik 2 any trace of the 'anguish' mentioned by Mengelberg in his programme. The atmosphere is one, at least at first sight, of tenderness and childlike serenity.[139] The style escapes all definitions, although its distanced lyricism casts an immediate spell, if only because it is so inscrutable. The appearances of an 'Idyll' are preserved, but ambiguity reigns,[140] a lyricism which seems loath to take itself seriously,[141] and remains much of the time 'objective'. This is not a serenade, but 'a serenade about all serenades'.[142] Of course past times are evoked with old-fashioned figurations and 'quaint' sonorities such as plucked strings and wind ensembles, but the musical substance is at once so Mahlerian and so new, as unforeseeable in its entirety as in its detail, that it confuses and disconcerts the unprepared listener. The lost world which is the apparent object of yearning appears unreal, imaginary, almost like that of the marionettes in the Trio of the Sixth Symphony. There are indeed surges of melancholy and outbursts of genuine 'sentiment' (for instance in bar 156, but more obviously in bars 211 ff., 236–57, and 314–27), but they are invariably cut short by the return of 'reality' in the form of stylized figures, regular rhythms, and quaint sonorities. In the œuvre of a composer who is usually known for his extreme subjectivity, the second Nachtmusik is undoubtedly unique if only because of its impersonal, objective, tone.

The plucked string instruments, although they lack volume in the orchestral context, were for Mahler indispensable: Schoenberg points out that the guitar was 'not used just for effect', but that 'the entire movement is based on its sonority. It belongs to it from the start, a living organ in the piece: not perhaps the heart, but the eyes, their gaze giving the face its characteristic aspect. We are very close here, but in a modern context, to the classical composers who built whole works and movements on the sonority of a particular instrumental group.'[143] Mahler's guitar was to have glorious progeny in Schoenberg's *Serenade* Op. 24 (1923), Webern's *Pieces for Orchestra* Op. 10 (1913) and Stravinsky's last ballet, *Agon* (1957), and even Boulez's *Marteau sans Maître*.

After a few bars of introductory refrain,[144] the clarinet presents, over harp and guitar chords, the characteristic accompaniment (stylized birdsong, as Davison and other authors have called it), which will later become part of the theme itself (bars 13–14). The first subject (A) is next presented by the horn and the oboe. A varied form of the refrain (solo violin and woodwind) introduces the second element as a reply (B, violins: bars 28 ff.). The third refrain (solo cello, then solo violin, bars 35 ff.)

---

[139] To my mind, there is in this respect something in common between this movement and the opening Allegro of the Fourth, whose simplicity is just as deceptive.

[140] Jungheinrich compares it with the Adagietto of the Fifth Symphony, but the nature of the expression in that movement seems much more subjective ('Katastrophe', 194).

[141] Except perhaps for the brief episode beginning at bar 203.

[142] Davison, 'Nachtmusik II', in Zychowicz, *Symposium*, 93.

[143] Arnold Schoenberg, 'Stil und Gedanke', in *Gesammelte Schriften*, i. 18. Schoenberg had perhaps paid tribute to this Nachtmusik in his *Kammersymphonie* Op. 9, and in particular by quoting bars 9 and 10 of the Mahler (figure 38, 41 in the small score), ultimately with insistence (figure 43 ff.). Admittedly he could not have heard the Seventh played by an orchestra when he was writing his *Kammersymphonie*, but he might well have read the score that Mahler gave to Zemlinsky when he asked him to make a piano reduction, probably in 1905, or early in 1906.

[144] Jungheinrich suggests naming it, like the last of Schumann's *Kinderszenen*, 'Der Dichter spricht' (The poet speaks), or 'Once upon a time' ('Katastrophe', 194).

announces a repeat of A whose dactylic motifs give rise to imitations in the woodwind, and to a fourth refrain, this time very much varied. The concluding element (C), which is in fact a new variant of A, has the character of an Abgesang (*Graziosissimo*: bars 56 ff.).[145] It is supported by repeated notes on the guitar and accented syncopations in the violins and violas. Once again, the oboe (and later the flute) take up the main theme (combined with C for solo violin) and the episode ends with a codetta with a *melancolisch* beginning and an accelerated end, a *veloce* descending figure interrupted at the end of a bar. There follows a long moment of quiet expectation (bars 99 ff.) where only the principal dactylic motif (quaver-semiquavers) remains of the theme. Chains of fifths are heard low in the strings,[146] then rise slowly by semitones, as if the instruments were trying to tune. This is the beginning of the second, modulating, section which, as seen above, acts as a kind of development and introduces new elements. The main one (E^1) is stated (bars 187 ff.) by the horn and solo cello. It is of course related to the preceding themes but its final phrase, in B flat minor (bars 211 ff.), has a more subjective feeling that comes as a surprise in such an oddly 'objective' context. After a return of E^1 and a short climax, the Serenade resumes its quiet course (bars 259 ff.), with its refrain, and the whole of the opening section is freely restated.

A restatement of C leads to a first climax (bars 247 ff.) which is interrupted after a few bars by held chords, pianissimo, and a return of the refrain, somewhat lengthened and altered. Once again the Serenade resumes its course with dactylic rhythms and a new line in the violins. Guitar and mandolin play an important role in the next episode (bars 295 ff.) which gains power and momentum in a quicker tempo (bars 319 ff.) preparing for the main climax in the movement. Theme C rises chromatically to the heights (violins and flutes), with agitated rising arpeggios and descending 'sighs' (variants of the 'bird' motif which was incorporated in the melody at bar 319).[147] But the return of theme A and its dactylic rhythm in the basses restores the calm rhythm in the basses restores the calm (bar 328), even before the high violin trills have risen chromatically to a stratospheric C. The high C *pianissimo subito*, is at first held, then seven times repeated (*morendo. Staccatissimo*). This is the beginning of one of the greatest codas ever penned by the supreme master of coda-composition that Mahler always was. The musical fabric slowly breaks up, while dream birds twitter in the flutes' treble range, and the clarinets, *piano*, tenderly recalling their own bird motif accompaniment of A. The filigree of sound is at its most consummate in the final page, with repeated high Fs, staccatissimo and pianissimo, from the muted violins, the last scraps of the bird accompaniment motif in the bassoon, and a long trill in the clarinet's low register, during which everything fades and blurs in calm repeated chords, first in the low strings, then in guitar, horns, and bass clarinet. The clarinet trill eventually comes to rest on a final languid grupetto, *ersterbend*, a reminiscence, perhaps, of the one that concludes the Adagio of Schumann's Second Symphony, or is it perhaps a premonition of the last bar in Mahler's future Ninth?

[145] Donald Mitchell has observed that this motif (bars 56 to 59) is prefigured in the Finale of the Sixth Symphony (bars 581 to 597) and that the resemblance becomes even more striking in bars 236 to 251 of the same movement (DMM2, 42).

[146] Hans Swarowsky considers these open fifths as a motif, and names it D. Richard Specht describes them as 'the harp of the great nameless Minstrel' (RSM2, 301).

[147] Davison notes that these expressive climaxes strain 'the stylised gestures of the "serenade" form' ('Nachtmusiken', 56).

(e) Rondo-Finale

Key: C major (the first bars are in E minor and several of the verses reach distant keys).

Time signature: 4/4, 3/2, and 2/2 (bar 87, then bars 197 to 290); alla breve (bars 268 to 403), then 3/2 and 2/2 (bars 404 to 538); then finally 4/4 again (to the end).

Tempo: *Tempo I: Allegro ordinario; Maestoso* (bar 7); *Sempre l'istesso tempo* (bar 53); *Gemessen! Nicht Schnell!* (Measured! Not fast!) (bar 87; *Grazioso* (bar 100); *Immer noch Tempo II* (Immer 2/2, *aber Pesante*) (bar 120), etc. (see synopsis below).

Rhythm: Most of the movement is binary, except for the *Grazioso* 'interpolations', in 3/2, which explicitly evoke the rhythm of a rococo minuet.

Duration: 18 minutes (see above. William Ritter gives the same duration).

Mengelberg's programme: 'Fifth movement: No more shadows, no more spectres, no dead, only human beings living in the full light of day. They work, they travel, they struggle, they construct: their life is full in every respect. The central idea of this movement is: activity.'

Analysis: Two recent analyses, by Bernd Sponheuer's (49 pp.)[148] and Hans Swarowsky's,[149] differ in a number of significant ways which will be summarized below. These very differences are proof of the extreme complexity of the structure of this movement. In a substantial article, John Williamson has examined Mahler's harmonic procedures, and in particular the role of deceptive cadences in this Finale.[150] But the most illuminating analysis published of this movement is undoubtedly the most recent one, by Martin Scherzinger (20 pp., 1995).[151] It lists with telling detail and admirable clarity the reasons why this extraordinary movement has disconcerted even some of its most unprejudiced listeners. Instead of identifying with the letter 'I' the introductory motif, as I do above, Scherzinger includes it among the five different segments or themes included in the opening section, each associated with different instrumental groups:

No. 1 (bars 1–6): timpani,
No. 2 (chorale-like: bars 7–14): trumpet,
No. 3 (with *Meistersinger* quotation: bars 15–22): strings and brass,
No. 4 (bars 23–7): horns and strings,
No. 5 (in fanfare style, amalgam of motives from 1 & 2: bars 38–51): trumpets.

Scherzinger notes that each of these themes is longer than the preceding one and that they are increasingly derived from previous motifs, while cadences separating them become gradually more pronounced. Another important feature, he points out, is that 'some of the less important structural moments, such as the opening section, are marked with forceful cadences, while structurally weightier sections tend to peter out or are suddenly interrupted with blocks of new material. Functional cadential figures are thus continually brought into question,

---

[148] Bernd Sponheuer, *Logik des Zerfalls* (Schneider, Tutzing, 1978), 353.
[149] Ibid. 353 and 151. See above.
[150] John Williamson, 'Deceptive cadences in the last movement of Mahler's Seventh Symphony', *Soundings*, Cardiff, 9 (1982), 87 ff.
[151] 'The Finale of Mahler's Seventh Symphony: A Deconstructive Reading', *Musical Analysis*, Oxford, 14 (1995): 1, 69 ff.

their roles paradoxically reversed.'[152] This is undoubtedly one of the causes of the uneasiness or malaise engendered by this movement.

Here is Hans Swarowsky's summary of the overall scheme:

Refrain
Verse   } First section: bars 1 to 119
Variation

Refrain
Verse   } Second section: bars 120 to 267
Variation

Refrain
Verse   } Third section: bars 268 to 445
Variation

Variation
             } Fourth section: bars 446 to 590
Refrain

The apparent simplicity of the structure is deceptive. However, things become complicated as soon as one tries to sort out the motifs and note their variants and relationships. Hans Swarowsky suggests it might be tempting to regard the first section as an exposition, the second as a varied exposition, the third as a *Durchführung*, and the fourth as a recapitulation, followed by a coda. However, closer examination does not confirm this hypothesis, and Swarowsky chooses instead the notion of a vast perpetual *Durchführung*, ceaselessly producing new forms from beginning to end.[153] Here, slightly modified according to the usual practice in this book,[154] is Swarowsky's synoptic table:

Bars	Themes and Motifs	Tempos and Time signatures	Keys
REFRAIN 1 (or RITORNELLO 1)			
1–6	Introduction: I^1 (bars 1 and 3), I^2 (bars 2 and 4); I^3 (bars 5 and 6)	*Tempo Primo* (*Allegro ordinario*)	E minor

---

[152] *Musical Analysis*, 83.

[153] Sponheuer also suggests a sonata form, but an entirely different one (Exposition: bars 1 to 154; *Durchführung*: bars 155 to 268; Recapitulation: bars 269 to 305). In my view, this synopsis does not conform to the reality of the music because the A^5 Ritornello (bars 269–305) is the only one that has a developmental character. In Sponheuer's synopsis, it would be placed at the beginning of the recapitulation (op. cit., 379).

[154] As before, the main thematic elements of the refrain are referred to as A and A′, and the letter B is applied the second theme (or verse) designed to create an impression of contrast. The three thematic elements of the introduction will henceforth be named I^1, I^2, and I^3. The episodic themes (E^1 to E^5) appear from the second variation on, and are derived from each other. The main theme of the first movement, which returns in the coda, is named AA. Swarowsky's analysis also contains a table of musical phrases and his suggested metronome tempos.

Bars	Themes and Motifs	Tempos and Time signatures	Keys
7–14	Themes A: element A^1	*Maestoso*	C major
15–22	Theme A: element A^2 (strings and horn) and A^3 (woodwinds)		
23–37	Themes A′ comprising A$'^1$ (bars 23–6); A$'^2$ (bars 27–30); A$'^3$ (bars 31–4)		
38–52	Conclusion (I^1,I^2,I^3, A^2)		
VERSE 1 (or SECONDARY THEME 1)			
53–78	Theme B (3rd bar: I^2)	*Sempre l'istesso tempo* *Behaglich* (comfortable)	A flat major
REFRAIN: Variation I			
79–86	(A^2, A^3)		C major
87–99	A^1 Combinations 1 (A$'^1$, A$'^2$, A$'^3$, I^3)	*Gemessen.* *Nicht schnell* (measured. Not fast) 3/2 and 2/2	D major
100–5	E/Combinations 2 (E^1, A^1)	*Grazioso* 2/2	D major
106-19	A′/Combinations 3 (A$'^2$, A$'^3$, A$'^4$, I^1/I$'^3$)	*Nicht eilen. Pesante* (do not hurry)	
REFRAIN II			
120–7	A^1	2/2	C major
128–35	A^2		
136–42	A$'^1$, A^4, A$'^3$	*Gemessen*	
143–52	I^3, A	*Nicht eilen (aber immer 2/2)* (do not hurry, but still 2/2)	
VERSE II			
153–88	B	*Etwas zurückhaltend* (hold back a little)	A minor
REFRAIN: Variation II			
189–96	A^2, A^3 (as introduction)	4/4	C major
197–209	Combination 1a (A$'^1$, A$'^2$, A$'^3$, A$'^4$, I^1)	Tempo II. 3/2 and 2/2	
210–19	A′/Combination 1b (A$'^1$ + B)	*Nicht eilen.* *Recht gemessen.* (do not hurry, very measured) 2/2	
220–30	E/Combination 2a (E^1)	*Grazioso* 3/2	A major
231–40	E/Combination 2b (E^2, B, E^1/A^3)	*Recht gemessen* (Very measured) *Quasi Andante*	

(cont.):

Bars	Themes and Motifs	Tempos and Time signatures	Keys
241–8	E/Combination 2c (E^2, B, A'^1, E^1, A'^3)	*Grazioso.* *Wieder gehalten* (again held back)	D flat major
249–59	A': Combination 3a (A'^1, I^1, A'^2)	*Fliessend* (flowing) 2/2 and 3/2	A major
260–7	A'/Combination 3b (transition)	*Unmerklich drängend* (imperceptibly speeding up) 3/2	

REFRAIN III: development

Bars	Themes and Motifs	Tempos and Time signatures	Keys
268–77	A^1, E^3, A'^1 I^1	Tempo 1 (*Halbe wie die Viertel des Tempo 1*) (minims same as the crotchets of Tempo 1) 2/2, 3/2, 4/2	C major
278–90	A^2, A'^1, E^1, I^1	*Fliessender* (more flowing)	
291–306	A'/A^1, E^1, A'^1, A'^2, A'^3, A'^4, I^1, I^2	*Tempo Primo* 4/4	A major

VERSE III

Bars	Themes and Motifs	Tempos and Time signatures	Keys
307–31	B (with A^3, I^2, etc.)		G flat major
332–59	Id		

REFRAIN: Variation III

Bars	Themes and Motifs	Tempos and Time signatures	Keys
360–7	A^1	*Tempo I subito*	B flat major
368–89	A'/combination 1a (A', E^4, A'^2)	*Sempre l'istesso tempo*, (alla breve)	
390–401	A'/combination 1b (transition)	*Unmerklich drängend*	
402–10	E/combination 2a (E^1, E^4, A'^1)	*Poco più mosso*	
411–29	E/combination 2b (E^1, A^1, A'^3, A^1)	*Meno mosso.* *Tempo II*, then *etwas gemessener*, etc.	C major
430–8	A' combination 3a (E^1, A'^1, A'^2)	*Andante, sehr gem essen* (very measured) 3/2 and 2/2	
429–45	A' combination 3b (A'^1, A^4)	2/2	

REFRAIN: Variation IV

Bars	Themes and Motifs	Tempos and Time signatures	Keys
446–54	A^1	*Wieder wie vorher.* *Plötzlich* (Once again. As before. Suddenly) 4/4	D major
455–61	E/combination 1 (AA, E^5, $A'1$)	*Nicht schleppen* (Do not drag)	D minor

Bars	Themes and Motifs	Tempos and Time signatures	Keys
462–75	(E³, AA)	*Fliessend* (flowing)	C sharp minor
476–85	(AA, A'¹)	*Pesante*	C minor
486–91	A'/combination 2 (A'¹, E⁵, AA, A'²)	*Flott* (lively) 3/2	B major
492–505	(E⁵, AA, A'¹)	2/2	B flat major
506–16	E/combination 3a (E¹, AA)	*Feierlich* (solemn)	D flat major
517–38	E/combination 3b (E⁶, A'¹, B, I¹)	*Plötzlich wieder a tempo II* (suddenly a tempo II) 3/2	C major
REFRAIN IV			
539–45	A (and I¹, I², A¹)	*Tempo primo*, 4/4	
546–53	A², A³		
554–7	A'¹	*Pesante*	
558–65	A¹		
566–80	Combination (concluding) (I¹, A'³, A¹)		
581–90	Combination (AA, A³, I¹)	*A tempo*, then *Drängend* (driving)	C major

The chief difference between this synopsis and that of Sponheuer lies in the 'episodic' themes. Sponheuer calls B '*Episodenthema* 1' and E '*Episodenthema* 2'. I have chosen Swarowsky's designation because E is not a true theme, but a motif varied five times and always superimposed on another. Because Sponheuer does not acknowledge some of the refrains as variations, he counts eight Ritornellos, three B episodes, and two C episodes (E by Swarowsky's system). Scherzinger lists an opening statement and seven Ritornellos, and only one development passage (bars 269–90). Sponheuer's analysis is less clear in characterizing episodes, motifs, and their combinations, as well as the element of variation fundamental to this Rondo.

The above synopsis reveals the staggering complexity of this movement. Arnold Forchert[155] notes that the refrains are varied every time they appear, that the three verses are thematically related not only to each other, but also to the refrains, and that in the first three the differences prevail, while the fourth sums up the content of the previous three and the last reverts to the form of the first.[156] Whatever the movement's formal complexity, he sees it as an alternation of two principal elements, one *festlich* in the manner of *Die Meistersinger*, with brass predominating, and the other characterized mainly by woodwind and strings. The contrasts in colour thus obtained seem to him deliberately archaic, recalling the concertino and ripieno of early

---

[155] 'Zur Auflösung traditioneller Formkategorien in der Musik um 1900', in *Archiv für den Musikwissenschaft*, 32 (1975): 2, 85 ff.

[156] Forchert, like Sponheuer, clearly regards bars 210 to 268 and bars 400 to 445 as verses (as well as the three listed in the table above).

Italian music. Given the extreme variability of the tempo,[157] the metre, and even the keys, and given the relationships existing from the outset between certain motifs[158] and the variants that ceaselessly arise, the task of the analyst here is exceptionally difficult.

'Was kostet die Welt!' (Everything has its price!) is the way Mahler himself characterized the insolent humour of this movement, full of capricious reversals, feline smiles, feigned innocence, and contrapuntal artifice. As in the Ländler of the Ninth Symphony, two principal tempos alternate: an Allegro in 4/4 time and a more measured 3/2 (sometimes 2/2) that becomes a parody of a minuet and that continually interrupts the initial merriment. The first motif (I^1) stated by the timpani, is taken up by the brass. Its second bar (I^2) is simply the double reiteration of a melodic third. It will reappear very frequently later on, like the Introduction's opening key of E minor,[159] which is a third above C major. Trumpets and horns share the task of stating the principal theme (A) whose second element (A^2: strings and horn), superimposed upon a brilliant figure in the woodwind (A^3), insolently quotes the rising scale motif (with contrary motion in the basses) of the Prelude to *Die Meistersinger* (bars 3 and 4).

The diatonic broken-scale motif that follows (A'^1, violins and horns: bar 23, Pesante) has been fiercely criticized by several commentators[160] as being a reminiscence of the 'Weiber Chanson' from Lehar's *Merry Widow*. It henceforward furnishes material for most of the verses. It is followed by a second (A'^2: bars 27 and 28), then a third (derived from the first: bars 31 and 32), characterized mainly by its two minims, later restated many times. The short concluding element (A'^4: bars 35 ff.) is finally superimposed on one of the former ones (A^2) in the bass. The refrain concludes in the most striking manner possible, with a codetta that weaves a garland of whirling semiquavers around the preceding motifs (I^1, I^3, A'^1, A'^3). Without modulating, but by a simple juxtaposition of keys with the note C, common to both tonic chords and used as a pivot, Mahler moves into A flat major for the first verse (or B section), in a neorococo, pastoral style, with ceremonious curtseys and bagpipe effects.[161] All the future B sections are to share its relaxed character. Less polyphonic and dense than the others, they provide a deliberate contrast.[162] A much curtailed return of theme A

---

[157]   Since it is impossible to reproduce all the markings in the table above, only the main ones are given.

[158] A'^1, in particular, is simply a rhythmic variant of I^3.

[159]   Some writers have seen this as an allusion to the first movement.

[160]   However their chronology is faulty, for Mahler completed his Seventh Symphony at the end of the summer of 1905, and *The Merry Widow* was first performed in December of the same year, and only became a success after several weeks' run. Redlich (HFR 204) finds this B theme 'dangerously close to the Waltz from *The Merry Widow*'. Ruzicka speaks only of 'effects borrowed from the domain of operetta' (*Herausforderung*, 111) while Sponheuer (*Zerfall*, 368) claims that theme A^1 'strikingly' resembles the waltz in question. When asked by me to identify the 'Waltz', Sponheuer acknowledged that only the 'Weiber Chanson' in the operetta's second act could be compared with one of Mahler's motifs. Alexander Ringer ('Ende Gut', 307) mentions in the same context the Aria *Schlösser die im Monde liegen* from the 'enormously successful' operetta *Frau Luna* by Paul Lincke, dating from 1899. The similarity between A'^1 and I^3 is obvious. In the dotted form (A'^1 and A'^3), it plays a vital role later. Considering the importance of this 'anachronistic' par excellence, 'neo-classical' motif, it should be pointed out that it was already present in the Waltz episode of the Scherzo (bar 55).

[161]   Redlich notes a strong 'Slavonic flavour' in theme B (Introduction to Eulenburg pocket score, p. viii). Scherzinger finds a close relationship between this chord of the flattened submediant (A flat) with the tonic chord with augmented fifth (G sharp) in the penultimate bar (bar 589). In his view, this is 'a true deceptive cadence which, paradoxically, brings the movement to a close'.

[162]   The second bar of theme B (oboe) is identical to the motif in thirds in bar 2 of the Introduction (I^2).

(horns and trumpets) with its 'furious' passage (this time in the strings) merges into the first 'Variation' (or development) of the refrain, of which I shall note only the principal features. The most striking of these is the *Grazioso* episode (bar 100) where A′ (varied rhythmically in the manner of I^3) is superimposed on an 'archaic' minuet motif (E^1) with trills and mordents, again inspired by rococo music. The return of the refrain that follows (bar 119) leads to a development, based on the various elements of A, but also containing the 'curtseys' from B (bar 154). Dotted rhythms predominate, and the texture becomes so rich that a practised ear is needed to follow all the voices.

The refrain that follows (bar 189) makes its appearance in the distant key of D flat, but returns to the opening key after two bars. The second development (Variation II) is more complex than the previous one, still combining elements from A and B, but involving the new theme E^1. This soon assumes a new form (E^2) without losing its minuet rhythm. D major has been succeeded by A (bar 220) and then by D flat (the key in which the refrain began: bar 241). Once again in A major, the strings in unison play about with the broken-scale motif (I^3 or A'^1: bar 249), supported by the principal element of the opening rhythm (I^1), and the episode ends in a flurry of scales and arpeggios turning in upon themselves (with the melodic thirds of I^2 in the horns). It is interrupted by a furious descending scale, itself cut short by the third refrain (bar 268). This is immediately deflected from its course by the insistent rhythm (I^1) and by another episodic theme (E^3: horns). The polyphonic and motivic work becomes denser as the excitement increases. The tension subsides with the return of verse B (in G flat major: bar 307), combined with theme A^3 (strings and winds). The insistent 'curtseying' of B; the *Flatterzunge* on the flutes; and the trills, more numerous and obtrusive than ever, heighten the anachronistic, neo-classical effect. Respecting the original key relationship,[163] the refrain reappears in B flat and introduces the third development, in variation form, leading directly to the last one, as shown on the synopsis above. The unison string passage (A'^1/I^3, combined with I^2), is gradually invaded by the rhythm of I^1 (horns: bar 376) and underscored by the bass drum and cymbals, in a near-quotation of the 'janissary music' in Mozart's *Entführung*. Soon, a new version of E (E^4, on the strings: bar 382) leads once more to another flurry of scales and arpeggios, which is cut short once again by a furious, triple forte descending scale, and a reprise of the minuet (in its E^4 form, followed by E^1) ever more satirical, this time in the trumpets. It is again cheerfully developed, pianissimo, with trills and portamenti. But the end is now near, announced by the trumpet which stubbornly superimposes the main fragment of the opening Rondo theme over that of the minuet.

The final string unison passage (A'^1/I^3), pianissimo (Andante, bar 434), sums up all the main fragments of A, whose *Meistersinger* (see bar 21) motif is taken up again by the brass. The beginning of the fourth refrain (bar 446: D major) leads to the most modulatory episode in the whole of the movement (D, C sharp minor, C minor, B major, B flat major, D flat). Now the reappearance of the main theme of the opening Allegro, played on four horns, has been well prepared and appears logical.[164] It is superimposed on E^5

---

[163] It will be recalled that he return of the refrain in C major followed the exposition of the first verse, in A flat major.

[164] Few commentators have found this return of AA genuinely triumphant or climactic. Davison calls it 'a witty attack on the confidence of Wagner's aesthetic idealism' and 'an ironic commentary upon its naivety' ('Nachtmusiken', 77). For Scherzinger ('Finale', 80), 'the references to the first theme of the first movement . . . have the function of breaking the cycle of internal references and bringing the movement to a close'; for

and I^3.[165] After descending all the keys of the chromatic scale, the development is suddenly interrupted by the most startling break of all: the return of the minuet episode pianissimo (on strings) made even more startling by a jump to D flat from C. This is the most unexpected event in the whole movement because the previous massive tutti had insistently declaimed the opening theme (in the trumpets), and seemingly announced the final apotheosis. Instead, the broken scales, portamenti and trills of the minuet episode appear more anachronistic than ever (bars 517 ff.). However this is only a short insertion, which holds back the conclusion only by a few bars. A new descending scale (in D flat) leads abruptly to the refrain in its initial form (C major, woodwind alone, with the timpani). After the first bars of A′, the reprise takes a sharp turn. The rising fourths from the beginning of A are several times taken up by the basses, first in quavers, then in crotchets, and finally in semibreves, while theme A keeps returning in the brass and woodwind. Finally, the opening theme of the Symphony (AA) prevails (horns, woodwind, and low strings), with the motif I^3. The whirl of the final bars (motif A^3, decorated with twisting semiquavers) is cut short by a tonic chord with augmented fifth, immediately followed by the perfect triad.

In this endlessly fascinating and often disconcerting Rondo, this is music about music which celebrates the impossibility of any real victory or of any return to the innocence humanity yearns for rather than a definitive victory over the forces of night.[166] Some of the disappointment of modern commentators might be ascribed to the excessive, almost comic enthusiasm of Mahler's first advocates. In 1913, Richard Specht wrote: 'But all of this opens into immensity, spreads its wings, when the timpani break forth in turbulent merriment and a glad, sunlit, light-hearted joy speaks out of every note of this blustering C major; the jubilant sound of market day, the high spirits of the *Meistersinger*—although not so much Nuremberg folk as good Austrian *Meistersinger* who suddenly let fly for all they're worth at the book of rules.'[167]

'Night is over, day is dawning', Paul Bekker added a few years later. 'With timpani, fanfares and bells in a radiant C major. No more twilight, no more struggling out of the dark, no more intimations of dawn-worship, as in the first movement. Victorious consciousness, free of doubt, a blessed surrender to brightness. . . . Mahler here attains the pinnacle of life-affirming confession. . . . The tragedy of our battle with fate, of the contradiction between world and individual, is overcome through the knowledge of the unity of One with All.'[168] At a time when our knowledge of Mahler has progressed so far, and when we have learned to admire him otherwise and for other reasons, it is no longer possible to regard this Finale simply as a new 'Hymn to Joy'. This would be to miss Mahler's irony and ambiguity which strongly colours many pages of his music.

Nevertheless, the negative attitude of the post-Second World War generation towards

---

'by this point there have been such an abundance of derived motives and thematic references that their origins and significances have become obscure'.

[165] Redlich likens the final form of E (E^5) of bars 454 ff. to the chorus of 'blessed youths' in the Eighth (second movement, bars 402 ff.).

[166] See above, Vol. i, Appendix 2, on the Fifth Symphony, Adorno's remarks about the Rondo Finale of the Fifth, which are also relevant to that of the Seventh.

[167] RSM2, 303.

[168] BMS 260 and 265. Paul Bekker considered also that the course begun in the Funeral March of the Fifth reached its optimistic conclusion in this Rondo-Finale and that Mahler had arrived at 'a new awareness' with 'such elemental force that it can barely be perceived by the physical ear'.

this movement seems to me no less excessive. For Hans Ferdinand Redlich, Mahler 'stuck too stubbornly to a rigorous symphonic scheme'[169] and used in this Rondo 'the least distinguished [thematic material] ever to emerge from his pen'.[170] As for Adorno, he speaks of 'that ominously positive element that . . . ruins the Finale':[171] 'One will scarcely be able to deny an impotent disproportion between the splendid exterior and the meagre content of the whole. Technically the fault lies with the steadfast use of diatonicism, the monotony of which was scarcely to be prevented, in view of such ample dimensions. The movement is theatrical: only the stage-sky over the too-adjacent fairground meadow is as blue as this. The positivity of the *per aspera ad astra* movement in the Fifth, which surpasses even this Finale, can manifest itself only as a *tableau*, a scene of motley bustle; perhaps the Finale of Schubert's great C major Symphony, the last abundant work of symphonic positivity to be written, already tends secretly towards operatic performance. The limpid soaring of the solo violin in the first measure of the fourth movement of Mahler's Seventh, solace that follows like a rhyme the mourning of the tenebrous Scherzo, commands more belief than all the pomp of the Finale. Mahler in one place gently mocks it with the epithet *etwas prachtvoll* (rather pompously), yet without the humour breaking through. The claim that the goal has been reached, the fear of aberrations *après fortune faite*, are answered depressingly by endless repetitions, particularly of the minuet-like theme. The tone of strained gaiety no more actualises joy than the word *gaudeamus*; the thematic fulfilments announced too eagerly by the gestures of fulfilling do not materialise.'[172]

In the same year, 1960, Deryck Cooke spoke of a 'grandiose but unconvincing conclusion' and was sorry to have to say that 'Mahler had for once written the thing he most detested—*Kapellmeistermusik*'.[173] Donald Mitchell (1963) found that the Rondo's 'unusually long stretches of purely diatonic invention' rendered the work weak and enigmatic.[174] Marc Vignal wrote of 'complete compositional failure'.[175] Karl Schumann (1972) saw in this Rondo 'a gigantic caricature of the pomposo style at the turn of the century, a bizarre summary of orchestral effects, rather in the manner of the American Charles Ives'.[176] In short, this Rondo Finale has had very few supporters since the Second World War, that is to say, since Mahler began to acquire the reputation he deserved. Admittedly Schoenberg, in his celebrated correspondence with the New York critic Olin Downes, quoted the theme of the first verse, in A flat, as evidence of the 'creative force' of a melody.[177] Erwin Ratz (1960) spoke of the 'vital gaiety' of this 'rousing' Finale and regarded the Seventh as 'the most positive' of the three instrumental symphonies. Such radiant C major music, he thought, could only have been

---

[169] Redlich recalls Alma's description of Mahler cruelly 'tortured by doubts' before the première of the Seventh, in Prague, but, as seen below, her statement does not correspond to the truth (see below, Vol. iiii, Chap. 2). [170] Introduction to Eulenburg pocket score, p. viii.

[171] TAM 137; TAMe 101.

[172] TAM 180; TAMe 137. The passage following this one in the text has already been quoted above (see Vol. ii, Appendix on the Fifth).

[173] Deryck Cooke (1960), *Gustav Mahler, An Introduction to his Music* (Faber, London, 1980), 91.

[174] See 'Mahler's enigmatic Seventh', in *The Listener*, 69 (1963), 649.

[175] Marc Vignal, *Mahler* (Le Seuil, Paris, 1966), 125 ff.

[176] Karl Schumann, *Das kleine Mahler Buch* (Residenz, Saltzburg, 1972), 83.

[177] Bars 56 to 61. See Arnold Schoenberg, *Briefe*, ed. Erwin Stein (Schott, Mainz, 1958), 274 (and Faber, London, 1964), 262. Schoenberg recalls here that Webern continually played and sang this melody, as well as the one from the beginning of the Serenade (bars 5 to 17 and bars 56 to 66).

conceived before the 1914–18 war, but he takes his analysis of Mahler's most contro-versial movement no further. One of the few modern advocates of this movement as a hymn of triumph, Constantin Floros, has suggested a possible literary key, a chapter in *Also sprach Zarathustra* entitled 'Seven Seals', in which Nietzsche evokes the concept of the 'eternal return' in the form of a rondo. He quotes the loud ringing (*starkes Glockengeläute*) of the bells in bars 360 to 367 in a chorale-like passage as possible evidence for such a Nietzschean reference. In the interview which Mahler had in 1906 with Bernard Scharlitt (already quoted several times above), he spoke of *Zarathustra* as a work 'symphonically conceived', and this shows that the poet-philosopher's work had lost none of its appeal for him.

The first writers to listen differently to the Finale belong to the post-war 'metacritical', generation.[178] In a Mahler anthology which appeared in 1977, Hans-Klaus Jungheinrich and Peter Ruzicka (born in 1948) each published articles on the subject of the Seventh and its Finale. Jungheinrich acknowledges that, at first sight, the Finale gives the impression of regressing, of returning to 'a long discredited brandishing of tonal strength' and to the use of 'exhausted' musical material that has become 'historically false'. But for him, the discovery of 'triviality' by Pop Art casts a new light on it.[179] The very term 'Allegro ordinario' shows that Mahler was aware of 'composing on more than one level' so that, in this context, C major sounds like 'a quotation, a compositional procedure implying a criticism of itself'. C major is not a 'victory', but 'the stigma of the deep ques-tionable nature of the symphonic conception'. Thus 'the jubilant C major passages of the Finale of the Seventh, saturated in timpani', put an end to 'the subjective expressive power of the individual more insistently and definitely' than the destructive hammer blows of the Sixth. Beyond the moments of explicit parody and deliberate 'banality', these C major crescendos are 'a slap in the face to "serious" symphonic construction', an announcement of 'the end of the symphonic', a proof that 'what was cannot now be as it was. . . . Even the nature sounds from previous symphonies seem in this Finale to be similarly dragged in, stripped of their power by bald triviality: the apotheosis of self-destruction. Mahler says No to symphonic development and to tonality; in this definitive rejection lies, however, a hope for musical meaning. What Mahler wrote after the Seventh could scarcely be any more radical.'[180]

Peter Ruzicka acknowledges that the refrain affirms an 'attitude consciously turned towards the positive' but sees in the choice of key a 'gestural "allusion" shaking its own credibility to the roots', just like the marking *Allegro ordinario*.[181] In Ruzicka's opinion, Mahler knew perfectly well that it was no longer possible to affirm anything at all in C major. Strauss's C major (in the *Domestica* and *Zarathustra*) had been inspired by an 'unfortunate exhibitionism' whereas Mahler's C major expresses 'a considered doubt, a self-jeopardy, above all a jeopardy in future symphonic concep-tion'. This music 'denies itself'. There is no page of the Finale that does not contain a demonstrable 'allusion', an 'objet trouvé' and the brutal A flat chord following the 'utter cliché' of the first refrain's conclusion shows straightaway that 'what went before' was 'mere outword show'. The string episodes, the reminiscences of serenades, mili-tary music, distorted chorales, gypsy music: all this prefigures the playing with styles

---

[178] See above the distinction drawn by Sponheuer between the 'critical' and 'metacritical' generations of critics.   [179] Jungheinrich, 'Katastrophe', 190.   [180] Ibid. 198.
[181] Ruzicka, *Herausforderung*, 109 ff.

that followed the 1914 war, so that this Finale is really 'the most experimental, and the most compositionally advanced, that Mahler ever wrote'.[182] Ruzicka suggests that the Finale as a whole is perhaps nothing but a 'parody of the established order, a documentary summation of and confrontation with unreflective positiveness, a kind of inventory of the musical environment that was in the process of falling apart.[183] . . . But the critical element in this music, its sting, results from the superabundance of ever-changing points of view, and from the seeming lack of credibility, occasioned by the stringing together of brief exposures that each time present themselves as alien.' Ruzicka goes so far as to compare these procedures with 'pop art collages', and considers that the return of the work's opening theme in the final bars in no way produces a sense of apotheosis, but rather one of 'compressed' (*gepresst*), 'alienated', 'unreal' (*verfremdet*) and disordered accumulation. Thus, concludes Ruzicka, 'we should speak rather of an apotheosis of self-destruction'. 'Mahler's pioneering role in music history, as in the history of perception, is that he suddenly ripped apart and brought to light the antagonisms of a time of fragmentation, of questioning and of deep-seated doubt, lying silted up in the musical materials available. Even if, in doing so, he was motivated by a subjective intention of reconciling things that, historically, could no longer be reconciled, what he actually did can be seen objectively as an attack upon the previously strong taboo concerning aesthetic unity.'[184] Thus, Ruzicka sees Mahler as a precursor of the music of today, where everything is 'suspended and brought into question'.[185]

In his thesis, dated 1985, Peter Davison sees the Seventh Symphony as a 'series of unresolved dualisms, which operate on many levels'. For him, 'the narrative and architectural concepts of form and the work's non-realisation of its immanent implications are a calculated ambiguity which reflect the artist's attempt to find a coherent interpretation of his subjective experience. Mahler does not begin to synthesize in the traditional symphonic way; that is a fallacious ambition. Here is an enigmatic, self-confessed failure, a work which sets out to be incomplete, unsettling. This can be diagnosed as a genuine aesthetic failure, or even overlooked for pragmatic reasons, which explains the Seventh's problematic reception. . . . But by the standards of human aesthetics, the work ends in disarray, because the incompatible mood and tonal range of the work are assembled in close proximity.'[186]

It is obvious that nowhere else in Mahler are 'breaks' in the natural flow of the music, or contrasts of sonority and dynamics so brutal and paradoxical, changes in tone more sudden, sonorities more crude, or 'vulgarities' more apparent. One of the leading post-war composers, Mauricio Kagel, has defended this Finale with equal warmth. Beyond the problems of the form he finds in it music 'of extraordinary beauty' and 'an astonishing pursuit of variation in its most rebarbative aspect, comparable with bovine rumination'. For him, Mahler, with his 'false proportions' and his instinctive desire to 'develop those things which had, until then, been left aside', succeeds in expressing 'something entirely new'. Mahler remains 'profoundly touching' where his

---

[182] Ibid. 112. Ruzicka gives a music example here, the brutal transition from the first refrain to the first verse, in A flat.   [183] Ibid. 112 ff.   [184] Ruzicka, *Herausforderung*, 113.

[185] Here Ruzicka quotes an example of 'destruction' and 'allusion' comparable to those of Mahler's Rondo-Finale. It is taken from one of his own works, *In processo di tempi* (1971).

[186] Davison, 'Nachtmusiken', 80.

communication is indirect, where he shows 'how to proceed in order to achieve emotion' with the precision of a scientist, or where he winds up 'communicating by purely acoustic means'.[187] Pierre Boulez, who has conducted many performances of this symphony and has also recorded it, also holds the Finale in high regard. For him, the two outer movements of the Symphony have far more weight than the middle movements which, despite their value as compositions, remain 'genre pieces'. The essential problem of this last movement, Boulez believes, remains that of interpretation, where a great many moments of parodic, and obviously heterogeneous nature, have to be blended.[188]

In his book which examines all Mahler's symphonic Finales, Bernd Sponheuer restates Adorno's much publicized condemnation of the Rondo-Finale of the Seventh. He distinguishes the 'orthodox' approach (Specht, Bekker, etc.) from the 'critical' (Adorno, Redlich, etc.) and the 'metacritical' (Ruzicka). Typical of Ruzicka's attitude, for Sponheuer, is his statement that the Rondo's gaiety is simply a 'critical montage of various forms of false musical perception'.[189] At this stage Sponheuer reserves judgement, which in his view can only be based on the results of a careful study of the movement. This takes the shape of a thirty-six page analysis whose outlines I have summarized earlier, after which Sponheuer begins by criticizing the form of the Finale as 'theatrical' and 'synthetic'. He goes on to express the view that the notion of parodic intentions, of 'persiflage', 'cannot be taken seriously'. Mahler was clearly seeking to 'infuse life into the old idea of the symphonic Finale' and into 'the commonplace of the joyous Rondo-Finale' at a time when both forms were in obvious contradiction to the historical situation. The joyous Rondo had, so to speak, disappeared since Beethoven, from symphonic music in any case, and had only survived in salon music in the form of the *Rondo brillant*, while being replaced by symphonic Finales of serious character. 'Like all restorations,' Sponheuer continues, 'this one founders on the irreconcilable contradiction in its own genesis. This can be seen in the disproportion of the compositional workmanship itself, which despite being tightly bound to the conception and basic formal structure of the old Finale seems no longer able to bring to it any substantial strength, or to deny the subsequently developed possibilities of modern symphonic technique. On the contrary, it takes refuge precisely in these: in pompous overblown musical gesturing that cannot hide its hereditary link to *Die Meistersinger*, in the rhetorical eloquence of advanced procedures in orchestration, in the abundant spread of images and musical idioms, incorporating historical quotations and reminiscences from the realm of folk music, in the calculated brilliance of surprise musical effects, and finally in the superficial attempt at a cyclic raising of the stakes, the use, in other words, of a new Finale convention arising from completely different premises and whose intensifying effect can plainly not be done without. The traditional joyous Rondo-Finale cannot withstand the forced intrusion of modern techniques intended specifically to guarantee a festive cheerfulness: we wind up with a dramaturgically induced, operatically glittering final tableau, a magical-musical illusion of a happy world vanished as surely as the old Finale itself, or rather having just as little reality, by this time, as the cloudless blue of the stage sky suspended over

---

187 Communication to the author (Sept. 1983).
188 Communication to the author (Oct. 1983). 189 Sponheuer, *Zerfall*, 362.

it.'[190] Sponheuer's view is surely correct in one respect: whether or not one considers this Finale successful as a piece of music or a symphonic Finale, no one can pretend that it solves the immanent tensions of the work, as Mahler's other symphonic Finales do. Since the Seventh is the most objective, disillusioned, lucid, critical work by Mahler, it was to be expected that its most assertive movement would also be the most ambiguous of all. Mahler admitted having set about to celebrate the triumph of the 'full light of day' over darkness. Yet daylight, as a symbol, can have at least two different and almost opposite meanings: either healthy *joie de vivre*, activity, or what Mahler himself named the 'Lebenstrudel', the bustle, the confusion, the empty excitement of daily life on earth, or in Adorno's words, the 'Weltlauf'.

Few people today would deny that this Finale belongs to the same family as the ironic Scherzo of the Second Symphony, the droll Scherzo of the Third, a family whose later members were to be the Scherzo and Rondo-Burleske of the Ninth. To the 'vulgar' or 'folk' episodes so evident in the first movement of the Third, it adds two new elements, the 'anachronistic' (the minuets) and the 'learned' (the polyphonic sections prolonging those of the Rondo-Finale of the Fifth). The 'joyous', 'boisterous' tutti of this new symphonic 'Humoreske' appear particularly ironic when one recalls Mahler's own ambiguous relationship with the 'people'. His deep love for mankind, his strong feelings of compassion for any form of human suffering often gave way to a no less strong aversion to the noisy rejoicing of the revellers in Maiernigg,[191] the soldiers of the Landro barracks in Schluderbach,[192] or the members of the Trenker family in his summer home in Toblach.[193]

No other movement by Mahler has aroused such controversy, which reflects the internal 'dissonances' of this Finale. Its Rabelaisian verve will continue, long into the future, to surprise, shock, and disconcert some and fascinate others, because Mahler flouts all rules, all limits, all habits and all traditions, particularly those he seems to want to revive. For in this formidable kaleidoscope of sounds, motifs, nuances, musical situations, musical styles, heaven turns to hell, day to night, joy to pain, laughter to a grimace, incense to sulphur, the Te Deum to carnival music, gold to lead. But the fascination of this music lies in its very excesses and paradoxes.

Mahler had undoubtedly set out to compose a paean of praise, to celebrate the triumph of light and day over darkness and chaos.[194] But it is equally obvious that the parodic elements introduce an element of derision and of caricature. Adorno, who refuses to take any of Mahler's affirmations—and particularly the Eighth—seriously, considers it even part of his greatness[195] that Mahler should have been so ubiquitously ambiguous, above all in his moments of optimism. However, Sponheuer's emphasis on the affirmative function of this Finale seems more surprising in view of his thorough knowledge of Adorno's writings on Mahler, for Mahler was, despite his literary and philosophical leanings, above all a musician. The primary aim of this Finale was after

---

[190] Ibid. 400.

[191] See BGA, no. 91 (3 July 1904).

[192] BGA, no. 141, undated (22 June 1905).

[193] BGA, no. 282 (27 June 1908); no. 318 (7 July 1910); no. 321 (7 July 1910).

[194] 'It is my best work,' Mahler wrote to Emil Gutmann at the beginning of 1908 of the Seventh, 'and of preponderantly cheerful character' (MBR1, no. 343; MBR2, no. 387. See below, Vol. iiii, Chap. 2).

[195] See above, Vol. ii, the section of Appendix 2 concerning the Fifth, and in this volume the section concerning the Eighth Symphony.

all to end the Symphony with a virtuoso piece made all the more indispensable by long lyrical episodes in the first movement and the two Nachtmusiken.[196]

The most interesting remarks about the Rondo-Finale are undoubtedly those made by Martin Scherzinger. They deserve to be summarized here because they reveal more clearly than ever before the reasons why this movement has disappointed and bewildered so many commentators. James Zychowicz was one of the first, in 1989, to suggest that: 'If the Finale does not fit some of the analytical models with which it is compared, it may be that the method of analysis rather than the music is at fault.'[197] In the course of his analysis, Scherzinger lists some of the Rondo's most provocative features, particularly 'the deeply ambiguous way in which its diatonicism is harnessed in the service of discontinuity and is made rather to challenge than to support tradition'. The 'ambiguities of the Rondo-Finale can never be finally pinned down', he adds. 'They indicate those moments when the syntax of the music falters, gestures beyond itself or simply disintegrates, suggesting an inexhaustible context of meaning.'[198] Scherzinger points out that 'the lack of a clearly identifiable development section (customary in a movement of this size), together with the persistent cadencing (though not even the cadences necessarily coincide with structural points of the movement),[199] serve to undermine rather than underscore the overall logic of the Finale. . . . The form has been robbed of much of its developmental function. The overall structure is more sequential than developmental in character. Nonetheless, the conventional (even archaic) triadic fanfare-melodies of the ritornello, as well as the persistent formality and conventionality of the cadencing, suggest that a backward (historical) glance is implied and that the music is relating itself in some way to a different era. . . . But it does so in a highly modern way. By exposing the shell of a form, but denying it the developmental function that is customarily associated with it, the composer creates a new tension. . . . The Finale challenges tradition precisely by making its own grinding logic—the denial of its ordinary functions—progressively more audible.'[200]

One of Scherzinger's remarks applies to the Finale as well as to the Second Nachtmusik,[201] that 'the same material returns with a different role . . . throughout the movement'.[202] He also underlines the 'harmonic implications which fail to be fulfilled',[203] the many overlaps between the different sections,[204] the proportions between sections that are 'out of kilter', the unmotivated eruptions, the duplicitous manner in which 'the roles of the various sections are reversed and transformed'.[205] Scherzinger's conclusion must be quoted in full because it summarizes his original view of this most disconcerting movement: 'The ambiguous interplay between sections is replicated on several levels: between metrically stable and metrically unstable passages, between functional and non-functional harmonic progressions, between

---

[196] It is likely that the Rondo-Burleske of the Ninth was initially intended to have the same function in the structure of the symphony.

[197] Zychowicz, 'Ein schlechter Jasager: Considerations of the Finale of Mahler's Seventh Symphony', in Zychowicz, *Symposium*, 98 ff.

[198] Scherzinger, 'Finale', 75.

[199] Williamson makes the same point in the article quoted above. Like him, Scherzinger shows that cadences often occur either prematurely or too late.   [200] Scherzinger, 'Finale', 76 ff.

[201] See above my summary of de la Motte's analysis of Nachtmusik 2.

[202] Scherzinger, 'Finale', 77.   [203] Ibid. 82.

[204] For instance at bar 79, when the ritornello begins in the home key before the material of the A flat section has resolved (Ibid. 83).   [205] Ibid. 78.

chromatic and diatonic passages, between expectations that are fulfilled and those that are undercut, between motives that are developed and those that are repeated, between sections that are clearly delimited by cadential figures and those that simply peter out, between the organic and the episodic, between the intra- and the extra-textual, and between the supplemental and the actual. There is also a sense in which the movement brings to the surface something about the tonal language that has nothing to do with increased chromaticism or the innovations of Schoenberg. The latter developments are predicated on an idea of evolution, on the notion that the tonal language has "inherent tendencies" which are susceptible of development. In Mahler's Rondo-Finale, however, there are numerous *types* of ambiguity; no level can be followed consistently throughout. There is neither a single *telos*, nor is the movement a mere sequence of sections; rather the very idea of *telos* and sequentiality are put into a dialogue with each other. As a result, the act of interpretation itself is foregrounded; the listener is drawn into the text. The strategic juxtaposition of the various traditional form-creating devices— that is, the act of presenting them 'out of phase' with each other—casts the devices themselves in a new light. It is by disclosing these devices, in other words, that their inadequacy is exposed.'

Thus Scherzinger's message is that the Finale of the Seventh is one of the most difficult and original of Mahler's compositions, one whose complexities will not soon be exhausted and completely understood. In the light of this article, some of the praise and condemnations lavished on this Rondo appear besides the point. It seems just as absurd to ignore its fundamental ambiguity and praise it to the skies as a modern 'Ode to Joy' as it is to denigrate it because Mahler failed to revive a form from the past, which is tantamount to investing him with neo-classical intentions which were never really his. What the Finale's detractors have probably wanted to attack, without always admitting it, is the musical material itself, and particularly the stylistic 'reminiscences, allusions or quotations',[206] more numerous than usual and of diverse origins. Adorno's insistence, and Sponheuer's after him, upon the weakness of the melodic substance, is to my mind surprising because only its manner of use is relevant. In the previous symphony a deliberate use of thematic material simply as building blocks was already noticeable, as was the effect of a compositional will (at the time it was seen as impotence) that refused to acknowledge the resistance of matter, or the laws of 'nature', in its determination to raise a monumental edifice. This argument, which is bound to result from a close study of the Finale of the Sixth, has not, however, been brought in to defend that of the Seventh, even though the intention of 'being joyful' is just as manifest there as was the tragic intention of the preceding symphony. Joy, in this movement, is a 'theme', just like 'night' in the Nachtmusiken. Mahler had long since opened the well-guarded doors of symphonic art to material from all origins, and had justified in advance the many 'intrusions' in this movement. They are no more and no less shocking than those in the first movement of the Third Symphony, which likewise contains 'joyful' and 'vulgar' elements that are clearly second-hand. Surely the important thing is that once again Mahler, the architect and craftsman, was able to build a unified structure from naturally disparate elements. Despite all the surprises and contrasts that can appear disconcerting at first sight, Mahler's technique has never been more masterly. In my view, the fascination exercised by this Finale on those who have

---

[206] See de la Grange, 'Reminiscences, Allusions, or Quotations', in Hefling, *Mahler Studies*, 122 ff.

learned to love it is above all musical. Sponheuer's refusal to acknowledge the ironic or parodic nature of many elements is all the more surprising since Mahler had many times before written 'music about music', or, to use Adorno's language, music that is critical of itself, and of culture.

'Free as one can only be who has not himself been entirely swallowed by culture, in his musical vagrancy he picks up the broken glass by the roadside and holds it up to the sun so that all the colours are refracted.'[207] In this memorable image, Adorno has perhaps provided us with the best possible key to the puzzling superabundance of sounds and colours in this Finale. Nowadays, the Seventh appears to us to be a decisive step along the road leading straight from the earlier Rondo-Finale (in the Fifth) to the Rondo-Burleske of the Ninth, a movement which does not seem to have disconcerted posterity because it is usually regarded as a satire of the *Alltag* (run of the mill), a stylized parody of its bustle, and an indispensable counterpart to the lyricism and other humours of the work. Thus the concept of 'collage' does not need to be invoked to explain the breaks and intrusions in the Rondo of the Seventh. E. T. A. Hoffmann's Kapellmeister Kreisler, and his 'death-defying leaps from one extreme to the other, which break the heart' will do,[208] to quote one of Mahler's favourite literary models. The omnipresent, fundamental split in his music, source of its ambiguity and richness, is definitely a strength not a weakness. In the Rondo-Finale, as in all the movements of the Seventh, Romantic irony has been transformed and sharpened by, and for, a machine-age in which the *Alltag* has become ever more intrusive.

In Mahler's own personality, there also was an authentically affirmative and positive aspect which has attracted much less attention than the others. In his daily life, gloomy meditation occupied only rare, private, and secret moments, even if it played a considerable role in his work. That this hyperactive man should have wanted sometimes to celebrate activity in his music, the happiness of creating, the sheer joy of making music, the straightforward enjoyment of the craftsman, is in no way surprising. As a conductor, Mahler achieved some of his greatest successes in optimistic or dionysiac music like the Finales of Beethoven's Fifth and Ninth Symphonies. Yet his music continues to be considered mainly as anguish-ridden, pessimistic, even morbid. This is perhaps another reason why this Rondo-Finale is regarded as a philosophico-musical setback: the fact that in it Mahler was not seeking to express 'great' thoughts.[209] It reveals him once more as a powerful architect of huge musical structures and large forms of vertiginous complexity. To deny this Finale's value is to refuse to listen to it as one of the boldest, most forward-looking pieces of music written before the 1914 war, and to allow oneself to be put off by its audacity, its insolence, and its superabundance, in other words it is an attempt to apply to it criteria as out-of-date as the 'cheerful classical rondo' itself and therefore to adopt a frankly reactionary attitude. Admittedly it was in the following symphony, the Eighth, that Mahler really gave to the world the 'Ode to Joy' of which he, like others before him, had dreamed. Meanwhile he had indeed produced a brilliant and original *Humoreske* illustrating the theme of rejoicing with a real scorn of convention. This doubly provocative act turned even people of goodwill against him.

---

[207] TAM 54; TAMe 36.

[208] Hoffmann, *Lebens-Ansichten des Katers Murr* (Winkler, Munich, 1961), 415.

[209] The brevity of Mengelberg's comments concerning this movement patently shows his unspoken disappointment.

EIGHTH SYMPHONY IN E FLAT MAJOR (1906).

Composition, preliminary programmes

Mahler himself, in a letter to his wife, told the story of the Eighth Symphony's composition in Maiernigg during the summer of 1906.[1] It was unlike anything else in his experience as composer. He went into the Häuschen on the first day of his vacation and was 'seized by the Spiritus creator' which 'shook and lashed me' for eight weeks during which he felt as if the new work was, so to speak, being 'dictated' to him. Two preliminary 'programmes' have survived, and they were surely drafted at the same time as the first musical sketches. The first was as follows:

1. *Hymn Veni Creator*
2. *Scherzo*
3. *Adagio Caritas*
4. *Hymn: die Geburt des Eros*[2]

An Adagio (in B major) subtitled *Caritas* had appeared several years earlier, in the initial plan of the Fourth Symphony[3] and had later been replaced by the G major Adagio. The new work was to end with a 'hymn' of unknown text, and Constantin Floros has suggested that this might well have been the final section of the 'classical Walpurgisnacht' in *Faust* Part II,[4] in which the birth of Eros results 'from the collision of Fire and Water, the most spiritual and the most elemental', and the Sirens sing: 'So let Eros reign, who all things began.'[5] According to Floros, Mahler was trying to achieve a synthesis between the Christian Pentecost hymn and the 'humanist' end of the Walpurgisnacht, but failed and eventually decided not to use the latter text. As for the last three movements in the 'programme', Richard Specht and Paul Bekker find traces of them in the three sections of the ultimate Finale.[6] The intended *Caritas* Adagio was never composed, and the Adagio introducing the second movement of the Eighth assumed quite a different character. Ultimately it was in the last scene of *Faust* Part II that Mahler found the synthesis he was seeking between the Christian *Caritas* and Goethe's humanist *Eros*, first cause of all.

The second 'preliminary programme' appears with a musical sketch, which also belonged to Alma, a first pencil version, in F sharp major, of the opening twenty-eight bars of the 'Veni creator':[7]

I. *Veni creator*
II. *Caritas*
III. *Weihnachtspiele mit dem Kindlein*
      (Christmas games with the child)
IV. *Schöpfung durch Eros. Hymne*
      (Creation through Eros. Hymn)

---

[1] See above, Chap. 6.

[2] This sheet, which formerly belonged to Alma Mahler, is mentioned by Paul Bekker (BMS 273). Its present location is unknown.   [3] See above, Vol. ii, Appendix 2 on the Fourth Symphony.

[4] Part II, 2nd Act, lines 8432 to 8487.

[5] 'So herrsche denn Eros, der alles begonnen' (line 8479). See also the letter Mahler wrote to Alma in the summer 1910 (BGA, no. 303, undated, probably 8 June 1910; see also Vol. iiii, Chap. 7).

[6] RSM2, 306; BMS 273.

[7] Alma later bequeathed this 'programme' sketch to Gustav Beer, president of the American League of Authors and Composers from Austria (ALACA), River Vale, New Jersey. Its present location is also unknown.

On the back of this second programme, Mahler wrote: '8th Symphony, August 1906;[8] The first idea (*Einfall*), kept for my Almschl. Spiritus creator.' Another preliminary musical sketch, this one for the 'Chorus mysticus', used to belong to Alban Berg in Vienna. Surprisingly enough, it is written on lavatory paper.[9] Mahler's initial aim was undoubtedly, as before, to create a new symphonic 'universe', but one quite different in conception and spirit from the Second and the Third Symphonies. Once more he dreamed, like many nineteenth-century composers before him, of following in the path of Beethoven's Ninth and bringing a message to all humanity. From here it was a short step to the idea of giving an unprecedented dimension to the symphony by making it a synthesis of all forms—symphony, cantata, oratorio,[10] motet, Lieder cycle—; and all styles—homophonic/polyphonic, harmonic/contrapuntal; also of combining in it all the techniques of composition, both strict and free. As we shall see below, there was also the idea of writing a vocal symphony, a symphony FOR chorus and orchestra, where the human voice would be of prime importance. But Mahler wanted to go one step further: the Second and Third Symphonies had already been exceptional in their dimensions and the resources they used. To give expression to his cosmic vision, it was now necessary to go beyond all previously known limits and dimensions. As he proudly wrote to Willem Mengelberg: *'these are planets and suns revolving'*.[11] There is nothing surprising about the appearance of such a huge work when viewed in the context of the period. The idea of the 'crowning work', the 'magnum opus' (*Hauptwerk*) was in the air.

But Mahler's ambition did not stop there. During his lifetime, music had become fully aware of its past. The new symphony developed in Mahler's mind as a summary and synthesis of the history of music, starting from the fifteenth century and the Flemish polyphonists who had played an essential role in the music of the Austrian Empire, and to whom Mahler had several times alluded in his correspondence. Not only does the strict counterpoint of the 'Veni Creator' recall their work: the use he makes of vocal timbre, melody and harmony to reflect the meaning of the words—in the 'Infirma nostri corporis' for example—harks back to the traditions of Renaissance and baroque music, as does the use of a rising motif for the 'Accende lumen'. By using a double mixed chorus, Mahler also established a link with the antiphonal music of Venice—also popular in Austria at the beginning of the baroque period—and with Bach's *St Matthew Passion*. With its continual antiphonal effects, which are not clearly perceptible in a normal concert hall where the two choruses have to be placed too close to each other, the Eighth Symphony looks back, beyond Bach, to the Venetian works written for the church of San Marco by the Gabrielis and others.

As seen above, Mahler composed the huge work in record time. On 21 June, he wrote to his friend Fritz Löhr requesting him to translate two verses of the 'Veni

---

[8] In 1906, Mahler as usual left Vienna on 20 June. Since he later claimed to have been seized by the Creator Spiritus from the first day of his holiday, this sketch dates in fact from June and he later got the date wrong when dedicating the sheet to his wife.

[9] TAM 57. This document, with the staves drawn in by hand, belongs to the Alban Berg Foundation in Vienna. It includes the first five bars of the 'Chorus mysticus', with the harmonic progressions noted in four parts.

[10] Concerning Mahler's synthesis in the Eighth of the oratorio form (*Reihungsform*), symphonic form (*Entwicklungsform*), and dramatic form (*mythische Kreisform*), see Hermann Danuser, 'Der Goethe-Interpret Mahler', in *Gustav Mahler: The World listens, Muziek und Wetenschap*, Dutch Journal for Musicology, 5 (1995–6): 3, 277.　　　　[11] MBR1, no. 306; MBR2, no. 360, already quoted.

Creator' and asking him how two words ('paraclitus diceris') should be scanned. He also inquired about the existence of 'a beautiful translation, maybe one that rhymes',[12] which means that he had not yet remembered Goethe's translation. On 18 July, when Mahler wrote once again to Fritz Löhr, he had already composed a large part of the 'Veni Creator'. This time, he asked his friend for a complete 'authentic' text of the hymn, along with the translation of the passage 'Infirma nostri corporis, Virtute firmans perpeti' and the two lines beginning 'Per te sciamus', for the 'damned old hymnbook' ('verfluchte Kirchenschmöker') he had at his disposal 'does not seem completely reliable'.[13] To the Graz critic Ernst Decsey, he told the story in detail:

Working away at it he noticed that the music was spilling over the limits of the text, like water out of an overfull bowl; in other words, the structural conception of the music did not coincide with the verses. He complained about this to a friend, and the friend—a philologist—pointed out to him that that was only natural, since the text that he was working with was incomplete, about one-and-a-half-verses were missing. Mahler lost no time in ordering the full text from Kapellmeister Luze in Vienna. When the hymn arrived, he noticed to his great surprise that the words fitted the music exactly, that it was his feeling for form which had made him write too much: each of the new words fitted without effort into the whole.[14]

Susanne Vill, who has devoted several paragraphs of her book to a discussion of the various versions of the Latin hymn, has attempted to identify the 'missing' verses. She believes that Mahler originally had set the liturgical version quoted below, which is the one most often used.[15] So the missing verses (probably Stanza 7 in his version),[16] fitted perfectly with an orchestral episode he had already composed. This filled him with deep pride, confirming his impression that during the summer he had been the agent of higher forces, or, better still, 'an instrument played by the universe'. Soon the text of the last scene of *Faust* Part II occurred to him as ideally suited to the second part of the symphony. When it was finished he sent triumphant notifications to a number of his friends.[17]

TEXTS

If we are to believe the passage by Constantin Floros referred to above, and if the idea of the Hymn to Creation through Eros was indeed inspired by a scene in *Faust* Part II, Mahler did not need to look far before deciding to use the closing scene from the same play for the second part of the Eighth. There already existed a link between the great German poet and the Christian Pentecost hymn, for at the end of his life Goethe

---

[12] MBR1, no. 269; MBR2, no. 354, undated, postmarked 21 June 1906.
[13] MBR1, no. 270; MBR2, no. 356. See below, under the heading 'Texts'.
[14] EDS1, 353 ff.
[15] See below, under the heading 'Texts'.
[16] According to Vill, the second half of Verse 3 (in the original), 'Tu rite promissum Patris, | Sermone ditans guttura' was probably missing in the text Mahler had in hand and he finally gave up the idea of inserting it. [17] See above, Chap. 6.

translated it into German verse, and the translation appears in his complete works.[18] In choosing a text as universally known and admired as the final scene of *Faust* Part II, Mahler was making an exception to his own rule of never setting to music first-rate poems, which he regarded as complete in themselves. However, Goethe in a sense led him to it, having given this final scene the form of a cantata or oratorio with texts explicitly attributed to solo singers and choruses, and achieving a poetic vision so vast, so general, so universal even, that it explicitly demanded a musical setting. Other composers had already accepted Goethe's challenge, Schumann setting the scene to music in its entirety, and Liszt the final 'Chorus mysticus'. Mahler now set about incorporating the whole of this scene into a vast symphonic entity, borrowing many of the motifs he had used in the opening 'Veni Creator', and making of Goethe's scene a serene affirmation of his deepest beliefs.

The 'Veni Creator'

Heinrich Lausberg, in a scholarly article about the Pentecost hymn 'Veni Creator',[19] claims that it was written on the occasion of a synod in Aachen in 809 by Raban Maur, or Hrabanus Maurus, a Benedictine monk and prelate living in Mainz, where he died in 856. A pupil of Alcuin and of Saint Martin of Tours, master and organizer of the Abbey of Fulda, and then archbishop of Mainz, Maurus was later given the title of 'Praeceptor Germaniae'. He wrote several works, notably the encyclopaedia *De Universo* or *De Rerum Naturis* and a teaching treatise for the use of monks, *De Institutione Clericorum*. However, his most famous work by far is the 'Veni Creator', the hymn that celebrates the coming of the Holy Spirit to the apostles on the day of Pentecost. As Deryck Cooke has written:

The hymn *Veni Creator Spiritus* is more than a humble Christian prayer for personal salvation in another world. It is concerned with Pentecost—the great moment of inspiration, when the Holy Ghost descended and spoke in many tongues through the mouths of the Apostles, and was interpreted by Peter in the words of the prophet Joel: 'Your sons and your daughters shall prophesy, your old men shall dream dreams, your young men shall see visions'. In other words, it is concerned with the time when the Christian faith itself was at its most dynamic, and it suggests the march of men towards higher things: it addresses the Creator Spirit as *Dux*—leader—and contains the lines: 'Scatter the foe; with Thee as our leader going before us, may we shun all that is evil'.[20]

It should first be noted that, as usual, Mahler made many small changes in this text beyond the simple repetition of words or lines. The most important is the omission of

[18] It is dated 'Weimar, 10 Apr. 1820'. Goethe sent it two days later to his friend, the composer Karl Friedrich Zelter, together with a message asking him to set it to music, 'so that it could be sung by a chorus, every Sunday in front of my house'. The hymn is mentioned several times in the poet's correspondence. He calls it, among other things 'ein Appel an das allgemeine Weltgenie' and adds in a later text: 'The splendid church hymn, "Veni Creator Spiritus" is actually an appeal to genius; hence its powerful appeal to intellectually active and able people too.' See *Maximen und Reflexionen*, no. 182, quoted by Dieter Borchmeyer, in 'Gustav Mahlers Goethe und Goethes Heiliger Geist', *Nachrichten zu Mahler Forschung*, 32 (Oct. 1994), 18 ff.

[19] See Heinrich Lausberg, 'Der Hymnus *Veni Creator Spiritus*', in *Jahrbuch der Akademie der Wissenschaften in Göttingen 1969*, Göttingen (1969), 26 ff., quoted by Constantin Floros, *Gustav Mahler*, Vol. iii, *Die Symphonien* (Breitkopf, Wiesbaden, 1985), 210 ff., English version, 338, n. 21.

[20] Deryck Cooke, 'The Word and the Deed, Mahler and his Eighth Symphony', in *Vindications: Essays on Romantic Music* (Faber & Faber, London, 1982), 114.

the second half of verse 3 of the original (perhaps missing in his copy of the hymn), 'Tu rite . . .',[21] and then the switching of the two halves of verse 4 (which is no. 3 in Mahler's version). After the fifth verse of the original (where Mahler replaces 'noxium' by 'pessimum') comes the first part of the original verse 3 ('Tu septiformis') and then the sixth verse, which Mahler shortens by omitting words ('atque' and 'Te utrius'). As for the stanza 'Da gratiarum munera', it occurs only in the Munich manuscript of the hymn. The final verse, or 'Doxology' (Prayer to the glory of God) replaces that of Maurus (quoted here below in a footnote) in the Roman manuscript. Mahler kept the same number of verses as are found in the liturgical original—seven (see below). This number has a symbolic meaning. It alludes to the seven gifts of the Spirit, which, according to Isaiah 11: 2, are spirit, wisdom, knowledge, counsel, strength, insight, and fear of the Lord.[22]

Many writers have speculated as to which verses were missing from the text Mahler had with him when he started to compose the 'Veni creator'. Stefan Strohm suggests that the missing stanza was the one not traditionally used in the liturgical text ('Da gratiarum', Mahler's second-last).[23] Mahler would then have composed music for both this verse and the second part of the recapitulation without having the text before him.[24] Susanne Vill believes that the music Mahler composed without text, adding the text only when he received it from Vienna, is that of the second episode in the reprise ('Da gaudiorum munera, at bars 441 ff.). She feels that Mahler felt compelled to write a long orchestral episode at this point so as to preserve the natural symmetry of the sonata form.[25] Strohm and Vill both emphasize the rigour with which Mahler here observed the criteria of the form, notably in the proportions of the three sections, exposition (168 bars), development (184 bars, plus 54 bars of fugato), recapitulation (82 bars), and coda (92 bars). Adapting the liturgical text to this traditional structure must have been so difficult that it is easy to imagine how, at the time when he still lacked one of the verses, he could have felt the need to compensate for its absence by writing a longer orchestral interlude.

A copy in Mahler's hand of the text of the 'Veni creator' has survived.[26] It comprises, written in ink, stanzas 1 and 2 of the original, then the first half of the fourth stanza ('Accende lumen') followed by the seventh,[27] the 'Doxology'. Added in pencil on the right side of the page are the second half of the fourth verse ('Infirma nostri corporis') and the third ('Tu septiformis', including the two lines that Mahler dropped). The sixth ('Per te sciamus')[28] is also on the right side of the page, at the bottom, but it is written

---

[21] The first half of this verse is inserted by Mahler *after* verses 4 and 5. According to Stefan Strohm ('Die Idee der absoluten Musik als ihr (ausgesprochenes) Programm', *Schütz-Jahrbuch* 4/5, 1982–3 (Bärenreiter, Kassel, 1983), 82) Mahler dropped the lines because he found them 'obscure both in form and content'.   [22] See Floros, *Symphonien*, 218.

[23] The first two lines of this stanza are put the other way round in the text quoted by Richard Specht in his analytical monograph (Universal Edition, 1912, p. 7, and RMS2, 277).

[24] See Susanne Vill, *Vermittlungsformen verbalisierter und musikalischer Inhalte in der Musik Gustav Mahlers* (Schneider, Tutzing, 1979), 138.   [25] Vill, *Vermittlungsformen*, 138.

[26] Bruno Walter Collection, LPA, New York.

[27] Mahler definitely wrote *noxium*, as in the original, and not *pessimum*.

[28] On the back of this sheet are two short poems from the *Knaben Wunderhorn*, one in Latin: 'Dormi Jesu, mater ridet' (Hempel edition, Vol. ii, 613) with the note '1st Trio: alto', and the other in German: 'Steht auf ihr lieben Kinderlein' (ibid. 583) followed by '2nd Trio, soprano'. These texts were probably intended for the movement 'Weihnachtsspiele mit dem Kinderlein', which Mahler eventually dropped. The first of these poems was set to music by Webern in his *5 Canons on Latin Texts*, Op. 16 (no. 12). Above 'paraclitus diceris' Mahler wrote the same words in reverse order, as they appear in some versions of the Latin hymn *Veni Creator*.

in ink. On the other hand Mahler's last stanza but one, the one which was presumably added after he received the fuller version of the text, 'Da gaudiorum premia', is missing from this copy.[29]

THE USUAL LITURGICAL TEXT[30]	MAHLER'S TEXT	ENGLISH TRANSLATION	BARS
1. *Veni, Creátor Spíritus,*	*Veni creator spiritus*	Come, Holy Ghost, Creator come,	1–45 (Theme A)
Mentes tuórum vísíta	*Mentes tuorum visita,*	From Thy bright heavenly throne.	
Imple suprena gratia	*Imple suprena grátia*	Come, take possession of our souls,	46–80 (Theme B)
Quae tu creásti péctora!	*Quae tu creasti pectora.*	And make them all Thine own.	
2. *Qui Paráclitus díceris,*	*Qui Paraclitus diceris,*	Thou who art called the Paraclete,	80– 90
Donum Dei altíssimi,	*Donum Dei altissimi,*	Best Gift of God above,	
Fons vivus, ignis, cáritas,	*Fons vivus, ignis, caritas*	The Living Spring, the Living Fire,	91–108
Et spiritális únctio.	*Et spiritalis unctio.*	Sweet Unction, and True Love!	(108–22 *Veni creator*)
			122–41: Interlude
3. *Tu septifórmis múnere,*	*Infirma nostri corporis*	With Thy strength which ne'er decays	142–68 (Theme C)
Dextrae Dei tu dígitus,	*Virtute firmans perpeti.*	Confirm our mortal frame	
Tu rite promíssum Patris,			
Sermoné ditans gúttura.			
			169–217: Interlude
	(Infirma nostri corporis)		218–53 (Theme D)
	(Virtute furmans perpeti)		
			254–61: Interlude
4. *Accénde lumen sénsibus:*	*Accende lumen sensibus,*	And guide our minds with Thy blest light,	262–89 (Theme E)
infúnde amórem córdibus:	*Infunde amorem cordibus.*	With love our hearts inflame	
Infírma nostri córporis			
Virtúte firmans pérpeti.			
5. *Hostem repéllas lóngius,*	*Hostem repellas longius,*	Far from us drive our hellish foe,	290–307
Pacémque dones prótinus:	*Pacemque dones protinus.*	True peace unto us bring,	308–11
Ductóre sic te praevio	*Ductore sic te praevio,*	And through all perils guide us safe	312–32
Vitémus omne nóxium.	*Vitemus omne pessimum.*	Beneath Thy sacred wing.	
	Tu septiformis munere,	Thou who are sevenfold in Thy grace,	333–49
	Dextrae paternae digitus!	Finger of God's right hand,	
6. *Per te sciamus da Patrem,*	*Per te sciamus da patrem,*	Through Thee may we the Father know,	349–66
Noscámus atque Fílium,	*Noscamus filium*	Through Thee the Eternal Son,	
Te utriúsque Spíritum	*Credamus spiritum*	And Thee, the Spirit of them Both	
Credámus omni tempore,	*Omni tempore.*	Be worshipped for all time.	
			366–412: *Accende*
			413–41 *Veni creator*

---

[29] Susanne Vill (*Vermittlungsformen*, 136) suggests several possible sources for this verse, which Stefan Strohm locates in a Munich manuscript of the hymn. On the original structure of the 'Veni Creator', which Mahler changed considerably, also see Stefan Strohm, 'Programm', 84.

[30] This version of the hymn, which is clearly the one Mahler had before him during his first week in Maiernigg, is quoted in full by Vill (*Vermittlungsformen*, 135 ff.) from the following source: *Antiphonale monasticum*, 518 ff. Mahler set it to music verbatim, except for the second half of the third stanza ('Tu rite promissum . . .'). His 7th stanza ('Da gaudiorum premia') comes from another version of the hymn. However, in some versions of the hymn, the last stanza or 'Doxology' reads as follows: 'Praesta hoc, Pater plissime | Patrique compar Unice | Cum Paracleto Spiritu | Regnans per omne saeculum'. Mahler's 'Doxology' seems to originate from Roman manuscripts. (See Stefan Strohm, 'Programm', 91.)

THE USUAL LITURGICAL TEXT	MAHLER'S TEXT	ENGLISH TRANSLATION	BARS
STANZA TAKEN FROM THE MUNICH MANUSCRIPT (see above)	*Da gaudiorum praemia,* *Da gratiarum munera.* *Dissolve litis vincula,* *Adstringe pacis foedera*	Give us the heavenly joy Give us Your divine grace, Appease our human quarrels	442–74
			475–88: *Ductore te praevio* 488–507: Interlude
7. *Glória Patri Dómino, Natóque, qui a mórtuis*	*Gloria Patri Domino, Natoque qui a mortuis, Deo sit gloria*[31] *Et filio qui a mortuis*	All glory to the Father be, And to the risen Son;	508–80
Surréxit, ac Paráclito, In saeculórum sáecula, Amen.	*Surrexit, ac Paraclito In saeculorum saecula.*	The same to Thee, O Paraclete, While endless ages run.	

The last Scene of Faust, Part II

Goethe published *Faust: A Fragment* in 1790, at the age of 41. He did not publish the complete version of Part I (*Faust: The first Part of the Tragedy*) until 1808. He had decided as early as 1797 to divide the work into two parts, and had already written sketches and notes for various scenes in Part Two. He did not complete the second part until 1831, the year before his death at the age of 83. At the end of Part II Faust is an old man, blinded by Care, but undeterred. He has found the ultimate wisdom which he has sought for so long. In his final soliloquy he speaks of his ambitions as governor of a territory granted to him by 'the Emperor'. It is a swampy coastal strip and constantly under threat of flooding by the sea. He will drain it and make it secure by strengthening its sea defences. (Goethe was deeply impressed by the disastrous floods that swept over the Netherlands in 1825.) Faust urges his overseer (Mephistopheles) to recruit workers by the hundred to push forward his land reclamation project:

> Here there shall be an inland paradise:
> Outside, the sea as high as it can reach,
> May rage and gnaw, and yet a common will,
> Should it intrude, will act to close the breach.
> Yes! To this vision I am wedded still,
> And this as wisdom's final word I teach:
> Only that man earns freedom, merits life,
> Who must reconquer both in constant daily strife.
> In such a place, by danger still surrounded,
> Youth, manhood, age, their brave new world have founded.
> I long to see that multitude and stand
> With a free people on free land!
> Then to the moment I might say:
> Beautiful moment, do not pass away!
> Till many ages shall have passed
> This record of my earthly life shall last.
> And in anticipation of such bliss
> What moment could give me greater joy than this?

[31] These two lines were added by Mahler, making the 'Doxology' more explicit than in the original text of the stanza, using the same words but replacing 'Domino' with 'Deo', and 'Nato' with 'Filio'.

With these words, Faust 'sinks back' and dies. A tragic death? But he has succeeded in discovering 'wisdom's final word'. A triumphal death? He has seen a vision of paradise on earth. But it is a land in which man must earn his freedom, merit his life, 'in constant daily strife!'. Contradiction, ambiguity? But he has learnt to accept the apparent paradoxes, and dies a serene death, confident that

> Till many ages shall have passed,
> This record of my earthly life shall last.

Confident of such immortality, he seems to have forgotten his pact, his wager with the Devil. If one reads Faust's last words before he dies, one can only conclude that he dies believing he has found the final answers to his questions. Is he the victim of an illusion?

Mephistopheles says he is, claims Faust's soul and waves over his corpse the record of the wager signed by Faust with his own blood in Part I. God intervenes, through his angels, and rescues Faust's 'immortal part' from Mephisto's minions. This conclusion announces both the dawning of a new world, in which all man's aspirations will be fulfilled, and the validity of human unquietness, despite all its aberrations.

In 'Mountain Gorges', the final scene of Part II, anchorites 'at various heights among the clefts of the mountain side' praise Nature as the manifestation of divine love. They greet a procession of three repenting women. They are hovered over by the Mater gloriosa, whom they entreat to have mercy on them for their sins. They ask her to have mercy also on a fourth repentant sinner ('formerly named Gretchen'). She in turn implores the Virgin Mother to forgive her for the joy she feels that her former lover is now coming back to her at last, and asks that she may be allowed to teach him how to enjoy heavenly bliss, now that he is shedding his earthly bonds. The Mater gloriosa summons Gretchen to 'higher spheres'; 'he must sense you to find the way'. So Faust, through the mediation of the forgiving Gretchen ascends to Heaven. Dr Marianus tells all the repenting sinners to look up to the tender, forgiving countenance of the Virgin, Mother, Queen . . . Goddess. And the Chorus Mysticus finally generalizes the salvationist message for all mankind: 'Eternal Womanhood draws us on high!'

Goethe's conclusion of the Faust story is enigmatic. Faust has at no time asked for redemption. Gretchen, more sinned against than sinning, is the one who pleads for divine forgiveness—for them both. The angels carrying Faust's 'immortal part' have repeated Goethe's alternative formula for salvation: 'He who strives on and lives to strive, can earn redemption still.' No attempt has been made to give 'strive' a moral content.

The male characters in this last scene are symbols and abstractions. The Magna Peccatrix, on the other hand, is the Evangelist Luke's so-called 'fallen woman' of whom Christ said: 'She has loved much, and will be forgiven much.' The Mulier Samaritana is borrowed from St John the Evangelist, while Maria Aegyptiaca is a legendary saint from Egypt, miraculously converted after a depraved life. In the Mater gloriosa are combined the Christian Virgin Mary and the pagan symbol of the 'Mother Goddess'.

Goethe's Text	English Translation[32]	
CHOR und ECHO	CHORUS and ECHO	CHORUS
Waldung, sie schwankt heran,	Woods, hitherwavering,	*Poco Adagio*
11845 Felsen, sie lasten dran,	Rocks, cliffs, downburdening,	(E flat minor)
Wurzeln, sie klammern an,	Roots close to roots they cling,	bars 167–218

---

[32]   The translation is by David Luke (Oxford University Press, World's Classics, Oxford, 1994).

GOETHE'S TEXT	ENGLISH TRANSLATION	
CHOR und ECHO	**CHORUS and ECHO**	CHORUS
Stamm dicht am Stamm hinan.	Trunk to trunk neighbouring.	
Woge nach Woge spritzt,	The rushing waters leap,	
Höhle, die tiefste, schützt.	The sheltering caves are deep.	

11850 Löwen, sie schleichen stumm-   Lions prowl round us, dumb
freundlich um uns herum,   Gentle and shy to come
Ehren geweihten Ort,   Into this holy place,
Heiligen Liebeshort.   Sacred to love and grace.

PATER ECSTATICUS	**PATER ECSTATICUS**	BARITONE SOLO
Ewiger Wonnebrand,	Joy of immortal fire	*Moderato*

11855 Glühendes Liebeband,   Lovebond of hot desire,   (E flat major)
Siedender Schmerz der Brust, Heart's seething agony,   bars 219–55
Schäumende Gotteslust!   Godspring of ecstasy!
Pfeile, durchdringet mich,   Arrows, pierce through me now,
Lanzen, bezwinget mich,   Spearpoints, subdue me now,

11860 Keulen, zerschmettert mich Clubs, strike and break me now;
Blitze, durchwettert mich!   Lightnings, unmake me now!
Dass ja das Nichtige   All that is vain and void
Alles verflüchtige,   Let it be all destroyed:
Glänze der Dauerstern,   Shine, star, for evermore,

11865 Ewiger Liebe Kern!   Love's everlasting core!

INTERLUDE
bars 256–65

PATER PROFUNDUS	**PATER PROFUNDUS**	BASS SOLO
Wie Felsenabgrund mir zu Füssen	The rocky precipice below	*Allegro appassionato*
Auf tieferm Abgrund lastend ruht,	Weighs on a chasm still more deep;	(E flat minor)
Wie tausend Bäche strahlend fliessen	A thousand streamlets shine and flow	bars 266–362
Zum grausen Sturz des Schaums der Flut,	Down to the foaming flood's dread leap;	

11870 Wie strack, mit eignem kräftigen Triebe, By its own energy ascending   1st stanza
Der Stamm sich in die Lüfte trägt: The tree thrusts skywards straight and tall: bars 266–324
So ist es die allmächtige Liebe,   All this shows forth the love unending
Die alles bildet, alles hegt.   That shapes all things and shields them all.
Ist um mich her ein wildes Brausen,   How wild a roar is this, as if

11875 Als wogte Wald und Felsengrund,   The forest shook, the abyss were stirred!
Und doch stürzt, liebevoll im Sausen,   Yet the great torrent from the cliff
Die Wasserfülle sich zum Schlund,   Pours down like love, its sound half-heard,
Berufen, gleich das Tal zu wässern;   To the valley's thirst; and by and by
Der Blitz, der flammend niederschlug,   Lightning has struck, its flame makes clean

11880 Die Atmosphäre zu verbessern,   The poisoned air, the sultry sky
Die Gift und Dunst im Busen trug: Where swollen thunder-clouds have been;

ORCHESTRAL
INTERLUDE
bars 363–84

Sind Liebesboten! Sie verkünden,   These are love's messengers! They tell
Was ewig schaffend uns unwallt.   Of power all-making, all-surrounding.
Mein Innres mög es auch entzünden,   Oh let it burn in me as well!   2nd stanza

11885 Wo sich der Geist, verworren-kalt,   Bonds of dull sense, my mind confounding,   bars 339–62
Verquält in stumpfer Sinneschranken Torment and chill me: oh release
Scharfangeschlossnem Kettenschmerz!   Me from these chains that bind so tight!
O Gott, beschwichtige die Gedanken,   Oh God, between my thoughts make peace
Erleuchte mein bedürftig Herz!   And to my needy heart give light!

(*cont.*):

GOETHE'S TEXT	ENGLISH TRANSLATION	
		ORCHESTRAL INTERLUDE bars 363–84

<table>
<tr><td>

[PATER SERAPHICUS
11890 Welch ein Morgenwölkchen schwebet
Durch der Tannen schwankend Haar?
Ahn ich, was im Innern lebet?
Es ist junge Geisterschar.

</td><td>

[PATER SERAPHICUS
Something hovers through the swaying
Pine-trees' tresses: who can tell
What it is? A cloud of daying!
In it youthful spirits dwell.

</td><td>

(Passage not set
to music by
Mahler)

</td></tr>
</table>

CHOR SELIGEN KNABEN Sag uns, Vater, wo wir wallen, 11895 Sag uns, Guter, wer wir sind! Glücklich sind wir: allen, allen Ist das Dasein so gelind.	CHORUS OF BLESSED BOYS Father, say, what is this place? Kind friend, is it you who call? Here we feel such happiness: Life is gentle to us all.
PATER SERAPHICUS Knaben, Mitternachtsgeborne, Halb erschlossen Geist und Sinn, 11900 Für die Eltern gleich Verlorne, Für die Engel zum Gewinn! Dass ein Liebender zugegen, Fühlt ihr wohl: so naht euch nur! Doch von schroffen Erdewegen, 11905 Glückliche! habt ihr keine Spur. Steigt herab in meiner Augen Welt-und erdgemäss Organ! Könnt sie als die euern brauchen: Schaut euch diese Gegend an! 11910 Das sind Bäume, das sind Felsen, Wasserstrom, der abestürzt Und mit ungeheuerm Wälzen Sich den steilen Weg verkürzt.	PATER SERAPHICUS Mortal children, midnight-born, Minds half open, sense half dead, From your parents' arms soon torn, To the angels given instead. You have felt a lover near you: Come to him! But, happy few, Earth's rough journey was to spare you And to leave no mark on you. Enter into me, come down now Into my earth-worldly eyes: You can use them as your own now. Look at this strange paradise! These are trees, and those are rocks; There a waterfall that gushes Wildly from the height—it strikes Its steep path, and down it rushes.
SELIGE KNABEN Das ist mächtig anzuschauen; 11915 Doch zu düster ist der Ort, Schüttelt uns mit Schreck und Grauen: Edler, Guter, lass uns fort!	BLESSED BOYS It is sad and gloomy here Though these sights are great to see: We are stirred with dread and fear. Noble father, set us free!
PATER SERAPHICUS Steigt hinan zu höhrem Kreise, Wachset immer und unvermerkt, 11920 Wie nach ewig reiner Weise Gottes Gegenwart verstärkt! Denn das ist der Geister Nahrung, Die im freisten Äther waltet: Ewigen Liebens Offenbarung, 11925 Die zur Seligkeit entfaltet.]	PATER SERAPHICUS Rise to higher spheres and grow Imperceptibly, as stronger Still God's presence there will glow, Pure, eternal, dimmed no longer; For the spirits' nurture reigning In that free ethereal zone And their blessed hope sustaining, Is eternal Love made known.] [33]

---

[33] The monologue of Pater Seraphicus, and his dialogue with the Blessed Boys (lines 11890 to 11926) are not set by Mahler.

GOETHE'S TEXT	ENGLISH TRANSLATION	
ENGEL	**ANGELS**	
Gerettet ist das edle Glied	This noble spirit saved alive[34]	(SCHERZO?)
(11935) Der Geisterwelt vom Bösen:	Has foiled the Devil's will!	WOMEN'S CHORUS
Wer immer strebend sich bemüht,	He who strives on and lives to strive	*Allegro deciso*
Den können wir erlösen!	Can earn redemption still.	(B major)
Und hat an ihm die Liebe gar	And now that love itself looks down	bars 385–420
Von oben teilgenommen,	To favour him with grace,	
(11940) Begegnet ihm die selige Schar	The blessed host with songs may crown	(sung simultaneously
Mit herzlichem Willkommen.	His welcome to this place.	with the →)
CHOR SELIGEN KNABEN	**CHORUS OF BLESSED BOYS**	CHILDREN'S
Hände verschlinget	Dance ring-a-ringing,	CHORUS
Freudig zum Ringverein!	All of us hand in hand	
Regt euch und singet	Joyfully singing,	
Heilge Gefühle drein!	Dance, sacred brother-band!	
11930 Göttlich belehret,	Heed that wise teaching!	
Dürft ihr vertrauen;	Him you revere,	
Den ihr verehret,	Pure hearts upreaching	
Werdet ihr schauen.	Shall see him here.	
		ORCHESTRAL
		INTERLUDE
		bars 421–35
		PRELUDE
		bars 436–42
DIE JÜNGEREN ENGEL	**THE YOUNGER ANGELS**	WOMEN'S CHORUS
Jene Rosen, aus den Händen	Holy penitents who gave	*Molto leggiero.*
Liebend-heiliger Büsserinnen,	Roses of their love to scatter,	*Scherzando*
Halfen uns den Sieg gewinnen,	Helped us so in our great matter,	(E flat major)
11945 Uns das hohe Werk vollenden,	As we fought this soul to save,	bars 443–520
Diesen Seelenschatz erbeuten.	Helped us gain this noble prize.	
Böse wichen, als wir streuten,	Devils fled before our eyes,	
Teufel flohen, als wir trafen.	Hell's dark spirits shrank back daunted	
Statt gewohnter Höllenstrafen	As we smote them with unwonted	
11950 Fühlten Liebesqual die Geister;	Heaven-fire of love's hot rain;	
Selbst der alte Satansmeister	Even old Satan felt that pain	
War von spitzer Pein durchdrungen.	Penetrate his master-mind.	
Jauchzet auf! es ist gelungen.	We won! Rejoice, all angelkind!	
		ORCHESTRAL
		INTERLUDE
		bars 520–32
DIE VOLLENDETEREN ENGEL	**THE MATURER ANGELS**	MIXED CHORUS
		and SOLO
Uns bleibt ein Erdenrest	An earthbound, immature	*Wie die gleiche*
11955 Zu tragen peinlich,[35]	And fragmentary,	*Stelle im 1. Teil*
Und wär er von Asbest,	Fireproof yet still impure	(Like the same
Er ist nicht reinlich.	Burden we carry.	passage in the
Wenn starke Geisteskraft	When spirit-energy	1st part)
Die Elemente	Captures the physical	bars 533–80

[34] The word '*euch*' is added by Mahler. He also puts the Angels' Chorus *ahead* of the Chorus of Blessed Boys, which precedes it in Goethe's text.

[35] Here Mahler repeats the word 'Uns' before 'zu tragen'.

(cont.):

GOETHE'S TEXT	ENGLISH TRANSLATION	
11960 An sich herangerafft,	Elements powerfully,	Quotation from
Kein Engel trennte	No force angelical	'*Infirma nostri*
Geeinte Zwienatur	Can loose the subtle bond	*corporis*'
Der innigen beiden:	That has allied them:	
Die ewige Liebe nur	Only the Love beyond	
11965 Vermags zu scheiden.	Time can divide them.	

DIE JÜNGEREN ENGEL	THE YOUNGER ANGELS	WOMEN'S CHORUS
Nebelnd um Felsenhöh[36]	Spirits in nebulous	*Im Anfang noch*
Spür ich soeben	Motion advancing	*etwas gehalten*
Regend sich in der Näh	Round this vertiginous	(Holding back
Ein Geisterleben.	Rock-peak are dancing.	slightly at the
11970 [Die Wölkchen werden klar:]	[Now the cloud brightens: see,] [37]	beginning)
Ich seh bewegte Schar	A happy company	
Seliger Knaben,	Circling together, new-	
Los von der Erde Druck,	Freed from earth's burden—they	
Im Kreis gesellt,	Are blessed children, who	
11975 Die sich erlaben	In the spring's beauty here,	*Allmählich flotter*
Am neuen Lenz und Schmuck	In this new higher sphere	(Gradually faster)
Der obern Welt.	Rejoice and play.	(E flat major, then
Sei er zum Anbeginn,	Let him first be with these:	G major)
Steigendem Vollgewinn	To joy's, to truth's increase	(Doctor Marianus
	That is his way.	enters at bar 604/
		line 11978: see
11980 Diesen gesellt!		below)

DIE SELIGEN KNABEN	THE BLESSED BOYS	CHILDREN'S
Freudig empfangen wir	Gladly we welcome this	CHORUS and
Diesen im Puppenstand;	Chrysalid-aspirant:	TENOR SOLO
Also erlangen wir	Ours now his heaven-bent	*Allegro deciso*
Englisches Unterpfand.	New metamorphosis.	(B major)
11985 Löset die Flocken los,	Thus from his close cocoon	bars 604–38
Die ihn umgeben!	We set him free:	
Schon ist er schön und gross	With angel-life so soon	
Von heiligem Leben.	How fair is he!	

DOCTOR MARIANUS	DOCTOR MARIANUS	TENOR SOLO (with
Hier ist die Aussicht frei,	How wide a view up here,	women's chorus, then
11990 Der Geist erhoben.	The soul to lift!	children: see above)
Dort ziehen Fraun vorbei,	What women now draw near?	
Schwebend nach oben.	Upwards they drift,	
Die Herrliche, mitteninn,	And in their midst, with stars	
Im Sternenkranze,	Crowning her splendour,	
11995 Die Himmelskönigin:	I see heaven's Lady pass—	
Ich sehs am Glanze.	Those lights attend her.	
Höchste Herrscherin der Welt,	Queen and ruler of the world!	TENOR SOLO
Lasse mich im blauen,	In this deep blue sky,	*Sempre l'istesso*
Ausgespannten Himmelszelt,	In thy tent of heaven unfurled,	*tempo*
12000 Dein Geheimnis schauen!	Show me thy mystery!	(E major)
Billige, was des Mannes Brust	I must love thee as a man,	bars 639–723

---

[36] Here Mahler changes the order of the words.   [37] Mahler does not set this line.

GOETHE'S TEXT	ENGLISH TRANSLATION	
Ernst und zart beweget	And my heart's emotion	
Und mit heiliger Liebeslust	Gives what sacred love I can:	
Dir entgegenträget!	Spurn not my devotion!	
12005 Unbezwinglich unser Mut,	We who fiercely fight for thee,	
Wenn du hehr gebietest;	Conquerors at thy bidding,	
Plötzlich mildert sich die Glut,	Gentle lovers we can be	
Wie du uns befriedest.	If thou hear our pleading.	
Jungfrau, rein im schönsten Sinn,	Purest Virgin, noblest Mother,	TENOR SOLO and
12010 Mutter, Ehren würdig,	Queen of our election,	MIXED CHORUSES
Uns erwählte Königin,	Goddess yielding to none other	*Sehr langsam.*
Göttern ebenbürtig.	In thy great perfection!	*Molto devoto*
		(Very slow)
		(E flat major)
		bars 724–57
[Um sie verschlingen	[Cloudlets surround her	(passage not set
Sich leichte Wölkchen:	Light as the elements:	by Mahler)
12015 Sind Büsserinnen,	These are her penitents,	
Ein zartes Völkchen,	Sorrowing and tender.	
Um ihr Kniee	Drinking the ether,	
Der Äther schlürfend,	Needful of mercy,	
Gnade bedürfend.]	Suppliants besiege her.] [38]	
		ORCHESTRAL
		INTERLUDE
		Poco più mosso:
		bars 758–79
		PRELUDE
		780–804
12020 Dir, der Unberührbaren,	Though inviolate, exempted	CHORUS II
Ist es nicht benommen,	In thy peerless glory,	*Äusserst langsam.*
Dass die leicht Verführbaren	Thou mayst listen to their story	*Adagiosissimo*
Traulich zu dir kommen.	Whom sweet sin has tempted.	(Extremely slow)
In die Schwachheit hingerafft,	They were weak, in thee they trust;	(E major)
12025 Sind die schwer zu retten:	Who shall save them now?	bars 804–44
Wer zerreisst aus eigner Kraft	Who can break the chains of lust?	
Der Gelüste Ketten?	Who will help but thou?	
Wie entgleitet schnell der Fuss	Easily the foot can slip,	
Schiefem, glattem Boden!	Slide to swift destruction,	
12030 [Wen betört nicht Blick und Gruss,	[Ardent eye and flattering lip	
Schmeichelhafter Odem?]	Breathe such strong seduction.] [39]	
CHOR DER BÜSSERINNEN	CHORUS OF PENITENT WOMEN	20 SOPRANOS
Du schwebst zu Höhen	In the transcendent	FROM
Der ewigen Reiche;	High regions soaring,	CHORUS II
Vernimm das Flehen,	Lady resplendent,	*Fliessend* (Flowing)
12035 Du Ohnegleiche,	See us adoring,	(B major)
Du Gnadenreiche!	Hear us imploring!	bars 844–67
MAGNA PECCATRIX	MAGNA PECCATRIX	SOPRANO I
Bei der Liebe, die den Füssen	By the love that on thy glorious	(B major)
Deines gottverklärten Sohnes	Son's feet shed a balm so tearful,	bars 868–905
Tränen liess zum Balsam fliessen	While the Pharisee's censorious	

---

[38] Mahler does not set this stanza.   [39] These two lines are not set to music.

(cont.):

GOETHE'S TEXT	ENGLISH TRANSLATION	
12040 Trotzt des Pharisäerhohnes,	Thoughts despised that homage fearful;	
Beim Gefässe, das so reichlich	By the fragrance poured so gladly	
Tropfte Wohlgeruch hernieder,	From the jar of alabaster,	
Bei den Locken, die so weichlich	By my hair that softly, sadly	
Trockneten die heiligen Glieder—	Dried thy sacred limbs, oh Master—	
MULIER SAMARITANA	MULIER SAMARITANA	ALTO I
12045 Bei dem Bronn, zu dem schon weiland	By that well where once they tarried,	(D flat major,
Abram liess die Herde führen,	Flocks by Abraham's shepherds tended,	then E flat)
Bei dem Eimer, der dem Heiland	By the cooling draught I carried	bars 906–56
Kühl die Lippe durft berühren,	Which his dear parched lips befriended;	
Bei der reinen, reichen Quelle,	By that pure rich fountain flowing	
12050 Die nun dorther sich ergiesset,	Now through all the world, unceasing,	
Überflüssig, ewig helle	Ever in abundance growing,	
Rings durch alle Welten fliesset—	In its brightness still increasing—	
		ORCHESTRAL
		INTERLUDE
		bars 957–69
MARIA AEGYPTIACA	MARIA AEGYPTIACA	ALTO II
Bei dem hochgeweihten Orte,	By the holy place where they	*Immer fliessend*
Wo den Herrn man niederliess,	Laid to rest our Saviour mortal,	(Still flowing)
12055 Bei dem Arm, der von der Pforte	By the arm that barred my way	(G minor)
Warnend mich zurückestiess,	As I dared approach its portal;	bars 970–1016
Bei der vierzigjährigen Busse,	By my forty years awaiting	
Der ich treu in Wüsten blieb,	Pardon in a desert land,	
Bei dem seligen Scheidegrusse,	By my last and blessed greeting	
12060 Den im Sand ich niederschrieb—	Written on the burning sand—	
ZU DREI	ALL THREE	TRIO IN CANON
Die du grossen Sünderinnen	Such great sinners find a place	*Sehr fliessend,*
Deine Nähe nicht verweigerst	Near thee, by the condescension,	*beinahe flüchtig*
Und ein büssendes Gewinnen	And their penitent intention	(Very flowing,
In die Ewigkeiten steigerst,	Grows into eternal grace:	almost hasty)
12065 Gönn auch dieser guten Seele,	This good soul, who only once	(C, A, F, major)
Die sich einmal nur vergessen,	Went astray and scarcely knew it,	bars 1017–93
Die nicht ahnte, dass sie fehle,	Also seeks thy mercy—show it	
Dein Verzeihen angemessen!	As befits her innocence!	
		ORCHESTRAL
		INTERLUDE
		bars 1094–103
UNA POENITENTIUM	UNA POENITENTIUM	SOPRANO II
	(*formerly named* GRETCHEN)	(D major)
Neige, neige	Virgin and Mother, thou	bars 1104–129
12070 Du Ohnegleiche,	Lady beyond compare, oh thou	
Du Strahlenreiche,	Who art full of glory, bow	
Dein Antlitz gnädig meinem Glück!	Thy face in mercy to my great joy now!	
Der früh Geliebte,	He whom I loved—oh see,	
Nicht mehr Getrübte,	He is undarkened, he	
12075 Er kommt zurück.	Comes back to me!	
		ORCHESTRAL
		INTERLUDE
		bars 1130–40

GOETHE'S TEXT	ENGLISH TRANSLATION	
SELIGE KNABEN	**BLESSED BOYS**	CHILDREN'S
Er überwächst uns schon	How soon with limbs of might	CHORUS
An mächtigen Gliedern,	He has outsoared us!	*Unmerklich frischer*
Wird treuer Pflege Lohn	We nurtured him aright,	(Gradually livelier)
Reichlich erwidern.	He will reward us.	bars 1141–85
12080 Wir wurden früh entfernt	Out of life's music all	
Von Lebechören;	Too soon death plucked us,	
Doch dieser hat gelernt:	But he has learnt it all;	
Er wird uns lehren.	He will instruct us.	

DIE EINE BÜSSERIN	**UNA PENITENTIUM**	SOPRANO II (with
Vom edlen Geisterchor umgeben,	(GRETCHEN)	CHILDREN'S
12085 Wird sich der Neue kaum gewahr,	Ringed by that noble spirit-chorus,	CHORUS)
Er ahnet kaum das frische Leben,	This neophyte of life unknown,	*Allegro* (with
So gleicht er schon der heiligen Schar.	Scarcely awake, and strange before us,	reprise of '*Er*
Sieh, wie er jedem Erdenbande,	Already makes our form his own.	*überwächst uns*
Der alten Hülle sich entrafft	See, how all earthly bonds discarding	*schon*')
12090 Und aus ätherischem Gewande	He casts his outworn husk aside,	bars 1186–212
Hervortritt erste Jugendkraft!	And an ethereal raiment parting	*Nicht schleppend*
Vergönne mir, ihn zu belehren:	His youth steps out refortified!	(Do not drag)
Noch blendet ihn der neue Tag!	O Lady, grant me now to teach him!	(B flat major)
	He is dazzled still by the new day.	Reprise of '*Imple*
		Superna gratia'
		ORCHESTRAL
		INTERLUDE
		bars 1243–8

MATER GLORIOSA	**MATER GLORIOSA**	SOPRANO SOLO
Komm, hebe dich zu höhern Sphären!	Come! Into higher spheres outreach him!	*Sehr langsam*
12095 Wenn er dich ahnet, folgt er nach.	He must sense you to find the way.	(Very slowly)
		(E flat major)
		bars 1249–76

DOCTOR MARIANUS	**DOCTOR MARIANUS**	TENOR SOLO and
Blicket auf zum Retterblick,	Gaze aloft—the saving eyes	CHORUSES
Alle reuig Zarten,	See you all, such tender	*Hymneartig*
Euch zu seligem Geschick	Penitents; look up and render	(Hymnlike)
Dankend umzuarten!	Thanks, to blest renewal rise!	(E flat, then E major)
12100 Werde jeder bessre Sinn	May each noble spirit never	bars 1277–383
Dir zum Dienst erbötig!	Fail to serve thee; Virgin, Mother,	
Jungfrau, Mutter, Königin,	Queen, oh keep us in thy favour,	
Göttin, bleibe gnädig!	Goddess, kind for ever!	
		ORCHESTRAL
		INTERLUDE
		bars 1384–448

CHORUS MYSTICUS	**CHORUS MYSTICUS**	CHORUSES and
Alles Vergängliche	All that must disappear	SOLOISTS
12105 Ist nur ein Gleichnis;	Is but a parable;	*Sehr langsam*
Das Unzulängliche,	What lay beyond us, here	*beginnend*
Hier wird's Ereignis;	All is made visible;	(Very slow at the
		beginning)

(*cont.*):

Goethe's Text	English Translation	
Das Unbeschreibliche,	Here deeds have understood	(E flat major)
Hier ist's getan; [40]	Words they were darkened by;	bars 1449–528
12110 Das Ewig-Weibliche	Eternal Womanhood	
Zieht uns hinan.	Draws us on high.	

Quoting Goethe's text in full enables us to see that Mahler's changes are few and slight. The biggest one is the dropping of the character of Pater Seraphicus and his dialogue with the Blessed Boys (lines 11890 to 11925).[41] A number of additions and repetitions of words arise where the text has to fit music already in existence. 'Euch' is added after 'Hände verschlinget' (line 11926) for metrical reasons, because Mahler has this text sung at the same time as the passage that follows it; the 'uns' also added before 'Zu tragen peinlich' (line 11955) is needed to alter the number of feet so that the line can be tailored to a musical episode taken from the first movement, 'Infirma nostri corporis'. In the angels' chorus (lines 11966 ff.), several lines are reversed, and line 11970 is dropped.[42] At line 11990 (bar 604) the tenor sings his invocation over the chorus's last three lines (lines 11978–80), and then over the 'Chorus of blessed boys' (lines 11981 ff.). He is not alone until 'Höchste Herrin' (line 11997). According to Susanne Vill, who has examined the first proofs of the score, corrected by Mahler, music was originally written for the passage 'Um sie verschlingen' (lines 12013 to 12019), but Mahler cut this episode 'for reasons of length, and partly because of the visual metaphor'.[43] Here and there, the choruses and the soloists overlap, one entering before the other is finished (for example at bar 604 ff.). Rudolf Stephan observes that the passage where Mahler does most violence to the text is 'Uns bleibt ein Erdenrest' (bar 532, line 11954) and on to the entrance of Doctor Marianus (bar 604). He uses the music of 'Infirma nostri corporis', from the first section, at the price of repetitions of words or half-lines, and of some switching around. All the last part of Dr Marianus's monologue ('Dir, der Unberührbaren': lines 12020 ff.) is given to the chorus. In the 'Chorus mysticus' the treatment of the text is also very free, as might be expected in such an apotheosis.

---

[40] Hermann Danuser notes that Goethe's text, in most editions, reads 'ist es getan' but that Goethe corrected his own text in an earlier version of the text as 'ist's getan' (Danuser, 'Interpret', 279).

[41] As Rudolf Stephan has shown in 'Zu Mahlers Komposition der Schlussszene von Goethes Faust' (see H. Kühn and G. Quander (eds.), *Gustav Mahler: Ein Lesebuch mit Bildern* (Orell, Füssli, Zurich, 1982), 137), the omission of this character and his monologue somewhat alters the sense of the children's chorus 'Hände verschlinget' which, in the original, took the form of thanks for the 'divine lesson' of Pater Seraphicus. On the other hand, this text is later sung along with the angels' chorus 'Gerettet ist', to which it replies. Susanne Vill has observed that by omitting this third Pater, Mahler does away with the symmetry of characters, where four men (the three fathers and Doctor Marianus) were opposite four women (Una Poenitentium, Magna Peccatrix, Mulier Samaritana, and Maria Aegyptiaca) with the Mater gloriosa in the centre, perhaps because this symmetry was only really observable on stage.

[42] Mahler's order of lines is as follows: 11967, 11966, 11969, 11968, 11972, 11971. Rudolf Stephan notes that Mahler changed certain words for reasons of diction, notably 'beweget' to 'bewegt' and 'träget' to 'trägt' (lines 12002 and 12004). At line 12050 he changes 'fliessest' into 'fliesst' but fails to modify the previous 'ergiesset' (bars 934–5) for the sake of the rhyme.

[43] Vill, in *Vermittlungsformen*, 152, quotes in a footnote the various melodic lines of this episode, which Mahler dropped in the proofs. It contains 26 bars for chorus (between bars 763 and 764). Later on, a reprise of 'Jungfrau, rein in schönsten Sinne' (28 bars for chorus between bars 844 and 845 of the score) is also dropped, as well as the melody of 'zu höhern Sphären' (bars 1249 to 61) and 'alle reuig Zarten' (bars 1280 to 1283).

MANUSCRIPTS AND VERSIONS

Apart from the sketches of 'programmes' noted above, and the corrected proofs also mentioned above,[44] only one complete autograph score of the Eighth Symphony is known. It used to belong to Alma Mahler,[45] and is now in the Bayerische Staatsbibliothek in Munich.

REVISIONS; EDITING

The first piano score of the Eighth appeared in time for the first rehearsals, in April 1910. Mahler as usual made changes to the score after the first rehearsals (which took place in June). It is thus extremely fortunate that the complete set of proofs mentioned before, retouched by him in August 1910, survives, as well as a score written out by a copyist and also bearing numerous corrections in Mahler's hand. A second, corrected, piano score (this time with a dedication to Alma) appeared in October the same year. Some of the orchestral parts, for strings only, were published in June 1910, that is to say before the première. They had been corrected by Mahler after the June rehearsals, and the definitive version appeared in September. The other orchestral parts were published between November 1911 and February 1912.

GENERAL OUTLINE; CONCEPTION; TECHNIQUE

The overall structure of the Eighth Symphony is exceptional, even unique, in Mahler's output, because all the themes throughout belong to families,[46] and are derived from a few rhythmic and melodic cells. A great deal of the thematic material is common to both sections:

When one tries to grasp that these two sections of the Eighth Symphony are nothing other than one single extraordinarily long and broad idea, a single idea conceived, contemplated and mastered at a stroke, then one stands amazed at the power of a mind which, even when young, was fit for unbelievable things, and which here achieves the seemingly impossible (*das Unwahrscheinlichste*).[47]

Indeed, looking at the whole of this vast work, springing so plainly from a single impulse and a single source, one has the impression that Mahler wanted to compensate

---

[44] Those of the second part belong to the Universal Edition but are deposited in ÖNB, Vienna. Those of the first part, which used to be in Alma's collection, belong to the Vienna Stadtbibliothek. Some extra instrumental parts, notably one for the glockenspiel (at number 81 in the second section) are written on separate sheets.

[45] However, two separate autograph pages of orchestral score are in BGM, one of the passage 'Tu septiformis' (bar 343 in the score) down to 'credamus' (bar 354, and one from the second section, starting with 'Gleichnis' (bars 1512 to 1527).   [46] See the thematic table below.

[47] Schoenberg, 'Stil und Gedanke', in *Aufsätze zur Musik* (Fischer, Frankfurt, 1976), 23.

for the dissimilarity of the two texts (the medieval Latin hymn, and Goethe's mystic and romantic scene) through a thematic unity never before or since encountered in his music. From the point of view of key, the work is exceptionally stable, with the opening key of E flat major recurring continually. Harmonically, then, this symphony shows a certain regression in relation to the previous works. It is as if Mahler wanted to carve his profession of faith in granite.[48] Arnold Schoenberg had this to say about this characteristic feature of the 'Veni Creator' movement:

How often this movement comes back to E flat major, on a chord of the fourth and sixth for instance! I would have told any student not to do it, and suggested that he find another key. And yet incredibly: here it is right! Here it works! Here it could not be otherwise. What have the rules got to say about that? It is the rules that need to change![49]

In other areas this symphony shows undeniable enrichment in Mahler's style, and not because of the counterpoint, even though the polyphonic skill of the 'Veni Creator' is perhaps unsurpassed since Bach and the masters of the Renaissance (a fairly astonishing standard for the 'bad' student in counterpoint classes at the Vienna Conservatory to have attained). Mahler's real triumphs here are strictly compositional, and find expression in the systematic use of the 'deviation' (*Abweichung*) or 'variant'. From the Eighth onward, Mahler's music is characterized by continuous evolution of the thematic material, which becomes supple and mobile, always recognizable yet always different. As Adorno noted, its transformations never detract from its expressivity: the reverse of what often happens with classical variations. Thus, for example, the first theme of the second movement, in the basses, is made up of the first two notes of the opening motif ('Ve-ni') followed by a rising motif borrowed from the theme 'Accende lumen'. Thus, again, the 'Love theme' marking the entrance of the Mater gloriosa is in fact an avatar of the melody played by the winds as early as the third bar of the second movement. Here and there, by frequent thematic references to the first movement, Mahler stresses the link between the words and ideas expressed in Faust and in the 'Veni creator'.[50] In effect the entire work is dominated by the 'Veni creator' theme, whose eloquence and epigrammatic conciseness do not at first reveal its rhythmic complexity (three changes of metre in four bars!). The first three notes (E flat–B flat–A flat) have the same unifying role as those in the *Lied von der Erde* (A–G–E) and Ninth Symphony (F#–A–B). And they later dominate the final apotheosis in each of the movements.

It has often been observed, as a further eccentricity, that the work is divided into two parts of unequal size. Undoubtedly this is unique in Mahler's output, but so is the symphony itself! In reality, the second section may appear a succession of strongly contrasted episodes, determined by the text. Under these conditions, all Mahler's craftsmanship and architectural genius are needed to hold the work together. The first Mahler commentators made out an Adagio, a Scherzo, and a Finale within the second movement. From Ortrun Landmann's excellent analysis I shall borrow a structural notion of this second movement that is a little different, but in my view closer to reality.

---

[48] Deryck Cooke, programme note for a concert by the Liverpool Philharmonic (29 May 1964), 9.
[49] Schoenberg, 'Stil und Gedanke', 15.
[50] I have noted these quotations, as and when they occur, alongside the text above.

FORM AND CHARACTER

The double meaning, subjective and objective, that Mahler discerned in the final scene in Goethe's *Faust* is explained by him in a letter to his wife quoted below.[51] His philosophical comments do much to justify and explain the very unusual structure of the Eighth, a perfectly coherent ensemble composed of two wings as dissimilar as possible, like the two texts themselves, which belong to two languages, two cultures, and two epochs far removed from each other. Mahler in no way sought to soften this contrast. On the contrary, he intensified it by treating the 'Veni Creator' as a Latin hymn, mostly contrapuntal, in an almost ecclesiastical style, but cast in the mould of traditional sonata form. The style owes little to Bach, whose main choral works Mahler nonetheless never ceased to study and admire, but more perhaps to the 'recherché' polyphonies (*ricercare*) of the Renaissance. The second section is, on the other hand, a sort of free fantasy, German Romantic and sometimes even impressionist in spirit, and far more homophonic than polyphonic. However, unity derives not only from the similarities of the thematic materials, but from the fact that the work as a whole expresses one single and abiding idea, and moves powerfully forward towards its monumental conclusion. The result of Mahler's great design can at first seem like a huge cantata, but it is in fact a symphony in the full sense of the term. A symphony *for* and not *with* soloists, choruses, and orchestra, in which the voices, treated in a thoroughly instrumental fashion, expose and develop the core thematic material. It is also the only Mahler symphony that is 'objective' rather than 'subjective', optimistic rather than pessimistic. It is the first of his works in which there is no 'music about music',[52] no stylized, distant echoes of birdsong, military marches or Austrian dance rhythms. Here, Mahler wished to answer all questions, dissolve all doubts, overcome all the uncertainties of the human condition. As Schoenberg pertinently noted, such a 'glorification of the highest joys is only possible for one who knows that such joys are no longer for him, and who has already resigned himself'.

In an article about the Eighth, Clytus Gottwald[53] observes that Mahler not only succeeds in 'linking Christian and Faustian Utopias, but in representing them as two aspects of one Utopia, intensely human', and that the 'Veni Creator' motifs dominate the whole of Part II, starting with the first bars of the Prelude.[54] Adorno finds no trace in this movement of a classical symphonic pattern of movements but acknowledges nevertheless that it is 'no mere string of contrasting solo songs and choruses, but is fed by a powerful underground developmental stream, a "symphony": as is *Das Lied von der Erde* with which it so strangely converges'. As we shall see below, Adorno has reservations about the affirmative and optimistic message of the Eighth, as with the Finales of the Fifth and

---

[51] See below, Vol. iiii, Chap. 5, the letter Mahler wrote to Alma in June 1910.

[52] See Henry-Louis de La Grange, 'Music about Music in Mahler: Reminiscences, Allusions or Quotations', in Stephen Hefling (ed.), *Mahler Studies* (Cambridge University Press, Cambridge, 1997), 122 ff.

[53] 'Mahlers Achte', in Peter Ruzicka (ed.), *Mahler: Eine Herausforderung* (Breitkopf, Wiesbaden, 1977), 208.

[54] It is used there both in the bass ostinato and in the flute melody. Gottwald also observes that, although Stravinsky was so scornful about the Eighth in 1913 (see below, Vol. iiii, Chap. 7), the end of Mahler's work served as model for the end of his *Symphony of Psalms*.

Seventh symphonies. He concludes: 'All is poised on a knife-edge, uncurtailed Utopia and the lapse into grandiose decorativeness. Mahler's danger is that of the redeemer.'[55]

On the other hand, Deryck Cooke does not question Mahler's powerful affirmation. He sets it against the previous funeral marches in Mahler's symphonies, which 'lament the burial of humanistic hopes', and he adds:

But being a product of the later, disillusioned humanistic period, Mahler was acutely conscious of the insufficiency of humanism, in its pure, godless aspect, owing to the insufficiency of man himself. In consequence he revived, from a new standpoint, the earlier attitude of Beethoven's Choral Symphony, attempting a new fusion of humanism with religious belief; and for the expression of this belief he turned to the central musical symbol for the Christian faith which had been handed on to him by the devout Bruckner—the chorale. In several of Mahler's symphonies, march and chorale appear side by side, or are transformed one into the other, or are even fused into a single thematic idea. And so much of his music, far from being concerned with abstractions, or with vague metaphysical ideas, is simply an existential meeting-place for humanism and faith in God—for the Deed and the Word. It is a place where a bold attempt is made to erect a spiritual bridge over the abyss of nihilism, of a kind which may be the way forward for disillusioned modern man, who can hardly hope to return to the unreflecting childlike faith that made possible the music of a composer like Bruckner. This is particularly true of the Eighth Symphony of 1906, which may be regarded as the Choral Symphony of the twentieth century, as Beethoven's Ninth was that of the nineteenth century.

In the Eighth Symphony, the Word and the Deed are set side by side, both in the text and in the music. The old Catholic hymn *Veni Creator Spiritus*, which Mahler used for the first part of the symphony, is actually an invocation to the Word—to the Holy Ghost of Christianity, as Creator Spirit. And the text of the symphony's second part—the final scene from Goethe's *Faust*—may be described as the free rendering of the Catholic Latin of the Word into the humanistic German of the Deed. The salvation of Faust's soul symbolizes the indemnification of his humanistic quest, in spite of its failure; and this is granted because, as the angels sing: 'He who ever striving drives himself onwards, that man we can redeem'. And likewise, in the music, the two great symbols are the Brucknerian chorale, standing for the Word, and the nineteenth-century brass-band march, standing for the Deed.

But there is a strange thing here, which reveals Mahler's profound artistic and human originality. We should expect the musical and verbal symbols to go simply in harness together—as they actually do in Beethoven's Choral Symphony, where the lines concerning the brotherhood of man become the basis of the march-music, while the words 'Seek your Creator above the starry firmament' are set to a kind of self-abasing religious hymn. But in Mahler's Eighth, the verbal and musical symbols are crossed with one another, to amazing effect. It is the setting of the *Veni Creator Spiritus*—the Word—that is the great striding triumphal march in the humanistic tradition; and it is the final scene of Goethe's *Faust*—the Deed—which is based on a religious chorale, and reaches its climax with that chorale. This extraordinary artistic cross-fertilisation can mean only one thing: that the symphony offers a multiple symbol of the humanising of religion and the spiritualizing of humanism—and the fusion of both into one faith. The Word becomes the Deed: in other words, the God the symphony addresses is not the static God 'out there', but the dynamic God 'in here'—in man's inner being: but it addresses this God, not as man's projection of his own ideal self—the purely human God of Feuerbach—but as the immaterial and intangible Creator Spirit which inspires and impels man's questing aspiration. . . . Goethe, by his recourse to Christian symbolism at the end of his great drama, was clearly intent on stressing the truth that man has need of God for the achievement of his aims; and Mahler's chorale backs him in this. But

---

[55] TAM 186; TAMe 142. On this subject, see also John Williamson, 'Mahler and the Veni Creator Spiritus', in *Music Review*, 44 (1983): 1, 25.

Mahler lived during the later period of humanistic self-doubt; and by bringing back on the orchestra alone the theme of his triumphal march to end his great symphony, in a new form which reaches up imperiously to the heights, he was evidently concerned with reminding us of the converse and complementary truth: that God—whoever or whatever God may be—has need of man for the fulfilment of the dynamic creative force of things.[56]

Clytus Gottwald also underlines the dynamic aspect of Mahler's faith, symbolized by the repetition of the word 'hinan',[57] set apart from its context, at the very end of the work: this displacement 'radically changes it into a call on its own, in no way contemplative, but thoroughly active here and now, as a Faustian device on the road to utopia'. From the point of view of form all commentators have stressed the conjunct use, in the first section, of all sorts of contrapuntal techniques together with sonata form (inspired by the sonata fugues of Beethoven more than by the fugues of Bach), and also the march rhythm and rondo elements found in the exposition of the three themes. Nevertheless, we have seen that it is the technique of the variant that is most striking. The introduction to the second section recalls, to some extent, the Adagio of the Fourth Symphony, which was also presented as a series of variations over a continuous bass.[58] Ortrun Landmann observes that, just as the keys of E flat and E major predominate in the Second, Third, and Fourth symphonies, in connection with the supernatural, so these two keys prevail in the Eighth. In her view, the Mater gloriosa theme (bars 780 ff.) 'comes close to banality' when first stated over simple chords for harps and harmonium, but is later 'ennobled and revalued' in the developments that follow.

THEMATIC MATERIAL; CYCLIC PROCEDURES

There can be no question here of listing all the 'cyclic procedures' of the Eighth Symphony, as the whole of it constitutes a single musical organism, drawing the unity of its content from a small number of melodic cells. Thus, for example, the first theme of the second section, the ostinato in the basses, is made up of the first two notes of the opening theme of the symphony, followed by a rising motif borrowed from the theme 'Accende lumen'. Thus, too, the 'Love theme' accompanying the entrance of the Mater gloriosa is an avatar of the melody played in the winds in the third bar of the orchestral introduction. Here and there, as we have seen, Mahler in the second section takes up a more or less complete episode from the first, to emphasize the similarity of situations or ideas. For example, we find 'Amorem cordibus' in 'Hände verschlinget euch' (I, bars 370 ff.; II, bars 385 ff.), both sung by the children's chorus; 'Infirma nostri corporis' in 'Uns bleibt ein

---

[56] Deryck Cooke, 'The Word and the Deed, Mahler's Eighth Symphony', in *Essays in Romantic Music* (Faber, London, 1982), 113.

[57] Prefix (or suffix) denoting a movement away from the person speaking. The repetition of the word *ewig* has also been much noted (bars 1486 to 1497), as it anticipates the same repetition at the end of the *Lied von der Erde*. Thus, as Rudolph Stephan notes, Mahler is celebrating the *Eternal* Feminine rather than the Eternal *Feminine*.

[58] Ortrun Landmann, 'Vielfalt und Einheit in der Achten Sinfonie Gustav Mahlers: Beobachtung zu den Themen und zu Formgestalt des Werkes', in *Beiträge zur Musikwissenschaft*, 17 (1975): 1, 33.

Erdenrest' (I, bars 142 ff.; II, bars 533 ff.); 'Imple superna gratia' in 'er ahnet kaum das frische Leben' (I, bars 46 ff.; II, bars 1213 ff.); 'Accende lumen' in 'Zieht uns hinan' (I, bars 262 ff.; II, bars 1467 ff.). As we have also observed, the entire conclusion of the second part, and of the symphony as a whole, is permeated and ruled by the second motif of the 'Veni creator' (bars 5 ff., trombones), which is simply a rhythmic variant of the first. Among links that are less obvious, but no less symbolic, can be noted, at bar 396 in the second part, the first appearance of the complete 'Accende' theme (E), on the words:

> Wer immer strebend sich bemüht,
> Den können wir erlösen
> (He who strives on and lives to strive
> Can earn redemption still.)

suggesting that light, the divine spark, the supreme revelation, comes only to those who 'strive'.

After the first theme, 'no resistance should be left in the hall': Richard Specht imagines Mahler using these words to anticipate the effect of the opening statement of the Eighth Symphony.[59] Exceptional as is this work in Mahler's œuvre, many thematic resemblances with other works of his have been noted in it. One of the most obvious ones links the 'Accende' theme, with a large family of rising melodies, the Resurrection theme of the Second, the opening theme of the Fourth, the Adagietto (and Finale) of the Fifth, etc.

ORCHESTRATION; SOLO VOICES

The orchestral forces required to perform the Eighth are large (though not as large as those required by Schoenberg for his *Gurre-Lieder*, the orchestration of which was completed in 1911). In addition to the strings, they include 6 flutes (with at least 2 piccolos); 4 oboes and cor anglais; 3 clarinets in B flat, 2 in E flat (at least), and a bass clarinet in B flat; 4 bassoons and contrabassoon; 8 horns; 4 trumpets; 4 trombones; 1 tuba; abundant percussion, including 3 timpani, bass drum, cymbals, tamtam, triangle, and low-pitched bells; glockenspiel; celesta; piano;[60] harmonium; organ; 2 harps (at least); and one mandolin (at least). In addition, a group of 4 trumpets and 3 trombones is to be placed separately from the main body of instruments, and Mahler recommends doubling the first desks of woodwind in very large halls where the numbers of choristers and strings are accordingly augmented. As always, the aim of his orchestration is to make the slightest detail audible, even during the most powerful tutti. There are also numerous passages of chamber music, orchestrated with the greatest lightness and economy of means.

As for the solo voices, it should be noted that the tessitura of the sopranos is particularly high, and that they frequently rise to high C (even the choral sopranos have

---

[59] RSM2, 315.

[60] The piano and the glockenspiel were added during the Munich rehearsals. (See below, Vol. iiii, Chap. 7, the conclusions to be drawn from various reviews regarding the resources used for the Munich première.)

several high Cs).[61] The alto parts call for no particular remarks, and their solos are fairly brief. The role of the tenor is singularly extended in the second section. For the Doctor Marianus solo a very full, almost heroic voice is needed, to be heard above the massed choruses. Yet his part includes quite a number of piano and pianissimo passages. The bass part is one of the most risky, because of the succession of big melodic leaps in the Pater Profundus solo.

ANALYSES

Unlike the Sixth or the Ninth, the Eighth Symphony has never been a favourite subject for analysts. The oldest texts are by Edgar Istel (18 pp., 1910)[62] and Richard Specht (48 pp., 1912 and 28 pp., 1913)[63] and their contemporaries Hermann Kretschmar (3 pp., 1913)[64] and Paul Bekker (37 pp., 1920).[65] After the Second World War, a long analysis by Deryck Cooke appeared in an English concert programme (25 pp., 1964).[66] The work has also been analysed by Ortrun Landmann (14 pp., 1975),[67] Susanne Vill (24 pp., 1979),[68] Rudolf Stephan (9 pp. in octavo, 1982; 30 pp., 1983),[69] and finally Constantin Floros (24 pp., 1985)[70] and Theodore Bloomfield (12 pp., 1988).[71]

A very substantial analysis of the first movement has been published by John Williamson.[72] For this first movement, all modern commentators accept the sonata-form outline already put forward in Mahler's lifetime. But the second part was regarded by Richard Specht as being divided into three parts, an Adagio (the opening chorus, and the solos of the two Paters, bars 1 to 284), a Scherzo (from 'Gerettet ist das edle Glied' up to and including the solo of Dr Marianus: bars 285 to 779) and a Finale (from the entrance of the Mater gloriosa: bars 780 ff.). Paul Bekker[73] held a similar view but started the Finale a little earlier, at the first appearance of Dr Marianus ('Hier ist die Aussicht', bar 604). The fact that there are such differences of opinion indicates that

---

[61] During rehearsals for the Viennese première in 1912, Bruno Walter made a typically Mahlerian remark to his choruses: 'All the sopranos have a C! The ones without it should sing it as well!' (Mary Komorn-Rebhan, *Was wir von Bruno Walter lernten* (Universal Edition, Vienna, n.d. [1913]). This brochure merits more attention than it has received, notably for the advice it provides concerning the performance of the Eighth Symphony. Bruno Walter attended most of the Vienna and Munich rehearsals, and thus knew better than anyone how Mahler wanted the Eighth performed.

[62] *Mahlers Symphonien, Meisterführer* no. 10 (Schlesinger, Berlin, 1913).

[63] The first is in a brochure published by Universal Edition in 1912, the other in RSM2, 304.

[64] *Führer durch den Konzertsaal* (Breitkopf, Leipzig, 1913), 811. This short article questions the title of symphony and the joining of Latin and German texts. It criticizes the work as a whole for being 'very uneven' and 'often spoilt by over-elaboration'. [65] BMS 209.

[66] Royal Liverpool Philharmonic Symphony Society, programme for a concert on 29 May 1964.

[67] Landmann, 'Vielfalt', 29. [68] Vill, *Vermittlungsformen*, 130.

[69] See Rudolph Stephan, 'Zu Mahlers Komposition der Schlussszene von Goethes Faust', in Werner Breig (ed.), *Schütz Jahrbuch 4/5, 1982–3* (Bärenreiter, Kassel, 1983), 73 ff., and Kühn and Quander (eds.), *Gustav Mahler: Lesebuch.*

[70] In Floros, *Gustav Mahler*, Vol. iii: 'Die Symphonien', 210 ff.

[71] See 'The Contrasts of Mahler's Eighth Symphony', in Evelyn Nikkels and Robert Becqué (eds.), *A Mass for the Masses: Proceedings of the Mahler VIII Symposium Amsterdam 1988* (Nijgh & Van Ditmar, Universitair Pers Rotterdam, Rijswijk, 1992), 167 ff. [72] Williamson, 'Veni Creator', 25.

[73] BMS 290.

the division is somewhat arbitrary. Ortrun Landmann,[74] in her substantial and convincing analysis of the Eighth Symphony, divides the different episodes of Geothe's text as follows:

1. Description of the landscape; presentation of the Paters; entrance of the angels with the soul of Faust (up to 'die ewige Liebe', line 11965).
2. We approach the sphere of the Mater gloriosa; Dr Marianus and the children start to take care of Faust's soul (up to 'Göttern ebenbürtig', line 1212).
3. Principal episode: appearance of the Mater gloriosa; prayers of the three sinning women and of Gretchen (from line 12075).
4. Faust's soul blossoms; the Mater gloriosa pronounces redemption; hymn to the action of grace (up to 'Göttin, bleibe gnädig', line 12103).
5. Chorus Mysticus: final commentary.

Landmann asserts that the division exactly fits the formal scheme it suggests, comprising: Episode 1: Exposition. Episodes 2 to 4: Development in three sections. Episode 5: Epilogue. The elimination of any recapitulation seems normal, in that the text itself never once looks back and the development sections are already substantial. As for the orchestral introduction, it is to be seen as a transition and as 'an entracte belonging with the second section'. Landmann also divides the various themes into families according to their rhythmic and melodic character, and emphasizes that the first movement is entirely dominated by the sonority of the choruses, while the orchestra participates in a more consistent manner in the unfolding of the second.[75] Landmann notes, finally, that Mahler's most important change to Goethe's text concerns the end of the monologue of Dr Marianus ('Dir, der Unberührbaren', line 12090), which Mahler gives to the chorus and places after the entrance of the Mater gloriosa.[76]

As before in these pages, the analysis below will be brief. I have chosen a method slightly different from the one previously used, because of the extreme complexity of the variant techniques in this work. Thus I have reproduced below a thematic inventory of about thirty music examples, which in my view is indispensable for making the text understandable and illustrating the numerous procedures of variants, augmentation, diminution, transformation, and quotation, let alone the subtler rhythmic and melodic relationships. As seen above,[77] Mahler spoke in the presence of Schoenberg's disciples after the first Viennese performance of his orchestral Lieder, of his ideal of a

---

[74] Landmann (in 'Vielfalt', 31) observes that no other Mahler scherzo is in four-time (or *alla breve*, as is often the case here), even though the one in the Sixth mixes 4/8 bars with others in 3/8 or 3/4. And while all of them have a form of their own, a blend of sonata and rondo, the alleged Scherzo of the Eighth is quite free, even at times disjointed.

[75] In 'The Chorus in Mahler's Music', in *Music Review*, 43 (1982): 1, 33, Zoltan Roman notes that in the first movement, only 100 bars out of 580 are without voices (i.e. 17.2 per cent of the movement) while, in the second, the orchestra plays alone for 602 bars out of 1572 (i.e. 38.3 per cent of the movement). In the first movement, 99 bars are given to solo voices and 204 to the chorus, while the proportions are reversed in the second, 484 bars for the chorus against 337 for the soloists. Roman also notes that the choral writing in the Eighth is 'normal' with one exception: if the registers of the outer voices, the sopranos and basses, are stretched both high and low, the registers of the tenors and altos are stretched upwards only. Even their lowest notes are high, so that 'light and clarity' reign in the middle voices, in accordance with the principles Mahler followed in his orchestration, at least from the Fourth Symphony onward.

[76] As we have seen, the two last lines of this stanza ('Wen betört nicht Blick . . .', lines 12030 and 12031) were dropped by Mahler.   [77] See above, Chap. 2.

musical unity that was absolute, with development springing tree-like from a single mother-cell. Never did he come closer to this ideal than in the Eighth, where the whole of the material is derived from a small number of motifs, often related to each other. My classification by families is modelled on Ortrun Landmann's. However, for the first part of the work, whose sonata form fits the most traditional outline, I have added the same system of letters that I have consistently used so far, that is to say, A for the principal theme, B for the second theme, and C for the concluding theme (along with D and E for the two new themes in the development). These letters have the advantage of immediately drawing attention, in the second part, to the numerous passages where material or episodes from the first are quoted.

For the *Faust* scene, I have reproduced below the sonata plan discerned only by Ortrun Landmann, for I consider that the division into three 'movements' does not stand close examination. If the distinction between 'sections' corresponds to an obvious reality, the role of the themes themselves, within this form, seems to me to be not very clearly defined. Their most characteristic trait is that they are derived one from another and that they mostly originate in those of the first movement. Among the novel aspects of this symphony, is the way in which Mahler several times anticipates a new motif by using it as a counterpoint to a previously existing one, for example in the eighth bar of the first movement (in the violins, theme C, 'Tu paraclitus diceris', is superimposed on A^1), or in bars 131 ff. (theme D, 'Infirma nostri corporis' from the beginning of the development, is superimposed on A') or again in bars 275 ff., where the new children's chorus's melody 'Amorem cordibus' (no. IV/3 in the table below) is superimposed on A', in the basses, and then on 'Accende' (E), in the second chorus. At the end of the movement, the main 'Veni creator' theme, combined with E ('Accende') and with the new motif from the second section, serves as the musical substance for the 'Doxology', 'Gloria patri', while the separate brass take up the two latter motifs and then an augmented, magnified, and triumphal version of A^2.

(a) Erster Teil (First part): Hymnus: Veni, Creator Spiritus

Composition: See below.

Key: E flat major (with the second theme in D flat and the third in D minor, etc.). See the table below.

Time signature: With the exception of the principal theme, which is characterized by changes of metre, and of a few bars that introduce the development, the movement as a whole is in 4/4.

Rhythm: March (but without military effects).

Tempo: *Allegro impetuoso; etwas gemässigter, immer sehr fliessend* (a little more moderate, still very flowing), for the second theme; *etwas gehalten* (slightly held back), for the third.

Duration: 30 minutes at the Munich première, according to Julius Korngold.

Form: Few movements in Mahler's work give such a strong impression of predetermination or seem so far removed from the 'novelesque' conception of form defined by Adorno. John Williamson even asks whether this might not have been the reason for Adorno's dislike of this movement.[78] He also points out the

---

[78] Williamson, 'Veni Creator', 34.

paradox involved in evoking a 'state of being' (faith) through thematic formulae generally associated with becoming (march music). In his view, the movement succeeds nevertheless in producing a 'static' effect thanks to the treatment of keys, all centred on E flat major, and to the use of a single principal theme, all tension arising, in terms of form, from the cry of 'Accende lumen'.[79]

Bars	Themes and Motifs	Tempos	Keys
Exposition 1			
1–45	Theme A^1(2–5); A'(5–7); A^1 and A''(8–10); A^2(22–5) 'Veni creator'	*Allegro impetuoso*	E flat, B flat, E flat major
46–107	Theme B^1 (with A',A^2); B^2 (or A'': bar 80), B'	*Etwas gemässigter, immer sehr fliessend* (a little more moderate, still very flowing)	D flat, A flat, (B flat major)
107–22	Theme A^1 (with B^1) 'Veni Creator'	*Sempre a tempo* *Pesante*	E flat major
122–34	Interlude/orchestra (A', A^1, A'', D)	*Tempo primo*	
135–41	Prelude/orchestra (A', A'', D)	*Noch einmal so langsam* (as slow again)	D minor
141–68	Theme C (A^1, B, A', B^1) 'Infirma nostri corporis'	*Etwas gehalten* (slightly held back), then *sehr ruhig* (very calm)	E flat major
Development			
1st section			
169–216	Prelude/orchestra (A^{1}inverted, A')	*Tempo I. Allegro, etwas hastig* (rather hurried)	A flat major (C sharp minor F, D, C, B major)
217–61	Theme D (var. of A') (A^1, B^1)	*Noch einmal so langsam als vorher* (again as slow as before)	C sharp minor F, D, C, E major
2nd section			
262–311	Theme E (variant of A') (A', A^1, A^{2}and IV/3) 'Accende lumen'	*Mit plötzlicher Aufschwung* (surging suddenly)	E, D, E major, E minor
3rd section			
312–412	Double Fugue (A', A^2, E, then B^1: bars 385 ff.) 'Praevio te Ductore'		E flat, A, A flat, B flat, A, E major

---

[79] Ibid. 35. The writer nevertheless sees in this movement an extension of the polyphonic methods often used in the *Rückert-Lieder*, and a forerunner of the tonal stability in the first movement of the Ninth Symphony. In his opinion, the unity of materials and structure differentiates the 'Veni Creator' from the sonata-form movements in the previous symphonies.

BARS	THEMES AND MOTIFS	TEMPOS	KEYS
RECAPITULATION (abridged)			
413–41	Theme A¹ (A′, A″, A², B²=A″)		E flat major
	'*Veni creator*'	*Gehaltener* (held back more)	B flat major
441–74	A′, A″, B¹	*Wieder tempo* (tempo again)	A flat major
	'*Da gaudiorum premia*'		
474–93	A′, A²		
	'*Ductore praevio*'		
CODA			
494–518	Theme C (A′, D, D augmented)	*Breiter* (broader)	E, E flat major,
	'*Gloria Patri*'	*Wieder frisch* (brisk again) *Pesante*	D flat major, B flat minor and major
519–40	Theme A (B′, C, A²)	*Tempo primo*	B flat major
	'*Gloria sit Domino*'		E flat major
541–80	(A, A′, E, A²⁾	*Fliessend* (flowing) *Unmerklich in Halbe übergehen* (moving imperceptibly into minims).	

After one bar of introduction, where the organ establishes the reigning key of E flat by a simple tonic chord, the two choruses in unison invoke, fortissimo, the Spiritus Creator. On the last bar of A¹, a variant of the theme, here diminished and abridged, is recalled in canon, first by the trombones, then by the trumpets. The second phrase, where the two choruses have a dialogue, is decorated with a new countermelody (A″: 'O creator'), in a typically 'contrapuntal' style, and rises gradually to high in the soprano register. It leads to a concluding episode, written in tighter polyphony,[80] which is in fact a new variant of A¹. As the cadence draws nearer, the energy of the dotted rhythms subsides. It is now that the solo soprano, soon joined by the other soloists, states, in D flat, the second, 'consolatory' theme, 'Imple superna gratia'.[81] Before the end of the first verse, two elements from the opening (A′ and A² inverted) are woven into the polyphony. The second verse, in A flat, is given to the chorus (with tenor and soprano soloists), after which the motif A² serves as a transition together with the second element (B² 'qui paraclitus', previously called A″, when it was a counterpoint to the opening theme). Here is confirmation of the tendency already emphasized, to an overall unification through the use of common motifs and fragments.

After this lyrical episode, which is full of antiphonal effects and eloquent oppositions between soloists and choral masses, the initial key returns for a new variant of the first theme, again divided between the two choruses, but this time mixed with elements of the second. Even in this movement, where the form is completely predetermined, the

[80] John Williamson compares this short episode with certain transitional passages in the Fifth Symphony (for example, the one starting at bar 157 of the second movement), where 'heightening of harmonic tension is combined with a high degree of polyphonic complexity' ('Veni Creator', 29).

[81] Hans Ferdinand Redlich finds a close affinity between this theme and a motif from Bruckner's 'Te Deum'. See also Constantin Floros, 'Von Mahlers Affinität zu Bruckner', in *Bruckner-Symposion 1986* (Linzer Veranstaltungsgesellschaft, Linz ,1989), 109 ff.

principle of the 'irreversibility' of time is respected, each of the new 'characters' bringing to the tale a new element that makes it impossible genuinely to turn back.

An interlude serving as an introduction to the development now amplifies and transforms the various components of A. Here the fragmentation of the theme, the sonority of the low bells, and the long tremolo on the timpani cast the first real shadow over the music. Over a moving groundwork of chords (strings and winds) the first theme remains present (horns, then trombones), but it metamorphoses again into a new version, varied and diminished, which is actually an anticipation of theme D in the development. In the episode 'Infirma nostri corporis' Mahler, with his usual genius for inventing new combinations of timbre, suggests human frailty and mortality with the somewhat weak, blurred sonority of the altos and tenors, singing pianissimo fairly low in their register. Yet the motifs that create this uneasy atmosphere, supported only by a tracery of triplets (on A^2) in the violins (soon taken up by violin solo) are nothing but a variant of A^1. This is one of the earliest appearances of those long 'heterophonic' embroideries, those ethereal garlands given by Mahler to a solo instrument with the instruction to 'ignore the beat'. They will now appear more and more frequently in his late works. In the second phrase, for choruses and solo sopranos a cappella, A' reappears in the basses in inverted form, while the second half, 'firmans virtute', again mixes with B^1 and A^2 It is prolonged by an expressive melisma in quavers, sung by the sopranos, after which the chorus completes the exposition, still piano, with an inversion of A' (I/2a).[82]

An interrupted cadence (the B flat of the basses suddenly falling to B natural in bar 169) brings back the quick tempo (*Etwas hastig*: rather hurried) and the restlessness of the preceding interlude. It will prevail throughout the orchestral introduction to the development. The low-pitched bells (always a symbol of transcendence in Mahler), the tremolos on the timpani and the fragmented themes reappear, together with irregular metres[83] and dotted rhythms that, high in the strings, pizzicato, take on a mocking, somewhat caricatural character. This 'negative' atmosphere eventually dissolves, however, in a series of high pianissimo chords (flutes and violins tremolando) recalling those of the 'bridge' in the opening Allegro of the Sixth. The tempo slows down, and these same chords serve as accompaniment to theme D ('Infirma nostri corporis'), introduced by the bass soloist (bar 218). As seen above, it is in fact a new variant of A', in which the rising seventh becomes an octave. From the third bar on, a fragment derived from B (tenor, then alto: 'firmans perpeti') is added to the others in the new theme. At the end of the verse, which is entirely performed by the soloists, A' reappears in the orchestra in its initial form for a brief interlude which, in seven bars, prepares the unforgettable surge in E major[84] of the

---

[82] John Williamson draws a parallel between this 'counter-statement' and the much longer one in the first movement of the Second Symphony.

[83] John Williamson recalls that irregular metres are also found in the episodes of delirium in the last act of *Tristan und Isolde*, when the hero's reason is obscured, as well as in the *Gesellen-Lieder* and the first Scherzo of the future Tenth Symphony. He sees in this episode of the Eighth an example of 'amorphous music' or musical 'prose', in a style related to the theatre. In his view, its character is closer to that of the servants' scene in *Elektra* than to that of the 'Veni Creator'. Mahler seems to him to 'temporarily lose hold of the movement's structure', but thus creates 'a flat background against which the central climax may stand out' ('Veni Creator', 32).

[84] Hermann Danuser emphasizes Mahler's choice of E major, in a movement written predominantly in E flat, to suggest transcendence in such moments as 'Accende lumen' in Part I; 'Höchste Herrin' (bars 639 ff.); and the appearance of the Mater gloriosa (bar 780) in Part II (Danuser, 'Interpret', 177).

divine light on the words 'Accende lumen', declaimed in unison by all the vocal forces combined.[85] Like the opening theme, this motif (E or IV/2) begins with a rising fourth which then falls. It is followed by four rising notes already characteristic of a large body of Mahlerian themes.[86] It symbolizes a powerful upwards impulse and is thus particularly apposite. A few bars later, the children's chorus makes its first entrance ('Amorem cordibus' IV/3) with another joyful song, whose various elements will play a critical role in the second movement. The tone grows more and more determined, even threatening, as the march rhythm accelerates. Over an ostinato of descending quaver scales in the basses the second chorus launches: 'Hostem repellas' (Drive away our foe),[87] while the sopranos twice, first with a leap of a ninth, then a falling seventh, utter the war cry 'Hostem', reproduced a few bars further on with even more insistence (this time, the falling interval is an eleventh) at 'Pacem'. The third and last section of the development is a double fugue of tremendous complexity, corresponding to the most 'bellicose' episode in the hymn: 'Ductore sic te praevio' (Guide us safe).[88] Its forward momentum, right up to the second episode in the re-exposition, is irresistible. Into the polyphonic web come, successively, A' (and its reverse), A^2, sometimes in its original form, sometimes augmented, and then crotchet elements from B. The composer's contrapuntal skill and invention seem literally inexhaustible. The fugue ends in a powerful unison, with the seven principal soloists declaiming an augmented variant of A^2, 'Per te credamus omni tempore' (with A' in the bass). Next the 'Accende lumen' section (E) is resumed by the first chorus, in its original key, with A' in the basses of the second. A new fugal passage now elaborates these two themes, with A^2 joining in. The latter dominates the final bars of the development and leads directly, within the same impulse, to the recapitulation by all vocal forces of the 'Veni creator' section.

As the synoptic table above shows, this return is considerably abridged. Thus the fragment A^2, substance of part of the development and in particular of the fugue, is excluded, so that we move straight to B^2 ('Tu paraclitus'). The episode that follows,

---

[85]   John Williamson ('Veni Creator', 31) feels that Mahler weakens his climax by his use of the words 'Accende lumen' in the preceding development.

[86]   Notably the theme of the Finale of the First, the resurrection theme in the Second, the opening theme of the Fourth, the Adagietto of the Fifth, the Alma theme in the Sixth, etc.

[87]   Floros, in a study of the affinities between Mahler and Bruckner, has pointed out that the melodic line of this passage is characterized by a series of falling fourths also found in other motifs of the movement and stemming from Bruckner's 'Te Deum', where it plays the role of a generative cell. The similarities between the 'Te Deum' and the 'Hymn' also extend to the use of archaic-sounding open fifths, to the general architecture of the movements and to the climate of jubilant affirmation that pervades them. As seen above (Vol. i, Chap. 17), Mahler was particularly fond of this 'Te Deum', which he conducted several times during his stay in Hamburg.

[88]   John Williamson emphasizes the combination, in this fugue, of 'elements of heterophony with the appearance of Bachian counterpoint'. He also observes how rare fugal episodes are in the symphonic literature prior to Mahler, after the famous example of the Finale in Mozart's 'Jupiter' Symphony. He places the final fugue of Beethoven's Ninth in the context of variation form, and prefers to link Mahler's fugue with the one in the Finale of Bruckner's Fifth Symphony. Mahler, like Bruckner, attempts to 'mate orthodox polyphony with standard motivic-polyphonic development'. Williamson also notes that the triple exposition of the principal subject is more or less regular up to figure 49, and that it is followed by a sort of codetta, then by an intermediate section (from figure 50). Procedures of augmentation, diminution, and stretto are used up to figure 55. But from this figure on, once the 'Accende lumen' reappears, the idea of a fugue completely disappears, despite 'contrapuntal references' (Williamson, 'Veni Creator', 31).

'Da gaudiorum', takes its material from both A′ and B¹. This latter element, combined with A² and with a final inverted variant of A¹ (with a ninth replacing the rising seventh: I/2a), leads to a last orchestral interlude, where the dotted rhythm of A′ becomes dactylic. The jubilant 'Doxology' (theme D), loudly intoned by the children's chorus ('Gloria Patri Domino') is taken up, in augmentation, by the two solo sopranos, over a descending-scale ostinato in the choruses (a variant of A²) that heralds the peroration. The opening theme dominates the entire conclusion, but the level of invention, both in terms of sonorities and counterpoint, remains so rich that there is an impression not of repetition but of inexorable progress towards the ultimate goal. In the last moments, an ensemble of trumpets and trombones, placed apart from the main orchestra,[89] triumphantly reintroduce, in canon, the 'Accende' motif (E),[90] while a victorious rising scale runs through all the registers of the orchestra and the choruses, from the deepest to the highest. The final 'Gloria in saeculorum saecula' is simply a long and powerful plagal cadence, during which the isolated brass ensemble plays A² for the last time.

(b) ZweiterTeil (Second Part). Schlusszene aus 'Faust' (Final scene of 'Faust')

Composition: See above.

Key: E flat major (the Introduction is in the minor, and the rest of the movement modulates freely and frequently, often into E major, as in the first part). (See below.)

Time signature: The introduction is in 4/4 and the first chorus is in 6/4. The rest of the movement is alla breve, except for the 'Pater profundus' solo (4/4), the chorus's 'Uns bleibt' (4/4 until bar 579), Gretchen's solo ('er ahnet', bars 1213 to 1243, 4/4) and the last chorus ('Alles Vergängliche' 4/4).

Rhythm: Always binary.

Tempo: *Poco Adagio, etwas bewegter* (a little faster), etc. See below.

Duration: At the première, according to Julius Korngold, 55 minutes.

The longest symphonic movement Mahler ever composed is made up, like Goethe's text upon which it is based, of a great many more or less distinct episodes. As indicated above, not only is a great deal of the thematic material borrowed from the first part, but there are several passages from it that are quoted almost literally.[91] The orchestral introduction presents, in the manner of an operatic overture, four episodes, namely the chorus and the solos of the two Patres, and the march of the angels ('Ich spür' soeben': bar 580). In the thematic inventory and the synoptic table below, the thematic links with the first part are very obvious. The identification of the motifs or cells *a, b, c, d, e,* and *f* is especially necessary as these micro-elements are common to several themes. Seen in its entirety, this long finale sets out from the sombre key of E

[89]   In the autograph fair copy of the score (Bayerische Staatsbibliothek, Munich), next to 'Isoliert postiert' (placed apart [from the main orchestra]) Mahler wrote 'in die Höhe' (in the heights).

[90]   Danuser notes that, since this motif is again utilized extensively as the thematic substance of the Introduction and the first choral section of Part II, the coda 'looks forward' to Part II, while the return of the 'Veni Creator' motif at the end of the work 'looks back' towards the beginning of the Symphony (Danuser, 'Interpret', 281).   [91]   See above, Cyclic Procedures.

flat minor and finishes in the radiant light of this same key in the major. The first episode, and the first chorus, which it announces, unfold in a mysterious half-light, with short thematic fragments and an orchestration as spare as that of the *Rückert-Lieder*. By contrast, all choral and orchestral forces without exception take part in the final apotheosis. Yet the very same theme, at first cut up, broken by silences and rhythmically hesitant, becomes in the epilogue a powerful chorale, symbol of peace and fulfilment.

Bars	Themes and Motifs	Tempos	Keys
INTRODUCTION (orchestra)			
1–56	IV/2a (ostinato), V/1A, V/1a (anticipating the first chorus)	*Poco Adagio*	E flat minor
57–96	V/1a, V/1b, V/1A (anticipating the Pater ecstaticus solo)	*Etwas bewegter*	
97–146	V/3, V/1a and IV/2A, V/3 and V/1b, V/1a and V/1b (Pater profundus solo and Theme of the angels' march: '*Nebelnd um Felsenhöh*')	*più mosso*	
147–66	Coda: V/1c (var. of IV/3), V/1b		
EXPOSITION			
1ST PART (167–384)			
167–218	V/1A and 1a, IV/2a Chorus: '*Waldung, sie schwankt*'	*Wieder langsam* (slow again)	E flat minor/ major
219–65	V/1a and 1b Baritone: Pater ecstaticus: '*Ewige Wonnebrand*'	*Moderato*	
266–362	V/3 and IV/2a Bass: Pater profundus: '*Wie Felsenabgrund*'	*Allegro appassionato*	E flat minor (C flat major)
362–84	Postlude (orchestra) V/3, V, 1/A		
2ND PART (385–539)			
385–436	E or IV/2A, IV/2, IV/3b Women's chorus: '*Gerettet ist*' Children's chorus: '*Hände Verschlinget*'	*Allegro deciso*	B, G, E flat major
436–520	VI/1, VI/2, VI/3, VI/1a, VI/4 Women's chorus: '*Jene Rosen*'	*Scherzando. Molto leggiero*	E flat major
520–39	Postlude (orchestra) E (IV/2), VI/1, VI/2a		
3RD PART (540–79)			
540–52	Prelude (orchestra) I/1a and I/2, III/2, A (I/1a, 2a)	*Schon etwas langsamer* (already somewhat slower)	D minor E flat major

Appendix 2: History and Analysis

(cont.):

BARS	THEMES AND MOTIFS	TEMPOS	KEYS
552–79	Theme C (I/1a), then I/2a Chorus: '*Uns bleibt*' and Alto solo	*Wie die gleiche Stelle* *im I. Teil* (like the same passage in Part I)	

DEVELOPMENT

1ST SECTION
(580–779)

580–604	V/3, V/1c, IV/3b Chorus: '*Ich spür*' *Soeben*'	*Im Anfang noch etwas* *gehalten* (still slightly held back at first)	E flat major
604–38	IV/3b Women's chorus, then children and tenor solo: '*Hier ist die Aussicht*'	*Noch etwas kecker* (still a little livelier) *Allegro deciso*	G, B major
639–723	IV/2a, IV/1, *f* Tenor solo: '*Höchste Herrin*'	*Sempre l'istesso tempo*	E major E flat major
724–57	V/2, IV/2a, E, *f* Tenor and Chorus: '*Jungfrau Rein*'	*Sehr langsam* (very slow)	E flat major
758–79	Interlude IV/2a, V/2	*Poco più mosso*	E flat–E major

2ND SECTION
(780–1248)

780–803	Prelude (orchestra) V/2 (related to A'')	*Adagissimo* *Äusserst langsam* (Extremely slow)	E major
804–24	V/2 Men's chorus: '*Dir,* *der Unberührbaren*'		
825–844	V/4 Mixed chorus '*Wer zerreisst*'	*Langsam. Schwebend* (Slow, Floating)	
844–67	V/2 Sopranos / Chorus II and Soprano solo II '*Du schwebst zu Höhen*'	*Fliessend* (flowing)	B major
868–905	V/2a, VI/1 Soprano I: Magna Peccatrix '*Bei der Liebe*'		B, G sharp minor E flat major
906–56	VI/1 Alto I: Mulier Samaritana '*Bei der Bronn*'	*Immer dasselbe Tempo* (still the same tempo)	B flat minor E flat major
957–67	Postlude (orchestra) VI/1		
968–1016	VI/3 and /1, V/2a Alto II: Maria Aegyptiaca '*Bei der Hochgeweihten*'	*Immer fliessend* (Still flowing)	G minor
1017–93	VI/1, VI/2, V/2a Trio of the Penitent women: '*Die du grossen*'	*Sehr fliessend, beinahe* *flüchtig* (Very flowing, almost hasty)	C major, A, F major

BARS	THEMES AND MOTIFS	TEMPOS	KEYS
1093–103	VI/1a with VI/4, V/2 Prelude (orchestra)	*Sich etwas mässigend* (A little more moderate)	D major
1104–29	V/2, E (IV/2) Soprano II: Una poenitentium '*Neige, neige*'		
1130–7	Postlude (orchestra) V/2, VI/1a		
1138–85	V/2, V/2a, *b* Children's chorus: '*Er überwächst uns*'	*Unmerklich frischer* *werden* (Imperceptibly faster)	
1185–212	VI/1, S, *f* Children's chorus: id. Soprano II: Una Poenit.: '*Vom edlen Geisterchor*'	*Allegro*	B flat major
1213–48	B, III/1, III/2, I/1, I/2 Soprano II: Una Poenit.: '*Er ahnet kaum*' Quotation of '*Imple*'	*Wie die korrespondierende* *Stelle im ersten Teil* (Like the corresponding passage in the first part)	B flat major
3RD SECTION **(1249–420)**			
1249–76	V/2, IV/2A, E Soprano III and chorus Mater gloriosa: '*Komm*'	*Sehr langsam. Dolcissimo* (Very slow)	E flat major
1277–383	V/A and V/2A, V/1a, V/A, V/2, V/4, V/2 Tenor and choruses: Dr Marianus '*Blicket auf*'	*Hymneartig* (Hymnlike)	E flat major, C minor, E major
1384–420	Postlude (orchestra) V/A, IV/2a, IV/1	*Fliessend* (flowing)	E flat major
EPILOGUE **(1421–572)**			
1421–48	Prelude (orchestra) IV/2, IV/1	*Langsam* (slow)	
1448–528	V/1a, V/2 (augmented), V/1a Choruses and soloists: '*Alles Vergängliche*'	*Sehr langsam beginnend* (Very slow at the beginning) *Schon bewegter*, etc. (Already getting faster)	
1528–72	Postlude (orchestra) A' (I/2), I/2a	*Fliessend* (Flowing)	

The opening bars of the orchestral introduction evoke, without exactly reproducing it, the first chorus which is to come. The rhythm is different, as are the orchestration and the motif completing the flute theme, which disappears from the chorus's accompaniment. The similarity of atmosphere with the *Rückert-Lieder*, or with the second and sixth Lieder in *Das Lied von der Erde*, is very striking. Motif *a* is also the one that served as leitmotiv in the Lied 'Um Mitternacht'. The same bass ostinato (IV/2a) will play a decisive role in the second section, which anticipates the Pater ecstaticus solo, but is not found in the accompaniment to this solo. The third episode, in the minor, announces and sums up the solo of the second Pater. Next, the bass ostinato, extended into a minor version of the Pater ecstaticus theme (VI/1c), later used by the angels at the beginning of the development ('Ich spür' es soeben'). This motif is also used to introduce the first chorus, where it is given to the basses as a whole without losing its ostinato character.

In the song of the anchorites, the writing for men's chorus (the altos join in, but only for the last phrase), the way in which Mahler suggests the 'echoes' in the text without resorting to strict canon, and the fervent yet disturbing and mysterious mood, have been admired by all commentators. Rudolph Stephan observes that the silences placed between the notes of the phrases derive from the natural pauses in the text itself and that they play a vital role. Motif *a* characterizes the melodic substance. Yet although, at the beginning of the introduction (bar 4), it opened the flutes' theme, it is now present only in the second bar of each phrase and in their 'echoes'. Mahler succeeds here in defining through music not only the words, but 'the situation, the scene, the content and the meaning'. Arising from the echoes, the asymmetry of the phrases adds to the effect of tension and mystery. The transition to the first solo is made by a brief, homophonic, solemn chorale-like passage in the major, 'Ehren geweihten Ort', followed by two echoes of the ostinato, low in the strings, pizzicato. It is this which provides all the material for the Pater ecstaticus solo (variant of V/1a), a solemn hymn with four verses of eight lines, and one of ten. But the difference in atmosphere, character, and orchestration, as well as endless changes of detail, give an impression of perpetual renewal. The last concluding falling motif is taken up in turn by the violins and violas, in quavers, then triplets, and then crotchets. Thus they prolong the last phrase of the song, while the trumpets play the 'Accende' theme (E or IV/2) from the first part in its original form. The descending motif which concluded the preceding solo is still present in the solo of the second Pater, whose main feature is the rising melodic leaps (octave, then tenth, then eleventh) which make it a daunting bravura aria for the bass, and symbolize the character's burning aspiration, his 'torture', and the 'savage roaring' that surrounds him. All this is also reflected in the chromaticism of the melody (very rare in this work), in the expressive grupetto and in the 'Parsifalian' sonority of the repeated chords. The triplet figure that ended the first two phrase sections of the corresponding episode in the introduction now forms part of the accompaniment, reflecting its origin in the first section (bars 83, 100, 144, etc.). The expressive climax is reached with the words 'allmächt'ge Liebe' (bar 285) where a theme from the first section is heard again (IV/2A), a theme which is from now on present for a long portion of the scene.

The solo ends in C flat major,[92] after which a short interlude gathers speed and leads to the first angels' chorus, in B major. The chorus of the 'Blessed boys', 'Hände verschlinget euch', soon superimposed on it, reproduces the 'Amorem cordibus' from the first section (themes IV/2A and IV/3). This is the beginning of the 'Scherzo' section identified by Specht and Bekker, where a new family of 'twisting' themes is established, with flute staccatos, trills, and string pizzicati. The central *Scherzando* episode, on 'Jene Rosen', is sung in thirds on a new rising theme (VI/2) by some of the female voices in

---

[92] Danuser ('Interpret', 280) emphasizes the reappearance of the 'Accende' motif from Part I in the last words of this solo: 'erleuchte mein dürftig Herz' ('to my needy heart give light').

the first chorus. The episode concludes with joyous shouts of 'Jauchzet auf!', but the atmosphere of naive good humour persists throughout the postlude. This leads to a slower tempo and a return of the sequences of chords which, in the first movement, introduced the episode 'Infirma nostri corporis'. The chorus of the 'More perfect angels' (altos and tenors: 'Uns bleibt ein Erdenrest') is in fact a fairly literal quotation of this episode,[93] with the same triplet embroidery (variants of II/1, here given first to viola then to solo violin). However, the 'consoling' alto solo ('Kein Engel trennte') is extended and amplified: it does not end until the first bar of the ensuing chorus of the 'Younger Angels'.

The lighter female voices in the second chorus next take up the joyous march theme from the end of the Introduction ('Ich spür' soeben'). As seen above, the central character of the second section, Dr Marianus, enters in G major before the end of this chorus, but Mahler requires him, for the moment, simply to 'accompany' the female voices. A few bars later, as the tenor begins to sketch what will soon become the 'love theme' (V/2), the children's chorus performs the 'Blessed boys' song (IV/3b), which begins like the preceding one ('Freudig empfangen wir': IV/3b, variant of IV/3), with the tenor still 'accompanying'. He is first heard as soloist in his passionate invocation to the Mater gloriosa ('Höchste Herrin der Welt', bars 639 ff.), in E major, during which the rapid tempo is maintained and the 'Love theme' further takes shape.[94]

The end of this solo is emotionally irresistible ('plötzlich mildert sich') as, with theme E being played on the solo cello, the soloist, who must be capable, elsewhere, of heroic singing, sings first piano, then pianissimo and legato. Even more moving, a few bars on, is the moment where the basses in the first chorus imitate the soloist's prayer in ecstatic chords ('Jungfrau, rein im schönsten Sinne'), while the solo violin floats above with the 'love theme' at last prefixed by its opening sixth (S), over an ethereal background of viola tremolos and soft horn chords.

Theme E (still in the horns) serves as a transition towards E major and the apparition of the Mater gloriosa. A simple held chord, on the harmonium, and arpeggios on the harp now accompany the 'love theme' in its complete form, in the violins (V/2) pianissimo. This tender, sinuous melody recalls the Adagietto of the Fifth, while looking forward to the epilogue of *Das Lied*. Soon the men in the second chorus enter, accompanying the theme with calm pianissimo chords and imitating its rising impulses. They pass it to the sopranos of the first chorus, who twice fervently repeat the opening bars (VI/4: 'Wer zerreisst'). After singing in unison with them, the second soprano soloist (the soul of Gretchen) emerges, and prepares the entrance of the Magna Peccatrix with a new variant of the 'Love theme' (V/2a). In the same tempo, but in B major instead of B flat minor, the solo that follows (by the Mulier Samaritana) brings back the mood of the earlier *Scherzando*, with the 'twisting' themes that previously characterized the angels (VI/1). The solo ends in E flat major with a brief interlude, in which the trumpets play E (VI/2), now followed by its new conclusion (f). The G minor solo of Maria Aegyptiaca retains the same motifs and the same joyful atmosphere. Next, the three voices which have just been heard separately join together in a canonic trio (based on V/2a and still accompanied by the twisting motif VI/1). At the

---

[93] However, the orchestration is different, and the passage is written in 4/4 and not, as before, in *alla breve*.

[94] Similarly, in Das Lied, the glorious 'Lebensthema' towards which the whole movement aspires gradually takes form from bar 460 on.

end of the episode, they converge and sing in unison ('Gönn' auch'). Their phrase is completed by the third sinner (Maria Aegyptiaca), in the key of D major which will be that of the penitent's solo (Una poenitentium). This is preceded by a prelude where the mandolin makes its first appearance, in unison with the flute (still VI/1) and delicately accompanied by woodwind chords, violin trills, and harp arpeggios, a sound background of unique refinement and expressivity. The same delicacy characterizes the whole of the accompaniment to Gretchen's solo, 'Neige, neige, du Ohnegleiche', where the love theme is found in the form given to it earlier by the violins. Now Faust's soul has reached the higher spheres, where the 'Blessed boys' greet it with a new song of joy: 'Er überwächst uns schon' (mixing the rising scale motifs of E, the rhythm R, soon to be heard again in 'Blicket auf', and the cell f). The 'Love theme' reigns serenely (violins, then oboes) over clarinet arpeggios, bassoon chords, and crystalline octaves in the piano and celesta,[95] after which the children's chorus, divided in two, and then some of the sopranos of the second chorus, resume, in imitative form, the rising scale b of 'Accende' (E).

The tempo quickens (*Allegro*, bar 1186), and the key of E flat succeeds that of D, while the children, on VI/1, again take up the verse 'Er überwächst uns schon', but on a new melody derived from IV/3b and from 'Freudig empfangen wir'. Now the voice of the second soprano (Gretchen) appears above those of the children, in an episode leading to her last solo, 'Er ahnet kaum', which fairly faithfully reproduces, in B flat major, the second thematic element of the first movement, 'Imple superna gratia'. This time, however, the subsidiary voices are in the orchestra. As before in B^1, the trumpets and horns soon evoke A^1 and A', pianissimo in the violins. The ending, however, is not the same as that of B^1, but takes all its substance from the codetta of the exposition in the first movement (bars 1233 ff., quoting bars 113 ff. of the 'Veni creator').

After a perfect cadence in B flat, in a tempo which is now 'slow' again, then 'very slow', the horns play E in imitative form, preparing the solo of the Mater gloriosa,[96] again in E major. Her rising, then falling melody is surrounded by countermelodies, first I/2, then the 'Love theme' high in the violins, with an aureole of celesta tremolos, harp chords and harmonics, then chords on the harmonium and tremolos on the strings. Next, 'Accende' (E), passes from the trumpet to the horn, pianissimo. Over gentle ecstatic chords from the second chorus ('Komm!'), Doctor Marianus sings his final solo, 'in the manner of a hymn' ('Blicket auf'), in which the principal role is played by a new rising motif in dotted rhythm (a variant of 'Jene Rosen' or of the last bar of I/2a: 'Auf zum Retterblick', bar 1291). The same soloist delivers the first complete statement of the theme of the coda ('Alles Vergängliche': derived from V/1a). The end of the episode is given to the chorus ('Blicket auf' and f). First it amplifies the 'Love theme', then another passage from earlier on, 'Wer zerreisst' (bar 825: V/4), which will dominate the entire coda. It is brought to an end by the orchestra, in the same exalted mood (at the climax, bars 1392 ff., the trombones declaim triple fortissimo the opening motif A'). The following bars revert to the calm mood in a passage governed by the same motif, 'Blicket auf', and by A' which is gradually transformed

---

[95] From bar 1164, the rising theme in the violins, taken up by the children's chorus doubled by cellos, irresistibly recalls the Resurrection theme in the Second Symphony.

[96] Mahler wanted a third soprano with a voice of crystalline purity to sing the all-important lines where the Mater gloriosa calls Gretchen to ascend to paradise, adding that Faust will follow her.

into a bass ostinato. The coda is prepared by twenty-eight bars pianissimo in which arpeggios are played drop by drop on celesta, piano, and harps, while the piccolo's falling motif is carried on by the clarinet, which stops in mid-register.[97] The spareness of the material and the transparency of the orchestration here look forward to the corresponding passage in the coda of *Das Lied von der Erde*.

Wie ein Hauch (like a breath) is Mahler's notation for the first bars of the 'Chorus mysticus'. The solemn chorale theme is already known, having been stated at 'Auf zum Retterblick'. It is the final avatar of the initial bass ostinato (IV/2a) and its countermelody (V/1A). The tendency to modulate from E flat to E major that has been noted throughout the symphony is once again confirmed in the middle of the first phrase, whose harmonization is both subtle and original. The second stanza ('Das ewig Weibliche') commences in D flat. Much of the effect is produced not only by the crescendo which swells very slowly up to bar 1506, but also by the rising motifs (*b*) played over a chromatically or diatonically descending bass line, while the note values gradually lengthen in the melody (crotchets, then minims, then semibreves, up to bar 1494). The effect of this unforgettable apotheosis comes also from the masterly use of solo voices and from the manner in which they join or contrast with the chorus. At bar 1478, the 'Love theme' is taken up by the sopranos of the first chorus, after which its initial motif (*e*) is twice exclaimed fortissimo by the men's voices on the word 'Ewig'.

As the final chorus reaches its climax, in A flat major, Mahler achieves a further degree of intensity by a surprisingly simple device. Whereas the whole orchestra, and notably the blaring voice of the brass, has taken part in the powerful crescendo marked in the preceding bars, it suddenly falls silent at the moment at which all vocal forces declaim 'Alles Vergängliche ist nur ein Gleichnis', supported only by the organ, as if the gates of paradise had suddenly opened before the crowds of the blessed. They sing the first two bars of the theme with the scale motif (*b*) which rises, in imitations. After a pause as dense as the tumult that precedes it, the voices break out again with 'zieht uns hinan' and then just 'hinan', while the horns and trombones symbolically recall the end of Gretchen's song, 'Der früh Geliebte, nicht mehr Getrübte' (bars 1117 ff.), and then the 'Accende' theme (E). At the chorus's last bar, the isolated brass ensemble enters with a grandiose evocation, in long note values, of the 'Veni Creator' (A'), whose seventh soon becomes a ninth (E flat, B flat, C).[98] The rising fragment (I/2a) has the last word in the immense triumphal turbulence that fittingly concludes the 'Chorus mysticus' and the symphony itself.

In an article called 'Mahler as Goethe Interpreter', Hermann Danuser, after studying Mahler's highly complex mechanisms of self-quotation, interrelation, reuse of melodic cells, symphonic procedures which unite the parts into a whole, concludes:

If we now look more closely at the two parts we begin to perceive a veritable network of relationships permeating the whole of the work. . . . This main theme ['Veni Creator'] is the basis not only of the first part, but also—transformed—of the second. The result is a broadly spread

---

[97]   The falling motif on the celesta (bars 1421 ff.), next played by the two wind instruments, is not listed in the thematic inventory below, but has appeared as early as the conclusion to the Pater Ecstaticus solo (bars 256 ff.).

[98]   This final motif, repeated again twice by the brass in the last bars, retains the presence of the sixth degree of the scale (C) right into the final chord on E flat major, recalling the role it has already played at the end of several previous works (notably 'Ich bin der Welt') and the Adagio of the Fifth) and which it will later play at the end of *Song of the Earth*.

system of thematic transformation, the details of which are too complicated to describe here, but the return at the end of the second part to the start of the work is unmistakably clear. . . . In the actual poetics of the Eighth Symphony, however, the rich experience of the middle instrumental symphonies seems to have been remembered. . . . The creative power he [Mahler] summoned up in the early sketch for the first movement and the Finale of the work and which remains invoked in the Pentecostal hymn, is accordingly confirmed in the work itself. . . . This [Adorno's negative view of the work's affirmation][99] seems however, in the light of the Goethe composition in the Eighth Symphony, to be unjustified. Music with a philosophical message (*Weltanschauungsmusik*) has generally laid claim to speak on behalf of all mankind, and Mahler's Eighth achieves this, since the poems are symphonically composed and transformed to a structure of musical relationships which is aesthetically unified.[100]

Coming at the dawn of a century of doubt and unrest, of uncertainty and reassessment, a work such as the Eighth was bound to provoke countless misunderstandings. People were beginning to understand that one of the results of man's impressive achievements, particularly in the realm of science, would be to plunge him deeper into self-doubt than ever. But it was precisely this uncertainty, this malaise, that provoked the powerful affirmation of the Eighth. It was most likely the scepticism of his time, the 'weakness of our bodies' ('Infirma nostri corporis'), that spurred Mahler on to proclaim his confidence in the eternal nature of the human spirit, and to renounce the tragic vision he had so often before embodied. He was conscious from the start that this work was exceptional in character, as witness these passages from two letters he wrote in August 1906:

I have finished my Eighth Symphony. It is the grandest thing I have done yet, and so peculiar in content and form that it is really impossible to write anything about it. Try to imagine the whole universe beginning to ring and resound. These are no longer human voices, but planets and suns revolving.'[101] . . . It is a gift to the nation. All my previous symphonies are just preludes to this. In the other works everything is still subjective-tragic—this one is a great joy-bringer.[102]

Alas, the misfortunes of the summer of 1907 brought Mahler back to the harshest realities of earthly life, not only because death struck the flesh of his flesh, but also because his departure from the Opera made him conscious of the frailty of all human enterprise. His subsequent works took on a completely different character. Perhaps for this very reason, the first modern exegetist to understand the universal dimension of Mahler's music, Theodor Adorno, expressed doubts about the validity of the 'triumph' the work celebrates, and the 'joy' it 'dispenses'. He claimed that in Mahler's Hymn 'Veni Creator Spiritus' 'there are passages where the impossibility of making a start turns into violence, as if wilfully asserting that the start had been a success. But there is no stronger argument in Mahler's favour than his impatience with the affirmative nature of the "magnum opus" (*Hauptwerk*). And it was the very idea of affirmation that he found suspect.'[103] A brilliant paradox, if ever there was one, but to my mind rather

---

[99] Here Danuser inserts Adorno's passage quoted in part below: 'The Holy of Holies is empty. . . . But the invocation ['Veni Creator'] is addressed, according to an objective sense of form, to the music itself. That the Spirit should come is a plea that the composition should be inspired. By mistaking the consecrated wafer of the Spirit for itself, it confuses art and religion . . .' (TAM 182 ff., TAMe 138 ff.).

[100] Danuser, 'Interpret', 281 ff.

[101] See above, Chap. 6, and MBR1, no. 306; MBR2, no. 360, of 18 Aug. 1906. Although I have already quoted from this letter, I have found it useful to quote it again here.

[102] Ibid. and RSM2, 304.

[103] Adorno, TAF 229 ff.; TAFe, 91.

futile. Adorno adds elsewhere: 'The dogmatic content from which it [the Eighth] borrows its authority is neutralized in it to a cultural commodity. In reality, it worships itself. . . . The Holy of Holies is empty. . . . The invocation is addressed to music itself.' In Adorno's eyes, Mahler was above all glorifying 'the collective social manifestation that he felt sounding through him as an absolute', and 'identifying with the attacker'.[104]

Even the juxtaposition of the two texts has been considered suspect, 'almost absurd', by the German philosopher Hans Mayer:

> The two parts of the Eighth Symphony represent . . . two worlds: one, definitely gone, that is cited as a thing rejected, and the other, also gone in fact, namely the world of late Goethe, to which, through intuition and spiritual union, a path still seems to be open. Seen thus, the unity of this 'Symphony of a Thousand' appears as unresolved parataxis: a togetherness which in reality is antithesis . . . The domineering composer changed the meaning not only of the *Faust*, but above all of the Latin hymn. The result was a musical work of total theological and poetic misappropriation.[105]

Mayer concedes that Mahler succeeded in achieving 'a new relationship between literature and music'. Nevertheless he regards him as a 'literary dilettante':[106] 'Mahler is not a religious, certainly not a Christian, artist. He belonged to the *Jugendstil* in the sense that, in his hands, religious motif degenerated, for the most part, into aesthetic ornament.'[107]

Another modern commentator, Clytus Gottwald, thinks the Eighth calls not on 'the spirit on high' but on the spirit 'that combatively takes form in the works of man'. His view is that the counterpoint in the first movement is chiefly aimed at 'defining spirit as that of man who transforms himself through his own work',[108] and that it thus has very much the same meaning as that attributed to the 'affirmative' Finale of the Fifth. He agrees with Mayer in claiming that Mahler had already altered the Christian message of Klopstock's Ode in the Finale of the Second Symphony, by adding lines which suggest that man himself can become the instrument of his own salvation.[109]

True to the views summed up earlier concerning the Finales of the Fifth and the Seventh, Adorno disbelieves the optimism of the Eighth. Within the development of the first movement he even perceives 'the abyss of the wicked and fallible' that 'yawns even in musical terms, protecting the Hymn from the insipidly edifying'.[110] In his particular dialectic, the weakness thus discerned amid the impetuous affirmation is to be regarded as a merit, not a fault. A more recent writer, Stefan Strohm, adds to Adorno's words:

> Because Mahler's music aims at unbroken and pure sound, it stays true to the idea that man is only the fragile mirror of the absolute. Mahler's music is Passion music through and through, its

---

[104] TAM 183; TAMe 138 ff.

[105] Hans Mayer, 'Gustav Mahler und die Literatur', in *Musik-Konzepte: Sonderband Gustav Mahler* (July 1989), 150 ff.

[106] Adorno contradicts Mayer's view in an article entitled 'Zu einem Streitgespräch über Mahler', (*Gesammelte Schriften*, Vol. xviii (Suhrkamp, Frankfurt, 1984), 244 ff.). In his opinion, Mahler succeeded through music in overcoming the stylistic break between the texts of the two movements, and created a 'harmony of a higher order'. Yet he adds: 'There cannot be one person taking art seriously who has not, at some time or other, revolted against Mahler' (because of these two texts) (ibid.).

[107] Mayer, 'Literatur', 150 ff.

[108] Clytus Gottwald, 'Die Achte', in Ruzicka, *Herausforderung*, 204.

[109] Mayer, 'Literatur', 150 ff.   [110] TAM 184; TAMe 140.

breakthroughs (*Durchbrüche*) are often of the negative kind: they open not on heaven but on the abyss. They are breakdowns, depicting the crucifixion idea of the death of God in contemporary form, speculative Good Fridays: all is empty and dead. And beyond this thought the music achieves an awakening out of the dream of the void into the burgeoning Here-and-Now. The central idea in Jean Paul's poem[111] most exactly describes the composed content of the essential Mahler: that the finite and the infinite are not separate, that the finite is not devoid of the absolute, that the absolute leans painfully towards the finite; there is a christological heritage in this idea. The spirit not blurring into eternity, but seen as the finite that yields itself up in Mahler's or Jean Paul's works, is the answer . . . This then is the second argument against the reproach of blasphemy: Mahler's music is aware of finiteness (*Endlichkeit*).[112]

Another writer, Adolf Nowak, interprets Mahler's 'Veni Creator' as 'postulatively striving' rather than 'affirmatively giving assurance'. It expresses, in his view, 'a fervent yearning towards the essence of things: like a plant towards the light, the crane towards its home, man towards freedom (in the words of the hymn, towards light and love). Faust's ascension in the last scene results from such an aspiration.'[113] But Nowak is unable to understand

how anyone could hear in this hymn only a prayer for musical inspiration. There is hardly any music whose formal process is so strongly imbued with striving in Goethe's sense: it is there in the thematic ideas not rounded off, categorized or held in metrically proportionate relationships; and in the formal procedures of transformation (*Verwandlung*), the *Durchbruch*, and the freeing of themes, as they arise in exposition, from their self-containment (*Fürsichsein*). When, in the final bars of the second part, the opening theme is powerfully sounded, it must surely be heard that this theme, in its text, is a prayer: *Veni creator*. At the end of the work stands the prayer that the transformation accomplished in Faust and specified in the musical process may become human reality. The final transformation of Faust as a transformable phenomenon is death. That death is a transformation and not the end is the meaning of the Hymn as text and as the musical realisation of the spirit of metamorphosis.[114]

Such an abundance of interpretations, commentaries, and exegeses clearly demonstrates the fascination exercised by the Eighth Symphony, today more than ever. There are indeed good reasons to wonder why a composer born in an age of scepticism should in the Eighth have needed so loudly to proclaim his faith. Given the character of most of Mahler's earlier and later works it is obvious that its blinding light, unclouded affirmation, and triumphal codas were bound to be questioned. Adorno was not alone in casting doubt on the Eighth's 'affirmative' message. Still today, it is mistrusted by many, especially by what I would call the 'intellectuals' among the Mahlerians. It is the fate of deeply popular, sincere works to be disbelieved by sceptical scholarly spirits: the Eighth worries them and makes them uncomfortable, conditioned as even they are perhaps by the traditional idea of Mahler as an introspective composer whose preferred mood was dark and even tragic. But should we really conclude because of this, as Adorno seems to do, that this most affirmative of Mahler's works is the least successful, or anyway the least Mahlerian, that it is musically and artistically inferior to the others, or worse still that, in order, perhaps, to win public

---

[111] The writer is here referring to a passage in the *Erstes Blumenstück* in Jean Paul's *Blumen- Frucht- und Dornstücke* (Berlin edn. of 1841, 315). See above, Vol. i, Appendix 2 on Symphony No. 1.

[112] Stefan Strohm, 'Programm', 81.   [113] Ibid. 94.

[114] Adolf Nowak, 'Mahlers Hymnus', 96, and, also in *Schütz Jahrbuch 1982–3*, 'Fragen zu Mahlers VIII. Symphonie', 71 ff., by Friedhelm Krummacher.

favour, Mahler made concessions, that he was insincere, and in any case defeated by the immensity of his theme?

Sceptics should perhaps be reminded that a powerful current of optimism, of deep metaphysical hope, runs through all Mahler's music, even his saddest works like the *Kindertotenlieder* or *Das Lied von der Erde*. The resigned, serene mood in which both of these works end is only reached through suffering, grief, and farewell. The Eighth knows nothing—or very little—of the darker sides of human existence. But what in fact does it set out so triumphantly to announce and to celebrate? None of the exegeses quoted from above seems to me to have asked the fundamental question about the nature of the message that Mahler wished to deliver to mankind at large.

That he wanted to make such a break with his past and to forget the pessimism of the 'Tragic' Sixth is obvious, since he speaks of his previous symphonies as 'mere preludes' to the Eighth. There is surely nothing surprising about that in a musician who in his everyday life always claimed the right to say one thing one minute and the opposite the next, and refused to accept the slightest criticism for doing so. But Mahler also turned his back on the ambiguous optimism of the Finales of the Fifth and the Seventh Symphonies, and even on the symbolic, childlike 'heaven' of the Fourth. With the Eighth he wished to compose at last an 'objective' work, a 'Freudenspender', a 'gift of joy to the nation',[115] a work <u>without</u> negative or gloomy elements, a work in which victory would be assured from the first bar. One could argue that the strength of the affirmation was provoked by the anguish, the uncertainty of a time from which Mahler wanted forcibly to free himself, at least in this work.

However, he also needed to express another essential aspect of his nature—that he was a believer, and that he too knew moments of joy and certainty. In the Eighth, he wished to address the masses and to express his faith in mankind, and to do so in a twentieth-century language that owes nothing, or very little, to other monumental Masses such as Bach's in B minor or Beethoven's in D. In Roller's presence he admitted that the Eighth was perhaps the Mass he would never be able to bring himself to write because he couldn't compose music to the Credo.[116] Yet the Eighth is, to my mind, a Credo, and a glorious one. Mahler's obstinate, categorical rejection of contemporary materialism and rationalism was always one of the basic traits of his personality. He never tired of expressing it in the strongest possible terms. It is the starting point for his whole conception of life, which cannot be regarded as pessimistic except to the extent that he believed that the 'here below' can only be an imperfect reflection of the 'hereafter'. The Eighth simply confirms a belief which pervades all Mahler's other works. The 'Veni Creator' movement has nothing of a prayer about it. It is from the start triumphant proclamation. With unshakeable confidence in the eternal nature of the human spirit, Mahler addresses the immaterial, intangible 'Creator Spiritus', who inspires and motivates the human quest.

It is, however, in the second part, the final scene of *Faust*, that the essential message of the work unfolds. Mahler never ceased to read Goethe, and was steeped in his thinking. His friend Siegfried Lipiner was a noted Goethe scholar. Mahler's many conversations with him had undoubtedly enlightened him as to Goethe's aims and

---

[115] 'Ein Geschenk an die Nation', see Richard Specht, Gustav Mahler, 2nd edn. (Schuster & Loeffler, Berlin, 1918), 304. Richard Wagner also spoke in 1856 of his Ring cycle as 'a gift to the Nation'.
[116] RBM 26.

intentions in *Faust*. Five days before his death, Goethe said that the key to *Faust* lay in the following lines:

> Wer immer strebend sich bemüht
> Den können wir erlösen.
> (The man who strives and never gives up the struggle
> Him we can redeem.)

and he added:

In these lines is contained the key to Faust's salvation: in Faust himself an ever loftier and purer activity right to the end, and from above Eternal Love coming to his aid. This harmonizes perfectly with our religious views, according to which we do not obtain heavenly bliss through our own strength alone, but with the assistance of divine grace.[117]

As seen above, the basic idea of *Faust* seems to be activity rather than love, quest rather than conquest. The hero's ultimate redemption proves the validity of human discontent since, at the end of the quest which has led him very far indeed from all the traditional paths to salvation, Faust is nonetheless greeted by the Mater gloriosa herself. Like Mahler, Goethe himself had doggedly pursued the Faustian ideal of '*pushing back the confines of our ignorance*' through knowledge and culture. His interests, like Mahler's, ranged everywhere, even to subjects as far removed from his literary activity as zoology, botany, optics, and medicine. He did not conceive of heaven as being eternal repose, or beatific contemplation. In 1827 he wrote at the age of 78:

I must confess that I should not know what to do with eternal beatitude unless it also presented me with tasks to carry out and difficulties to overcome[118] . . . Let us continue to work, until we, in our turn, either before or after one another, are summoned by the Spirit of the Universe to return into ether. And may the Master of Eternal Life not deny us new activities, like those in which we have already been put to the test! . . . The Entelechean Monad must maintain itself in ceaseless activity.[119]

For Goethe, then, the idea of immortality was intimately linked with that of activity:

Man should believe in immortality; he has a right to it; it is in conformity with his nature . . . To me the eternal existence of my soul necessarily arises from my idea of activity; if I work on incessantly till my death, nature is bound to give me another form of existence when the present one can no longer sustain my spirit.[120]

For Mahler, too, activity was the guiding principle of life. The reason he gave Ferdinand Pfohl for believing in the hereafter was akin to that of Goethe: 'for it [that is to say, faith in the hereafter] is within us and everything within us exists with more certainty than anything lying outside our human inner selves'.[121] At the time of writing the Eighth Symphony Mahler had begun to believe in reincarnation in its most dynamic and demanding form. As he explained to Richard Specht: 'I must live in an ethical way so

---

[117] Goethe, *Conversations with Eckermann*, June 1831: 'In diesen Versen ist der Schlüssel zu Fausts Rettung enthalten. In Faust selber eine immer höhere und reinere Tätigkeit bis ans Ende, und von oben die ihm zu Hilfe kommende ewige Liebe. Es steht dieses mit unserer religiösen Vorstellung durchaus in Harmonie, nach welcher wir nicht bloss durch eigene Kraft selig werden, sondern durch die hinzukommende göttliche Gnade.'   [118] Goethe, letter to Friedrich von Müller, 23 Sept. 1827.

[119] Goethe, letter to Carl Friedrich Zelter, 19 Mar. 1827.

[120] Goethe, *Conversations with Eckermann*, 4 Feb. 1829.   [121] FPM 21.

that my Self, when it returns, will be spared part of the journey and will find its existence not so difficult. That is my moral duty.'[122] Just as Goethe had intimations of 'an ever loftier and purer activity', so Mahler spoke of 'the great aspiration towards the accomplishment of purification that progresses through each reincarnation.' He then went on to explain to Specht another of his convictions drawn from Goethe's work:

Every wrong done to me is a wrong done to the whole universe, and affects the World Spirit (or whatever you want to call the central being of the world). . . . If I hurt my little finger, my whole functioning is disturbed. The same thing is true on a larger scale, although I don't want to picture myself as the little finger of the Cosmos. Goethe wrote endlessly about this.[123]

Likewise André Gide writes of Goethe: 'That we are responsible for everything we do, that each of us depends on everything and everyone else, and that no one can behave as though he alone mattered: that is the conclusion he finally comes to.'[124] It was to my mind in Goethe that Mahler found this conviction of belonging to the universe. Like Goethe, he did not regard man as 'fallen', and believed that he was 'accountable only to himself'. The text that he added to Klopstock's Ode in the Finale of the Second Symphony powerfully affirms this. André Gide might have been writing of Mahler when he said of Goethe:

The only God he recognizes merges with nature: the All, of which he, Goethe, is part. And it is as a part of the divine All that Goethe honours and esteems himself. His individualism is a part of his worship, and his duties towards himself are derived from his duties towards God, whom he seeks and finds everywhere in the Cosmos, and not by shutting his eyes to the outside world.[125]

Like Goethe's, Mahler's *Weltanschauung* was influenced by Plotin's Neoplatonism and Spinoza's Pantheism, far more than by Christianity or Judaism.[126] Like Goethe, Mahler did not reject the visible, the tangible, and showed an almost mystic confidence in Nature. This feeling, which already pervades the Third Symphony, is by no means foreign to the Eighth, nor could it be: man like Goethe's redeemed hero, Faust, must draw ever closer to the Soul of the world, the final Unity from which each individual life emerges and into which each life continually tends to merge anew. Mahler, with Goethe,

---

[122] 'Deshalb muss ich ethisch leben: um meinem Ich, wenn es wiederkommt, schon jetzt ein Stück Weges ersparen und um ihm sein Dasein leichter zu machen. Dahin geht meine sittliche Pflicht, ganz gleichgültig, ob mein späteres Ich davon weiss oder nicht und ob es mir danken wird oder nicht' (RSM2, 39).

[123] 'sondern nur auf den grossen Zug zum Vollendeten; zu der Läuterung die in jeder Inkarnation fortschreitet. . . . Jedes Unrecht, das mir angetan wird, ist ein Unrecht am ganzen Universum und muss den Weltgeist (oder wie immer man das zentrale Weltwesen nennen mag) schmerzen. Wenn ich mich am kleinen Finger verletze, so tut es mir weh, nicht nur dem kleinen Finger, und ich bin an meinen Funktionen gehindert. Ganz ebenso ist es im Grossen; wenn ich mich auch nicht als den kleinen Finger des Kosmos fühlen darf. Goethe hat darüber Unendliches gesagt . . .' (ibid).

[124] André Gide, preface to Goethe's complete plays (Pléïade edition, Gallimard, Paris, 1942), p. xv: 'Que chaque geste nous engage, que chacun dépend de tout et de tous, et que l'homme ne peut se comporter en "cavalier seul", voici ce dont il se persuade . . .'

[125] André Gide, ibid., pp. xix: 'Le seul Dieu qu'il reconnaisse se confond avec la Nature; c'est le Tout, dont lui-même, Goethe, fait partie. Et c'est en tant que partie du Tout divin que Goethe se respecte et s'honore. Son individualisme est compris dans son adoration et ses devoirs envers soi-même découlent de ses devoirs envers Dieu. Si Dieu ne lui fait pas défaut, c'est qu'il le cherche et trouve partout dans le Cosmos et non point en fermant les yeux sur le monde extérieur.'

[126] See Hermann Danuser, 'Interpret', 270 ff.

preached the dynamic virtues he never ceased to practise himself: movement towards the infinite, even by way of error; purification through experience; victory over oneself; acceptance of life and its limitations; the true sanctity of practical activity directed towards a definite end; solidarity among men; and finally love as the law of the world.

But Goethe's Eros was not only love—although love is a leitmotiv of the last scene of *Faust*, Part II—[127] it was also the symbol of inexhaustible activity, of courage, of harmony in remaining true to the earth, of self-mastery in the acceptance of reality. It was this Eros that Mahler conceived as the creative force in his earliest plan, and that later he recognized as the very principle of his symphony (in the words he scribbled under the musical phrase that Alma had written out from memory and sent him).[128] However, the second part of the Eighth Symphony celebrates repose, death as the ultimate transformation, using as a symbol the figure of the Mater gloriosa, the 'eternal feminine' which here can be compared with other Mahlerian symbols such as the 'eternal life' of the Second Symphony and the 'earth' of *Das Lied*. Yet, contrary to appearances, this is a triumph through effort, a humanist triumph such as that summed up by Goethe shortly before his death in the following terms: 'Through use, teaching, reflection, success, failure, encouragement, resistance and still more reflection, the organs of a human being unconsciously bring together in free activity, the acquired with the inborn, producing a unity that astounds the world.'[129]

No doubt Mahler himself would have strongly opposed any attempt at explaining the meaning of the Eighth. Like him, Goethe declared that explanations of a work of art are useless, even harmful, and always diminish its impact.

Only have the courage to give yourself up to your impressions, allow yourself to be delighted, moved, elevated, nay, instructed and inspired for something great; but do not imagine all would be lost, if one could not find in the depths of a work some idea, some abstract thought. . . . I am rather of the opinion that the more incommensurable, and the more incomprehensible to the understanding, a poetic production is, the better it is.[130]

This could be Mahler speaking! Is Goethe's advice not worth following? Should we not, while listening to the Eighth, indulge without afterthoughts in the sheer physical pleasure procured by the torrents of sound of the 'Veni Creator' and of the final Hymnus, or in the neo-baroque contrapuntal proliferations of the double fugue, whose simultaneous lines and antiphonal refinements fill our ears with ten times, a hundred times more notes than our minds can take in?

As seen above, Mahler himself considered that one of his greatest innovations was to have used true symphonic methods, in composing FOR solo voices and chorus. His original and wholly modern use of solo voices and chorus, with an unsurpassable

---

[127] Danuser has made a list of lines, in Goethe's scene and Mahler's Part II, in which love is mentioned (ll. 11852–3, 11865, 11871–2, 11924–5, 11938–9, 11950, 11964–5, 12003–4, 12110). He also notes that each of these moments in the Symphony stands out, either 'thanks to a cadence, a cantilena, or a certain melodic feature'. (Danuser, 'Interpret', 274).

[128] Alma's quotation from memory of a passage from the second movement of the Eighth was corrected by Mahler in Salzburg, where he had received it (see above).

[129] Goethe, letter to Wilhelm von Humboldt, written five days before his death, on 17 Mar. 1832: 'Die Organe des Menschen durch Übung, Lehre, Nachdenken, Gelingen, Misslingen, Förderniss und Widerstand und immer wieder Nachdenken verknüpfen ohne Bewusstsein in einer freien Tätigkeit das Erworbene mit dem Angeborenen, so dass es eine Einheit hervorbringt welche die Welt in Erstaunen setzt.'

[130] Goethe, *Conversations with Eckermann*, 6 May 1827.

mastery of sonority, colour, timbre, and acoustics, has not as yet inspired a detailed study, but it merits one. It would be rewarding to examine more closely Mahler's writing for 'the most beautiful instrument of all'[131] his use of such magical effects as, in Part II, the entry of the chorus, with simple triads as a background to Dr Marianus's prayer to the Mater gloriosa;[132] or the echo effects in the opening section of the same movement; or the 'Infirma nostri corporis' passage in the first part. Ultimately, it is the basic theme of the 'Veni Creator' (E♭–B♭–A♭), symbolizing man's progress towards a higher truth, that dominates the entire work and gives it its unity.

In the Eighth, Mahler at the same time affirms his rejection of materialism and his faith—not naive, not 'decorative', but deeply tinged with mysticism—in the divine spark shining in every human being. He in his turn accomplished the loftiest and most ambitious design of most nineteenth-century composers: to speak to the people, to the 'nation', to the whole human race, in a language accessible to all. In doing so he carried out one of the boldest endeavours ever made in music, and reached the furthest point of the monumental, choral symphonism initiated by Beethoven's Ninth and Berlioz's *Requiem*, and already carried forward by Mahler in his own Second. Since then, other composers have followed in his footsteps, attempting to erect cosmic cathedrals fit for the century that has conquered space. So far, no one seems fully to have succeeded. For this reason, the Eighth is invariably chosen to celebrate great occasions such as the opening of a large concert hall or an international festival, causing the hearts of a multitude to beat as one. Thus Mahler's enterprise must be considered entirely successful, and his Eighth has truly become de facto the only twentieth-century equivalent of Beethoven's Ninth.

Admittedly, the loftier the building, the more reinforced its design has to be, if only in deference to the architectural laws that keep it from collapsing. The Eighth has been criticized for a certain monotony arising, perhaps, from the prevailing binary rhythms. (This criticism is in part attributable to the rhythmic symmetry of Goethe's lines.) It is obvious that Mahler consciously used the 'tempus perfectum' of tradition, the rhythm of unswerving certainties. However that may be, listening to the Eighth, the ear has much else to listen to, and rhythm appears as only one element in an indivisible whole. The rhythmic symmetry is amply compensated for by the prodigious fecundity of the musical invention, the epic sweep, and the sovereign technical mastery that make this work fully equal to those that precede and follow it.

Mahler's last two finished works, *Das Lied von der Erde* and the Ninth Symphony, have perhaps put the Eighth somewhat into the shade. Their intense subjectivity and overwhelming expressivity opened up new horizons and drew the attention of the musical public away from the less frequently heard Eighth. Our modern propensity to fit everything into categories makes us dislike whatever is exceptional. Yet are not all Mahler's symphonies exceptional in one way or another, exceptional in their context, their thought, their expression, their form, their techniques, or even their style? After

---

[131] See above Mahler's statement to Richard Specht about the composition of the Eighth (*Grazer Tagespost*, 14 June 1914).

[132] Second movement, bar 724. Hermann Danuser singles out many other striking features of Mahler's choral writing, for instance the use of the Children's chorus for the 'Blessed Boys', as opposed to the mixed chorus for the angels, thus allowing a more flexible handling of the text. He also points out Mahler's use—for the first time homophonically—of soloists, children's chorus, and the complete mixed choruses, unaccompanied, in the last bars of the Coda (bar 1506 ff.).

completing *Das Lied* and the Ninth Mahler poured a huge amount of energy into preparing the première of the Eighth. He knew that it not only conveyed a message, but also opened new paths to the music of the future, if only in its use of 'variant' procedures, which here moves significantly the perpetual variation of the Viennese school, towards the continuous development that eshews the slightest backward glance in the musical argument, an ideal which Mahler pursued intermittently since the beginning of his career as a composer. In the Eighth, Mahler's 'variant' procedures achieve a unity which is not only technical, but also philosophical, a synthesis of the unique and the whole.

The huge audiences which, then and now, never fail to greet its performance with the utmost possible enthusiasm are surely not conscious of Mahler's unique technical and compositional feats, yet their unanimous applause awarded him in 1910 his last and most complete recompense as a composer. Likewise today's performers of the Eighth are assured of being rewarded for their efforts and are always grateful to a composer who incites them to outdo themselves and who gave the full measure of his genius in celebrating the eternal values behind the transient (*Vergängliche*) and the incomplete (*Unzulängliche*) of which our earthly life is made up.

FIRST PART

FAMILY I:
(Characterized by great rhythmic energy, dotted rhythms, cells Q^1 and Q^2 (rising and falling fourth) and by the dotted rhythm R. As well as the themes proper, two cadential elements, K^1 and K^2, are indicated.)

(Sop. solo) su-per-na su - per - na su - per - na gra - ti - a (Organ, Horn)

FAMILY II:

Also very sharp in outline. (First appearance as countermelody to A.) Cells: Q^1, R, and S (rising sixth).

(Vl. I)

Qui pa-ra - cli-tus di - ce-ris
(Sop. I/II soli)

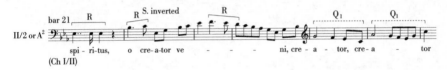

spi - ri-tus, o cre-a-tor ve - - - ni, cre - a - tor, cre-a - tor
(Ch I/II)

FAMILY III:

Lyrical, singing, contrasted with I and II. Cells Q^2, R, and S nevertheless serve to establish a common bond.

Im - ple su-per - ne gra - ti-a, gra-ti-a, quæ tu cre - a sti
(Sop. solo)

Imp - le su - per - - - na
(Sop. solo)

FAMILY IV:

Again more or less related to family I. As well as the cells already known, motifs *a*, *b*, and *f* appear.

Link established between families IV and V by the combination of IV/2 and V/2.

(Cellos, Bns.)

In - fir-ma, in - fir-ma, nos-tri cor-po-ris Fir - mans per - pe - ti
(Bar. solo) vir - tu - te per - pe - ti

SECOND PART

FAMILY IV (continuation of the preceding):

FAMILY V:

New transformations of IV. V/1a comes from IV/2 and is indirectly derived from family I, by a and b; V/1a is particularly linked to IV/2 and IV2a. New motifs: *d* and *e*.

FAMILY VI:

New variant of IV. It appears frequently in the form of an ostinato figure below VI/2 to 4 (as IV/2a did earlier below themes of Family V).

APPENDIX 3

The Vienna Opera in Mahler's Time

CHARACTERISTICS OF THE HOFOPER AUDITORIUM IN 1907

There are 1,500 seats, with standing room for 500 in the pit and in the third and fourth circles. Women are not admitted to the standing places in the pit.

DIMENSIONS OF THE STAGE

Width of proscenium arch	14 m.
Height of proscenium arch	11 m.
Depth of stage (2 m.: forestage)	27 m.
Width of the stage (wall to wall)	29 m.
Space available for scenery	23 m.
Height of stage from floor to upper flies	28 m.
Depth below stage in five tiers	12 m.

A basic fixed curtain, grey-green in colour, hangs down too far and limits visibility to a height of 7.5 m., even though the proscenium arch is 11 m. high. Sets are designed for this height, and the perspective established on this basis, with the result that grand spectacle is impossible: the spectator always has a sense of things being skimped and squashed, which considerably damages the effect.

As well as this fixed curtain there is a moveable curtain which can descend to 4 m. above the stage. The forestage curtains are lined with cork to deaden sound, so that people in the auditorium do not hear noises on stage during the intervals.

The stage has eight areas; the width of the slips varies from 1 m. downstage to 1.75 m. at the back. The battens for each area contain, as well as the usual incandescent lamps, four arc lamps, each of 1,200 candlepower. The reflectors for the battens are placed exactly above each one, an arrangement preferable to the usual one because the light reflected down in this way is much more intense.

The back of the stage is huge: 23 m. long, 13 m. wide, and as high as the rest of the stage. It encompasses a great metal practicable 4 m. high and as wide as itself. This practicable can be moved backwards and forwards and be placed just in front of the doors of two upper corridors which face each other at the centre of either side of the back of the stage. This is very useful in certain deep designs like the second act of *Lohengrin* where the procession, emerging from one of the corridors, descends at a distance of 39 m. from the footlights.

The back of the stage is also used in *Aida* for the act with the trumpets, and in the ballet *Excelsior.* The gradient of the stage is 2%. The first metre of the forestage slopes down sharply, and is edged with grey carpeting designed to lessen the glare of the footlights into the performer's eyes. The carpeting has an odd appearance.

The stagehands operate from the first service corridor, generally on the 'côté cour', called *Stadtseite* (town side or opposite prompter or stage-left) as opposed to *Burgseite* (castle side or prompter side or stage-right).

The stage manager, Richard Bennier, has undertaken radical transformations of the stage, following a system of his own invention. But this lengthy task can only proceed as and when new grants are made to him, and only during the two months when the opera house is closed, from 22 June to 18 Aug. [1907].

His sytem derives from the 'Asphaleia' (Greek: protection) system drawn up by Gwinner of Vienna and Burghard of Budapest, and installed in the Budapest Theatre. It can be summed up as follows: an electric motor of about 10 horsepower activates movable metal traps in such a way that a whole slip can be lowered up to 2 m. or raised, either entire or in a dozen fragments or steps, as high as 4 m. The trapdoors of these false slips are operated in the same way, by a five-horsepower motor.

This is a very ingenious conception, but very expensive. Each area will cost almost 80,000 kronen. At this time only the eighth area has been completed.

At the back of the stage, a lift operated by a little three-horsepower motor and capable of lifting a weight of 1,200 kilos communicates with the stores below.

As a security measure only one person, the below-stage foreman, has keys to the motors. Richard Bennier has just patented a system to do with the electrical transmission: by lowering resistances, a saving of 40% can be made. The chief electrician sits at a sort of tiny keyboard with which he can vary all lighting effects *ad infinitum*. The rigging loft at the Vienna Opera has to be completely changed. The upper flies at this time are an impenetrable tangle of wooden beams, ropes, and wires: on the court side [stage-left] wires can even be seen brushing against the wooden lattice-work of the upper flies, which must be a fire hazard.

Backstage on the court side of area zero (*Nulgasse*) there is a curious machine: a writing or reading desk whose upper part bears several stops marked: rain, wind, storm, etc. A répétiteur follows the score and, at the appropriate moment, pulls the necessary stop.

The vapour used for stage effects is not released under pressure. In the last scene of *Don Giovanni* this silent vapour is of considerable effect.

For ordinary performances 57 stagehands and 9 electricians are used. For big spectacles it is possible to call on a further 36 stagehands.

About thirty operas are constantly at the ready in the theatre stores, along with two big ballets and five small ones. The outlying warehouse at the end of the Prater holds in reserve fifty more operas and almost as any ballets; many sets or parts of sets serve for several operas. Old material with no further regular use is burnt.

The auditorium has a very sophisticated system of heating and air conditioning. Powerful ventilators pump in anything from 40,000 to 120,000 cubic metres of air per hour through three conduits (one of them under the orchestra stalls), maintaining an overall temperature of 15 to 16 degrees centigrade even in summer, for there is hydraulic machinery for cooling the air.

From Eugène d'Harcourt, *La Musique actuelle en Allemagne et en Autriche-Hongrie* (Durdilly, Paris, 1908).

REPERTOIRE OF THE VIENNA OPERA UNDER MAHLER
(1 MAY 1897 TO 31 DECEMBER 1907)[1]

Abbreviations

Cond. conductor
M. Mahler
M/ number of performances conducted by Mahler
PR first performance at the Hofoper
NE Neueinstudierung (revival involving complete reworking)
NI Neuinszenierung (new production)
s/d stage-design
T/ total number of performances under Mahler's tenure
WA Wiederaufnahme (revival with a few short rehearsals)

This list does not include ballets and *divertissements*. The titles of French, Italian, and German operas are given in their original language. For a small number of unfamiliar works like *Les Dragons de Villars*, the German title is also given. For names of composers and translations of titles, see the index at the end of this volume. Several operas have two sets of figures. The first one concerns the number of performances *before* a *Neueinstudierung*, *Neuinszenierung*, or *Wiederaufnahme*. The distinction between *Neueinstudierung* and *Neuinszenierung* is not always easy to make because Roller sometimes took elements from older staging and modified them. Sometimes he designed only the costumes.

ABREISE (Die) (d'Albert), PR: 28 Feb. 1905 (cond. M.) (M/5) (T/8).

AFRICAINE (L') (Meyerbeer), WA: 4 Aug. 1897 (cond. M.) (M/1) (T/19).

AIDA (Verdi), WA 29 Apr. 1898 (cond. Mahler) (M/12) (T/35); NI: 11 May 1903 (cond. M., s/d Lefler, Brioschi) (M/2) (T/49).

AM WÖRTHER SEE (Koschat), WA: 18 Aug. 1898 (cond. Hellmesberger) (T/6).

BALLO IN MASCHERA (Un) (Ein Maskenball) (Verdi), NE: 5 Mar. 1898 (cond. Fuchs) (T/8); NE: 19 May 1906 (cond. Walter) (T/21).

BÄRENHÄUTER (Der) (S. Wagner), PR: 27 Mar. 1899 (cond. M.) (M/14) (T/20).

BARBIERE DI SIVIGLIA (Il) (Rossini), (T/4); NE: 25 Dec. 1906 (cond. M.) (M/2) (T/12).

BARTERED BRIDE (The) (Die verkaufte Braut) (Smetana), (M/1); NE: 20 Sept. 1899 (cond. M., s/d Brioschi) (M/10) (T/56).

BOHÈME (La) (Leoncavallo), PR: 23 Feb. 1898 (cond. M., s/d Brioschi) (M/6) (T/6).

BOHÈME (La) (Puccini), PR: 25 Nov. 1903 (cond. Spetrino, s/d Brioschi) (T/61).

BUNDSCHUH (Der) (Reiter), PR: 13 Nov. 1900 (cond. M.) (M/4) (T/5).

CARMEN (Bizet), (T/20); NE: 26 May 1900 (cond. M., s/d Brioschi) (M/6) (T/85).

CAVALLERIA RUSTICANA (Mascagni), (T/131).

CONTES D'HOFFMANN (Les) (Hofmanns Erzählungen) (Offenbach), PR: 11 Nov. 1901 (cond. M., s/d Brioschi), (M/8) (T/108).

---

[1] Mahler was only appointed Deputy Dirctor in July 1897, and full Dirctor on 8 Oct. However, from the date of his debut on (11 May), his influence on the repertoire became predominant.

CORREGIDOR (Der) (Wolf), PR: 18 Feb. 1904 (cond. M., s/d Roller) (M/5) (T/7).

COSÌ FAN TUTTE (Mozart), NI: 4 Oct. 1900 (cond. M., s/d Brioschi) (M/7) (T/8); NI: 24 Nov. 1905 (cond. M., s/d Roller) (M/6) (T/1).

DAME BLANCHE (La) (Die weisse Dame) (Boieldieu), NE: 4 Oct. 1898 (cond. M.) (M/7) (T/11); WA: 15 Feb. 1902 (cond. M.) (M/3) (T/13).

DALIBOR (Smetana), PR: 4 Oct. 1897 (cond. M., s/d Brioschi) (M/21) (T/23).

DÄMON (Der) (*The Demon*) (Rubinstein), PR: 23 Oct. 1899 (cond. M.) (M/5) (T/5).

DAS WAR ICH (Blech), PR: 28 Feb. 1905 (cond. M.) (M/3) (T/5).

DJAMILEH (Bizet), PR: 22 Jan. 1898 (cond. M.) (M/19) (T/19).

Don Giovanni (Mozart), (M/2) (T/9); NI: 21 Dec. 1905 (cond. M., s/d Roller) (M/14) (T/16).

DONNA DIANA (Reznicek), PR: 9 Dec. 1898 (cond. M.) (M/7) (T/7).

DONNE CURIOSE (Le) (Die neugierigen Frauen) (Wolf-Ferrari), PR: 4 Oct. 1905 (cond. M., s/d Roller) (M/10) (T/12).

DOT MON (Der) (Forster), PR: 28 Feb. 1902 (cond. M., s/d Brioschi) (M/3) (T/11).

DRAGONS DE VILLARS (Les) (Das Glöckchen des Eremiten) (Maillart), NE: 21 Apr. 1899 (cond. Fuchs) (T/13).

ENTFÜHRUNG AUS DEM SERAIL (Die) (Mozart), NI: 29 Jan. 1906 (cond. M., s/d Roller) (M/16) (T/18).

ERNANI (Hernani) (Verdi), NE: 2 Oct. 1902 (cond. Walter) (T/6).

ES WAR EINMAL (Zemlinsky), PR: 22 Jan. 1900 (cond. M.) (M/11) (T/12).

EUGENE ONEGIN (Tchaikovsky), PR: 19 Nov. 1897 (cond. M., s/d Brioschi) (M/20) (T/20).

EURYANTHE (Weber), NI: 19 Jan. 1903 (cond. M., s/d Roller) (M/4) (T/5); NE: 19 Jan. 1904 (Mahler version) (M/5) (T/5).

EVANGELIMAN (Der) (Kienzl), (T/34).

FALSTAFF (Verdi), PR: 3 May 1904 (in German), (cond. M., s/d Roller) (M/6) (T/13).

FAUST (Margarethe) (Gounod), (M/4) (T/90).

FEDORA (Giordano), PR: 16 May 1900 (cond. Schalk) (T/3).

FEUERSNOT (R. Strauss), PR: 29 Jan. 1902 (cond. M., s/d Brioschi) (M/3) (T/11); NE: 5 June 1905 (cond. M.) (M/1) (T/1).

FIDELIO (Beethoven), (T/20); NI: 7 Oct. 1904 (cond. M., s/d Roller) (M/19) (T/25).

FILLE DU RÉGIMENT (La) (Donizetti), NE: 6 Sept. 1899 (cond. M.) (M/2) (T/4).

FLAUTO SOLO (d'Albert), PR: 28 Nov. 1906 (cond. Schalk, s/d Roller) (T/4).

FLEDERMAUS (Die) (J. Strauss), (M/1) (T/91).

FLIEGENDE HOLLÄNDER (Der) (Wagner), (M/4); NE: 4 Dec. 1897 (cond. M., s/d Brioschi) (M/7) (T/51).

FRA DIAVOLO (Auber), NE: 29 Sept. 1899 (cond. M., s/d Brioschi) (M/8) (T/14).

FREISCHÜTZ (Der) (Weber), NE: 21 Oct. 1898 (cond. M.) (M/13) (T/43).

GOLDENE KERUZ (Das) (Brüll), NE: 6 June 1902 (cond. Schalk) (T/4); WA: 4 June 1907 (cond. Schalk, s/d Brioschi) (T/5).

GÖTTERDÄMMERUNG (Die) (Wagner), (M/1); NE: 4 Sept. 1898 (uncut version) (cond. M., s/d Brioschi) (M/9) (T/43).

GUILLAUME TELL (Wilhelm Tell) (Rossini), (T/40); NI: 11 May 1905 (cond. Spetrino, s/d Brioschi) (T/8).

GUTE NACHT HERR PANTALON (Grisar), (T/2).

HAMLET (Thomas), (T/2).

HANS HEILING (Marschner), (T/13).

HÄNSEL UND GRETEL (Humperdinck), (T/57).

HEIMCHEN AM HERD (Das) (Goldmark), (T/3); WA: 25 Apr. 1898 (cond. Hellmesberger, s/d Brioschi) (T/17).

HUGUENOTS (Les) (Die Hugenotten) (Meyerbeer), (T/1); NI: 29 Oct. 1902 (cond. M., s/d Brioschi) (M/8) (T/40).

IOLANTHE (Tchaikovsky), PR: 22 Mar. 1900 (cond. M., s/d Brioschi, Brughart, Kautsky) (M/8) (T/9).

IPHIGÉNIE EN AULIDE (Gluck), NI: 18 Mar. 1907 (cond. M., s/d Roller) (M/5) (T/6).

JUIF POLONAIS (Le) (Erlanger), PR: 4 Oct. 1906 (cond. Walter, s/d Brioschi) (T/3).

JUIVE (La) (Halévy), NI: 13 Oct. 1903 (cond. M., s/d Brioschi) (M/2) (T/19).

KÖNIGIN VON SABA (Die) (Goldmark), (T/7); NE: 29 Apr. 1901 (cond. M., s/d Brioschi) (M/3) (T/44).

KRIEGSGEFANGENE (Die) (Goldmark), PR: 17 Jan. 1899 (cond. M.) (M/4) (T/6).

LAKMÉ (Delibes), PR: 14 Nov. 1904 (cond. Walter, s/d Roller) (T/26).

LEGENDE DER HEILIGE ELISABETH (Die) (Liszt), WA: 19 Nov. 1898 (cond. Schalk) (T/10).

LOBETANZ (Thuille), PR: 18 Mar. 1901 (cond. Schalk, s/d Brioschi) (T/6).

LOHENGRIN (Wagner), (M/19) (T/33); WA: 27 Dec. 1900 (cond. Schalk) (T/62); NI: 27 Feb. 1906 (cond. Schalk, s/d Roller) (T/28).

LOUISE (Charpentier), PR: 24 Mar. 1903 (cond. M., s/d Brioschi) (M/8) (T/24).

LUCIA DI LAMMERMOOR (Donizetti), NE: 9 Oct. 1899 (cond. Luze) (T/6); WA: 31 Oct. 1903 (cond. Spetrino) (T/15).

LUSTIGEN WEIBER VON WINDSOR (Die) (*The Merry Wives of Windsor*) (Nicolai) (T/2); NI: 4 Oct. 1901 (cond. M., s/d Brioschi) (M/10) (T/26).

MADAMA BUTTERFLY (Puccini), PR: 31 Oct. 1907 (cond. Spetrino, s/d Roller) (T/14).

MANON (Massenet), (T/23); NE: 26 May 1905 (cond. Schalk, s/d Brioschi) (T/17).

MARTHA (Flotow), NE: 4 May 1901 (cond. Brecher) (T/7).

MEISTERSINGER VON NÜRNBERG (Die) (Wagner), (T/10); NE: 26 Nov. 1899 (uncut version) (cond. M., s/d Brioschi) (M/10) (T/72).

MIGNON (Thomas), (M/5) (T/83).

MUETTE DE PORTICI (La) (Die Stumme von Portici) (Auber), NE: 27 Feb. 1907 (cond. Walter, s/d Roller) (T/5).

NACHTLAGER IN GRANADA (Das) (Kreutzer), NE: 6 June 1898 (cond. Fuchs) (T/6).

NORMA (Bellini), NE: 24 Jan. 1898 (cond. Richter) (T/11).

NOZZE DI FIGARO (Le) (Die Hochzeit des Figaro) (Mozart), (M/31) (T/36); NI: 30 Mar. 1906 (cond. M., s/d Roller) (M/13) (T/16).

OPERNPROBE (Die) (Lortzing), PR: 10 Feb. 1899 (cond. M., s/d Brioschi) (M/8) (T/25).

ORPHÉE ET EURYDICE (Gluck), (T/7).

OTELLO (Othello) (Verdi), (T/4); NE: 3 May 1907 (cond. Zemlinsky) (T/5).

PAGLIACCI (Leoncavallo), (T/137).

PIQUE DAME (Tchaikovsky), PR: 9 Dec. 1902 (cond. M., s/d Brioschi) (M/13) (T/30).

POSTILLON DE LONGJUMEAU (Le) (Adam), NE: 4 Feb. 1904 (cond. Schalk) (T/5).

POUPÉE DE NUREMBERG (La) (Die Nürnberger Puppe) (Adam), NE: 24 Apr. 1899 (cond. Fuchs) (T/1).

PROPHÈTE (Le) (Meyerbeer), (M/1) (T/15); NE: 5 Mar. 1907 (cond. Walter) (T/6).

RHEINGOLD (Das) (Wagner), (M/11) (T/19); NI: 23 Jan. 1905 (cond. M., s/d Roller) (M/9) (T/23).

RIENZI (Wagner), NI: 21 Jan. 1901 (cond. M., s/d Brioschi) (M/2) (T/27).

RIGOLETTO (Verdi), NE: 20 May 1899 (cond. Fuchs) (T/36).

ROBERT LE DIABLE (Robert der Teufel) (Meyerbeer), NE: 20 Mar. 1898 (cond. Fuchs) (T/13).

ROMÉO ET JULIETTE (Gounod), NE: 21 Nov. 1897 (cond. Hellmesberger) (T/14).

ROSE VOM LIEBESGARTEN (Die) (Pfitzner), PR: 6 April 1905 (cond. M., s/d Roller) (M/7) (T/18).

SAMSON ET DALILA (Saint-Saëns), PR: 11 May 1907 (cond. Walter, s/d Roller) (T/7).

SIEGFRIED (Wagner), (M/12) (T/49).

SPEZIALE (Lo) (Der Apotheker) (Haydn, arr. Hirschfeld), PR: 10 Feb. 1899 (cond. M., s/d Brioschi) (M/6) (T/7).

TANNHÄUSER (Wagner), (M/4) (T/20); NE: 11 May 1901 (uncut version) (cond. M.) (M/4) (T/69).

TRAVIATA (La) (Verdi), (T/10).

TRISTAN UND ISOLDE (Wagner), (M/16) (T/18); NI: 21 Feb. 1903 (cond. M., s/d Roller) (M/21) (T/27).

TROMPETER VON SÄKKINGEN (Der) (Nessler), (cond. Hellmesberger) (T/17).

TROVATORE (Il) (Verdi), NE: 26 Oct. 1900 (cond. Schalk) (M/1) (T/48).

WAFFENSCHMIED (Der) (Lortzing), NE: 4 Jan. 1904 (cond. M., s/d Brioschi) (M/4) (T/7).

WALKÜRE (Die) (Wagner), (M/11) (T/36); NI: 4 Feb. 1907 (cond. M., s/d Roller) (M/5) (T/14).

WERTHER (Massenet), NE: 12 May 1906 (cond. Schalk) (T/7).

WIDERSPENSTIGEN ZÄHMUNG (Der) (*The Taming of the Shrew*) (Götz), NI: 3 Nov. 1906 (cond. M., s/d Roller) (M/8) (T/9).

WILDSCHÜTZ (Der) (Lortzing), NE: 27 Jan. 1900 (cond. Luze) (T/5).

ZAIDE (Mozart, arr. Hirschfeld), PR: 4 Oct. 1902 (cond. Walter, s/d Brioschi) (T/3).

ZAR UND ZIMMERMANN (Lortzing), NE: 11 Sept. 1897 (cond. M.) (M/15) (T/28).

ZAUBERFLÖTE (Die) (Mozart), WA: 16 Oct. 1897 (cond. M.) (M/31) (T/34); NI: 1 June 1906 (cond. M., s/d Roller) (M/8) (T/12).

MAHLER'S SINGERS AT THE HOFOPER

Abbreviations

a   alto
b   baritone
bs bass
m   mezzo-soprano
s   soprano
t   tenor

The dates indicate commencement and termination of contracts with the Vienna Opera.

Men

BERTRAM Theodor, b (01.09.01–19.09.01).
BORUTTAU Alfred, t (01.09.05–21.08.06).
BREUER, Hans, t, and stage-director (11.08.00–31.08.29).
BROZEL Philipp, t (01.09.07–31.08.08).
DEMUTH Leopold, b (01.06.98–04.03.10).
DIPPEL Andreas, t (01.08.93–31.07.98).
FELIX Benedikt, b (16.02.83–31.01.12).
FRAUSCHER Moritz, bs (01.08.99–31.07.04).
GRENGG Karl, bs (01.08.89–28.02.03).
HAYDTER Alexander, bs (01.09.05–11.02.19).
HESCH Wilhelm, bs (01.08.96–04.01.08).
HORWITZ Willibald, bs (01.04.80–31.03.09).
KURZ-STOLZENBERG Karl, t (01.09.06–31.08.08).
LEUER Hubert, t (01.08.04–1920).
MAIKL Georg, t (01.09.04–31.08.41).
MARIAN Ferdinand, bs (01.04.96–30.06.21).
MAYR Richard, bs (01.09.02–31.08.35).
MELMS Hans, b (01.10.92–10.03.04)
MOSER Anton, b (01.09.03–29.11.09).
NAVAL Franz, t (01.08.98–30.04.02).
NEIDL Franz, b (20.07.90–31.07.04).
PACAL Franz, t (15.08.98–14.08.05).
PREUSS Arthur, t (15.02.99–15.02.15).
REICH Karl, bs (01.09.05–31.08.11).
REICHENBERG Franz von, bs (01.06.84–30.04.04).
REICHMANN Theodor, b (01.06.83–08.04.89 and 01.09.93–22.05.03).
RITTER Josef, b (01.08.91–31.07.06).
SCHITTENHELM Anton, t (15.08.75–15.08.03).
SCHMEDES Erik, t (01.06.98–31.08.24).
SCHRÖDTER Fritz, t (01.05.85–31.05.15).
SEMBACH Johannes, t (01.10.04–31.07.07).
SLEZAK Leo, t (15.09.01–31.08.12 and 15.09.17–31.08.34).
SPIELMANN Julius, t (01.08.98–28.02.99).
STEHMANN Gerhard, b (16.09.99–06.07.26).
STOLL August, b, and stage-producer in name (20.10.84–12.07.18)
VAN DYCK Ernest, t (01.10.88–30.09.00).
WEIDERMANN Friedrich, b (01.09.03–30.01.19).
WINKELMANN Hermann, t (01.06.83–31.05.06).
WISSIAK Wilhelm, bs (01.01.05–15.02.08).
ZAWILOWSKI Konrad von, bs (01.05.04–30.04.07).

Women

ABENDROTH Irene, s (01.09.94–31.08.99).
BAIER-LIEBHARDT Ida, m (01.04.80–31.03.06).
BEETH Lola (01.08.98–31.07.01).

BLAND Elsa, s (01.06.05–31.05.08).
CAHIER Sarah, a (01.04.07–15.09.11).
DRILL-ORRIDGE Theo, a (01.02.06–01.02.16).
EHRENSTEIN Luise von, s (01.09.89–30.11.99).
ELIZZA Elise, s (01.10.95–30.08.18).
FELLWOCK Ottilie, a (11.08.98–31.07.99).
FELSER Frida, s (01.09.05–17.08.06).
FLADUNG Irene von, s (01.09.06–31.03.07).
FÖRSTEL Gertrud, s (01.09.06–31.01.12).
FÖRSTER-LAUTERER Berta, s (01.10.01–30.09.13).
FORST Grete, s (01.09.03–15.09.11).
FORSTER-BRANDT Ellen, s (01.05.87–30.04.06).
GUTHEIL-SCHODER Marie, s (01.06.00–30.04.27).
HILGERMANN Laura, m (01.03.00–28.02.02 and 01.09.02–1920).
KARIN Anita, s (01.10.00–30.09.01).
KAULICH-LAZARICH Luise, a (01.02.78–31.01.06).
KITTEL Hermine, m (01.08.01–31.08.31).
KIURINA-LEUER Berta, s (01.09.05–30.06.21).
KORB Jenny, s (01.01.00–31.01.01).
KURZ Selma, s (01.08.99–31.01.27).
KUSMITSCH Karoline, a (01.06.98–30.04.02).
MICHALEK Margarete, s (01.09.97–31.08.10).
MILDENBURG Anna von, s (01.06.98–30.04.16 and 01.01.19–1920).
PAALEN Bella, s (01.09.07–01.09.37).
PETRU Josie, a (01.09.02–31.08.07).
POHLNER Jenny, s (01.08.97–31.07.18).
RELLEE Leonore, m (01.08.99–31.07.00).
RENARD Marie, s (01.10.88–31.01.00).
SAVILLE Frances, s (08.12.97–28.02.03).
SCHUBERT Betty, s (01.09.02–16.08.05).
SEDLMAIR Sophie, s (01.01.97–31.12.07).
SEEBÖCK Charlotte, s (01.08.05–31.08.07).
TELEKY Emmy, s (15.09.96–31.07.97).
WALKER Edith, a (01.08.95–22.09.03).
WEIDT Lucie, s (01.09.02–31.08.27).

THEATRE REFORM? [BÜHNENREFORM?]
BY ALFRED ROLLER[1]

Daily life has become much more exciting than it was, while the theatre in general is correspondingly more boring. At least so it seems. Perhaps just by contrast. Because

---

[1] Article published in the journal *Der Merker*, 1:5 (1909), 193 ff., tr. by Meredith Sutcliffe.

of this, people concerned with the theatre now give more attention than they should to its secondary aspects. To design for example, about which much more has been said and written than is helpful for its development.

And everyone has his say!

It has often struck me that when someone who does not deserve a hearing starts to talk about art, he always excuses himself by saying: 'I know nothing about music (or "painting", or "poetry"), but I think that...' before giving of his wisdom. Only when people talk about the theatre do they omit the introductory excuse: in this area every-one considers his opinion to be valuable and justified. It would be very interesting if someone were clever enough to explain why this is so.

For myself I am convinced that the problems of theatre reform will be solved not through theoretical discussions but through a great many experiments, and that in particular, anything visual artists have to say about the essentials of this matter will be either self-evident or totally incomprehensible. If you wish to hear me out, you will have to be content with the following peripheral and incidental observations.

Would it not be better to reflect on what theatre was at the start, and on what we have made of it in the course of time? And to ask, above all, whether in its present form it is still viable and healthy? Could it not be that the travelling theatre was healthy and right, and that all permanently established theatre is merely decadent? To be in a different place every three weeks, startling the Philistine, giving him the excitement he longs for, preserving the sense of the exceptional! A thespis-car, what fun!

But a permanent theatre! Serving up the exceptional 300 times a year! For every good performance of a work of art must be in some way exceptional. But that I mean that it should stand out from ordinary daily life and project beyond it.—This is what has always drawn people to the theatre, this view into another world that excites, stirs, uplifts, unnerves, diverts, in any case engages! If the theatre becomes merely a part of ordinary life it gradually loses this attraction.

I know that the theatre also functions as a social manifestation and as a business. But these aspects are of secondary interest if we are to consider the possibility of investing it with new life.

So: a sacred and festal art, or a permanent institution for edification and entertain-ment?

Certainly I would not like to hear *Tristan* or *Figaro* or *Fidelio* every day of the week; and probably every great work of art is someone's *Tristan* or *Figaro* or *Fidelio*.

Repertory theatre seems to me to be simply a mistake. Admittedly Gustav Mahler was able to show that sacred festival performances [*Weihefestspiele*] of works in the repertory are possible. But he imposed this through his own inordinate strength, quite against the tendency of his organization.

It would be rash to suppose, for example, that there could ever exist the thousands upon thousands of strong personalities that our current abundance of permanent theatres requires. And what is to interest us on stage, if not strong personalities? Occasionally perhaps just the beautiful sound of a voice or the agility of a virtuoso. But in the long run? And what, if not boredom, can be dispensed by all those countless others who have chosen the stage as their calling? Chosen! There it is.—If, in earlier times, many people were driven to the theatre by the narrowness of bourgeois life— nowadays, most have chosen the stage deliberately. In earlier times they were wild [*durchgängerisch*] spirits, marked creatures whose perpetually precarious lives lent them a feckless charm. But these numerous honest persons on the stage today, learned owner-occupiers, professionals, and businessmen: can they bring us the extraordinary, which is what we expect from the theatre? Good citizens and hardworking people just like them are sitting in the stalls: the public is familiar with them through its own daily experience. Why should it bestow special attention on them as soon as they put on make-up and bright clothes, and why would it believe them when they speak great or terrifying or sweet words? Or when they sing their parts more or less correctly?

So why do we stick to a kind of orchestral activity which seems no longer to be viable? Granted, new and contemporary forms are continually arising, but in their lack of tradition they are naturally not exalted enough to meet with serious encouragements or to win favour with the cultivated! Isn't a good film to be preferred to a bad performance of Schiller?

Our theatre fails to satisfy the more serious part of its public, so in order to restructure it, one first sets to work on stage-design. But is this not the wrong way around? Production is, after all, the art of presentation, never an end in itself: an altogether secondary thing, ineluctably taking its principles and rules from the work itself, and having no guiding principle other than that of fulfilling the quite particular, often unique requirements of that work. So what can it mean to be seeking a new production method? 'Do you favour stylization, or illusion?' one is continually asked, 'three-dimensional sets or backdrops?'—just as at table one is asked 'Would you like white wine or red?' No choice is actually possible in these questions; they are answered within the work that is to be produced. But one must know how to read and listen one's way to this answer! Each work of art carries within itself the principles of its production.—Rules and methods established today can be stood on their head by a poet who comes along and creates a work tomorrow. Should he be prevented? In Shakespeare the décors were orally explained. Genius can look after itself. Admittedly we are vulgar enough to throw in naturalistic sets along with his abundant imagery.

The truth is that production today is at the same point as it was 100 years ago. In fact it has regressed from there; for in those days writers and musicians were well aware that theatre is performances (*Spiel*), and they well knew the stage for which they were writing and composing, whether they were sacred festivals or slapstick comedies. Today the one writes for an arena, the other for a tiny auditorium, a third would prefer his works performed in the open, or with a cyclorama that suggests the open, while most, when they write or compose, barely think about the stage at all, only about our bad theatrical habits. Let us also not forget that three quarters of the repertory in our theatres consists of works from the past. And all these works, which came into being in such varied circumstances, are performed in the self-same theatrical space. Is it a wonder that full justice is done to none of them, and that their impact is weak?

What is more: if anyone took the trouble to draw up plans of these spaces called for by our writers in their stage directions, some very remarkable architecture would result! In very few writers have I found a clear notion of the spatial structures in which their plots are to unfold.

Gordon Craig looks forward to a time when painters and designers will write their own plays; I would be satisfied if the writers of today's works would simply think in terms of a particular stage and its requirements. Some do. But how few they are! And how rarely does a newish work find its effectiveness increased through performances! For a strong theatrical effect, in the best sense of the words, depends entirely on the combined action of all elements on the stage.

The strange play put on last summer by young Kokoschka in the open-air theatre of the Kunstschau was probably not a great literary achievement; I am no judge of that. But the complete originality of the visual and poetic intention it showed, the forethought as to the given physical circumstances under which it was to be played, produced a theatricality, in the best sense, whose power was irresistible, and of which even a small portion would have been enough to save many of the new works put on in recent years, some perhaps of high literary quality, from failure.

Singers and actors, too, generally see things in terms of the old proscenium arch stage [*Kulissenbühne*]. Whether the set represents the primeval forest, or a drawing room, or the North Pole, they stand either 'right' or 'left' (on exactly the same spot each time) or 'take the centre'—obviously because on our stages, whether decorated by this principle or that, nothing else is possible, and because what the writer had commanded them to sing or say can probably best be sung or said from these particular favourite places. And people imagine that a theatrical renaissance can proceed from a renaissance in theatre design!

The indifference shown by our writers towards the physical and practical requirements of the stage, the disparity of the assumptions about staging that emerge from their works, the lack of connection between the average actor or singer, and the design of his surroundings: all this simply indicates that we do not really possess a living theatrical form of our own, that we are still using our scoffed-at inheritance, the proscenium arch stage, which is just variously dressed up and titivated, not genuinely transformed.

The panoramic horizon, three-dimensional sets, adjustable horizons, rotating stages, swivelling stages, pneumatic bellows, pneumatic fire, electric light, diffused lighting, chemical fog, painted flats, travelators, and all our other extravagantly praised 'modern achievements in theatre technique' that continually excite the press and public, are in fact simply masks and disguises for the old proscenium arch stage. The disease started with 'closed sets'; after that there was nothing for it but to drain the cup to the dregs and to exploit and exhaust all the possibilities offered.

So Reinhardt was quite right, in his *Midsummer Night's Dream* and subsequent productions, to take all these attempts at elaboration of the proscenium arch theatre to their logical conclusion, thus leaving the way open for genuinely new forms in the future.

In any case, why does the public not resolve wholeheartedly to support experiments being made in many places by individual artists in the direction of a new theatrical form? Because of weakness and sentimentality. Many people would like a new, more satisfying form of performance, but without relinquishing their old familiar stage picture. They declare themselves unable to do without theatrical illusions. Then, armed with binoculars and glasses, they do everything they can to break down that illusion. And when they succeed they are shocked, like children reaching after soap bubbles who cry when the suds get into their eyes.

It is not a matter of some artist or other discovering a new way of using our traditional stage which can then be followed by every hack: it is a matter of writers, public, and designers together becoming aware of the basic sense of all theatre as performance, and discarding outworn forms, trusting in our own ability to create new ones.

No 'stage reform', then, but 'theatre reform'!

It is a matter of resolutely turning our backs on frivolity and our accustomed vulgarity (known as 'tradition') in order to achieve a theatre that will live once more, where what happens on stage frankly signifies, rather than being, or pretending to be.

And when we have our own living literary and musical theatre, then at last we shall know how the great works of the past should be performed today.

Theoretical discussions will not bring us nearer this goal: only a prodigal outlay of work and countless serious experiments.

Visual artists can only say: 'Let us try!'

THE THEATRICAL WORKS OF ALFRED ROLLER

BDT	Berlin, Deutsches Theater
BKO	Berlin, Komische Oper
BLT	Berlin, Lessingtheater
BNS	Berlin, Neues Schauspielhaus
BSO	Berliner Staatsoper
BAF	Bayreuth, Festspielhaus
BZS	Berlin, Zirkus Schumann
DHT	Dresden, Hoftheater
MFA	München, Festsaal des Ausstellungsparkes
MKS	München, Königliche Schauspielhaus
MNF	München, Neue Musikfesthalle
NY.DT	New York, Deutsches Theater
NY.MET	New York, Metropolitan Opera
PGO	Philadelphia, Grand Opera
SFD	Salzburg Festspiele, Domplatz
SFF	Salzburg Festspiele, Festspielhaus
SFR	Salzburg Festspiele, Reitschule
SKK	Salzburg, Kollegienkirche
SST	Salzburg, Stadttheater
SKT	Stockholm, Kunliga dramatiska Teatern
WAT	Wien, Akademietheater
WBT	Wien, Burgtheater
WDV	Wien, Deutches Volkstheater
WHO	Wiener Oper (Kaiserliche und Königliche Hofoper until 1918)
WSO	Wiener Staatsoper after 1918
WRS	Wien, Redoutensaal
WSS	Wien, Schönbrunner Schlosstheater
WTJ	Wien, Theater in der Josefstadt
WVO	Wiener Volksoper

(Original titles, in German, Italian, and French.
For translations, see the index at the end of this volume.)

1903	WAGNER	TRISTAN UND ISOLDE	WHO
	PUCCINI	LA BOHÈME	WHO
	WOLF	DER CORREGIDOR	WHO
1904	VERDI	FALSTAFF	WHO
	DELIBES	LAKMÉ	WHO
	BEETHOVEN	FIDELIO	WHO
	WAGNER	LOHENGRIN (First Act)	WHO
1905	PFITZNER	DIE ROSE VOM LIEBESGARTEN	WHO
	WOLF–FERRARI	DIE NEUGIERIGEN FRAUEN	WHO
	WAGNER	DAS RHEINGOLD	WHO
1906	MOZART	DON GIOVANNI	WHO
		LE NOZZE DI FIGARO	WHO
		DIE ZAUBERFLÖTE	WHO
		DIE ENTFÜHRUNG AUS DEM SERAIL	WHO
	WAGNER	LOHENGRIN (2nd and 3rd Acts)	WHO
	GÖTZ	DER WIDERSPENSTIGEN ZÄHMUNG	WHO
	SCHILLINGS	DER MOLOCH (not performed)	WHO
	HOFMANNSTHAL	OEDIPUS UND DIE SPHINX	BDT
1907	HAUPTMANN	KAISER KARLS GEISEL	BLT
	MINKUS–DELIBES	RÜBEZHAL (Ballet)	WHO
	WAGNER	DIE WALKÜRE	WHO
	GLUCK	IPHIGÉNIE EN AULIDE	WHO
	ROSSINI	IL BARBIERE DI SIVIGLIA	WHO
	PUCCINI	MADAMA BUTTERFLY	WHO
1907	BEETHOVEN	FIDELIO	NY.MET
	SCHILLER	WILHELM TELL	NY.DT
1908	WAGNER	SIEGFRIED	WHO
	BITTNER	DIE ROTE GRET	WHO
	D'ALBERT	TIEFLAND	WHO
	MÉHUL	JOSEPH ET SES FRÈRES	WHO
1909	WAGNER	GÖTTERDÄMMERUNG	WHO
	STRAUSS, R.	ELEKTRA	WHO
	GOETHE	FAUST I	BDT
1911	GOETHE	FAUST II	BDT
	STRAUSS, R.	DER ROSENKAVALIER	DHT
	SOPHOCLES	OEDIPUS REX	BZS
	AESCHYLUS	THE ORESTEIA	BZS
			MFA
	HOFMANNSTHAL	JEDERMANN	BZS
			MNF
			WBT
1912	GOETHE	EGMONT	BNS
	WAGNER	DER FLIEGENDE HOLLÄNDER	WHO
	SCHREKER	DAS SPIELWERK UND DIE PRINZESSIN	WHO

	HOFMANNSTHAL	JEDERMANN	WBT
	BÜCHNER	WOYZECK	MKS
1914	WAGNER	PARSIFAL	WHO
1916	STRAUSS, R.	SALOME	WVO
	SHAKESPEARE	A MIDSUMMER NIGHT'S DREAM	WDV
	SCHÖNHERR	VOLK IN NOT	WDV
1918	SOPHOCLES	ANTIGONE	WBT
	GOETHE	DIE NATÜRLICHE TOCHTER	WBT
1919	PFITZNER	PALESTRINA	WSO
	STRAUSS, R.	DIE FRAU OHNE SCHATTEN	WSO
	WILDGANS	DIES IRAE	WBT
	BEER–HOFMANN	JAKOBS TRÄUME	WBT
	UNRUH Franz von	EIN GESCHLECHT	WBT
1920	SCHREKER	DIE GEZEICHNETEN	WSO
	WEINGARTNER	DIE DORFSCHULE	WSO
		MEISTER ANDREA	WSO
	MOZART	COSÌ FAN TUTTE	WSO
	SHAKESPEARE	MACBETH	WBT
		HAMLET	WBT
	SHAW	THE HEARTBREAK HOUSE	WBT
	HOFMANNSTHAL	JEDERMANN	SFD
1921	KORNGOLD	DIE TOTE STADT	WSO
	BITTNER	DIE KOHLHAYMERIN	WSO
	MOZART	DON GIOVANNI	WSO
	CLAUDEL	L'ÉCHANGE	WBT
	HOFMANNSTHAL	JEDERMANN	SFR
	MOZART	DON GIOVANNI	SST
	STRINDBERG	THE DREAM PLAY	SKT
1922	STRAUSS, R.	DIE JOSEPHS-LEGENDE	WSO
		FEUERSNOT	WSO
	SCHUMANN	CARNAVAL	WSO
	SHAKESPEARE	CORIOLANUS	WBT
	VIDRAC	LE PAQUEBOT TENACITY	WBT
	WILDGANS	KAIN	WBT
	BEER–HOFMANN	DER GRAF VON CHAROLAIS	WBT
	MOZART	LE NOZZE DI FIGARO	WRS
		COSÌ FAN TUTTE	WRS
	ROSSINI	IL BARBIERE DI SIVIGLIA	WRS
	CALDERÓN–HOFMANNSTHAL	DAME KOBOLD	WRS
	GOETHE	CLAVIGO	WRS
		STELLA	WRS
	MOZART	COSÌ FAN TUTTE	SST
		LE NOZZE DI FIGARO	SST
		DIE ENTFÜHRUNG AUS DEM SERAIL	SST
	CALDERÓN–HOFMANNSTHAL	DAS SALZBURGER GROSSE	
		WELTTHEATER	SKK

1923	Puccini	Manon Lescaut	WSO
	Shakespeare	Antony and Cleopatra	WBT
		The Winter's Tale	WBT
	Calderón	L'Alcade de Zalamea	WBT
1924	Beethoven	Die Ruinen von Athen	WSO
	(Arr. R. Strauss)		
	Wagner	Rienzi	WSO
	Strindberg	The Ghost Sonata	WAT
	Shakespeare	The Taming of the Shrew	WSS
	Schiller	Kabale und Liebe	WTJ
1925	Wagner	Der fliegende Holländer	WSO
	Shakespeare	A Midsummer Night's Dream	WBT
	Mozart	Die Entführung aus dem Serail	WRS
	Rossini	Angelina	WRS
1926	Puccini	Turandot	WSO
	Lessing	Minna von Barnhelm	WBT
	Goethe	Egmont	WBT
			BKO
	Mozart	Die Entführung aus dem Serail	WST
1927	Beethoven	Fidelio	WSO
	Rossini	Il Barbiere di Siviglia	WSO
	Strauss, R.	Intermezzo	WSO
	Romains	Le Dictateur	WBT
1928	Puccini	Manon Lescaut	WSO
	Stravinsky	Oedipus Rex	WSO
	Rossato-alfano	Madonna Imperia	WSO
	Strauss, R.	Die Aegyptische Helena	WSO
	Mell	Das Nachfolge	WBT
		Christi Spiel	WBT
	Goethe	Iphigenie in Tauris	WTJ
			SST
1929	Rabaud	Marouf, savetier du Caire	WSO
	Strauss, J.	Eine Nacht in Venedig	WSO
	Strauss, R.	Der Rosenkavalier	WSO; SFF
	Frank	Karl und Anna	WBT
	Schiller	Wallenstein	WBT
1930	Verdi	Simone Boccanegra	WSO
	Kaiser	Die Bürger von Calais	WBT
	Hauptmann	Die Jungfern vom Bischofsberg	WAT
	Gluck	Iphigénie en Aulide	SFF
	Mozart	Le Nozze di Figaro	SFF
	Strauss, R.	Die Aegyptische Helena	PGO
	Verdi	Aida	PGO
	Wagner	Lohengrin	PGO
1931	Heuberger	Der Opernball	WSO
	Strauss, R.	Die Frau ohne Schatten	WSO

	MOZART	IDOMENEO	WSO
		LE NOZZE DI FIGARO	WSO
	WAGNER	SIEGFRIED	WSO
		GÖTTERDÄMMERUNG	WSO
	GOETHE	STELLA	SST
1932	WEBER	DER FREISCHÜTZ	WSO
	VERDI	DON CARLOS	WSO
	SUPPÉ	BOCCACCIO	WSO
	HEGER	DER BETTLER NAMENLOS	WSO
	GOETHE	FAUST I, FAUST II	WBT
	SCHILLER	DER RÄUBER	WBT
	MELL	DAS SCHUTZENGELSPIEL	WBT
	STRAUSS, R.	DIE FRAU OHNE SCHATTEN	SFF
1933	VERDI	MACBETH	WSO
	MOZART	DIE ZAUBERFLÖTE	WO; SFF
	STRAUSS, R.	DIE AEGYPTISCHE HELENA	WSO
		ARABELLA	SFF
1934	WAGNER	DER FLIEGENDE HOLLÄNDER	WSO
	BITTNER	DAS VEILCHEN	WSO
	MELL	DAS SCHUTZENGELSPIEL	WBT
		DIE SIEBEN GEGEN THEBEN	WBT
	GOETHE	GÖTZ VON BERLICHINGEN	WBT
	STRAUSS, R.	ELEKTRA	SFF
		DER ROSENKAVALIER	BSO
	WAGNER	PARSIFAL	BAF
1935	SHAKESPEARE	KING LEAR	WBT
		ANTONY AND CLEOPATRA	WBT

APPENDIX 4

Two Letters of Siegfried Lipiner Addressed to Mahler

The following letters have survived in typewritten copies among Alma's papers (UPL, Philadelphia). They were written in 1902, after the disastrous dinner party of 3 January 1902 (BGA, 124, see above, Vol. ii, Chap. 12), during which Alma (and Mahler) behaved outrageously towards some of Mahler's oldest and dearest friends.

The guests that evening were Anna and Carl Moll, Justine and Arnold Rosé, Siegfried Lipiner and his second wife Clementine, Albert and Nina Spiegler (she had been Lipiner's first wife), Anna von Mildenburg, and the Secession painter, Koloman Moser. Feeling she was under scrutiny by a group of Gustav's old friends (of whom she was already jealous <u>because</u> they were his old friends)—a situation which required tact, diplomacy, discretion, and modesty on her part, Alma perversely decided that she couldn't care less what they thought, about her, about Mahler's music, or about things artistic in general. To make matters worse, Mahler had broken all rules of etiquette and retired with her after dinner to the next room for an embarrassing length of time, failing several times to respond to Justine's entreaties to return.

The first letter is obviously a reply to one of Mahler's, in which he had attempted to explain and defend her behaviour. This letter can no longer be found; it was probably destroyed in 1945, when the top floor of Alma's house on Steinfeldgasse was severely damaged by a bomb. Lipiner was obviously writing in a state of extreme agitation, wounded to the quick by Mahler's explanations even more perhaps than by his and Alma's behaviour during the dinner party. It is a unique and fascinating commentary, written by one of his oldest friends, on Mahler's character and behaviour. It shows how angry and even insulting he could be when encountering dissent, and how he could then become cold and contemptuous towards those who had disagreed with him instead of attempting to understand their arguments. His method of healing the breach was to say he had forgotten all about it, while remaining supremely unaware that the people he had humiliated found it impossible to do so.

The second letter was no doubt written some time later, after the two friends had met and attempted to solve their disagreement.

FIRST LETTER

[January 1902]

Dear Gustav,

In order to be able to write at all—and I must unfortunately insist in this—please let's get one thing clear: I'm going to keep off the subject of 'love'. My heart overflows with bitterness when I talk to myself about it—as sometimes happens: <u>to you</u> I shan't mention it. Just behave towards me and others decently and if possible fairly, from time to time as far as I'm concerned even unlovingly—as you regularly react, with the most extreme coldness when one only scratches you—the skin of 'love' gives off quite a different humour—as you behave even when one does not scratch you (by which I don't mean 'offend', but for example saying something which for the slightest of reasons you find disagreeable at the time)—so behave as people normally do towards their 'friends'. That's an area which I know a bit about; living there is uncomfortably hot; you in any case in the cooler zone will be able to stand it longer than I—I'm on the edge of it and <u>can't</u> stand it much longer. I am not talking about how you behave to <u>me</u>, but in general; I am the least concerned. I've experienced with you <u>things I can't forget</u> (quite insignificant things—mere 'words', I'm such a pedant, like Fritz, 'sensitive', etc.). But <u>now</u> I am not speaking of my own feelings. I could say a lot about them, in particular things which could make your behaviour to me seem better than it is: everything that's involved in it, how much is concealed behind it. But if our relationship rubs along even tolerably well, it's thanks entirely to me. I have also developed the habit of keeping quiet when I can plainly see you thinking: 'You have no idea, my dear Siegfried, how little you matter to me, you and all the others!' That doesn't often happen, but when it does, then one <u>knows it</u>. Don't shift the blame on to your irritability; I don't overlook the part that <u>that</u> plays, but I hardly notice it; I am <u>not</u> sensitive (you are—more than most!)—but there is a difference in the way this or that person behaves when they are irritated. What I'm talking about is the deep, lasting, everlasting coldness—and you are absolutely dumbfounded by my saying this, I know. It would be a good thing if for a time you behaved really badly, with completely naked selfishness: the veil would then be torn away. But don't, please, play the gracious, patronizing master, who, when things are going smoothly is so nice and can even be generous, but then somehow every now and again behaves differently—<u>why</u> is for him to decide. Lackeys nowadays are conceited enough not to think, as their counterparts did in the good old times: The gracious Master has quite unjustly treated me badly, but he soon forgets it and is nice to me again! In all seriousness you once said to me, when we were discussing a stupid outburst of yours against me: 'And immediately after, I forget all about it.' That, you know (it happened last year), and things like that, really make me see red.—For you in the last analysis people are not <u>persons</u>, they are <u>things</u>. You throw someone away, <u>for no reason at all</u>, then pick him up again—or not, as the case maybe—and everything is in order again. And in every situation that matters at all, and towards everybody, that is how you behave. You make no exceptions. Even the pretence that it might in some cases be different is easy to see through. My experience in this respect has been particularly fortunate, as I have said. And that is precisely why I can say these things.—Let me also tell you that I am an idiot for whom <u>only what people say</u>—what comes straight out of them—is important. What you might ever have <u>done</u>—to others or to me—that I could overlook. But not anything you <u>said</u>. (If you had ever called me a scoundrel perhaps, I would count that as a <u>deed</u> and overlook it). Indeed: even the 'good' deeds don't matter. 'For by your words you will be acquitted, and by your words you will be condemned', as the New Testament says. Of course it was Christ who said that; it is quite anti-Jewish.

But there is one thing that counts as much as your words: and that is certain quite inconspicuous ways of behaving which seem unimportant and for that reason are almost never recognized by you for what they really are. There is also something unconscious about them, something that stems from your nature, and that you therefore take for granted. I'm not writing a thesis, so let's say no more on that. But the 'something' which recently so embittered me, and continues to do so, is one such piece of behaviour. My embitteredness, as your letter makes clear, will not disturb your affection for me. I shall be forgiven, have already been forgiven, and your affection is undiminished. But it has never for a moment occurred to you to reflect that I and all of us (they all think as I do) are not Fritz, as you so generously and tactfully put it—I can hear exactly the tone of voice you use on such occasions, when you're not saying <u>directly</u> what you mean, and would not wish us in this case to take you at your word—and that it might be worthwhile trying to find out from the others whether, because of 'the few moments' absence' (as you put it), they really are so upset and Siegfried so embittered. I'll break off here to make some incidental observations—that I have much too much love (not specially for you) and much too little presumption, to 'make allowances' for you; that on that evening you could not possibly have been particularly embarrassed (even as regards the physical aspect you could be reassured and in any case the doctor's intervention and my encouragement were not entirely unsuccessful); that you had been seeing Alma every day, and, knowing that you were free to be with her as much as you wanted, you had absolutely no grounds for as it were in desperation snubbing everybody by paying attention only to her; and that while we might have understood it if on the grounds of some possible irritation you had thrown an ink pot at everyone's head, the way you did behave was incomprehensible. But stick to your way of looking at it; I can't change my opinion—and you certainly can't.

It's Alma I must talk about. It's something I absolutely must get off my chest, for since that evening I'm through with her. And that's final as regards any future intercourse between us. Perhaps I don't matter enough to you—perhaps none of us do, for me to talk to you like that without giving other reasons. Perhaps she <u>alone</u> satisfies your needs. I am sure, solely from what I know of your personality, that there are moments when you throw us all away, i.e. you say: 'Don't worry, we shall manage very well together, just the two of us.' Just as you with your own inimitable coldness and the irony which positively makes my flesh creep, already spoke to me of the 'old hens' who worry so much about you, i.e. Nina, who for your sake makes herself more ill than she is, e tutti quanti,—tiresome, useless people who busy themselves with your affairs. But there are also other moments when they are the dear old friends. And after all, when one is defending <u>oneself</u>—or, with their permission, <u>others</u>—against the impermissible, one is entitled to talk; so, I'm talking. Fortunately it only concerns me theoretically: Moll kept me, in spite of my reluctance, so long to himself that I was later too tired even to make the attempt to speak to Alma; besides, I 'knew' her already. So, it's a question of the others, that is to say the women.

Your fiancée had already said earlier, with a reference to the coming 'getting acquainted' party: I don't like meeting with gossipy old ladies (or: women, it's all the same). I wouldn't be surprised if a Viennese girl, one of the common sort, said something like that, but a better-off natural girl would show some shyness, some curiosity, some happy pride in her engagement when she entered the circle of her future acquaintances, the friends of her husband, without worrying much about whether they were old or young and like other young girls but from your fiancée we were entitled to expect not only that she would abhor such an unnatural, superficial, callous attitude, but that she would enter into a circle of people whom through you she already <u>knew</u>, in the best sense of the word, to be <u>your old and treasured friends,</u> and would show cordiality, pleasure, and confidence and everything that goes naturally, indeed inevitably with such an occasion,—not the morally obligatory but a naturally spontaneous respect for you, indeed love for you, should have made her greet those poeple with special warmth and want to really get to know them. But she doesn't like meeting old women. So that finishes us, in every sense of the word.

It is certainly not shyness, but lack of shyness which prompts her to say such a thing.—Embarrassed! Shy! (You write that, so I can speak about it.) One is constantly meeting people one never knew before,—how ridiculous! And she must very often have already been in such a situation! A few words, sincerely spoken, sincerely answered, and all embarrassment and feelings of strangeness have gone; <u>she knows that</u>—as everybody does who has had any experience at all of meeting people. And because one is so 'embarrassed', so 'shy', one cannot get to know anybody—is that it? For how is that supposed to happen, if one keeps away from those people? and if during the whole evening one does not exchange a single word with the old women, with Albert? You showed me the passage in a letter in which she wants to sit next to me and in which she talks about the 'criterion' (she doesn't understand the word). Earlier she spoke in the same way of the tribunal and such things. I could hardly contain myself as you showed me those words. From the thought that would occur to a natural, modest girl: 'Ah! what impression shall I make on them!' this, and that other earlier remark, is the complete opposite. One can't imagine anything more unnatural, <u>more insincere</u> and at the same time more stupid. That's not shyness, it's lack of shyness. Who gives her the right to speak so condescendingly of the tribunal? where does she get that ironic mood from? What right has she to assume that these people are going to sit there, cold and judgemental, like critical old women? How can she dare to say such things? That is the peevish tone of someone who is predisposed to avoid meeting people whom one must respect, predisposed to find it disagreeable that she will be 'judged'—and who expresses her displeasure in inelegant and outrageous terms. A shy, embarrassed person would not dare so to offend against the canons of good behaviour which come naturally to decent people that she leaves the people who have come to her (instead of as would be right and proper she to them) simply sitting there and waiting, and stays away for about an hour (ask Albert) not 'a few moments'—a lack of manners, a gross insult which—that's the main thing—one simply accepts as a matter of course!! instead of telling her future husband, to whom it never occurs to think that he has invited those people precisely to help her, how she should behave. At table Nina was sitting next to you not knowing which way to look; she couldn't interrupt your whisperings with Alma (during which the really necessary, indeed all the discreet happenings since yesterday could have been discussed); you ignored her almost completely, and Alma did too, naturally; <u>and yet you were sitting there as the physical link between them!</u> After the meal you both go out; and when finally—after two fruitless reminders by Justi—the persons whom one had come solely and precisely to see deign to come in again, the future husband sits between mother-in-law and fiancée—then quite casually there fall from Alma's lips a few words, a few scraps of recognition of the physical presence of Anna sitting beside her; <u>neither Gustav nor Alma take the slightest notice of the guests</u>, and that went on from the beginning to the end of the getting-to-know-each-other evening! A splendid schooling for the in my opinion so far totally unschooled Alma. One doesn't have to trouble about other people; that suited <u>her</u>, and you ratified it. If you had just once taken some notice of the existence of Nina and the others and had stood up so that someone else could get to her (or she to someone else, which of course would have been asking too much). But even apart from Alma, how could you ignore everyone in that way? Why did you invite us? But I didn't want to talk about you. Only it would be amusing one day to see how you would react when someone else—and in this case you were the master of the house!—were guilty of only a hundredth of that!

I've always had the shivers when Alma was around and she has always given me the impression of being not an embarrassed person, but someone coldly indifferent, presumptuous, and derogatory: and precisely because it was not directed at <u>me</u> I can say it. It would be hard to find among much more capable and qualified judges one who in front of Reni's chief painting could dismiss with an unspeakably laughable scornful gesture a master whom she knew nothing about. She took one look—'what's it supposed to represent?' Someone explained: immediate reaction—contempt. Nor would it be easy to find someone who could find no more to say about the *Symposium*[1] than: 'I just had to keep laughing.' (I should have to say a lot more to show you how unbelievable that is—and, apart from the lack of maturity and the misunderstanding; what a lack of every natural feeling for greatness and respect of every kind this undeniably reveals!) I kept all these thoughts not only from you but from myself until that evening the impression of coldness and all that will always make her <u>alien</u> to me was confirmed. And again, and a thousand times: it was to your own friends whom you esteem so highly that she behaved like that! Has she really a deep relationship to you, and are you not letting yourself be deceived by <u>words</u> which do not arise spontaneously, but through the situation and—I know this from you—in the most senseless and demoralizing way are provoked by <u>you</u>?

When it comes down to it, I too belong to the fussy old hens.

Yours,

S.

SECOND LETTER

[January 1902 (after the preceding letter)]

Dear Gustav,

Perhaps I'm wrong: obviously discussions won't help here, but put me to shame by doing something, let us get along with each other again as before, without mentioning—or if possible remembering recent events (insofar as you alone are concerned); but be human and (the really important thing) behave like someone who thinks he is simply obliged to do so—and after a time perhaps I'll say: 'Someone who, like Gustav,

---

[1] Lipiner is alluding to Plato's famous Dialogue.

can be like that must always have been like that, that's his true character: I was wrong, I was, if not mad, at least blinded—perhaps over-excited by being right for a moment, etc. I think you are capable of understanding this suggestion and of facing up to it in a manly way: if I am not wrong, then let us happily get on with it—with humour. After all: who are we? and what's so important about opinions—even about the best of friends? If you can alter my opinion you will make me happy—and the devil must take it if you can't manage that for someone who has been so longing for it—if I have done you wrong.—I don't bear a 'grudge', 'hurt' would be a better way of putting it; only I hate anything 'sentimental'—what you darkly hint at as your 'incognito' (even before me—as you say), that too you will get rid of—for why should we put up with being in any sense 'incognito' to each other? If you ask for concealing (for that's how I under-stand it) your ethical value from me, then you are being unfair to me. Don't do it—even if some sort of feeling of shyness prompts you to—show yourself, speak out; and gener-ally when in future we get round to talking about you, I would like to leave the talking to you, preferably to have a fully positive <u>exposition</u>, precisely to get rid of the incog-nito.—But please if possible, get one thing out of your system—something that is very strong in you—contempt for people. Hate can hide love, and can above all be justified; contempt is diabolical, and always wrong and unjustified. So much of what you in this area believe to be <u>unworldly</u> is with you only a nuance of contempt for people. Only someone like that can treat even 'worried' friends ('worried', as you are and perhaps not diligent enough in expressing that worry) as you have done. You will just have to accept it when I say. 'His superior lordship has spoken as we have and worse, and would not like (now that he's home and dry) our approval—and is displeased if we don't jump to obey, indeed to anticipate, his command; this displeasure is enough to prompt him to throw people away (that's the word for it!: 'What do they want then? Why are they poking their nose in?' that was the tone. . . . Since you so often repeat certain words of mine, take me at my every word. I will do penance for every one of them if your future behaviour, which I shall allow to have retrospective validity, proves me wrong. From now on and in future I will accept all the blame if only you will make it <u>possible</u> for me to do so.

But you must not swim out and drown—and that we must discuss—if with that 'must' you don't consider that I am perhaps overstepping the bounds.

Yours always,

S.

APPENDIX 5

Analysis of Alma Mahler's Handwriting

Handwriting test 134 carried out by Margarete Bardach von Chlumberg in Vienna on 18 December 1918[1]

GRAPHOLOGICAL FINDINGS

The handwriting of a very generous, vivacious, impressionable personality.

Writer is highly intelligent and mentally alert, has fertile imagination in artistic matters, a very versatile and exciting emotional and nervous life, unusually lively but changeable voluntary pursuits predominantly literary interests.

She is capable of enthusiasm, ambitious to a high degree, vain, headstrong in thought and deed, generous, has a great variety of prospective intentions, breadth of vision, freedom in her opinions, a certain effusiveness in thinking and feeling.

Writer has a strong liking for the original and unusual, aesthetic tastes sometimes bordering on the bizarre; can be tactful and sensitive.

She is warm-hearted but not without a sharper side, is governed by moods and superficial impressions, believes that it is important to keep up appearances, which shows itself in her behaviour and whole lifestyle; is not very adaptable.

She is very self-assertive, proud, frank, but very reserved about things which affect her personally.

A person with pronounced individuality and independence of mind.

Margarete von Bardach

ADDITIONAL NOTES

Outwardly remarkable, inwardly interesting. Exceptional elegance: attributes an unusual degree of importance to elegance; decked out with jewellery, particularly well

---

[1] Any pretence that these pages are a serious attempt at character analysis solely on the basis of handwriting becomes doubtful after the first page. The second and third pages seem to be based mainly on Margarete Bardach's direct knowledge of and personal acquaintance with Alma Mahler. Many passages read like an *apologia pro vita sua* by Alma herself and could be based on conversations during which Alma treated Mrs Bardach more as a friendly psychologist than as a graphologist. It is curious that there is no mention of Alma's major problem with handwriting, that of legibility. Mahler constantly complained that he was unable to read her writing. The original typewritten copy of this text is in the Alma Mahler collection in UPL. Alma wrote at the beginning of the first page 'Meine Schrift' (My writing) and underlined a number of passages with heavy, double lines.

cared for in every respect; posture, gait, movements *comme il faut*; particularly striking choice of shoes, hats, manicure and so on. Very aristocratic, something majestic in her manner and appearance, similarly her friends and her lifestyle, money drips from her fingers. The same in sports: riding, fencing, coach-driving. And since she is afraid she could lose the power she exerts, she is now trying to step up still further her outward elegance. Her chief concern seems to be to stave off any decline. As a result of the effect she has on those around her she is constantly bombarded with compliments, she stands out whether she wants to or not. She has no peace, since people run after her.

She has gone through a lot, big experiences are behind her, and now a second flowering is beginning. Having terminated one life, a new life is beginning for her. Had already given up hope, but is now taking an interest in things, although sadness still breaks through from time to time.

Colossal pride, at times amounting to arrogance. Proud of herself her advantages, of the impression she makes. Since she is spoilt her strong will, which has become a desire to dominate, will tolerate no opposition. Was basically very good, and if life had not spoiled her she would have become a modest, good-natured person. She is, as an examination of her life, as the development of her qualities shows, the victim of her own beauty. Hence she always found her satisfaction in domination. She could not fully satisfy this with a man and always needed a chorus of envious and admiring men and envious women, otherwise she felt that life was dull. Wants to be idolized and have everyone lying prostrate at her feet. The marriage was a happy once, since her husband encouraged her efforts to achieve this and offered her the appropriate framework for it. She chose a man in a corresponding situation, of whom she could be proud. Now feelings were decisive, then satisfaction. But signs that she was not happy. Signs of mental struggles.

She has artistic taste, but again the same motivation: Art mainly regarded as something for her class of person, as a worthy framework.

She put up with a lot of flattery, but was only interested in someone who did not run after her. It might be possible that she could now take a deeper interest in someone. Her development now seems to be progressing and she is finding it hard, perhaps because the development seems difficult—and new to her. For she is capable of a passionate attachment, and in that case would have to be interested in a person who was something special. These are signs that she is beginning a new life. Not that she has got a new focus of interest. Up to now she has not found anything, one can see disappointment, but she is looking for someone who can influence her. A turning-point seems to have arrived. Everything that she found left her cold. She has now got as far as knowing what she is looking for, doesn't waste her time any more with eccentricities, is looking not just for big, outward things in someone, but heart and mind. The ideal husband for her would have to be someone who was calm but also a dreamer. In any case she could never accept being in poor circumstances and would rather put an end to things. Highly nervous but organically sound, quick to assess situations, knows how to react to any eventuality, can always think of the right thing to do, very ready-witted, thinks fast and to good purpose; nevertheless no eccentricities.

She is in a certain way the victim of her own advantages, since these mislead her into demanding things which seldom come together in this world, and drive her to drastic presumptuousness. She was originally in love with her own husband, but then cooled off. No great calm pain which she can control, but thrown hither and thither as if at sea. Must have suffered much from women, among whom she rarely had friends, has a sharp tongue for anyone who offended her.

tr. by Roy MacDonald Stock

SELECT BIBLIOGRAPHY

As in Volume ii, this list includes mainly books and articles either published in recent years, or used extensively in Volume iii. Other sources not included here are mentioned in the footnotes. For a more comprehensive list of books, newspaper articles, and publications concerning Mahler, see the three reference works by Bruno and Eleonore Vondenhoff, Simon Michael Namenwirth, and Susan Filler mentioned in the Preface of Volume ii.

Abendroth, Walter, *Vier Meister der Musik (Bruckner, Mahler, Reger, Pfitzner)* (Prestel, Munich, 1952).

Albrecht, George Alexander, *Die Symphonien Gustav Mahler. Eine Einführung* (Niemeyer, Hameln, 1992).

Anbruch, Musikblätter des, Mahler issues, 2: 7–8 (Universal Edition, Vienna, Apr. 1920); 12: 3 (Universal Edition, Vienna, Mar. 1930).

Appia, Adolphe, *Die Musik und die Inszenierung* (Bruckmann, Munich, 1899).

Arc, L', Mahler issue, 67 (L'Arc, Aix-en-Provence, 1976).

Bahr, Hermann, *Meister und Meisterbriefe um . . . ,* ed. Joseph Gregor (Bauer, Vienna, 1947).

Baker, Evan, 'Alfred Roller's production of Mozart's "Don Giovanni": A break in the scenic traditions of the Vienna Court Opera', Ph.D. thesis (New York University, 1993).

Barsova, Inna 'Rouskaia Premiera Vosmoi Symphonii Mahlera', *Sovietskaia Mouzyka* (Apr. 1984), 55–60.

Bauer-Lechner, Natalie, *Recollections of Gustav Mahler,* ed. Peter Franklin, trans. Dika Newlin (Faber, London, 1980).

Beetz, Wilhelm, *Das Wiener Opernhaus 1869–1945* (Central European Times, Zurich, 1949).

Bekker, Paul, *Die Sinfonie von Beethoven bis Mahler* (Schuster & Loeffler, Berlin, 1922).

Berger, Frank, *Gustav Mahler: Vision und Mythos* (Freies Geistesleben, Stuttgart, 1993).

Bethge, Hans, *Die Chinesische Flöte* (Inselverlag, Leipzig, 1907).

Bie, Oskar, *Die moderne Musik und Richard Strauss* (Giegel, Leipzig, 1907).

Blaukopf, Kurt, *Gustav Mahler oder die Zeitgenosse der Zukunft* (Molden, Vienna, 1969).

—— *Mahler: A Documentary Study* (Oxford University Press, New York, 1976).

—— and **Herta,** *Mahler: His Life, Work and World* (Thames & Hudson, London, 1991).

—— *Die Wiener Philharmoniker* (Zsolnay, Vienna, 1986).

Blessinger, Karl, *Mendelssohn, Meyerbeer, Mahler: Drei Kapitel Judentum in der Musik als Schlüssel zur Musikgeschichte des 19. Jahrhunderts* (Hahnefeld, Berlin, 1939).

Böke, Henning, 'Gustav Mahler und das Judentum', *Archiv für Musikwissenschaft*, 49: 1 (1992), 1–21.

Botstein, Leon, 'Music and its public: habits of listening and the crisis of musical modernism in Vienna, 1870–1914', Ph.D. thesis (3 vols., Harvard Univ. Cambridge, Mass., 1985).

Brod, Max, *Gustav Mahler: Beispiel einer deutsch-jüdischen Symbiose* (Ner-Tamid-Verlag, Frankfurt, 1961).

Carr, Jonathan, *The Real Mahler* (Constable, London, 1977).

Carrol, Brendan G., *The Last Prodigy: A Biography of Erich Wolfgang Korngold* (Amadeus, Portland, Ore., 1997).

Chord and Discord, i, 10 issues (Bruckner Society of America, New York, 1932–9): ii, 10 issues (Bruckner Society of America, New York, 1940–63); iii, 2 issues (Bruckner Society of America, New York, 1969 and 1998).

Cooke, Deryck, *Gustav Mahler (1860–1911): An Introduction to his Music* (BBC, London, 1960).

—— *Gustav Mahler: An Introduction to his Music* (Faber, London, 1980).

—— *Vindications: Essays on Romantic Music* (Faber, London, 1982).

Danuser, Hermann, *Gustav Mahler and seine Zeit* (Laaber Verlag, Laaber, 1991).

—— (ed.), *Gustav Mahler: Wege der Forschung* (Wissenschaftliche Buchgesellschaft, Darmstadt, 1992).

Davison, Peter, 'The Nachtmusiken from Mahler's Seventh Symphony: Analysis and Reappraisal', Ph.D. thesis (Univ. of Cambridge, 1985).

Decsey, Ernst, *Musik war sein Leben: Lebenserinnerungen* (Hans Deutsch, Vienna, 1962).

—— *Die Spieldose* (Tal, Leipzig, 1922).

Del Mar, Norman, *Mahler's Sixth Symphony* (Eulenburg Books, London, 1980).

Diepenbrock, Alphons, *Verzamelde Geschriften* (Het Spectrum, Utrecht, 1950).

—— *Brieven en Documenten IV*, ed. Eduard Reeser (Martinus Nijhoff, The Hague, 1974).

Effenberger, Rudolf, *Fünfundzwanzig Jahre Dienstbarer Geist im Reiche der Frau Musika* (Gesellschaft der Musikfreunde, Vienna, n.d.).

Eggebrecht, Hans Heinrich, *Die Musik Gustav Mahlers* (Piper, Munich, 1982).

Ekman, Karl, *Jean Sibelius* (Kustannusosakeyhtiö, Helsinki, 2nd edn. 1935).

—— *Jean Sibelius: The Life and Personality*, trans. Edward Birse (Knopf, New York, 1938).

Farga, Franz, *Die Wiener Oper* (Franz Göth, Vienna, 1947).

Feder, Stuart, 'Gustav Mahler, Dying', *International Psycho-Analytical Review*, 5: 125 (1978), 125–48.

Filler, Susan, *Gustav and Alma Mahler: A Guide to Research* (Garland, New York, 1989).

Floros, Constantin, *Gustav Mahler*, i. *Die geistige Welt Gustav Mahlers in systematischer Darstellung* (Breitkopf & Härtel, Wiesbaden, 1977), ii. *Mahler und die Symphonik des 19. Jahrhunderts in neuer Deutung* (1977); iii. *Die Symphonien* (1985).

—— *Gustav Mahler: The Symphonies* (Amadeus Press, Portland, Ore., 1993).

—— Gustav Mahler: *Visionär und Despot* (Arche, Zurich, 1998).

Franklin, Peter, *The Life of Mahler* (Cambridge University Press, Cambridge, 1997).

Fried, Oscar, 'Erinnerung an Mahler', *Musikblätter des Anbruch* 1 (1919): 1, 16 ff.

Fülöp, Peter, *Mahler Discography* (Kaplan Foundation, New York, 1995).

Gradenwitz, Peter, *The Music of Israel* (Norton, New York, 1949).

Graf, Max, *Wagner Probleme und andere Studien* (Wiener Verlag, Vienna, 1900).

—— *Geschichte und Geist der modernen Musik* (Humbold, Stuttgart, 1953).

—— *Jede Stunde war erfüllt: Ein halbes Jahrhundert Musik- und Theaterleben* (Forum, Vienna, 1957).

Grasberger, Franz, *Richard Strauss und die Wiener Oper* (Schneider, Tutzing, 1969).

—— (ed.), *Die Welt um Richard Strauss in Briefen* (Schneider, Tutzing, 1969).

Greisenegger, Evanthia, and Wolfgang, and Pausch, Oskar (ed.), Alfred Roller und seine Zeit (Böhlau, Vienna, 1991).

Greisenegger, Wolfgang, 'Alfred Roller: Neubedeutung des szenischen Raumes', *Studia Musicologica Academiae Scientiarum Hungaricae*, 31 (Budapest, 1988), 271–81.

Gutheil-Schoder, Marie, *Erlebtes und Erstrebtes, Rolle und Gestaltung* (Krey, Vienna, 1937).

Hahn, Reynaldo, *Thèmes variés* (Janin, Paris, 1946).

Hansen, Mathias, *Gustav Mahler: Reclams Musikführer* (Philipp Reclam jun., Stuttgart, 1996).

Harcourt, Eugène d', *La Musique actuelle en Allemagne et en Autriche-Hongrie* (Durdilly, Paris, 1908).

Harten, Uwe (ed.), *Bruckner Symposion: Bruckner, Liszt, Mahler und die Moderne*, Internationales Brucknerfest Linz, Sept. 1986 (Anton Bruckner Institut, Linz, 1989).

Hartungen, Harmut von, 'Der Dichter Siegfried Lipiner (1856–1911)', Ph.D. thesis (Munich, 1932).

Hauptmann, Gerhart, *Tagebücher 1897–1905* (Propyläen, Berlin, 1987).

Hefling, Stephen E., (ed.), *Mahler Studies* (Cambridge University Press, Cambridge, 1997).

Hellsberg, Clemens, *Demokratie der Könige* (Schweizer Verlaghaus, Zurich, 1992).

Hevesi, Ludwig, *Altkunst Neukunst, Wien 1894–1908* (Konegen, Vienna, 1909).

Heyworth, Peter, *Conversations with Klemperer* (Gollancz, London, 1973).

—— *Otto Klemperer: His Life and Times*, i. *1885–1933* (Cambridge University Press, Cambridge, 1983).

Hoffmann, Rudolf Stephan, *Erich Wolfgang Korngold* (Stephenson, Vienna, 1922).

Holde, Artur, *Jews in Music* (Owen, London, 1959).

Istel, Edgar (ed.), *Mahlers Symphonien* (Meisterführer No.10; Schlesingersche Buch- und Musikhandlung, Berlin, n.d.).

Jülg, Hans-Peter, *Gustav Mahlers Sechste Symphonie* (Musikverlag Katzbichler, Munich, 1986).

Karpath, Ludwig, *Lachende Musiker* (Knorr & Hirth, Munich, 1929).

Kennedy, Michael, *Mahler* (Dent, London, 1974).

Klemm, Eberhardt, 'Zur Geschichte der Fünften Sinfonie von Gustav Mahler', *Jahrbuch Peters 1979* (Aufsätze zur Musik, Leipzig, 1980), 9–116.

Klemperer, Otto, *Klemperer Stories, Anecdotes, Sayings and Impressions of Otto Klemperer* (Robson Books, London, 1980).

Kolleritsch, Otto (ed.), *Gustav Mahler: Sinfonie und Wirklichkeit* (Universal Edition, Graz, 1977).

Korngold, Luzi, *Erich Wolfgang Korngold,* ed. Elisabeth Lafite (Österreichischer Bundesverlag, Vienna, 1967).

Kralik, Heinrich, *Die Wiener Philharmoniker* (Frick, Vienna, 1938).

—— *Das Buch der Musikfreunde* (Amalthea, Zurich, 1951).

—— *Gustav Mahler,* ed. Friedrich Heller (Lafite, Vienna, 1968).

Kraus, Hedwig, and **Schreinzer, Karl** (eds.), *Statistik der Wiener Philharmoniker 1842–1942* (Universal Edition, Vienna, 1942).

Krebs, Carl, *Meister des Taktstocks* (Schuster & Loeffler, Berlin, 1919).

Kühn, Helmut, and **Quander, Georg** (eds.), *Gustav Mahler. Ein Lesebuch mit Bildern* (Ein Buch der Blerliner Festwochen, Orell Füsseli, Zurich, 1982).

Kunz, Otto, *Richard Mayr* (Bergland, Vienna, 1933).

La Grange, Henry-Louis de, 'Mahler Today', *The World of Music,* 11 (Bärenreiter, Kassel, Mar. 1969): 2, 6–17.

—— 'Mistakes about Mahler', *Music and Musicians,* 21 (Oct. 1972): 2, 16–22.

—— 'Mahler and Schönberg: Tradition und Revolution', *Bruckner Symposion* (Linz, 1986), 15–24.

—— (ed.), *Colloque International Gustav Mahler,* Jan. 1985 (Association Gustav Mahler, Paris, 1986).

—— 'Mahler and the Metropolitan Opera', *Studia Musicologica Academiae Scientiarum Hungaricae,* 31 (Budapest, 1989), 253–70.

—— 'Gustav Mahler auf der Suche nach der verlorenen Unendlichkeit', *Gustav Mahler: Leben, Werk, Interpretation, Rezeption,* Int. Gewandhaus Symposium, 1985 (Peters, Leipzig, 1990).

—— 'Berlioz und Mahler: Vom musikalischen Roman zum Sphärengesang', in Peter Petersen (ed.), *Musikkulturgeschichte,* Festschrift für Constantin Floros (Breitkopf & Härtel, Wiesbaden, 1990).

—— 'Mahler and France', in Matthias Theodor Vogt (ed.), *Das Gustav-Mahler-Fest-Hamburg, 1989* (Bärenreiter, Kassel, 1991), 229–46.

—— *Vienne: Histoire musicale,* ii, *1848 à nos jours* (Coutaz, Arles, 1991).

—— *Vienne une histoire musciale* (Fayard, Paris, 1995).

—— 'Auf der Suche nach Gustav Mahler', in Hermann Danuser (ed.), *Gustav Mahler: Wege der Forschung* (Wiss. Buchges., Darmstadt, 1992), 30–68.

—— 'Mahler and France', in Donald Mitchell and Andrew Nicholson (eds.), *The Mahler Companion* (Oxford University Press, Oxford, 1998).

—— 'Music about Music in Mahler: Reminiscences, Allusions, or Quotations?' in Stephen E. Hefling (ed.), *Mahler Studies* (Cambridge Univesity Press, Cambridge, 1997), 122–68.

Lea, Henry A., *Gustav Mahler: Man on the Margin* (Bouvier, Bonn, 1985).

Lieberwirth, Steffen (ed.), *Gustav Mahler, Leben—Werk—Interpretation—Rezeption.* Gewandhaus-Symposium, Gewandhaus-Festtage 1985 (Peters, Leipzig, 1990).

Louis Rudolf, *Die Deutsche Musik der gegenwart* (Müller, Munich, 1909).

Mahler, Alma, *Gustav Mahler: Erinnerungen und Briefe* (1st edn. Allert de Lange, Amsterdam, 1940).

Mahler, Alma, *Gustav Mahler: Memories and Letters*, trans. Basil Creighton (Murray, London, 1946).

—— *Alma Mahler-Werfel: Tagebuch-Suiten 1898–1902*, ed. Antony Beaumont and Suzann Rode-Breymann (S. Fischer, Frankfurt, 1997).

Mahler, Gustav, *Mahler Feestboek* (6 and 21 May 1920) (Concertgebouw, Amsterdam, 1920).

Mahler Vereinigung Hamburg (ed.), *Gustav Mahler 'Meine Zeit wird kommen': Aspekte der Mahler-Rezeption* (Dölling & Galitz, Hamburg, 1996).

Martner, Knud, *Gustav Mahler in Konzertsaal: Eine Dokumentation seiner Konzerttätigkeit 1870–1911* (KM-Privatdruck, Copenhagen, 1985).

Marx, Joseph, *Betrachtungen eines romantischen Realisten* (Gerlach & Wiedling, Vienna, 1947).

Mengelberg, Rudolf (ed.), *Das Mahler-Fest. Amsterdam, May 1920* (Universal Edition, Vienna, 1920).

Metzger, Heinz-Klaus and **Riehn, Rainer** (eds.), Musik-Konzepte Sonderband, *Gustav Mahler* (Pribil, Munich, 1989).

—— (ed.), *Gustav Mahler: Der unbekannte Bekannte*. Musik-Konzepte 91 (Edition Text+Kritik, Jan. 1996).

Meysels, Luciano O., *In meinem Salon ist Österreich: Berta Zuckerkandl und ihre Zeit* (Herold, Vienna, 1984).

Mitchell, Donald and **Nicholson, Andrew** (eds.), *The Mahler Companion* (Oxford University Press, Oxford, 1998).

Mittag, Erwin, *Aus der Geschichte der Wiener Philharmoniker* (Gerlach & Wiedling, Vienna, 1950).

Moderne Welt: Mahler issue, ed. Ludwig Hirschfeld, 3 (Vienna, 1921–2): 7.

Mooser, Aloys, R., *Souvenirs, Genève 1886–1896, Saint-Pétersbourg 1896–1909* (Georg, Geneva, 1994).

Morrison, Julie Dorn, 'Gustav Mahler at the Wiener Hofoper: A Study of Critical Reception in the Viennese Press (1897–1907)', Ph.D. thesis (Evanston, Ill., vol. i, 1996).

Müller, Karl Joseph, *Mahler: Leben—Werke—Dokumente* (Piper-Schott, Mainz, 1988).

Musical, Revue du Châtelet, n. 9, 'Mahler et la France', H. L. de La Grange (ed.) (Paris, Feb. 1989), by Alain Surrans, Nathalie Brunet, Mac Vignal, Henry-Louis de La Grange, Gérard Pesson, William Ritter, Guihelm Tournier.

Musik, Die: Mahler issue, ed. Bernhard Schuster, 10 (Schuster & Loeffler, Berlin, 1910–11): 18.

Namenwirt, Simon Michael, *Gustav Mahler: A Critical Bibliography* (3 vols., Harrassowitz, Wiesbaden, 1987).

Nebehay, Christian M., *Ver Sacrum 1898–1903* (Tusch, Vienna, 1975).

Nemeth, Carl, *Franz Schmidt: Ein Meister nach Brahms und Bruckner* (Amalthea, Vienna, 1957).

Neumayr, Anton, 'Gustav Mahler', *Musik und Medezin. Chopin. Smetana. Tschaikowsky. Mahler* (Sachbuch Jugend & Volk, Vienna, 1995), 191–230.

Niemann, Walter, *Die Musik der Gegenwart* (Schuster & Loeffler, Berlin, 1913).

Österreichische Musikzeitschrift: Mahler issue, 15 (Vienna, 1960): 6.

Osthoff, Wolfgang, 'Hans Pfitzners "Rose vom Liebesgarten": Gustav Mahler und die Wiener Schule', *Festschrift Martin Ruhnke* (Hänssler, Neuhausen-Stuttgart, 1986), 265–93.

Partsch, Erich Wolfgang (ed.), *Gustav Mahler: Werk und Wirken. Vierzig Jahre Internationale Gustav Mahler Gesellschaft* (Vom Pasqualatihaus, Vienna, 1996).

Paumgartner, Bernhard, *Erinnerungen* (Residenz, Salzburg, 1969).

Pausch, Oskar, ' "Mahlerisches", in den Rollerbeständen der Wiener Theater-sammlung', *Studia Musicologia Academiae Scientiarum Hungaricae*, 31 (1989), 343–52.

Perger, Richard von, *Fünfzig Jahre Wiener Philharmoniker: 1860–1910* (Fromme, Vienna, 1910).

Pfitzner, Hans, *Reden, Schriften, Briefe* (Luchterhand, Berlin, 1955).

Pickett, David Anniss, 'Gustav Mahler as an Interpreter: A Study of his Textural Alterations and Performance Practice in the Symphonic Repertoire', 3 vols. Ph.D. thesis (Univ. of Surrey, 1988).

Pott, Gertrud, 'Die Spiegelung des Sezessionismus im Österreichischen Theater', Ph.D. thesis (Vienna, 1970).

Pringsheim, Klaus, 'Erinnerung an Gustav Mahler', *Neue Zürcher Zeitung* (7 July 1960), 2322.

Rauchhaupt, Ursula von (ed.), *Die Welt der Symphonie* (Polydor International, Westermann Verlag, Hamburg, 1972).

Raupp, Wilhelm, *Max von Schillings* (Hanseatischer Verlag, Hamburg, 1935).

—— *Eugen d'Albert: Ein Künstler und Menschenschicksal* (Koehler & Amelang, Leipzig, 1930).

Redl, Renata, 'Berta Zuckerkandl und die Wiener Gesellschaft. Ein Beitrag zur Österreichischen Kunst- und Gesellschaftskritik', Ph.D. thesis (Vienna, 1976).,

Reed, Philip (ed.), *On Mahler and Britten. Essays in Honour of Donald Mitchell on his Seventieth Birthday* (The Boydell Press, Woodbridge and The Britten-Pears Library, Aldeburgh, 1995).

Reeser, Eduard, *Gustav Mahler und Holland: Briefe* (IGMG, Universal Edition, Vienna, 1980).

Reich, Willi (ed.), *Gustav Mahler: Im eigenen Wort. Im Worte der Freunde* (Arche, Zurich, 1958).

Richolson-Sollitt, Edna, *Mengelberg spreekt* (Kruseman, The Hague, n.d.).

Robert, Gustave, *La Musique à Paris 1898–1900*, v–vi (Delagrave, Paris, 1901).

Rolland, Romain, *Musiciens d'aujourd'hui* (Hachette, Paris, 1922).

—— (ed.) *Richard Strauss et Romain Rolland: Correspondence, Fragments de Journal* (Albin Michel, Paris, 1951).

—— *Fräulein Elsa: Lettres de Romain Rolland à Elsa Wolff* (Albin Michel, Paris, 1964).

Ruzicka, Peter (ed.), *Mahler: Eine Herausforderung, ein Symposiom* (Breitkopf & Härtel, Wiesbaden, 1977).

Salten, Felix, *Gestalten und Erscheinungen* (Fischer, Berlin, 1913).

Samuels, Robert, *Mahler's Sixth Symphony: A Study in Musical Semiotics* (Cambridge University Press, Cambridge, 1995).

Schadendorf, Mirjam, *Humor als Formkonzept in der Musik Gustav Mahlers* (Metzler, Stuttgart, 1995).

Schiedermair, Ludwig, *Gustav Mahler* (Seemann, Leipzig, 1900).

Schiedermair, Ludwig, *Musikalische Begegnungen* (Staufen, Cologne, 1948).

Schiff, David, 'Jewish and Musical Tradition in the Music of Mahler and Schoenberg, *Journal of the A. Schoenberg Institute*, 9 (1986): 2, 217–31.

Schlüter, Wolfgang, *Studien zur Rezeptionsgeschichte der Symphonik Gustav Mahlers*, Ph.D. thesis (Technische Universität, Berlin, 1983).

Schmidt, Leopold, *Aus dem Musikleben der Gegenwart* (Hofmann, Berlin, 1909).

—— *Erlebnisse und Betrachtungen* (Hofmann, Berlin, 1913).

Schmitt, Theodor, *Der langsame Symphoniesatz Gustav Mahlers* (Fink, Munich, 1983).

Schneider, Gunter, 'Egon Wellesz über Gustav Mahler', *Österreichische Musikzeitschrift*, 40 (1985): 12, 637 ff.

Schoenberg, Arnold, 'Gustav Mahler', 'Stil und Gedanke', *Gesammelte Schriften*, i, ed. Ivan Vojtěch (Fisher, Frankfurt, 1976). 'Gustav Mahler', *Style and Idea* (Philosophical Library, New York, 1950) (Leins, Tübingen, 1966).

—— *Briefe*, ed. Erwin Stein (Schott, Mainz, 1958).

—— 'Banalität und Genie. Zum 100. Geburtstag Gustav Mahlers', *Forum*, 79/80 (Vienna, 1960): 7, 277–80.

Schrott, Ludwig, *Die Persönlichkeit Hans Pfitzners* (Atlantis, Zurich, 1959).

Schuh, Willi (ed.), *Richard Strauss, Jahrbuch 1954* (Boosey & Hawkes, Bonn, 1953).

—— *Richard Strauss: Jugend und frühe Meisterjahre. Lebenschronik 1864–1898* (Atlantis, Zurich, 1976).

Schünemann, Georg, *Geschichte des Dirigierens* (Brietkopf & Härtel, Leipzig, 1913).

Schuschitz, Elisabeth Désirée, 'Die Wiener Musikkritik in der Ära Gustav Mahler 1897 bis 1907: Eine historisch-kritische Standortbestimmung', Ph.D. thesis (Vienna, 1978).

Seidl, Arthur, *Moderne Dirigenten* (Schuster & Loeffler, Berlin, 1902).

—— *Moderner Geist in der deutschen Tonkunst* (Bosse, Regensburg, 1912).

—— *Aufsätze, Studien und Skizzen* (2 vols., Bosse, Regensburg, 1926).

Silbermann, Alphons, *Lübbes Mahler-Lexikon* (Lübbe, Bergisch Gladbach, 1986).

Slezak, Leo, *Mein Lebensmärchen* (Piper, Munich, 1948).

Smoley, Lewis M., *Gustav Mahler's Symphonies: Critical Commentary on Recordings Since 1986* (Grenwood Press, Westport, Conn., 1996).

Specht, Richard, *Mahler, Symphonie VI: Thematischer Führer* (Kahnt, Leipzig, 1906).

—— *Das Wiener Operntheater: Erinnerung aus 50 Jahren* (Knepler, Vienna, 1919).

—— *Mahler. Symphonies, I, II, III, IV, VII: Thematic Analyses* (Univresal Edition, Vienna, n.d.).

Sponheuer, Bernd, *Logik des Zerfalls: Untersuchungen zum Finalproblem in den Symphonien Gustav Mahlers* (Schneider, Tutzing, 1978).

Stahmer, Klaus Hinrich (ed.), *Form und Idee in Gustav Mahlers Instrumentalmusik* (Heinrichshofen, Wilhelmshaven, 1980).

Stauber, Paul, *Das wahre Erbe Mahlers* (Huber & Lahme, Vienna, 1909).

Stefan, Paul, *Das neue Haus* (Strache, Vienna, 1919).

—— *Bruno Walter* (Reichner, Vienna, 1936).

—— and Heinsheimer, Hans (ed.), *25 Jahre Neue Musik: Jahrbuch 1926 der Universal Edition* (Universal Edition, Vienna, 1926).

Steinert, Heinz, 'Der Skandal Gustav Mahler: Der Mythos von der Vertreibung Mahlers aus Wien', *Adorno in Wien* (Gesellschaftskritik, Vienna, 1989), 77–95.

Stephan, Rudolf (ed.), *Gustav Mahler: Werk und Interpretation: Autographe, Partituren, Dokumente*, Catalogue of Exhibition held at the Heinrich Heine Institut, Oct. 1979 to Jan. 1980 (Volk Verlag, Cologne, 1979).

—— 'Zu Mahlers Komposition der Schlussszene von Goethes Faust', *Vom musikalischen Denken* (Schott, Mainz, 1985), 98–104.

—— 'Mahlers letztes Konzert in Berlin: unbekannte Briefe Mahlers', *Festschrift Rudolph Elvers zum 60. Geburtstag* (Schneider, Tutzing, 1985), 491–503.

—— (ed.), *Mahler-Interpretation: Aspekte zum Werk und Wirken von Gustav Mahler* (Schott, Mainz, 1985).

Storck, Karl, *Die Musik der Gegenwart* (Metzlersche Verlagsbuchhandlung, Stuttgart, 1922).

Strauss, Richard, and Hofmannsthal, Hugo von, *Briefwechsel* (Atlantis, Zurich, 1952); English trans. Hans Hammelmann and Ewald Osers (Random House, New York, 1961).

—— and Rolland, Romain, *Correspondence: Fragments de Journal* (Albin Michel, Paris, 1951).

Stuckenschmidt, Hans Heinz, *Schönberg. Leben, Umwelt, Werk* (Atlantis, Zurich, 1974).

Stuppner, Herbert (ed.), *Mahler in Toblach, Mahler Festwoche 1981–1988* (Unicolpi, Milan, 1989).

Swarowsky, Hans, *Wahrung der Gestalt* (Universal Edition, Vienna, 1979).

Thomas, Walter, *Richard Strauss und seine Zeitgenossen* (Langen-Müller, Munich, 1964).

Trenner, Franz (ed.), *Richard Strauss: Dokumente seines Lebens und Schaffens* (Beck, Munich, 1954).

Van Leeuwen, Jos, *A 'Mass' for the Masses: Proceedings of the Mahler VIII Symposium, Amsterdam 1988* (Universitaire Pers, Rotterdam, 1992).

Vestdijk, Simon, *Over Gustav Mahler* (Meulenhoff, Amsterdam, 1994).

Vignal, Marc, *Mahler* (Le Seuil, Paris, 1966; 2nd revised edn. 1977).

Vill, Suzanne, *Vermittlungsformen verbalisierter und musikalischer Inhalte in der Musik Gustav Mahlers* (Schneider, Tutzing, 1979).

Vogt, Matthias Theodor (ed.), *Das Gustav-Mahler-Fest Hamburg 1989, Bericht über den Internationalen Gustav-Mahler-Kongress* (Bärenreiter, Kassel, 1991).

Vondenhoff, Bruno, and Eleonore, *Gustav Mahler Dokumentation* (Schneider, Tutzing, 1978).

Vondenoff, Eleonore, *Sammlung: Ergänzungsband zur Gudstav Mahler Dokumentation* (Schneider, Tutzing, 1983).

—— *Samlung: Zweiter Ergänzungsband zur Gustav Mahler Dokumentation* (Schneider, Tutzing, 1997).

Wagner, Cosima, *Briefwechsel mit Prinz Ernst zu Hohenlohe Langenburg* (Cotta, Stuttgart, 1937).

—— *Das zweite Leben: Briefe und Aufzeichnungen 1883–1930* (Piper, Munich, 1980).

Wagner, Manfred, *Alfred Roller in seiner Zeit* (Rezidenz, Salzburg, 1996).

Walter, Bruno, *Gustav Mahler* (1st edn. Reichner, Vienna, 1936; 2nd edn. Fischer, Berlin, 1957; 3rd edn. *Gustav Mahler: Ein Porträt*, Heinrichshofen, Wilhelmshaven, 1981; English trans. James Galston, with biographical essay by Ernst Krenek, Greystone, New York, 1941; revised, ed., and trans., by Lotte Walter Lindt, Knopf, New York, 1958).

Walter, Bruno, *Thema und Variationen* (Fischer, Berlin, 1950; trans. James A. Galston, Knopf, New York, 1946).

—— *Briefe 1894–1962* (Fischer, Frankfurt, 1969).

Weber, Horst, *Alexander Zemlinsky* (Lafite, Vienna, 1977).

Weiss, Günther (ed.), *Neue Mahleriana: Essays in Honour of Henry-Louis de La Grange on his Seventieth Birthday* (Peter Lang, Berne, 1997).

Wellesz, Egon, *Arnold Schoenberg* (Tal, Leipzig, 1921).

—— *Die neue Instrumentation* (2 vols., Hesse, Berlin, 1928).

—— and **Emmy,** 'Mahler', in Franz Endler (ed.), *Egon Wellesz, Leben und Werk* (Zsolnay, Vienna, 1981), 21–5.

Werba, Robert, 'Mahlers Mozart-Bild (I–VIII)', Mozartgemeinde, Wiener Figaro (Vienna, 1975–9).

—— 'Marginalien zum Theaterpraktiker Gustav Mahler: Aspekte seiner regielichen und dramaturgischen Tätigkeit an der Wiener Oper im Spiegel der Kritik', *Studia Musicologica Academiae Scientiarum Hungaricae*, 31 (Budapest, 1989), 371–88.

Wiesenthal, Grethe, *Der Aufstieg: Aus dem Leben einer Tänzerin* (Rowohlt, Berlin, 1919).

—— *Die ersten Schritte* (Rowohlt, Berlin, 1947), 181.

Wiesmann, Sigrid (ed.), *Gustav Mahler in Wien* (Belser, Stuttgart, 1976).

Williamson, John G., 'The Development of Mahler's Symphonic Technique with Special Reference to the Compositions of the Period 1899 to 1905', Ph.D. thesis (Liverpool, 1975).

Williamson, John, 'Liszt, Mahler and the Chorale', *Proceedings of the Royal Musical Association*, 108 (1981–2), 115–25.

—— 'Deceptive Cadences in the last movement of Mahler's Seventh Symphony', *Sounding*, 9 (1982), 87–96.

—— 'The Structural Premises of Mahler's Introductions: Prolegomena to an Analysis of the First Movement of the Seventh Symphony', *Music Analysis*, 5: 1 (Mar. 1986), 29–57.

—— 'Mahler and Veni Creator Spiritus', *Music Review*, 44 (Feb. 1983): 1, 25–35.

Witeschnik, Alexander, *Musizieren geht über probieren: Die Geschichte der Wiener Philharmoniker in Anekdoten und Geschichten* (Paul Neff, Vienna, 1967).

Zuckerkandl, Bertha, *Ich erlebte fünfzig Jahre Weltgeschichte* (Bermann, Stockholm, 1939).

—— *Österreich intim* (Propyläen-Ullstein, Frankfurt, 1970).

Zweig, Stefan, *The World of Yesterday* (Viking Press, New York, 1943).

—— *Die Welt von Gestern* (Fischer, Berlin, 1977).

Zychowicz, James (ed.), *The Seventh Symphony of Gustav Mahler: A Symposium* (Univ. of Cincinnati, 1990).

INDEX

Compiled by Joan Dearnley

Notes 'n' are included in the page locators only where there are no other references to the subject within the text on the page.
The titles of musical works and books are listed under the name of the composer or author.